A PLUME BOOK

THE FILMMAKER'S HANDBOOK

STEVEN ASCHER's acclaimed films include *So Much So Fast*, which premiered at the Sundance Film Festival, and *Troublesome Creek*, which was nominated for an Academy Award and won the Grand Jury Prize and Audience Award at Sundance (both films made with his wife, Jeanne Jordan). He has taught filmmaking at Harvard University and at the Massachusetts Institute of Technology. His awards include the Prix Italia, a George Foster Peabody Award, and he was nominated for a Director's Guild of America Award. His website is www.WestCityFilms.com.

EDWARD PINCUS's films include *Black Natchez*, *Panola*, and *Portrait of a McCarthy Supporter* (all made with David Neuman). His pioneering work in personal documentary led to *Diaries: 1971–76*. He founded the Film Section at the Massachusetts Institute of Technology and later taught filmmaking at Harvard. His awards include a Guggenheim fellowship, and he is author of the widely used *Guide to Filmmaking*. He is currently a commercial cut-flower grower in northern New England and is working on a new film, *The Axe in the Attic*.

THE FILMMAKER'S HANDBOOK

A COMPREHENSIVE GUIDE FOR THE DIGITAL AGE

THIRD EDITION

Steven Ascher and Edward Pincus

Drawings by Carol Keller and Robert Brun
Original Photographs by Ted Spagna
and Stephen McCarthy

COMPLETELY REVISED AND UPDATED BY STEVEN ASCHER
WITH CONTRIBUTIONS BY DAVID LEITNER

A PLUME BOOK

PLUME

Published by Penguin Group • Penguin Group (USA) Inc., 375 Hudson Street, New York, New York 10014, U.S.A. • Penguin Group (Canada), 90 Eglinton Avenue East, Suite 700, Toronto, Ontario, Canada M4P 2Y3 (a division of Pearson Penguin Canada Inc.) • Penguin Books Ltd., 80 Strand, London WC2R 0RL, England • Penguin Ireland, 25 St. Stephen's Green, Dublin 2, Ireland (a division of Penguin Books Ltd.) • Penguin Group (Australia), 250 Camberwell Road, Camberwell, Victoria 3124, Australia (a division of Pearson Australia Group Pty. Ltd.) • Penguin Books India Pvt. Ltd., 11 Community Centre, Panchsheel Park, New Delhi – 110 017, India • Penguin Group (NZ), 67 Apollo Drive, Rosedale, North Shore 0745, Auckland, New Zealand (a division of Pearson New Zealand Ltd.) • Penguin Books (South Africa) (Pty.) Ltd., 24 Sturdee Avenue, Rosebank, Johannesburg 2196, South Africa

Penguin Books Ltd., Registered Offices: 80 Strand, London WC2R 0RL, England

First published by Plume, a member of Penguin Group (USA) Inc.

First Printing, June 1984
First Printing (second edition), March 1999
First Printing (third edition), August 2007
10 9 8 7 6 5 4 3 2

CIP data is available.
ISBN 978-0-452-28678-8

Printed in the United States of America
Set in Janson Text
Designed by Eve Kirch

For Jordan

For Jane

CONTENTS

It's not easy being a filmmaker. It's not easy getting the money, making the movie, or finding an audience when the film is done. Some things never change. But one thing is changing all the time: technology. Astonishing developments in video and film equipment and techniques have transformed moviemaking. You can do things today that only a few years ago would have been impossible, or impossibly expensive. But as high technology becomes more accessible, there's a hidden cost—it takes a lot of energy and time to understand and keep up with it all.

When I was writing the second edition of this book in 1998, I knew that some of the content would become dated shortly after the book came out. That was not the case when Ed and I wrote the first edition in the early 1980s. That edition, about tried-and-true filmmaking on celluloid film, remained pretty current for nearly fifteen years. Right now, the pace of change in video and computer technology is so rapid, some things in this book could be dated before you get to the end of this sentence.

Though a website is easier to update, a book has certain advantages. You can take it with you to the top of a hill. From there, you can get a view of the filmmaking world that stretches out below, and use the book to help you decide where you want to go and how to get there. Once you start the journey, you'll need a lot more detailed and up-to-the-minute advice on local routes and customs, which you'll get from websites, online bulletin boards, user manuals, and conversations with other filmmakers and professionals.

There have always been two worlds captured by moviemakers: the fictional and the nonfictional. The fiction film creates a world before the camera. A story is written and characters act out the events to make the film. In the documentary, filmmakers attempt to show the world as it is. From the dawn of cinema, circa 1900, the French contrasted the films of Lumière, who filmed his baby eating breakfast and a train arriving at the station, with those of his contemporary Meliès, the magician, who created stories, costumes, and special effects for his films. On the one hand, there is the difference between documentary and fiction; on the other, the difference between the filmmaker finding magic in the real world and creating it for the camera. This book is for both kinds of filmmaking.

In a sense, all moviemakers start out as independents. More often than not, the novice must become versed in all aspects of production—shooting, sound recording, editing, raising money, and distribution—simply because there's no one else to perform these tasks. Learning all the facets of filmmaking has advantages no matter what your future career is in movies. The best cameraman or -woman is one familiar with the needs of the sound recordist and editor, and vice versa. Producers and directors can benefit enormously by understanding all the tasks taking place on the production. Whenever industry terms are used in this book to identify a specific craft—editor, director of photography, camera operator, recordist, and so on—it is for convenience and not necessarily to encourage the division of these roles.

The book presents technical information of practical value, introducing key terms and concepts while trying not to overwhelm you with technical jargon. You'll find information on equipment and techniques used by students and by working professionals. Even if you can't yet afford some of the items discussed, it's useful to have a grasp of some of the things you'll need to know if you work in the industry.

For help with the first edition, thanks go to Mark Abbate, Benjamin Bergery, David Brown, Michael Callahan, Elvin Carini, Claude Chelli, Alfred Guzzetti, Ned Johnston, Rudolph Kingslake, Dennis Kitsz, Steve Kuettel, David Leitner, Mark Lipman, Ross McElwee, Robb Moss, Sami Pincus, and Moe Shore.

For help with the second edition, thanks also to Richard Bock, the Bueermanns, Frank Coakley, Sandra Forman, Victoria Garvin Davis, Len Gittleman, Peter Gloeggler, Sam Kauffmann, Julie Mallozzi, Eric Menninger, Michael Phillips, Adam Schatten, and Tim Spitzer. Also to Rob Brun and Stephen McCarthy for wonderful illustrations and photographs. Bob Doyle provided invaluable help with the video chapters.

For the third edition, particular thanks to David Leitner whose encyclopedic expertise and lucid prose helped interpret the digital world. His contributions improved the book enormously and prevented many errors; those that remain are mine. Thanks also to Dan Coplan, Patrick Gaspar, Greg McCleary, Matt McMakin, Graeme Nattress, Bill Weisman, and to researchers Joshua Weinstein and Luke Gasbarro. Ned Johnston and Andy Young shot some great photographs.

Thanks to the many people, too numerous to mention, who graciously supplied information or pictures.

Jeanne Jordan, my filmmaking partner and wife, has made me a better filmmaker, and made this a better book. For Jeannie, storytelling is the important thing and technology is only of interest, as she says, on a "need-to-know basis." In a world where people can become obsessed with the latest equipment, software, or gizmo, Jeannie is proof that great filmmaking comes from the filmmaker, not the tools. Our son, Jordan Ascher, is a constant reminder that people growing up in a digital world not only aren't intimidated by new technology, they welcome and expect it. To both of them, all my love and gratitude.

S. A.
April 2007

THE
FILMMAKER'S
HANDBOOK

CHAPTER 1

Introduction to Video and Film Systems

This book is about making movies, whether they are dramatic features, documentaries, music videos, corporate videos, multimedia projects, TV programs, commercials, or home movies. Actually, "movie" isn't the right term to describe all types of productions; no single word is. You could call them "motion pictures," but that has echoes of Hollywood hype (especially when preceded by "major"). Sometimes the name we use for a production has to do with how it's made. For example, if you say you're making a "video" people will probably assume you're shooting with a video camera, not a film camera.[1] But often the name has more to do with how the end product is distributed. A documentary shown in a theater might be a "film," but if you saw the same thing on television you might call it a "show" or a "program." A two-hour drama may begin life as a "picture," be called a "feature" when shown at a festival, a "release" in theaters, a "movie" when broadcast on television, a "video" or "DVD" by the sales clerk at your local store, and a "full-length download" or "video podcast" on the Internet.

This confusion about names reflects how diverse the many forms of production and distribution have become. There was a time when a "film" was photographed on celluloid film, edited on film, and shown on film. Though that is still possible, it's likely that the same production today will be shot in high definition video, or in a digital file format using a *digital cinematography* camera; then digitally edited and finished with effects; and then released in a wide variety of exhibition formats, including film projection, digital projection, analog broadcast television, HDTV, computer files for Internet downloading, and recorded media, such as DVDs.

Because movies can now be created, manipulated, and shown in all sorts of ways, the old distinctions between filmmakers, videomakers, and digital video artists no longer apply. In the wake of the digital video revolution, all formats and approaches now pass through a computer at some point. This is why the term *workflow*, borrowed from IT (information technology) to describe the careful step-by-step management of a complex project, now popularly refers to strategies for managing digital video production, editing, and finishing.

The first edition of *The Filmmaker's Handbook* was about film only. The second edition added video. In this third edition, digital technologies are discussed as

---

1. Unless of course you're making music videos, which are often shot on film.

much as or more than film. This is not because film is "dead." However, as the power and reach of digital media grow and the costs fall, more and more filmmakers will turn to digital first. Even those who shoot film will make extensive use of digital tools in the course of production, postproduction, and distribution.

This book is written from the point of view that media makers will reach for whatever tools suit them best to record, edit, and display their work. Their toolset can include film, digital video, and computers in any number of configurations.

Which brings us back to the problem of names. Given the expansiveness of the media-making process, what shall we call the work being produced? As this is *The Filmmaker's Handbook*, we'll call the end product a *film* or a *movie*. This is for convenience only, and is not meant to suggest any limitations in terms of the media, formats, or equipment used to make or distribute the production.

This first chapter is intended as an overview of the moviemaking process, an outline of techniques and equipment.

Making a Movie

The technical, creative, financial, and social aspects of filmmaking are tightly interwoven, perhaps more so than in any other art form. The more you understand about all these aspects of production, the better prepared you'll be for the challenges of making a movie and getting it seen.

Movie production ranges from a multimillion-dollar, big-screen Hollywood epic to a home video of a child's birthday. Although movies vary widely in terms of budgets, number of personnel, and intended audiences, many of the processes used to create movies are similar for all types of productions. Moviemaking tasks can be divided chronologically into *preproduction*, *production*, and *postproduction* periods.

Fig. 1-1. Moviemaking is a collaborative art. (Fletcher Chicago/Egripment USA)

Preproduction is the time for planning and preparation. Research is done, a topic is chosen. For fiction projects, a *treatment* may be written in preparation for a *script*. Documentaries may start as a written proposal outlining what is to be filmed. The filmmaker (or producer) draws up a *budget* of the movie's estimated cost and arranges for financing. For higher-budget projects, this usually involves soliciting investors, distributors, grants, or a television contract. Lower-budget projects are often self-financed, sometimes with the hope of recouping costs after the movie is finished. During the preproduction period, the *crew* is assembled and *locations* (the sites where the movie will be shot) are scouted. For some projects, *sets* may be built in a studio and *casting* is done to choose actors.

The production period essentially begins when the camera rolls. This is sometimes called the start of *principal photography*. Since movie equipment can be expensive, it is often rented for the duration of production, or only on the days it is needed. Lower-priced gear may be purchased outright. *Additional photography* or *pickup shots* are scenes filmed separately from the main production or after the main shooting is done. The material that's been filmed may be viewed during production, on set, or elsewhere. The traditional film term for the footage recorded by the camera is *rushes* or *dailies*, because the film is processed at the lab as fast as possible for daily viewing (these terms can also be used for video, which doesn't need to be processed). Rushes are unedited, though often not all the footage that was shot gets printed, copied, or viewed.

The postproduction period (often just called *post*, as in, "We're scheduled for eight weeks of post") generally begins once the principal shooting is completed. On some films, the editor works during production, cutting as soon as each scene is shot, which may give the director and crew feedback in time to make corrections. On other projects, editing starts after the shooting stops. Editing is done to condense what are typically hours of raw film or video footage into a watchable movie. It is usually in the editing room that the project can be seen in its entirety for the first time. Movies are often substantially rearranged and reworked during editing. Documentaries often find their structure and shape in the editing room, not from a preplanned script. The first edited version of a movie is the *assembly* or *string-out* (all the scenes in order). The assembly is condensed into a *rough cut*, which is then honed to a *fine cut*. When a satisfactory version is complete (called *picture lock*), the various stages of *finishing* take place. This may include *scoring* with original music or adding prerecorded music; *sound editing* (to clean up and enhance the sound track); *sound mix* (to balance and perfect the sound); and creating titles and any visual effects that weren't done earlier.

When a movie that was shot on film is finished, *prints* are made, which are copies of the film that can be shown in screenings. If a movie was shot on video and is intended for theaters it may be transferred to film, sometimes called a *film-out*. All movies, regardless of whether they were shot on film or video, are eventually distributed in some form of video. A copy of a videotape is sometimes called a *dub* (duplicate copy) or *clone* (exact digital copy). The movie may also be transferred to disc, such as DVD.

Finally, the movie is *released* or *distributed*—sent out into the world to find its audience. There are many types of distribution, aimed at different markets. *Theatrical release* is the goal of most feature films. A theatrical run may take place in *first-run movie houses* or smaller, specialized *art houses* which are often part of a *specialty chain*. *Television distribution* may include traditional broadcast television, cable TV, or satellite. *Educational* or *A-V (audio-visual)* distribution usually implies selling or renting videos to schools and libraries. *Home video* release is selling or renting videos either directly to consumers or through retail outlets. *Video-on-demand* (*VOD*) and *pay-per-view* (*PPV*) are distribution methods that bridge the gap between television and home video sales by allowing viewers to select and/or pay individually for programming when they want it. *Multimedia projects* are generally computer-based, *interactive* programs that allow the user to control or respond to the program. Both multimedia and *linear* (noninteractive) productions may be distributed to consumers on disc (such as CD-ROM or DVD) or over the Internet. Downloading of TV shows from websites and streaming of video clips via the popular Flash file format are the beginnings of *IPTV* (*Internet Protocol Television*), which some say is the future of television.

A given project may be distributed through all of these channels or in various combinations; moreover, because movies are increasingly distributed in a global marketplace, issues of multiple languages, technologies, and venues must be dealt with. Many decisions you make while you're producing a movie affect what kind of distribution is possible, and you must try to anticipate distribution goals from the very start of your project.

The Moving Image

A film or video camera has a lens that focuses an image of the world onto a light-sensitive piece of film (see Fig. 1-32) or a light-sensitive electronic chip (see Fig. 1-3). This part of the process is much like a still camera. But how do we capture *movement?* The impression of continuous movement in a motion picture is really an illusion. A film or video camera records a sequence of still images (frames) in rapid succession (see Fig. 1-2). In film, the standard frame rate is 24 *frames per second*, written 24 *fps*. When the images are then displayed one after another on a screen (for example, a theater screen or a TV), if the frames in the sequence change from one to the next quickly enough and the differences between them are not too great, the brain perceives smooth, realistic motion. This effect brings the magic of motion to film, video, and flip books.

Fig. 1-2. All motion pictures—in film or video—are made up of a series of still images that appear to move when shown rapidly, one after the other.

Traditionally, this illusion has been explained by something called *persistence of vision*, which is based on the idea that the eye retains an impression of each frame slightly longer than it is actually exposed to it. According to this theory, when each new frame is displayed, the eye blends it with the afterimage of the previous frame, creating a smooth transition between them. There are many problems with this explanation (for example, afterimages move with your eyes if you look left or right, they don't stay in place on the screen).

A perceptual illusion called *beta movement* describes one situation in which viewers interpret successive still images as motion. A static shot of a ball is flashed on the left side of a screen, then on the right side, and viewers see it as moving from left to right. Think of a lighted ticker tape–style sign in a store, on which messages seem to scroll from left to right across the display.

The full picture of how the brain and eye actually perceive motion is still under debate.[2] What we do know is that for a realistic viewing experience we need to create the illusion of both smooth motion and consistent illumination. If the images change too slowly from one to the next, the illusion falls apart. Instead of smooth motion you see jerky, stop-start motion, and instead of continuous illumination, the screen may appear to *flicker* (get brighter and darker as the images change). For more on this see Judder and Strobing, p. 361.

VIDEO SYSTEMS

Camera and Recorder Basics

We've just seen that the concept behind motion picture recording is to capture a series of still images and then play them back. Let's look at how this is done in video.

The video camera focuses its image on the flat surface of a solid-state electronic chip which is sensitive to light. This chip is the camera's *sensor* or *imager*. There are two types of sensor chips: *CCD* (*charge-coupled device*) and *CMOS* (*complementary metal oxide semiconductor*). CCD has been the most common chip used in video cameras, although CMOS is catching up. People often use "sensor" and "CCD" interchangeably. You can also just call it a *chip*.

The surface of a CCD or CMOS sensor is divided into a very fine grid of spots or sites called *pixels* (for picture elements). Each pixel in the chip is in some ways like a tiny light meter that reads the brightness of the light at that spot. When a pixel is struck by light, it creates and stores an electric charge. The more light that strikes it, the more charge builds up (this process can be compared to a bucket filling with rainwater, see Fig. 5-15). A given sensor may have millions of pixels in a chip that is less than an inch across. To capture the whole picture, the charge of each pixel in the grid is read at an instant in time and the output from all the pixels together is processed into the *video signal*, which puts the picture information into a format that can be recorded and displayed.

A video frame is displayed as a series of thin horizontal lines called *scan lines*. This pattern of scan lines is called a *raster* from the Latin word for rake; a video frame is literally a raked image. Different video systems use different numbers of scan lines.

NTSC (*National Television System Committee*) video is the traditional analog broadcasting system used in North America and parts of Asia, including Japan, South Korea, and Taiwan. NTSC video has 525 lines per frame and the frame rate is about 30 fps (29.97 fps, to be precise).

The *PAL* (*Phase Alternate Line*) standard is used in the U.K., Western Europe,

---

2. Articles on the problems with persistence of vision by Joseph and Barbara Anderson can be found on the Web.

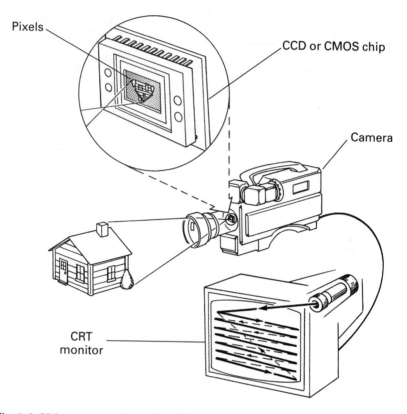

Fig. 1-3. Video camera and monitor. The camera's lens focuses an image of the world onto the sensor, which converts it to a video signal. The CRT monitor shown here "paints" the image on the screen following a pattern of lines called the *raster*. (Robert Brun)

Australia, parts of Asia, and parts of South America. PAL has 625 lines and the frame rate is exactly 25 fps.[3]

Today's CCDs and CMOS sensors, with their pixel structure, capture an entire frame all at once like a film camera, but many of them also borrow a technique from tube cameras called *interlace scanning*, in which only half of the scan lines are recorded at a time (see Progressive and Interlace Scanning, p. 12).

In the earliest days of television, the only way to preserve the image from a live TV camera was to record it on 16mm black-and-white film using a *kinescope*, basically a special camera aimed at a small, high-resolution TV display. In 1956 the *videotape recorder* (*VTR*) was introduced, which records on magnetic tape. VTRs are sometimes called *tape decks*, or just *decks*. Later tape decks use tape in cassettes, although the term *videocassette recorder* or *VCR* is usually reserved for machines used by the consumer in the home. More recently, video recording is also done directly to computer hard drives, to various forms of optical discs like DVDs, and to

---

3. In France and Russia, video is produced in PAL but broadcast in SECAM (*Séquentiel Couleur à Mémoire*), which has the same frame rate and number of lines.

Fig. 1-4. Camcorder. The JVC GY-HD110 records HDV and DV. Accepts detachable lenses. (JVC Professional Products)

reusable digital media cards using Flash memory. When a camera and recorder are combined in one unit, it's called a *camcorder*.

Video can be viewed on a *monitor*. Types of flat-screen monitors include *liquid crystal display* (*LCD*), which is what many computers use, and *plasma* screens. Video can also be projected on a large screen using LCD technology or *Digital Light Processing* or *DLP* which uses thousands of tiny micro-mirrors (for more on monitors, see p. 197).

The traditional analog video monitor is based on the *cathode ray tube* or *CRT*. Typical older TVs are CRTs. Inside a CRT monitor, a cathode ray gun fires a stream of electrons at the back of the video screen (the side opposite from the one you watch). The inside of the screen is coated with a phosphor surface that glows when it is excited by the ray of electrons. The ray "paints" the image on the screen, line by line. The higher the current of the ray, the brighter the screen glows.

So, to review, let's track the steps of how the video system translates an image of the world to the TV screen: First, the image is projected by the camera lens onto the camera's sensor. The brighter areas in the image create a higher electric charge at the pixels in those areas of the sensor. The higher charge eventually results in a higher electrical current sent to

Fig. 1-5. Videotape recorder, or VTR. Panasonic AG-DV2500 records and plays DV and plays DVCAM. (Panasonic Broadcast)

those areas of the monitor, which produces a brighter glow in that part of the screen. The brightness of the video signal is called *luminance* or *luma*.

Analog Versus Digital

Until the 1980s, most video and audio production was done with analog equipment. In analog tape recorders, continuously changing video or audio signals are recorded as continuously changing amounts of magnetism on tape. Today, most new recording equipment is digital. In digital recorders, the video or audio signal is converted to a set of numbers that can then be stored in various ways (for more on how digital works see p. 372 for audio and p. 208 for video).

Fig. 1-6. Sony XDCAM HD high definition cameras and decks. (Sony Electronics, Inc.)

There are many advantages to digital recording. Once sounds or images are in digital form, a whole world of possibilities is opened up for storing, editing, manipulating, and transmitting them. And you can achieve high quality at lower cost.

Analog equipment can produce excellent results too, but analog recording has a particular problem when it comes to making copies (which is a frequent need during production and distribution). When you make a copy of an analog tape (called a *dub*), noise can build up and other distortions can be introduced. On a sound recording, this may be noticeable as a low hiss during quiet passages. In video, copying can cause increased grain or contrast in the image. After several *generations* (making copies of copies) this can be a real problem. Copies of digital recordings, on the other hand, can be perfect clones, with no difference between the generations.[4]

Despite the advantages of digital, it's important to remember that just because something is digital doesn't necessarily mean it sounds or looks good. While the digital process is capable of high quality, it's perfectly possible to make a low-resolution, low-quality digital recording (and this is often done deliberately for various reasons).

---

4. Though not all digital copies are clones, and in some situations adding generations digitally *does* degrade the recording.

There is still a great deal of analog equipment in use today—the transition to an all-digital world will take some time. Almost all digital video equipment includes some analog components, such as CCD or CMOS sensors (yes, they're analog) or analog microphone inputs on a camcorder or digital audio recorder. It's common to convert sounds and images back and forth between analog and digital forms when needed, though there is some quality loss each time you do.[5] Ideally, once the video and audio are in digital form, they should stay in the digital domain for as much as the production process as possible.

A note on terminology: There are many video formats that are digital. One particular digital video format called DV, for "Digital Video," uses economical ¼-inch videotape along with a type of digital signal compression also called DV. It's best known as the format used in MiniDV camcorders. In this book, the term digital video is used to refer to *all* digital formats, and DV means that particular format.

THE VIDEO FORMAT

Video format refers to how many lines or pixels form an image, the basic shape of the picture, how a signal is processed or compressed along the way, what medium it's recorded onto, what broadcast standard is used, and a host of other technical aspects of how video is captured, transmitted, or reproduced. There are many formats in use today—so many that even professionals get confused trying to keep track of them all. Part of the confusion is due to the transition from older analog standards to newer digital ones. Whereas the original 1953 NTSC broadcast standard contained only *one* format, today's *ATSC (Advanced Television Systems Committee)* standard defines eighteen different format variations for digital TV broadcast in the U.S. and some other former NTSC countries.

Though various video formats are defined by their key differences, they all have a lot in common. Let's look at the different ways that video formats capture images and sound.

Fig. 1-7. Canon Elura consumer DV camcorder. (Canon U.S.A., Inc.)

How Many Pixels: Standard and High Definition

A digital video image is formed by a rectangular grid of pixels (see Fig. 5-16). Each pixel represents the brightness (and color, if any) of that part of the image. The *frame* is all the pixels that can be seen in the picture (these are known as *active pixels*). It helps to visualize the pixel grid as a set of horizontal lines or rows stacked

5. There can also be quality loss when converting between different digital formats.

on top of one another, since that's how the picture information is processed. As described above, rows of horizontal pixels form horizontal lines called *scan lines*, and the total pattern of all the lines together is called the *raster*.

Video formats differ in how many pixels and how many lines they have (see Fig. 1-8).

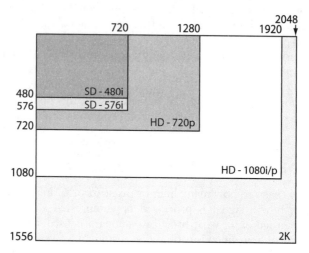

Fig. 1-8. Pixel counts. This shows the number of pixels in standard definition 480i (NTSC countries) and 576i (PAL countries), high definition 720p and 1080i/p, and a full 2K scan. Note that for CCD or CMOS sensors, pixel count is not the same as physical size (a high definition camera might have a sensor that's smaller or larger than the sensor in a standard definition camera). As shown here, NTSC- and PAL-based formats have different pixel counts, but when viewed onscreen, the shape of their frames is actually the same (which is accomplished by using different-shaped pixels).

Digital *standard definition television* (also called *SDTV*, *SD*, or *standard def*) has the smallest number of pixels of the broadcast formats. In NTSC territories, the standard definition frame is a rectangle of about 480 active horizontal lines, each 720 pixels wide (this is often indicated as 720 x 480 and pronounced "720 by 480"). In PAL territories the SD picture has 576 active horizontal lines, also 720 pixels wide.

High definition television (*HDTV*, *HD*, or *high def*) uses more pixels per frame. How many more? There are two flavors of HD. The original HD format is 1920 x 1080 (1080 horizontal lines, each 1920 pixels wide). This format has a total of around two million pixels or 2 megapixels (Mpx). A smaller HD format is 1280 x 720, which is a little less than 1Mpx.

Why do we care about the number of pixels? As the pixel count goes up, so does the ability to record fine detail in the image, allowing for a clearer, sharper picture. Formats that have more pixels are considered higher *resolution* (there are other factors that contribute to resolution, as well). On a very small screen, you might not be able to see a big difference between SD and HD. But the larger the screen size, the worse SD looks: There may be an overall fuzziness or lack of detail and you may see the individual pixels, which makes the picture look "digital" and not natural. High definition formats allow you to display the image on a bigger screen while still maintaining sharpness and clarity. Bigger screens give a more cinema-like viewing experience.

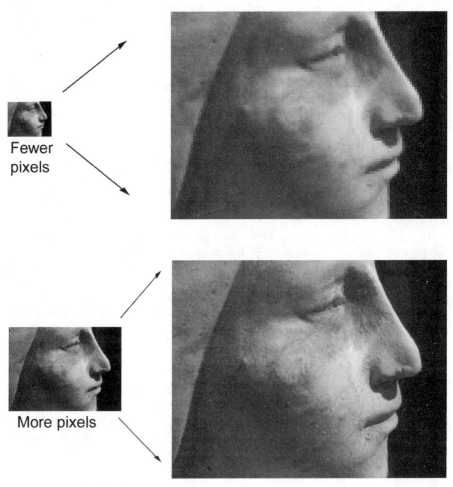

Fig. 1-9. (top) When you enlarge a low-resolution image, it starts to look unsharp. You may begin to see individual pixels and unwanted artifacts like the jagged line on the edge of the nose. (bottom) When a higher-resolution image is enlarged, it retains more of its sharpness and clarity. This is one reason why high definition video looks better than standard definition, especially on a big screen.

When it comes to an *actual* cinema experience—widescreen projection in a large theater—there are digital motion picture formats that use even higher pixel counts than HD video. Sony's SXRD *digital cinema* projector can display a *4K* format (4096 pixels wide by 2160 high). At this resolution, digital capture rivals (or surpasses, according to some) the resolution of 35mm film.

Converting between formats that have different pixel counts is sometimes called *scaling* or *rescaling*. Going from low resolution to high resolution is *upconverting*, *upscaling*, or *up-resing* (pronounced "up-rezzing" and sometimes spelled with a *z*). Going the other way is *downconverting*, *downscaling*, or *down-resing*. When material shot in high definition is downconverted to standard definition, the footage will generally look better than material that was originally shot in SD. Standard definition footage that is upscaled to HD will never look as good as material that originated in high def.

DIFFERENCES WITH ANALOG. Analog video formats don't use pixels the way digital formats do. Each analog frame has a pattern of horizontal lines, but each scan line is continuous and not broken up into individual pixels. A tube-based analog camera (used from the origins of TV until the early 1990s) captured brightness levels all the way across a scan line, then briskly returned to the left side, moved down one line, then scanned across again, somewhat like the motion of a typewriter. This is similar to the way your eye takes in a paragraph of written text. When the thin electron beam in the tube camera reached the bottom of the screen, it returned to the top and started over. This is still how analog CRT monitors display video (see the monitor in Fig. 1-3).

In a similar fashion, analog broadcast signals received by your TV at home describe continuously scanned lines, not rows of pixels. While NTSC creates a total of 525 scan lines, only 483 are *active lines*—that is, visible on screen. (It's worth noting—and you'll be reminded again—that strictly speaking, the terms "NTSC" and "PAL" refer only to *analog* formats, not digital formats that have similar frame size and frame rate, even though most people use the terms loosely to mean either analog or digital.)

PAL and SECAM create a total of 625 horizontal scan lines (576 active), which means they enjoy higher vertical resolution than NTSC.

Progressive and Interlace Scanning

When a modern CCD or CMOS camera uses *progressive scanning*, all the pixels of each frame are captured at the same instant in time. Progressive scanning is similar to the way a film camera exposes an entire frame at once, then moves on to the next frame. Processing one whole frame at a time is very simple, very clean.

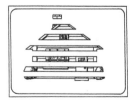 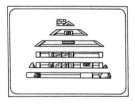 

Field 1   Field 2   Complete frame

Fig. 1-10. Interlace. Each field contains half the horizontal video lines. When the two fields are shown rapidly one after the other, the eye integrates them into one complete frame with all the lines. (Robert Brun)

An earlier method, still in wide use, is *interlace scanning*. Interlace dates back to the first days of NTSC when television systems were too slow to capture and transmit an entire frame at time—it was just too much information.[6] With interlace, only half the frame is recorded or broadcast at a time. The camera starts at the top of the picture and works its way down, capturing odd-numbered lines (1, 3, 5, 7 . . .), while skipping the lines in between. This is the *upper field* (also called the *odd field*). It then returns to the second line from the top and records the other half, the even-numbered lines (2, 4, 6, 8 . . .), all the way to the bottom. This is the *lower* or *even field*.[7] The two fields follow each other rapidly, and together they make one frame. When watching a TV, the reassembled half frames create a smooth video image.

Since there are two fields for every frame, NTSC, which operates at about 30 fps, can also be thought of as 60 fields per second. PAL runs at exactly 25 fps and fields are scanned at twice that rate—50 fields per second.

While interlace cameras are common, many feel that progressive scan (sometimes called *pro scan*) cameras are superior. To grasp the advantages of one you have to understand the disadvantages of the other.

The problems with interlace include, for starters, that you're seeing only half

Fig. 1-11. Interlace artifacts. Each interlace field contains only half of the horizontal lines. In this image you're seeing both fields together. Notice how the man in the foreground has moved between the two fields. You can see how each field has half the resolution, with obvious *edge tear* or *combing* along the edge of his shirt. The diagonal line behind the man in the background reveals an undesirable stairstep pattern called *aliasing* (which may also occur, to a lesser extent, with progressive formats). See also Fig. 18-8. (Stephen McCarthy)

6. If you think about it, broadcasting half frames to cut bandwidth in half was the original form of video compression.

7. In many formats, like DV, the lower fields are recorded first. See Field Order, p. 572.

the lines at a time, which means lower resolution.[8] Interlace creates various *artifacts* (flaws or irregularities in the image). One artifact is that diagonal lines in the scene can end up looking like jagged stair steps on TV (see Fig. 1-11). This is called *aliasing*.[9] Another artifact called *twitter* happens when thin horizontal lines appear to vibrate or flicker as they move up or down in the frame. This is often visible in the text of a credit roll at the end of a movie.

Another motion artifact comes from the fact that cameras that use interlace scanning capture the odd scan lines first, then the even lines, which, upon playback, causes the parts of the image formed by the first field to appear a split second earlier in time than the parts captured by the second field. You can see this effect in slow-motion playback or freeze-framing of interlaced video frames, especially in the case of rapidly traveling objects that move laterally. Figure 1-11 shows both fields of an interlaced frame together. Notice how the man in the foreground has moved between the first field and the second, causing the edge of his body to have a torn, jagged look (this is called *edge tear* or *combing*). Edge tear doesn't happen with static (nonmoving) images. For shots with camera or subject movement, edge tear can reduce resolution when the video is playing at normal speed. If the video is slowed down (say, for sports replays) or frozen (for still images), edge tear can become much more bothersome.

When interlaced video is converted to progressive or is output to film, the picture needs to be *deinterlaced*. This is done by blending two fields together (or sometimes just discarding one of them) to create a single progressive frame. This is when motion artifacts like edge tear can be a real problem, and deinterlacing can result in lower resolution or strange-looking motion (for more on deinterlacing, see p. 720).

With progressive formats, most of these problems don't happen at all and aliasing is much minimized. Furthermore, modern display devices like LCDs, DLPs, and plasma screens are inherently progressive, so footage shot with a progressive camera plays nicely on them with no deinterlacing necessary. Progressive also works better with the compression used in digital broadcasting. There are many situations in which video needs to be resized, repositioned, or converted to different resolutions. These tasks are much easier to do at high quality if you're working with progressive. Similarly, if you're planning a transfer from video to film, progressive is a much better source.

As a rule, it's easy to convert progressive video to interlace if needed. It's harder to convert interlace to progressive with good results.

There *are* some potential drawbacks of progressive. Shooting in progressive makes the camera less sensitive, typically requiring an additional stop of light (twice as much) to get proper exposure. Compared to interlace, progressive requires more *bandwidth* (a fatter data "pipe") which can put more demands on recording, editing, and broadcasting equipment.

---

8. Though only half the pixels are seen at once, the resolution isn't cut in half—it's slightly better than that (about 70 percent of the full progressive resolution). When an interlace system displays, say, line 3 of the raster, it actually calculates that line by averaging together lines 2 and 3, which improves resolution a bit. This also improves low light sensitivity.

9. The term *aliasing* may also be used to mean any kind of distortion caused by not having enough digital samples to accurately record picture or sound.

Since most video equipment in use around the world is still interlace—though this is changing fast—working in progressive often requires finding ways to be compatible with it. As an example, a common technique for recording a progressive-scan image is to embed it in an interlace pattern that can be played on standard interlace decks and TVs (for more on this, see Working with 24p, p. 564).

When world video technology evolves and everything is progressive (as it should be), interlace, invented in the 1920s, will not be missed.

The Frame Rate

The number of frames recorded each second affects how motion appears on screen. Modern digital cameras may offer a choice of frame rates, but the legacy of different broadcast systems has imposed standard frame rates that filmmakers must work with (or work around).

The NTSC system used in North America and Japan was designed to run at 60 fields per second because the electric power in wall outlets in these countries runs at 60Hz. The original black-and-white TV signal was 60 fields, or 30 frames, every second.

In 1953, color TV was introduced, and to keep the new system compatible with the old one, a technical quirk required that the existing 30 fps frame rate be lowered by 0.1 percent. This made NTSC's *actual* frame rate 29.97 fps. For simplicity's sake, when people talk about this rate they often round it up to 30. In countries where NTSC is the rule, if you see a scanning rate expressed in a whole number, that's usually for convenience, and the actual frame rate is 0.1 percent lower. That is, 30 really means 29.97 and 60 fields per second really means 59.94 fields. 24 fps is a special case. In the case of most video cameras in these territories, 24 really means 23.976 fps (often written 23.98 fps). Unfortunately, there *are* times when 24 fps really means *exactly* 24 fps (such as when shooting with film cameras or with the latest digital cinematography cameras, see p. 606). To avoid confusion, it helps to be as precise as you can.

Happily, in the rest of the world where PAL and SECAM are the rule, 25 fps is *exactly* 25 fps and 50 fields per second is exactly 50 fields.

For more on the look of different frame rates and choosing one for your production, see Frame Rate and Scanning Choices, p. 97.

The Shape of the Video Frame

Aspect ratio is a term used to describe the shape of the picture, the ratio of the frame's width to its height (see Fig. 1-12). Unlike film, video possesses only two aspect ratios, 4:3 and 16:9.

Traditional standard definition television has an aspect ratio of 4:3, which means four units wide by three units high. In video this is pronounced "four by three" and is sometimes written 4 x 3. In film, the same thing is described as 1.33, the quotient of 4 divided by 3.

Widescreen video is 16:9, pronounced "sixteen by nine" or "sixteen to nine," or written as 16 x 9. In film, the same aspect ratio is described as 1.78. Standard definition video can be either 4:3 or 16:9. All forms of high definition are 16:9.

Increasingly many video cameras possess 16:9-shaped sensors. Most of these are capable of shooting a widescreen 16:9 image and recording it in a standard

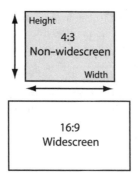

Fig. 1-12. The aspect ratio is the width of the frame divided by its height. Non-widescreen video has an aspect ratio of 4:3, and widescreen is 16:9.

Fig. 1-13. High definition widescreen CRT monitors. (Sony Electronics, Inc.)

definition 4:3 frame. There are several ways this can be done. For more on aspect ratio, see p. 87.

How Color Is Recorded

Inside your eyeballs are cones, natural sensors that allow you to see color. One type of cone is sensitive to red light, another to blue light, and the third to green. When you look around a room, every color you see is a mix of red, green, and blue light in different proportions.

The sensors in a video camera also measure the relative amounts of red, green, and blue light in the image. Actually, a CCD or CMOS chip "sees" only in black-and-white (it measures only brightness) but it can be tricked into reading color. One method, used in single-chip color cameras, is to fit tiny red, green, and blue filters over individual pixels. In the generally superior three-chip color cameras, a beam-splitting prism behind the lens divides the incoming image into separate red, green, and blue (RGB) components and sends each to a separate sensor (see Fig. 1-14).

RGB, COMPONENT, AND COMPOSITE COLOR. Capturing color sounds like an easy process—just record each red (R), green (G), and blue (B) signal from the sensor. Indeed, computers natively create and reproduce RGB signals, in which information about the three colors is simply recorded and processed in three separate paths. This method is known as *RGB color*. This is also used in professional digital still cameras that capture uncompressed images (called *RAW* files).

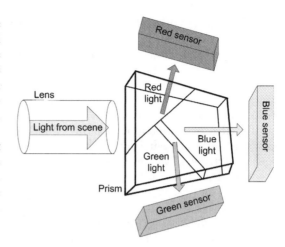

But video uses a different method that originated years ago. Black-and-white TV had a single brightness signal called *luminance*. When color was introduced, two color signals called *chrominance* (or "color difference") were added. Nearly all video today, analog and digital, is based on this technique of encoding the camera's original RGB signals into one luminance (brightness) and two chrominance (color) signals (see Fig. 5-9).

Fig. 1-14. In a three-chip camera, light entering though the lens strikes a prism which divides it into its red, green and blue components. Each is captured by a separate sensor.

The three encoded signals are called *component* signals. Videotape formats which maintain separation of these signals are called *component video*. Digital component tape formats include D-1, Digital Betacam, DV (including DVCAM and all forms of DVCPRO), HDV, and HDCAM. Betacam is an analog component tape format.

It's not uncommon these days to hear people refer to "RGB component video" when they mean RGB. In this book, *component video* means a true video signal which contains separate luminance and chrominance components that can be recorded to a VTR. Keep in mind, though, that both component video and RGB systems represent a component signal approach to electronically capturing motion images. They maintain high-quality color because the color components are processed in *separate* streams; this allows the cleanest color and highest-quality image.

In *composite video*, which is the basis of traditional NTSC and PAL analog broadcast television, the video component signals are further combined (which is also called encoding) into *one* signal that can travel on a single path. Composite can be thought of as "video soup," since all the color and brightness information, as well as audio and sync signals, are mixed together into a single electronic signal. Composite video makes recording and broadcasting simpler, but results in a marked loss of image quality.

These days composite video is found mainly in analog television and VHS video. Both component video and RGB are common in high-end consumer systems. Digital broadcast, cable, and satellite exclusively use component signals, as do digital cameras and disc players.[10] Eventually, composite video will become obsolete.

See p. 192 for more on composite and component systems.

---

10. D2 and D3 are digital tape formats that are composite, but they are becoming obsolete.

COLOR SAMPLING. In the RGB color system just discussed, all of the color information captured by the camera can be recorded and displayed. For motion picture production, the most sophisticated HD cameras, such as Sony's HDC-F950 (used for *Star Wars: Episode III*) and Grass Valley's Viper FilmStream, can output uncompressed RGB signals, with no color data reduction or encoding of any kind. The drawback is that these cameras produce an enormous amount of data to be processed and stored.

To reduce the amount of data, most digital video cameras make use of the fact that when looking at fine details, the human eye is much more sensitive to brightness than to color.[11] High-end component video cameras throw away half of their color pixels (which reduces the color detail and data by half compared to luminance) and most viewers can't see that anything's missing—this is how we're used to looking at video.[12]

A shorthand has developed to describe this technique of throwing away color information: *4:2:2.* If all of the camera's luminance signal is recorded (represented by "4") but only half of each of the chrominance signals ("2" and "2"), then what do we have? We have the costly D-1 format, the gold standard of standard def digital video—for years the best there was.

Economical formats like DV are designated 4:1:1 or 4:2:0 and record only one quarter as much color information as brightness data. Again, in a typical viewing experience most people can't see the difference. In fact, the range of color values (the *color gamut*) in DV is the same as in 4:2:2 video, there's just less color information in the fine details. However, this lowered color sampling may make it more difficult to do special effects like green screen work (see Fig. 14–24).

By comparison, RGB systems with no data reduction are 4:4:4 and the data rates (before compression, if any) can be upwards of 600 Mbps, or 24 times the rate of DV.

For more on color sampling see p. 196.

What Do You Call That Format?

As you've noticed, there are an awful lot of numbers and letters thrown around when talking about video. It's easy to get confused, and the situation isn't helped by the fact that different people use different letters and numbers to talk about the same thing.

These days, the most common notation used to describe a format is:

- the number of active horizontal lines per frame (say, 480 or 1080),
- followed by *p* or *i* (for progressive or interlace),
- followed by the number of scans per second (the frame rate or field rate).

So, a format indicated as *720p/24* tells us that the frame has 720 horizontal lines, scanned at 24 progressive frames per second. PAL video is sometimes called 576i/25 (576 lines, interlaced, at 25 fps).

11. The eye registers most picture detail in the green part of the color spectrum, and green makes up over 70 percent of the luminance signal.
12. Note that this step would never be accepted in still photography!

However, with interlaced formats, often it's the *field rate* not the frame rate that's indicated (remember, there are two fields for every interlaced frame). So the same PAL format can be written 576i/50. This is the convention you'll find in this book (using the frame rate for progressive and the field rate for interlace.) NTSC video would be written 480i/60.

In ads, articles, and equipment manuals, notation varies in small and large ways. For example, 1080p/24 may be written 1080/24p. Sometimes people don't indicate the frame or field rate at all. PAL may be called just 576i, since people know it runs at 25 frames per second.

Sometimes when people are talking about the motion and look of video they'll just refer to the frame or field rate *without* the frame size, such as 24p or 60i.[13]

As noted earlier, NTSC and PAL are broadcast formats that use analog composite signals. To talk about *digital* NTSC or PAL doesn't really make sense. However, for convenience many people use these terms to refer to digital video that has roughly the same frame size and rate. So you'll hear people refer to NTSC DV when they mean digital video that's 720 x 480 at 29.97 fps.

No one said this stuff is simple, and don't feel bad if you're confused! Believe it or not, these terms will sort themselves out as you use them.

Fig. 1-15. A Steadicam being used to shoot from an awkward spot. (The Tiffen Company)

---

13. And, as mentioned on p. 15, when you see 60i it really means 59.94i. As for 24p, in NTSC countries it usually means the video rate (23.98p) but sometimes it's the film rate (exactly 24p).

DIGITAL COMPRESSION

As time goes on, consumers and content providers expect ever-higher quality and definition from their video systems. The problem is that high definition video in its native state involves lots and lots of digital data that has to be captured, stored, and transmitted. Working with all that data can be expensive because it calls for big storage devices, fast computers, and high-speed connections for broadcasting or Internet distribution.

At the same time, consumers and content providers want formats that are affordable, easy to work with, and flexible enough to display on screens big and small.

To balance these two needs we have *digital compression*.

The goal of compression is to shrink digital video and audio data down to a smaller size while maintaining picture and sound quality. After images and sound have been compressed, they take up less storage space on tape or on computer disks. This allows us to use smaller, cheaper camcorders (production), load more footage into an editing system (postproduction), or fit a longer movie onto a disc for playback at home (distribution).

A crude analogy to compressed video is instant coffee, which is made by taking brewed coffee and removing the water to make a powder that's compact and easy to store. To drink it, you have to add the water back, restoring the coffee to something close to its original form and (hopefully) taste.

With digital compression, video and audio signals are compressed into a smaller package for storage and transmission. When it's time to view or listen to them, they must be decompressed (expanded). The intent is that the decompressed video will resemble the original as closely as possible. Compression schemes are called *codecs* (from *co*mpressor/*dec*ompressor or *co*der/*dec*oder).[14]

There are many different codecs in use. Some are designed to maintain the highest picture quality, others to shrink the amount of data as much as possible. Most try to do both to some extent. If you've ever downloaded music from the Internet you've worked with an audio codec such as *Mp3* or the superior *AAC*. These codecs shrink the size of the original music file to speed up downloading and allow you to store more songs on your music player. As codecs evolve, engineers are finding ways to make files smaller while maintaining better quality.

One way to compare video formats is to look at how much data they create (the *data rate* or *bit rate*). This is often measured in *megabits per second* (*Mbps or Mb/s*). For example, to record or playback uncompressed standard definition video requires about 172 Mbps, while the compressed DV25 format uses only 25 Mbps. The data rate depends in part on the size of the frame and other factors, as well as how much the video is compressed (if at all) before it's recorded. The amount of compression is often indicated as a ratio between the original size of the video/audio data and its compressed size. For example, the DigiBeta format uses 2:1 compression (cutting the data rate in half) for a bit rate of about 90 Mbps. Uncompressed video would have a 1:1 ratio.

People often assume that the greater the compression (and thus the lower the

---

14. Sometimes a codec is a software-only mathematical formula called an *algorithm*, and sometimes the algorithm resides in a chip also called a codec.

data rate) the worse the material will look or sound after it's decompressed. But there has been remarkable progress in recent years and some codecs that are very compressed—called *lossy*—are capable of astonishingly high picture and sound quality. Since the mid-1990s, for instance, MPEG-2 compression has made possible DVDs, ATSC digital TV broadcasting, and lately the HDV format, while newer, more efficient MPEG-4 codecs like H.264 are finding widespread use in streaming SD and HD on the Internet.

With other codecs—called *lossless*—a side-by-side comparison of uncompressed video and the same material after it has been compressed and decompressed by the codec shows virtually no difference. Examples include Sony's high-end HDCAM SR compression (MPEG-4) and Avid's DNxHD compression.

Codecs that employ a high degree of compression may require a lot of computing power to get the job done, which can make working with them slow, depending on your equipment. It's important to understand compression and have a feel for the codecs currently being used because compression plays a key role in what video format you choose to work in, what camera you use, how you edit, and how you distribute your movie.

For more on compression, see p. 222.

SOUND RECORDING FOR VIDEO

Most video sound recording is done right in the camera—the sound is recorded with the picture to tape or disk. Different cameras and video formats have different configurations of soundtracks. Most formats allow for two audio channels. Some formats allow you to record four separate tracks. For some productions, having multiple tracks can provide great flexibility, since you can assign different

Fig. 1-16. Two-person video crew. The sound recordist carries a boom microphone and a mic mixer, shown here connected to the camera by a cable. (Stephen McCarthy)

microphones to different channels. When it comes to distribution, having four tracks allows you to send out a movie for international use in two different versions (for example, a version with narration and one without). Regardless of what format you use to shoot your movie, postproduction almost always involves transfer to another format for mastering. So even if you shot the film with a two-channel DV camera, you could bump up to a four-channel format during editing and then release as a 5.1-channel DVD (see p. 654).

Most camcorders have a microphone or (also called a *mic*—pronounced "mike") built into the camera or mounted on it. On-camera mics are simple and convenient, but often result in poor sound, since the microphone is often too far from the sound source for optimal recording. Professionals generally use separate mics, which can be placed nearer the subject. The audio from the mic may be fed to the camcorder or VTR through a cable or by using a wireless transmitter. When there's a sound recordist on the crew, microphones are usually fed first to a mixer, which allows easy monitoring of sound levels and blending of multiple mics. Recording sound in the camera along with the picture is called *single system recording*.

Sound may also be recorded *double system* (sometimes called *dual system*), which means using a separate audio recorder. This may be done for a feature or concert film to achieve the highest quality, or because multiple audio tracks are needed. Sometimes this is done because the camera or format has poor recording capability or as a backup, in case there are problems with wireless transmitters, for example. Before you can work with the footage, sound from the audio recorder has to be married to the picture (synched up). This is often done in the editing system prior to editing.

See p. 383 for more on audio for video camcorders.

TIMECODE

Timecode is a digital time-stamp added to each video frame upon recording.

Since every frame has its own unique timecode number, or *address*, you can use it to quickly find images and sounds according to their timecode. Precise frame location is what makes nonlinear editing possible. Most digital video cameras and some audio recorders generate and record a timecode signal whenever they're recording. Because the timecode count advances with each frame, you can also easily determine the running time of a shot or of an entire film.

Timecode looks like an advancing digital clock that counts hours, minutes, seconds, and frames. For example, 03:25:45:10 would be three hours, twenty-five minutes, forty-five seconds, and ten frames. These numbers are normally invisible but can be machine-read and displayed in various ways during recording or playback. In addition, timecode can be *burned in*—superimposed or incorporated into a little window over the picture (see Fig. 1-17). This can be helpful when people using different playback devices must refer to the same clips.

The SMPTE/EBU timecode in use today was standardized in the 1970s. In the United States and other NTSC countries, it is known as *SMPTE* (*Society of Motion Picture and Television Engineers*) timecode—pronounced "simpty." SMPTE

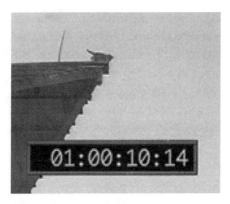

Fig. 1-17. Timecode. Shown here burned-in on screen.

timecode has a *timebase* of 29.97 fps and is used for all video with that frame rate, including HD.

In Europe and those parts of the world where the PAL broadcast standard predominates, the *EBU (European Broadcasting Union)* timecode is used, which has a timebase of 25 fps. A third variant of SMPTE/EBU timecode, used in 24p video recording and sometimes in film cameras, offers a timebase of 24 fps.

Analog consumer formats like VHS don't accommodate timecode in shooting. Some consumer digital formats use a simplified proprietary timecode that may be incompatible with other manufacturers' equipment. Material without timecode can still be edited, but certain operations can become more difficult (depending on the editing system); in some cases footage can be *post-striped* with timecode for editing.

For more on timecode, see p. 203.

COMPARING VIDEO FORMATS

This section will serve as an outline of common video formats. For more on choosing a format to work with see Chapter 2. If any of the terms below are unfamiliar, see earlier in this chapter and check the index.

THE EVOLUTION OF FORMATS. Video formats are constantly being invented, changed, and dropped as better formats arrive on the scene. Like buying a computer that may be outdated a few months after you get it, when you invest in a video format (either because you're purchasing gear or simply using it to shoot a project) you need to remember that a new, better format may be just around the corner. The upside is that video systems keep getting smaller, cheaper, and more powerful. The downside is that formats and equipment become obsolete. The movie you shoot today may need to be transferred to another format in several years when you can no longer find playback equipment in the old format.

At one time, format choices were few, and camera choices centered on what size tape they recorded to. Nowadays, cameras may offer a choice of formats, or different flavors of a given format, and may record to tape or directly to hard drives or memory cards. All this makes it hard to talk about formats in a simple way, and it's not helped by the fact that by the time you finish reading this paragraph, new cameras and formats will have been introduced.

It used to be that *all* video production was done in standard definition, and as of this writing, there is still a vast infrastructure of cameras, editing, and broadcast equipment that support SD. As time goes on, there is increasing pressure to produce and distribute work in high definition, and a lot of SD equipment will disappear.

HIGH END VS. LOW END. When manufacturers design and market a piece of equipment they generally try to target a certain type of user. The user categories are not exact, but in descending order of quality there is: broadcast, professional/industrial, prosumer, home/consumer. The assumption is that professionals will pay top prices and can handle complexity, while consumers want something cheap and easy to use. Revolutions have been made, particularly by independents, in seizing tools intended for the lower end of the market and showing that they can produce professional-quality work. Footage shot with an inexpensive prosumer camera can sometimes look surprisingly like footage from a $40,000 professional rig if it's well shot and well lit and the sound is good. On the other hand, it's often true that you get what you pay for, and a high-end camera can provide more control and a better image.

When comparing formats, take a look at the data rate. Generally speaking, formats that are more compressed (i.e., that have a low data rate) are more affordable. The cameras are smaller and less expensive; you can store more material on a tape or hard drive; editing equipment can be simpler too. The highest-end equipment tends to use the least compression (and thus has high data rates) and is often preferred when the footage will be shown on a big screen. However, when deciding on a format, bear in mind that some formats that operate at a high data rate may be within your budget and, by the same token, formats that are less expensive and more compressed may still have excellent sound and picture quality.

MAKING CONNECTIONS. When comparing formats, another thing to consider is the technology used to connect pieces of equipment, such as the cable connection between a video deck and a hard drive. This is also related to the data rate. Connections that can pass a lot of data in a given amount of time are said to be *high bandwidth*. With formats that have a low data rate, you can use inexpensive, low bandwidth connections; higher data rates call for a fatter "pipe" to move all that information.

When the DV format was first introduced, one of the innovations was the use of *FireWire* (*IEEE 1394*, also called *iLINK*) technology. A FireWire cable allows a direct digital two-way connection between devices (for example, between a camera and an editing system or VTR). A single FireWire cable takes the place of numerous video, audio, and deck control cables normally used for input and output (see Fig. 1-18). FireWire connections are simple, inexpensive, and easily installed on most computers.

Formats with data rates that are much higher than DV require higher

Fig. 1-18. The single FireWire cable to the camera at left replaces all the cables pictured at right for video, audio, and deck control. (Bob Doyle)

bandwidth connections, which may add cost or complexity. *SDI (serial digital interface)* connections are used for uncompressed standard definition signals. *HD-SDI (high definition serial digital interface)* may be used for HD video. For more on these and other connections, see p. 216.

STANDARD DEFINITION DIGITAL FORMATS

Standard definition cameras in NTSC territories like North America and Japan record 525 lines, but only 480 "active" lines are actually visible. This is called 480i, which means an interlaced frame of 720 x 480 pixels.[15] In PAL territories like Europe, Australia, and parts of Asia, standard definition cameras record 625 lines with 576 active lines. This, in turn, is called 576i, with an interlaced frame size of 720 x 576 pixels. Some SD cameras can record progressive as well as interlace. All cameras record in 4:3 aspect ratio and many can shoot in widescreen 16:9 as well.

Formats labelled D-1 through D-10 are accepted industry-wide as world standards.

Fig. 1-19. Panasonic AG-DVX100B. This DV camcorder can shoot 60i and 24p.

15. ITU-R 601 video, used in the D-1 format and for conventional NTSC broadcast, is 720 x 486.

DV, Digital 8, DVCAM, and DVCPRO

DV (Digital Video) records an excellent component digital image on a very small tape cassette. Introduced in the mid-1990s, DV revolutionized independent and multimedia production. Suddenly, for a few thousand dollars filmmakers could shoot and edit with gear that rivaled or surpassed analog equipment costing tens of thousands more. Before long, DV-originated material found its way into the broadcast world and, once transferred to film, into theaters.

The basic DV codec (also called DV25 for its 25 Mbps data rate) uses 5:1 compression with 4:1:1 color sampling (the PAL version is 4:2:0). The quality of the DV picture can be *very* good, but it depends a lot on the particular camera. When shown on large screens, DV material may show artifacts caused in part by the compression. Also, if you plan to do a lot of visual effects, the 4:1:1 or 4:2:0 color subsampling is not ideal, since it represents a loss of picture detail.

The consumer version was originally called DVC (digital video cassette) but is usually referred to as *MiniDV* for the small cassettes intended for small cameras (the tape itself is about 6mm wide, or ¼ inch). Sony's *Digital8* cameras record the same codec to 8mm videotape, useful for people who already have a movie collection on analog Hi8 tapes (see p. 39).

For broadcast and professional use, Sony makes DVCAM and Panasonic makes DVCPRO. Both of these formats use the same 25 Mbps codec and ¼-inch tape as MiniDV, but have certain professional enhancements. The tape goes through the camcorder faster, reducing the chance of *dropouts* (momentary loss of recording). DVCAM and DVCPRO cameras accommodate MiniDV-sized tape cassettes and many accept a full-sized cassette shell that's several inches larger and can hold more tape (see Fig. 2-8). The professional-grade cameras allow more control over things like timecode settings than many MiniDV cameras. Panasonic's DVCPRO decks can play DV and DVCAM tapes (the MiniDV tapes require a cassette adapter). Most DVCAM machines cannot play DVCPRO cassettes.

Some DVCPRO cameras can also do progressive recording (see p. 12).

All of these formats can be used with simple FireWire connections.

DVCPRO50 and D-9

Panasonic makes camcorders that combine two 25 Mbps DV codecs to record in DVCPRO50 (sometimes called DV50), a 50 Mbps format with superior 4:2:2 color sampling and an image quality that rivals Digital Betacam but at lower cost. Compression is 3.3:1. DVCPRO50 tape travels twice as fast through the camcorder, which means that a cassette will last half as long compared to shooting DVCPRO25. Like DV25, DVCPRO 50 can also be used with FireWire.

JVC makes camcorders in the *D-9* format (sometimes called *Digital S*), which record DV50 to a special metal-particle ½-inch tape in a VHS-sized cassette. Some D-9 decks can play back analog S-VHS as well.

Digital Betacam

Sony's *Digital Betacam* format (also called *DigiBeta* or *D-Beta*) is a high-quality ½-inch tape format based on the familiar Betacam cassette. DigiBeta records with 4:2:2 color sampling, which makes it good for effects work, and uses 2:1 lossless compression (about 90 Mbps). Most people can't see the difference between 2:1 and uncompressed video.

DigiBeta was one of the earliest professional digital formats (the first to use SDI connections); it can record four uncompressed PCM audio channels and is used very widely around the world for both production and postproduction. Often projects shot on lower resolution SD formats are finished on DigiBeta. The cost and size of the DigiBeta camcorder and its compact ½-inch tape cassettes make it a tool for professionals; even so, the camera is easily hand-holdable (see Fig. 10-14).

Betacam SX and MPEG IMX (D-10)

Sony's *Betacam SX* and *MPEG IMX* are also ½-inch tape formats based on the familiar Betacam cassette, but use MPEG-2 compression. SX employs a type of MPEG-2 compression (for more on MPEG-2, see p. 224). This technique yields visually seamless results for newsgathering, the intended purpose of SX. The higher quality IMX format, also called D-10, uses only I-frames to bring the advantages of advanced compression while sidestepping the editing obstacles created by ordinary MPEG-2 interframe compression.

Betacam SX uses a 25 Mbps MPEG-2 codec, and MPEG IMX uses a 50 Mbps MPEG-2 codec. Both use 4:2:2 color sampling. Some IMX decks play Digi-Beta and Beta SP tapes as well as IMX. MPEG IMX camcorders offer progressive scanning.

XDCAM

The same MPEG IMX codec is also used in Sony's optical disc–based *XDCAM*, an example of a newer generation camcorder that combines several formats into a single system. XDCAMs can record in MPEG IMX at 30, 40, or 50 Mbps for highest picture quality, or you can switch to DVCAM at lower quality for longer recording times.

The XDCAM format records to blue-laser optical discs (based on the consumer Blu-ray standard) housed in a cartridge that can be popped out of the camera and into a deck (see Fig. 1-23). The cartridge can also be put in a drive unit to transfer the data to a laptop, hard drive, or network. Sony claims the XDCAM format is more robust than tape and provides a lot of versatility for recording, editing, and broadcast (see also XDCAM HD, p. 31).

Postproduction Formats: D-1, D-2, D-3, D-5

There are several professional digital cassette formats that have been used primarily for postproduction.

Sony's *D-1*, introduced in 1986, was the first format capable of recording uncompressed component video. It uses 8-bit precision with 4:2:2 color sampling. The D-1 cassette uses ¾-inch tape and offers four tracks of uncompressed PCM audio. Many people incorrectly use the term D-1 video to mean component digital video.

Partly because D-1 is expensive, other formats such as Panasonic's D-5 have replaced D-1 for high-quality production and postproduction. D-5 is also uncompressed 4:2:2, but it is 10-bit, offers eight audio channels, and 120 minutes of continuous recording. (There is also a high def version, D-5 HD; see p. 30.)

Ampex's D-2 and Panasonic's D-3 are obsolete composite formats and should be avoided.

HIGH DEFINITION DIGITAL FORMATS

There are two basic types of high definition video: 1080i (1920 x 1080 pixels, interlaced) and 720p (1280 x 720 pixels, progressive). True 1920 x 1080 is sometimes called *full raster* since this is the largest frame approved for broadcast, but many cameras that work in 1080i record less than the full 1920 pixel width. 1080i HDCAM and HDV camcorders, for instance, record only 1440 pixels across. Such sub-sampling is one of several techniques used to squeeze huge HD signals onto small-gauge tape formats. At a higher-quality level and data rate than 1080i, some production is now done in 1080p.

All HD cameras shoot in 16:9 widescreen aspect ratio.

HDV

When the DV format was introduced in the mid-1990s, it provided an affordable way to record compressed, standard definition video to a very small tape cassette. DV quickly became enormously popular with filmmakers working on a tight budget. HDV is the high definition equivalent. *HDV (High Definition Video)* records to the same MiniDV cassettes as DV, and the signal is sent through the same FireWire as DV. The magic trick was to use a more efficient MPEG-2 compression instead of DV compression. Targeted originally at consumers, HDV makes high definition production surprisingly affordable and has caught on very fast with professionals.

There are two flavors of HDV. Both use 4:2:0 color sampling, in which only a quarter of the original color samples are preserved.

- HDV-1, introduced by JVC, is 720p (1280 x 720, progressive). HDV frame rates include 25p, 30p, 50p, and 60p, although JVC has added 24p for professional applications. JVC calls the format ProHD.

Fig. 1-20. Canon XL H1. Records HDV and DV and can output uncompressed HD. (Canon U.S.A., Inc.)

- HDV-2, introduced by Sony and used also by Canon, is 1080i (1440 x 1080, interlaced). Frame rates include 50i and 60i. Both Sony and Canon camcorders also offer 24, 25, and 30 fps rates, which simulate progressive capture (for more on this, see p. 104), and some newer Sony camcorders, such as the HVR-V1U, can do actual 24p.

HDV camcorders available at this time will record *either* 1080i or 720p, not both, and may not do all the frame rates listed above. All will internally downconvert and record standard definition interlaced video (480i or 576i) to MiniDV, which often looks better than material shot on comparably priced standard def DV cameras. Some can also capture progressive SD at frame rates including 24p, 25p, 50p, and 60p. Sony HDV camcorders, for instance, can at the same time record HDV to tape and output a downconverted MiniDV signal with matching timecode via FireWire.

HDV uses a form of MPEG-2 compression with a long "group of pictures" or GOP (for more on this, see p. 224). HDV-1 uses a 6-frame GOP and HDV-2 uses a 15-frame GOP. In the latter case, this means that among each group of 15 compressed frames, only one frame actually exists. In other words, HDV is highly compressed. The 1080i version is compressed about 22:1 for a data rate of 25 Mbps. The 720p version starts with fewer pixels and requires less compression—17:1— for a data rate of 19.7 Mbps. However, bear in mind that in either case you are recording an HD picture that has a lot more pixels than SD at a data rate the same or lower than plain old standard def DV25. There's no free lunch, and this amount of compression can create issues in shooting, sound recording, and editing (see p. 225). Nevertheless, HDV represents a quantum leap in picture resolution from DV at a price that's not a lot higher.

DVCPRO HD

Panasonic's DVCPRO HD format is a 100 Mbps high definition format with 4:2:2 color and 6.7:1 compression. It uses DV *intraframe* compression, meaning that each frame is individually compressed for simplified editing and postproduction (in contrast to MPEG-2 and HDV, which compress long GOPs; see p. 225). Like DV25, it is friendly to laptop editing if you have adequate storage available. Think of it as DV25 times four.

DVCPRO HD is the format of Panasonic's versatile Varicam camcorder, which can record at frame rates from 1 to 60 fps using the same size tape cassettes as standard def DVCPRO camcorders. Panasonic's smaller HVX200 camcorder employs the DVCPRO HD codec too, but captures to P2 Flash memory cards instead of to tape (see Fig. 2-9).

Fig. 1-21. Panasonic AG-HVX200. Versatile camcorder can record high definition DVC-PRO HD to P2 memory cards and standard definition DV to tape. (Panasonic Broadcast)

Although most Panasonic HD camcorders are native 720p, DVCPRO HD can also handle 1080i. In either case, DVCPRO HD horizontally sub-samples. In 720p, full-raster 1280 x 720 is recorded as 960 x 720; and in 1080i/60 and 1080p/24p, full-raster 1920 x 1080 is recorded as 1280 x 1080. In spite of this, DVCPRO HD is considered by many an ideal choice for economical HD postproduction and mastering. Both 720p and 1080i DVCPRO HD formats are readily sent through FireWire.

D-5 HD

D-5 HD, based on ½-inch tape cassettes, is Panasonic's highest-quality HD mastering format with data rates up to 235 Mbps. A D-5 HD recorder can be switched between an 8-bit mode that uses 4:1 compression and a 10-bit mode that compresses 5:1. D-5 HD accommodates all 1080-line HD formats at a full HD raster of 1920 pixels, as well as 720-line HD formats. D-5 is an industry workhorse.

D-9 HD

D-9 HD is a high definition version of JVC's ½-inch D-9 format which, much like DVCPRO HD, records at 100 Mbps using the DV100 codec with 6.6:1 compression. It offers eight audio tracks.

HDCAM and HDCAM SR

Sony's HDCAM records HD video on ½-inch Betacam-style cassettes. HDCAM cameras and camcorders capture 1080 lines in both interlace and progressive formats. The HDCAM signal recorded to tape is sub-sampled 1440 x 1080 with 3:1:1 color, using 7:1 compression for a data rate of 140 Mbps. Introduced in 1997, it was the first practical HD camcorder format.

Fig. 1-22. Sony HDW-F900R. High-end HDCAM camcorder. Produces 1080 HD at a variety of frame rates, including 24p. (Sony Electronics, Inc.)

Sony's later CineAlta family of HDCAM cameras, camcorders, and decks are designed to record at true 24p and are often used for high-end productions intending to transfer to 35mm film. (24p is almost always actually 23.98p in NTSC countries for compatibility with 29.97-based equipment used in SD postproduction and broadcasting.) CineAlta's other frame rates include 25p, 30p, 50i, and 60i.

In 2003, Sony introduced its highest-quality videotape format ever, HDCAM

SR (superior resolution)—440 Mbps, no pre-filtering or sub-sampling, only mild, lossless MPEG-4 compression of 4:4:4 RGB or component 4:2:2 HD video. A quantum leap above the original HDCAM, it's increasingly popular as an HD mastering format. First used as a field format in the making of *Star Wars: Episode III*, it is gaining popularity in Hollywood production. Because there is no HDCAM SR camcorder, Sony has made a small, portable HDCAM SR deck that mounts atop a CineAlta F950 camera to resemble a 400-foot 35mm film magazine, or at the rear of the camera for Steadicam use.

Fig. 1-23. Sony's XDCAM camcorders record to blue-laser discs contained in a dust-resistant cartridge. (Sony Electronics, Inc.)

XDCAM HD

Sony's XDCAM HD format uses the same single-sided, Blu-ray–based disc as standard definition XDCAM to capture 1080i/60 and 1080p/24. It employs long-GOP MPEG-2 at a choice of three data rates: 18 Mbps (variable bit rate), 25 Mbps (constant bit rate, functionally equivalent to HDV), and 35 Mbps (variable bit rate). The higher data rates provide best quality.

Like HDV, horizontal resolution is sub-sampled to 1440. XDCAM HD camcorders are fairly compact and economical and as of now use ½-inch CCDs instead of the ⅔-inch CCDs that have been more common on professional cameras. Sony nonetheless includes them in its high-end CineAlta HD camera family.

Use of blue-laser discs for HD mastering is unproven at this time, although Sony intends postproduction applications for XDCAM HD.

DNxHD

In 2004, Avid introduced a free "Open Standard" compressed HD codec, DNxHD, for both 8-bit and 10-bit 4:2:2 high definition up to 220 Mbps, including frame rates of 720p, 1080i, 1080p/24. What set DNxHD apart is lossless 2:1

compression and a full HD raster of 1920 horizontal pixels—no horizontal sub-sampling. Avid intends DNxHD to become a mastering compression format for post-production. Industry reaction has been positive, although DNxHD is so far found mainly in Avid editing and finishing products and in Ikegami's EditcamHD camcorder, which uses DNxHD to capture to removable 120 GB hard disk cartridges called FieldPaks or 8 GB RAMPaks.

JPEG2000

Grass Valley's tapeless Infinity camcorder records 10-bit SD and HD at all standard resolutions and frame rates, with a choice of codecs including DV25, MPEG-2, and a new intraframe codec, JPEG2000, the same compression chosen by Hollywood for theatrical digital projection. Grass Valley's inclusion of JPEG2000 in a camcorder is an industry first. Among its many advantages, the JPEG2000 codec is scalable and allows you to select data rates from 25 Mbps to 100 Mbps, giving you a lot of flexibility. Because JPEG2000 is wavelet-based—a different approach to compression than DV or MPEG-2—dropouts appear as fuzzy, out-of-focus patches instead of blocky, checkerboard patterns.

Fig. 1-24. Rev Pro media (hard disk cartridge) and drive. (Iomega Corporation)

Is JPEG2000 a format however? Tapeless capture requires new ways of thinking. To capture JPEG2000 files, the Infinity camcorder offers two slots for consumer-grade compact Flash memory, an internal bay for Iomega's innovative REV removable hard disk (see Fig. 1-24), and connectors for SDI, HD-SDI, FireWire, Gigabit Ethernet, HDMI (for direct digital display), and USB 2.0. Grass Valley calls this approach "IT-centric." (IT stands for information technology.) In other words, Infinity is a network-friendly computer shaped like a camcorder. Hard drives are the most likely recording medium for JPEG2000.

AVCHD and AVC-Intra

AVC, or Advanced Video Codec, is another name for the H.264 standard popularized by Apple. MPEG-4 AVC compression is twice as efficient as MPEG-2. Both consumer and professional camcorders use AVC.

The consumer version is called *AVCHD*. This is the consumer industry's answer to the tapeless HD recording trend that's reshaping the professional landscape. Some AVCHD camcorders use conventional—and cheap—DVD-R discs and others record directly to an internal hard drive. The creators of the AVCHD format,

Fig. 1-25. These Sony camcorders record high definition AVCHD as well as standard definition MPEG-2. (left) The HDR-UX1 records directly to a DVD in the camera. (right) The HDR-SR1 records to an internal hard drive. (Sony Electronics, Inc.)

Sony and Panasonic, recognize that it holds key advantages over HDV, being non-linear, dropout-proof, and mechanically simpler because there's no tape. AVCHD uses an 18 Mbps variable bit rate interframe compression to capture a full-raster image at 1920 x 1080 pixels—no horizontal sub-sampling like HDCAM, DVCPRO HD, and HDV—at 8-bits and 4:2:0. Frame rates include 1080i, 720p, and 1080p/24 (the latter is not included in the HDV standard), plus a choice of uncompressed PCM audio or lossless Dolby Digital AC-3 audio for multichannel surround.

AVC is being used at the pro level in Panasonic's P2 camcorders that record what Panasonic calls *AVC-Intra*. Unlike AVCHD's interframe compression, AVC-Intra uses intraframe compression (I-frames only, see p. 225), which makes editing and processing simpler. It provides highly efficient 10-bit encoding, with quality comparable to DVCPRO HD at half the data rate, so you can get twice as much material on a P2 card. The AVC-Intra codec has two modes: 100 Mbps, (very high quality, comparable to D-5 HD) and AVC-Intra 50 Mbps for high quality at a lower data rate. AVC-Intra is a promising codec that some believe is poised to become very popular in the industry.

DIGITAL CINEMATOGRAPHY SYSTEMS

What we call "video" today originated as broadcast television technology. In other words, all present video formats are descended from broadcast standards for things like pixel counts, line counts, and frame rates.[16] This legacy has resulted in a number of technical compromises.

To sidestep those compromises, a newer generation of electronic motion picture cameras called *digital cinematography cameras* has arrived. Think of them as digital still cameras that operate at 24 fps. Instead of using video formats, they capture images as a chain of uncompressed or compressed still images. "Digital cinematography" refers to high-quality acquisition using non-video 2K and 4K formats

---

16. The exception is the relatively recent adoption of the 24 fps frame rate for video. However, nearly all video camcorders with 24 fps capability can convert 24 fps to standard video frame rate for output.

Fig. 1-26. Digital cinematography camera. Arriflex D-20 has a Super 35–sized CMOS sensor and accepts standard PL mount 35mm cine lenses. It can output RAW data, 4:4:4 RGB, and other formats. (Arriflex Corporation)

on productions that previously would have been shot on film, often for theatrical release. Digital cinematography projects are often destined for transfer to film (also known as *film-out*) and may be shot at 24p or 25p. Some of the HD cameras discussed above can also be used for this purpose.

At the high end of cost and quality, there are camera systems designed to emulate the look and feel of 35mm motion picture cameras. Some of these have very large single CCD or CMOS sensors—as large as a 35mm film frame—allowing the use of 35mm film–style lenses, for the traditional feature film look (see p. 85). Many of them use high-bit-rate data formats (such as 4:4:4 log formats) that are not intended for direct viewing, but are used as "electronic intermediates" to provide a great deal of flexibility in post for creating different looks.

Camera systems with a large single sensor include the Dalsa Origin, which features a 35mm-sized CCD, optical viewfinder, and use of PL-mount film lenses; the Panavision Genesis, which features a 35mm-sized CCD, electronic viewfinder, use of existing Panavision 35mm film lenses, and a docking Sony HDCAM-SR recorder; and the Arri D-20, which features a 35mm-sized CMOS, optical viewfinder, and use of PL-mount lenses.

Camera systems with three conventional ⅔-inch CCD sensors and video B4 lens mounts include the Sony HDC-F950 and Grass Valley Viper FilmStream, which has a unique CCD architecture featuring a mechanical shutter that provides native widescreen aspect ratios in both 16:9 and 2.37:1 (no anamorphic lenses required). Both cameras output 4:4:4 RGB. The Sony 950 records to an HDCAM-SR VTR. The Viper records to a Venom FlashPak solid state recorder.

Note that of the above camera systems, only the Dalsa Origin is capable of 4K images. The Genesis, D-20, Sony 950, and Viper produce 1920 x 1080 images derived from HD video technology.

There are a number of small companies designing lower-cost digital cinematography cameras that are about the size of a 16mm handheld camera, each featuring a single CMOS sensor and PL-mount for use of film lenses. These include Silicon Imaging, Phantom, and RED and offer very high-quality images.

RECORDING TO DRIVES, DISCS, AND MEMORY CARDS

The job of a digital video camera is to turn light into digital data. How do we record and store that data? Traditionally, video was recorded just to videotape. Now there are a number of other options. For more on using these systems, see Choosing Media for Recording and Storage, p. 74.

HARD DRIVES. A *hard disk drive recorder* (*HDD*) is a portable hard drive system for recording video. Some HDDs are lightweight and can be mounted on a camera or attached separately to the operator's belt via a FireWire. These can be set up to capture video, audio, and timecode in the format used by your nonlinear editing system. The files can then be imported into the editing system much faster than tape, saving time in the editing room. Focus Enhancements, which customizes its DV/HDV FireStore HDD recorders for use with camcorders from JVC, Panasonic, and Canon, calls this idea *direct-to-edit* (*DTE*) technology.

Fig. 1-27. Hard disk drive (HDD). The Sony HVR-DR60 can be mounted on a camera. (Sony Electronics, Inc.)

In some cases, recording to an external hard drive may allow longer recording times, or recording at a higher resolution than permitted by a camera's internal tape drive. In the case of Sony HDV camcorders, simultaneous downconversion and recording to SD with matching timecode is possible using a portable HDD connected by FireWire.

The HDD recording system found in Grass Valley's Infinity camcorder makes use of Iomega's removable REV 35 MB hard disk cartridge (see Fig. 1-24). At heart a consumer technology (there is also a professional REV PRO version), the REV cartridge contains a single 2.5-inch platter and spindle motor. The heads are built into the camera. Think of REV as a high-density floppy that's hard.

For high-end production are hard drive systems like Directors Friend or S.two's DFR (Digital Field Recording), which capture huge uncompressed 10-bit streams from digital cinematography cameras. These are hefty appliances, with stacks of drive arrays for security (see p. 219).

As capacity rises and prices drop, large hard drives are increasingly used in post-production and distribution—individually and in networks. HDDs are also used in the home to record TV programming from cable or other sources. Another name for this is *digital video recorder* (DVR). DVRs generally record compressed video, using MPEG2 or other codecs. TiVo is a well-known example.

For more on the use of HDDs in shooting, see pp. 74 and 125. For more on use of hard drives in editing, see p. 510.

DVDS AND OPTICAL DISCS. *Digital Video Discs* or *DVDs* (also called *Digital Versatile Discs*) were introduced in the mid-1990s as a format for watching videos at home. Using MPEG-2 compression, DVDs offer component color, multiple soundtracks, and much improved resolution compared to VHS and quickly became the format of choice for distributing standard definition videos.

Camcorders that record directly to DVDs have been generally restricted to consumer models, intended as a convenience for shooting and viewing home movies. The AVCHD format described on pp. 32–33, however, is poised to find professional application. Professional camcorders already use other forms of optical discs, notably Sony's XDCAM camcorders that record to blue-laser disc cartridges.

There are two competing formats for the new generation of high definition DVDs. Both of them include support for MPEG-2, MPEG-4 (H.264), and VC-1 (formerly Windows Media 9). Specs call for compatibility with HD at 1920 x 1080 HD (50i, 60i, and 24p); 1280 x 720 HD (50p, 60p, and 24p); and SD at 720 x 576/480 (50i or 60i).

The *Blu-ray* disc format is endorsed by companies such as Sony, Apple, Panasonic, and Dell. Single-layer Blu-ray discs can hold 25 Gigabytes and dual-layer discs can record 50 GB, which is about five to ten times the capacity of a standard DVD. Larger capacities are expected. The *HD DVD* format is endorsed by companies such as Microsoft, Toshiba, and Intel. It has lower capacity (15 GB for single-layer, 30 GB for dual-layer).

For consumers, DVDs are simply a handy way to watch movies. When people buy a feature film on DVD, the disc already has compressed video recorded on it. As discussed, standard definition DVDs use MPEG-2 compression.

For filmmakers, DVDs serve multiple functions. You can *burn* (record) compressed SD video using MPEG-2 (or other codecs) so your movie can be played on typical DVD players. You can also burn HD to a standard DVD using H.264 (MPEG-4), although at this moment playback is limited mostly to computers. Additionally, in many parts of the world, the Video CD format, or VCD, is popular for burning video to *compact discs* (*CDs*). Because VCDs use MPEG-1 compression, the quality is lower than DVD (it looks more like VHS) but CD-Rs are dirt cheap and CD burners common. With appropriate software, VCDs are easily played on a computer.

Filmmakers frequently use DVDs as a storage medium for uncompressed video, audio, still images, or text. Likewise, you can use CDs to burn music (using Mp3 or other codecs) that can be played on a car CD player, or you can use them to store many other types of computer files. DVDs and CDs are both forms of *optical discs*; DVDs have much larger capacity. For more on making DVDs, see p. 560.

Various types of *Magneto-Optical* (*MO*) discs are sometimes used in audio post-production; these can be used as "digital dubbers" for sound editing and mixing and can also be used for video.

FLASH MEMORY CARDS. Some newer cameras and audio recorders are capable of recording to Flash memory cards, which are a reusable, solid-state storage device with no moving parts. Types of Flash memory cards include *CompactFlash*, *Secure Digital*, Sony's *Memory Stick*, and Panasonic's *P2 cards*. Flash memory cards are small, require less power than a hard drive or tape mechanism, and are more resistant to the physical shocks and dirt of a challenging location environment.

To record to a card, you insert it (or several cards) in the camera or audio recorder. When a card is full, you remove it and download to a hard drive or other storage device. The card can then be erased and reused.

Like recording directly to hard drives, using Flash memory allows you to move quickly from shooting to editing by copying files from the card to the editing system. Some cards can be inserted in a PCMCIA slot in a laptop or easily connected to any computer with an adaptor. For video production, Flash memory is still expensive for the amount of storage, but prices are coming down. For more on working with memory cards, see p. 74.

ANALOG FORMATS

Both the present and the future belong to digital, but there is still an enormous amount of analog equipment being used productively (though relatively little is still being manufactured). There are also untold hours of material—fifty years' worth—recorded on analog tapes that may or may not get transferred to digital as time goes by.

2-inch Quad and 1-inch Type-C

In 1956, Ampex Quadruplex videotape machines running 2-inch-wide tape on open reels successfully made the first electronic recordings of live broadcast TV. Editing was another matter, requiring a razor blade and tape, and it would take another decade for SMPTE timecode to be invented, but this dinosaur format remained the dominant medium of broadcast TV for more than twenty years, well into the 1970s.

In 1976, SMPTE standardized a 1-inch reel-to-reel videotape format designed to replace 2-inch. Called 1-inch Type-C, it remained an industry workhorse into the late 1990s despite the fact that it was an analog composite format.

¾-inch U-matic

In 1969, Sony introduced the world's first videocassette recorder to the consumer market, where it promptly failed because of its high cost. But U-matic was embraced elsewhere, in Hollywood for instance, as a portable means of viewing film dailies and rough cuts, so Sony revamped ¾-inch-wide videotape as a professional offline format.

U-matic's *color under* signal is neither composite nor component—its two chrominance components are combined into a single chroma signal (like the signals that an S-Video, or "separate video," connector provides; see p. 194). As a result, each generation of dubbing causes red detail to bleed, as well as other distortions. Not a pretty sight.

Yet ¾-inch was still in common use in industrial and broadcast applications until only very recently.

Betamax

In 1975, in another stab at the consumer market, Sony introduced a miniaturized version of U-matic, the ½-inch Betamax. Some will remember the 1980s videotape format war—Betamax lost out to JVC's VHS—but few probably realize that the smaller Betamax cassette became the basis for the wildly successful professional Betacam family of formats, up to and including HDCAM.

VHS and Super VHS

VHS (originally Vertical Helical Scan, later Video Home System) launched about a year after Betamax with a key advantage: three-hour tapes versus one-hour for Betamax. Technically Betamax was better, but VHS won over the home video market. By 2003, DVD overcame VHS in popularity, but there remain millions of VHS machines out there, not to mention home recordings and pre-recorded films.

Like U-matic and Betamax, VHS is an analog format using the color under recording technique mentioned above, with its characteristic color bleeding when making dubs. In image quality alone, VHS is the worst format of the three. It further degrades when recorded at slow speeds—LP (long play) or SLP (super long play). VHS decks with hi-fi (high fidelity) recording provide excellent sound quality, however.

Super VHS (S-VHS) systems provide a significant increase in horizontal resolution of 400 lines (luminance only, not chrominance) compared to 240 lines of standard VHS. S-VHS is an S-video system that is higher in quality than composite, but not up to component quality (see p. 194).

Fig. 1-28. Canon Hi8 and 8mm analog camcorder. (Canon U.S.A., Inc.)

Video8 and Hi8

In the mid-1980s, *8mm* tape was introduced. Despite smaller tape cassettes and camcorders, Video8's image quality matched that of Betamax and VHS. In the late 1980s, *Hi8* (*high band* Video8) brought enhanced horizontal resolution (400 lines), although it remained a color-under format with poor dubbing characteristics. Today's Digital 8 cameras (see above) can play analog Hi8.

Betacam and Betacam SP

Introduced in 1982, Sony's *Betacam* camcorder and videocassette format revolutionized video field production. The original Betacam format used a ½-inch cassette to record an analog component video signal using a unique dual-track approach: The luminance signal is recorded to one track, and the two color difference signals are recorded to a separate but parallel track.

Betacam SP (superior performance) came along in 1986, improving horizontal resolution to 340 lines by use of metal-particle tape. Betacam SP also provided four audio tracks: two standard longitudinal tracks and two high-quality FM tracks embedded in the video signal (Hi8 had FM tracks too).

For many years, Betacam was the tool of choice for *ENG* (*electronic news gathering*) and *EFP* (*electronic field production*). While Sony no longer makes analog Betacam cameras, many are still in use. A good Betacam camera produces results similar to a good DVCAM camera.

VIDEO EDITING

Digital Nonlinear Editing

Virtually all video and film editing today is done with *nonlinear editing* systems (*NLE*). A nonlinear editor is computer software that allows you to edit and manipulate video much like the way a word processing program allows you to write, cut, paste, and format text. In nonlinear editing, video and audio data are stored on hard drives for instant access. A nonlinear editing system often includes a deck (or sometimes a camera) to bring material in or out of the system; a computer; hard drives for storage; and an external monitor for viewing (see Fig. 1-29). NLEs range from professional HD systems, with all the bells and whistles that cost tens of thousands, to simple programs like Apple's iMovie, which consumers can run on a basic laptop.

Video editing has evolved through several generations of technology (see Editing on Tape, p. 42). Editors who worked with earlier, more cumbersome methods may still find themselves amazed at how powerful nonlinear editing is, and how it frees the filmmaker's creativity. Nonlinear editing gets its name because it is unlike traditional tape editing systems that force you to start at the first shot of the movie and edit in a straight line (linearly) to the end. With nonlinear systems you can work on any scene at any time, with the freedom to expand, shorten, or change it as you like. With an NLE you can instantly search through the footage for a particular shot or quickly save different versions of a scene for later reference. Many of the time-consuming tasks of editing are automated so that the editor can concentrate on the movie itself.

In linear tape editing, working with audio is particularly unwieldy. In the past,

Fig. 1-29. Nonlinear editing. Michael Tronick A.C.E on the set of *Gone Baby Gone* with an Avid Xpress Pro editing system. (Michael Phillips)

editors working with tape didn't even attempt some kinds of sound manipulations because they were so hard to do. Nonlinear systems make it easy to do complex sound editing and processing. In fact, there are nonlinear systems specifically designed for sound work, which are called *digital audio workstations* or *DAWs*.

There may be some drawbacks to nonlinear editing. Because nonlinear editing has the reputation of being "fast" and because some editing systems are expensive, editing schedules are sometimes made very short. Editors can find themselves cheated out of the "thinking time" they need to structure and refine a movie. Also, because changes can be easily made until the last minute, indecisive moviemakers can get trapped in a morass of endless possibilities.

WORKING WITH AN NLE. To begin editing on an NLE, load the footage from the camera onto the editing system's hard drives. If the camera you used in the field recorded to digital videotape, then loading that material into the NLE is called *capturing*. If the camera recorded DV, MPEG, JPEG2000, or RAW sequence files to hard drive, optical disc, or Flash memory, then loading that material into the NLE is called *ingesting*. If your camera recorded to analog tape, then the footage has to be converted to digital form before it can be stored on the NLE; in this case bringing the footage in is called *digitizing*.[17]

Sometimes the total amount of footage you shot exceeds the storage capacity of your system's computer drives. When this happens, you can work on material in

17. Not all nonlinear editing systems are set up to digitize analog material.

Fig. 1-30. Online editing suite. Avid Nitris nonlinear system. (DuArt Film and Video)

smaller chunks. Another approach is to capture at a lower resolution, which sacrifices image quality but increases the system's storage capacity. Some systems can work with *proxy images*, which are of very low resolution.

How you work with an NLE depends in part on the resolution of your original footage, how powerful your editing system is, and what you plan to do with the finished movie.

For example, if you're working on a school project, you might shoot with a DV camera and do all your editing on a low-cost NLE. Even basic NLEs can do video effects, create titles, and do some degree of sound balancing or mixing. A finished movie can then be output from the system back onto tape, exported as a computer file, or burned to a DVD.

However, if you're doing a project for broadcast, you might do the majority of your editing on a mid-powered NLE, then finish the project on a high-end NLE that's better equipped for color correction, graphics, and output to high-quality tape formats. This way of working is known as an *offline/online* workflow. The offline NLE is used to find the movie's structure and put the shots in their proper order. Fine-tuning the color and sound are usually not top priority during the offline edit. After the offline is done, you move the project to a facility with an online NLE that has all the scopes, monitors, and decks needed to do the final polish. To transfer the project from one machine to another, a computer file can be generated that contains all the information about where each shot starts and stops, what tape it came from, and any effects that have been applied.

The audio may be sent to yet another system for mixing (usually in a specialized sound studio), then brought into the online system or put directly on the final tape.

Another situation that calls for an offline/online approach is when you're working in a high-resolution format that exceeds the capabilities of your NLE: For example, if you had shot HDCAM and your NLE lacks the storage capacity or processing power to handle uncompressed high definition video. In this case, you might dub the HDCAM tapes to standard definition DVCAM and do your offline edit with a low-cost DVCAM deck and NLE. After you complete the offline edit, you then move to an uncompressed HD editing system and conform the original HDCAM tapes to the edit you created in the offline.

Editing on Tape

For many years, all video cameras recorded to videotape, and all video editing was done by rerecording from one piece of tape to another. Traditional tape editing has now been largely replaced by the nonlinear editing systems just discussed. Nevertheless, tape continues to play an important role in video editing. Tape is still widely used for shooting, so it's used as the source for bringing footage into the editing system. Tape is also used after editing to store the finished movie. Many terms and concepts of nonlinear editing come from tape editing, so it's helpful to understand it.

The idea of tape editing is based on using two tape machines (see Fig. 14-7). One is a player, in which you put the footage from the camera. Using an edit controller—a device with frame-accurate control of both machines—you search through the footage until you find the first shot you want to use. You mark the beginning and end of the shot, then play it on the player while rerecording it on a

Fig. 1-31. Tape editing suite. (Sony Electronics, Inc.)

second machine that contains the editing master tape. Once that's recorded, you move on to the next shot. This way, you build up the movie on the master tape, one shot at a time. Again, this is why tape editing is called *linear*—you start at the beginning of the movie and go in a straight line to the end.

The concept of offline/online editing got its start with tape editing, but with tape it's done differently than with nonlinear. In the 1970s and 1980s, computer-controlled ("online") editing systems were developed using expensive, high-quality tape machines. Online tape editing is particularly ill-suited to long-form projects, which can require a lot of costly editing time and a lot of searching back and forth through the tapes, possibly damaging them. So, to first do an offline tape edit, the source tapes are dubbed (copied) to a lower-cost format. In the 1980s, it was common to shoot in Betacam SP and dub to ¾-inch U-matic tape for the offline; today an HD tape might be dubbed to an SD format like DVCAM. These offline tapes are called the *worktapes* (or *workdubs*). It's imperative that the worktapes have the exact same timecode as the originals, either recorded in a timecode track or at least displayed in a window on screen (see Fig. 1-17).

The worktapes are then edited with relatively inexpensive, lower-quality offline tape decks. Because the original camera tapes and the worktapes have the same timecode, once we identify a shot we want on the worktape, we can easily find the same shot on the original tape. The end product of offline tape editing is a list of every shot in the movie with the timecode address of the beginning and end of each shot. This is called an *edit decision list*, or *EDL*. The EDL is brought from the offline system to the online system, where the movie you created in the offline edit is re-constructed using the high-quality camera original tapes.

Tape-to-tape editing is far less common today, but editing from an NLE to a tape machine is done all the time: for example, when outputting the finished movie from an NLE to create the master tape for later duplication.

The chief drawback of tape editing is that it is difficult to later change the order of shots. You can't simply remove or add a shot from the middle of the master without leaving a hole or covering up other shots you may want. The solution is either to start over from the beginning or to rerecord part of the master onto a new tape (a new master), make changes, then record the rest. This is not only slow, but with analog formats, the image can degrade every time you make a copy of a copy (adding generations).

The traditional tape online session takes place in a high-priced video post-production facility with high-end equipment. The online editor needs to know a lot of engineering to operate the machines. As time goes on, online editing equipment is becoming less expensive and more user-friendly; it is increasingly possible for moviemakers to do onlines in their own workplaces.

For more on nonlinear and tape editing, see Chapter 14.

FILM SYSTEMS

The Camera and Projector

As discussed earlier in this chapter, the principle behind motion pictures is to record a series of still frames rapidly—one after another—and then display them on a screen rapidly, one after another (see p. 4).

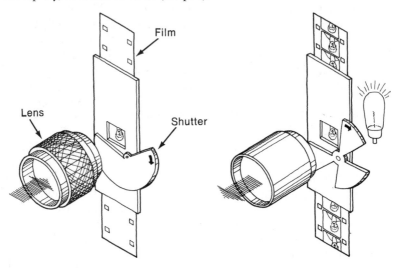

Fig. 1-32. The camera and the projector. The camera (left) draws in light to capture an image of the world on film; the projector (right) throws the image back onto a screen. (Carol Keller)

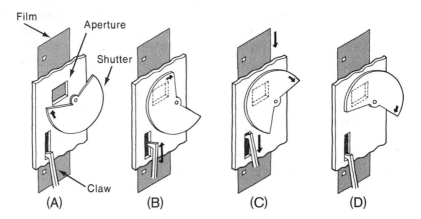

Fig. 1-33. The shutter and intermittent movement. (A) The claw holds the film in place during exposure. (B, C) The shutter rotates to block light from the film while the claw moves up to pull down the next frame. (D) The claw freezes in position to hold the next frame steady for exposure. (Carol Keller)

The film camera works by focusing light from the scene to be captured onto a small rectangular area of photographic film. After each rectangle (*frame*) is exposed to light, a *shutter* blocks off the light. The camera's *claw* then pulls more film into position and holds it in place. The shutter opens again, allowing light to strike the fresh frame of film. This stop-start process is called the camera's *intermittent movement*. The camera is loaded with a roll of film that may be 50 to 1,000 feet long. Each *camera roll* records thousands of frames.

The film projector operates on the same principle, but rather than focusing light from the scene onto the film, it projects the photographed image onto a screen using a bright lamp behind the film path. As long as the projector runs at the same speed as the camera, motion will appear normal. Sometimes cameras are run at a higher speed so that motion will appear slowed down (*slow motion*) in projection. See p. 357 for more on camera speeds.

The Film Format

While all film cameras expose images in essentially the same way, the size and shape of the image produced vary with the camera type. The first movies, made in

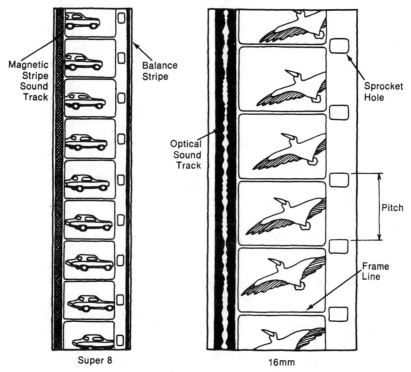

Super 8   16mm

Fig. 1-34. Each still image on the film is called a *frame*. Successive frames are divided by the *frame line*. The claw advances the film by engaging a sprocket hole, or perforation. The 16mm film print shown here has an optical sound track and the Super 8 film has a magnetic stripe sound track. Note the different sprocket hole positions in the various formats. (Carol Keller)

the 1890s by Thomas Edison, were shot on *cellulose nitrate*–based film that was about 35mm wide. Nitrate film is highly flammable and becomes explosive as it deteriorates with age (much of the first version of Robert Flaherty's *Nanook of the North* was destroyed by a fire from cigarette ash). Nitrate has since been replaced by the more stable *cellulose acetate* base and in some cases by indestructible polyester. The 35mm gauge remains the most commonly used in theatrical filmmaking.

In the 1920s, 16mm film was introduced as an amateur format. The area of the 16mm frame is only one quarter of that of the 35mm frame and when projected side-by-side, looks grainier and less sharp. World War II gave rise to professional use of 16mm, as the U.S. military commissioned lightweight 16mm Bell & Howell cameras and projectors for field use. With technological improvements in cameras, lenses, and film emulsions in the late 1950s, 16mm became widely used in professional filmmaking. In the early 1970s, *Super 16* was developed. Unlike regular 16mm, Super 16 has only one row of perforations. By extending the image almost to the edge of the film into the area formerly occupied by the second set of perforations, Super 16 allows a 40 percent larger image to be recorded for each frame (see Fig. 1-40).

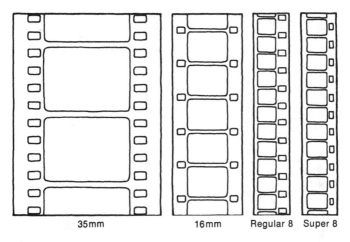

35mm   16mm   Regular 8   Super 8

Fig. 1-35. Comparison of film formats. (Carol Keller)

In 1932, 8mm cameras were introduced that used 16mm but with twice as many perforations (*Double 8mm* or *Regular 8mm*). You would insert a 25-foot load in your camera, shoot until the 25 feet were used up, then flip the spool, and reload the film from the tail end so that another 25 feet of 8mm images could be photographed along the opposite edge. After developing, Double 8mm was slit down the middle to create two lengths of 8mm film.

In 1965 Kodak introduced *Super 8* film that was 8mm wide, but with smaller, repositioned sprocket holes that made room for an image 50 percent larger than regular 8mm. Super 8 was pre-loaded into easy-to-use cartridges that made threading the camera a thing of the past.

Super 8, once the prime format for home movies, now has limited use among artists and music video producers.

Aspect Ratio and Film

A film's *format* refers to the width of the film material itself (the film *gauge*), as well as the size and shape of the image that's recorded on it. The 16mm and Super 16 formats use film of the same gauge (16mm), but the size and shape of their frames are different. The shape of the frame is described by the proportions of its rectangle: the width of the frame divided by the height is the *aspect ratio* (see Fig. 1-12). A rectangle four units wide and three units high is the standard for several formats (including regular 8mm, Super 8, 16mm, and both NTSC and PAL). This aspect ratio is 4:3 ("four by three"). In film world, that ratio is usually expressed as 1.33:1 (spoken as "one three three to one," or just "one three three").

1.33:1   1.85:1   2.35:1

Fig. 1-36. Film can be shot at a variety of aspect ratios (see Fig. 1-12). Widescreen formats call for a different approach to image composition. (Carol Keller)

In 35mm, the full frame for sound film has an aspect ratio of about 1.33:1 and is called *Academy aperture*, named for the Academy of Motion Picture Arts and Sciences that defined it. Though the Academy frame was standard for feature films in the early twentieth century, it is no longer used for films shown in theaters. Theatrical features are generally widescreen, with an aspect ratio of at least 1.85:1 and often as wide as 2.40:1.

For more on aspect ratio and widescreen formats, see p. 87.

COMPARING FILM FORMATS

As a rule of thumb, as the size of the format increases, so do the cost, the image quality, and the size and weight of the camera. When a large area of film emulsion is used for each exposure, the grain and imperfections of the film detract less from the image. In the 35mm camera, about 12 square inches of film are exposed each second; in 16mm only about 2.5 square inches are used.[18] When a 16mm frame is projected on a modest 8-by-10-foot screen, it must be enlarged about 100,000 times. To fill a screen of the same size, a Super 8 frame must be magnified more than 300,000 times. This is why theatrical features are usually shot on 35mm or 65mm film (although independent films often originate on smaller formats). For more on how format size affects picture quality, see p. 82.

The film image is affected not only by the format but also, in order of increasing

18. This is comparing 35mm Academy frame to regular 16mm. Standard 1.85 aspect ratio 35mm film exposes about 9 square inches each second.

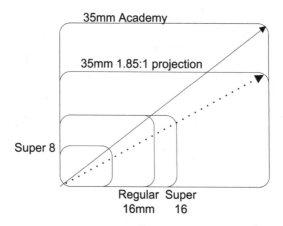

Fig. 1-37. Relative frame sizes of various film formats. The solid diagonal line shows that three of the formats have the same aspect ratio. The dotted line shows that Super 16 and 35mm 1.85 projection have nearly the same aspect ratio.

consequence, by the particular camera being used, the lenses, and the choice of camera negative (called *film stock* or *raw stock*). A film camera will produce vastly different results depending on choice of both film stock and processing.

Most professional filmmaking is done with color negative film stocks. Upon developing, negative stocks render a scene with reversed tonalities and colors; that is, what was light in reality is dark on the negative, what was green in reality is magenta on the negative (see Fig. 7-2). When the *camera original* (the film that actually went through the camera) is negative, it must be printed on *positive* film stock to be viewable in a projector. Sometimes films are shot with *reversal* film stocks. Like slides in still photography—also reversal—they show a normal image as soon as they're developed. Prints made from color reversal camera films show noticeably more grain and contrast than prints made from color negative stocks. Back when TV news was shot on film, reversal was preferred because it could be shown immediately after processing with no printing needed. Editing reversal original saves time and money, but runs the high risk of scratching the film. Not all stocks are available in all formats.

Super 8

Super 8 cameras are cheap, portable, and easy to use. Film is inserted in pocket-sized cartridges. Many Super 8 cameras are equipped to record sound in camera, but magnetic-striped film stock capable of sound recording is no longer made by Kodak. Super 8 was once the format of choice for home movies but video now owns that market. Super 8 is becoming obsolete and most equipment is only available secondhand.

The people still shooting on Super 8 are a dedicated group of enthusiasts who covet old cameras and relish the particular look and feel of Super 8 film. Super 8 footage has found its way into music videos, commercials, and even feature films (both ultra-low-budget films and high-budget movies, such as Oliver Stone's work

Fig. 1-38. Beaulieu Super 8 sync sound camera. (Pro8mm, Inc.)

with cinematographer Robert Richardson, including *The Doors* and *JFK*). Super 8 is used in school settings to give students an opportunity to work with film.

Traditionally, all Super 8 shooting was done with reversal Ektachrome or Koda-chrome (now discontinued by Kodak) that could be projected directly without making a print. Pro8mm in Los Angeles has created a line of color and black-and-white negative stocks by using a film-cutting machine to load professional 35mm film emulsions into Super 8 cartridges.

Rather than edit or distribute films in Super 8, most people transfer to video and/or blow up (enlarge) to 16mm or 35mm.

Aside from cost, why shoot Super 8? When used with some film stocks, Super 8 cameras may offer much of the flexibility of a small-format video camera and with a distinctive film image. But Super 8 can also offer "deficiencies" that filmmakers may be seeking. Sometimes a rough, grainy image is desired, perhaps as a stylistic touch or to simulate the look of old movies. Instead of trying to degrade a 16mm or 35mm image, filmmakers may shoot on one of the grainier, more contrasty Super 8 stocks.

16mm and Super 16

During its life span, 16mm has gone through enormous changes. Starting as an amateur format (once considered "spaghetti" by pros), the portability of 16mm cameras made them the tool of choice for TV news and documentaries. The grainy, handheld 16mm look is still associated with some sense of documentary "realism." In the 1970s and 1980s, 16mm cameras and stocks improved greatly, and 16mm was used extensively for TV documentaries, low-budget features, animation, and avant-garde films. At one time, 16mm projectors were found in virtually every school.

By the mid-1990s, video had replaced 16mm for low-budget and industrial productions, and 16mm as a distribution format had pretty much disappeared. By the mid-2000s, standard 16mm was on its way out too (having already disappeared in Europe a decade earlier). Nevertheless, with newer, technically advanced color negatives, Super 16 is capable of a rich image that rivals 35mm and remains popular for higher-budget documentaries, TV pilots and series, commercials, and low-budget features. As a measure of confidence in the future of Super 16, Arriflex in 2006 introduced an entirely new, state-of-the-art Super 16 camera system, the Arri 416. But as high definition continues to gain traction in professional and consumer use alike, it will undoubtedly replace film for many of these uses.

Fig. 1-39. Aaton XTRprod camera. Adapts for regular 16mm and Super 16 filming. Versatile and exceptionally well balanced for handheld work. (AbelCineTech)

Films can be easily made in 16mm by a two- or three-person crew and even by an adroit solo filmmaker, but somewhat larger crews are the norm. Because so many projects are now done in video, used 16mm equipment can often be purchased at a great discount.

Universities and film festivals may still show films in 16mm, but more commonly films that originated on 16mm are transferred to video or are blown up to 35mm for distribution. Properly shot Super 16 films can look superb when blown up to 35mm (such as *Leaving Las Vegas*). In Europe almost all made-for-TV movies are Super 16.

Since digital broadcasting, HDTV, and theatrical 35mm projection systems are widescreen, it is advisable to shoot Super 16 rather than regular 16mm when video or 35mm exhibition is the goal. The Super 16 frame has an aspect ratio of 1.78:1, which is very close to widescreen video's 16:9, so a transfer to HD or widescreen SD formats can be done with negligible cropping (see Fig. 1-40). When blowing up to 35mm, you can create prints at 1.66:1 or the much more common 1.85:1. In either case, a Super 16mm negative will blow up with less grain and need less enlargement and cropping than standard 16mm (for more on aspect ratio conversions, see p. 87).

Keep in mind that Super 16 is an origination format for film blowup or video transfer. If you need to make a standard 16mm print, you will have to optically recenter and crop the image to create room for the sound track, which is not cheap.[19] Some cameras (like Aatons) can be switched between regular 16mm and Super 16. Lenses designed for Super 16 can be used for standard 16mm, but the reverse is often not the case. If in doubt, it is always wise to first test standard 16mm lenses for vignetting when used with a Super 16mm camera (see p. 169).

The decision to shoot a feature in Super 16 instead of 35mm may be made on the basis that production costs are lower, crews are smaller, and film stock is less

19. Or you could skip the optical step and make lower-cost contact prints, but you'd have to put up with one side of the frame being cut off.

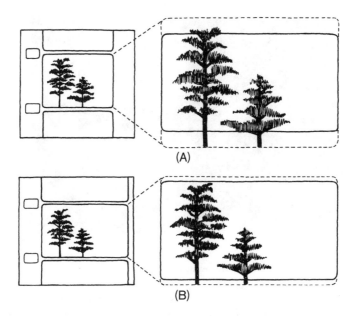

Fig. 1-40. Blowing up 16mm film to 35mm. (A) When regular 16mm is blown up to wide-screen 35mm, the image must be significantly cropped. (B) By using the area normally reserved for the optical sound track, the Super 16 frame closely approximates the 1.85:1 widescreen aspect ratio. Very little of the Super 16 image is lost when the blowup is made. (Carol Keller)

expensive in 16mm. This has to be weighed against the cost of the eventual blowup to 35mm.

For more on blowups from 16mm and Super 16, see p. 679.

35mm

The standard format of feature films, as well as television commercials and TV movies not shot on video, is 35mm. Traditional 35mm cameras are heavy, cumbersome, and expensive. These cameras are usually supported on tripods or dollies because of their bulk and the importance of having a steady image on a large theater screen. The newer generation of lighter, hand-holdable 35mm cameras and stabilization devices, such as the Steadicam (which enables the operator to carry the camera smoothly; see Fig. 9-25), provides greater mobility and allows more nimble filming techniques to be used in feature films. (Steadicams are also used in 16mm and video production.)

In general, the highest-quality equipment, techniques, and lab services are available for 35mm production, for which film budgets usually run in the millions. Due to the bulkiness of the equipment and the complexity of projects done in 35mm, crews of about eight to more than a hundred persons are employed.

The standard 35mm frame is four perforations high. Some 35mm cameras are set up for the *three-perf* 35mm format, which uses a frame that is only three perforations high. Because less film is needed for each frame, this results in a 25 percent

Fig. 1-41. 35mm camera. Panaflex Millenium. (Panavision, Inc.)

savings in the cost of film stock and processing. This format is well suited to 1.78:1 (16:9) capture and is popular for production of TV series filmed in Los Angeles. Three-perf looks the same as four-perf when transferred to 16:9 video and can be optically printed to the standard four-perf format for film distribution at the conventional 1.85:1 aspect ratio.

Less common but facing renewed interest is *two-perf* 35mm. Two-perf was introduced as the *Techniscope* format by Technicolor in Rome in the early 1960s. This was done because, compared to normal 35mm motion picture lenses, the anamorphic lenses needed to horizontally squeeze a panoramic 2.40:1 frame (also called 2.35, 2.37, CinemaScope, or 'Scope) into a squarish four-perf 35mm frame are heavy, awkward, and optically slow. Why not instead use a regular 35mm format lens, shoot on a two-perf 35mm frame half the normal height with the same aspect ratio as an unsqueezed anamorphic frame to begin with, then blow up the result to a standard CinemaScope squeezed negative? The result could be printed and projected as conventional CinemaScope. Benefits include a 50 percent cost savings in film stock and processing, a quieter camera, and mags that last twice as long. Not bad.

A number of classic films were indeed shot in two-perf, including George Lucas's *American Graffiti* and spaghetti Westerns such as *The Good, the Bad, and the Ugly* and *Once Upon a Time in the West*. Today the *digital intermediate* (D.I.) process makes it a snap to scan a two-perf original 35mm negative, then record it back out to squeezed four-perf 35mm negative. Aaton has designed a new compact 35mm camera that switches between four-, three-, and two-perf.

Large Formats

There are a number of widescreen formats used primarily for feature films. Some high-budget films are shot in 65mm, which is then shown in theaters using 70mm prints (the added width is used for sound tracks). *Lawrence of Arabia* and *2001: A Space Odyssey* demonstrate the stunning detail and rich image of this format. The 65mm negative is reduced to 35mm for smaller theaters.

Even larger are the IMAX and Omnimax formats, which run 65mm film *horizontally* through the camera, creating an image that spans fifteen perforations per frame instead of 65mm's five. These are shown on huge, enveloping screens in specially constructed theaters. (Omnimax is designed for domed screens.) The image is spectacular.

SOUND RECORDING FOR FILM

Most films have sound tracks; even silent films were intended to be shown with musical accompaniment. Through the years there have been numerous sound recording technologies used for shooting films. Unlike video cameras, which typically record audio right in the camcorder, most modern film cameras do not record sound. Virtually all filmmaking is done with double system recording, which means using a separate audio recorder to record sound to tape, hard drives, or memory cards.

Fig. 1-42. Recordist's sound cart with recorder, mixer, and digislate. (Pawel Wdowczak/ Denecke, Inc.)

Before portable recording equipment became available, most sound films were made in the studio under controlled conditions. The soundstage was acoustically isolated from distracting noises, and the bulky recording equipment was permanently mounted in place. When it was necessary to film on location, there was usually no attempt made to record a high-quality sound track. Instead, the film would be *looped* afterward in the sound studio. Looping, sometimes called *dubbing*, involves cutting scenes into short, endless loops that the actors watch while respeaking their lines. Today, dialogue replacement may be done to fix sound that was badly recorded, or when the dialogue is to be rerecorded in another language. *ADR* (*automatic dialogue replacement*) is now done with more sophisticated equipment than were the old film loops.

In the 1950s, advances in magnetic tape recorders made it practical to record sound on location. From the 1960s through the 1980s, classic portable ¼-inch reel-to-reel recorders made by Nagra and Stellavox were the rule. By the 1990s, light-weight *DAT* (*digital audiotape*) cassette recorders were in common use on film sets. Today, various digital audio recording devices are taking over the industry. *File-based recorders* create audio files that are recorded to hard drives, memory cards, and/or optical discs; they provide a lot of flexibility, multiple audio channels, and save time in editing.

The smallest, least expensive film cameras are noisy and are intended for shooting without sound (though sound can be added later). These cameras are sometimes called *MOS* (see p. 340), or *wild cameras*. Confusingly, the term *silent camera* is sometimes used to mean an MOS camera, and sometimes means one that is quiet enough to be used for sound filmmaking. Audible camera noise on the sound track can be disastrous, especially in nondocumentary projects. Most good sound cameras are extremely quiet.

Synchronous or *sync* (pronounced "sink") sound, also known as *lip sync*, matches the picture in the way you are used to hearing it: When the actor's lips move on the screen, you hear the words simultaneously. *Nonsynchronous* or *wild sound* is not in sync, or matched to the picture, in this way. Some films use wild sound exclusively, such as travelogues that have only narration and a musical background. Wild sound can be recorded with any tape recorder and then transferred for editing (see below).

Because sync sound requires precise alignment of sound and picture, only cameras and audio recorders equipped for sync sound work can be used. Most modern sound cameras are crystal-controlled (*crystal sync*) to operate at a precisely fixed speed (usually 24 fps). In both picture and sound, speed must be regulated exactly because even tiny fluctuations in speed (if uncorrected) result in the sound becoming out of sync with the picture. In that case, the picture of the actor's lips moving might appear before or after we hear the sound of his words.

A microphone or mic is used to capture sounds and send them to the sound recorder. In double system recording, the camera and sound recorder are generally not attached to each other, so the microphone can be positioned close to the sound source for good recording, regardless of where the camera is. See Chapters 10 and 11 for more on sound recording.

FILM EDITING

From the beginning of filmmaking, movies were edited by cutting rolls of film into pieces (individual shots), arranging the shots in the desired order and length, and reattaching them into rolls. Celluloid film was literally cut and spliced back together, which is why editing is also called *cutting*.

In the 1990s, a sea change took place in the way films are edited. Instead of cutting on film—using film editing equipment—most filmmakers today transfer their film footage to video and do their editing with computer-based, nonlinear editing systems (NLEs, see p. 39). Nonlinear video editing has a lot of advantages over

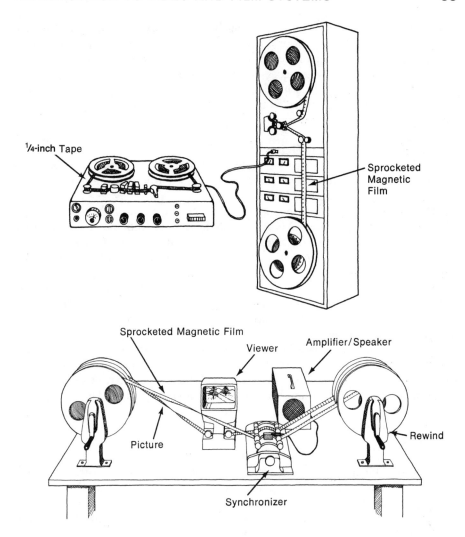

¼-inch Tape

Sprocketed
Magnetic
Film

Sprocketed Magnetic Film

Viewer

Amplifier/Speaker

Picture

Rewind

Synchronizer

Fig. 1-43. In traditional film editing, sound recorded in the field (shown here recorded with a ¼-inch tape deck) is then transferred to sprocketed magnetic film for editing. (bottom) The mag film can then be edited with the picture in frame-for-frame correspondence. (Carol Keller)

editing on film: You have much more control, you can try out visual effects, create titles, do more sophisticated sound editing, and easily output video copies of the edit when you need them.

Given the benefits of nonlinear video editing, why would anyone still cut on film? There are a number of reasons. If you're making a movie that will be shown on film in theaters, working with film gives you a better sense of what it will eventually look like on screen, and allows the cinematographer to better judge lighting and exposure during production.[20] On big-budget features, sometimes the editing is done in video, but a film print is cut alongside for test screenings. Film schools may encourage cutting on film to learn film craft. Some filmmakers believe that the tactile experience of joining pieces of film is an important part of creating a film. Also, there are costs involved in transferring to video and acquiring video equipment; if you already have film editing gear, cutting on film can sometimes be a cheaper route.

Editing Film on Video

When a production is to be shot on film and edited in video, there are many options and technologies available. The process can be fairly simple or quite complex depending on what route you choose.

During the production of the movie, the *camera original* film (the film that actually went through the camera) is sent to the laboratory to be processed and then transferred to video. When the transfer comes back, it is called *video dailies* or *rushes* (because on large productions it is rushed back and viewed every day; small films may not get such good service).

Sound recorded in the field must be combined with the video, in the proper place so that it is in sync with the picture. (This is called *synchronizing the rushes* or *synching up*.) Synching may take place when the dailies are transferred to video or afterward in the editing system.

Once the dailies are loaded into the NLE and the sound is in sync, editing can begin. Working with an NLE to edit a movie that was shot on film involves most of the same procedures as editing a movie shot on video. There may be certain differences stemming from the frame rate, how the audio is handled, and how the project will be finished.

When you're done editing, there are a few options for finishing and distributing the movie:

- It may be finished in standard definition video or HD and distributed solely on video (broadcast TV, cable, DVD, etc.). In this case, though film was used for shooting, the movie becomes essentially a video production.
- It may be finished in SD or HD video and then transferred to 35mm film (called *film-out*) for projection in theaters.
- The project may be edited in video, but finished by scanning the original negative into a digital file format to create a *digital intermediate* (D.I.), from which a new film negative and 35mm prints are made. This is an expensive option that provides a lot of image control (see p. 713).
- The project may be edited in video, but finished by returning to the original film negative and making traditional film prints (see next page).

As noted above, there are many ways of doing these tasks. For more, see Chapters 15 and 17.

---

20. That said, digital systems that allow cinematographers to calibrate color and exposure on video are improving and offer a new way for them to communicate to the postproduction team their intentions for the image.

Traditional Film Editing

Even though fewer projects today are edited the traditional way, and film editing equipment is getting harder to find, it's valuable for filmmakers to understand conventional film editing, since some of the methods and equipment continue to be used.

In traditional film production, the camera original footage is sent to the lab for processing and then a *workprint* is made—that is, a positive print of the original negative. The workprint is sent back to the production as dailies; this prevents damage to the original, which is stored at the lab.

In preparation for editing, the sound recorded in the field is rerecorded or transferred to *magnetic film*, also called *mag*, *mag stock*, *stripe* (in 35mm) or, in some cases, *fullcoat*. Mag has the same dimensions and sprocket holes as 16mm or 35mm picture film, but it has a magnetic oxide like that used in sound recording tape. Editing is then done with two strands of material (picture and sound) that are both sprocketed and can be lined up, frame for frame. Before editing, the dailies must be synched up. This is usually done by cutting and placing the mag alongside its corresponding workprint. Once the rushes are in sync, the two strands are then *edge coded* by mechanically printing the same *ink numbers* on the edge of each strand. Edge code allows pieces of sound and picture to be quickly identified and put back in sync at any point in the editing process.

During editing, sound and picture can be freely cut and combined. The editor can add, rearrange, or remove images or sounds anywhere in the movie. Often, several sound tracks are built. Multitrack editing machines can play two or more tracks in sync with the picture (see Fig. 15-7); this permits the editor to add music, narration, and sound effects to the sync sound.

During the editing process, you should occasionally watch the film on a bigger screen than the one on the editing machine. In order to project a double system film (with picture and separate sound track) you can either use a *double system projector* (see Fig. 13-2) or arrange for an *interlock screening* in a mix studio or theater that can interlock the projector with one or more *dubbers* that play the mag.

After editing is complete and the picture is locked, a sound mix is done to rerecord all the various sound tracks onto one final track. The pristine camera original is cut to match the edited workprint (called *negative matching* or *conforming*). Prints can then be made directly from the original negative or from a *duplicate negative* (often called *dupe neg*) made from a special *master positive* (often called *interpositive* or *interpos*), which is itself a protection copy of the original.

The movie may call for various kinds of image transitions or manipulations. Simple transitions are done while making the print—such as *dissolves* (where two images meld into each other) or *fades* (where the image appears from or disappears into darkness). More complex effects, called *opticals*, must be done in a separate step using an *optical printer*. Opticals include effects like *freeze frames* (where motion stops like a still photo) or *wipes* (where one image seems to push another off screen). Lettering for titles and credits is traditionally shot with a special camera onto a separate piece of film. The title rolls are then printed with the original negative. Color correction (also called *grading* in Europe) is done by a *color timer* (or *grader*), who views each scene in the film and estimates the correct printer settings for red, green, and blue exposure.

All the steps of making a film print are time-consuming and involve a certain amount of trial and error. Typically, lab personnel do the titles, opticals, and color corrections and then the director and/or director of photography view them in the *first answer print* (sometimes called a *check print*). Any adjustments are then made and additional *corrected prints* are struck. The feedback process between the lab and filmmakers may take days, weeks, or months to produce a finished print acceptable to the filmmakers.

After all the adjustments are done, a *release print* is made. The sound track is now combined with the picture; prints with sound tracks are called *composite* or *married prints*.

Film editing methods are discussed in Chapters 15 through 17.

CHAPTER 2

Before You Begin Production

This chapter is an attempt to corral in one place some of the production and technical questions to consider before you even begin your movie. Technology has evolved to the point that we have an enormous number of options in the equipment and techniques we use. The theory is that more choice makes us happier, but too much choice can be a real burden. The number of decisions filmmakers must make about formats, camera settings, editing procedures, software, and distribution can be oppressive, and many people feel bewildered by them.

Particularly in film and videomaking, we live in a transitional time with enormous changes between how things used to be done, how they're done now, and how they'll be done in the near future. Knowing the history, staying alert to current developments, and keeping an eye to "future proofing" your production are all important parts of planning your path. Internet user groups, forums, and digital video websites are excellent resources for the latest developments and practices.

Before you begin any project, you have to make some fundamental choices about what equipment and methods you'll use. Though you may prefer or be forced to work in one format exclusively, it is increasingly common to shoot in one or more formats, edit in another, and release the movie in several others. It helps to consider the three stages of the filmmaking process separately, while also keeping in mind the whole.

1. *Acquisition.* How will you record picture and sound? Will you shoot video or film? Which format(s); which camera?
2. *Postproduction.* How will you edit? What kinds of picture or sound manipulations will you need to do? What technologies will you use?
3. *Distribution.* Where do you want to show the movie? What kind of steps do you need to take in advance to be sure the movie is suitable for these outlets?

The choices you make affect how the movie gets made, how it looks, how much it costs, and where you can show it when you're done. All of these issues are deeply interrelated, and the discussion below circles back on some topics to examine them from more than one angle. Most items here are also discussed elsewhere in the book, and if any terms are unfamiliar, check in other chapters.

WORKING BACKWARD
FROM DISTRIBUTION

There are a number of decisions you can best make by considering the end product you hope to create and working back from there. Some people create movies for their private use, but for most filmmakers, the goal is not just to make a film, but to get it shown to audiences. How that happens depends in part on the choices you make: aesthetic, practical, technical, and commercial. There are many gatekeepers along the way who will decide whether to finance, buy, or show your movie. Depending on your goals, you may encounter gatekeepers in the form of funders, festivals, distributors, theater bookers, broadcasters, galleries, or school systems. Each will have certain criteria that influence whether they accept or reject your film. Some may not have a fixed set of rules about what they'll take, but each has certain expectations.

Educate yourself about the world you want to work in. Research what projects have been successful recently in whatever area of filmmaking you're interested in. Read case study articles ("how we made our movie") to learn about what kinds of financing, technology, or production methods were used. Go to festivals and theaters to see what's current. Visit museums and galleries. Watch TV. Get a sense of production values of successful films and how audiences respond. Read the "trades"—industry papers, magazines, and websites—to find out about what kinds of projects are getting produced and distributed.

The point is not to imitate what's out there at the moment (though Hollywood has made an industry of that). Hopefully, you'll make your film as fresh and original as you can. In fact, people who pattern their work too closely on recently successful films often find that the public and the gatekeepers are looking for something completely different by the time their film comes out. Short-term trends about what's hot can prove meaningless because for most projects there's a delay of months or years between when the movie is planned and when it's completed. Look for things that inspire you and give you ideas, then take your best guess about what the world will be like when you finally release your film.

When it comes to technology, you have a lot of options to choose from. If you're aiming for a particular outlet (say, cable or broadcast television) there will be expectations about what formats are acceptable and certain technical specs you'll need to meet. Many broadcasters have websites with technical and production requirements, and things like standard program lengths.[1]

In choosing a camera or format, some filmmakers like to work at the cutting edge of technology (often thought of as the "bleeding edge" for the problems you may encounter). Other filmmakers feel more comfortable with the tried and true. Are there long-term technical trends that might affect your film? For example, there are currently millions more standard definition television sets in the world than high definition, which might be an argument for working in SD. But the

---

1. Such as the PBS Red Book in the United States, available online, which details policies and deliverables.

industry is moving toward high def, retailers are pushing HDTVs, and broadcasters are increasingly offering high def programming. It's reasonable to assume that your options for showing a film in the future will be greater if it's shot in HD rather than SD. During this time of transition, some filmmakers are choosing to shoot on HD, but edit and finish in SD, with the idea of returning to the original HD recordings at a later date to create an HD version.

New forms of distribution create new markets and income streams. Keep an ear to the ground for what's coming so you can take advantage. Distribution contracts sometimes refer to "formats now known or hereafter devised" as a way to lay claim to developments yet to come. The Internet has the potential to fully democratize distribution, removing the gatekeepers altogether. However, while posting your film on a website may make it available to viewers, there are still the hurdles of attracting an audience to watch the movie and ensuring that you get paid when they view it. Some things don't change, and whenever money is involved, the gatekeepers are never far behind; filmmakers will always need to find a way to work with them.

For more on the business aspects of distribution, see Chapter 19.

THE BIG SCREEN AND THE SMALL(ER) SCREEN

The past fifty years have seen a war of technology between the big screen (theaters) and the small screen (TV). When television started stealing audiences from the theaters in the 1950s, cinema fought back with widescreen formats (see below), color, and multichannel surround sound. Before long, TV answered back with color, then its own versions of surround sound. Now, 16:9 widescreen TV is common, and flat-screen TVs have increased in size to the point that some can provide a more cinema-like viewing experience in the home. Even a blockbuster Hollywood film will be seen by far more people sitting on couches at home than by people sitting in theater seats. Even so, only the theater offers the communal experience of watching with a large audience, on an enveloping screen in a dark room, away from the distractions of daily life.

The term "small screen" used to be understood as meaning broadcast television typically viewed on a modest-sized box in the living room. Now screens for personal viewing range from enormous wall-mounted displays to inch-wide cellphones. The source of the programming can be satellite, cable, DVD, hard drives, the Web, or any number of other storage and transmission technologies. For a filmmaker, it's hard to know where or how your work will be seen or how you should prepare for that. The next fifty years will see increasing convergence between the large and smaller screens, and if you're producing mainly for one, you'll need to take the others into account.

Theatrical Exhibition

Projection on a large screen puts tremendous demands on the image because any defects, graininess, shakiness, or lack of focus will be greatly enlarged and have the potential to disturb the viewing experience. Traditionally, feature films for theaters have been shot in 35mm film. For the feature film industry, this has meant that many of the tools of production, techniques of postproduction, and projection systems of theaters have been geared toward 35mm film (or even larger film formats).

Fig. 2-1. Large-screen projection puts particular demands on image and sound quality. (Film-Tech.com)

Though there have been exceptions—low-budget features blown up from 16mm, super 16mm, and video (more on digital video below)—it's important to recognize how important the 35mm standard has been for audiences worldwide. Even if they can't describe why the picture looks the way it does, people generally know when they're watching a real "movie" shot on 35mm. The 35mm look has to do with the tonal range, the clarity of the image, the grain structure, the frame rate, lenses, and other aspects (see the "Look" of the Movie, below). Obviously, films shot in 35mm can look very different from one another, and may employ a variety of film stocks, lenses, or filters in order to achieve different looks. But there are certain qualities in common—qualities that we particularly identify with fictional stories.

From an artistic point of view, this is not to say that 35mm is necessarily *better* than other formats. The films of John Cassavetes that were shot with a handheld 16mm camera would not be better if shot in 35mm. The look of a low-resolution DV camera may be perfectly suited to the movie you're making. And even the 35mm image has certain characteristics, such as graininess, unsteady projection, and motion artifacts (jerkiness during fast pans or wagon wheels that appear to spin backwards), that aren't by definition "good"; they're just very familiar and deeply intertwined with our collective experience of going to the movies.

Some people who shoot in digital video have no interest in emulating the look of 35mm film. They may be trying to deliberately distance themselves from Hollywood styles, or they may be seeking the unique characteristics of video. For others, the concerns of story, content, cost, and convenience are so much more pressing than the look or visual style that they'll shoot with whatever format they can get their hands on.

On the other side of the coin, some feature filmmakers are drawn to high definition video because they feel the HD image can approximate the look of film. As discussed earlier, HD technology comes in various flavors, ranging from economical HDV camcorders using MiniDV tape to advanced HD cameras like the Grass Valley Viper that output huge uncompressed RGB signals for big-budget feature production. As HD acquisition becomes increasingly affordable, most filmmakers shooting video for big-screen release are using some form of HD.

Since the 1950s, theatrical films have been in widescreen. If you're producing for theatrical exhibition, plan on an aspect ratio that's at least 16:9 (see p. 87).

Another key consideration if you're aiming for theatrical release: Thousands of theaters in the world are equipped with 35mm projectors. Digital projection is catching on, and the number of theaters equipped with digital video projectors is growing rapidly. But as of this writing, if movies for theatrical exhibition are not available as 35mm film prints, they can face limitations in terms of where they can be shown. There are also still a few major film festivals that require entries to be projected on film. Blowing up or transferring material shot in 16mm or video to 35mm can produce excellent results if done carefully with the right equipment. But a blowup can represent a significant portion of a low-budget film's costs (see p. 68). If you're contemplating doing a transfer to 35mm from video or 16mm, it's prudent to wait until you're sure theatrical distribution is really going to happen for your project before spending the money.

Digital Television

For decades, broadcast TV was pretty straightforward in terms of formats. It was always analog, standard definition, interlaced, and non-widescreen (4:3). In North America, the NTSC broadcasting standard is 525 lines at 29.97 fps. Both the European PAL and French SECAM broadcasting standards are 625 lines at 25 fps. As of this writing, most over-the-air broadcasts worldwide are in one of these three formats, and a great deal of programming is broadcast this way.

ATSC FORMATS

Resolution	Frame Rates	Aspect Ratio	Pixel Format
HIGH DEFINITION			
1920 x 1080	24p, 30p, 60i	16:9	square
1280 x 720	24p, 30p, 60p	16:9	square
STANDARD DEFINITION			
704 x 480	24p, 30p, 60i, 60p	4:3	nonsquare
704 x 480	24p, 30p, 60i, 60p	16:9	nonsquare
640 x 480	24p, 30p, 60i, 60p	4:3	square

Fig. 2-2. ATSC formats. Digital television broadcast in the United States includes these formats. 60i means 30 fps, interlaced.

Enter *Digital Television (DTV)*. The idea of DTV is to replace analog TV broadcasting with a new, flexible digital technology capable of transmitting up to four different standard definition channels in compressed form in the same signal space, or bandwidth, as a single conventional 6 MHz analog TV channel. It is also possible to transmit in the same 6 MHz channel a high definition signal along with several standard def signals. You can see why broadcasters, anticipating additional income from advertising in the new channels, might welcome DTV.

What are the advantages of DTV to the consumer? Unlike analog TV, which is susceptible to ghosting and multiple images caused by signal path reflections, DTV reception is crystal clear. There is no "snow" when the digital signal grows weak, as is the case with poor analog reception. With digital broadcasting, the signal is either cleanly displayed or nothing is displayed (though occasionally digital errors do creep in). In this respect, over-the-air DTV resembles digital cable TV, which also employs MPEG-2 compression to squeeze as many channels as possible into a cable company's available signal pipeline.

Also like digital cable TV, over-the-air DTV can be either standard definition or HD. It's important to emphasize this fact, because many mistakenly believe that DTV means HD. It doesn't. In fact, a TV station can continue to produce analog programming in standard definition and digitize it for digital broadcasting at the last possible moment, at the point of transmission. Put another way, DTV is not a production system or tape format but a *transmission* system. Any format can be used to create programming for DTV.

In the United States at least, broadcasters have a choice of which SD and HD formats they broadcast in. For example, as of this writing, CBS and NBC have chosen 1080i for their high definition programming, while ABC and Fox are going with 720p. Again, it's important to note that not all DTV programming is HD. For a while, in fact, much of it will be SD.

Initiating free, over-the-air digital TV broadcasting has proven to be no trivial matter. On the broadcaster's end, investment in new transmitters and antennas is required. On the consumer's end, new rabbit ears and rooftop antennas are necessary (both virtually extinct at the end of the analog era), as well as new TVs capable of decoding a digital signal, or, in the case of older analog TVs, added boxes with decoders.

In the United States, digital broadcast television is known as *ATSC (Advanced Television Systems Committee)*, after the organization that set the technical specs. ATSC was adopted in 1996 to replace analog NTSC. ATSC-compatible equipment is required to handle 18 different format variations at both 30 fps–based frame rates and slightly slower NTSC-compatible 29.97 fps–based frame rates. (Some describe this as 36 different format variations. See Fig. 2-2.) ATSC can also broadcast SD in 4:3 or 16:9 aspect ratios, and in both SD and HD using either interlace or progressive scanning. ATSC uses MPEG-2 video compression (like standard definition DVDs, satellite, and digital cable TV) and Dolby Digital AC-3 audio compression for 5.1 audio channels (see Chapter 16).

ATSC was originally supposed to take over completely from NTSC by 2006 (ending the analog era) but adoption is taking longer for various reasons, including slower-than-expected consumer purchasing of new TVs with ATSC receivers (though this is changing rapidly with the surge in popularity of flat-screen TVs), a sluggish build-out of DTV transmitters by TV stations, and delays achieved by special-interest groups.

EUROPEAN DTV. In Europe, DTV has made greater inroads. The European digital broadcasting standard known as *DVB* (*Digital Video Broadcasting*) was adopted by a multinational consortium in the mid-1990s. By 2003, Berlin became the first TV market to switch off analog PAL broadcasts entirely. Like ATSC, DVB utilizes MPEG-2 compression but it differs in key respects. While ATSC describes land-based (terrestrial) broadcasting only, DVB standardizes signal delivery across all platforms including satellite, cable, and even handheld phones. As a result, there are extended DVB standards known as DVB-T (terrestrial), DVB-S (satellite), DVB-C (cable), and DVB-H (mobile handheld).

Most DVB broadcasting has been standard definition until recently. However, European interest in HD is growing, and the DVB standards-setting body has embraced H.264 (MPEG-4) compression for delivery of both standard and high definition. H.264 is designed to permit a high-quality image to be scaled to high and low resolutions and frame rates for large and small screens (see p. 228).

LAPTOP TV. As if these developments weren't epochal enough, mobile "laptop TV" is being actively introduced in Europe and Asia using DVB-H or a rival technology called *DMB* (*Digital Multimedia Broadcasting*), which also uses H.264 compression. The transmission system used by ATSC does not lend itself to mobile reception, so prospects for mobile DTV in the United States are less promising. However, mobile viewing is an idea whose time has come—who doesn't watch video on computer screens these days?—and your work will certainly be viewed this way in years to come.

Other Sources

Regardless of what happens with digital broadcasting, there are other forms of distribution that offer different opportunities, both in terms of technology and how you get your movie to audiences.

VHS cassettes created a revolution when they were introduced in the late 1970s by allowing consumers to watch a wide range of movies at home on their own schedule. DVDs upped the ante with far better picture and sound quality, multiple languages, and extras, such as the director's commentary and "making-of" videos. DVDs are now a major revenue source for many films, and newer high definition videodisc formats like HD-DVD and Blu-ray are raising the stakes once again. DVDs are also proving to be an important aftermarket for programming that has already aired on TV.

Internet streaming of films in the past has been plagued by low-quality video and the problem of having to watch while sitting at a computer. Codecs like H.264 (MPEG-4) and VC-1 (formerly Windows Media 9) are making it possible to get much higher quality video through a broadband Internet connection, and the signal can be fed to a Web-enabled TV in your living room.

From a distribution standpoint, these technologies provide a way for filmmakers to get their films to viewers without going through the commercial machinery of broadcast television, theatrical exhibition, or traditional distributors. An independent with no support from a large company can set up fairly easily to sell discs online or provide the movie itself for downloading. Some producers have made a lot of money selling DVDs with the help of a *fulfillment house* that takes the orders, processes the payments, and ships the discs. Marketing still remains a challenge.

Small-Screen Viewing

As discussed above, when movies are intended for a big screen, there's an advantage to shooting in a high-resolution format. When they're intended for a small screen, the benefit is smaller but still significant.

It used to be the received wisdom that if you knew your movie would only be streamed as highly compressed MPEG-1 video on the Web or viewed on a tiny monitor, perhaps for a computer-based multimedia project, then HD didn't offer a lot of advantage in image quality, and it certainly increased costs. This is because when high resolution images are shown on a small screen, the eye cannot perceive fine detail. Look at Fig. 5-16 on p. 211: These images are very low resolution, but when viewed from far enough away, they begin to look sharp. In terms of fine detail, the smaller the screen (and the larger the distance between the viewer and the screen) the less benefit you get from shooting HD.

But there remain benefits to shooting in high-resolution formats even when viewed on small screens, including the "over-sampling" of image detail for better reproduction of medium-resolution details, wider color gamut and less color compression—all of which can often be "felt" by the viewer even on a small display viewed at close distance. (If you've ever seen a black-and-white Ansel Adams photograph reproduced in a magazine, itself not capable of matching the fine detail or tonal scale of the original print, it's likely you nevertheless felt the superior image quality of the original.) These benefits also apply when shooting high-end standard definition formats such as Digital Betacam or DVCPRO 50 with a progressive-scan camera.

With the one-two punch of cheap consumer HD formats like HDV and improved compression technologies for streaming HD like H.264 and VC-1 (both

Fig. 2-3. Cell-phone video. In *Sunset Boulevard*, silent film star Norma Desmond says, "I *am* big, it's the pictures that got small." This is a lot smaller.

utilized in HD-DVD and Blu-ray disc formats), there's a trend toward editing and viewing HD-originated material on computer monitors that match or exceed HD resolution and that are designed to be viewed up close, not at a distance like TVs. (In terms of resolution, computer monitors left standard definition TV in the dust years ago.) Even smallish laptops can now display compressed HD images.

So with network TV in the early stages of ceding ground to "networked TV," perhaps the only thing that can be said for sure is that whether you're producing in HD or SD, the ultimate viewer may well be watching something that looks a lot different than what you produced. Many TVs automatically change the shape, color, and resolution of the images you've worked hard to create. Many viewers will be watching on a small or low-resolution TV, and may be squinting to make out details that were so bold and beautiful in the editing room. This is taken to the extreme when films are distributed in a form that can be viewed on cell phones or iPods. Some companies are producing content expressly for these devices, and they do offer additional distribution channels and revenue streams for other types of programming. However, for some filmmakers, the idea that people are watching their movies on a microscreen while walking down the street or riding the subway gives them the willies.

PRODUCTION PLANNING

Chapter 19 covers topics like fund-raising and hiring crews and actors. Chapter 9 has ideas about organizing and planning shoots. Below are some things to think about when planning the production as a whole.

Workflow

As noted in Chapter 1, *workflow* is a term borrowed from information technology to describe the careful step-by-step management of a complex project. Applied to film and digital video, it refers to the sequence of steps or tasks needed to accomplish a goal in production, editing, or finishing. For example, if you shoot DV and record on tape, your postproduction workflow will include capturing the video from the tape to a hard drive before you can start editing. However, if you record directly to a hard drive in the field, your postproduction workflow is simplified and you can start editing immediately because you've already captured the footage.

Particularly now that there are so many technologies and ways of doing things, it's important to plan out your workflow in advance. Often, choices you make at the beginning commit you to a certain workflow later on. The best workflow choices harmonize the steps of production, editing, and finishing, so that time is saved and money is not wasted on fixing mistakes in post.

Perhaps the best way to prepare a project workflow is to talk to people at each step of the production process and find out before you start how they like to work and what they need to do their jobs. If you're shooting film, visit the film lab, meet the color timer or telecine colorist and ask their advice about using the latest film stocks and formats. If you're shooting video or film, ask the postproduction facility how they want material delivered, what kind of timecode they need, or any particular audio requirements. Discuss detailed strategies of online conforming and color-correction with your editor and your post house. The value of talking to people in advance cannot be overstated! Don't go blindly into decisions that may leave you regretting them later.

Upfront Versus Back-end Costs

Almost every film is made under pressure. There's never enough time or money. Even if there's an ample budget and schedule, the work has a way of taking every penny or minute available. Often, movies are started with less than the full budget in hand, with hopes of raising the rest of the money later. Filmmakers figure they'll get something *in the can* (that is, through production but not necessarily all the way through postproduction) and worry about the rest later. This may be the only way to get into production, and if done responsibly, can be a smart strategy. Particularly if you don't have a strong track record (but even if you do), backers, distributors, and broadcasters often want to see something concrete before they commit to a project.

Nevertheless, there can be pitfalls to this approach. One is the instinct to defer expenses as long as possible. As an example, this sometimes leads feature film-makers to shoot video (cheaper upfront) than film (expensive upfront but possibly cheaper to finish) even if the net cost for the project may be higher in video (more on this below). Filmmakers may have the strategy of paying the minimum for things out of pocket with the hope of getting a distributor to pick up finishing costs at the end. Keep in mind that most expenses that are "paid" by the distributor are actually deducted from your share of the film's revenue, so you're really choosing between paying now or being paid less later.

Similar arguments can be made about shooting HD versus SD, or renting high-quality equipment versus cheap but convenient alternatives, or hiring an experienced crew versus novices. It's good to keep your initial budget low, but you may pay for it in the end with unanticipated costs. These can stem from corner-cutting decisions like not taking enough time on the set to get good lighting; not trying to fix poor audio on the spot (which may be unfixable later), or using nonprofessional equipment that creates subsequent postproduction problems.

Obviously, you can only afford what you can afford. By talking to people and getting experience you'll learn where it makes sense to scrimp, and where it doesn't.

SHOOTING FILM VERSUS SHOOTING VIDEO

As high definition video improves, it's beginning to rival the look of film, which is the *original* high definition medium. At the same time, most film productions now incorporate a lot of video technology. The lines that separate film and video are blurring. Going into a new production, why choose one over the other? Let's examine some of the production and financial questions.

Cost

On a per-minute basis, film is a lot more expensive than video. That is, an hour of tape costs much less than sixty minutes of film, especially when you count film stock, processing, synching the audio, and making workprints and/or transferring to video for editing. However, when you consider the whole budget, film isn't *always* much more expensive. For example, on a per-day basis, you may be able to rent a film rig for less than a high-end video equipment package. So if your production will take place over many days, there may be savings in camera rentals if you shoot film. Similarly, if you can be frugal in how much footage you shoot (say, restricting yourself to only a few takes for each shot in a drama) the higher cost of film won't be as much of a problem.

Fig. 2-4. Small video crew. Including, at right, videographer, assistant, and dolly grip. (From the *Better & Better* series with Elizabeth Hepburn. Photo by Arledge Armenaki.)

You also need to factor in distribution. If you shoot in digital video and plan to do a film-out to 35mm for theatrical release, you'll be looking at $30,000 to $80,000 for the video-to-film transfer. If you shoot on film, you can make a release print for much less than that. Of course, if you're shooting video and only releasing on video then the cost structure changes.[2]

Convenience

Generally, video is a lot easier to shoot than film. If you're working alone or with a small crew, video is simpler and more portable. Tape is cheap and comes in long, easy-to-load cassettes so shooting video can be much more relaxed. You can take more risks with things that might or might not work out. On a drama, you

2. And if you're shooting film but making a "digital intermediate," that will raise the cost of film considerably. See Chapter 18.

can keep the camera rolling between takes if you want, which can help keep energy and concentration up. If you're interviewing someone for a documentary, and the subject takes a long time to loosen up, you can keep shooting until he does, without fretting about the cost. That said, shooting a lot of footage isn't necessarily better than shooting less. Having vast amounts of material to wade through in the editing room can be a real burden. Students can get beneficial experience from learning the discipline of shooting film, and the planning and control it requires—skills you may not get if you shoot only video (for more, see The Shooting Ratio, p. 320).

Interestingly, the Flash memory cards (like Panasonic's P2) used by some newer video cameras instead of tape are often limited to only a few minutes of recording before the card needs to be downloaded. This workflow brings to video something akin to the inconvenience of having to change film magazines on a film shoot.

For recording sound, film shooting involves using a separate audio recorder. This is called *double system* recording and allows the sound recordist a great deal of freedom to get close to the sound source or even to go off and record at another location, completely independently of the camera. But there are disadvantages too: If you're shooting alone, a separate audio recorder can be awkard to operate. Double system recording also means extra time in post to sync up the audio before editing.

When shooting video, audio is usually recorded in the camera (*single system*). This can be much more convenient, especially for solo work. However, if there is a sound recordist on the crew, he or she will usually be connected to the camera by a cable or by wireless transmitters. It is also possible to shoot video double system with a separate audio recorder (more on this below).

The video image requires no processing and can be instantly viewed on a monitor— a great convenience for the director or client. The tape can be checked right away after the shot if needed. Many film productions are done with a *video assist* (also called a *video tap*), which allows you to view and/or record a video image of what the camera is shooting. This allows you to check the action but it's not the same as seeing what the film stock is actually capturing (see Video Assist, p. 247).

Some Image Considerations

Shooting video sometimes requires less lighting than film, because many video cameras are slightly more sensitive than film stocks and also offer several additional stops of electronic gain to work with. On the other hand, because film stocks handle a high contrast range better than video cameras, there are times when you may need *more* lighting for video, for instance to reduce the contrast range of a scene in bright sunlight or when shooting an interior against bright sunny windows.

SLOW MOTION. In the past, film was the only option for shooting slow motion. As discussed on p. 357, for really smooth slow motion you need to shoot many frames per second; until recently only film cameras could achieve these frame rates. Now there are video cameras such as Panasonic's Varicam and HVX200 (see Fig. 1-21) that, when shooting a 24 fps project, can operate at decreased or increased frame rates, up to 60 fps. Shooting 60 fps for a 24 fps project slows motion by a factor of 2.5. While not in the same league as an Arriflex SR High Speed 16mm film camera, which can achieve 150 fps, it's often effective for gentle slo-mo effects

Fig. 2-5. Arriflex 16SR Highspeed. A similar SR is available for standard-speed operation. This camera is reflex, with quick-change magazines. (Arriflex Corporation)

involving people. For higher frame rates—good for capturing flying bullets or explosions—there are now digital file–based cameras like the Cine SpeedCam, which can capture SD images up to 1000 fps. Others can capture HD and beyond at similar rates. What's exciting about these electronic high-speed camera systems is that playback is instant. No waiting around to screen the results from the film lab. As a result of instant feedback, on-the-spot adjustments can often be made to perfect the shot through multiple takes. You can't do that with film. Even so, on some video productions critical slo-mo shots (say, big explosions) are done on film, which still proves cost-effective.

TIME-LAPSE. When film cameras are used for time-lapse shooting (used to make events that take hours or days appear to happen in seconds) you can't view instant playback. Many newer tape-based and file-based video camcorders now provide a true single-frame time-lapse capability. Tape-based camcorders with this ability incorporate a picture cache board—similar to Flash memory—that accumulates 5 to 15 seconds of video captured one frame at a time, which is then laid off to tape while the cache card begins to fill again. Alternatively, camcorders with non-linear media, such as hard drives, optical drives, and Flash memory, can easily write a single frame to media as it's recorded. As a result of the ease of creating stunning time-lapse shots in digital video, this technique is growing in popularity and is now often seen in everything from TV dramas to indie documentaries. For more on time-lapse, see p. 359.

Future-Proofing
Film is an established technology that, while continuing to be refined, hasn't fundamentally changed in many years. Video technology, on the other hand, has

been going through a period of explosive growth, and formats that are hot today are likely to be obsolete before too long. One argument for shooting film is that a production shot on celluloid may have better shelf life and adapt better to new video technologies as they come along (helping "future-proof" the movie, as Kodak would say). When it comes to long-term archival storage, it's hard to guess how many years in the future any given video recording will still be playable. Over time, the glue (called a binder) that attaches the recordable metal oxide layers of videotape to its polyester base will deteriorate. When this happens, the oxide begins to flake off. Recordable DVDs (like DVD-R) suffer a different problem: Their data is contained in photosensitive dyes that fade over time, just like film. What happens to a DVD when key data is lost—a directory or header file? You get a shiny coaster to put under your drinks. If film breaks, you lose a couple of frames.

In theory, film can withstand the passage of time better. But individual stocks and storage conditions make a big difference. There are black-and-white negatives from the 1930s that still look wonderful, while some color films from the 1980s are already faded beyond fixing.

CHOOSING A CAMERA

Many factors go into choosing a video or film camera. With film, the first question is usually, what format do you want to shoot in (16mm or 35mm)? With video, you may ultimately choose between competing formats based on things like the capabilities of particular cameras or what editing equipment is available. This and the following three chapters can serve as a reference for what features and formats you may want for your production.

In both film and video, camera size is a key consideration. The cost of a production is often tied closely to the size of the camera. If you're shooting with a 35mm Panavision camera, you'll need a sizable crew to lug it around. If you're working with a DV camera, on the other hand, you might need only a cameraperson. If you're shooting a documentary alone or with a small crew, a small camera that can be tossed into a shoulder bag can be a big asset.

The size of a camera affects how people respond to the production. In documentary shooting, big cameras often draw attention ("What TV station will this be on?") or may make subjects uncomfortable. A small camera that looks a little like a consumer model (or *is* a consumer model) sometimes helps you fly under the radar and avoid raising suspicions. On a feature film, a small camera may make some people think it isn't a "real" (that is, Hollywood) film. At times this can be a help—for example, if people can see you're working with a small budget, they may be more understanding when you can't pay them a lot. At other times, you might not be taken as seriously. As technology develops, small is often seen as cool.

From the cameraperson's standpoint, small cameras have advantages and disadvantages. Small, prosumer, or consumer cameras may not have the features or accept the accessories that professionals rely on to do their job. You may find your creativity hampered by the lack of manual controls or the inability to choose lenses or other devices. Some people love shooting with a little camera that can be cradled in the hands, floated above the ground, or fit into small spaces. But when you hold

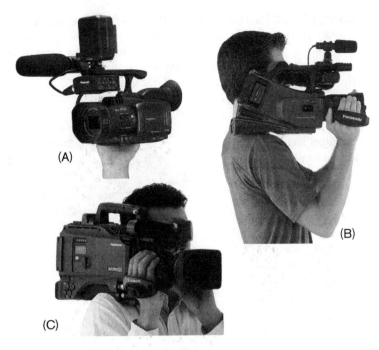

Fig. 2-6. (A) A small, handheld camera is light and portable, but can be hard to hold steady. (B) This camera perches on the shoulder, which increases steadiness, but a lot of the weight is on your right arm, which can get tiring. (C) A camera that balances on the shoulder can be steadier and sometimes more comfortable for handheld work, even if it's heavier. Panasonic models shown: AG-DVC30 with infrared light for night shooting, AG-DVC60, and AJ-SPC700. (Panasonic Broadcast)

a small camera up to your eye, all the weight is on your right arm. For handheld shooting, this can make steadiness difficult and can be very tiring after a few hours of shooting. A heavier, longer camera that balances on the shoulder may be easier to work with. But beware of a camera that has a shoulder rest or brace but doesn't really balance on the shoulder—your arm still has to hold it up. Some camerapeople like to wear a body brace for handheld work; others find that cumbersome.

Generally speaking, the size of a video camera correlates with the size of its sensor, which has an impact on the look of the image it records (the same is true with film cameras and the film gauge). See p. 148.

MANAGING DATA IN PRODUCTION AND POST

Digital video creates a lot of digital data to be recorded, processed, and stored. From the get-go, you need to consider which technologies and techniques you'll use, as they affect many aspects of production and postproduction.

Choosing Media for Recording and Storage

Not too many years ago, a typical video camcorder recorded only one format onto a particular size tape cassette—end of story. Today, many cameras offer a variety of formats and ways to record them. Choices you make in production have an impact on the quality of the recording and on your workflow.

When thinking about digital video recording, it helps to remember that digital video is just a form of computer data stored in files, whether on a tape, hard disk drive (HDD), optical disc, or a solid-state memory card like a CompactFlash or a Panasonic P2 card. Video files are a whole lot bigger than text files, but the basic operations of storing, copying, and moving them aren't so different from what you might do with word processing files on your home computer.

Fig. 2-7. Wafian HR-1 Direct-to-Disk high definition video recorder. Records Cineform Intermediate codec in both .AVI and .MOV formats. (Wafian Corporation)

SHOOT WITH TAPE OR GO TAPELESS? Videotape originated in the analog era and continues to be a useful medium for recording digital video. Among the benefits of tape cassettes are that they're relatively cheap; they can be quickly loaded and unloaded from a camera; they're lightweight; and they can be used for long-term storage. Unlike a hard drive, a tape cassette is not a piece of "equipment"; so, for example, if you shoot footage for someone else, you can give them the tape and not have to worry about getting the drive back later.

Tape has some clear disadvantages too. A crease in an analog tape can create rolling break-up in the image. Dropouts can result from bad contact between the tape and the recording or playback heads, resulting in momentary horizontal white lines in analog playback or blocky colored patches in digital playback. The good news is that recent digital tape formats like HDV, which spreads compressed video

Fig. 2-8. DVCAM tape cassettes. The small cassette is MiniDV size. The larger shell holds more tape and can be used with larger professional cameras. (Sony Electronics, Inc.)

Fig. 2-9. P2 cards. These Flash memory cards are about the size of a credit card and are available in various storage capacities. (Panasonic Broadcast)

over multiple frames when recording and utilizes powerful error correction, are fairly resistant to dropouts. Tape stocks have also improved, notably those using multiple-layer technology.

With non-tape media you don't have to worry about dropouts. They no longer

Fig. 2-10. Portable hard disk drive. This Panasonic battery-powered unit can be used in the field to download P2 cards (the card slot is visible on the front) and then connected to an editing system as an external disk drive. (Panasonic Broadcast)

exist, since there are no heads in physical contact with magnetic media. And compared to a videotape camcorder with its delicate tape transport and spinning head drum assembly, there's very little mechanism to wear down or break. Indeed, in the case of the P2 card, there's no mechanism at all. This means that HDD, optical disc, and Flash memory camcorders should prove considerably more durable. (Note, however, that it is still possible for a disk sector to fail or for a data sector to fail in a P2 card.) FireWire and USB 2.0 hard drives and CompactFlash and PCMCIA cards are off-the-shelf commodities that get cheaper all the time.

There can be drawbacks to recording to hard drives in the field. During a shoot, hard drives require power and can add weight or bulk to the camera. Whether recording to a laptop or HDD, you have to deal with short, stiff FireWire cables that restrict mobility and sometimes even cause FireWire glitches during recording or copying.

SAVING TIME IN EDITING. On the editing side, file-based non-tape media can free you to edit without a tape deck or camera as part of the editing system, which can be an enormous cost savings and make for a more portable NLE. You can insert P2 cards directly into any laptop with a standard PCMCIA (also known as a PC card) slot, while portable FireWire drives can be attached to any laptop with a FireWire port.

With tape, before you can edit on a nonlinear system, the material on the tape needs to be "digitized" (if the original is analog) or "captured" (if the original is digital) to a hard drive. On some projects, this isn't a problem; in fact, it's a blessing. Having a chance to review the tape and then transfer into the NLE only the material you plan to use (if disk space happens to be an issue) can help you organize the material, even if it does take a bit longer. But sometimes you need to edit during the shoot or immediately after. In those situations, file-based recording directly to a hard disk drive, optical disc, or solid-state memory card can get you editing faster, at least in theory.

Why in theory? On the face of it, recording directly to nonlinear media should speed up the postproduction workflow because it eliminates the step of digitizing or capturing, which typically happens in real time (an hour of material takes at least an hour to capture). With file-based recording, you can connect the media directly to the NLE and get right to work . . . that is, if the NLE accepts the camera's native file format with no file translation, transcoding, or rendering. The reason this is noteworthy is that with the swelling number of new tape and file formats, there have been instances of popular NLEs that won't accept, at least at first, a new format or file type or frame rate. It's important to research file format compatibility all the way from production to post and finishing, to be sure the method you're planning will work. The devil is in the details, as ever.

Also note that while direct recording to nonlinear media eliminates digitizing or capturing, it has no impact on the time-consuming next step of logging: the task of breaking down and labeling clips.

PROTECTING DIGITAL DATA. Direct recording to nonlinear media introduces a new concern, namely, "what is the master recording?" HDDs and P2 cards are meant to be reused, not labeled and carefully stored like recorded videotape masters. A single 8 GB P2 card holds only 8 minutes of 1080i HD; when it's full it has to be copied to a laptop, external hard drive, or Panasonic's portable hard drive storage device, the "P2 Store" (see Fig. 2-10). If you've ever copied the contents of an entire hard drive to another hard drive, you know that it takes considerable time. Maybe not as long as digitizing or capturing from a videotape— although in the tense atmosphere of a shoot it can seem as long. Next, before you wipe forever clean the P2 card, you want to be absolutely sure that you have copied intact working files to the backup device, because your footage is costly if not impossible to replace. Often this means that someone is assigned the responsibility of first playing back and inspecting the copied files—in real time, of course—before the P2 card is recycled. So much for the big time advantage over digitizing or capturing.

When an HDD or memory card attached to the camera fills up, you need an empty drive standing by plus some additional media to download the first drive or card to (depending upon your workflow strategy). In the case of P2 cards, extra P2 cards must be on hand to replace the one being copied, to ensure a steady supply of recordable media to the camcorder. If you can afford enough P2 cards, this shouldn't be too limiting, but if you have only a few, you may need to stop shooting for several minutes to download from the cards.

When a laptop or P2 Store fills up, a second file transfer of the same footage becomes necessary, which has to be figured into the workflow. Some productions also take an additional precaution and make a second complete backup to DVDs or to additional hard drives. When working with rerecordable nonlinear media, bulletproof backup is an absolute requirement—even if an extra person or assistant on the set is needed.

To get the best of both worlds, some people record simultaneously to tape and to an HDD—the HDD gets them editing faster and the tape goes to long-term storage in the archive. Sony HDV camcorders, for example, can record HDV internally to a MiniDV cassette and simultaneously output the same HDV signal via FireWire to a compact HDD, such as the popular FireStore disk recorders made by Focus Enhancements. Focus Enhancements, incidentally, has collaborated with JVC, Canon, and Panasonic to tailor 100 GB FireStore disk recorders to their respective HDV and DVCPRO HD camcorder lines (see Fig. 3-10).

As of this writing, optical disc recording is limited mostly to professional camcorder systems like Sony's XDCAM and XDCAM HD (both Blu-ray based) and the new consumer AVCHD format which uses cheap DVD-R discs. In both cases, disc drives are integral to the camcorders and play/record decks (although AVCHD discs are readable in any standard tray-based computer DVD drive).

LONG-TERM STORAGE. For long-term storage, memory cards remain wildly expensive. While hard drives with their delicate mechanisms are of questionable long-term archival value, they have found favor as an affordable "bit bucket" to store project files and media, especially as the cost per gigabyte has plummeted. The most economical approach is the use of "bare" 3.5-inch drives. These are ATA (also called IDE) or newer, hot-swappable SATA drives without fancy cases, power supplies, or FireWire bridges—add-ons that jack up the cost of individual hard drives. Instead, do-it-yourself filmmakers buy bare drives off the Internet and mount them in removable enclosures that contain power, data cables, and a FireWire chipset. Bare drives can be swapped in and out of a single enclosure, turning 500 GB hard drives into, in effect, big data cartridges.

The latest generation of DVDs for HD recording and playback—Blu-ray and HD DVD—may also provide an affordable answer, if not necessarily a fast one. In this workflow, instead of archiving *everything* (including all the bad takes as you generally would with tape) you might store only selected takes. Why? A MiniDV tape contains 11 GB of digital video while a standard DVD holds only 4.7 GB. You would need three DVDs to copy one full MiniDV tape. By comparison, a single-sided, single-layer HD DVD holds 15 GB—the equivalent of about one MiniDV tape—and a Blu-ray disc, 25 GB—about two MiniDV tapes. Now can you see why tape remains cost-effective?

And then there's the new *Holographic Versatile Disc* (*HVD*), which uses two lasers to store 300 GB on the same discs Blu-ray uses—the equivalent of 27 MiniDV tapes! (Naturally, there's already a rival format.) HVD promises 40 times the DVD transfer speed and an eventual 3.9 terabyte capacity. This format is backed by Panasonic and Fuji Photo (they make media) and is of intense interest to Hollywood because an entire Digital Cinema feature release might conceivably fit on a single disc. From a long-term archival perspective, however, there remains one nagging concern about each one of these recordable disc formats: Like color film, they all rely on organic dyes that fade due to aging and warm temperatures.

Thinking About Compression and Workflow

See the discussion of compression on p. 20 before reading this.

We've seen that shooting digital video requires processing a lot of digital data. The more resolution the camera is capable of, the more data you've got to deal with.

Inside the digital video camera, as signals are sent from the camera's sensors into its processing circuits, the resulting component digital video signal is not yet compressed. This is the cleanest, highest-quality form of the picture. But to record uncompressed video, especially in high definition, requires a lot of storage and an expensive recorder. On some high-end productions, the budget is large enough to justify recording uncompressed in order to get the very best picture quality. But on most productions, uncompressed just isn't practical, and may not provide much benefit (that is, depending on how your movie is to be shown, you may not see much difference between working in uncompressed and using some compression).

As discussed in Chapter 1, different cameras and formats compress the video different amounts before recording it. Generally speaking, the systems with the least compression provide the highest quality and are most expensive to work with, and the systems that use a lot of compression are smaller and more affordable. One reason manufacturers offer so many different systems is that productions vary considerably in their relative priorities of quality, convenience, and cost. If you can afford it, there are advantages to shooting with as little compression as possible. On the other hand, a highly compressed system may suit your needs well. As time goes on and codecs improve, you'll be able to work at lower data rates (more compressed) without sacrificing quality.

Some cameras may offer various options for compression. If you're able to work with an external recorder you may have even more. For example, some affordable

HDV cameras record highly compressed HDV within the camera, but can output full baseband (uncompressed) analog component HD or uncompressed digital HD via an HD-SDI link or an HDMI cable to a deck or hard drive.

Another variation on this theme is Panasonic's HVX200 camera, which can record to both P2 memory cards and MiniDV tapes. The camera will capture high definition DVCPRO HD (which is somewhat compressed) and DVCPRO50, but only to the P2 cards. If you want to record to the internal MiniDV tape mechanism, you're limited to standard definition DV. This is because tape heads capable of recording at the data rates necessary for HD would have cost more than the camera.

As you move into postproduction, you have more options about compression. If you shot in a relatively uncompressed, high-data-rate format and want to edit in that format, you'll need a lot of storage and a powerful, relatively expensive editing system. This can be a particular problem with high definition.

On many productions, to save money and storage, footage is downconverted or compressed prior to editing. For example, HD tapes might be down-resed to standard definition DVCAM to allow an offline edit on an inexpensive DV editing system. After the editing decisions are made in the offline, you finish on an HD online system. One disadvantage of this particular workflow is that while you're offline editing you won't be able to see the image in its full resolution. Alternatively, you could offline with a compressed HD codec.

In another type of postproduction workflow, camera footage is *decompressed* before editing (making the files *larger*). Since HDV compression can create issues in editing and effects, some filmmakers prefer to decompress it or transcode to a less compressed codec like DVCPRO HD or ProRes 422 prior to editing.

In finishing your project, you'll face yet more considerations about what format to create the master in, and how to manage up- or down-conversions from that master for distribution. See Chapter 14 for more on editing and finishing issues.

Workflow decisions about compression through the production chain have a whole array of pros and cons that you can best evaluate by talking with people in both production and postproduction and doing research on the Internet.

THE IMPORTANCE OF SOUND

In filmmaking, *sound quality is often more important than picture quality*. This may seem counterintuitive, but you can test it yourself. First watch a scene that's well lit and in focus but has distant, scratchy, rumbling sound with dialogue that's hard to understand. Then watch a scene that's very underexposed and maybe a little out of focus, but has pristine audio with crystal-clear voices. After a minute or two, the first scene becomes truly irritating; the second one, though not ideal, is at least watchable.

On many productions a misguided priority is placed on image over sound. For example, the director of photography may be given hours to light the set; then, at the last minute, the sound recordist is told to slide a microphone in wherever there's room—as long as it doesn't cast any shadows. Or, a filmmaker may spend thousands to get a high-resolution camera, only to shoot with a cheap on-camera mic.

For a fiction film, sound recorded poorly on the set can be remedied by re-recording the dialogue later in a studio (called *ADR—automatic dialogue replacement*). Even on an otherwise well-recorded movie, ADR may be necessary for scenes shot in noisy locations or where mics are impractical. ADR, of course, takes money and time.

On a documentary, ADR is not done (even if it could be, most would argue it *shouldn't* be). Many a great documentary scene has been abandoned on the cutting room floor because of unintelligible sound.

Sound recording and editing is discussed in Chapters 10, 11, and 16. But there are several aspects to sound that you should consider before you begin production.

Microphones

When it comes to recording the human voice, there's no substitute for getting close to the source. Miking from a few feet away usually allows you to capture the voice clearly, without too much competing background sound.

Professional sound recordists often use a microphone boom that can be positioned close to the person talking, and may use a directional mic that reduces background noise (see Chapter 10). Another solution is to put a wireless mic on the main person(s) talking; a wireless lapel mic can be hidden under clothing, or, for some documentaries, clipped on a tie or shirt.

With video camcorders there's a temptation to use the mic that is built-in or mounted on the camera. On-camera mics can be useful for run-and-gun situations, or when the subject is very close to the camera. However, if you plan to shoot your movie mostly with an on-camera mic, be aware that there will be many situations where you'll get bad sound. The camera is usually farther from the subject than is optimal for audio, and it's often pointed at something other than the sound source. Also, on-camera mics often pick up camera or handling noise. Avoid them when you can! Even if you're filming alone, a wireless mic or sometimes a handheld mic can be a big improvement.

The Recording System

As discussed above, film is always shot double system. When shooting video, sound may be recorded in the camera or it may also be recorded double system. When choosing a video camcorder, look into its sound recording capabilities. Few if any camcorders record sound that is of as high quality as professional sound recorders because professional sound recorders have expensive preamps and processing optimized for first-rate audio. But many camcorders record sound that is almost as good, typically 48 kHz, 16-bit digital audio, the same as DAT and many other digital recorders. Many indie features and documentaries have been successfully made with in-camera audio.

On occasion, a particular camcorder or video format results in audio that is of lower quality. For example, while nearly all digital video formats from MiniDV to HDCAM record uncompressed 16-bit PCM audio, the HDV format uses a "lossy" audio compression called MPEG-1 Audio Layer II (MP2). Its high bit rate of 384 Kbps—typical Mp3s found on the Internet are 128 Kbps—somewhat makes up for its "perceptual coding" technique which leaves out what it thinks you can't hear, and as a result HDV sound quality is considered "near CD" and "perceptually lossless." Some filmmakers, especially those making dramatic feature films, prefer instead to use portable flash- or disc-based recorders to record uncompressed audio while shooting HDV.

As another example, MiniDV camcorders record standard 16-bit, 48 kHz audio but some have a setting for recording lower-quality 12-bit, 32 kHz audio—a nonprofessional sample rate that should be avoided when quality counts.

Talk to audio recordists or postproduction mixers to get advice about your setup. For professional results, you may decide to use different camera settings, a different camera, or a separate audio recorder. When you shoot video double system, you gain a certain flexibility, but there may be added complexity on the shoot and you also need to account for the additional time you'll need to sync the sound and picture during editing.

Music

Music is a powerful force in movies. It can have a huge impact on the audience's emotions and energy. It can also have a huge impact on your budget. Filmmakers often plan scenes around their favorite song, or find themselves shooting a scene in which a cool tune is playing in the background. Unless you have deep pockets, beware!

If a character in your film plays or sings a song, you'll need to clear the rights to it with the song's publisher. To use a prerecorded song by a popular artist (whether it's playing in the scene or added in editing) you'll need to license it from both the publisher and the record company. This can cost thousands or tens of thousands of dollars. Never commit yourself to using a song (for example, by having a character perform it) without finding out first if you can clear and afford it. Even a tune as ubiquitous as "Happy Birthday" is copyrighted and needs to be licensed.

If you're shooting a documentary, it's generally a good idea to avoid radios or other music sources while you're filming. Turn them off when possible. (It also makes cutting easier if no continuous music exists in the background.) Even musical cell-phone ringtones could cause legal hassles.

There is an exception, however, which applies mostly to documentaries. The legal concept of copyright includes the idea of "fair use," which permits limited use of unlicensed audio and video materials under specific circumstances.

There's more on music editing in Chapter 16 and on the legal aspects of clearing music and fair use in Chapter 19.

The Sound Mix

Early sound recordings were monophonic—just one audio channel. Then stereo (two channels) became standard. Now some sound systems have five or more channels. Having a multichannel sound mix can enhance your distribution opportunities, especially if theatrical release is anticipated, but it adds complexity and cost to finishing the film. If you want or need a multichannel mix, budget for it and plan ahead (particularly in editing, but even in shooting). See Chapter 16 for more on mixing.

THE "LOOK" OF THE MOVIE

How a movie looks has an enormous impact on what the movie means to the audience. Marshall McLuhan said, "The medium is the message," and there is no doubt that the medium itself plays a large part in how we understand a movie's content and experience its emotional impact. There are cultural traditions that associate certain technologies and styles with certain types of movies. As discussed above, the dramas we're used to seeing in theaters are closely associated with the look of 35mm film shot with a large crew, careful lighting, and sophisticated dollies and other equipment to move the camera smoothly. In contrast, television news stories since the 1970s typically have the look of handheld, standard definition video, often shot with harsh, camera-mounted lights. Clearly, there is a noticeable difference in terms of the emotional "feel" and texture of the two formats/looks.

In a simplistic way, the crisp, bright video look makes news and sports feel "real." But the same look can make TV dramas (like soap operas) seem "fake"— that is, instead of allowing the audience to enter into the dramatic world the show is trying to create, the video image makes us aware of the "reality" of a bunch of actors walking around on sets. Higher budget dramas have traditionally been shot on film in order to capture a richer, softer feel that allows viewers to "suspend disbelief" and enter into the fictional world of the movie. Much television production, from news to soaps, is already migrating to HD.

Over time, certain looks and styles can become clichés. At one time, so many documentaries were shot using grainy 16mm film and shaky handheld camerawork that their look became associated with "documentary." When fiction films try to simulate a documentary look they often resort to handheld, shaky camerawork and bad lighting. Meanwhile, documentary forms have evolved, and many nonfiction films have beautiful lighting and fluid, elegant camerawork.

Styles are continually being borrowed and traded between different genres of filmmaking. As technologies and tastes develop, there is an ever wider range of looks and styles possible. How audiences interpret those looks and styles keeps changing too, as new films explore different combinations.

As a filmmaker, you have at your disposal many tools and techniques to create different looks and moods. Your toolkit includes: how you record the movie (such as what camera, what lens, what format); all the things that take place in front of the camera (such as performances, lighting, sets, costumes, makeup); and things done in postproduction (including editing, sound work, color correction, music).

Quality is important. Many movies have been dragged down by inattention to the technical aspects of filmmaking. But it's worth keeping in mind that for audiences, it's usually the story that comes first. If viewers feel emotionally or intellectually involved in a film, they can be quite forgiving of an imperfect image. And if they're not interested in the film, style alone won't make them love it. At the Sundance Film Festival, for example, the movies that get the most attention (and awards) are often not the slickest, most perfect films, but the most interesting, compelling ones. For some films—experimental films, for example—style and texture can be especially important; but even so, as you make stylistic choices, be sure they serve the film, not the other way around.

Let's examine some of the factors that go into particular looks. Some of these things can be experimented with or changed on a shot-by-shot or scene-by-scene basis. Others you may need to commit to before you start shooting, and stick with that choice to the end.

COLOR AND SENSITIVITY TO LIGHT

Video and film cameras are tools for capturing an image of the world that can then be projected on a screen. That screen image may look a lot like the scene as it appeared in real life, or it may look very different, depending in part on the camera, the way it is adjusted, and other factors. For example, if you're shooting film, different film stocks have very different color and contrast reproduction. Some tend to reproduce colors in muted, pastel shades while others produce a palette of richer, more saturated hues. Similarly, video cameras may record color with very different tonalities; sometimes the color rendering is adjustable, but not all video cameras are flexible in this way.

Color and the response to light are complex topics and are discussed more in Chapters 5, 7, and 8. But it's worth thinking about these things when deciding on the camera system you'll use to shoot your movie. ("Camera system" in this sense is meant to include the whole package, including the camera, its internal adjustments, its lens, and the recording format or, for a movie camera, the film stock.)

Low-Light Shooting

Film and video camera systems vary widely in their sensitivity to light. Some can record an acceptable image using the light level of a normal home or office; others require much brighter movie lights. The camera's ability to handle low light can have a big impact on your production style and budget. If you can shoot with available light (whether it's daylight or artificial) or a minimal amount of movie lights, you'll be able to work faster, more efficiently, and more freely. Low-light sensitivity can make a huge difference if you need to shoot outdoors in the evening or on the street at night. Any time you're filming real people going about their lives, it's far preferable to not *have* to light them. There are many times you'll want to add lights for artistic reasons (more on this below), but if your camera can get enough basic exposure without a lot of added lighting, your shoot will be easier and you'll have the option of capturing the natural feel of the locations where you shoot.

When you're choosing a camera or a film stock, look into its low-light performance. Talk with knowledgeable people who have worked with it. As a rule of thumb, video cameras with larger sensors tend to have better sensitivity than video cameras with smaller chips. A video camera's sensitivity depends in part on the frame rate (slower rate requires less light) and also whether you're shooting progressive or interlace (interlace usually requires less light for the same frame rate). The camera manual or advertising may list the minimum amount of light needed (this may be indicated in *lux*, see p. 289). But ads and generalities aside, it's worth doing tests to see how the camera actually performs.

Most video cameras have a *gain* setting that can increase low-light sensitivity; a little gain boost can often help, but too much gain can introduce electronic *noise* to the image (see p. 134). Similarly, there are high-speed film stocks designed for low-light shooting that tend to be grainier than other stocks. You may or may not object to the graininess.

With cameras that have detachable lenses, the choice of lens can make a big difference in how much light you need to shoot (see p. 162).

Handling High Contrast

Pay attention not just to the *minimum* amount of light the camera needs, but also to its ability to handle a wide *range* of brightness in a scene. Most scenes you'll want to shoot contain areas that are much brighter or darker than other parts of the scene. All camera systems are significantly more limited than your eyes in being able to see details in both bright areas and shadows at the same time (see Fig. 7-14). Camera systems also vary in their ability to handle these high contrast scenes. A film stock that can capture detail in shadows and bright areas at the same time is said to have wide *latitude* or *exposure range*. In video, the same idea might be described by saying the camera can handle a large *dynamic range*. In the past, film cameras were capable of much greater range than video cameras. In fact, one of the giveaways that something is shot on video is often that the *highlights* (bright areas of the scene) are burned out, leaving bleached-out white areas. On some earlier television shows, the exteriors (outdoor shots, which tend to have high contrast) were shot on film, while the interiors (where the contrast can be controlled with lighting) were shot on video.

Video cameras have improved significantly in their dynamic range and ability to handle high contrast. This is one area where larger, more expensive video cameras with sophisticated image processing circuits often outperform smaller, cheaper ones. Some cameras have adjustable *gamma settings* that can be used to reduce contrast and try to emulate a film camera's response to light (see p. 185). Experiment with different gamma settings to create different looks.

The better your camera handles high-contrast scenes, the faster you'll be able to work and the less lighting you'll need. If the range of brightness in a scene is too great for your camera, there are a number of steps you can take (see p. 478).

It's worth noting here that careful lighting can work wonders to elevate the image produced by a low-end camera, and poor lighting will look bad even with the priciest camera. For more on lighting (and the use of light from natural sources), see Chapter 12.

SHARPNESS AND FOCUS

The word "resolution" can have different meanings, but it's often used to talk about how much *information* a format can record. In a high-resolution image, fine details appear sharp and distinct; in a low-resolution image they may be blurred, or not visible due to artifacts in the picture (see Fig. 1-9). Different video and film formats vary in their resolution. High-resolution formats—like 35mm film and HD video—can capture details in a scene with sharpness and clarity. Certain types of shots or subject matter reveal differences in resolution more than others. For example, a wide shot of a landscape with a lot of detail will look dramatically better in high definition, while a closeup of a face might look fine in either standard or high definition.

High-resolution formats put more demands on your shooting technique. If your subject's out of focus in HD, you're *really* going to notice it. Thankfully the latest HDV and DVCPRO HD camcorders have a "magnify" or "focus assist" or "expanded focus" button that momentarily enlarges the viewfinder image for more precise focusing. Nevertheless, if possible bring a good-sized, high definition monitor to check focus on any HD production.

It would seem logical to assume that more sharpness is a good thing—and it often is—but the effect of sharpness on the look of your movie is something to consider closely. First of all, it's quite possible for the image to be *too* sharp. With very high resolution you may see things you don't want to—like every blemish on an actor's face, or the telltale imperfections that let the audience know your sets are just sets. Sometimes the picture just looks *too* crisp. On many dramas, diffusion filters (see p. 305) and other techniques are used to soften the image, to make things feel a little less real and create some mood. Romantic scenes and historical dramas are often made to look more gauzy than sharp. In these cases, filmmakers working in high definition formats are deliberately throwing away some resolution.

With video formats that aren't high-resolution, certain tricks are used to boost the apparent resolution. For example, increasing contrast can often make an image seem sharper than it really is. Video cameras have a *detail* or *enhancement* circuit that can put a light or dark edge or halo around people and objects to get them to pop out more in the picture (see Fig. 3-14). Particularly with low-end cameras, the detail setting may be too high, and the image takes on a very electric, video-like look. This can work fine for things like sports, but may look cheap if you're trying to achieve a more subtle feel. If possible, find a camera with user-adjustable detail settings and experiment with the look you like (see Chapter 3).

LENS QUALITY. Experienced filmmakers know that lens quality is paramount. The image is created by the lens in the first place, after all, and can't be any better than the lens is. When shooting high definition, it should come as no surprise that lens quality is even more critical. SD lenses costing tens of thousands of dollars are often considered insufficiently sharp to shoot HD. An irony of the HDV revolution is that for a fraction of the price of a good HD lens you can now buy an entire high definition camera with lens. Of course, making a camera that inexpensive results in compromises. No matter what format you're working in, if your camera accepts detachable lenses, keep in mind that using a higher-quality lens will noticeably improve the image the camera is capable of. You may want to rent or borrow a good lens (or set of lenses) for your shoot.

Depth of Field

Many dramas aim for a look that has very shallow depth of field (see Fig. 2-11). Depth of field is discussed in Chapter 4, but the effect of shallow depth of field is that you can easily set up shots in which people are sharp and the background and/or the foreground is out of focus. Isolating people from their surroundings in this way can be a very powerful tool, useful in both fiction and documentary. It can both create a mood and allow the filmmaker to use *selective focus* to draw the

Fig. 2-11. Depth of field. In both shots, the camera is focused on the girls. (top) This shot has enough depth of field so that the foreground and the background are both in focus. (bottom) This shot has shallower depth of field, and only the girls are in sharp focus. It's easier to create a shot with shallow DOF using a video camera with a large sensor, or a film camera with a large film gauge like 35mm. (Ned Johnston)

audience's attention to different elements in the frame. This is one of the key factors that characterize the look of the classic 35mm feature film.

Many factors go into controlling depth of field, some of which can be adjusted shot by shot while you are filming. But your choice of camera is also important. The larger the film format, or for video cameras, the larger the sensor, the easier it is to achieve shots with shallow depth of field (see Fig. 4-6). So, for example, if you

Fig. 2-12. P+S Technik MINI35 Digital Image Converter allows you to mount cine lenses on a variety of small-format video cameras to achieve the angle of view and depth of field of a 35mm film camera. (P+S Technik)

shoot with a video camera with a ⅓-inch chip, you'll find it harder to create shots with shallow depth of field than if you use a bigger camera with a ⅔-inch sensor. Filmmakers trying to shoot a low-budget feature with a small DV camera may find that some of the shots they have in mind are difficult to get. Of course, if you seek a deep focus look with great depth of field (see Fig. 9-12), the small chip or film gauge will help you.

There are devices that allow you to use lenses for 35mm film cameras (PL-mount) and even Nikon lenses on standard video cameras. The most common design involves an internal ground glass. The 35mm lens focuses an image on the ground glass, and an internal relay lens projects the ground-glass image onto the video camera's sensor. This delivers to the video camera the same depth of field and angle of view that a 35mm film camera would receive. These adaptors are especially popular for use with smaller MiniDV and HDV camcorders. The best known are P+S Technik's PRO35 and MINI35, Redrock Microsystems' M2, and Kinomatik's MOVIEtube. With these, you can approximate the 35mm look in terms of depth of field and angle of view, while shooting small-format video.

ASPECT RATIO CHOICES

See the discussions of aspect ratio on p. 15 and p. 47 before reading this section.

For many years, both in film and in video, the shape of the frame was a rectangle, four units wide by three units high. In the video world, that's called 4:3; in the film world, the same thing is expressed as 1.33:1. Today, that's often called *non-widescreen*.

Cinema was the first to move to a wider screen image. In *widescreen* formats, the

Film or video frame

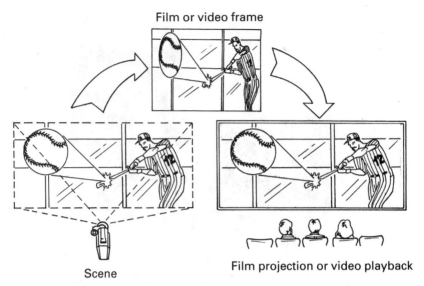

Scene   Film projection or video playback

Fig. 2-13. A widescreen image can be *squeezed* (compressed horizontally) to record it on a non-widescreen film or video format. It is then *unsqueezed* for widescreen viewing. In film, the squeezing process is done with anamorphic lenses on the camera and projector. In video, normal lenses are used and the image is compressed electronically. (Robert Brun)

rectangle is narrower (see Fig. 1-36). Though widescreen makes it sound like you're getting more (it's wider, right?) another way to think of it is that for the same width the picture is not as high. In fact, in some formats, the widescreen look is achieved by masking off the top and bottom of the frame (more on this later).

Many movies viewed in American theaters are made to be shown at 1.85:1, which is a widescreen aspect ratio. European theatrical films may be made for projection at 1.66:1, which, for the same height, is not quite as wide as the 1.85:1 image. In video, widescreen usually means 16:9, which is the equivalent of 1.78:1, making it just slightly less wide than the cinema standard 1.85 for the same height. Some very widescreen theatrical films are shot at 2.39:1 (sometimes written 2.35:1 or 2.4:1), popularly known as CinemaScope or 'Scope.

Different aspect ratios call for different approaches to composing your shots, which can affect your choice of locations, the way you move the camera, art direction, and blocking of action (see p. 93).

Though 4:3 is still used for television, the future belongs to widescreen. All HD formats are 16:9 and most new TV sets are configured to this proportion. If you have any plans for your movie to be shown in theaters, you should shoot widescreen. Before you start shooting you need to decide which aspect ratio you want to work in, and how you're going to achieve that. Depending on the camera and the format, there are various alternatives that can affect the resolution of the image, the postproduction workflow, and the way the movie is shown.

Widescreen Options for Video Cameras

HD cameras have 16:9 sensors and record to one of the HD formats, all of which have a 16:9 pixel raster—so it's widescreen from start to finish.

Many SD cameras can shoot in 16:9 or 4:3, but in either case the image is recorded to the SD raster which is 4:3. Different SD cameras use different methods to capture and record the widescreen picture. Described below are the main methods used in standard definition cameras, and some of the tradeoffs involved.

WIDESCREEN CHIPS. Many newer professional and higher-priced prosumer standard definition cameras have chips that are in 16:9 aspect ratio (see Fig. 2-14).[3] With true 16:9 sensors there's no compromise of resolution when you shoot widescreen.

Fig. 2-14. Camera sensors. The CCD chip at left is non-widescreen 4:3 format. CCD at right is 16:9 widescreen. The photo has been enhanced to show the chips' light-sensitive area. (Sony Electronics, Inc.)

So how do you store the 16:9 image on a 4:3 frame? An *anamorphic* process is used.[4] The camera *squeezes* the picture horizontally before recording so it will fit in the squarer 4:3 frame. If you take the anamorphically squeezed image and look at it on a non-widescreen monitor, everything looks squished horizontally, people look too tall and skinny and circles become vertical ovals (see Fig. 2-13). To view the picture properly, you need a widescreen monitor that can unsqueeze (stretch) it horizontally, essentially pulling the sides out to restore the 16:9 aspect ratio.[5]

The anamorphic image recorded from a camera with a 16:9 sensor uses all the pixels in the frame and is called *full-height anamorphic* (*FHA*) or sometimes *full-height, squeezed*. Full-height anamorphic with a 16:9 chip is the highest-quality, most professional way to record widescreen in SD. Finished videos in full-height anamorphic format are the optimal way to supply a widescreen image for display on a widescreen monitor. If you work in full-height anamorphic, you'll need a widescreen monitor to see the image properly.

If you need to show your movie on a non-widescreen monitor (which are still

3. Some newer chips are have a more square shape than 16:9 but have enough extra pixels to record both 16:9 and 4:3 in native resolution.

4. Anamorphic is an optical term that properly refers to film camera lenses with a special cylindrical lens element to squeeze a super-wide CinemaScope image into a standard rectangular film frame. Digital video has borrowed this term to describe the electronic squeezing of 16:9 images.

5. Some 4:3 monitors can display the anamorphic image properly not by stretching the sides, but by squeezing down the top and bottom to restore the 16:9 shape (creating a letterbox).

widely used) you'll have to letterbox the picture (see below), which may add time or expense. Many broadcasters require that you deliver finished widescreen movies in full-height anamorphic (material that isn't FHA can be converted in editing; see below).

SD cameras with 16:9 chips can be switched to 4:3 for shooting non-widescreen. There are several ways for a camera to accomplish this, but the most common technique is to simply omit the right and left sides of the 16:9 chip in favor of the 4:3 image in the center, thereby reducing the horizontal angle of view by about 25 percent and making your lens effectively a little less wide-angle (see p. 148).

DIGITAL STRETCH. Many older or lower-priced standard def cameras have non-widescreen 4:3 chips. Some of these use a method called variously *digital stretch*, *digital 16:9*, or *squeeze mode* to capture at a widescreen aspect ratio. At the sensor, the horizontal lines on the top and bottom of the image are masked off (so you capture a 16:9 rectangle in the center of the chip) and the picture is then vertically stretched to full-height anamorphic before recording. This full-height anamorphic image can then be easily displayed on a widescreen monitor. But the FHA picture you get with digital stretch is lower-resolution than what you'd get with a true 16:9 chip. To use the example of a 480i camera: With a native 16:9 chip you'd be capturing the full 480 horizontal lines from the sensor, but with digital stretch you're capturing only 360 lines in the middle, and then electronically stretching them to fill the frame. So vertical resolution is reduced by about 25 percent.

The loss of resolution with digital stretch is not as bad with progressive formats as with interlace. Digital stretch may look just fine for your purposes. However, if you have to use a camera with a 4:3 chip, bear in mind that digital stretch may result in lower resolution than using an anamorphic adaptor (see next page) and some people argue that it is better to shoot 4:3 and create the widescreen frame in post (see next page). When shooting digital stretch, with some cameras the image appears as a 16:9 letterbox in the viewfinder, which is much preferable to cameras that display it as a squeezed anamorphic picture, which makes framing and composing your shots difficult.

LETTERBOX MODE. Some cameras offer the option of creating a 16:9 image simply by adding black bars on the top and bottom of the 4:3 picture. There's nothing anamorphic here. This degrades the resolution much like digital stretch since you're only using 75 percent of the horizontal scan lines. The picture can be shown on a non-widescreen monitor, and will appear as a typical letterboxed image. If you aim to show the movie *only* on a non-widescreen monitor, this can be convenient.

When shown on an HD widescreen monitor, things get a little unpredictable. Some monitors will recognize the letterbox and essentially perform a digital stretch in the monitor, both horizontally and vertically, filling the screen with a properly proportioned image.[6] Some monitors will not compensate for the letterbox, and will display the image with black bars on the side *and* top (which leaves the picture a lot smaller than the full-screen size).

6. It would probably depend on the particular camera and monitor whether you're better off having the digital stretch done in-camera or by the monitor.

It is possible to remove in-camera letterboxing by doing a vertical stretch in postproduction to create a full-height anamorphic image, which will play normally on a widescreen monitor.

ANAMORPHIC LENS ADAPTOR. On some cameras, a special anamorphic lens can be mounted in front of the camera's lens to squeeze the image horizontally, allowing you to record an anamorphic 16:9 image on a 4:3 chip. Popular anamorphic adaptors for MiniDV cameras were made by Century Optics, now a division of Schneider Optics, and the former U.K. company Optex, now out of business. (You can sometimes still find these used adapters for sale.) Panasonic also introduced an anamorphic adaptor for its popular DVX100 MiniDV camcorder. (The wide-angle adaptor in Fig. 4-16 can give you an idea of what a front-mounted adaptor looks like.)

Canon now makes an optical anamorphic adaptor for 16:9 cameras that creates an FHA image in a 16:9 raster which, when unsqueezed, produces 2.39:1 widescreen.

The advantage of using an anamorphic adaptor is that, as with shooting with a widescreen chip, all of the horizontal lines of the sensor are used, so there's no loss of vertical resolution.

However, anamorphic adaptors can be tricky to work with. They need to be precisely aligned vertically so you squeeze the image only in the horizontal axis and maintain focus. They add weight and can limit your ability to zoom. They also may lower resolution somewhat just from the optics of the glass.

The image you record is full-height anamorphic, which looks squeezed and skinny. Some cameras can be fitted with anamorphic lenses in the viewfinder or LCD screen to unsqueeze the picture while you're shooting; without this, it isn't easy to frame your shots.

SHOOT 4:3, CREATE 16:9 LATER. Some people feel that the best way to get a 16:9 picture with a camera that has a 4:3 sensor is to just shoot the full 4:3 image and create a letterboxed or full-height anamorphic version during postproduction. They argue that this gets the maximum resolution from the chip and that the image processors for doing the digital stretch in post are much better than what most low-end cameras can do internally. It also leaves open the option of repositioning the frame up or down, or releasing a full-frame 4:3 version later.

To shoot this way, you have to be able to visualize the edges of the 16:9 frame while looking at a 4:3 image in the camera viewfinder. Film cameras can usually display precise markings in the viewfinder so you know the exact boundaries of the frame, but low-end video cameras usually don't. Some monitors can display a variety of widescreen frame lines. Without this you could try to shoot a framing chart and mark the 16:9 frame on a monitor, but framing will not be exact, which could be a real drawback.

The same principle can be used for shooting widescreen at aspect ratios higher than 16:9. For example, George Lucas has used HD cameras that natively capture 16:9, but he extracted a 2.39:1 widescreen image by cropping the top and bottom.

Widescreen Options for Film Cameras

As you can see in Fig. 1-37, the full frame of several film formats is 1.33:1 (which is the same as 4:3). This includes Super 8, 16mm, and 35mm. Hollywood films were shot in 1.33 in the early days, but by the 1950s, filmmakers shooting 35mm for theaters had switched to widescreen formats.

16MM AND SUPER 16. There are still some people making low-budget features for blowup to 35mm who will shoot standard 16mm, despite the fact that all commercial 35mm projection is widescreen. Working in standard 16mm, you must expose the entire 1.33 frame, but you can choose to frame for video's 16:9 or film's 1.85. Film cameras can be fitted with 1.33 viewfinders that have markings for a widescreen frame (see Fig. 6-7). During shooting, those lines are considered the top and bottom of the frame. Later, during blowup to 35mm, it is possible to have the excess image on top and bottom masked out in black as a guide to 35mm film projectionists to align the 1.66 or 1.85 image vertically in the projector's own 1.85 mask. This is particularly helpful if the top or bottom of the 1.33 image—the parts not meant to be seen in projection—contain boom mics or cables on the floor. Alternatively, sometimes filmmakers intentionally keep the top and bottom of the 1.33 frame "clean" so that the full frame, uncropped, can be used in video transfer to make a 1.33 image. In this case, the 35mm blowup is not masked for projection, because for video transfer a 35mm blowup makes a superior transfer element to 16mm. In this case, the filmmaker must cross his or her fingers that every projectionist properly aligns vertically the SMPTE countdown at the head of each print. Otherwise the image will project too high or too low on the 1.85 screen—a big problem when subtitles are involved. For more on blowups from 16 to 35mm see p. 679.

If you're using 16mm as a high definition acquisition format for movies that will ultimately be distributed in SD or HD, a widescreen aspect ratio is now generally called for. If you shoot standard 16mm, the reframing issues described above apply equally. Compared to film blowup, however, there are many avenues for reframing to widescreen in video, including at the NLE stage.

35MM FORMATS. In shooting 35mm, a similar process of exposing the entire 1.33 frame but framing for 1.85 widescreen is common, particularly in made-for-TV movies. When the film is projected, the area outside the 1.85 central letterbox is matted out by a mask in the projector. This technique is sometimes used when it's necessary to generate a separate 4:3 version of a theatrical film for video or television, but cinematographers dislike the practice because it ignores their precise 1.85 widescreen compositions. The arrival of 16:9 video formats (a half century after film went widescreen) has been welcomed by cinematographers for this reason.

Traditional 35mm frames are four perforations in height, but as described in Chapter 1, a three-perf-high frame that is virtually identical in aspect ratio to 16:9 has caught on in Hollywood's TV production community (see p. 51). Not only does this new format save 25 percent in camera film costs but it provides an ideal framing for HD. Boom mics can now kiss the top edge of the frame for better audio instead of flying high above to avoid being seen in full-frame 1.33 transfers. It remains mostly a format for TV production or digital intermediate finishing, where it can be output to conventional four-perf.

For film formats wider than 1.85, anamorphic lenses are used. These are film camera lenses with a special cylindrical lens element that optically squeezes a super-wide frame by a factor of two so that it will fit on a conventional 35mm film negative (see Fig. 2-13). Anamorphic film systems are called *'Scope*. Normal, nonanamorphic lenses are called *spherical*, and nonanamorphic prints are called *flat*.

Because of their increased weight and special construction, anamorphic lenses are more challenging to use. Because horizontal angle of view is doubled by the anamorphosing element, to obtain the same angle of view you would get with a normal 35mm lens, you have to use an anamorphic lens of twice the focal length—which means depth of field is less, so anamorphic lenses require very accurate focus pulling. These lenses aren't fast, either. Experienced DPs generally won't shoot wider open than T4, so faster film and more lighting is needed. But because the anamorphic format uses the largest area of any four-perf 35mm format, grain is tightest, projection is brightest (no masking in projector gate), and the result is glorious on the big screen.

Because of the unique challenges of anamorphic lenses, two widescreen alternatives have arisen, both featuring normal spherical lenses, which are lighter, faster, sharper, and cheaper.

Super 35mm is a format that uses a wider camera negative area—the size, in fact, of the original silent film frame before its right edge was trimmed to make room for a sound track. Shooting Super 35mm involves a lot of costly hoops to jump through in postproduction. You shoot a four-perf high image, then severely crop the top and bottom to produce a 2.39:1 frame, then optically squeeze the image on an optical printer to produce a 'Scope negative from which you make prints for conventional anamorphic projection.

If you look at the narrow 2.39:1 area on a Super 35mm negative, you'll realize that much of the four-perf "real estate" is wasted. In fact, the 2.39:1 frame would fit nicely on a frame only two perfs high. This would confer many benefits: Magazine loads would last twice as long, the camera would be quieter, film costs would be cut in half. This is the idea behind two-perf 35mm, originally called Techniscope, as described on p. 51.

Converting from One Aspect Ratio to Another

Whether you work in video or film, widescreen or non-widescreen, there will be situations in which you have to accommodate other aspect ratios. For example, your widescreen film may be seen on non-widescreen TVs. Or you may want to incorporate 4:3 footage into a 16:9 production. Different forms of distribution call for different aspect ratios, and if you're converting from one to another it helps to think ahead. This discussion will address 4:3 and 16:9 but the same principles apply to other widescreen formats as well.

FROM WIDESCREEN TO NON-WIDESCREEN. Because many people own 4:3 televisions, if you make a movie in 16:9 you may need to prepare a version that can be shown on a 4:3 screen. Converting from 16:9 to 4:3 can be done in a number of ways.

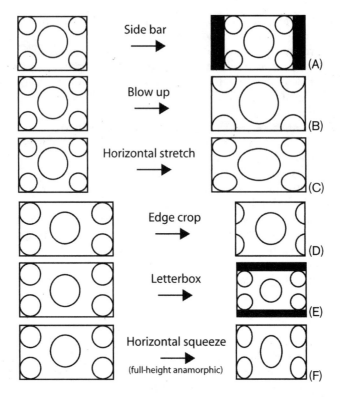

Fig. 2-15. Converting from one aspect ratio to another. When going from a non-widescreen format to a widescreen format: (A) you can place the non-widescreen frame within the widescreen frame with bars on either side; (B) you can enlarge the smaller frame, cropping the top and/or bottom edges and sacrificing some resolution; (C) you can stretch it horizontally, causing a distorted picture. When converting from a widescreen format to a non-widescreen format, you can: (D) crop the left and/or right sides; (E) letterbox the shot, preserving the whole frame but making it smaller; (F) squeeze the image horizontally. Horizontal squeeze is commonly used to record widescreen images anamorphically on non-widescreen film and video formats (the full-height anamorphic picture is later un-squeezed to restore the original widescreen frame).

Letterboxing means showing the entire 16:9 image inside of the 4:3 screen, with black bars on the top and bottom (see Fig. 2-15E). If the original was 16:9, letter-boxing involves scaling down the 16:9 image to fit within the 4:3 screen. If done poorly, this can reduce resolution, particularly in the case of interlaced formats. Letterboxing has become widely accepted, however, despite viewers who object to the black bars and feel that the image looks too small. Even talk shows in the United States are now broadcast letterbox.

Another approach is called *edge crop* or *center crop*. Here, a 4:3 rectangle is cut out of the center of the frame (see Fig. 2-15D). Some cameras with widescreen chips offer edge crop as an output option. Edge crop may arbitrarily cut off impor-tant action—someone talking on the edge of the widescreen frame may not even be visible on screen. To reduce this problem, *pan and scan* may be used. With pan and scan, the position of the 4:3 crop is adjusted on a shot-by-shot basis or even within a shot with the intention of keeping key action on screen. This is done during editing or post and may introduce artificial "camera" movements that the director never intended.

The third method, sometimes called *squeeze mode*, is to squeeze the picture horizontally, creating an anamorphically distorted picture in which people look tall and skinny and circles become vertical ovals (see Fig. 2-15F). Sometimes at the beginning or end of an old feature film that was otherwise converted via pan and scan, a broadcaster will show the credits squeezed so you can read all the titles. This is *not* a good way to watch a whole program.

FROM NON-WIDESCREEN TO WIDESCREEN. Say you have a movie or some footage shot in 4:3 standard definition and want to convert it to 16:9, either as part of an upconvert to HD, or for display in SD on a widescreen monitor. There are several options; none is ideal.

One approach is to center the 4:3 picture within the 16:9 frame with black bars on either side. This is variously called *pillarbox, windowbox, curtained,* or *sidebarred* (see Fig. 2-15A). The advantage of pillarbox is that the entire 4:3 frame is preserved, with no loss of resolution or added distortion. There are, however, a few disadvantages. For one, the picture may seem too small since it doesn't fill the frame. Some broadcasters won't allow pillarbox. If you're using pillarbox to convert some footage that will be incorporated into a 16:9 movie that will ultimately be letterboxed, that footage can end up as a little 4:3 rectangle with black bars on *all* sides; called *postage stamp*, it's something to avoid.

Another issue with pillarbox is that some widescreen TVs are set to recognize the black bars and then stretch the image horizontally, distorting it (see Fig. 2-15C). Sometimes instead of black bars, a textured or neutral background of some sort is put behind the 4:3 image in editing to fill out the frame and create the sense that the whole frame is being used.

Another approach for converting 4:3 is to enlarge the image so it fills the 16:9 frame (see Fig. 2-15B). This is perhaps the most common technique and results in a 25 percent loss of resolution. It also means cropping the top and/or bottom of the picture. If this is done during an editing session, the frame can be positioned up or down on a shot-by-shot basis to avoid cropping out important details. This is much like pan and scan and is sometimes called *tilt and scan.*

Another approach, which is done automatically by some broadcasters and TVs, is to stretch the 4:3 image horizontally by 33 percent (the opposite of squeeze mode described above). The resulting anamorphic distortion makes circles look like horizontal ovals and people look heavier than they are (see Fig. 2-15C). Some TVs apply more distortion to the edges of the frame than the center (called *panorama mode*) in hopes of disguising it a bit. The stretch method fills the screen with picture—supposedly satisfying consumers—but filmmakers who have carefully crafted their images may find the distortion disturbing. It's common to see programming stretched on airport or restaurant TVs, and many people probably aren't even aware of it.

How Aspect Ratio Affects Your Shooting

All this discussion of aspect ratios is to prepare you to think about how your choices affect the production from start to finish, and particularly to help you while you're shooting. Let's look at that part now.

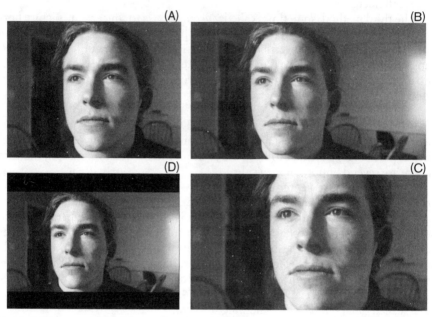

Fig. 2-16. Composition and aspect ratio. (A) The 4:3 non-widescreen frame is well suited to a close-up of a face. (B) Shooting the same subject at the same size in 16:9 widescreen includes a lot more of the background, which needs to be taken into account. (C) If you shoot tighter to show the same amount of background as in A, the frame crops out the forehead and chin. (D) When B is letterboxed, the framing doesn't change, but everything looks smaller.

One thing you can say for non-widescreen 4:3, it's well suited to the proportions of the human face. A closeup of a person talking can fill the frame nicely (see Fig. 2-16). If you shoot a close up of a face 16:9, you have a choice between cutting off the forehead, or shooting wider and seeing a lot more of the background. When you're shooting widescreen, you need to pay more attention to positioning the person in the space of the room, and to the other things that are visible around and behind the person. When you're selecting locations, *dressing* them (place objects or props), and choosing your camera angles, be sure you're making good use of the widescreen frame. If you're filming a single character, you'll often want to counterbalance the person in the frame with objects or perhaps with lighting.

Widescreen formats are well suited to wide shots with more than one character or where landscape is being featured. Widescreen formats work well in the cinema because even things that are relatively small in the frame are easy to see when enlarged on the big screen. When widescreen films are shown on a small TV, details can often disappear. The shot from *Lawrence of Arabia* in which a camel rider appears as a spec on a vast expanse of desert and comes toward us is suspenseful and glorious when shown in the theatrical Super Panavision 70mm prints at 2.20:1 aspect ratio. The same shot letterboxed on a standard definition TV leaves you wondering for quite a while what (if anything) is going on.

If you anticipate releasing a version of your movie in a different aspect ratio, keep that in mind when framing shots and blocking action. How you adjust depends on what format you're shooting and what kind of conversion you'll do.

If you're shooting widescreen 16:9 and plan to make a letterboxed 4:3, you know the entire frame will be visible in the 4:3 version, but everything will be smaller. If there's some element that's crucial for the audience to see or read in the scene, make sure it's big enough in the frame to still be legible when scaled down in the letterbox.

If you're shooting 16:9 and will be making a 4:3 version by doing edge crop, be careful not to position important elements too close to the left and right edges of the screen (or, if you're doing pan and scan, you can use one edge or the other but not *both* at the same time). For example, it often looks good in 16:9 to have one character on the far left and one on the far right. Once converted to 4:3, one of them will probably be cut off. A classic problem occurs when someone enters frame from the left or right of the 16:9 version and on the 4:3 version you hear them before they enter the 4:3 frame.

When doing edge crop, the frames of the 16:9 and 4:3 version share a "common top and bottom," so the *headroom*—the distance from the top of someone's head to the top of the frame—is the same for both. But the sides are different. You can't be expected to put all the action in the center of the frame, but bear in mind the cropping that may happen later. As of this writing, the BBC (British Broadcasting Corporation) asks that when shooting 16:9 you *protect* for 14:9, a compromise that forces you to keep the action a little closer to the middle.

When shooting in a 4:3 format that you plan to convert later to 16:9, the two versions will share "common sides" but you need be concerned with the cropping of the top and bottom of the frame. If you're converting to 16:9 by enlarging the image (see Fig. 2-15B), you'll be cutting out the top and/or bottom of the picture. This means when shooting you should leave enough room above and below the action so you don't lose key details after the conversion. Sometimes filmmakers concentrate so much more on the narrower widescreen frame that they forget to protect the top and bottom of the frame from things like microphone booms that appear unintentionally in the 4:3 version.

FRAME RATE AND SCANNING CHOICES

Not that many years ago, choosing a frame rate was a no-brainer. If you were shooting film, you shot at 24 frames per second. If you were shooting video in North America, it was NTSC 60i (30 frames per second, interlaced) and in the U.K., Asia, and Europe it was PAL 50i (25 frames per second, interlaced). Though these are still widely used frame rates, things have gotten a lot more complicated. You have more choices about frame rates and whether to shoot interlace or progressive. These choices can have a big impact on the look of your movie, your shooting style, and your postproduction and distribution options. Before reading this section, see pp. 12–15 in Chapter 1. The ideal way to read this section would be with a camera in hand to try out different settings.

To understand your options, it helps to know some history.

24 fps Film

In the silent era, film cameras were hand-cranked at about 16 frames per second. Movies used to be called *flickers* (later *flicks*) because the image on the screen flickered (got brighter and darker). When talkies were introduced in the late 1920s, film cameras and projectors were motorized, and the standard speed was increased to 24 fps to accommodate sound. This reduces flicker, but even at 24 fps the light would appear to flash on and off if projectors weren't equipped with extra blades (see Fig. 17-11). The projector essentially flashes each frame on the screen twice or three times, with an instant of darkness between. This gives an apparent "flash rate" of at least 48 flashes per second, which is fast enough so we perceive the illumination as continuous and not flickering.

Over the years, we've come to associate 24 fps with the cinema experience. The look of Hollywood feature films is integrally tied to that frame rate. But shooting only 24 frames each second is a relatively slow "sample rate" in terms of the slices of time that are recorded. This reveals itself in several ways.

First, when a camera runs at 24 fps, the standard amount of time that each frame is exposed to light is 1/48th of a second. This is slow enough that when a person moves across the frame quickly, they will be blurred while they are in motion (see Fig. 2-17). Audiences are used to this particular *motion blur*; they may even like it— it's part of the "film" look.

Fig. 2-17. Motion blur. (left) When the subject or camera moves quickly, there is motion blur within each frame that looks natural in film or video footage. (right) Shooting with a higher shutter speed reduces motion blur, which allows you to grab sharper still frames but can make motion seem choppy at some frame rates.

Another result of shooting 24 fps is that motion isn't perfectly continuous. There's a characteristic unsmoothness that you may not be consciously aware of (until you see a side-by-side comparison with footage shot at a higher frame rate).

However, you can become *very* aware of it if the camera pans (pivots horizontally) across a landscape too quickly: The objects in the landscape will not appear to move smoothly across the screen, but instead seem to jump or stutter from one position to the next. This is called *judder* or *strobing*. It happens when camera or subject movement is too fast, and it destroys the illusion of continuous movement (and gives viewers a headache). There are shooting techniques that help minimize strobing, such as throwing the background out of focus, tracking with a moving subject, and not panning too fast (for more on judder, see p. 361).

Shooting film at a higher frame rate (like 30 fps) for projects destined for video can reduce judder. This is sometimes done for high-end TV commercials. But faster frame rates burn up more film each second, costing more money.

Many filmmakers like the 24 fps look, but it's worth remembering that in terms of its *temporal* (time) qualities, it's a relatively slow frame rate that may cause the motion artifacts just discussed, which is why some people *don't* prefer it for video.

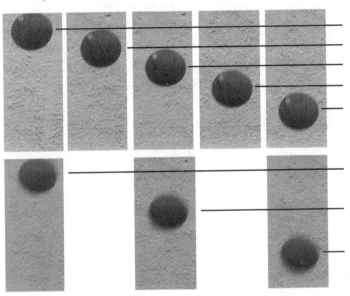

Fig. 2-18. Frame rate and the smoothness of motion. (top) Consecutive frames of a basketball falling. (bottom) The same action shot at a slower frame rate: Now there are fewer frames in the same amount of time, and the ball moves farther between frames, which can increase the chance of choppy motion or judder. Note also that the slower frame rate typically has a slower shutter speed—resulting in more motion blur in each frame—which can help make the increase in judder less noticeable.

50i/60i Video

If video could be displayed at 24 fps on a CRT monitor it would appear to flicker, just as film would flicker if the projector didn't have extra blades, as described above. In video, like film, if we repeat each frame twice but flash each one for half as long we can reduce the sensation of flicker without changing the feel of the motion or the running time of the movie.

In NTSC's traditional 30 fps interlace scanning scheme, first the odd lines are scanned and recorded, then the even lines. What does dividing each NTSC frame into two fields accomplish? Among other things, each field of odd or even lines represents 1/60th of a second. We perceive no flicker on the monitor as a result of this more rapid 60i ("i" for interlace) refresh rate. In the meantime, our eyes blend the odd and even fields back into continuous frames (we don't detect individual fields, or "half frames," being broadcast). So 30 fps NTSC video matches the flicker-free appearance of 60 fps. PAL and SECAM CRTs with their lower 50i scan rate are somewhat susceptible to the appearance of flicker, especially when the viewer looks to the side, not directly at the TV image.

One benefit of 50i and 60i video is that judder is reduced. Things can move in the frame and the camera itself can move more quickly without risk of judder since fields are captured at a rate of 50 or 60 per second (see Fig. 2-18). In some sense, the look of 60i is more "realistic"—it's closer to the way we normally perceive motion. It's also the scanning rate we've grown accustomed to from years of broadcast television. As noted above, 50i and 60i have been the standards for video and television programming, including sports, news, documentary, and corporate videos for many years.

Whether you prefer the more film-like look of 24p or 30p (see below) or the traditional video look of 60i is a matter of taste and what's appropriate for your production.

25p/30p Video

As discussed on p. 12, film is inherently "progressive"—the entire frame is recorded at once. The same is true of progressively scanned video formats: 25p means video progressively scanned at 25 fps, which is a frame rate sometimes used in countries where PAL has been the standard. It's quite similar to 24 fps film in terms of its rendering of motion. Indeed, productions shot on film in these countries are often shot at 25 fps.[7]

The 30p progressive frame rate is sometimes used in countries where NTSC has been standard. While it is faster than 24p or 25p, it still captures some of the feel of film's motion (but has less motion blur). Like all other progressive frame rates, there are no interlace artifacts. However, you can sometimes get objectionable judder at 25p and 30p. To reduce judder at 30p, some cameras, such as JVC's HDV cameras, have a motion-smoothing feature that blends two successive 60p frames to create one 30p frame with residual traces of both images.

Upon output, cameras that shoot 25p or 30p typically divide the frame into two fields that are then recorded as a conventional 50i or 60i signal. This reduces flicker, maintains the same motion rendering, and allows you to play and edit the video on standard 50i/60i equipment. This technique is called *segmented frame* (see p. 104).

Panasonic suggests one use of 30p for situations where you need NTSC-compatible output with easy conversion to still frames, such as videotaping of legal documents or police evidence recording. They also recommend it as a capture

---

7. Or they're shot on film at 24 fps and then sped up by four percent to 25 fps when transferred to video.

mode for "streaming video or downloadable video or as a component of flash animations, due to its very high efficiency in compressing to a low bit rate, and compatibility with computer graphics software applications."

One caveat about shooting 30p: If you plan to distribute in PAL or SECAM territories, it's not easy to transfer from 30p to 50i with good quality.

50p/60p Video

For people who like the smoother motion of 50i/60i but don't like the interlace artifacts—stairstep jaggies that accompany fine detail, temporal displacement of detail between fields—there are formats that record 50p and 60p. At 60 progressive frames a second you get motion that's more continuous with no edge tearing or other interlace weirdness. Compared to 24 fps, 60p produces much less movement blur when the camera or objects in the frame move (because the exposure time is much shorter). This can be a benefit for sports and other material where you want to capture all the action and be able to get good slow motion and crisp freeze frames (more on that below). The key drawback, of course, is that it requires twice the bandwidth, bit rate, or storage media compared to 60i. Plus you need a display capable of keeping up with 60p.

24p Video

Sony and Panavision started developing the first 24p HD camcorder, the HDW-F900, in response to a 1977 request from George Lucas, who was in the early planning stages of *Star Wars* Episodes I, II, and III. Twenty years later, Lucas was testing prototypes. Panasonic brought the costs of 24p down to earth in 2002 with the introduction of the standard definition MiniDV DVX100. Besides Sony and Panasonic, with its 24p Varicam series and breakthrough HVX200 P2 camcorder, JVC too has supported 24p. They introduced the first true 24p HDV camcorder, the HD100, in 2005.

Many filmmakers (especially those in NTSC countries) were thrilled to finally have the ability to capture the feel of film-like motion in video. For video acquisition of footage that will ultimately be transferred to film, 24p is particularly useful (it's a very clean transfer, one progressive video frame per film frame) and it's increasingly popular for movies that will remain in video from start to finish.

In terms of motion, 24p video comes with many of the same advantages and disadvantages of 24 fps film. When shot at the standard shutter speed of $\frac{1}{48}$ of a second, it has the same movement blur of film, and the same discontinuous motion. It may have somewhat worse strobing problems, however. This is because judder is most noticeable on parts of the frame that are sharply in focus and, as discussed above, it's often harder in video to work at shallow depth of field, where you can throw the background or foreground out of focus (since video cameras usually have smaller sensors than the exposed image area of 35mm film cameras).

Though some video cameras are capable of recording at *exactly* 24 fps (which may be used for projects destined for film), in North America they are usually set to run 0.1 percent slower, to 23.976 fps, to match the NTSC frame rate of 29.97 fps (see The Frame Rate, p. 15). Why should we care about NTSC when shooting 24p? Aside from editing systems that can play back 24p at exactly 24 fps, most 24p production in North America and other NTSC territories still relies on conventional monitors, switchers, decks, recorders, and other equipment that run only at 29.97 fps. Compatibility with existing equipment was required for rapid acceptance of the new 24p camera technology. So when people talk about 24p, that's usually a convenient way to refer to 23.976 progressive frames a second (which is often rounded to 23.98 fps in writing and conversation). When you get into production, it's important to be specific about which frame rate you mean.

Different cameras handle 24p differently; many do not simply record 24 progressive frames a second. There are various strategies used by different manufacturers. Which method you use affects the image recorded as well as your postproduction workflow.

24p NATIVE. Some video cameras can record 24 fps "natively," which in this case means simply recording 24 progressive frames a second. For example, Panasonic's HVX200 camera can record "24pn" to P2 memory cards. This is simple and straightforward and provides an easy path to edit and finish in 24p.

Recording 24p natively allows you to record 20 percent more material on a drive or a tape compared to the pulldown methods described below. However, if you need to record the footage to a traditional NTSC 60i or PAL 50i format, then one of the pulldown methods needs to be applied. Most cameras and decks capable of shooting native 24p can apply pulldown on output, which is useful for monitoring or rerecording.

24p NORMAL PULLDOWN. Since 60i has been a standard for so long in NTSC countries and there is a vast amount of 60i equipment in use, manufacturers felt that 24p would be most useful if it could be played on existing decks and monitors. Many cameras use a technique of embedding the 24p stream in a 60i recording that can be viewed and edited on any NTSC-compatible equipment.

It happens that we have a lot of prior experience translating 24p to 60i, since for years every movie shot on film and shown on TV has gone through a similar process. When a film is transferred to video it's run though a *telecine*, which is a machine that scans the film frames and records them to video (see p. 696). Using a process called *2:3 pulldown* (also called *3:2 pulldown*), every four film frames are recorded to five video frames (see Fig. 14-30). By distributing each group of four film frames over five video frames in this way, the speed of the movie doesn't change, motion looks normal, and the resulting video can be edited like any other 60i video.[8] You also have the option of doing a *reverse telecine* process (also called *reverse pulldown*) to extract the 2:3 pulldown when bringing the telecined video into a nonlinear editing system, to recreate the original footage at 24 fps if you need it.

Many video cameras use a similar technique to convert 24p to 60i. The 24p video signal is processed within the camera so that every group of four frames is translated into five frames of 60i that can be recorded on tape or disk. If you're planning to finish your movie on video at 60i, then using *24p normal* is a good pulldown choice; you'll get the look of film motion and can edit in the normal way you would with 60i.

---

8. Actually, when film is converted to 60i, the speed *is* reduced by 0.1 percent (see p. 706). This does not happen when 24p video (actually 23.98p video) is converted to 60i.

To see how 24p normal works, take a look at Fig. 14-30. You'll notice that Frame "A" from the 24 fps stream at the top is transferred to both fields of Frame "1" in the 60i stream. Frame "B" goes to both fields of Frame "2" *and* to the first field of Frame "3." Frame "C" is transferred to two fields (split between Frame "3" and Frame "4") and Frame "D" goes to three fields. This pattern or *cadence* is why normal pulldown is also called 2:3 or 2:3:2:3. The point of this whole operation is to create six extra frames every second, bringing us from 24 fps to 30 fps.

24p ADVANCED PULLDOWN. As just noted, normal pulldown works well for movies shot in 24p that are finished in 60i video. But on some projects, the goal is a 24 fps end product: You might be making a 24p DVD, or transferring to film or making a Web movie at 24 fps. In this case, a pulldown pattern called *24p Advanced (24pA)*, originally introduced in Panasonic's DVX100 but adapted by others, offers some benefits and some drawbacks.

Say you decide to shoot 24p and have your finished movie run at 24 fps. If you shoot with 24p normal pulldown, you need to do a reverse pulldown process in the editing system to recover the 24p frames from the 60i video you recorded. If you're working in a compressed format like DV, HDV, or DVCPRO HD this requires decompressing the video. Why? Notice in Fig. 14-30 that Frame "C" from the 24p recording is split into Frame "3" and Frame "4" in the 60i stream. In order to reconstruct Frame "C" we must decompress the video, combine the "C" field from Frame "3" with the "C" field from Frame "4" and then recompress the video again for storage. This is not ideal—it degrades the quality and results in unnecessary storage.

To avoid this, some cameras can record a different pulldown pattern. Instead of the normal 2:3:2:3, we use the "advanced" cadence 2:3:3:2. Note in Fig. 14-32 that Frame "1" in the 60i stream is made up of two fields from Frame "A" and *nothing else*; it is a complete, whole frame. Similarly, Frame "2" contains two fields from Frame "B" and nothing else. The same is true for Frames "4" and "5." So we can easily play back the original four frames of the 24p video simply by deleting Frame "3" from the sequence. This is very clean and no decompression is needed. When you shoot 24p Advanced, a *flag* is recorded in the video that tells the editing system to recognize the 2:3:3:2 pulldown, ignore Frame "3," and capture only the other four complete frames.

Shooting in 24p Advanced results in a higher quality capture into the editing system and reduces the amount of data you need to store by 20 percent. It also lightens the load on the computer processor during editing. It can result in a better end product if you plan to distribute in a 24 fps format.

However, 24p Advanced has other consequences. First, 24pA is not meant to be shown as is, directly from the camera tapes. If you play a 24pA tape before removing the pulldown, motion may look unsmooth and somewhat jerky.[9] 24pA can be thought of as a kind of intermediate format that's not designed to be watched directly prior to editing.

Second, 24pA material is intended to be edited at 24 fps. If you plan to combine 24pA material with 60i material, one of them will usually have to be converted to the other's *timebase* (frame rate). The editing implications of 24pA are discussed

---

9. This is not the usual judder from the 24 fps frame rate, but results from the Advanced pulldown.

more on p. 564, but be aware that if you're releasing on 60i, or working on a project that uses a lot of existing 60i material, then 24p advanced may be a disadvantage. If your editing system doesn't support 24pA, shooting with it isn't recommended.

There are various work-arounds and conversion methods if you shot in 24pA but would rather have 24p normal, or if you have 60i material to bring into a 24 fps movie (see p. 571).

OTHER FORMS OF 24p. The two pulldown methods just described have something in common: They take four frames of 24p and create ten fields of 60i. There's another pulldown pattern that accomplishes the same thing: 2:2:2:4. This is a pulldown used in some cameras and editing systems that can result in motion that may look more irregular or jumpy than the other cadences.

Another method is Panasonic's multiframe rate system used in their Varicam, which can shoot 4 to 60 fps by embedding all of these rates in a 60p stream. (A similar but more limited system is used in their HVX200.) The system works by flagging certain frames to be repeated or skipped in playback, depending on the frame rate you choose. For example, if you shoot 30p it records two identical 60p frames at a time and ignores one of them during playback, giving you 30p. Recording at 24 fps is accomplished with 2:3 pulldown.

PROGRESSIVE SEGMENTED FRAME. Contrary to common misunderstanding, *progressive segmented frame (PsF)* is not a frame rate or format but simply a method of recording 24p HD.[10] It has no impact whatsoever on the appearance of a 24p image upon playback. Also called just *segmented frame (sF)*, Sony introduced 24PsF with the original 24p F900 HDCAM camcorder as a way to integrate 24p recording with existing 50i/60i equipment.

With PsF, the entire frame is captured in one exposure at the camera's sensor and then split into two fields, each with half the horizontal lines, prior to recording. So, 24PsF is recorded essentially as though it were 48i (see Fig. 14-33). But the difference between PsF and interlace is that both fields are captured *at the same instant in time* (instead of one field being exposed after the other, as would be the case with interlace). On playback from a 24 PsF deck, the "segmented frames" display on a CRT HD monitor as if they were 48i fields, but the interlace artifacts like edge tear or aliasing are nowhere to be seen. In postproduction, you can recombine the two fields to remake the original, single progressive frame with no artifacts (which you might do, for example, for a film-out).

If 60i video is needed from 24 PsF, conventional pulldown is done prior to output, with the segmented frames again treated as fields.

The segmented frame method can be used with a variety of frame rates, including 25p and 30p.

FRAME MODES. There are a number of cameras that don't shoot true 24p, but offer various "fudged" methods that try to simulate something like it. Manufacturers may claim that these look a lot like 24p, but there are important differences. Some Sony HDV camcorders like the Z1 and A1 offer a *Cineframe 24* mode.

10. As described earlier, 24PsF is usually 23.98 PsF in NTSC countries.

The camera's sensor captures 60i, from which fields are selected to try to simulate the motion of 24p. But how to get 24 slices of time from 60? Put another way, how to turn 2.5 fields into a single frame? It can't truly be done. But Cineframe 24 (sometimes written 24F) applies a tangle of frame doubling, blending, and faux 2:3 pulldown to create a gumbo that some find acceptable as a substitute for true 24p— for instance, for DVD authoring. However, the motion is uneven, which any attempt at a reverse pulldown will readily reveal to the discerning eye. This is a consumer-oriented feature to create a particular look in a 60i recording, but it should not be confused with true, professional 24p. It should not be used for blowup to 35mm or bump-up to HDCAM for the festival circuit.

Sony's *Cineframe 30* and *Cineframe 25* modes function in 60i and 50i camcorders, respectively, by dropping one field and doubling the other—the same technique found in slow shutter speed effects in Sony camcorders. This creates the motion feel of 30p and 25p but at half the vertical resolution (since you're recording only one of each two fields). The loss of resolution may or may not bother you depending on the application.

Canon's XL H1 HDV camcorder offers a 24F mode too, but it's entirely different from Sony's CineFrame 24. Like Sony's HDV camcorders, the XL H1 employs interlace CCDs, but in Canon's 24F mode they are clocked at 48i, not 60i like Sony. In other words, although not true progressive scan, the XL H1 applies the correct timebase to its simulated 24p. Next, in its digital signal processing, the XL H1 blends each pair of 48i fields to synthesize a single 24p frame with as little visible temporal displacement of detail as possible. For output, the XL H1 then creates progressive segmented frames (24 PsF), adds 2:3 pulldown, and outputs the result as 1080i from its HD-SDI port. While impressive to many, it's important to keep in mind that the XL H1's 24F is a simulation of 24p and cannot deliver the vertical or temporal resolution of true 24p.

Cameras from other manufacturers have various types of frame modes to simulate progressive recording or frame rates in which they don't really operate. Experiment with them to see if you like the look, but ask questions about how they work so you'll know whether they might cause problems for you later.

SHOOT 50i; CONVERT TO 24p LATER. Filmmakers in PAL countries are familiar with shooting at 50i (25 fps, interlaced), which can be converted to 24 fps during editing or afterward (it may be easiest in these countries to complete the edit in 25 fps and do the 24 fps conversion later).

Before 24p cameras were available, feature filmmakers in NTSC countries often worked in 50i PAL when doing projects shot in video but finished on film. The reason was that in standard definition, PAL has higher vertical resolution than NTSC and its 25 fps frame rate is close enough to 24 fps to convert comfortably. (In HD however, 1080/60i and 1080/50i share the same resolution.)

The conversion from 25 fps to 24 fps can be done by slowing the footage down by 4 percent. The effect this has on motion is usually not bothersome (and often not detectable, although some directors will dispute this), but the sound will drop in pitch, so voices and music will sound too low. A pitch correction can be done to the audio using audio software (such as Pro Tools) to bring it back up to normal. Note that what works for pitch-shifting typical voice frequencies sometimes causes distortion in high frequencies found in music. There is a certain amount of art to pitch-shifting, so consult with your audio mixing facility when considering this path.

The resulting 48i video can then be deinterlaced to create 24p.

Converting from One Frame Rate to Another

Your choice of frame rate should be based mostly on the look you hope to achieve. But your choice will affect your workflow and can also have an impact on distribution. These days there are sophisticated standards conversion systems from companies like Teranex and Snell & Wilcox that can convert anything to anything and do it well. For example, if you shoot 60i, it's fairly easy to convert to 50i for distribution in PAL countries.

However, standards conversion can be expensive and often there are "gotchas." As always, the more you understand in advance, the better. For instance, 30p does not convert easily to 50i. And PAL converts to NTSC with better quality than NTSC to PAL. Which is why many Hollywood TV shows continued to shoot film for years. They knew that transferring from 24 fps film to PAL was superior to standards-converting NTSC to PAL. Indeed, there is a long tradition of converting 24 fps film to all formats of video. For this reason, some people prefer to shoot in 24p video (or transfer from film to 24p) to create a "universal master" from which 24p, 25p, 50i, and 60i can be relatively easily created for different distribution outlets.[11] Before choosing a frame rate, explore your options down the line. Talk to post facilities. They have abundant experience in this area.

COPING WITH TECHNOLOGY

Surviving the Format Wars

So, you're setting out to make a movie, and you have to decide about equipment, formats, frame rates, whatever. As we've seen, there are many ways to go— too many, really. Your choices will be somewhat limited by the equipment you have or can afford. You may face difficult tradeoffs that force you to sacrifice one option for another. And when you ask for advice, be prepared to hear different people argue passionately for or against any given choice. Some of these people will know what they're talking about and others will be equally as sure of themselves.

It would seem that any disagreements about formats and settings could be settled by a simple test to see which looks best. But it's often not that simple.

As an example, consider the choice in high definition between 1080i (1920 x 1080 pixels, interlaced) versus 720p (1280 x 720 pixels, progressive). The advocates for 1080i argue that it absolutely looks better due to its higher resolution. The other side argues that the difference in pixel count isn't that great, because given the interlace of 1080i you're seeing only half of the horizontal lines at a time. For them, the advantages of progressive are clear and 720p is the winner.

---

11. However, going from 24p to PAL usually involves a change in speed and pitch (see p. 607).

Fig. 2-19. A format is rarely just a format. This image was shot in 16mm, transferred to Di-giBeta, dubbed to DVCAM, exported as a TIFF file, up-resed and deinterlaced in Photoshop, then printed in black and white. A lot of film and video footage goes through a similarly complex path from acquisition to display. You can go crazy trying to control how each stage changes the picture. (Stephen McCarthy)

But these kinds of arguments are rarely about just one thing (so far we've been talking about both resolution and the differences between interlace and progressive). How about frame rate? Are you comparing 1080i/60 with 720p/30? If so, part of what you're looking at is the different way motion is rendered at 60i versus 30p. How about compression? Are you comparing the output of an HDV camera with one that records in DVCPRO HD? Maybe what you're seeing is due in part to the compression. And then there's the monitor and playback equipment. Are you seeing the format in its native form? Modern LCD and plasma displays have a fixed resolution and will convert incoming signals to it (which means upconverting or downconverting from the source). The disc or tape player may be adding pulldown or deinterlacing the picture (and it may be doing this well or badly). There may be lovely color in the original recording that's lost on a monitor incapable of displaying the full tonal range.

As if all these considerations weren't enough, there's also the simple truth that the exact same format, frame rate, and compression can look good when shot and displayed with well-designed professional equipment and appear a lot worse with cheap consumer gear.

It can seem overwhelming to account for so many factors. But to understand what you're doing and why, you need to be a critical thinker and try to examine one factor at a time. For example, using just one camera and one monitor, experiment with different frame rates. Get to know the different feel they produce. Then, when you see the output of another camera, you'll have a sense of whether it looks the way it does thanks to the frame rate or some other factor. And when you find something you like, try watching it in different environments—on small screens and large—to see how it holds up.

It's easy to get caught up in numbers. Filmmakers and consumers always want to know which is the "best" format, camera, or TV. Preferably, they'd like a simple numbered scale or ranking to compare "A" to "B." As we've seen, there are many numbers used to quantify different things (such as frame size, color depth, compression, and so on) but the numbers are sometimes more misleading than helpful. What your eye perceives can't be boiled down to a meaningful number. Sometimes an image that "should" look inferior according to the numbers actually looks great. People develop prejudices based on old assumptions or how much something costs and then are shocked by a new technology that performs better than anything before in its price range. A format or camera may be just fine for your purposes even if another is technically "superior."

In the end, it's not the numbers that matter, it's what you see and hear. Over time you'll learn to interpret why something looks and sounds the way it does, so you can decide if it's right for you, or what you might do differently.

The Cost of Independence

As digital technology becomes more sophisticated, filmmakers are expected to understand and work with some really complex tools. These tools put a great deal of power in your hands, but require a lot of attention when you might rather concentrate on other things.

As digital equipment and software become more affordable, it becomes technically possible for one person to shoot and edit a movie, do the color correction and sound mix, create the titles, effects, and everything else. Working this way can be a real boon: It saves time, money, and hassle and gives the filmmaker unprecedented creative control. But it entails some losses. When you're no longer interacting with the professionals who would have otherwise done the sound mix, color correction, graphic layout, and such, you lose the benefit of their expertise. Technology can be democratizing, but it can be isolating too.

CHAPTER 3

The Video Camcorder

This chapter is about the basic operation of video cameras and recorders used in production. Please read first the overview of video recording in Chapter 1. The use of lenses is discussed in Chapter 4 and a more detailed discussion of video recording is in Chapter 5. See Chapters 10 and 11 for microphones and audio recording for video. Much of this chapter applies to both digital and analog camcorders, but it is written with the assumption you are probably using either an all-digital camcorder, or at least one with digital components.

Overview of the Digital Camcorder

The video camcorder combines a video camera and recorder into one convenient unit. Many camcorders have a mechanism for recording to videotape (a videotape recorder or VTR). Some have provisions for recording to memory cards, hard disk drives (HDDs) or optical discs. The smallest, lightest camcorders have a single

Fig. 3-1. The video camcorder. Panasonic HVX 200. (Panasonic Broadcast)

body and are called *one-piece* units. Some camcorders are *dockable*, which means the camera and recorder can be separated if necessary (handy if one part breaks down). In studio settings, instead of camcorders, several cameras can be used with one or more separate VTRs. Regardless of the physical package the camera and recording mechanism are in, all camera/recorders share certain elements:

1. *The lens.* Forms an image of the scene on the camera's sensor(s). Most lenses have controls for the focus of the image, the brightness of the image (using the *iris diaphragm*), and the magnification of the image (using the zoom to change focal length). On some cameras the lens is built into the camera; on others it is detachable and different lenses can be used.
2. *The sensor.* Light-sensitive electronic chip that converts the light coming through the lens into electric charges. Either a CCD (charge coupled device) or CMOS (complementary metal oxide semiconductor) type of imager. A CCD outputs analog signal voltages, a CMOS usually outputs signals already converted to digital bits. See Fig. 2-14.
3. *DSP.* Digital Signal Processors convert the signal from the sensor to digital form if it isn't digital already. Other tasks: adjust color and tonal reproduction; set frame rate and the length of exposure (using the *shutter*); adjust the sensitivity of the sensor (using the *gain* control); manage and store a range of complex parameters.
4. *The viewfinder.* A small monitor (TV screen) that allows you to see what you're shooting or playing back. Some cameras have both a viewfinder and a separate fold-out video screen.
5. *The recording system.* Stores the video signal on tape, hard drive, or other media.
6. *Audio recording.* Most camcorders have built-in or attached microphones and provisions to plug in external mics. The recording level (volume) of the sound must be adjusted before shooting (see Chapters 10 and 11).
7. *The power supply.* Cameras can be run on rechargeable batteries or by plugging into an AC power supply.
8. *Timecode.* Critical for many aspects of postproduction (see p. 203). Most modern cameras have timecode capability.

Many consumer camcorders are designed for the "point and shoot" user and are highly automated. Some won't even let you adjust key settings. Since control of focus, exposure, and color is part of the creative process of shooting, it's often not an advantage to have these things set automatically. Professional camcorders are generally not so automatic or at least provide manual overrides. If you hope to capture high-quality images and sound, it's important to know which automatic settings can be trusted, and when you need to make adjustments manually.

PICTURE CONTROLS

Viewfinders and Monitors

To look at the video image, we use a *monitor*.[1] The viewfinder is a small monitor mounted on the camera that allows you to see the image you're shooting. Professionals often work with a larger, separate monitor as well, which permits others to watch too. For years, camcorders were equipped with black-and-white CRT viewfinders (see p. 198); these used to be the sharpest but newer color LCD (liquid crystal display) viewfinders can be very sharp. Many camcorders have both eye-piece-style viewfinders and fold-out LCD screens (see Fig. 3-1). Fold-out screens have advantages and disadvantages. They allow you to hold the camera away from your face and in positions that would be difficult with a standard viewfinder. They also make viewing playback easier, especially when more than one person want to watch. But they can drain the battery faster and may be hard to see in bright daylight. They are also a poor tool to use to judge focus or exposure. Newer fold-out LCDs may also have touch-sensitive camera controls instead of mechanical buttons and switches on the camera body.

Viewfinders and other types of monitors are essential for checking how the shot is framed and if the focus, exposure, and color are correct. However, it takes experience to learn when you can trust the picture and when you should take what you're seeing in the viewfinder with a grain of salt. Some examples:

Fig. 3-2. Consumer DV camcorder showing LCD. (Canon U.S.A., Inc.)

- When you're shooting, view-finders and monitors show you the video as it comes out of the camera, but they don't tell you what is actually being recorded. So if there are problems with the tape or recording device, you'll find out only when you stop recording and watch playback.
- The edges of the frame that you see in the viewfinder or monitor may be different than what the audience will see. See p. 331 for discussion of TV cutoff and p. 87 for aspect ratio.
- Exposure, color, and contrast may look quite different in the viewfinder than what is actually being recorded.

---

1. What's the difference between a monitor and a TV? A TV usually has a built-in *tuner* that allows you to receive broadcast television channels over the air or through a cable. Monitors allow you to input video directly from a camera or deck and usually have no tuner. These days, most TVs also have direct video inputs. For more on different types of monitors, see p. 197.

The more you work with any given camera or monitor, the better you'll be able to translate what you're seeing in the viewfinder to what's really being recorded. The ultimate picture reference is a high-quality studio monitor in a dimly lit room.

Moviemakers who place too much reliance on field monitors and camera viewfinders are often surprised (sometimes pleasantly, sometimes not) by what they see on a better monitor.

Camera viewfinders can be set to display information about things like battery power, timecode, audio levels, and tape remaining (see Fig. 3-6). This info can be very useful, but sometimes having all that text on or around the screen is distracting. Also, there's a natural tendency when shooting to avoid positioning things in the frame where they'll be hidden by the data displays. (Later, when you see the image on a monitor with no data overlays you may wonder why certain parts of the frame look empty.) Most cameras allow you to turn off the data when you want.

Adjusting the Viewfinder

With the exception of some consumer cameras, most viewfinders and monitors have adjustments for brightness, contrast, and color (when applicable). Adjustments made to the viewfinder or monitor affect only what you see in the monitor itself—they have no affect on the video that's being recorded. However, if the monitor is not "set up" properly, you won't be able to evaluate the image correctly and this may lead you to make other changes (in exposure, lighting, focus) that *will* affect the actual recorded video. It's very important to set up a monitor before beginning work by adjusting the brightness, contrast, and color. See Appendix A for instructions.

Some viewfinders have a *peaking* or *detail* adjustment that helps you focus by putting a fine white edge around things that are sharply in focus. If you set the peaking high, as you turn the focus ring on the lens, objects will really pop in the viewfinder when you've got them in focus.[2] One problem with setting the peaking very high is that the white edges can make it harder to judge the lighting and exposure. Often a medium setting is a good compromise.

Some cameras allow you to quickly magnify part of the image as a focusing aid. This can be particularly helpful in HD, where focus is especially critical. Many cameras have a *zebra indicator* that highlights areas in the frame that may be overexposed (see Fig. 3-6). For more on use of zebras, see The Video Camera's Response to Light, p. 177.

VIEWFINDER FOCUS. If your camera is equipped with a typical eyepiece (tube-like viewfinder), you must focus the viewfinder for your eye before shooting. This is done with the focus or *diopter* adjustment on the viewfinder. This has no affect on the focus of the image being recorded through the camera lens; rather, it allows you to make the tiny monitor screen in the viewfinder as sharp as possible for your eye. Everyone's eyes are different and you should reset the viewfinder focus anytime someone else has been using the camera.

With the camera on, turn or slide the viewfinder focus adjustment until the scan

---

2. This can be especially helpful when you're working with a camera that has its internal detail set low; see p. 137.

lines or printed characters on the screen are sharp. If your camera generates *bars* (a test signal), they provide a sharp image to look at while focusing the eyepiece. It is important that your eye be relaxed and not straining to focus. Only when your eye relaxes most—at infinity focus—should the diopter be adjusted to achieve viewfinder focus. If done properly, you can then shoot for hours without eyestrain.

Fig. 3-3. Sony HVR-V1U. Shoots HDV, including 1080/24p. Also DVCAM and DV. Uses CMOS sensors. (Sony Electronics, Inc.)

Modern video viewfinders are very wide in diameter (they have a large "exit pupil"), so you can easily wear glasses while hand-holding a video camera and take your eye away from the viewfinder eyecup anytime you want while shooting. This is definitely not the case with film cameras, where the eye must be pressed tightly against the eyecup to prevent light leakage down the viewfinder's optics, which will cause film fogging.

On some cameras you can flip the magnifying lens out of the way for more comfortable distance viewing. Some people who wear glasses prefer to shoot this way. If the camera's diopter won't compensate for your vision (if you are astigmatic and don't wear glasses), you can switch to contact lenses for shooting.

Setting the White Balance

Video and film cameras need to compensate for the color of light so that the image doesn't come out with an unintended blue or yellow color cast. When shooting video, adjusting the camera to the color balance of the light is called *setting the white balance*.[3] Before reading this section, please see the discussion of color temperature on p. 297.

Most places you go, your eye and brain adjust to the lighting to make the overall color of light appear white. But in actuality, every different lighting environment, indoors and out, has a different color balance. For example, daylight is relatively blue, while typical bulbs used in the home are by comparison yellow/red. The sensors in many video cameras are designed so that light of about 3200°K—close to bulbs used at home—will look natural as "normally" processed by the camera. 3200°K is actually the color temperature of professional tungsten movie lights. If

---

3. In film, the similar issue of the suitability of a film stock for certain lighting conditions is usually talked about in terms of *color temperature* or *color balance*.

all you did was shoot under studio lighting, the 3200°K setting would be all you needed. But since the color of light from scene to scene often varies from 3200°K, we need a way to adjust the white balance accordingly. Say you were shooting indoors using tungsten lighting and then decided to step outside and take a shot of the street. Tungsten lighting has a lower color temperature (it is more yellow/red) compared to the daylight. If no adjustment were made, the shot outside would be very blue; skin tones and anything red in the scene would look cold and unnatural. By adjusting the white balance, we make white objects look white on screen. Most video cameras give you three ways to set white balance: by using factory presets; by adjusting the white balance manually; or by letting it set itself automatically.

USE OF WHITE-BALANCE PRESETS. Many cameras have a white-balance switch with a "*preset*" position for 3200°K. Some cameras label this position "tungsten" or "indoors." Professional and prosumer video cameras usually have a mini-toggle switch with three positions: preset, A, and B (see Fig. 3-4). Preset is the position for the factory-preset white balance, and the A and B positions are memory settings for manual white balances created by the camera operator (described on the next page).

In many newer cameras the mini-toggle "preset" position can be changed from 3200°K (indoor tungsten lighting) to 5600°K (outdoors) by making a selection in the menu settings or with user-assignable buttons. (by convention, 5600°K is an average for outdoors but is only a crude approximation of the actual color temperature at any given moment: Imagine all of the permutations of yellow sun, blue sky, amber sunset, gray cloud cover, etc.) Selecting 5600°K for the preset position is useful if most of your shooting is in daylight or under daylight-balanced lighting like HMIs, or LEDs and fluorescents balanced to 5600°K. Many cameras now allow you to tweak the factory-preset color temperature of each setting to your liking.

Fig. 3-4. Some image controls on a Sony camera: Gain; Output, including color bars and Dynamic Contrast Control (see p. 184); White balance (preset and two user-settable memory positions).

On some professional cameras, the difference between 3200°K and 5600°K is too great for the circuits to handle by themselves without introducing unwanted noise. These cameras have a built-in filter wheel. When used in conjunction with the 3200°K white-balance preset, the "5600K" position on the wheel inserts an orange filter, which warms up the light coming through the lens before it reaches the sensor. (This filter is similar to the 85 filter used for tungsten-balanced films. It cuts down the light intensity by about ⅔ of a stop; see p. 298.)

Is it a good idea to use the factory preset white balance? One argument for using presets is that every scene need not be corrected for identical whites. In nature, white is rarely simply white. Think of parchment under candlelight. It should be warm, not pure white. Look at figurative paintings and you'll rarely see white applied as colorless white. The tinting of white has graphic and emotional power. If you shoot video under candlelight with 3200°K preset, whites will indeed look warm and yellowish. However, if you do a manual white balance (see below), the warmth will be removed and white will be rendered white.

Another argument for using presets is that exact balance during the shoot may not be necessary. Color correction in NLEs and post has become so accessible and effective that the fussiness of white-balancing for every minor change in the prevailing light has given way to a practice akin to the way cinematographers shooting film handle the situation: by choosing an overall tungsten- or daylight-balance, then doing scene-to-scene color correction later in the lab, after the edit is assembled and a print is ready to be made. Even so, some videographers prefer to get the white balance as close to optimal as they can while shooting.

For years it was thought that the use of the white balance presets in video was for amateurs or those too lazy to properly white-balance, but in truth many top professionals now swear by it. Experience will dictate whether you want to use presets for some or all scenes, do a manual balance instead, or embrace the convenience and compromise of automatic white-balancing (see p. 117).

MANUAL WHITE BALANCE. Many professionals reset the white balance by hand for every new lighting condition. For example, scenes lit by household bulbs, tungsten movie lights, fluorescents, sunlight, or shade (no direct sun, just skylight) can all have a different color balance. Whenever the lighting changes they "do a white balance" by holding a white card or piece of white paper in the same light as the subject, zooming in so the card fills most of the frame, then pushing the camera's white balance button.[4]

When white-balancing, the camera's circuits adjust the relative strength of the red, green, and blue signals coming from the sensors until the white card looks white on video (if white objects look white, then the other colors will look natural too). It does no good if the white card isn't reflecting back the same light that's falling on the subject, so be aware of light sources that hit the subject but not the card, or vice versa. Also make sure you're exposed properly for the scene before doing the white balance. If you're not sure about your exposure, switch the lens into auto-iris mode. Let the camera decide exposure. If the camera doesn't have enough light to white-balance properly, it will indicate this in the viewfinder.

It's okay if the white paper has black text as long as, when zoomed in on, the white predominates. In documentary situations, any white object in the prevailing light of the scene will do—like a white shirt or a white wall. A neutral gray card or truly gray object will also work in a pinch. In some cameras the white-balancing circuit center-weights the frame, so that if your white card fills at least the central portion of the frame the white balance will still work. Experiment with your camera.

As noted above, most professional video cameras have a mini-toggle switch that

---

4. Confusingly, on some cameras the button that performs a manual white balance is labeled "auto white balance." This should not be mistaken for settings that continuously and automatically alter the balance (see Automatic White Balance, p. 117).

offers a white-balance memory with two positions, A and B. You can set these to any color balances you'd like. Maybe you're shooting a documentary and one room is lit with dim reddish tungsten bulbs, while another is lit with greenish cool white fluorescents. Once you've done a white balance in each room, a flip of the switch is all it takes to toggle between the optimum white balances for each one. Even when the camera is powered down, the white-balance memory will retain these custom settings.

Many larger professional cameras and camcorders use a built-in filter wheel with "CC" or color correction filters. A Sony HDW-F900, for instance, has four filters: 5600K, 3200K, 4300K, and 6300K. This 5600K filter used with the preset (see p. 114) often works fine in daylight, but you may still want to do a manual white balance with the filter in place to fine-tune the color. When clouds cover the sun and the color temperature becomes more blue, perhaps the 6300K filter is the place to start.

On some lower-cost cameras there isn't a button for doing a manual white balance, but you can let the camera set itself automatically on the white card, then press "hold." Whether you're shooting in daylight or tungsten, it's always a good idea to compare the preset white-balance settings to the white balance you do manually—sometimes the preset just looks better. As mentioned earlier, on some cameras you can even adjust the color temperature of the presets to get a look you like.

If you're using a color viewfinder or monitor to judge the white balance, be sure that it's properly set up first (see Appendix A). Sometimes even after white-balancing, the overall color balance seems too cool or too warm. This could be a problem with the way the monitor is adjusted or it may be simply the way the camera's electronics work. For example, some Sony cameras have a tendency to balance on the cool side. You could just shoot that way and plan to do color correction during post, but many cinematographers prefer to get the color as close as possible while shooting. In general, skin tone looks better if slightly too warm rather than too blue.

One solution is to use a filter over the lens to warm up skin tones and the overall balance. You can use screw-on filters or a matte box (see Fig. 8-9). An 81B filter adds a mild amount of warming and an 812 warms a bit more. Remember you must put the filter on *after* you do the white balance, otherwise the camera will try to remove the warming effect of the filter.

If you can't or don't want to use filters, a simple, low-tech trick is to "fool" the camera by doing a white balance on a nonwhite object. If you balance on a piece of pale blue paper, the camera will try to make the blue appear white, which will warm the entire image (alternately, you could do the white balance with a blue filter over the lens). Macie Video (macievideo.com) makes a "cool warm card" with panels of different shades of blue; one approximates the effect of an 81B filter, another simulates an 812.

If you're using lighting, you can do a normal balance using white light, then put colored warming gels on the lights (see Chapter 12).

For shooting a scene that has light sources of different color temperature, see Mixed Lighting, p. 480.

Fig. 3-5. Iconix high definition camera and control unit. The camera head is a little bigger than a golf ball and can be used for hard-to-reach camera angles and point-of-view shots. Outputs most flavors of HD and SD. (Iconix)

AUTOMATIC WHITE BALANCE. All consumer camcorders and increasingly many professional ones have the ability to set the white balance continuously and automatically with no user input. This is sometimes called *auto white balance* or *auto tracing white balance (ATW)*.

On some cameras, auto white balance works surprisingly well. Experiment with yours to see how you like it. In run-and-gun situations, having quick, automated white balance can be very convenient. For some reason, certain prosumer cameras produce a better, more neutral balance when on automatic than when set manually.

However, there are reasons why pros usually don't leave the white balance on auto. Usually the auto feature needs a few seconds after a lighting change to make its adjustment. Some systems get confused by very bright light or by light sources such as fluorescent or mercury vapor. But even if the automatic feature is working perfectly you can end up with inconsistent results. Say you're shooting a person in tungsten light, then change position to shoot the same person from a different angle that reveals a window in the background. The auto white balance will try to compensate for the bluer window, making the skin tone warmer in the second shot. With the change in the skin tone, the two shots may not cut together well.

Color balance is a creative element in shooting and when possible it's best to control it yourself.

BLACK BALANCE. Professional cameras have a *black balance* feature, which ensures that black is truly black with no color cast. A black balance should be done if the camera is new or hasn't been used for a while or if the temperature has changed significantly. On some cameras it's recommended to black-balance after changing shutter speed or switching between progressive and interlace recording.

To black-balance, press the black-balance control. If your camera doesn't close the iris automatically, cap the lens or close the iris if it closes all the way to "C." Afterward, it's not a bad idea to do a new white balance.

Setting the Exposure

Setting the exposure on a video camera usually begins with adjusting the iris (see p. 150) to control how much light comes through the lens. On some cameras this is done by turning the iris ring on the lens (turn toward the lower *f*-numbers to increase exposure). On other cameras there is no mechanical iris in the lens; instead you control exposure with a knob or button on the camera body. It's an advantage to use a camera that allows you to smoothly adjust the iris up or down; avoid cameras that have clicks or detents in the setting, which can make for jarring changes when done during a shot.

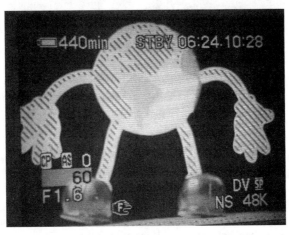

Fig. 3-6. Data in the viewfinder. You can choose to display lots of information about battery level, timecode, lens settings, and menu choices. Sometimes all the clutter blocks what you want to see. The zebras (stripes) shown here indicate overexposure.

How should you set the exposure? The simplistic answer is: so the picture looks good. With too much exposure, the scene will look very bright and washed out. The brightest parts will have no detail at all—just blown-out areas of undifferentiated white. With too little exposure, the scene will be murky and dark—the darkest parts of the scene will appear as masses of undifferentiated black (see Fig. 7-22).

To start, make sure the viewfinder or monitor is properly adjusted (see Appendix A). Then set the exposure so the balance between light and dark is as pleasing as possible. The most important elements of the scene—often people's faces—should have sufficient detail and be neither washed out nor murky. Overexposure can be a particular problem with video. Washed-out areas of the frame often look objectionable and may "bloom" or spread into other parts of the frame. Even so, sometimes you have to let a bright sky or window burn out if you hope to see detail in darker parts of the frame.

In some situations, there simply may be not enough light to shoot, or there may be too great a range between the bright and dark parts of the scene to get a pleasing image (see Fig. 7-14). There are several solutions, including using lights or repositioning or adjusting the camera. As a rule of thumb, scenes that are slightly underexposed are easier to fix in post than scenes that are grossly overexposed, so it's usually best to slightly underexpose rather than overexpose.

This discussion of exposure is deliberately simplified. For more precise and specific ways to adjust exposure, see Forming the Video Image, p. 177.

AUTOMATIC EXPOSURE CONTROL. Many video cameras (and some film cameras) have the ability to set the exposure automatically. *Autoexposure (AE)*, sometimes called *auto-iris*, has improved in recent years; some cameras offer sophisticated programmable control. Autoexposure can be helpful in some situations, particularly for fast-moving documentary scenes. But though many beginners prefer the supposed security of AE, many professionals avoid it when possible because it can result in inconsistent exposures or jarring exposure changes.

The autoexposure system works by measuring the brightness of the scene through the lens, and choosing an exposure setting that it thinks will work. Depending on the particular camera, its settings, and the amount of light, the AE system may try to adjust the iris and/or the gain (see p. 134) and/or the shutter (see p. 134). Changes to each of these can affect not only the exposure, but other aspects such as noise and how motion looks. More advanced cameras should permit you to select which of these functions to make automatic. For example, there may be a setting that allows you to use just *auto-iris control* or *auto-gain control* (AGC). If you want to experiment with automatic exposure, it's a good idea to start by setting the gain and shutter manually, and then see the effect of auto-iris alone.

One issue with automatic exposure is that the AE system doesn't necessarily know which part of the scene you're interested in. Dark or light backgrounds can be a particular problem. If you shoot someone against a bright background or with backlighting, the camera reads all that brightness and closes down the iris, darkening the scene and often throwing your subject into silhouette. Some cameras have a *backlight feature* that compensates by increasing the exposure a stop or more or an *AE shift* setting to increase or decrease exposure a set amount. (See Fig. 7-22 for more on backlight.) Some cameras allow you to select the part of the frame on which to base the automatic exposure, and this is a big help in getting the exposure you want.

AE systems often make exposure adjustments when none is needed. Say you're shooting your subject and a person with a dark sweater crosses the frame close to the camera, between you and the subject. Normally, you would want the exposure to remain constant—you don't want the exposure of the subject and background to change when the person walks by. AE, however, may open the iris as the dark sweater passes through the frame. Similarly, if you pan the camera (turn it horizontally) across a group of dark and light objects, the brightness of the background may change unnaturally as the camera passes the various objects.

Automatic exposure control works best in scenes that are front-lit (where the light comes from behind the camera position), that have relatively uniform backgrounds, and where the subject and background are neither excessively bright nor dark. AE can be of enormous help in "run-and-gun" documentary situations when your subject changes locations rapidly, and it can work acceptably in scenes where the lighting is even.

Autoexposure will generally prevent you from overexposing, so some videographers let the auto-iris initially set the exposure, then lock the setting in place by switching to manual control. Many prosumer camcorders have an "iris lock" or "exposure lock" button on the side that toggles the auto-iris on and off—when you press the button, auto-iris is on; when you press a second time, the iris is locked at that exposure. Professional video camera zooms have a similar button on the lens handgrip that momentarily enables auto-iris for as long as it is held down. Using this function, you might, for instance, let auto-iris get a reading of a wide shot of the scene, or you might zoom in on the most important part of the frame. In either case, let the iris adjust, lock it in place, then set the zoom where you want.

Setting the Focus

Before you shoot, you need to focus the camera's lens on what you're shooting. This is discussed in Focusing the Image, p. 151. Most professional cameras allow you to focus manually by turning the focus ring on the lens. As discussed in Adjusting the Viewfinder, p. 112, some cameras have a peaking feature in the viewfinder to assist you in seeing proper focus. Some cameras also allow you to magnify the viewfinder image so you can see focus more clearly.

AUTOFOCUS. Many camcorders have autofocus capability. Some consumer cameras rely on autofocus and are difficult or impossible to focus manually. Autofocus works by analyzing the image and adjusting the lens to maximize contrast and sharpness. Some autofocus systems work quite well, and can be handy in various situations, including times when you can't look through the viewfinder or when focusing it difficult. Many cameras offer three focus modes: full manual; full automatic (with continuous autofocus adjustment); and manual with instant focus readjustment when you push and hold a button (similar to iris lock). This last mode can be very useful, especially with LCD viewfinders in which it may be hard to see precise focus. Point the camera at the subject, press the focus button, and let the camera lock focus at that point. Then you can frame the shot as you like. This method can result in very accurate focus, particularly when the camera and subject aren't moving.

However, using the camera in continuous autofocus mode can produce unwanted results, particularly in scenes where there's movement or unusual framing.

One problem is that the autofocus system may not focus on the things you want to be in focus. Say you're shooting a man close to the camera who's looking at a mountain in the distance. Normally, the filmmaker should control whether the man or the mountain is in better focus. Using autofocus, however, the camera will usually choose whichever part of the scene is centered in the frame. Sometimes there's nothing of interest in the center. Say you're positioned at the head of a table, shooting two people talking to each other on either side of the table. Autofocus may try to focus on the wall behind them. When the camera and/or subject are moving, autofocus can sometimes track the action well, but other times it will make focus changes when none is called for. Autofocus systems do a certain amount of "hunting" to find proper focus, though recent cameras respond a lot faster than older models. Situations that may throw off autofocus include low light, shooting through glass or other material (like a scrim or a fence), bright backlight, and horizontal stripes.

Because focus is one of the key creative controls in shooting, continuous auto-focus should be used only if absolutely necessary.

THE VIDEO RECORDER

The sensor in a video camera converts light into an electrical signal (see Camera and Recorder Basics, p. 5). Different camera systems employ different methods of recording that signal on tape, hard drive, optical disc, or other storage media. For an overview of recording media, see p. 35 and p. 73.

THE VIDEOTAPE RECORDER

For many years, the standard way to record video in a camcorder has been on videotape using the built-in videotape recorder (VTR). The basic principles of recording on tape are similar for audio and video. (For audio, see p. 371. For digital video recording on tape or disk, see p. 208.)

A VTR is basically a machine for imparting a changing magnetic field to metal-oxide tape and then reading it back again. To record the video signal, the VTR sweeps its *record heads* across the tape as the tape moves past them. The heads are electromagnets that magnetize tiny particles on the tape according to the strength of the changing video signal. When you play the tape back, the heads respond to the magnetized tape particles and convert the fluctuating magnetic field back to an electrical signal, which after being processed into a video signal can be displayed as a picture again.

The Tape Path

When you insert a tape cassette into the VTR, a mechanism inside the machine opens the front of the cassette, pulls the tape out, and wraps it around the head drum, which is a fast-spinning cylinder containing various *heads* for recording, playback, or erasure (see Fig. 3-7). Other fixed (stationary) heads for audio and control tracks may be positioned inside the VTR along the edge of tape path. A *capstan* and *pinch wheel* (see Fig. 10-5) actually pull the tape along. The VTRs for different video formats differ widely in the way the heads are arranged and in many other aspects of the system.

Erasure

The erase head clears the tape of any signal prior to recording. This head is essentially an electromagnet that randomizes the magnetic pattern of the tape particles. Older or cheaper VTRs have only a fixed, full-track erase head that erases all the video and audio tracks. Most camcorders and other VTRs are equipped with *flying erase heads*, allowing you to edit or rerecord material without breakup (glitches) between sections. Flying erase heads are mounted on the rotating head drum and can begin or end erasure cleanly at a selected point. In some machines, they allow you to erase video without affecting linear audio tracks.

The Head Drum and Tape Speed

Videotape wraps diagonally around a fast-spinning cylindrical *head drum* out of which the heads protrude slightly. VTRs have two and often many more heads embedded in the rotating drum. During recording, each head sweeps a diagonal path across the tape, magnetizing a short swath (called a *helical scan*). Just as one head

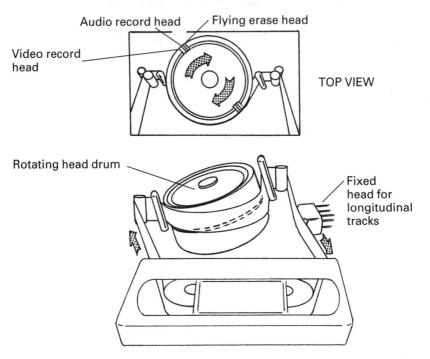

Fig. 3-7. Simplified view of the tape path and heads. Video formats vary widely in the configuration of the heads and the tape path. (Robert Brun)

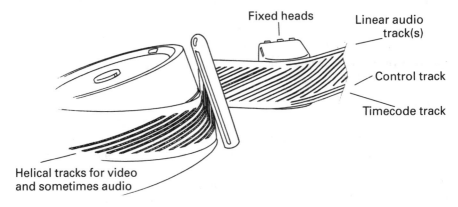

Fig. 3-8. The rotating heads record helical tracks while fixed (stationary) heads record the linear (longitudinal) tracks sometimes used for audio and/or control track signals. Track and head layouts vary by format. (Robert Brun)

finishes its swath, another head rotates into position to begin its swath. Sometimes when viewing an analog tape you can see at the bottom of the TV screen the *head switch*, a fuzzy line in the picture where the signal switches from one head to another.

The total speed at which the heads travel across the tape (*write speed*) is a combination of the speed of the tape and how fast the heads are spinning against the moving tape. Increasing the write speed offers various advantages. In analog recording, you get a better quality signal at high tape speed (which is why, for example, long play or extended play modes in VHS result in poorer quality than standard speed). In digital formats, higher tape speed can result in fewer dropouts (see below). The only reason to use slow tape speeds is so you can record more time on the same length tape. Some VTR formats use very fast rotating heads *and* a slow-moving tape to allow high quality and long record times. DV heads rotate at an amazing 9000 rpm.

Other Tracks

All videotape formats record the video signal in diagonal tracks (helical scans) across the surface of the tape using the rotating heads. In the case of MiniDV, DVCAM, and DVCPRO, for instance, ten diagonal tracks equals one frame of video. Each of the ten tracks also includes a small section set aside for audio, for timecode, and for timing (control) of tracks.

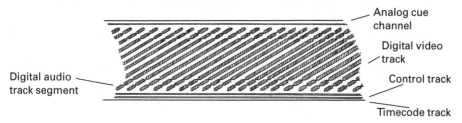

Fig. 3-9. Digital videotape track layout. Individual formats differ in the number, type, and position of tracks (Robert Brun).

Analog VTRs record their control track instead along the edge of the tape using a fixed magnetic head. Analog control track pulses can be thought of loosely as electronic sprocket holes, which guide the video playback. Tracks recorded along the edge of videotape like this are called *longitudinal* or *linear* tracks (see Fig. 3-8). In analog formats, longitudinal tracks are used also for recording audio and timecode. (For more on audio tracks, see p. 383.) In most digital formats, as in the DV examples above, audio, timecode, and control tracks are embedded in the diagonal tracks along with video.

Tape Recording Problems

If the heads become clogged with tape particles or dirt, they won't make good contact with the tape. The resulting image may be noisy (*video snow*) or contain many dropouts (momentary loss of recording that may appear as white pixels or horizontal white or black lines). With MPEG-2 formats, a single dropout can affect a group of frames. To clean the video heads, get a *head-cleaning cassette* and read the instructions for use. It is typical to run it like a tape through the machine for about ten seconds. Never rewind or reuse the head cleaner. Some people clean the heads on a regular basis; others only when the heads are obviously dirty (as indicated by bad recordings).

For persistent clogs, get head-cleaning fluid and a cleaning swab (not a Q-Tip). With no tape in the deck, clean the rollers and the tape path. Swab very gently over the heads horizontally along the tape path. Do not rub up and down (perpendicular to the tape path). It is very easy to damage the heads, so avoid manual cleaning if possible. Humidity can also cause recording problems. Avoid steamy locations when possible. In winter, when bringing a cold camera into a warm house, allow it to warm up in a sealed plastic bag to avoid condensation. When shooting in cold weather, try to keep the camera warm. Frozen tapes should be warmed before use. A hair dryer on low heat or air setting is sometimes used to warm or dehumidify equipment.

Tape Stock

Like audiotape, videotape is composed of a *base* or backing material (polyester) that provides the dimensional strength and stability, and a thinner, magnetically sensitive layer that actually records the video signal. The magnetic layer was once made up primarily of ferric (iron) oxide. Now manufacturers make a variety of formulations for the magnetic layer, ranging from various oxides to higher-quality "metal" tapes that have no oxide. The word *oxide* is sometimes used to mean standard-grade tape; at other times people use it just to refer to the magnetic layer in general.

Metal tapes come in two varieties: metal particle (MP) and metal evaporated (ME). In MP tape, microscopic cigar-shaped iron particles are individually coated to prevent oxidation and are applied in several layers to the base. In ME tape, cobalt is evaporated in a vacuum chamber and allowed to condense onto the surface of the polyester base. These special procedures make metal tapes considerably more expensive to produce. But both possess a higher magnetic *coercivity* (how strong a magnetic signal can be recorded) and *retentivity* that enable much higher recording densities than simple oxide tape. (In fact, MP tape made Hi8 possible in the late 1980s, while ME tape made MiniDV possible in the 1990s.)

All digital formats today use either MP or ME tape. The format determines which metal tape is required. For instance, MiniDV and HDV require ME tape, while Panasonic's DVCPRO formats use MP tape and Sony's DVCAM format uses ME tape. It is important not to use MP tapes in devices designed for ME tapes, as the two metal tape surfaces possess different friction characteristics and head wear will be affected. ME tape is usually the more costly.

As video formats have become smaller and record more data on narrower and shorter tapes, the quality of the tape stock has become more critical. A higher-quality tape will have fewer defects and allow you to record with less noise and dropouts (in analog formats you may also get clearer color and better detail). But picking a tape stock is not like picking a film stock. Film stocks vary in terms of basic color palette, contrast, and sensitivity to light. In video, the camera itself determines these things. The same video stock serves equally well for recording color or black-and-white, in daylight or indoor illumination, in PAL or NTSC.

Because tape stocks continually evolve, ask a professional for advice on picking a stock. Some manufacturers offer "mastering" stocks for top quality (and top price). Talk to people and check out online user groups for suggestions. If you are renting a camera, the rental house will often have a preference. Low-quality tapes may shed their oxide, clogging the heads and causing dropouts. Different tape manufacturers use different types of lubricants that may not interact well; many people recommend finding one brand you like and staying with it (or at least cleaning the heads between brands).

Cassettes come loaded with different-length tapes. Often, longer tapes are less expensive per minute of running time, and allow you to make fewer tape changes while shooting. On the other hand, sometimes long-playing cassettes contain tape stock with a thinner base. These stocks may be more vulnerable to stretching and breaking and should be used with care. One consideration on cassette length: If a tape gets lost or damaged, you suffer less if it's short. Losing a half hour of footage is bad enough; losing three hours is a whole lot worse.

Though tape stock is reusable, many feel that each pass through the VTR adds to the likelihood of dropouts or other defects. Professionals generally only use fresh, virgin tapes for critical camera recordings, using the best-quality tape stock they can afford. On the other hand, each pass of the tape along the spinning head drum effectively polishes the tape's surface, and some argue that head contact is improved. If you must reuse a tape, especially a metalized digital tape, don't lose sleep over it. Digital error correction is remarkably forgiving. Relative to all the costs of production, tape is usually very cheap. Don't scrimp. You can find good prices shopping online and save by buying in lots of ten or more.

Some digital cameras allow the operator to record additional information about shots (such as which are the good takes), which may save time if you can't do other kinds of logging in the field. This is particularly helpful for fast-paced news-gathering and editing. Sony's Cliplink system for DVCAM requires a cassette with a chip embedded in it. If you don't plan to use this feature you can save money by getting DVCAM or MiniDV cassettes with no chip.

STORING TAPE STOCK. Improperly stored videotape can deteriorate in various ways, including becoming brittle, stretching, or losing its magnetic charge. To maximize usable life, keep tapes away from any magnetic fields (including electric motors). Store them in spaces that would be comfortable for humans—Sony recommends medium humidity (neither very dry nor very moist) at temperatures from 59° to 77°F. Tapes should be fully wound or rewound and stored upright. No one knows exactly how long newer tape formulations will hold up. Since all tape formats eventually become obsolete, it's a good idea to transfer important archive masters to a new format every several years. DVD and other optical disc formats may make better archive media than DAT and other tape formats—although some argue that fading dyes in recordable DVDs create archival problems too. Let's hope that better archival solutions are waiting down the road.

HARD DRIVE, OPTICAL DISC, AND MEMORY CARD RECORDING

Newer digital cameras may permit recording to hard drives, optical discs, or Flash RAM memory cards instead of, or in addition to, tape. This may save time in postproduction, provide flexibility during the shoot (allowing instant playback of takes, longer record times, recording at a higher data rate/resolution) or other benefits. See p. 35 for an overview of these systems, and p. 73 for considerations of working with them. Systems vary in terms of available codecs, file formats, and other factors.

Some camera systems have internal disc drives, such as Sony's Blu-ray optical disc–based XDCAM (see Fig. 1-23) or Grass Valley's Infinity, which features Iomega REV removable hard disks (see Fig. 1-24). These cameras record to insertable disc (or disk) cartridges that can be popped out of the camera and into a drive bay in the editing system. You may have a choice of codecs (for example, MPEG-2 or DV) at various data rates. Some of these systems can also simultaneously record a very low-resolution and a full-resolution version of your material. This allows you to do *proxy editing* in the field with the low-res version on a laptop before returning home where you then configure a full-resolution version of the edit in a higher-powered editing system.

Fig. 3-10. Hard disk drive for recording directly to file. Firestore FS-100 supports DVC-PRO HD, DVCPRO 50, DVCPRO 25, and DV recording formats. Can record in several file formats for compatibility with different editing systems. (Focus Enhancements)

Many cameras can be used with an external hard drive, such as one of the Fire-Store products (see Fig. 3-10). These hard disk drives (HDDs) can be used much like a VTR, with record and playback capabilities at the push of a button. With certain camera/drive combinations, you can slave the drive to the camera, so it starts and stops when you press the camera trigger. If you record on the drive in the same file format used by your editing system, you can easily drag files from the HDD into your editing system, or in some cases edit directly from the HDD. Different editing systems use different file wrappers to package the video/audio data (see p. 220); the HDD may offer choices such as AVI, Quicktime, or OMF. Check to make sure you're using the right file format for your editing system. If the proper format isn't supported you'll need to do the extra step of converting the files while importing them into the editing system before you can work with them.

You may be able to record directly to a laptop, depending on your needs and the capability of your laptop. A software product such as Serious Magic's DV Rack (see Fig. 9-13) allows you to record DV, HDV, and DVCPRO HD via FireWire to a laptop using a variety of on-screen displays including a picture monitor with underscan, color bars, waveform monitor, vectorscope, and audio meters.[5] There are also various external drive configurations for high data-rate uncompressed or HD formats.

Some cameras record to solid-state Flash RAM memory cards or sticks. These are small, lightweight, and slip easily into the camera and then into a laptop (see Fig. 2-9). As of this writing they are relatively expensive and of limited capacity, but both of those problems will ease over time. When a card fills up, you can download it to a hard drive or other storage system (see Fig. 2-10).

OPERATING THE CAMCORDER

Before you shoot, be sure to charge and/or check the batteries (see Batteries and Power Supplies, p. 130.) Set the timecode, if any (see Timecode, p. 203). For information on audio recording, see Audio in the Video Camcorder, p. 383, as well as Chapters 10 and 11. We'll assume here that audio is ready to go. When you're ready to start shooting, make sure the viewfinder is focused for your eye, and that you've checked or set the white balance, exposure, and camera focus (see pp. 111–121). If you're recording on tape, insert a fresh tape cassette.

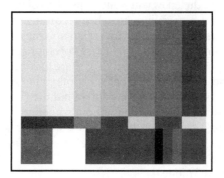

Fig. 3-11. SMPTE color bars (also see Appendix A).

BARS AND TONE. Since the analog era, it has been a professional practice to record 30 seconds of color bars and audio reference tone at the beginning of every camera tape, using the camera's color bar generator and an audio test tone from the camera or the sound mixer (see Appendix A and Reference Tone, p. 421). In part, the idea is to roll far enough into the tape to avoid any dust and to provide bars and tone for video and audio calibration later on. If you're shooting an analog tape format such as Betacam SP, bars and tone are used to adjust video and audio levels properly when the tape is dubbed or digitized into an NLE.

5. DV Rack is Windows-only.

In digital video, levels are encoded into the digital stream and do not need adjustment or monitoring during copying or cloning. Recorded color bars and tone are therefore of use mostly when an analog step exists, such as digitizing into an older NLE that can't accept a DV signal via FireWire, or adjusting a video monitor which requires an analog video input (unless it uses DVI or HDMI digital video inputs, but as of this writing, these are relatively scarce).

So, bars and tone on every camera tape may be expected professionally, but may not actually be that useful for digital cameras.[6] If you're working for yourself, you won't miss recording bars on each cassette when shooting, for example, a digital documentary involving hundreds of cassettes for editing on an NLE. You should record at least ten seconds of *something* at the head of each tape (to provide preroll for the editing deck—see below) and you may want to put bars on at least some cassettes as an aid in adjusting picture monitors on location or in the NLE.

If instead of tape you are recording to hard disk, optical disc, or Flash memory, there can be no concern about dirty tape ends or preroll. Whether you wish to include a short segment of color bars and audio test tone will depend on the same considerations just described.

THE CAMERA TRIGGER. All cameras have a trigger to start and stop the VTR or disk/disc recording device (push once to go into "record" mode, push again to stop). Get in the habit of checking the record indicator in the viewfinder to make sure that you're *actually* rolling when you think you are. It's surprisingly easy to get off cycle, and push the button thinking you're starting the camera when actually you're stopping it (and when you check the tape later, you're shocked to find you've recorded none of the takes you wanted, just lots of nothingness in between). This painful possibility is especially acute when recording to Flash memory such as Panasonic's P2 cards, as the camcorder makes no noise upon start-up or operation (the silence is why sound recordists love P2). Professional tape-based camcorders have a two- or three-position power switch (or there may be more than one switch) to allow you to put the camera in different states of readiness. In one state, power is supplied to the camera so you can see through it, but the tape is not threaded in the VTR and the head drum is not spinning. This is sometimes called "save" mode. In another state, the tape is threaded, the heads are spinning, and the tape will start recording immediately when you push the trigger (sometimes called "standby" or "operate" mode). The names vary from machine to machine, and not all camcorders have a true "save" mode.

"Standby" mode should be used when recording is imminent. It allows you to roll tape instantly and generally ensures a clean transition from one shot to the next. However, when you are paused between shots, the "standby" position drains the battery faster and can wear down the tape or heads if you park in the same spot on the tape too long. Going to "save" mode disengages the tape and stops the heads from spinning. This conserves power and cuts down wear and tear, but when you are ready to shoot, the camera takes a few seconds to come up to speed. If there is fast-breaking action, it's probably best to leave the camera in "standby." If you know it will be several minutes between shots, switch to "save" or power down the

6. Bars and tone on finished master tapes are still considered essential.

camera completely (most cameras automatically switch to "save" after a little while).[7] Of course, if you're recording to Flash memory cards, these considerations don't apply.

The *tally light* in the viewfinder indicates when you're recording, or, for a switched, multicamera shoot, when the camera is being selected ("*taken*"). There is usually a tally light on the outside of the camera so everyone knows when you're recording. For documentary work, many filmmakers turn it off or put a piece of tape over it.

PRE-RECORD CACHE. Some cameras have a *pre-record* (also called "loop" or "retroloop") system that continually stores about five to ten seconds of material when the camera's on but not rolling. Then, when you hit the trigger, the recording begins five to ten seconds *before* you pressed start. It's like having your own personal time machine! A special random access memory board in the camera, called a *pre-record cache* (also called *video cache* or *picture cache*), makes this possible. On some cameras it is an option, on some cameras it is built in. External disk-based systems like DV Rack and FireStore disk recorders can add this capability to cameras that lack it. Several seconds of prerecord can be especially useful in unpredictable documentary situations.

This same RAM video cache also makes possible single-frame *interval recording* (known in film as time-lapse) in tape-based camcorders. A tape-based camcorder can accumulate single frames over a long period of time until the video cache becomes full, then automatically lay off its contents of five to ten seconds of time-lapse to tape in one burst of recording. A long time-lapse can be achieved by allowing the camera to accumulate several such segments.

CLEAN CUTS FROM SHOT TO SHOT. Digital camcorders are generally designed to provide seamless transitions between shots. If you press stop at the end of one shot, then press start again, the new shot begins without a glitch. However, when recording to analog tape, some situations can cause a brief breakup in the image between shots due to a break in the control track. This may happen even in a digital camcorder if you power the camera down, switch to "save" mode, take the tape out of the camera, or play back a shot to check it. If you do any of these things, you can still ensure a glitch-free transition. Some cameras have an *end search button* (professional cameras often have a *return button* marked "RET"); these will pause the camera at the very end of the last shot, ready to begin the new shot with continuous control track. On consumer cameras, often if you just play to the end of the last recorded shot and press stop while still on the shot, the camera can pick up from there, recording smoothly into the next shot.

There are other reasons as well why you might not have continuous timecode and/or control track from one shot to the next. You might be using an older camera, or you might be using time-of-day timecode (see p. 206). In any of these cases, it's a good idea when beginning a new shot to let the camera roll for five to ten seconds after pressing start before any action begins. This *preroll* time is needed in editing for VTRs to lock to the timecode or control track. With some tape-based

---

7. On some cameras you can set how long the camera waits before going into "save" mode.

cameras and editing systems, and with some HDV cameras or other formats that use interframe compression (see p. 223), the recording or playback doesn't become fully stable until a few seconds after the beginning of the shot, so it's never a bad idea to leave some preroll time after you push the trigger before calling "action" or start shooting. Similarly, it's prudent to wait a few seconds after the scene stops before stopping the camera.

PROTECTING AND LABELING MATERIAL. A note about reviewing takes on the set: If you decide to go back and check something you just shot for performance or technical reasons, be *very* careful to make sure you return to the end of the tape before recording again. Many hearts have been broken by cuing to the wrong spot and unintentionally burning a good take. Some cinematographers refuse to rewind on set for that reason (though without checks you then run the risk of being unaware of a head clog or other problem). Fortunately, newer hard drive and memory card recording systems can prevent you from accidentally recording over your material (although they introduce the possibility of other calamities, like deleting entire clips by mistake).

When you've finished recording a tape, remove it from the VTR and immediately slide the record lock on the cassette to prevent accidental erasure (on older tape formats this can be a removable plastic button). XDCAM cartridges and P2 cards have similar record lock tabs. Label all tapes, cartridges, and Flash memory cards (if there's room to mark them) before shooting or immediately after. Indicate the name of the project, the production company, the date, the cassette number (if tape), the starting timecode (if any), and if tape, be sure to write "camera original" or apply the manufacturer's premade sticker.[8] It often helps to write some notes about the content as well. See Chapters 9, 13, and 14 for more on logging and note-keeping.

BATTERIES AND POWER SUPPLIES

All electronic gear needs power to run. For a shoot to go smoothly, you must have power when you need it.

AC Power Supplies

For interior work, you can use an *AC power supply*, which is plugged into the wall. (In the U.K., wall current is called the *mains*.) With AC power, you never run out of juice, but your mobility is limited by the cable. When shooting in a foreign country, keep in mind that different countries have different types of power (see Electric Power, p. 484). The AC power may be supplied at 120 or 240 volts at a line frequency of 50 or 60 Hz. In some places what comes out of the wall isn't AC (alternating current) at all. Many power supplies and battery chargers can accommodate

---

8. *Never* label a cassette using masking tape or other tape. It can easily jam in a deck.

different types of power (either automatically or with a switch). In some cases, you have to convert the power to a different standard before plugging in (see p. 485). Check the manual that came with your equipment.

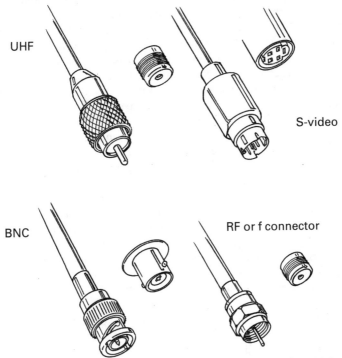

Fig. 3-12. Common video connectors. Also see Figs. 5-14, 10-12, and 10-30 for other connectors used for video and audio. (Robert Brun)

Battery Power

For shooting in the field, and when portability is important, rechargeable batteries are used to power the camera. Most camcorders and film cameras use *on-board* camera-mounted batteries that range from several ounces to a few pounds. Battery belts and packs can also be used, especially for larger cameras. Batteries have to be managed carefully so you don't run out of power when you need it.

There are several types of rechargeable batteries. *Nickel-cadmium* (*NiCad*) batteries have been a widely used type of camera battery. Other battery formulations gaining popularity include *nickel-metal-hydride* (*NiMH*) and *lithium-ion* (*Li Ion*), which are more expensive and supply more power than a NiCad in a smaller, lighter package. *Lead acid* batteries (what cars use) are heavy for the amount of power they supply. These may be used for powering lights directly or sometimes for camera power using a car's interior accessory outlet (cigarette lighter socket).

Estimating your battery needs with a film camera is relatively straightforward. Consult others or check the manual to determine how much film your camera will shoot per battery. If you know how much film you plan to shoot, you know how many charged batteries you need for the day.

Because video cameras (and audio recorders) use power whether they're actually recording or merely standing by with the circuits on, it's harder to estimate battery needs. You could spend hours rehearsing actors with the camera on, then run out of power just before you start to record. You can determine how much continuous recording time a battery will supply, then figure you'll need power for at least two to three times longer—for the time when you're looking through the camera but not actually recording. It's better to be safe than sorry, so bring plenty of batteries and a charger if you can. With consumer or prosumer camcorders, its usually a good idea to use larger, *extended batteries* instead of the small ones that usually come with the camera. With larger, professional cameras you may have a choice between a heavy, high-capacity *brick* or smaller battery packs. The lighter batteries won't run as long, but if you'll be hand-holding the camera, they may save your back.

You can nurse batteries along by powering down the camera or by going into "save" mode when not recording (but it's probably not worth powering down for less than a few minutes' break). Avoid rewinding tapes when you're trying to save battery power. Check batteries often during use to determine how much capacity is left. Newer cameras and batteries often have a display that indicates how many more minutes of use the battery has in it. Bear in mind that most rechargeable batteries will put out their full rated voltage until just before they're depleted (at which point the voltage drops sharply), so battery checks may not give much prior warning of low charge. For cameras that need 12 volts to operate, many people prefer to use batteries rated at 14 volts to get the most capacity out of the battery before the 12V cutoff point is reached. Batteries should be checked under load (with the camera running) if possible.

Batteries put out much less power when they're cold. For cold-weather shooting, keep the battery warm until you're ready for it or get an extension power cable so you can keep the battery inside your coat while shooting. Camera-mounted lights (and video taps on film cameras) consume a lot of power. It's always safer to run them off their own battery (separate from the camera's) to be sure you can keep the camera going even if the other systems run out of juice. A battery belt or battery pack makes a good auxiliary supply. On an expedition where normal battery charging is difficult, consider a solar-powered charger or a lithium, high-capacity, nonrechargeable expedition battery.

For many types of smaller equipment that consume less power (including audio recorders, microphones, and wireless transmitters), nonrechargeable batteries are sometimes preferred because they may allow longer continuous service without changing the batteries (though rechargeable AA and AAA batteries have improved greatly in recent years). Alkaline batteries provide more power than standard cells. Lithium and other expensive types are better yet. When replacing any battery, be sure the polarity is correct (that is, the plus-minus orientation of each cell). If the equipment uses several batteries together, never replace less than a full set. Reversed or dead cells will drain the others.

Battery Charging and Maintenance

There are many types of batteries and chargers, so be sure to read the manual that comes with your equipment. Generally, the more power a battery puts out, the more time it needs to charge. Some chargers are designed to switch off when the battery is fully charged. With others, you must unplug the battery when done. Overcharging a battery can destroy it. If the charger isn't one that automatically shuts off, unplug a battery if it feels hot.

Slow chargers are the least expensive, and can take up to sixteen hours depending on the system. This can make it hard to keep batteries fully charged if you're on the road or shooting every day. *Fast chargers* may work in as little as an hour, and can make all the difference for recharging during a shoot. Sometimes not all the cells in a battery get full on a fast charge. Some electronic chargers are designed to do a quick charge and then go into *equalize* mode, topping off all the cells. Most rechargeable batteries will slowly lose their charge just sitting on the shelf. Be sure to recharge just before a shoot. Even better, get a charger that will maintain a full battery for months by delivering a continuous *trickle charge*. A good trickle charger may also extend the life of the battery.

Some chargers double as AC power supplies for the camera—very handy when all your batteries are dead and you don't have time to recharge. On the other hand, some consumer chargers are designed to work *only* with a battery that's in the camera, which is a real disadvantage when you want to be charging a dead battery while shooting with a second, fresh one.

Charge a depleted battery as soon as possible after use and charge batteries every few months if unused. Batteries retain their charge best in a cool place: 0° to 10°C is ideal. However, never try to charge a cold or frozen battery. Warm it up to room temperature first. As noted above, cold batteries put out less power when you use them. Don't charge batteries if the temperature is above 110°F.

There is a lot of debate about the concept of battery memory. Some people claim that if a NiCad battery is repeatedly discharged only partway and recharged, it will eventually lose its ability to store a full charge. Anton Wilson (of Anton/Bauer, makers of widely used batteries) points out that this memory effect happens only if the battery is discharged to *precisely* the same amount each time, and that even then the problem can be corrected by a few full discharge/slow-charge cycles. To avoid any memory issues with NiCad and NiMH batteries, discharge the battery fully each time you use it (until the low battery warning comes on in the camera) and rotate through your batteries by starting with a different one each day. Li Ion batteries have no memory effect at all.

Overdischarging can harm a battery as much as overcharging. Most video cameras will shut off before overdischarging a NiCad, but a lighting fixture will drain it past the safety point.

Rechargeable batteries have a limited life both in terms of age and the number of discharge/charge cycles. You should expect to get around 400 to 600 cycles from a NiCad or NiMH battery and around 1000 cycles from a NiMH before the battery won't hold a full charge. You can often replace just the cells in a professional battery pack, saving the cost of buying a whole new battery.

ADVANCED CAMERA FEATURES

Camera Sensitivity

Camera sensors have improved greatly in their sensitivity to light. Even a consumer camera may be usable in light as dim as candlelight, though the image-rendering won't be ideal. Most cameras have a *gain* or *sensitivity* switch that boosts the camera's sensitivity for low-light shooting. Increasing gain also increases noise in the image, which looks a bit like graininess in film. Video gain is measured in dB (decibels). A typical gain switch might include settings for 0, +3, +6, +9, and +18 dB. Boosting gain 6 dB doubles sensitivity, equivalent to opening up one stop. (In film terms, this is like doubling the ASA or pushing one stop.) Switching to +18 dB is like opening up three stops. Usually, small increases in gain can improve the image in low-light situations without introducing too many image defects, but higher increases may show noticeable noise and should be used only if necessary (such as the *hypergain* setting in some cameras that can look like a snowstorm of noise). Experiment with your camera.

For extremely dark scenes, some cameras can record *infrared* (and may be equipped with an infrared on-camera "light"; see Fig. 2-6). Infrared responds to heat, not visible light, and the image looks unnatural; but with it, you can shoot scenes too dark to shoot otherwise. You may like the weirdness of the look. Sony calls its consumer infrared system *NightShot*.

In sunlit scenes, there is often too much light for the sensor. Even with the lens iris closed down to minimum aperture, the image may be overexposed. Professional cameras are often equipped with an internal filter wheel, which may offer a choice between settings at 5600K, 5600 + ¼ ND, and 5600 + 1/16 ND. The first position inserts an orange filter for daylight that warms the light and cuts down the intensity by not quite half (⅔ stop; see Color Conversion Filters, p. 301). The second position adds a neutral density filter (see Neutral Density Filters, p. 302) which cuts the light to ¼ its previous level (this is a .06ND which cuts out 2 stops). The last position cuts the light to 1/16 (a .12ND or 4 stops). Some cameras just have ND filters with no color correction, which can be very handy when you want to reduce the light without changing the color balance (for example, to allow opening the iris to reduce depth of field).

Some cameras have a position on the gain switch that *decreases* sensitivity, for instance to −3 dB. This can be used for overly bright situations. Since reducing gain also reduces noise, some cinematographers use the lowered gain setting whenever possible. Both neutral density filters and lowered gain can be used to shoot at a wider iris for shallower depth of field (see p. 151).

Frame Rate and Shutter Speed

A video camera is really a machine for capturing a series of still images (that is, frames; see p. 4). How many frames are captured each second is the frame rate. For a discussion of frame rate options, see p. 97.

If you've done much still photography, you probably know that still cameras have a *shutter speed adjustment* that controls how long the film or digital chip is exposed to light when you press the trigger. You might use a high shutter speed (short exposure time) for shooting sports when you want to freeze fast-moving action (see Fig. 2-17). You might use a slow shutter speed (long exposure time) in a dark scene when you need to collect as much light as possible to get enough exposure on the film or chip.

Most video cameras also have a shutter speed adjustment. This controls not how many frames are taken each second (that's the frame rate), but the length of time the sensor collects light while each frame is being captured. The standard shutter speed is determined in part by the frame rate: generally speaking, *the standard shutter speed is half the frame rate.*

Fig. 3-13. Mighty Wondercam shoulder pod can be used to steady a camera that doesn't balance on the shoulder. Shown with Sony HVR-Z1U camcorder, which records 1080i HDV as well as DVCAM and DV and has a widescreen chip. (Videosmith, Inc.)

For example, if you're shooting PAL at 25 fps, the default shutter speed on the camera will usually be 1/50th second. If you're shooting interlaced video, two fields are scanned for every frame. So shooting NTSC at 30 fps (also known as 60i) results in 1/60th second standard shutter speed.

There are times when you might want to use a higher shutter speed. Some cameras are capable of shutter speeds up to 1/10,000 second or more (the faster the shutter speed, the shorter the exposure). Why use a higher shutter speed? In a normal film or video image, any motion in the frame (whether caused by the camera or the subject movement) will cause a certain amount of blur (see Fig. 2-17). This blur looks natural at normal playback speed, but if you plan to slow the footage down or display still frames, you can make each frame crisper by using a higher shutter speed. This is might be done in order to analyze sporting events. Increasing the shutter speed can be used to create a deliberately choppy mood for an effect. However, using high shutter speeds can cause certain image problems (see p. 361). For more on slow motion, see p. 357.

Because high shutter speeds cut down the exposure, you'll need to compensate for increasing the shutter speed by opening the iris, increasing the gain, or adding more light. Very high shutter speeds are usually only feasible in bright light. In a situation where you deliberately want to reduce exposure so you can open the iris to achieve shallow depth of field, you might increase the shutter speed (see p. 151).

Slower shutter speeds produce more motion blur and are sometimes used for a more gentle, dreamy effect. Some cameras have a *slow shutter mode* that allows you to select shutter speeds that are longer than one frame or field: for example, $\frac{1}{15}$-, $\frac{1}{8}$-, and $\frac{1}{4}$-second shutter speeds when shooting 60i. This way, a single exposure effectively stretches across multiple frames. If there's any camera or subject movement there will be blurring and trails. You might like this as a special effect, but if not, use a good tripod and avoid any camera or subject movement. In static shots you can use a slow shutter to gain exposure when there isn't enough light to shoot otherwise. Be aware that some cameras—Sony's, for instance—use field doubling to accomplish slow shutter speeds, in which one field in each frame is discarded and the remaining field is doubled. This cuts vertical resolution in half compared to normal video frames, although given the blurring of the slow shutter speed, it is often hardly noticeable.

Some cameras have various shutter modes to simulate the look of 24p (see Frame Modes, p. 104).

Shooting computer and video monitors can be challenging if the *refresh rate* (scanning rate) of the monitor doesn't match the frame rate of the camera, which results in a frame bar or uneven screen illumination. Some cameras have a special shutter control that allows you to dial the shutter speed up or down in very small increments to try to match the scanning rate of the camera to the monitor. Sony's system is called *Clear Scan;* Panasonic calls theirs *Synchro Scan.* See Chapter 18 for more on shooting monitors.

Camera Sensors

The sensor of a video camera is the light-sensitive chip that captures the image inside the camera (see Fig. 1-3). In modern cameras, the sensor is generally either a CCD or CMOS. Each type has its advantages, and there are subtypes of CCDs (such as IT, FIT, Hyper HAD, and so on) that offer improvements to increase sensitivity and decrease image defects. CMOS chips, which unlike CCDs have their own signal processing built in, have been rapidly improving in recent years.

It used to be true that cameras with three chips (one each for red, green, and blue) produced better images than single-chip cameras. In a three-chip camera, an internal prism splits the light into the three color components (see Fig. 1-14). Some three-chip cameras also use a *pixel shift* technique to increase resolution by offsetting the red and blue sensors by half a pixel from the green sensor to effectively double the number of discrete image samples. Some camcorders, like Sony's Z1, do this in a horizontal direction only, while others, like Panasonic's HVX200, pixel-shift both horizontally and vertically. Pixel-shifting is a venerable technique that has been used in professional cameras for decades because it can produce very good results.

While three-chip cameras have certain advantages, such as light sensitivity, today some of the highest-end cameras use single chips (as do some of the lowest-end cameras). These include Panavision's Genesis, Arriflex's D-20, and Dalsa's Origin. Like digital still photography cameras, single-chip digital cinema cameras predominantly use a *Bayer pattern* filter on a huge sensor (the size of a 35mm film frame) to separate red, green, and blue light. A Bayer filter contains microscopic red, green, and blue filters—one per pixel—in a repeating pattern like this: RGBG— which provides twice as many green pixels as red or blue.

With a three-chip video camera, some light is lost in the prism and you must use a lens specifically designed for that type of prism, limiting your choice of lenses. With single-chip cameras there is no prism (just like in digital still cameras). This simplifies the optical path and allows use of high quality PL-mount film lenses designed for 16mm and 35mm film cameras.

Not too long ago, most professional cameras had ⅔-inch chips (about the size of the 16mm film frame). Now, smaller cameras may have ½-, 1⅓-, ¼-, or even ⅙-inch chips. As a rule, larger chips have an advantage: They're more sensitive and have lower noise and less bothersome artifacts. Packing the one or two million pixels needed for high-resolution HD formats into a tiny chip is an enormous technical challenge. Even so, when evaluating a camera, look at its total performance (how the image looks, how the camera handles low light, and so on) and don't just judge by chip size.

The size of the sensor affects the angle of view afforded by a lens of a given focal length (see Focal Length and Format, p. 148). This can have implications for depth of field and your shooting style (p. 85).

Camera Setup

Numerous adjustments and settings within the camera's electronics affect the color, contrast, and sharpness of the image. Some of these settings are user-adjustable; others need to be done by a technician. When you get a new professional or prosumer camera, it's a good idea to have a technician fine-tune the settings and explain to you their purpose and use.

Some cameras have a *scene file* capability that can store a variety of settings and combinations, which you can choose for different looks. Some cameras accept a *setup card*, which is an insertable memory chip that can be programmed to adjust various aspects of the picture, including contrast and color balance. A setup card can be used to try to make a video camera mimic various film stocks. The card can be set to a cameraperson's preference, then brought from shoot to shoot when the exact same type of camera is used, or it can be used to ensure consistency on a multicamera shoot, again when the same type of camera is used. Note that if the same type of camera is used but each camera has a different type of lens, the lens differences cannot be accounted for by use of scene files unless there is a scene file for each lens that takes into account the differences.

GAMMA. In video, gamma refers to the contrast of the image, particularly in the midtones. Gamma has a big impact on the feel of the image and whether details are visible in shadows or highlights. Many prosumer and professional cameras offer a choice of gamma settings. For example, Panasonic's HVX200 allows you to select between gamma modes such as "Low," "High," and two "Cine-like" settings. For more on gamma and contrast, and choosing a gamma setting, see p. 185.

DETAIL. Before reading this, see Sharpness and Focus on p. 84. *Detail* (sometimes called *enhancement, edge enhancement, sharpness,* or *aperture correction*) is a setting that affects the apparent sharpness of a video image (see Fig. 3-14). Many cameras have a menu setting for detail (this is for the recorded image, *not* a viewfinder adjustment). When detail is set too high, there is a crisp, clear outline around objects, making them stand out boldly with a kind of electric "ringing" effect.[9] When detail is set very low, the image may seem soft or unsharp. (You cannot truly add sharpness that doesn't exist to an image. When detail is low or turned off, that is, in fact, the true resolution of the video image.)

Fig. 3-14. Detail or enhancement. (top) A shot made with a Sony DSR-500 camera with detail set to minimum. (bottom) Detail set to maximum. Notice the artificial white edge around the numbers on the clock and other objects.

9. The detail setting doesn't actually improve the ability to see fine details. It doesn't increase resolution, it just makes shapes pop out more—which fools the eye into seeing things as sharper.

Generally speaking, setting the detail high feels "video-like" and setting the detail lower is more "film-like." TV news footage is often shot with a crisp, enhanced look. Shots made with low detail can sometimes look mushy, but your eye gets used to the mellower, subtler look. Depending on your camera, what you're shooting, and your preferences, you may like more or less detail, but overuse of enhancement should be avoided. (This works exactly like the Sharpen or Unsharp Mask filters in Photoshop. If you use Photoshop, over-apply either of these to a still image to get an idea of what setting the detail circuit too high does to your video image.) If you're planning to do a film-out or upconvert to a higher-definition video format, it's recommended to keep the detail settings mid to low, if not turned off entirely. (Some camcorders won't allow the detail circuits to be completely turned off.) When in doubt, less detail is safer than more, since it can be added later but it can't be removed. However, bear in mind that on some cameras, setting the detail too low can make the image look out of focus.

Ideally, detail should be adjusted with the help of an experienced technician, but if your camera has a menu setting for detail and you want to try it yourself, be sure to check the results on a familiar monitor you trust, and try projecting on a big screen as well. Something that looks good in a small monitor may look very different when projected big. Experiment with the *detail level* (it may be called *sharpness*) and the *vertical detail*. On some cameras changing to a cine gamma (see p. 188) automatically reduces detail. Keep in mind that the detail setting within the camera is completely separate from the detail or peaking adjustment in the viewfinder. In fact, if the camera detail is set low, you may want to set the viewfinder peaking high to help you focus.

There's another setting on some cameras labeled *vertical detail frequency*. On some Panasonic cameras, for example, you can set this to "thin," "mid," or "thick." When cameras record in standard definition progressive mode, they can capture fine horizontal lines without artifacts. Setting the vertical detail frequency to thin or mid will capture the most resolution (and is preferable for progressive displays and/or film-out). However, when the footage is displayed on an interlaced monitor, the same fine horizontal lines can seem to flicker (twitter) or cause Moiré patterns that seem to vibrate. Using the thick setting sacrifices resolution but helps prevent these problems on interlaced displays.

CHROMA. The *chroma* setting affects how saturated colors are. High chroma means bright, deep colors; low chroma means pale, desaturated colors. Very saturated colors may look appealing on a small monitor, but are sometimes too vibrant on a bigger screen. Your choice of gamma setting will also have an effect on chroma. For more on color, see p. 192.

If you're not a video tech or a DIT (digital imaging technician) with experience in adjusting color matrix parameters, it's always prudent to avoid experimenting with color settings. The camera's default settings usually can be relied upon to produce attractive images, and hue, saturation, and the like can be easily adjusted later, at the NLE or color-correction stage, when the likelihood of working with a large, finely calibrated monitor in a controlled visual environment is greater.

Digital Signal Processing, Effects, and Stills

Digital cameras have a growing assortment of sophisticated image controls and features in addition to the ones mentioned above. *Digital signal processing (DSP)* encompasses a wide range of image manipulations a digital camera may be able to do. For example, some cameras have a *skin detail* feature that can target skin tones and soften the texture for a more flattering look while leaving the rest of the image sharp. Some cameras can capture a previously recorded image and superimpose it in the viewfinder, allowing you to re-create a setup recorded earlier. Some cameras can record camera settings for each shot, aiding in reviewing or re-creating shots.

Many video cameras have a range of capabilities for in-camera visual effects. These may include generating titles, doing fades and dissolves, in-camera editing, colorizing, posterizing, or otherwise distorting the image. Consult your camera's manual for details. In general, it is far better to do these effects in postproduction than in the camera. Many cameras are also capable of interval recording or shooting individual frames, allowing you to do time-lapse or animation work (see p. 360).

Some cameras allow you to capture a still image and record it to a memory card or on a tape. This can be useful in a pinch, perhaps while location scouting. But you'll get a far better still image from a digital camera designed to take still photographs than from a camcorder that also has this capability, even if the camcorder's sensor can capture stills in a progressive format (with all the scan lines) instead of an interlaced format (which will be half-resolution because the still can only be made from only one field). HD camcorders will producer better-looking stills than SD thanks to their higher pixel count, but will still fail to match dedicated still cameras. Ever tried composing a vertical frame with a camcorder?

CHAPTER 4

The Lens

This chapter is about lenses for both film and video cameras. The lens is the eye of the camera system. To create the kinds of images you want, it's important to understand the basic characteristics of lenses and how they gather light. Generally, film cameras accept interchangeable lenses, allowing you to select the best lens for a given shot. Professional and some prosumer video cameras usually also accept interchangeable lenses, while consumer and other prosumer cameras may have fixed lenses, so your choice of camera will be based partly on the lens it has.

Photographic lenses are generally made of several pieces of glass, called *elements*. Some of these elements are cemented together (*compound elements*) and then mounted in the lens *barrel* (housing). The lens gathers light rays from the subject and bends them to form an image in the camera.

FOCAL LENGTH AND PERSPECTIVE

Focal Length

If we take a light source at infinity—a star will work fine, but anything at a great distance can serve as "infinity"—the lens will focus the rays at a point behind the lens. This point falls on the *focal plane*, and the lens is said to bring the star into focus in the focal plane (see Fig. 4-1). In a film camera the film normally rests in the focal plane when it is exposed; in a video camera, the CCD or CMOS sensor will be in the focal plane. (Because most lens concepts are identical for film and video, in this chapter the terms "film" and "sensor" will be used interchangeably to mean the surface where the image is formed.)

The *focal length* measures the power of a lens to bend light rays coming from the subject. The shorter the focal length, the greater the bending power and the closer the focal plane is to the rear of the lens. The focal length of a lens is defined as the distance from the lens (actually, the *nodal point* of the lens) to the focal plane when the lens is focused on an object at infinity. Lenses are identified by their focal length. *Prime lenses* (also called *fixed focal length lenses*) have only one focal length.

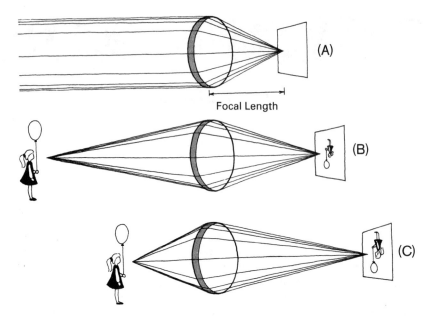

Fig. 4-1. Focal length. (A) The rays from a point source of light at infinity are parallel when they strike the lens. The distance from the lens to the focal plane (where the rays are brought back to a point) is the *focal length*. (B) The photographic lens forms an upside-down image flipped from left to right. (C) The closer an object is to the lens, the farther from the lens the rays converge and the larger the object appears on the film. (Carol Keller)

Zoom lenses have a range of focal lengths, allowing you to change focal length during a shot. Focal length is usually expressed in millimeters or, more rarely, in inches (1 inch is approximately 25mm).

For each shot, the cinematographer decides how large the subject should be in the frame. For example, should the shot include the whole body or should the face fill the frame? There are two ways to increase the size of the subject in the frame: You can either move the camera closer to the subject or use a longer focal length lens (see Fig. 4-2). If we view a scene with two lenses, the lens with the longer focal length will reveal less of the scene and will make any object in its field of view appear larger. This lens "sees" the scene through a narrower angle—the longer the focal length, the narrower this *angle of view*.

Focal length is directly proportional to the size any object will appear on film or video. If we double the focal length (keeping the distance to the subject constant), the subject will appear twice as large on film. The size of the object is inversely proportional to its distance from the camera—that is, if we double the distance, we halve the size of the subject on film (see Fig. 4-3). At 10 feet, a 50mm lens yields the same size subject as a 25mm lens does at 5 feet.

Perspective

As just discussed, there are two ways to control the size of an object in the frame: change the distance between camera and subject or change the focal length. Does it make a difference if you move the camera closer to the subject rather than use a lens

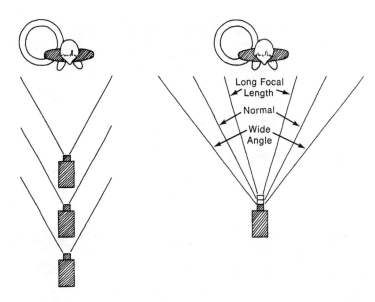

Fig. 4-2. Angle of view and focal length. (left) Keeping the angle of view constant, moving closer to the man (dollying in), makes him appear larger. (right) Keeping the camera in the same position while using increasingly longer focal lengths also makes the man larger but decreases the angle of view. See the results in Fig. 4-3. (Carol Keller)

of a longer focal length? Figure 4-3 illustrates that it does. When you change focal length to enlarge part of a scene, it's like enlarging a detail from the image. Both foreground and background objects become larger to the same relative extent. In other words, if the focal length is doubled, all the objects in the frame double in size on film.

On the other hand, as the camera is moved closer, the relative size of foreground and background objects increase at different rates. Objects closer to the camera become larger faster than objects farther from the camera. In the first set of photographs in Fig. 4-3, the camera is moved closer to the subject. The building in the background does not increase in size nearly as much as the man in the foreground. If you move twice as close to an object, the object doubles in size on film, but objects in the background increase by less than that.

Perspective may be thought of as the rate at which objects become smaller the farther they are from the camera. In Fig. 4-3, as the camera moves in toward the subject, the man increases in size at a rate faster than that of the building, increasing the feeling of depth and making the man appear relatively far from the building. However, in the other set of pictures we can see that if we change only the focal length and don't move the camera the perspective doesn't change. Although the image is magnified, the relationship between the man and the building remains the same. By cropping out closer objects, the space appears flatter and the foreground and background seem compressed.

By altering both focal length and camera-to-subject distance, the cinematographer can control perspective. Coming in closer and using a wide-angle lens exaggerates distances, while moving back and using a lens with a long focal length

Fig. 4-3. Zooming compared to dollying. When you start at the same position (top), you can move the camera closer (the two photos at left) or zoom in (the two photos at right). In the zoom, everything gets proportionally larger—the man and the building double in size. In the dolly shot, at left, the man doubles in size but the building stays about the same size. (Compare how many windows are visible in the bottom pair of photographs.) (Ted Spagna)

compresses distances. An image is said to have natural perspective when the perspective appears similar to what one would see if standing at the camera position. Lenses of "normal" or medium focal length generally yield images of natural perspective. A 25mm lens is considered normal for 16mm cameras or video cameras with ⅔-inch sensors (for other formats, see Focal Length and Format, below).

Lenses of appreciably shorter-than-normal focal length are called *wide-angle* or *short focal length lenses*. A rough rule-of-thumb is that wide-angle lenses are about half the focal length of normal lenses (50 percent), while lenses below about 35 percent of normal are *extreme wide angle*. Lenses with a focal length appreciably longer than normal are called *long focal length* or *telephoto lenses*. Lenses longer than about 150 percent of normal focal length are considered telephoto.

Perspective Effects

As discussed above, the farther the camera is from the subject, the flatter or more compressed the perspective; that is, objects of different distances from the camera do not appear greatly different in size on film. With a long focal length lens, distant objects do not appear as small as you might expect (see Fig. 4-4). This effect is easily observed when a race is filmed head-on with a long focal length lens. The runners seem to be closer to one another than they actually are, and although they seem to be running hard, they don't appear to be making much progress. This illusion occurs because of the great distance to the subject and the use of a long focal length lens. A very long lens can make the world seem almost flat or two-dimensional.

Wide-angle lenses are apt to exaggerate depth; the distance between foreground and background seems greater than you would expect, objects far from the camera seeming too small in relation to the objects closer up. This phenomenon is sometimes called *wide-angle lens distortion* or *perspective distortion*. Although you may not find exaggerated perspective pleasing, it is, in fact, not "distorted," and, when the image on screen is viewed from up close, the perspective seems natural. As you get even closer to the screen, the perspective flattens. If you tend to sit close to a movie or TV screen (and not because you're nearsighted), you probably prefer compressed perspective; if you sit far from the screen, it may be because you prefer more depth in the image.

You can use a wide-angle lens to make a room seem larger. However, if someone is near the camera and moves toward it, he will appear to move unnaturally fast. In general, use a wide-angle lens to exaggerate the speed of any movement toward or away from the camera. A wide-angle lens on a moving vehicle pointed in the direction of the movement strongly suggests speed, especially if objects sweep past near the lens. Use a wide-angle lens to emphasize heights; for example, shoot down from the top of a building or shoot a person from below. Perspective effects are accentuated when there are objects both in the close foreground and distant background. A distant landscape or seascape with nothing in the foreground will show perspective less.

Fig. 4-4. Compression and exaggeration of depth. (top) The long focal length lens makes the foreground and background appear close together. The cars look flat, packed together and close to the distant sign. (bottom) In this still from *Citizen Kane*, a feeling of deep space is created, in part, by using a short focal length lens. (Ted Spagna, RKO General)

PERSPECTIVE IN THE CLOSE-UP. When you shoot a head-and-shoulder close-up with a wide-angle lens, the camera must be fairly close, which exaggerates depth. The nose will seem too large, and the ears too small and too far from the front of the face. Such close-ups are usually used for comic or eerie effect. If the subject moves toward the camera, the nose grows in size. A hand movement in the direction of the camera seems too fast, the hand itself too large. Faces in profile and motion perpendicular to the lens's axis show this exaggeration of perspective less.

If you film at the most common filming distances—about 5 feet or more from the subject—you don't have to worry about exaggerating facial features. For close-ups of faces, it is better to err on the side of flatter perspective (a longer focal length lens at a greater distance). However, when perspective is too flat, intimacy is lost and the viewer may feel distant from the subject (see Fig. 4-5).

Fig. 4-5. Close-ups with different focal length lenses. (top) A head-and-shoulder close-up made with a wide-angle lens from very close to the subject results in distorted facial features—foreheads and noses can appear too large and the face too wide. (middle) A medium-length lens from a middle distance gives a feeling of dimensionality without looking unflattering. (bottom) Shooting with a long focal length lens from far away compresses the features, flattening the face. Although this lens sometimes creates a feeling of distance or remoteness, it's not unflattering. Note also reduced depth of field that throws the background out of focus. (Ned Johnston)

Focal Length and Format

With experience, cinematographers learn which focal lengths will achieve the effect they're looking for. For example, when shooting a typical interview with a 16mm film camera, a range of focal lengths from about 10mm to 50mm will allow everything from a medium shot of the subject to a close-up of the face. Or, for a long shot of a stream of people flowing down a sidewalk, a 150mm lens will provide really compressed perspective. Once you get comfortable shooting in any format, you'll begin to have an instinctive feel for roughly what length lens you need in various situations, and what angle of view each focal length provides.

When you shoot with a different film or video format, keep in mind that the angle of view afforded by any focal length lens changes according to the size of the image being exposed within the camera (that is, the size of a video camera's sensor or, in a film camera, the size of the film frame in the gate).

With film cameras, the image produced by a 16mm camera with a 25mm lens is about the same as what a 35mm camera produces with a 50mm lens (note an approximate doubling between the formats). The same angle of view in Super 8 would require about a 14mm lens.

With video, it's not the recording format but the size of the camera's CCD or CMOS sensor that matters. The ⅔-inch sensor found on many larger professional video cameras is just slightly narrower than the 16mm film frame.[1] To get the same angle of view of the lenses just mentioned, a video camera with a ⅔-inch sensor would need a 22mm lens. A camera with a ½-inch sensor would need about a 16mm lens.

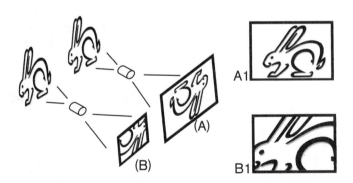

Fig. 4-6. Focal length and format. (A) A shot made with a video camera with a large sensor. (B) A shot made with the *same focal length lens* on a camera with a smaller sensor captures only part of the image compared to A. A1 and B1 show how the images will appear on screen. Comparing the two, you can see that the smaller sensor results in a more blown-up image (as though you zoomed in). If you wanted the same angle of view with the smaller sensor, you'd need a wider-angle lens. The same principle applies to different film camera formats (which is why a 50mm lens on a 35mm film camera produces the same angle of view as a 25mm lens on a 16mm film camera).

---

1. The ratio between the Super 16 film frame and a ⅔-inch video chip is about 1.33. So a 10mm lens with a ⅔-inch video sensor has about the same angle of view as a 13.5mm lens in Super 16.

The wider the actual image recording area on the piece of film (or the larger the video sensor), the longer focal length lens you need to produce the same angle of view (see Fig. 4-6).

This is why formats with a large recording area (like 35mm film) have less depth of field for the same angle of view than, say, 16mm film or ⅔-inch video sensors, making it easier to shoot shots with very shallow focus (see below for more on depth of field).[2] A shot taken with a video camera with a ⅔-inch chip will have roughly half the depth of field of a shot taken with a camera with a ⅓-inch sensor that has the same angle of view and *f*-stop.[3]

Once you learn how various focal lengths look in one format, you can translate those numbers when working in another format. Appendix E gives you the relationship of focal length to angle of view in various formats. Consumer and prosumer video lenses often don't even indicate the focal length, because the manufacturers assume you won't know how to interpret it, or they indicate it as a "35mm equivalent" for people who have worked with 35mm still cameras.

ANGLE OF VIEW AND ASPECT RATIO. Standard definition video cameras that have a 16:9 sensor will have about 25 percent narrower angle of view when switched to 4:3 mode (it will look as though you zoomed in slightly). A similar thing happens when you extract a 4:3 image from the center of a 16:9 HD shot using edge crop (see Fig. 2-15D). In either situation, what *was* your widest angle lens when working in 16:9 will appear less wide (narrower angle of view) in 4:3— you lose the edges of the shot.

THE LIGHT-GATHERING POWER OF THE LENS

F-Stops

The lens gathers light from the subject and projects its image on the film or on the video camera's sensor. The light-gathering power of the lens is called the *speed* of the lens. It is expressed as an *f-number* (*f-stop*, or *relative aperture*), which is the ratio between the focal length of the lens and its diameter (the aperture):

$$f\text{-number} = \frac{\text{focal length}}{\text{lens diameter}}$$

The *f*-number essentially tells us the light-passing power of a lens. As the lens diameter increases, so does the amount of light that passes through the lens. As the focal length increases, the light is dispersed over a greater area and the amount of light available for exposure to the film or video sensor decreases. The *faster* a lens, the more light it lets through; the *slower* a lens, the less light. Lenses of about *f*/2 (that is, the diameter of the lens is one half the focal length) are usually considered fast.

2. In theory, you could get equivalently shallow depth of field with a small format film or video sensor, but you'd need a very wide aperture (low *f*-number) and many lenses just aren't fast enough.
3. This is a rule of thumb; other factors come into play.

Inside most lenses is the *iris diaphragm*, which can close down to control the amount of light that the lens lets through. The iris is a mechanical device, usually made of overlapping blades (see Fig. 4-7), which can be set to form a large or small hole or *aperture (lens aperture)*. It functions similarly to the iris in the eye. In dim light, the eye's iris opens to admit more light, and in bright light it closes down to let less light pass through.

f/11   f/4   f/2.8

Fig. 4-7. Iris diaphragm. As the blades of the iris open, more light passes through the lens. (Carol Keller)

A formula similar to the one that describes the speed of the lens is used to express the light-gathering power of the lens at any iris diaphragm opening. The *f*-number, or *f*-stop, is the focal length of the lens divided by the diameter of the aperture. The standard series of *f*-stops, or *f*-numbers, is:

$$1, 1.4, 2, 2.8, 4, 5.6, 8, 11, 16, 22, 32$$

The distance between consecutive numbers is called a *stop*. On most professional lenses, the *f*-stops are engraved on a ring on the lens barrel. Each stop represents the halving (or doubling) of the amount of light that the lens passes. At high *f*-numbers, the iris is more closed and less light passes through. As the ring is turned toward the lower numbers (*opening up*), the iris opens; conversely, as the ring is turned to the higher numbers (*stopping down* or *closing down*), the iris closes. For a lens set at *f*/4, for instance, opening up a stop would mean setting the lens at *f*/2.8 (which doubles the amount of light for exposure), and closing down two stops from *f*/4 would mean setting the lens at *f*/8. Remember, opening the lens three stops lets eight, not six times more light in (each stop doubles the previous amount). See Fig. 7-18 for intermediate *f*-stops.

Lens manufacturers generally engrave the focal length, serial number, and speed of the lens (widest relative aperture) near the front element. The speed is sometimes written as a ratio; 1:1.4 would be an *f*/1.4 lens.

The standard technique for setting the *f*-stop is to open the lens to its widest opening and then stop down to the selected opening without passing it. This avoids any play in the iris that, in some lenses, can cause a full stop error at the smaller apertures.

T-Stops

Particularly when shooting film and using a light meter to calculate exposure, it's important to know how much light is *actually* passing through the lens to the film. The *f*-stop is a geometric relationship between focal length and aperture and doesn't take into account how much light is lost within a lens. Each air-to-glass surface within the lens reflects some light. A zoom lens may have more than 15 elements and can lose a significant amount of light to internal reflections. A *T-stop* accounts for this loss (T is for "true" stop or "transmission"). The T-stop is defined as the equivalent to an *f*-stop of a perfect lens (a perfect lens transmits all the light it gathers with no internal losses). Thus, on a perfect lens, the *f*-stop and T-stop are identical. On a zoom lens that loses a full stop internally (that is, a 50 percent loss), setting the lens to *f*/8 would result in the same exposure as T11. Note that the T-stop is always a higher number than the *f*-stop.

Some cine (movie) lenses are calibrated in both *f*-stops and T-stops (sometimes the *f*-stop in white on one side of the iris diaphragm ring and the T-stop in red on the other side). Many lenses are marked only in T-stops; others only in *f*-stops. Be sure to check the lens you're using. With prime lenses, the difference between *f*-stops and T-stops is usually less than ¼ stop—not enough to upset exposure calculations. With zoom lenses, the difference is usually greater. One zoom might have the widest aperture marked as *f*/2, but the T-stop could be T2.5, which means this lens loses ⅔ stop in transmission.

If the lens is marked with T-stops, use them to calculate film exposures even though the light meter is marked in *f*-numbers (see Chapter 7). For depth of field calculations (see below), use *f*-stops.

Video Cameras and *F*-Stops

With some consumer and prosumer video cameras, the iris adjustment is made in discrete steps instead of continuously, which is a real disadvantage when making changes during a shot (adjustments are sudden, not smooth).

With video lenses, the difference between *f*-stops and T-stops is complicated by the additional light lost in the camera's internal optics. However, T-stops are not usually a concern in video, since most people set the exposure according to video levels, not with a light meter. See Chapter 12 for a technique of using a light meter for video.

FOCUSING THE IMAGE

Depth of Field

Nearly all lenses have provisions for focusing the image. On most lenses, you turn the lens barrel to focus. Most professional lenses and some prosumer lenses have distance markings on them. When shooting a portrait of a man ten feet from the camera, you can set the barrel to 10 feet and the man will be brought into sharp focus.

In an ideal (theoretical) lens, there is only one subject plane in focus—everything in front of or behind this plane is out of focus. In the case of the portrait, if the man's eyes were exactly 10 feet from the camera, his nose and ears would be out of focus. Fortunately, with real lenses the area that looks in focus is more generous. A zone (called the *depth of field*) extends from in front of the subject to behind the subject, delineating the area of acceptable sharpness (see Fig. 4-8). In other words, the depth of field is the zone, measured in terms of near distance and far distance from the camera, where the image appears acceptably sharp.

Fig. 4-8. Depth of field. The lens is focused on the man in both photographs. (left) The depth of field is not adequate to make the foreground and background appear sharp. (right) The lens has been stopped down, and the entire picture now appears sharp. (Ted Spagna)

Depth of field is not an absolute. There is no clear demarcation between parts of the image that are sharp and those that are blurry and out of focus. Instead, there is a gradual transition between the two. Even the idea of "acceptable sharpness" is relative. It depends on many factors, including the film or video format, the type of film, lens filters, and lighting. For more on how depth of field varies with different film and video formats, see p. 148.

What "In Focus" Means

To understand depth of field, it helps to understand what being "in focus" or "out of focus" actually means. A point in the subject or scene is considered in *critical focus* when it registers as a point on film or video (see Fig. 4-9). All of the points in the subject that are in critical focus make up the *plane of critical focus* (also called the *plane of primary focus*). Any point that is nearer or farther from the camera than this plane registers as a circle instead of a point in the image. This circle is the *circle of confusion*.

When circles are sufficiently small or far enough away, they appear to the eye as points (you can check this by making a circle on a piece of paper and viewing it from a distance). The depth of field is determined by the region on either side of the plane of critical focus where points in the subject are circles so small that they appear to the viewer as points (and thus appear to be in sharp focus).

We use depth of field to define what parts of the subject are acceptably sharp, but as noted above, "acceptable sharpness" depends on many things. In part, the eye perceives sharpness in a relative way. For example, if you shoot with a low-resolution format (or use a diffusion filter to soften the image), the apparent depth of field is greater since *nothing* is particularly sharp. High definition video formats tend to have less depth of field than standard definition formats because they are capable of producing a very sharp image.

One of the key considerations in focusing and depth of field is how much the image is magnified (points start to look like circles when you enlarge them.) Something that looks sharp on a small TV screen may look out of focus when the same image is projected on a large theater screen. Depth of field will seem smaller on the big screen.

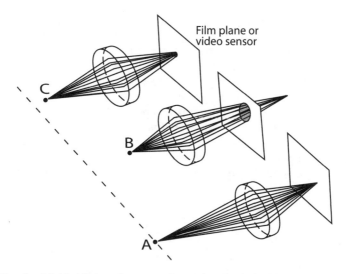

Film plane or
video sensor

Fig. 4-9. Depth of field. All three lenses are focused at the dashed line. (right) Point A is on the line and the rays of light converge to a point at the film plane. This is in sharp focus. (middle) Point B is closer to the lens so the rays of light form a circle (*circle of confusion*) where they hit the film. This is out of focus. (left) The rays of light from point C also form a circle, but it's small enough to appear as a point to the eye. This seems in focus to the viewer and thus C is within the depth of field. The same principle applies for a video camera; substitute the sensor for the film in the description above.

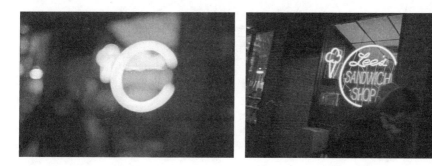

Fig. 4-10. Out of focus and in focus. Point sources of light appear as circles when they're out of focus.

In general, the more you magnify an image, the softer (less sharp) it looks (see Fig. 1-9).

Controlling Depth of Field

There are two ways to control depth of field: change the size an object appears in the image (*image reproduction ratio*) or change the *f*-stop.[4] The larger an object is

4. With some consumer or prosumer camcorders there aren't *f*-stop markings on the iris, but adjusting the iris still means changing the *f*-stop.

reproduced, the less the depth of field. You can make an object appear larger by moving the camera closer and/or by using a longer focal length lens (if you're using a zoom lens, zoom in). You might want to decrease depth of field for a portrait in order to throw the background out of focus. You might want to increase depth of field for a large group portrait, in which case you move the camera farther away from the subject and/or use a wider-angle lens.

Stopping down the *f*-stop (using a smaller aperture) increases depth of field (see Fig. 4-11). The iris can be stopped down if you add light to the subject, use a faster film (see Chapter 7) or increase video gain (see Chapter 3). You can open the iris when there is less light on the subject, when you use a slower film, when you use a neutral density filter (see Chapter 8) or when you increase shutter speed (see Chapters 3 and 6).

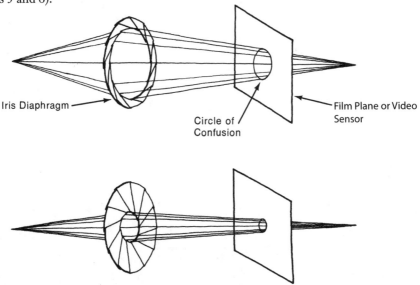

Iris Diaphragm

Circle of Confusion

Film Plane or Video Sensor

Fig. 4-11. Stopping down the lens increases depth of field. (top) Circle of confusion at wide aperture. (bottom) As the iris diaphragm closes, the diameter of the cone of light gets smaller and so the circle of confusion is smaller. (Carol Keller)

To minimize depth of field, open the iris, move closer or use a longer focal length lens. To increase depth of field, stop down, move farther away, or use a wide-angle lens (also see Split-Field Diopters, p. 167). Long focal length lenses at close focusing distances and with wide apertures (for example, at *f*/2) yield the least depth of field, whereas wide-angle lenses at far distances and stopped down (for example, at *f*/16) give maximum depth of field. A 25mm lens set at *f*/2 when focused at 4 feet has a total depth of field of 7 inches (about half a foot).[5] At *f*/11, total depth is 6 feet. If the same lens were set at *f*/2 but focused at 10 feet, total depth of field would be over 5 feet. In other words, moving farther back, stopping down, or doing both increases depth of field dramatically.

It's commonly thought that wide-angle lenses have more depth of field than

---

5. With a 1/1000-inch circle of confusion.

longer focal length lenses. They do, but not as much as cinematographers tend to think. In a typical shooting situation, you find you don't have enough depth of field to keep your subject in proper focus, so you consider going to a wider-angle lens and getting closer to the subject, with the goal of keeping the subject the same size in the frame. For example, you change from a 50mm lens at 10 feet to a 25mm at 5 feet. Will the wider-angle lens give you more depth of field? For close distances like this, the difference is negligible, and you will not improve the situation. However, for the zone *outside* the depth of field, for example when the background extends out to infinity, the wider angle lens will make the background less blurry than the longer focal length lens. For this reason, when cinematographers want to throw a background out of focus, they reach for their long focal length lenses.

Although depth of field increases as the iris is closed down, the sharpest images are not obtained with small iris openings. Many lenses are sharpest when stopped down two to three stops from their widest aperture (see Lens Sharpness, p. 170).

Setting the Focus

For feature films and other controlled filming situations with large crews, setting the lens focus is often done by measuring the camera-to-subject distance with a tape and then adjusting the lens using the distance markings on the lens barrel. For documentary or other uncontrolled shooting, focus setting is generally done by eye, looking through the viewfinder to determine proper focus. Some film and video cameras have provisions for automatic focus control (see Setting the Focus, p. 120).

WHERE TO FOCUS. Focus is one of the creative aspects of image making. You can use focus to draw the viewer's attention where you want. However, if something important is out of focus, the viewer may feel annoyed or uncomfortable. Generally, when someone is speaking, he or she should be in focus, unless another person's reaction is more important. For close shots, a rule of thumb is to focus on the subject's eyes.

A properly constructed lens focuses on a plane perpendicular to the direction of the lens. For example, suppose you want to focus on a group of people for a portrait and want them as sharp as possible at 10 feet from the camera. Should they be lined up along the arc of a circle, so that they are all 10 feet from the lens? No, only the person directly on line with the lens should be 10 feet away. All the others should be in the same plane, perpendicular to the axis of the lens.

If you are focused on a subject, you will have roughly twice as much depth of field behind the subject as in front of it. Thus, if two objects are at different distances from the camera, focusing at a point halfway between them will not render the two objects equally sharp. You should instead focus on a point one third the distance from the closer to the farther object (see Fig. 4-12). If one object is at 10 feet and the other at 40 feet, the split focus distance is 20 feet (that is, 10 feet in front and 20 feet behind).[6] Use this rule only if there is sufficient depth of field to render both objects sharply.

---

6. A more accurate (although complicated) formula for split focus is:

Split focus distance = (2 × nearest distance × farthest distance) / (nearest distance + farthest distance). This formula gives 16 feet for the above example.

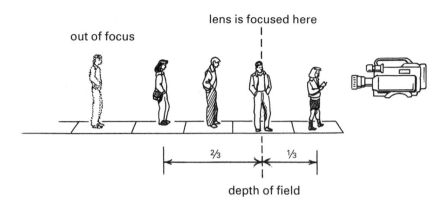

Fig. 4-12. Split focus. Depth of field extends about twice as far behind the plane at which the lens is focused as in front. (Robert Brun)

For a shot in which the camera and/or the actors' movements are planned (blocked out), you should rehearse focus changes (*follow focus*). A camera assistant or focus puller often changes (*pulls*) focus during the shot. Follow-focus devices (sometimes remotely controlled) are available to make it easier to pull focus and repeat moves precisely (see Fig. 4-13). Place tape or make chalk marks on the floor to cue the actors or the focus puller. Put tape on the lens distance scale and mark settings with a Sharpie for a homemade follow-focus device.

TAPE FOCUS. On some productions, and for some shots, an assistant measures distances with a 50-foot tape or electronic measuring device. The distance is measured from the film plane (marked on many cameras by an engraved Φ on the camera housing) to the chosen plane of critical focus. Measurements can also be made to the near and far points that must be in focus; then, if there is adequate depth of field, calculate the split focus distance and set the focus accordingly. For wide-angle lenses, tape focusing is often more accurate than eye focus. Cinematography Electronics makes the "cine tape measure" that gauges distance to the subject ultrasonically and gives a digital readout at the camera. Tape focus doesn't work if your lens doesn't have distance markings, and the lens must be properly collimated for the focusing scale to be accurate (see Depth of Focus, p. 173).

FOCUS IN THE VIEWFINDER. In many shooting situations, focusing by eye through the viewfinder is preferable to tape focus. With small crews or when the action is uncontrolled, it may be impossible to use a tape. Eye focus is often faster and is usually more accurate with long focal length lenses or in other situations where depth of field is shallow.

Be sure the viewfinder's diopter is adjusted properly to your vision before focusing either a video camera (see Chapter 3) or a film camera (see Chapter 6). To focus the camera lens, rotate the focus ring or other focus control until the subject is brought into sharpest focus. If the camera is not running, "go through" focus once or twice—that is, rotate the focus ring past the point where the image is sharpest, stop and then rotate back to the point of sharpest focus.

Many camcorders allow you to increase the detail or peaking in the viewfinder,

Fig. 4-13. Arriflex 16SR 3 equipped with follow focus knob, matte box, extended view-finder for tripod or dolly work, and video assist. (Arriflex Corporation)

or to magnify portions of it, which can be a big help in seeing focus (see p. 112). You may also want to use the camera's autofocus to find focus (but don't leave it on auto; see p. 120).

With film cameras, focus with the lens iris at the widest aperture to keep the viewfinder bright, to minimize depth of field, and to see the image pop in and out of focus better. With video cameras, opening the iris beyond normal exposure will not help.

When focusing a zoom lens, remember that depth of field will be minimized at the longest focal length (zoomed in). To focus the lens, zoom all the way in, set focus, then zoom out to whatever focal length you like. If you focus instead at a wider focal length (where depth of field is greater), the subject will usually go out of focus when you zoom in. (Sometimes when the subject is very close to the camera, this method doesn't work because when you zoom in, the depth of field can no longer accommodate the subject.)

If, while shooting, the image is sharp at wide angle but goes out of focus when zoomed in, it probably means you didn't focus at long focal length as you should have. If the image becomes seriously out of focus when zooming out from long focal length to wide angle, it may mean the lens is not properly seated (see The Lens Mount, p. 171).

When pulling focus during a shot, you obviously shouldn't open the iris or do too much "going through" focus as described above. If an unrehearsed focus pull must be done while the camera is rolling, documentary filmmakers often zoom in quickly, refocus and zoom back to the selected focal length. This "focusing zoom" is generally edited out.

With some video cameras and digitally controlled zooms, you can preprogram zoom and focus and exposure settings and have the camera automatically transition from one to the other for very fluid moves, including very slow moves that are hard to do manually.

Whenever you're shooting, always have a general idea of how much depth of field you're working with. For example, if you're using a wide-angle lens stopped down to a high *f*-number, you know you have a lot of depth of field, so focusing is less critical. Using the hyperfocal distance (see below) can help you estimate when refocusing is necessary.

Because of the increased sharpness of HD compared to SD, focus is particularly critical when shooting HD. When shooting with video cameras, focus and depth of field can be judged in the viewfinder or monitor (and a large, sharp monitor can help a lot). When using film cameras, some viewfinders provide a better sense of focus and depth of field than others (see Chapter 6). Ground-glass or fiber-optics reflex viewfinders give a rough idea of the depth of field; aerial image finders give almost none. In general, any small film or video viewfinder image tends to exaggerate depth of field. If something looks out of focus in the viewfinder, it will be out of focus when recorded on film or video. But a sharp viewfinder image is not a guarantee that the picture will look sharp on screen.

Depth of Field Charts

Depth of field charts (see Appendix C) and calculators give an estimate of the depth of field. For a given focal length lens, you cross-reference the distance the lens is focused at, the lens aperture (*f*-stop) and the circle of confusion to find the near and far extent of depth of field.

Charts and calculators are designed for a "generic" reading of depth of field, but the particulars of your lens, the film or video format, or individual shots can result in actual depth of field that is as much as 15 to 20 percent different. Depth of field calculations are properly made from the front nodal point of the lens, which varies with lens design. Typical charts and calculators don't take into account individual lens variations, possibly throwing off readings at close focusing distances (the lens manufacturer's charts, however, should compensate for this). Some lenses have rough depth of field guides engraved opposite the *f*-stop ring. Use only *f*-stops, and not T-stops, in depth of field calculations.

To provide a reference point for sharpness, a permissible *maximum* circle of confusion is chosen for different formats (sometimes called the *circle of least confusion*). To use a depth of field chart, you need to choose what circle of confusion you want to work with; see Appendix C. For example, in 16mm a permissible circle of confusion of $\frac{1}{1000}$-inch or $\frac{1}{2000}$-inch is often used.

As noted above, don't think of depth of field—or DOF charts—as an absolute. There are always variables like the recording format (in a high resolution film or video format, depth of field is reduced, since the eye has a sharp reference point that makes areas that are out of focus more obviously soft) and the distribution format (theatrical projection calls for a smaller circle of confusion than small-screen TV broadcast).

The Hyperfocal Distance

For any lens at a particular focal length and *f*-stop, the closest distance setting such that the far limit of depth of field extends to infinity is called the *hyperfocal distance* (see Appendix D). When the lens is set at the hyperfocal distance, depth of field extends from half that distance to infinity (infinity may be written ∞ on lenses and charts). For example, a 25mm lens at *f*/8 has a hyperfocal distance of 10 feet (based on a 1/1000-inch circle of confusion). When the lens is focused at 10 feet, the depth of field extends from 5 feet to infinity. The hyperfocal distance is also the near limit of depth of field when the lens is focused at infinity.

The hyperfocal distance setting is quite handy when focusing is difficult. If you set the lens at the hyperfocal distance, you don't need to worry about focus unless the subject comes closer than one half the hyperfocal distance. Of course, the remarks about depth of field not being an absolute apply here as well, and to use the hyperfocal distance chart you must choose an appropriate circle of confusion for your work.

Some very wide-angle lenses (and some very cheap lenses) have no provisions for focusing. These lenses are usually prefocused at the hyperfocal distance of the widest aperture. Consult the manufacturer's data sheet to find the closest focusing distances at the various *f*-stops.

CHOOSING A ZOOM LENS

The *zoom lens* offers various focal lengths in one lens. Focal length may be changed during a shot (*zooming*) or between shots. Zoom lenses are larger, heavier, more delicate and more prone to flare and distortion than fixed focal length (prime) lenses. Zoom designs have improved to the point that some high-quality zoom lenses are as sharp as primes. This section is about choices in zoom lenses. For techniques of shooting with zooms, see p. 355.

The zoom is sometimes the only lens used on a production, so the choice of which one you use is important. With video cameras that have permanently mounted lenses, you may choose the camera in part for its lens. When selecting a lens (or camera/lens combination) there are various criteria to take into account.

Zoom Range

Zoom lenses vary in their range of focal lengths. Zooms are designated by their zoom range (for example 10–100mm) or the widest focal length times a magnification factor (for example, 10 x 9.5 is the same as 9.5–95mm). Because the angle of view afforded by any particular focal length lens depends on the film or video format you're shooting, you need to know what gauge film or what size video sensor your camera has in order to evaluate what the range of focal lengths really means visually (see Focal Length and Format, p. 148). Sometimes consumer video lenses indicate only a magnification factor (10X) and you can't easily tell exactly what the range is.

Having a good wide-angle lens can make a big difference in many shooting situations, particularly in documentary work or whenever you're shooting in close quarters or want to capture wide vistas or deep focus shots. To take the example of a 16mm film camera (or a video camera with a 2/3-inch chip), having a lens that goes to less than 9mm opens up a whole range of possible shots (and ways that the

Fig. 4-14. Fujinon video-style lens with attached zoom motor. Standard definition 20 x 6.4 lens, which means a generous zoom range from 6.4 to 128mm or (with built-in 2x range extender) from 12.8 to 256mm. (Fujinon, Inc.)

camera can interact with the film subjects) that can't be done if your lens reaches only to 10mm or 12mm. Shooting people in cars or around a dinner table often requires a really wide lens (even 5.5mm or 6mm can be helpful). A difference of a couple of millimeters at long focal lengths is trivial, but at short focal lengths is very noticeable (a 9.5mm lens is about 25 percent wider than a 12mm). Many consumer and prosumer video cameras are really deficient in the short focal lengths and need to be used with a wide-angle adaptor (see below).

Long focal lengths allow you to capture small details in the landscape or create shots with highly compressed perspective. Shooting at long focal lengths requires that the camera be very steady on a tripod (see Telephoto Lenses, p. 164). Having both long and short focal lengths in one lens gives you tremendous flexibility and allows for extreme zoom shots that range from a tight closeup to a distant, wide view in one shot. Some video cameras have a *digital zoom* feature that magnifies the image beyond the range of what the lens does optically. This is like enlarging the pixels using a digital video effect. It lowers the resolution and should generally be avoided.

Fig. 4-15. Fujinon cine-style digital cinema lens. Wide-angle zoom, 13 x 4.5, which means a wider angle but more limited 4.5–59mm range compared to the lens in Fig. 4-14. Cine lenses typically have larger gear teeth for items like zoom motors and follow focus attachments, and better markings for zoom and focus. (Fujinon, Inc.)

CHANGING THE ZOOM RANGE. Some zoom lenses can be fitted with a wide-angle attachment to convert to a zoom range of shorter focal lengths. A .8X wide-angle converter could be used with a 12–120mm lens to make it 9.6–96mm. As a rule, these attachments don't affect aperture or focus settings and may not significantly impair the image (converters that require you to refocus when you zoom are lighter and more compact but are much less useful).

Fig. 4-16. Century Double Aspheric .6X wide-angle adaptor mounts on the front of lens. With this adaptor, you can't zoom during shots, but there are other Century adaptors that permit full zooming. (Fletcher Chicago/Schneider Optics)

Rear-mounted lens attachments, such as *range extenders,* change the relative aperture and reduce the speed of the lens. For example, a 2X range extender converts a 12–120mm zoom range to a 24–240mm and changes an *f*/2.2 aperture to an *f*/4.4. Aberrations are also magnified and may make the image unacceptable. Stopping down does minimize most of the aberrations, but stopping down to *f*/8 is the equivalent of *f*/16 when using a 2X extender.

Many video lenses have a built-in 1.5X or 2X range extender that can be set by switching a lever. Doing so provides longer focal lengths, but sacrifices some image quality and lens speed. Front-mounted range extenders don't change relative aperture, but sometimes they vignette at the shorter focal lengths. Range extenders are also used with prime lenses.

Fig. 4-17. Extreme wide angle shot taken with Century .55X Super Fisheye adaptor. Note barrel distortion causing trees to appear curved. (Fletcher Chicago/Schneider Optics)

Zoom Lens Speed

The widest aperture f-stop and T-stop are an important part of zoom lens designations. Faster lenses allow you to shoot in lower light (though using very wide apertures limits depth of field and lens sharpness; see Depth of Field, p. 151 and Lens Sharpness, p. 170). The Angenieux f/1.1, 16–44mm T1.3 designation tells us this lens is f/1.1 at its widest aperture. Its equivalent T-stop is T1.3 (it loses about one third of a stop), thus, it is a very fast lens with a limited zoom range of 16–44mm (2.8 x 16 tells us its magnification factor is only 2.8).

In order to achieve high speeds, some zoom lenses are designed to maintain their widest aperture only at wide angle. When shooting with the iris fully open or nearly so, as you zoom in these lenses *ramp* f-stop (darkening the image). For example, the Fujinon 20 x 6.4 zoom (6.4–128mm) is a very fast f/1.4 from 6.4mm to 90mm but ramps to f/2 at 128mm. This means that if you were to shoot wide open at f/1.4 at 50mm and then zoom to 128mm, you'd lose a full stop of light at the long focal length. Generally, it's undesirable to zoom across a range that loses more than one third of a stop. When this lens is stopped down to f/2, the f-stop is constant across the zoom range and there are no problems. Some lenses have detents that prevent zooming at focal lengths that will change the f-stop. When shooting film, calculate exposure with T-stops, since some zooms lose almost a full stop in transmission.

Minimum Focus Distance

Being able to focus on a subject that's close to the camera can have a big impact on your shooting style. There are many situations where you want to get in very close to the subject; a common one is shooting the driver of a car from the passenger seat. The need to get close is particularly an issue in documentary work where the relative position of camera and subject is often not under your control.

The *minimum object distance (MOD)* is the closest an object can be to the lens and be in focus. Some zooms focus down to 2 feet, some even down to their front element. Others focus only to 6 feet or more and need closeup diopters or must be switched into macro mode for close focusing (see p. 165 for more on these items). To give you greater flexibility in shooting, ideally a zoom should focus to around a couple of feet or less with no additional attachments or adjustments.

Front Element and Barrel

The diameter of the front element affects what size filters, lens shade, or matte box you can use (see Chapter 8). Particularly when you're using more than one lens, it helps if both lenses accept the same size attachments (you may need adaptor rings).

On some zooms, the front part of the lens barrel rotates for focusing. On others, the outermost part of the lens remains fixed, which is important when mounting polarizing or graduated filters that should not be rotated once they are positioned. If you are using a matte box, this is not an issue (see Chapter 8).

On cine-style lenses, the focus ring often rotates farther than on video-style lenses, which helps with critical focusing. Also, the gear teeth are spaced differently on film and video lenses, which is a concern when using external focus devices or motors.

Zoom Lens Problems

Some zooms change magnification noticeably when you focus (called *breathing* or *pumping*). This is more common with video lenses than cine lenses. Avoid these lenses if you can.

Check zoom lenses for vignetting with the lens wide open, at the shortest focal length and the distance scale at infinity (see Chapter 8). The lens shade or matte box should also be checked with the lens set at the closest focusing distance.

Before you use a zoom lens, zoom back and forth several times to distribute the lubrication in the mechanism. Some manual lenses have "zoom creep"—the lens zooms by itself. In this case, bring the lens to a technician for repair, but a temporary solution is to fit a wide rubber band, not too loose or too tight, around the zoom ring and barrel to create a little friction.

Zoom lenses often have less depth of field than primes of equivalent focal length. This is only important at close focusing distances; use the manufacturer's depth of field charts in such instances.

PRIME LENSES
FOR SPECIAL USES

Fast Lenses

For low-light shooting, prime lenses are available that are faster than most zooms. Though lenses are generally less sharp when used with the iris wide open, some primes are optimized for shooting this way. For example, for HD cameras there are the Zeiss-Distagon DigiPrime lenses, which are mostly T1.6 (about a third of a stop slower than *f*/1.4) and come in focal lengths including 3.9mm, 5mm,

10mm, 20mm, 40mm, and 70mm. They use aspherical elements, which are expensive but make these lenses sharp even when shooting wide open.

Fig. 4-18. Panavision Primo prime lenses. (Panavision)

Depth of field can be very shallow when the lens is wide open at common camera-to-subject distances. Focusing can be difficult. Using high-speed, wide-angle lenses makes night shooting far easier because of the great depth of field of wide-angle lenses at common filming distances.

Telephoto Lenses

Telephoto lenses (also called *tele-lenses*) are, loosely speaking, about 50 percent longer than normal lenses for the format; for example, a lens greater than 35mm for a 16mm camera or greater than 70mm for a 35mm camera would be considered telephoto. True telephotos are of a sophisticated design that allows them to be physically shorter than their focal length would imply.

Telephoto lenses render the subject large even at great distances, providing extreme compression of perspective. The camera crew can be unobtrusive and can work a safe distance from dangerous events. Since they have little depth of field, telephotos are useful for throwing a distracting background out of focus. When you want a dramatic focus pull, use a long focal length lens.

You can simulate a moving camera shot by using a telephoto to track a subject moving laterally to the lens (that is, pan with the subject from far away). The tracking pan keeps the subject's size constant in the frame and makes it appear that the camera is dollying. Akira Kurosawa often used these tracking pans in his samurai movies to simulate the free movement through space usually achieved with a dolly shot—the longer the focal length, the more sustained the effect.

Telephotos longer than 150mm tend to be fairly slow, though there have been improvements in recent years. *Catadioptric* lenses use reflecting mirrors and achieve long focal lengths in a very compact design. They are usually in the *f*/8 range and employ neutral density filters in place of an iris diaphragm for exposure control.

Telephotos are extremely vulnerable to camera vibration. A camera may function perfectly well with shorter focal lengths but reveal vibrations with a 300mm lens. You should use a lens support or cradle with long telephotos to minimize vibration and to avoid straining the lens mount; use a very steady tripod and do not handhold the camera (but see Image Stabilization Devices, p. 353). Heat waves often show up in landscape telephoto shots, which can be avoided by shooting in the morning before the ground has heated up. Distant scenes may be overexposed due to atmospheric haze; use a haze filter and stop the lens down one half to one full stop. Tele-extenders may be used to increase focal length, but keep in mind the limitations discussed in Changing the Zoom Range, p. 161. Inexpensive telephotos are like tele-extenders, often using optics that are not much more sophisticated than a magnifying glass. Spherical and chromatic aberrations are serious on these lenses, but stopping down minimizes their effects.

CLOSE FOCUSING

Some zoom lenses focus no closer than 3 feet from the subject. Prime lenses often focus closer. The closer the subject is to the lens, the farther the lens must be from the film plane to focus. Specialized *macro lenses* allow you to bring very close objects into focus. Often macro lenses can yield an image reproduction ratio of 1:1, that is, the image size is the same as the subject size—a thumbtack would fill the standard video frame. Many video lenses have a built-in macro mechanism, which allows for close focusing but may cause the focus to shift while zooming.

Many lenses can be extended farther from the film plane by the use of *extension bellows* or *extension tubes*. Bellows permit a wider range of focusing distances and greater magnification and are faster to adjust than tubes. Extension tubes and bellows work best with normal or slightly long focal length lenses. If they are used with a zoom lens, the zoom will not remain in focus across its range, and the results are often not sharp.

When the lens is far from the focal plane, less light strikes the film and an exposure compensation must be made (the engraved *f*-stops assume the lens is about its focal length distance from the film plane). Generally, no exposure compensation need be made until the subject is closer than ten times the focal length of the lens—for example, closer than 250mm (10 inches) with a 25mm (1 inch) lens. Video cameras will make the exposure compensation automatically, as will film cameras with behind-the-lens meters (like most Super 8 cameras). Lighting can be a challenge when the subject is inches from the lens.

Close-up Diopters

Close-up diopters or *plus diopters* are supplementary lenses mounted in front of the lens like a filter. Also called *Proxars* (actually a brand name) these permit closer focusing with all lenses, including zooms, and require no exposure compensation. Plus diopters come in varying strengths ($+\frac{1}{2}$, $+1$, $+2$, etc). The higher the number of a plus diopter, the closer you can focus. As power increases, however, the quality of the image deteriorates. It's better to use a longer focal length lens with a less powerful diopter than a shorter focal length with a more powerful diopter. For best results, close down the lens a few stops. With a close-up diopter mounted, the focus scale on the lens is no longer accurate, so focus by eye through the viewfinder. Also, you can no longer focus at infinity.

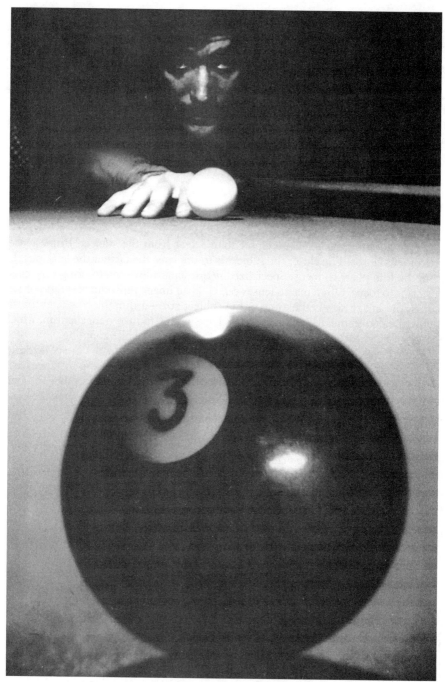

Fig. 4-19. Extreme depth of field is possible in carefully set-up shots with a split-field diopter mounted on the lens. The nondescript field between the two billiard balls obscures the border between the two halves of the diopter. (The Tiffen Company)

The convex side of the diopter should face the subject. If an arrow is marked on the diopter mount, face it toward the subject. Diopters may be combined to increase power. Place the higher-power diopter closer to the lens, and make sure the glass surfaces of the diopters don't touch. A +2 diopter combined with a +3 diopter has the same power as a +5 diopter.

Split-Field Diopters

Split-field diopters are usually half clear glass and half close-up diopter. These diopters allow half the frame to be focused on far distances and half to be focused at close distances. Frame the distant objects through the clear glass, the close ones through the plus diopter. The area between the two parts of the diopter will be out of focus and, for the shot to be successful, should be an indeterminate field (see Fig. 4-19). Carefully compose the shot on a tripod. If the diopter is used in a matte box, it may be positioned so that an area greater or less than half the frame is covered by the plus diopter.

Fig. 4-20. Tilt-focus lens. Tilting the lens allows you to position the plane of focus at an angle to the camera instead of perpendicular to it. Can be used to bring an angled subject into even focus or to create out-of-focus effects. Similar to using a split-field diopter but without a hard dividing line. (Schneider Optics)

LENS QUALITY AND CONDITION

At the start of production on a feature film, lens tests are generally done to ensure that the lenses being used are sharp, working properly, and well matched to each other. On smaller productions there may not be time or resources to do tests

Fig. 4-21. *Vivre sa Vie* (*My Life to Live*), Godard's 1962 film. Anna Karina is backlit with window light. Note how the extensive flare obscures the border between her hair and the window. (Corinth)

or to choose among several lenses. On all productions, be vigilant about scrutinizing the image for defects that may come from lens problems. When shooting film, this means projecting the rushes on a good screen and watching carefully. When shooting video, it means viewing on a high-quality monitor. Unfortunately, on many productions, footage is viewed on bad video monitors, low-resolution tape formats, or editing systems that may mask lens problems.

Even expensive lenses vary in quality, which becomes apparent in use and can be checked by a lens technician. When you purchase a lens, if possible, take a few of the same model lens to a technician, since significant differences may exist from sample to sample. Small bubbles, which are often visible in a lens element, usually do not affect quality. Small surface scratches on used lenses do not affect performance, unless they are fairly numerous, in which case they lower image contrast. A chip in a lens element severely impairs the image by scattering light. All the controls on a lens should move smoothly, and nothing should rattle when you shake the lens. There should be no play in the iris diaphragm. A lens that has been hit hard should be tested by a technician.

Traditionally, lenses for standard definition video cameras were made to lower technical standards than cine lenses for film cameras, and were cheaper. High definition video cameras put tremendous demands on lens design, because of the need for high resolution with a relatively small sensor size (the smaller the image size, the harder it is to maintain that quality). This is why high-quality, professional HD lenses often cost as much as the camera.

LENS ABERRATIONS. Centuries before the invention of lenses, painters used a *camera obscura* (literally, "dark room"), which is a dark room with a small hole in one wall that looks out onto an exterior landscape. The landscape is projected on the opposite wall. Reduced in size, this concept is the *pinhole* (lensless) *camera*. Using a lens in a camera increases brightness and sharpness, but introduces aberrations in the image. Lens aberrations are distortions in the formation of the two-dimensional image by the lens. Common aberrations include: *curvature of field* (if the lens is perpendicular to a wall, either the edges or the center of the frame will be sharp but not both); *chromatic aberration* (light rays of different colors bend at different angles, decreasing image sharpness and creating a rainbow-like fringe on some objects); and *astigmatism* (vertical lines focus in a different plane than horizontal lines). *Geometric distortions* are most apparent when a grid is photographed. *Barrel distortion* causes the grid lines to bow away from the center; *pincushion distortion* will make them appear bowed in.

Nearly all aberrations, except distortion, are most apparent when the lens iris is wide open or nearly so, and they limit lens sharpness (see p. 170). As the iris is stopped down, the effect of the aberrations becomes less pronounced. Prime lenses have built-in correction for curvature of field, but zoom lenses have less correction at the same focal length (and zooms tend to have worse chromatic aberration due to more glass elements).

VIGNETTING. *Vignetting* is an optical phenomenon in which less light reaches the edge of the image than the center. Vignetting, in the loose sense, refers to any loss of light toward the edges of the frame. This often occurs when lenses from a smaller format are used in a larger format (for example, lenses for 16mm cameras often do not completely cover the film area for super 16 or 35mm cameras). Vignetting is most apparent when the lens is wide open and the distance scale is set at infinity (and, in the case of zoom lenses, at the widest angle). If a lens shade or matte box cuts off picture area, it too is said to "vignette."

LENS SHARPNESS. Defining lens sharpness presents the same problems as defining film sharpness, which is discussed fully in Chapter 7. Resolution, contrast, acutance and modulation transfer function (MTF) are all used in lens evaluation (see p. 214). Resolution charts do have a special use in lens testing; although they have all the limitations discussed in Chapter 5, they are useful for judging if a particular lens has been badly constructed or damaged. For example, improperly centered lenses show more resolution on one side of the image than they do on the other.

Diffraction, an optical phenomenon, occurs when light passing through a small hole scatters and renders the image unsharp. Iris openings of $f/16$ or smaller may cause noticeable loss of sharpness. Diffraction is a function of the absolute size of the aperture (the f-stop is a relative aperture—the ratio between aperture and focal length); thus wide-angle lenses especially become less sharp when stopped down. While long focal length lenses may stop down to $f/32$ without problems, some wide-angle lenses only close down to $f/11$ to prevent loss of sharpness at the smallest openings.

A lens is said to be *diffraction limited* when its sharpness is limited (at particular f-stops) only by diffraction, thus showing no aberrations at those f-stops. Most lenses are sharpest when stopped down two to three stops from the widest aperture. For example, an $f/2$ lens would be sharpest around $f/4$ to $f/5.6$.

Because lens sharpness is limited at the wide apertures by aberrations and at the very smallest apertures by diffraction, you should try to shoot at middle apertures when possible. To avoid shooting at the smallest apertures, use a neutral density filter (or a slower film stock) so you can open the iris a few stops. Some people think there is a contradiction in the idea that sharpness decreases at small f-stops while depth of field increases. Sharpness, however, refers to how clear the image can be, whereas depth of field tells us the relative sharpness of objects at different distances from the camera.

To get the most out of a sharp lens, you need to use a sharp film stock or high resolution video format. However, particularly in video, a sharp lens can often vastly improve the look of a format that is lower resolution than the lens (cheap lenses make any format look bad). By the same token, HD cameras require very sharp (and expensive) lenses to capture the resolution they are capable of. As you can imagine, much of lens evaluation is subjective. The cinematographer may just like the look of a particular lens or favor a lens and format combination. In small-format film and video cameras the tendency is to maximize image sharpness, but in 35mm, which can achieve great sharpness, many cinematographers prefer a softer, more diffuse image.

FLARE. Lenses are made of multiple pieces of glass—elements—and the more elements, the more reflections take place within the lens, which add an overall exposure to the image, thus lowering contrast. Zoom lenses are particularly vulnerable. This flare is particularly noticeable when a light source is photographed; for example, when someone is standing in front of a bright window. Flare diffuses the image, lightens the blacks, increases the appearance of grain, decreases sharpness, and often softens the edges of backlit figures.

Nearly all modern lenses have anti-reflective coatings on their elements to minimize flare. One rule of thumb for checking coatings is that the more colors you can see reflected in the front elements of the lens, the more efficient the coating will be.

The front element of the lens often picks up stray light from bright objects or other light sources even when the light source is not in the frame. This may cause flare and internal reflections of the iris diaphragm to appear in the image as bright spots in the shape of the iris opening. If the front element of the lens is viewed from in front of the camera and you can see reflections from light sources, there will be some flare in the image. The solution is to use a deeper lens shade or matte box or to flag the light source (see Chapter 12). Since flare adds exposure to the film, it sometimes affects the exposure calculation (see Chapter 7).

Flare is generally considered a phenomenon that deteriorates the quality of the image, a form of system noise. On the other hand, you may like the effects of flare. It was considered an artistic breakthrough when Jean-Luc Godard's cameraman, Raoul Coutard, in the early 1960s, pointed the camera lens into large café windows in interior shots and "degraded the image with flare" (see Fig. 4-21).

THE LENS MOUNT

Many consumer and prosumer camcorders have permanently mounted zoom lenses. Although this prohibits the use of other lenses, it allows for an accurate and sturdy mount. Most other cameras accept interchangeable lenses. The *lens mount* is the system that allows the lens to be attached to the camera. The camera is equipped with a certain mount and accepts lenses of the same mount. With some mounts, adaptors can be used to join otherwise incompatible lenses and cameras. Whenever changing lenses or using lens adaptors, be sure the lens is properly seated and collimated before shooting (see p. 173).

Film Camera Mounts

The *C mount* was at one time the most common 16mm lens mount. It is a simple screw mount that is not particularly strong, nor designed for very close tolerances, and it is not desirable for zoom lenses, heavy lenses, or very wide-angle lenses. Adaptors allow lenses with a variety of mounts to be fitted onto a camera that accepts C mounts, but you cannot adapt a C mount lens to a camera that takes, for example, an Arriflex or Aaton mount.

The Bolex Rx mount is a variant of the C mount that is specially designed to accommodate the change in back focus on the Bolex camera equipped with a behind-the-lens viewfinder prism. Prime lenses of less than 50mm and zoom lenses in Rx mount should be used only on these Bolexes and not on other cameras.

Arriflex lens mounts have evolved over time. The *Standard* mount was replaced by the *Bayonet* ("Arri bayo") mount. Newer cameras are equipped with the *PL* (*positive lock*) mount. The earlier mounts can be used on PL-equipped cameras (with adaptors), but PL lenses will not fit on cameras equipped with the other mounts.

Many other manufacturers have their own mounts, including Aaton, Mitchell, Cinema Products (CP) and Eclair. Panavision lenses can be used on Panavision cameras and on Arriflex and other cameras modified for the Panavision mount. Lenses may be manufactured with *neutral mounts*, allowing you to install the proper mount for your camera. Adaptors are available to accept a variety of 35mm still photography lenses with cine (film) cameras and some video cameras.

THE LENS TURRET. Before the advent of high-quality zoom lenses, 16mm cameras often had turrets that would accept two or three lenses. Take care that a wide-angle lens does not include in its field of view a long focal length lens mounted on the same turret. A divergent turret, like the one on the Arriflex S (see Fig. 4-22), permits you to mount a slightly greater range of lenses. When you rotate the turret, grasp the turret grips and never the lens. Although turrets are not as stable as single-lens mounts, the Arriflex S and Eclair NPR have very stable turrets.

Fig. 4-22. Arriflex 16S with three prime lenses on a divergent turret. The camera has reflex viewing with a mirror shutter, a registration pin, and high-quality optics, but it is very noisy. This camera accepts 100-foot internal loads (pictured) or an external magazine. (Arriflex Corporation)

Video Camera Mounts

Most professional video cameras and some prosumer models accept detachable lenses. The lenses used must be appropriate for the size of the sensor. For example, a lens for a ⅔-inch chip needs to cover a larger area than one designed for a ½-inch chip. Three-chip video cameras employ a beam-splitter prism assembly in the camera and lenses are designed for particular prisms. Because of this, video lenses should be used only with the appropriate camera (some cameras have a menu setting to accommodate different lens types).

To take the example of the Fujinon A22x7.8BERM-28 lens designation, A indicates this is for a ⅔-inch sensor, B indicates camera manufacturer and correlates to flange focal distance, E indicates internal range extender, R means servo zoom, M means manual focus and 28 indicates camera type. Different manufacturers use different code letters.

Some video cameras, such as certain Canon models, accept 35mm still photography lenses, opening up a wide range of lens options.

Devices such as the P + S Technik image converters allow the use of 35mm cine and still lenses on video cameras. There are versions for cameras that accept detachable lenses and models for small-format video cameras that have permanently mounted lenses (see Fig. 2-12). These can provide the angle of view and depth of field associated with the lens as it would appear on a 35mm film camera, even though the camcorder has a much smaller image recording area.

Among the newer generation, high-end, single chip cameras, some accept lenses designed for 16mm or 35mm film cameras with the proper mounts or adaptors. Many use the industry-standard PL mount.

LENS SEATING AND COLLIMATION

Depth of Focus

Depth of focus is the tolerance in the accuracy of the mounting or seating of the lens on the camera. Never confuse depth of focus with depth of field. Depth of focus is an area *behind* the lens (inside the camera). It refers to the very small distance on either side of the focal plane where the film or video camera's sensor can be situated and still record an acceptably sharp image. The greater the depth of focus, the more leeway you have for a lens that is mounted slightly too close or too far from the film or sensor. When a lens is mounted improperly it's said to be *out of collimation* or that the *back focus* is off.

Depth of focus increases as the iris is stopped down. However, unlike depth of field, it is least in wide-angle lenses. This means that a fast wide-angle lens needs to be very accurately mounted. On some lenses, even tiny pieces of dirt on the mount can throw off focus.

If a prime lens is not properly seated, its focus scale will not be accurate and a tape-measured focus setting will be inaccurate. Although focusing through the viewfinder will correct this error, an improperly seated lens might not be able to focus to infinity.

If a zoom lens is not properly seated, it will go out of focus as it is zoomed out to wide angle. The lens may focus well at long focal lengths where depth of focus is considerable (although there is little depth of field), but, as the lens is zoomed to wide angle, tolerances become more critical and the picture may go out of focus. If the image goes out of focus when zooming in from wide to telephoto, it means you probably didn't focus properly. If it goes out of focus when zooming out from telephoto to wide-angle, it probably means the lens is out of collimation.

In an emergency, an improperly seated zoom can still be used as a variable focal length lens (that is, for changing focal lengths between shots), especially at the longer focal lengths.

Flange Focal Distance and Back Focus

The distance from the focal plane to the lens mount flange is called the *flange focal distance* or *depth*. This is essentially a measure of whether the camera's portion of the lens mount (the lens seat that receives the lens) is set to the standard distance. On a film camera, depth can be measured with a depth gauge inserted into the lens port to measure the distance between the lens seat and the film plane. The tolerance in the depth is measured in ten-thousandths of an inch and is usually adjusted by a technician. On some cameras, the depth can be adjusted in the field.[7]

Different camera systems have a different specified depth, but if the depth is set correctly, you should be able to use many different lenses (assuming they are set up to specs) without problems.

The distance between the rear element of a lens and the film plane (or video sensor) is the *back focus*. Every lens has a specified back focus. We can think of the lens mount as having two parts: the female part (lens seat) that is attached to the camera and the male part that is attached to the lens. For the back focus to be correct, the female part of the mount must be set correctly (the depth) and the male part must be attached to the lens correctly relative to the rest of the lens barrel and the glass lens elements.

Back focus is measured with an optical device called a *collimator*. For a film camera, a test image is projected through the front of the lens and bounced off the film and viewed through the collimator. When the lens focus ring is set at infinity, the test target should be in sharp focus, indicating that the lens is properly collimated. With film cameras, collimation is generally tested and adjusted by a lens technician. However, there is a simple check you can do yourself, which should be performed at the beginning of a shoot, or when using a new lens or camera, or in the field if you suspect the lens may be damaged or out of whack (see below).

With video cameras that have detachable lenses, back focus can be often be adjusted in the field by the camera operator (see p. 175).

Checking Collimation—Film Cameras

There's a simple test to check the accuracy of a reflex focusing system and the seating of a zoom lens. Put a starburst lens focus chart on the wall (see Fig. 4-23). Point the tripod-mounted camera at the chart from about 10 feet away. Zoom in all the way, filling the frame with the test pattern. Focus the lens carefully. Use only enough light so that the iris can be set wide open. Beginning at the longest focal length, hold for a few seconds, and then zoom to wide angle, stopping for a few seconds at different focal lengths. Project the developed film on a good-sized screen to ascertain that the chart stays in focus throughout the zoom. If not, the camera's focusing system must be checked; the lens may need to be reseated or repaired, or this error may be caused by a behind-the-lens filter (see p. 309). If you don't have a focus chart, you can tape a piece of newspaper to the wall, draw a black line down

---

7. With some 35mm cameras, the depth is checked during the shoot on a regular basis and adjusted if necessary. In 16mm, this adjustment is not commonly made in the field.

Fig. 4-23. Focus chart. Get a full-size chart or use this one in a pinch. (Schneider Optics)

the middle of it, and shoot it from a 45-degree angle. Focus on the line and zoom out as described above. On projection, the line and the region on either side should be in focus.

Checking Back Focus—Video Cameras

The collimation on some video lenses must be set by a technician. However, some lenses have a *back focus adjustment* that you can check or reset when necessary. Put the camera on a tripod and view the image with the sharpest, biggest monitor you can find. Put up a starburst focusing chart or a newspaper as described above. Use only enough light (or use filters) so that you can set the iris wide open. Zoom in on the chart and focus the lens, then zoom out to the widest angle. Loosen and adjust the back focus lever until the image is as sharp as possible. Touching *only* the zoom control, zoom in. If the image is not sharp, refocus the lens using the front focus ring, *not* the back focus adjustment. Zoom out and reset the back focus again if necessary. Repeat this process until one lens focus setting produces a sharp image at both telephoto and wide angle, then tighten down the back focus adjustment.

This should be close to the dot or other marking for the standard position on the back focus adjustment.

CARE OF THE LENS

When possible, remove lenses from the camera when shipping, and pack them in fitted, foam-lined cases. Shocks, prolonged vibration, and extreme heat can loosen a lens element. Keep the lens mount clean. Both camera and lens mating parts must be free of dirt and dust to ensure proper seating of the lens, especially zoom and wide-angle lenses. If necessary, clean the mount with a soft cloth.

When a lens is not in use, cover the front element with a lens cap to protect it from dust and fingerprints. Use a rear element cap when the lens is not on the camera. Some people like to keep a clear, daylight filter in place at all times to protect the front element (see Chapter 8).

Dust on the Lens

Dust on the lens lowers contrast. It may be blown off with a rubber syringe (available at any pharmacy) or with small containers of compressed air (like Dust-Off). Avoid compressed air that may have oil droplets in the spray. Tip the lens down when blowing dust off. Some cinematographers use their breath to remove dust, but take care not to blow saliva on the element, since it is harder to remove than dust.

If air doesn't remove all the dust, use a clean camelhair brush, reserved for the sole purpose of lens cleaning. Avoid touching the bristles, since oil from the hand will transfer to and remain on them. An alternate method is to fold photographic lens tissue over itself several times, tear off an edge and lightly brush the element with the torn edge. Do not rub a dry element with the lens tissue; you may damage the lens coating.

Fingerprints on the Lens

Oil and fingerprints are more difficult to remove and, if left on the lens, can etch themselves into the coating; remove them as soon as possible. First, remove dust from the lens as described above. Use photographic tissue—not eyeglass or silicone-coated tissue, which may damage the coating. Never rub tissue on a dry lens. Breathe on the lens to cause condensation. Rub the tissue as gently as possible, using a circular motion combined with a rolling motion to lift any dirt off the element. To avoid grinding grit into the coating, continually use a clean portion of the tissue. Whenever the condensation evaporates, breathe on the lens again.

For particularly stubborn fingerprints, apply a drop of lens-cleaning solution to the tissue (not directly to the lens). Take care that the solution does not come into contact with the area where the element meets the barrel, as it may loosen the element. After moistening the element, use a dry tissue as described above (rubbing only a moistened lens).

CHAPTER 5

The Video Image

This chapter provides more technical information about video recording in production and postproduction. For the basics of video formats, cameras and editing, see Chapters 1, 2, 3, and 14.

FORMING THE VIDEO IMAGE

THE VIDEO CAMERA'S RESPONSE TO LIGHT

On p. 84 you'll find simplified instructions for setting the exposure of a video camera when shooting. Let's look more closely at how the camera responds to light so you'll have a better understanding of exposure and how to achieve the look you want from your images.

The camera's sensor can be thought of as a device for converting light into a electrical signal (see p. 4). Generally speaking, the more light that strikes the sensor, the higher the voltage of the signal. But to look more closely at the relationship between light and the resulting video signal, we can draw a simplified graph like the one in Fig. 5-1. The amount of light striking the sensor increases as we move from left to right.[1] Look at the line marked "A." Note that below a certain amount of light (the far left side of the graph), the system doesn't respond at all—this is the *black clip* level. Then, as the exposure increases, there is a corresponding increase in the signal. Above a certain amount of exposure, the system again stops responding. This is the *white clip* level. You can keep adding light, but the signal won't get any stronger.

This is somewhat like a characteristic curve for film (see Fig. 7-4). When the exposure for any part of the scene falls below the black clip level, that area in the image will be undifferentiated black shadows. Anything above the white clip will be bright and washed-out white. For objects in the scene to be rendered with some detail, they need to be exposed between the two.

---

1. By the "amount of light" we mean *exposure*, which is determined by the amount of light in the scene, the setting of the lens iris, filters being used, and the setting of the electronic shutter.

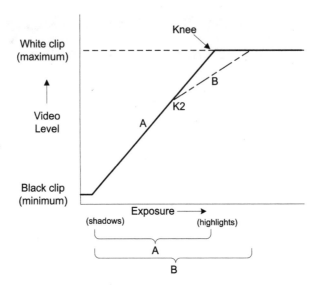

Fig. 5-1. The video camera's response to light. The horizontal axis represents increasing exposure (light) from the scene. The vertical axis is the level of the resulting video signal that the camera produces. Line "A" shows that as the light increases, so does the video level until the white clip is reached, at which point increases in light produce no further increase in video level. With some cameras, the knee point can be adjusted down (K2) with a less steep response curve to the right of that point (Line "B"). Note how this extends the "highlight handling" ability of the camera compared to "A." This graph is deliberately simplified.

The response curve helps explain why the world looks very different to the naked eye than it does through a video camera. Your eye is more sensitive to low light levels than most video cameras are—with a little time to adjust, you can see detail outdoors at night or in other situations that may be too dark for a camera. Also, your eye can accommodate an enormous *range* of brightness. For example, you can stand inside a house and, in a single glance, see detail in the relatively dark interior and the relatively bright exterior.

Both film and digital video are much more limited in the range from bright to dark that they can capture with any detail (called the *exposure range* or *dynamic range*). When shooting, you may have to choose between showing good detail in the dark areas or showing detail in the bright areas, but not *both* at the same time (see Fig. 7-14). Kodak estimates that many of their color negative film stocks accommodate a usable ten-stop range of brightness (a contrast ratio of about 1000:1 between the brightest and darkest value), although color negative's S-shaped characteristic curve can contain an additional 4+ stops of information in both ends of the "S." A Kodak test of 5245 color negative, for instance, once measured seventeen stops latitude.[2] Historically, tube-based analog video cameras were able to handle only a limited range, some as low as about five stops (40:1), but new high-end digital cameras capture an exposure range of around ten stops and digital cinematography cameras like the Dalsa Origin claim twelve stops.

2. The stock used—5245, E.I. 50—has been replaced by improved Kodak Vision2 5201.

The image in Fig. 7-22 was shot with film; the middle shot shows a "compromise" exposure that balances the bright exterior and dark interior. With video it is often harder to find a compromise that can capture both; instead you may need to expose for one or the other (more on this below).

To truly evaluate exposure range we need to look at the film or video system as a whole, which includes the camera, the recording format, and the monitor or projection system—all of which play a part. For example, a video camera's sensor may be capable of capturing a greater range than can be recorded on tape, and what is recorded on tape may have a greater range than can be displayed by a particular monitor.

Measuring Digital Video Levels

We've seen that the digital video camera records a range of video levels from darkest black to brightest white. This range is determined in part by what is considered "legal" by broadcast standards. We can think of the darkest legal black as 0 percent digital video level and the brightest legal white as 100 percent (sometimes called *full white* or *100 percent picture white*).

The actual range the camera is capable of actually goes beyond what is legal. For example, the point at which bright whites are clipped off is usually somewhat above 100 percent. A digital video camera takes video levels from black to white and assigns a number or code to each one (see Digital Recording—How It Works, p. 208). In eight-bit component digital video (which includes most digital video formats up to and including HDCAM) darkest black is set at a digital coding level of 16 and brightest legal white at 235. You can see in Fig. 5-8 that there are some codes below black (*super black* or *blacker-than-black*) and above white (*super white*) that are reserved for signals lower or higher than the legal broadcast range. These levels may still be used in recording as long as they're corrected before the finished movie is aired.

Many video cameras have a viewfinder display called a *zebra indicator* (or just *zebra*) that superimposes a striped pattern on the picture wherever it exceeds a preset level (see Fig. 3-6). A zebra set to 100 percent will show you where video levels are at or above maximum and are being clipped (or are close to it). Some people like

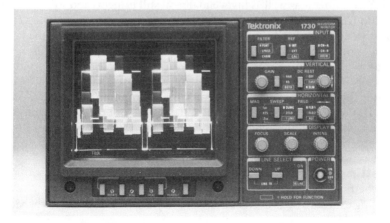

Fig. 5-2. Waveform monitor. (Tektronix)

to set the zebra lower (at 85 to 90 percent) to give some warning before highlights reach 100 percent. If you use the zebra on a camera that's not your own, always check what level it's set for.

A *waveform monitor* gives a more complete picture of video levels (see Fig. 5-2). Waveform monitors were originally developed to display analog video levels in *IRE* (*Institute of Radio Engineers*) units of measurement.[3] The range of active video equals 100 IRE units. Waveform monitors that display digital video use an identical scale, except that units are expressed in simple percentages instead of analog IRE units. For digital video formats, 0 percent represents absolute black and, at the other end of the scale, 100 percent represents peak white level. A waveform monitor is a valuable tool on any shoot in addition to, or as part of, a picture monitor, and is frequently used in postproduction to ensure that black levels are set correctly and luma and chroma levels are legal.

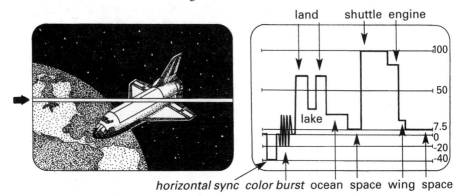

Fig. 5-3. The waveform monitor display of a single horizontal line (at left) shows video levels across the picture. The 7.5 IRE black level shown here is for NTSC analog video only. (Robert Brun)

A display called a *histogram* is found in the viewfinder of some newer CMOS-based video cameras as well as high-end digital still cameras and some software applications (see Fig. 5-4). An active histogram is a dynamically changing chart that displays video levels from 0 to 100 percent from left to right along the horizontal axis and a pixel count along the vertical axis. In a dark scene, the histogram will show a cluster of tall bars toward the left, which represents a high concentration of dark pixels in the image. A bright highlight will cause a tall bar to appear on the right side. By opening and closing the iris, the distribution of pixels will shift right or left. If you know that you want to favor dark detail or bright highlights (or both), this can be helpful in deciding where best to place exposure—which is how digital still photographers use histograms.

Setting Exposure—Revisited

See Setting the Exposure on p. 118 before reading this.

Setting exposure by eye—that is, by the way the picture looks in the viewfinder

---

3. IRE units divide the 1-volt analog video signal into 140 equal parts, with the sync signal occupying a range of minus 40 to 0 IRE, blanking (for beam retrace) at 0 IRE, and peak white at 100 IRE.

or monitor, is the primary way many videographers operate. But for the picture to be a reliable indicator of exposure you need a professional monitor, which needs to be set up properly, and the viewing conditions need to be right. For example, there shouldn't be too much ambient light falling on the screen (see Appendix A). You also need some experience with how the monitor image will ultimately look when recorded and played back.

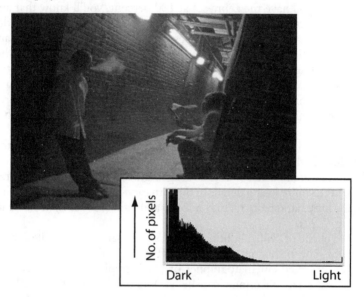

Fig. 5-4. The histogram of this shot shows that dark tones predominate, with few midtones and only a small spike of highlights (from the lights in the background). This shot might be considered underexposed, but as a night shot it feels appropriate. The lights in the background accentuate the cigarette smoke, and provide contrast with the dark foreground.

By using the camera's zebra indicator or another of the measurement tools mentioned above you can get more precise information to help you set the level.

The goal is to adjust the iris so the picture is as pleasing as possible, with good detail in the most important parts of the frame. If you close the iris too much, the picture will look too dark and blacks will be *crushed* and show no detail. If you open the iris too much, the highlights will be *compressed* and the brightest parts of the scene will be blown out. As noted above, there is a white clip circuit that prevents the signal from going much above 100 percent, although many recent camcorders capture up to 109 percent.[4] Say you were shooting a landscape, and exposing the sky around 100 percent. If a bright cloud, which would normally read at 140 percent, came by, the white clip will cut off (clip) the brightness level of the cloud somewhere between 100 and 109 percent, making it nearly indistinguishable from the sky.

In most video productions, you have an opportunity to try to correct for picture

4. The absolute maximum (109 percent) is called the *peak white level*. How highlights get clipped is also affected by the gamma and knee settings; see below.

exposure in postproduction when doing color correction. Given the choice, it's better to underexpose slightly than overexpose when shooting since it's easier in post to brighten and get more detail out of underexposed video than to try to reclaim images that were overexposed on the shoot. Once details are blown out, you can't recover them.

One method for setting exposure is to use the zebra indicator to protect against overexposing. If you have the zebra set at 100 percent, you'll know that any areas where the zebra stripes appear are being clipped or are right on the edge. You might open the iris until the zebra stripes appear in the brightest areas and then close it slightly until the stripes just disappear. In this way, you are basing the exposure on the highlights (ensuring that they're not overexposed) and letting the exposure of other parts of the frame fall where it may. If you're shooting a closeup of a face, as a general rule no part of the face should read above 100 percent (or even close) or else the skin in those areas will appear washed out in a harsh, unflattering way.

However, sometimes, to get proper exposure on an important part of the scene you must allow highlights elsewhere in the frame to be clipped. If you're exposing properly for a face, the window in the background may be "hot." The zebra stripes warn you where you're losing detail. In this situation you may be able to "cheat" the facial tones a little darker, or you may need to add light (a lot of it) or shade the window (see Fig. 7-22).

It's an old cliché of "video lighting" that it's necessary to expose flesh tones consistently from shot to shot, at a particular IRE level or lighting contrast ratio. Tell this to an experienced cinematographer or photographer, or any portrait painter for that matter, and they'll cringe in disbelief. Video lighting got off to a bad start—a legacy of bland TV studio lighting handed down by video engineers with pocket protectors and waveform monitors who didn't know Stieglitz from Toland from Caravaggio.[5] As in film or photography, exposure of faces in video should serve the needs of dramatic or graphic expression. (Unless you're lighting the local news anchorperson, which you probably aren't.)

The old rules about "proper" exposure of flesh tones at around 65 IRE units are outmoded (if not racist). Average "white" skin is a stop brighter than the 18 percent gray card that approximates average scene brightness that auto-iris circuits aim for (see Understanding the Reflected Reading, p. 278). Black skin, on the other hand, runs a wide gamut of brightness levels. Furthermore, in a dark night scene, at what levels should light or dark skin tones be (see Fig. 5-4)? The reality is that people move through scenes, in and out of lighting. Lighting is dynamic, never static. Momentary use of auto-iris is a good way to spot-check what the camera thinks the best average exposure should be, but don't neglect to use your eyes and creative common sense too. If the auto-iris had its way, the world would always be the average brightness of an 18 percent gray card, even at night.

With today's digital video cameras, you have nearly ten stops of dynamic range. Use 'em. For inspiration regarding the creative limits to which digital video exposure—particularly HD—can be pushed these days, watch the newest dramatic series

---

5. In case you didn't know, either: Alfred Stieglitz, pioneering American art photographer; Gregg Toland, cinematographer (*Citizen Kane*); Michelangelo da Caravaggio, Italian Baroque painter.

on network or cable television for the latest trends in lighting. You may be in for some surprises.

UNDERSTANDING AND CONTROLLING CONTRAST

As we've seen, the world is naturally a very contrasty place—often too contrasty to be captured fully in a single video exposure. For moviemakers, contrast is a key concern, and it comes into play in two main areas:

(A)

(B)

(C)

(D)

Fig. 5-5. Thinking about contrast. (A) This image was captured with enough latitude or dynamic range to bring out details in the shadow areas (under the roadway) and in the highlights like the water. (B) This image has compressed shadow areas (crushed blacks), which can happen when you set the exposure for the highlights and your camera has insufficient dynamic range to reach into the shadows. (C) This shot has increased overall contrast; shadows are crushed and the highlights are compressed (note that details in the water are blown out). Notice also the greater separation of midtones in the sidewalk (the two types of paving stones look more similar in B and more different in C). Though increasing the contrast may result in loss of detail in dark and/or light areas, it can also make images look bolder or sharper. (D) If we display image C without a bright white or dark black, it will seem murky and flat despite its high original contrast. Thus the overall feeling of contrast depends both on how the image is captured and how it is displayed.

- *Shooting.* Can you record pictures that have good detail in important parts of the frame? Are some parts so dark they're lost in the shadows and other parts so bright that details are blown out? This depends in part on the range of brightness in the scene, the exposure range of the camera and how the exposure is set during recording.
- *Display.* When the recorded pictures are played back on a monitor or on a screen, does the range of tonalities reproduce the important details? Does the tonal range express the visual "feel" you're trying to convey? This depends in part on how the video was recorded, any contrast adjustments that were made during postproduction, and the settings and capabilities of the display device.[6]

Contrast is important because it's both about *information* (are the details visible?) and *emotion* (high-contrast images have a very different feel and mood than low-contrast images). Contrast can be thought of as the separation of tones (lights and darks) in an image. The greater the contrast, the greater the separation between the tones. Low-contrast images—images without good tonal separation—are called *flat* or *soft* (*soft* is also used to mean "not sharp"). Low-contrast images are sometimes described as "mellow." High contrast images are called *contrasty* or *hard*. An image with good contrast range is sometimes called *snappy*.

Let's look at some of the factors that affect contrast and how you can work with them.

Highlights and Overexposure

When you go into the world with a camera, you're constantly dealing with situations in which the contrast range is too great. You're shooting in the shade of a tree, and the sunlit building in the background is just too bright. You're shooting someone in a car, and the windows are so blown-out you can't see the street.

In film, there tends to be a fairly gradual transition from areas that are normally exposed to parts that are overexposed; the shoulder of the tonal scale reproduction curve is relatively "soft" (see Fig. 7-4). In video, the camera's response to light can cut off abruptly at the white clip level—one object can be normally exposed and a brighter object next to it completely overexposed and lacking detail. To compensate, many video cameras use a *soft clip* or *knee-compression* circuit. The soft clip compresses the highlights in a nonlinear fashion akin to film, bringing down the level of bright areas (see Fig. 5-1). Parts of the scene that would otherwise be overexposed can be retained with some detail.

On some cameras you can adjust the *knee point* to improved highlight handling. One Panasonic camera lets you set the knee to begin compressing at 80 percent, 90 percent, or 100 percent (80 percent will result in the most compression). Sometimes if the knee correction is too aggressive (that is, starting too low on the curve) highlights may seem too compressed, the image may seem to lack enough contrast, and normally bright whites may seem dull.

Professional cameras may have a *dynamic contrast control* (*DCC*, a Sony term, see Fig. 3-4) or an *automatic knee* function that automatically increases highlight

---

6. One key aspect of the display device is its contrast ratio; see p. 202.

compression for contrasty scenes that have high brightness backgrounds, and decreases it when not needed. Experiment with this feature to see how it can preserve some highlight detail, although the outcome is often subtle. Many videographers simply leave it on all the time.

When the lighting contrast of a scene exceeds the camera's ability to capture it, there are a number of things you can do (see Controlling Lighting Contrast, p. 478).

Video Gamma

The line marked "A" in Fig. 5-1 represents a CCD or CMOS sensor's response to light. It is perfectly straight ("linear"). Because the response of the human eye isn't linear and the image reproduction of CRT monitors isn't linear either, video cameras have always compensated by adding a default *gamma correction* to the signal after it leaves the sensor.

Most professional and many prosumer cameras these days allow you to choose, for creative purposes, the overall gamma correction you'd like to see on screen (see Fig. 5-6). This is often driven by an attempt to mimic a "film look" for video. In-camera gamma is now widely understood to incorporate both the default gamma correction and additional manipulations for artistic ends.

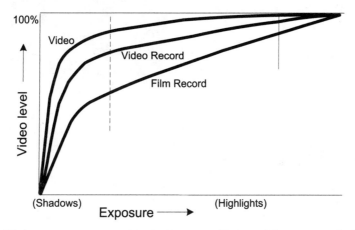

Fig. 5-6. Three gamma curves used in the Panasonic Varicam. The curve marked "Video" is a conventional video gamma. When the Varicam is switched to film mode, you can select "Video Record" for playing back images with a wider dynamic range that emulates a film look more than conventional video does. Or you can choose "Film Record" for securing the widest dynamic range for video images intended for actual output to film. Compare to Fig. 5-7.

Changing the gamma has a noticeable effect on which parts of the scene show detail and on the overall mood and feel of the picture. Setting the gamma high creates an image that can look crisp and harsh. This has the effect of compressing the highlights (losing detail in the bright areas) and stretching the blacks (see Fig. 5-7A). Colors look more saturated and intense when the gamma is high. Setting the gamma low creates a picture that looks flat and muted. It extends the upper

(A)  (B)

(C)

Fig. 5-7. These images were made by setting the master gamma in a Sony DSR-500 camera to maximum (A) and minimum (B). Notice that A has an overall bright feel with good shadow detail (stretched blacks) but very compressed highlights (virtually no detail outside the window). B, on the other hand, is darker overall and has much less compressed highlights (there's a lot more detail outside the window). If you shot with the settings of B, the image would likely look too dark. However, in postproduction, B can be color corrected to C, which is brighter, with good shadow detail but still retaining more detail in the highlights than A. These examples are deliberately extreme. Be sure to discuss gamma with experienced persons before choosing a setting.

dynamic range, allowing you to see more gradations and detail in the bright areas that would otherwise overexpose, while compressing shadow detail (see Fig. 5-7B). Low gamma tends to soften or desaturate colors.

To see why this is, we can look at how the camera converts differences in scene brightness to differences in video levels. This kind of input-to-output relationship is sometimes called a *transfer function*. We can plot gamma on a graph.

In film, gamma is the slope of the straight-line (linear) middle section of the film's characteristic curve (see Fig. 7-4). A 1:1 film gamma—no contrast gained or lost—has a slope of 45 degrees. High gamma (steeper than 45 degrees) means high image contrast; low gamma (below 45 degrees) means low image contrast. Simple!

In video, gamma doesn't refer in such a simple way to how tones in the image are reproduced. Video gamma indicates the *contrast of the midtones*, which is the middle range of tonalities between deep shadows and bright highlights, but video gamma isn't a linear function as it is in film. Graphically it's a contrast *curve* that affects tonal reproduction quite differently in shadows, midtones, and highlights.

To understand this difference, look at Fig. 5-6, which represents the three gamma curves available on the Panasonic Varicam. The horizontal axis represents increasing amounts of exposure (light) from the scene. The vertical axis shows the resulting video level produced by the camera. Note that the beginning and end point of the three curves is the same. This is because in traditional broadcast video, the values for 0 percent black and 100 percent white are anchored in place at the ends of the curve. Only the middle section, or midtones, can be stretched away from the straight diagonal line. Imagine grasping a piece of plastic with both hands and gently bending. It will bend from the middle. Video gamma similarly bends from the middle.

Notice that the curve marked "Video" rises quickly in the shadows, providing good separation of tones (good detail) in the dark parts of the scene. However, as we move to the right, the curve becomes almost horizontal. This means that increases in brightness in the brightest parts of the scene will produce almost no increase in video level. Thus this curve compresses the highlights, showing little detail there.

Now let's compare the curve marked "Film Record." This rises much less steeply in the shadows and is substantially lower in the midtones. If you run your finger along the dashed vertical line you can see that the "Film" curve produces much less level than the "Video" curve at that point—in other words, midtones are darker. As we move to the right, however, the "Film" curve continues to rise gently in the highlights. Now run your finger along the dotted vertical line in the highlight area. The "Video" curve is nearly flat here, but the "Film" curve is still rising, capturing highlight detail that might be blown out with the "Video" curve.

Talking about gamma in video cameras can be tricky. For one thing, language is imprecise. Some people would say the "Video" curve in Fig. 5-6 has more contrast than the "Film" curve. However, contrast is often thought of as the separation of tones, and as we just saw, the "Video" curve provides *greater* separation of tones in the shadows and *less* separation in the highlights. So it has more contrast and less contrast in different parts of the scene! Another problem is that while the "Video" curve is said to have "increased" gamma compared to the "Film" curve, the numerical value of the slope of the "Video" curve at any point in the midtones—called *point gamma*—is actually lower. So it's easy to get confused, and you may find the same curve marked "low" gamma or contrast by one manufacturer and "high" by another.

Some people choose to experiment with gamma settings on location, while others prefer to alter the look of the image in post under more controlled conditions. For the former, there are default settings specified by video standards (ITU-R 601 for SD and ITU-R 709 for HD; see p. 195). For the latter, different types of stories or scenes might call for different settings. Digital video cameras make selecting alternative gammas easy by using stored values from lookup tables (LUTs, see p. 720) in memory. Professional and prosumer digital cameras also provide for the use of *setup cards* to store preprogrammed or user-selectable gamma settings, allowing you to transfer settings from one camera to another or reproduce different effects in different scenes.

If you want to experiment with gamma, you should determine the gamma for your project (or for a scene) after shooting tests, talking with technicians and film-makers and, if you're considering doing a film-out, with a tape-to-film transfer facility. Please note that different makes of cameras vary greatly in how gamma settings affect the image (they use differently shaped, proprietary gamma curves) and, as discussed above, even in what the settings are named. Look closely at the manual and especially at the results to know what you're getting!

Here are some general considerations:

NORMAL GAMMA. The basic default gamma correction for broadcast video cameras produces a gamma of about 0.45 or .05 to compensate for the high 2.5 gamma of CRTs. Since the gamma of the eventual video image that you see on a TV screen is the product of the camera's gamma multiplied by the gamma of the display, the overall transfer characteristic of the camera/CRT combination is about 1.1 to 1.2—a little more contrasty than the original scene but more appealing to the eye given typical TV viewing conditions.

Normal gamma has an overall bright, intense feel with relatively rich, saturated colors. For sports and news, this traditional SD video look gives a vibrant look. At the same time, it is a relatively high gamma that also results in the most limited exposure range—highlight detail is lost. However, compared to old-style broadcast cameras, today's digital video cameras are vastly better in handling dynamic range, and the "factory setting" normal gamma in newer cameras may be enhanced to reflect this. Manufacturers of TV cameras, after all, want their products to be known for a distinctive look, which drives sales. With HD cameras the normal gamma must conform to the prescribed ITU 709 gamma curve, which will produce a good result on various types of displays, but subtle gamma manipulations can be added to the mix, as well.

REDUCED GAMMA. Reducing the gamma darkens midtones, lowers highlight contrast, and extends the dynamic range, allowing you to capture more detail in bright areas that would otherwise overexpose. It also produces a mellower, softer look. This is thought to have a more filmlike look (hoping to emulate the look of film transferred to video) and on some cameras this is labeled as a "cine gamma" setting. The middle curve in Fig. 5-6 is the Panasonic Varicam's "Video Record" setting that offers a more filmic look than normal gamma, but it is intended for productions that will be shown as video (though it can also be used for film-out). Some people like this setting; others think it looks a bit flat and desaturated.

CINE OR FILM GAMMA. On some cameras *cine gamma* or *film gamma* simply means a version of the reduced gamma setting just described, which produces a picture that can be shown as is on video.

However, on some cameras cine gamma is a setting that provides *very* low contrast and *extreme* dynamic range. This allows you to capture detail far up into the bright areas that would normally overexpose and deep into shadows. The intent is to provide a great deal of detail and flexibility for color correction in post and especially for doing a film-out (where proper contrast will be restored by the film stock). However, the picture will look dull and dark on a typical video monitor. The Varicam's "Film Record" setting in Fig. 5-6 provides this kind of look. In fact, the dynamic range captured by the Varicam in this mode is far greater than what a typical video monitor can reproduce; Panasonic makes a "gamma box" which can bring the midtones into a more normal range for on-the-set monitoring.[7]

In a similar vein, digital cinematography cameras can also produce an image that looks flat and dull prior to downstream color and gamma correction. Grass Valley's 3-CCD Viper produces a 1920 x 1080p 4:4:4 RGB signal of this type called FilmStream, while Arriflex's D-20 in film mode uses a single sensor with Bayer color filtration to capture 2K images in the RAW data format. RAW files in particular can be thought of as a digital intermediate element (see p. 718) that needs first to be de-mosaiced into 2K files or HD, then corrected and converted to a broadcast- or projection-standard video format. The good part is that as long as you don't overexpose, there's a wealth of extra detail, spanning from highlights to shadows, that you can work with in post to create the final look.

Black Level

The broadcast legal minimum video level is called the *black level*. This is the darkest black, the level the camera puts out when the lens cap is on (also known as *reference black*). Black level is important because it sets the bottom of the tonal range. If the black level is elevated, instead of a rich black you may get a milky, grayish tone (see Fig. 5-5D).[8] Without a good black, the overall contrast of the image is diminished and the picture may lack snap. Having a dark black can also contribute to the apparent focus—without it, sometimes images don't look as sharp.

The black level is where the black clip takes effect. Nothing in the scene can be darker than this black. But it is also possible to have a scene in which nothing even approaches black (for example, a shot of a piece of white paper).

In digital video, the world over, reference black is 0 percent video, also known as *zero setup*. When you're recording digitally, or transferring from one digital format to another, the nominal (standard) black level is zero.[9]

ANALOG NTSC SETUP. In analog NTSC video *only*, the black level is raised to 7.5 IRE units. This dates back to the early 1940s, intended as a small safety margin to separate video black from the 0 IRE blanking level. Today this added level is known as *setup* or *pedestal*. This 7.5 IRE setup does *not* apply to digital video (SD or HD), analog PAL, or "NTSC-J" used in Japan and Korea. It applies *only* to analog NTSC video used in North America, the Caribbean, parts of South America, Asia, and the Pacific.

Unfortunately, setup causes a lot of confusion when going between digital and analog worlds. Say you're using an analog monitor to look at analog NTSC tapes (perhaps Beta SP). The Beta deck outputs standard NTSC analog video with the 7.5 IRE setup and you adjust the monitor with color bars to look correct and

7. According to Panasonic, without the gamma box a normal monitor will display only the upper five stops of a ten-stop dynamic range.

8. If you turn the brightness control up on an analog monitor you can see the effect of elevated blacks.

9. As shown in Fig. 5-8, zero percent video level corresponds to digital code 16 in an 8-bit system.

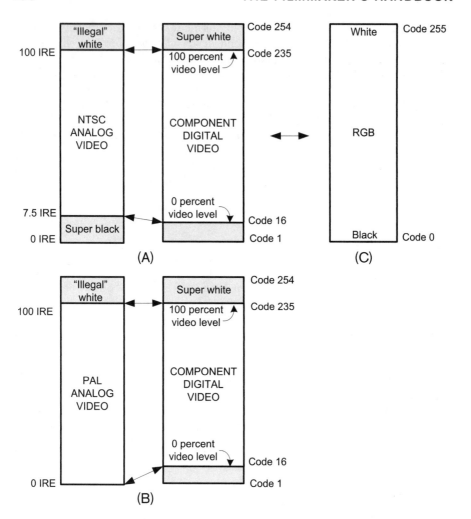

Fig. 5-8. Converting between different video systems. (A) In NTSC analog video used in North America, the darkest black is 7.5 IRE. When converting to component digital video, this 7.5 IRE setup must be removed so that the darkest blacks fall at 0 percent level in digital. When going the other way, setup must be added to bring blacks up to 7.5 IRE. Note that both analog and component digital can accommodate levels that are higher than 100 percent, which may be "illegal" for broadcast. (B) In both PAL and the Japanese version of NTSC, there is no setup and the darkest blacks are at 0 IRE. This converts simply to 0 percent video level in digital. No setup need be added or removed when moving between systems. (C) The 8-bit RGB color used in computer systems puts the brightest white at digital code 255 and the darkest black at code 0. Note that this is a greater range than 8-bit component digital where white is at code 235 and black is at code 16. This can result in some problems, such as bright tones or colors that look fine in an RGB graphics application but are much too bright when imported to component video; or images that look fine in component that look dull or dark when converted to RGB or displayed on an RGB computer monitor. Fortunately, some systems compensate automatically and others offer manual adjustments when moving between RGB and component. (Graeme Nattress)

everything is normal. Now, you decide to look at a digital tape, and you plug the same monitor into the analog output of a digital DV tape deck. The monitor is still expecting to see video levels with 7.5 IRE setup, but digital black is the equivalent of 0 IRE, so the signal coming out of the DV deck makes the blacks look too dark and the overall contrast seem too harsh. *This is not supposed to happen*, because all digital video devices sold in the U.S. market are supposed to automatically add 7.5 IRE setup to their analog output, as required by the NTSC standard. But sometime around the late 1990s, with the introduction of MiniDV devices with FireWire digital-to-digital connections—in which 7.5 IRE setup doesn't exist—the manufacturers of DV equipment (not coincidentally, mostly Japanese) pulled a fast one. They simply omitted 7.5 IRE setup from the analog output of many of their prosumer camcorders and decks.

It's true you can compensate for this by turning up the brightness control on the monitor (see Appendix A). And some professional monitors offer a choice of 0 IRE setup or 7.5 IRE setup for analog input, assuming you know where to look in the monitor's menu. But what about the millions of normal NTSC TV sets in the world's largest TV market (the United States) which expect to receive a standard analog signal with 7.5 IRE setup when Dad plugs in the MiniDV camcorder to playback Junior's graduation?

Simply put, all analog NTSC (except in Japan) is expected to have 7.5 setup for proper image reproduction. A professional digital deck may have a menu setting to *add setup* to the analog output for use when viewing on an analog monitor (many monitors are still analog) or when rerecording the video to an analog NTSC deck (for example, when making a VHS dub of your movie).

Unfortunately, many popular MiniDV camcorders and digital decks do not add 7.5 IRE setup upon analog output. (Sony's DSR-11 and DSR-20 DVCAM decks, for instance.) A *proc amp* (either a stand-alone unit or one built into a capture card) can used to add setup when needed. Again, keep in mind that if you use a *digital* connection (such as FireWire or SDI) between a deck, a computer, and/or a monitor, no NTSC setup is needed.

Most prosumer MiniDV digital video cameras that have a menu setting to add 7.5 IRE setup do so to the analog output of the camera. However, some MiniDV camcorders incorrectly add setup between the sensor and the recorder. Which means that you will record a raised black level of 7.5 to the digital video. This is wrong! Digital video should never have an elevated NTSC 7.5 black level; it would then be incompatible with normal digital video. If you have any doubts about your camera, make sure you have it set to 0 setup when you're recording. If you notice that the blacks in the picture seem milky or gray, this may be a tip-off that setup has been incorrectly added.

If you are recording *from* an NTSC analog source to a digital deck, you will want to *remove* setup, to bring the black levels down from 7.5 IRE to 0. This is usually done automatically, as the digital deck expects an incoming NTSC signal to contain standard 7.5 setup.

BLACK STRETCH/COMPRESS. Some cameras have a *black stretch* adjustment that can be set to increase or decrease contrast in the shadow areas. Increasing the black stretch a little brings out details in the shadows and softens overall contrast. On some cameras, the darkest black can be a bit noisy, and adding some black stretch helps elevate dark areas up out of the noise. Sony's HD camera HDW-F900 has a *black gamma* setting which can be used to increase shadow detail without changing the absolute black level, and without affecting midtones.

On some cameras there is a separate *black compress* setting, which you could use to darken and crush shadow areas. Because you can always do this in post, it's a good idea not to throw away much shadow detail in shooting.

Tonal Range

We've seen that having a good black helps the overall contrast. The same is true of a bright white. If you compose your shots so that everything in the frame is near the bottom of the tonal scale, the video image displayed as video can sometimes look murky. (The video image transferred to film is a different story.) Even for a dark night shot, it may help to have *something* bright in the picture (a streetlight, a streak of moonlight) to provide the eye with a range of brightness that, in this case, can actually make the darks look darker (see Fig. 5-4).

That said, there *are* times when you want to limit the tonal range. For example, you might use smoke or a low-contrast filter to soften contrast by bringing up the dark tones to gray. In this case the darkest black level may be quite elevated.

BROADCAST STANDARDS

Setting video levels is partly a means to getting a pleasing picture and partly dictated by the engineering requirements of the prevailing broadcast television system. You have more flexibility if the movie is not going to be broadcast. When you submit a program for broadcast, or even for finishing in a postproduction house, a technician will scrutinize it for proper luma and chroma levels (for more on levels, see Color Correction, p. 573). Something that looks fine to you may not pass muster for technical reasons. The term *broadcast quality* comes from requirements for the video *signal*, not the way the picture looks. And then there are the requirements for *audio* levels and phasing. When preparing a show for broadcast, consult a technician and discuss any potentially problematic equipment or scenes in advance.

VIDEO COLOR SYSTEMS

Color Systems

Be sure to read How Color Is Recorded, p. 16, before reading this section.

The camera's sensor (or sensors in a three-chip camera) generates three distinct color signals—red, green, and blue (RGB). From these three color signals, the camera "encodes" a monochrome *luminance* (*luma*) signal, represented with the letter Y, that corresponds to the brightness of the picture, as well as two "color difference" signals called *chrominance* (*chroma*).[10] Your color TV later decodes the luma

---

10. In SD video, $Y = 0.299R + 0.587G + 0.114B$. Note that by far the most brightness information is contained in the green component.

and chroma signals and reconstructs the original RGB signals, which it displays. If you happen to have a black-and-white TV instead, you're watching the luma signal alone.

The gamut or range of colors that an imaging system can reproduce is called its *color space*. How color space is translated into RGB signals, which are then encoded, processed, and routed through the video system, has a big impact on the quality of the picture and on what types of equipment you can use together. Four major methods are currently in use:

RGB. In a simple RGB system, the three colors are kept separate using different paths for R, G, and B signals. RGB color offers a wide gamut of hues and is used in computer displays and some high-bandwidth video systems. Because the three color components are kept in separate channels, RGB is sometimes called *component color*, which should not be confused with the digital video component system discussed below. RGB in fact is not technically video, if video is defined by its

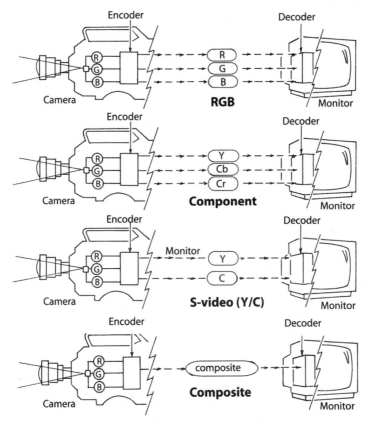

Fig. 5-9. RGB, component, S-video, and composite video systems vary in the paths they use to convey the video signal from one piece of equipment to another. For systems that use multiple paths, the signal is sometimes sent on multiple cables and sometimes the various paths are part of one cable. See text for explanation. (Robert Brun)

relationship to broadcast standards. RGB handles brightness values differently than component video, so there may be translation issues, for instance, when moving between the RGB color of a computer graphics program and the component color of a video editing program (see Fig. 5-8C).[11] It's interesting to note that high-bandwidth cameras that capture full 4:4:4 RGB, such as Sony's HDC-950, use HDCAM SR videotape recorders to capture RGB as digital video instead of as DPX files. Electronic capture of RGB motion images is still in its infancy.

COMPONENT VIDEO. In a component video system, as noted above, there are three signal paths: one for luminance (Y) and two chrominance or *color difference signals* (R minus Y; B minus Y). This *component video* signal structure is widely—though inaccurately—referred to as *YUV*. Component video is used in all current digital video formats because it provides a high-quality image with excellent color reproduction and requires less data to record and transmit than RGB.

The proper way to indicate digital component video is YC_BC_R (the analog version is YP_BP_R). However, you often find YC_BC_R interchanged or confused with YUV; Y,R-Y,B-Y (generic shorthand for component video); or sometimes *YIQ* (analog NTSC).

When signals are separately routed, component and RGB connections can require between three and five cables. It's more common today, however, to use single cables that digitally route together all three components at the same time. These include SDI (Serial Digital Interface), HD-SDI, FireWire, and fiber-optics links, increasingly popular in high-end production (see Fig. 14-28).

S-VIDEO. *S-video (Separate video)* is also called *Y/C*. This is not so much a video system as two-path method of routing the analog luminance signal separately from the two chrominance signals. It provides poorer color and detail than true component video, but is noticeably better than composite. It was introduced in the 1980s with "color-under" recording formats like Hi8, S-VHS, and ¾-inch SP (and their predecessors, 8mm, VHS, and standard ¾-inch) which merge the two chrominance signals into a single chroma signal that is channeled apart from the luminance signal through all stages of signal processing. Many types of gear (such as monitors or DV cameras) have S-video inputs or outputs, and these are always a superior choice over a composite input or output.

COMPOSITE VIDEO. With composite video, the luminance and two chrominance signals are matrixed (encoded) into *one signal* that can be sent down a single path, such as a coaxial cable or a broadcast signal. This has long been used for analog broadcast PAL and NTSC. Composite video has the lowest-quality image of all the color systems. Composite signals can introduce a number of image defects such as *dot crawl* (which makes thin lines seem to be moving) and *color bleeding* (also called *smearing*, in which colors spread out beyond the area where they should be). The color red can be particularly problematic with composite.

---

11. Particular attention has to be paid to how bright values are treated (RGB allows for brighter whites than component) and to which colors are broadcast legal (some RGB brightness levels and saturated colors are not legal in component broadcast video). Many graphics and compositing applications allow you to limit color selection to legal broadcast values.

Composite connections between pieces of equipment are convenient because you need only one video cable. Many different types of gear have composite inputs and outputs (often labeled simply "video in" and "video out," see Fig. 14-11). This can be handy for, say, monitoring a camera on a shoot. However, given the problems with composite video, avoid composite recording formats and connections when quality is important.

Note that even if you record component digital video (say, DV), your equipment may have connections that allow you to input or output using other signal types. However, if the signal is sent through one of the lower-quality methods (S-video or composite) it will not gain quality by later going to component.

Digital Color Standards

To make digital video consistent worldwide, the International Telecommunications Union (ITU) defines certain standards. As a filmmaker, there are three in particular you may come in contact with.

ITU-R 601. Also known by its full name, *ITU-R Rec BT. 601, Rec. 601* or the older *CCIR 601*. This standard defines the color values used in uncompressed, interlaced, standard definition component digital video. Although many people use *"601 video"* as a general term to mean uncompressed standard definition digital video compatible with 525-line NTSC in North America (sometimes called *D1 video*, because it was the basis of the original uncompressed D1 tape format), ITU-R 601 equally defines uncompressed digital 625-line PAL.[12] ITU-R 601 also specifies a range or gamut of acceptable (legal) colors.

ITU-R 709. Also known as *ITU-R Rec BT. 709, Rec. 709* or *CCIR 709*. ITU-R 709 is a newer standard for high definition video. It has a similar color gamut to 601 video and to PAL, though brightness values are somewhat different. Transferring material shot in 601 to 709 may cause some color shifts. Cameras and other video equipment may have settings to choose 709 color space, which is the HD standard.

Over time, ITU-R 709 will likely prevail over standard definition 601 color space for new production, but for now many monitors, whether CRT (SMPTE-C phosphors) or LCD, conform to the 601 specs. Many HD productions, for instance, use monitors that are 601 compliant. It gets even more confusing when you consider that many current HD cameras can also output SD. Which color space are they using? Moreover, while Panasonic's DVCPRO HD cameras use 709 color space for HD (what do they use for SD capture?), HDV cameras can be either 601 or 709 and, of course, they capture both SD and HD.

It's a very good thing that the 601 and 709 color spaces are as close as they are.

xvYCC. A new color standard is *xvYCC* (shorthand for extended-gamut YCC color space for video applications). This standard, sometimes called *x.v. color*, is based on the 709 standard, but extends the color range beyond the capabilities of CRT monitors and other conventional displays. With almost twice as many

12. Which is to say that 601 video has a frame size of 720 x 486 with 4:2:2 component color sampling. The PAL version has 720 x 576 pixels. Both have 720 luminance and 360 chrominance samples per line and share a 13.5 MHz luminance sampling frequency.

colors, more natural and vivid color reproduction is possible. xvYCC is used in some new consumer cameras and displays and may be used in pro gear as well. It's supported by HDMI 1.3 connections and cables.

Color Sampling

See Color Sampling, p. 18, before reading this.

When we look at a picture or the world, our eyes (assuming we have good eyesight) can perceive subtle distinctions in brightness in small details. However, the eye is much less sensitive to color gradations in those fine details. Because of this, smart engineers realized that if a video system records less information about color than brightness, the picture can still look very good, while cutting down the amount of data. This can be thought of as a form of compression.

As discussed above, most digital video cameras use component color. In this system there are three components: Y' (luma), C_B and C_R (both chroma). When the signal from the camera's sensor is processed, some of the color resolution is thrown away; how much depends on the format.

To see how this works, look at a small group of pixels, four across (see Fig. 5-10). In a *4:4:4* ("four-four-four") system there are four pixels each of Y, C_B and C_R. This provides full color resolution. Only some high-end video systems use 4:4:4 component color and very few cameras do. (However, RGB color described above is always 4:4:4.)

In 4:2:2 systems, a pair of adjacent C_B pixels is averaged together and a pair of C_R pixels is averaged together. This results in half as much resolution in color as brightness. Many high-quality component digital formats in both standard and high definition are 4:2:2. For example, ITU-R 601. This reduction in color information (also called *chroma subsampling*) is virtually undetectable to the eye.

Some formats reduce the color sampling even further. In a 4:1:1 system, there are four luma samples for every C_B and C_R, resulting in one-quarter the color resolution. This is used in the NTSC version of DV. While the color rendering of 4:1:1 is technically inferior to 4:2:2, and the difference may sometimes be detectable in side-by-side comparisons, the typical viewer may see little or no difference. However, for titles and graphics, blue- or green-screen work or special effects, 4:2:2 is usually preferable. This is in part because previously sharp borders between colored areas can become somewhat fuzzy or diffuse in 4:1:1. Often, projects that are shot in a 4:1:1 format like DV are finished on a 4:2:2 system that has less compression.

Another type of chroma sampling is 4:2:0, used in HDV and PAL DV. Here, the resolution of the chroma samples is reduced both horizontally and vertically. Like 4:1:1, the color resolution in 4:2:0 is one-quarter that of brightness, and the same caveats apply (though people have reported very successful green screen work with 4:2:0 HD formats).

Some people can get very wrapped up in comparing cameras and formats in terms of chroma sampling, praising one system for having a higher resolution than another. Take these numbers with a grain of salt: The proof is in how the picture looks. Even low numbers may look very good. Also, bear in mind that chroma sampling applies only to resolution. The actual gamut—the range of colors—is not affected.

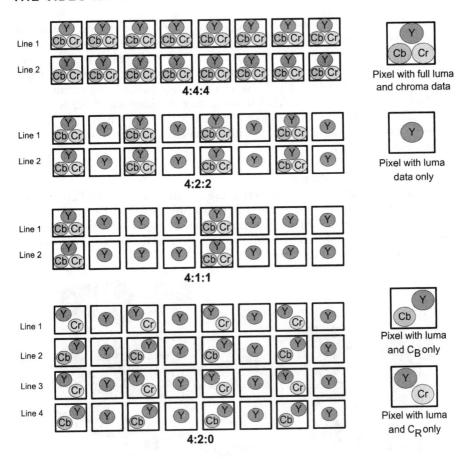

Fig. 5-10. Color sampling. In a 4:4:4 system, every pixel contains a full set of data about brightness (Y) and color (C_B and C_R). In 4:2:2 and 4:1:1 systems, increasing amounts of color data are thrown away, resulting in more pixels that have only brightness information. In the PAL DV version of 4:2:0 shown, pixels with Y and C_R alternate on adjacent lines with ones that have Y and C_B (other 4:2:0 systems use different layouts).

VIDEO MONITORS
AND PROJECTORS

See Camera and Recorder Basics, p. 5, and Viewfinders and Monitors, p. 111, before reading this section.

On many productions, a lot of attention and money goes to finding the best camera, doing good lighting, creating artful production design, etc. All in the service of creating a picture that looks great and captures the intent of the filmmakers.

But when showing the work in video, all that care can be undone by a display device that's not up to the task. There are numerous reasons why a given monitor or projector may not show the picture the way it should (see below). As a moviemaker, you can control some aspects of the viewing experience (such as what type of equipment you use yourself and how you set it up). In screening situations, always do a "tech check" beforehand to make sure anything adjustable is set correctly. Unfortunately, once your movie goes out into the world, you have no control over how it looks and viewers will see something that may or may not look the way you intended it.

Types of Displays

These days, video displays are everywhere and there are many different types. The following are some of the main varieties available. Many of these technologies are available in different forms: as flat panel screens (except CRT); as video projectors (which shine on a screen like a film projector); or as rear-projection monitors. CRTs are analog; the rest are digital.

Fig. 5-11. Sony's Luma series of professional LCD video monitors. (Sony Electronics, Inc.)

CRT. *Cathode Ray Tube (CRT)* technology is what's behind the traditional TV set dating back to the beginning of broadcasting (see Fig. 1-3). For decades, CRTs were the only game in town; now, many manufacturers are discontinuing them in favor of lighter, flat-panel displays. Even so, high-quality CRTs continue to offer the best color and contrast reproduction of any monitors. Some CRTs are capable of multiple resolutions.

LCD. *Liquid Crystal Display (LCD)* monitors use a fluorescent backlight to project through liquid crystal molecules. The brightness of a pixel is controlled by sending a voltage to it, darkening the pixel to prevent light from shining through. LCDs are very thin and can offer good color reproduction; good blacks are a problem through, and shadow detail may be crushed. Contrast, however, is constantly improving and major broadcast manufacturers are beginning to introduce reference-quality LCD video monitors (see below).

Some LCDs are limited in their viewing angle: If you sit *off axis* (to the side) the image may be darker. LCDs have no burn-in effect (see below).

PLASMA. Plasma screens are flat panel displays that use tiny red, green, and blue pixels filled with a rare gas that gives off light when excited with electricity (similar to fluorescent light). Plasma screens can be very large, with a wide viewing angle. They have good contrast, color, and black levels. They tend to be heavier than LCDs.

Some plasmas can suffer from *screen burn-in*, which causes the screen to retain brightness values from static images held for a long time (for example, if you constantly watched letterboxed movies, the shape of the letterbox might appear as shading on an otherwise bright screen).

DLP. *Digital Light Processing* (*DLP*) displays use millions of microscopic mirrors to direct light through colored filters. The mirrors switch on and off thousands of times a second. DLP monitors and projectors are capable of excellent color, contrast, and resolution and can support fully digital connections with no analog conversion necessary. Instead of using three DLP imagers and RGB filters to create full color, recent low-cost DLP projectors have introduced a single DLP chip with a fast-spinning color wheel for excellent color reproduction and compact size.

Fig. 5-12. Panasonic DLP projector. (Panasonic Broadcast)

OTHERS. *LCOS* (*Liquid Crystal on Silicon*) is similar to LCD technology and is used for video projectors. JVC calls their version D-ILA and Sony call theirs SXRD. Both claim that LCOS totally eliminates the *screen door effect* (on some LCDs, the pixel grid is visible in the image, as though viewing through a screen door). Sony has introduced a 4K SXRD projector for Digital Cinema use. *HTPS* (*High Temperature Poly-Silicon*) is a technology used in some LCD projectors; it's fairly inexpensive with good color and contrast. A newer illumination technology, *Light Emitting Diode* (*LED*) systems, offer a very wide color gamut and good stability. *OLED* (*Organic Light Emitting Diode*) displays are another newer thin-film display technology that may someday replace LCDs. When an electrical current is applied, OLEDs phosphoresce, providing their own illumination. They are bright, offer excellent color and contrast, and can be made cheap and light.

Computer, Video, and Broadcast Monitors

Clearly, there are numerous display technologies in use. As a moviemaker, you need to be aware that, even within one type of technology, all monitors are not created equal and you need the right type for the job you're doing.

Fig. 5-13. Matrox Axio NLE. In the setup shown here, two LCD computer monitors are used for the editing interface and a CRT video monitor displays the picture. (Matrox Electronic Systems, Ltd.)

Computer monitors are designed to show the output of a laptop or desktop computer and may be connected to the computer with an analog VGA cable, a digital DVI cable (Digital Video Interface), or a digital HDMI cable (High Definition Multimedia Interface, a successor to DVI, see Fig. 5-14). You may be using a computer monitor as part of a nonlinear editing system. Computer monitors typically operate in RGB color space (see above). If you're producing something that will be seen only on cell phones, iPods, or computer monitors, such as a Flash video or Internet-only MPEG video, then a computer monitor can serve as a picture reference. However, if you're doing something for broadcast or distribution in video, a computer monitor should not be used as a picture reference. Even if the computer monitor is very good, broadcast video will usually look flat (low contrast) and dark on a RGB computer monitor (see Fig. 5-8). Both the color values and the gamma are wrong for video. Other aspects of the picture may be off as well.

Instead, you should view the video on a professional *video monitor*. A video monitor should have analog inputs for component video ($Y'P_BP_R$), S-video, composite video, or digital inputs in various forms (see below). You can feed a video monitor with the output from a camera, a deck, or a video capture card or external video interface on an editing system. Video monitors display the image in component video color space and will show titles and graphics the way they will appear when the movie is broadcast or projected. Sometimes a computer monitor that has separate video inputs can double as a video monitor, but this is usually not a good idea.

A *broadcast monitor* is essentially a high-quality video monitor capable of reproducing the full range of color to meet broadcast standards, with the kinds of controls and settings necessary to adjust the image properly. One particularly helpful control is the *blue-only* switch for accurate color adjustments (see Appendix A).

When doing critical tasks like color correction (or, when shooting, evaluating lighting and exposure) *only* a broadcast monitor should be used (even better, use a high-end *reference monitor*). Consumer TVs generally do not deliver consistent, controlled results; only with a broadcast monitor can you make the most realistic and accurate assessment of what the picture actually looks like.

As time goes by, new forms of distribution and display are coming into use, and the distinctions between these types of monitors will break down somewhat. For example, consumers are increasingly watching video over the Internet or from DVDs on computer monitors. So filmmakers need to judge how their work looks on all sorts of displays. The good news is that consumer and computer monitors are improving, and the different technologies are converging.

Some Monitor Issues

RESOLUTION AND SCANNING. Flat panel displays have a fixed number of pixels, which is their *native resolution* (you can find it in the monitor's manual) and they are at their best when playing video with the same number of pixels. If the monitor will accept video with different resolutions, the picture will be scaled to that size. If you play video that has a higher resolution (more pixels), some detail will be lost and some of the picture area may actually be cut off. If you input video that has a lower resolution, you won't gain detail. Instead, the monitor will do *line doubling* or pixel interpolation to fill in the missing pixels (see Frame Size, p. 720).

There are various devices that can convert from one format or resolution to another for monitoring. For example, if you're editing HD video and only have an SD monitor, there are capture cards or external boxes that can downconvert to SD in real time (see p. 508).

Most flat panel displays and digital projectors use progressive scanning. If you input interlaced video, the player or monitor will deinterlace, which may cause artifacts. The other side of that coin is that if you shoot in an interlaced format, there can be interlace artifacts, such as twitter, that appear *only* on an interlaced CRT display (you won't see them on progressive flat screen display)—so if you have only an LCD or plasma screen there could be image issues *you* won't see but others may.

The *response time* of an LCD monitor is critical; if it's too slow, fast movement may cause ghosting or streaking.

COLOR. Getting accurate color reproduction is one of the trickiest aspects of monitors and projectors. There are two aspects you need to be concerned with. One is *hue*, technically called *phase*, which is like dialing into place all the colors on a color wheel. Small errors in hue adjustment will throw off NTSC colors in a big way.[13] The other aspect is *saturation*—how pale or rich the colors are—which is controlled by the chroma setting. See Appendix A for instructions on setting up a monitor.

Note that for high definition using HD-SDI, there is no phase adjustment, nor are phase adjustments needed for component analog RGB signals. However, HD monitors often display SD too, and sometimes the phase control is not disabled

---

13. Adjustment of phase only exists in NTSC; PAL, which stands for *Phase Alternation by Line*, cancels phase errors.

when HD is displayed as an analog component signal. Also, when using an NTSC standard definition monitor to display HD downconverted to SD, phase *does* need to be adjusted. On the other hand, some HD monitors, particularly LCD models that rely mostly on digital SDI and HD-SDI inputs, have done away with the phase control altogether, even for composite analog inputs. It's always a good idea to both study a new monitor's manual and test the monitor to verify its functionality.

There are newer, high-end digital *reference monitors* that claim to be able to reproduce colors accurately and consistently over time and from monitor to monitor without adjustment. The need for this kind of standardization can't be overstated. As things stand now, many monitors and projectors you encounter will be poorly adjusted, and many aren't even capable of reproducing all the colors in your video. But until the world is brimming with perfect digital monitors, keep those color bars handy.

CONTRAST RATIO. The range from the darkest black to the brightest white that a monitor can reproduce is critical (see Understanding and Controlling Contrast, p. 183). Manufacturers express this as a *contrast ratio*, such as 800:1. The higher the better, but be skeptical of the numbers in the ads; they are often fudged.

Be sure to set black level (brightness) and contrast as described in Appendix A. The screening environment also plays a role in contrast. If there's too much light in the room (and on the screen), you won't get a good black. If the room is *totally* dark, contrast may seem harsh. A dim ambient light often works best with consumer monitors.

ASPECT RATIO. Playing widescreen video on a non-widescreen monitor, and vice versa, can cause issues. This is affected by the monitor and how the video itself is prepared (see p. 87). Another consideration is whether the video and the monitor both use square or nonsquare pixels (see p. 213).

CONNECTIONS. Often, video recorders and players offer a variety of output options through different connectors. For example, a player might have composite and component outputs. Always use the highest-quality signal path possible. See Video Color Systems, p. 192, for a ranking of some of the options you may have. If the monitor has digital inputs, it's usually preferable to go digital out from the player to the monitor rather than use analog connections. For example, use a DVI connection or an HDMI connection, which supports uncompressed video and audio between player and monitor or other gear. However, with some equipment, direct digital connections are not available. See p. 216 for more on digital connections.

Professional monitors often allow you to *loop through* the signal—going into the monitor and out to another monitor or recorder. If the monitor is the last or only item on the line, be sure it is *terminated* properly (see Appendix A).

Fig. 5-14. Data and video connectors. (A) Hi-speed USB 2.0 male A connector. (B) USB 2.0 Mini B connector. (C) FireWire (IEEE 1394) 4-pin. (D) FireWire 6-pin (the two extra pins supplies power). (E) DVI connector. (F) HDMI connector. (Belkin Corporation)

TIMECODE

The idea of timecode is simple: to assign a number to every frame of picture or sound. Timecode is a running 24-hour "clock" that counts hours, minutes, seconds, and frames (see Fig. 1-17). Timecode enables many different aspects of production and postproduction and is pretty much essential for serious video and audio work. Timecode comes in a few different flavors, which can sometimes be confusing.

Types of Timecode

In all video timecode the frame count depends on the frame rate you're working in.

For example, when shooting at 30 fps (either 30p or 60i), timecode can advance as high as 23:59:59:29 (twenty-three hours, fifty-nine minutes, fifty-nine seconds, and twenty-nine frames). One frame later it returns to 00:00:00:00. Note that since there are thirty frames per second, the frame counter only goes up to :29. This timecode system is called *SMPTE nondrop timecode*. Many people just refer to it as SMPTE (pronounced "simpty") or "nondrop" (often written "ND"). This is standard, basic timecode often used in North America and places where NTSC has been standard.

In Europe and other parts of the world where PAL video has been standard, video is often shot at 25 fps (25p or 50i). Here, *EBU timecode* is used, which has a similar 24-hour clock, except the frame counter runs up to :24 instead of :29.

DROP FRAME TIMECODE. One of the joys of video is that with several formats, the frame rate is just slightly slower than what you might think it is (by 0.1 percent). For example, 30 fps NTSC video is actually 29.97 fps (which is to say, 60i is really 59.94i). When you shoot 24p video, that usually means 23.976p. This is described on p. 606.

You can't see the 0.1 percent reduction in speed, but it affects the overall running time of the video. Say you watch a movie shot at 29.97 fps that has nondrop timecode, and click a stopwatch just as it begins. If you stop the stopwatch when the video timecode indicates one hour, you'd see that actually one hour and 3.6 seconds has gone by. The nondrop timecode is not keeping real time. This discrepancy is no big deal if the movie is not intended for broadcast. Nondrop timecode is often used for production.

Because broadcasters need to know program length very exactly, *drop frame* (*DF*) timecode was developed. This system drops two timecode numbers every minute so that the timecode reflects real time.[14] A program that finishes at one hour drop frame timecode is indeed exactly one hour long. With drop frame timecode, no actual frames of video are dropped and the frame rate doesn't change. The only thing that's affected is the way the frames are counted (numbered). This is a point that confuses many people. Switching a camera from ND to DF has no affect on the picture or on the number of frames that are recorded every second. The only thing that changes is the way the digits in the timecode counter advance over time.

Many television-bound programs are done with DF code. Many editing systems can work with either drop or nondrop, and shooting with nondrop doesn't prevent you from finishing with drop. Mixing drop and nondrop code in the same project can sometimes cause problems. DF timecode is usually indicated with semicolons instead of colons between the numbers (00;14;25;15) or with a semicolon just before the frame count (01:22:16;04).

24p TIMECODE. If you're shooting and editing at 24p frame rate, you may be using 24-frame timecode (the frame counter goes up to :23).

You want to avoid drop frame timecode in 24p mode because the dropped timecode numbers can make it harder to do pulldown removal in the editing system. Many cameras in 24p will not record DF for this reason.

How Timecode Is Recorded

Most digital video cameras generate timecode in some form. The timecode may be embedded in the video recording, or included with the digital video file as metadata (see p. 219).

One way to record timecode is to embed the data in each video frame, outside the picture area. This is *vertical interval timecode* (*VITC*, pronounced "vit-see"). One advantage of VITC for tape recording is that it can be read by the VTR even when the tape is not moving (very useful for editing). VITC does not use up any audio

---

14. The :00 and :01 frames are dropped every minute, unless the minute is a multiple of 10 (no frames are dropped at 10 min., 20 min., etc). Thus, the number following 00:04:59:29 is 00:05:00:02. But the number following 00:09:59:29 is 00:10:00:00.

tracks but must be recorded at the same time as the video and cannot be added later (except during dubbing to another tape).

On some videotape formats, there is a *longitudinal track* (*LTC*) just for timecode. With some video decks, the LTC is readable during high-speed shuttle but VITC isn't. Some formats allow you to use one of the audio tracks for code. Longitudinal and audio timecode can be added or changed even after the video has been recorded. The *address track* on a ¾-inch U-matic VTR is reserved for code but must be recorded with the video.

With analog tape formats, timecode degrades when copied from tape to tape. Use a *timecode generator* to regenerate the code while dubbing and be sure it is sync-locked to the video.

Consumer or prosumer equipment sometimes uses nonprofessional timecode systems, such as RC timecode. These systems may limit your ability to interface with professional equipment.

ADDING CODE TO A NONCODED TAPE. If you plan to do an online edit, it is virtually impossible without timecode. If the original footage was shot without code (or the code is messed up), often the simplest solution with digital formats is to rerecord on another digital deck that records proper code. For example, with DV you could do a FireWire transfer to another camera or deck, which would mean no quality loss. Or you could capture into an editing system and play out to a recording deck.

With small-format analog tapes, you may want to *bump up* the original footage to a timecode digital tape format. For example, footage shot in Hi8 might be transferred to DV, with timecode recorded during the transfer. The DV tapes would then become the masters.

Using Timecode in Production

Most digital consumer camcorders offer very little control over timecode (there may be only one mode and that code may automatically start at zero every time you put in a tape). All professional cameras and many prosumer models allow you to preset the starting code and may offer a choice of timecode options. Different productions call for different choices.

RECORD RUN MODE. The simplest timecode mode is called *record run*, which advances whenever the camera is recording. When recording to tape in record run mode, you can stop and start the camera as much as you want, but the code should advance on the tape uninterrupted from beginning to end.[15]

On most professional and prosumer cameras you can *preset timecode* to select the starting code. If you are using tapes less than an hour long, you might start the first at one hour (1:00:00:00), then start the second tape at two hours (2:00:00:00) and so on. That way, the timecode on each tape is different, which helps keep things organized in editing. However, as long as you keep track of each tape or disc, having two with the same code isn't a big problem (and is unavoidable if you shoot a lot of

---

15. Powering down, rewinding the tape, removing, and replacing the tape may cause timecode breaks or discontinuities, see below.

material on a project). Many cameras allow you to set *user bits* (*U-bits*), which are a separate set of data recorded with the timecode and can be used to identify camera roll numbers, the date, or other information. Be sure to use U-bits if the timecode on any two tapes is the same.

TIME-OF-DAY AND FREE RUN MODES. On some cameras, you can shoot with a *time-of-day* (*TOD*) clock recorded as timecode. TOD code can be useful if you need to identify when things were filmed, or may be used when more than one camera is shooting at the same time. A similar system is sometimes called *free run mode*, which advances every second whether the camera is running or not, but can be set to start at whatever number you preset.

TOD code can create a number of issues, which are explained below in Avoiding Timecode Problems. One issue is that TOD code is discontinuous whenever you stop the camera (because when you start up again, it will jump to the new time of day). Another problem can occur if you shoot the same tape on different days. Say you finish the first day at four in the afternoon (16:00:00:00 code). You start the next day at eleven in the morning (11:00:00:00 code). When you edit this tape, the edit controller will find the lower code number after the high number, causing problems. Using TOD code will likely result in several tapes having the same code numbers, so try to put the date or tape number in the U-bits. You can avoid some of these problems with camcorders that have a *real time mode* that puts the time of day in the user bits (if you need it for reference) but uses record run mode for the regular timecode.

MULTICAMERA SHOOTS. On productions when more than one video camera is being used at the same time, you may want to have them running the exact same timecode to facilitate editing.

With cameras that can generate and accept an external timecode source, one technique is to run a cable from the timecode-out connector of one camera (the master) to the timecode-in on the second camera (the slave). Some cameras can import timecode via the FireWire connector. The master camera should be started first, then the slave. Make sure the two are running identical code before starting the take.

If you don't want the cameras wired together, you may be able to *jam sync* one camera with the code from another or from a separate timecode source (such as Ambient's *Lockit box* or Deneke's *Syncbox*, see Fig. 11-18). The cameras are then used in free run mode and should maintain the same timecode. However, timecode may drift slightly over time, so you may need to rejam the cameras every few hours to keep their timecode identical.

Even with the same timecode, two or more cameras may not be perfectly in sync with each other for editing or live switching. For perfectly matched editing from one to the other, the cameras should be *genlocked* together. This can be done on professional cameras by running a cable from the video-out connector on one camera (or from a separate sync source) to the genlock-in connector on the other. With HD cameras, genlock is properly called *tri-level sync*. There are Lockit and Syncboxes that can generate tri-level sync and timecode, to permit genlocked shooting with cameras not tethered to a wire.

See Timecode Slating Systems, p. 438, for using timecode with audio recorders and film cameras.

Avoiding Timecode Problems

You can think of timecode as an organizational tool for keeping track of your material and locating it later. If you plan to do any editing, timecode is more than that: It's a crucial part of how the editing system retrieves video and audio data when needed. When recording to tape, there are certain ground rules to follow.

REPEATING TIMECODE. You never want to have a situation in which the same timecode number occurs on a single tape in more than one place. A common way this can happen is with some DV cameras that reset the code to 00:00:00:00 every time you remove or insert a tape. You shoot part of a tape, take it out, then put it back in to finish recording it. When you're later searching for that great shot of a guitar player that starts at timecode 00:12:12:00, you find instead a shot of drummer with the same code. This can create nightmares in editing.

With most camcorders you can avoid this whenever there's an interruption in code by rewinding the tape into the last previously recorded shot and playing to the end of it (*record review* or *end search* on the camera may do this automatically). Then, when you start the new recording it will pick up where the timecode ended before (see Operating the Camcorder, p. 127). Some cameras have a *regen (regenerate) timecode* setting; this will continue the timecode already recorded on tape (as opposed to using "preset," which will usually start where you have it set). Regen should be used when shooting with a tape that was partially recorded before.

Some people using low-end gear like to *prestripe* a tape with continuous code before shooting (by recording a whole tape with the lens cap on, then rewinding it prior to the shoot). While this may work, it increases wear and tear on the equipment and on the tape (increasing the chance of dropouts) and generally isn't necessary. Prestriping is often used in editing, however (see Chapter 14).

TIMECODE BREAKS. As discussed above, if you shoot carefully in record run mode you can record a whole tape with continuous, ascending timecode. This gives you the most flexibility in editing to capture material in small or large chunks and not lose anything. However, wherever there are breaks in the timecode, when you bring the material into the editing system, a new clip will be created at the break (see p. 526). When using time-of-day code, timecode breaks happen whenever you stop the camera (because the timecode jumps to a new time when you start recording again). Another way to cause a break is if you aren't careful and leave a gap after, say, rewinding the tape to check a take (see p. 129).

Timecode breaks aren't necessarily a big problem, but they can be annoying, especially if you're shooting a lot of short shots. If you know there's a break in code, be sure to leave five to ten seconds of preroll time after you start recording before calling "action." One solution for a tape that has timecode breaks or many short shots is to dub it to a new tape with continuous timecode before editing.

TIMECODE OUT OF ORDER. You want to avoid a situation in which a higher number timecode precedes a lower number on the same tape. This can happen when using time-of-day code (see above) or if you preset the code for an hour tape to start at 23:30:00:00 (because it would finish at 00:30:00:00). Editing systems expect the numbers on a tape to be *ascending* and get confused if a high number comes before a low number.

If you absolutely can't avoid this happening, make sure you note it carefully on the tape box or in the log for later reference.

DIGITAL VIDEO RECORDING— HOW IT WORKS

The Basic Idea

Before digital recording existed, there was analog. In analog recording, changes in light or sound are represented by a changing electrical signal. When a singer holds a microphone and starts to sing louder, the electrical voltage in the wire coming from the microphone increases. We can say that changes in the electrical signal are *analogous* to changes in the sound. If we use an analog tape deck to record the singer, those electrical changes are translated yet again into changes in magnetism on the tape. All these translations can introduce distortions and reduce the quality of the recording. When you copy an analog recording (and then make a copy of the copy) yet more distortions are introduced and the quality is reduced further.

The idea of digital recording is to express changes in light or sound as a set of binary numbers, ones and zeros, that represent those changes as precisely as possible. We can then transmit, record, and copy those basic digits with—we hope—no translation errors. The copy can be as good as the original.

As a very simplistic idea of how digital transmission can be superior to analog, think of the "telephone" game kids sometimes play. A group of people sit in a circle and the first person whispers a phrase to the person on the right. Then that person whispers it to the next, and so on around the circle. Say, in this particular game, we use a musical tone instead: A woman plays a note on a piano, a B flat. The man next to her hears it, and tries to hum it to the next person. His pitch isn't perfect and neither is the next person's, and by the time you get around the circle the note sounds a lot different than what came out of the piano. This is the "analog" version of the game.

In the "digital" version, the woman doesn't play the note, but writes "B flat" on a piece of paper. The man copies what she's written (and checks that it's the same as the original); then the guy next to him copies and checks it again, and so on down the line. By passing along this written version of the note, when it comes fully around the circle, we can still know *exactly* what that note is and play it again on the piano.

Digital recording works by *sampling* the audio or video signal at regular intervals of time; each sample is a measurement of the voltage at that one moment in time. That measurement is converted to a number that can be recorded on tape or on disk (converting the voltage to a number is called *quantizing*). Once the number is recorded, we can pass it along, much like the written B flat in the game, and reproduce it exactly even after many copies have been made.

In digital systems, all numbers are expressed in *binary code*, which uses a series of ones and zeros. (The number 5 would be 101 in binary.) Each digit in a binary number is a *bit* (101 is thus a three-bit number). By convention, eight bits together make a *byte*.

The entire process of converting a video or audio signal to digital form is called *digitizing* and is done by an *analog-to-digital* (*A/D*) converter, which is usually an internal chip or card. To view the picture or hear the sound, we need to convert it back from digital to analog form using a *digital-to-analog* (*D/A*) converter.

The process of recording video digitally shares a lot with recording audio, but there are differences. Let's look at video first. Digital audio recording is described on p. 372.

Digital Video Recording—With Buckets

See Camera and Recorder Basics, p. 5, before reading this section.

Let's look at how a digital video camera converts light to a digital recording. The camera's sensor is a grid of thousands or millions of pixels. Each pixel is a receptor that collects light (*photons*) when the shutter is open. To use a simple analogy, we can think of each pixel as a tiny bucket that collects raindrops (see Fig. 5-15). We put out a large number of buckets in a grid, uncover them (opening the shutter) and rain falls into the buckets. Then we cover them again (close the shutter) and measure exactly how much fell into each bucket.

In the actual camera sensor, each pixel gets a different amount of light depending on whether it's in a bright area of the picture or in shadow. The *sampling* aspect

Fig. 5-15. Digital video recording—the bucket version. (left) Buckets placed on the ground in a grid pattern collect different amounts of rainwater depending on where they are in the scene. This is akin to how pixels in the camera's sensor collect different amounts of electric charge after being struck from light from the scene. (right) These two buckets have the same amount of water. The measurement scale on the upper bucket only has four levels, so the water level would be considered either 2 or 3, introducing a half-unit error (there's no such thing as 2½ in digital). The scale on the lower bucket has eight levels, so we can say the water level is precisely 5 units with no error. In the digital equivalent, the scale on the lower bucket can be thought of as having greater *bit depth* or *precision*.

of digital video takes place both in *space* (light is measured only where the pixels are) and in *time* (light is collected only during the time the shutter is open).

Returning to the water buckets, let's imagine that along the side of each one there's a numbered scale, with zero at the bottom and four at the top. We can walk from bucket to bucket, writing down the water level in each according to that scale: for a half-full bucket we'd record a number 2; a full bucket would be a 4. We now have a list of numbers that describes how much water is in every bucket in this large array of buckets. We've converted the pattern of rainfall to numbers. This is *quantizing.*

If we wanted to, we could set up an identical set of buckets somewhere else, fill them with water according to our list of numbers and reproduce the original pattern of rain.

This is essentially how digital imaging works. The pixels are struck by different amounts of light and respond by creating different amounts of electrical charge. The A/D converter measures the charge of each pixel and converts it to a number.[16] That digital number (after a lot of digital signal processing) can then be sent to a video monitor and converted back into light.

For a high-fidelity recording, we want to be able to reproduce the original scene as closely as possible. One key factor is how many pixels (buckets) we use; more on that below. Another factor is how precisely we measure the level of each one. In our rainwater example, the scale on the side of each bucket has four levels. But what if the water level in one bucket were exactly halfway between level 2 and level 3? In digital systems, you can only record whole numbers, so we'd have to score what was actually a 2½ as either a 2 or a 3—introducing a rounding error that makes our recording inaccurate (see Fig. 5-15).[17]

For more precision, we could use buckets that had a finer scale, say from zero to eight. Now we could score that same water level as precisely a 5, with no error. This is the concept of *bit depth* or *precision.* A two-bit system gives us four levels on the scale; a three-bit system gives us eight levels. The more levels (bits) we have, the more precisely and accurately we can measure the water in each bucket.

One more thing about buckets: once they're full, they overflow and stop collecting rain. When a pixel has absorbed all the photons it can handle, it becomes overexposed and stops responding. This is what happens when you exceed the exposure range of the camera (see p. 177).

PIXELS AND RESOLUTION

The Pixel Array

The digital video frame is made up of a lattice or grid of pixels. As discussed in Chapter 1, video formats differ in their number of pixels and in the number of

---

16. The sensor's job of translating light energy to electrical energy is an analog process (even in a digital camera). With a CCD chip, the sensor downloads the charge from one row of pixels at a time, sending the signal to the A/D converter. In a CMOS chip, every pixel does its own A/D conversion and the data comes off the chip already digitized.

17. This is a *quantizing error.*

Fig. 5-16. (top) A relatively low number of pixels forms a coarse, low-resolution image. (middle) Using more pixels in a finer grid produces a higher-resolution image. (bottom) This image has the same number of pixels as the middle image but the bit depth is only three bits per pixel instead of eight. Note the discontinuous tonalities. Try viewing these images from a distance to see how they appear sharper. Compare with Fig. 12-26. Also see Fig. 1-9.

horizontal lines the pixels are arranged in (see p. 9). Take a look at Fig. 5-16. The top image is divided into a lattice of fairly large pixels in relatively few horizontal lines. The middle image has far more pixels in the same area and more horizontal lines. The middle image is capable of capturing finer detail—its *resolution* is higher.

If the number of pixels is too low, the image will look unsharp, and other artifacts may be introduced. One such defect is aliasing, which can produce a moiré pattern or cause diagonal lines in the frame to look like jagged stair steps (see Fig. 1-11).

If the number of pixels is high enough, the eye can't even discern that the image is divided into pixels at all. Compare Fig. 12-26, which is the same image with yet more (and smaller) pixels. HD video formats have higher resolution than SD formats in part because they have more horizontal lines and more pixels.

Interestingly, our ability to judge resolution in an image is related to how large the image appears. Try viewing Fig. 5-16 from several feet away and notice how the images appear sharper from that distance. Author Charles Poynton notes that viewers tend to sit far enough away from a video monitor so that the pixels and scan lines are invisible. With an HD screen you can sit much closer without seeing the pixels—so the screen takes up more of your field of vision, creating a more enveloping experience. As a crude comparison, notice that you can get very close to Fig. 12-26 and it still looks fine, whereas you have to stand a long way back from the middle image in Fig. 5-16 to try to get the pixels to disappear and make the image look continuous.

Bit Depth

We've seen that resolution can be increased by increasing the number of pixels. We can also improve resolution by measuring the brightness of each pixel more precisely. Remember the buckets and how we could measure the water level more precisely with a finer scale?

Eight-bit video systems can distinguish between 256 different brightness values for each pixel. With sixteen-bit systems, there are 65,536 gradations. The more gradations, the finer the detail you can render and the greater the dynamic range between black and white. Greater bit depth particularly facilitates any manipulation like color correction or recovering shadow detail that involves stretching image tones.

In Fig. 5-16, the middle image uses eight bits, while the bottom image (which has the same number of pixels) has only three bits per pixel. Notice how the shading on the wall and on the man's face is relatively continuous in the middle picture and is blocky and discontinuous in the lower picture (this discontinuity is called *banding* or *posterization*).

The bottom image in Fig. 5-16 has no more than eight levels of brightness from black to white—you can count each level on the wall. Clearly, this is very unlike the way the scene appeared in reality. Unsurprisingly, you won't find any three-bit camcorders on the market.

Many video formats use 8 bits, a few have 10- or 12-bit precision, and some high-quality HD systems use 16 bits. Increasing the number of bits beyond a certain point isn't necessarily directly visible to the eye. However, there are various types of video processing (such as effects work and color correction) where any digital errors get multiplied, so having more precision helps prevent visible artifacts. The downside of using more bits is that it means more data to process, store, and transmit.

Pixel Shape

Not all pixels are created equal: the shape (proportions) depends on the format. The pixels in computer video systems and HD video formats including 720p HDV are square (see Fig. 5-17). However, the pixels used in SD video formats, and in 1080 HDV, are rectangular (nonsquare). NTSC 601 non-widescreen video uses pixels that are slightly taller than they are wide. PAL 601 non-widescreen video has pixels that are slightly wider than they are tall.

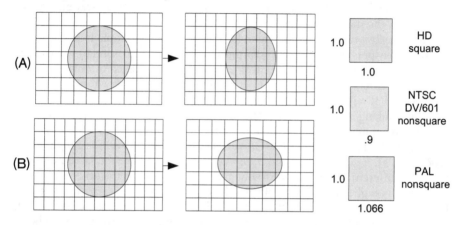

Fig. 5-17. Pixel aspect ratio. When converting between formats or systems that have different shaped pixels, the image can become distorted if adjustments aren't made. (A) An image created in a square pixel format (such as HD or any computer graphics application) can look horizontally squeezed when imported into NTSC-based formats, which use tall, nonsquare pixels. (B) An image created in an NTSC-based format can look horizontally stretched when shown on a computer monitor (which displays square pixels) or imported into a computer graphics application. Note that settings vary, and some systems compensate automatically, so your results may not be distorted or may be distorted in different ways. The pixel aspect ratios indicated on the right are for non-widescreen formats.

Pixel shape can be described as a number: the *pixel aspect ratio* (*PAR*). It's the ratio of pixel width to height, like the way display aspect ratio is expressed (see Fig. 1-12). Non-widescreen 601 and NTSC DV have a pixel aspect ratio of .9; for widescreen it's 1.2. PAL non-widescreen is 1.066; widescreen is 1.42. Both 1080 HDV and DVCPRO HD are 1.33.

If you work in only one format, pixel aspect ratio is usually not a major concern. Most editing systems make the necessary adjustments when you input video from the camera. However, if you are working with a mix of formats that have different PARs, or are creating graphics in an application like Photoshop, you need to be aware of it. Figure 5-17 shows that a ball originating in a square pixel format looks horizontally squished when shown in a format with narrower pixels. Similarly, if you create titles in a graphics program and import them into your video they could become distorted if not built and converted correctly. To avoid image distortions, consult the manuals of your graphics and editing software when combining material with different pixel aspect ratios.

Resolution and Sharpness

The *resolution* of a video image refers to its ability to reproduce fine detail. When fine detail is rendered clearly, an image will usually look sharp to the eye. But sharpness is a complicated topic. There are many factors that play a part in apparent sharpness. These include the measurable fine detail of the image (resolution), the contrast of the picture (higher contrast images tend to look sharper than low), and the distance from which we are viewing it (the farther away and smaller an image is, the sharper it looks).

Particularly when comparing video formats or cameras, people look for numerical ways to express resolution and sharpness. All of them are useful to some extent, but none of them perfectly correlates to the actual experience of *looking* at video footage. If camera X has 10 percent better numbers than camera Y, it won't necessarily look that way on screen.

When talking about resolution, the first thing to consider is the frame size, particularly the number of horizontal lines. Standard definition DV has 480 horizontal lines of pixels; high definition HDCAM has 1080. HDCAM is thus a higher resolution format. Even so, you could have two formats that have the same number of lines, but different resolution due to one being interlaced and the other progressive (the latter is higher resolution). Bit depth or precision plays a part too: a ten-bit format has a higher resolution than an eight-bit format with the same pixel count.

When comparing two cameras that record the same frame size, there can be differences in resolution due to the particular sensor, compression, lens, or other factors. There are various methods used to evaluate sharpness based on measuring what can be seen in the picture.

One technique is to look closely at a test pattern of finely spaced vertical lines. The higher the resolution of the format, the smaller and more tightly packed the lines can be and still be distinguishable. As Joe Kane puts it, "How small can a picket fence be in size and still have the individual slats show up?" The measurement is called *TV lines per picture height* (*TVL/ph*). "Per picture height" means that instead of counting lines all the way across the frame, we measure only the same distance as the height of the picture. This allows comparisons between widescreen and non-widescreen images.

Don't confuse TV lines with the horizontal scan lines described above, or with the line-pairs-per-millimeter measurement used to evaluate film stocks. If someone says, "DV has a resolution of 500 lines," that person is referring to TV lines per picture height. TV lines are a rather inexact, simplified way to discuss resolution.

Another measurement system called *MTF* (*Modulation Transfer Function*) is perhaps more useful. MTF looks at a pattern of alternating black and white lines, specifically measuring the contrast between them. While TV lines per picture height measures only the *top limit* of resolution (which may not be that critical when images are viewed from far away), MTF looks at the how the image holds up across a whole *range* of lines, from thick, widely spaced bars (low frequencies) to the finest lines (high frequencies). When the lines are relatively wide, any video system can

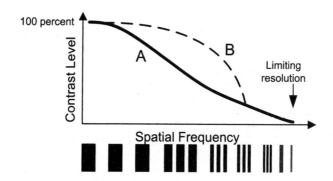

Fig. 5-18. An MTF (modulation transfer function) chart shows how well an imaging device (such as a lens) or a combined system (such as a lens plus a video camera, or a lens plus a film stock) can reproduce the contrast between black and white bars. On the left, the bars are far apart and the contrast is 100 percent. As we move to the right, the bars are thinner and more closely spaced; eventually they appear to blend together into gray (0 percent contrast). This point is the limiting resolution, expressed in line-pairs per millimeter (similar to TV lines/picture height in video). System A can distinguish finer details than System B and has higher resolving power. However, B has better contrast in the middle range, which, for audiences viewing images from a distance, may make it look sharper.

recognize that the black lines are deep black and the white lines are bright white. (This is high contrast or "one hundred percent modulation.") But as the lines get very narrow, blurring across the borders between the lines makes the black bars lighter and the white bars darker, which reduces contrast. If the lines are so narrow that they exceed the resolution of the system (this is the TVL/ph) they all appear as gray. MTF can be used to compare lenses, cameras, film stocks, recording format, displays, or a combination of any of the above as a complete imaging system. The MTF of any single element in an imaging system is simply multiplied by the MTF of other elements to determine overall system MTF.

Bear in mind that even if a format or camera is theoretically capable of a certain resolution, many things can conspire to reduce resolution, including a low-quality lens, poor focus, or an unsharp monitor. Also note that sometimes a *less* sharp image looks better than an apparently sharp one (see p. 84.)

WORKING WITH DIGITAL DATA

While movies are about characters and stories, the tools of moviemaking are increasingly about creating, moving and storing digital data. Not that long ago, file formats, digital connections, and disk storage were mostly of concern for editing and postproduction. But today, many people are recording directly to a hard drive from the camera, connecting equipment digitally, and needing to choose file formats at the start of production. Even if you don't consider yourself a computer wiz, a little knowledge of basic concepts and common equipment can help you navigate this world.

You can think of digital audio and video as a stream of digits: ones and zeros. Different formats create different sized streams. If data were water, imagine that the data stream produced by standard definition DV could flow through a thin garden hose. By comparison, uncompressed high definition 1080p might need a thick fire hose to move the data fast enough. The amount of information flowing every second is the *data rate*. The term *bandwidth* is also used to talk about data rate. Bandwidth is like the diameter of the hose. A high bandwidth connection can pass a lot of data quickly (high-speed Internet connections are called *broadband*). A connection with low bandwidth, or low *throughput*, has a relatively narrow hose.

In Appendix B, you can see a comparison of different formats and how much data they generate. Data rates are often expressed in megabits per second (Mbps). You will also see them as megabytes per second (MBps—note the capital "B"). There are eight bits in a byte, so a megabyte is eight times bigger. To review basic digital quantities: A kilobyte (KB) is 1,000 bytes; a megabyte (MB) is 1,000 KB and is often referred to as a "meg"; a gigabyte (GB) is 1,000 MB and is called a "gig"; and a terabyte (TB) is 1,000 GB.

DIGITAL CONNECTIONS

When you work with cameras, monitors, computers, and editing systems there are many situations where you need to connect pieces of gear together; say, connecting a video deck to a computer for editing. You may have several options depending on the equipment, the video format, and what you're trying to do. It's easy to get confused when talking about these connections because several factors can be involved.

1. The original recording itself: what format it's in, and the data rate being used.
2. The output and input options of the equipment you're using: A DV camera, for example, might be able to output your recording as component DV or as analog, composite NTSC. Or a video capture card might be able to output the same HDV recording as compressed HDV, as uncompressed analog HD, or as downconverted digital SD.
3. The actual cables and connectors between machines: In some cases, one type of connector can carry only one of the options; in others, the same cable might be used for different formats.

As for the first item, you'll find a listing of some widely used formats starting on p. 23. For the second item, you find the video color systems, and their relative advantages and disadvantages on p. 192. Regarding number three, here is a listing of some of the main types of connection systems and cables and their uses:

USB. USB is a common connector found on computers. The original USB 1.1 has a maximum data rate of 12Mbps, which is too slow for video. The newer Hi-Speed USB 2.0 is much faster (rates up to 480 Mbps) and has some video uses (like backing up data) but is not efficient enough for many applications, such as editing.

FIREWIRE (ALSO CALLED IEEE 1394 OR i.LINK). FireWire connections are found on many consumer and prosumer cameras and computers. A single FireWire cable can carry video, timecode, and deck control information (see Fig. 1-18 and Fig. 5-14). FireWire devices can be *daisy chained*, from one to another, connecting up to 63 different devices in a line. FireWire is an Apple term for what's defined officially as *IEEE 1394*. Sony's name for the same thing is *i.Link*.

People often think of FireWire cables as a way to connect DV equipment, but many other formats can be used with FireWire, including HDV, DVCPRO and DVCPRO HD, and uncompressed SD.

The original FireWire system is capable of 400 Mbps and is called FW400. A newer version, FW800 is twice as fast and is found on some computers and hard drives.

FW400 connectors come in 4-pin and 6-pin styles (the 6-pin has two pins to carry power); FW800, connector has 9 pins. With the right cable or adaptor you can connect a FW400 device to a FW800 device, but the speed will only be 400 Mbps.

SDI, HD-SDI, AND DUAL LINK. *Serial Digital Interface* (*SDI*) is used widely in professional video equipment. SDI can carry 8- and 10-bit 4:2:2 standard definition video with up to eight channels of digital audio. Sometimes referred to as *SMPTE 259M*, this connection is capable of a data rate up to 270 Mbps. SDI cables have BNC connectors at their ends (see Fig. 3-12).

HD-SDI is a faster version, up to 1.485 Gbps, capable of carrying component high definition video. Also known as *SMPTE 292M*.

For higher speeds, both SDI and HD-SDI can be used in *dual-link* configurations (with two cables). The very high-end HDCAM-SR camera, which records uncompressed 4:4:4 high definition video, uses a dual-link HD-SDI connection between camera and recorder.

HDMI. *High Definition Multimedia Interface* is a poor man's HD-SDI that originated as a consumer standard (see Fig. 5-14). HDMI supports uncompressed 1920 x 1080, 4:2:2 component or 4:4:4 RGB, and eight channels of audio.

SDTI AND HD-SDTI. *Serial Data Transmission Interface* (*SDTI*) is used to carry compressed video at 270 Mbps. *HD-SDTI* can carry compressed HD at the same rate. SDTI can be used to transfer material faster than real time.

ETHERNET. Some newer equipment has the ability to communicate and send files over the internet through direct *Ethernet* connections to a camera or computer. If you have a DSL modem in your home, you're probably familiar with the Cat. 5 Ethernet cable and connector. The Grass Valley Infinity camera has a *gigabit Ethernet* connection that can handle data rates up to 1,000 Mbps.

HARD DRIVE SYSTEMS

Hard drives are used in the field to capture material from the camera, and in editing and postproduction to store video, audio, and graphics. As we've seen, video formats vary widely in their data rate. Hard drives vary in their ability to handle high data rates: There are differences between types of hard drives, models within a certain type, and between different ways of grouping or configuring drives. When you choose a hard drive system, make sure it's up to your needs in terms of throughput, *seek time* (how fast data can be accessed) and capacity. In editing, hard drives should be able to handle not just the basic data rate of the format, but multiple streams of video for situations when you're displaying more than one image at a time. The following is a brief rundown of some drive technologies. Be sure to consult knowledgeable people before choosing drives or setting up a system.

Hard Drive Types

Hard drives can be installed in or attached to a computer using various technologies. The *interface* or *bus* that connects the drive(s) and the computer determines in part how fast the connection is, how long cables can be, and how many drives can be grouped together. The following are some of the main interface types as of this writing.

ATA DRIVES. *ATA drives* (also known as *IDE drives*) are used widely in computers and make for affordable internal storage (within the computer case). Larger computer cases have room for additional ATA drives inside.

SATA DRIVES. *Serial ATA (SATA)* drives are a newer technology with improved performance over ATA at around the same price. These can be added externally to a computer with a SATA PCI Express (PCIe) card. SATA II is a newer, faster version.

FIREWIRE DRIVES. A FireWire drive is simply an ATA (IDE) or SATA drive with a small FireWire "bridge" board mounted in a single hard drive enclosure. They are easy to set up and relatively inexpensive. (Often when a FireWire drive fails, it is the FireWire bridge that has burned out, not the drive itself. Many edits have been saved by moving the hard disk from a failed FireWire drive to another FireWire enclosure with a good FireWire bridge.) As discussed above, FireWire connections come in FW400 and FW800 versions.

SCSI. SCSI (pronounced "scuzzy") drives offer high performance and can be grouped together in high-capacity configurations. SCSI drives have been a common way to provide fast storage for editing systems for almost two decades. They are more complex to use and more expensive than FireWire.

FIBRE CHANNEL. Fibre channel is a newer type of interface that offers high data rates and the ability to add many drives or devices together, with long cables between computer and drives. Fibre channel drives can be quite expensive.

Storage Systems

When high speed and/or high storage capacity is needed, hard drives can be grouped together to improve performance. When more than one user needs to share access to the material, drives can be connected in a network.

RAIDS. Several drives can be operated together as a single unit in a *RAID (Redundant Array of Inexpensive Disks)*. RAIDS can be configured in various ways to serve different purposes. When information is spread across multiple drives (called *striping*) it increases the data transfer rate. With striping, the system alternates between more than one disk at a time when writing and reading data, avoiding bottlenecks. RAIDS can also be used to protect against drive failures or corrupt data by *mirroring*, where the exact same data is placed on two drives at once (you can use just one drive if the other goes down).

There are several different RAID configurations or levels, which are aimed to maximize performance or safety or to balance both needs. For example, RAID 0 just involves striping, and is good for boosting speed and getting the most storage space. RAID 3 and 5 use both striping and mirroring to provide redundancy (for safety) while improving speed.

Fig. 5-19. A RAID is several drives grouped together to improve performance or data integrity. Avid VideoRAID in five-drive tower. (Avid Technology, Inc.)

NETWORKS. There are many situations in which it's helpful for several users to access stored video and audio from different workstations or locations. For example, in a postproduction facility, an editor could be cutting a movie while special effects work is done on the same files, while the sound editor is using the same material to prep for the mix.

Many technologies are used to network computers and storage devices together. A *local area network* or *LAN* can be used to transfer files between systems, and is sometimes fast enough for editing. A *storage area network* or *SAN* is a more versatile and expensive solution that allows multiple users to work from the same files. Apple's Xsan and Avid's Unity systems both use fibre channel and are complex systems requiring expert setup.

The least expensive but often sufficient method is to physically carry portable drives (such as FireWire drives) from machine to machine as needed. This low-tech solution is known affectionately as "sneakernet."

FILE FORMATS AND DATA EXCHANGE

The digital revolution has a lot to do with sharing information between different systems. Something as basic as buying dinner with a credit card means that several computer systems exchange information about who you are, how much you owe, and how to transfer the money from your account to the restaurant's.

The revolution in digital video and postproduction is also fueled by information exchange between systems. And there is a lot of information to be exchanged! For example, a digital video camera doesn't just record the pixels that make up each frame, but also lots of data about things like the frame rate, timecode, audio, and sampling rate. As another example, a digital editing system doesn't simply play one shot after another, but works with all sorts of associated information, including how to color-correct the shots, how to transition from one shot to the next, how loud to play the audio, and what shape the frame should be.

We can divide all this information into two groups. The pictures and sounds themselves are the *media* (sometimes called the *essence*). All the other information about how to play or edit the media, or create effects with it, is called the *metadata*. Metadata is data about data. If making a movie were like baking a cake, the media files would be the ingredients and the metadata would be the recipe.

To make movies, we need ways to transfer both the media and the metadata from a camera to an editing system, from one editing system to another, or from a disc to a video player. There are several file formats that serve as "wrappers" or containers to bundle the media and metadata together to make it easier to work with them.

When you shoot video with a digital camera, the video is compressed with a codec (see Digital Compression, p. 222). For example, you might record using the DV or DVCPRO HD codecs. When you record DV to tape in the camera, the video is stored in raw DV stream files. But when that material is transferred to a hard drive, say for editing, it is usually wrapped inside another file that contains both the media (the DV codec) and the metadata. There are various wrapper formats available. Some are designed to be open exchange formats, allowing you to conveniently transfer media and metadata from one platform to another. Other wrappers are proprietary and work only on certain systems or with certain applications. In some cases, you might have video wrapped in one format, and need to unwrap it and convert to another wrapper format in order to work with it on your system.

Wrappers are used in both production and postproduction. In an ideal world, projects could be edited on any system in any format, then have the video, audio, and metadata wrapped so that the project could be transferred to any other system for display or for further work. That level of universal, seamless interchange is not yet available.

Some Common Wrappers

QUICKTIME. *QuickTime* was developed by Apple but is usable on Macs and PCs. QuickTime is a wrapper format that can contain a number of different codecs, depending on what you're working with, along with many types of metadata. QuickTime is supported by a wide range of players and applications. QuickTime files normally have the extension ".mov." QuickTime Pro, an upgrade from the free software, can be handy for converting media files from one format to another. For the latest developments with QuickTime go to Apple.com.

WINDOWS MEDIA. Microsoft's container format has evolved and had various names, including Video for Windows and Windows Media. Like Apple, Microsoft has built a large media creation and distribution system around Windows Media. Files have the extension ".avi." For more, see Microsoft.com.

MXF. *MXF* (*Material Exchange Format*) is a wrapper used in cameras and editing systems to facilitate transfer of a wide range of media files and metadata from one system to another. MXF files can contain a variety of codecs, including MPEG-2, DV, and DVCPRO HD. As one example, Sony's XDCAM wraps MPEG-2 files in the MXF format and offers the potential to include such metadata as voice notes from the cameraperson, or GPS location information.

AAF AND OMF. *AAF* (*Advanced Authoring Format*) shares many aspects of MXF and is also an open format for exchanging media and metadata between different applications or systems. AAF grew out of an Avid format called *OMFI* (*Open Media Framework Interchange*), which is often referred to just as *OMF*.

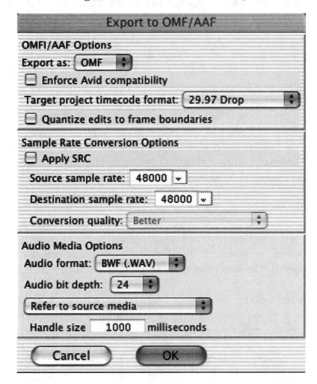

Fig. 5-20. DigiTranslator converts and exchanges OMF, AAF, and MXF audio files, video files, and sequences through Pro Tools. (Digidesign)

AAF is often used in postproduction as a way to transfer project elements such as video, audio, graphics, animation, and effects from one application to another. For example, AAF can be used to export sound files from a nonlinear editing system to a digital audio workstation in preparation for a sound mix. For more on this process, see Chapters 14 and 16.

XML
The *XML Interchange Format* is not a wrapper or a way to move media exactly, but it's a tool used to describe data in one application using plain text so it can easily

be understood by another. Final Cut Pro uses XML, as Apple puts it, "to describe every aspect of a Final Cut Pro project—from clips, bins, and sequences, to edits and transitions, effects, color correction settings and keyframes. Using XML provides an open, transparent, plain text format that anyone can read and manipulate with a wide range of tools." As one example, XML is used to convert audio level settings in an NLE to text that can be understood by an audio editing program. The audio editing program then converts the text to its own system of setting audio levels and, voilà, your audio levels have been preserved as you move on to your mix.

DIGITAL COMPRESSION

See Digital Compression, p. 20, before reading this section.

Though digital compression is a complex topic, the idea behind it is simple: Take some video or audio, use a codec to compress it into a smaller package, then decompress it again when you want to view or hear it. Ideally, after going through this process, the material looks and sounds as good as it did originally.

Starting from the camera's sensor, there is a long chain of events from recording to editing to broadcast. Forms of compression can happen at every stage.[18] One of the first things that happens in most cameras is that the raw RGB data from the sensor is processed into component video, reducing the color information in a way that normally isn't noticeable to the viewer (see Video Color Systems, p. 192). Different formats throw away different amounts of color data.

At this point, we have what's called *uncompressed* or *baseband video*.[19] Uncompressed video uses a lot of data; how much depends on the format (see Appendix B). Uncompressed is the top quality the format is capable of. However, uncompressed video requires so much storage and processing power that it just isn't practical in most digital cameras. Uncompressed video is often used in editing and finishing, however.

To compress the video prior to recording, a codec (compression/decompression algorithm) is used. Some codecs are standardized for an entire format. For example, the DV codec is employed in all DV cameras; no matter which manufacturer made your camera, the video it records should be playable with DV from other cameras (even so, some cameras do a better job of compressing than others). Other codecs are proprietary to one company or a group of companies and, if they're good codecs, are intended to get you to buy that company's gear (for example, you won't find Panasonic's DVCPRO HD on a Sony camera). Codecs can be hardware—a chip for example—or they can exist wholly in software.

Some codecs don't degrade the image at all. With *lossless compression*, you can decompress the video and get a picture that has perfect fidelity to the original before

18. The word compression can have several meanings in film, video and audio. The digital data compression being discussed here should not be confused with compressing audio levels (see p. 649) or video levels (see p. 184).

19. Note that what is called "uncompressed" video has really already been compressed somewhat in the conversion from RGB to component color space, which discards some of the chroma information.

you compressed it. *Lossy compression*, on the other hand, throws away information that can never be restored. In practical use, almost all codecs are lossy but can still look great to viewers. Some codecs can be used at different levels of compression, so the same codec could look very good at a light compression setting, and look worse with heavier compression. If you've worked with digital stills, you may be familiar with the JPEG file format (file names have .jpg extension) which allows you to select how much compression you want: The greater the compression, the smaller the file, and the lower the quality. Several video codecs are based on JPEG.

COMPRESSION METHODS

Different codecs use different techniques to compress video. These are some of the main methods.

Compressing Within a Frame

All codecs compress individual frames. In other words, they take each video frame one at a time, and delete some of the data while trying to preserve image quality.[20] This is called *intraframe compression* or *spatial compression*. Intraframe means "within the frame."

Most intraframe codecs use a process called *DCT* (*discrete cosine transform*). Versions of DCT are used in DV, DVCPRO, DigiBeta, HDCAM, and other formats. Basically, DCT involves analyzing the picture in 8 x 8 blocks of pixels called *macroblocks*. It then uses sophisticated formulas to delete repetitive information and compact the data.

Another intraframe compression process called *wavelet*, used for both video and audio, is gaining popularity. Hollywood's Digital Cinema Initiative adopted wavelet-based JPEG2000 for theatrical distribution partly because any dropouts cause the affected area to turn soft in focus instead of blocky, as DCT codecs do. For production, Grass Valley's Infinity camcorder uses JPEG2000 with MXF file wrappers.

Different codecs compress the data by different amounts. For example, DigiBeta compresses about 2:1; DV uses heavier compression, about 5:1. The more compression, the greater the chance of artifacts, such as the "mosquito noise" that can sometimes be seen in DV images as dark or light pixels around sharp edges and text.

With intraframe compression, each frame stands on its own, independent of the others. This speeds up the compression/decompression process, and makes editing much simpler. However, intraframe compression alone creates files that are larger than if interframe compression is also used (see below).

Compressing a Group of Frames

Video images can be thought of as existing in three dimensions. Two of them are in space: the horizontal and vertical dimensions of the frame. The third dimension

---

20. With interlaced formats, this may be done on a field-by-field instead of a frame-by-frame basis. DV uses adaptive *interfield* compression: If little difference is detected between two interlaced fields in a frame, the DV codec will compress them together as if they were progressive to save bits.

is time. The intraframe compression we just looked at compresses data in the first two dimensions. *Interframe compression* analyzes a string of frames over time and finds ways to delete repetitive information from one to the next (interframe meaning "between frames"). This method is also called *temporal* (relating to time) *compression.*

To get the idea of interframe compression, try looking at some video footage in slow motion. You'll notice that very often, not much changes from frame to frame. An extreme example is a "locked off" (nonmoving) shot of an empty, windowless room. You could shoot for an hour and the first frame you recorded and the thousands that follow would be identical. Rather than record each of these individually, we could save a lot of space if we could somehow record just one frame with instructions to keep repeating it for an hour.

Obviously, most video footage has some movement, and some has a great deal, so we can't just repeat frames. However, codecs that use interframe compression look for anything that stays the same from frame to frame—even if it moves somewhat—and finds ways to reuse the data it already has stored rather than trying to store a whole new frame every time. Interframe compression works by looking at a group of frames together (referred to as a *Group of Pictures* or *GOP*). The first frame in the group is recorded normally. But for several of the frames that follow, instead of storing a whole picture, the codec only records the *differences* between the frame and its neighboring frames. Recording only the differences between frames takes a lot less data than recording the actual frames themselves.

MPEG-2 is a very widely used interframe codec. MPEG-2 is the basis for an impressive number of production, distribution, and transmission formats, including HDV, XDCAM, DVDs, cable TV, digital satellite, and ATSC broadcasting.

In MPEG-2, each GOP has three types of frames (see Fig. 5-21).

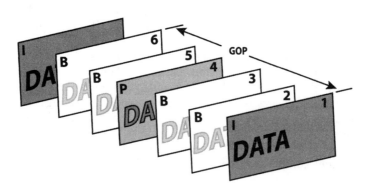

Fig. 5-21. Interframe compression means compressing several frames in a group (a *Group of Pictures* or GOP). Only the I-frame is independently stored; the P- and B-frames are calculated based on neighboring frames. The P-frame has about half as much data as the I-frame and the B-frames have one quarter; compared to I-frames, they require more computing time to generate or view them. Pictured here is a six-frame GOP used in the 720p version of HDV. The 1080i version uses a 15 frame "long GOP." The longer the GOP, the greater the compression, and the more computing time and power that's required to work with the material.

- *I-frames* (*Intra-frames*) are independent frames that get fully recorded. I-frames are compressed using intraframe compression as described above. I-frames can be thought of as solid anchors that begin each GOP. They can be reproduced by themselves without reference to any other frames.
- *P-frames* (*Predicted frames*). P-frames have about half as much information as an I-frame. The P-frame contains only the differences between itself and the previous I-frame or P-frame. In playback, the codec uses those instructions to rebuild what the P-frame should look like.
- *B-frames* (*Bi-directionally predicted frames*). B-frames have about one-fourth the information of an I-frame. A B-frame is made up of the differences between I- or P-frames that come before *and* after (sometimes B-frames are called "between frames"). This is done by storing a group of frames in memory, making all the calculations, then outputting the frames and instructions in proper order.

Different MPEG-2 formats use a different length GOP. The length of the GOP impacts how the compressor handles motion and complexity: the longer the GOP, the more you can compress the data, but that means more processing power to keep up with the calculations. The 720p version of HDV, for instance, uses a 6-frame GOP; the 1080i version uses a longer, 15-frame GOP.

As a filmmaker, what does all this mean for you? Well, the upside of interframe compression is that it results in more efficient compression and more convenient storage. It makes a low-cost HD format like HDV possible in the first place.

The downside is that it can create problems in shooting, editing and distribution. Different versions of MPEG-2 and other codecs that use interframe compression behave differently, so these problems may or may not apply to the system you're using. But it helps to understand some of the potential underlying issues, discussed below.

SHOOTING AND EDITING WITH MPEG-2 AND OTHER INTER-FRAME CODECS. In shooting, problems may result from the way MPEG-2 handles footage that has a lot of complexity or action. As discussed, the codec is always looking for redundancy (repetition) between frames. When things don't change much (remember the locked off shot of the room?) the codec has very little to do. But when things change a lot, the compressor can get overwhelmed by all the data (the more change, the harder it is for the codec to generate all those P- and B-frames). A shot that has a lot of detail and motion—for example, a tree branch with fluttering leaves or a wide-shot of a stadium full of cheering fans—could cause the picture to momentarily break up into blocky, noisy artifacts. On the whole, though, HDV makes very respectable HD images with few conspicuous flaws, which is why it has quickly become so popular.

In editing, a long GOP creates other challenges. In a certain sense, the P- and B-frames don't fully exist (at least they aren't completely stored); they have to be generated every time you want to look at one. This puts a lot of demand on the editing system when you view or edit individual frames. If you make a cut *within* a group of pictures, the system has to insert a new I-frame and build a new sequence of I-, P- and B-frames before the footage can be output (you can't start a GOP with just P- and B-frames; you always need an I-frame to begin the group).

However, while the editing of a long-GOP MPEG-2 is not as straightforward as intraframe formats such as DV, popular NLEs (including Final Cut Pro HD and others) have demonstrated that "native" HDV editing is readily accomplished. Final Cut Pro HD, for example, uncompresses HDV on the fly to provide live HD for desktop display in the viewer and canvas, and nearly simultaneously recompresses the same HD back to HDV as it passes the playhead. This enables real-time viewing and editing (but not viewing on an external broadcast video monitor without a converter).

The problem arises when you've edited your 1080i HDV movie and you're ready to export it from the NLE. To export as HDV, Final Cut Pro HD must first reestablish the 15-frame GOP structure along the entire length of the project. Depending upon the muscle of your Mac's CPU and the amount of RAM you have, this begins a rendering process (also called *conforming*) that can take hours if not days if the work is of feature length or contains many effects layers. Heaven forbid you have a crash in the meantime.

There are several work-arounds to this obstacle. Matrox makes a small adapter box called MXO that accepts the DVI signal ordinarily sent directly to the computer monitor and converts it on the fly to HD-SDI, analog HD, or downconverted SD via SDI. In other words, with MXO all you have to do to get real-time uncompressed HD or SD output without massive rendering is to hook up an HD or SD recorder to the converted DVI output. Almost too good to be true.

Fig. 5-22. Matrox MXO. The output adaptor in the foreground connects to the DVI output of a Mac to provide real-time HD-SDI from an HDV timeline without rendering. Also provides hardware acceleration of HDV and DVCPRO HD effects and real-time HD to SD downconversion. (Matrox Electronic Systems, Ltd.)

The second work-around is to avoid editing HDV altogether. (See What Format or Resolution to Edit In?, p. 516.) This work-around can take two paths. You can ingest long-GOP HDV into your NLE, then transcode it into an intraframe format such as DVCPRO HD for simpler editing and output. This will consume roughly four times the disk space, but may be well worth it. Side benefits include conversion of HDV's 4:2:0 color sampling to 4:2:2 and conversion of lossy MPEG-1 Audio Layer II to lossless PCM audio. After rendering any effects, further rendering of DVCPRO HD for output is not necessary.

Another method is that, upon ingest, you can transcode HDV to any of a number of "intermediate codecs" designed as I-frame substitutes for MPEG-2 long-GOP formats. As discussed on p. 522, intermediate codecs provide nearly lossless conversion from lower or higher data rate formats and produce excellent results on screen. Alongside Apple's own Apple Intermediate Codec for Final Cut Pro HD, CineForm has introduced excellent intermediate codecs. Apple's ProRes 422 is another I-frame codec for editing and finishing.

HDV was the first interframe, long-GOP MPEG-2 format used in camcorders—a sort of proof of concept, if you will. In the beginning, long-GOP MPEG-2 was poorly understood and rumors flew that dropouts in 1080i HDV would destroy 15 frames (half a second) of video. What proved to be the actual case, instead, is that MPEG 2's long-GOP structure spreads data from 15 frames over the span of each GOP in such a way that individual dropouts cause significantly *less* impact than they do on a single frame of DV. So following on the solid success of HDV are newer long-GOP MPEG formats like XDCAM HD and the disc-based AVCHD, both of which employ similar GOP lengths to HDV.

Compared to HDV, the intraframe compressions used in formats such as DV and DigiBeta are very simple and straightforward. They only have I-frames, and their codecs make no attempt to take into account what happens before or after each frame. They're also longer in the tooth, dating back further in time. MPEG codecs are more sophisticated and therefore more efficient. So is there a way to have our cake and eat it too? The answer is that there are indeed forms of MPEG-2 (including Sony's 50 Mbps MPEG IMX) and MPEG-4 (such as Panasonic's AVC-Intra for P2) that use a one-frame GOP, which is sometimes called *I-frame only*. The advantages of I-frame only include fewer artifacts and much simpler editing and processing. H.264, part of the MPEG-4 standard, is considered to be twice as efficient as DV, taking up half the storage for the same quality of image, even in I-frame-only mode (see AVCHD and AVC-Intra, p. 32).

Constant and Variable Bit Rates

We've seen that shots with a lot of detail or motion require more data to process than ones that are relatively simple or static. With some codecs, the same amount of data is recorded for every frame, regardless of how complex it is. For example, the data rate of DV is 25 Mbps no matter what you're recording. This is a *constant bit rate (CBR)* format.

Some formats, however, allow for a higher data rate on shots that are complex or active, and reduce the data rate for scenes that are less demanding. These are *variable bit rate (VBR)* formats. VBR encoding is more efficient: it provides more data when you need it, less when you don't. It can result in fewer artifacts and smaller file sizes. The problem with VBR is that it requires more processing power and time to accomplish. In postproduction (for example, when creating DVDs) VBR compression is sometimes done in a two-pass process: in the first pass, the system analyzes the entire movie to gauge where high and low data rates are called for; in the second pass the codec actually does the compressing.

An interesting example of a camcorder design that exploits both CBR and VBR is found in Sony's XDCAM HD camcorders, the PDW-F330 and PDW-F350, which record 1080i/60 and 1080p/24 using long-GOP MPEG-2 with a choice of

18 Mbps (variable), 25Mbps (constant, functionally equivalent to HDV), and 35 Mbps (variable).

A FEW COMMON CODECS

There are numerous codecs, and new ones are always being developed. Some are employed in camera formats, some are used primarily in editing, and others are used mostly for distribution. Some codecs are used in all three areas.

See Comparing Video Formats, p. 23, for camera formats and the codecs they employ, including DV, DVCPRO, DVCPRO HD, HDV, and others. Below are just a few other codecs used in video production and postproduction.

MPEG-2

MPEG-2 has been around since the early 1990s and is still widely used. (See Compressing a Group of Frames, above, for a basic idea of how MPEG-2 compression works.) MPEG-2 provides superb picture quality, all the way up to HD, and supports widescreen. It comes in a number of flavors (there are different *profiles*, each of which have various *levels*) which may behave differently and may not be compatible (a system that can play one may not be able to play another). As mentioned above, it is the codec used in standard definition DVDs and is also one of three mandatory codecs for both HD-DVD and Blu-ray. It is used extensively in digital broadcasting and cable.

Several camera systems use MPEG-2 for HD. Some offer a choice of data rates/quality levels. HDV cameras use a form called MPEG-2 TS (*transport stream*). This allows for a lot of compression but makes real-time editing difficult, and results in lowered quality if the material has to be compressed a second time. Sony's XDCAM HD cameras record another form, MPEG-2 ES (*elementary stream*).

H.264

H.264 is a newer codec that's making a big splash. Also known as *AVC* and *MPEG-4, Part 10*, this codec is twice as efficient as MPEG-2 (which means you can get the same quality at up to half the data) and will likely replace MPEG-2 in many applications. H.264 is very *scalable*, which means you can use the same codec for high-quality needs like HD projection and for very low-resolution cell phones. H.264 does require considerable processing power to encode, which means much computing time to create the compressed files. H.264 was originally viewed as a delivery codec (used for distribution) and is supported by many newer systems, including digital broadcasting and QuickTime. It is also one of the three mandatory codecs for both HD-DVD and Blu-ray. To take advantage of H.264's doubled efficiency, Panasonic created an I-frame-only version which they call "AVC-Intra," for use with their P2 cards as an alternative to DVCPRO HD (see p. 32 for more on AVC-Intra and AVCHD).

Windows Media Video

VC-1, standardized as SMPTE 421M, is the codec used in Microsoft's *WMV* (*Windows Media Video*). As of this writing, *Windows Media 9* is the most recent version of their media player system. VC-1 is a competitor to H.264 and offers many of the same advantages. It, too, is very scalable and can be used for high- and low-quality applications. VC-1 is one of the three mandatory codecs for both HD-DVD and Blu-ray.

Avid DNxHD

Avid introduced DNxHD compression as a free "open standard" in 2004 to allow HD to fit more easily within an SD environment. Uncompressed 10-bit SD requires about 200 Mbps. By comparison, DNxHD supports high definition at 220 Mbps for 10 bit (6:1 compression) or 8 bit (4:1 compression) 720p/60, 1080i/60, or 1080p/24p. It also supports 145 Mbps HD at 8 bit and a low data-rate 36 Mbps HD version for offline editing. All within a standard MXF file wrapper and available across the entire line of Avid editing products. On the camcorder side, Ikegami's HD Editcam uses DNxHD for lossless 2:1 compression and can capture more than an hour of 1920 x 1080 HD at 24p with a 120 GB FieldPak2 hard disk.

Apple ProRes422

Apple has introduced ProRes 422 compression for editing with Final Cut Pro HD. It provides a very high-quality HD image at data rates lower than uncompressed SD. It supports SD and full-resolution HD (both 1920 x 1080 and 1280 x 720) at 4:2:2 color sampling with 10-bit precision. ProRes 422 is an I-frame only codec with variable bit-rate encoding for efficient editing. Normal quality is targeted at 145 Mbps, and there is a high-quality (HQ) version at 220 Mbps. This codec can be used to streamline editing of long-GOP formats like HDV and XDCAM HD. Apple is positioning it as a kind of universal codec into which many other formats can be converted for editing and finishing.

JPEG2000

In 2005 Grass Valley's Infinity camcorder introduced wavelet-based intraframe JPEG2000 to production. Using MXF file wrappers, Infinity generates .j2k bit streams at 25, 50, 75, or 100 Mbps, which it records to removable Iomega REV PRO hard drives (see Fig. 1-24). As described above, JPEG2000 is the same compression adopted by Hollywood's Digital Cinema Initiative for theatrical projection. This compression is very new and people don't have a lot of practical experience with it as yet, but many find it extremely promising.

CineForm Intermediate

CineForm is a young company that makes basically one product: variations of the CineForm Intermediate codec, a wavelet-based "digital intermediate" codec that lends itself to efficient compression of high-end HD, 2K, and 4K moving images. It is software-based and compatible with Adobe Premiere Pro 2.0, Sony Vegas, and Final Cut Pro HD. CineForm Intermediate is used in the Wafian hard disk recorder (see Fig. 2-7). CineForm created the first real-time HDV editing and later introduced CineForm RAW for Digital Cinematography cameras with a large single sensor and a Bayer pattern filter for color, which generate 2K or 4K RAW files. CineForm enjoys a reputation for first-rate codecs.

CHAPTER 6

The Film Camera

An Overview of the Camera

The motion picture camera has the following components:

Fig. 6-1. Arriflex 16mm BL. The film chamber door and magazine lid are open to reveal the film path. The feed roll is 400 feet of core-loaded film. The pressure plate is open to show the film gate. The camera has a mirror shutter for reflex viewing. (Arriflex Corporation)

1. *The lens:* focuses light from the world onto the film.
2. *The lens mount:* receptacle where the lens is attached to the camera (see Chapter 3 for the lens and lens mount).
3. *The viewfinder:* allows the camera operator to see what image is being recorded on the film.

4. *The film chamber:* a light-tight compartment that holds the film before and after it is exposed to light. Many cameras use a detachable magazine to hold the film.

5. *The motor:* supplies the power to run the film past the lens for exposure.

6. *The film gate and claw:* The claw pulls down each frame of film for exposure and holds it steady in the film gate during exposure.

7. *The shutter:* blocks light from the film when it is moving between successive exposures.

The unexposed film (*raw stock*) is loaded into the camera from the *supply* or *feed reel*. The film passes through the film gate for exposure and is spooled on the *take-up reel*.

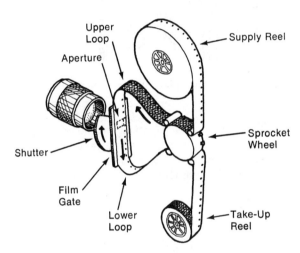

Fig. 6-2. Simplified camera. (Carol Keller)

THE FILM GATE AND SHUTTER

The Film Gate

In the *film gate*, the raw stock is exposed to light that comes through the lens. The gate is composed of two plates that sandwich the film. The plate between the lens and the film is the *aperture plate*. The *aperture* itself is a rectangle cut out of the aperture plate, through which light from the lens shines. The aperture's edges define the border of the image on the film. The base of the film rests on the other half of the gate, the *pressure plate*, which holds the film flat during exposure. Super 8 cartridges and some quick-change magazines (see Camera Film Capacity, p. 242) have a built-in pressure plate that is not part of the camera's body.

THE CLAW. Most cameras and projectors have a *claw* or *shuttle* that advances the film, frame by frame, in the gate. The claw engages a perforation in the film and pulls the film forward one frame (the *pulldown*). After exposure, the claw engages the next frame and pulls it down (see Fig. 1-33).

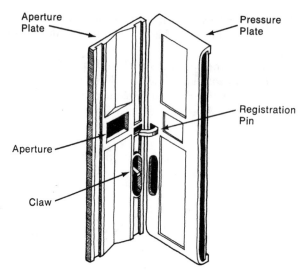

Fig. 6-3. Film gate with open pressure plate. Not all cameras use registration pins. (Carol Keller)

It's critical that the film be held *absolutely* steady in the gate or else the image will not be steady when projected on screen. Some cameras have a *registration pin* to help ensure steadiness during exposure. The pin enters a perforation while the film is stopped in the gate and holds it motionless.

THE INTERMITTENT. The claw is on an *intermittent* (that is, a noncontinuous or stop-start) movement that allows the film alternately to stop in front of the aperture and then to move on. Since the film roll is moving continuously through the camera, there must be some slack between the intermittent claw and the constantly moving feed and take-up reels to prevent the film from tearing. On most cameras and projectors, *loops* are formed between the film gate and the *sprocket wheel*—which drives the film—to provide the needed slack.

Loops must be accurately formed. If they're too small, the film may tear or chatter. When a camera jams, it usually "loses its loop." If the loops are too large, they may rub against the camera housing and scratch the film. See your camera's manual for proper loop size.

The Shutter

After each frame of film is exposed to light coming through the lens, the shutter must close to block the light while the next frame moves into position in the gate. The film must be completely at rest before the shutter opens again for the next exposure. If the shutter does not block the light when the film is moving, the image will be blurred. The simplest kind of shutter is a rotating disc with a section removed.

A circle may be represented by 360 degrees. The shutter opening is the number of degrees open in the disc. The 180-degree shutter, a half-moon in shape, is used in many cameras, particularly in 16mm.

SHUTTER SPEED AND EXPOSURE. *Exposure* is determined by two elements: the intensity of light that passes through the lens and the time each frame is exposed to the light. The reciprocity law simply says: Exposure = Intensity × Time. Doubling exposure time is equivalent to doubling intensity. The halving and doubling of light intensity are measured in *stops* (see Chapter 4). If you close down the lens by one stop, you must double the time of exposure to keep exposure constant.

Standard film speed is 24 frames per second (fps). A camera with a 180-degree shutter admits light to the film half the time (the disc is half open) so the exposure time (the shutter speed) is $\frac{1}{24}$ x $\frac{1}{2}$ = $\frac{1}{48}$ second (which we usually round off to $\frac{1}{50}$ second). As a rule of thumb, most film cameras have a shutter speed of about $\frac{1}{50}$ second when operated at 24 fps, but check your camera to determine the angle of its shutter opening. The general formula for any shutter opening and camera speed is:

$$\text{Exposure time (shutter speed)} = \left(\frac{1}{\text{speed in fps}}\right) \times \left(\frac{\text{angle of shutter opening}}{360}\right)$$

For shutter openings less than 180 degrees, the shutter speed is faster than $\frac{1}{50}$ second. For example, a 135-degree shutter at 24 fps yields a shutter speed of $\frac{1}{24}$ x $\frac{135}{360}$ = $\frac{1}{64}$ (approximately $\frac{1}{65}$ second).

In general, longer exposure times have advantages: They decrease the possibility of judder (see p. 361) and they mean that less light is needed for proper exposure. However, if the exposure time is very long, there will be excessive motion blur in the image (see Fig. 2-17).

THE VARIABLE SHUTTER. On cameras equipped with a *variable shutter*, the shutter angle can be narrowed to change the shutter speed. Narrowing the angle reduces exposure time. A 90-degree shutter, for example, gives a shutter speed of about $\frac{1}{100}$ at 24 fps (using the formula just given for shutter speed). Closing the shutter reduces the exposure, allowing high-speed film to be used outdoors or allowing the lens to be opened to decrease depth of field or to shoot at a selected *f*-stop (see Chapter 4).

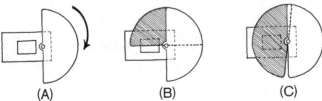

(A)   (B)   (C)

Fig. 6-4. Variable shutter. (A) A 180-degree shutter shown fully open. The small rectangle represents the aperture. (B) To close the shutter, an adjustable disc (shaded) swings out; shown here, it forms a 90-degree opening. (C) The shutter is almost completely closed. (Carol Keller)

A variable shutter that can be closed down while the camera is running allows exposure changes in the middle of a shot. For example, when the camera moves from a sunlit to a shaded area within a shot, it's often necessary to change exposure.

The iris diaphragm of the lens can be changed, but this would change the depth of field and may be more noticeable than shutting down the variable shutter. If the variable shutter can be shut down continuously to 0 degrees with the camera running, in-camera fades and dissolves can be created. If variable shutters are used for exposure control, you risk judder in the image if there is a great deal of camera or subject movement (see p. 361). On cameras with a variable shutter, always check that the shutter is properly set before every day's shooting. If someone else has used the camera, the shutter opening may have been narrowed.

CAMERA SPEED AND MOTORS

The first cameras were cranked by hand. The camera operator would hum a popular song of an appropriate tempo to approximate the filming speed. On modern cameras, either a spring-wound or electric motor drives the film through the camera and controls the rate at which the film moves.

Standard Speed

Standard worldwide theatrical film projection speed is 24 fps, and unless special effects are desired, it is assumed that the standard running speed of a film camera is also 24 fps (also known as *sound speed*). However, as the filmmaking world has become more complex, there are certain situations in which 24 fps is not used as the basic speed.

Fig. 6-5. Speed control on Beaulieu cine 8 camera. (Pro8mm, Inc.)

1. In Europe and other places where PAL video has been standard, film footage intended primarily for transfer to video is shot at 25 fps to match the video frame rate (see Chapter 15). Even theatrical films may be filmed at 25 fps to simplify postproduction; however European theatrical film projection is typically 24 fps.
2. Film is sometimes shot at 23.976 fps. This is 0.1 percent slower than standard 24 fps and matches the video "24p" rate in NTSC countries. This may

be used to simplify video postproduction on a film project, or when the film footage needs to keep sync with a video camera, or sometimes when filming music videos to maintain sync with prerecorded music (see p. 428). This speed is sometimes also used for filming video monitors (see Chapter 18).

3. In NTSC countries, film is sometimes shot at 29.976 fps. This may be done when filming TV monitors. Filming at 29.97 or 30 fps is occasionally done for footage intended for video transfer as a way to increase the clarity of the image, especially if the video will be run in slow motion or be freeze-framed. If you shoot at 29.97 or 30 fps and don't transfer to video at that rate, motion will be slowed down.

4. Certain camera speeds can cause problems with some HMI, fluorescent, and other discharge-type lighting (see p. 452).

When the *camera speed* (or *frame rate*) matches the projection speed, movement on the screen looks natural. When the camera speed increases, more frames are filmed each second. When film shot at high speed (say, 40 fps) is projected at the normal speed (24 fps), action is slowed down (*slow motion*). Conversely, if you film at a slower speed, say 8 fps, and then project at normal speed, movement is sped up—in this case, three times as fast.

When you change camera speed, you need to make an exposure compensation, since the exposure time is different. Consult a frame-rate/exposure chart or use the formula for shutter speed specified above. In general, if you double the frame rate, you lose a stop of exposure, so compensate by opening the lens one stop. If you cut the frame rate in half, close the lens by a stop.

For a discussion of slow motion and time-lapse shooting, see p. 357.

Camera Motors

Most cameras today have electric motors powered primarily by rechargeable batteries (see Batteries and Power Supplies, p. 130).

In order to be used for sync sound filming (see p. 54), the speed of the camera must be very precisely controlled. Most modern cameras used for sound work are equipped with crystal-controlled motors, which use a very stable crystal oscillator to ensure accuracy. These cameras drift in speed less than one frame in several hours, longer than any roll of film. Some cameras have precise crystal control over a wide range of speeds. Others are crystal at 24 or 25 fps and are less precise at other speeds. Some older cameras have governor-controlled motors, which are not as accurate; these can sometimes be used with a cable between camera and sound recorder, or can sometimes be retrofitted with a crystal.

Some cameras are not intended for sound work. Sometimes called MOS or *wild cameras*, nonsync cameras may have variable-speed motors or governor motors. These cameras are often small, light, and noisy. Some wild and sync cameras can be run in reverse for reverse motion shots, for example, when spilled water appears to be sucked back into its container. This effect can also be achieved by shooting double-perf film with the camera upside down. In the latter case, to reverse the motion, project the film tails out (that is, the last frame first).

Some nonsync cameras use spring-wound motors, which are wound by hand prior to the shot. Their chief disadvantage is that they run out of power after about

(A)

Fig. 6-6. (A) Bolex H16 Reflex 16mm camera. Beam-splitter reflex with nondivergent lens turret. Shown here with zoom lens and automatic exposure system. Spring-wound motor capable of single-frame operation. This camera accepts 100-foot internal loads or an external magazine. It has a 135-degree variable shutter. (B) Bolex H16 EBM 16mm camera. An electric motor runs the camera. Pictured here with accessory pistol grip and 400-foot detachable magazine, it also will take 100-foot internal loads. 170-degree fixed shutter. (Bolex)

(B)

a thirty-second shot. These are very light and low cost. They need no batteries and are safer in explosive environments since they are less likely to produce a spark.

SPEED CONTROLS AND INDICATORS. Many cameras can be fitted with an external speed control to allow precise speed selection over a wide range of speeds (see Fig. 9-28). Most crystal cameras have a warning system when the camera is not holding crystal speed. You can also get an external speed-checking device, such as the Cine Check. Some wild cameras have tachometers to indicate approximate speed. To determine its accuracy, use a speed checker, or run a premeasured length of film through the camera and time it with a stopwatch.

VIEWING SYSTEMS

The *viewfinder* allows you to see what is being recorded on film. Most modern cameras use a *reflex viewfinder*, which allows you to see through the lens (the *taking* lens). Some older or lower-cost cameras employ a *nonreflex viewfinder* that is separate from the taking lens. These generally give a less accurate representation of what is being filmed. Some cameras have no viewfinder at all and rely on finders attached to the lens. The oldest-style reflex system was found in 35mm where the camera operator, his head covered by a dark cloth, viewed a dim image through the back of the film.

THE REFLEX VIEWFINDER

Modern reflex cameras divert light coming through the lens to a viewfinder where the image is projected on a *viewing screen*. Many newer cameras have *fiber-optic viewing screens*, which use a bundle of glass fibers to bring the image to the viewfinder. Fiber-optic screens are bright and allow you to see if the image is properly focused across the whole image.

Some cameras use a *ground-glass viewing screen*. Ground-glass screens are generally darker than fiber-optic screens, especially when the lens is stopped down (see Chapter 4). *Aerial image* systems often have a clear viewing screen with a circle in the center of the image for focusing (see Fig. 6-7). The central disc may be a ground-glass or a range finder. *Range finders* are usually *split image* or *microprism*: In the former, you focus by aligning the two parts of the image; in the latter, you focus by making the texture of the microprism disappear. Center-focusing viewfinders have disadvantages compared to viewing screens that show focus across the whole image. First, the viewfinder gives no impression of depth of field. Also, you may need to focus on a point that is not in the center of the frame, so changing focus in the middle of a shot can be difficult.

Composition in the Viewfinder

Most viewfinders are marked for the standard *projector aperture*, which is a slightly smaller frame than the *camera aperture* (which is the entire frame that is actually recorded on film). The difference between the two is significant only in very

Sound Recording Level   Battery Test   End of Film Indicator

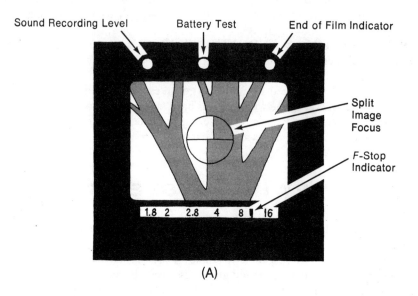

(A)

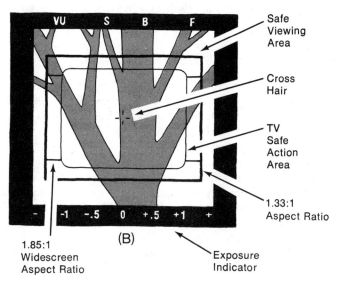

Fig. 6-7. Viewfinder screens. (A) An aerial image typical of Super 8 reflex cameras. The split-image range finder here shows that the image is out of focus. (B) A ground glass typical of 16mm cameras. Note the safe viewing area, which provides warning of things just outside the frame. Horizontal marks near the edge of the frame indicate top and bottom frame lines when shooting for 1.85:1 widescreen aspect ratio. Viewfinders sometimes have indicators for lens aperture, out-of-sync warning, and end-of-film warning. On some 35mm cameras, the viewfinder includes a magnification system to enlarge the frame for critical focusing, and a lens to unsqueeze an anamorphic image. (Carol Keller)

detailed work. Some viewfinders display an area that is even larger than the camera aperture and give you advance warning when objects, such as the microphone boom, are about to enter the frame, which is very helpful. Because video monitors usually cut off the edges of the full image, many viewfinders are etched with a TV safe action area (see Fig. 9-10). See p. 331 for more on TV cutoff and working with widescreen formats.

The Mirror Shutter

In some cameras, light is diverted from the lens to the viewfinder screen by a *mirror shutter*. The mirror, either part of the shutter itself or rotating in synchronization with it, alternately allows all the light to hit the film, and then, when the shutter is closed, all the light to go to the viewfinder (see Fig. 6-8). One advantage of a mirror shutter system is that when each frame of film is exposed, no light is lost to the viewfinder, so in critical low-light situations you have as much exposure as possible. One disadvantage of mirror shutters is that when the camera is running, the viewfinder image flickers, since light only goes to the viewfinder about half the time. On better-designed systems, the finder is brighter and the flicker less annoying.

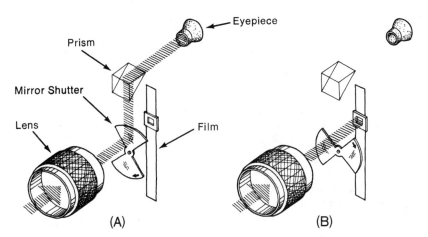

Fig. 6-8. Mirror shutter. (A) With the shutter closed, all the light is diverted to the viewfinder. (A) With the shutter open, all the light strikes the film and exposes it. Compare with Fig. 6-9. (Carol Keller)

One paradox of the mirror shutter is that you see an image in the viewfinder when the shutter is closed, but the viewfinder image goes dark when each frame of film is actually exposed. In some situations this can be misleading. For example, if you film a gunshot and see the flash of the gun in the viewfinder, it may not actually appear on film. Systems are available to synchronize gun triggers to the camera shutter. If you film under strobe lights—at a dance, for example—the flashes you see in the viewfinder are exactly the ones that will *not* be photographed. Some strobing rates read well on film (for example, those around ten to fifteen flashes per second). If the rate is too slow, there may not be enough frames exposed; if the rate is too fast, too many frames will be exposed and the strobing effect may be lost.

Beam-Splitter Reflex

In an alternate design for reflex viewing, a partially reflecting mirror (*pellicule*) or a prism with a partially reflecting mirror (*beam-splitter*) in the light path diverts some of the light to the viewfinder, letting the balance hit the film (see Fig. 6-9). This system is used in most Super 8 cameras. Anywhere from one third of a stop to a full stop of light (depending on the camera) goes to the finder and does not contribute to exposing the film. This avoids flicker, but the exposure loss can be serious in low-light filming. If the prism is in the camera body, an exposure compensation for the light loss is usually made by altering the shutter speed used for exposure calculation. For example, some 16mm Bolex cameras have 135-degree shutters (⅟₆₅ second at 24 fps), but the Bolex manual suggests that an exposure compensation be made by using an "effective" shutter speed of ⅟₈₀ second with your light meter. In Super 8 cameras with built-in light meters, the exposure compensation is made automatically (see Chapter 7).

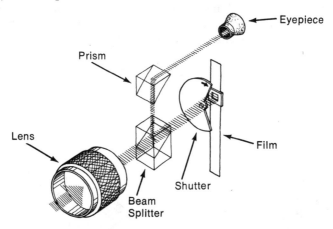

Fig. 6-9. Beam-splitter reflex. Some light is always diverted to the viewfinder, making it unavailable for exposing the film. The beam-splitter prism may be internal to a zoom lens or may be part of the camera. (Carol Keller)

Because of the light loss, the beam-splitter reflex is rarely found in new 16mm and 35mm equipment.

The Diopter Adjustment

The viewfinder eyepiece on reflex cameras can correct for the cameraperson's near- or farsightedness. Make sure the *diopter* adjustment on the eyepiece is adjusted every time someone new uses the camera. The diopter does not affect the actual focus of the image on film, but it does affect your ability to see if the image is in focus.

If your system has a ground-glass, partial ground-glass or fiber-optic screen (most 16mm and 35mm cameras do), adjust the diopter as follows: Remove the lens or open the iris diaphragm on the lens. Point the camera at a bright area; the sky or a bright wall will do. (If viewing through a lens, throw the image out of focus as much as possible.) Rotate the eyepiece *diopter adjustment ring* (on some finders it is a push-pull) until the grains of the ground-glass (on fiber-optic screens use the etched frame line) are as sharp as possible. If there is a locking device, lock the setting in place. The eyepiece is now adjusted.

On reflex cameras that have an aerial image in place of a ground-glass (many Super 8 cameras), the diopter adjustment is more critical, since you are calibrating the focusing system. To adjust this system: Zoom the lens out to the longest focal length, open the lens aperture wide, and focus the lens at infinity. Find a distant object that you can focus on (like a building far away) and focus the eyepiece until the object is as sharp as possible. Lock the adjustment and the eyepiece is adjusted.

If you wear eyeglasses while shooting, adjust the diopter with your glasses on. Wearing eyeglasses during shooting makes it difficult, if not impossible, to see the whole viewfinder image. If possible, adjust the diopter for your eyes without glasses or wear contact lenses. If the camera's diopter adjustment is not strong enough to correct your eyesight, a correction lens can be mounted in some eyepieces.

The Eyepiece

To prevent stray light from entering the eyepiece and traveling through the reflex system in reverse and fogging the film, viewfinders have light traps that shut light off from the finder. During filming, your eye usually seals off stray light. When you are filming without looking through the viewfinder, close the light trap or place something against the eyepiece. This problem is most serious with beam-splitter systems, especially if there is a light source behind the camera. On some cameras, the light trap can be set so that it opens when you press your eye up against the eyepiece and closes when there is no pressure on the eyepiece.

Some cameras have illuminated viewfinders that highlight the frame line, which can be a boon for shooting dark scenes. Condensation from your breath on a cold day can be a real problem. Some cameras offer heated viewfinders. Some people apply a little anti-condensation coating to the viewfinder (never use this on the taking lens).

The eyepiece is usually fitted with a rubber eyecup that cushions the eye (or eyeglasses) and helps seal out stray light. A foam or chamois cover will make it more comfortable. Covers get lost and dirty, so carry spares.

Reflex Viewfinder Placement

Most camera designs favor right-eyed viewing, but some finders can extend out for left-eyed viewing. Test yourself to see if you favor one eye over the other. With both eyes open, point at an object. Then alternately close your left and right eye. The favored eye's vision will correspond best to that of both eyes. Although most people are right-eyed, this group does not seem to comprise as large a majority as right-handed people do. Try to cultivate viewing with your right eye, as many viewfinding systems will permit only right-eyed viewing. Also, right-eyed viewing on most cameras provides a less restricted view of the surroundings. Documentary filmmakers often develop the ability to look through the viewfinder with the right eye, keeping the left eye open to see what is happening outside the frame.

For tripod- or dolly-mounted cameras, use a viewfinder that extends to the back of the camera (see Fig. 4-13). For shoulder-mounted camera rigs, the ideal position of the viewfinder is close to the film plane (*zero finder*), since this generally allows the camera to be optimally balanced. Cameras used in both tripod and handheld work should ideally have interchangeable finders.

Some viewfinders swivel for viewing in awkward positions—for example, if you are kneeling on one knee with the camera on the other or if the camera is pointed backward over your shoulder. Orientable finders (also called dovetail or erect image finders) maintain an upright image even when the finder is rotated (see Fig. 8-9).

CAMERA FILM CAPACITY

Magazines

Some small cameras are designed to be used with film loaded on spools that mount inside the camera body. But most cameras use *magazines* (*mags*), which are detachable film chambers (see Figs. 6-1 and 6-11). The standard 16mm magazine is 400 feet, which runs 11 minutes at 24 fps (36 feet per minute). Some 16mm cameras accommodate 200- or 1200-feet mags. Aaton makes an 800-foot mag that accommodates 800-foot film rolls. In 35mm, a 1000-foot mag holds about 10 minutes of film (35mm runs at 96 feet per minute). Some 35mm cameras have 200-, 400-, 500-foot or other size magazines. Large-capacity mags weigh more but allow more shooting between reloads.

Fig. 6-10. Aaton 35-III. Hand-holdable 35mm camera with quick-change magazines. (AbelCineTech)

Some magazines, like Mitchell mags, mount on top of the camera and are made up of a feed compartment in front of a take-up compartment. A variant of this is called a displacement magazine, like the 400-foot mag for the Arriflex 16 BL (see Fig. 6-1). Here the feed and take-up are together in one smaller chamber. *Coaxial magazines* often mount behind the camera body and have the feed and take-up

Fig. 6-11. Magazine for Aaton 35-III camera is open, showing feed and take-up in same compartment. (AbelCineTech)

chambers side by side (see Fig. 4-13). Coaxial mags have the advantage of being lower profile for shooting in tight spaces and they don't change the camera's balance as the load moves through the camera, which can be an advantage for Steadicam work. Generally, if the magazine has separate compartments for feed and take-up, this facilitates threading, unloading partial rolls, and dealing with problems.

In *quick-change magazines*, such as all Aaton mags and Arri 16SR mags, much of the camera mechanism and the pressure plate are part of the magazine itself. This makes each mag more expensive and heavier, but has the tremendous advantage that once magazines are loaded with film, they can be clipped on the camera with no additional threading. This can make all the difference in documentary shooting when the action won't wait for you to reload. Even in dramatic shooting, minimizing the time for mag changes can be important. Most quick-change mags are of a coaxial design.

Loading Magazines

Magazines may be loaded with film prior to the day's shoot and then reloaded as necessary. Feature filmmakers may have a photographic darkroom available either in a studio or a truck. More typically, mags are changed using a *changing bag*, which is a lightproof, double-layered, double-zippered fabric bag (see Fig. 6-12). Look for a clean, dry place to work with subdued light. Some people like to work on a table or flat surface. You can work on the floor, but this may introduce dirt. Some changing bags have a kind of tent-like design that gives you room to work with big mags. Some people prefer to load 16mm mags on their lap; your legs help keep things from sliding around. Also, a lap is good for many locations (like outdoors) where a good, clean surface may not be available.

Cleanliness is essential, because any dirt on the film may lodge in the gate (see

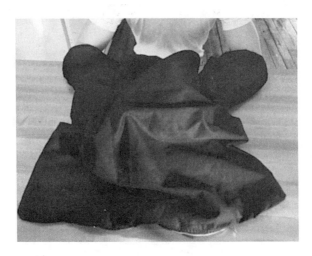

Fig. 6-12. A changing bag functions as a portable darkroom. (Ted Spagna)

Checking the Gate, p. 250). Some people like to blow mags clean with a can of compressed air (like Dust-Off), a tank of nitrogen, or even a rubber bulb syringe. Be careful with any compressed gas: Avoid blowing dirt into cavities in the mag or camera; also, the cold, expanding gas can damage mirror shutters. Some people prefer to clean mags with a paintbrush reserved for this purpose. You can also grab bits of dirt with a piece of tape, sticky side out, wrapped around a finger.

Before loading, the changing bag should be examined for rips or tears. If you find one, do a temporary repair with gaffer's tape or discard the bag. Turn the bag inside out and brush it clean with your hand. When not in use, zipper the bag closed and, if possible, keep it in a cover. When you're in the bag, bring the sleeves above the elbows to avoid light leaks and don't work in direct sunlight: use the shade of a tree or go inside.

Develop a standard operating procedure for loading mags so you won't get confused under pressure. Remove the moistureproof tape from around the film can before putting it in the changing bag. You can hang the tape on the wall near you and reuse it to seal up cans (though black camera tape is preferred for this purpose as a signal that the roll is exposed). Hold the can closed and put it in the bag; you can put the can under the mag to make sure it doesn't accidentally open while you're closing up the bag.

Once you've zipped up the changing bag with the film and clean mag inside, and gotten your hands in, you can open the film can. The end of the film will usually be taped down. Don't lose track of this tape! It might end up jamming the camera. If you stick it on the inside of the can you'll know where it is. You can reuse it to tape up the film after it is exposed.

On some magazines, you just have to slip the film into the feed side in the dark and then can do most of the threading outside the bag with the lights on. Be sure the feed roll pulls out smoothly. If the roll fights you or makes noise when pulled, it's probably not seated properly. Never pull hard on any film roll or you might cause cinch marks.

Nearly all raw stocks are supplied emulsion-in (see Fig. 7-10). Some magazines take up emulsion-in and others, emulsion-out.

Many mags have a post to accept a standard 2-inch plastic core. When film is taken up on a core, attach it as shown in Fig. 6-13. Wind the film around the core several times in the direction it takes up, and make sure there is no bump where the film fits into the slot on the core (you may have to refold it). Generally, the camera gate should be brushed or blown clean before attaching the fresh mag. Make sure all loops are the right size (you can count the frames) and be sure they are centered properly so they don't bind or rub. Generally, you should check the gate every time you change mags or more often (see p. 250).

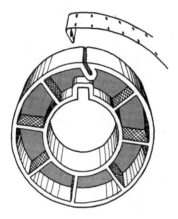

Fig. 6-13. Attaching the film to take-up core. Fold the film over itself and insert it in the slot. Position the slot as illustrated—angled against the direction of the take-up to keep the film from slipping out. Rotate the core to wind up several turns of film. Some magazines take up emulsion face-in and others face-out. (Carol Keller)

Some mags use a "core adaptor," which is a mechanical core that clamps shut on the film when you slide a lever. These have two disadvantages: It's easy to accidentally leave them in the film when unloading; and many labs prefer that film be delivered with a core in it.

Run a few feet of film through the camera to make sure everything is running smoothly. If you hear a fast ticking sound, your loops may be off. If you hear a low, slow rubbing sound, the film roll may have dished in the feed side, and needs to be gently pressed flat. Sometimes a firm slap with the palm of your hand on the side of the mag (take it off the camera first) will stop a roll from rubbing. With mags that have separate feed and take-up compartments, you can run the camera with the take-up side open to see if everything is okay, and check that the film is not being scratched (see p. 251 for scratch test).

Labeling and Managing Magazines

After the mag is loaded, a piece of tape should be put across the latches to prevent accidental opening. The edges of the magazine covers are sometimes a source of light leaks that may fog film, especially with old equipment. Taping the magazine with camera tape along the length of the lid ensures against leaks (see p. 252 for a light leak test).

The magazine should be labeled with a piece of tape or a sticker to identify its contents:

1. The type of film (e.g., 7248).
2. The emulsion and roll number from the film can's label (see Fig. 7-9); this is useful if there are problems later.
3. The length of the roll (e.g., 400 feet)
4. The camera roll number (e.g., CR 55); this should be marked only *after* the mag is on the camera.
5. The mag's number or serial number (useful if scratches are found later).
6. The date.

In documentary shooting you may not have time to get everything down. Items 1, 3, and 4 are essential. Some people use color-coded tape for different types of stock. Never label two camera rolls with the same number!

Have on hand spare cores, cans, and black bags for *short ends* (the unshot portion of a partially filmed roll). When unloading exposed film, tape up the end of the roll and be sure the black bag is neatly folded before closing and retaping the can. Be sure to mark the can clearly as exposed. See Chapter 17 for labeling the can after the film is exposed and Chapter 7 for handling, storing, and shipping film stock.

When magazines are reloaded during a shoot, some people prefer to unload the exposed film, remove it from the changing bag, and then go back in with the fresh stock. This avoids any confusion. With mags that have separate feed and take-up compartments, it's faster to clean the empty feed side, put the mag and fresh stock in the changing bag, load the feed side and—while you're still in the bag—unload the exposed film into the can you just emptied.

Magazines are often emptied at the end of the day's shooting and should be emptied before air travel. When unexposed film is put back in a can (*recanned*), it should be labeled as noted above, except without the camera roll and mag numbers. Mark "unexposed/recan" and put the name of the person unloading in case there are questions later.

SPARE MAGAZINES. Have at least one extra magazine. This lets you change mags if problems develop and allows you to load the next roll before it's needed, saving time at what might be a crucial moment. When you use two different raw stocks (for example, a slow-speed film for interiors and a high-speed for exteriors), the extra magazine makes both immediately available. On a feature film it is common to have five or more mags. Some documentary crews load up a lot of film at the beginning of a day's shoot so they can do without a magazine changer and keep the crew size to a minimum. In two-person documentary crews, a few spare magazines can be carried by the sound recordist or assistant—usually two quick-change mags or three or four regular mags.

Daylight Spools

Film in 16mm and 35mm is supplied on cores (*darkroom load*) or *daylight spools* (see Fig. 6-14). Spool-loaded film for 35mm is generally only available in 100-foot spools, while 16mm film may be supplied on 100-, 200-, and 400-foot spools. You don't need a changing bag for daylight spools, but load them in subdued light since bright light could fog the edges of the film. Integral head and tail leaders protect the unprocessed film from stray light. The way the unexposed film is wound on the spool helps prevent stray light from penetrating to the inner layers. After shooting, the film is not as protected. If the camera runs out of film during a shot (run-out shot), unload the film in a changing bag to protect the tail of the shot.

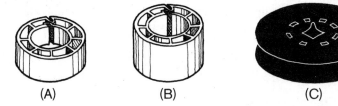

(A)   (B)   (C)

Fig. 6-14. Cores and daylight spool. (A) 16mm core. (B) 35mm core. (C) 16mm, 100-foot daylight spool. (Carol Keller)

Most 16mm magazines have both core and spool adaptors (sometimes you re-move the core adaptor to mount a spool). Though most magazines will accept day-light spools of up to 400 feet, spools are heavier than darkroom loads and may scrape against the side of the magazine, creating an annoying noise. Sometimes darkroom loads are spooled down onto daylight spools for use with small, spool load cameras. This will result in reversed key numbers (see Chapter 7) if the film is not rewound once before spooling. Some labs will do this for you.

Super 8 Cartridges

Super 8 Cartridges are lightproof, but you should still avoid exposing them to direct sunlight. Don't break the cartridge's moistureproof foil until you load the camera. A notch in the plastic cartridge automatically sets the ASA number on many Super 8 cameras with automatic exposure. When using Pro8 negative stocks, it may be necessary to manually carve out the notch for proper ASA and filter set-tings on certain cameras. On many cameras, the footage counter resets to zero when the film compartment door is opened. Be sure to write down the footage if you open the door to check the gate or change film in the middle of a cartridge.

OTHER CAMERA FEATURES

Video Assist

A *video assist* (also called a *video tap*) diverts some light from the film camera to an attached small video camera that allows you to watch the image on a monitor and/or record it on video. Video taps can be valuable for allowing the director or others to see the shot, for reviewing takes, and for logging or even editing footage prior to processing. A video assist can be crucial for Steadicam, crane, or car shots in which the operator cannot look through the camera. However, there can be some drawbacks. The image is a low-quality approximation of what is being recorded on film, and often misrepresents what the image will eventually look like.

Since you're not actually seeing the film, you can't know about a host of film problems, including scratches or even a run-out. And video taps consume a lot of battery power (when possible run them on a battery separate from the camera).

The video cameras used for the assist vary in sensitivity and quality. Most video taps get their light by shunting off light from the camera's viewfinder (making the viewfinder image darker). Some taps actually replace the finder. Many video taps produce a flickering image because, like the camera viewfinder, the tap only gets light half the time—when the mirror shutter is closed. There are newer, "flicker-free" designs that store the image when the shutter is closed and replay it when the shutter is open, filling in the time that would otherwise be dark. Another system uses a pellicle (like a beam-splitter reflex viewfinder; see p. 240) to divert light before it reaches the shutter. The video image is better, but the film loses some light.

See p. 616 for editing the image recorded from a video assist.

Sound Dampening

Camera noise on the sound track can be annoying in a documentary or disastrous in a fiction film. Even when filming without sound, a noisy camera can be disruptive. Noise calls attention to the camera and can distract subjects or alter animal behavior when doing nature filming.

High-end 16mm and 35mm cameras designed for sync-sound work are usually very quiet. Camera manufacturers often rate cameras intended for sync-sound shooting according to a noise level expressed in decibels (dB; see Chapter 10). Shooting outdoors or in noisier locations allows the use of a noisier camera. Since much of 35mm cinematography is done on a soundstage where there is virtually no background noise, standards for a quiet camera are more stringent. Cameras have

Fig. 6-15. Camera with white barney, rubber lens shade, and French flag (small card on articulated arm for preventing lens flare).

to be in good repair to be really quiet. On some cameras, most of the noise comes from the magazine. Slightly shrunken film chatters in some cameras more than in others. High-frequency sounds may be more bothersome than low, rumbly sounds.Camera noise can be dampened with a *barney*, which is a soft cover, sometimes made of lead foam (see Fig. 6-15). Barneys are often custom-fitted for the camera, allowing access to controls. Barneys may cover the whole camera or just the magazine. In a pinch, a heavy coat or a sound blanket (see Chapter 11) can serve as a makeshift barney. White barneys are sometimes used to reflect sunlight and keep the film cooler in hot weather. The *heater barney* is a battery-operated camera cover that keeps the camera warm when filming in very cold weather.

An old sound-dampening device is the *blimp*, which is a hard, soundproof camera housing. Underwater housings are available for cameras in all gauges for filming underwater or in very wet locations.

In-Camera Timecode

Timecode can be very useful in production and postproduction. Some newer film cameras can expose timecode along the edge of the film, which can be read after the film is developed (see Fig. 6-16). The Aaton/Panavision system uses both Arabic numerals ("man-readable") and a matrix of dots (machine readable). The Arriflex system uses a barcode instead.

Many cameras are not equipped for internal timecode can still use timecode using timecode slates. See Chapter 11 for use of timecode during shooting and Chapter 18 for timecode in film-to-tape transfers.

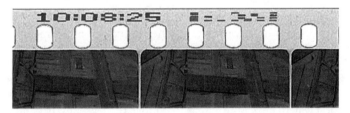

Fig. 6-16. In-camera timecode. The camera exposes the timecode along the edge of the film. The AatonCode system uses both human-readable numbers and a machine-readable matrix of dots. (AbelCineTech)

Multiple-Format Cameras

Some cameras are capable of shooting more than one format. For example, suitably equipped Aaton and Arriflex 16mm cameras can shoot either 16mm or Super 16. The camera must have a Super 16 gate, the proper viewing screen, and the lens must be shifted over (recentered on the frame) when changing between formats. Many 35mm cameras have a number of interchangeable gates and viewing screens for different aspect ratios and formats. Bear in mind that a lens designed for one format won't necessarily cover the full frame of a wider screen format. For example, Super 16 lenses will cover the 16mm frame, but the reverse is not necessarily true (see Chapters 1, 2, and 17 for more on 16mm and Super 16).

In-Camera Effects

Some cameras can make in-camera effects, such as fades and dissolves. In 16mm and 35mm, effects are generally created in the laboratory during the printing stage, so few cameras have this feature (some Bolexes are an exception). Some Super 8 cameras have back-winding capabilities for dissolves and multiple images.

You can create multiple images by exposing the same section of film two (*double exposure*) or more times. Be sure to compensate to avoid overexposure. The rule of thumb is to underexpose each image one stop. However, if a light scene is to be double-exposed, it may have to be further underexposed (since it will bleach out a darker scene), whereas a dark scene may need to be exposed normally without any underexposure.

Do in-camera fades by closing down a variable shutter to 0 degrees. Merely stopping the lens iris down will generally not produce a totally black image, and the changing depth of field may be noticeable. Make dissolves by overlapping a fade-out with a fade-in. A frame counter in addition to a footage counter is needed for dissolves, or for making any precise in-camera effect. The matte box is also used for some in-camera effects (see Chapter 8).

CAMERA TESTS AND MAINTENANCE

Of the following tests, checking the gate is done regularly while shooting. The other tests are often done before a shoot, when checking out a camera from a rental house or other equipment supplier.

CHECKING THE GATE. Dirt or bits of emulsion often lodge in the camera aperture and are exposed as a shadow on the edge of the picture ("hairs in the gate"). A good way to check the gate is to remove the lens and, from in front of the camera, examine the edges of the aperture with a lighted magnifier. You need to manually inch the motor forward so that the mirror shutter is open, giving you a clear view of the aperture and the film behind it. Some people prefer to check the gate through the lens. This takes practice and works well only with long lenses. Open the iris all the way, focus to infinity, and set a zoom to telephoto. Use a small flashlight to look around the edge of the frame. The advantage of this method is you're less likely to introduce dirt while checking the gate (in a dusty location, for example). The disadvantage is that all the lens settings have to be reset and you still have to take the lens off if there's dirt.

To clean the gate, carefully insert an *orangewood stick* (sold as cuticle sticks for nail care in drugstores) and lift the dirt out of the frame. Never insert anything metal and don't touch the mirror shutter or any of the optics. Compressed air may damage the mirror. Don't forget to inch the motor forward after cleaning to close the shutter and return the mirror to viewing position. You can inch the film forward a few frames or run it a bit and check again to be sure the dirt is really gone.

How often should you check the gate? The answer depends on the camera, the cinematographer, and the project. On a feature, the gate should be checked whenever a new film roll is begun and at least before the camera is moved from one setup to another. Some people check the gate after every take, or every good take (printed takes). Once you find a hair, you have the unpleasant task of trying to guess how long it's been there, so the more often you check, the safer you are. On a documentary, you may only have time to check once a roll. Hairs are more critical in 16mm—where the edge of the gate forms the edge of the image—than in some 35mm formats where the full Academy gate may give you some extra clearance from the part of the frame you're actually using. The gates on some cameras seem to naturally stay fairly hair-free, such as many Aaton and Panavision cameras. Dirty locations and soft film emulsions require more attention to the gate. Do everything you can when loading and cleaning magazines to avoid or remove dirt that might otherwise end up in the gate.

SCRATCH TEST. Run a few feet of film through the camera, and remove the film from the take-up reel. Examine the footage for surface scratches by holding the film obliquely toward a light source. To locate the cause of a scratch, mark the frame in the aperture; unload the film; mark where the scratch begins; thread the film with the first marked frame in the aperture, and note the location where the scratch begins. Then clean the gate, rollers or other scratching surfaces. Test for scratches whenever checking out a camera or magazine for the first time, and check occasionally during use. Keep some short ends around for scratch testing, but use only film that hasn't run through a camera gate before.

REGISTRATION TEST. *Registration* refers to the steadiness of the image— the camera's ability to expose each frame in the same place relative to the sprocket holes. Bad registration causes the image to jiggle and gives audiences eye strain. To check registration, mount the camera on a steady tripod and tape a lens's zoom ring so it doesn't move, and then don't touch the camera. With negative film, photograph a black cross or grid on a white wall; with reversal, shoot a white cross on a black field. Underexpose by about a stop to compensate for double exposure. Wind the film back to the beginning, move the camera slightly and photograph the cross again. (In 35mm you must mark the frame in the gate when you start so you can place it in the gate to start the second pass.) Having moved the camera, there is now a small amount of space between the two images of the cross. On projection, the less the movement of the crosses with respect to each other, the better the registration.

Another test of registration, particularly in 16mm, can be done with any footage you've shot. During projection, shift the frame line adjustment of the projector so the frame line can be seen. If the frame line seems to get thicker and thinner (to breathe), registration is poor. A lot of jiggle between the frame line and the edge of the screen is more likely an indication of poor registration of the projector than a problem with the camera (when you start to look for it, it's shocking how unsteady many projectors are).

FRAME LINE TEST. The frame line in 16mm should bisect the perforations (see Fig. 1-34). To test a camera, fold a strip of exposed and developed film over itself, place pins through the perfs, and check that the frame lines are perfectly in line with each other. The projector frame line adjustment can correct for a consistently misplaced frame line. Problems arise, however, when you use two different cameras (or purchase stock footage) with a dissimilar frame line.

TESTING VIEWFINDER ACCURACY. To check the accuracy of the viewfinder, mount the camera on a tripod. Get a test chart or make one with numbered rectangles with the proper aspect ratio (1.33:1 for standard 16mm; 1.85 for standard widescreen 35mm) nested within one another. Carefully align the viewfinder with one of the rectangles, photograph and check for accuracy. The only discrepancy on a reflex finder should be between camera aperture and projector aperture.

TESTING RETICULE POSITION. Viewfinders like those on zoom lenses with auxiliary finders have a mask or reticule that defines the outlines of the frame. To check for proper orientation, place the camera on a flat surface (say, a solid table) and align the frame edge with the table edge. The two should be parallel. If they are not, adjust the reticule. On some zooms, it is a simple adjustment.

LIGHT LEAK TEST. Light leaks show up on developed camera original as uneven fogging extending outside the picture area. If you detect light leak in your footage, it may come from poor handling when loading or unloading the magazines. To check a camera for light leaks, load it with unexposed raw stock and mark or expose the frame in the aperture. Move a bright light source (held a few inches from the camera) around from every angle, develop the film and check for edge fogging. If edge fog is found, reload the footage, placing the marked frame in the aperture. Edge fog at any point locates the source of the light leak. When shooting, it's generally good practice to tape the edges of a magazine to reduce the chance of light leak.

OTHER TESTS. See Chapter 4 for lens focusing tests that may discover faults in the camera viewfinder or the adjustment of the lens mounting. Always check rushes for any defects (see Chapter 17) and immediately troubleshoot (search for the fault). An image with total vertical blurring is a sign of a lost loop in the camera. Partial vertical blurring is a sign of a shutter timing error: The frame has been exposed while moving. The whole image moving in and out of focus (*breathing in the gate*) usually calls for pressure plate adjustment. These last three problems can also be caused by a malfunctioning projector, which should also be checked. Investigate any image flicker or unevenness in exposure.

Camera Quality

Accurate registration in a camera is a sign of good mechanical design, but it does not measure its sturdiness, nor how well it will keep to its original specifications. The quality of workmanship often determines whether a camera will become noisier with age or break down often, but reliability is also a question of design. Seek advice on specific cameras from filmmakers who have field-tested the equipment and from camera rental houses. Some cameras are easier to repair than others. Modular designs (with replaceable units) permit easy field repair.

Camera Care

Keep the camera clean. Don't blow compressed air into the aperture or places where dirt can become lodged. Never use metal to scrape emulsion from the gate. You can use alcohol on a cotton swab to remove emulsion deposits, but take care not to leave any cotton fibers. Acetone damages some plastics. Use magazine covers, lens socket caps, and body caps to keep dust out of camera openings.

Don't run a camera without film at speeds higher than 24 fps.

Hand-carry a camera on a plane if you can rather than checking it as baggage. When shipping, use rugged shipping cases, and detach the lens before shipping. Place all delicate equipment in foam-lined and fitted cases. Secure the camera on a car seat rather than leave it loose on the car floor or in the trunk where it will be subject to more vibration.

When you use a battery belt connected to the camera by a cable, be careful not to rest the camera on a surface and walk away, pulling the camera along behind you (sounds like obvious advice, but you'd be surprised how often it's been done). Use a coiled cable to minimize the risk. When you rest the camera on a table, don't let the lens extend over the edge where it may be hit by an unwary passerby.

Obtain the manufacturer's operation and maintenance manual for special information on oiling and overhaul instructions for your camera. Check whether any special lubrication is required for cold weather filming. Try to assemble a group of tools and spare parts for field repairs.

Shooter's Ditty Bag

Typical items in a cinematographer's (or assistant's) bag:

Changing bag
Camelhair brush
Compressed air in a can
Clean paintbrush
Spare cores, cans, black bags
Depth of field calculator
Light meter(s)
Marking pens (Sharpies)
50-foot measuring tape
Grease pencil
Screwdrivers
Jeweler's screwdrivers
Adjustable wrench
Electrical multimeter
Crocus cloth for removing
   burrs

Camera tape; white and black
Magnifying lens with light
Orangewood sticks
Lens tissue
Lens cleaning fluid
Small flashlight
Slate with color chip chart
Swiss Army knife
Small LCD video monitor
Chalk
Needlenose pliers
Set of Allen wrenches
Tweezers
Soldering iron, wire
Camera oil or grease

CHAPTER 7

The Film Image

U nexposed film is called *raw stock*. After you choose the film gauge—Super 8, 16mm, or 35mm—the raw stock determines much of the look of the film. Consult with filmmakers or the laboratory for advice on obtaining the look you want.

PROPERTIES OF THE FILM STOCK

Developing the Image

The top layer of the raw stock, the *emulsion*, consists of the light-sensitive material *silver halide crystals* suspended in gelatin. The crystals vary in size, the larger ones being more sensitive to light. Exposure to light forms a *latent image* in the emulsion. The latent image becomes visible when the film goes through the *developer*, a solution that reacts chemically with those silver halide crystals that have been exposed and reduces them to *metallic silver*, which is opaque to light. At a later stage in the development process, crystals that have not been exposed to light are removed from the emulsion by another solution, the *hypo* or *fixer*.

The areas of the emulsion most exposed to light end up with the greatest con-

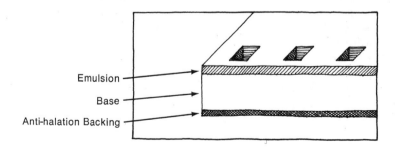

Fig. 7-1. A cross section of film. The anti-halation backing, which on some stocks is between the emulsion and base, is removed during processing. (Carol Keller)

centration of metallic silver. These are the densest, most opaque areas; they appear dark when you project light through them. Conversely, areas that receive little light end up with less metallic silver and are relatively transparent. This is a *negative film* (see Fig. 7-2). On the negative, all the brightness values in the original scene are reversed: What was dark in the scene becomes light (transparent), and what was light becomes dark (dense).

The emulsion rests on a binder that allows it to adhere to a firm, flexible support material, the *base*. All currently manufactured stocks have a *safety base*, usually of cellulose triacetate (*acetate*), that is not flammable. Some stocks are also available on a synthetic polyester base, such as Kodak's ESTAR, which is thinner and stronger than acetate. Standard cement splices do not work on polyester; splicing is done with either tape or a special fusion splicer. Polyester base film is sometimes used for high-speed cinematography. Release prints and intermediates (see Chapter 17) made on polyester can withstand rougher handling and take up less storage space.

Bright light can pass through the emulsion, scatter in the base, reflect off the back of the film, and re-expose the emulsion; this is known as *halation*. Most camera stocks incorporate an *anti-halation backing* in the emulsion to absorb these unwanted light rays. Even so, a bright light source in the subject will sometimes show a halo in the image due to halation.

The Negative-Positive Process

In the process discussed above, the exposed raw stock became a negative image of the photographed scene after development. If you make a print from the negative, using essentially the same process to reverse the tonalities again, you end up with a *positive* of the original scene. In the positive, bright areas of the scene end up light (transparent) and dark areas end up dense. Thus you reverse the tonalities of the original scene twice to produce an image that looks normal. The negative-positive process is, at this time, the standard for film development in 16mm and 35mm filmmaking.

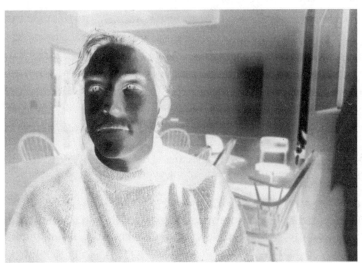

Fig. 7-2. The negative. Figure 12-26 shows the positive image. (Stephen McCarthy)

The Reversal Process

Reversal film uses a different development process from negative and yields a positive image that can be directly projected without the need of a print (like a slide in still photography). If desired, a reversal print can be made of the reversal original to yield a print in one step. Reversal was once the standard process in Super 8 and 16mm. Though reversal is still used, negative film is now used much more often.

The key to the reversal process lies in the development of the image. The film is exposed to light in the camera to form a latent image. As in the negative process, the developer reduces the silver halide of the latent image into metallic silver. Whereas in the negative process the remaining (unexposed) silver halide crystals are washed away in the hypo, in reversal development the metallic silver is removed by immersing the film in a bleach, leaving the unexposed silver halide crystals, which are still light-sensitive, in the emulsion. The film is then uniformly exposed to light (or immersed in a chemical fogging agent), exposing the remaining silver halide. It is then redeveloped in a second developer, and fixed again in the hypo. Thus, light areas in the subject build up heavier densities that get bleached away, leaving relatively little silver halide behind. When these areas are then exposed to light and developed, they leave a transparent region on the film. After processing, light areas of the subject end up transparent on the film and dark subject areas build up greater densities on the film and are more opaque (see Fig. 7-3). In this way, the reversal process maintains the relative brightness values of the original scene.

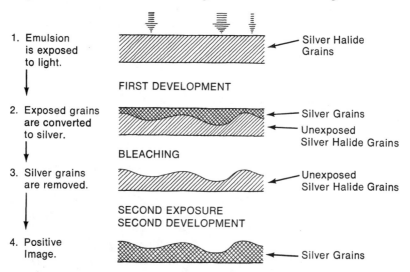

Fig. 7-3. Reversal development. A cross section of the emulsion shows the various steps in processing. The arrows at top represent varying degrees of exposure. (Carol Keller)

The Characteristic Curve

A basic knowledge of characteristic curves will help you understand the practical aspects of exposure, which are discussed in detail later. The *characteristic curve* for an emulsion is a graph that shows the relation between the amount of light that exposes the film and the corresponding density built up in the film. To plot the curve, the film is exposed to progressively greater amounts of light in constant increments. The film is then developed, and the densities are measured. For negative stocks, the greater the exposure, the greater the density, whereas for reversal, the greater the exposure, the less the density. Exposure is plotted along the horizontal axis and density along the vertical axis (see Fig. 7-4).

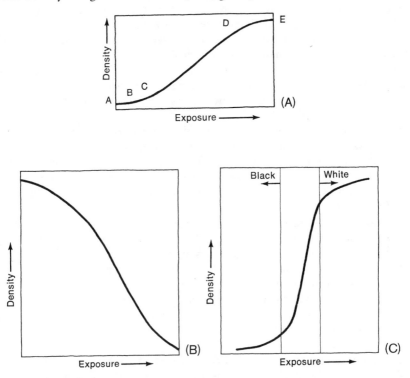

Fig. 7-4. Characteristic curves. (A) A simplified black-and-white negative characteristic curve: Point A is the base-plus-fog density; B to C is the toe; C to D is the straight line portion; D to E is the shoulder. (B) Characteristic curve for reversal film. The greater steepness of the curve shows the higher contrast of reversal stock. (C) A very high contrast black-and-white negative stock used for titles. (Carol Keller)

Even when the film receives no exposure, *some* density is built up. The base itself has some density (it absorbs some of the projected light), and the development process adds an overall light *fog* to the film (some unexposed silver halide gets converted to metallic silver). This is the minimum density of the film. For black-and-white film, it is called *base-plus-fog* and for color film *D-min* (for *minimum density*).

In the negative process, increases in exposure don't start to increase the density above base-plus-fog until the *threshold* of the emulsion, the point where the curve starts to rise, is reached (point B in Fig. 7-4A). Even though a dark area in the scene emits some light, if it falls below the threshold of the film, it won't produce any change in the density. Deep shadows produce minimum density and will appear in a positive print as undifferentiated black with no detail.[1]

1. In video, the equivalent concept is that any dark areas that fall below the black clip level won't be visible (blacks are crushed).

The *straight line section* of the curve (point C to point D in Fig. 7-4A) is the portion where a given change in exposure produces a constant change in the density. This is normally where we want to expose as much of the scene as possible.

The *toe* of the curve (point B to point C) is the area of lowest densities—usually the darkest shadows that show some detail—where constant increases in the exposure do not lead to proportional increases in density. The densities here increase more gradually than they do in the straight line section; the slope in the toe is thus less steep (slower rising) than in the straight line section. The *shoulder* (point D to point E), like the toe, is a flatter curve than the straight line section. Again, constant increases in exposure do not lead to constant increases in density. At point E, increases in exposure do not cause any increase in density. This is the maximum density (*D-max*) possible in this film.[2]

If an area of the subject gets exposed high on the shoulder, differences in brightness will not be recorded as significant differences in density. For example, a white wall may be three times as bright as a face, but if both expose high on the shoulder, the difference in their densities will be insignificant (highlights are *compressed*). In a positive print, this area will appear as an undifferentiated white (*blocking of the highlights*).

Shadows will show no detail if they fall near the film's threshold, and highlights will show no detail if they fall too high on the shoulder. Generally, for correct exposure, the important parts of the subject that should show good tonal separation must fall on the straight line section. Shadow and highlight values may fall on the toe and shoulder, respectively, but, if you want some detail, they should not be too close to the outer limits. When you are filming, there are many ways to control exposure in order to control where on the characteristic curve parts of the subject will fall (see Exposure and Film Stocks, p. 289).

Characteristic Curves for Color Film

Modern color film stocks are composed of three emulsion layers; each layer is similar to a black-and-white film emulsion. The top layer is sensitive only to blue light (and records the blue *record*, or blue part, of the scene). The second layer records the green record; the bottom, the red record. All the colors rendered by the film are created from a combination of the record of these three *primaries* (see Chapter 8 for further discussion of primaries).

Incorporated into each of the three emulsion layers of a color stock is a distinct group of *dye couplers* that release dyes of the appropriate color during development (see Fig. 7-5). The more exposure a particular emulsion layer receives, the greater the density of the metallic silver in that layer and the more color dye that remains after development. Most of the metallic silver, along with the unused dye, is bleached away during developing. The three color layers will be recorded with the dye color of each layer's complementary color (see Chapter 8). The blue, green, and red record will be recorded with dyes colored yellow, magenta, and cyan, respectively.

Because of imperfections in the absorption of color dyes, additional colored dye couplers are incorporated into the emulsion of color negative films. They form a

2. The video equivalent is the white clip level.

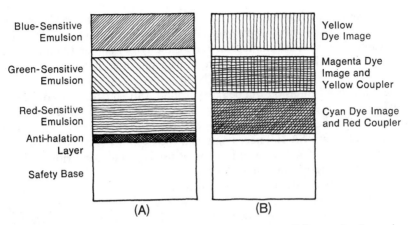

Blue-Sensitive Emulsion — Yellow Dye Image

Green-Sensitive Emulsion — Magenta Dye Image and Yellow Coupler

Red-Sensitive Emulsion — Cyan Dye Image and Red Coupler

Anti-halation Layer

Safety Base

(A)   (B)

Fig. 7-5. Color negative before (A) and after processing (B). Yellow and red couplers are found in the green- and red-sensitive emulsions to compensate for deficiencies in color absorption of the magenta and cyan dyes. (Carol Keller)

color *masking* to compensate for unwanted dye absorption. The masking gives color negative its characteristic overall orange appearance. Reversal films have dyes that absorb their complementaries more accurately and thus have no need for color masking.

A color emulsion is represented by three curves, one for each emulsion layer (see Fig. 7-6). The curve closest to the horizontal axis (the red curve in Fig. 7-6) represents the color most susceptible to underexposure, and the highest curve (the blue), the color most susceptible to overexposure. Underexposure or overexposure of only one of the layers can cause a color cast in underexposed shadow or overexposed highlight areas.

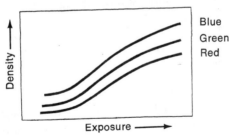

Density

Exposure

Blue
Green
Red

Fig. 7-6. Characteristic curve for color negative. The three curves represent the three layers of a color emulsion. (Carol Keller)

Film Speed and ASA

The *speed* of a stock is a measure of its sensitivity to light. The "faster" a film stock, the less light it needs to produce an acceptable exposure. The *exposure index* (*EI*) expresses the speed as a number that can be used with light meters to help determine proper exposure. The film manufacturer recommends an exposure index for each stock that may be given in the form of an *ASA number* (American Standards

Association, now American Standards Institute or ANSI). The metric equivalent is a *DIN number* marked with a degree sign. An *ISO number* (International Standards Organization) gives the ASA number first, then the DIN number. On the label for Eastman Kodak stocks you will find the exposure index indicated in this format (see Fig. 7-9). EI 500/28° means ASA 500, DIN 28.

A medium-speed emulsion will be rated around ASA 100. ASA speeds below 50 are usually considered slow. Fast or high-speed emulsions are rated ASA 200 or higher. Doubling the ASA number means that the film will be twice as sensitive to light. A film rated at ASA 100 needs only half the exposure (that is, one stop less) than a film rated ASA 50. The faster film can be used in conditions with less light or to allow a smaller iris opening on the lens.

Black-and-white emulsions are sometimes rated by two exposure indexes, one for tungsten illumination and the other for daylight. The tungsten rating is generally about one third of a stop slower than the daylight rating, representing the emulsion's lower sensitivity to the red end of the spectrum.

Color film stocks are also rated with one EI for tungsten light and one for daylight. Here the implication is that you will use a filter for one type of light, and some light will be absorbed by the filter. For example, a tungsten-balanced stock rated ASA 500 will be rated ASA 320 for use in daylight with an 85 filter (see p. 298).

The manufacturer's recommended exposure index is intended as a starting point. It is not unusual for cinematographers to rate the film at a slightly different ASA (see The Light Meter and Exposure Control, p. 275, for more on varying the EI).

CONTRAST OF THE IMAGE

Contrast measures the separation of tones (lights and darks) in an image. The higher the contrast, the greater the separation between tones (see Fig. 7-7). See Understanding and Controlling Contrast, p. 183, for an overview, and for how contrast and gamma apply to video. In film, many of the concepts are very similar, though gamma is defined differently.

Two Aspects of Contrast

Low-contrast images are called "flat." High-contrast images—with good tonal separation—are called contrasty or hard. An image with good contrast range has "snap."

To visualize the idea of tonal separation, imagine two parts of a scene that have somewhat different brightness (say, the bright side of the man's face and the shadowed side in Fig. 7-7). With low contrast (left image) the dark and light tones are close together; with high contrast (right image) the tones are much more different, there's more separation between the dark and the light. Also see Fig. 5-5.

The following are two key factors that affect how the eye perceives contrast:

GAMMA. The steepness of the film's characteristic curve (mathematically, the *slope*) indicates the amount of contrast at any point on the curve. The steeper the

Fig. 7-7. Varying degrees of contrast. (left) Low-contrast image looks flat and dull. Note muddy blacks and lack of bright whites. (center) Normal contrast. (right) High-contrast image has bright whites and deep blacks but lacks midtones. Note loss of detail on bright side of face and dark sweater. (Stephen McCarthy)

curve, the higher the contrast, and thus the greater the separation of tones. *Gamma* (γ, defined as the slope) is a measure of the steepness of the straight line section of the characteristic curve. Increasing gamma means increasing the contrast of tonalities that fall on the straight line section.

The straight line section is steeper than either the toe or the shoulder portions, so areas of the subject that are exposed on the straight line section will show more tonal separation (contrast) than areas that fall on the toe or shoulder.[3]

An example of very high gamma can be found in a photocopy of a photograph (similar to the right-hand image in Fig. 7-7). A characteristic curve of a photocopy would have a very steep straight line section—almost vertical (the reversal equivalent of Fig. 7-4C). Dark areas in the original are rendered black, and slightly lighter areas are rendered white; nothing prints gray (no midtones).

With video systems, "gamma" refers particularly to the contrast of the midtones. Video gamma curves have a different shape than film curves, resulting from the different ways the two systems respond to light.

WHITE AND BLACK VALUES. Even if an image has high gamma, if it doesn't have a bright white and a rich black, the overall contrast will probably seem low to the viewer. There are several ways to demonstrate this. If you turn the brightness control up on a video monitor, this raises the black level (blacks become gray); the contrast seems reduced, even though the gamma doesn't change much. As an example of an image that lacks both a dark black and a bright white, see Fig. 5-5D. Thus, it's not only gamma but also the range from black to white—sometimes called the *contrast range*—that determines an image's overall contrast.

There are many factors that may lessen contrast. A low-contrast lens or flare in

3. The tonalities in the straight line section are "stretched" and those in the toe and the shoulder are "compressed."

the lens (see Chapter 4), either in the camera or projector, can make the image look flat. During projection, any stray light in the room will also cause loss of overall contrast. For example, suppose the darkest part of the screen reflects 1 unit of light and the lightest 100 units, making the overall ratio 100:1. If someone opens a door and lets 2 units of light cover the screen, the darkest area now reflects 3 units (2 + 1) and the lightest 103 (100 + 3), a ratio of about 34:1, which is a significant drop in overall contrast.

Force Processing and Gamma

Gamma depends on both the nature of the particular film stock and the way it's developed at the lab. Laboratories often talk about developing to a particular gamma. A higher gamma results from increasing the time or temperature of development. Increasing gamma also increases the sensitivity of the film to light (it raises the ASA number; see p. 259), and, when done for this purpose, is called *force processing* or *pushing*.

Force processing may be used when there is insufficient light to shoot. For example, a film rated ASA 100 is exposed as though it were rated ASA 200 to effectively double its sensitivity. The lab is then instructed to "push one stop" to compensate for the underexposure by increasing development time. Some stocks can be pushed one to three stops, but force development increases graininess, sometimes to a degree that makes the image unacceptable. Consult the lab on particular stocks.

When you're force processing, change ASA speed on the light meter for exposure calculations. When pushing one stop, double the ASA number; when pushing two stops, multiply it by four.

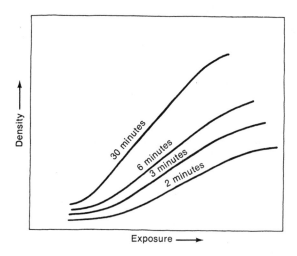

Fig. 7-8. Force processing. As the development time increases, the characteristic curve becomes steeper (contrast increases)—because the brighter parts of the scene (right side of graph) respond more to increased development than the darker parts. Fog level also increases with development time. (Carol Keller)

Pushing increases contrast because areas in the scene that fall on the straight line section and the shoulder increase in density more than those on the toe (see Fig. 7-8). Middle tones and highlights will show significant increases in density. So midtones in the scene that would have otherwise been underexposed get a boost from pushing.

However, pushing does not generally raise the threshold of the film, so shadow values that fall on the toe will not significantly increase their densities. That means pushing will not result in much more detail in the shadows. When we are concerned with "seeing into the shadows," stocks with long flat curves do best; pushing helps little. One way to change the film stock's response to shadow value is through flashing (see below).

When reversal stocks are pushed, the blacks often become muddy and look grayish (a lower D-max).

Bleach Bypass

Another way to increase contrast in development is to use the *bleach bypass process* (sometimes called *skip bleach*). The film is processed without the bleach that would normally cause the silver grains to be removed. Metallic silver is left in the emulsion along with the colored dyes. The result is increased contrast, desaturated colors, and washed-out highlights. Some cinematographers use this process to create a special look. This should only be undertaken with tests and the lab may not guarantee the results. If you are transferring to video and then making a digital intermediate or film-out (see Chapter 18), you may be able to achieve many of these effects digitally without doing bleach bypass in processing.

Reducing Contrast in the Film Stock

Gamma can be increased via force processing, which affects the rendering of bright areas in the scene more than it does the dark areas. Gamma can be lowered by *underdeveloping* (*pulling*) the film in the lab. Pulling reduces film speed, grain, and contrast. If this is planned, the film is overexposed during shooting, then underdeveloped to the same degree. For example, you might rate the film at half its normal ASA (use ASA 50 for a film normally rated at ASA 100), then instruct the lab to pull by one stop. With some stocks, pulling can result in a rich image with subtle shading. Be sure to check with the lab first; not all stocks can be successfully pulled and the lab may not perform this service (and will usually charge extra if they do). Pulling is sometimes done for footage that is accidentally overexposed in shooting.

Another way to reduce contrast is by *flashing*, a process in which the film is uniformly exposed to a dim light either before (*preflashing*) or after (*postflashing*) the scene is photographed. This exposure raises base-plus-fog density (or, in reversal, it lowers D-max) and increases the exposure of shadow areas, but it has little effect on the bright areas. It thus lowers the contrast between shadow and highlight values.

The effect of flashing is similar to the screening room example given above. On negative film, two units of exposure from the flashing may double a shadow density while having almost no effect on higher densities. The contrast range of the image is thus reduced.

The Arriflex VariCon unit is a device that mounts in front of the camera lens like a matte box and reflects a low-level white or colored light into the camera. Unlike postflashing, using the Varicon lets you see and adjust the amount of flashing while filming. Any color used affects the shadow areas but generally not the faces (midtones). The Panaflasher is a Panavision unit that flashes the film in the camera magazine, but you can't see the effect in the viewfinder.

When two stocks of different contrast are used on the same film (especially when they are used for the same scene), the contrastier stock is sometimes flashed to better match the lower-contrast film. Flashing also provides detail in some shadow areas that would otherwise be rendered as black, since it may give them enough exposure to be boosted over the threshold. Flashing can thus be used like pushing to increase the sensitivity of film to light. Unlike pushing, however, it does not increase contrast and it affects the darker, rather than the lighter, areas of the scene. Do not expect much increase in film speed—depending on the stock, at most a half stop or so. Print stocks may also be flashed.

You may not like the way flashing increases graininess, desaturates colors, and imparts a milkiness to the image, especially in the shadow areas. Be sure to consult your lab and make tests before flashing footage. As noted above, this effect may be achievable—at least in part—in video without requiring changes in shooting or processing.

SHARPNESS

Definition, or *sharpness*, expresses the degree of clarity in an image. There are several physical measurements that more or less correspond to the viewer's evaluation of sharpness.

Resolution

Resolution, or *resolving power*, is the ability to record fine detail in the image. Resolution in film is measured by photographing a test chart with sets of parallel lines in which the space between the lines is equal to the thickness of the lines, the thickness progressively diminishing. The image is then examined under a microscope to determine the greatest number of lines per millimeter that can be distinguished. Don't confuse resolving power with measurements of resolution used in video (see Chapter 5).

Resolving power is of limited use for predicting the viewer's evaluations of sharpness, since those perceptions are highly dependent on the contrast in the image—the higher the contrast, the sharper the image appears. An image may have a very high resolution, say, 100 lines/mm, but will not appear to be sharp if the contrast is excessively low. Bear in mind that resolution measures small details that may not be as important to the eye as larger areas in the image.

Modulation Transfer Function (MTF)

MTF measures the "noise" in an imaging system. If you were to examine a small area of the image, you would see that some of the variations in light and dark are caused by differences in brightness in the scene. However, some of the variations are caused by lens or film imperfections that result in light spilling from a lighter to a darker area. MTF measures the loss of image quality due to graininess, light scatter in the film emulsion, and aberrations in the camera or projector lens.

To measure the MTF, a test pattern of alternating light and dark strips, with distance between the strips decreasing, is photographed on film. As the light and dark areas become closer, the emulsion tends to average out the light and dark, and the contrast range of the original pattern is decreased.[4] For more on MTF, see p. 214.

Resolution and MTF can be used to evaluate any part of an imaging system (for example, film, lens, or projection), but MTF alone can predict the sharpness of a combination (say, lens and emulsion) from the MTF of each component.

Graininess and Granularity

The photographic image is composed of small grains of metallic silver, or, in the case of color films, masses of dye that occupy the areas where metallic silver formed during the development process. When a single frame is enlarged, it will show the roughness caused by these grains or dyes. The viewer's perception of this roughness is called *graininess*, and the objective measurement that attempts to quantify it is known as *granularity*.

Granularity is measured by exposing and developing a sample and examining density variations at great magnification. A count of these variations gives a numerical value expressed as *RMS granularity*. A difference of 6 percent is barely noticeable.

Graininess is usually considered to be an undesirable element of a film system, but different grain structures create a look that in some stocks, even those with high granularity, may be considered pleasing. You may like a sharp, clear grain in black-and-white. Some grain structures on color film look beautiful, while others merely impair the image.

Every emulsion has a built-in graininess for any particular development process. In general, faster films are made up of larger silver halide crystals and thus appear grainier. Fine-grain emulsions are usually found in slower film stocks. Kodak has reduced graininess in fast stocks with "T-grain" technology. T-grains are flatter, so sensitivity is increased because more of the grain is exposed to light; but since grain mass is not increased, the appearance of grain does not increase. Black-and-white reversal films often exhibit less grain than negative films, because the larger, more light-sensitive grains are exposed first and then washed away during the bleaching stage, leaving the finer grains behind.

Graininess in black-and-white is fundamentally different from graininess in color. Black-and-white grains are made of metallic silver, which is opaque to light. In color film, the grain pattern results from uneven distribution of silver grains that are replaced by transparent dyes during development. Generally, slightly overexposing color negative film results in less graininess, whereas in black-and-white overexposure causes an increase in graininess. Color negative films are significantly less grainy than comparable-speed color reversal emulsions.

Storage conditions of the raw stock or exposed undeveloped film can affect graininess. High temperatures or long storage periods increase fog and grain. Force processing also makes the image grainier.

---

4. *Acutance* is a measure of how well the film can reproduce any knife edge transition from black to white.

Graininess varies with subject matter. It is most easily seen in large areas of uniform density. A blue sky that is not overexposed will show more graininess than a landscape. Color negative usually shows the most grain in uniform shadow areas that do not print as deep black. Sharp images divert the eye from the grain: Graininess is most apparent in blurry images. Since grain position changes from frame to frame, grain seems to move or "boil" during projection, making it more noticeable. Granularity does not measure this dynamic aspect of graininess.

CHOOSING A RAW STOCK

As you prepare to shoot a movie, you select which stock or stocks to use for the project. There are many options, and new stocks are constantly being introduced. Seek advice, do tests, and find out what stocks were used for movies that have a look that you like. For the latest listing of available film stocks, check out the manufacturers' websites (see Bibliography).

How film stock will ultimately perform depends on the choice of stock, the exposure, processing, and filters used, among other things. Kodak's Look Manager System is a digital tool that can help previsualize various choices on a laptop using test stills shot with a digital camera.

Many films are still printed the old-fashioned way, from the camera original film to print stock (or to an intermediate first; see Chapter 17). However, today many movies shot on film are transferred to video and all subsequent distribution in video and film comes from the video master (see Editing Film on Video, p. 605). Working in video opens up many opportunities to change the color, contrast, grain, and look of the image digitally. This workflow can have implications for production. For example, Kodak's Vision2 HD color scan film is intended *only* for digital scanning, and can emulate the look of several other Kodak stocks. It can be used as a high-speed or lower-speed stock, in tungsten or daylight without a filter. No matter what stock you use, you can manipulate the image digitally in post during the telecine session or after. If you anticipate a workflow that includes making a digital intermediate or film-out, this should be considered when you choose your raw stock.

Black-and-White Versus Color

Today, most motion pictures, distributed in film or video, are in color. Audiences expect color. Black-and-white may have associations of being old-fashioned or historical. However, because black-and-white is now relatively unusual, it can also command attention. Black-and-white films made in the "color era" have a unique place; for example, Martin Scorsese's *Raging Bull*.

The ascendancy of color in the film industry makes it difficult to find laboratories that do high-quality black-and-white work. Black-and-white, when properly handled, can be exhilaratingly beautiful, but good contrast is the key to this beauty. When the blacks turn muddy or there are no clear whites, the image looks dull. On the other hand, a print with too much contrast has a short tonal range and looks harsh.

Part of the aesthetic challenge of black-and-white is to render the world through the range of gray tones from black to white. Some people think black-and-white gives a realistic look, while others feel that it presents an abstract image of the world. Lighting tends to be more difficult because there is no color contrast to give snap to the image. For example, in black-and-white, a green leaf and red apple may photograph as the same gray tone, whereas in color they would be strongly differentiated. The Hollywood lighting style for black-and-white includes a rim light to separate the subject from the background (see Chapter 12).

Films that mix black-and-white and color generally must be printed on color film stock; color-balancing color print stock to achieve a pleasing black-and-white look can be tricky. Movies can be shot in color and then made monochrome during or after the transfer to video.

Black-and-white films have longer storage lives (color dyes fade) and using black-and-white film may lower production costs. However, some TV broadcasters will not air a contemporary black-and-white movie. Distribution for black-and-white movies is generally more difficult.

Negative Versus Reversal

Most movies are made with negative stocks. There are more stocks available in negative than in reversal. Negative can handle a greater range of lighting conditions and is more forgiving of exposure errors. It is much easier to make a quality print with good sound in negative than in reversal. Labs offer more options and services for negative; some don't handle reversal at all. In short, if you're thinking of starting a project in 16mm or 35mm, think first of negative.

Nevertheless, there are certain advantages to reversal. If you want to minimize costs, you can shoot reversal and project or edit it without making a print. The traditional Super 8 home movie is reversal original (though negative Super 8 is now available). However, projecting or editing the original puts it at great risk of scratching and should not be done for important projects. If you plan to edit and distribute in video, you might just as well start with negative.

Manufacturers include "chrome" in the name of the stock to indicate color reversal—Ektachrome, Fujichrome, etc. Most reversal stocks are made for direct projection of the original with a 5400°K light source and may appear slightly red on a projector with a tungsten bulb (see Chapter 17). A reversal original often looks wonderful, but when a print is made the contrast increases and the image looks hard and grainy. This is particularly a problem in black-and-white. There are low-contrast companion printing stocks for color reversal, but they usually do not produce a good optical sound track. Printing from an internegative can help. Maintaining a low lighting contrast ratio during shooting (see Chapter 12) will result in better contrast in the prints.

Reversal film is easier to handle than negative film. Its emulsion is usually more resistant to scratches. Dust prints as black on reversal, which is much less noticeable than the white sparkle that results from dust in the negative-positive system. Reversal also allows for selective workprinting, since you can examine the original and cull unwanted footage.

Film Speed

Film speed is often the key element in the selection of the raw stock. In general, the faster the speed, the more flexibility you have. Not only is it easier to shoot in available light, but supplementary lighting need not be as bright, cutting lighting costs and creating a better environment for the actors. High-speed film stock allows the lens to be stopped down to increase depth of field. On the other hand, high-speed films may produce a poorer-quality image, with more grain and less sharpness (though there are exceptions). As a rule of thumb, select the slowest film that allows you either to shoot at a preferred f-stop (this is the usual practice in studio production) or to get an adequate exposure in situations where you can't use lights (often very important in documentaries). At this time, the range of standard color negative films extends from ASA 50 to 500. Documentary cinematographers who shoot in unpredictable available light situations often look for the fastest film of acceptable quality. On many productions, two or more stocks are used: a slow speed for exteriors and higher speeds for interiors or night work. Do tests to ensure that the stocks you want to use intercut well. Often, two different stocks are used for the same movie, but look too different to be intercut in the same scene.

PUSHING. Film sensitivity can be increased with forced processing (pushing, see Force Processing and Gamma, p. 262). Different stocks respond to pushing with radically different results; some show unacceptable graininess when pushed even one stop. A stock that responds well to force processing gives you flexibility when encountering unexpected low-light conditions.

Daylight Balance Versus Tungsten

For complete discussion of color balance and film stocks, see Chapter 8.

Film stocks are generally made to be used without a filter with either tungsten illumination (professional lighting at 3200°K) *or* daylight. Eastman Kodak uses the letter T or D after the ASA number to indicate the type (100T film is ASA 100, tungsten). Fuji uses a similar system. Films balanced for tungsten light can be used in daylight with a filter (usually an 85 filter). Similarly, films balanced for daylight can be used in tungsten light with a different filter (80A).

If you plan to shoot *exclusively* in daylight (either outdoors or in a window-lit interior), then it makes sense to use daylight-balanced film. However, because the 80A filter cuts out two stops of light, this can cause problems when you shoot indoors with tungsten illumination. Two stops are a lot to lose when you're lighting a scene—you need four times as much light to compensate. (Of course, you could use daylight-balanced lighting units such as HMIs; see Chapter 12.)

For most filming situations, it's generally a better idea to order tungsten-balanced film. This allows you to shoot indoors with a minimum amount of artificial light (since no light is lost to the filter). When you shoot outside, the ⅔ stop lost by 85 filter is usually not a problem. In fact, often you need additional ND filters to cut the light level down even more. In some situations you can shoot tungsten-balanced film outdoors with no filter (see Chapter 8).

Contrast and Film Stocks

Compared to high-contrast film stocks, low-contrast stocks have a longer, more gently sloped characteristic curve and can handle a greater range of brightness in the scene (they have greater exposure range or latitude; see p. 290). Generally, the slower a stock is, the greater its latitude will be—but not always. Negative stocks have greater latitude than reversal. When you film an interior scene that includes bright windows, a film with a small exposure range will usually not be able to show detail in both the dark interior and the bright window (see Fig. 7-22). Some film stocks are designed to be especially sensitive to the darker areas, "reaching into the shadows" to provide good detail at the low end of the curve.

It's important to think about contrast in terms of the several linked steps that bring the image from the camera to the audience. Most negative camera stocks are designed with reduced contrast (gamma), which, when printed on more contrasty release print stock, will produce an image of pleasing contrast. As discussed above, most reversal stocks are made for direct projection without making a print first. The high overall gamma looks correct on the original, but prints often look too contrasty.

Some stocks are designed especially for direct transfer to video. These feature low contrast (great exposure range) and color rendering that is well matched to the telecine. See Chapter 18 for more on contrast and video transfer.

Color Reproduction

Every film stock has a particular *palette*, or range of colors or tones it creates on screen (analogous to the palette from which a painter selects paint). The colors you see on screen stem partly from what's in front of the camera (sets, costumes, lighting, filters) and partly from what's in the camera (the stock). Different manufacturers design their films for different looks. Different laboratories may make the same stock appear quite different in terms of color, grain, and sharpness. Often, higher-contrast stocks tend toward deeper, more saturated color.

PACKAGING, HANDLING, AND PURCHASING

Most cameras use *core-mounted* film. The film roll is wound around a plastic hub (the core) and must be handled only in darkness (see Fig. 6-14). Some cameras accept *daylight spools*, which are solid metal reels that allow the film to be loaded in light. See Camera Film Capacity, p. 242, for a detailed discussion of roll lengths and camera loading procedures.

Film stocks have a multidigit identification number (see Fig. 7-9). The Kodak film in the illustration has the number 5279-184-1704. The film type is 5279; the "52" tells us this is a 35mm stock. If it were 16mm, it would start with "72" instead (7279). Experienced filmmakers often refer to stocks only with the second two digits, as in, "give me two rolls of 79." The second part of the number (184 in the example) is the emulsion batch number. For consistency, many filmmakers prefer to buy only film from a single batch, though with improved quality control that may not be necessary. When each batch of film is manufactured, it is first created in wide rolls, which are cut down into many smaller rolls for sale. The last part of the number (1704) is the roll number and part of the roll from which this piece of film was cut. It's a good idea to note the entire number as a check against potential problems (see p. 245).

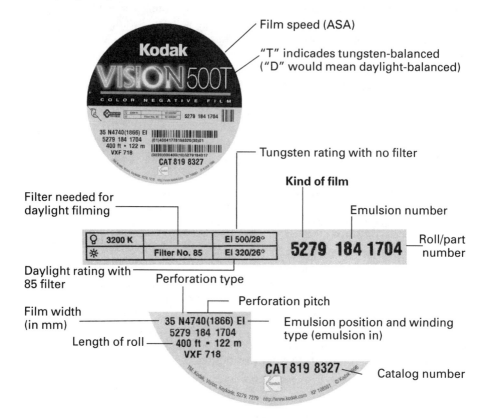

Fig. 7-9. Film label and enlarged details. This label is for Kodak 5279 color negative film, also called Vision 500T (now discontinued). Kodak's newer Vision2 500T film is renumbered 5218. (Eastman Kodak Company)

Perforations

Super 8 film is perforated on one side (*single-perforated*, or *single-perf*), while 35mm film is perforated on both sides (*double-perforated*, or *double-perf*). Film in 16mm may be single- or double-perforated (see Fig. 1-35). Double-perf film can be used in any camera and has a slight advantage over single-perf when cement splicing the original. When shooting Super 16 you must use single-perf.

The *pitch* of the perforations is the measured distance from the bottom of one perforation to the bottom of the next perforation (see Fig. 1-34). A 16mm camera original for high-speed cameras sometimes has a slightly longer pitch and may be marked "high speed" on the label.

Different camera formats use a different number of perfs for each frame. For example, the standard 35mm frame spans four perfs, but there are also three-perf and two-perf formats (see Chapter 1). However, both formats use identical 35mm film stock.

Windings

Raw stock perforated on one edge and wound with the emulsion side in has two possible windings, designated *winding A* and *winding B* (see Fig. 7-10). Camera original is almost invariably in winding B. Stock in winding A is generally used only by laboratories for printing.

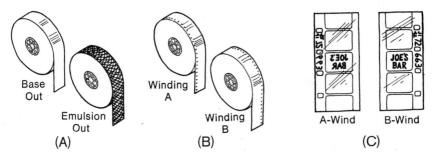

Fig. 7-10. Emulsion position and winds. (A) Film can be wound base-out or emulsion-out. (B) Single-perforated film, wound base-out, can be winding A or winding B, depending on the position of the perforations as shown. (C) With the base facing you, B-wind film reads properly through the base, while A-wind film will be reversed or flipped. Note that the key numbers usually read the same as the image. Compare with Fig. 17-2. (Carol Keller)

There's another laboratory use of these terms that often leads to confusion: *A-wind* and *B-wind* are used to distinguish whether the picture "reads correctly" (that is, not flipped left to right) when viewed facing the emulsion side (A-wind) or when viewed facing the base (B-wind). An easy way to remember this is that *B*-wind film reads correctly through the *base*. B-wind is also called *camera original position*.

Key Numbers and Edge Identification

Along the edge of 16mm and 35mm film, the manufacturer exposes a latent image with information such as the name of the manufacturer, the film identification number, and a running footage count. This information is readable after the film is processed, and can be printed from the negative to another piece of film (when making a workprint, for example). The numbers that track the footage are called *key numbers* or *latent edge numbers*. Key numbers allow each frame of film to be identified by number and are indispensable for conforming the original (see Chapter 17).

Today, most film stocks also have a machine-readable bar code version of the key number. This is generically called *keycode* (Eastman calls its system KeyKode; Fuji calls its MR Code). When editing film on video, keycode is tremendously useful because it allows the telecine and other machines to automatically identify and find each frame of film (see Chapters 15 and 18).

In 16mm, key numbers are printed every half foot (20 frames). When counting frames in 16mm there is a dot at the beginning of the number, which is the *zero frame reference mark*. In Fig. 7-11, you can see the dot to the left of the letter "M" in the key number M69 1234 7880. This is the frame that should be considered exactly 7880. The next frame going toward the tail (in the direction of 7881) would be 7880 + 1. The frame on the other side of the mark going toward the head (in the direction of 7879) would be 7879 + 19.

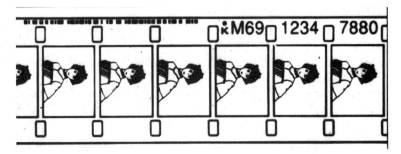

Fig. 7-11. 16mm key numbers and KeyKode. (Eastman Kodak Company)

In 35mm, key numbers are printed every foot (16 frames for standard four-perf cameras). There is also a midfoot key number to help identify short pieces of film; this is located 32 perforations from the main number. When counting frames in 35mm, the zero-frame reference dot immediately follows the last four digits of the key number. Thus, for the key number KJ 23 1234 5677, the frame where the dot falls is 5677. The next frame going toward the tail (in the direction of 5678) would be 5677 + 1. The frame on the other side of dot (going toward the head) would be 5676 + 15.

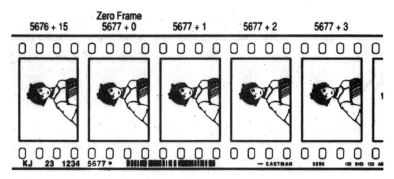

Fig. 7-12. 35mm key numbers and KeyKode. (Eastman Kodak Company)

Unfortunately, there are now so many types of coding and numbering schemes in filmmaking that the names (and concepts) can be easily confused. Here are some things that key numbers and keycode are *not*:

1. Ink edge numbers (sometimes also called "edge code," "Acmade numbers," or just "edge numbers"). Generated by a machine that stamps an ink number on film workprint and mag sound to aid in synchronizing (see p. 602). Some labs also use ink numbers on the negative.
2. In-camera timecode. Generated by some cameras and exposed on the edge of the film during shooting (see Fig. 6-16).
3. Video (telecine) timecode. Generated during the film-to-tape transfer for use in video editing; not printed on the film (see p. 702).

For more on key numbers and timecode, see Chapters 17 and 18.

Handling Film Stock

Unprocessed film undergoes change over time. There is a gradual lowering of speed and contrast and an increase in the fog level. Color films are particularly vulnerable, since the changes may occur at different rates in the three emulsion layers, causing a color shift that may not be correctable in printing. Poor storage conditions not only cause changes in the emulsion's photographic properties, they can also change the film's physical condition (for example, brittleness and shrinking).

High relative humidity (greater than 70 percent) can damage labels and cartons and produce rust on metal cans. As long as the original moistureproof tape seals the can of raw stock, humidity is less of a problem.

Eastman Kodak recommends using raw stock within six months of purchase. Avoid heat when storing film. The lower the temperature, the slower the aging process. At high temperatures, change occurs rapidly. An automobile left in the sun can heat up above 140°F (60°C), and film in the car can undergo significant changes in a matter of hours. Similarly, stock left on a radiator will show significant deterioration in a short time.

If storing film for up to three months before use, keep it below 55°F (13°C) at relative humidity of 60 percent or lower. Put it in a refrigerator if the storage area is too warm. Whenever storing film for more than three months, put it in a freezer, ideally at 0° to −10°F (−18° to −23°C). Since relative humidity in a refrigerator or freezer is very high, pack film in plastic freezer bags to control humidity. After you remove the stock from cold storage, allow it to come to room temperature before breaking the moistureproof seal. This prevents condensation and spotting on the stock. Minimum warm-up times are 1 to 1½ hours for Super 8 and 16mm stocks and 3 to 5 hours for 35mm. If the day is particularly warm and humid, increase the warm-up period.

Once the seal is broken, expose the film as soon as possible, and then, after exposure, have it processed as soon as possible. If processing must be delayed, avoid high temperature and humidity, since the latent image is even more vulnerable than the unexposed stock to deterioration. If the cans are resealed with the moistureproof tape, a household refrigerator may be used to store the film, although a freezer at 0°F is preferred. Though not recommended, we have found that some exposed stocks maintained an excellent image when frozen for more than a year prior to processing.

Kodak recommends storing processed film in a cool, dry place, at 70°F (21°C) or lower. Though often impractical, long-term storage for color film is ideally at 36°F (2°C) or lower. For the ultimate protection against color dye fading, make black-and-white separation positives.

Static electricity discharges can expose raw stock and cause lightning-like streaks or blotches on the processed film. Low temperature and low humidity increase the possibility of static discharge. Black-and-white stocks are more susceptible than color. Improvements in stocks have made the problem less common now; in the past, cameras had to be grounded at times to avoid the problem. You can help avoid static discharge by giving raw stock removed from cold storage adequate warm-up time and by rewinding raw stock at slow speeds.

AIR TRAVEL. When traveling through airports, beware of X-ray machines! Unprocessed film can tolerate some X-ray exposure, but excessive amounts will increase the fog level and grain. Kodak says that X-ray machines used for carry-on baggage shouldn't cause noticeable damage to most films. However, as the threat of terrorism increases, so do the intensity and number of scans in a typical trip. X-ray exposure is cumulative, so repeated X-ray inspections are most problematic, especially for high-speed films. Sometimes you do best by hand-carrying the film and asking for a hand inspection at the gate. However, some inspectors will demand to look inside the film cans! Bring a changing bag in case it's needed. Sometimes you can contact the airport manager in advance to get a manual inspection.

In the past, one solution was to pack the film in a cooler lined with lead foil and send it as baggage. However, newer baggage X-ray machines are far more powerful (and damaging to the film) than the ones used to inspect hand-carried items.[5] Kodak recommends never shipping unprocessed film as checked baggage on commercial airlines. Check the X-ray policies of commercial couriers and mail carriers. Consider using an export company or customs broker to ship the film and do all the paperwork. Another possibility is to process the film in the area or country where you're shooting. Be sure to label film (PHOTOGRAPHIC MATERIALS—NO X-RAY). Normal X-ray inspection shouldn't damage film that's already been processed, audio- or videotapes, or digital memory.

Purchasing Raw Stock

Order raw stock from the manufacturer's catalog by catalog number and stock name. For example, ordering Kodak Vision2 500T film allows numerous further possibilities, but the catalog number 1289578 identifies the stock as 5218, 35mm, 400 feet on core, emulsion in, standard perforations.

Use fresh raw stock. Order it to arrive a week or so before it is needed rather than months in advance. As discussed above, many people prefer to order stock with the same emulsion number to guarantee uniformity. If you encounter a raw stock of an unknown age, the manufacturer can tell from the emulsion number when it was manufactured. Of course, this tells you nothing about its past storage conditions. Some manufacturers and supply houses can deliver stock overnight if you run out during a shoot.

It's often possible to purchase raw stock that was ordered by another customer and never used. There are businesses that buy and sell unexposed stock. Generally, they will allow you to return defective stock. Test a roll by sending fifteen or twenty feet of unexposed stock to the lab to be developed and checked for increased fog, which, if present, is a sign of poor storage or possible exposure to airport X-ray machines. Buy previously owned stock of the same emulsion number to avoid having to test each batch. Raw stock less than three months old sells for about 15 to 25 percent off list price, and less if the stock consists of short-ends (parts of complete rolls). Stock older than three months is cheaper, but you may be pennywise and pound foolish. The stock is only one of many costs.

5. With some newer X-ray machines, the lead foil automatically triggers a more intense and damaging ray on the film.

THE LIGHT METER
AND EXPOSURE CONTROL

Many of the ideas in this section build on concepts introduced in Properties of the Film Stock, p. 254.

Exposure

When you're filming a scene, there is no single "correct" exposure. We might say that a scene is properly exposed when the image on film looks pleasing to the eye and important elements in the scene are shown with sufficient detail. If a close-up of a person's face is significantly overexposed (that is, too much light is allowed to strike the film), the face on screen will look too bright and facial details will be washed out. If the shot was seriously underexposed, the projected image would look very dark and muddy. In both cases, facial details are lost—either because they are washed out or because they are indistinguishable from parts of the emulsion that have received no exposure at all.

When shooting negative film, the negative is exposed in the camera and then a positive print (or video transfer) is made to view the image. Compare the negative image in Fig. 7-2 with the positive in Fig. 12-26. You can see that the dark parts of the positive image (the man's sweater and the doorway on the left side) are quite thin and transparent on the negative. The light parts of the scene (the bright side of his face and the splash of sun on the back wall) show up in the negative as dark and relatively dense (thick or opaque). For an area in the scene to be rendered with good detail on a positive print, that area in the negative needs to be sufficiently dense and detailed. Areas where the negative is too thin and transparent will have relatively little detail in the positive print. In this image, the sweater or the doorway might be considered "underexposed" in the sense that they show up on the positive print as very dark and lacking much detail. However, in the context of the whole picture, this lack of detail seems natural. The most important part of this scene is the man's face, and as long as his skin tone appears naturally bright and rendered with good detail, other parts of the scene can be allowed to go brighter or darker. Thus, "correct" exposure means identifying what's important in the scene and exposing that properly.

If important details are visible on the film after processing, shots that are slightly too bright or too dark can be corrected when the film is printed or transferred to video. In general, reversal stocks are less forgiving of exposure errors than negative stocks. When shooting with color negative stocks, you want to avoid significant *under*exposure because the resulting negative will be thin and without detail. When shooting reversal stocks, significant *over*exposure will result in the film being thin and lacking in detail. With both negative and reversal, the goal is to expose in the *middle* of the range, to capture detail in both the bright areas (the *highlights*) and the dark ones (shadows), so the overall exposure seems natural and pleasing.

Exposure and Incident Light

The exposure of an object on film is related to the amount of light *falling on the object*—that is, the *incident light*. Incident light can be measured with an *incident light meter* that has a translucent plastic hemisphere (or *hemispherical diffuser*), which simulates the light-gathering ability of a typical three-dimensional subject—specifically, the human head. The incident meter is held at the position of the subject (or in the same light) and is *pointed in the direction of the camera*. The meter averages together the light coming from the front, the sides and, to a lesser extent, the back of the subject.

Fig. 7-13. (left) The reflected meter is pointed at the subject from the direction of the camera. (right) The incident meter is held in the same light as the subject and pointed toward the camera. (Carol Keller)

Many cinematographers use incident meters almost exclusively. Incident light readings are quick and easy to do, and they usually result in proper exposure of facial skin tones. Faces, especially in close-ups and medium shots, are often the most important element in the frame.

INCIDENT METERS AND CONTRASTY SCENES. Some scenes contain a great range of incident light. Consider the example of filming people by a building on a sunny day. If you take an incident reading near the people in the shadows, and then set the exposure accordingly, the people in the sun are likely to be drastically overexposed. Conversely, if the incident reading is taken in the sun, the people in the shadows will be underexposed. This can happen to varying degrees with all film stocks. The reason is that the range of brightness in the scene (the lighting contrast; see p. 447) exceeds the film's sensitivity range (latitude or exposure range; see p. 290).

Fig. 7-14. A scene with high lighting contrast. (left) If you take a light meter reading in the sunlit area and expose accordingly, the shadow area is underexposed. (right) If you take your reading in the shadows, the sunlit area is overexposed. (center) A compromise exposure, slightly underexposing the figures in the shadows. Film stocks vary in their ability to handle high-contrast scenes.

In Fig. 7-14, the figures in the foreground are lit by direct sun and the figures in the background above them are in shadow. Had you witnessed this scene with your naked eye (and a dramatic scene it was), you would have had no problem seeing detail in both the shadow and sunlit areas. This is because the eye's retina has a great range of sensitivity and your iris constantly adjusts the amount of light that strikes it. Film stocks, however, have a much narrower range of sensitivity. The image on the left is exposed for the sun. The image on the right is exposed for the shadows. The image in the center is a compromise exposure that attempts to split the difference.

Other approaches to this contrast problem include adding light to the shadow areas to reduce contrast or using a lower-contrast film stock that has greater latitude.

Exposure and Reflected Light

An object's exposure on film is more fully described as resulting from the *total amount of light reflected by the object* in the direction of the camera's lens. This is determined not only by incident light but also by what percentage of the incident light is reflected by the object (that is, its *reflectance*). Subject reflectance is determined by color and surface texture; a dark-colored, textured object reflects less light than a light-colored, smooth one does. For example, a dark wool sweater in the sun (low reflectance, high incident light) might produce the same amount of exposure as a bright white car in the shade (high reflectance, low incident light). That is to say, their *brightness (luminance* or *intensity*) is the same.

To see how reflectance relates to incident light, look at the middle image in Fig. 7-14. Of the figures in the background, the tiger and the figure in the middle received equal amounts of incident light, but the white, reflectant tiger produces more exposure than the dark clothes of the man next to him.

The amount of light reflected by the subject can be measured with a *reflected light meter*. This meter requires more care to use properly, but it can give more precise readings than the incident meter, especially for subjects whose reflectance is not near that of facial skin tones. It can also be used in certain situations, like filming through a window, where the incident meter would be useless. The reflected meter is *pointed at the subject* from the camera position (or closer). The reflected reading must always be interpreted and never taken at face value.

UNDERSTANDING THE REFLECTED READING. When film is exposed, developed, and then projected on a screen, it can produce a range of tonalities from dark black (where the film holds back the projector light) to bright white (where most of the light shines through). The tone in the middle of this range is called *middle gray*. Reflected light meters are designed so that if you take a reading of any uniform object and then expose the film accordingly, the object will appear as middle gray on film. So, if you take a reading of an "average" subject, it will appear in the middle of the tonal range when projected on screen and it will look natural. But what if the subject isn't average? Say you take a reflected reading of a black cat. This will result in the cat appearing on screen as middle gray—which means the cat will be unnaturally bright and other objects in the scene will probably be very overexposed. So, if you want dark objects to appear dark, you must give them less exposure than the reflected meter reading of the object would indicate. Similarly, for light objects to appear light, they must be given more exposure than the meter suggests.

A *gray card*, or neutral test card, is a piece of dull gray cardboard that reflects 18 percent of the light that strikes it. This card is intended to represent an indoors object of "average" reflectance. If you take a reading of the gray card and expose the film accordingly, the tonality of objects in the scene will usually look natural on film—neither too light nor too dark.

Gray cards are available at photographic or film supply stores. It's a good idea to carry one. Keep it protected in an envelope. As an experiment, set up a gray card facing the camera from several feet away. Use an incident meter to take a light reading at the card (remembering to point the meter toward the camera). Now take a reading of the card with a reflected meter (pointing it toward the card from a few feet away). The two readings should be the same.

Since Caucasian skin is about twice as reflectant as the gray card—having about 35 percent reflectance—you could just as well base an exposure on a reading of skin tone, as long as you remember to give the film twice as much exposure as the meter indicates. This is normally done by opening the iris diaphragm one stop (see p. 284 for other types of skin).

LIGHT METERS

Meter Types

Light meters, or *exposure meters*, may be either handheld or built into the camera. Some meters can take *both* incident and reflected readings. Some of these work quite well; others are designed primarily for one type of reading and are inferior for the other. Some reflected meters have a sliding or detachable translucent plastic bulb (hemispherical diffuser) for incident readings, but the diffuser is much smaller than the ones found on true incident meters and does not respond as well to side and back light. Similarly, some incident meters have detachable parts so they can be converted for reflected readings; these may have too-large angles of acceptance (see p. 281) compared to true reflected meters. If possible, get a meter of each type (which also provides a backup if one breaks).

The most useful meters give you a direct reading of *f*-stops when you push a button (see Fig. 7-16). Less useful are meters that require you to find the *f*-stop using a calculator dial on the meter (time is precious when shooting). Some direct-reading meters (like the older-style Spectra) use a set of slides that must be inserted to key the meter to the film and shutter speed settings. Slides are easy to lose and may not be available for the particular film stock and processing combination you are using.

Most light meters operate with a photoelectric cell that generates electricity when light strikes it. Some meters use this electricity to deflect an indicator needle. These meters may be less expensive and require no batteries. Most modern meters have a digital readout and use batteries (either more expensive button-type photo batteries or inexpensive AA cells). Digital meters are more rugged than meters with needle mechanisms and some are more accurate. All meters are generally most accurate in the middle of their operating range. Readings at the lower end of the scale tend to be the least precise. Light meters may have a zeroing adjustment and/or a battery check. It's a good idea to have a technician check your meter periodically.

Fig. 7-15. Analog direct-reading Spectra incident light meter. The upper scale reads foot-candles, the lower reads *f*-stops. Requires slides; the tab of the ASA 32 slide is visible at top. (Simon Associates)

Fig. 7-16. Digital meter. Shutter speed and ASA are keyed into the meter and then *f*-stops can be read directly. (Konica Minolta Corp.)

Reading the Meter

In controlling exposure, you are regulating the amount of light that strikes each frame of film. The amount of light is determined by how long the shutter is open (the shutter speed, determined by the shutter angle and the camera speed) and how much light passes through the lens during this time (affected by the iris diaphragm setting, the filters in use, light loss in the lens, and light loss in the viewfinder optics). Usually, the meter is set to compensate for all the other factors, then the light reading is used to determine the proper iris setting (that is, the *f*-number) for a particular shot.

For typical film cameras, the shutter angle is about 180 degrees and, when run at sound speed (24 fps), the shutter speed is about ⅟₅₀ second. The shutter speed for any camera can be found in its instruction manual or can be easily calculated if you know the shutter angle (see Chapter 6). If you change the camera speed (for example, to produce slow-motion effects), you will alter the shutter speed.

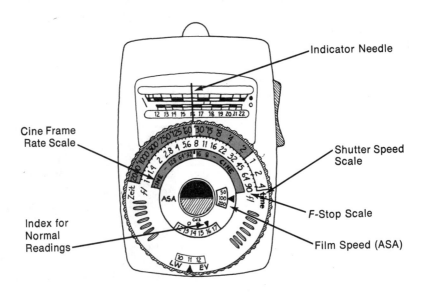

Fig. 7-17. Calculator dial found on Gossen Luna Pro reflected/incident meter. The film speed window indicates that the meter is set for ASA 100 film. The light reading (16) is set opposite the triangle in the window just below the ASA setting. A camera with a 180-degree shutter run at 24 fps has a shutter speed of 1/50 second (50 can be found on the time scale between '60 and '30). The *f*-stop is read opposite this point. Alternately, the *f*-stop could be read opposite the 24-fps mark on the cine scale (found between 32 and 16). The meter indicates a reading between *f*/5.6 and *f*/8. (Carol Keller)

The meter must be set to the proper film speed (ASA) for the film stock you are using. Remember to compensate for filters you may be using (for example—when shooting in daylight with tungsten-balanced color film—see Chapter 8). Cameras with built-in meters usually compensate for filters automatically, and, in Super 8, the ASA and shutter speed may be set automatically as well (see Chapter 6). With direct-reading meters, the shutter speed is also set on the meter so that f-stops can be read directly when the trigger is depressed (see Figs. 7-15 and 7-16).

On meters with calculator dials, the indicator needle is read against a numbered scale. Set this number on the calculator dial. You will find the shutter speed on the *shutter speed scale* (sometimes labeled *time* or *zeit*), which is marked in fractions of a second ('60, '30, etc.). You can then read the f-stop opposite the proper shutter speed. With cameras equipped with 175- or 180-degree shutters, you may find it easier to read from the *cine scale*. This is marked in frames per second (64 fps, 32, 16, etc.) and usually has a bold mark at 24 fps, corresponding to $\frac{1}{50}$-second shutter speed. After you have thus determined the f-number, you can set the lens's iris accordingly.

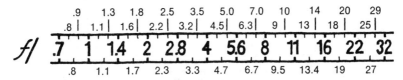

Fig. 7-18. Intermediate values on the f-stop scale. Above the scale are one-third stop increments; below the scale are half-stop increments. (Carol Keller)

In most circumstances, it doesn't pay to be more precise than about one third of a stop when calculating exposures; few meters are accurate enough and few film stocks (especially negative stocks) will show the difference.

VIEWFINDER OPTICS. With cameras that have internal beam-splitter viewfinders (for example, most Super 8 cameras and the 16mm Bolex), some light is diverted from the film to the viewfinder (see Fig. 6-9). When you use a *handheld light meter* rather than a built-in one, do not set it to the *actual* shutter speed (based on shutter angle and frame rate); instead, use an *effective* shutter speed that compensates for light lost in the viewfinder. The effective speed is always faster. On some Bolexes at 24 fps, actual speed is $\frac{1}{65}$ second, effective is $\frac{1}{80}$. Your camera's manual should indicate the proper setting.

F-STOPS AND T-STOPS. *F*-stops do not take into account light lost internally in a lens, whereas T-stops do (see p. 150). When you use a professional zoom lens marked in T-stops (sometimes a red scale on the opposite side of the iris ring from the f-stops), use the T-stops instead of the f-stops for all exposure calculations. Ignore the fact that light meters are marked in f-stops. T-stops should also be used whenever you are filming with more than one lens.

The Angle of Acceptance

All meters built into still and movie cameras are of the reflected type. Built-in, through-the-lens meters may average together the light from the entire frame (called *averaging meters*), they may read only the light from objects in the center of the frame (*spot meters*; see Fig. 7-19), or they may read the whole frame, giving more emphasis to the center (*center-weighted meters*). Consult your camera manual to find out what part of the frame the meter reads.

A few cameras, like the Canon Scoopic, have built-in meters that do not read through the lens. This meter is comparable to having a handheld meter attached to the camera.

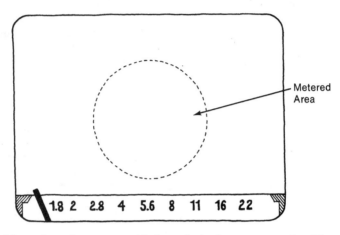

Fig. 7-19. Metered area in a camera with through-the-lens spot metering. The relative size of the metered area varies from camera to camera. (Carol Keller)

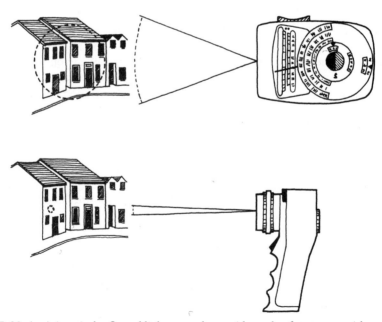

Fig. 7-20. (top) A typical reflected light meter has a wide angle of acceptance (about 40 degrees here) and averages areas of differing brightness. (bottom) A spot reflected meter (pictured here with a 5-degree angle of acceptance) can isolate a small area in the subject. (Carol Keller)

Handheld reflected meters have a window over the photocell that allows light to enter from an *angle of acceptance* (usually between 15 and 60 degrees). Some meters are designed to simulate the angle of view of a "normal" lens, but the meter may read a wider or narrower area than the lens you are using. All the light reflected by objects within the angle of acceptance is averaged together, so if you are trying to read the light from an individual object, it is necessary to get close to it (but be careful not to cast a shadow with the meter or your body). Handheld *spot meters* are simply reflected meters that have a very narrow angle of acceptance, often 1 degree or less. They can be used to read the light from small areas at a greater distance. Cameras with zoom lenses and built-in, through-the-lens meters can be zoomed in for variable-angle spot metering.

TAKING READINGS

The Incident Reading

Because the incident light meter is easy to use and renders skin tones consistently, it is preferred by cinematographers in many filming situations. As previously discussed, the incident light meter measures the amount of illumination falling on the subject rather than the light reflected by it. For many scenes, taking an incident reading is faster than using a reflected meter. Incident meters are preferred when studio lighting is used because they conveniently indicate how much light is contributed by each light source. In this case, the hemispherical diffuser may be replaced with a *flat disc diffuser* that can more easily be aimed at one light at a time. Incident meters are often advantageous in those situations in which it is difficult to approach the subject to take a reading. If the subject is fairly far

Fig. 7-21. Spot meter. This meter has a 1-degree angle of acceptance, approximately the angle of view of a 550mm lens on a 16mm camera. (Konica Minolta Corp.)

away outdoors, you can take an incident reading from the camera position (assuming it is in the same light), and—unlike a reflected reading—it won't be thrown off by large expanses of sky or other extraneous elements. Unlike the reflected meter, the incident meter is useless when you film something that *emits* light (like a television screen), when you film through something that *filters* light (for example, a tinted car windshield), or whenever the meter cannot be placed in the same light as the subject.

Often, the part of the scene that is most important to expose correctly is skin tone. Incident meters are not affected by extraneous elements in a scene, and are therefore very good for exposing skin tones consistently. Nevertheless, there are many instances when the incident reading must be interpreted and not used directly.

Often it is necessary to "bias" or "weight" an exposure reading to compensate for important parts of the frame that are especially light or dark. Say you are filming someone in the snow. The normal incident reading would expose the person's face well, but the snow, because it is so reflective, would probably overexpose. As a general rule, if important subject matter is especially reflective (a white car, for example), close the iris a half to one stop from the incident reading; if it is especially dark and absorptive (dark clothing), open the iris by the same amount. You may also decide to adjust the exposure for creative purposes; for example, if you want a person lurking in the shadows to look dark, close the iris from an incident reading taken in the shadow.

The Reflected Reading

The reflected light meter can give the filmmaker a more complete idea of the exposure of various elements in a scene. Many people are familiar with the idea of reflected readings from doing still photography with cameras equipped with built-in meters. Still cameras often have averaging meters or center-weighted meters. You take a reading of the whole scene, set the exposure, and shoot. This kind of reflected reading can work fine for "average" subjects, particularly if they are front lit (the light coming from behind the camera). But a single reflected reading of the whole scene can cause the subject to be poorly exposed if the subject or the background is particularly light or dark, or if the light is coming from behind the subject. For movies, there is the added consideration that the framing of the picture may change significantly *during* the shot.

Whenever you use a reflected meter, always ask yourself if the area of the scene that you're pointing the meter at is important. Base the exposure on the most important areas, and use readings of other areas to give you a sense of the overall range of brightness in the scene. If the range of brightness (the contrast) of the scene is very great, you may need to take steps to lessen it.

Also ask yourself how you want the area you're reading to look on film. As discussed above, the reflected reading of an object will cause that object to appear on film in the middle of the tonal range. If you're reading an object that's near to average reflectance (like the 18 percent gray card), then the meter reading will result in that object looking natural on film. But if the object you're reading should look relatively dark on film, you need to give it less exposure than the meter indicates (usually by closing down the iris—that is, using a higher *f*-stop than the one indicated on the meter).

CLOSE-UPS AND MEDIUM SHOTS. In medium shots and close-ups of people (see Fig. 9-5), it's important that facial skin tones be exposed correctly. To take readings directly from the subject's face, put the meter close enough so that other areas are excluded from the meter's field of view. Be careful not to block the light or cast shadows with your body or the meter. If your skin tone is similar to your subject's, you can read the back of your hand instead, as long as it is in the same light. Since Caucasian skin is about twice as reflective as the gray card, you must give it about twice as much exposure as the meter indicates to render it appropriately light on film. Thus if the meter reads *f*/8, open up the iris to *f*/5.6. Black skin is usually less reflective than the gray card. You might stop down the iris a half stop for medium black skin, a full stop for darker black skin (a meter reading of f/8 would then be exposed at f/11). Some people have black skin that is extremely dark and absorptive and may require more exposure compensation.

You can easily find out exactly how much to compensate for your skin tone or the skin of your subject by comparing a reflected reading of the skin with an incident reading (or a reflected reading of a gray card) taken in the same light. If the reading of your hand reads, say, f/5.6, and the incident reading is halfway between f/4 and f/5.6, you know to open the iris a half stop from a reading of your hand. You have thus "calibrated" your hand as a portable gray card.

Faces are normally lit so that part of the face is bright and part is in shadow. In general, if compensations are made as above, the exposure should be based on a reading of the brighter side. However, if the light comes from the side, more than half the face may be in shadow. You may want the dark side to remain dark. But if it's important to see more detail in the shadows, you might increase the exposure a half to one stop from the exposure used for the bright side. (For exposing faces that are fully backlit see Backlight, p. 286.)

One way to expose skin tones with a reflected meter is to use an 18 percent gray card. Angle the gray card halfway between the subject and the main source of light and take a reading from about six inches away with the reflected meter. This is essentially a measure of the incident light (since the gray card has the same reflectancy in every situation), and it should produce about the same reading as an incident light meter.

While these methods can get you consistent exposure for skin tones, it should be noted that there are many situations in which skin tone is *deliberately* exposed brighter or darker from shot to shot or scene to scene. You might start with your meter reading, then open or close the iris to achieve the effect you want.

WIDE SHOTS. In wide shots, landscapes and scenes where people do not figure prominently, instead of basing the exposure on skin tone, it's often better to take a reading of the average amount of reflected light in the scene. To do this, point the meter (or the camera, if you are using a built-in meter) at the scene from the camera position. If you are shooting outside, a bright sky will tend to throw off the reading; angle the meter downward somewhat to avoid reading too much of the sky. In general, you should avoid pointing the meter at light sources. An averaging meter with a wide angle of acceptance can take in the whole scene and give you an average just by pressing the button. A spot meter, on the other hand, will fluctuate wildly as you scan it across highlight and shadow areas, so you will need to calculate the average. Some meters will store readings in memory, helping you to find the average.

One approach is to take readings of the brightest and darkest areas where you want to see detail and base your exposure on the average between them. When calculating the average between readings of bright and dark areas, you are not looking for the mathematical average, but one that is expressed in f-stops. Thus, the average of two readings (say, f/2 and f/16) is the stop halfway between the two (f/5.6), not the mathematical average $(2 + 16)/2 = 9$. Meters like the Gossen Luna Pro indicate light readings on a numbered scale, which can be averaged in the familiar way and then converted to f-stops.

REFLECTED AND INCIDENT READINGS TOGETHER. Spot readings of specific areas can be useful for fine-tuning an exposure based on an incident reading or on an average reading of the whole scene. For example, you might take an incident reading near the subject, then scan around the scene with a reflected meter to get a precise reading of particularly bright or dark areas of the subject or background. (You could also do this with an incident meter.) If important areas are reading much brighter or darker than the subject, you can then bias or weight your exposure to compensate, as described above. One rule of thumb says that to see detail in the shadows, they should not read more than two stops or so darker than the exposure you're using. Thus if the lens is set for the main subject at $f/5.6$, the shadows should fall around $f/2.8$. Different film stocks vary in their ability to register shadow detail (see Exposure and Film Stocks, p. 289).

Backlight

Light that comes from behind the subject in the direction of the camera is called *backlight*. Backlighting is often encountered outdoors when shooting in the direction of the sun or when shooting people in cars, or indoors when the subject is positioned in front of a window or a bright wall. Usually when you expose a backlit subject, it is desirable for the shaded side of the subject to appear *slightly* dark, which it is, but not so dark that the person appears in silhouette with no facial detail (see Fig. 7-22).

If you base the exposure on a typical reflected light meter reading from the camera position, the meter's angle of acceptance will include a great deal of the background. The meter then assumes that the subject is very light; it indicates that you should stop down quite far, throwing the person into silhouette. A rule of thumb to prevent silhouetting in this case is to open the iris one and a half stops above what the meter indicates (for example, open from $f/8$ to halfway between $f/4$ and $f/5.6$). Some film and video cameras have a backlight button that does just that.

A more precise exposure calculation can be done by taking an incident reading or by getting very close to the subject to take a reflected reading of the shaded part of the face. Be careful to block any backlight from striking the meter directly. Since you do want the face to appear slightly dark, close the iris about a stop from the exposure you would normally use for the skin tone. For example, when exposing Caucasians with a reflected meter, the same effect can be gained by exposing at the f-number that the meter indicates (*without* the usual compensation of opening the iris one stop).

In backlit settings, it is common to have one exposure for wide shots that include a lot of the bright background and another for closer shots where shadow detail may be more important. The latter might be opened up a half stop or so more than the former.

Special Exposure Conditions

Setting exposure may involve a series of compromises, especially when areas in the scene vary greatly in their brightness. If you're interested in seeing detail in bright areas, keep the iris slightly further stopped down; if detail in shaded areas is important, open up a little more.

Fig. 7-22. A backlighting problem when shooting toward a window. (top) Exposed for the interior, the outside is overexposed. (bottom) Exposed for outside, the woman is silhouetted. (middle) A compromise exposure, slightly underexposing the woman. (Stephen McCarthy)

FLARE. If you're filming in the direction of a strong light source that's shining directly into the lens (for example, against a very bright window or into the sun), you may pick up lens flare from light that reflects within the lens (see Fig. 4-21). Zoom lenses are prone to severe flare. Flare tends to fog the film, desaturating colors and increasing overall exposure. If there's no way to block this light with your hand or a lens shade, keep in mind that flare can increase exposure a half stop or more. When flare is severe in backlit situations, you may want to close the iris a half stop in addition to the correction you made for backlighting.

SNOW OR SAND. When you film people on a sunny beach or in a snowscape, a typical reflected reading from the camera position will be thrown off by the bright background. For close-ups and medium shots, use an incident meter or take a close reflected reading of skin tone in the normal way. If good reproduction of the snow or sand is important, decrease this reading by a half to one stop (especially for wide shots).

NIGHT SCENES. As long as some bright highlights, such as street signs, storefronts, or narrow areas of street light, are visible, large areas of the frame can be rendered dark in night scenes. Similarly, if there are bright facial highlights recorded on the film, then the general exposure of the face can be lower than normal. (See Fig. 5-4 and Special Lighting Effects, p. 482.)

DISTANT LANDSCAPES. Haze, which may not be apparent to the eye, increases the exposure of distant objects on film. In hazy conditions, use a skylight or haze filter on the camera. Use a spot meter to average distant highlight and shadow areas, or, with an incident meter, decrease the exposure a half stop for front-lit scenes, or about a stop for side-lit scenes.

PARTIALLY OVERCAST SKIES. Thick clouds passing in front of the sun can decrease exposure by three stops and change the color temperature of the light. Don't forget to open the iris to compensate for the former. In controlled filming situations, sometimes a frame is mounted above the subjects (an *overhead*) to hold thin diffusion material, which helps minimize the difference between sun and clouds (see Chapter 12).

SUNRISE AND SUNSET. For sunrise or sunset shots in which the foreground scene is mostly silhouetted, take a reflected reading of the sky but not the sun directly. Closing down the iris from this reading may deepen the color of the sun, but it will also make the landscape darker. When possible, bracket exposures by using the reading you think is correct, then shoot with a half to one stop more, then the same amount less. If scenes are front-lit by a red rising or setting sun, no 85 filter need be used with tungsten-balanced color film. Backlit scenes may look blue without it.

FLAT COPYWORK. For discussion on flat copywork see Preparing Film Titles, p. 673.

Built-in Meters and Automatic Exposure Control

Reflected light meters are built into most Super 8 cameras and some 16mm cameras. Usually they read through the camera's taking lens. Built-in meters can be convenient, particularly if the light changes while you're shooting, but they have a number of drawbacks. If you have only a built-in meter, you lack the ability to take incident readings and you must carry the camera around to take readings, which can be awkward.

In most Super 8 cameras, the ASA and shutter speed settings on the light meter are keyed automatically by the film cartridge and the camera speed selector (see Chapter 6). If the meter indicates that there is insufficient light for filming, you may decide to push-process the film to increase its speed (ASA). However, if you push one stop, the meter's reading (if any) will be one stop too low for the film.

It can sometimes be unnerving to see how the through-the-lens reflected reading changes during a shot. Say you're shooting someone against a dark background, zooming in from wide shot to close-up. The exposure should remain unchanged, but the through-the-lens reading will be very different at the end of the shot than it was at the beginning. It takes practice to know when to ignore the meter.

AUTOMATIC FEATURES. Cameras with built-in meters may allow the filmmaker to choose between manual and automatic control of the aperture. Automatic exposure control is available in most Super 8 cameras and some 16mm cameras. See Automatic Exposure Control, p. 119, for a discussion of this feature.

Measuring Foot-Candles and Lux

Filmmakers often need to measure the intensity of light in absolute terms (a reading of *f*-stops is relative to the shutter and film speed being used). One *foot-candle* is the intensity of light emitted by a "standard candle" at a distance of one foot. (Lightbulbs are sometimes rated in candle power.) *Lux* are the metric version of foot-candles. Cinematographers often instruct a crew to light a set to a certain number of foot-candles; a total film "system," including camera, lens, and film stock, is sometimes evaluated in terms of how many foot-candles or lux it needs to operate.

Foot-candles can be measured with an incident meter. Some meters will read directly in foot-candles, others have a conversion chart on the back to calculate them. Shooting ASA 100 film at standard shutter speed with the lens set to *f*/5.6 requires about 260 foot-candles of light.

EXPOSURE AND FILM STOCKS

Beginners usually think about exposure on the basic level of "did the picture come out?" In some ways, that question never goes away, but experienced cinematographers understand that exposure is fundamental to their art, and that it offers opportunities to create a wide range of effects on film. Exposure choices depend on the particular scene and the film stock you're using.

Exposure Range

Perhaps the biggest challenge when exposing either film or video is accommodating the fact that the range of brightness in many scenes exceeds the camera's ability to faithfully record it. A common example is shooting an interior scene with bright windows visible in the background. Your eye can easily adjust to both the dim interior and the bright exterior; however, film and video systems cannot handle this much contrast in one exposure. You might have to choose between exposing for either the interior or the exterior, but can't count on both being rendered with detail (see Fig. 7-22).

As discussed above (see Contrast of the Image, p. 260, and Contrast and Film Stocks, p. 268), some stocks can accommodate a great range in scene brightness, rendering both bright highlights and deep shadow with good detail. Such stocks are said to have great *latitude* or *exposure range* (see below for more on latitude). A stock's latitude is determined by the length of the straight line portion of the film's characteristic curve (see The Characteristic Curve, p. 256). You can determine the exposure range of a stock by shooting tests, asking the lab, or checking the manufacturer's data sheet (often available online). Color negative has about a nine- or ten-stop range; most reversal films have closer to five or six stops. Traditionally, video cameras have had a more limited exposure range than negative film stocks, but some newer cameras may have a similar range.

With a reflected light meter, you can check the difference in *f*-stops between important light and dark areas in the frame. If the brightness range of the scene is too great for the film stock, it may be necessary to recompose the shot, add light, flash the film, change an actor's costume or makeup, or redecorate the set (see Controlling Lighting Contrast, p. 478).

Exposure Error

Cinematographers always want to know, "How much can I be off in my exposure and still get an acceptable image?" The answer depends in part on the latitude or exposure range of the stock (see above). The larger the stock's exposure range, the more error that can be tolerated. But the amount of acceptable error also depends on what you're shooting: The higher the lighting contrast in the scene, the less leeway you have.

As an example, imagine shooting an outdoor scene with areas of bright sun and deep shadow. With proper exposure, you might just be able to capture detail in the brightest areas and the shadows. But if the exposure were increased even slightly, the highlights might be pushed into the shoulder of the characteristic curve and lose detail. Similarly, if the exposure were decreased, the dark areas would now fall on the toe of the curve and no longer show detail.

Now imagine shooting the same scene on a cloudy day. The contrast range between highlights and shadow is now much smaller, so all the areas of the image fall on the straight line portion of the curve, far from the toe or shoulder. You might be able to increase or decrease exposure a few stops without losing detail.

With an average subject, color negative stocks might allow one to one and a half stops of underexposure or two or more stops of overexposure. A color reversal film might have only a stop or less leeway at either end. Some degree of exposure error can be corrected during video transfer and/or printing.

Confusingly, the word *latitude* is used to mean both the total exposure range and the degree of acceptable error (in the latter case, it is sometimes called *exposure latitude*). If someone says, "This stock has a latitude of ten stops," they mean the total exposure range the stock is capable of. If they say, "You have two stops of latitude on the overexposure side," they're talking about exposure error. As discussed above, latitude as a measure of acceptable exposure *error* depends not only on the exposure range of the stock, but on the contrast of the particular scene.

Exposure and Image Quality

As noted above, color negative stocks generally look better when slightly overexposed and reversal stocks do better if slightly underexposed. An underexposed negative is thin and transparent. When it's printed, the printer light has to be set very low (see Chapter 17), which results in increased grain and the blacks becoming milky. To get a rich black in the print, you need to be able to punch plenty of light through during printing. If faces are properly exposed (and thus dense enough on the negative), then a bright printer light can be used that will produce a rich black in the shadows and help suppress grain. This is why it's important in night scenes, for example, to have *some* bright highlights in the frame. If the highlights are properly exposed, then you can use a bright enough printer light to make the dark parts of the frame look dark and clean. But if *everything* is dark and underexposed in shooting, the printed image will be murky and grainy, and color will be muted.

Some cinematographers routinely overexpose color negative slightly (about a half stop or so) in order to get richer, more saturated colors and less grain. Black-and-white negative, on the other hand, becomes grainier with overexposure. Color reversal produces richer, more saturated colors when it is slightly underexposed.

When shooting color negative specifically for video transfer, bear in mind that while overexposure decreases grain, it requires a higher video gain in the telecine, which increases noise (and noise looks a lot like grain!). When shooting 35mm negative for transfer, overexposure is generally not recommended. However, 16mm can still be overexposed up to a stop.

Gross over- or underexposure should be avoided. When negative or reversal film is greatly overexposed, highlights bleach out, faces look pasty, and deep blacks are lost. "Printing down" when the lab makes a print from overexposed negative *may* yield a bright white and a rich black, but will usually not restore much detail in the highlights. Printing overexposed reversal usually requires sacrificing a bright white. In general, correct exposure uses the full range of densities and results in an image of good contrast.

Exposure Control

In brief, you have the following means of controlling exposure at your disposal.

1. *Film speed.* Aside from the choice of raw stocks, film speed can be altered via force development (pushing) and sometimes via underdevelopment (pulling). A film that is properly exposed in the highlights but contains areas of underexposed shadow can sometimes be helped with flashing.
2. *The lens.* The iris diaphragm is the primary means of exposure control. Neutral density filters can be used to avoid overexposure or for opening the

iris to a selected *f*-stop (to control depth of field or maximize lens sharpness). Polarizing filters, and, in black-and-white, contrast filters can be used to alter the exposure of various elements in the scene (see Chapter 8).

3. ***Shutter speed.*** Cameras equipped with variable shutters can be set to increase and decrease exposure time, but this may affect the smoothness of motion. Changing the camera speed (frame rate) affects exposure time, but also affects the speed of motion (see Chapter 6).

4. ***Ambient light.*** Light on the scene, or on selected parts, can be increased with artificial lighting fixtures or with reflectors that reflect sunlight. Neutral density and colored filters can be placed over lights and windows, and lightweight cloth nets can be used to cut down the amount of light falling on a subject (see Chapter 12).

EXPOSURE AND VIDEO CAMERAS. As a point of comparison, it's useful to note which of these tools of exposure control are available when shooting video. In the above list, item number one is obviously not applicable to video. However, in its place there is the gain setting, which can increase or decrease the camera's sensitivity. For item number three, many video cameras have an adjustable shutter, and some allow you to change the frame rate (camera speed). Everything else in the list applies equally to film and video.

CHAPTER 8

Color and Filters

The first part of this chapter is about the basic principles of color for both film and video systems. The second part is about color- and image-control filters that can be used with film or video cameras.

COLOR

Primary Colors and Complementaries

If a red light, a blue light, and a green light all shine on the same spot, the spot will appear white. You can think of white light as made up of these three colors, called the *additive primaries*, and expressed as:

$$red + blue + green = white[1]$$

Red and blue light together yield a purple-red color called magenta. Blue and green light produce a green-blue color called cyan, and red and green together produce yellow.

$$red + blue = magenta$$
$$blue + green = cyan$$
$$red + green = yellow$$

Cyan, magenta, and yellow are the *subtractive primaries*; that is, they are made by subtracting one of the additive primaries from white light. For example, if the red component is taken away from white light, cyan (blue + green) is left:

$$cyan = blue + green = white - red$$

Similarly,

$$magenta = blue + red = white - green$$
$$yellow = red + green = white - blue$$

---

1. People familiar with painting may think of the primary colors as red, blue, and yellow. This is a different color system. Mixing all colors in paint produces black. Mixing lights of all colors produces white.

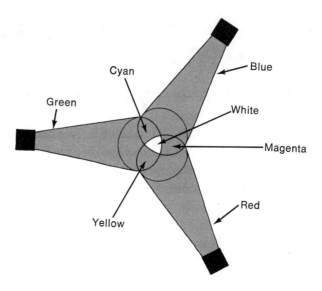

Fig. 8-1. Additive color. Spotlights of the additive primaries—red, green, and blue—form white light where all three overlap. Where any two overlap, the subtractive primaries are formed. (Carol Keller)

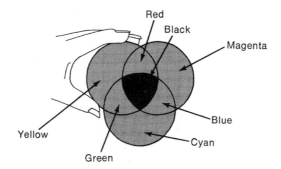

Fig. 8-2. Subtractive color. If you view white light through yellow, cyan, and magenta filters, you get the additive primaries where any two overlap and black where all three overlap. (Carol Keller)

Each additive primary has a *complementary color*, a color that when added to it produces white. From the above three equations, you can see that cyan is the complement of red, magenta the complement of green, and yellow the complement of blue. A filter works by passing the components of its own color and absorbing its complement. A yellow filter thus passes its components (red and green) and absorbs its complement (blue).

The eye is more sensitive to the green portion of the light spectrum than to the red or blue parts. To create light that appears white, the three colors are not mixed in equal proportion. In video, a signal that is a mixture of 72 percent green, 21 percent red, and 7 percent blue will appear white on screen.[2] Because more visual information is conveyed in the green component, the green sensor in a three-chip video camera, or the green light in a film printing report, are of special importance.

Color in Film and Video Systems

We use various terms to describe colors. The *hue* is the base color (such as red, green, etc.). *Saturation* describes how pure the color is. Saturation can be thought of as the absence of white; the more saturated a color is, the less white it has in it. Very saturated colors are intense and, particularly in video, may seem to spread or bloom. Desaturated colors are pale; very desaturated colors are almost monochrome (black-and-white). Experiment with a color video monitor or TV to get a sense of changing color values. A TV's hue or tint control changes the base color, and the "color" control varies the saturation (see Appendix A).

Many factors influence our perception of color. For example, the same color will seem more saturated when surrounded by a black border than a white border.

Standardizing Color Reproduction

There are many opportunities for color values to change (intentionally or not) between the time you shoot a scene and the time that scene appears in a finished film or video. Whenever film or video material is printed or dubbed or transferred from one format to another, the color may change, either because a technician adjusted it or because of the inherent nature of the system. Analog NTSC (sometimes called "Never Twice the Same Color") video is particularly notorious for shifting color values.

There are various ways to measure color and to try to keep it consistent.

In video, standardized *color bars* can be recorded on a tape and used to adjust color reproduction on monitors when the tape is played back (see Appendix A). For analog formats, color bars may be used to maintain color balance when digitizing material into an editing system. With digital formats, the color should remain unchanged when cloning tapes, copying files, or capturing to an editing system, regardless of bars.

To measure the standard color values in the bars, a *vectorscope* is used (see Fig. 8-3). A color's hue is indicated by the position of the signal around the circular face of the vectorscope. The saturation (chrominance level) is indicated by the distance from the center (closer to the edge means higher chroma). When setting up a tape to bars, the phase (hue) and chroma level (saturation) are adjusted until the six dots are centered in the six little boxes around the circle.[3]

When shooting film, color scales (chip charts) are sometimes filmed along with the slate to aid in timing (color balancing) film or video dailies. Perhaps more useful is to shoot an 18 percent gray card (see p. 278). A patch of bright white and dark black next to the gray can help too. Lab personnel will adjust printing or telecine machines to make sure the gray card is reproduced at proper exposure without any color cast, which should make all the other colors fall into place in terms of hue (see Fig. 8-4).

2. This is for high definition ITU-709 color space; standard def NTSC ITU-601 is about 59 percent green, 30 percent red, and 11 percent blue.

3. This is for NTSC video.

Fig. 8-3. Vectorscope. (Tektronix, Inc.)

Sometimes you shoot with nonstandard lighting to create a certain effect. For example, you might use colored gels for a firelight effect or a nightclub scene. If you shoot the gray card under standard (uncolored) tungsten light, and *then* turn on the gelled lights, you have a better chance of getting the color you're looking for in the workprint or video dailies. Increasingly, DPs are using digital stills to show the lab and postproduction team the color and effects they are trying to achieve.

Fig. 8-4. Shooting a gray card so color balance and exposure can be set correctly in the telecine. Shown here with Aaton Greyfinder system. (AbelCineTech)

COLOR TEMPERATURE

The human eye adjusts to most lighting situations so that the color of the light source appears to be white. However, a light source will appear colored if it is strongly deficient in one or more of the primaries. Daylight appears bluer than tungsten light when the two are seen together. For example, if you stand outside on an overcast day and look through a window into a room lit by typical household incandescent (tungsten) bulbs, the interior light will seem relatively yellow compared to the bluer daylight. However, if you go in the room, your eye will adjust so that the tungsten light appears white.

Although the eye accepts a broad range of light sources as white, different light sources are, in fact, composed of unequal amounts of the primaries. The reddish cast of sunset and the blue of an overcast winter day occur when one of the components of white light clearly predominates. Unlike the human eye, color film stocks and video camera sensors are designed for light of a *particular* color balance. If the light source differs in its color balance (the proportions of the primaries), the video camera or film stock will not provide natural rendition of color—unless compensations are made electronically or by using filters. In order to judge how much compensation is needed, we need a way of measuring the color components of the light source.

If a piece of metal is heated, it first becomes red in color ("red hot"). Heated to a higher temperature, the metal starts to become blue and then white ("white hot"). You can correlate the temperature of an ideal substance, called a *black body*, with the color of the light it radiates when it is heated to different temperatures. This color temperature is measured in degrees *Kelvin*, which is a temperature scale equal to Celsius (centigrade) minus 273° (absolute zero).

Standard tungsten studio lamps have a color temperature of 3200°K (read "degrees Kelvin" or just "Kelvin"; color temperatures are often written without the degree sign, but it's used in the book for clarity). A lower color temperature light source has a larger red component, while a higher color temperature source has a larger blue component. Light sources and images are thought of as being warm or warmer as they move toward red (think of red in fire), and cold or colder as they move toward blue (think of the icy blue light of an overcast winter day). Some people get confused by the fact that *colder* blue light reads higher (*hotter*) on the Kelvin temperature scale.

APPROXIMATE COLOR TEMPERATURES
OF COMMON LIGHT SOURCES

Light Source	*Degrees Kelvin*
Match flame	1700
Candle flame	1850–2000
Sunrise or sunset	2000
40- to 60-watt household bulbs	2800
100- to 200-watt household bulbs	2900
500-watt household bulbs	3000

APPROXIMATE COLOR TEMPERATURES
OF COMMON LIGHT SOURCES (continued)

Light Source	Degrees Kelvin
Studio tungsten lights	3200
Photofloods and reflector floods	3200–3400
Fluorescent warm white tubes*	3500
Sunlight one hour after sunrise or one hour before sunset	3500
Early-morning or late-afternoon sunlight	4300
Fluorescent daylight tubes*	4300
Blue (daylight) photofloods	4800
White flame carbon arc	5000
Summer sunlight, noon, Washington, D.C.	5400
Xenon arc projector	5400
Nominal photographic "daylight"	5500
Average daylight (sunlight and blue sky)	5500–6500
HMI lamps	5600
Overcast sky	6000–7500
Summer shade	8000
Summer skylight with no sun	9500–30,000

*Conventional fluorescents have a discontinuous spectrum and thus do not have a true color temperature. The temperature indicated is a rough equivalent. Fluorescents made expressly for film and video use, such as Kino Flo lamps, are available in 3200° and 5500° versions.

Video Cameras and Color Temperature

With video cameras, adjusting the camera for light of different color temperatures is called *white balancing*. This is discussed in Setting the White Balance, p. 113.

Film Cameras and Color Temperature

When a color film emulsion is manufactured, it is balanced for a light of a particular color temperature. The color temperature of the light source should approximately match the film in order to reproduce natural color. Unlike the human eye, which accepts a wide range of color temperatures as white (or colorless), color film will have a color cast unless the color temperature of the source of the illumination roughly matches the color temperature for which the film was balanced.

TUNGSTEN BALANCE. Film stocks balanced for 3200°K are called tungsten-balanced, or Type B tungsten.[4] When tungsten-balanced films are shot with daylight illumination, the excess blue in daylight can overexpose the blue layer in the emulsion, giving a bleached-out, bluish look to the film. To prevent this, an

4. Some film stocks for still photography and amateur use are balanced for 3400°K, the color temperature of some photofloods (see Chapter 12). These are called Type A tungsten but are now rarely used for movies.

85 conversion filter is normally used (see Color Conversion Filters, p. 301). However, some color negative stocks have sufficient latitude to allow filming in daylight without an 85 filter (which can be helpful in low light or when there isn't time to put on a filter). Shooting without the 85 decreases the film's latitude. Color reversal always needs the conversion filter, since the lab cannot adequately compensate in the print. Consult the lab for advice.

DAYLIGHT BALANCE. Film stocks balanced for color temperatures around 5500°K are considered daylight-balanced. Daylight is made up of both direct sunlight and skylight, which is bluer. Shady areas with no direct sun can often have very bluish light, since they are illuminated mostly by skylight. Daytime color temperature varies from 2000° to well over 10,000°K. During sunrise and sunset, as the light of the sun becomes redder, the color temperature drops until it is far below tungsten. When daylight-balanced films are shot with tungsten illumination, a conversion filter is usually used (see p. 300).

See p. 268 for further discussion of tungsten- versus daylight-balanced films.

Off-Balance Color Temperature

If the color temperature of the light source doesn't match the film's color balance (or a video camera's white balance) you can do one or all of the following: filter the lens (see p. 300); filter or change the light source (see Chapter 12); accept a color cast in shooting and make corrections as necessary later in printing (see Chapter 17) or during video color correction (see p. 573). Some scenes demand a color cast—candlelight, firelight, sunset, and night scenes, for example. You may also want a color cast for other artistic effects.

Some scenes contain a great range of color temperatures. For example, when shooting indoors with illumination coming from both tungsten lights and windows (see Mixed Lighting, p. 480).

Differences in color temperature are more significant at the lower color temperatures. The difference between 3000°K and 3200°K is noticeable, while the difference between 5400°K and 5600°K is not very significant.

Measuring Color Temperature

The color temperature of a source of illumination can be read with a *color temperature meter*. A *two-color meter* measures the relative blue and red components of the light, while a *three-color meter* also measures the green component. A two-color meter is adequate for measuring light sources of continuous spectral emission, including tungsten, firelight, and daylight. For light sources such as fluorescents and mercury arc lamps, you should also measure the green component with a three-color meter.

Color temperature meters are more often used when shooting film than video, since in video you can see the color on the monitor. Most lighting situations don't require a color temperature meter, as it is enough to know the approximate color temperature of a light source. Large differences can be corrected by a filter (see p. 300) and smaller differences can be corrected in postproduction. Color negative film, in particular, allows for a very wide range of color corrections.

Color meters prove most handy when balancing the color temperature of different light sources (see Chapter 12). For example, the meter can measure if adequate compensation has been made by putting gels on windows to match the color temperature of tungsten light fixtures. Use a two-color meter to measure the decrease in color temperature of tungsten light when there is a voltage drop or to measure the change in color temperature in early morning or late afternoon. If a sequence is shot over several days or weeks, but is supposed to appear as the same time period in the finished film, the meter can be used to match the light balance from day to day.

The color temperature meter is sometimes used with a set of filters for color temperature compensation (see below). Filter the light source or lens to change color

Fig. 8-5. Color temperature meter. (Konica Minolta Corp.)

temperature. Some meters read in degrees Kelvin, while others read in mired values (see Color Compensating Filters, p. 306). Point the meter at the light source as you would do with an incident meter (see Chapter 7).

FILTERS

Lens filters are used in shooting for a variety of reasons. Some are used to make a scene look "normal" on film or video (that is, close to the way the scene appeared to the naked eye). Others are used to create special effects. In some cases, filtration must be done in the camera to achieve the look you want. However, as video technology has gotten more sophisticated, some filter effects that were traditionally done on the shoot are now done in postproduction. This also applies to projects shot on film that are finished on video or via a digital intermediate. Leaving some of the adjustments to video post can help you shoot faster without worrying about getting everything just right on the shoot.

Filter Factors

All filters absorb some light, and compensation must be made for the loss of light to avoid underexposing the film or video image. The *filter factor* is the number of times exposure must be increased to compensate for the light loss. Each time the filter factor doubles, increase the exposure by one stop. Manufacturers supply filter factors for each of their filters.

If you know that a filter decreases exposure by one stop (a filter factor of 2), compensate by opening the lens one stop. When two or more filters are used simultaneously, the filter factor of the combination is the product of each of their factors. If one filter has a factor of 4 and the other a factor of 2, the combination will have a filter factor of 8 (4 x 2). To compensate, open the iris 3 stops.

When shooting video, any light loss from a filter will become apparent as you look through the viewfinder. Be sure to set the exposure with the filter in place on the lens.

When shooting film, you can divide the filter factor into the ASA number to calculate exposure directly from the exposure meter. If you were using a filter with a filter factor of 4 with a film rated ASA 100, the meter could be set at ASA 25 (100 divided by 4) and the exposure calculated directly. In this case, don't open the iris beyond what the meter indicates. Film stock data sheets list filter requirements and factors for various light sources.

FILTERS FOR FILM CAMERAS

Color Conversion Filters

When you expose daylight-balanced film under tungsten illumination or tungsten-balanced film in daylight, you should generally use a *conversion filter*.

Since tungsten film in daylight appears blue, you will want to warm up the daylight to match tungsten illumination. Filters that warm up a scene are red or yellow. Most cinematographers identify these filters by their Kodak Wratten filter numbers. The 85 filters have a characteristic salmon color. A #85B (or simply, *85B*) is designed to convert daylight for use with standard 3200°K tungsten-balanced color negative films and Type B reversal films. An 85 filter (sometimes called a *straight 85*) can be used for shooting Type A reversal films (balanced for 3400°K) in daylight. Most people use a straight 85 for typical 3200°K color negative, since Kodak recommends it and the difference between an 85 and an 85B is insignificant. The 85 has a filter factor of 1.6 (⅔ stop loss).

Daylight-balanced film shot under tungsten illumination will appear red-brown, so add blue. The 80A conversion filter is blue. An 80A converts most daylight films (balanced for about 5500°K) for use under 3200°K illumination. The 80A has a filter factor of 4 (a loss of two stops).

Color conversion filters are used so frequently that cinematographers tend to think of film speeds in terms of the ASA that compensates for the filter factor. Manufacturers will list a color negative balanced for tungsten as ASA 100 for tungsten light and ASA 64 for daylight with an 85 filter (100 divided by filter factor 1.6 is approximately 64). Conversion filters are often used in combination with neutral density filters (see Neutral Density Filters, p. 302).

Filters for Black-and-White

A set of filters is made primarily for black-and-white film. These filters are used mostly to darken a sky or to change the relative exposure of two differently colored objects that would otherwise be recorded as similar tonalities.

Red and green objects that are equally bright may photograph in black-and-white as the same gray tone. Because filters absorb their complementary color and transmit their own color, photographing the red and green objects with a red filter makes the green object darker than the red (since the red filter absorbs much of the green light).

The sky can be darkened using graduated neutral density filters and polarizers (see below). Black-and-white film allows the use of several differently colored filters to darken a blue sky but not a white, overcast sky. As red and yellow filters absorb blue, they will darken a blue sky. Unlike the effect with a polarizer, the darkening doesn't change as you move the camera, so the camera may be panned without worry.

Some of the most commonly used black-and-white contrast filters are: Wratten #8 (K2; yellow or light orange) for haze penetration, moderate darkening of blue sky, and lightening of faces; and Wratten #15 (G; deep yellow) for heavy haze penetration, greater sky darkening, and, especially, aerial work and telephoto landscapes. The red filters (for example, #23A, #25, #29) have increasing haze penetration and increasing power to darken skies. The #29 can make a blue sky appear black with prominent white clouds. The green filters also darken the sky, but make foliage lighter. Blue filters lighten blue skies and blue objects and increase haze and ultraviolet effects.

Presumably, these filters could be used for shooting black-and-white (monochrome) video, but this is not usually done.

FILTERS FOR BOTH FILM AND VIDEO CAMERAS

Haze Control

Unlike the human eye, film and video are sensitive to ultraviolet light. Atmospheric haze scatters large amounts of ultraviolet light, making the haze appear heavier when shooting distant landscapes. To minimize this effect, use a *UV* or *1A* (*skylight*) *filter* with both black-and-white and color work. The UV is clear to slightly yellow in color, while the 1A is slightly pink. The filter factor is negligible, and no exposure compensation need be made. Haze filters have no effect on fog and mist because these atmospheric effects are composed of water droplets and are not the result of the scattering of ultraviolet rays.

The 1A filter is useful to warm up the blue cast caused by ultraviolet light present in outdoor shade, which is especially noticeable when snow scenes are filmed. Since the 1A and haze filters don't significantly affect exposure and, in general, have no unwanted photographic effects, they're useful in protecting the front element of the lens in difficult environmental conditions—for example, in salt spray or sand. Some filmmakers leave this filter in place at all times.

Neutral Density Filters

Neutral density (*ND*) *filters* are gray in color and affect all colors equally. They are used to reduce the amount of light passing through the lens without affecting the color. They allow you to open the lens to a wider aperture to reduce depth of field, to shoot at an aperture that yields a sharper image or to shoot at all if the light level exceeds the film stock or video camera's ability to handle it.

Neutral density filters are generally marked in increments of .1ND, which is equivalent to one third of a stop; .3ND is one stop, .6ND two stops, and 1.2ND four stops. When you combine ND filters, these numbers should be added, and not multiplied as is done with the filter factor. Sometimes ND filters are marked 2X or 4X, in which case you are given the filter factors (one and two stops, respectively).

ND filters are often combined with color conversion filters for daylight filming when you want to reduce the amount of light. For example, an 85N3 combines an 85 filter with one stop of neutral density (the decimal point is dropped when ND filters are used in combination with other filters or sometimes for gels used in lighting).

When shooting film, an ASA 100 tungsten-balanced film would have a daylight exposure index of ASA 32 with the 85N3. Similarly, an 85N6 (two stops of neutral density) would give the film a daylight ASA of 16.

Many video cameras have a built-in ND filter and/or combination ND and 85 filter. See Camera Sensitivity, p. 134.

Graduated Filters

Graduated filters (also called *grads* or *wedges*) have one section neutral density and one section clear. The transition from dense to clear can be abrupt or gradual (filters with a smooth transition from dense to clear are sometimes called *attenuators*). Grads are primarily used to darken a sky that would otherwise bleach out and show no detail. Grads can be used to make day-for-night scenes more realistic by darkening the sky. Some grads have a color, such as orange to heighten a sunset effect.

Fig. 8-6. Graduated filter. Shown here off the camera, a grad can be used to selectively darken or color the sky. Grads vary in the sharpness of their transition from dark to light. (Stephen McCarthy)

Grads should be used with a matte box (see p. 307). The larger the filter you use, the more freedom you will have to position it correctly. Position the neutral density portion to cover the sky, and align the graduated region with the horizon line or higher. If you're working with great depth of field (say with a wide-angle lens at small apertures), the grad itself may be too sharply in focus to achieve the effect you want. Keep it as close to the lens as possible and use a soft-edged grad if stopped down.

Selectively darkening the sky or any portion of the frame can also be done in postproduction, either in a telecine or in video post. One advantage of using a grad on the camera is it may prevent the sky from being grossly overexposed (burning out cloud details, for example) which might not be correctable in post.

Polarizing Filters

Aside from graduated filters and special effects, the *polarizer* is the only way to darken a sky when shooting in color. A polarizer is somewhat like a neutral density filter in that it affects all colors equally. The difference is that it selectively cuts down light oriented in a single plane—that is, polarized light. On a clear day, some of the light from the sky is polarized, as is light reflected from glass and water, but not metal. Polarized light can be progressively eliminated by rotating the polarizer. Reflections from glass and water can sometimes be totally eliminated, but be careful not to overdo the effect; otherwise, a car may look as though it has no windshield or a pond as though it is dry.

Fig. 8-7. (left) Without polarizer. (right) With polarizer filter. The polarizer minimizes the reflections from the windshield. (Schneider Optics)

As you move the camera, the orientation of the polarizer to the light source may change, altering the amount of light that is filtered out. The exposure of an object may thus change during the shot. When the polarizer is used to darken the sky, this change is particularly noticeable when the camera pans. Maximum darkening of the sky occurs with the filter oriented at right angles to the sun. When it is pointed toward the sun or 180 degrees away (the sun directly behind), the polarizer has no effect. Similarly, polarized shots taken at different angles to the sun may not edit together well, since the sky will appear different from one shot to the next. Clear blue skies can most easily be darkened with the polarizer. The hazier the sky, the less noticeable the effect will be. An overcast sky, whether in color or in black-and-white, can be darkened only by a graduated filter.

The polarizer has a filter factor varying from 2 to 4 (one to two stops), depending on its orientation and the nature of the light in the scene. Side lighting and top lighting, when the sun is at right angles to the polarizer, may require a compensation of two or more stops.

When shooting film, calculate exposure compensation by taking a reflected light reading through the polarizer, with the polarizer oriented as it will be on the lens.

When shooting video, set the exposure with the polarizer in place and oriented as it will be for the shot.

Diffusion Filters

Diffusion filters soften hard lines and are often used to minimize facial lines and blemishes. They are sometimes used to indicate a dream sequence or a historical sequence or just make the image a little mellower or less harsh. As diffusion increases, flare from bright areas creeps into adjacent areas. A diffusion effect can be achieved by stretching silk or nylon stocking material in front of the lens or over the rear element (see below for discussion of mounting filters behind the lens).

Fig. 8-8. (left) Without diffusion. (right) With diffusion filter. Diffusion filters soften fine detail and cause light sources in the frame to spread. (Stephen McCarthy)

Tiffen's Softnet filters have netting material laminated within a glass filter. Black net or dot pattern diffusion filters don't affect contrast; white net filters do soften contrast. Diffusion filters generally require no exposure compensation, though net material may cut out some light. Wherever a net is mounted, keep it as close to the lens as possible and check that the net pattern is blurred and not in focus on the image. Use a good lens shade or matte box to keep stray light from striking a diffusion filter directly.

In 35mm film and HD, a softened image is often desirable. In 16mm, and most SD video formats, the image is softer to begin with, and diffusion should be used sparingly unless an exaggerated effect is desired. Sometimes diffusion or nets are used in video to soften the image slightly and give it more of a "film" look. You can evaluate the effect in a good monitor (though it may look different on a larger screen).

The same diffusion will seem more pronounced through a long focal length lens than with a short focal length lens, so you may want to use less diffusion when zoomed in for a close-up if you're trying to match the look of a wide shot.

Various methods can be used to soften or diffuse an image in video post.

LOW-CONTRAST FILTERS. *Low-contrast (low-con) filters,* available in several grades, reduce contrast without softening lines or reducing definition as much as diffusion filters. Low-cons affect the shadow areas particularly, by smearing the highlight areas into the shadows. Colors are less saturated and the overall look is softer. There are a few variants of low-contrast filters, including Tiffen's Pro-Mist and Ultra Contrast filters. No exposure compensation is required when using low-con filters.

Fog Filters

Fog filters are available in various grades to simulate everything from light to heavy fog. In general, the more contrasty the scene, the stronger the fog filter needed. With too strong a filter, objects may lose so much contrast that they become invisible. Fog filters are sometimes used for heightened mystery or romanticized flashbacks.

In natural foggy conditions, objects tend to become less visible the farther away they are. Most fog filters do not simulate this effect, so try not to photograph objects too close to the camera or let a subject move toward or away from the camera during a shot. Double fog filters lower image definition less than standard fog filters do. There's no exposure compensation for fog filters, though slight overexposure can increase the fog effect.

Special Effects Filters

There are filters (sometimes called vari-burst) that will take light sources in the image and break them up into spectral colors. Star filters break bright highlights into stars of four, six, or eight points, depending on the type of filter you select. The filters may be rotated to position the directions of the points. Other filters are available that break the image into multiple repeating images of various patterns.

Split-field diopters are discussed in Chapter 3.

Color Compensating Filters

Generally, major color corrections are made during shooting, and fine-tuning of the color is left for postproduction. There are times, however, when specific color adjustments may be made via filtration on the lens: for example, when shooting with certain discharge-type light sources such as fluorescent, mercury vapor, or sodium vapor lights (see Chapter 12); to compensate for off-balance color temperatures when shooting reversal film for direct projection; or when you want to create a specific color effect, such as a sepia look for scenes intended to look old.

Sometimes a little warming is done with a camera filter to provide a more appealing look. The Tiffen 812 filter has the nice effect of improving skin tones without making the whole scene look too red; it can also be used to make a cloudy day seem less cold. When using an 812 with a video camera, be sure to white-balance *without* the filter in place, or the camera will undo the filter's effect.

For film shoots, precise color adjustments are sometimes made with a set of *color-compensating (CC)* or *light-balancing* filters. The most advantageous system in common use assigns a *mired value* to every color temperature. To convert from one color temperature to another, subtract their mired values. If the result is a positive number, use yellow filtration to warm the scene, as yellow increases mired value and decreases the color temperature. A negative number calls for blue filtration to decrease mired value and raise the color temperature. Unlike in degrees Kelvin, where a difference of 100°K is more significant at 3200°K than at 5500°K, mired values indicate a constant shift across the scale.

Mired values can be used to measure any red-blue color shift. When you put gels on windows to lower the color temperature from 5500°K (mired value 182) to 3200°K (mired value 312), a gel with a +130 mired value is needed (an 85 gel is close enough, with its mired value of +131). If you want the daylight to appear cooler than the tungsten interior light, use a gel that doesn't lower the color temperature as much. A gel called a half 85 (mired value +81) lowers the color temperature to 3800°K, so that the window light will appear bluer than the 3200°K interior lights. (Consult a professional reference like the *American Cinematographer Manual* for mired values of typical light sources and filters and for the Kodak Color Compensating filter system.)

MATTE BOXES AND LENS SHADES

Use a lens shade (see Fig. 4-14) or matte box (see Fig. 8-9) to prevent stray light from hitting the front element and causing flare. If you look at the front of the lens and see the reflection of any light source, there is the potential for flare. A deeper matte box or shade gives better protection. Matte boxes are often adjustable and should be adjusted as deep as possible without vignetting the image. Similarly, use a lens shade as deep and narrow as possible. Long focal lengths allow for a narrow shade. The shades for extreme wide angle are often so wide that they offer little protection from stray light. A French flag (see Fig. 6-15) can be set to cut light sources that the lens shade or matte box miss. When light sources are in the scene you're filming, sometimes you can shade the source itself to minimize flare (see Chapter 12).

Matte Boxes

Matte boxes have slots that accommodate one or more filters. Often one of the slots rotates for filters such as polarizers, split-field diopters, and special effects filters. Glass filters are expensive; with a matte box, one set of filters can be used for different lenses. Gelatin filters can be mounted in frames that fit into the slots.

You can use mattes in the matte box for special effects; for example, a keyhole matte simulates looking through a keyhole. A mask that blocks half the frame in one shot and the other half when the film is exposed again lets an actor play two roles in one shot. These effects can also be done in post.

Matte boxes often mount on *front rods*, which extend from the camera to support the lens, the matte box, and/or other accessories. Some matte boxes are fairly large and may be too intimidating in documentary settings. If the front element of the lens does not rotate during focusing, a lightweight matte box can sometimes be attached to the lens itself. A thick *optical flat* (clear glass) in the matte box can help suppress camera noise. A *lens doughnut* is sometimes needed as a seal between the lens and the back of the matte box, to keep light from entering from behind.

Fig. 8-9. Matte box mounted on front rods. Shown with Aaton XTRprod camera. (Abel-CineTech)

CHECKING FOR VIGNETTING. To check for vignetting, make sure you can see into each corner of the frame. Place a pointed object—a pencil or finger—parallel to the front surface of the lens, and move it toward each corner of the image. If you cannot see the end of the object through the viewfinder because the corners are dark, there is vignetting. Try this test at close focusing distances and, with a zoom lens, at its widest angle. This test can also be made at the focusing distance and focal length for each particular shot.

Lens Shades

A glass filter can usually be mounted between the lens and the lens shade. On some shades a filter can be dropped in place. Some shades have provisions for rotating a filter. Lens shades are available in metal, hard plastic, and soft rubber. Rubber shades are collapsible and cause less shock if inadvertently hit. Lens shades often act like a megaphone, increasing camera noise in the direction of the subject. Rubber shades minimize this effect. Rectangular lens shades work more efficiently for their size but can be used only on lenses with nonrotating focusing mounts.

Mounting Glass Filters

Most special effects filters are used in front of the lens. If the orientation of the filter matters, a matte box or a lens with a nonrotating front element will make things simpler.

Glass filters are the most expensive, but they are also the most durable and can be cleaned of fingerprints, dust, and the like. It doesn't make sense to use an expensive lens with a poor-quality glass filter that may impair the image, so use high-quality filters. Gels sandwiched between glass are generally of lower quality. Dyed glass filters should have an anti-reflective coating (*coated filters*). You can check the quality of the filter with a collimator; if there is a noticeable loss of resolution, use a higher-quality filter. To avoid an unwanted optical phenomenon known as *Newton's rings*, don't mount two or more glass filters so that their surfaces touch.

Some cinematographers like to keep a glass filter over the front element of the lens to protect it from scratches or from poor environmental conditions, such as sand or salt spray. Use a high-quality coated filter. Clear, IA, or haze filters will not alter image color or tonal rendition to any serious extent.

Glass filters may be square shaped for matte boxes or round for mounting on lenses. They come in a variety of sizes, sometimes designated in millimeters and sometimes by *series size* in Roman or Arabic numerals. Different lenses may take different-sized filters.

ADAPTOR RINGS. Most lenses accept an *adaptor ring* that screws into the area around the front element or slips over the barrel for mounting glass filters in front of the lens. The filter of appropriate size is then secured with the lens shade or another adaptor ring. A *retainer ring* lets you mount two filters. Use *step-up rings* to mount a large filter on a smaller lens.

To remove tightly screwed retainer rings or extension rings, use light pressure. Too much pressure distorts thin rings from the round, making removal more difficult. A solvent such as carbon tetrachloride may be needed for a particularly stubborn ring. In general, whenever you screw threaded rings, be careful to screw them properly (cross-threading damages the threads). If you need to force a threaded ring, this is probably a sign of misthreading.

Behind-the-Lens Filters

Colored and neutral density filters may be placed either in front of or behind the lens. Some cameras have a behind-the-lens slot for gels, and there are adaptors for mounting gels on the rear of the lens. When a gel is mounted behind the lens, it refracts light and moves the focal plane back about one third the thickness of the gel. If the lens is wide-angle (about 12mm or wider in the 16mm format) and the aperture wide, depth of focus is so narrow that the image may be thrown out of focus. If you plan to use behind-the-lens filters, have the flange focal distance adjusted by a technician to compensate for the change. You must then always use a clear gel (UV 1A or 2A) when not using another filter.

Gels are extremely vulnerable to scratching and crimping. Dust can sometimes be blown off but cannot be wiped off. Cut the gel carefully to size, so that it fills the gel holder completely and won't shift while filming. Handle gels in paper or only by their edges, preferably with tweezers. Gels are the least expensive filters and fade the fastest and should be fairly fresh. Store them in a cool place to increase shelf life.

Serious problems can occur when you use gels behind the lens. The closer the gel is to the film or video sensor, the more likely it is that physical imperfections and dust will show up in the image. The longer the focal length of the lens or the more a lens is stopped down, the greater the chance of gel defects showing up in the image. On some film cameras the gel is placed behind the reflex mirror shutter, which keeps the viewfinder bright but doesn't show whether the gel has shifted out of place or not. Check cameras with behind-the-lens slots often to make sure that no one has inserted an unwanted gel, or that a gel has not shifted or become damaged.

As discussed above, sometimes nets or stocking material are mounted behind the lens for a diffusion effect. These do not affect the collimation the way gels do, but must be used with care to be sure they don't come off or damage the lens or camera. Rubber bands or special *transfer tape* (also known affectionately as *snot tape*) that has a rubber cement–like adhesive can be used to attach the net to the lens.

CHAPTER 9

The Shoot

The first part of this chapter is about planning and preparing to shoot your movie. The second part is about camerawork and directing, for both narrative (fiction) and documentary. Because shooting a movie draws on all the skills and techniques of filmmaking, in some sense all the other chapters in the book are relevant to this one. More specifically regarding the choices made by the director or camera operator, it's important to have an understanding of cameras (Chapters 3 and 6), lenses (Chapter 4) and editing (Chapter 13).

PREPARING FOR THE SHOOT

Preparing well for your shoot can mean the difference between an organized, productive filming experience and a chaotic, haphazard one. Actually, shooting movies is almost always chaotic—there are an enormous number of things going on at once, decisions being made, events out of your control—but if you're prepared, and lucky, it will be a kind of controlled chaos that results in getting the footage you need while staying close to your schedule and budget and keeping everyone relatively happy.

Preparation can take many different forms. For a director, it may mean previsualizing the action and camerawork. Alfred Hitchcock prepared so meticulously—working out the entire film beforehand—that he claimed that shooting was an uneventful execution of the movie he'd already seen in his mind.

For a producer, preparation means hiring a good team and making sure the resources needed are available on time. No matter what budget you're working with, there are always financial pressures, and you may not be able to deliver what's on everyone's wish list. Knowing which things you can do without—and which you can't—is part of the producer's skill.

For the director of photography, preparation means having the equipment you need, knowing how to use it, and being confident that it's working. Together with the director you'll have worked out a visual style and, depending on the shoot, planned individual shots, angles, and lighting.

Some shoots can be planned to the nubs; others have to be highly improvised in the moment. As a Roman philosopher said, "Luck is what happens when preparation meets opportunity." Two thousand years later, it's a tired cliché, but still useful for film shoots.

STORY AND SCRIPT

Script Preparation

Narrative films often begin with a story or treatment. Then a more detailed screenplay (script) is written. What stories you choose to tell, and how you structure them, is up to you and beyond the scope of this book. There are many screenwriting guides (see Bibliography). It's important to put the script in standard page format (in terms of margins and headings) since it's expected by actors and executives, and, especially if you're a novice, you want to show that you understand industry practice. You can use a scriptwriting program like Final Draft or just use a word processor.

When writing a script to be read by potential funders or actors, it's a good idea to keep camera direction and *blocking* (the actors' movements) to a minimum. The reader should experience the movie as it will play on screen and not be burdened by the mechanics of how it's put together. However, as you approach production, a *shooting script* should be prepared that includes numbered scenes, more detailed camera angles, and more specific action notes. The director will also draw up his or her own notes about details of shot coverage and blocking.

Before you go into production, every scene and description in the script should be considered for its financial and technical implications. You can hire a production manager or other experienced person to draw up a budget based on what's written. It's one thing to script a shot where the camera flies over the ocean and comes to rest on an extreme close-up of your character on the beach, but unless you can afford a helicopter and the time to execute the shot (or have the means to do this as a digital effect), take it out of the script. Similarly, be sure the total number of scenes and locations is within your budget. See p. 319 for more on script breakdown.

When you read the screenplay of a movie you admire, or recall the dialogue in a memorable scene, it's sometimes surprising how few words are used. Powerful moments in films are often made up of looks, actions, and relatively terse exchanges rather than long stretches of expository dialogue. Novice (and experienced) filmmakers often find in the editing room that scenes play better with much less dialogue than was written (see Chapter 13). This is in part because of pacing, and in part because some things you might think need to be explained actually play better when the audience makes the connections themselves. Be sure to read through every line of dialogue *aloud* before going into production. This is often best done with the actors (see below). There's no better time to trim dialogue and entire scenes than before you shoot!

Another consideration in preparing the script is estimating how long the finished film will run. You may want to hit a standard length, such as ninety minutes or two hours, and you may be required to if a contract calls for it. There's a general assumption that scripts in standard layout run about a page a minute. Dialogue scenes are more predictable than action scenes in terms of the relationship of page length to running time. Even so, some dialogue is delivered as rapid-fire repartee and some is slow and filled with pauses. You can estimate running time by speaking the lines with a stopwatch.

You may want to have a lawyer or script service vet the screenplay for any potential legal issues. For example, if you have a character named Roy Cornelius who lives on Houston Street in New York, you'll want to check that there isn't a real person with that name on that street. If the script calls for a specific piece of music to be performed or used, that will also need to be cleared. For more on legal and clearance issues, see Chapter 19.

Rehearsal and Previsualization

If you were setting out to design an environment that fosters creativity and relaxed, fresh thinking, a film shoot would *not* be it. On a typical day, if you're not already behind schedule, you will be if you stop too long to ponder. Not to mention the fact that there may be hordes of people busily executing the ideas as planned, who won't be happy when you decide to change *everything* at the last moment.

There are many ways to explore, experiment, rehearse, and previsualize before you actually go into production.

Having a group of actors read through the script gives you a chance to hear the dialogue and get ideas for direction. Reading with the actual actors who will play the parts can be a productive time to work out scene ideas and to form relationships. Some directors insist on rehearsal time. Director Mike Leigh uses rehearsal as a time when the actors can actually shape the story and dialogue. Other directors prefer that actors do the material fresh on the shoot with little prep. There are benefits to rehearsing in a separate space prior to the pressures of production, but sometimes you just have to rehearse in the moment on the set.

The physical aspects of the set or location are an integral part of how the scene is blocked and shot. Sometimes the physical space is designed or modified according to how you want to play the scene, and sometimes you're on location and just have to use what you've got. It's very helpful for a director to spend some time in the space to plan the scene. Often this is best done with the art director, director of photography, and others to block out set design, props, camerawork, and lighting (see below). Shoot stills and/or video for later reference.

Drawing up simple sketches of camera angles and blocking can be extremely helpful as a way to plan and as a tool for communicating with the crew (see Fig. 9-1). The DP may also want to make charts of lighting setups.

Storyboards are shot-by-shot drawings of how the action and camerawork are supposed to play on screen. These can

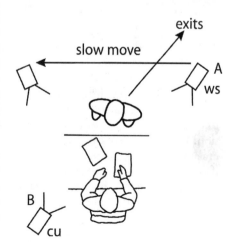

Fig. 9-1. Making simple sketches of blocking and camera angles is a good way to plan scene coverage.

be particularly useful for effects shots and complex setups where many people may be needed to make the shot work. A storyboard artist may draw them or you might make sketches yourself. Computer storyboarding programs, such as StoryBoard Quick and StoryBoard Artist, may save time and can be helpful if you lack drawing skills (see Fig. 9-2).[1] Some directors use detailed storyboards as a way to previsualize a scene; others find them limiting. Often there are many changes between the storyboard and what is actually shot and edited into the movie.

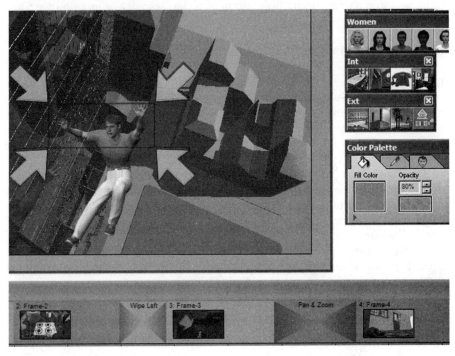

Fig. 9-2. Storyboards can be created with programs like StoryBoard Artist. (PowerProduction Software. www.storyboardartist.com)

Some filmmakers like to rehearse not just the actors but the entire movie, including shooting and editing. Francis Coppola and others have used video as a tool to essentially shoot a rough draft of a movie (or scenes) and edit prior to production. You might go out with a small-format video camera and experiment with camera angles, moves, dialogue, or blocking. Cut it together and see how it flows. Even if you can't shoot the real locations or real actors, you'll get ideas, which you'll either use for the movie, or you'll realize—with plenty of time to make a new plan—that you want to do something completely different.

---

1. Computer programs can also simulate a camera moving through a physical space, showing you what the camera would see as it moves. These can be used as a way to plan set construction or to build a CGI shot.

THE CREW AND LOCATION

Production Tasks

The following is a brief description of the roles of key members of a large Hollywood-type film production unit, which gives an idea of the range of tasks involved in a movie shoot. The use of terms like cameraman is not meant to imply that the job is performed by a male.

The *producer* raises the money for a production and often creates the "package," which may include the script (*literary property*), the director, and the actors. The producer is responsible for the budget and the overall production and can hire and fire personnel. The *director* is responsible for the production unit, translating the script into visual terms, and directing the actors. In some television productions, the producer's functions overlap with those of a film director.

Fig. 9-3. The large production unit on location. A production still from *Lady Tubbs* (Universal, 1935) shows a tripod-mounted, blimped camera on a platform that serves as a dolly and can be pushed along the tracks by the grips. Note the microphone boom and the reflectors used to fill in the harsh shadows created by the sun. (Universal Pictures)

The *director of photography* (*DP* or *DoP*), also called the *cinematographer*, *first cameraman*, or *lighting cameraman*, composes the shots, plans camera movements, and decides how to light scenes, usually in consultation with the director. On small units, the DP may operate the camera, but on large units, the *camera operator* or *second cameraman* sets the controls and operates the camera during a take. The *first assistant cameraman* (*1st AC*) operates the follow focus, checks the gate for dirt, and manages the camera equipment. The *second assistant* or *clapper loader* operates the slate, loads film, and keeps the camera report sheet.

On a digital cinematography or video shoot, job descriptions are somewhat different, as there's no film to load or gates to check, but include other responsibilities, such as managing tapes or data files, setting up monitors, and so forth. A *DIT* (*digital image technician*) may be on the crew to adjust camera parameters and supervise recording.

The *gaffer* and a crew of *electricians* place the lights as directed by the DP. The *best boy* or *second electric* assists the gaffer in setting up lights and cables. The *grips* move things around, place props, and build scaffolds and other rigging for cameras or lights. The *dolly grip* pushes the dolly. The sound department is run by the *sound recordist* or *mixer*, who records the sound and directs the *boom operator*, who maneuvers the microphone, sometimes assisted by a *cableman*.

The *script supervisor* is responsible for continuity and making sure shots match in everything from weather to hairdo and that everything has been shot from the angles called for in the script. The *first assistant director* (*1st AD*) maintains order on the set, makes sure the needed actors and crew are present, and controls extras in crowd scenes. The second AD assists in these tasks.

The *second unit* is usually responsible for stunts, crowd scenes, battle scenes, and special effects—essentially those scenes that are shot without sound. These scenes have their own director and camera crew.

The *unit production manager* (*UPM*) does a breakdown of scenes so that they can be filmed as economically as possible. The UPM is responsible for the relation between the production and outside labor and suppliers. He or she works with the first AD to keep the production on schedule. A *line producer* performs similar tasks in a supervisory role. A *production coordinator* handles details such as shipping, transport, and lodging. A *location manager* or *scout* finds locations as needed and helps arrange logistics.

Production design, art direction, set construction, props, makeup, hairdressing, costume design, wardrobe on the set, and countless other jobs are specialized tasks that each require one or more people to perform them. *Production assistants* (*PAs*) are low-paid "gofers" (go for this, go for that) who do all sorts of underappreciated tasks. Don't confuse PAs with APs (*associate producers*).

Production stills (photographs of the actors or crew on the set) are shot by a *still photographer*. On a production of any size, do not neglect to have production stills made; they are invaluable in promoting the film and are difficult to create after the production is finished (see Chapter 19).

Job responsibilities vary by country and by type of production. On union productions, union rules determine much of standard industry practice. The crew is divided into departments (camera, sound, art, etc.), each with a department head, and there are rules about what duties fall within or outside a given job's jurisdiction. For example, the camera crew often cannot touch a lighting fixture. On nonunion or smaller productions, there may be significant overlap in responsibilities, and one person may be called on to perform a variety of tasks.

Crew Size

While big studio productions are made with the full-sized crews just discussed, many dramas are shot with much smaller crews. Some documentary filmmakers like to shoot alone, working unobtrusively with a small video camera. A small documentary crew might consist of a cameraperson and a sound recordist, with either or both functioning as director. A third person may be needed to manage equipment, drive the car, help set up lights, and run errands. In documentaries, the smaller the crew, the better the access to the subjects being filmed and the less disruption to their lives.

In all types of productions there can be advantages to small crews. Aside from keeping the budget lower, small crews can move quickly and gain access to certain locations, such as city streets, small houses, or mountaintops that would be difficult for larger crews. Finding the right crew size is a balancing act. If the crew is too small for the complexity of the production, crew members get overburdened and the work becomes inefficient and slow. However, as crew size grows, there is a kind of instant multiplying effect: More people require more support (cars, meals, accommodations), which requires more people.

See p. 729 for the business aspects of hiring crew.

Casting

For any production that involves actors, casting is vital. Finding actors who are not just right for their roles but who also work well as an ensemble can make all the difference. If the casting is good, the director's job is enormously easier. If the casting is bad, a great script and director may not be able to save the project.

Professionals usually work with a casting director or a casting agency that has files on hundreds of actors and conducts regular auditions for new talent. For a Hollywood picture, a talent agency might assemble a "package" of lead actors for a project. Casting websites can give you quick access to a pool of actors in various cities. Beware of actors' *headshots* (posed photos)—they can be very misleading. Some producers hold open auditions, advertised to the general public; if you do this, be prepared to find a few undiscovered gems and a lot of people who have little experience and less ability.

For a dramatic feature, having some name-brand stars may enable you to get financing and is a boon for marketing. Many stars have been known to appear in low-budget films if the script is good and the number of days required is small.

Depending on the production, you may have a choice whether to work with union or nonunion actors. Union actors are generally more experienced and expensive, though they may defer their salaries for students. For more on unions and hiring actors, see p. 730.

It's essential to videotape auditions—you won't be able to trust your memory after seeing dozens of people. You want to find out how well actors take direction, so ask them to try their lines a few different ways. Often, it's best to have people audition in pairs. Pay attention not just to line readings, but to how actors handle themselves when they're *listening*. A major part of acting is nonverbal.

Location Planning

Whenever possible, locations should be scouted in advance; the British call it *doing a recce* (from "reconnaissance"). For a documentary, the director and cinematographer might just do a quick check to see what they'll need to work at the location. For a drama or other more controlled shoot, the production manager, designer, and/or art director may also come along to evaluate what must be built or changed. Bring a still camera and/or video camera to record the layout of the space. A video camera or *director's finder* (a small handheld finder for viewing a scene at different focal lengths) is useful to block out shots. The location should be checked for a variety of needs:

1. *Direction.* Is the space adequate for shooting? Are the rooms cramped or is there enough space to get the camera back away from the action? If a dolly will be used, is there room for the tracks? Are the walls, furniture, or artwork usable for your movie or will they need to be changed? Any problems with views out windows? For an exterior location, will there be a problem with crowd control?

2. *Lighting.* What is the natural light and how is it expected to change over the time of the shoot, from morning to night? How much artificial light will you need? Are the ceilings high enough to hide lights out of frame? How much electric power is there; will generators or other sources be necessary (see Chapter 12)?

3. *Camera.* Will any special lenses be needed (for example, a wide-angle for small spaces)? Can the usual camera supports be used or will you work handheld or with a Steadicam? Will you need to adjust camera, filters, or film stocks due to high or low light levels?

4. *Sound.* Is the location quiet enough to shoot? Is it under an airport flight path or near a highway? Do the floors squeak when you walk on them? Is the space too reverberant (see Chapter 11)?

5. *Production support.* Is there adequate parking or can permits be obtained to reserve more? Are there enough bathrooms? Are there staging areas where equipment, wardrobe, and makeup can be set up separately from the shooting area? Will you need fans or air conditioners to keep the space from getting too hot? Is the location difficult to find?

Finding a good location that suits all your needs is difficult. Often, filmmakers will shoot exteriors in one place, and the interior that is meant to represent the inside of that building in an entirely different place. If the production budget will support it, shooting in a studio can solve many of the typical problems of locations. Even on a low-budget production, a quiet space, a few *flats* (movable walls), and some props can take you a long way if you have good lighting and clever art direction.

You may need a location release, a permit, or an insurance bond to shoot at some locations (see Chapter 19). Many states have film bureaus that will help you obtain permits and scout locations.

SCHEDULING AND BUDGETING

Script Breakdown and Scheduling

As you prepare for shooting, every scene in the script is broken down for the production elements required. A *script breakdown sheet* lists the people and resources needed for each scene, including cast (both principal players and extras); crew; stunts; props; wardrobe; makeup/hair; vehicles; special effects and equipment; music; and so on. The *production board* (also called *production strip board*) is a chart with strips of paper for each scene, color coded according to whether the scene is interior or exterior, day or night. Strips can be moved around to form the schedule and modify it as necessary. This organizational system can also be done on a computer with software like Movie Magic's EP Scheduling (see Fig. 9-4).

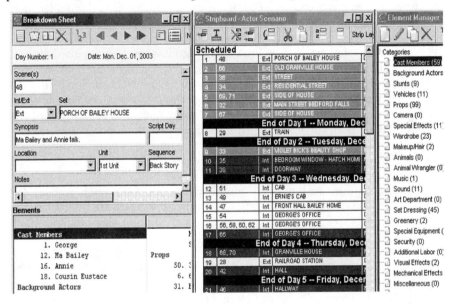

Fig. 9-4. Movie Magic's EP Scheduling. (left) A breakdown sheet for each scene with talent, props, and equipment needs. (middle) Stripboard for planning the shooting schedule. (Entertainment Partners)

Production scheduling is a complex task that takes experience to do well. The goal is to maximize efficiency and make the best use of time when you have a particular actor, are at a particular location, or have particular crew members on board.

A key question is how much to shoot in the sequence of the story versus shooting in whatever order will save the most time and money. With some stories, there may be benefits to working chronologically. For example, a film about two people meeting and developing a relationship may be performed more naturally by actors who are just getting to know each other in the early scenes and have the experience of the shoot behind them for later scenes in the movie. However, shooting in sequence is often a luxury you can't afford. Typically, you need to film all the scenes that occur in one location at the same time. It's just too inefficient to return to the same place to set up multiple times.

The production team will work faster and get more comfortable with one another after working together a while, which argues for shooting relatively easy scenes first, then doing scenes that are more complex technically (or, for actors, emotionally) later on. Actually, crews often go through an arc: Things are bumpy at first, after a while they get into a groove, and then, as exhaustion sets in, they get more ragged.

You need to plan for the unexpected. If you're shooting an exterior on Tuesday, be prepared if it rains to shoot the interior that was previously scheduled for Thursday. Have a backup schedule in case an actor gets sick or some special equipment breaks down. Duplicate wardrobes and props allow the production to continue even when a prop has been misplaced or a shirt has gotten dirty. Backup locations allow you to continue if plans fall through.

It's always tricky to estimate how long it will take to shoot a scene, especially if you don't have a lot of experience. Professional productions have standard expectations about how many pages are shot per day; the pace is faster for television than for studio film productions. Dialogue scenes may go faster than action scenes that require many camera setups (lots of short scenes often take longer than a few long ones). The pace of shooting is usually dictated by the budget. If you can afford only two days at a location, you'll have to get the scenes there done in that time even if it means compromising the original plan. It's not uncommon to go into a shoot with a long list of camera setups on the schedule, then pare the list down to bare essentials as the time—and, often, the light—run out.

Key considerations are how many hours each day you work, and how many days each week. If you're working with union talent or crew, there are rules governing this and financial consequences if you go overtime. Nonunion shoots have the same issues, but negotiations have to be done on an individual basis.

On some productions, everything is shot during the period of principal photography. On others, time is left in the schedule for *reshoots* (often after editing has begun) or for the occasional *pickup shot* needed to fill in a gap or transition. ADR may be needed to replace dialogue before the mix (see p. 492). It's smart to anticipate these thing by building it into the schedule and your contract with the actors.

See Chapter 19 for more on budgeting and business arrangements.

The Shooting Ratio

When drawing up a budget and a plan, the question arises: How much material is going to be shot? The total amount of footage shot is invariably greater than the length of the final edited movie. The ratio of total footage filmed to final footage (*the shooting ratio*) varies widely by type of movie, budget, and director's style. An unscripted documentary might be shot at 40:1 or higher, while a carefully planned fiction film might be on the order of 5:1 or 15:1. These estimates may mean nothing for your particular production or way of working, as you may like to shoot much more or much less depending on your style and the demands of the project.

On a drama, the footage shot will depend on several factors: the length of the script; how many scenes there are; the number of different camera angles (setups) required; how many takes of each need to be shot. Sometimes directors shoot a whole scene in wide shot, then reshoot the whole scene again in close-up to give the most flexibility in editing. This results in a higher shooting ratio than if you decide in advance that you'll only film, say, the opening and closing of the scene in wide shot and do the bulk of the dialogue in close-up. By "pre-editing" in this way you'll save time in the shoot and reduce the amount of footage; you'll also reduce your options in the editing room somewhat.

No matter how predictable you assume the action, the unexpected always seems to happen: changes in the weather, flubbed lines, or technical difficulties with picture or sound. Additional takes are invariably needed in acted work, and documentary is always unpredictable.

One of the biggest factors in the shooting ratio is whether you're shooting video or film. Film is obviously expensive, so there's always pressure not to shoot too much. Video is much cheaper on a per-minute basis, so people tend to shoot it at a much higher ratio than film. When you shoot film, you have to edit in your head and make every foot of film count. With a video camera, it's almost harder to turn it off than to just keep shooting. The benefit of video is a more relaxed feeling on the shoot. You can take bigger risks in terms of trying things out, letting actors play around with a scene, or not stopping and restarting everything between takes. With unpredictable documentary scenes, video may allow you to capture things that you couldn't afford to shoot with film.

However, there can be real problems with shooting too much. First is the extra cost for stock and processing (yes, even video may have processing costs due to dubbing, downconversion, or storage). Also there may be added production time and hassles in the editing room. Managing a project that has hours and hours of material can be a headache and may require many days simply to view and log the footage. When cutting individual scenes, video camerawork can often be too relaxed and rambling. Shots may have no particular beginning or end, and may be impossible to cut. It's interesting to note that students who first learn how to shoot on film tend to shoot more carefully and thoughtfully than those who started with video.

With experience, you will find the ratio that's right for your style of working.

ORGANIZING EQUIPMENT

Equipment Prep

Equipment for a shoot may belong to you, people you hire, a rental house, or a school or other institution (see Renting Versus Buying Equipment, p. 731). Prior to the shoot, the *equipment package* needs to be assembled and tested to be sure everything's working. For camera tests, see Chapters 3, 6, and 7. For audio equipment, see Chapter 11. The night before the shoot, make sure that replaceable batteries are fresh and rechargeable batteries are charged (see Chapter 3).

If you're traveling to the location, use solid shipping cases to protect the gear in vehicles or planes. Many people prefer to hand-carry the camera itself and delicate lenses or audio gear on planes (see p. 176). Bring batteries when hand-carrying; inspectors may demand that you operate the equipment to show it's legit. See p. 274 for shipping film.

Having your equipment and supplies well organized and easily accessible is extremely important. In the pressure of a shoot, you want to be able to quickly put your hands on whatever you need. When shooting with a large crew and plenty of support vehicles, things can be divided into many cases or storage containers. However, when you need to pack light for portability—and especially when working alone—having the right amount of gear in the right cases makes a huge difference. Particularly for documentary work, you'll want a soft shoulder bag or belt bag for tapes and batteries and such that you can wear while shooting. Portabrace makes a nice case for small video cameras that has a detachable inner bag for run-and-gun situations and the main bag (for protecting the camera) is compact enough that you can wear it while shooting if you have to (see Fig. 11-1).

A Field Package

The following is a basic list of equipment for a professional field shoot in video or film. Depending on your camera and production style, you may need more or less stuff. All items are discussed elsewhere in the book.

VIDEO CAMERA

Camera with zoom lens
Soft camera case
Tripod with fluid head and spreader
Three or four batteries, with charger
AC power supply
Wide-angle adaptor
Field monitor
Cables for camera-to-monitor
    connection plus spares (often
    BNC-to-BNC cables)

AUDIO FOR VIDEO

Shotgun (hyper-cardioid) mic
Lavalier mic; assorted clips
Wireless transmitter and receiver
Fishpole mic boom with shock
    mount
Zeppelin windscreen or Softie
Field mixer
Headphones
Cables for mic-to-mixer and
    camera-to-mixer connections
    (often XLR-to-XLR)

FILM CAMERA

Camera body and zoom lens
Two or three magazines
Three batteries and charger
Tripod with fluid head, spreader
Wide-angle adaptor or prime lenses
Lens shade or matte box with support
85 and ND filters; close-up diopters;
    polarizer
Barney; French flag
Zoom lever or motor
Light meters, changing bag
Camera tape and other accessories
    (see p. 253)

AUDIO FOR FILM OR DOUBLE SYSTEM VIDEO

Audio recorder
Mics, boom, and windscreen
Slate; timecode generator
Headphones
Field mixer, if needed
Mic cables and spares

LIGHTING AND GRIP

Lighting units, spare bulbs
AC power cables; cube taps or
   power strips
Gels, CTB, and CTO (small sheets
   for lights, large rolls for windows)
Spun and/or other diffusion
Collapsible reflector
Assorted clamps, clips, hangers
Clothespins, sash cord, etc.
Gaffer's tape; black wrap
Dimmers

OTHER LIGHTING AND GRIP

C-stands with arms
Sand or water bags
Flags, silks, nets (various sizes)
Foam-core or white bounce cards
Dolly; curved and straight
   track and wedges (if applicable)
Apple boxes
Sound blankets
Overhead with silk, net and solid
Photofloods; fuses
Tie-in cables and boxes

COMPOSITION AND SHOT SELECTION

SCENES AND TAKES

A script is divided into a series of *scenes*—a scene is an event that takes place in one setting in a continuous time period. However, when someone walks from one room to another and the camera is moved to a new location, it is often considered two separate scenes in the script. A *sequence* is generally a scene or a series of scenes that make up a unit. For example, you might refer to the "baptism sequence" in *The Godfather*, which includes a scene in a church intercut with a series of scenes of murders being committed around the city.

A scene may be made up of a single *shot* (such as a wide shot of the entire action) or it may be divided into several shots or *camera angles* (or just *angles*) that will eventually be edited together (such as matching close-ups of two actors talking to each other).

Various *takes* are filmed, each trying to capture a particular shot. For example, "Scene 8, Take 14" is the fourteenth attempt to capture Scene 8 in the script. Letters can be used to indicate a particular angle called for in the script. "Scene 8B, Take 4" is the fourth attempt to get the second camera angle (B) of Scene 8. Another way to notate it would be "Scene 8, Shot 2, Take 4."

During production, every time the camera is moved to a new spot to get a different scene or camera angle is considered a new *setup*. The *daily production report* on a feature tracks how many setups were filmed that day. Changing setups often implies not only changing camera position, but changing lighting and other aspects as well.

Take (or *camera take*) refers to each section of footage from the time the camera begins shooting until it is turned off. Shot is sometimes used to mean camera take and sometimes to mean the edited take—that is, the portion of the take used in the edited version of the movie. To confuse things further, scene sometimes means shot (as in, "scene-to-scene color correction"). Usually the context distinguishes the meaning.

Types of Shots

Shots are divided into three basic categories—the *long shot* (LS), *medium shot* (MS), and *close-up* (CU). The long shot includes the whole body of the person in relation to the environment, usually taken from fairly far away from the subject. A wide view of a landscape is sometimes called a long shot or a *wide shot*. The *establishing shot* is a long shot that defines the basic space or locale where events will take place. The medium shot is not too detailed, includes part of the subject and usually includes people from head to knee or from waist up. The close-up shows a detail of the scene; in the case of a person, it is a head-and-shoulder shot. A "two-button close-up" shows everything from the face down to the second button on a person's shirt. In a *big close-up*, just a face fills the screen, or in an *extreme close-up* (ECU) part of a face or a small object fills the screen—for example, a watch or a fly.

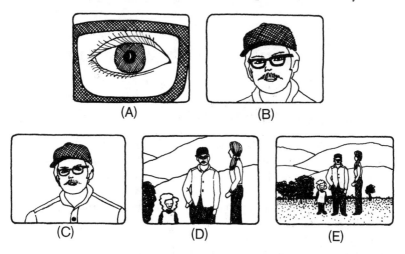

Fig. 9-5. Shot division. The categories are not exact. (A) The *extreme close-up* fills the screen with a small detail. (B) The *big close-up* fills the frame with a face. (C) The *close-up* includes the head and shoulders. (D) The *medium shot* includes most of the body. When two people are shown in medium shot, it is a *two shot*. (E) The *long shot* includes the whole body and the surroundings. (Carol Keller)

Two shots taken from opposite angles are called *reverse-angle shots*. A conversation between two people is often shot with each person alone in the frame in three-quarter profile. When the scene is edited, we see one person looking left, then the other looking right. This shooting-editing style is called *angle-reverse-angle*. These shots are typically close-ups, but the back of the other person may be visible. Often, the speakers are matched in size and are in the same relative position on the screen (see Leading the Action and The 180-Degree Rule, p. 326). Angle-reverse-angle cutting is often contrasted with the *two shot*, which is a single shot of two actors from the front showing them from the knees up (*knee shot*) or waist up. The *point-of-view* (POV) shot is taken from someone's or something's vantage point. It can be taken from behind an actor over his shoulder or at the position of his eyes. POV shots also include shots from extreme vantage points, such as from directly overhead (*bird's-eye view*).

The shooting and editing of *static* or *locked-off shots* (that is, shots taken with no camera movement) can be contrasted to that of moving camera shots. A camera pivoting from a single point can *pan* (move in a horizontal axis left or right) or *tilt* (pivot in a vertical axis up or down). If the support that's holding the camera can be raised, this may be *pedestal* up or *boom* up or *crane* up. If the support is on wheels, you can make a *dolly* or *tracking shot*. You could move from a long shot to a medium shot in a single take (for more on dolly shots, see p. 348).

Whether you use static or moving camera shots, the parsing or dividing of the action into various shots (instead of shooting an entire scene from one camera position in a single shot) helps both in shooting the scene and editing it. *Coverage* refers to how many options have been provided by the director in terms of different camera angles and takes. Having multiple camera angles available in the editing room allows you to change the pace of the scene, direct audience attention to different aspects, and edit around mistakes (see below and Chapter 13). If a scene is covered with only one or two angles or takes, options are limited. Many an editor has lamented a director's lack of coverage.

One logical and traditional way to break down a scene is to move from a long shot to a medium shot to a close-up. This orients the audience to the physical space and the progression of increasingly tight shots suggests forward movement into the scene, as though the camera is delving deeper into the action. When a scene goes wider, from a medium shot to a long shot, we expect action on a larger scale (for example, a new arrival in the scene) or a leave-taking from the action (as might happen at the end of a movie). Nevertheless, contemporary audiences are used to a wide variety of cutting styles and the traditional rules about the relationship of shots don't always apply.

Composition

Each shot is *composed* or *framed* in the camera viewfinder. When you film from a script, each shot is *blocked out*, or planned, before the take. In unscripted work, framing and movement are improvised based on both what is seen through the viewfinder and what is seen and heard outside the frame.

The notion of composition comes from easel painting and in part from still photography, and refers to the arrangement of objects within the frame—their balance and tensions. Composition in motion pictures is quite different, since objects move within the frame (subject movement) and the frame itself can move (camera movement). Furthermore, one shot is edited next to another, creating an entirely new set of tensions and balances through time.

Because a shot often reveals its meaning through motion, it's possible to have strong film composition without well-composed still frames. Composition that is dynamic usually resolves tension by the use of subject or camera movement or through editing. A frame that seems off balance at first may fluidly become better centered as it develops. Or the off-balance quality itself may be used as an interesting pictorial element.

Although there are no set rules for composition, there are expectations that compositions create, and that may be used to surprise the audience or to confirm or deny their expectations. For instance, camera angles from below are used to suggest the importance, stature, and height of the subject. In horror films, compositional imbalance in the frame often suggests something scary lurking outside the frame. These days, gross imbalances may be used simply to add flavor, particularly in commercials.

Objects should be placed naturally in the static frame. Don't compose so important objects or people are so close to the edge of the frame that they seem to "fight" with it. Keep objects comfortably within the frame or use the edge to cut them off decisively and to direct attention to important areas of the frame. Avoid large dead spaces, and don't lose the subject in a mass of irrelevant details. Be attentive to what's directly behind the subject, such as plants that may seem to be growing out of the person's head.

The *rule of thirds* is a rough compositional guide to help you avoid placing important areas of interest dead-center in the frame, which may result in a dull image. Instead, position important areas one-third of the screen width from either side or one-third the screen height from the bottom or top. Accordingly, in close-up or medium close-up shots, place the subject's eyes one-third of the screen height from the top (the nose will then be roughly centered in the frame). In medium shots, place heads about a third of the way down from the top of the frame. Keeping in mind the above, it must be pointed out that exceptions are legion.

Leading the Action

Whenever a subject has a definite movement toward the edge of the frame, place the subject closer to the edge from which he is moving (see Fig. 9-6). For example, if you track someone running from left to right, frame him closer to the left side of the frame as if to leave room for running on the right. If the shot continues for some time, the runner can advance in the frame (still leaving room at the right) to suggest forward movement. Similarly, someone in profile looking off screen to the right should be framed closer to the left side of the frame, leaving space on the right.

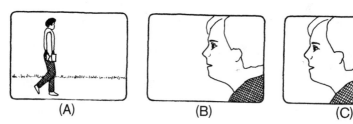

(A)   (B)   (C)

Fig. 9-6. Leading the action. (A, B) Leave more room on the side of the frame toward which the action points. (C) The void at the right throws the frame off balance, and you expect something to happen (for example, the man may be attacked from behind). (Carol Keller)

The 180-Degree Rule

Screen direction refers to the right or left direction on screen as seen by the audience. If a subject facing the camera moves to his left, it is screen right. The *180-Degree rule* (also called the *director's line* or the *line*) tells how to maintain screen direction when different shots are edited together. If a subject is moving or looking in one direction, in general it's best not to let screen direction change when cutting to the next shot. For example, when watching football on television, the blue team is seen moving from screen left to screen right. If the camera were now to shift to the opposite side of the field, the blue team would appear to be moving in the opposite direction (that is, their screen direction has changed from right to left). It's likely that the audience would be confused. To avoid this confusion, TV crews generally keep their main cameras on one side of the field, and, when they use a camera position from the opposite side of the field, a subtitle may be flashed on the screen saying "reverse angle."

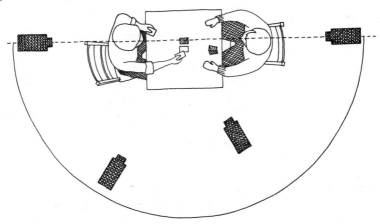

Fig. 9-7. The 180-degree rule. If all the camera positions are kept on one side of the sight line, screen direction will be preserved in editing. (Carol Keller)

To help plan your shots, imagine a line drawn through the main line of action—be it a moving car, a football field, or the eye line of a conversation. If all camera setups are on one side of the line, screen direction will be preserved from shot to shot. Shots *on* the line (for example, someone looking directly into the camera or a shot from the end zone in the football example) are considered neutral and can go with shots on either side of the line.

During a take, the camera can move across the line with minimal disorientation. But if later in the editing room you don't use the shot where the camera crosses the line, you may have to violate the 180-degree rule. Rule violations may disorient the audience, but rarely are they disastrous. Sometimes inserting a neutral shot minimizes disorientation. The problem is most serious when screen direction itself has been used to construct the space of the scene. For example, in an angle-reverse-angle scene of two people talking, they must be looking in opposite screen directions when there is a cut from one to the other, otherwise they will not appear to be talking to each other. Similarly, chase sequences depend on screen direction to establish whether one car is chasing another or if the two are headed toward each other.

Screen direction issues can sometimes apply to shots that aren't even in the same scene. For example, documentary interviews are often filmed so that one subject is facing camera left and a subject with a contrary opinion is facing right. Cut together, there's a sense of opposition or contrast in the framing as opposed to the uniformity that would result if each were looking to the same side of the lens.

Sometimes there are two different lines of action and there is no way to avoid breaking the rule. For example, a couple is talking in the front seat of a moving car in a scene that is shot angle-reverse-angle. When the driver is shot, the background is moving left; but when the passenger is shot, the background is moving right. Since the relation of the couple is most likely the key element of the scene, draw the line of action along their eye line to preserve their screen direction in the editing.

Continuity

In the grammar of film shooting and editing, there's often a need to create the illusion of continuous time. That is, to join shots filmed at different times in such a way that the audience sees them as a continuous, uninterrupted flow. Contemporary filmmaking styles sometimes dispense with this illusion and simply cut from one moment to the next, which audiences have come to accept. However, many types of movies and scenes call for *continuity*, and it's important to understand how to maintain it (also see Chapter 13).

Usually several takes of the same scripted action are shot, in part because actors blunder or crew members make technical errors, and in part because by shooting different camera angles you can minimize the chance of discontinuities in the edited sequence. Even if you plan to shoot the action in one take, allow for an overlap of action from one shot to the next in the scene to be sure there won't be temporal discontinuities in the editing. For example, say the script calls for a wide shot of a man getting in a car and slamming the car door, followed by a close-up of his face. Shoot the wide shot all the way through the slamming of the door. When you start the close-up, shoot the action from a point *before* the first take ended, including the slamming of the door. This gives the editor options to cut the two shots together at several different points without discontinuity. (Note: The two shots should usually be taken at different angles to make a smoother cut and to minimize any slight discontinuities.)

The same problem arises in documentary, but an overlap of action is usually only possible in scenes where people repeat the same actions several times (for example, when cooking or chopping wood).

A *cutaway* is a shot away from the main action that can be used to cover discontinuities or to condense the action. For example, when shooting a politician giving a speech at a rally, a shot of a woman in the audience could be considered a cutaway or a *reaction shot*. In editing, the cutaway can be used to smoothly join one part of the speech with another. You cut from the politician (in sync sound) to the woman and back to the politician at a later part of the speech. Without the cutaway, the condensed speech would be more obviously discontinuous.

When a character walks off camera, the viewer generally accepts a time jump when the next shot begins with him later on. For instance, if someone walks off frame toward the door, a cut to the same person walking down the street or sitting at a restaurant doesn't seem discontinuous. When panning or tracking with a moving subject, it's usually a good idea to let him walk out of frame at the end of the shot to provide more options in editing.

There are many ways to cover or show discontinuities in time. Say you're shooting a character painting a picture and you want to show her starting with a blank canvas and then in the next shot show her putting the last touch on the finished work. To simply cut from one wide shot to another would probably seem too severe. The routine solution is to dissolve from one shot to the other. Another possibility is to do a *reveal*. The first shot ends as a wide shot. The second shot might begin with a close-up of her face and pull back (either by zoom or moving camera) to reveal the finished painting.

In both documentary and fiction shooting, always try to have in mind what shot you can cut the present one with. In a two-way conversation, a close-up of one person will almost invariably cut next to a close-up of the same size of the other person (assuming the 180-degree rule is observed), but two close-ups of the same person at the same size can rarely cut smoothly together. Whenever you feel there will have to be a cut made to another shot, change camera angles and focal lengths to make continuity editing easier.

When shooting, ask yourself how the shot you're taking might work with the other shots you've gotten or need to get. Do you have enough coverage—that is, have you provided enough options for editing? Have you got cutaways? Do you have an establishing shot? Have you got interesting close-ups? See Style and Direction, p. 332, for more on coverage and shooting styles.

Errors discovered while viewing rushes or during editing often necessitate pickup shooting, which entails going back to get additional shots to fill in a sequence. A documentary crew might return to get a cutaway from a car window, or, in a fiction film, there might be a need for a reaction shot of an actor. Take stills of sets, lighting setups, makeup, and costumes to help match shots that may need to be redone. Many DPs (or their assistants) keep detailed notes about lenses, camera angles, and lighting to facilitate reshoots.

Other Elements in the Dynamic Frame

The focus may be "pulled" from the background to the foreground to shift audience attention. Some filmmakers consider this technique mannered unless it is used to follow a movement. Selective focus is used to accentuate a portion of the subject. In a close-up, it's usually advisable to focus on the eyes. A *tilt-focus lens* (see Fig. 4-20) allows you to tilt the plane of focus. Lighting may be changed within a shot; for example, car headlights might suddenly illuminate a person.

Shots tilted sideways (tilted horizon line) are called *Dutch angle* or *canted* and are sometimes used, often in medium close-up, to add tension to a static frame (see Fig. 9-8). Sometimes one tripod head is mounted perpendicularly on another to allow the camera to be smoothly tilted from side to side while tilting forward and back (see Fig. 9-9).

Cinematographers often shoot at an angle that reveals as many sides of the object as possible in order to enhance the feeling of depth. For example, a building filmed head-on reveals one side; shot from an angle it reveals two sides; and shot down and at an angle it reveals three sides. Use familiar references to establish scale. An enormous boulder will seem larger if there is a person in the frame.

Hollywood directors frequently use camera angle, camera movement, and lighting to create a feeling of deep space in the image. This allows them to clearly distinguish foreground from background and exclude large areas of unmodulated

Fig. 9-8. Dutch angle from *Citizen Kane*. Note the strong diagonal lines in the frame. (RKO General)

black or white. European directors in the 1960s and 1970s often emphasized the flatness of the screen through their use of lighting and camera angle, sometimes shooting perpendicularly to a wall or allowing large areas of the frame to be overexposed or underexposed.

Composition in the Monitor or Viewfinder

There's an expression in computer-speak, "what you see is what you get." Unfortunately, when framing up a shot in a video or film camera, what you see is often *not* what you get. That is, the image that's ultimately delivered to the audience may look a lot different than the one you're seeing, not just in color or exposure, but also in the shape of the frame and where the edges of the picture are. Depending on

Fig. 9-9. The Cartoni dutch head enables you to mount a second fluid head perpendicular to the first, allowing side-to-side as well as front-to-back tilts. (Cartoni)

how the movie is distributed and displayed, some or all of your audience may be seeing a different aspect ratio or they may see the same aspect ratio, just not all of the picture. It's a real trick in shooting to try to compose for the frame you're seeing while keeping in mind the different ways it may get transformed.

TV CUTOFF. A television screen will usually not display the entire video frame. For example, if you feed non-widescreen (4:3) video to a typical non-widescreen, 4:3 TV, the TV will usually crop out the outer edges of the picture. This is called *TV cutoff* or *overscan*. It is actually intentional on the part of the TV manufacturers who fear their product will look worse if viewers ever see beyond the edge of the picture, so they enlarge the picture a bit so it more than fills the screen. All monitors do this somewhat, but consumer TVs are the worst. Cutoff can also happen when widescreen video is shown on widescreen monitors.

Because the viewer may not see the edges of the frame, remember when shooting to avoid positioning anything crucial too close to the edges of the viewfinder frame (top, bottom, or sides). TV cutoff is inconsistent from one TV to another—you can't *count* on how much the edges will get cut. Something undesired—like a microphone in the corner of the shot—may or may not show up.

The camera viewfinder should be able to display a *TV safe action* frame as a guide to show which parts may be cropped. The *TV safe title* area is even closer to the center of the picture to protect text and titles that have to be readable (see Fig. 9-10). Some monitors are switchable between *underscan*, which shows you the entire image, and *overscan*, which shows you typical cutoff. Underscan will show you when unwanted things are definitely out, and also what the image may look like when shown on the Web (Web video typically doesn't have cutoff).

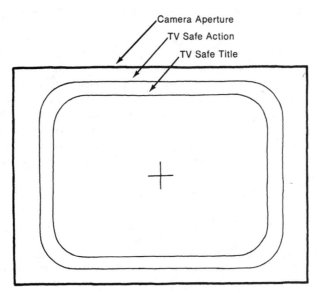

Fig. 9-10. TV safe action and safe title areas for non-widescreen 1.33:1 (4 x 3) film or video. If you're planning to extract a 16:9 image later (see Fig. 2-15B) the top and bottom of the 16:9 frame will be fairly close to the TV safe action line. (Carol Keller)

WIDESCREEN AND NON-WIDESCREEN FORMATS. If you shoot in a widescreen format, you need to consider what will happen if your movie is shown in a non-widescreen format or display. Similarly, if you shoot non-widescreen, the footage may get converted to widescreen at some point. To understand what's involved, read the discussion of aspect ratio starting on p. 87 and particularly How Aspect Ratio Affects Your Shooting on p. 96.

If you're shooting in a widescreen format, use a viewfinder marked with widescreen proportions. Some film cameras have interchangeable viewing screens or ground glasses in different aspect ratios, such as 1.66, 1.85, and 2.35. Some viewfinder screens show different formats nested within each other, so shots can be composed from the center out, thus guaranteeing that important parts of the scene are visible in each format. This also helps you to "protect" every aspect ratio from undesired things like microphone booms. However, trying to frame for different-shaped frames can lead to poor compositions. It's like an artist trying to paint a canvas that may later have the edges snipped off!

As discussed in Chapter 2, there are different methods of converting from one aspect ratio to another, and you need to be clear in your mind which one will be used. For example, if you're shooting typical 16:9 HD widescreen and plan to downconvert to SD non-widescreen using edge crop (also called center crop), the widescreen picture in the viewfinder and the eventual non-widescreen cropped version share a common top and bottom but not common sides. In this case, you should remember to keep crucial action away from the sides. If pan and scan will be used, you have more flexibility.

STYLE AND DIRECTION

Style in movies, as all art forms, is continually evolving. At any given time, different types of movies make use of various conventions in shooting and editing. The conventions shift over time for a variety of reasons: A stylistically new film will spawn imitators; changes in technology make new techniques possible; ideas are borrowed from one type of moviemaking and applied to others. What follows is a deliberately sketchy history of some styles used in moviemaking, and some thoughts on directing, as a stimulus to thinking about the relationship of style and shooting possibilities. See the sections Some Film Theory and Cutting Styles in Chapter 13.

DOCUMENTARIES

Documentary Styles
In documentary filmmaking, some of the key stylistic questions relate to how much the filmmaker attempts to control or interact with the subjects, and to the way information is conveyed in the movie.

Some of the first motion pictures were made by Thomas Edison in the 1890s. These were "documentaries" in the sense that a camera was set up to record actual events, such as the death of an elephant. Or the Lumière brothers' *Train Coming into a Station* (1896), which is a single, continuous shot of a train arriving (and which reportedly caused pandemonium because audiences thought the train was really coming at them).

The style adopted by U.K. documentarians such as John Grierson in the 1930s and 1940s is a kind of hybrid that can involve staged events and real people (non-actors). Because the cameras and the sound recording equipment were heavy and hard to move around, action was often produced and orchestrated for the camera. Scenes could be scripted and shot much like a narrative film. Many of these films use a "voice of God" narration—the authoritative male voice that provides factual information and often spells out the message intended for the viewer to take from the film.

In the 1960s, lightweight 16mm cameras were introduced that could record sync sound with portable tape recorders. With the advent of handheld cameras, new access to locations and people's lives was obtained. Jean Renoir spoke of the heavy studio camera as an altar to which actors had to be brought. The handheld camera could now go out into the world instead of the filmmaker bringing the world to the camera. *Cinema vérité* (also called just *vérité* or *direct cinema*) films attempt to spontaneously react to events and capture life as it is lived. With a small crew and enough time for subjects to get comfortable, the filmmaker can become very unobtrusive. Unself-conscious subjects will reveal to the camera how they really live and self-conscious subjects will reveal themselves in how they choose to perform. Many of these films use no narration or interviews and attempt to minimize the sense that the material has been influenced or interpreted by the filmmaker.

In the 1970s, a "personal documentary" movement emerged. In these movies, filmmakers explore their own lives, or shoot others with the explicit acknowledgment of the camera's presence and the filmmaker's role in interpreting events for the audience. Rather than seeking an illusion of objectivity, these films embrace a subjective and personal view, and are often narrated by the filmmakers themselves.

In the 1980s and 1990s, nonfiction programming grew in popularity on network television. Magazine-style shows such as *60 Minutes* are structured around short segments in which a correspondent is the guide and narrator of a particular story. These productions have their roots in journalism. The correspondent is seen interviewing subjects and doing *stand-ups*—telling the story directly to the camera. These shows usually contain some amount of "vérité-style" footage in which people are seen living their lives or doing their jobs. This footage is often referred to with the antiseptic term *B-roll*. B-roll is noninterview material that is often only allowed to play for a few seconds in sync sound. Then the location audio is dipped down and the picture becomes a bed over which to lay narration.

Today, nonfiction films are made using all of these styles, or combinations of them. When you embark on a documentary project, you need to determine the stylistic framework for the movie. In what ways will the audience learn about the subject? By watching events unfold in a vérité-style approach? By seeing interviews with the subjects or hearing them over other footage? By seeing interviews with "experts" commenting on the subjects? Will there be a narration (also called *voice-over*)? If so, is the narrator a disembodied voice or someone also seen on screen (either a subject, the filmmaker, or a correspondent)?

Often the film's topic will dictate style. Documentaries about past events generally use a combination of interviews (*talking heads*) and archival material (*stock footage*). Often this is combined with present-day footage of locations where events took place. Sometimes *reenactments* of past events are shot using actors. This footage may be shot in a stylized way to avoid being too literal; for example, actors might be filmed without any dialogue or perhaps not showing their faces. Of course, the more screen time devoted to reenactments (and the more dialogue they contain) to closer you get to the hybrid genre *docudrama*, which exists somewhere between documentary and fiction.

SCRIPT OR NO SCRIPT. Historical and issue-based films often begin with research, followed by a script or detailed treatment. Sometimes "pre-interviews" are done to determine what someone will say (more or less) before they're filmed. The film is structured as much as possible in the writing, and the footage shot in the field or acquired from other sources is intended to illustrate a set of ideas that have already been laid out.

One of the reasons television tends to favor correspondent- and interview-based productions is that they can be produced on a short schedule. Interviews can be done and stand-ups scripted fairly quickly. The interview *bites* (responses) are edited together with B-roll. It's not unlike writing a newspaper piece.

This is in contrast to documentaries in which the shooting *is* the research. Contemporary stories that are still unfolding often call for a much more spontaneous approach. You should have an idea of what you're looking for, and focus on particular story threads, but often it's in the shooting that you find what the arc of the story is. Some stories have an obvious arc—a film about an election, for example.

What's called "reality TV" is a loose genre of programming in which "real" people engage in competitions, are thrown into pre-planned situations, or are challenged with various tasks. While the dialogue may not be scripted, the idea is to shoot a defined event that takes place in a short shooting period, and can be edited into a digestible hour or half-hour episode.

When you make documentaries about real people living their lives—without trying to "direct" them or structure what they do—you're never sure what's going to happen or when. Many a filmmaker has completed weeks, months, or years of shooting with no idea if enough of a story has emerged to make a film. Then it may take an extended period in the editing room to weave together a coherent piece. But the payoff to this risky approach is in the power of stories that develop over a long period of time, in which characters change and grow, are born or die. The result can be a complexity and depth that can't be achieved any other way.

Filming Real Life

Documentary film provides a uniquely rich opportunity to experience how other people live their lives. There's a particular thrill about seeing dramatic moments unfold, knowing that they're spontaneous and unscripted. Creating the environment in which people will reveal themselves with a camera present is part of the documentarian's art.

The more that the people you're filming trust you, the more comfortable they'll be in front of the camera. Filmmakers use different approaches to building trust.

Some like to spend a long time with their subjects before filming begins, to give everyone a chance to get to know one another. If you do so, you can expect many moments when you'll wish you had your camera. Regardless of when you start filming, spending some personal time together when the camera's not rolling (sharing a meal or a cup of coffee) is an important part of learning about and getting comfortable with your subjects and their learning about you.

You should discuss with your subjects what kind of film you're making and where you plan to show it. You may want to talk with them about what's okay to shoot and what's not. Some filmmakers have the subjects sign a release at the outset, granting permission to use whatever is filmed (see Talent and Appearance Releases, p. 741). Others wait until later. From a journalistic standpoint, it's not a good idea to give subjects a formal right of approval over what gets used in the film and how it's edited (you're making the movie, not them).[2] However, you may or may not want to offer to show them the film before it's done to get their response. Public exhibition of a film can have an enormous impact (both positive and negative) on the subjects' lives, which you need to consider seriously as you shoot and edit. In some situations, people will let you film them only if they have some input in the process.

Once production begins, keep the crew small and use as few lights as possible, so the shooting is relaxed and low-key. When you start shooting, don't make a lot of commotion. Some camerapeople like to keep the camera on their shoulder or in position much of the time so there's not a big distinction between the times they're shooting and when they're just waiting. On a video camera, turn off the tally light that announces when you've pulled the trigger. When shooting film, keep slates quiet or do tail slates (though this may increase costs in the telecine). The point is not to be sneaky, but to make the filming process as subtle as possible, with a fluid transition between shooting and not shooting.

Using wireless mics can be particularly useful in documentary. When the subject wears a mic, they're free to roam where they want without a soundperson sticking a mic boom in their face. Be sure to show them where the mute button is so they can have privacy when they want it.

Though people may be self-conscious at first, the fact of the matter is that being filmed over a period of time can be quite boring—the novelty wears off quickly. This is what you want—for your subjects to go about their lives without worrying about what you're shooting. Some filmmakers try to become a fly on the wall and interact very little with their subjects. Others are friendly and conversational when they're *not* shooting, but silent when the camera's rolling. In some filmmaking styles, the conversation between filmmaker and subject continues the whole time. It's up to you.

Shooting Uncontrolled Scenes

For the cameraperson, filming real people without controlling what they do takes a special combination of sensitivity, luck, and quick thinking. Perhaps more than any other kind of shooting, cinema vérité filming requires that the camera

---

2. Some broadcasters may consider the film compromised if the subjects have control or if it feels like a puff piece promoting a group or individual.

operator think like a director and an editor, all while spontaneously reacting to changing events. The tendency while shooting is to concentrate on the central action or person talking; remind yourself that the audience may also need to see the context (wide shot) and reactions from other people in the scene. Think about the sequence as a whole. Ask yourself if you've gotten enough coverage. Though you don't yet know how the sequence will be edited, try to provide multiple options for editing and shots you think might make interesting beginnings or endings. The audience will be seeing the scene through *your* eyes, so always have them in mind while you shoot.

Fig. 9-11. A small LCD monitor can be mounted on the camera, or used as a portable "director's monitor" for mobile shooting. If you plan to use an LCD monitor as a reference for color and contrast, be aware that low-quality monitors (and ones that lack a blue-only switch for setup) may misrepresent what you're actually getting. (Panasonic Broadcast)

It's especially important to think of individual shots and camera movements as having a shape, with a beginning and end. Novices, especially when shooting video, tend to move the camera constantly, which makes the footage very hard to cut. When doing a camera movement (whether it be a zoom, pan, dolly, or walking shot), it's often a good idea to begin with a static frame that is held for a few seconds, then transition into the movement, and glide to a stop on another frame and hold that a few seconds. The editor may cut out the static beginning and end, but at least he or she will have them if needed.

A few documentary filmmakers, notably Frederick Wiseman, have a style in which scenes often play out in nearly real time with relatively little cutting within the scene. This can allow human interactions to unfold in a natural way.

Far more commonly, scenes as edited on screen must play much faster than the actual event took in real time. The filmmaker must find a way to shoot so that time can be condensed. This means judiciously shooting the action so that the editor can cut out the uninteresting parts and weave together the essential parts. Take the example of shooting two people talking over dinner. The meal might take two hours in real time and run two minutes in the edited movie. If the camera remained locked in a two-shot the entire time, the sequence would be almost impossible to cut. Instead, get a variety of angles, some two-shots, some close-ups. Be sure to shoot ample footage of the person *listening* as well as the person talking. An over-the-shoulder shot taken from behind the person talking shows the relationship of the two subjects without showing moving lips; this can be very useful in the editing room. Similarly, when shooting someone on the telephone, try to get some angles from behind or where the phone's mouthpiece blocks the camera's view of the person's lips. When shooting someone playing an instrument, be sure to get neutral shots in which no fingering or hand position is visible.

Shooting Interviews

There are various approaches to the use of interviews. In a typical news or journalistic piece, they may be the primary source of content and take up much of the screen time. In some films, interviews are woven in with other types of footage and feel more like an opportunity for conversation or storytelling than for information delivery. In some films, the audience never sees the interview; instead, the filmmaker edits the audio and uses it as voice-over, to give the sense that the character is narrating the movie.[3]

A key issue when doing interviews is whether the interviewer's voice will be heard in the edited interview. That is, will the audience hear the questions and follow-ups (as is common when a correspondent does a magazine piece), or will they just see the subjects' responses edited together (which is typical when there's no host or filmmaker shown or heard on screen)? Doing interviews when the questions *won't* be heard creates a unique, somewhat bizarre dynamic that takes some practice to pull off smoothly. You need to get the person talking, but not exactly *to* you (since you don't exist in the conversation). You may have the urge to respond, to reassure the person that what they're saying is interesting, but you can't make a sound—at least while they're talking. Some things that may help:

- Set a relaxed tone at the outset. Have the subject talk to you and try to ignore the camera. Tell them it's okay if they need to stop to think, or to redo a question. (You might, however, *want* to put them on the spot.)
- Explain that your voice won't be in the piece, which is why you may be nodding but not responding when they talk.
- It can be awkward if they answer questions the audience doesn't hear. If you ask, "Where were you born" and all they say is, "London," you'll have a problem in the editing room. Instead, ask them to incorporate your question into their answer ("I was born in London") or at least ask them to respond in full sentences.
- Don't let them say, "As I said before" or refer to earlier conversation. There's no way to know what order the material will be used, or if you'll use both bites. Every statement should stand on its own. If you're not part of the piece, don't let them refer to "you" either.
- Filmmakers differ in how much to let people talk during the interview and how much to try to influence how they phrase things (it also depends on the

3. If you know *for sure* that you only want the audio from the interview, recording only with an audio recorder can sometimes put people more at ease. Or use a video camera but point it away.

project). Long, run-on sentences may be unusable. Always be listening for how you can edit what's being said, to shorten it while retaining the meaning. Some people have a knack for speaking in long strings of dependent clauses that are simply uneditable. You may want to stop and ask them to say the same idea more succinctly, or to address the content in separate short bits instead of one long chunk. Often, the first time someone answers a question is the freshest. If you need to do a "re-ask," change the focal length of the lens so you can edit the first part of one answer with the second part of the other, if you want.

Sometimes interviews feel more natural if the subject has a physical activity to do or is in a familiar setting. The background and setting can be used to tell the audience something about the person. Another approach is to use a neutral backdrop to provide consistency from one subject to the next. A textured cloth or black (*limbo*) backdrop can be brought from location to location, but if there are many talking heads, a uniform backdrop may become dull. Sometimes interviews are filmed in front of a green screen, with the background added in postproduction (see Chroma Keys, p. 543). This opens the door to all sorts of imagery—including motion shots—in the background. Keyed backgrounds sometimes feel artificial, but when appropriate can be really interesting.

CAMERA ANGLES AND MOVES. For sit-down interviews, usually the interviewer sits close to the camera so the eye line of the subject is toward the lens but not directly into it (which can sometimes feel awkward). When positioning the subject, be attentive to screen direction—try to alternate setups with subjects facing screen left with those facing screen right (this is classically done for people with opposing opinions). When the interviewer is to be shown on camera, or if there is more than one camera, sometimes one camera angle is from the side, to get more of a profile shot. Filmmaker Errol Morris uses what he calls the "interrotron," which is basically a teleprompter (see Fig. 9-29) that projects his face on a screen in front of the lens, so the interviewee can look directly *into* the lens while talking to him. On-camera hosts or correspondents generally look directly *to camera* when addressing the audience.

Some filmmakers shoot interviews with no camera movements during shots, but zoom in or out to vary the focal length between shots. This allows cutting in or out of the material without ever having to cut during a zoom, which some people find objectionable. However, a well-timed zoom can enhance an interview by bringing the viewer closer for important or emotional material, or pulling back to capture, say, interesting hand gestures. If the zoom is gradual and properly timed to the phrases of speech, cutting opportunities should not be too limited.

Sometimes interviews are filmed with a dolly-mounted camera to keep some sense of movement throughout. Curved track can help you maintain the same distance from the subject while moving around. Timing is everything, since even a slow dolly move will reach the end of the track before long. It may just be luck if you're moving in the right direction at the right place at the right time.

When more than one camera is used, as is typical with news and magazine shows, one can hold a more conservative, wider shot while another is more active. Shooting interviews with multiple cameras provides a lot of flexibility for editing and avoids the fake reaction shot problem that happens when there's only one camera and the interviewer is shown "reacting" to something filmed much earlier. (For a great example of this, see James Brooks's comedy, *Broadcast News*).

If lower-third subtitles will be used to identify subjects (see p. 501), be sure to leave room at the bottom of the frame.

DRAMAS

Narrative Styles

In fiction and other scripted filming, one of the director's prime concerns is where to place the camera. On a broader stylistic level, the director must plan how individual shots relate to the action of the scene and to the juxtaposition of other shots through editing.

In the deep focus shot (see Fig. 9-12), the whole frame is in focus. The meaning of the scene thus develops in the deep space of the frame. The camera movement, subject movement, dialogue, lighting, costumes, and so forth all contribute to the forward movement of the film. The long take—that is, a shot of long duration— allows the action to unfold in real space and underlines the fact that the shot's meaning comes from filming, not from editing.

Fig. 9-12. Deep focus shot from *Citizen Kane*. A wide-angle shot with both foreground and background in focus allows the action to develop within the frame. (RKO General)

This staging of the shot, or *mise-en-scène*, is contrasted with *montage*, in which meaning and forward movement are conveyed through editing, through the juxtaposition of various shots that by themselves may contain less information or content. When the action of a scene is captured in many shorter shots, the filmmaker has an opportunity to control pacing and to direct the audience's attention in ways that may not be possible with longer takes. Montage also opens up the possibility of constructing entirely new meanings by suggesting connections between shots that otherwise might seem unrelated (for more on montage, see Chapter 13).

André Bazin, the French film critic often credited as the decisive influence on the French New Wave, thought it characteristic of advanced film directors of sound pictures to be concerned with mise-en-scène, with the integrity of the photographed space. If you think of dangerous stunts, it is easy to grasp the visceral effect of seeing the events photographed rather than constructed. Among all the silent filmmakers, Buster Keaton seemed to understand best the power of unmanipulated space. His stunts, often performed in long shot, were clearly incredible feats. Much of the attraction of unmanipulated documentary is its ability to convince the viewer that what is seen on the screen actually occurred.

On the other hand, when audiences "suspend disbelief" and enter into the world of the movie, a carefully constructed edited sequence can deliver enormous emotional impact or bring out otherwise buried meaning. Staging and editing should not be thought of as opposites but as two stylistic tools at the filmmaker's disposal.

The first dramatic filmmakers approached motion pictures as an extension of theater. A story would be acted out in front of a fixed camera. Though the early silent films of the 1900s were not actually shot on a proscenium stage, the camera's relationship to the action was much like a theatergoer's view of a stage play. D. W. Griffith is credited with first exploiting the power of the close-up. The camera comes in close to reveal nuances of an actor's expression, creating a new relationship between audience and actor, necessitating a new, more subtle style of acting. The silent cinema defined the basic vocabulary of the film image. Today, shots taken without sound are referred to as *MOS*. The story goes that when the German directors came to Hollywood in the early 1930s, they referred to silent footage as "mit-out-sprache" (a kind of fractured German for "without speech"), hence MOS.

Hollywood sound films until the 1950s generally were shot in studios using a conservative shooting/editing style. Scenes are first filmed all the way through in master shots (relatively wide-angle, continuous takes). Then close-ups are filmed, if needed. The edited scene begins with the wide establishing shot to ensure that the audience is well oriented and comfortable in the setting before cutting to the closer shots. From this evolved a "traditional" style of covering a two-person scene using four camera angles: a master shot, a two-shot, a close-up of one character, and a reverse of the other. A radical exception to this style is found in Robert Montgomery's *Lady in the Lake*, which was filmed with a subjective, point-of-view camera that is meant to reveal what the audience would see if they were inside the protagonist's head.

In the 1960s and 1970s, as the general culture loosened up, so did narrative style in many films. The old dictates of master shot/close-up coverage gave way to a freer form shooting that assumes that audiences have the visual sophistication to understand a scene that might be played in, say, only an extreme close-up. John Cassavetes experimented with a style that seems to merge documentary and narrative sensibilities. To the audience, both the acting and the camera work may appear spontaneous and improvised. The usual notions of "coverage" give way to scenes that flow organically from one moment to the next. It has become increasingly popular to shoot dramas in a documentary style. This may be done to add a sense of "realism" to a fictional or semifictional story or as a parody of documentaries ("mockumentaries," such as the wonderful *This Is Spinal Tap*).

The 1980s brought the music video. Made by and for a generation that was raised watching TV, music videos introduced a new lexicon of quick cutting and the juxtaposition of wildly differing types of imagery. Stylistic touches exploited in music videos and TV commercials have found their way into many other types of movies; these techniques include deliberately shaky camera work, distorted images, fast cutting, and intentional jump cuts (see Chapter 13).

Today, narrative films combine elements of all these styles. Many mainstream Hollywood or TV dramas are very straightforward stylistically, employing a style that will not "intrude" on the storytelling. Independent dramas tend to take more risks, but more often what sets them apart is the kind of stories they tell, rather than the fundamental visual language of shot selection and editing.

Narrative Shooting

When a movie is made from a script, the filmmaker has the possibility of pre-planning the action and the shots. See Rehearsal and Previsualization on p. 313.

Fig. 9-13. Shooting a scene. With Serious Magic's DV Rack software, video and audio can be monitored on a laptop and recorded as well. (Serious Magic)

See Composition and Shot Selection, p. 323, for more on framing and coverage.

Blocking the camera and actors is a kind of choreography. Keep the image as dynamic as possible. Be attentive to the depth of the space you're shooting in, either to show it or let actors move through it.

When shooting dramas or documentaries, try to put yourself in the mind of the audience. What do you want them to see, and how? How do you want the scene to unfold? Use blocking to *reveal* things rather than to merely show everything up front. Use mystery to your advantage. Some shots are most interesting for what they *don't* show.

Perhaps the best way to think about the shooting and editing style is to watch movies and note which scenes work especially well or badly. To understand the relationship of camerawork to editing, it can be particularly instructive to watch films with the sound off.

When filming a two-way conversation using paired close-ups, be attentive to balancing the composition of the two angles (though they don't have to be identical). When shooting one actor's close-up, it's a good idea to set a microphone for the off-camera actor as well—the performances from these takes can sometimes be better than the on-camera takes. Higher-budget films often shoot with two cameras simultaneously in this situation.

Getting a take exactly right is expensive and, for long takes, very difficult. One saying has it that the best takes are the first and the tenth (the advantages of spontaneity versus practice), but the production's budget may not permit ten takes.

Always shoot at least two good takes of any shot to have a backup in case the first one gets damaged or has unnoticed problems. Some directors like to review each good take on video after shooting it; this can slow production down a lot. However, it's generally a good idea to check the best takes before breaking down a camera or lighting setup and moving on to the next one. Use a log or camera report to keep track of good (*circled*) takes and backups (see below). Inexperienced directors tend to shoot more takes and more circled takes. When something goes wrong in the middle of a take (*busted take*) try to reset quickly ("back to one") without a lot of chatter and keep the momentum and concentration going.

Make sure to cover for mistakes. While the beginning and end of a take may be good, the middle may have an error or just be too slow on the screen. Shoot a reaction shot or a cutaway as editing insurance even if you don't intend to use it. You may want one continuous take, but, too often, surprise errors show up during editing and it is essential to be able to cut around them. Even if a long take is good, you may need to cut the sequence or film shorter and your beautiful three-minute shot now becomes a burden.

Both the order of scenes in the original script and the overall length of the movie are often changed substantially in the editing room. Keep this in the back of your mind as you plan your coverage. Don't paint yourself into a corner so that shots and scenes can be put together only *one* way.

Looking at dailies is a good way for the director, cinematographer, and others to evaluate the footage as it gets shot, preferably on a relatively large screen. Some directors invite actors to attend dailies screenings; others prefer that actors not see themselves and get self-conscious. Uncut dailies don't look like polished movies—

they're repetitive, rough, and often messy. It takes experience to see the potential in the raw footage.

On some productions, the editor cuts scenes as they're shot, which can be a good feedback mechanism for the director. You'll either know things are working or you'll see where adjustments need to be made or even when scenes need to be reshot.

On the Set

As much as films vary stylistically, directors vary in their style of working with actors and in the tone they set for the talent and the crew. Some like to plan and control every line and gesture. Others, such as Robert Altman, like to create an environment in which actors are encouraged to experiment with their roles. Some like to discuss deep psychological motivation and others are more interested in basic blocking and line readings. As noted above, some directors see rehearsal as a chance to work out ideas with the actors; others prefer to go into the shoot with as much spontaneity as possible.

Whatever your style, do what's necessary so actors can deliver their best performance. Actors are often extremely vulnerable to disruptions of mood and should be treated with respect and deference. Only the director should give performance instructions to actors; anyone else wishing to communicate should tell the director. Particularly in intimate or difficult scenes, some actors prefer that crew members not even make eye contact with them while the camera is rolling (in some scenes it may be best to clear the set of unneeded crew). Avoid shouting and arguments in front of the actors (or anyone else for that matter) and don't involve them unnecessarily in your technical business. Make sure they have a comfortable space to go to off the set to relax.

Rehearsal is done both for the actors and for the crew. The actors' blocking will affect the lighting and the camerawork (and vice versa). You may want the actors to take part in working out the blocking but don't make them stand around while the lighting crew does its work (that's what *stand-ins* are for). Marks for the camera or the actors to hit are "spiked" with a piece of tape on the floor. Keep in mind that once lighting, props, and dolly tracks are set, your flexibility to change things is limited.

See Operating the Recorder, p. 437, for a standard protocol for starting the camera and calling action.

It's very helpful for the director to get a headphone feed from the sound recordist to hear how dialogue sounds as it's actually being recorded. A wireless link is best.

When a dramatic shoot is done with a live video monitor, there's a tendency for some directors to bury themselves in "video village" (the place where monitors and playback equipment are located, sometimes under cover when shooting outside). This can leave actors feeling isolated. And when video village is filled with a lot of people kibitzing over the video monitor, you can easily end up with a "too many cooks" problem.

Fig. 9-14. Kibitzing in video village.

SUPPORTING AND MOVING THE CAMERA

The Tripod

The *tripod* is a three-legged camera support. The camera mounts on the *tripod head*, which sits on the tripod's *legs*. Heads designed for motion picture work are able to *pan* (short for *panorama*), which is to rotate the camera horizontally, or to *tilt*, which is a vertical rotation. *Friction heads* for tripods are the cheapest, but they make it hard to pan smoothly. *Fluid heads* have a built-in hydraulic dampening device to make panning much easier. Their light weight and ease of operation make them the best for small crew work. Large cameras are sometimes used with *geared heads* that use two gear wheels to control movement (see Fig. 9-16). These are heavy and expensive and take experience to use, but can produce very smooth, repeatable movements.

Tripod heads have locks that prevent inadvertent movement. The lock on the tilt movement is very important, since the camera and tripod can fall over if there is an unintended tilt. Heads have an adjustment for the amount of drag or dampening for panning (it's easier to pan smoothly when the head "sticks" a little). Most heads have a balancing mechanism, either a spring affair or a forward/back adjustment. When the camera is properly positioned and balanced, it should not move when the head is unlocked.

Modern tripods often have lightweight aluminum or carbon fiber legs. Standard legs will telescope out to around 6 feet, and *baby legs* raise to around 3 feet. Dual-stage legs have three sections, allowing them to go lower than single-stage legs while reaching the same height or higher (see Fig. 9-18). The *high hat*, used for low-angle shots, does not telescope and is often attached to a board. A *table stand* can be useful for small cameras (see Fig. 9-17). Tripod legs and heads are rated by the weight they support; don't use a camera heavier than the rating.

Level a tripod so that the horizon line is parallel to the top or bottom of the frame. Unleveled tripods result in canted shots and tilted pans. To level a tripod, extend one of the legs (loosen the leg lock and tighten at the proper length); extend the other two legs but don't tighten them yet; hold the tripod in a vertical position and press down on it until the legs are even, and then tighten all of them. Point one of the legs in the direction that you will shoot the camera, and place the other two legs to approximate an equilateral triangle. With a ball-in-socket head,

Fig. 9-15. Fluid heads are the most versatile and easiest to operate. This Sachtler head has seven-step pan and tilt drag controls and a quick-release plate that attaches to the camera and can be snapped on and off the head. The top surface slides forward and back for balance. (Fletcher Chicago/Sachtler Corp. of America)

loosen the ball and move the head until the bubble on the attached spirit level is centered. If the tripod has no level, use architectural horizontal or vertical lines to level the camera. If the camera is not pointed up or down, align a true vertical with the vertical edge of the frame; or align a true horizontal, viewed head-on, with the top or bottom of the frame.

Quick-release mechanisms save an enormous amount of time mounting and releasing the camera from the tripod head without having to screw and unscrew the connection each time. Avoid tripods that lack a quick release plate.

Tripod legs often have a point or spike at each toe that can be secured in dirt or sand. A *spreader* (also called a *spider* or *triangle*) is a three-armed device that spreads from a central point and clamps to each tripod leg; this prevents the legs from sliding out from

Fig. 9-16. Geared head. Arrihead 2 shown with Arriflex 535B 35mm camera. (Arriflex Corporation)

Fig. 9-17. A folding table stand can be useful for grabbing a steady shot indoors or out. Tucks under the camera when shooting handheld. Sony PD-150 DVCAM camera with wide-angle adaptor and lens shade. (Sony Electronics, Inc.)

under the tripod head. A spreader that remains attached to the tripod even when stored for travel saves a lot of setup time. A spreader that attaches midway up the legs instead of at ground level can be helpful when shooting outdoors or on uneven surfaces.

Fig. 9-18. (left) Tripod legs with "above-ground" spreader can have an advantage when shooting on uneven surfaces. (right) Dual-stage legs (note three sections on each leg) can often go both lower and higher than comparable single-stage legs. (Miller Camera Support)

When shipping or transporting a tripod, loosen all locks and drag mechanisms on the fluid head so the head is free to move in its case.

A *rolling spider* or *tripod dolly* (a spreader with wheels) facilitates moving the camera between shots. Don't use it for dolly shots except on the smoothest of surfaces. When no spreader is available, a four-foot by four-foot piece of rug can be used. You can tie rope or gaffer's tape around the perimeter of the legs for an improvised spreader.

Some tripods (usually made for still photography) have devices for elevating the center of the tripod. On some tripods this extension may contribute to the unsteadiness of the image; it's usually better to extend the legs. If additional height is needed, mount the tripod on a platform. On larger productions *apple boxes*—strong, shallow boxes of standard sizes—are put together to make low platforms. Apple boxes are available in full, half, and quarter size.

Heavy-duty suction cups and clamps allow you to attach cameras to vehicles and other surfaces. The surface must be fairly flat, smooth, clean, and dry to use suction cups. If the camera is mounted on a moving vehicle or in a precarious spot, be sure to tie it down with safety lines.

Fig. 9-19. Super Grip uses a suction mount with vacuum pump and can be attached to cars, windows, and nonporous surfaces. Car mounts should be set up by experienced persons using safety lines when possible. (Fletcher Chicago/Alan Gordon Enterprises)

If you'll be shooting for extended periods on a tripod or dolly (see The Moving Camera, p. 348) it's very helpful to have a viewfinder extension (with a leveler; see Fig. 1-41) or, for a video camera, a rear-mounted monitor. Remote controls for the lens and camera are available for both video and film cameras. Some mount on the tripod handle; some extend from the lens or camera directly or on cables (see Fig. 9-26). When shooting from a tripod or dolly, it can often be difficult to reach the lens or camera switch without them.

PANS AND TILTS. Whenever possible, plan and rehearse pans and tilts. Adjust the tripod so the front leg points in the direction of the lens to maximize the amount of room behind the camera. On very wide-ranging pans, you may have to cross over a tripod leg, which is not easy to do without practice.

Pans work best when motivated by a subject moving through space. Panning with a moving subject makes the rate and movement of panning natural. Panning to follow a subject is sometimes called tracking, but this should not be confused with the tracking shot where the camera itself moves through space (see below). However, panning with a long focal length lens can be used to simulate a moving camera shot (see Telephoto Lenses, p. 164).

The most difficult pans are across landscapes or still objects, as any unevenness in the movement is evident. These pans must be fairly slow to avoid judder or strobing (see p. 361). The *swish pan*, a fast pan that blurs everything between the beginning and end of the movement, also avoids the strobing problem.

Panning is sometimes thought to be the shot most akin to moving your eye across a scene. If you look from one part of the room to another, however, you will see that, quite unlike the pan, equal weight is not given to all the intermediate points in the visual field. Viewers tend to read images from left to right, and scene compositions should take this into account. Therefore, pans generally cross still landscapes from left to right, as though the world unfolds in this way.

Cinematographers sometimes say that shots with camera movements like pans, tilts, zooms, and dolly shots are supposed to start from a static position, gradually gain and maintain speed, and then slow down to a full stop. This rule is often honored in the breach, and shots appear in films with constant speed movement.

Keep in mind that the larger the movie is projected, the more exaggerated any camera movement will be. A quick pan or shaky camera may be far more disorienting or objectionable on a large screen than on a small one.

The Moving Camera

When the camera moves through space, the viewer experiences the most distinctly cinematic of the motion picture shots. The moving camera is perhaps the most difficult and often the most expensive shot in the cinematographer's vocabulary. These shots are called *dolly*, *tracking*, or *trucking* shots: When the camera moves in, it is called *dolly in* or *track in*; when the dolly moves out, *dolly out* or *track out*. If the camera moves laterally, it is called *crabbing* or *trucking* (for example, *crab left* or *truck right*).

A wheeled vehicle with a camera support is called a *dolly*. The *doorway dolly* is basically a board on rubber wheels with a simple steering mechanism; this is a lightweight, portable, and inexpensive dolly. You can place a tripod on it and anchor it with sandbags. The *western dolly* is a larger version. Though these dollies are steerable, they can't move laterally like a crab dolly.

A dolly with an integral *boom* provides up-and-down (vertical) movement, which adds enormously to the lexicon of possible shots. A *jib arm* can be used with a tripod and/or a dolly for up-and-down or side-to-side movement. Jib arms are harder to control than built-in booms, but they can provide extended reach for high angle shots. If the support can reach great heights, it is called a *camera crane*. Industrial "cherry pickers" (like a telephone repair truck) may be used to raise the

Fig. 9-20. Dolly with boom permits vertical as well as horizontal movements. (J. L. Fisher, Inc.)

Fig. 9-21. Doorway dolly. Lightweight, affordable, basic dolly. (Matthews Studio Equipment, Inc.)

Fig. 9-22. Miller Projib. Compact jib arm for studio and location work. Jib arms are often mounted on a dolly. (Miller Fluid Heads)

Fig. 9-23. Briefcase dolly. Can be used with straight or curved track or on bare floor. The dolly platform folds up, becoming a thin carrying case for travel. (Fletcher Chicago/ Egripment USA)

camera up high for a static shot, but they don't have the proper dampening for a moving shot that ends with the camera motionless.

Most dollies can be run on plywood sheets or smooth floors. Use air-filled tires when running on pavement. Large tires, especially when underinflated, give smoother motion on rougher surfaces. For the smoothest, most repeatable movements, use a dolly that runs on tracks. Track comes in straight and curved sections of various lengths that can be combined as needed. Track can be used indoors or out, but needs to be carefully positioned and leveled with *wedges* to produce bump-free, quiet movements. A little lubricant helps stop squeaks. Some dollies can be switched from flat wheels to *bogey wheels* for track.

There are substitutes for professional dollies—wheelchairs, shopping carts, children's wagons, a pushed automobile. Don't secure the camera rigidly to most of these improvised dollies. Hand-holding often insulates the camera from vibrations.

The person pushing the dolly (the *dolly grip*) becomes an extension of the camera operator and needs just as much practice and finesse to get the shot right. Keep this in mind when hiring your dolly grip.

Even if you don't plan to do moving shots, having the camera on a dolly with a boom can save a great deal of time on the set, allowing you to quickly put the camera in positions that would be slower or impossible to do with a tripod.

Shooting from a Moving Vehicle

When you need a tracking shot that's faster than what you can get from a dolly, use a motorized vehicle. A vehicle, especially if it is equipped with a shooting platform, is extremely versatile. In general, the larger the car, the smoother the ride. Automatic transmissions are preferable, since manual shifting may create a jerky movement. Keep tire pressure low to smooth out the ride. If you're not using a professional camera vehicle, it's usually best to hand-hold the camera to absorb automobile vibrations. It's easiest to achieve smooth camera movement if the car's speed remains constant, and most difficult if the vehicle goes from a stop into motion.

Shooting in the same direction as the moving vehicle results in the motion appearing normal on the screen. Shooting at right angles to the direction of the vehicle makes the car appear to be going roughly twice as fast as it is. At intermediate angles, the speed is between these extremes. Wide-angle lenses increase apparent speed and long focal length lenses can decrease apparent speed (see Perspective Effects, p. 145). To determine how fast the vehicle will appear to move on the screen, take into account the lens focal length, the angle of shooting, and the speed of the vehicle. With film cameras and some video cameras you can shoot at a higher frame rate to smooth out unevenness in the ride.

The Handheld Camera

The handheld camera was first experimented with during the silent era, especially in the films of Dreyer, Clair, Vigo, and Vertov, as well as in various MOS sequences during the studio era of sound film, such as when James Wong Howe shot a boxing sequence on roller skates. However, not until the early 1960s, with the New Wave in France and cinema vérité films in the United States, was the potential of the handheld camera realized. Not only could the camera now capture new subject matter in new locations, but handheld shooting, at its best, imparted electricity to the image. Handheld shooting is often best in unscripted situations—whether a documentary or with improvised acting. The extreme mobility of this camera permits following the action, achieving a feeling of intimacy impossible in a tripod- or dolly-mounted camera.

A skilled cameraperson can hand-hold with real steadiness, maintaining mobility but keeping the image very stable. On the other hand, sometimes the reason a handheld camera is used is to bring a "documentary" feel to the footage, in which case a little bit of shakiness may be desired.

TIPS FOR HANDHELD SHOOTING. Shoulder-mounted cameras are the steadiest, because the operator's body braces the camera and dampens vibrations (see Fig. 2-6). Cameras that are held in front of the eye, like many small-format video cameras, are more difficult to hold steady and can start to feel heavy after hours of shooting.[4] Cameras that don't balance on the shoulder can be used with a body brace. Braces are available for small video cameras that increase stability but still require you to support the front of the camera (see Fig. 3-13). Heavy, unbalanced cameras like the Arriflex BL need a brace, but the brace takes all the weight. A brace does encumber you and prohibits you from responding as quickly to unpredictable events. Some cinematographers feel the brace imparts a mechanical feel to the shooting, but for those situations where the mobility of the handheld camera is needed and the action is predictable, a brace may work out well.

You should memorize which way to turn the lens controls for focus, aperture, and zoom. Make up your own memory aid such as "pull to bring infinity close and bright," which means (assuming the lens is operated with the left hand) pull counterclockwise for farther distances (infinity), to open up the aperture (bright) and to zoom in closer. The controls on your lens or camera may be completely different, so you may need to make up another memory aid for your rig.

To shoot a handheld camera over extended periods of time, it helps if you're in good physical shape. Find a comfortable position for shooting by practicing before you begin. Some people shoot with one foot in front of the other, others with their feet shoulder-width apart. Don't lock your knees; if you like, keep them slightly bent. Stand so you can smoothly pan in either direction and move forward or backward. For filming while walking, walk Groucho Marx–style, with your knees bent and shuffling so that the camera doesn't bob up and down.

When you film without a script, avoid excessive zooming and panning, which could produce results that are unwatchable and uncutable. To get in the rhythm, students should try counting slowly to six without making any camera movements.

When you shoot while walking backward, have someone (say, the sound recordist on a small crew) put his hand on your shoulder and direct you. Some camera eyepieces or monitors swivel so that you can walk forward with the camera pointing backward. Try cradling the camera in your arms while walking and shooting; use a fairly wide-angle lens, positioned close to the subject and keep in stride. Put the camera on your knee when shooting the driver in the front seat of a cramped car.

To steady a static shot, lean against a person or a support, such as a car or building. When shooting landscapes or scenes with strong architectural elements, any jiggles become obvious due to the stillness of the subject. Consider using a tripod or putting the camera on a surface for these shots.

Documentary filmmaking creates some of the most difficult follow-focus situations, as the camera-to-subject distance constantly changes in unpredictable

---

4. Especially when you add items like a hard disk recorder or a wireless receiver. Consider mounting those items on your belt or putting them in a small shoulder bag with wires to the camera (see Fig. 11-1).

ways. When careful focusing is not possible, zoom to a wider angle to increase depth of field and move the distance ring to the approximate position. As your skill increases, it will become easier to pull something directly into focus by looking through the viewfinder. As previously said, remember that the wider the angle of the lens, the less annoying any camera jiggle will be in the image (see Chapter 4).

Image Stabilization Devices

Image stabilization devices can be used to lessen unwanted camera vibrations and jiggles. These range from devices built into a camera or mounted on the lens, to handheld or body-mounted devices, to helicopter and other vehicle mounts, such as the Tyler mount and the Wescam system.

Fig. 9-24. The Fig Rig (shown here with inventor, director Mike Figgis) can be used with small cameras for control, stability, and mounting accessories. (Bogen Imaging, USA)

THE STEADICAM. The Steadicam, Glidecam, and other similar devices allow the camera to be mounted on a harness worn by the camera operator that absorbs most shocks, enabling smooth movements. The camera movements possible are similar to those from a dolly, but these devices permit much faster setups, shooting in tighter quarters, and significantly increased mobility. Any vehicle—automobile, boat, helicopter—can achieve dolly-smooth movements. Pans, tilts, running shots, and shots going up stairs can be made with the subtlety of the moves of the human body without any handheld jiggles. With a Steadicam, you don't look through the camera's viewfinder but, rather, at a small video monitor that displays a through-the-lens reflex image. Although you can respond to unplanned subject movement (unlike a dolly, for which each shot must be blocked), response is slower than that of the shoulder-mounted camera. Also, Steadicam or Glidecam shots have a floating smoothness that some people find more mechanical and less exciting than well-done handheld shots.

Fig. 9-25. Steadicam. The camera floats smoothly, isolated from shocks or jarring with springs in the support arm. The operator wears a harness and watches a small monitor mounted on the Steadicam. Steadicam and Glidecam also make smaller, handheld systems for small cameras. (The Tiffen Company)

The Steadicam must be set up specifically for each camera and requires that film cameras be equipped with a video tap. Film cameras with vertically mounted magazines or coaxial magazines (see p. 242) work best, since the camera's center of balance remains more stable during a take. The operator needs special training and plenty of practice.

The implications of these devices for dramatic films are monumental. Not only does it add to the repertory of dolly-like shots, but, more important, it creates new relationships between filmmaker and location and between filmmaker and actors. Quick, inexpensive setups relieve the pressure on actors and crew. The use of image stabilization devices in a documentary can be effective for tracking or establishing shots. For filming people in more intimate settings, however, the equipment may be too intrusive.

There are various smaller devices designed to smooth out camera movement for small-format video camcorders, including Steadicam Junior and Handyman 1000. These are handheld, with no body brace. With practice, these can provide smooth moves in some shooting situations.

OTHER IMAGE STABILIZERS. Some video camcorders have built-in image stabilization devices that can reduce camera shake with handheld shots. *Electronic image stabilization (EIS)* digitally processes the video image to reduce image shake, which may reduce image quality. *Optical image stabilizers*, which are used with some film and video cameras, use a device on or in the lens to dampen vibration and shake. Experiment to see whether you like the effect of the stabilizer. Some devices add a slight lag to intentional camera movements, giving an unwanted floating effect.

To stabilize large movements (for example, when shooting from a boat) a *gyroscopic stabilizer* can be mounted on a tripod to compensate for motion in the camera platform. Some image stabilization can be done in postproduction.

ZOOM LENS TECHNIQUES

The choice of zoom lenses is discussed on p. 159. This section is about shooting styles with zooms.

The Zoom Effect

Zooming changes the image significantly and, unless it is handled well, can be quite disruptive. The classic, graceful zoom starts up slowly, reaches the desired speed, and gradually slows to a stop. There are also times when a "pop" zoom that jumps suddenly from one focal length to another may be desired.

Novices tend to zoom too often ("zoom-happy"), which can be quite annoying. Zooms are most effective when they are motivated and deliberate, not random.

As discussed earlier, some people feel that all zooms should come to a stop before a camera cut. However, there are many instances of effective cuts while the camera is still zooming, especially if the zoom is slow.

If you don't like the zoom effect, but want to zoom within the shot to change focal length, you can hide it with another camera movement—for example, a pan. "Burying" a zoom in a pan can make the zoom almost invisible.

Manual and Motorized Zooms

For a slow, smooth zoom, use a motorized zoom. Almost all video lenses have built-in zoom motors. External zoom drives are available for cine-style lenses used with 16mm and 35mm film cameras and some HD cameras. Zoom motors usually have a range of speeds. It's helpful to have a very fast speed to reset the lens even if you don't plan to use that speed in the shot; fast speeds may be available only on more expensive lenses.

It's *very* important that the zoom control be able to accelerate smoothly from a stop and feather smoothly back to a stop. Sometimes an external zoom control has a more delicate rocker switch than a camera's built-in switch. When shooting on a dolly or tripod, you'll want an external control mounted on the handle of the tripod head so you don't have to reach around to the lens. Some video cameras, like some Sony HDV cameras, can be pre-programmed to execute a smooth move from one focal length to another.

Some filmmakers prefer a manual (nonmotorized) zoom, which puts you in direct contact with the "feel" of the zoom. Most professional ENG (video-style) lenses can be switched to manual mode with a switch under the zoom control. Manual zooming allows you to respond more quickly to fast-changing action. It can also be used for a deliberately "rougher" shooting style.

Fig. 9-26. External zoom controls can be useful for tripod and dolly work when it's hard to reach the lens or camera controls. On some models, the rocker switch for zooming provides better control than the switch on a camcorder. The VariZoom unit on the right has focus and iris control in addition to zoom. (VariZoom Lens Controls)

Some lenses can accommodate a zoom lever for manual zooming that extends perpendicularly from the zoom ring; the longer the lever, the smoother the zoom can be. Long levers can produce smooth, relatively slow zooms on a tripod but are awkward when used with a handheld camera. Detachable drag mechanisms are available that adjust the resistance of the zoom. Jerkiness in the zoom shows up more in the projected image than it does in the viewfinder.

Zoom Versus Dolly

Some people object to the zoom effect because the viewer is brought closer to (or farther from) the filmed subject without changing perspective. In zooming, the entire image is magnified equally (see Fig. 4-3), similar to when you approach a still photograph. In a dolly shot, the camera moves in toward the subject and the perspective changes; objects also pass by the side of the frame, suggesting to the viewer that he or she is physically moving into the space.

The moving camera creates a feeling of depth in the space. The zoom tends to flatten space and can call attention to the act of filming itself. Some filmmakers like this feature and will use the zoom to pick out a significant detail in the subject.

Zooming in the opposite direction of subject or camera movement results in a treadmill effect. If an actor runs toward the camera but the lens zooms back, the viewer feels as though the actor has made no progress. Similarly, if you shoot out of a car's front window and zoom wider, the viewer will feel as though the forward movement is disrupted. In *Vertigo*, Alfred Hitchcock combined zooming in one direction and moving in reverse to simulate the feeling of vertigo. The camera appears to move down a staircase and the lens simultaneously zooms back to keep the size of the field constant. Although the viewer sees the same subject matter, the perspective is exaggerated (since the camera moves closer), evoking the sensation of dizziness due to height. Steven Spielberg used a similar effect in *Jaws*, dollying in one direction while zooming in the other.

SLOW MOTION, FAST MOTION, AND JUDDER

SLOW MOTION

Slow motion can be used to analyze motion or even to call attention to motion itself. In Leni Riefenstahl's *Olympiad*, a film of the 1936 Olympics in Berlin, the movements of the athletes are broken down and extended in time with slow motion, letting the viewer see things unobservable in real time. Televised sports events often show replays in slow motion ("slow-mo") to analyze the action. Slow motion extends real time, sometimes giving an event more psychological weight. A character's death may occur in an instant, yet be the most important moment in a film. In countless films the protagonist's death is shown in slow motion, extending the time of death to give it greater emotional emphasis.

Slow-motion effects can be achieved in two ways: by running the camera at higher than regular frame rate; and by shooting at normal speed and then slowing the footage down later during postproduction. There can be a noticeable difference between the two methods.

When the camera runs fast, you are capturing many continuous frames in a given period of time (say, 80 frames in a second). This makes the slowed action seem smooth and continuous on projection or playback. This technique is also called *overcranking*.

However, when a film or video camera is shooting at normal speed (say, 24 or 30 frames a second), and you then slow the footage down in post, motion may appear discontinuous and jerky. The slow-motion effect is achieved in post by repeating each frame two or more times, then moving to the next frame. There will be a slight jump when you move to each new frame.[5] Also, the normal motion blur that takes place with any camera and/or subject movement—which is invisible at normal projection speeds—will be more pronounced when normal footage is slowed down (see Figs. 2-17 and 2-18). This effect may be desired, or at times it may just look inferior to true slow motion shot with a camera running at a higher frame rate.

At one time, only film cameras could be used for overcranking. Now various video cameras can also be used to shoot up to 60 fps or more (see Slow Motion, p. 70). When shooting film, the higher the frame rate, the more film you use every minute. High frame rates also result in shorter exposure times, which require more light.

High speeds can be also used to minimize the effect of unwanted camera jiggle and vibration. When the camera is handheld or on a moving vehicle, faster camera speeds lengthen the distance between jerky or uneven movements and

5. This can be minimized in video by using frame blending; see p. 545.

make the image seem steadier. Of course, any subject movement will also be in slow motion.

High-Speed Cameras

Sometimes very high frame rates are needed for an effect or to capture or analyze fleeting events. If you want to see individual water droplets slowly crashing on the ground or a bullet shattering glass, use a high-speed camera (and preferably strobe lighting). Speeds higher than 250 fps are rarely needed in nonscientific filming. A camera speed of 250 fps stretches one second of real time into more than ten seconds of film time.

Fig. 9-27. Locam II high-speed reflex camera. Shoots at speeds up to 500 fps. Shown with a shoulder brace for handholding. (Redlake Corp.)

High-speed film cameras with intermittent-type movements can run up to around 500 fps. Cameras that run up to 10,000 fps do not use an intermittent movement. Instead, the film runs continuously and a rotating prism forms the individual frames. At 10,000 fps, one second of real time is stretched into six and a half minutes.

High-speed filming implies very short exposure times, which usually requires a lot of light (and a fast stock for a film camera or a sensitive chip for a video camera). Some cameras can be operated at normal speed and then ramp up to high speed when the key action begins and automatically adjust the exposure.

FAST MOTION

Most film cameras and some video cameras can be operated at slower than normal frame rate (called *undercranking*). This results in each frame being exposed for a greater length of time. For example, shooting at 12 fps gives one stop more exposure than filming at 24 fps. This can be used to advantage in scenes where the light level is too low for exposure at normal speed and there is no movement in the scene—for example, when filming exteriors at night. Keep in mind that any motion, like car headlights, will seem sped up. If shooting film in a dark church interior at 12 fps, you might have actors walk at half speed, or move the camera half as fast as usual so the movement will appear normal in projection. If you take undercranked footage and slow it down in postproduction, you can get an interesting ghost-like effect.

Though undercranking produces a slower shutter speed, it should not be confused with shooting at normal frame rate, but opening an adjustable shutter (see p. 233 and p. 134).

Chase sequences can be undercranked to make motion appear faster and more dangerous. The sped-up motion of silent film comedy was, supposedly, the result of an unintentionally undercranked camera on a Mack Sennett set. You can get this effect by filming at about 16 to 20 fps and then projecting at 24 fps.

Time-Lapse

With significantly slower speeds, time is proportionally sped up. In *time-lapse*, the sun can set, a flower can blossom, or a building can be demolished and another constructed in a few seconds (sometimes called *pixilation*). For very condensed time, you need a camera that can make single-frame exposures. Some film and video cameras have this option, which may be called interval recording (see p. 71). Some cameras can do time-lapse with an *intervalometer* (an animation motor may also be needed for some film cameras). Intervalometers vary from relatively simple devices that allow you to set the frame rate for a given time period, to highly sophisticated devices that can vary camera speed at set times, change the exposure, switch on lights, signal a malfunction, and turn on the coffee pot.

Some filmmakers are using digital still cameras to create time-lapse footage and stop-motion animation. Tim Burton's *Corpse Bride* was shot with a Canon digital SLR still camera. This is an inexpensive method for capturing very high resolution images with a camera much smaller than comparable film or video cameras.

Finding the right frame rate for a time-lapse sequence takes some experimentation. Start by estimating how long you want the finished sequence to run on screen. From this you can figure the total number of frames to expose. Say you want to film a sunset that takes two hours and have the shot run 10 seconds in the movie. For this example, let's assume this is a film or 24p video project. Hence, 10 seconds x 24 fps = 240 frames. This means you need to expose an average of 2 frames per minute during the sunset. It's a good idea to start shooting sometime before and continue after the main action to provide flexibility in editing.

Exposures may be programmed for one or several frames at a given time interval or at varying intervals. The fewer exposures at a time and the farther apart, the more jumpy or staccato the motion will look. Single-frame exposures are often slower than the normal camera shutter speed. Very slow shutter speeds for each exposure will increase motion blur. You can use this effect to turn car lights at night into colored streaks.

Some time-lapse sequences look best without changing the lens iris or exposure time over the sequence. In this case, base the exposure setting on the light reading at the most important part of the sequence. You could also "ride" the exposure, changing it manually or by using automatic features in the camera or intervalometer.

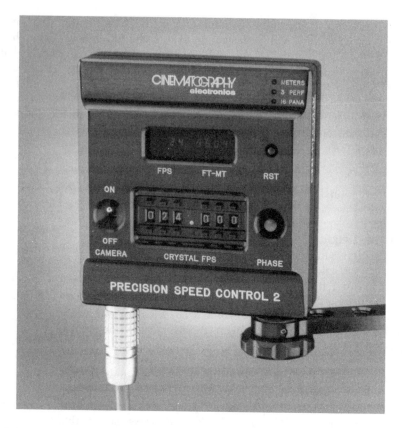

Fig. 9-28. Precision speed control. Allows frame rates from 1 to 159.999 frames per second in .001 fps increments. Has phase button for shooting video monitors. (Cinematography Electronics Inc.)

In some situations an auto-iris can extend the usable length of the sequence if the light is changing. In others, it might fight with the effect you're looking for: a sunset might look too silhouetted, for example.

Often, a wide-angle lens produces the best time-lapse effect. A wide shot of traffic at a certain frame rate might produce a shot that looks like a fast-moving river of cars; any single car might be seen moving from one side of the frame to the other. However, if you used a telephoto lens to get a long shot of the same scene at the same frame rate, you might end up with a shot that showed individual cars popping into one frame and disappearing in the next. An interesting effect can be had by walking or dollying the camera, shooting a frame or two every step.

Most nonlinear editing systems can speed up shots to create time-lapse sequences from footage shot at normal speed.

Animation

Animation can be seen as a variant of time-lapse photography. A series of paper drawings or paintings on acetate (*cel animation*) are done with slight changes between the images. A few frames of one drawing are exposed, then the next one is filmed. On projection, the art seems to "move." This technique can also be used for "Claymation" and other pixilated shots of real objects that seem to move by themselves.

Today, animation is often generated digitally, but traditional animation can be done with an animation stand and film or video camera capable of single exposures. Motion-control animation stands such as the Oxberry allow you to program moves across an animated or still image. Motion-control film and video setups have been used to do moves on photographs, for rock-steady, precise zooms and pans. However, today it's usually easier to scan artwork and do the moves in an editing system (see Stills, p. 548).

JUDDER OR STROBING

All motion pictures are based on the illusion that a series of still images, when shown one after another, will appear to have movement. For the illusion to work and for motion to appear smooth, the changes from one image to the next can't be too great. With typical interlaced video, 50 or 60 images (fields) are recorded every second, which tends to result in fairly smooth-looking motion on screen. However, when you shoot film or progressive video at 24 fps, there are fewer images every second, and the changes between frames when either the camera or the subject moves can be greater (see Fig. 2-18). If something moves too quickly, to the audience it can look as though the object is jumping or skipping from one position to the next rather than moving smoothly and continuously. This irregular movement is sometimes called *judder, strobing,* or *skipping.* It can give the viewer eyestrain or a headache. Judder is something to pay attention to when shooting at slower frame rates (like 24 fps) and sometimes even when shooting at higher frame rates when an adjustable shutter is set to a very fast shutter speed.

Judder most often appears in pans, especially fast moves across strong vertical lines. The higher the image contrast or greater the sharpness, the more likely that judder will occur. To minimize strobing when shooting, there are various guidelines or tricks. A rule of thumb is to allow at least five to seven seconds for an object to move from one side of the screen to another. This applies both when the camera pans or when the subject moves through a stationary frame. If the camera moves or pans *with* a moving subject, the viewer concentrates on the person and is less likely to notice judder in the background. In this situation, use shallow depth of field if possible and focus on the subject, letting the background go soft. Avoid panning across high contrast scenes that have strong vertical lines. Fast swish pans are usually not a problem. You can get charts of safe panning speeds for different camera and lens settings.

Footage shot with cameras that have relatively small sensors (including HD and SD video and 16mm film) may appear to judder more than footage shot with 35mm film cameras in part because shots in 35mm typically have shallower depth of field, making it easier to throw the background out of focus. Using a slow shutter on a video camera (for example, $\frac{1}{24}$ second) may reduce judder. Judder or flicker often appears more severe in a camera viewfinder than it will when the image is seen on screen.

A phenomenon related to strobing, and frequently referred to by the same term, is often noticed when the wheels of a moving vehicle on the screen seem to be stopped or to be traveling in reverse. This occurs when exposures happen to catch spokes at the same position in consecutive frames (thus, the wheels seem stopped) or catch them in a position slightly behind so the wheels appear to be spinning in reverse.

OTHER ASPECTS
OF PRODUCTION

Wardrobe, Makeup, and Set

An actor's wardrobe, makeup, and hair can have a huge impact on the look of the movie and on the character's presence on screen. Don't overlook the importance of good makeup and wardrobe as well as set decoration. In some documentary settings it's not appropriate to deal with these issues, but in others—such as shooting interviews—you can choose the setting, make suggestions for wardrobe, and apply some minimal makeup.

Guidelines for clothing also apply to wall treatments, furniture, and other items on the set.

In general, it's a good idea to avoid very bright or very dark clothing, especially when shooting video. White shirts often burn out (overexpose) when the camera is set for proper skin tones. Pastel or off-white shades work better. Video reacts badly to some colors or patterns; this is especially a problem with NTSC. Avoid fine patterns like checks and stripes, which can cause moiré patterns. Bright reds may smear (chroma bleeding).

Avoid shiny surfaces or jewelry. Washable *dulling spray* or even a little dry soap can be applied to bright items, or lights can be flagged (see Chapter 12) to minimize reflections. When shooting people with glasses, light them from high above or to the side to avoid kicks in the glasses.

Applying makeup is an art and needs to be tailored to individual faces. Facial shine, caused by sweating under hot lights, is a common problem that is easily remedied with a little translucent face powder, which can be brushed on actors or interview subjects and will be totally invisible. Apply the powder first to the brush, not directly to the skin, and touch up faces whenever you see shine. Many cinematographers carry powder in their ditty bag.

Prompters and Cue Cards

Actors may forget their lines. Correspondents or on-camera narrators may be asked to speak long passages directly to the camera. Lines can be written on *cue cards*. When a host or correspondent reads to camera, her eye line must be directed as close to the lens as possible so she won't appear to be reading. A low-budget technique is to cut a hole in the center of the cue card for the lens. A better solution is to use a *teleprompter*, which mounts in front of the lens and displays written copy from a computer (see Fig. 9-29). Teleprompters may limit camera mobility and usually require a solid camera support. Some actors are adept at using an *ear prompter*, which is a pocket-size recorder that transmits to a miniature receiver that fits in the actor's ear. The actor reads his lines into the prompter prior to the take; then during the take he hears the words played back while he speaks to the camera (this only works for scenes in which no one else talks). It takes practice to talk while listening, so don't let the talent try this for the first time on the shoot.

Fig. 9-29. Teleprompter. A monitor displaying the script faces up, projecting the copy into a partially reflecting mirror surface so it can be read by the person being filmed. The camera shoots from behind the mirror. This lightweight ProPrompter model can be used for handheld work. (Bodelin Technologies Inc.)

PREPARING FOR POSTPRODUCTION

As you move from production to postproduction, it's important to organize the material that was shot and keep good records of what went on during the shoot. You'll need to identify how footage is to be processed. On a film shoot that could mean lab processing, workprint, and/or video transfer. On a video shoot, that could include dubbing, downconverting, or capturing into a nonlinear editing system. Once you're in the editing room, you'll want to be able to quickly find every bit of picture and sound that was recorded.

Keeping a Log

Several different kinds of logs or reports are used in production. The most basic, often used for video shoots, is a listing of what's been shot and where to find it. It's easy enough to create your own log form by making a table with a word processing program. The log includes information on:

- Date and location.
- Tape number, or disk, drive, or card number. Never have two tapes or film rolls with the same number. Use letters if necessary.
- Scene number and/or description.
- Take number (if any).
- Timecode start for each take. (Usually the starting timecode of the next take tells you the ending timecode of the previous take, but some people note both start and stop codes.)
- Indicate if the take was good; any performance or content notes.

Fig. 9-30. For logging in the field, the Scriptboy provides a writing surface with built-in timecode display. The transmitter sends timecode wirelessly from the camera. (Vortex Communications, Ltd.)

Devices such as Scriptboy can provide a wireless remote readout of the camera's timecode to aid the person logging (so they don't have to keep bugging the cameraperson for timecode numbers). When practical, timecode can also be superimposed on a video monitor for the logger.

In unscripted documentary work there tends to be little time for detailed logging. It's important to write down notes whenever you can, at least at the end of every day, indicating what has been shot and which roll or film or tape covers what.

Camera and Sound Reports

When shooting film, the camera assistant fills out a *camera report* that indicates every take on a given roll of film, including the length of the shot and any remarks (see Fig. 9-31). Good takes are normally circled. This tells the lab which takes to print and/or transfer to video. See Processing the Original, p. 659, for instructions needed when sending film to the lab for processing and Video Dailies, p. 699, for instructing the lab on the video transfer.

When double system sound is recorded for film or video shoots, the sound recordist may fill out a *sound report* (see p. 412).

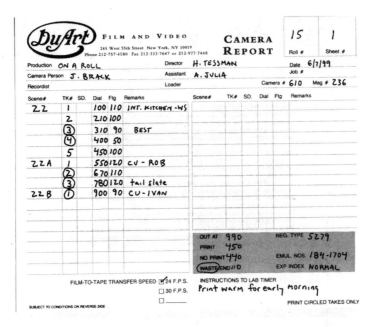

Fig. 9-31. The camera report accounts for every take on each camera roll. The best takes are circled. In 35mm, usually only circled takes are printed. (Form by DuArt Film and Video)

Continuity Script

For feature films and other scripted work, the script supervisor creates a marked script to show what camera angles were used to cover each page. This *continuity script* serves as a reminder of what coverage has been shot and needs to be gotten, and tells the editor what shots were filmed during production (see Fig. 9-32). Notes may also be made about lenses used and distances for each shot, as well as other continuity issues. Sometimes camera reports include lens settings.

Some systems can upload script information to the telecine shot log to help organize video clips by their content (see Shot Logs, p. 705).

An HD Checklist

As noted above, when film is sent to the lab for processing and video transfer, a detailed set of instructions is sent with it so the lab understands what to do. When shooting video, a similar set of instructions may be needed if you're sending video material to be dubbed or converted prior to editing. Even if the footage is going directly to the editor, it's important to keep track of how things were recorded and to plan how postproduction will be done (see Chapter 14 for more on postproduction workflow).

What follows is a checklist for an HD shoot. Your equipment or shoot may be simpler, but even if some items don't apply to you, the list may help you think about options.[6]

6. Thanks to Bill Weisman, who made the list from which this was adapted.

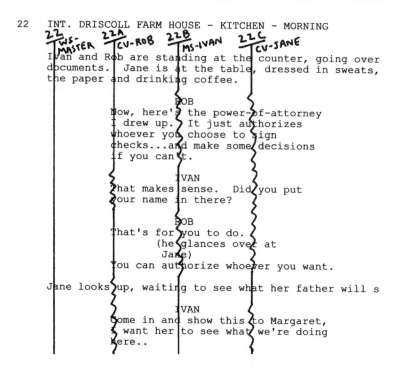

22   INT. DRISCOLL FARM HOUSE - KITCHEN - MORNING

Ivan and Rob are standing at the counter, going over
documents. Jane is at the table, dressed in sweats,
the paper and drinking coffee.

                    ROB
          Now, here's the power-of-attorney
          I drew up. It just authorizes
          whoever you choose to sign
          checks...and make some decisions
          if you can't.

                    IVAN
          That makes sense. Did you put
          your name in there?

                    ROB
          That's for you to do.
                    (he glances over at
                    Jane)
          You can authorize whoever you want.

Jane looks up, waiting to see what her father will s

                    IVAN
          Come in and show this to Margaret,
          want her to see what we're doing
          here..

Fig. 9-32. Lined script. Each vertical line indicates a different camera angle or shot that was filmed. Zigzag portions indicate off-camera dialogue or action. The script is normally marked by the script supervisor during the shoot.

Recording:

1. What camera was used?
2. What frame rate was used (23.976, 24, 25, 29.97, 30, 59.94, 60)?
3. Interlace or progressive (1080p, 1080i, 720p, 720i, 480p, 480i)?
4. Timecode: Did you record non–drop frame or drop frame? Free run/time-of-day or record run?
5. How many audio channels were recorded on the camera?
6. Did you shoot double system with a separate audio recorder? Did you jam sync the camera to the audio recorder? Did you use a smart slate or clock-it box?
7. Do you have any footage at different frame rates (undercrank or over-crank)? Did you record this on a separate tape, disc, or card?

If you're making SD downconverted tapes for editing:

1. What format are you downconverting to?
2. Do you want letterbox, full height anamorphic, or 4:3 edge crop on the downconverted tapes (see Fig. 2-15)?
3. Do you want drop frame or non–drop frame timecode on the SD tape (not applicable for PAL)?

4. Do you want the timecode burned in (window burn)? Do you also want the original camera timecode burned in? (For example, if you shot 24p HD and are downconverting to 60i SD, the 24 fps and 30 fps timecode will be different; see Fig. 15-19.)
5. How many audio channels do you want on the SD tapes? (For example, if recording to DVCAM you can have two channels of high quality 48 kHz audio, or four channels of lower quality 32kHz audio. You may need only two channels.)
6. When do you need the downconverted tapes?

Postproduction workflow:

1. Will the master tapes or files be cloned or backed up? Where will the masters and backups be stored? (Don't put them in the same place!)
2. What edit system will be used for the offline? The online?
3. Are you shooting with or combining any other formats?
4. What format will you be mastering to?
5. Is the final product for TV, film, and/or DVD? (If for TV, will you have an HD master and an NTSC or PAL 4:3 master?)

CHAPTER 10

Sound Recording Systems

This chapter is about sound and the audio recording equipment used for both film and video. Many of the principles that apply to one type of system are relevant to others. See Chapter 11 for discussion of the sound recordist's role and recording techniques.

SOUND

What we hear as sound is a series of pressure waves produced by vibration. A violin, for example, works by vibrating air rapidly back and forth. When you pluck the string, it makes the body of the violin vibrate—when it moves one way, it *compresses* the air (pushes it) in that direction; when it moves the other way, that pressure is temporarily reduced. Sound waves travel through the air and cause your eardrum to *oscillate* (move back and forth) in response to the sound. Like ocean waves breaking on a beach, sound waves alternately press forward and recede back.

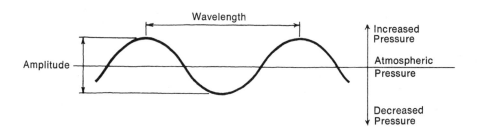

Fig. 10-1. Graph of a simple sound wave at an instant in time. The height of the wave (or *amplitude*) corresponds to loudness. The distance from one peak to the next (the *wavelength*) corresponds to the sound's frequency. (Carol Keller)

Loudness

The *loudness* or *volume* of a sound results from the amount of pressure produced by the sound wave (the *sound pressure level* or *SPL*). Loudness is measured in *decibels* (*dB*), which are used to compare the relative loudness of two sounds. The softest audible sounds occur at the *threshold of hearing*. The volume of normal conversation is about 65 dB above threshold, thus its sound level is said to be 65 dB. The *threshold of pain* is at about 130 dB, equivalent to the noise of a jet passing within 100 feet.

When we work with recording systems, sound level is expressed in dB units that reflect the electrical voltage (see below). With audio in a recording system, if we increase a sound's level by 6 dB, it will sound about *twice* as loud. For more details, see Setting the Recording Level, p. 414.

Dynamic Range

For any passage of sound—be it music, speech, or noise—the difference in volume between the quietest point and the loudest is called the *dynamic range*. The dynamic range of a symphony orchestra is about 80 dB, which represents the difference in volume between the full group playing fortissimo and a single violin playing very softly. Actually, the dynamic range of the orchestra is somewhat lessened by the shuffling and coughing of the audience, which may be louder than the quiet solo violin.

Dynamic range is a term used in evaluating audio systems. The human ear has a dynamic range of 130 dB between the thresholds of hearing and pain. High-quality analog tape recorders have a dynamic range of 70 dB or higher between the loudest sounds that can be recorded without audible distortion and the low-volume sound of the tape noise. Tape noise, or hiss, is always present in analog recordings and, like the shuffling sounds of the symphony audience, it determines the lower limit of the dynamic range (the *noise floor*). The dynamic range of a tape recorder is sometimes called the *signal-to-noise (s/n) ratio*. The "signal" is the sound we want to record; the "noise" may be tape hiss or system noise from the amplifiers and circuits in the recorder and the microphone.

With digital recorders, tape noise is virtually eliminated (though there can still be other types of noise). Digital recorders usually have much better dynamic range—up to about 100 to 120 dB or more.

Frequency

Musical notes are pitches; the modern piano can produce pitches from a low A to a high C. The lower notes are the *bass*, the higher ones the *treble*. What is perceived as pitch is determined by the *frequency* of the sound wave. Frequency is a measure of how frequently the waves of sound pressure strike the ear—that is, how many cycles of pressure increase/decrease occur in a given length of time. The higher the frequency, the higher the pitch. Frequency was formerly measured in cycles per second; now the same unit is called a *hertz* (*Hz*). Musical notes are standardized according to their frequency. Orchestras usually tune up to concert A, which is 440 Hz. Doubling this or any frequency produces a tone one *octave* higher.

The male speaking voice occupies a range of frequencies from about 100 to 8,000 Hz (8 kHz). The female speaking voice is slightly higher, ranging from about 180 to 10,000 Hz. The ear can sense low frequencies down to about 20 Hz, but these sounds are very rumbly and are felt throughout the body. At the other extreme, sounds above 20,000 Hz are audible to dogs and bats, but seldom humans. For more on working with voice in postproduction, see Frequency Range and EQ, p. 651.

When sound volume is low, the ear is much more sensitive to midrange frequencies (2,000 to 4,000 Hz) than to low or high frequencies. Thus, a low-frequency sound seems quieter than a middle-frequency sound if they have the same sound pressure. Some audio equipment has a "loudness" control that increases the low bass when the volume is down to compensate for this deficiency. When sound volume is high, the ear responds much more evenly to all frequencies of sound; low, middle, and fairly high frequencies of the same sound pressure all seem equally loud.

Tone Quality and Harmonics

All naturally occurring sounds are made up of a mixture of waves at various frequencies. A violin string vibrates at a basic frequency (called the *fundamental*), as well as at various multiples of this frequency. These other frequencies are called *harmonics* or *overtones*, and they are usually quieter than the fundamental. With tones that sound "musical," the frequencies of the harmonics are simple multiples of the fundamental. Most other sounds, such as a speaking voice or a door slam, have no discernible pitch; their harmonics are more complexly distributed. The relative strengths of the harmonics determine tone quality or timbre. When a man and a woman both sing the same note, their voices are distinguishable because the man's voice usually emphasizes lower harmonics than the woman's. Pinching your nose while talking changes, among other things, the balance of harmonics and produces a "nasal" tone quality.

Frequency Response

Frequency response is used to describe how an audio system responds to various frequencies of sound. As noted above, at low volume the ear favors middle-frequency sounds, and at high volume its frequency response is more even or flat. A good audio recorder is capable of providing a fairly *flat* frequency response throughout the frequency range of human hearing.

Because all sounds incorporate a spread of frequencies, if you change the frequency response of your equipment by increasing or decreasing the response to low, middle, or high frequencies, you can change the character of the sounds. The bass and treble controls on a radio do this to some extent; most people like to turn the bass up in dance music to make the rhythm, carried by low-frequency instruments such as the bass guitar and bass drum, seem more powerful. *Equalizers* (see Fig. 16-15) are often used to alter the frequencies of sounds during recording or after. With an equalizer, you could boost low frequencies to make, say, a truck engine sound deep, rumbly, or menacing, or you could boost the high frequencies of a piano to make its sound "brighter." If we diminish high frequencies without changing the bass, the effect is like putting cotton in your ears: The sound is muddy and dull.

Telephones have a fairly limited frequency response, which is centered on the middle frequencies needed to understand speech. In movies, the sound of someone talking through a phone can be simulated with an equalizer by cutting the low and high frequencies and boosting the midrange.

HOW AUDIO IS RECORDED

This section is about how analog and digital recording works—the fundamental process of capturing and storing sound. Though most recording is done digitally these days, it's important to understand analog because it's still very much a part of the process.

ANALOG AUDIO RECORDING

In simplest terms, the idea of analog recording is to convert sound energy in the air to magnetic energy, which can be stored on tape. When the tape is played back, the process is reversed to reproduce sound (see Fig. 10-2).

The *microphone* responds to sound waves by producing electrical waves that have essentially the same character in terms of frequency and amplitude. Most modern microphones employ an extremely light *diaphragm* that can move with the slightest variations in sound pressure. Mics vary in the way the moving diaphragm generates electricity. The common *dynamic microphone* that comes with some home audio recorders is also called a *moving-coil* microphone because it has a very light coil of wire attached to the diaphragm. When the diaphragm moves back and forth, the coil moves past a magnet and creates an alternating electric current that flows through the wires in the coil. Thus, sound pressure is translated into electric pressure, or *voltage*.

This voltage travels from the microphone to a *mic preamp (preamplifier)*, which increases its strength, and may supply the mic with power. Then it goes to the magnetic *recording head*. A recording head is an electromagnet, not unlike the ones used in metal scrap yards or that kids sometimes play with. When electricity passes through the head it generates a magnetic field. The head is a C-shaped piece of metal with wire coiled around it. On its front is an extremely narrow opening called the *gap*. The head completes a flow of energy: Advancing and receding sound waves become electrical waves, which finally result in a magnetic field that is oriented first in one direction and then in the opposite.

Magnetic tape is made up of a thick support material or *base* and a thin emulsion that stores the information. Tape emulsion is called *oxide* and contains small particles of iron. Each piece of iron is a miniature bar magnet with distinct north and south poles. When a particle of iron passes the gap in the recording head, the magnetic polarity of the particle aligns itself with the magnetic field at the head. When the tape moves on, it maintains that alignment. Since the magnetic field is always alternating back and forth, any given stretch of tape contains groups of particles that alternate in their alignment. The orientation of the particles corresponds to the original sound in this simplified way: The louder the sound, the more particles will be forced to line up the same way; the higher the frequency, the closer together the alternating groups will be.

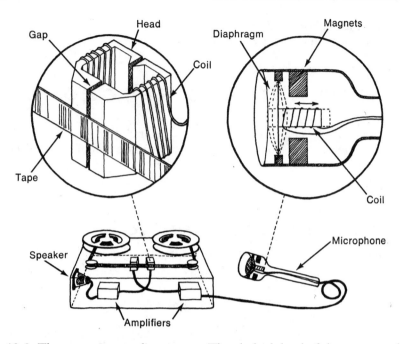

Fig. 10-2. The magnetic recording process. The playback head of the tape recorder is shown in a cutaway view (the width of the gap is exaggerated for clarity). The microphone cutaway shows the components of a dynamic microphone. (Carol Keller)

When you play back the tape, it is passed over the same head, or a similar playback head. Now the magnetic field stored in the iron particles creates an electric current in the wires coiled around the head. This signal is amplified and sent to a loudspeaker, which acts like a moving-coil microphone in reverse. Instead of the microphone's diaphragm, the speaker employs a paper cone that is connected to the coil. When current passes through the coil, it moves the cone, which in turn pushes the air to produce sound pressure waves. If you stand in front of a large bass speaker, you can both hear and *feel* the sound waves generated by the paper moving back and forth.

DIGITAL AUDIO RECORDING

Before reading further, see The Basic Idea, p. 208.

The way digital audio is recorded is similar in many respects to the analog audio process described above. First of all, microphones and speakers are analog, so sound is captured and reproduced using the same equipment regardless of the recording format (the same microphone could feed an analog or digital recorder). The difference is in the way digital recorders process and store the sound.

With analog recording, sound is converted to a voltage; the voltage is converted to a magnetic field, which is then stored on tape. In digital audio recording, we start the same way: Sound is converted to a voltage. Then the *analog-to-digital (A/D) con-*

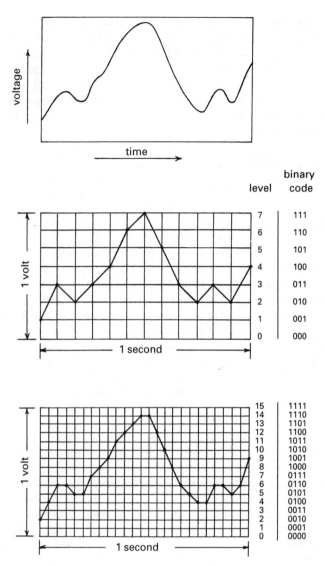

Fig. 10-3. Digital recording. (top) The original analog signal. Note that the voltage level changes continuously over time. (middle) To record the signal digitally, we take *samples* (measurements) at regular time intervals (the vertical lines). The level of the signal at each sample is measured according to a level scale (the horizontal lines). The total number of units in the scale is determined by the *number of bits* in the system; a three-bit system is pictured here. Samples can only be measured in *one-unit increments*. A measurement that falls between, say, level two and level three must be rounded down to two or up to three. (bottom) By taking more samples in the same period of time (higher *sample rate*) and using more bits per sample, we can make a higher-resolution recording. Pictured here is a four-bit system with twice the sampling rate as the middle graph. Now the scale has finer gradations, allowing us to measure the signal more precisely. Note that this curve better approximates the shape of the original analog signal. (Robert Brun)

verter processes the sound by repeatedly measuring the voltage level (*sampling* it) and converting those measurements to numbers (*quantizing*). This two-step process is the heart of digital recording. The quality of the recording depends how *often* we sample the voltage and how *accurately* we measure each sample.

Once we have the sound expressed as digital data we can then store it on tape, hard drive, or in other media. The basic concepts of sampling and quantizing are quite similar for both video and audio recording. If you understand one, it can help you make sense of the other.

Sample Rate

The first part of the digitizing process is to take a series of samples or measurements of the sound level. Take a look at Fig. 14-21, which shows an audio waveform (a visual representation of a sound). You can see that it's constantly changing (oscillating). High-frequency signals change very fast and low-frequency sounds change more slowly. To accurately measure the level of high-frequency sounds we need to take samples more frequently than for low sounds.

As a simplified example, imagine you're making popcorn and want to count how fast the kernels are popping. When you start heating the popcorn, kernels pop only every few seconds, so you can take your time counting them (low frequency). But as the corn heats up, many kernels start popping every second, so you have to count much faster to get an accurate count.

High frequencies are of particular concern because without them, a recording may have poor quality and sound muddy or dull.[1] A Swede named Henry Nyquist proved that the sampling rate has to be at least *twice* the maximum frequency we hope to capture. Because humans can perceive sounds up to about 20,000 Hz (20 kHz), a digital audio recorder needs to sample at least 40,000 times a second (40 kHz) to capture that range of frequencies.

Different digital audio recorders use different sample rates. Too low a sample rate results in *aliasing*, with poor high-frequency reproduction. The higher the sample rate, the better the frequency response and quality. Increasing the sample rate also increases the amount of data that needs to be stored.

CDs have a sample rate of 44.1 kHz (this rate is sometimes referred to as "CD quality" and is often used for music). Many video cameras and recorders use 48 kHz, which is a standard professional sample rate. Very high-quality recorders used for high-end production and music recording may operate at 96 kHz or even 192 kHz. Some DV cameras can be operated at 32 kHz—a low sample rate that compromises quality.

Bit Depth or Precision

Sample rate is an expression of how often we measure the audio signal. *Bit depth* or *precision* refers to how accurately we measure each sample.[2]

To get the idea of bit depth, consider this simple example. Say you had to measure people's height with a stick. The stick is one foot long and you can only record

---

1. If a video recording lacks high frequencies, fine detail in the picture may be lost, making it appear unsharp.
2. Bit depth is also called *bit length* and *word length*.

the height in one-stick increments. So, you could measure a six-foot-tall man very accurately (six sticks). But when you measure a woman who's five feet, six inches tall, you either have to record her height as five sticks or six sticks—either way, you're off by half a foot.

Now, imagine that we do the same thing with a shorter stick that's only six inches long. We can still measure the man's height precisely (twelve sticks). And when we measure the woman, now we can be just as accurate (eleven sticks).

Digital systems use a measurement scale to record the voltage of each audio sample. The scale has a number of levels. In an 8-bit system there are 256 levels.[3] Each level is the equivalent to our "sticks." The quietest sound could be given the level 1 and the loudest would be given level 255. But there's no such thing as a fraction of a level. If the signal level fell midway between 125 and 126, it would be rounded down to 125 or up to 126. Either way, that would introduce an error that could degrade the sound. In the digital audio world, that's called a *quantizing error*; it's a form of noise.

For greater precision we could use more bits. In a 16-bit system (which is fairly typical in professional video cameras) there are 65,536 levels. Now we can measure different voltage levels much more accurately and reproduce sounds more precisely. The more bits used for each sample, the higher the quality and the lower the noise. However, increasing bit depth, like raising the sample rate, increases the amount of audio data to be processed and stored.

Some high-quality recording systems use 20 bits or 24 bits or more. Even though you might not be able to hear the difference between 16 bits and 24 bits, when digital audio gets processed during postproduction, errors get multiplied, so more precision keeps the sound cleaner in the end.[4] Often, 16-bit recordings are converted to 24 bits for mixing.

Keep in mind that using more bits doesn't mean recording *louder* sounds. As you can see in Fig. 10-3, the one-volt maximum signal is divided into eight levels in the middle graph and sixteen levels in the lower graph. The maximum level is the same in both. However, an interesting thing happens at the *bottom* of the scale where the very quietest sounds are recorded. Sounds that are lower than the first level will disappear entirely from the recording (they will be recorded as zero). This is the *noise floor*. But if we use more bits, the first level is now lower, and we may be able to catch quiet sounds that would have been too low to register before. This reduces noise and increases dynamic range.[5]

Resolution and Sound Quality

Together, the sample rate and bit depth contribute to the *resolution* of a digital audio recording. Low-resolution recordings may sound "gritty" or overly crisp ("cold"). When the recording can't capture the subtleties of the original sound, artifacts result, which may be disturbing to the ear. High-resolution recordings

3. Digital systems use binary (base 2) numbers, and each digit is a *bit*. Eight bits is 2^8, which is 256.

4. When the sound level is very low—near the noise floor—there is a noticeable difference between 16-bit and 24-bit recording.

5. Systems that use *dither* actually allow you to hear sounds *below* the lowest level. Dither is a special form of low-level random noise. Generally, dither should be used when converting from a high bit depth to a lower one (such as converting 24-bit to 16-bit).

sound more faithful to the original sound source in terms of frequency response, dynamic range, and lack of noise. In the 1950s, vinyl LP records were considered "hi-fi" (high fidelity). Today, our standards for fidelity are a whole lot higher.

Recording and Transmitting Digital Audio

Once audio has been digitized, we can record it on hard drives, memory cards, or tape. With digital audio or video, it's very easy to move data around because you only need ones and zeros to represent any value.[6] A number can be transmitted from one place to another by sending a series of electrical pulses: send an *on* pulse for the ones, send an *off* pulse for the zeros.

This is why digital recordings on tape are so much more "robust" than analog recordings. To record an analog signal, you have to capture and store in the tape *tiny* variations in magnetic levels. With digital, the signal has only two possible levels: completely on or completely off (representing ones or zeros). The tape has a much simpler and cruder job: record either "full on" or "full off."

Tape noise is a problem with analog recordings because very quiet sounds may be lost in the noise of the tape. Digital systems generally don't have a problem with tape noise because even quiet sounds are recorded with pulses that are either full on or full off, so there's no confusion about what is signal and what is tape noise (however, as we've seen, there are still other types of noise in digital).

Digital tape recorders use rotating heads as in a video camcorder (see Fig. 3-8) instead of the fixed (stationary) heads used in analog tape recorders.

TYPES OF AUDIO RECORDERS

Today, film- and videomakers have a wide range of options for recording audio. When shooting video, sound is usually recorded right in the camcorder. Different cameras and video formats have different audio capabilities. On some video shoots—and on all film shoots—sound is recorded on a separate audio recorder. Audio recording technology has evolved a great deal. Until the mid-1990s, most professional sound recordists on film shoots used analog tape recorders with ¼-inch-wide tape; the Nagra recorder was the industry standard. Later, *DAT* (*digital audio tape*) became popular. Today, most recordists are moving toward a range of digital machines that record directly to audio files stored on hard drives, Flash memory cards, and/or optical discs.

The quality of an audio recording depends in part on the recording format and the settings used, and in part on the quality of the particular recorder. Even a good digital format may sound noisy if the recorder has poor microphone preamps. Before choosing a system, talk to recordists and read reviews.

6. In binary, a number like 250 would be 11111010.

DIGITAL AUDIO RECORDERS

Types of Digital Recorders

Digital audio recorders offer high quality in a small, light package and have had a huge impact on audio, video, and film production. There are many types of digital systems used for field production that record to a variety of media (the distinctions between them are fluid since many can record to several different types of media).

Fig. 10-4. Digital audio recorder. Sound Devices 722 is a file-based audio recorder that can record to an internal hard drive, CompactFlash cards, or external FireWire drives. (Sound Devices, LLC)

- *Hard drive recorders.* These have an internal hard disk drive for recording. After recording, audio data is exported to an external drive (often via FireWire) or by burning a CD or DVD. Hard disk recorders record directly to file so they permit instant playback of any take in the field and provide very fast ingest of files into an editing system with no capturing needed (simply drag and drop).
- *Laptop recorders.* A variant of hard drive recorders, this method combines a device that has mic inputs and preamps with software for feeding digitized audio to a laptop hard drive. Controls for setting level and other items may be part of the physical hardware or done with software on the laptop. May not be as portable for handheld recording as some more compact systems.
- *Flash memory recorders.* These record to solid-state memory cards, such as *Compact Flash (CF)*, *PCMCIA cards* (like *Flash ATA*), and *MemoryStick.* No moving parts, so the machine is very quiet and may be useful for harsh physical environments with a lot of jostling (hard drives don't like to be treated roughly). Some are very small. These also record directly to file, so have the same benefits as hard drive systems for easy playback and quick ingest of files. With some equipment, the flash memory or PCMCIA card may be taken out of the recorder and inserted into a laptop or desktop editing system.
- *DVD or CD recorders.* These record to optical discs. Some record to DVD-RAM, about half the size of a conventional DVD. Same benefits of recording direct to file.

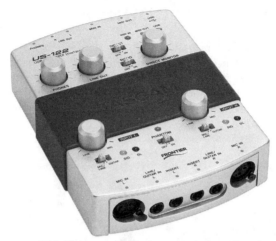

Fig. 10-5. Mic preamp. This Tascam unit allows you to input microphones (via XLR connectors with phantom power) and output digital audio via a USB cable to a laptop or other computer recording system. (TASCAM)

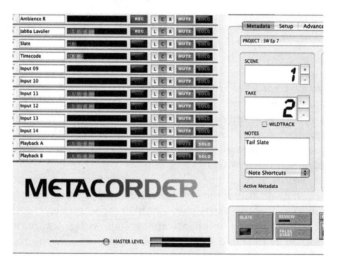

Fig. 10-6. Metacorder field audio recording software designed for film and video shoots. (Gallery)

- **Digital Audio Tape (DAT).** DAT machines use tape cassettes that are a little smaller than typical analog audio cassettes. DAT was once an exciting improvement over analog tape, but is less so today, as it's a linear tape format without the benefits of recording directly to file. Sony and other manufacturers have stopped making DAT machines. *ADAT* is a system for recording eight tracks of digital audio to an S-VHS cassette; used in the music industry.[7] *DA-88* machines record eight digital tracks to Hi8 cassettes and are still used to deliver final mix stems in the TV industry.

7. ADAT is also a protocol for eight-track digital recording that can be used with other recording media.

Fig. 10-7. TASCAM HD-P2. Records file-based digital audio to CompactFlash cards or external drives via FireWire. (TASCAM)

Fig. 10-8. DAT (digital audiotape) recorder. This machine is no longer made, but many DAT units are still in use. (Fletcher Chicago/Sony Electronics, Inc.)

- *Magneto-optical discs.* There are various systems for recording audio to MO discs. One of the best known is Sony's *MiniDisc*. MiniDiscs look a bit like 3.5-inch floppy discs and some of the recorders are not much bigger. They use the proprietary Sony ATRAC codec to record compressed but very good quality sound. There are full-sized MiniDisc recorders with professional features, but MiniDiscs are not widely used for film and video production.

Audio File Formats

Hard drive and Flash memory systems may give you options in the file format of the audio files created in recording. A standard file format for professional video and film field production is *BWF* (*Broadcast Wave Format*). BWF is based on the common Microsoft WAVE (.wav) audio file format but includes an extra "chunk" of information about such things as timecode, date and time, bit depth, sample rate, and so on.[8] This added information is called *metadata* (see p. 220); compared to formats that don't carry metadata, BWF files offer big advantages for managing postproduction workflow.

There are two flavors or modes of BWF that handle multitrack recording differently. *BWFm* (*monophonic*) creates separate mono files for each channel of audio. So, if your recorder can record to four channels simultaneously, when using BWFm you'll get four separate files (they can still be grouped by file name and metadata). Depending on the system and the recording, the files can be put in sync in the editing system either manually or automatically.

BWFp (*polyphonic*) is the other version. Using BWFp, the four channels would be recorded as a single file, with all the tracks interleaved. This is similar to how standard stereo .wav files for music combine the left and right channels in one file. BWFp simplifies editing, but not all editing systems can handle it (or may need a separate tool or application to prepare the files for ingest into the editing system).

BWF includes support for uncompressed PCM audio as well as MPEG compressed audio.

Some recording systems will record to other formats, including AIFF (.aif) and SDII (Sound Designer 2) and/or compressed formats such as .mp3 or AAC.

Before choosing a file format, be sure to discuss it with the postproduction team!

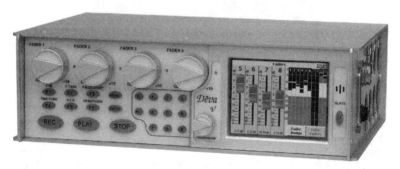

Fig. 10-9. Zaxcom Deva V is a high-end, file-based recorder that records to internal hard drive, DVD, and to external drives via FireWire. Records up to ten audio tracks. (Zaxcom, Inc.)

Recorder Setup

Given the wide variety of technologies and recording systems, it's beyond the scope of this book to go into detail on each. Some general considerations:

SETTING SAMPLE RATE AND BIT DEPTH. Most newer digital recorders offer a choice of sample rate and bit depth (see p. 374). Most video camcorders record audio at 48 kHz at 16- or 20-bits. A setting of 48 kHz/16-bits is, as of this writing, standard for TV and film delivery and may be the best choice if

---

8. Standard WAVE files have the extension .wav. BWF files can have either .wav or .bwf. Some software can't read the metadata in the BWF file header and will play only the audio using the extension .wav.

you're using camcorder audio along with sound recorded separately. However, if you're working with a separate recorder that supports it, you may choose to record at higher resolution. Recording at 24 bits is increasingly common for high-end production. As noted above, increasing either setting will increase the amount of data to be stored (and reduce the amount of time you can record on the media you have).

FILE STRUCTURE AND NAMING. Depending on your system, you may need to format or initialize disks or Flash memory in preparation for recording. You may create a "session" or folder for the day's work, or for each scene. Or you may use a different directory structure for organizing the audio files. Files are easy to lose track of, so good organization will help you stay sane.

You may have a choice about the scheme for naming files. One naming system with mono BWF is: 075BT0005_2.BWF. This would be Scene 75B, Take 5, Track 2. If there are multiple tracks, each has the same file name but the number after the underscore (_2) indicates which track it is so you can put them together later. The recorder will automatically increment the file name/take number each time you press "record." You can't have two files with the same name in the same folder. Depending on the system, a very long take may exceed the maximum file size. Some systems will automatically split the recording over multiple files which can be seamlessly joined in editing.

BWF files are stamped with the time of creation, so check that the recorder's clock is set correctly.

TIMECODE. Some digital recorders are equipped for timecode. See Timecode, p. 203, and Timecode Slating Systems, p. 438.

Recording

Many digital recorders have familiar controls like a typical tape deck's transport controls ("record," "play," "fast forward," "pause") even though there may be no tape and nothing is actually moving.

Setting the recording level is discussed on p. 414.

Many digital recorders have a *prerecord* function (also called a *record buffer*). This magical feature captures sound from *before* you press record. Here's how it works. When the machine is on, even if it's in "pause," it's *always* recording, and saving the latest ten seconds in a buffer.[9] When you press "record," it begins the recording with what's stored in the buffer, allowing you to capture audio ten seconds before you pressed "record." This can be useful for documentary recording, where you may not start recording until you hear something interesting but by then you've missed the beginning of the sentence. When recording for film shoots, some telecines need five to ten seconds of preroll time before the take begins (see Chapter 18); using prerecord you can capture the preroll automatically. Or, as one recordist put it, even if you're busy eating a donut when you hear the director call "action!" you can still get the first part of the take.

Some recorders have buttons that permit you to mark preferred takes (circle takes) for later reference as well as blown takes (false starts to be deleted).

---

9. The size of the buffer varies between machines and may depend on sample rate.

Monitoring

All recorders have headphone jacks. Many will allow you to choose different modes such as mono (all tracks in both ears) or L/R (left channel in left ear only, right channel in right ear only). On a multitrack recorder there may be an option to *solo* one track alone.

On all recorders, you hear the sound as it is processed in the recorder, just prior to being recorded. Some recorders also offer *confidence monitoring*, which means listening to the actual *recorded* sound from tape or file. On a tape recorder, the headphone switch might have two positions: "Direct" (or "Source") and "Tape." The benefit of listening to the recorded sound is that you can be sure everything is recorded satisfactorily, and that there aren't problems with the tape or file. The disadvantage is that the recorded sound may be delayed by up to several seconds, which can be a bit disorienting for the recordist.

Fig. 10-10. Zaxcom ZFR100 is a highly compact Flash memory recorder that can receive timecode wirelessly from the video camera, allowing automatic start-stop when the camera rolls and automatic syncing in postproduction. (Zaxcom, Inc.)

Digital and Analog Connections

Digital field recorders have analog mic inputs for attaching microphones and analog line inputs for recording from other analog sources (see Mic and Line Level, p. 401).

They also have analog outputs for sending the audio to headphones and to various types of analog equipment, such as an amplifier, analog mixer, or a speaker system.

However, when sending the audio to another *digital* system (such as a digital mixer or another recorder), it's almost always preferable *not* to use the analog outputs, because that means converting the digital audio to analog and then back to digital again (which can degrade the quality).

For editing purposes, the simplest solution with file-based recorders is to do a file transfer to the editing system from the recorder's hard drive or Flash memory or to burn a data CD or DVD. However, there are many situations where you want to connect equipment digitally before or after recording when a file transfer isn't appropriate.

To pass digital audio data back and forth, professional audio recorders often have digital inputs or outputs that use the *AES* format (also called *AES3* or *AES/EBU*). AES cables use XLR connectors (see Fig. 10-30) or, for the *AES3id* version, BNC connectors (see Fig. 3-12).

The consumer version is called S/P DIF. S/P DIF cables are either *coaxial* (electrical) and use RCA jacks, or *optical* and use a *TOSLINK* connector (see Fig. 10-12). Many types of consumer equipment such as DVD players use S/P DIF.

When using any of these systems, be sure to use high-quality cables designed for this purpose, not conventional analog audio or video cables. You can go from a machine with an AES output to one with a S/P DIF input (or vice versa) with the proper adaptor.

Digital recorders use a precise timing signal called *word clock*. When two digital machines are connected via AES or S/P DIF, there shouldn't be any variation be-

Fig. 10-11. MOTU Traveler provides four mic inputs and a total of twenty channels of analog and digital inputs and outputs. A full-featured interface for recording to a laptop in the field. (MOTU, Inc.)

tween the two word clocks. In this situation, one machine may be designated the word clock master and the other the slave to synchronize them.

Another way to transfer audio digitally between video cameras and decks is to use an SDI link (see p. 217); several audio channels can be embedded in the SDI signal.

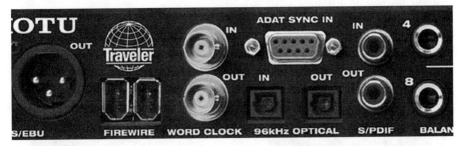

Fig. 10-12. The rear panel of the Traveler provides a good view of various connectors used for digital audio. From the left: XLR (used here for AES/EBU); FireWire; BNC; 9-pin (used here for ADAT), Toslink (for S/P DIF optical); RCA (used here for S/P DIF coaxial); ¼-inch phone jack for balanced analog input. (MOTU, Inc.)

Archiving Audio Recordings

Like all types of digital recordings, digital audio presents problems when it comes to long-term storage or archiving. If you used a hard drive or Flash memory recorder, you'll need to store the data on other media (possibly another hard drive, DVD, CD, or DLT). If you used a DAT machine, the audio is already on tape and can be easily stored, but DAT tapes may suffer degradation of signal over time and are not considered a good archive medium. All archive formats suffer from the problem that, as time passes and technology advances, it gets harder to find older-style equipment that can play or read it.

AUDIO IN THE VIDEO CAMCORDER

See Sound Recording for Video, p. 21, before reading this section.

On most video shoots, the camcorder itself is the audio recorder. The audio recording capabilities depend on the particular camera and on the video format. For the basics of operating a camcorder, see Chapter 3. For instructions on setting the audio level, see p. 414.

Mics and Inputs

Consumer and prosumer camcorders usually have a built-in microphone and professional camcorders typically provide a mount for attaching an external mic. On-camera mics can be very handy when working alone or for quick setups but they are often too far from the subject to record good sound and can have other disadvantages (see The Microphone, p. 390).

The built-in mics on consumer camcorders often record in stereo (splitting the sound into left and right channels; see Stereo Recording, p. 431). This can be fine for informal recording and for gathering ambient sound or effects that you want in stereo. You may also like the feel of stereo sound. However, keep in mind that on professional productions, dialogue is typically recorded in mono, even if the movie is ultimately released in stereo or multichannel sound (see Chapter 16). When using an on-camera mic with a prosumer or professional camcorder you might use a mono mic and record to *one* of the channels.

Another concern with consumer camcorders is that the mic inputs may have only mini-phone jacks (see Fig. 10-30) and have no provision for higher quality mics that use professional XLR cables or that need phantom power (see below). You can get an external preamp unit with professional connectors (and phantom power if needed) that mounts on the bottom of the camera (see Fig. 10-13).

Fig. 10-13. If you have a consumer camcorder and want to use professional mics that have XLR connectors there are a number of products available. This Beachtek unit mounts under the camera and has two balanced mic or line inputs. (Beachtek, Inc.)

Sometimes even on a good quality prosumer or professional camera, the mic preamps and audio circuits are noisy or have other defects. Recordists usually prefer to use a separate field mixer (see p. 400) to power the mics and control the volume, using a line-level connection into the camera (see below).

Wireless microphones can be connected directly to the camera or through a mixer (see p. 400).

Number of Audio Channels

Every video format can record at least two channels of audio which can be used for recording two separate mono tracks or one pair of stereo tracks. For typical field production, you might put a boom mic on one channel and a wireless mic on the other.

Some formats offer more tracks. Digital Betacam can record four audio channels. HDCAM SR can handle twelve tracks. Recording on multiple channels provides more flexibility later, by keeping separate mics separate and not mixed together. However, managing multiple channels on videotape can add complexity to the process. If you want to record many tracks (perhaps for a five-channel surround-sound recording) you may have an easier time using a separate hard-drive audio recorder and recording directly to file.

Audio Quality

The quality of sound recorded on a video camcorder depends on several factors.

As mentioned above, even cameras shooting the same format can differ in the mic preamps, level control, and other audio processing that takes place before the sound is even recorded.

With digital cameras, one must consider sample rate and bit depth (see above). This tends to be determined by the recording format, but there may be options. For example, DV typically records two channels of audio using a 48 kHz sample rate at 16-bits. Some DV cameras will also record four channels of audio at 32 kHz at 12-bits. The second option provides much lower quality and should be avoided.

Most video formats use 48 kHz sampling. Bit depth varies by format: DV, DVCAM,

Fig. 10-14. Wireless receiver mounted on a camcorder. (Sony Electronics, Inc.)

DVCPRO HD, and HDV use 16-bits, which is a common bit depth in today's cameras; Digital Betacam and HDCAM use 20-bits; HDCAM SR uses 24-bits.

Many prosumer and most professional cameras can record uncompressed audio. This is usually indicated as *PCM* or *linear PCM* audio tracks. Uncompressed is preferred as the highest quality. Some formats compress the audio to save storage space. Some HDV cameras record compressed audio using MPEG-1 Audio Layer 2 compression at 384 Kbps. This lowered quality may work fine for you, although with some projects it may be better to record uncompressed (see The Recording System, p. 80).

ANALOG VIDEO FORMATS. As a rule, analog videotape has more noise and lower quality than most digital formats. The poorest audio is recorded with the longitudinal or linear audio tracks that run along the edge of the tape. Some analog formats can also record higher-quality tracks as part of the video. For example, the stereo hi-fi tracks in VHS, S-VHS, and Hi8, and the AFM tracks in Betacam SP (channels 3 and 4) benefit from the higher write speed of the rotating video heads and can sound very good. These tracks have to be recorded at the same time as the picture.

THE ANALOG TAPE RECORDER

The benefits of digital recorders are great enough that relatively few analog machines are now being made. However, a lot of them are still around. The Nagra recorder has played a venerable role in the industry and records excellent quality sound. Several items discussed below apply to *any* type of tape recorder—analog or digital.

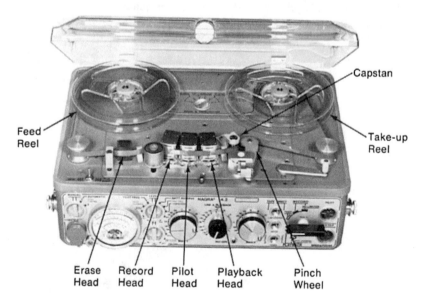

Fig. 10-15. Nagra 4.2 This ¼-inch tape recorder served as a standard for the industry. (Nagra USA)

The Tape Path

Most analog audiotape recorders used for film or video have the following components: a *feed* or *supply* reel of tape; an *erase head* that cleans the tape of any distinct magnetic pattern; a *record head* to record the audio signal; a *pilot head* or a *timecode system* for speed-control information; a *playback head* to reproduce the audio; a *capstan* and *pinch wheel* to move the tape forward; and a *take-up* reel to store the tape. On some machines, a single head is used for recording, playback, and sometimes pilot as well. On *reel-to-reel* (also called *open reel*) recorders, the feed and take-up reels are separate. On cassette decks, they are enclosed in a cassette.

Erasure

The first head in the tape path is the erase head, which clears any magnetic signal present on the tape. Erase heads work by exposing the tape to an inaudible, very high-frequency tone. On most recorders, the erase head turns on when the machine is switched to "record" mode. Care must be taken not to erase a tape accidentally.

Although most erase heads work very well, some recordists prefer to use a bulk eraser to clean (*demagnetize*) recorded tapes before reuse. Using a bulk eraser may lower tape noise slightly, and it certainly removes any confusion between new and old sound. Bulk erasers, like most other kinds of demagnetizers (also called *degaussers*), involve exposing the tape or other object to a powerful, alternating magnetic field. To use any kind of demagnetizer, turn it on while the tape or magnetized object is several feet away. Move the tape onto the eraser slowly while rotating the tape. Rotate the tape around a few times, keeping it flat, and remove the tape slowly, still rotating. Larger format material, like 16mm mag stock, should then be turned over and erased again. As you remove the tape from the demagnetizer, it's imperative that you pull it away *very slowly* (one or two inches/second), especially when the two are within a couple of feet of each other. Only after the tape or object is at arm's length from the demagnetizer should you turn off the machine. Turning it on or off when the tape is close will leave the tape more magnetized than it was at the start.

Bear in mind that the permanent magnetic field of an unshielded loudspeaker can partially erase a tape, so never store tapes on a speaker.

Recording

For a discussion of setting the recording level on analog recorders, see p. 414.

TRACK POSITION. Some audio recorders used for film and video record monaural, or mono, sound (that is, one channel only) on a track that spans the full width of the tape. Some recorders use at least two audio tracks. This may open up possibilities for stereo recording or using multiple microphones. Some stereo recorders also have a center track between the two audio tracks that may be used for cuing information. On most professional recorders, tapes cannot be "turned over" to get twice the recording time, the way some cassettes are.

BIAS. Like film stocks, magnetic tape stocks have a threshold below which weak, low-energy signals will not be recorded. In order to boost the audio signal above this threshold, the recorder mixes in a *bias* current. Bias itself is not audible, but if its level is badly adjusted the effects are. If you're getting poor-quality recordings or if you switch to a new type of tape, the bias should be checked. Afterward, use the tape stock for which the machine is adjusted.

EQUALIZATION. *Equalization* refers to balancing various parts of the audible spectrum—boosting or diminishing certain frequencies relative to others. One type of equalization, called *pre-equalization*, or *pre-emphasis*, is used in the tape recorder to improve its ability to record high-frequency sounds. Different tape speeds and stocks require different amounts of pre-emphasis. Most high-quality recorders have an equalization switch (sometimes labeled "EQ") that has settings for various tape speeds or stocks.

Other types of equalization are discussed below and in Chapters 11 and 16.

Playback

Some recorders have one head that doubles as both a record and playback head. Without a separate playback head, when you listen through headphones while recording you hear the sound *before* it gets to the tape. Some recorders have a separate head just for playback, which allows for confidence monitoring (see above). A *slight* change in volume between what you hear direct and what you hear off the tape is normal and is usually no cause for concern; a large change may mean dirty heads or other problems.

Head Care

Magnetic heads must be kept clean and free from magnetic charge. They must not be too worn and must make good contact with the tape as it passes. The first sign of a dirty, worn, magnetized, or improperly adjusted head is the loss of high-frequency sounds—recorded material sounds muddy or dull.

Heads should be cleaned with commercially prepared head cleaner, which dries instantly, or with isopropyl (rubbing) alcohol. Buy some head-cleaning swabs or use a Q-Tip that has been twirled in your fingers to ensure that no hairs come off and lodge in the tape path. Heads should be cleaned at least every few tapes to remove accumulated oxide.

Heads can become magnetized over time. Some recordists demagnetize the heads regularly, others wait until poor sound quality indicates they are probably magnetized. Have an experienced person show you how to demagnetize heads; beginners often increase the magnetic charge by doing it incorrectly. Always turn off the recorder before demagnetizing. Use a hand *degausser* (sometimes called a *defluxer*), not the tiny pencil type used for erasing sections of tape or a large bulk eraser, which may affect parts of the recorder (such as the meter) that are supposed to be magnetized. Slowly move the degausser to within ¼-inch to ⅛-inch of the head; slowly wave the tip of the degausser along and then across the head slightly; then retract it slowly (see precautions on erasure, p. 387). The R. B. Annis Company (1101 N. Delaware Street, Indianapolis, IN 46202) makes an excellent hand degausser as well as a magnetometer, which helps you determine if the head is actually magnetized.

When a magnetic head becomes worn, the gap gets wider and its response to high frequencies is impaired. If the face of the head is not perfectly parallel to the tape path or if the face is parallel but the head is tilted to the side, the effect is the same. The terms used for various types of head alignment include *height*, *zenith*, *rack*, and *azimuth*. If the heads are excessively or unevenly worn, have a technician check them for possible replacement or realignment.

Speed Control for Sync Recording

For an audio recorder to be used for sync sound film or video work, the speed of the playback must be precisely controlled. Digital recorders are generally accurate enough, but with analog, even a high-quality tape recorder, if not specially adapted for sync work, will have speed variations that will cause the picture and sound to go out of sync. Different speed control systems are based on the idea of recording a clock-like or pulsed signal on the tape. On playback, the tape is controlled so the pulses are played at exactly the same speed they were recorded (called *resolving*).

The classic speed control system is Nagra's *neopilot* (or just *pilot*) tone. On a Nagra 4.2, the pilot is recorded right in the audio track without interfering with the sound. Some analog cassette recorders have been modified for sync work by devoting one of the audio tracks to pilot, using a *crystal* in the recorder to generate the pilot tone.

The Tape Transport

On most recorders, the tape is pulled along by a *capstan*, which is a smooth, vertical cylinder that is rotated by a motor. A rubber *pinch wheel* holds the tape snugly against the capstan as it rotates. If the capstan has dirt on it, or if the motor is malfunctioning, *wow* or *flutter* may result. Wow is any irregularity or variation in the speed that repeats less than ten times per second, and flutter is any variation that repeats faster than that.

Rollers and capstans should be kept clean. Don't let the pinch wheel remain pressed against the capstan for more than a few hours if the tape is not rolling or a flat spot may result. This happens on some recorders when the machine is left in "pause" mode.

When batteries weaken, the tape may slow down during recording. When this tape is played back with fresh cells, the sound will be speeded up (voices take on the familiar "chipmunk" sound). Sometimes such recordings can be salvaged by capturing the audio in a digital audio workstation and speeding it up.

TAPE SPEED. Most ¼-inch tape recorders offer a choice of two or three tape speeds: 3¾, 7½, and sometimes 15 inches per second (ips). Generally the faster the speed, the smoother the tape runs (that is, less wow and flutter). Faster speeds increase dynamic range, reduce audible noise, and improve the recorder's response to high-frequency sounds. The standard for most movie work is 7½ ips; 15 ips is used for critical music recordings.

The Tape

Magnetic tape is made up of a thick *base* and a relatively thinner *emulsion* or *oxide* that actually stores the magnetic information. Most tape oxides are made of iron, also called ferrous oxides. Various other more expensive emulsions, including chromium dioxide, or CrO_2, and "metal" formulations may offer lower noise and better frequency response. Special tape formulations are more often used for analog cassette recorders than for ¼-inch recording in which tape noise is less of a problem. With ¼-inch recording today, the choices in tape stock are very limited.

A common analog tape problem is *print-through*, which occurs when the sound on one layer of tape becomes imprinted on the next layer out on the reel, causing a slight echo that can be heard during quiet moments before or after loud sounds. Print-through is mostly noticeable on material recorded at quiet locations where there is no background sound to mask the echo. It can be minimized by storing the tape tail-out on the reel, by keeping the tape in cool locations, and by rewinding it every now and then.

Noise Reduction

Many analog tape recorders and video camcorders are equipped with *noise reduction* units such as one of the Dolby systems. There have been several different versions of Dolby noise reduction, including A, B, C, and SR (Spectral Recording). Dolby C works by boosting the level of mid- and high-frequency sounds as they are recorded and then diminishing their level in playback, leaving the sound signal normally balanced. Tape hiss is also a high-frequency sound; however, since it is inherent in the tape, it is not affected by the Dolby during the recording. It is diminished, though, when the Dolby reduces the high frequencies in playback.

If a recorder has a noise reduction unit, you should generally use it. Tapes recorded with noise reduction *must* be played back with it, on a machine that employs the same system. Always indicate on the tape box whether a recording was made with noise reduction and which system. Tapes made without noise reduction should not be played back with it or the sound quality will be degraded (for example, with Dolby C, high frequencies may be lost).

There are several Dolby multichannel and digital audio systems (see Chapter 16).

THE MICROPHONE

Microphone Types

There are a few basic types of microphones used for film and video production.

Condenser microphones are used extensively. They are often quite sensitive and some are expensive. Condenser mics use a capacitor circuit to generate electricity from sound, and they need power supplied to them to work. Power may come from batteries in the microphone case, on the mic cable, or in the recorder itself. *Electret condenser* mics employ a permanently charged electret capacitor. They can be made very cheaply and may require no power supply.

Dynamic or *moving-coil microphones* are typically used by musical performers, amateur recordists, and many professionals. They are simpler and less sensitive than condensers, but usually quite rugged and resistant to handling noise and they require no batteries or special power supply.

Fig. 10-16. Electro-Voice 635 omnidirectional dynamic microphone. Simple and durable. (Electro-Voice)

Directionality

Every mic has a particular *pickup pattern*—that is, the configuration of directions in space in which it is sensitive to sound.

Omnidirectional or *omni* microphones respond equally to sounds coming from any direction.

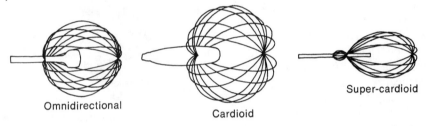

Fig. 10-17. Representations of the directional sensitivity of omni, cardioid and super-cardioid microphones (not drawn to the same scale). These indicate each mic's response to sound coming from different directions. Imagine the omni mic at the center of a spherical area of sensitivity; the diaphragm of the cardioid mic is at about the position of the stem in a pattern that is roughly tomato-shaped. Though the lobes of sensitivity are pictured with a definite border, in fact sensitivity diminishes gradually with distance. (Carol Keller)

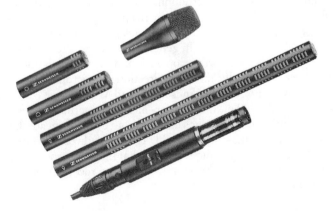

Fig. 10-18. Sennheiser K6 modular condenser microphone system. The powering module is at bottom (works with internal batteries or phantom power). Interchangeable mic heads range in directionality from super-cardioid to omni. (Sennheiser Electronic Corp.)

Cardioid mics are most sensitive to sounds coming from the front, less sensitive to sounds coming from the side, and least sensitive to those coming from behind. The name derives from the pickup pattern, which is heart-shaped when viewed from above. *Hyper-cardioid* microphones (sometimes called *in-line, short-tube shotgun,* or *mini shotgun*) are even less sensitive to sounds coming from the side and behind. *Super-cardioid* microphones (*long-tube shotgun* or *shotgun*) are extremely insensitive to any sounds not coming from directly ahead. However, some hyper- and super-cardioid mics have a certain amount of sensitivity to sound emanating from directly behind as well. Because the names for these microphone types are not entirely standardized (one company's "hyper-cardioid" is another's "super-cardioid"), be careful when you select a microphone.

Bidirectional mics have a figure-eight pickup pattern with equal sensitivity on either side; these mics may be used in a studio placed between two people talking to each other.

Boundary microphones (sometimes called *PZM* or *Pressure Zone Microphones*) are mounted very close to a flat plate or other flat surface and may have a hemispherical pickup pattern. These are sometimes used for recording a group of people when the mic can't be close to each speaker, or when recording music (mounted on a piano, for instance).

Manufacturers print *polar diagrams*—graphs that indicate exactly where a microphone is sensitive and in which directions it favors certain frequencies. It's important to know the pickup pattern of the mic you are using. For example, many people are un-

Fig. 10-19. Mounted on a flat surface, a boundary mic uses the surface to boost its audio response. (Audio-Technica, U.S., Inc.)

aware of the rear lobe of sensitivity in some hyper- and super-cardioid mics, which results in unnecessarily noisy recordings (see Fig. 10-20).

Hyper- and super-cardioid microphones achieve their directionality by means of an interference tube. The tube works by making sound waves coming from the sides or back of the mic strike the front and back of the diaphragm simultaneously so that they cancel themselves out. In general, the longer the tube is, the more directional the mic will be. For proper operation, don't cover the holes in the tube with your hand or tape. Usually, the more directional a microphone is, the more sensitive it will be to wind noise (see Windscreens and Microphone Mounts, p. 395).

Contrary to popular belief, most hyper- and super-cardioid mics are not more sensitive than cardioid mics to sounds coming from directly ahead; they are *not* like zoom lenses; they don't "magnify" sound.[10] However, directional mics do exclude more of the competing background sound, so that they can produce a good recording at a greater distance from the sound source—as recordists say, the "working distance" is greater.

---

10. *Parabolic mics,* which look like small satellite dishes (sometimes used at sporting events), actually *do* have a magnifying (amplifying) effect.

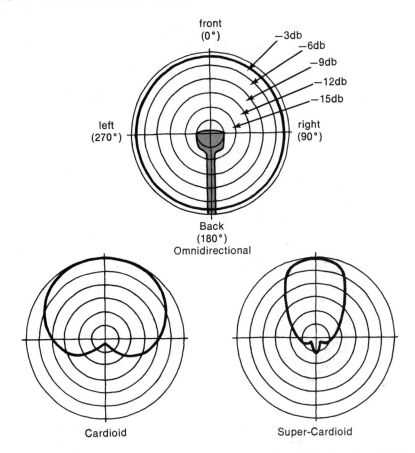

Fig. 10-20. Polar diagrams indicating the sensitivity of omnidirectional, cardioid, and super-cardioid microphones. Imagine each diagram as a cross section of the mic's sensitivity, with the microphone lying along the vertical axis (as the omni mic is here). The microphone's diaphragm would be positioned at the center of the graph. (Carol Keller)

One disadvantage of highly directional mics is that you may encounter situations in which it's hard to capture important sounds within the narrow lobe of sensitivity. A classic case is trying to record a two-person conversation with a super-cardioid mic: When the mic is pointed at one person, who is then *on-axis*, the other person will be *off-axis*, his voice sounding muffled and distant. Panning a long microphone back and forth is an imperfect solution if the conversation is unpredictable. In such cases, it may be better to move far enough away so that both speakers are approximately on-axis. Unfortunately, the best recordings are made when the microphone is close to the sound source.

Microphone Sound Quality

Microphones vary in their frequency response. Some mics emphasize the bass or low frequencies, others the treble or high frequencies.

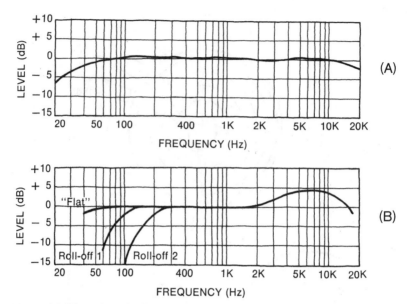

Fig. 10-21. (A) The relatively flat frequency response of a good-quality audio recorder. Where the graph drops below the 0 dB line indicates diminished response. (B) A microphone frequency response curve. This mic is more sensitive to high frequencies. The three parts of the curve at left represent increasing amounts of bass roll-off controlled by a built-in, three-position switch (see p. 429). (Carol Keller)

    The frequency response of a microphone or recorder is shown on a *frequency response graph* that indicates which frequencies are favored by the equipment. Favored frequencies are those that are reproduced louder than others. An "ideal" frequency response curve for a recorder is flat, indicating that all frequencies are treated equally. Many mics emphasize high-frequency sounds more than midrange or bass frequencies. Recordists may choose mics that favor middle to high frequencies to add clarity and *presence* (the sensation of being close to the sound source) to speech. Some mics have a "speech" switch that increases the midrange ("speech bump"). In some situations, a mic that emphasizes lower frequencies may be preferred. For example, a male vocalist or narrator might like the sound coloration of a bassy mic to bring out a fuller sound. A large-diaphragm mic, like the Neumann U-89, can be used for a "warm" sound.
    Sometimes recordists deliberately *roll-off* (suppress) low frequencies, especially in windy situations (see Chapter 11).
    When you purchase a mic, check the frequency response graph published by the manufacturer. An extremely uneven or limited response (high frequencies should not drop off significantly before about 10,000 Hz or more) is some cause for concern.
    One of the things that distinguishes high-quality mics is low "self-noise"—the mic itself is quiet and doesn't add hiss to the recording. The better the recorder, the more likely you are to notice mic noise.

The microphones that come with recorders and cameras are often not great and may need to be replaced. Set up an *A/B test* where you can switch from one mic to another while recording. However, you may find that you prefer the sound of the less expensive of two mics. An A/B test is especially important if you need two matched microphones for multiple mic recording (see Chapter 11).

Windscreens and Microphone Mounts

The sound of the wind blowing across a microphone does not in the least resemble the gentle rustle of wind through trees or the moan of wind blowing by a house. What you hear instead are pops, rumble, and crackle. When recording, don't let wind strike a microphone (particularly highly directional mics) without a *windscreen*. A windscreen blocks air from moving across the mic.

A minimal windscreen is a hollowed-out ball or tube of *acoustifoam*—a foam rubber–like material that does not muffle sound (see Fig. 9-17). This kind of windscreen is the least obtrusive and is used indoors and sometimes in very light winds outside. Its main use is to block the wind produced when the mic is in motion and to minimize the popping sound caused by someone's breathing into the mic when speaking.

For breezier conditions, a more substantial windscreen is needed. Many recordists carry a soft, fuzzy windscreen with built-in microphone mount, such as the Rycote Softie (see Fig. 10-23). A Softie can also

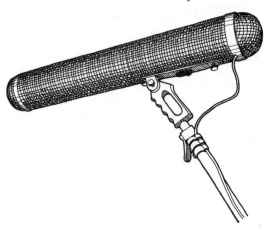

Fig. 10-22. A zeppelin windscreen for a shotgun mic, shown with a pistol grip and mounted on a microphone boom. (Carol Keller)

be used to cover a camera mic. For heavier wind, a windscreen called a *zeppelin* can be used.[11] Like its namesake, this is large and tubular; it completely encases the mic. In strong winds, an additional sock-like, fuzzy covering can be fitted around the zeppelin. A good windscreen should have no noticeable effect on the sound quality in still air.

When you are caught outside without an adequate windscreen, you can often use your body, the flap of your coat, or a building to shelter the mic from the wind. Hide a lavalier under clothing or put the tip of a wool glove over it (see below). Often, a bass roll-off filter helps minimize the rumble of wind noise (see Chapter 11). Omni mics may be the least susceptible to wind noise.

Besides wind noise, microphones are extremely sensitive to the sound of any

11. In the U.K., windscreens are called "wind shields," and zeppelins may be called "blimps."

Fig. 10-23. (left) Rycote rubber shock mount and pistol grip. (right) Rycote Softie wind-screen works well in windy conditions. (Rycote Microphone Windshields, Ltd)

moving object, such as hands or clothing, which touches or vibrates the micro-phone case. *Hand noise*, or *case noise*, becomes highly amplified and can easily ruin a recording with its rumbly sound. The recordist should grip the microphone firmly and motionlessly, grasping the looped microphone cable in the same hand to pre-vent any movement of the cable where it plugs into the mic. Even better, use a pis-tol grip that has a shock mount (usually some form of elastic or flexible mounting) to isolate the mic from hand noise (see Fig. 10-23).

In many recording situations, a *fishpole* (collapsible) boom should be used to en-able the recordist to stand away from the action (see Fig. 9-13). A shock mount will isolate the mic from hand or cable noise on the boom.

Lavalier or Lapel Microphones

Lavalier microphones (*lavs*) are very small mics generally intended to be clipped on the subject's clothing.[12] Also called *lapel mics*, these are often used with a wireless transmitter (see below) or may be connected by cable to the recorder. Most TV news anchors wear one or two lavs clipped on a tie or a blouse. Lavaliers are quite unobtrusive and are easy to use when there isn't a sound recordist. Lavs are often used for interviews because they can result in clear, loud voice tracks. They're use-ful for recording in noisy environments because they're usually positioned so close to the person speaking that they tend to exclude background sound and the rever-beration of the room. However, this also results in a "close" sound, which some-times sounds unnatural. Many professional recordists don't like using lavs and prefer the sound from a good cardioid or hyper-cardiod mic on a boom because it's more natural, more "open," and doesn't risk clothing or body noises. In some situa-tions, recordists like to record with a lavalier on one track and a boom mic on an-other, to get both good voice and some background sound; avoid mixing both mics on the same track in the field.

---

12. Lavalier used to refer to a larger type of mic designed to be hung on a cord around the subject's neck. These are rarely used today.

Most lavaliers are omnidirectional, although hyper-cardioid lavs are available. Many have a flat frequency response. However, when you clip a mic on someone's shirt you may get too much bass (from being right over the chest cavity) and not enough treble (since the mic is out of line with the speaker's mouth). Some lavs have a midrange speech bump (see Microphone Sound Quality, p. 393) to compensate.

A good position for a lavalier is in the middle of the chest at the sternum (breastbone). For subjects wearing a T-shirt or a sweater, sometimes the mic is clipped on at the collar. The problem with collar placement is it may be too close to the subject's voice box and may cause sound variations if the subject turns his head away from the mic. If the subject is looking generally in one direction (perhaps for an interview), put the mic on that side of his collar.

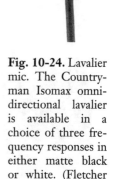

Fig. 10-24. Lavalier mic. The Countryman Isomax omnidirectional lavalier is available in a choice of three frequency responses in either matte black or white. (Fletcher Chicago/Countryman)

Often it is preferable to hide the mic; for shooting dramatic material, it's essential. Clip or tape the mic under clothing, but listen carefully for case noise caused by the cloth rubbing on the mic. Silk and synthetic fabrics are the worst for noise; cotton and wool are often fine. Small frames or cages are available to provide separation between the cloth and the mic. You can improvise with some rolled-up tape to prevent rubbing (see Fig. 10-25). Leave enough slack in the cable so that the body movements don't pull on the mic; make a small loop in the cable for strain relief and tape or clip it in place.

Sometimes you can get better sound by hiding a lav in the subject's hair or a hat. Carry some moleskin or surgical tape for taping mics to skin.

For more on using lavaliers, see Chapter 11.

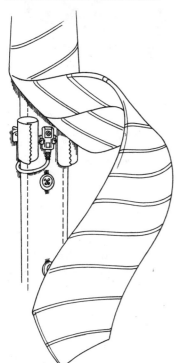

Fig. 10-25. Hiding a lavalier. To prevent cloth from rubbing on the mic, one technique is to use rolled-up gaffer's tape. Some recordists like to hide the mic under a tie's knot. Most recordists prefer not to place mics under clothing whenever possible. (Robert Brun)

Wireless (Radio) Microphones

To allow the camera and subject greater freedom of movement, a *wireless*, or *radio, microphone* can be used. A wireless isn't really a mic at all, just a radio transmitter and receiver. In a typical film or video shoot, a lavalier mic is clipped on the subject, plugged into the concealed transmitter that's about the size of a pack of cards. A receiver mounted on the recorder or camera picks up the signal with a short antenna. Wireless sound quality may not be as high as with *hard-wired mics* (mics connected by cables), but some wireless systems are excellent and are used regularly in professional productions. High-end systems can cost thousands, although much more affordable wireless systems costing a few hundred dollars are surprisingly good. Some systems are digital, others analog, and some combine both technologies.

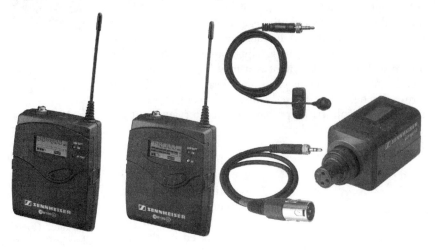

Fig. 10-26. Wireless mic. Sennheiser Evolution system with bodypack transmitter, receiver, lavalier mic, XLR cable, and plug-on transmitter for handheld mics. This affordable UHF wireless system offers a wide choice of frequency bands so you can avoid radio interference. (Sennheiser Electronic Corp.)

Using a wireless opens up many possibilities for both fiction and documentary shooting. You never need to compromise camera angles for good mic placement, since the mic is always close to the subject but out of view. In unscripted documentaries, there are great advantages to letting the subject move independently, without being constantly followed by a recordist wielding a long microphone. Some people feel uncomfortable wearing a wireless, knowing that whatever they say, even in another room, can be heard. As a courtesy, show the person wearing the mic where the off switch is. Some recordists object to the way radio mics affect sound

Fig. 10-27. Lectrosonics wireless receiver with super-miniature transmitter. Lectro makes some systems for the DV market, but many are very high-quality, expensive units for pros. (Lectrosonics, Inc.)

perspective: Unlike typical sound recording, when the subject turns or walks away from the camera wearing a wireless, the sound does not change.

A wireless transmitter and receiver can be used for many purposes: to connect a handheld mic, a standard boom mic, or a mic mixer to the camera or recorder; or to transmit timecode or a headphone feed on the set.

Wireless transmission is not completely reliable. Depending on the physical obstructions and competing radio transmissions in the area, wireless signals may carry up to several hundred feet or they may be blocked altogether. Many newer wireless systems operate in the UHF bands, which may have less interference than VHF bands. It's important to find a transmitting frequency that isn't being used by a local television station or taxi company (unless you want the sound of a cabbie in your movie). Newer wireless systems usually offer a choice of frequencies (and are called "frequency agile"). Talk to a recordist or dealer to find the frequencies that are likely to be interference-free in the area where you're shooting; lists of open frequencies should be available on the Web. Some radio mics are sold with a particular subset of frequencies; get the band that works best in your area.

When there's interference or loss of signal, you can get a loud noise on the track. Some systems broadcast on more than one frequency simultaneously to avoid breakup. "Diversity" radio mics use multiple antennas for the same reason. Inexpensive consumer wireless systems can get interference from many household sources. Avoid electric motors, computer monitors, and other electronic interference. Make sure the *squelch* control is properly adjusted to prevent noise when the radio signal is lost.

Always position the receiving antenna as close to the transmitter as possible. If the signal breaks up, experiment with different antenna positions. Make sure the transmitter antenna is straight. Some systems use very short stub antennas and some use longer ones. Run a long one around the belt line or up the subject's back (clip it on clothing near the shoulder and hide it under a coat or sweater; use a rubber band between the clip and the antenna for strain relief). Antennas sometimes work best if dangled away from the body.

Check and/or replace transmitter and receiver batteries every few hours.

Most professional wireless transmitters use a limiter (see p. 423) to prevent excess volume levels. Many models have a level adjustment and some have a light to indicate excess volume. With the subject speaking normally, turn the level up until the light flashes often, then turn it down a bit (for more on level adjustments, see Chapter 11).

Wireless receivers can be mounted directly on a camera with various brackets or plates. For handheld work with a small camera, this may increase the camera's weight noticeably, especially when more than one receiver is used.[13] You can also put receivers on your belt or in a shoulder bag with a wire to the camera (see Fig. 11-1). It's important to match the output level of the receiver to the audio input on the camera or recorder. Some receivers work at line level, others at mic level, and some are switchable. For more on this, see Mic and Line Level, p. 401, and Gain Structure, p. 423.

---

13. Zaxcom makes a wireless system that can transmit two audio channels to one receiver, lightening the load a bit.

AN ALTERNATIVE TO WIRELESS. There are some very small recorders that can be placed on the subject to record independently of the camera. These include MiniDisc recorders and some small Flash memory recorders, such as the Zaxcom ZFR100 (see Fig. 10-10). These could be used if you don't have a wireless, if you don't have enough transmitters, or if radio reception is poor. You need to sync the audio in editing (see Recording Double System for Film and Video, p. 434). The ZFR100 can be controlled wirelessly with the camera's timecode signal, allowing remote start and stop from the camera and auto syncing in the editing room.

Field Mixers

A *field mixer* or *microphone mixer* allows you to take inputs from various audio sources, combine and control them, and then output the signal to a camera or recorder. A mic mixer could be used to control a single boom mic (see Fig. 1-16) or to balance multiple mics (such as combining a wireless with a boom mic). Sometimes when recording a person giving a speech in a lecture hall, instead of using your own mics you get a house feed from the facility's public address system. A field mixer can be used to control that signal before recording it.

Fig. 10-28. Portable microphone mixer. Shure FP33 stereo mixer is usually mounted in a carrying case. See Fig. 1-16. (Shure Brothers, Inc.)

Most mixers have two or more input channels to control the level of different inputs and one or more master faders to control the level of the combined output. Many mixers have a tone generator for recording a reference tone (see p. 421). For more on mixer controls, see p. 630.

Microphone Power

The electric power needed to run a condenser microphone may come from a battery in the mic or on the cable. Power may also come from the mic preamp (sometimes called just a "mic pre") in the camera, recorder, or mixer; the most common version of this method is 48-volt *phantom power* (the mic input is often labeled "+48V"; see Fig. 10-29).[14] Phantom power frees you from carrying an extra set of often expensive batteries for the mic. Always check that your mic is compatible with the power supply before plugging it in or you could damage the mic (dynamic

---

14. Another flavor of phantom power is 12V *T-power*.

mics and some condensers—especially those that have their own batteries—should not be used with the +48V setting).

On some recorders, if the microphone input is set up for phantom powering, it will not accept dynamic mics or condensers that have their own power; but on many machines it can be switched either way. Phantom powering sometimes involves rewiring microphone cables to reverse or "flip" the phase, making them not interchangeable with normally wired cables.

AUDIO CONNECTIONS

Microphones, mixers, and recorders can be connected in various ways. Not all are compatible and may need an adaptor or device to make the connection work. It's worth learning the names of connectors used for audio cables. All connectors have male and female forms; the male is sometimes called the *plug*, the female, the *jack* (see Figs. 10-12 and 10-30).

Mic and Line Level

The audio inputs on many cameras and recorders can be switched between *mic level* for taking signals directly from microphones and *line level* for connecting other types of audio equipment. Professional gear may have a three-way switch: "line," "mic," and "mic +48V" (see above). On some machines, there are separate sets of inputs and outputs at mic and line level. Some systems have a *trim control* to tweak the level of an input up or down to better match the source to the recorder.

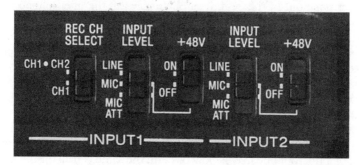

Fig. 10-29. Audio input selector on a Sony camcorder. Note choice of input level including Line, Mic, and Mic ATT (short for attenuator, this reduces the level by 20 dB for loud situations). When mic input is selected, you can choose +48 volt for condenser mics that require phantom power or select Off for self-powered condensers and dynamic mics. (Sony Electronics, Inc.)

If you have a choice, it's generally advantageous to use line inputs and outputs to connect mixers, recorders, and wireless receivers. The line level is much stronger than mic level and is less susceptible to interference. Never plug a line-level signal into a mic-level input or damage could result. If you plug a mic-level signal into a line-level input, the signal will be weak, but you may be able to boost it enough to be usable.

Another thing to keep in mind is that line level comes in a professional version (+4 dBu) and a lower-powered consumer version (which may be indicated as -10 dBv.)[15] This means that if you plug the line output of a consumer camera into the line input of a professional deck, the signal may be too quiet and possibly noisy. Going the other way (from the line output of a professional machine to the line input of a consumer machine), the signal may be too loud and possibly distorted. A *line pad* or *attenuator* can be used to reduce signal level. Also, professional line outputs are usually balanced, while consumer line outputs are usually unbalanced (see below).

Balanced Cables

Interference and hum from nearby power lines, automobile engines, fluorescent lights, and radio stations can be a problem. The best solution is to use a microphone and recorder that are connected by a *balanced cable*. In a balanced mic cable, the two wires of a standard cable are enclosed in a sheath-like third wire that insulates them from electric interference (see Fig. 10-30). Balanced cables can usually be recognized by the three contacts, instead of two, in the connectors at either end. Most professional audio gear that has balanced inputs or outputs uses either XLR cables or cables with three-contact ¼-inch plugs (also known as *TRS* for *Tip, Ring, Sleeve*). If a piece of equipment has only RCA or mini-connectors, these are not balanced inputs. If you connect a balanced mic cable to an unbalanced cable or unbalanced input using an adaptor, the signal will not be balanced.

Whenever you get electrical interference, try moving the recorder or the cable to another position. In the field, it can help to wrap the microphone cable, especially the connectors, or even the recorder, in aluminum foil. Sometimes when you connect two pieces of equipment, a low (50 Hz or 60 Hz) humming sound results if either piece is plugged into the AC wall current. If this happens, connect a ground wire between the case of one machine and the case of the other or ground them both to a common point.

Impedance

Impedance is a measure of the resistance of any audio device to the flow of electric current. Impedance, sometimes represented by Z, is measured in *ohms*. The impedance of a microphone may be low or high; the same is true for the microphone input on the mixer or recorder. Usually, professional microphones with XLR connectors have low impedance. It is important to use a low-impedance mic with a low-impedance mic input, or a high with a high. Exact matching is not necessary.

Historically, low impedance was 600 ohms (often written 600 Ω) or less, while high-impedance devices were around 10,000 (10k) ohms or more. Today many mics and camera inputs have impedances in the 100 Ω to 2,000 Ω range and most modern mics, cameras, and recorders should work fine together.

Low-impedance equipment is preferable because it allows you to use up to

---

15. The consumer version is actually about 12 dB lower than pro level (it uses a different dB scale).

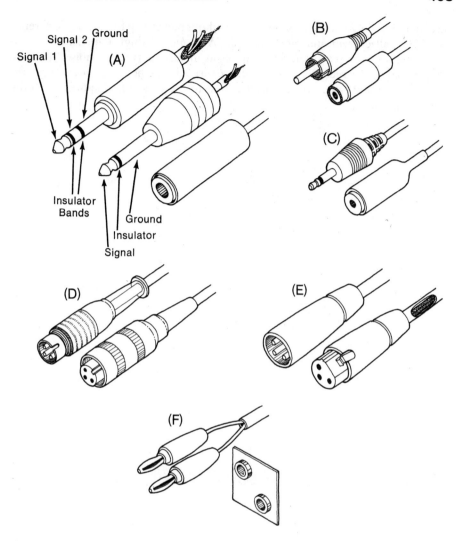

Fig. 10-30. Audio connectors. (A) ¼-inch males and female. A three-contact (also called TRS) stereo plug is at left, a two-contact (TS) mono plug is in the center. The three-contact version can be used for balanced cables. (B) *RCA* or *phono* male and female. (C) *Mini-phone* or simply mini male and female. This is a miniaturized version of the ¼-inch connector (diameter is ⅛-inch instead of ¼-inch). There is a stereo version of this plug, recognizable by the two black insulator bands (see A). (D) Three-pin *Tuchel* male and female. The sleeve on the female engages the threads on the male. This Tuchel is a variant of a *DIN* connector. (E) Three-pin *XLR* or *Cannon* connectors. The male and female snap together. Both XLR and Tuchel connectors may have more than three pins. The female XLR is pictured with the insulation cut away to show the balanced or stereo cable with the two signal wires encased in the sheath-like ground. (F) *Banana* plugs and jacks. For more audio and video connectors, see Figs. 3-12, 5-14, and 10-12. (Carol Keller)

several hundred feet of microphone cable without picking up hum and interference from AC wall current and radio stations. With *high-Z* (high impedance) equipment, lengths over six to ten feet may result in various types of noise. If you're using an old mic or recorder and impedances are mismatched, use a *matching transformer* on the mic cable. Try to put it closest to the piece of equipment with the higher impedance.

CHAPTER 11

Sound Recording Techniques

This chapter is about methods of audio recording for video and film. See Chapter 10 for discussion of audio recording equipment.

PREPARING FOR A SHOOT

GATHERING GEAR

Lists of useful audio equipment for a video or film shoot appear on p. 322. Here are some considerations in choosing audio equipment.

Recorders and Formats

When shooting video, the choice of camcorder or VTR format is usually driven by picture needs, but it clearly has an impact on sound as well. In selecting a system, you must consider: How many audio tracks do you need? Does the camcorder allow manual adjustment of audio levels? Can you use external mics? Are there professional mic connectors (such as XLR) or will you need adaptors? If you're working with a sound recordist, will you need a mic mixer so he or she can control levels? Does the camera record audio in a highly compressed format or with a low sample rate that might compromise quality?

For film or double-system video shoots, the recordist has more freedom in choosing a recorder. This decision should be made on the basis of what features are needed, the cost, and how postproduction will be done. You must choose between digital and analog, with timecode or without. Many of the questions mentioned above apply here as well. How many tracks do you need? Can you easily input professional-type mics? If recording digitally, what format will you use? How will files be exported from the recorder for archive and postproduction? Do you have enough storage media? How will the deck be powered in the field? Do you need a shoulder case? Are the controls easily readable in daylight? Sometimes when a recorder is too small, or has badly arranged controls, it may be hard to use in high-pressure situations.

Spare batteries, fuses, and an AC power connection for the recorder should be kept on hand.

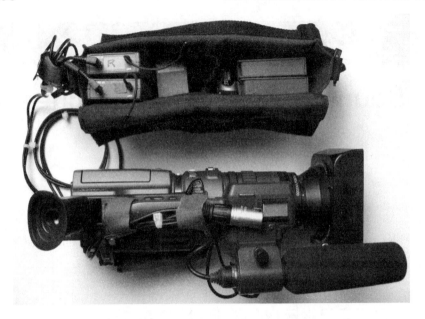

Fig. 11-1. A shooting kit. Portabrace makes a small shoulder pouch that's just the right size for spare tapes and batteries. Shown here, two wireless receivers are connected by cables to the camera, but sit in the pouch to keep the weight off the camera. A hard disk drive could be carried in a similar way.

Microphones

Unless you can carry several mics, your choice of a primary microphone is very important. Many recordists prefer a somewhat directional microphone (a hyper-cardioid, like the Sennheiser ME-66), which can exclude some background sound but is excellent for general uses. This type of mic is good for unpredictable documentary or dramatic scenes. Some recordists prefer a super-cardioid (long shotgun) mic, like the Sennheiser MKH-70. This mic allows you to stand farther back from the subject and is good for isolating voices in noisy environments, such as a train station or a parade. Some long shotgun mics are very big and awkward. In documentary work, subjects can find them intimidating. Also, a long shotgun is often too directional for recording in tight quarters (see Directionality, p. 391).

Modular microphone systems allow you to use one power supply with several heads of varying directionality (omni, cardioid and hyper-cardioid; see Fig. 10-17). This provides a great deal of flexibility. There are modular systems at both ends of the price range.

Always try to have at least one backup microphone and cable as insurance. If the second microphone is more directional or less directional than your primary mic, you'll have more flexibility. Lavalier mics (see p. 396) are very small, pack easily, and can be used for general recording in some situations.

In many shooting situations, a microphone boom is essential to allow the mic to be positioned close to the sound source while keeping the person holding the mic out of the shot. Typically, recordists carry extendible booms that can be adjusted for each shot. Studio mic booms are mounted on a pedestal to relieve the boom person of the considerable fatigue that results from holding a boom all day. For smaller, mobile crews, borrow a stand from a lighting kit and get a bracket so you can mount the boom on it; this is particularly useful for situations such as sit-down interviews or scenes in a drama in which actors aren't moving.

In some documentary scenes, the boom may be too big or intrusive. The mic can be handheld (with or without a pistol grip shock mount) for more intimate situations. A short table stand for the mic can be handy at times.

Headphones

The choice of headphones is also important. For controlled shooting situations, it makes sense to get headphones that have good fidelity and closed ear pads that fit around the ear. These block any sounds coming directly to the recordist without having gone through the microphone first, so you can be sure of the recording without being misled by other sounds around you. Open headphones are lightweight and more comfortable. They usually rest on top of the ear (*supra-aural*). With these, you may not hear some defects that will be apparent on a better sound system. Sometimes sound leaking out of these headphones may be picked up by the mic.

One problem with headphones that fit around the ear for unstaged documentary filming, especially when a directional microphone is used, is that the recordist

Fig. 11-2. (upper left) Headphones with closed earpads. (upper right) Headphones with open earpads. (bottom) Mono earpiece shown with mono connector; stereo-to-mono adaptor (so you can hear both channels from the camcorder); and right-angle adaptor (so the plug doesn't stick out from the camcorder).

can hear only sounds he or she expects to hear; if someone speaks outside the mic's range of sensitivity, the recordist will not hear or react to it. Some documentary recordists just put the headphone over one ear so they can better relate to people and react to events.

Some camcorders have a small speaker at the operator's ear. All cameras can be used with a wired earpiece that goes in one ear. These allow you to respond to what's going on around you and are not obtrusive. They aren't great for close monitoring of the sound (it's easy to be fooled by what you hear in the *other* ear that's hearing the scene without the earpiece) but you'll hear major problems like breakup or loss of audio.

Stereo headphones should be used with a mono adaptor when you are recording only one channel of audio so that you can hear it in both ears. Some headphone outputs can be switched to mono for that purpose. A mono earpiece may need a stereo adaptor if you're recording stereo so you can hear both channels.

Other Equipment

A typical professional video package includes a field mixer (see p. 400). Get a *breakaway cable* with a *headphone return* line in it. This allows the recordist to monitor the sound coming from the camcorder (as a check that the signal is really there), and breaks apart easily so the camera and sound recordist can separate quickly.

One or more wireless microphone systems (see p. 397) will greatly increase your mobility and flexibility for both film and video shoots.

Fig. 11-3. External DVD burner. Addonics model can transfer data stored in ten different types of Flash media directly to DVD or CD, or record video to disc via a USB port. (Addonics Technologies, Inc.)

Recordist's Tools and Supplies

Having a few tools at hand can mean the difference between easily finishing a shoot and canceling it. Many repairs are very simple. After phoning and consulting a technician, even inexperienced persons can often make adjustments or isolate what needs to be repaired or replaced.

For any system:
> Permanent felt-tip marker (e.g., Sharpies)
> Small roll of gaffer's tape
> Spare batteries for recorder and mic
> Sound report sheets or log

For video recorder or DAT:
> Head-cleaning cassette

For digital recorder:
> Flash memory cards
> CDs or DVDs for backup
> External FireWire drive

For open-reel or analog recorders:
> Head-cleaning fluid or isopropyl (rubbing) alcohol
> Cotton swabs or head-cleaning sticks
> Spare take-up reel and reel retainer nut
> Single-edge razor blades (for breaking tape)

For repairs:
> Swiss Army knife with scissors
> Screwdriver handle and detachable blades: two sets, medium and jeweler's size
> Small needle-nose pliers with wire-cutting edge
> Small volt/ohm meter ("multitester")
> Battery-operated soldering iron, rosin-core solder
> Short length of light wire
> Fuses for the recorder or camera
> Head demagnetizer (for analog tape heads)

Preparing the Recorder

Equipment should be checked thoroughly before using. This is especially important if it has been transported, used by someone else, or come from the rental house. School equipment is more likely to be malfunctioning than working properly. Many recordists check their equipment whenever they arrive at a new location for shooting. The preparation you do depends a lot on the particular technology you're using. If anything in this list is unfamiliar, look elsewhere in this chapter and in Chapter 10.

1. *Clean the heads.* This should be done as a matter of course for analog recorders (see p. 388); for camcorders and DAT machines, it may not be necessary unless there's evidence of a problem. For hard drive and memory card recorders, this does not apply.

2. *Check the batteries.* If possible this should be done with the machine rolling in "record" position to see how the batteries read under load. Many rechargeable batteries will read fairly high on the meter until they are ready to give out, then the voltage drops sharply, so be prepared if the reading seems at all low. See Batteries and Power Supplies, p. 130, for more on managing batteries.

3. *Check the settings.* There are numerous settings; here are a few to check: Is the limiter or AGC on or off? If recording digitally, what about sample rate,

bit depth, file formats? Scan through physical switches and menu selections. Check the manual if you're unsure about any settings.

4. ***Timecode and/or pilot.*** For a timecode-capable deck, make sure that the timecode can be properly recorded and played back. On analog sync recorders, check that the pilot signal is actually being recorded on tape.

5. ***Microphones.*** Do you have cables? Windscreen? Various clips for lavs? Are the recorder inputs set correctly for mic level (and phantom power if needed)? Wireless mics should be checked for clear radio channels (without interference) and fresh batteries.

6. ***Test the audio.*** Do a test recording, which you can erase when you begin recording for real. Check the meter. Make sure you can move the level control without causing static. If not, moving the control rapidly back and forth a few times can help. Set the headphone level adjustment, if there is one. Gently move the recorder, cable, and microphone while listening through headphones to be sure there are no loose connections. This should not produce noise or static. Play back the recording and listen carefully for any defects. If the sound is muddy on an analog deck, try cleaning the heads. If the sound doesn't improve, this may indicate that the heads need demagnetizing.

If you can't get the recorder to work properly, systematically isolate various components. Try a different mic or mic cable; plug the mic into a different input; make sure the recorder is not in "pause"; check the AC/battery power switch (if there is one); try running the recorder on AC power; try cleaning the battery contacts with an eraser or grit-free abrasive, and so on.

Before going out to shoot, coil up excess cabling and fasten with Velcro cable ties (see Fig. 11-4). Make the recorder and/or mixer package as neat and compact as possible. It's much easier to concentrate on recording if you can move without getting tangled up. For handheld work, carry the recorder on the side of you that allows easiest access to the controls and the meter, and put some padding under the strap to spread the load. Wear soft-soled shoes and clothing that doesn't rustle.

Fig. 11-4. Cable tie. This Velcro fastener can be used to keep coiled cables under control. (Fletcher Chicago/The Rip Tie Company)

Recordists on feature films often use a *sound cart* as a platform for mounting the recorder, mixer, and accessories that can be wheeled between setups (see Fig. 1-42).

THE SOUND RECORDIST'S ROLE

The sound recordist is responsible for placing the microphones (although someone else may hold them), operating the recorder or mixer, and making sure that the quality of the recording is good. For staged (controlled) work, the recordist, who is sometimes called the *mixer*, can usually experiment with various mic positions and monitor the level of a rehearsal before shooting begins.

On video shoots, the recordist usually does not control the camcorder, but he or she must ensure that the sound actually recorded in the camera is acceptable. When possible, this means monitoring from the camera with headphones and/or doing periodic playback to check the recording.

For unstaged documentary shooting, the recordist should be alert and attentive to the action and not be glued to the meters. With time, your judgment will make you less dependent on the meter.

Recordists should be respectful of actors or subjects when placing body mics. Some recordists bring a newspaper to the set and pretty much tune out when they're not recording. Try not to "disappear" on set. Staying alert will help you and others do their jobs. On some sets, people in the sound department are treated like second-class citizens. The recordist may be forced to find mic positions only after all the lighting and blocking is done, making his job harder. He may also be blamed for airplanes flying over and the dog barking next door.

Communication

On all productions, crew members must communicate with each other. The camera operator must be able to signal to the recordist (or boom person) that he is in the frame, and the recordist must be able to indicate his need to change position. Sometimes in documentary work, only the recordist can hear whether a scene is worthy of being filmed. For all of these reasons, the filmmakers should have a set of signals with which to communicate silently. If these are hand signals, they should be sent with minimal commotion, so as not to disturb actors or documentary subjects. This requires that crew members watch each other as well as the action. The recordist, or whoever is operating the microphone, should not position himself on the camera operator's blind side (which is usually the right), and the camera operator should frequently open her other eye so that she can see the recordist while shooting. This is most important when filming improvised or unstaged action. After a crew works together for a while they begin to predict each other's needs, and eye contact precludes the need for hand signals.

If circumstances are such that a good-quality recording can't be made, the recordist should say so. If an airplane makes a take unusable, tell the director when the take is over (some directors want you to signal the problem during the take; smart directors will be looking at you as soon as they hear the plane). The director must decide whether to try to salvage a take with ADR or other postproduction cures (hence the solution for every conceivable production problem: "We'll fix it in the mix!").

Organization and Logging

It's generally part of the recordist's job to organize and label tapes or other recording media, to prepare the media to be recorded, and to keep a report or log of what's been recorded.

LABELING AND MANAGING MEDIA. Videotapes should be clearly labeled with the name of the production title, production company, tape number, date, frame rate, timecode type (drop or nondrop), timecode start, reference tone level (see below) and any special track assignments (such as LAVALIER CH. 1., BOOM MIC CH. 2).

Whenever a separate audio recorder is used, in addition to the above information, also indicate the camera roll or tape number, name of recordist and, when applicable, sample rate, bit depth, timecode frame rate (also indicating drop or nondrop), tape speed, and/or type of sync signal (for example, 60 Hz pilot). This information can additionally be spoken into the microphone and recorded.

When recording audio to file with a hard drive or Flash memory system, care must be taken in organizing file names, keeping track of drives, memory cards, or optical discs, making backups, and all the other details that will prevent the disaster of losing irreplaceable recordings due to carelessness or a corrupted file.

If recording to tape, develop a system to keep track of which tapes have been recorded and which are fresh (if you reuse tape, it is especially easy to get confused). Cassettes have little record-inhibit tabs that should be pushed in after recording to prevent accidental rerecording. Analog audio cassettes have small tabs on the edge opposite the one where you see the tape that can be punched to prevent accidental recording. These tabs can be plugged up or taped over later if you want to rerecord the tape.

When shooting film and recording on audiotape, whenever a camera roll is changed partway through the sound roll, an announcement should be made on the tape.

A reference tone should usually be recorded at the head of every videotape, audiotape, or other recording. This is discussed on p. 421.

For double-system recording, slates are generally used to sync sound and picture and to provide information on scene and take number. See Recording Double System for Film and Video, p. 434.

LOGGING. For a video shoot, someone may be assigned to keep logs of each take (see Keeping a Log, p. 363). On a double-system film or video shoot, the sound recordist often keeps a *sound report*, which is a written log of each take, noting the length, any problems, and whether the director considers the take good or bad (similar to the camera report in Fig. 9-31). On some productions, a *sound take number* is given each time you record audio (and is included on the slate). This identifies each piece of sync and wild sound. Since sound take numbers advance chronologically throughout the production (unlike scene numbers), in conjunction with the log, they aid in locating pieces of sound and picture. When recording to file using a hard drive or Flash memory recorder, the system may automatically assign a take or event number to the file name or user bits.

When recording to file, some systems can convert information in the BWF file including scene/take, time of recording, and other info to a text file such as an Avid Log Exchange file (ALE; see p. 705 for more). This can be used instead of a handwritten sound report, printed out, and/or imported into the editing system.

In unstaged documentary work, there's no time for meticulous log keeping. Instead, if a separate audio recorder is being used, the sound person should record a quick message after every shot or two, describing what was filmed, if there were problems with the slate, and so on; this can save a great deal of time in the editing room. It's a good idea to keep an informal log, listing the contents of each sound roll or group of files.

If you're recording to tape, record an announcement before sections of *wild sound* (sound recorded without picture); in some cases you may want to record wild sound to a separate tape, especially if a telecine transfer will be done. You may also want to make a verbal note when MOS shots (shots without sound) are filmed.

RECORDING TECHNIQUE

Basic Strategy

The general objective in sound recording is to place the microphone close enough to the sound source to produce a loud and clear sound track. A good track should be easily intelligible, should lack strongly competing background sounds, unpleasant echo, or distortion, and should be reasonably faithful to the tone quality of the original sound. Once a good recording is in hand, you have a great deal of freedom to alter the character of the sound later as you choose.

The ideal placement for many mics is between one and three feet in front of the person speaking, slightly above or below the level of the mouth. If the microphone is directly in line with the mouth, it may pick up popping sounds from the person breathing into it. A windscreen helps. If a directional mic is too close, it will bring out an unnatural bass tone quality. This is the *proximity effect*, which results from the particular way low frequencies interact with directional microphones. If a microphone is too far from the subject, background sound (*ambient sound*) often competes with or drowns out the speaker's voice. Also, undesirable acoustic qualities of the recording space, such as *echo* and *boominess*, become more noticeable (see Acoustics of the Recording Space, p. 425).

The microphone's position is almost always compromised by the camera's needs. It's important, however, that the sound source be solidly within the pickup pattern of the mic. Generally a boom mic will be brought in from just above the camera's frame, as close as possible without getting in the shot. The boom operator should practice during rehearsals. Be attentive to mic shadows—you may need to move away from a light to avoid them. Ask the camera operator for a frame line before the shot begins so you know how far in you can go.

Keep in mind that sound, like light, diminishes in intensity with the square of the distance (see Fig. 12-6). Thus, moving *twice* as far from the sound source diminishes the sound to *one quarter* of its previous level. If the recording level of the sound seems low, especially with respect to louder background sounds, you must get closer to the sound source and not attempt to correct the problem by turning the level way up.

Many beginners think the recordist should try to capture all sounds in a general fashion, standing back from, say, a party, a conversation, or a street scene to record all the sounds together. The result of such recordings is usually an indistinct blur. The recordist should instead select individual sounds and get close enough to record them clearly. If an overall mix of sounds is desired, it may be necessary to put together several distinct tracks later. For documentary filming in noisy conditions, you may need to get closer to the subject than you feel comfortable doing. A few experiences with scenes ruined by bad sound will help overcome shyness.

Another approach to a noisy situation is to use a lavalier mic on the subject with a wireless transmitter to get the mic in close while allowing the recordist to stand back.

Whenever you put a mic very close to the sound source it minimizes both ambient sound and the natural reverberation of sound reflecting in the recording space. In some situations, a close mic sounds artificial. For example, if the camera is filming a distant long shot and the mic is very close, the recording will lack the proper *sound perspective*. Although distorted sound perspective is found regularly in movies, you may not like it. To correct this, the recordist could move farther back, but at the risk of sacrificing clarity. Alternatively, during the sound mix you could lower the level and maybe use equalization and a little reverb to give a sense of distance to the sound (see Chapter 16). Similarly, any missing ambient sounds can be added later by mixing in additional tracks. These kinds of effects are usually handled better under the controlled conditions of sound editing than they are while making a live recording. You can always *add* background sounds, distance effects, and equalization during sound editing and mixing, but nothing can make a noisy, echoing, or weak recording sound pleasing and clear.

SETTING THE RECORDING LEVEL

One of the recordist's key jobs is controlling the volume of the recording. The loudness of sound as it passes through a camera or audio recorder is called its *level* or *gain*; this is adjusted with a control labeled *volume*, *gain*, or *level*. This control is sometimes called a *pot* (short for *potentiometer*). All prosumer and professional cameras and audio recorders have a manual control to set the recording level (some consumer cameras only have auto control). In a typical recording situation, you're controlling the level of one or more microphones.

Setting the level isn't hard. In the simplest terms, *you want to record sound as loud as you can without it being too loud*. But to know what that really means, you need to understand a few things about the nature of sound, what meters do, and the workings of your digital or analog recorder. Please see Sound, p. 368, and How Audio Is Recorded, p. 371, before reading this section.

Understanding Sound Level

Figure 11-5 shows a simplified representation of the level of a sound signal over time. Notice that the level is always changing, with peaks and valleys. The lower black line represents the *average level*. This corresponds most to how our ears perceive the *loudness* of sound.

Yet, there are peaks that rise quite a bit higher than the average. The upper black line shows the highest limit of the peaks. Peaks often come and go very quickly, so the ear may not fully perceive their loudness. However, we are very concerned with how high the peaks are because recording equipment can't tolerate peaks that are too high.

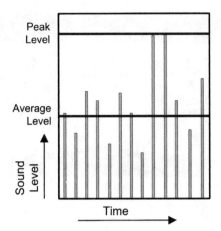

Fig. 11-5. Sound levels over time. Typical sounds contain volume peaks that are higher than the average level (how much higher depends on the sound).

The relationship of the average level to the peak level varies with the type of sound. With a "normal" male speaking voice, the peaks might be 8 to 10 dB higher than the average. With short, percussive sounds like a hammer, jangling keys, or a chirping bird, the peaks might be up to 50 dB higher than the average—a much bigger ratio.

When recording sound, we need some way to measure or meter the sound level.

The classic meter for analog equipment is the *VU (volume unit) meter*, which is found on both inexpensive and costly recorders (see Fig. 11-6). If a meter has a needle and is not identified otherwise, it's probably a VU meter (some VU meters use lights or LEDs instead of a needle). VU meters read the *average* sound level, so they provide the best reading of how loud things *sound*.[1] VU meters give an accurate reading of steady signals that don't have sharp peaks (like steady reference tones or a violin playing a long, slow note). However, VU meters are designed to respond relatively slowly to changes in sound level (you can think of the needle as being fairly "heavy"), which means that quick peaks, called *transients*, can pass by without deflecting the meter much (see Fig. 11-7). This is the problem with VU meters—they don't give a good reading of how high the peaks are.

Enter the *peak-reading meter*. Unlike the VU meter, the peak meter responds almost instantaneously to quick surges in volume and provides a reading of the *maximum* sound level. VU meters give too low a reading for fleeting sounds, like the aforementioned hammer or keys, because the volume peaks have passed by the time the needle is finished responding. The peak-reading meter, on the other hand, responds quickly enough to give an accurate reading of sounds of short duration. However, the drawback of peak meters is that the level on the meter may not correspond as well to perceived loudness. A recording with lots of quick peaks that shoot up high on the peak meter may *sound* the same as one that lacks those peaks and reads much lower on the peak meter.

1. It's worth noting that true VU meters are very costly, and the typical meters found on inexpensive gear only approximate a real VU response.

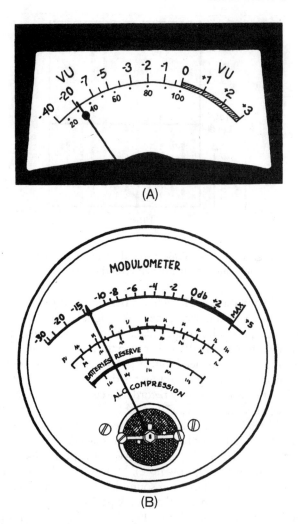

Fig. 11-6. (A) VU meter. (B) Modulometer on Nagra 4.2. Sound level is read on the top scale. (Carol Keller)

Peak meters come in various forms: an LED display; the *modulometer* found on a Nagra recorder. The *PPM* (*peak program meter*) widely used in Europe responds to transients faster than a VU meter but slower than a true peak reader (because distortion from super-short peaks may not be audible).

Many audio peaks come and go so fast that you can't actually see them on a meter. Peak meters may have a *peak hold* function, to let the meter linger a bit at the highest peaks so you can read them.[2] Some meters combine a VU meter with a peak indicator light, giving you the best of both worlds.

---

2. How quickly a meter responds to a peak, and then releases afterward is called its "ballistics." PPMs, for example, are defined by very specific ballistics, and there are a few different flavors of PPMs.

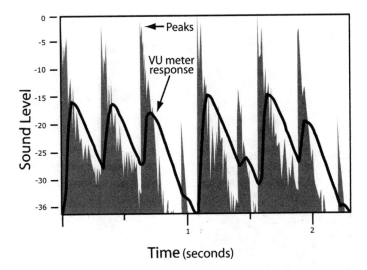

Fig. 11-7. Peak level and the VU meter. The gray area represents the sound level of a drum beat, with its short, percussive peaks. The black line is the response of a VU meter. Note that the VU meter lags behind the actual spikes in level, and doesn't rise as high or drop as low as the quick peaks and valleys. The VU meter indicates an average level that gives a good sense of how loud something sounds, but is often significantly lower than the actual peaks. (From http://en.wikipedia.org/wiki/VU_Meter)

Average and peak: Keep these two concepts in mind when you record sound. We care about the average level because that's closest to how things sound. And we care about peaks, because a signal with too much level causes recording problems (as described below). Meters can help you if used correctly, but in the end, your ears tell you more about level than a meter can.

Digital Level

The peak meters found on digital cameras or recorders typically start at 0 dB at the top of the scale and range down to a negative number like –60 or less at the bottom (see Fig. 11-8). In digital recording, 0 dB represents *all* the digital bits being used; there is nothing higher. This is *full scale*. The units on the meter are marked as "dB" and represent *dBFS* or *decibels full scale*. You could think of them as decibels *below* full scale—the number tells you how close you are to the top. You *never* want the signal to actually reach 0 dB because anything above this level will be clipped and distorted.

As a general rule, you want to record the signal as high (loud) as you can. This provides the best dynamic range and keeps the sound signal as far from the noise floor as possible. In film and video production, sound levels are always readjusted during editing and mixing, so even if you record a sound loudly in the field, you can always make it quiet later if that's called for (see Fig. 11-9).

So, the goal is to set the level in the camera or recorder relatively high, without letting the signal reach 0 dB. How best to do that depends on your equipment, the sound, and your preferences.

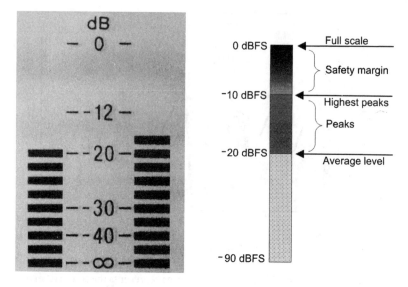

Fig. 11-8. (left) Digital peak reading meter found on Sony camcorder. The left channel reads −20 dBFS. (right) Rough guidelines for setting the level during field recording. Different situations call for different levels.

With professional recording for broadcast in the United States, the level is often set so that the average level of voices or music on the peak meter reads around −20 dBFS or so and the loudest peaks don't go above −10 dBFS. This leaves a safety margin of 10 dB before reaching the top, in case of any sudden, hotter (louder) peaks (see Fig. 11-8). If you're looking for a simple rule to follow, this should work fine in most situations.

With consumer and prosumer machines that have more noise and less dynamic range, the level is sometimes set higher, to stay farther away from the noise floor. The average level may be set to −12 dBFS, which leaves less *headroom* or safety margin in case of a loud peak.[3] You might use this level when capturing tapes into an editing system, as you can redo anything that goes too high.

Many recordists use a limiter as a matter of course with digital recordings to protect against high peaks (see p. 423).

Digital meters often have a clipping indicator or "over" light to show when peaks hit 0 dB; sometimes these light up just *before* you hit 0. Some systems *only* have a peaking indicator. In this case, turn the level up until the light comes on frequently, then reduce the level until the light stops flashing on. Some digital equipment has VU meters (see p. 420).

With any recorder, be attentive to the type of sound and how high the peaks are.

---

3. The idea of "safety margin" as used above is the difference between the highest peaks and the maximum level the system can record without distortion. "Headroom," however, is usually defined as the difference between the *average* signal level and the system maximum. If you're recording the average program level at −20 dBFS with peaks up to −10 dBFS, you have 20 dB of headroom, but only 10 dB of "safety margin."

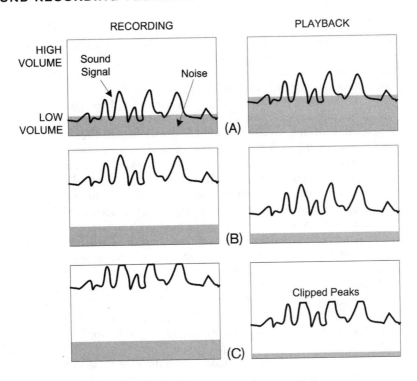

Fig. 11-9. Setting the recording level. The sound signal is what we want; the interfering noise could come from the recording system, the recording environment, or, with analog recorders, tape noise. (A) If the sound signal is recorded at a low level—near the level of the noise—when the volume is increased to a medium level in playback, the competing noise gets louder too. (B) If the signal is recorded as loudly as possible without over-recording, you can lower the volume in playback and the noise level will diminish as well. (C) If the level is set so high in recording that the signal is distorted, it will still be distorted in playback even if the level is reduced later (note the clipped peaks).

If you're filming a scene of two characters having a fight, the dialogue might go from low mumbles to loud shouts (with a few smashed dishes along the way). In situations like this in which dynamic range is high, you might want to keep the level lower than normal to protect against unexpected peaks. This is a situation in which a good limiter can help.

On the other hand, when you're recording something very even and predictable, you can nudge the level higher without risking over-recording.

If your recorder has an adjustment for headphone volume, set it at a comfortable level and leave it there. This will help you record consistent levels, and when you're in a situation in which it's difficult to watch the meter, it will help you to estimate proper recording level by the way things sound in the headphones.

Analog Level

With analog tape recording, the same rule applies as for digital: You want to record sounds as loudly as possible without over-recording. However, the rule is interpreted slightly differently.

Analog machines typically have a VU meter (or a version of one) with a scale that goes from about −40 VU to +3 or +6 with a bold change in the color or thickness of the markings at the 0 VU point (see Fig. 11-6).

For normal recording, the level should be set so that the highest deflections of the meter read up to 0 VU. Though most recordists are careful to avoid letting the needle pass the 0 dB mark, it's usually the case with analog recording that occasional, loud peaks can go to +3 or even more without causing problems. With analog tape recording, there isn't a fixed top level as in digital, where the sound is *sure* to be distorted. When there's too much level, all the particles in the tape become magnetized (called tape *saturation*), and the sound may become crackly or harsh or seem to break up. The actual point of over-recording and distortion is really determined by the type of sound, the recorder's amplifier, and the tape being used. Some sounds may read a few decibels above the zero point without serious distortion, some will distort, and some will not be badly harmed by the crackle and breakup produced (a gunshot, for example).

Another difference with analog is at the lower end of the scale, where quiet sounds are recorded: There's a lot more noise. All magnetic tape has inherent noise. Even a *virgin* tape straight out of the package will play back a hissing noise. When sound is recorded on tape it must be louder than the tape noise to be audible. Ideally it should be a lot louder so that the tape noise can be heard only as a quiet background during pauses in the sound signal. Both digital and analog recordings can have noise from the physical space where the microphone is, and from the circuits in the mic and the recorder—but only analog has a problem with *tape* noise.

Overall, compared to digital recording, with analog you can be a little less worried about over-recording but you should be a little more careful about not recording things too quietly.

If you're using a VU meter, keep in mind that the actual peaks will be higher than the meter indicates (see Fig. 11-7). So if you're recording percussive sounds like the hammer, chirping bird, or jangling keys, don't turn the level control way up to try to get them to read high on the scale. Many types of sounds will record just fine even though the VU meter is only in the middle or even lower part of its range.

Some analog machines have peak-reading meters. With Nagra's modulometer, a typical recording might be in the −8 to −1 dB range; this is easy to remember because the needle will be roughly in a vertical position. If the level goes above 0 dB, lower it somewhat.

Whether you use a VU meter or a peak-reading meter, many analog recorders only inform you of the level of the signal as it goes to the record head, not what is *actually taking place on the tape*.[4] Tape stocks vary in noise and saturation levels. Whether or not you are under- or over-recording can only really be determined by listening to the tape playback with good headphones or a good speaker.

4. Nagras are an exception; you can switch the headphones and meter to "tape" for confidence monitoring.

Reference Tone

To help ensure that recordings are played back at the proper level, a *reference tone* (also called a *line up tone*) is recorded at the beginning of a tape or session. This helps you or others calibrate the playback level to match the level of the original recording. Many pro or prosumer recorders, mixers, and cameras have a *tone generator* or *oscillator* that can make a steady tone, typically at 1 kHz. You may have a choice of tone level, often between −12 dBFS and −20 dBFS. The idea is to use a tone level that corresponds to the average level at which you recorded (the *program level*). Though the idea is simple enough, it can get complicated because of different types of equipment and different styles of recording.

- As noted above, a standard approach for professional digital video recording in the United States is to record the average program level around −20 dBFS with peaks no higher than −10 dBFS. In this case, set the reference tone to −20 dBFS. This is a level that postproduction houses and broadcasters are used to working with and should result in fairly consistent levels. The −20 tone equates to 0 VU on a VU meter.
- When using a VU meter, tone is typically set at 0 VU. Peaks are not allowed to exceed +3 or sometimes +6 dB.
- When using a Nagra recorder, tone is typically set at −8 dB on the modulometer.
- In Europe and the U.K., −18 dBFS is often used instead of −20 dBFS as the reference level; peaks are kept under −10 dBFS.[5]
- As noted above, sometimes people record at −12 dBFS average level with prosumer cameras (and also sometimes with editing systems or in other postproduction situations with mixed tracks). In this case, use a line up tone at −12 dBFS. However, if you do so, a dub house or broadcaster may think the peaks are too high, or, if they don't bother checking and just assume the tone was recorded at −20, they may make the sound too low.

It is *very important* when recording a reference tone that you indicate in writing (and sometimes as a spoken message on the tape) what level the tone is recorded at, how high the peaks are above it, and what kind of meter you used. If you use a nonstandard tone, be sure to discuss it with anyone involved in postproduction sound or dub work.

Reference tones are just that—a reference. Just because a tone is recorded at the start of a tape or program doesn't mean the levels are correct throughout.

Some Recording Guidelines

In general, recordings sound better if the level is not changed in a noticeable way during the recording. This may mean, for example, setting the level at a compromise position between the loud and soft voices of two people talking. (Another solution might be to move the microphone closer to the soft-spoken person.) Try to anticipate surges in volume, choosing perhaps to under-record slightly an orator

---

5. In Europe, meter layouts vary. Reference tone may be +4 on a BBC PPM meter or 100 percent on a peak meter.

whose every sentence is greeted with loud cheers from the audience. This is another situation where a good limiter could be helpful (see below).

Often, a certain amount of level adjustment (called "riding the gain" or "riding the pot") is called for. Try to make level changes between lines of dialogue, not during them; if you have to reset during a line, adjusting the level gently and not suddenly will be less disturbing.

Try to maintain consistency in your tracks. If you're recording a scene in a drama, try to keep the characters at roughly the same level so they can be edited together without a lot of level changes.

When recording a single mic with a two-track (or more) recorder or camera, some recordists use the second track as insurance against over-recording. Record the mic on one track at full level. Also route the mic to the second track, but set the level on this track -6 dB lower (or even lower than that). This second track is used only if the first one is too hot. Be sure to write down that you've done this and record the reference tone on the second track at normal level *before* turning the level down.

When quiet sounds seem under-recorded, don't turn the level control beyond three fourths of its full range, as this will usually add system noise. Instead, get closer to the sound source. If extremely loud sounds (like live rock music) require that the level control be set at less than one fourth of its range, this too may degrade the sound signal. If this is the case, get an *attenuator*, or *line pad*, to place on the cable between the microphone and the recorder (some mics and recorders have built-in attenuators, see Fig. 10-29). The attenuator cuts down the strength of the signal.

Automatic Level Control

Many audio and video recorders are equipped with some form of automatic control of recording level. The names for the various types of automatic systems are not entirely standardized. Some types work better than others, but often the effectiveness depends more on the sophistication of the particular camera or recorder than on the type used.

AUTOMATIC GAIN CONTROL. *Automatic gain control (AGC)* or *automatic level control (ALC)* works by automatically choosing a predetermined recording level. If the sound signal coming in is too quiet, it will be boosted; and if it is too loud, the gain will be reduced. AGC requires no attention on the part of the operator, and it can be quite effective for straightforward recording in which the sound level doesn't vary too much. However, some AGC devices don't handle sudden volume changes well. Say you're recording someone in a kitchen. While he speaks, the level is fine, but when he stops, the AGC responds to the quiet by boosting the gain, bringing the sound of the refrigerator to full prominence. AGCs sometimes have a slow *release time*, and if a sudden, loud sound occurs while someone is speaking, the recording level will drop, reducing the level of the dialogue, and return to normal some moments later.

For all these reasons, AGC gets a bad rap. Indeed, some AGCs are not very good and in most situations a competent recordist setting the level manually can do much better. However, some AGCs work well and can be a real lifesaver if you're shooting alone or in a challenging situation. Test your own system and judge for yourself.

LIMITERS AND COMPRESSORS. A *limiter* is another form of automatic control that allows you to control the basic recording level; the limiter kicks in to reduce the level only if you're in danger of over-recording. Limiters often cut in fairly sharply when the sound level gets too high, protecting against sudden volume peaks (see Fig. 16-14).[6] Some limiters work so well that they're virtually "transparent" (unnoticeable); others can produce an unnatural, flattened effect in the sound.

Some wireless mics and other systems have limiters with a flashing LED indicator instead of a meter. Turn up the gain until the indicator lights up, showing that the limiter is cutting in; then decrease the level a bit until the limiter operates only on the loudest peaks.

Limiters can be very helpful for scenes in which sound levels change suddenly. They're especially useful for digital recording where too much level is a particular problem. Limiters can be a kind of insurance policy against hot peaks, but if they're relied upon too heavily (that is, if the recording level is set so high that the limiter is constantly working), the sound may lose much of its dynamic range and seem flat and without texture. Some pros use them; others avoid them.

A *compressor* is another method used in various audio systems (including some wireless mics) for dealing with excess level. Compressors reduce the level by a certain ratio (say, 2:1 or 3:1), which compresses (reduces) the dynamic range of the sound. A *compressor/expander* (sometimes called a *compander*) compresses the dynamic range during recording—to accommodate any loud volume peaks without over-recording—and then expands the dynamic range again during playback.

For more on compressors and limiters see Level and Dynamic Range, p. 648.

Gain Structure

There are many situations in which you want to use two pieces of audio gear together. For example, using a wireless mic with a camcorder. It's important to coordinate how the level is set in each, especially with analog connections. *Gain structure* or *gain-staging* refers to the process of setting the level correctly through the whole audio chain.

As a rule, you want the upstream item (say, the wireless receiver) set to output at normal full level (*unity gain*) but not so high that the sound is distorted. If you feed too low a level from the wireless to the camera, the camera will need to boost the signal, raising the noise level. If you feed a signal that's too hot, the signal will be distorted from that point forward.

In shooting, it's common to use a microphone mixer (field mixer) with a camera or audio recorder (see p. 400). Most mixers have level controls for individual channels and a master fader that controls all the tracks together. Especially when using only one channel, you generally want to avoid situations in which the channel is set low but the master is set high, which may add noise. Set the channel at a healthy level, then use the master to fine-tune the level.

---

6. The threshold point where a limiter cuts in and how much it limits the sound level varies among systems and is sometimes adjustable.

When using a field mixer, typically the recordist wants to set things up so he or she can control the level from the mixer, knowing that the camera will record correctly. Ideally, the field mixer should output to the camera using line level (see p. 401). Make sure any AGC is turned off in the camera. Turn on the mixer's tone generator and set it to 0 VU on the mixer's VU meter.[7] Then adjust the gain on the camera so the tone reads –20 dBFS on the camera's digital meter (but see p. 421 for more on reference tones). Now the recordist can adjust the level during the shoot using the mixer's meter and level control. You should still try to monitor the audio output from the camera with headphones, and check the camera's meter from time to time. The same concepts apply when using a mixer with a separate audio recorder.

LOCATION SOUND

Ambient Sound

Ambient sounds are the background sounds that surround any recording space. They can come from birds, traffic, waves, refrigerators, fluorescent lights, stereos, and the like. The best way to minimize their effect, when possible, is to eliminate them entirely. Don't shoot the birds, but do turn off refrigerators and air conditioners, and close windows facing out to the street.[8] When possible, locations should be chosen with ambient noise in mind. Try not to set up shoots underneath an airport flight path or by a busy highway. Sometimes you can get permits to block off a street while you are shooting; otherwise, plan to shoot at a quiet time of day. Heavy *sound blankets* (furniture packing pads) can be used to dampen noisy windows or air vents. These can be clipped and hung on grip stands to make a quieter space near the actors or subject.

Ideally, audible background sounds should remain consistent throughout a scene. Consistency is important for editing, since much condensing and rearranging of the movie's chronology are done at that time. An editor needs the freedom to juxtapose any two shots without worrying that the background tone may not match. The audience will tune out the gentle ambience of an electric fan, but will be aware of it if it pops in and out in every other shot. If you begin shooting a scene with the window closed, don't open it during the scene. In situations where you can't control some background sound (a neighbor's auto, for example), record some of the offending sound alone in case during editing you need to cover sections of the scene that lack it. In some cases, an inconsistency in the background sound will seem logical and doesn't need to be disguised.

Make every effort to turn off or lower any music that is audible at the filming location. Discontinuous music is a glaring sign that the chronology of shots has been changed. Recording music may also create copyright problems (see Chapter 19). If ambient music can't be eliminated, or if it is part of the scene you are filming, plan your editing around it when you shoot.

---

7. On some mixers the tone is not adjustable. Also, not all mixers have VU meters.

8. Many a crew has driven off from a location forgetting to turn the fridge back on. Recordist Frank Coakley suggests putting your car keys in it when you turn it off to remind you.

Always record thirty seconds or so of *room tone* at every location. Have everyone be quiet and stop moving while you record. Even if nothing in particular is audible at the location, every site has its distinct room tone, which is very different from the sound of pure silence or dead tape. Room tone—an expression that refers to outdoor sound as well—is used in editing to bridge gaps in the sound track, providing a consistent background.

Acoustics of the Recording Space

The size, shape, and nature of any location affects the way sound travels through it. An empty room with hard, smooth walls is acoustically *live*, reflecting sound and causing some echoing. Bathrooms are often very acoustically live; sound may reverberate in them for a second or more before dying out (try singing in the shower). A room with carpets, furniture, and irregular walls is acoustically *dead*; sound is absorbed or dispersed irregularly by the surfaces. Wide-open outdoor spaces are often extremely dead, because they lack surfaces to reflect the sound. Test the liveness of a recording space by clapping your hands once or giving a short whistle and listening to the way the sound dies out.

The acoustics of a location affect the clarity of the sound track and the loudness of camera noise. It's hard to hear clearly in an overly live room (a *boomy* location), as high frequencies are lost and rumbly low frequencies predominate. If you've ever tried to talk in a tunnel, you know what it does to the intelligibility of voices.

There are a number of ways to improve an overly reverberant location. You can use a directional mic and move closer to the sound source. A room can be deadened by closing curtains or by hanging sound blankets on stands and spreading them on the floor. Avoid positioning a microphone near a smooth wall where it will pick up both direct and reflected sound; echo may be increased or sound waves may cancel each other, weakening the microphone's response. This may also occur when mics are mounted on a short table stand over a smooth, hard surface. Avoid placing the mic in a corner or equidistant from two or more walls where reflected sound may

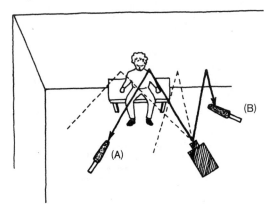

Fig. 11-10. Microphone positioning. Directional microphone positioned at (A) is pointed right at reflected noise from a film camera. Microphone positioned at (B) will reduce pickup of both direct and reflected camera noise. (For clarity in the illustration, the microphones are shown farther away from the subject than is optimal.) (Carol Keller)

cancel or echo. Sometimes boominess can be reduced by filtering out low-frequency sounds below about 150 Hz (see Bass Filters, p. 429).

If a space is too live, even a quiet camera's noise will sound loud. When you point the mic away from the camera, you often are aiming at reflected sound bouncing off a wall. When this happens, deaden the space with blankets, move closer to the subject, or use the pickup pattern of the mic to cancel out both direct and reflected camera noise.

Location Recording Problems

If you have to shoot in a noisy location, there are a number of things you can do. First, use a directional mic and get the mic as close to the source as possible. Always keep its pickup pattern in mind (see Fig. 10-20). Try not to let the subject come between the mic and a major noise source, like the street. Stand in the street to mic someone on the sidewalk; don't stand with your back to the buildings where you will pick up the sound of your subject and the street noise equally. With a super-cardioid microphone, if you can point the mic upward from below (or down from above), you can minimize street level background noise, including sound reflected off buildings.

Lavalier mics are often useful for noisy settings. These are especially effective for a single subject or even sometimes when two people are near each other (even though one person is wearing the lav, you can usually still record the other person; you may want to place the mic a little lower than normal to try to even out the two voices). Lavs can also be hidden, for example, in a piece of furniture.

Shooting a group of people at a dinner table or conference table can be difficult. A boom mic is hard to manage if the conversation is unpredictable (and can be really distracting if it swings around wildly trying to catch everyone who talks; using two booms can help). Sometimes you can place a couple of omni mics or lavs in the center of the table and go wireless to the camera or recorder. Or try using a boundary (PZM) mic (see Fig. 10-19). Some lavs have a bracket so they can be taped face-down on a surface as a kind of boundary mic. Be careful about the sound of objects being put down on the table. You may need to keep the mic off the table surface, or give people a cushion—say, a placemat for cups and glasses—to soften the noise of putting things on the table.

With film cameras (and some video cameras), camera noise is a big problem. Avoid pointing the mic at the camera or its reflected sound (see Fig. 11-10). Put a film camera in a barney (see Fig. 6-15) if needed.

MUSIC, NARRATION, AND EFFECTS

Recording Music

Some suggestions for music recordings:

1. It's often best to record music in stereo (if not with more channels). See p. 431 for more on stereo mics.

2. When you record an acoustic band or orchestra, try to find a mic placement that balances the instruments nicely. Often, a stereo mic slightly behind and above the conductor's position on a high stand is used as the master mic. With many instruments, the sound will radiate out and up, so getting the mic high helps. Hanging mics is another solution. Sometimes a second mic is added to capture a vocalist or soloist. You may also want to put mics elsewhere in the space to record on separate tracks or mix with the master. When you use more than one mic, be careful to avoid phase cancellation (see p. 430).

3. When you record an individual instrument, place the mic near the point where the sound is emanating (for example, the sound hole of a guitar or the bell of a saxophone).

4. When recording amplified vocalists or instrumentalists, you often want to put your mic by the loudspeaker, not the person. When you record a person at a podium, you may get better sound by miking the person directly, but you must get the mic very close. Often with amplified speeches or musical performances you can get a line feed directly from the public address system (or a band's mixing board) to your recorder. By doing this, you avoid having to place a microphone and you usually get good-quality sound (in the case of the band's mixer, you get premixed sound from multiple microphones).

5. Generally, you want to let the musicians control the volume. Avoid using automatic level control or making sudden manual adjustments to the recording level. Find the highest level that can accommodate loud passages in the music and then try to leave the level alone. For live performances, professional recordists sometimes attend rehearsals, follow the musical score, and make slight adjustments during rests or pauses between soft and loud passages. When recording music with a digital recorder, consider using a higher bit depth and/or sample rate. With analog machines, you generally want to use the fastest tape speed you can.

6. When shooting a musical performance, plan to record fairly long takes. Unlike a lecture that can be cut into short segments and spliced together, musical performance sound must be relatively continuous. The camera should get a number of cutaways that can be used to bridge various sections or tie together takes from different performances. Shooting with more than one camera helps ensure that you will have sufficient coverage. For cutaways, get some neutral shots (such as faces) that don't show fingering or specific hand positions, which can be used anywhere.

7. If you want to use an existing recording, do a digital transfer to capture directly to your editing system. You may need to convert to a different file format using Quicktime Pro or another program. Use uncompressed sources whenever possible.

8. If you plan to use music in your movie, you should be familiar with music copyright laws (see Chapter 19).

Music Videos and Music Playback Scenes

Music videos and scenes in movies that include performing to prerecorded music present some challenges to the sound recordist. Generally, the band will have already recorded the song, and the performers will lip-sync (sing along) with it for the video. The recordist is usually responsible for having equipment to play back the song. It's a good idea to also record a scratch track on the set, which will help in syncing the footage to the song, and will capture any on-set banter or other sound that may be wanted by the director.

VIDEO CAMERAS. Shooting to music playback with video cameras is fairly straightforward. The music should be played back on a stable, speed-controlled format such as hard drive, Flash memory, DAT, or good-quality CD player. Use a camera frame rate that won't require speed changes in postproduction. In NTSC countries, 23.976 fps and 29.97 fps should work fine. In PAL countries, you can use 25 fps. The singers' mouth movements captured on video should then match up to the song in postproduction. Some video cameras may drift slightly in speed. A sync generator may be used to keep the audio playback and the camera locked together. Even without it, if shots are kept relatively short, sync drift won't be apparent in the shot.

FILM CAMERAS. Shooting with a film camera for video release in NTSC countries can be somewhat trickier. If the camera is run at 24 fps, the film will be slowed down by 0.1 percent during the telecine transfer (see Chapter 18). Compared to the master recording of the song, the singers on video will then be moving their lips 0.1 percent too slow. One way to solve this is to run the camera at 23.976 fps or 29.97 fps. Shooting at 29.97 uses 25 percent more film, and is not appropriate if you're doing music scenes for a movie that is otherwise shot at 24 fps.

Another solution is to shoot at 24 fps and *pull up* (speed up) the music playback by 0.1 percent on the set. There are several digital and analog recorders that can be made to play exactly 0.1 percent fast.[9] Or, you can create a file in a DAW that's speeded up by this amount and play that on the set. The lip-sync singing is then done to the speeded-up song, but when the picture is transferred to video, it will drop down to the speed of the original song. Always consult with the transfer house or other professionals before shooting.

Recording Narration

Narration (*voice-over*) should generally be recorded in a soundproof booth in a studio, as any background sound in the narration may cause serious problems. Any noise in the recording will be especially noticeable in the movie as the narration cuts in and out. For a low-budget production, or if you have to record on location, you can build an enclosure with sound blankets and grip stands to try to isolate the narrator. Set it up as far from windows and outside noise (such as airplanes) as possible—basements sometimes work best. You might even try a big coat closet.

Be attentive to echoes from reflected sound, especially in the small space of a

---

9. An excellent resource on timecode and speed issues for music videos and many other situations is Wolf Seeburg's *Sync Sound for Film and Video* (see Bibliography).

recording booth. Even the stand used to hold the narration can create unwanted acoustic effects. Use a clip or small stand to hold the script. Narrators often like to use their hands when speaking, so it's better if they don't have to hold the script.

Often the mic is placed quite close to the narrator for a feeling of presence. Position the mic a few inches to the side and use a good windscreen to avoid breath popping. Listen closely while recording for breath sounds; redo takes if necessary. Many people like the warm, full sound of a large-diaphragm studio mic like a Neumann U87 or U89. For more on writing and delivering narration see p. 493.

Recording Sound Effects

Sound effects (SFX) are nonmusical, nonspeech sounds from the environment. The sounds of cars, planes, crowds, and dripping water are all considered effects. Effects usually have to be recorded individually. Don't expect to get a good recording of effects during scenes that involve dialogue. An effect may be difficult to record well either because of practicalities (positioning yourself near a jet in flight, for example) or because it doesn't sound the way audiences have come to expect it (for example, your recording of a running brook may sound more like a running shower). It can be better to purchase prerecorded effects from a sound library or mix studio (see Chapter 16) or to try to simulate an effect (crinkling cellophane to simulate "fire" sounds, for instance). There are many postproduction processes (reverb, speed changes, filtering) that can be used to create and enhance effects.

OTHER RECORDING ISSUES

Bass Filters

Many recorders, mixers, and microphones are equipped with filters that reduce the level of low-frequency sounds. These filters are variously called *bass cut*, *bass roll-off*, *high pass*, and *low-frequency attenuation (LFA)*. Some filters cut off bass fairly sharply at some frequency, say 100 Hz. Others roll off low frequencies more gradually, often diminishing them 12 dB per octave; thus, the filter might reduce 150 Hz somewhat, 75 Hz quite a bit, and 37 Hz almost entirely.

Filtering, also called *equalization*, is done to minimize the low-frequency rumble caused by such things as wind, traffic, machinery, and microphone-handling noise. The low-frequency component of these sounds is disturbing to the listener and can distort higher-frequency sounds. If low-frequency sounds are very loud, the recording level must be kept low to avoid over-recording, and this impairs the sounds that you really care about (like voices).

Microphones and recorders may have a two- or three-position bass roll-off switch. The first position (sometimes labeled "music" or "M") provides a relatively flat frequency response with no bass filtering. The next position ("voice" or "V") provides filtering below a certain frequency. If there is a third position, it rolls off bass starting at an even higher frequency (see Fig. 10-21). Do test recordings with the filter to judge its effect. On some mics, the "M" position is optimal for most recording, and the "V" position should be used only for excessive rumble or when the mic is very close to someone speaking. Sometimes the third position removes so much of the low end that recordings sound very thin and hollow. For this reason, it's usually best to avoid using a camcorder's "wind" menu setting.

There are two schools of thought on filtering bass: One is to filter as needed in the original recording; the other is to hold off as much as possible until postproduction. The first school argues that the low frequencies will be filtered out eventually, and a better recording can be made if this is done sooner rather than later. This must be weighed against the fact that frequencies rolled off in the original recording are not replaceable later. The sound studio has better tools and is a better environment in which to judge how much bass needs to be removed.

A prudent approach is to filter bass only when excessive rumble or wind noise requires it or when trying to compensate for a microphone that is overly sensitive to low frequencies. Then filter only the minimum amount to improve the sound. If filtering is done, keep it consistent in the scene.

Multiple Microphones and Multitrack Recorders

There are many situations in which you may want to use more than one microphone. Typical examples are when recording two people who are not near each other, recording a musical group, or recording a panel discussion. Many recorders have provisions for two microphone inputs, and some machines can record from microphone and line inputs simultaneously (mics can usually be fed into the line input with the proper preamp). A mic mixer allows several mics to be fed into the recorder. Try to get microphones that are well matched in terms of tone quality. Sometimes a filter can be used on one mic to make it sound more like another.

When recording with multiple mics, be careful to avoid *phase cancellation*. This occurs when the peak of a sound wave reaches one mic slightly before or after it reaches another mic, diminishing the strength and quality of the sound signal. In phase cancellation, the diaphragm of one mic is pushed by the sound pressure while the other mic is being pulled and the two signals cancel each other out. The rule of thumb for avoiding this is that the microphones should be at least three times farther from each other than the distance from each mic to its sound source (see Fig. 11-11). Directional microphones that are angled away from each other can often be placed closer together.

Start with one mic and watch the level on the audio meter when you plug in the second mic—the strength of the sound signal should be increased, not decreased. Sometimes two microphones are wired differently, so that even if the mics are placed correctly, they cancel each other anyway. When recording in stereo, phase cancellation is not always noticeable but becomes apparent when the two mics are combined (*summed*) to one mono channel.

When using multiple mics, when someone is *not* speaking, keep his mic level down to avoid unwanted noise; this is often difficult when recording unpredictable dialogue.

If the recorder has multiple tracks, this opens up various possibilities for multiple microphones. You can record both a boom mic and a lavalier separately. You can place two mics in different positions and choose whichever sounds best later. If different subjects have their own mics and recording channels, their lines of dialogue can be separated more easily for editing and mixing purposes. Director Robert Altman used recording systems with up to forty-eight tracks with wireless mics on individual

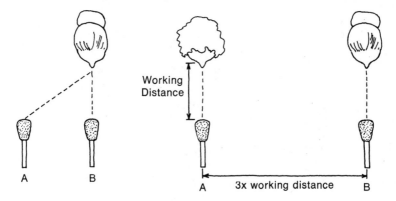

Fig. 11-11. Multiple microphones. (left) Distance from woman to microphone A is only slightly longer than distance to microphone B, leading to possible phase cancellation. (right) Separation between microphones is three times the distance from each mic to its sound source. Now the distance between microphone A and the woman at right is sufficient to minimize the chance of phase cancellation. (Carol Keller)

actors, each feeding a different channel. With this system, the actors can freely improvise, and everyone's lines will be recorded well, something that is almost impossible to do with only one mic and recording channel. Phase cancellation can often be avoided with multiple recording tracks, if the editor can choose the sound from one mic or another without trying to mix them together.

Having many tracks can be cumbersome for dailies screenings or for the picture editor. If you record to multiple tracks, you may need to create one or two *mixdown tracks* that combine the key dialogue tracks. Some multitrack recorders allow you to record a mixdown along with the individual source tracks.

Stereo Recording

Most video and audio recorders have at least two tracks and are capable of recording in stereo. Some camcorders are equipped with dual built-in mics that give some stereo separation between the left and right sides.

When movies are distributed to the public, in theaters, on TV, or as DVDs, they are in stereo (at least two channels) or other multichannel formats such as 5.1 channel sound (see Mix Formats, p. 654). However, it's important to make the distinction between *recording* in stereo on location and *releasing* the finished movie in stereo. For very many projects, dialogue scenes and the like are recorded in mono, even if those scenes will ultimately appear in a stereo sound track in the finished movie. A mono recording is made with one microphone (or more) on one audio track. It's very easy during the sound mix to place a "mono" sound either on the left or right side of the screen to create a stereo effect if needed.

Nevertheless, there are times when stereo recording is desired either for the entire production or for specific types of sound such as music, effects, or wide shots (perhaps to capture the sound of a horse moving from one side of the screen to the other).

There are various techniques for recording stereo. Stereo mics built into

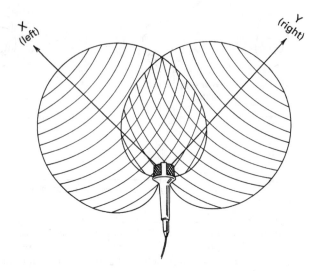

Fig. 11-12. Pickup pattern of a stereo mic in the X-Y configuration. Shown here, the two mic capsules are in one body. (Robert Brun)

camcorders usually employ the *X-Y* method (see Fig. 11-12). This uses two cardioid mics each pointed 45 degrees to the side (the two mic capsules may be in the same housing). The X-Y method is straightforward and simple, though when the two mics are separate—that is, not in the same case—mounting and controlling them must be done with care. It can sometimes be difficult to get the proper balance between the left and right side.

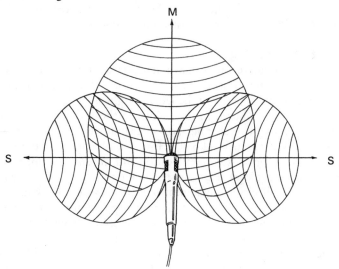

Fig. 11-13. Pickup pattern of a stereo mic in the M-S configuration. Shown here, the two mic capsules are in one body. (Robert Brun)

Some people prefer the *M-S* (*Mid-Side*) method. This also employs two mics: one with a cardioid pickup pattern and one with a figure-eight pattern (see Fig. 11-13). Mics like the Shure VP-88 have both mics built into a single housing. The cardioid mic picks up sound from the front and the figure-eight mic gets the left- and right-side image; each mic is sent to a separate track on the audio or video recorder. Later, the two tracks are "matrixed" through an M-S decoder to create the standard two-channel stereo effect.

Fig. 11-14. Shure VP88 microphone. Versatile mic that can output an M-S signal or can be switched internally to provide a stereo (X-Y) output with a choice between low, medium, or high stereo effect. Comes with a splitter cable for outputting the two channels. Use both output connectors for M-S or stereo output, or use just one in the M-S mode to record a mono signal from the cardioid capsule or the figure-eight capsule. (Shure Brothers, Inc.)

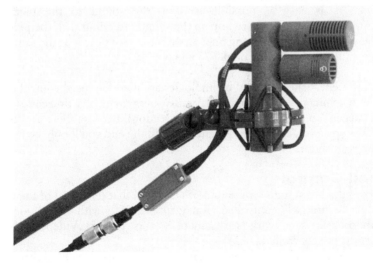

Fig. 11-15. Schoeps M-S setup showing separate cardioid and figure-eight mics that can be combined (matrixed) to create stereo. Schoeps makes very high-quality professional mics. (Posthorn Recordings, NY)

If you keep the M and S tracks separate throughout the editing process, you'll have more flexibility in the mix, because you can then adjust the relative balance of the mid, left, and right sound images, and you can isolate the mono signal from directly in front, if needed. However, by doing so, you won't be able to hear the stereo effect until after you're done editing (unless you have an M-S decoder in the editing room). Some M-S mics (such as the VP-88) allow you to output an X-Y (left-right) signal if you prefer; on some you can even choose how "wide" the stereo pattern is.

RECORDING DOUBLE SYSTEM
FOR FILM AND VIDEO

Double system (or *dual system*) recording means using a separate audio recorder from the camera. All film shoots are done double system; film cameras don't record sound. Video shoots are sometimes done with a separate audio recorder in order to record higher-quality sound or more audio tracks or to provide more mobility for the recordist than might be possible by recording sound in the video camera. In this situation, it's still recommended to record audio in the video camcorder as well, to serve as a scratch track for reference.[10]

When sound and picture are recorded in separate machines, there are two basic concerns:

- Ensure that both sound and picture can be played back at the same speed or frame rate, so they don't drift relative to each other during a shot.
- Make it as easy as possible to sync the sound to the picture in postproduction—that is, to line up the sound recording with the picture so that when we see something happen on screen we hear it at the same time. Synching up is discussed on p. 573 and p. 601.

Many different techniques and technologies are used for speed control and for making the synching process easier. Today, many of them involve timecode (be sure to read Timecode, p. 203, before reading this section). Because there are so many options, this topic can get confusing; remember, in the end you'll only be using *one* of them on your shoot.

Speed Control

To record double-system sync sound, it's essential that the speed of the camera and recorder be precisely controlled. Today, film cameras with crystal-controlled motors are used for sync work (see Camera Motors, p. 235). Video cameras are usually also crystal controlled.

As for audio recorders, most recent digital machines such as hard drive, compact flash, DAT, MiniDisc, and CD recorders should have speed control that's accu-

---

10. This could be done as a feed from the audio recorder or just by leaving the camera mic on.

rate enough for sync recording. In some cases there may be slight drift over very long takes, which is usually corrected easily in editing. For precise sync, some recorders can accept a reference signal from the camera.

Speed control with analog recorders is discussed on p. 389.

PULLDOWN. In certain situations the speed of the audio needs to be adjusted after recording. Perhaps the most common occurs while shooting film in NTSC countries when video transfer and editing are planned. Film shot at 24 fps will typically be slowed to 23.976 fps in the telecine (see p. 606). This means that audio recorded in the field must also be pulled down (slowed down) by the same 0.1 percent. This can be done in a number of ways.

When working with digital audio, speed adjustment may be done by manipulating the sample rate. Unlike film or video, digital audio doesn't really have "frames"—the recording is just a constant stream of data (samples). For example, when using a 48 kHz sample rate, the recorder creates 48,000 samples each second; then, in playback, the machine makes sure 48,000 samples are played back every second to maintain constant speed.

If you're planning to slow the audio 0.1 percent, with some recorders you can set the sample rate to 48.048 kHz. This creates 480 extra samples per second when recording. However, the recording is "stamped" as having the normal 48 kHz rate, so the playback machine plays back the usual 48,000 samples per second, making the sound 0.1 percent slower. This method has the advantage of requiring no sample rate conversion or analog transfer later, either of which take time and could degrade the quality.

However, if the project will be distributed on film, this may not be the best route. Pro Tools and other DAWs have a pulldown/pullup feature for material recorded with standard sample rates. Always discuss settings with the post team before recording.

Traditional Slates

Synching involves lining up the sound and the picture. It's much easier to do if there's a distinct event that can be seen clearly in the picture and heard on the sound track. For example, the closing of a car door might suffice. A *slate* is an event in sound and picture that can be used to facilitate syncing.

The traditional slating device—called variously a *slate, clapper board, clap sticks* or, simply, *sticks*—is literally a piece of slate on which information can be chalked, with a hinged piece of wood on top that makes a sharp noise when it makes contact with the board (see Fig. 11-16). Now slates are usually plastic. Information written on the slate includes the production company, name of film, director, DP, scene and take numbers, sound take number (if any), camera and sound roll numbers, and date. A small gray card (see Fig. 8-4) or chip chart will assist in color-correcting a film workprint or video transfer.

The clapper board is usually handled by an assistant who writes and reads aloud the scene and take numbers and/or the sound take number before snapping down the hinged part of the slate at the beginning of each take. The numbers are often written on pieces of tape that can be stored on the back of the slate and quickly stuck on the front as needed.

Fig. 11-16. Traditional clapper board slate. (Victor Duncan, Inc.)

Another slating device is the *slate light*, which is connected to the recorder. When its trigger is pushed, it flashes a small light (some flash consecutive numbers to identify takes) and it produces an audible beep. The slate light can be handy for documentary filming, although the light is sometimes hard to see in daylight. Slating can also be done by gently tapping the microphone once or twice or even by snapping your fingers within range of the recorder.

When you make any slate, it's imperative not to turn off the camera or recorder between the slate and the shot itself, as novices sometimes do. Make sure that the slate is clearly visible to the camera to avoid spending unnecessary time synching up. It's a good idea to say "slate" or "marker" into the mic to help the editor find the sound later.

When possible, do *head slates*, which are done at the beginning of the shot. Head slates speed the process of putting the sound and picture in sync in the telecine suite or editing room. *Tail slates*, done at the end of the shot, are sometimes preferable for unstaged documentary filming since they don't loudly announce to everyone that filming is about to begin; they may also be less disruptive for emotional, acted scenes. However, tail slates can slow down synching, especially in the telecine. Traditional clapper boards are usually held upside down to indicate a tail slate; the person slating should call out, "tail slate" or "end sticks" when doing so. If the film runs out before the last tail slate on a roll and the camera operator says "run out," you can use this as an approximate slate.

If either the camera or audio recorder miss a slate and you have to do it a second time, announce "second sticks" to alert the editor. In any situation, a gentle, quiet slate helps put actors or film subjects at ease. Generally, actors should not be rushed to begin the action immediately after the slate.

It takes longer, but it's usually not hard to put shots in sync without a slate (see Chapter 15).

OTHER SLATED INFORMATION. The term *slating* also refers to the recording of information on film or tape. MOS takes are slated, not for synchronization, but to identify the scene and take number at the head of the take ("MOS" should be written on the clapper board and the hinged bar should not be raised). It's a good idea to use a slate on all dramas—in film or video—even if not needed for synching. Each roll of film is normally slated at the head by shooting a card or clapper board with production name and company, camera roll number, date, and so on for a few seconds. Similarly, sound tapes are slated at the head with information on the roll number or the content.

Operating the Recorder

For staged work, there's a traditional protocol for beginning each take. The assistant director calls for quiet and then says "sound." The recorder is then started, and the recordist says "speed" when the machine is running smoothly. The AD then says "camera," and the camera operator calls "speed" or "rolling" when the camera has come up to speed. If slates are being used, they are done at this point; the AC reads off the scene and take numbers and calls out "marker." The director or AD then calls "action." Normally, the camera and recorder are not turned off until the director says "cut."

When doing slates, be sure the slate is shot so it's large in the frame and in focus. The numbers can be spoken aloud. Even when using a slateless system (see below), a clap stick with manual slates may still be done as a backup in case of timecode problems and for scene/take information.

When shooting film, some telecines require five to seven seconds of "preroll" before the slate or first usable audio. Consult the transfer house before you shoot to find out how much preroll, if any, they need. Make sure you let the recorder run the allotted time before the slate is done or the camera starts (and/or use prerecord to build in the preroll time; see p. 381).

In unstaged documentary work, it's important that the soundperson be ready to record at a moment's notice. If shooting appears imminent, the recorder should be put in the standby position (on some recorders this is done by pressing the "record" button, but not the "forward" button) and the recording level should be set. If the scene looks interesting, the recordist should not hesitate to roll. If the scene doesn't pan out, simply say "no shot" into the mic and stop recording. If the scene is good, the camera should roll. The first part of the scene that has no picture can usually be covered with another shot or a cutaway. There is no advantage to rolling vast amounts of sound, but often if you wait too long to start the recorder, the take will be useless (another situation where prerecord can help).

If your recorder is equipped with a separate confidence head, it's a good idea to monitor it and not the microphone directly (see p. 382). This allows you to check the recording quality and, for a tape recorder, whether you've run out of tape. Running out of tape or storage space on a Flash card is unnecessary and embarrassing. Some recordists routinely change tape or cards when the camera changes to a new roll/tape/card even if some recording time is remaining, which ensures adequate supply and means the camera crew won't have to wait for *you* to make a change later. If you don't have enough tape or media to complete a shoot, in emergencies you may be able to switch to a slower tape speed or lower sample rate, but don't forget to log this and to inform the person transferring the sound.

If shooting film that will be transferred to video for editing, it's generally a good idea to record or store all *wild sound* (sound without picture) separately so that they don't have to wade through it during the telecine session or when synching up.

TIMECODE SLATING SYSTEMS

The advantage of traditional slates is that they're low-tech and fairly foolproof. The disadvantage is that it can take a long time in the telecine or editing system to find the right audio and sync it up to the picture. By using timecode, synching can be done much faster, or even automatically. All timecode methods require at least that the audio recorder be able to record timecode (not all recorders can).

Timecode Slates

A *timecode slate* (also called a *digi-slate*) looks like a standard clapper board with a timecode display on its face (see Fig. 11-17). In one of the simplest ways of using a timecode slate, timecode is fed from the audio recorder to the slate. Any sync sound film camera or video camera can be used. Slates are done in the usual way, preferably at the head of the shot. When the clap sticks are lowered on the slate, the timecode at that instant is held on the display. In postproduction, the video or film frame where the clap sticks closed is paused on screen so the audio timecode at that moment can be read on the slate. That number is entered into the editing or telecine system, which locates that same timecode in the audio and, presto, the shot is in sync.

Fig. 11-17. Timecode slate. A "dumb slate" can display timecode sent from the audio recorder or other source. A "smart slate" incorporates its own timecode generator (see Fig. 11-18). (Denecke, Inc.)

In this method, timecode is sent to the slate from the audio recorder via a cable or a wireless link. With a *smart slate*, the slate has its own timecode generator. *Jam synching* means that one timecode source sets the other machine to its timecode. You can jam-sync the generator with timecode from the audio recorder or from another timecode source, and the slate and recorder should maintain the same free run/time-of-day code.

A timecode generator, such as Ambient's Lockit Box or Denecke's SB-T, can be used to jam-sync the slate and/or audio recorder.

AVOIDING TIMECODE SLATE PROBLEMS. Some people prefer smart slates because they require no connection between the slate and the audio recorder. On the other hand, this provides one more opportunity for timecode to go out of whack. A wireless transmitter can be used to send code from the recorder to a dumb slate (timecode reader only), which simplifies things somewhat, but requires a good wireless link.

As a safety precaution when using a timecode slate, be sure to record the sound of the clap sticks closing (the old-fashioned slate system) in case there's a problem with the code. Also be sure to frame the slate in the camera viewfinder *clearly* so the timecode numbers are big and easy to read.

Timecode generators tend to drift slightly over time. This can lead to sync errors if the timecode in a slate or camera differs from the timecode in the audio recorder. When using more than one timecode device, pick one of them to serve as the master clock and use it to jam-sync the other machines. Re-jam whenever devices are powered down or, in any case, no more than every few hours.

Audio Timecode Frame Rates

Most timecode-capable recorders offer a variety of timecode frame rates. The goal is to pick a frame rate for the audio timecode that will match or be compatible with the film or video timecode rate. Keep in mind that the audio timecode frame rate does not control the speed of the audio, it only affects how the timecode is recorded. Not all audio recorders can handle all timecode rates.

- *23.976 fps.* HD cameras that record "24p" in NTSC countries are often operated at 23.976 fps (also known as 23.98). This timecode is always nondrop (ND).
- *24 fps.* This frame rate (true 24p) may be used with both film and HD cameras when no transfer to NTSC video is expected.
- *25 fps.* This rate is used for PAL video.
- *29.97 fps, DF.* This is the standard drop frame rate for NTSC video for broadcast.
- *29.97 fps, ND.* This is the nondrop NTSC video rate. Sometimes also used for Panasonic HD cameras.
- *30 fps, ND.* This is a *true* 30 fps rate, *not* the same as 29.97, and is often used for film shoots where the picture will be transferred to NTSC video. After the 30 fps audio TC has been slowed down by 0.1 percent, it will match the 29.97 rate on the video transfer. This is a standard audio timecode rate used for film production in the United States.

- *30 fps, DF.* Same idea but drop frame. Sometimes used for long-form TV shows.

In some cases, the frame rate of the audio timecode is the same as the film or video frame rate. For example, for European film or PAL shoots where the camera is running at 25 fps, the audio TC is 25 fps. However, sometimes the audio rate is different than the camera's but still compatible. Film shoots in NTSC countries are usually done with the film camera running at 24 fps (which after transfer to NTSC video will be 29.97 fps). The audio TC is recorded at true 30 fps, which, after being pulled down 0.1 percent as described above, will then also be 29.97 fps.

Be sure to discuss any audio timecode choices with the lab, post house, and postproduction team before recording! Label all boxes, logs, and slate clearly with sound TC speed, drop or nondrop (as well as the usual items listed earlier). Shoot a test before beginning a production to make sure all systems are working.

Slateless Timecode Systems

In the methods described above, synching is done by visually reading the audio timecode on the slate at the moment the slate is closed. This can be done with film cameras that have no timecode capability. This can also be done with video cameras that generate timecode, but the video timecode may be different from the audio (which is to say 1:00:05:06 audio TC could sync up to 5:00:10:08 video TC—as long as we have a sync point, the numbers themselves don't have to be the same).

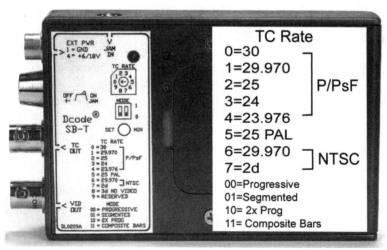

Fig. 11-18. Timecode generator. The Denecke SB-T reads, generates, and jams to all standard frame rates. Outputs timecode and video sync in PAL and NTSC, as well as tri-level sync for HD shoots. Enlargement shows available frame rates. (Denecke, Inc.)

However, if the film or video camera is recording the *same* timecode number as the audio recorder, then you don't need slates at all. In postproduction, the computer just locates the identical timecode numbers in video and audio; synching can be totally automated. This saves time on the set, as no slates are necessary, and saves time in the telecine or editing system when synching is done. There are no distracting slate claps to disturb actors or subjects, nor is footage wasted doing slates. The camera can start and stop at will, and as long as the recorder is running, you know you'll be able to quickly sync up the material. This can be useful for interviews in which you want to start and stop the camera while always rolling sound. This also makes it possible to quickly sync up footage from multiple cameras. For a concert shoot, you could have several roaming cameras and never need an audio or visual slate to find sync.

There are various ways to record the same code in picture and sound; which one you choose depends on the capabilities of your equipment.

FILM CAMERAS. Some film cameras can expose a running timecode display along the edge of the film (*in-camera timecode*). The *AatonCode* system (also used in Panavision cameras) exposes on the film a combination of human-readable numbers and a machine-readable matrix of dots (see Fig. 6-16). The Arriflex system uses a bar code. The camera's timecode is jam-synched to the audio recorder. In postproduction, properly equipped telecines can read the film timecode and automatically sync it to the audio code (see Chapter 18).

VIDEO CAMERAS. In one method, the timecode output from the video camera is connected by cable or wireless link to the timecode input of the audio recorder. This may allow use of record run timecode, which is often preferable. Some audio recorders can be slaved to the camera's timecode so they start and stop automatically when the camera does.

Another method is to use free run/time-of-day timecode and jam-sync the camera and audio recorder with the same TC source. This could be done by cable or with a timecode generator such as the Ambient or Denecke products mentioned above. This may be preferable when more than one camera is being used. For precise sync with more than one HD camera, you need to feed each camera the same timecode via the timecode input and feed tri-level sync via the genlock input.

There are numerous other methods of coordinating timecode between systems. Methods vary in terms of which unit is considered the timecode master and which is the slave, and how the timecode is conveyed from one to the other (wirelessly, by cable, or by a sync box).

Whatever system you use, be sure all the equipment is set the same way in terms of drop frame versus nondrop.

WHEN TIMECODES DON'T MATCH. Depending on your equipment and what you're trying to do, there may be situations where you *can't* have identical code in the camera and audio recorder. For example, when shooting HD at 23.976 fps, you may find that your audio recorder can't handle that rate. However, if you use 29.97 fps timecode in the audio recorder, you can jam the camera's 23.976 timecode to the recorder and the two will have identical code at the first frame of every second, even though the frames *within* each second are different. The two timecodes will stay in step with each other as long as you use 29.97 fps and *not* 30 fps code in the audio recorder (and avoid drop frame TC). Matching up different timecodes with different frame rates is called *cross jamming*.

Another approach is to use a product like an Evertz Afterburner on the camera to convert the HD timecode to 29.97 fps and jam *that* with the audio recorder. There may be a delay of a few frames between them, which can be corrected in post.

CHAPTER 12

Lighting

The Function of Lighting

Everything we do with cameras and lenses is about capturing light. Light is needed to register an image on film, or on a video camera's chip, but the lighting in a movie plays a much more complex role than just that. A scene may be lit by nature (the sun), with *available light* (using whatever natural or man-made light is already at the location), or with lighting fixtures that the filmmaker controls. The way a scene is lit influences both how we understand the scene—what we can see in it— and how we experience the scene emotionally.

Lighting directs the viewer's attention, since the eye is naturally drawn to bright areas of the frame. Lighting gives the audience cues about the time of day and season in which a scene takes place. The angle from which light strikes an object or a face affects how we see shapes and textures. Side lighting casts shadows that emphasize depth, dimension, and surface texture, while frontal lighting tends to flatten, compress, and smooth over features.

Qualities of light have a powerful effect on the mood of a scene. Painters are often celebrated for the way they manipulate light and create particular moods. Andrew Wyeth, for example, evokes the gray, quiet feeling of the Maine landscape with extremely flat and even illumination. Rembrandt creates a much more dramatic effect by using a "chiaroscuro" style, in which pools of light and shadow are used to obscure as much as they reveal of a subject. Think of the qualities of light over the course of a day. A bright morning sun can feel cheery and safe, while a moonless night evokes mystery or tension.

On feature films, lighting is usually a top priority. The actors and sets must look their best and the mood of the scene must be right. Lights are positioned carefully, consuming much time and expense. The director of photography is usually responsible for the lighting design, which is as important as his or her mastery of cameras and lenses.

In documentary production, light is sometimes a low priority, thought of less for its mood than for its exposure value. In some cases there's just no time for careful lighting. But sometimes good lighting takes no more time than bad. It may be as simple as using available light smartly.

In all productions, one of the key concerns is controlling contrast. Most natural and available light situations have a range of brightness that exceeds the film or video camera's ability to capture it. Often, lighting equipment is needed to make shadows less dark, or highlights less bright.

In the ongoing debate over which looks better, film or video, lighting often plays an important role. Because film is more expensive, people tend to do better lighting on film shoots. If the same care is used on video shoots, the difference between the two media is much smaller.

This chapter is written for film- and videomakers who may be working with a large crew or alone. For simplicity's sake, the person doing the lighting will be referred to as the DP (director of photography).

LIGHT

Look at a painting, photograph, or a scene in a movie that you think has interesting light. How is the painter or photographer achieving that effect? Start by identifying the light sources (you may not be able to see the source itself, just the light it produces). Examine each source for these factors that contribute to its effect in the scene:

1. What kind of shadow does it cast (crisp or diffuse)?
2. What angle is it coming from?
3. How bright is it (its intensity)?
4. How bright is it relative to other lights (the lighting contrast)?
5. What color is it?

When you're ready to shoot a scene, ask the same questions about the light sources. At times, you may specifically check, say, the angle or intensity of a given light. But at other times you will look at things more instinctively, evaluating the overall "feel" of the lighting but keeping these factors in the back of your mind.

Qualities of Light

The *hardness* of light is a way to describe the type of shadow it casts. *Hard light*, also called *specular light*, like direct sunlight on a clear day, is made up of parallel rays that produce clean, hard shadows that neatly outline the shapes of objects. Hard light is crisp and can sometimes feel harsh.

Soft, or *diffuse*, light is less directional. It's made up of rays going in many different directions and produces much softer, gentler shadows. The light on a hazy or overcast day is soft. It emanates from all parts of the sky at once. If it casts shadows at all, they are dull and indistinct.

Hard light can be produced artificially with *lensed* or focused lamps that emit a clearly directed beam. The spotlights used to single out a performer on stage are extremely hard. The light from a car headlight is quite hard. Hard light can be created with a fairly compact lighting fixture.

Because hard light casts very distinct shadows, it is used to delineate shapes. It brings out surface textures and can cast dramatic, sculpted shadows. The classic Hollywood look of the 1940s is based on fairly hard light sources. In a less flattering

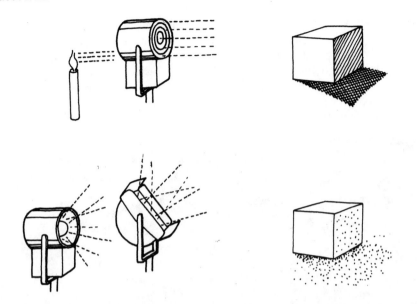

Fig. 12-1. (top) The relatively parallel rays of hard light cast a sharp shadow. (bottom) The scattered, more random rays of soft light cast a diffuse shadow. (Carol Keller)

use of hard light, news photographers often use a simple, hard light that creates sharp shadows across the face.

Soft light sources produce a broad and even glow, not a beam of light. Soft sources are usually indirect; that is, the light from the bulb is first bounced off a white or silvery surface before striking the subject. In a classic umbrella light (see Fig. 12-13), the bulb shines into the umbrella, which reflects back a wide, diffuse pattern of light. To soften the light from any bulb, we need to spread the light out and disrupt the parallel rays. Another way to soften light is to put some type of translucent material between the source and the subject, which is not unlike what a typical cloth lampshade does on a household fixture.

Soft light is relatively gentle and tends to smooth out features and textures. Traditionally, female actors are lit with soft light to disguise any facial wrinkles or imperfections. A single soft light off to the side can provide delicate modeling of curved surfaces such as the face, because of the way it "wraps around" the curve with gradual shading (hard lights produce shadows that are more sharp-edged). Some people feel that soft lighting is more "natural." This is true in some situations; for example, window light is often fairly soft and may cast gentle, soft shadows. On the other hand, direct sunlight streaming through a window is usually quite hard and casts hard, crisp shadows.

Directionality

As noted above, the direction or angle from which light strikes the subject influences how the subject appears on screen. Light coming from the general direction of the camera is called *front light*. *Front axial light* comes from very near the camera's lens; its shadows are mostly not visible from the camera position. Camera-mounted fixtures, such as flash units used on still cameras, provide front light, which illuminates all the visible surfaces of the subject. Full frontal lighting can be quite harsh and usually uninteresting, since dimensionality and surface texture are minimized. However, the flattening effect may be desired. Fashion models are often photographed with very frontal light, which makes their faces seem flawless and without dimension.

You can think of full frontal lighting as projecting from the number 6 on a clock

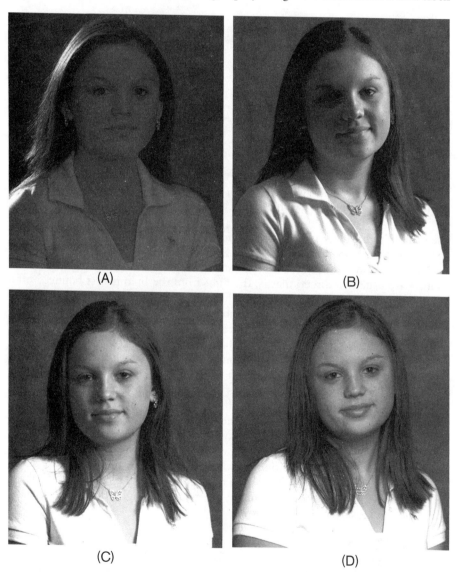

(A)   (B)

(C)   (D)

Fig. 12-2. Directionality of light. The subject is lit by one light. (A) Backlight or kicker. (B) Side light. (C) Three-quarter front light. (D) Full frontal light. (Ned Johnston)

face whose center is the subject. (Think of the camera as also positioned at the number 6.) *Offset* (the light at number 5 or 7) and *three-quarter front light* (around 4:30 or 7:30) can be used for portraiture when more shadowing is desired.

Full side light (around 3 or 9) provides good modeling and indication of texture (since texture is revealed by the pattern of tiny individual shadows visible from the camera position). Side light can be quite dramatic. It produces shadows that fall clearly across the frame and distinctly reveal the depth of various objects in space.

Backlight originates from behind (and usually above) the subject. It tends to outline the subject's shape and to differentiate it from the background. Backlight can produce a bright edge or halo on a subject's hair and shoulders. When backlight predominates, called *contre-jour*, it can create a moody and romantic effect. If the background is bright and no light falls on the camera side of the subject, the subject will be in silhouette.

We are also concerned with the *vertical* angle of light—that is, the height from which it strikes the subject. *Top light*, which shines down from directly above the subject, can make deep shadows in eye sockets. Gordon Willis used top light in *The Godfather* to cast menacing shadows in Marlon Brando's eyes. Top light can also make landscapes seem more two-dimensional, because few shadows are visible (think of sunlight at noon on a bright day). Most film lighting is done with the key lights angled about 40 degrees from the floor or slightly higher for the best modeling without casting excessive shadows. *Underlighting*, in which the light comes up from below the subject and casts shadows upward, occurs rarely in nature and is used in horror films to lend a ghoulish look to faces.

Lighting Contrast

Much of the mood or atmosphere of a lighting scheme is determined by the *lighting contrast*—that is, the relationship in light intensity between the brightly lit areas and the shadow areas. With great lighting contrast, there is a great difference in intensity between the bright areas and the deep shadows. With low lighting contrast (often achieved by using secondary lights to fill in the shadows), the lighting appears fairly flat and uniform throughout the frame. The degree of lighting contrast is often expressed numerically in terms of the *lighting contrast ratio* (see p. 478). Lighting contrast results from the relationship of the *key light* (which casts the primary shadows) and the *fill light* (which fills in the key's shadows). See below for more on these terms.

A *low-key* lighting design has high lighting contrast and a Rembrandt-like look, with dark shadow areas predominating over light areas. Low-key lighting is associated with night, emotion, tension, tragedy, and mystery. Film-noir movies, as well as *Citizen Kane*, are lit in moody low-key lighting; the dramatic feel of the lighting is well suited to the black-and-white image. With *high-key* lighting, the lighting contrast is low and bright tones predominate, making everything appear bright and cheery. High-key lighting is used for daytime scenes, comedy, and most studio-shot television shows. In a high-key lighting scheme, the light is evenly distributed around the set, which is convenient in situations in which several cameras are shooting simultaneously from different angles or when an actor must be able to move freely around the set without walking into deep shadows.

Fig. 12-3. The single candle produces fairly hard light (note the crisp shadows) and a very low-key lighting scheme with no fill illumination and deep shadows. (*The Penitent Magdalen* by Georges de La Tour, The Metropolitan Museum of Art, Gift of Mr. & Mrs. Charles Wrightsman, 1978)

Fig. 12-4. Light from the large window is fairly soft (note gentle shadow angled downward from windowsill). The lighting scheme is relatively high-key, but would be more so if stronger fill light were added from the right side of the frame. (*Young Woman with a Water Jug* by Vermeer, The Metropolitan Museum of Art, Gift of Henry G. Marquand, 1889)

Fig. 12-5. Lighting depends on the camera angle. From this side, the performer is backlit by the spotlight, with a very low-key, edge-lit look. If you shot from the other side, she would be front lit with a flatter, higher-key look. The camera on the crane directly above is seeing a side-lit shot of the keyboard. (Sony Electronics, Inc.)

The terms *high key* and *low key* are sometimes confusing, since the key light is actually lower in intensity relative to the fill light in high-key lighting designs. One way to distinguish the terms is to remember that actors in comedies are usually high-key personality types.

LIGHTING EQUIPMENT

Lighting equipment may be owned by the filmmaker, a production company or school, or it may be rented for individual shoots. Often the DP or gaffer (see p. 315) assembles a lighting package from a rental house according to the needs of each production or day's work.

Lighting Fixtures and Light Intensity

In the world of movie lighting, a lighting fixture may be called a *lighting unit, instrument, head,* or *luminaire*. The bulb is referred to as a *lamp* or *globe*; changing a bulb is *relamping*. Lighting units are identified by type and power consumption. A 5K spot is a 5000-watt (5-kilowatt) spotlight. Lights are balanced for tungsten (3200°K) unless stated otherwise. Don't confuse degrees Kelvin with use of "K" that indicates wattage.

On the set you'll find many names used for various pieces of equipment; some are based on manufacturers' names, others are nicknames used in different parts of the country or in different countries.

The brightness of a lightbulb is usually discussed in terms of wattage. *Wattage* is actually a measure of how much electric power is used (see Location Lighting, p. 483); some bulbs and fixtures put out more light than others for the same power consumption (that is, they are more efficient). In the case of two lights that employ the same type of bulb in the same fixture, a doubling of wattage implies a doubling of light output.

With the exception of certain focusing lighting fixtures, the intensity of illumination decreases the farther the subject is from a light. This is known as light *falloff*. The rule for typical open bulbs is that the falloff in intensity is inversely proportional to the *square* of the distance (see Fig. 12-6). Thus, moving an object *twice* as far from a lamp results in it being lit by *one quarter* the amount of light. Because of this, falloff is especially sharp when you are *near* the light source. Imagine a couch lit by a floor lamp at one end of the couch. A person sitting near the lamp could be lit four times as brightly as the person sitting next to him (an exposure difference of two stops). This difference will look even more extreme when captured on film or video. For even illumination, lights should be kept far away from the subjects so that slight changes in distance do not cause large changes in exposure. Soft light sources fall off more sharply than focused, hard light sources.

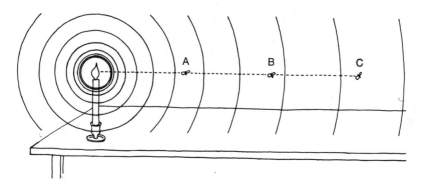

Fig. 12-6. The inverse square law. (1) Light falls off rapidly as you move away from the source: Moth B is twice as far from the candle as Moth A but receives one quarter the amount of light. Moth C is three times farther from the candle than moth A and receives one ninth the amount of light. (2) Light falloff is less severe when you are farther from the source: Moving from B to C is the same distance as moving from A to B, but the light falloff is much less (it falls off to about half the previous level instead of to one quarter). (Carol Keller)

BULBS

Bulbs differ in the type and color of light they emit. If you're unfamiliar with color temperature and its use in film and video, see Chapter 8. Further discussion of white balance and video cameras is on p. 113.

Household Bulbs and Photo Bulbs

Common household incandescent bulbs can be used with video cameras as long as the camera can get a good white balance. They can also be used for black-and-white film shoots. Their color temperature, however, is about 2900°K, so the light they produce looks yellow-orange instead of white on tungsten-balanced color film. Sometimes professional 3200°K lighting units are used for the primary illumination for a film or video shoot, and household bulbs are used in a table lamp or other practical fixture (see Lighting Styles, p. 467). In this case, though the household bulb may look yellow relative to the movie lights, it may seem natural in the scene. See Practicals, p. 460.

Photo bulbs are available that use tungsten filaments similar to those in household bulbs, but the light emitted is designed to match tungsten-balanced film. Both 3200°K and 3400°K versions are available. A bluer, "daylight-balanced" version (rated at 4800°K) can also be purchased.

Photo bulbs may be either *photofloods* or *reflector floods*. Photofloods look just like household incandescent bulbs. Reflector floods are mushroom-shaped with a built-in reflecting surface that projects a more directed beam of light. The R-40 is a commonly used reflector flood. Photo bulbs are the least expensive kind of artificial lighting for film, and they can be used with many home and amateur fixtures. They become very hot, however, and should be used only with fixtures that allow good upward ventilation. They are not very bright compared to other types of bulbs (about 1000 watts maximum) and their life span is short (often as little as five or six hours). After a few hours, photo bulbs darken from internal deposits, diminishing both the brightness and the color temperature, which may result in a reddish color cast.

Tungsten-Halogen Bulbs

Also called just *tungsten* or *quartz*, these bulbs employ a tungsten filament surrounded by halogen gas encased in a quartz glass bulb (see Fig. 12-11). Tungsten-halogen bulbs are the most commonly used bulbs for professional lighting instruments. The standard "tungsten" lighting unit is assumed to have a tungsten-halogen bulb rated at 3200°K. Tungsten bulbs are far smaller and more efficient than photo bulbs. The brightest ones are rated at about 20,000 watts. Unlike photo bulbs, they burn for hundreds of hours, do not diminish in brightness or color temperature over their life span, and are more resistant to breakage during transport. Tungsten bulbs become very hot and are used mostly in heavy-duty fixtures for maximum safety and control. However, there are screw-in bulbs that can be fitted in well-ventilated household fixtures. Finger oils damage quartz glass, so use gloves or paper when handling the bulb. If the glass is touched, wipe it with alcohol. Carry a metal clamp for removing hot bulbs. Since quartz bulbs can explode, never turn one on when you or anyone else is directly in front of the fixture.

As noted above, tungsten bulbs are rated at 3200°K for use with tungsten-balanced film. These bulbs, and any other tungsten-balanced source, can be raised in color temperature to better match daylight illumination with a blue *dichroic* filter or with blue gel material (see p. 465). This normally cuts the light's output by about half.

HMI Bulbs

Hydrargyrum medium-arc iodide (*HMI*, also called *metal halide*) bulbs are an efficient lighting source that produces daylight-balanced illumination (5600°K or
6000°K). HMIs put out three to four times as much light as tungsten bulbs for the
same amount of electric power used. This improved efficiency means that bright
lights can be run off a smaller power supply, possibly avoiding the need for special
power lines or generators. Trying to match daylight with a tungsten source requires
filters that cut out half the light; HMIs require no filters for daylight and are far
more efficient for daylight applications. HMIs also give off less heat than tungsten
lights, making them popular with actors and crews.

Fig. 12-7. HMI lights being used outdoors. Note the ballast unit (circled). HMIs are an efficient source of daylight-balanced illumination.

HMIs are generally operated using AC power (wall current) and require a *ballast*
unit to control the electricity going to the lamp. Most HMIs produce a pulsed light
that seems continuous to the eye, but may result in flicker in the film or video
image if used improperly.[1] To avoid flicker, the light pulses must be evenly distributed on each video or film frame. These are the guidelines:

1. Use a crystal-controlled camera. All video cameras and most sync-sound
    film cameras are crystal controlled.

1. Flicker means that some frames seem more brightly lit than others.

2. Use a very stable power supply. In most technically advanced countries, the frequency of AC current is very stable. Care must be taken when using generators (use a crystal-controlled generator) or when shooting in the third world.

3. Use a frame rate that is divisible into twice the AC frequency. Thus, in the United States and other countries where the AC power is at 60 Hz, a frame rate of 12, 15, 20, 24, 30, 40, or 60 can be used. At 24 fps, film camera shutter angles from 60 to 200 degrees will work fine, but a shutter angle of 144 degrees allows for the maximum variation if camera or power is slightly off speed. In countries with 50 Hz power, you can film at 10, 12.5, 16.666, 20, 25, 33.3, or 50 fps without danger of flicker. In these countries, a camera run at 25 fps can use any shutter angle. A film camera run at 24 fps can avoid flicker by using a 172.8-degree shutter.

4. For video cameras, when shooting in 60 Hz countries, a standard NTSC video frame rate of 30 fps (60i) can be used without flicker. In countries with 50 Hz power, PAL video cameras run at 25 fps (50i) should be flicker-free.

These principles apply to all AC discharge lamps, including some fluorescent tubes (see below), HMI, CSI, sodium vapor, and mercury vapor lamps (the latter two are often found in sports stadiums and parking lots; they may require special filtering for color balance).

If you need to shoot at other frame rates, there are *flicker-free* ballasts available that allow filming up to 10,000 fps. These may produce a high whistling sound in some settings.

Some HMIs can be battery powered. A 200-watt HMI puts out nearly as much light as a 1K tungsten unit (see Fig. 12-17).

Fluorescent Bulbs

Fluorescent lighting falls into two categories: standard fluorescent fixtures typically found in office and institutional settings, and specially designed fluorescent lighting units for film and video work.

CONVENTIONAL FLUORESCENTS. Standard fluorescent lighting fixtures are usually undesirable for film and video, but they may be unavoidable. The spectrum of light from standard fluorescent tubes is discontinuous and matches neither tungsten nor daylight illumination. There are several types of fluorescent tubes available (daylight, cool white, warm white) that vary in color. Daylight and cool white tubes may produce an unpleasant blue-green color cast. Some warm white bulbs, however, are fairly close to tungsten.[2]

As long as all fluorescent tubes in a scene are the same type, most video cameras can achieve an acceptable white balance (you may want to experiment with the "daylight" position on the white balance control). Film cameras can be used with

2. The newer energy-efficient *compact fluorescent* bulbs (CFLs) used in homes and businesses to replace tungsten bulbs have a wide range of color temperatures, but some are around 3000°K when they warm up.

Fig. 12-8. Kino Flo high-output, flicker-free fluorescent lights are available in true tungsten or daylight balance. (Kino Flo, Inc.)

filters on the lights or the camera to improve color rendition, such as using an 85 filter or FLB for tungsten films or FLD for daylight-balanced films. However, with many color film stocks, acceptable color balance can be achieved in the lab even if no filters were used. It's better to get a good exposure with no filter than to be forced to underexpose with a filter.

Fluorescent lighting causes similar but less severe flicker problems than HMIs (see above). Standard film and video frame rates of 24, 25, and 30 fps are fine. (In North America and other places 60 Hz power is used, the rule of thumb is simply not to use shutter speeds faster than ⅟₆₀ second; it's usually not necessary to have a crystal-controlled camera.)

Mixing fluorescents with other sources of light can cause problems (see Mixed Lighting, p. 480). Fluorescent fixtures at workplaces often shine straight down, resulting in overexposed hair and deep eye and nose shadows. Many DPs choose, whenever possible, to replace standard fluorescents with color-balanced tubes (see below) or to turn off the fluorescents altogether and relight with some other source. When shooting in supermarkets and other settings in which it's impractical to either turn off or replace existing tubes, a DP will sometimes use a professional fluorescent fill light fixture that uses the same tubes, to at least maintain consistency.

FLUORESCENTS FOR FILM AND VIDEO. Fluorescent lighting units are available that overcome the problems mentioned above. A wide range of fixtures are made by Kino Flo using high-frequency ballasts that are flicker-free and avoid the humming noise of standard ballasts. The KF55 tube is daylight-balanced at 5500°K and the KF32 is tungsten-balanced. Other manufacturers make fluorescent units as well. Banks of fluorescents can be used as key or fill lights. The light output is bright, soft, and very even. Individual tubes—sometimes very small ones—can be used for out-of-the way spots or can be built into a set.

There are also fluorescent tubes available that can be used with conventional fixtures but produce a true color that reads correctly with either film or video. The Optima 32 bulb is tungsten-balanced and the Vita-lite and Chroma 50 tubes are daylight-balanced. When shooting in an office or other institutional setting, a movie crew will often replace the existing tubes with these bulbs.

LEDs

A newer type of lighting unit for film and video uses *LEDs* (*light-emitting diodes*). These compact units can produce heat-free, silent light that can be dimmed from 100 percent to full off with no color shift (unlike many other types of light). Some can be switched between daylight and tungsten balance. See Fig. 12-9.

Fig. 12-9. Litepanels mini LED lighting system used for a car shot. LEDs are efficient lighting, available in daylight and tungsten balance, and are fully dimmable with virtually no shift in color. (Litepanels)

TYPES OF LIGHTING INSTRUMENTS

Lensed Spotlights

The most controllable kind of lighting unit is a focusing spotlight. Some spots have a *Fresnel lens* (silent *s*, pronounced "freh-NEL") in front of the bulb (see Fig. 12-10). These lights emit focused, parallel rays of light that don't spread out much or diffuse over distance. Most spotlights are focusable, which means the bulb can be moved back and forth relative to the reflector or lens to produce either a hard, narrowly directed beam of light (*spot* position) or a wider, more diffuse, less intense

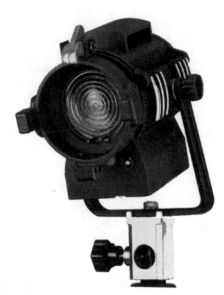

Fig. 12-10. LTM Pepper Fresnel. Compact, focusing lensed spotlight. Note Fresnel lens. (Fletcher Chicago/LTM)

beam (*flood* position). These, like most other movie lights, have a set of adjustable baffles called *barndoors*, which are used to block the beam from going where you don't want it (see Fig. 12-12).

Mole-Richardson makes a widely used line of studio equipment and you should learn Mole's names: a 5K lensed spotlight is a *senior*, while the 2K is a *junior*, and the 1K is a *baby* spot. A *baby junior* is a 2K in a small housing. A *tweenie* has a 650-watt bulb and a *mini* or *tiny* is only 200 watts.

Focusing, lensed spotlights are versatile and very controllable and are used extensively on typical movie sets. They may also be used on location shoots, particularly when the production is supported by a truck and a larger crew. However, lensed units are sometimes too heavy for a documentary being done with a small crew or involving a lot of travel. Some documentary DPs carry one or two lensed units and use mostly open-faced lights (see below).

Open-Faced Spotlights

Open-faced spotlights have no lens in front of the bulb. These are lighter and cheaper than Fresnel units and are often used on location and in small-scale filming. While these nonlensed instruments can be focused by moving the bulb from spot to flood positions, they are less controllable or "cutable" than lensed units (because the beam is not as sharp-edged), and the quality of light is not as hard.

Open-faced lights have various names. Mole's 1K is a *mickey*, Ianiro's is a *redhead*. A 2K may be a *mighty* or a *blonde*. Lowel's open-faced spots include the *omni-light* (maximum 500W) and the *DP light* (maximum 1K).

Fig. 12-11. Lowel DP open-faced spot. The quartz bulb is clearly visible. (Lowel Light Mfg., Inc.)

Nonfocusing Lights

There are a variety of lights that are not focusable. Some have lenses, some don't. *PAR lamps* (for *parabolic aluminized reflector*) are sealed beam lights that look like automobile headlights. PAR lights are available with different fixed lenses; some project a very narrow beam over great distances, others have a wider pattern. PARs may be used singly or in groups—typically, a grid of 2 x 3 or 3 x 3 lights on a frame (called *six lights* and *nine lights*, respectively). PARs put out a lot of light, and they can be used to simulate or augment sunlight, but they can be hard to control. *FAY* bulbs are PARs that incorporate a dichroic filter to produce daylight-balanced illumination. You can also get HMIs in sealed-beam configuration.

There are several types of nonfocusing, open-faced floodlights. *Scoops* are dish-shaped floodlights. *Broads* are rectangular and have a long tube-shaped bulb (see Fig. 12-12). Floodlights are sometimes used on the set as fill lights or to provide even illumination over a broad area. They can be hard to work with because the light tends to spill where you don't want it.

Soft Lights and Reflectors

The relatively hard light produced by a spot or a flood unit can be softened by placing some *diffusion* material in front of the unit. Diffusion spreads the light, disrupts the hard parallel rays, and cuts down the light's intensity. One of the most common types of diffusion is light fiberglass matting called *tough spun* or *spun* (for spun glass), which will not burn under the high heat of movie lights. There are many other types of professional diffusion, including translucent plastic sheets such as Lee 216 White Diffusion and the slightly milder Opal Tough Frost made by Rosco. Rosco's Soft Frost looks a bit like shower curtain material; because it's flexible, it won't rattle in the wind like some other diffusion material. Most types of diffusion are available in various grades, including full, ½ (medium), and ¼ (light). If placed far enough from the heat of the fixture, any number of materials can be used for diffusion, including thin cloth, silk, or rolls of tracing paper.

Fig. 12-12. Broad. Bardwell & McAlister 1000-watt Mini-Mac with four-leaf barndoor. Note the tubular bulb. (Bardwell & McAlister, Inc.)

Fig. 12-13. Soft lights. (left) Lowel collapsible soft light. (right) Umbrella reflectors. (Lowel Light Mfg., Inc.)

To obtain softer lighting, the light from the bulb can be bounced off a white or silvery surface; the larger the surface and the farther it is from the bulb, the softer the light. A *soft light* is a large, scoop-shaped fixture that blocks all direct light from the bulb so that only bounced light escapes. Studio soft lights are quite bulky, but there are collapsible models available that pack easily for travel.

A *soft box* encloses the bulb in a collapsible reflector with a soft diffuser over the opening. These can provide a very nice, soft light and are quick to set up and easy to use. Chimera makes popular soft boxes (called *lightbanks*) that can be mounted over a conventional spotlight with a *speed ring* adaptor. Lowel's RIFA light is a self-contained soft box (see Fig. 12-14). Chimera also makes *lanterns*, which have rounded or pancake shapes that can be used to provide a gentle glow by a subject or for even illumination over a dinner table. You can make your own low-cost lantern using a household paper Japanese lantern and an incandescent bulb.

Fig. 12-14. Collapsible soft boxes produce very soft, very even illumination and fold up for travel. Lowel Rifa Lights shown here. (Lowel Light Mfg., Inc.)

Soft lighting can also be created with a spot- or floodlight by bouncing the light off walls, ceilings or reflecting cards. *Foamcore sheets* are lightweight, rigid and make a versatile bounce board that can be easily cut and taped to walls or mounted on stands. White cardboard *show cards* are cheaper but are sometimes not rigid enough. Using foamcore or cards for fill lighting can be a good way to fill shadows from lights without creating new ones (see Fig. 12-27).

An extremely lightweight *space blanket* or a foil sheet can be taped shiny side out to make an excellent reflecting surface on a dark or colored wall, and it will protect the wall from burning. Another way to create soft light is to use a photographer's umbrella, which is silver or white on the inside. The lighting unit is mounted on the stem and is directed toward the inside of the umbrella. Umbrella reflectors fold to a compact size for traveling.

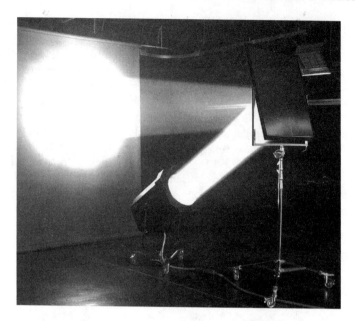

Fig. 12-15. A light source can be softened by bouncing it and/or by projecting it through diffusion material. Note that the xenon light source produces a very circular, focused, narrow beam of light. Shown here with Xeno Mirror reflector. (Matthews Studio Equipment, Inc.)

Generally, the reflecting surface should not have a color cast. However, sometimes a colored surface is used deliberately to create an effect. A reflector with a gold surface may be used to provide a warm fill light. Space blankets usually have a blue side that can be used to approximate daylight when bouncing tungsten lighting units.

Reflectors of various kinds are also used outdoors to redirect sunlight. This is commonly done to fill shadows on a sunny day. Usually you can get much more punch from a reflector than you can from a powered lighting instrument and it requires no electricity. Smooth, silvered reflectors provide relatively hard light, while textured silver or white surfaces are softer. Collapsible, cloth reflectors such as the Flexfill are popular for location shoots. They fold into a small disc for travel, and open to a larger circle with one side white and the other silver or gold. On windy days, all reflectors must be carefully steadied or the intensity of light on the subject will fluctuate.

Practicals

When a typical household table lamp is used on a movie set, it is called a *practical*. Practicals are often part of the set design. They may also be present in documentary shoots. Often a dimmer or diffusion material is used with a practical to cut down the intensity or at least minimize the light falling below or above a lampshade. You can get inexpensive dimmers that screw into the socket or plug between the power cable and the wall. If you're looking for more intensity from a practical, and use a photoflood or screw-in halogen light, be sure the fixture is rated for the wattage of the bulb and that there's adequate upward ventilation to prevent burning or melting. For more on working with practicals, see Lighting Wide Shots, p. 475.

Camera Lights and Handheld Lights

Camera-mounted lights are commonly used for news gathering or documentary (where they are sometimes called *sun guns*) and feature films (where they may be called *obie lights*, *eye lights*, or *bash lights*). A camera-mounted light is useful when the camera is moving because the unit moves with the camera and provides shadowless light on the subject. This shadowless light can be a blessing if it is filling the shadows cast by other, stronger lights. However, if it is the only light on the subject, it can be a curse, as full frontal lighting tends to be flat and harsh.

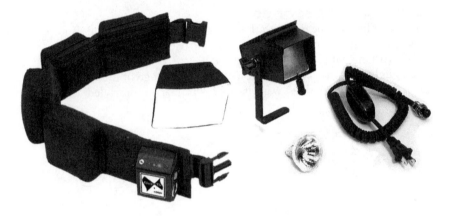

Fig. 12-16. Cool-Lux on-camera light with battery belt and diffuser. (Cool Lux)

Sun guns (originally a trade name that gained wide use) are often handheld and powered by battery. Even a standard tungsten spotlight can sometimes be fitted with a 30-volt bulb and powered with 30-volt battery pack or belt. One belt may run about 50 minutes with a 150-watt bulb, or 20 minutes with a 250-watt bulb. Lights and power packs vary in capacity, and most require several hours to recharge (see Battery Power, p. 131). When the batteries run down, light intensity and color temperature drop. Battery-powered lights are useful for scenes in cars; some can be run off the car battery by using an adaptor.

When a scene is lit with only one small light, it's not easy to make the lighting pleasant. With a handheld light, it's probably best to position the light a few feet to the side of the camera. The harsh shadows can be softened with diffusion on the light, although this sacrifices brightness. Some DPs bounce handheld lights off the ceiling or a wall, producing a very diffuse light. To maintain constant illumination, hold the unit steady. It's often best to have an assistant hold the light.

Fig. 12-17. Bron-Kobold 200-watt portable HMI with ballast unit. Can be used as a hand-held sun gun. (Bron-Kobold, USA)

Lighting Accessories

The art of lighting begins with the lights themselves, but the tools for controlling light are just as important. The lighting package includes many accessory items for working with light.

Spilled light, or just *spill*, is light usually from the edge of the beam that illuminates an area where you don't want it. Spill is primarily controlled with *barndoors*,

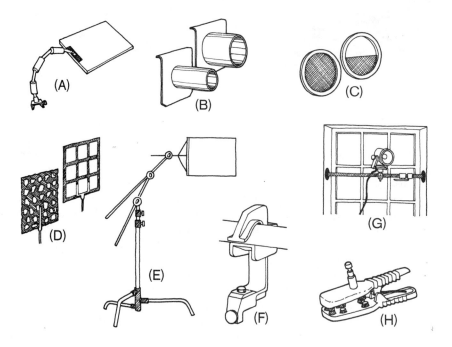

Fig. 12-18. Lighting accessories. (A) French flag. (B) Snoots. (C) Full scrim and half scrim. (D) Cookies. (E) Century stand with three gobo heads and flag. (F) Hanger for mounting on pipes or small beams. (G) Polecat mounted in window well. (H) Gator grip. (Representations are not drawn to same scale.) (Carol Keller)

which are adjustable flaps that mount on the front of the lighting instrument. Barn-doors come in two- and four-leaf versions, the latter providing more control. They can be opened wide or closed down to produce a relatively narrow beam of light. An even narrower beam can be made with a *snoot*, which is a cylindrical baffle that fits over a spotlight.

Flags, which are also called *cutters* or *gobos*, are either rectangular metal cards, dark cloth on wire frames, or pieces of cardboard. They are often mounted on stands to cut off unwanted spill. The farther the flag is from the light, the sharper its shadow will be.

French flags are small cards on a flexible stem often mounted on the camera as an effective lens shade to block light spilling into the front of the lens (see Fig. 6-15).

At times there is a need to flag off a light softly, creating a gradual transition from light to dark rather than having a hard shadow line. This may be done with a *net*, which is a piece of very thin, dark netting often mounted on a three-sided frame. Nets come in single and double thicknesses and can be used in multiple layers for increased shadowing.

Spill leaking from the back of a lighting unit can cause flare in the lens, or, if gels are being used, it can disrupt the lighting scheme with light of the wrong color. This spill can usually be blocked off with cards or flags. *Black wrap* is black aluminum foil that is very handy for controlling spill.

A *cucoloris* (usually called a *cookie* or *kook*) is a cutout piece of material placed in front of a light to cast a patterned shadow. Cookies are typically used to project the shadow of a window frame or venetian blinds. By adjusting the color and angle of a light projecting a window pattern you can suggest a mood or indicate the time of day. Sometimes an abstract, dappled pattern is used to break up a uniform expanse of wall or floor or to create a transition zone between sunlit and shaded areas. The shadow cast by any cookie or flag will be sharpest if it is placed closer to the subject than to the light and if the light source is hard.

Fig. 12-19. A silk being used to cut the bottom half of the light beam; this evens out the illumination close to and far from the light. The light is attached to the telephone pole using a poultry bracket. (Matthews Studio Equipment, Inc.)

There are many ways to reduce the intensity of a light. The simplest is perhaps just to move it farther from the subject. *Nets* can be used to shade or "feather" a light. *Silks* are white silk material mounted on frames like nets; they cut down the light while diffusing it somewhat (see Fig. 12-19).

Scrims are circular wire mesh screens that can be placed in front of a lighting unit, usually inside the barndoors, to reduce the intensity without changing the color temperature or the quality (hardness) of light. Inserting a scrim is the best way to reduce light intensity without changing anything else. A *single scrim* (usually indicated by a green frame) reduces the intensity about a half stop; a *double scrim* (red frame) cuts out a full stop. On a *half scrim*, half of the circle is left open. A half scrim can be used to solve the common problem that occurs when someone walks toward a light. Normally, as he approaches the light he'll become brighter. To even out the illumination, raise the lighting unit fairly high above the subject and point it down at an angle. Use a half scrim to reduce the intensity of the *bottom* of the light beam (which falls near the unit) without diminishing the top of the beam (which reaches into the distance). You could use a net or a silk to do the same thing (see Fig. 12-19). The word scrim also refers to a thin cloth used for diffusion.

Studio lighting is sometimes dimmed with *shutters*, which act like venetian blinds. *Dimmers* are used in the home and in theatrical lighting to regulate light intensity. Dimmers lower the voltage going to the light, which not only makes the light dimmer, but with tungsten lights results in the color temperature dropping as well (making tungsten lights more orange). There are some situations in which the lowered color temperature may seem natural (see Mixed Lighting, p. 480). LEDs and some fluorescents can be dimmed without changing the color.

There are hundreds of devices for supporting lights and mounting them on various surfaces. Lights are usually supported by stands, which are collapsible for transport. *Century stands* (*C-stands*) have low-slung legs at different heights that allow several stands to be positioned close together. *Gobo heads* with multiple locking arms can be positioned in endless ways. *Roller stands* have wheels that make it easier to reposition heavy lights.

A *gator grip* is a spring-loaded clip for attaching lights to doors, pipes, and moldings. A *C-clamp* with a *spud* to mount a light is more stable. A *polecat* is like an expandable closet bar. A heavier-duty version is the *wall spreader*, which allows you to run a piece of lumber, such as a two-by-four, between two walls. A polecat or a wall spreader can be used to hang lights near the ceiling without stands that might show in the scene. When shooting in offices or other rooms that have hung ceilings, a *scissors clip* allows you to mount lights right on the ceiling. A *wall plate* for mounting fixtures can be screwed or taped to vertical or horizontal surfaces.

Carrying several feet of opaque black fabric such as *duvetyn* ("doova-teen") can be extremely useful for creating limbo backgrounds, darkening a window, or placing on a table for product shots.

Other items for a lighting package include apple boxes (see p. 347), *sand bags* for stabilizing lights and stands, *stingers* (extension cords), gloves for handling hot lamps, and plenty of *gaffer's tape* (a gray fabric tape sold in equipment houses—*not* duct tape). See p. 322 for a typical lighting and grip package.

Colored Filters and Gels

A common way to change the color of light is to use *gels* (gelatine), which are made of flexible, transparent plastic that comes in small sheets and large rolls. Gels can be mounted on lights in gel frames or just attached to barndoors with clothespins.

Fig. 12-20. Open spotlight with attached gel frame. (Lowel Light Mfg., Inc.)

CTO (color temperature orange) gels are used to lower color temperature for converting daylight to tungsten-balanced light or otherwise warming a light source. *Sun 85* or ¾ *CTO* gels are roughly equivalent to an 85 camera filter (see Chapter 8) and are used to convert standard 5500°K daylight and HMI sources to tungsten. These filters cut out about ⅔ of a stop of light. Lee 204 and Rosco 3407 are full CTO gels that are slightly more orange and are used to convert skylight (6500°K) to tungsten.

CTB (color temperature blue) gels are used to raise color temperature and make any source bluer. Some blue gels are referred to as *booster gels*, since they boost the color temperature. Rosco 3202 and Lee 201 are full CTB gels, used to bring a 3200°K tungsten source up to 5700°K daylight. These cut out about 1⅓ stops of light.

Gels can be purchased in full, ¾, ½, ¼, and ⅛ intensity versions, from deep color to pale, to make large or slight changes in color for precise matching of light sources. The deeper the color of the gel, the more it cuts down the light intensity. Often the full CTB cuts out too much light, and a ¾ or ½ CTB is used instead, allowing a tungsten source to appear slightly yellow compared to daylight.

Gels are available in many other colors besides orange and blue. Sometimes the light from an HMI lamp seems *slightly* too blue; a ⅛ straw gel or a pale yellow may be used to "take the curse off" and warm the light a bit. There is a wide range of other colors for creating more theatrical effects.

Gels are also available in combination with neutral density (ND; see p. 302) or diffusion material. Blue Frost converts tungsten to daylight while adding diffusion—having both effects in one gel may prevent unneeded loss of light.

Gels should be replaced when heat from the lamp causes the center of the gel to become paler. Gels and the more rigid *acrylic filters* are often attached to windows to filter daylight (see Mixed Lighting, p. 480).

Another way to raise color temperature is to use a *dichroic* filter, sometimes called a *dike*, which is a special blue glass filter used to convert 3200°K tungsten sources to about 5500°K to match the color of daylight. These cut out about 50 percent of the light, reducing intensity by one stop. Dichroics are expensive, fragile, and must be fitted to a particular light.

Mounting Lights Safely

In close quarters a hot, falling light can do serious damage. Spread legs of a light stand wide for maximum stability. Weigh down light stands with sand or water bags or tape them down with gaffer's tape. When raising a light, use the lower, thicker extensions of a light stand before the thin, upper ones.

Fig. 12-21. Lowel Solo Kit. Location package includes two Omni-lights (650-watt maximum open-faced spots) and four Tota-lights (1000-watt maximum broads). Accessories include stands, flags with flexible stems, scrims, door/wall brackets, clamps, gel frames, reflector, and umbrellas. Everything fits into the carrying case. (Lowel Light Mfg., Inc.)

Tape all power cables neatly to the floor or put mats over them in high traffic areas so no one trips on them. Use plenty of good-quality gaffer's tape when you attach lights to a wall, and if you can, place lights where they won't strike anyone if they fall. Remember that tape loses its stickiness when hot. When possible, "safety" a hanging light by attaching a piece of sash cord or chain to a fixed point to catch the light if it drops off its mount. Gaffer's tape will often remove paint and wallpaper, so peel the tape back slowly as soon as possible after shooting to minimize damage.

LIGHTING TECHNIQUE

LIGHTING STYLES

Before beginning any movie that involves controlled lighting, decide on the lighting style you hope to achieve. The DP and director can look at movies, photographs, and paintings for ideas.

Like everything else, lighting styles have evolved over the years. Black-and-white feature films of the 1930s and 1940s were usually lit in a highly stylized way. The goal was not "realistic" lighting, but something that would heighten the drama and the glamour. These films were shot on studio sets that often had no ceiling and only two or three walls. Lights mounted outside the set on overhead grids and elsewhere struck the actors from directions that would be impossible in a normal building interior.

In many feature films today, lighting is intended to be more "naturalistic"—that is, like the kind of light one would find in the real world. Many lights may be used, but the intent is to simulate the light that might normally occur in the filming space, whether it be from sunlight or man-made fixtures. One way to help give lighting a natural feel is to make sure that the chief light sources seem "motivated." Motivated lights are ones that appear to come from a logical source. For example, actual window light may be used for illumination, or lighting instruments may be set up near the windows to give the illusion that the light comes from the windows.

Often a few household fixtures are placed in a scene as practicals. These may actually light the subject or merely act as motivation for light from professional lighting instruments.

Even if the goal is naturalistic lighting, usually liberties can be taken to improve the lighting of faces or achieve particular effects. Of course, many movies don't seek realism at all, and lighting is used to create a dramatic, expressive ambience.

The sensitivity of film stocks and video cameras has improved, and it's increasingly possible to shoot indoors entirely with available light without introducing any special lighting equipment. This can be a real boon for documentaries (see below). For fiction films, ironically, it sometimes takes a lot of light to make a scene look really *unlit*, the way it does to the naked eye. For example, you may be able to shoot an interior scene with just window light, but this may result in the windows being overexposed and the people appearing somewhat underexposed (see Fig. 7-22). To get a natural balance between the interior and exterior may require gels on the windows and/or a significant amount of light from inside (see Mixed Lighting, p. 480).

Documentary Lighting

Lighting a documentary can be tricky. You have to balance your desire for a certain style or look with the typical constraints of small crews, small lighting packages, and short shooting schedules. Interviews can be lit fairly fast, but providing good lighting for an uncontrolled scene in which people move around a large space, either at work or at home, often takes more time and equipment. Sometimes large spaces are lit with a few lights bounced off the ceiling. This may give you enough light for exposure and is fairly even. However, this kind of light is flat and tends to be "toppy"—that is, coming from above and causing dark shadows in the eye sockets.

When shooting unscripted scenes of people living their lives, consider the effect the lights have on your subjects. If you're filming intimate scenes of family life and other potentially delicate moments, you want to do everything you can to minimize the disruption caused by the film crew. Bright lights can create an "on-the-set" feeling, and people under the lights may feel like they should "perform" when the lights go on. Also, because it's hard to light an entire house or location, the use of lights transforms some areas into filming spaces while others remain living space. All of this may disrupt the natural flow of life that you hope to capture. Sometimes you can mount a few lights on the wall or ceiling and basically leave them in place for the duration of a shoot, turning them on when needed. The less light you use, the more mobile and unobtrusive you can be. But this may come at some sacrifice to the image quality. For every scene, you have to balance these concerns.

POSITIONING LIGHTS

A Basic Lighting Setup

A classic lighting technique is sometimes called *three-point lighting* because three basic lights are used to illuminate the subject: the key, fill, and backlight. Each light has a particular function. Even if many lights are used to cover a large set, each light plays one of these three roles.

KEY LIGHT. The key is the brightest light and casts the primary shadows, giving a sense of directionality to the lighting. The key may be hard or soft; the harder the light, the bolder or harsher its shadows will be. The key's shadows must be watched carefully for the way they interact with the subject. The key light is usually placed somewhat off the camera-to-subject axis, high enough up so that the shadow of the subject's nose does not fall across the cheek but downward instead. This height helps ensure that body shadows fall on the floor and not on nearby walls where they may be distracting.

FILL LIGHT. The main function of the fill light is to fill in the shadows produced by the key without casting distinct shadows of its own. Fill lighting is almost always softer than the key; it's usually created with a soft light fixture or a bounced spotlight. If the fill light emanates from a point close to the camera's lens and at the same level, its shadows will not be visible to the camera. The fill is generally placed on the opposite side of the camera from the key. Sometimes light is bounced off the wall or ceiling to provide flat, even fill over a broad area.

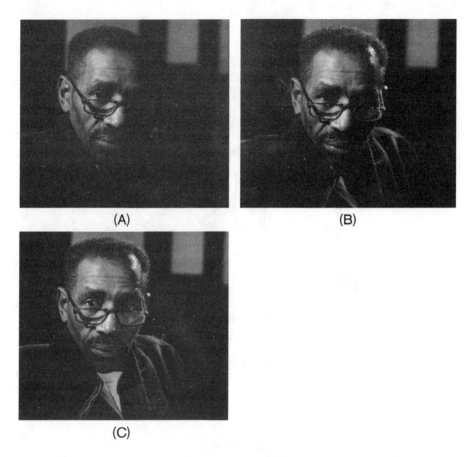

(A)   (B)

(C)

Fig. 12-22. Three-point lighting. (A) Key light only. In this shot, the key is quite far to the side. (B) Key plus backlight. The backlight separates the man from the dark background and brings out texture in his coat and hair. (C) Adding fill light from near the camera on the opposite side from the key brings up the light level primarily on the dark side of his face, making the shadows less severe. For another example of classic three-point lighting, see Fig. 4-5. (Stephen McCarthy)

BACKLIGHT. Backlights (variants are called *hair*, *rim*, or *edge lights*) are placed on the opposite side of the subject from the camera, high enough to be out of view. Backlight should generally be fairly hard, to produce highlights on the subject's hair. If a backlight is at about the same level as the subject and somewhat off to the side, it is called a *kicker*. Kickers illuminate the shoulders and the side of the face more than hair lights do. All backlights are used to give a bright outline to the subject, helping to separate the subject from the background and define shape.

SET LIGHT. In some situations, the key and fill lights adequately light the background. In others, a fourth basic type of light, the *set light*, is used to illuminate the background and selected objects. Sometimes parts of the set need to be given their own key, fill, and/or backlights.

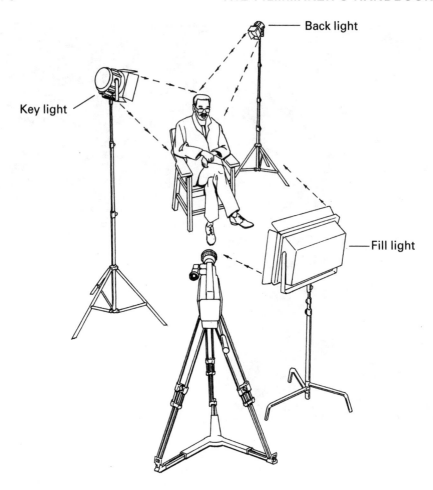

Fig. 12-23. A three-point lighting setup, similar to the one used for Fig. 12-22. (Robert Brun)

Lighting Faces

In medium and close shots that include people, the lighting on faces is extremely important. When lighting a set or location, if you know there will be significant close shots of people, the overall lighting should be designed to provide good facial lighting (even so, the lighting for wide shots will generally be tweaked or cheated somewhat when it comes time for close-ups). For the purposes of this discussion, let's assume you're lighting a single subject in a chair.

Start by positioning the key light alone, paying close attention to the shadows of the subject's nose and eye sockets. Every face is different; people with deep-set eyes and prominent noses will have more shadowing than those with flatter faces. The closer the key light is to the camera, the less shadowing there will be. Television news programs tend to be done with very frontal, flat lighting (see Fig. 12-2D). This is a functional lighting approach, and minimizes possibly objectionable shadows, but it may be dull. If the key is brought around somewhat to the side (three-quarter light), the face takes on more dimensionality (see Fig. 12-24). About 45 degrees from the camera is considered fairly standard for the key position. In Fig. 12-22, the key is positioned quite far to the side (almost 90 degrees) for a dramatic look. In this case, it is also fairly high to avoid reflections in the man's glasses.

Fig. 12-24. Frontal facial lighting. Key is slightly offset to provide some modeling. Nose shadow falls near the "smile line" from the side of the nose to the corner of the mouth. Though the lighting is fairly flat, the background is dimly lit, and thus provides strong contrast with the foreground figure. (*Portrait of Jacques Louis Leblanc* by Ingres, The Metropolitan Museum of Art, Purchase, Wolfe Fund, 1918)

Pay close attention to the way the eyes are lit. As the poet tells us, eyes are the windows to the soul. When you can't see the eyes, sometimes you feel like you can't see into the *person.* Generally, subjects face one side of the camera or the other. Often the lighting looks best if the subject is looking *toward* the key light (thus, if the subject is facing camera left, put the key light on the left side of the camera; see Fig. 12-26). This puts both eyes in the key light. If one eye is in shadow, the fill light can be used to bring up the illumination on that side (see below). Of course, you might choose to put one or both eyes in shadow to create a mysterious or spooky feel.

Fig. 12-25. Far-side key. Key light positioned on far side of subject produces a rim of light on the nose and brings out skin texture. Virtually no fill light in scene creates a low-key dramatic look, which could be used for a nighttime scene. In many situations it's most interesting when the camera shoots from the shadowed side of the face. (*Portrait of Martin Baer* by Johan Hagemeyer, The Metropolitan Museum of Art, Gift of the Estate of Johan Hagemeyer, 1962)

The key should generally be high enough so that the nose shadow falls down, not across the face (some DPs try to place the nose shadow on the "smile line," which extends from the nose to the corner of the mouth; see Fig. 12-24). The "standard" key is 45 degrees above the subject.

More dramatic effects can be achieved by moving the key very far to the side. In Fig. 12-25, the subject looks off screen into a light that might be meant to suggest a distant window or lamp. Here, the key is actually coming from the far side of the subject. His nose is rim-lit with strong shadows falling across his face (the camera side of his face is left quite dark). This kind of look is well suited to a very low-key nighttime scene (see Special Lighting Effects, p. 482).

Should the key light be hard or soft? It depends on how you want the audience to interpret the lighting. Direct sunlight is quite hard; indirect window light or the light of an overcast day is soft. You may like dramatic, crisp shadows or you may

Fig. 12-26. Window-lit scene. Nearby window provides key light. Light reflected from the wall on the right provides fill on the dark side of the man's face. A splash of light on the back wall reinforces the sense of sunlight. (Stephen McCarthy)

prefer a gentler look. Generally, some diffusion material (see Soft Lights and Reflectors, p. 457) should be used to help make the key less harsh. Hard light will accentuate skin defects, makeup, and lighting errors more than soft light. Soft light is more forgiving. One look that can be appealing is to use a quite soft key. The light will wrap around the face and you may need little or no fill light (see Fig. 12-26). Diffused lights do not "throw" as far as hard ones, so soft light sources need to be placed closer to the subject. For soft lights, as a rule, the larger the surface of the light source and/or the closer it is to the subject, the softer the light will be.

After the key has been placed, some DPs "rough in" the fill light, others go next to the backlight. Backlight should be used when needed, but it can seem artificial or stagy if overused. Backlight can be very important to provide separation between the subject and the background (see Fig. 12-22). Some scenes just look *dull* without a little backlight to add luster to the hair and put some bright "kicks" in the scene. On the other hand, sometimes the subject and the background have adequate separation simply because one is significantly darker or lighter than the other, and you don't really need a backlight (see Fig. 12-24). Some scenes are meant to appear lit only by one source, and backlight might spoil the effect (see Fig. 12-26). However, sometimes if a backlight is subtle, it can add a little shine without calling too much attention to itself (see Figs. 12-22B and 4-5).

Backlights should be placed high enough to avoid lens flare in the camera and angled down so that they don't strike the tip of the subject's nose. If a backlight causes flare or casts a noticeable shadow in front of subject, flag it off with the barndoors or a gobo.

The fill light is used to bring up the light level in the shadows cast by the key or the backlight. Put the fill light close enough to the camera so that it doesn't create a second set of shadows of its own. The difference in brightness between the shadows and the highlights is the lighting contrast. The contrast plays a big part both in how details will be reproduced in the film or video image and in the mood of the lighting. (See Lighting Contrast, p. 447.)

Sometimes, fill lighting is provided not by a separate lighting unit, but by a reflecting surface (this has the advantage of not casting another set of shadows). In Fig. 12-26, the wall on the right side of the room reflects back the sunlight, filling the shadows on the dark side of the man's face. In Fig. 12-27, a piece of white foamcore is used to simulate the same effect. A Flexfill or other reflector (see Soft Lights and Reflectors, p. 457) may be used outdoors to do the same thing. Often, a white reflector needs to be quite close to the subject to provide significant fill.

There are various other techniques and tricks used to improve facial lighting. A low-powered eye light is sometimes used to add a little sparkle to the eyes, giving the

Fig. 12-27. "Window-lit" scene. A lighting setup that might be used to simulate the light in Fig. 12-26. Key light is bounced for a soft look. Fill lighting is provided by a white card just out of frame to the right. A set light provides the sun effect on the back wall. Flags and/or a cookie might be needed to create the desired effects on the walls. (Robert Brun)

subject an alert or alluring look. An eye light should not be so bright that it washes the face out with flat fill. Sometimes nets are used to delicately shade the top and bottom of the face, focusing attention on the eyes and mouth. A dedicated light may be used to bring up the illumination on particularly dark or absorptive clothing.

Facial shine can be very distracting and can be avoided with a basic application of powder (see p. 362).

It should be noted that a certain amount of "relighting" can be done in video post. Particularly for a locked-off shot, it's not hard to shade off the background or selectively darken parts of the frame to create a more interesting look (see Fig. 14-36).

Lighting Wide Shots

Wide shots or long shots that show a large part of a set or location can be harder to light than close-ups because of the greater area to be covered and the problem of hiding lights and light stands. Wide shots often involve people moving from one place to another, which adds the challenge of providing good light in several different parts of the set.

Generally, wide shots should be lit to establish mood and to cover the actors' blocking (movements). Proper facial lighting is a lower priority. Keep in mind that the eye is naturally drawn to light areas of the frame. Thus, the area in which the actors move is normally lit slightly brighter than the background or extreme foreground. Flags or nets can be used to diminish the light falling on unimportant areas such as broad expanses of wall. Much of the mood of the shot is established by the relation between the brighter action area and the darker background. Try to maintain this balance when you change camera position or lighting.

When you light any scene, it's usually more interesting to have pools of light and areas that are relatively dark than to have flat, even illumination throughout the frame. Pools of light also create a greater feeling of depth; a corridor, for example, seems longer if bright and dark areas alternate. Use fill light to provide illumination between the brighter areas.

When subjects move closer and farther from a light, the illumination falling on them can change significantly (see Fig. 12-6). Sometimes a half scrim or other material can be used to even out the light (see Fig. 12-19). In general, using a brighter, harder light from a greater distance away from the action will result in more even illumination than a softer unit closer to the subject. Sometimes a very bright light positioned outside a window or on the far side of the room is the best way to keep interior action evenly lit.

For a naturalistic look, every location needs to be examined for appropriate "motivating" sources for the lighting. Most daytime scenes include light coming through a window. Actual window light may be used, but often it must be simulated because the sunlight would change during the course of filming. If the window itself is not visible, you can position the light source wherever seems plausible. You can bounce light off a large white card for an overcast or "north light" look or use a large, focused spotlight or PAR light to simulate sunlight streaming in. When simulating sunlight, a warming gel (CTO; see Colored Filters and Gels, p. 465) is sometimes used over the light. If tungsten light is mixed with actual window light, some filtering must be done (see Mixed Lighting, p. 480).

If household fixtures are being used as practicals in a scene, sometimes they can provide significant illumination. You can replace the bulb with a photoflood or a screw-in halogen bulb. Or, you may be able to use just a bright household tungsten bulb, but the color may read too red/yellow on film or video depending on what other sources are used and how the camera or film is color balanced. Many practicals can't handle much heat or electricity, and often a bright bulb makes the practical appear too bright on camera. The shade may overexpose, looking burned out. To seem natural, the lampshade of the practical should read about two to three stops brighter than the faces of nearby actors. This varies, of course, with the type of shade and fixture.

Often, the opposite approach is taken with practicals. Instead of trying to light the subject with them, they are treated simply as set dressing. Sometimes a low-intensity bulb or a screw-in dimmer is used to keep the light subtle. Neutral density gels or diffusion material can be hidden in the lampshade to dim down the shade or the spill coming out of the light. Then a professional lighting instrument is aimed in from off camera to simulate the light that would come from the practical. Be sure the instrument is flagged so it doesn't shine *on* the practical and cast a shadow—a dead giveaway.

Frequently, one light can be used to accomplish several functions. If two people are talking across a table, a light can key one person while it backlights the other.

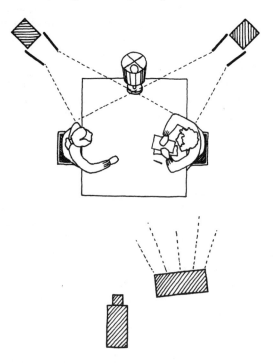

Fig. 12-28. Cross lighting. Each spotlight keys one subject and backlights the other. Lights are used in part to simulate practical illumination from the table lamp and are thus flagged off of it. Fill light is placed near the camera. (Carol Keller)

This is called *cross lighting* (see Fig. 12-28). When an actor moves through his blocking, a given light may change from a key light to a backlight.

Cinematographer Nestor Almendros (*Days of Heaven*) prided himself on being able to light a scene with as little as one or two lights. Many scenes require more lighting fixtures, but often, the fewer the sources, the cleaner the image looks. When there are many lights, you run the risk of many distracting shadows falling in different directions. To minimize this, keep actors away from walls, place them against dark rather than light walls, position furniture or props to break up the shadows, and use diffusion to soften secondary lights. Moving a light closer to a person will diffuse the shadow he casts.

Bright, shiny surfaces in the frame attract the eye and are usually undesirable. Glints or kicks can be diminished by repositioning a shiny object or by applying washable *dulling spray* or even soap. Sometimes you can get rid of the reflection of a light in a surface by raising or lowering the camera a few inches or wedging a little tape behind a picture frame to angle it away from the camera. Reflections from smooth, nonmetal surfaces such as plastic, glass, and water can be reduced by putting a polarizer filter on the camera. Avoid shooting glass or mirrors that will pick up the lights or the camera. If you have to film against white walls, take care not to overlight them. Usually, broad expanses of wall are broken up with pictures or furniture.

When a scene is to be filmed with both long shots and medium or close-up shots, it's common to determine the blocking, set the lighting, and shoot the long shots first. Then, as the camera is positioned closer to the subject, the lights can be cheated (moved) to maintain the general sense of the long shot while providing more desirable facial lighting. Close-ups are usually lit with slightly lower contrast lighting than long shots are so that facial detail will be clear. When the camera angle changes significantly, you can make many changes in the light without the audience noticing.

When shooting video, or when using a film camera with a video tap, watching the image in a monitor can help you light, but beware of small and poor-quality monitors. Make sure the monitor is set up properly (see Appendix A) and that there isn't light falling on the monitor screen. On film shoots, digital stills are sometimes taken to see how the light will look (although motion picture film may respond differently) and to aid in relighting in case the scene needs to be reshot. Stills are also very helpful for continuity purposes to record how props were arranged and how actors were dressed.

Before you shoot, scrutinize the frame to make sure no light stands or cables are visible. Be sure no lights are producing flare in the lens (stand next to the camera and look at the front of the lens; if you see any light sources in the glass, try to flag them off). Rehearse the shot to check that movements of the crew and especially the microphone boom don't produce visible shadows.

Lighting and Exposure

When setting lights, the question arises: How brightly should a scene be lit? On a feature film, many DPs try to work at a given f-stop consistently throughout the movie, which helps them judge lighting setups by eye. Lens sharpness for many lenses can be maximized by shooting at apertures about two stops closed down from wide open (on an *f*/2 lens, shoot around *f*/4). Higher or lower *f*-stops may be used to increase or decrease depth of field. As a rule, the discomfort of both crew and actors, or documentary subjects, rises with the amount of light.

CONTROLLING LIGHTING CONTRAST

As discussed in Chapters 5 and 7, both film and video systems have a limited ability to capture the range of brightness that the eye can see. When lighting a scene, you must pay close attention to the *lighting contrast* (see Lighting Contrast, p. 447). To the eye, scenes always have less contrast than they do as rendered on film or video. Shadows that look natural to the eye may be rendered as black and without detail. Bright highlights can easily overexpose and be rendered as areas of featureless white.

When shooting film, DPs may judge the lighting contrast just by the way it looks or with a light meter. When shooting video, it's possible to use a light meter, but often DPs on video shoots don't have one.[3] A good monitor can help you judge how the contrast looks on video, but a bad monitor may be worse than none at all. In general, video is less forgiving of high lighting contrast than film is. Web video handles contrast particularly badly.

If you have a light meter, measuring the *lighting contrast ratio* can help you determine the proper lighting contrast. This is the ratio of key plus fill lights to fill light alone (K + F : F). For a typical close-up, the lighting contrast is measured by reading the light on the bright side of the face (which comes from both the key and fill lights) and comparing it to the light in the facial shadows (which comes from the fill light alone). The measurements are most easily taken with an incident light meter, blocking or turning off the key light(s) to take the second reading. Some DPs prefer to use the incident meter's flat-disc diffuser when doing this to make it easier to isolate the light coming from individual sources.

If the bright side of the face is one stop lighter than the facial shadow, the ratio is 2:1. Two stops would be 4:1; three stops, 8:1. To the eye, 2:1 and 3:1 look quite flat, but this lighting contrast is considered "normal" by Kodak. This is a conservative standard. Kodak recommends that contrasts of 4:1 or higher be used for "special lighting effects" only, but it is common for filmmakers to work with these contrast levels. Low-key scenes, nighttime effects, and many outdoor sunlit scenes are shot at ratios much higher than 4:1.

For either film or video, you should use lighting contrast to create the mood and look that you want. If you choose a high lighting contrast, bear in mind that you may lose detail in shadow or highlight areas. How much you lose depends on the film stock or video camera, the exposure, and how the project is handled during

---

3. To use a meter with a video camera, you need to find the "exposure index" (EI) for the camera (as though it had an ASA/ISO number). Cinematographer Harry Mathias suggests this technique: Using a waveform monitor and a standard chip chart, point the camera at the chart and open the iris until the brightest white chip (peak white) reads 100 IRE units on the waveform (the middle gray "crossover" chip should read about 55). Then hold the incident meter at the chart (pointed toward the camera) and fiddle with the meter's EI or ASA setting until the meter indicates the *f*-stop the lens is set at. You will need to recalibrate if you change lenses or the shutter or the gain setting.

postproduction and distribution. As noted above, many video cameras have a more limited exposure range than most film stocks (see p. 178), so lighting contrast must usually be kept lower for video than film shoots.

As a rule of thumb, a film or video image will generally *pick up* contrast through the various stages of processing the footage and reproducing it. So if you start with a somewhat lower contrast, you may find the image has gotten "snappier" without you doing anything. You can generally *increase* contrast later if you find the image too flat, but if footage is originally shot with too much contrast, it may be difficult or impossible to recapture the lost detail afterward.

If the contrast seems too high, the fill light can be moved closer to the subject or a brighter fill light can be used. Alternately, the key light could be dimmed with a scrim or moved back. Lighting contrast should be evaluated with respect to all parts of the frame, not just the light and shadow on faces. Walk around the set or location with an incident or reflected meter, or point a video camera at various parts of the set to get a sense of the range of exposure in the scene. If the background is in deep shadow, it may need additional light to keep the overall contrast down. Or, if a window is too bright it may need a neutral density gel to darken it up a bit. A bright wall can be made darker by flagging the light off it, or using a net to gradually shade the light (often you want keep the light on the actors and darken the upper part of the wall above them). Actors or subjects may be asked not to wear very bright or very dark clothing, high-contrast props can be replaced, or set walls repainted in medium shades (see p. 362). In general, it's less disturbing if some areas of the frame are underexposed than if large or important areas are significantly overexposed.

CONTRAST VIEWING GLASSES. Some DPs set their lighting with the use of *contrast viewing glasses*, which are smoked glass monocles that cause the scene to appear to have higher contrast, more like the way it will appear on film or video. These glasses must be held to the eye only briefly, since the eye gradually adjusts, lowering the apparent contrast. It takes some experience to use these properly.

Lighting Contrast in Daylight

On a sunny day outside, the direct sunlight usually acts as the "key light." The "fill" is provided by skylight and, to a lesser extent, reflections from buildings, objects, and clothing. On a bright day, the lighting contrast is often too great for film or video. If you expose properly for the bright areas, the shadows end up looking very deep and harsh. A classic problem is shooting people at midday under a bright sun; the eye shadows may make it almost impossible to see their eyes. That's why hazy or lightly overcast days, with their lower lighting contrast, are often ideal for shooting people outdoors.

There are a number of solutions to the problem of shooting in sun. For an interview or close shot, you can use a white card or a small reflector such as a Flexfill to help fill the shadows. For a larger scene, a bigger reflector such as a shiny board with a silver or gold surface can also be used. Daylight-balanced lighting instruments can also be used, but it takes a lot of intensity to try to match the sun on a bright day.

Another approach is to try to diminish or soften the direct sunlight. An *overhead set* (also called a *butterfly*) is a pipe frame (often six by six feet or twelve by twelve feet) that can be placed over the action to hold either a *silk* to diffuse the light, a *scrim* to cut down the light without diffusing it, or a *solid* to block the light altogether. Overheads must be used carefully so that the shadow of the frame doesn't show in the shot, and neither does the brightly (and more harshly) lit background. The overhead must be held down securely when the wind blows. If sunlight is diffused in this way, it's easier to maintain consistency in the light over a day's shooting, since the material can be removed if a light cloud passes.

Whether or not you have reflectors or lights, try to use the angle of the sun to your advantage. When possible, put your subject in gentle shade near a building or by a tree. Don't shoot against a hot (bright) background like a bright sky or a white wall. Sometimes it's best to avoid shooting at all in the middle of the day when sunlight is the harshest.

When shooting in direct sun, if the sun is not directly overhead, changing the position of the camera and/or the subject will have a big effect on the contrast. If the sun comes from behind the camera (front lighting), contrast will be fairly low, but the subject may have to squint. Alternately, if the subject has her back to the sun, contrast will be fairly low on her face (all indirect light), but there may be a large contrast between her face and the background. If you now bring in a reflector from the camera-side of the subject, it will pick up the sun nicely and boost the illumination on her face.

When you shoot in cars or near windows, lighting contrast can be extremely high between the darker foreground interior and the brightly lit exterior (see Fig. 7-22). You might choose to add light to the interior or put neutral density gel on the windows. Without these steps, a compromise exposure is normally used.

LIGHTING AND COLOR

Mixed Lighting

Before reading this section, see the discussion of color temperature and filters for film and video systems in Chapter 8 and the discussion of video white balance on p. 113.

A video camera can render colors naturally in daylight or in tungsten light if it is properly white-balanced. Similarly, color film stocks can be used in *either* daylight or tungsten light and produce a pleasing color rendition with the proper filters. However, no video or film camera can shoot a scene that contains *both* daylight and tungsten light without rendering the former blue or the latter yellow/red relative to the other.

To take a typical example: You're trying to shoot an interior scene using window light, but there's not enough light for exposure, so you set up some tungsten movie lights to boost the light on your subject. If you balance the video camera for the tungsten light (or shoot tungsten film without a filter), the daylight from the windows will look very blue by comparison. If you balance the video camera for daylight (or use an 85 filter with tungsten film), the tungsten light will look much too warm (orange).

There are a few ways to deal with this problem. One is to make the tungsten light bluer, to better match daylight. This can be done with dichroic filters or full CTB (blue) gels on the lights (see Colored Filters and Gels, p. 465). However, this will reduce the lights' output by half or more. Also, when shooting tungsten-balanced film—and with some video cameras—an 85 camera filter is generally used for daylight, which cuts down the light intensity almost in half again.[4] This may not leave enough light to shoot.

In this situation, sometimes instead of using a full CTB gel on the lights, only a ¾ or ½ CTB is used. This lets more light through and results in the tungsten light appearing *slightly* yellow compared to the daylight, which can look very nice. Also, if you're shooting film, you could use a daylight-balanced stock that requires no 85 filter.

Another approach is to balance the video camera for the tungsten light (or use no filter with tungsten-balanced film), and filter the *window* light with orange gel or acrylic sheets. Gel comes in large rolls and is easy to transport. Tape it carefully to the windows or it will show in shots that include the windows. Gels crease easily, will reflect the lights if mounted sloppily, and are noisy in windy locations. Acrylic sheets, on the other hand, are inconvenient to carry, but they are good for mounting outside the window where they won't show. They are also optically sharper for shots that involve shooting *through* the window.

A sun 85 or ¾ CTO (orange) gel can be used to warm up 5500°K daylight to 3200°K tungsten balance. For dimming overly bright windows it can be very helpful to have some combination CTO–neutral density gels (for example, 85 N6, which brings down the color temperature and cuts an additional two stops of light; see p. 302). While a ¾ CTO gel will make daylight match the color of tungsten, sometimes you want the window to look a little blue by comparison, to maintain some of the natural difference between the interior and exterior light. In this case, use a paler gel, such as a ½ or ¼ CTO, on the windows.

If a location has large windows and is illuminated primarily with daylight, or when you're shooting outside, often the best solution is to use an HMI (see p. 452) or daylight-balanced FAY light (see p. 457), either of which will give you plenty of light output and requires no filter to match daylight (though a little warming gel often improves the look). You could also use a daylight-balanced LED.

However, if window light is insignificant in a scene, it is often easiest to block the daylight out altogether (using curtains, sound blankets, or show cards) and then light completely with tungsten.

MIXED FLUORESCENTS. See p. 453 for discussion of fluorescent lighting. Ideally, anytime you are shooting with fluorescent light, you should use Kino Flo or other true tungsten- or daylight-balanced tubes. However, if you are forced to shoot with conventional fluorescent tubes and plan to mix in daylight or tungsten sources, filtration is usually called for. Unfortunately, conventional fluorescents come in a variety of colors, so different gels are called for. Some fluorescents can be thought of as daylight with a green spectral element. Thus, window light can be filtered with Rosco's Windowgreen to match "cool white" or "daylight" fluorescents

---

4. With many color negative stocks you can get away with shooting in daylight without an 85 filter, and this is one instance where you may need to.

better; HMIs can be filtered with Tough Plusgreen and tungsten sources can be filtered with Tough Plusgreen 50.

Alternatively, the fluorescent tubes themselves can be filtered with Minusgreen to match daylight better or Fluorfilter to convert to 3200°K tungsten. Various gels come in sleeves that can be fitted over the fluorescent tubes, which reduce the green halo effect that sometimes occurs when fluorescent units are visible in a shot. If filtration is not possible, fluorescent lighting fixtures, such as the Molescent unit by Mole, can be brought in for additional light using the same type tubes that are already in the room. Mixing conventional fluorescent light with other sources and mixing various types of fluorescent tubes can be very tricky. A three-color color temperature meter helps (see Fig. 8-5).

Color Contrast

Differences in color between two objects (their *color contrast*) help us to tell them apart and determine their position relative to each other. In black-and-white, however, a red bug and a green leaf may be indistinguishable because their tonal values are the same (they reflect the same amount of light). Thus, when shooting in black-and-white it is usually necessary to use slightly higher lighting contrast than you would in color and to make sure that there is adequate shading and/or backlighting to differentiate various objects from each other. It is also possible to use color contrast filters on the camera to separate tonally similar areas (see Chapter 8).

Color contrast is also important when shooting in color because the shades and intensities of colors play a large part in setting the mood of a scene. The color scheme in a movie can be controlled in wardrobe planning, set design, and choice of film stocks or the setup of a video camera. To make colors appear more pastel or desaturated, you can use camera filters such as a diffusion or low-contrast filter. Underexposure and overexposure also affect color saturation (see Chapter 7). During video postproduction (and/or film-to-video transfer) you can make many adjustments both to color saturation and the reproduction of individual tones (see Chapters 14 and 18).

SPECIAL LIGHTING EFFECTS

Night-for-Night

Sometimes you can shoot at night without supplementary lighting, particularly on city streets. However, often you need to augment whatever existing light there is. When using lights to simulate a nighttime effect (such as moonlight or streetlight), use hard lighting fixtures in an extremely high-contrast, low-key lighting scheme. Lights should be used to produce sharp highlights or rim lighting with very little fill. Shadows should be crisp and not diffused. Create pools of light—not flat, even illumination.

When the light level is low, the eye is less sensitive to color. If you go out on a moonlit night, the landscape seems desaturated and slightly bluish. Often, lighting fixtures on movies are gelled blue to simulate moonlight. A pale grayish-blue often looks more natural; avoid an intense, saturated blue. Some DPs like to wet down streets and surfaces at night so that they reflect highlights.

Because night scenes can require many lights, especially for a wide shot, it is often better to shoot at the *magic hour* just before sunrise or just after sunset when there's enough light to get exposure on buildings and the landscape but it is sufficiently dark that car headlights and interior lights show up clearly. Although beautiful, the magic hour is fleeting, often lasting only about twenty minutes, depending on the time of year and your location. Rehearse and be ready to go as soon as the light fades. It helps to have some supplementary light on hand for additional fill in the waning moments and for shooting close-ups when it gets darker. When you shoot magic hour scenes with tungsten-balanced color film, an 85 filter should not be used. In general, avoid shooting the sky during the magic hour because it will look too bright, or use a graduated filter (see Fig. 8-6).

Day-for-Night
Hollywood invented the technique of shooting night scenes during the day, using filters and underexposure to simulate a night effect (the French call this *la nuit Américaine*—"American night"). *Day-for-night* often looks fake. It's easier in black-and-white where a red or yellow filter can be used to darken a blue sky (see Chapter 8). For color work, a graduated filter can be used. Ironically, day-for-night works best on bright, sunny days. Shoot early or late in the day when distinct sidelight or backlight casts long shadows that will seem like moonlight. Avoid shooting the sky and use intense lights in windows to make interior lights look bright relative to the exterior. Underexpose by two or three stops while shooting (after making the normal compensations for any filters). When shooting film, do not rely on trying to print down a normally exposed negative.

Rain, Smoke, and Fire
In order to be visible on film or video, rain, smoke, and fog should be lit from behind (see Fig. 5-4). Aim the lighting instruments as close to the camera as possible but flag them off so that no light shines directly in the lens and causes flare.

Sometimes firelight is simulated by placing an amber gel over the light and jiggling strips of paper or cloth suspended from a horizontal bar in front of the light. Even better, get a *flicker box*, which is an electronic device that allows you to dial up different rates of flicker. Sometimes DPs make fire effects (or simulate the light from a television) with very intense flickering and virtually no fill light, making the scene seesaw between very bright and very dark. In real life, that kind of flicker generally happens only if there's *no* other light in the room. In a typical room with a fireplace, or in a TV-watching environment, usually people have a least *some* other light on, and the flicker on people's faces from a fire or TV is usually subtle. Sometimes, the most convincing effects are done with two or more lights that can be flickered alternately.

LOCATION LIGHTING

The Location
Whenever possible, scout locations prior to filming to assess lighting needs, the availability of electric power, and to formulate a shooting plan (see p. 318). When scouting an interior location, bring a light meter and try to estimate the natural

light at various times of day (a compass can help you estimate the sun's path and calculators are available to determine it precisely). Bring a camera or a director's finder to block out actors' movements and camera angles. Determine what lighting package you need. If any windows need to be gelled, will you need a tall ladder to reach them? A day at a cramped location helps you appreciate why many movies are made in studios with high ceilings, overhead lighting grids, movable walls, air conditioning, and plenty of work space. Movie crews on location often break furniture and mar walls with lighting gear. You can save a lot of time by coming prepared with paint and repair supplies.

Electric Power

Lights for moviemaking consume a great deal of electric current. Before you shoot, try to determine if the location has enough power for your needs; otherwise, fuses or circuit breakers may blow, the production could be shut down, or a fire could erupt.

To estimate your power needs, use the formula: volts x amps = watts. You want to find the number of amps your lights will use, as this is what overloads circuits and causes fuses or breakers to blow when too many lights are put on one circuit. Standard household current in North America is delivered at about 110 volts, which can be rounded off here to 100. Every lamp is rated by the number of watts it consumes. In the home, a 75-watt bulb is typical, while, for filming, 1000 watts (1K) is more common. If you simply read the bulb's wattage and divide by 100, you get the number of amps the lamp requires (this formula includes a safety margin). A typical home circuit can handle 15 (or 20) amps, which is thus enough to run three (or four) 500-watt bulbs. Using any more lights will trip the circuit breaker or blow the fuse.

In Europe and most of Asia, the wall current is delivered at 220 to 240 volts. The same calculation can be done by dividing the wattage by 220 (or to make the math easier, and the safety margin greater, just divide by 200).

To determine how much power is available at the location, examine the circuit breakers or fuse box (often found in the basement). Count how many circuits there are and the maximum amperage of each one (amps are indicated with a number followed by "A"). Circuit breakers, which can be reset by flipping a switch when they are tripped, are found in most houses with newer wiring, but keep a few spare fuses in your lighting kit. Never replace a fuse with one of higher amperage, since the fuse is designed to blow before the wiring in the wall catches fire.

Often, circuits are labeled to indicate which rooms they are connected to. If not, plug lights into various wall outlets and turn the breakers off one at a time and see which lights go out.[5] Extension cables can be run to other rooms to distribute the load if necessary. Don't use thin, home extension cords, as they increase the load and may melt.

When too many lights or overly long cables are used, the voltage may drop (the equivalent to summertime brownouts), which lowers the color temperature of the lights. A 10-volt drop in supply lowers tungsten lights about 100°K. If there is no

---

5. You can also get an inexpensive device that you plug into an outlet, then wave a sensor over the circuit breaker to see which circuit is which.

window light and all light sources are on the same supply, this color change is usually correctable.

To get around this and other typical problems of location power supplies, professionals usually *tie in* to the electric supply as it enters the house and use their own set of circuit breakers and electrical distribution cabling. This should be done only by a trained electrician; in some places, a permit must be obtained and the electrician must also be licensed.

In outdoor locations, a generator ("genny") or a set of car batteries can be used for power. Honda makes a portable, low-cost, relatively noisy generator that puts out 45 amps (5500 watts). There are also large truck-mounted generators that are much more powerful and quieter. Ten 12-volt car batteries ("wet-cells") wired in series can run regular tungsten lights at normal color temperature. As the batteries weaken, the color temperature and light output drop.

WORLDWIDE POWER SYSTEMS. Household power in North America is supplied at 110 to 120 volts. It is *alternating current (AC)*—that is, it pulsates back and forth; it does so sixty times a second (60 Hz). As noted above, in most parts of the world power is supplied at 220 to 240 volts, alternating at a frequency of 50 Hz.[6]

Most AC equipment works equally well at frequencies of 50 or 60 Hz. However, clocks, some battery chargers, and other equipment will not run properly if the frequency of the current is incorrect. Tungsten lights work fine with either system, but AC discharge lamps, including HMIs and fluorescents, may be incompatible with the camera speed or shutter.

Virtually all equipment should be used only with the voltage it was designed for. Tungsten fixtures can be converted from one voltage to another simply by using a different set of bulbs. Some equipment may have a switch to select 110 or 220 volt use. Other equipment requires a voltage-changing device, of which there are two types. The *transformer* is relatively heavy for the amount of power (wattage) it can handle. It can be used with any equipment, but should not be overloaded. Transformers don't affect the frequency of the current. *Diode-type voltage changers* are extremely light (usually a few ounces) and, for their size, can handle much more power than transformers. They should be used only for lights. Since these work by converting AC current to DC, they should not be used with anything that is frequency dependent. Check with a technician on the requirements of your equipment.

While typical electric plugs in North America and most of Central America use two flat blades and sometimes a round grounding pin, outlets found in much of the rest of the world have a different configuration. Other systems use plugs with two or three round pins or angled blades. Adaptors are available to convert from one type to the other or you can replace the plugs on your equipment if needed.

---

6. Some countries, particularly in Central America, may supply power at 220 V but at 60 Hz.

CHAPTER 13

Picture and Dialogue Editing

My movie is first born in my head, dies on paper; is resuscitated by the living persons and real objects I use, which are killed on film but, placed in a certain order and projected onto a screen, come to life again like flowers in water.
— ROBERT BRESSON

Editing is the selection and arrangement of shots into sequences and the sequences into a movie. It's sometimes thought to be the most important element in filmmaking. On many films, the storyline is substantially formed or reformed in the editing room, sometimes "saving" the film.

The earliest filmmakers made films from one unedited camera take or shot. A few years later, it became obvious that shots could be trimmed and placed one after another, with the audience accepting that the action occurs in the same setting. The joining of two shots, with the abrupt ending of one shot and the immediate beginning of the next, is called a *cut*. When editing film, the word cut applies not only to the transition from one shot to another on screen, but also to the physical cutting and joining (splicing) of the film (hence editing referred to as cutting). In video, the term *edit point* is often used to indicate the point where a cut takes place. When editing on a video system, the *head* (beginning) of a shot may be referred to as the *In Point* and the *tail* (end) as the *Out Point*.

SOME FILM THEORY

Montage

Perhaps the most developed theory of film comes from the silent era and is called Russian *montage theory*. The word "montage" is derived from the French and means to "put together" or "edit." The Soviet filmmakers claimed that the ability to change images instantaneously was unique to film, and constituted its potential as an art form. In editing, the image can shift from one person's point of view to another's; it can change locales around the world; it can move through time. The Soviets, for the most part, looked at the shots themselves as meaningless atoms or building blocks and claimed that meaning first emerges from the images through the juxtaposition of the shots.

In the early 1920s, Lev Kuleshov, a Soviet film teacher, created experiments to show how the meaning of a shot could be totally altered by its context. He took a series of shots of Ivan Mosjoukine, a famous contemporary actor, looking at something off screen with a neutral expression on his face. He then constructed a few

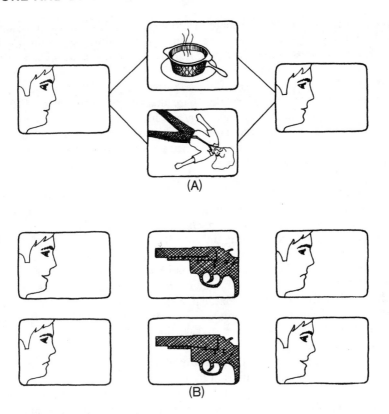

Fig. 13-1. Three-shot sequence. (A) The meaning of the actor's expression depends on the insert shot. (B) The meaning of the actor's expression depends on the ordering of the shots. (Carol Keller)

different sequences. In one sequence, he cut from a medium shot of Mosjoukine to a close-up of a bowl of soup and then back to a close-up of Mosjoukine. In the next sequence, the middle shot, called an *insert shot*, was replaced with a shot of an injured girl. Kuleshov's students commented that the last shot in each of the sequences, called the *reaction shot*, showed the actor's great acting ability to convey with subtlety hunger in the first sequence and pity in the next.

In another of the Kuleshov experiments, a sequence was constructed as follows: an initial shot of Mosjoukine smiling, an insert shot of a gun, and a reaction shot of Mosjoukine frowning. Kuleshov then rearranged the order: first the frowning shot, then the gun, and finally the smiling shot. In the first sequence, the actor's reaction seemed to be one of fear; in the second, one of bravery. The important point of these experiments is that the actor's expression is constant, but the viewer attributes changes in emotional states to him on the basis of the editing.

A girl looks off screen; there is a cut to a bomb blast and then a reaction shot of the girl. The audience assumes the girl is looking directly at the blast, even though the blast could have, in fact, occurred in another part of the world at another time. Sergei Eisenstein, the most renowned of the early Soviet filmmakers, claimed that film space was the constructed space of montage, not the space photographed in the shot. Film space was more than the simulation of real space; it could also be abstract. It is possible to cut from a shot of Kerensky, who was head of the Provisional Government and is a villain in Eisenstein's *October*, to shots of a glass peacock to suggest that Kerensky suffers from the sin of pride. There is no suggestion, however, that the peacock and Kerensky share the same physical space. Two shots, edited together, produce a new meaning, and film space allows for these kinds of metaphorical relationships between images. In addition to narrative content and metaphor, shots can be held together by abstract elements such as movement, tone, compositional weight, and image size.

Similarly, Eisenstein saw film time not as the duration of real movement but as the time set up by the rhythms and juxtaposition of montage. An event may take only a split second in real time, but, as its importance may be great, its duration should be lengthened in film. In *Potemkin*, Eisenstein extended time by showing a crying baby in a carriage teetering on the edge of a steep flight of stairs and then cutting to other shots before returning to the baby. Suspense is heightened by prolonging the event. Real time can also be condensed. Cutting from a horse race to a reaction shot of the crowd (a shot away from the main action is called a cutaway) and then back to the race allows a large portion of the race to be deleted. Similarly, a character's walk will seem continuous if you cut from him walking off screen to a point much further along in the action. Like film space, film time is also a construction created in editing.

Eisenstein also experimented with the montage of very short shots. In *Potemkin*, a sequence of brief shots of statues of lions in different positions cut quickly gives the illusion of their movement. A few frames of an attacking Cossack convey horror. There is no absolute rule for the minimum length of a shot; the minimum depends on the nature of the shot and the context. During World War II, it was found that plane spotters could recognize a female nude in one frame, but it took them much longer to recognize a Messerschmitt.

The directors in Hollywood never adopted the Soviet concept of montage in its broadest sense. In Hollywood, a "montage sequence" is a sequence of short shots that condenses a period of time. For example, the hero might be shown growing up through a sequence of five or six shots that show him at different ages. The aspect of montage that was accepted by Hollywood (indeed, the Soviets had discovered it in early American films) was the *three-shot sequence*—that is, actor looks off screen, cut to a shot from his point of view, and then cut back to the reaction shot. Alfred Hitchcock constructed *Rear Window* almost entirely using this cutting technique.

Today montage theory underlies much advertising and some experimental films. The juxtaposition of women, happy teenagers, and upbeat music with automobiles, soft drinks, and other products is used to manipulate consumers. In experimental films, the tradition of montage seems to find new life. In *A Movie*, Bruce Conner cut together *stock footage*—that is, footage purchased from a service (also called *library* or *archival footage*)—from widely disparate sources, ranging from pornography to newsreels, to form a unified whole. Music videos popularized a shooting and editing style with seemingly no rules about how images can be combined. Although the shots come from different times and places and are shot in vastly different styles, the viewer integrates them into a flow.

In Woody Allen's *What's Up, Tiger Lily?*, a Japanese action film is dubbed by

Allen to change the story line completely. It is not that the original film has lost its meaning. The joke is the ease with which meanings are changed by editing, in this case, by altering the relationship of sound and image.

See Style and Direction, p. 332, for a discussion of shooting and editing styles in drama and documentary.

CUTTING STYLES

Invisible Cutting

In its simplest form, editing is a guide to focus audience attention. The editing style should have its reasons and every cut a motivation. *Invisible* or *match cutting* usually refers to the construction of sequences (or scenes) in which space and time appear to be continuous. Usually both fiction and documentary sequences are match cut to appear continuous. On a film set, however, shots are rarely done in the order that they will appear in the final movie. It's the director's responsibility to shoot scenes with adequate coverage so that the editor can construct continuous sequences (see Continuity, p. 328). On a documentary shot with one camera, every cut alters continuous time, which may be disguised in editing or not, depending on the context.

There are various ways to make action seem continuous. If the eye is distracted, a cut becomes less noticeable; therefore, editors "cut on the action" (a door slam, punch, or coin flip) to hide a cut. The action draws the viewer's attention away from the cut and from any slight mismatch from one shot to the next. Overlaps of action allow the editor to cut just before or just after the action or on the action itself. Cuts tend to propel time forward and to pick up the pace. Sometimes the action looks too fast due to cutting, and the editor must include a few frames of action overlap between two shots.

Changing camera angle and focal length between consecutive shots disguises discontinuities and may make the cut "work"—that is, look as though it matches and is not jarring. Cutaways and reaction shots are tools that maintain continuity between shots that do not match. Cutting away from the main action to a reaction shot allows you to delete uninteresting dialogue or mistakes in the main action. Cutaways and reaction shots also allow the tempo of the film to be controlled through editing, which would be impossible with a continuous take.

The Jump Cut

The sequence of cuts that moves from long shot to medium shot to close-up is generally made up of match cuts. In other words, each of the cuts appears to occur in the same space and time period. A disconcerting mismatch between shots is called a *jump cut*. To cut from a shot of a person sitting to a shot of the same person standing in the same spot creates a noticeable jump in time. If the image size and angle don't change very much from one shot to the next (for example, two medium shots of the same person cut next to each other), the cut may appear to jump and feel unmotivated. A larger change in image size or angle can make the same cut in action seem natural.

The director Jean-Luc Godard, in the early 1960s, began to use the jump cut as a creative element in his filmmaking. He cut out what he felt were boring middle parts of shots or spliced together two close-ups of the same character with a definite jump in time. Not only did these jump cuts comment on the nature of film space, but they also created exciting rhythms that seemed to express the feeling of modern life.

The jump cut is also used for comic effect. In *A Hard Day's Night*, director Richard Lester showed the Beatles cavorting about the landscape in a series of jump cuts. Today, jump cuts are used widely in sequences where match cuts were traditionally used, and audiences have come to accept them as a routine part of the visual language of editing. However, keep in mind that jump cuts may not work, and it makes sense to cover yourself with alternate shots, cutaways, and the like, rather than be forced to resort to jump cuts to salvage a sequence. Sometimes a quick dissolve or a fade out/fade in is used to cover what otherwise would be a jump cut.

Screen Direction

A basic rule of film editing is to try to preserve screen direction at cuts (see The 180-Degree Rule, p. 326). Cutting from a shot of one person looking off screen to the right to a shot of another person also looking off screen to the right makes it appear that the two people are looking in the same direction rather than at one another. Much of the directional information in a chase sequence comes from screen direction.

When two shots violate the 180-degree rule and there is no shot available where the camera crosses the line, you can separate the shots with a neutral shot (for example, a shot taken on the line).

In editing, if a character walks off screen right, he should usually come in from screen left to appear that he is continuing on his walk. If he comes in screen right, he may seem to be returning to his previous spot. Screen direction to the right is usually accepted by audiences as meaning travel from west to east; to the left is travel from east to west. A plane flying from New York to Paris is typically shown flying left to right.

Joining Sequences

One traditional method of editing connects shots into a sequence with straight cuts and then brackets the sequences themselves with *fades* and *dissolves*. Fades work like theater curtains opening and closing on an act or like a sunset followed by a sunrise. Dissolves, on the other hand, suggest a closer connection between one sequence and the next. Like fades, dissolves convey the passage of time—sometimes short time gaps within a sequence and sometimes long periods, as when a close-up of a person dissolves into another close-up of the same person shown at a much older age. When dissolves are used within sequences to signal short time gaps, their only function often seems to be to avoid jump cuts. Sequences can also be joined by wipes, and many other visual effects (see Chapter 14).

In contemporary filmmaking, two sequences are typically joined with a straight cut (that is, one follows directly after the other with no dissolve or other effects). This sometimes creates the problem of distinguishing cuts *within* sequences—those that signal no significant time change—from cuts *between* sequences where there is a significant change of location or time. Filmmakers like Luis Buñuel and Alain Resnais like to explore this ambiguity. On the other hand, even with straight cuts there are many cues to signal the audience that the sequence has changed, including differences in sound level, lighting, color, dress, locale, image grain, or contrast. Even dream and fantasy sequences may be introduced with a straight cut, unlike in the American films of the 1930s and 1940s in which they would be signaled by eerie music and a *ripple* or *oil dissolve*. It's not unusual to see a contemporary movie with no effects other than a fade-in at the opening of the film and a fade-out at the end. Another way to join two sequences is to *intercut* them (also called *parallel editing*). For example, the perils of the heroine heading toward a waterfall in a canoe are intercut with the hero's race to arrive in time to save her (always just in the nick of time). We cut back and forth to develop two threads of action simultaneously.

DIALOGUE EDITING

Dialogue and Scene Structure

In both fiction and documentary, dialogue editing is part of shaping the basic story line. What gets said, and when, is a fundamental part of moving the story ahead. Careful editing of dialogue can have a big impact on individual sequences, even if the scene has been carefully scripted.

Unlike stage plays, which may include long speeches that work well when delivered to a live audience, film dialogue tends to work best when it's quite simple and spare. Images, facial expressions, and juxtapositions of editing should tell the story as much as dialogue, when possible. In documentary, even expository material usually plays best when pared down to essentials. For more on this, see Story and Script, p. 312.

When editing a scene, look for places where you can remove unnecessary dialogue. Sometimes you can begin the sequence after most of the setup has already taken place, doing away with unneeded exposition. Sometimes a pivotal line can be moved to the beginning of a sequence, allowing the rest to be made more succinct. Not every scene needs a beginning, a middle, and an end. Real people often speak with false starts, digressions, repetition, long pauses, or uninteresting detail; people on screen (whether they're in documentaries or dramas) generally need to be a lot terser to hold audience interest. Find places where a look from one character to another might replace dialogue. Let the audience fill in the details.

The use of simple cutaways is the most common method of condensing or rearranging speech. A three-shot pattern is used. While one person is speaking, we cut to a person listening or to another relevant shot. During the cutaway, the speaker completes one thought and the sound cuts to another sentence (to the audience this sounds like the normal flow of speech). Before the picture cuts back to the speaker's face, pauses, words, and whole sections of dialogue can be removed or added. The editor can construct any number of possible sentences from the collection of recorded words. Sometimes cutaways are not needed to condense dialogue: a match cut or jump cut may work just as well.

Cutting away from sync-sound dialogue can be a useful tool for providing a sense of dynamic flow in a conversation. Say you cut from one person asking a question to a shot of someone else responding. If the picture cuts from the first person to the second before the question is finished, the editing may take on a more natural, less mechanical feeling (see Fig. 14-23). Showing the person being spoken to, and not just the person speaking, can give the audience insights into the characters as well as clues on how to interpret what is being said. Hitchcock insisted that what is said on the sound track should contrast with what is seen. Cutaways may be chosen to provide an interesting counterpoint to the spoken dialogue.

When the sound cuts before or after a picture cut (instead of in sync with it) this is called a *sound overlap*, *split edit*, or *L-cut* (see Basic Sound Editing, p. 539). Sound overlaps play a big part in creating the illusion of continuity across cuts (see Sound and Continuity, p. 632).

Replacing Dialogue

It's essential that the audience be able to understand spoken dialogue. Bad sound and unintelligible dialogue can quickly alienate viewers and make them lose interest in the movie. Listen critically to your dialogue tracks and avoid using takes that are hard to hear (for more, see Evaluating the Sound Track, p. 632).

In fiction films, where the pacing of dialogue may be quite consistent from one take to the next, it's often possible to substitute the sound from one take with that of another (while keeping the picture from the original take). This can be used not only to improve sound quality, but to find better performances as well. Pauses between words usually need to be trimmed or expanded slightly to maintain sync. When location audio on feature films is unacceptable, dialogue tracks may be replaced using *ADR (Automatic Dialogue Replacement)*, also called *looping*. Actors are brought into a sound studio to redo their lines while watching repeating loops of picture. ADR can be slow and expensive. Often the timing is wrong or the voices sound "canned" and unnatural. The dialogue must be mixed properly with foleys or other sound effects to make the takes believable and to try to match them with the ones recorded on location. Software such as SynchroArt's VocAlign can automatically adjust the timing of a redone take to match the pacing of the original take. For more on this, see Chapter 16.

Cutting Dialogue Tracks

When editing dialogue, it's often necessary to separate words that are spaced closely together on the track. This is a skill that improves with practice. When editing with a nonlinear system, use the audio waveform display to help locate the beginning and end of a word (see Fig. 14-21). Sometimes you can't avoid clipping a word, which sounds jarring. Often, a two-frame crossfade can make an otherwise awkward cut sound natural. Some NLEs can cut within a frame (subframe editing), which may make a cleaner cut. Be attentive to breaths between words—avoid cutting in the middle of a breath. It's often better to leave the whole breath in place and fade it down quickly.

When editing 16mm or 35mm mag film, locating words can be trickier. You can run the sound slowly forward and back by hand (scrubbing). A useful aid is to put a piece of low-tack masking tape (sold in architectural supply stores) on the emulsion side of the track, beginning or ending on the frame you plan to cut. (The recorded track area on U.S. standard 16mm mag film is the top quarter of the film opposite the edge with sprocket holes.) This way you can try different versions of the cut without chopping the track to shreds. Be sure to remove any tape goo from the track or it will clog the heads.

Narration

Narration, or voice-over, is used in both documentary and fiction. It may be used to deliver information, provide the point of view of an unseen character, or allow an onscreen character to comment on the action.

Narration should be kept simple and clear—it shouldn't sound "written." When writing narration, practice speaking it aloud to be sure it sounds like natural speech. Avoid complex phrasing or vocabulary that will tax the audience's ability to understand.

Narration sometimes works best when woven in with sync sound from the scene. Look for places where you can float a line of narration, then bring up sync sound, then run another line of narration. This needs to be done carefully—if the narrator speaks over a close shot of someone else talking, it can sometimes be distracting.

Often, editors or directors record their own voices as a "scratch" narration during editing that will be replaced by the actual narrator after picture is locked. Many NLEs have a voice-over or direct recording tool that allows you to record a scratch narration straight to hard drive, while watching the picture if you want. This can be very convenient.

Narration recording sessions should be logged to keep track of good and bad takes; often you want to combine parts of several takes. Narration should either be recorded with timecode or transferred to a timecoded format after recording to facilitate editing.

Ideally, final narration should be recorded in a sound booth to get high-quality, clean sound with no background noise. Some narration sessions are done while watching the picture, but often this is not necessary. Instead, takes are timed with a stopwatch to make sure they are read at the right speed. See p. 428 for narration recording suggestions.

See Chapter 16 for editing music and other sound editing concerns. When editing in film, have the mag edge coded before you cut; see p. 602.

THE EDITING PROCESS

The editing process varies by type of production, type of editing equipment, and individual editors' preferences. Feature films are usually edited by one or more editors and a staff of assistants. Independent filmmakers or corporate videomakers may work alone. The editing schedule and budget determine many of the procedures used in the editing room.

The Editing Room

Editing rooms have their own rites and rituals. Work space is usually cramped, and there is often material stored from other productions. Make certain all the material for your project is clearly labeled with the (working) title of the production, the name of the production company, and the reel number. Store the camera original elsewhere (for example, at the laboratory vault or postproduction facility) until completion of editing. Make sure that camera original film footage or camera original master tapes are clearly labeled as such and that they are in a safe place!

The Editor and Assistant Editor

The editor, usually in consultation with the director or producer, decides how the movie is to be cut. In the traditional film editing room, the editor marks the shots to be cut and an assistant editor may perform the physical act of cutting. The assistant also keeps the logbook, synchronizes rushes, reconstitutes outtakes, and performs other tasks. In the past, this kind of relationship played an essential role in the training of new editors and provided useful feedback and aid to the chief editor.

With nonlinear video editing, the role of the assistant has been minimized on many low-budget productions. Once the material is captured into the editing system, the editor can do most tasks alone. On larger productions and feature films, assistants may be used to organize and capture footage, to maintain equipment, or to cut workprint, but often their work takes place at night or other times when the editor is not using the system. The diminished relationship between editor and assistant may lower postproduction costs, but it is also a loss to the editing process.

On some productions, media is stored on shared drives, and a number of people, including picture editors, dialogue editors, and effects creators, can all work on the project at the same time.

The Editing Log

Careful logging and recordkeeping during production can save a lot of time in the editing room. On a feature film, a script marked up by the script supervisor shows the editor which camera angles and takes were filmed for every part of the script (see Fig. 9-32). On a documentary, there may be a log of shots or topics discussed in an interview; verbatim transcripts are often made of any interview material. See Preparing for Postproduction, p. 363, for more on production logs and marking scripts.

In the editing room, a system should be put in place and a separate log created to allow the editor to quickly locate every bit of picture and sound. The *editing log* on a video project should include a list of all the camera original footage, with beginning and ending timecode and a listing of contents. Once the material has been captured into a nonlinear editing system, the bins and list management tools of the NLE can be used to organize, log, and locate shots (see Chapter 14).

On a film project, the editing log should list every roll of camera original, with beginning and ending key numbers and the contents. If the project is being edited on film, the log should correlate camera roll numbers, editing rolls (which may contain more than one camera roll), key numbers, and ink edge numbers. If the film project is being edited in video, a shot log will usually be generated in the telecine that correlates key numbers to timecode numbers (see p. 703); this log should be checked for accuracy when loading material into a nonlinear editing system (see p. 617).

For any project that involves use of a separate audio recorder, the log should list all production audio with timecode numbers, if applicable.

Selecting Shots

As useful as they are for organizational purposes, production logs can sometimes get in the way of editing judgments. On the set, directors indicate the takes they like, often having seen them only once. Sometimes the director may be attached to a shot because it was hard to get. The editor, on the other hand, can bring to the project a fresh set of eyes, unbiased by what took place during production. Some editors prefer *not* to view dailies with directors so they can form their own opinions about what works and what doesn't. In this case, the editor may put together a first cut from the script and then discuss it with the director. Similarly, though it saves money not to print or capture takes considered "bad" on the shoot, these takes can be a goldmine to the editor who may be looking for something very specific to solve an editing problem. A take with a bad line reading may make a perfect cutaway. The dead air before a slate may supply just enough room tone to fill a hole.

In his book *In the Blink of an Eye*, Walter Murch (who edited *Apocalypse Now*) talks about an interesting, unexpected drawback caused by the ability of nonlinear editing systems to instantly locate any shot from the log. In film and linear videotape editing, you're forced to wait and watch while fast-forwarding or rewinding to find a shot. NLEs save this "wasted" time, but may deprive you of some serendipitous discoveries—shots you weren't looking for that trigger new ideas for the cut.[1]

On documentaries, sometimes producers or directors go through a transcript marking up the bites they want, creating a script before editing begins. If done without actually watching the footage, this can be tremendously misleading, since something that reads well on the page may actually sound terrible, or can't be cut where you want because of the way the words were spoken. Also, working straight from a transcript can lead to visually dull editing.

All of these are reasons to avoid too much "preselecting" of material prior to real editing.

That said, it must be pointed out that on many projects, the edit is created almost entirely by preselection. The director may take home a screening cassette and create a *paper cut* or *paper edit*—a list of the selected shots in their proper order, identified by timecode. Starting with the paper cut, the editor then assembles the shots, tunes the transitions, and makes other adjustments. If your budget is limited, this technique can save a lot of time and money in the editing room.

Various logging programs are available that allow you to capture timecode and frame grabs of shots and shuffle them to the desired order (see Logging Clips,

---

1. When working on nonlinear systems, some editors like to create a sequence of all the unedited takes together, forming a "virtual tape" of rushes that can be easily viewed from beginning to end.

p. 522). Some directors like to assemble their preferred takes on their own NLE, then pass the sequence or EDL to the editor.

   PICTURE AND SOUND QUALITY. You must always try to translate what you see and hear on the editing system to what the audience will see and hear in the finished movie. Sometimes the editing system is not a reliable indicator of what the footage will look like. For projects that originate on film and are edited on video, the telecine video transfer may not capture details in the highlights or shadows that may be visible later when a more careful transfer is done. You may or may not be happy when you later see the hidden details. Be sure to check carefully for flash frames and nearby overexposed frames (see p. 597).

   Any project edited on an NLE may be captured for editing at low resolution to save storage space. If you do so, bear in mind that during editing, landscapes and detailed shots may be harder to read. Walter Murch talks about the tendency to use a lot of close-ups because they are easy to see on the editing system. Wide vistas or even medium shots that may ultimately look great when the project is finished at high resolution can seem paltry during editing with a small monitor. The need for good sound quality is noted above. Bear in mind that the small speakers and machine noise of many editing systems may mask a lot of detail in the original audio recording. You may not be able to hear problems or even desirable-but-quiet sounds (see Chapter 16).

From Rough Cut to Picture Lock

   To begin editing the movie, the unedited footage from the camera (dailies or rushes) is divided into shots you want to use (the *in-takes* or *ins*) and shots you put aside (the *outtakes* or *outs*).

   An *assembly* (also called a *string-out*) puts the shots in the order called for by the script. For unscripted material, an assembly may simply be all the sequences in chronological order. The *rough cut* is the first attempt at shaping the film. For scripted films, the assembly and first rough cut may be essentially the same thing. In a documentary, the rough cut may be made by shortening and reordering the sequences from the assembly. The editor usually attempts to put together the rough cut fairly quickly, worrying less about the pace of scenes and getting everything to work well, and concentrating more on establishing the overall direction of the work. Most editors prefer to edit rough cuts on the long side, in order to try out shots and scenes, even if they're questionable and likely to be cut out later. Rough cuts are often two or more times as long as the final film.

   As the movie continues to be edited and refined, you may have several rough cuts. One of the nice features of an NLE is that you can save different versions for comparison.

   When the basic scene order is in place and you start polishing individual sequences and transitions, this is called *fine cutting*. It's often easier to fine-cut and pace individual sequences after you've seen the overall flow of the rough cut. As you work, the rough cut becomes a *fine cut*. When you're done making changes to the picture, this is *picture lock* or *picture freeze*.

   Some people prefer to fine-cut from the start of editing instead of making a rough cut. Even though this approach requires more time to complete the first cut, you may be better able to judge the editing.

The two approaches have been compared to carving a work out of a mass of material versus building up a structure piece by piece. With experience, you'll find what works best for you.

Test Screenings and Feedback

Editing requires an intense, focused kind of thinking. You sit close to the screen and get deeply involved in large problems and tiny details. This is not a good environment to judge whether the movie is really working. You need to step back occasionally and see it from a different perspective.

For projects that will ultimately be shown on a big screen—either in film or large-screen video projection—it's imperative that you view the movie on a big screen during the editing process. The transition from small screen to large can be startling. Sometimes the pace of the movie seems to speed up and sometimes to slow down. Wide shots that may seem boring on the small screen suddenly reveal fascinating detail. Close-ups may seem overpowering when ten feet tall. Cuts that draw the eye's attention from one side of the screen to the opposite side may seem a little jumpy on the small screen and very jarring on the big one. If you can't get access to a big screen, at least make a tape or disc that you can take out of the editing room and view in a different setting.

Watching the movie with an audience is another important part of getting a fresh perspective. Even watching the movie with one person who is not part of the editing team will cause *you* to see it in a different way, with a different sense of the timing and content. Screenings can be very valuable to determine whether something in the movie is confusing, boring, or really doesn't work.

Filmmakers vary on the value of test screenings with large audiences. Some love to get feedback (or may be forced to get it by backers or studios). Some resent the idea of putting important, personal decisions to something that seems like a popular vote. Often, test audiences disagree with each other on which scenes should stay or be cut. One audience may laugh where another is silent. The differences in "temperature" between different audiences can be stunning (which you'll find as you screen the finished film as well). In the end, the filmmakers must make the editing decisions.

Another factor in test screenings is the problem of showing unfinished work. You can explain to an audience all you want about what a rough cut or a rough mix or uncorrected picture means, but even experienced professionals often lack the ability to imagine what the movie will be like when finished. For more on showing unfinished work to backers or distributors, see Chapter 19.

Finding the Right Length

If your movie lucks out in the combination of writing, direction, and editing, it could happen that the rough cut plays just fine at the length it was intended to. Congratulations, and enjoy the easy finishing process ahead.

For most projects, however, you'll face some tough decisions. The rough cut may be many hours long. Or the fine cut may seem too *short*. How do you find the right length for the project? Do you let the material dictate length, or do you try to cut it to a standard length?

Start by asking yourself what would make the best, tightest movie. If a movie is too long, audiences can turn on it, even if they liked it at first. Well-edited, taut

Fig. 13-2. Palmer 16mm Interlock Projector for double system projection with picture and mag film on separate reels. (W. A. Palmer Films, Inc.)

movies keep audience energy high and allow the ideas and emotions in the film to emerge clearly. Be hard on yourself—don't hold on to a sequence just because you're in love with it; only keep it if it really works in the context of the whole film. The advice to "murder your darlings" applies when paring down a rough cut.[2] If two sequences repeat the same idea or emotion, consider dropping one of them. If you can get away with starting a shot ten seconds later, trim off the head. It's easy for filmmakers who have nurtured material from script through production to feel attached to things the audience won't feel attached to in the least. Good editors have the ability to see the movie through the eyes of the audience, and to understand which shots and scenes are essential and which aren't. Sometimes ideas or plot points you cut out have a way of emerging subtly in other scenes, and don't need to be explicated.

Many filmmakers have had this experience: They finish a fine cut, declaring the movie finished and tight and done. Then, perhaps to fit a broadcast slot (see below), they begrudgingly have to cut some time out. They comb the film for every slack or wasted moment. In the end, they like the shortened version better. Barry

---

2. Attributed to many writers, it was probably said first by Sir Arthur Quiller-Couch in 1914. Next time you're losing an argument in the editing room with someone who doesn't want to drop a scene, you can say, "As Sir Arthur Quiller-Couch once said . . ." Note: You may then be asked to leave the room.

Sonnenfeld (*Men in Black*) remarked that he's one of the few directors whose director's cuts are sometimes *shorter* than the released version of the movie.

Be especially attentive to the first few minutes of the movie. Outside of a theater (where the audience is captive) some people will choose to watch the movie only if they're hooked in the first several scenes. On the other hand, if you start things out too quickly (in the first minute or so) you may lose people who haven't settled into their seats. If there are head titles (see below), consider developing the story visually under or between the titles—this keeps things moving even while people settle in.

LENGTH AND DISTRIBUTION OPPORTUNITIES. In determining length, you must also consider potential distribution. If you're making a feature film, typically these run about ninety minutes to two hours, give or take. If a film is only slightly over an hour, it may not be considered a "feature" for theatrical, festival, or broadcast slots. If a feature runs substantially over two hours, exhibitors (theater owners) get nervous because it means they can have fewer shows per day and broadcasters may want to cut the film shorter to fit a two-hour (or even 90-minute) program slot. Documentaries may be feature length, or they may be shorter. There are far more opportunities to show a one-hour documentary on cable or broadcast television than if the program is longer (even a series may sell to more markets if each show is an hour or a half hour). For any broadcast slot, you need to deduct time for station IDs and advertising or promotions. A "one-hour" program may run 58 minutes or a whole lot less, depending on the broadcaster's needs.

When producing something for an educational market, keep in mind the typical length of a class in whatever age bracket you're targeting. Sometimes a one-hour film is cut down to 20 to 40 minutes for educational distribution. Movies for young children are often 10 minutes or less to accommodate short attention spans.

For corporate and industrial projects, about 10 to 15 minutes is sometimes the longest that busy executives or workers want to spend watching a movie. For training pieces you must weigh how much information people can absorb and how much "seat time" they want to put in. Short and punchy is better than too detailed and long.

TITLES

Planning the titles and credits and placing them in the movie is part of the editing process (though the actual title design and production may be done after editing is finished). Titles and credits may be created by a professional designer at a title house or postproduction facility, or you can work them out on your editing system. Sometimes people shoot titles with physical objects or artwork—like shooting a wall with graffiti titles spray-painted on.

Some titles and credits appear as lettering over a plain background or other nonmoving graphic. Titles that appear over action (a moving film or video image) are called *supers* (for superimposition, see Fig. 13-3).

Fig. 13-3. Title tool from Avid Xpress. Text should stay inside the title safe area (the inner box). Drop shadows help separate text from the background. (Avid Technology, Inc./Joshua Weinstein)

When a name appears as static (nonmoving) lettering, this is considered a *title card*. If there are *head credits* at the beginning of the film, these are usually individual cards that fade in or cut in. Title cards may be supered or nonsupered, though some people use the term title card to mean a nonsupered title. End or tail credits may be done as cards, but more often they are done as a *credit roll*, in which a long list of names moves up from the bottom of the screen. Vertically moving titles are also called *scrolls* or *crawls* (though in video, crawl is usually used to mean a line of horizontally moving type). The advantage of a credit roll is that the various credits can be given equal screen time (whereas cards tend to favor the names at the top of the card) and the whole list can be read comfortably in less time. With cards, on the other hand, it may be easier to make changes or correct errors. Extensive head credits are common in Hollywood films (with the biggest star credits coming before the title), but lengthy head credits on a student film can seem pretentious. There is a generally accepted order for various credits, which is often stipulated in contracts or union rules. Be aware that some broadcasters have restrictions on how credits are done in terms of placement, length, and who can be thanked or credited. There may also be restrictions on including Web addresses.

Double- and triple-check for correct spellings and proper job titles, and make sure you didn't omit important credits!

Timing
A rule of thumb is to keep titles on screen long enough to read them aloud twice. Experiment with pacing. Overly slow titles may slow down the film and bore

the audience. Too quick titles may leave them frustrated. Another rule of thumb for credit rolls is that it should take about seven to twelve seconds for a line of text to travel from the bottom of the screen to the top; however, rolls may go slower on feature films and often go a great deal faster on TV programs.

Typeface and Placement

When choosing a typeface for the lettering, avoid fonts that have very narrow lines or serifs (the angled lines that extend from and ornament some type styles). The smaller the font size, the more likely it is that thin lines or elements will disappear on film or flicker or look noisy on video.

Usually, lettering should be no smaller than about ⅟₂₅ of total image height (that is, no more than 25 lines on screen at once). Maximum characters per line should be around 40 for most formats; in 35mm up to 55 characters may work. The longer the line, the harder it is to read quickly. When doing subtitles for dialogue, consider breaking the titles into two shorter lines rather than one long one.

Though feature films sometimes use titles that extend to the edges of the widescreen image, because many movies will at some point be shown on non-widescreen TV, it may be safer to prepare titles that fit within the 4:3 rectangle (see Aspect Ratio Choices, p. 87). Lettering should fit within the TV safe title area, which is smaller than the TV safe action frame (see Fig. 13-3).[3] Credit rolls often look best if centered on a central *gutter* with the job title extending to the left of the gutter and the name extending to the right. Look at movies for layout ideas.

Try to put superimposed titles over shots without excessive movement or complexity that might fight with the titles. Titles will make any camera jiggle especially noticeable. Supers should almost always be done with *drop shadows*, which rim the letters with a dark edge to separate them from the background. Supers used in documentaries to identify film subjects are sometimes called *lower thirds*, since they fall in the lower third of the frame. Often, lower thirds are set against a dark rectangular *pad* to help separate them from the background. If lower thirds are anticipated, be sure to shoot your subjects with enough room at the bottom of the frame to accommodate titles. If the project is distributed in foreign markets, you will be asked by broadcasters for a textless version of the movie so they can do foreign language titles. If you plan for this during post, you can create textless background elements on which titles can be added later.

In video, supered and nonsupered titles are easy to do. When finishing a film project the traditional way on film, supered titles may cost more than nonsupered titles, depending on the printing method used. For more on generating video titles, see p. 547. If you are shooting titles on film, see p. 673.

---

3. Of course, widescreen films are often letterboxed when shown on non-widescreen TV, in which case the whole frame is visible, but the titles will look smaller (see Fig. 2-15E).

CHAPTER 14

Editing Video

This chapter is about video editing. Mostly it's about nonlinear editing systems or NLEs (the term is used to refer both to the entire editing system and to the particular editing program—the software—it uses). Information is also included about tape-to-tape editing, which is less common today but continues to play a role.

See Chapter 1 for an overview of video editing concepts, Chapter 13 for a discussion of editing choices and styles, Chapter 5 for more technical aspects of video, Chapter 18 for transferring film to video and Chapter 15 for specific issues of editing film-originated material on video.

This is the best of times and worst of times for video editing. NLEs have matured to the point that some are amazingly easy to use. Today, even many kids have had a chance to shoot some video, capture it into a basic editing program, and make a little movie.

Meanwhile, on the professional side, there has been an explosion of formats, choices, and technologies. NLEs used in the industry have become amazingly sophisticated and powerful. The editor's role has expanded in some cases to include whole areas that used to be *someone else's* job (sound mixing, color correction, graphic design, computer repair, etc.). Professional NLEs sometimes seem like they have more controls and settings than a jet plane.

Filmmakers vary in their interest or ability to deal with technical stuff. Some editors with great filmmaking skills know very little about the systems they work on. Others are techno-geeks and proud of it. They want to know everything about the software and hardware and how to do the most complex tasks.

Whatever your level of interest or ability, try to find people who can advise you. Other filmmakers working with the same NLE can be a great resource. There are online user groups where you can post technical questions and find problems being discussed (see Bibliography). And when you're stuck, you'll find that just doing an online search with some key words turns up helpful solutions.

This chapter covers both basic concepts as well as some more specialized details (particularly later in the chapter). If a section gets too technical for you, skip ahead to the next one. Also, a disclaimer: There are far too many editing systems, ways of working, and different names for the same thing to cover them all. When it comes to working with *your* particular system, be sure to read the manual and consult the help section in the software. Remember that the same basic editing functions exist somewhere in each popular NLE. It's like driving a car—there are many designs, but the steering wheel, ignition, and pedals are the same all over the world.

NONLINEAR EDITING SYSTEMS

Before reading this, be sure to see Video Editing, p. 39, where key ideas are introduced.

Fig. 14-1. Nonlinear editing system. From left, CRT video monitor, computer monitors for the editing interface, computer, and video deck. This high definition Grass Valley Edius Pro system is shown with a high-end Sony HD deck. (Grass Valley)

Think of your NLE as a kind of factory. You put into it the raw materials: images and sounds from the camera, maybe graphics or music. You use the NLE to process all that material—to cut it, rearrange it, to balance the elements. When you're done, you ship the finished movie out of the factory in various forms: You might put it on videotape or on DVD or create a file to post on the Web.

A nonlinear editing system is basically a computer running specialized software. Various devices are attached or installed internally to get material in and out of the computer. Hard drives store the video and audio. And picture and sound monitors allow you to see and hear what you're working on.

COMPONENTS OF A NONLINEAR EDITING SYSTEM

Depending on your situation, you may be working on a system assembled by someone else, or you may be putting one together yourself. If you're getting your own, you can buy or rent the elements separately, or you may have a vendor sell you a *turnkey system* (a preassembled package). From a production standpoint, a huge benefit of NLEs is that they are relatively cheap (compared to the tape systems that preceded them), which allows filmmakers to own their tools and work where and

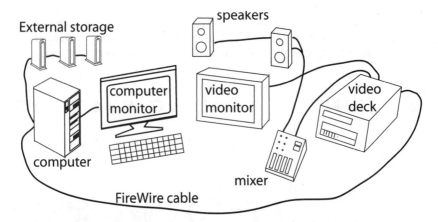

Fig. 14-2. A DV editing setup. Compressed digital video and audio travel between the computer and the video deck via the FireWire cable. The deck decompresses the signal and feeds analog video to the video monitor while sending analog audio to the mixer and speakers. Many other configurations are also common for NLEs.

when they want. On the other hand, it's shocking how fast a "hot" system can turn into a dinosaur. If you intend to buy, look into the cost and possibility of later upgrades. Good tech support from the manufacturer or dealer can be a big help, particularly if you're new to the nonlinear world. With some deals, tech support is included; with others you pay for it separately.

Because computer technology and NLEs change constantly, before making decisions check the NLE and hardware makers' websites and get recommendations from vendors and people working with the gear.

Software

While the hardware and equipment that goes with an editing system is important, the software application—the NLE program itself—has perhaps the biggest impact on your editing experience. There are numerous NLEs on the market that span a wide range of price and power. Many companies make them; the makers and products change on a regular basis. There are high-powered systems for the top of the professional postproduction market, more limited systems aimed at the corporate, multimedia, and independent markets, and very simplified programs for consumers.

Since the early 1990s, Avid's NLEs have played a leading role in the mainstream film and television industries. More recently, Apple's Final Cut Pro has gained popularity both with independent filmmakers and mainstream facilities. Adobe's Premiere Pro is also a key player with thousands of users worldwide. Home users have various low-cost, stripped-down programs to choose from, including ones from Ulead and Apple. NLEs are also made by Matrox, Sony, Canopus, Discreet, and many others. High-end professional systems often include the hardware and software as an integrated package.

How should you select an application? Start by talking with others who do the kind of work you're doing or want to do. Brand names are only part of the story because often the same company offers a range of products. Several companies, including Adobe, Apple, and Avid, offer their NLEs in a suite of applications, with integrated programs that do specialized tasks such as visual effects, graphics and title creation, music, audio mixing, and DVD authoring. Having these programs bundled together makes it easier to jump from one to another with the NLE as your base of operations.

One consideration in choosing an NLE is your computer and/or operating system (OS). Traditionally there has been a big split between applications like Final Cut Pro that run only on Mac OS and programs that run only on Windows (some run on both). Now that Apple is using Intel chips in Macs, you have more flexibility (if you own a Mac, you can also run Windows applications). NLEs and other applications are often designed for specific drivers and hardware; check manufacturers' websites for compatibility.

If you're working alone, or on in-house projects, you have more freedom in choosing an NLE. If you need to interact with outside production facilities and workers, try to use something standard in the industry or at least compatible. For example, you may have projects that you want to bring to a post house for finishing. If you and the post house are using software from the same maker it's easier to move the project over.

Another consideration is employment. If you hope to work in the industry it makes sense to get trained on the tools being used by professionals. Fortunately, most NLEs have a lot in common, so if you know one you can learn another without too much pain (well, a fair amount of pain). It takes a while to learn where the buttons and controls are, but the basic concepts are pretty much the same.

The Computer

When it comes to video editing, you can't have too much computing power. A high-performance machine can mean the difference between being able to concentrate on creative tasks or having to wait repeatedly while the computer renders (computes) effects, prepares your material for output, or simply chokes because it can't keep up with the data. The need for power is even more acute when working in HDV and HD.

When computer shopping there are several things to look for. First is the speed of the central processor (CPU) which is expressed in gigahertz. The faster the better, but speed costs money. Often a smart strategy is to get a computer near, but not at the top, of a manufacturer's line—it will still be fast but you won't pay extra for the absolute best. Many NLEs are designed for multiple processors and work best with dual or quad chips. If you're editing on a laptop, bear in mind that fast processors and multiprocessors (if available) add weight and heat and drain batteries faster. CPU speed (also known as clock speed) isn't the only thing that determines overall performance; also look at the on-chip memory caches (such as L2 and L3) and attached busses.

Another key item is RAM (Random Access Memory). Many tasks need lots of it. Sometimes adding more RAM can substantially improve the performance of a relatively slow computer. You can often find better RAM prices from aftermarket manufacturers (that is, *not* the computer maker). RAM comes in different sizes, types, and speeds, so make sure the RAM you get is right for your computer and comes from a reputable company.

Fig. 14-3. Editing with Final Cut Pro on a laptop. (DuArt Film and Video)

The video or graphics card drives the computer monitor(s). Video cards have their own processors and RAM. Ideally, get a card that will take some of the computing load off the CPU. Cards also differ in which types of monitor connections they support (such as analog VGA or digital DVI and HDMI) and whether they'll drive more than one monitor.

The computer is the heart of the NLE, but it only works when connected to other gear. You want a machine with lots of flexibility in terms of available ports for connections such as USB, FireWire, Ethernet, DVI, or HDMI (see Digital Connections, p. 216). Also look for the number of open expansion slots (especially PCI Express slots) into which you can put cards for various other connections.

You'll want a DVD burner for creating DVDs and importing and exporting any manner of other data.

It's extremely useful—if not essential—that the computer have a high-speed Internet connection, or at least be able to be connected when needed. You'll use the Internet for software updates, sharing files with others working on a project, downloading sound effects or stock footage, among many other uses. That said, be aware that anti-virus and firewall software can conflict with NLEs, which is why some editors choose *not* to be connected to the Web. (Mac OS X enjoys a well-known advantage here.) Make sure any anti-virus program you use is compatible with your NLE.

Input and Output

There are many different ways to get video and audio into and out of an NLE. Which methods you use depends in part on how the video was recorded in the first place and in what format. If the video was recorded on tape, you'll use a camera or video deck as a source. If it was recorded on hard drive or memory card, you can make a direct file transfer to the NLE's hard drives.

Similarly, your choice of output device depends on what end product you want to make (tape, file, or DVD).

The input/output device may be also used as a format converter. For example, a DV video deck could be used to convert an analog video source to DV while capturing to the NLE. If you plan to use any analog video it *must* be converted to digital using a deck, camera, or capture card before it can be used in an NLE.

Depending on how your system is configured, the input/output device may be part of the chain that allows you to view material on external monitors while you're editing (see Fig. 14-2). NLEs usually store video in compressed digital form while external monitors (a broadcast video monitor for picture and a speaker system for sound) typically require uncompressed digital or analog signals. Often, the input/output device (for example, a camera, deck, or capture card) is used to uncompress the signal and/or convert to analog for monitoring.

FIREWIRE CONNECTIONS. Most computers used for video editing have a FireWire port or can be easily fitted with one. A FireWire cable is a simple, inexpensive way to bring a variety of formats in and out of the computer including standard definition codecs like DV, DVCAM, and DVCPRO, and high definition codecs like HDV and DVCPRO HD. FireWire can be used to connect a camera, deck, or hard drive and the cable can carry video, audio, timecode, power, and device control information. When used with a conversion box (see p. 508) even uncompressed SD video can be sent over FireWire (for more on FireWire, see p. 217).

FOR MATERIAL RECORDED TO FILE. If your camera recorded to hard drive or memory card you can import those files to the NLE's drives or edit right off the memory card or drive used on the shoot (in some cases, a manufacturer-specific software driver is required). If the files weren't recorded with the proper wrapper format for the NLE—for example, QuickTime, AVI, or MXF—you may need to convert them (see p. 220). When copying files into the NLE, be sure to organize your folders and bins logically and carefully so you can find the shots you want quickly and don't have more than one file with the same name.

FOR MATERIAL RECORDED TO VIDEOTAPE. If the video you want to work with was recorded on tape, you could use your digital camcorder as a source to feed the NLE. For example, a DV or HDV camcorder can be connected with a FireWire cable (for small camcorders, 4-pin at the camcorder to 6-pin at the computer; see Fig. 5-14). This is most often done by filmmakers on a tight budget or when they're on the road. Usually a camcorder is not the best source for playing a lot of tapes: It's not designed for a lot of heavy shuttling back and forth, and fast-forwarding and rewinding is slow. On the other hand, some recent DV and HDV decks use the same transport mechanism found in cameras, so the difference can be moot. If you capture large sections of a tape without much shuttling for later breakdown and logging, camcorder playback can be a workable solution in some cases.

A video deck (VTR) is usually a better, more robust choice for input to and output from an NLE. Decks range from simple play-only machines to professional multiformat recorders. Most VTRs are fast and rugged enough for shuttling lots of tapes.

If your source tapes are analog, you'll need to convert the signal to digital before capturing into the NLE. When source tapes are VHS, Hi8, or Beta SP, typically a capture card or conversion box (see below) is used. Or you may be able to route the signal from an analog camera or deck through a digital camera or deck that can make the digital/analog conversion.

With analog decks, the quality of the deck can have an impact on picture quality upon playback. Things like unstable sync, poor head contact, or tracking errors can cause unstable playback and tearing of the image. However with digital formats you should be able to make a digital transfer to the NLE with no loss of quality regardless of the quality of the deck—so even a low-cost deck can serve you well.

In the simplest DV or HDV setup, the NLE can control the VTR using the same FireWire cable that carries the video. For many filmmakers this is a very workable setup and allows them to both capture from tape and record to tape while controlling the deck from the NLE. FireWire is totally accurate for capturing footage with timecode. However, FireWire deck control may not be frame-accurate when editing to tape. Professional VTRs often use *RS-422 serial device control*, which provides precise editing and allows insert editing. You need a deck with an RS-422 port (it's a 9-pin connector, similar to the one in Fig. 10-12). If you're using a Mac, you need to install a serial port on the computer. Other deck control protocols include RS-232 and LANC, which is sometimes used on consumer or prosumer gear.

CAPTURE CARDS AND CONVERSION BOXES. A number of products serve as an interface so you can bring various formats of video and audio in and out of the computer. Conversion boxes such as AJA Video System's IO or Avid's Mojo connect to the computer via FireWire cable (see Fig. 14-4). PCI card systems (also called *capture cards*) plug directly into the computer's PCI or PCI Express card slot and often include a *breakout box* (*BOB*) with various video and audio connections (see Fig. 14-5). Capture cards and boxes are made by Blackmagic Design, AJA, Matrox, and Avid, among others. These devices vary enormously in their capabilities and price; some of the functions that may be available include:

Fig. 14-4. Blackmagic Design's Multibridge Extreme is a versatile box that can convert in real time between analog and digital in SD and HD and between 720p and 1080i HD. It can downconvert from HD to SD and provide hardware support and monitoring for many types of NLEs. (Blackmagic Design)

Fig. 14-5. Matrox RT.X2 capture card provides real-time HDV and DV editing and effects. It can convert analog video to high-quality SD or HD I-frame 4:2:2 MPEG-2. Allows you to edit HD and SD in the same sequence in real time. The card mounts in the computer's PCI express slot. The breakout box on the right provides a FireWire connection and inputs and outputs for HD and SD analog video. (Matrox Electronic Systems, Ltd.)

- *Conversion between analog and digital.* If you have an analog source (composite, component, or S-video) the device converts to a variety of digital codecs. The device also converts *to* analog video from digital, which can be used to feed an analog monitor while editing.
- *Transcoding between digital formats.* The device can convert your video to different codecs at different data rates. Many cards offer proprietary codecs designed for efficient editing. This allows you to capture at a lower data rate for offline editing (see p. 514).
- *Up- and downconversion between SD and HD.* Some devices can take in HD or SD and output the other. They can also cross-convert between HD formats (such as between 1080i and 720p).
- *SDI connections.* The device allows you to input uncompressed ITU-601 standard definition via an SDI link or input high definition via HD-SDI from a video deck (see p. 217). The device may also provide SDI or HD-SDI output to feed a digital monitor.
- *HDMI connections.* The device allows you to input HDMI from a camcorder or output HDMI to a monitor (see p. 217).
- *Digital audio input and output.* The device may have connectors for digital audio formats such as AES/EBU (see p. 382).
- *Hardware acceleration.* Some devices are designed to take some of the processing load off the computer's CPU. This can provide more real-time effects (see p. 513) and make for a more streamlined editing experience. Some can output edited HDV with no rendering.

VIDEO SYNC GENERATOR. In some editing setups, the various pieces of equipment need a common signal so they all operate in sync with each other (called being *genlocked* together). For example, a VTR with serial device control needs to be fed the same sync signal as the NLE in order to perform frame-accurate edits. Video sync can be generated by a capture card or by an external *sync generator.* There are many terms used for sync, including *black, black burst, house sync, genlock,* and *reference.* Regular composite video contains sync, so often you can sync two devices by plugging the composite video output from one device into the *reference input* of another.

In the high definition world, the same concept is called *tri-level sync*.

Hard Drive Storage

The NLE stores digital video and audio files on hard drives. Having enough disk storage space is critical (see Storage, p. 519).

When choosing drives, pay attention to how much data they can move every second (their *data transfer rate* or *throughput*). The higher the data rate of the video format you're working in, the more speed you'll need (see Appendix B for examples). Because various video effects can involve playing more than one *stream* of video at a time (for example, a split-screen with two shots running simultaneously) you'll want fast disks that are capable of more than just the basic data rate of the format.

There are several types of hard drive interfaces (including SATA, FireWire, SCSI, and USB) that vary in terms of their speed. For high data rates, drives are often grouped into a disk array such as a RAID (Redundant Array of Inexpensive Disks). See p. 218 for drive types commonly used for video.

Though editing can be done on a computer with only one drive (such as a laptop), it's recommended that video and audio media not be stored on the same physical hard drive where the NLE application itself is installed. If your computer has open bays, you can add additional internal drives, which provide fast data flow. External drives have the advantage that you can bring them from system to system as needed. For DV and HDV work, many filmmakers attach relatively inexpensive FireWire drives to store the media. FireWire drives are *hot-swappable*, which means you can add or remove them while the system is running. Even so, be sure to *dismount* the drives (eject them from the desktop) before disconnecting or turning them off!

Although FireWire allows devices to be daisy-chained, you'll get better performance (fewer dropped frames) if the media drives are on a different bus—a digital signal path—than the deck or camera. Adding another FireWire controller card (set of FireWire connectors) to the PCI or PCI Express slot at the back of your computer isn't hard. FireWire controller cards are available on the Internet for less than the cost of a box of MiniDV tapes.

For productions that involve a team of editors and/or effects creators, having networked storage can greatly facilitate postproduction. See p. 219.

Picture Monitors

The computer monitor allows you to view the graphical interface that controls the NLE. Use the biggest computer monitor you can—or better, use two monitors—to get more screen "real estate" for all the information. Often, people put the bins (see below) on one monitor and the timeline on the other.

Keep in mind that a computer monitor usually can't display video correctly in terms of brightness and color values. This is explained in Computer, Video, and Broadcast Monitors, p. 200. Whenever possible, you should have a true NTSC/PAL or HD video monitor as part of your NLE setup.[1] The broadcast industry is

---

1. However, if you're working on a multimedia project that will be seen *only* on computer monitors, then use one as your picture reference.

transitioning from traditional CRT picture monitors—which still offer advantages in color and tonal scale reproduction—to LCD picture monitors, some of which are coming very close to CRTs in quality. Either of these types of monitors will do as long as they are professional video monitors with adequate controls and a blue-only mode (see Appendix A). Typically, the video signal is fed to the picture monitor from a VTR, a capture card, or a camera attached to the NLE (see Fig. 14-2).

If you're working in high definition and can't afford an HD broadcast monitor, there are two work-arounds. Some attached cameras, capture cards, and converter boxes can downconvert HD output to SD on the fly, meaning that an SD monitor can be used to view an HD project. While HD resolution can't be accurately displayed, color and contrast can. In another approach, various NLEs can output a full-screen, pixel-per-pixel HD picture viewable on a computer monitor. In this case, HD resolution can be accurately displayed while color and contrast can not. (Computer monitor color space is RGB; digital video including HD is YC_BC_R—for more on this, see Chapter 5.) Computer monitors with high enough resolution to view full HD—at least 1920 x 1080 pixels (or 1280 x 720 if you're editing 720p)—are a lot cheaper than video monitors of the same resolution. Final Cut Pro's full-screen viewing mode is called Digital Cinema Desktop. A 23-inch Apple Cinema Display has 1920 x 1200 pixels, just enough to display full HD. Though not as good as a true HD broadcast monitor, the image looks very good.

Audio Input and Monitoring

You'll need to hear what you're working on, and you'll want ways to bring sound from various devices into the NLE.

Audio monitor is a fancy term for a set of speakers. Often people use a pair of self-powered desktop speakers for editing. Get good speakers whenever possible. For more on speaker selection and the audio environment of the editing room, see p. 629.

Fig. 14-6. A small mixer is a helpful addition to the editing system for connecting audio equipment (like mics and tape decks) and controlling speaker volume. (Behringer)

It's very helpful to have a small *mixer* (see Fig. 14-6) as part of your editing setup. You can use it to record from a microphone or from other analog sources.[2] Often, the mixer is patched through a deck that performs the analog-to-digital conversion. The speakers are also run out of the mixer, which allows you to easily adjust the level and choose which channels you want to monitor.

A note about audio sync: If you're using a computer without an external video monitor, and are plugging speakers directly into the computer (or using internal speakers) audio sync will be correct—when you see, for example, a door close on screen, you'll hear it at the same time. However, in many NLE setups, the broadcast video monitor and the speakers are plugged into a deck, which is connected to the computer via FireWire connection (see Fig. 14-2). In this case, what you see on the broadcast monitor will be in sync with the sound, but the picture you see on the computer monitor may not be (you'll see the door close on the computer screen a few frames before you hear it). That's because it takes some time for the signal to get through the FireWire and deck to the speaker and external video monitor.[3] Regardless of your setup, it's very important while editing that you watch whichever picture is in sync with the audio!

HOW THE NLE PLAYS AND EDITS MEDIA

Media Files and Clips

To start work on an NLE, you load the video you want to edit into the system. This is variously called *capture*, *ingest*, *import*, or, for analog material, *digitizing*. If the camera recorded to a hard drive or memory card, ingest basically involves copying the files created by the camera to the NLE's drives (sometimes you can edit right off the drives or cards used on the shoot). If the camera recorded to tape, you'll use the NLE's capture tool to capture the video and audio from a VTR or camera (more on that below).

Either way you bring the material in, the video and audio files will be written to the NLE's hard drives. These captured chunks of video and audio are the *media files* or *source files*.

Media files are contained in a wrapper file format such as QuickTime (.mov), Windows media (.avi), OMF, MXF, or other formats (for more on wrappers, see p. 220). On some systems, the video and each channel of audio are captured as separate files; on others, they are wrapped together.

When each media file is captured, the NLE creates a *clip* to go with it. A clip is like a pointer that tells the NLE to go to that media and play it. The clip doesn't contain any audio or video data, it just refers to the media file that does.

The idea of "editing" using a nonlinear system is really just repositioning clips that tell the computer which media file to play next. Let's say we've captured three shots: A, B, and C. When we edit these three clips together in order, we're simply telling the computer to find the media for shot A, play it, instantly jump to shot B, play it, and so on.

---

2. If your computer lacks analog inputs, you can also record analog audio sources without a deck with an inexpensive A/D converter that plugs in a USB port, such as the Griffin iMic.

3. Some NLEs have an offset adjustment to compensate for this.

If we decide to shorten shot B and insert shot N before it, all we do is alter the "playlist." Now the computer is told to play shot A, then jump to N, then jump to B, but this time play less of the shot than it did last time. Even though we have re-ordered and changed the length of shots, the actual media files are not moved or changed. All we've done is altered the length and order of the clips that point to them. We can have many different versions of the movie with different clips point-ing to the same media or different parts of it. Clips can "reuse" the same source media as often as needed (unless this is a project that was shot and will be finished on film; see p. 620).

Real Time and Rendering

When an NLE can play clips in a sequence and jump instantly from one to an-other, we say that it is processing in *real time*. Depending on your system and what you're trying to do, there are occasions when the NLE may not be able to play or perform various effects in real time. Say, for example, instead of a hard cut between shots A and B, you decide to dissolve between them. The computer will play the end of shot A and meld it with the first few frames of shot B. If the computer can do this on the fly, that's a *real-time effect*. But with some effects, the computer can't do all the calculations fast enough. In this case, the effect must first be *rendered*, which means creating a new file (a *render* or *precompute file*) that contains the effect. If we render the dissolve between shots A and B, the frames that contain the A/B overlap become a render file that the NLE inserts between A and B in playback.

Generally speaking, the faster your computer and/or the lower the resolution of your video the more you can do in real time. When dealing with material that re-quires a lot of processing, many NLEs will reduce the picture quality on playback to try to stay in real time. (You always have the choice to stop and render when you want to maintain normal quality.) On some systems, various effects can be dis-played in real time on the computer monitor, but need to be rendered before they can be viewed on an external video monitor or played out to a VTR.

THE NLE AND WORKFLOW

Projects vary a lot in terms of the raw materials and the end products. You might have shot the movie with a cheap DV camera or a top-of-the-line profes-sional HD rig. Your ultimate goal may be a homemade DVD to share with friends, or a 5.1-channel surround-sound Digital Cinema production for screening in a 2,000-seat theater.

NLEs vary a lot too, in software and hardware. You might be running an old version of a consumer program on a slow laptop, or you might be working at a post house with the latest HD system with the fastest processor and terabytes of storage.

With each project, you need to chart out a workflow—a plan for how you're going to work with your materials and tools. As a rule, most filmmakers have three overarching needs: maintain the highest quality; find the fastest, most efficient route; save the most money. You can't necessarily achieve all three. (The old saying has it that among good, fast, and cheap you can have any two.)

With so many formats, editing systems, and ways of working, it's impossible to cover them all in a book like this. However, there are some standard ways of working based on what you're starting with, the capabilities of the editing system, and what end product you're aiming for.

The Idea of Offline and Online

The terms *offline* and *online editing* come from the days when video was edited exclusively on videotape, rerecording from one tape machine to another. In this traditional methodology, the camera tapes are dubbed to a lower-quality format and offline editing is done with relatively inexpensive offline editing decks (the original systems were called "offline" because the controller was not computerized). With these cheaper machines you can afford the time to shape and structure the movie. The offline edit is where you determine the "pattern" of the movie—every shot is cut to its proper length and is in its proper order. But at the end of offline editing you don't have a finished, high-quality tape—offline cuts often have poor image quality and rough sound. The goal of offline editing is to produce an *edit decision list* (EDL) which is like a construction blueprint that details the beginning and ending timecode of every shot used in the movie (see Fig. 14-39). You then take the EDL to an online editing suite, where the original, high-quality tapes are configured by timecode in the exact same way using expensive, online video decks. The end product of the online is the high-quality, finished master.

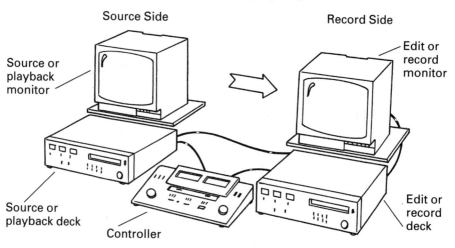

Fig. 14-7. Videotape editing. Material is played on the *source* deck and rerecorded on the *edit* or *record* deck. The *controller* operates both machines. Each side has its own monitor. (Robert Brun)

The terms offline and online continue to be used today, in the era of digital nonlinear editing. What do they mean now? We can see from the above description that, in one sense, "offline editing" means working on something that is not a finished product; the finished piece will be created later in the online stage. Offline and online are thus stages in the editing process. But in another sense, the idea of offline editing equipment suggests something that works at a lower or "draft" quality while online equipment is capable of "finished" or high quality. Today, these distinctions can become blurred. You might be able to use the same NLE to turn out an offline or an online product, simply by using different settings. Or your editing system might be capable of onlining a corporate DV project, but not an HD movie for television.

Many workflows used with NLEs involve offline and online stages; how those stages are accomplished varies widely. Though many nonlinear editing systems can generate an EDL, there are better, more powerful methods for making the transition from offline to online (for more on this, see From Offline to Online, p. 549).

A note about language: as you've probably already noticed, "offline" and "online" can be used as verbs ("We're offlining Tuesday"), nouns ("The offline is in my car"), and adjectives ("This is an offline deck"). In nonlinear editing, the terms can also be used to indicate whether or not media files are connected to the system and available for editing ("These clips are offline").

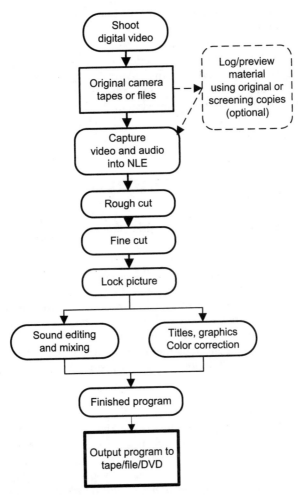

Fig. 14-8. An online workflow. In this scenario, all the work is done on one system. See Figs. 15-14, 15-16, and 15-17 for options when working with film-originated material.

An Online Workflow

Perhaps the simplest, most straightforward workflow is to capture the video into the NLE, edit it, and output it at the same resolution you captured it (see Fig. 14-8). This can be thought of as an online workflow (there is no offline), and is used for everything from simple student projects to professional projects of many kinds. With many digital formats, there's no loss of picture quality going in and out of the system. This workflow is convenient in the sense that you are working in one location on one machine with one set of tools, but it also means you're limited to the capabilities of your NLE or the other software you might have on your system.

An Offline/Online Workflow

There are many reasons you might choose an offline/online workflow. You may want to do an offline at "draft" quality because you don't have enough hard drive storage for full quality. Or you may want to online on a more powerful NLE with better software and faster hard drives. In Fig. 14-9, you'll see a possible workflow that involves shooting either HD or SD, capturing to one NLE system for offline editing, then moving to an online NLE for finishing. As shown in this flowchart, whether you shoot HD or SD, you can reduce offline storage needs by compressing to a lower data rate codec. Alternatively, with HD you can downconvert to SD prior to offline editing. Prior to the online edit, the original HD or SD camera tapes or files are recaptured to the online system at full resolution. In this workflow, audio is exported to a digital audio workstation for mixing at a sound studio. Other offline/online workflows could be done on one NLE in a single facility.

WHAT FORMAT OR RESOLUTION TO EDIT IN?

Some of the key decisions about workflow hinge on the resolution and data rate of the material you're editing and how that relates to the capabilities of your NLE. Virtually all digital cameras use a codec to compress the video before recording (see Digital Compression, p. 20 and p. 222.) Which codec is used (and at what data rate) depends on the format you're shooting and the particular camera. When you're ready to edit, and you want to capture what you've shot into the NLE, you may have choices about whether to edit with that same codec, convert to a different codec (called *transcoding*) or you may even decide to edit with uncompressed video.

Your choices will be influenced by the system you're working with, your budget, and your time. Even if not all options are open to you, it helps to understand the issues involved.

Native Editing

When an NLE can work in the same codec that you shot with (and therefore allow you to capture the video without changing it) it is said to handle that format "natively." Native editing means that there is essentially no quality loss when you import the video into the NLE, edit it, and then export it back to tape or file in the same format. The simplicity and ease of native editing are part of how DV created such a revolution for consumers and pros alike.

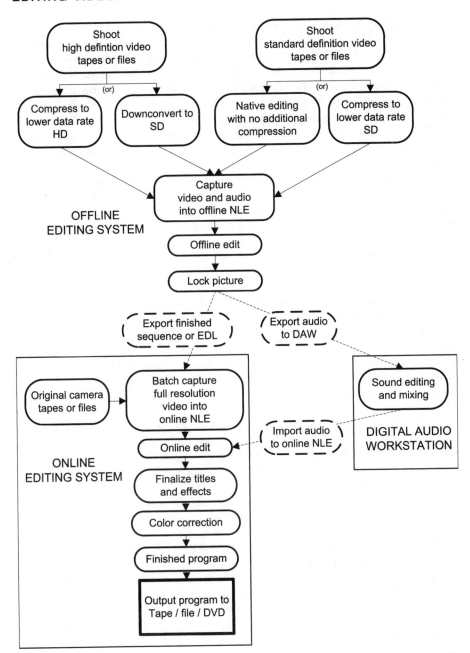

Fig. 14-9. An offline/online workflow using two nonlinear editing systems and a digital audio workstation. Whether you shoot HD or SD, you can reduce offline storage needs by compressing to a lower data rate codec. Alternatively, with HD you can downconvert to SD prior to offline editing.

Almost every NLE can work natively with the DV codec and most people edit DV that way. It's a very simple path to capture the video from a DV camera using a FireWire cable. This is essentially just a file transfer from the tape (or from a hard drive if you recorded originally on an HDD) to the NLE's hard drive. If all you do is cut and rearrange shots, the original files remain unchanged on the drives. After editing, you transfer the files back to tape (in their edited form) and the video looks just as good as it did originally, with no quality loss.

This same concept is the reason that we can make identical clones (copies) of most compressed digital formats with no loss between the original and the dubbed copy.

Native editing can be fast because no time is spent converting to another codec. If you're using a fairly compressed codec, such as DV or HDV, it can be cheap too, because no special capture card or drive array is needed. Native editing can be done in an online-only workflow. (You start at native quality and finish at native quality on the same editing system.)

Even so, at times, native editing isn't *completely* native.

When shots are only cut and rearranged in editing (called *cuts-only editing*) the video files remain compressed and there is no loss in quality. However, if you do other kinds of manipulations (like changing a shot's color or speed, dissolving between two shots, or adding text over a shot), these are accomplished by decompressing the video, making the changes, and then recompressing into a new file. Any time you're recompressing footage there is a risk of quality loss.

In most NLEs, all the changes or effects you do in the timeline are ultimately processed together in a single decompression/recompression cycle. However, sometimes footage is sent out to a separate application for compositing or effects, which can add compression cycles.

Generally speaking, the less compressed the codec is in the first place, the less the quality loss on recompression will be. DV material (which has 5:1 compression) will look a lot more like its native self after a few compression/recompression cycles than HDV material (which in the HDV-2 version has 22:1 compression and may suffer noticeably for the added generations).

As a general rule, it's best to keep decompression/recompression to a minimum, especially when there's a way to do what you want natively.

Editing with a More Compressed Codec

Appendix B shows the data rate and storage requirements of various formats and codecs. As you can see, there are big differences between some of them. For example, you'd need only 217 MB to store a minute of standard definition DV but it takes more than 9 GB to store a minute of uncompressed, 10-bit, full-raster HD—that's almost forty-four times more space on a hard drive. Since some formats are real data hogs, in various situations it makes sense to reduce the data rate before editing.

Generally this is done with an offline/online workflow. The video is converted to a more compressed codec or format while being captured into the NLE (sometimes the conversion happens before or after capture). You then do the offline edit. When you're done, you configure a high-quality version of the movie at the full, original data rate.

Many NLEs or capture cards offer a choice of codecs at different data rates; lowering the data rate generally lowers the picture quality, but some codecs look very good even at a low data rate.

Some systems offer codecs such as M-JPEG that can be used at various resolution levels. Resolution may be indicated as a compression ratio, such as 2:1 or 15:1. Higher compression (in this case, 15:1) means lower data rate.

Some systems allow you to capture only one field of an interlaced format, instantly cutting the data rate in half. Avid indicates single-field resolutions with an "s" after the compression ratio (such as 15:1s).

Certain codecs or settings deliberately sacrifice picture quality and are intended *only* for low data-rate offline editing. An example is Final Cut Pro's *Offline RT*, which uses the photo-JPEG codec at a smaller frame size than standard definition video.

Some camera systems support proxy editing, where an extremely low resolution proxy version of the material is generated in the camera and stored along with the normal recording. You can edit the low-res proxy on a laptop or send the files easily over the Internet to another location. Then you do an online edit at full resolution with the original media on a more powerful system.

The following are some of the reasons why you might want to work with a lowered data rate.

STORAGE. As just discussed, the higher the data rate, the more hard drive space you'll need to store material for editing. As storage gets cheaper, this is becoming less of a problem—it's easier to buy or rent more drives. However, if you think you won't have enough drive space, you can edit with a lower data rate.

Determining hard drive needs after filming is finished isn't hard. Consult Appendix B or sources such as your NLE's manual to determine how much storage you'll need per hour of material and multiply by the hours of video you have. Include some extra for graphics, music, and other files you'll add during editing and for the render files and timeline archiving that the NLE will create on its own. And keep about 25 percent of disc capacity unused. If you're just starting a project, estimating future storage needs is trickier. You could guess based on the length of the finished piece and the shooting ratio (see p. 320). Or you could multiply the number of shooting days by how much you plan to shoot each day.

If you have only enough storage to work on a small portion of your footage at a time, you may find your creativity hampered and various tasks will take longer. Even so, many people work by logging all the material, then capturing only the best takes or the stuff they want to work on first. You can always go back to the original tapes or files to search for other material as needed. Also, it's not hard to capture all the material for a scene or section of the film, then delete the unused portions after preliminary editing, freeing up disk space for other material (see Media Management, p. 578).

REAL-TIME PROCESSING AND NETWORKS. If you work at a high data rate and large frame size, your NLE may not be able to process in real time (see p. 513), causing delays that can interfere with the editing experience. Also, if you're sharing files with others in a network, high data rates may exceed the bandwidth of your network.

HD AND SD. Editing uncompressed HD puts huge demands on an NLE, both in storage and in processing. Many people work with NLEs that aren't equipped for uncompressed HD (or even uncompressed SD). One solution is to work in a compressed HD codec, such as DVCPRO HD. Doing so may or may not reduce the data enough for your system and needs. Avid's DNxHD codec includes an offline resolution that produces full-raster HD at 36 Mbps, hardly more than DV's 25 Mbps. Apple offers the *ProRes 422* format for HD at reduced data rates.

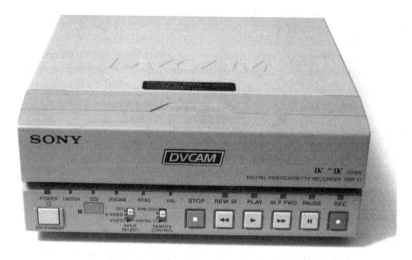

Fig. 14-10. The Sony DSR-11 is a basic deck for working with DV and DVCAM in NTSC or PAL.

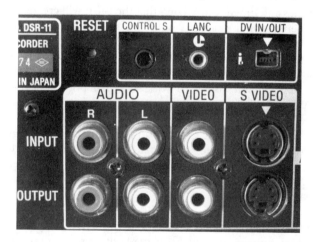

Fig. 14-11. The rear panel on the DSR-11 shows analog inputs and outputs for audio, composite video and S-video. The FireWire (iLink) connection ("DV In/Out") provides input and output for digital video and audio.

Some people choose instead to offline HD projects in SD. The downconversion can be done by a card, conversion box, deck, or camcorder during capture. (Sony's Z1, for instance, in playback can downconvert HDV to DV with matching time-code.) Another approach is to make a set of SD tapes or files from your HD material first, then capture those into the NLE (for example, you could dub HDCAM tapes to DVCAM).[4] You do the offline with a low-cost SD system, then do the on-line on an HD system.

Another issue with editing HD is that some editing systems aren't equipped for HD monitoring, which is expensive. This is discussed in Picture Monitors, p. 510.

Editing with a Less Compressed Codec

We've seen that using more compression can reduce demands on the editing system and be especially helpful for offline editing. Are there times when it helps to go the other way, to a *less* compressed codec or all the way to uncompressed?

STARTING AND FINISHING IN NATIVE RESOLUTION. If you're starting with a compressed codec like DV, DVCAM, DVCPRO 50, or DVCPRO HD and plan to *finish* on the same compressed codec, you generally won't improve quality by going to uncompressed video for editing. An example of this workflow would be to use a DV deck with an SDI link to convert DV (5:1 compression, 4:1:1 or 4:2:0 color sampling) to full uncompressed video (no compression, 4:2:2) before capturing to an NLE that can edit uncompressed video. If all you're going to do is recompress to DV when you're done, you're not gaining much advantage and you'll need a lot more storage. You're usually better off editing natively. However, if you intend to do extensive color correction or chroma keying (such as green screen), the doubled color resolution (from 4:1:1 or 4:2:0 to 4:2:2) is advantageous, as explained in the next section.

ONLINE EDITING. It's quite common to bump up from a compressed codec to something less compressed for the online edit and then finish in the less compressed format (this is often done at a post house that has the fast disk arrays necessary for uncompressed video). Thus, a project shot and offlined natively in DV (5:1 compression, 4:1:1 or 4:2:0 color sampling) might be finished at Digi-Beta resolution (2:1 compression, 4:2:2 color sampling). In this example a DV deck would be connected via SDI to a DigiBeta deck. The uncompressed SDI step would double the video signal's effective color resolution before recom-pression to DigiBeta, which then quantizes color at 10-bits instead of the original 8 for improved color bit depth. Improved color resolution and bit depth facili-tate color correction or chroma keying, with better results in the end. Titles also look better in a less compressed codec, so you're better off creating titles (or recreating them) at the higher data rate. Similarly, if you plan to upconvert from SD to HD, it's best to make (or remake) titles and graphics in HD. (With

---

4. A potential disadvantage of editing HD in SD is that the two have a different color space and pixel shape and may have a different frame rate, which can complicate postproduction. In some cases you can still edit at the same frame rate (see Working with Mixed Formats, p. 571).

many systems, titles built at one resolution can easily be rerendered at a higher one; see p. 547).

OFFLINE EDITING. There *are* some cases in which people choose to convert to a less compressed codec for offline editing as well. For example, because of its high compression, sometimes people convert HDV to a higher data rate codec before editing to avoid issues relating to quality loss after recompression (see above), the need to render ("conform") HDV before output, or because they plan to output in a format other than HDV anyway. One way to do this is to use a camera or deck to decompress the HDV to uncompressed HD and then, using a capture card or conversion box, capture into the NLE using a codec such as Apple's ProRes 422 or Avid's DNxHD. Alternatively, the HDV can be captured natively into the NLE, then transcoded to a less compressed HD codec such as DVCPRO HD or an *intermediate codec*.[5] Intermediate codecs streamline HD or HDV editing, offering significantly lower data rates than uncompressed, nearly lossless conversion from lower or higher data rate formats, and excellent results on screen. They include CineForm HD, Apple Intermediate Codec (AIC), and lossless AVI or QuickTime codecs. These are I-frame codecs that put less demand on the NLE than HDV or other interframe MPEG codecs. Your workflow would be to convert your material to the intermediate codec during or after capture, do the edit using the intermediate, then convert to another codec for output and distribution.[6] For more on this, see Compression Methods, p. 223.

CAPTURING AND ORGANIZING YOUR MATERIAL

Logging Clips

When the editor receives material from the production crew, the footage may be well organized and carefully logged as to what has been shot and which tapes or drives contain which scenes. Or the material may be a chaotic mess of undocumented footage with nothing but the date written on the tape boxes. It's essential that the editor organize the material as it's brought into the NLE so that any scene can be found easily when needed. The organization includes how the video is broken into individual clips to be captured, and how those clips are stored in the NLE for editing.

On some productions, everything that was shot is captured into the NLE; on others, the editor or assistant editor first logs all the material while noting which sections to capture (each section becomes a separate *master clip*). *Logging* means marking the *in point* (beginning) and *out point* (end) of each clip, giving the clip a name, identifying which tape or folder it came from, and adding any comments.

---

5. An application called HDVxDV can be used to transcode HDV to other codecs when used with Final Cut Pro.

6. As of this writing, AIC resets the timecode to zero at the beginning of each clip, which makes it impossible to accurately recapture from tapes later for a typical offline/online workflow (see below).

On a drama or other project that was shot with a script it's usually best to name clips by their scene/shot/take numbers.

Logging can be done with the capture tool of the NLE (see Fig. 14-13). Some people like to log on the fly, marking and naming each clip as it's being captured. Others like to log and capture in separate steps. First, you go through each tape, logging each clip and saving the clip information but not the media itself to the NLE. After you've logged everything, you do a *batch capture*, in which the NLE automatically captures the media for the clips as you've logged them (all you have to do is put in the right tape when requested). This process requires timecode (for more on this, see p. 526).

If you don't have access to the NLE for logging, there are stand-alone programs such as Imagine Products' HD Log that allow you to create a log before the edit, and import it into the NLE. HD Log can also be used with Panasonic's P2 cards to view, log, and name clips from MXF files.[7] For a low-cost, low-tech logging solution you can just use a word processor or spreadsheet program like Excel to create a four-column table with clip name, start and end timecodes, and reel number for each clip. Many NLEs can import that data for batch capturing. To screen your tapes, you'll need a deck or camera that can display timecode, or you could have a set of tapes made with burn-in timecode (see Fig. 1-17) to be able to see the numbers.

When logging, the question comes up: How long should a clip be?

Most important, you want to avoid clips that have a break in timecode or control track, so wherever there is a break, you should start a new clip (many NLEs can be set to automatically generate a new clip where breaks occur).

Some people like to make clips very long. Say you've shot an interview that goes for sixty minutes without stopping. You could capture that as one long master clip.[8] During capture or afterward, you can divide that into *subclips*, which are a convenient way to delineate sections within the master clip. You could mark subclips for each interview question and name them according to the question. Subclips could also be used to show where a certain character speaks in a dramatic scene.

Some people feel that capturing shorter clips makes organization easier. Also, it's not uncommon for files to become corrupted or have other problems. If your clips are very long you'll lose a lot (or have a lot to fix) if a problem occurs. That said, clips that are too short can be a pain. For example, cameras using time-of-day timecode may force a new clip at every camera stop—which can be really irritating if the shots are very short.

Some systems can do *auto scene detection* (also known as *scene extraction*), which may allow you to capture an entire tape in one pass. The system uses timecode or picture changes to find places where the camera stopped and mark new clips or subclips at each stop. This may or may not be better than marking clips yourself.

Organizing Clips

As clips are captured into the NLE, they can be grouped together for convenience in *folders* or *bins* (to see why they're called bins, see Fig. 15-8). You may want to put all the clips from a certain scene in one bin, keep edited sequences in an-

---

7. HD Log can also be used during a shoot to capture and play HD from a laptop.
8. The NLE may limit you to a certain maximum clip size, measured in gigabytes of storage.

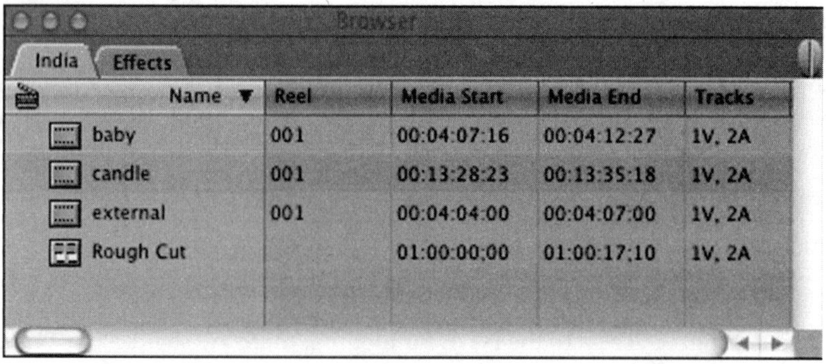

Fig. 14-12. This Apple Final Cut Pro browser shows one bin for the "India" project containing three source clips and one sequence ("Rough Cut"). (Apple, Inc.)

other, and so on. All the bins for a project are viewed in the *project window* or *browser* (see Fig. 14-12). This is your main tool for organizing all your video, audio, graphics, and titles.

The project window has columns for many types of data, including clip name, media starting and ending timecode, tape (reel) number, codec, etc. You can customize it with more categories, such as shoot date, location, or anything you like. By clicking on column headers you can quickly sort the clips in a bin to find, say, all clips from a certain tape or scene.

With most NLEs you can have the browser display text, or you can switch to a *frame view* that shows *thumbnails* (still frames) from each clip; some will even let you play the clip in motion. Editors can use the images to form a storyboard to visualize how the clips can be edited together.

Some NLEs can import the script and allow you to associate individual clips with lines from the script (called *script-based editing*), streamlining the process of finding clips as you work through the script. Other information from the shoot may also be imported into the NLE.

For a project that originated on film, you may need to track keycode numbers, in-camera or audio timecode, as well as camera roll, sound roll, and telecine reel numbers (see Telecine Event and Scene Management, p. 702). Though you could enter this data by hand, it can be automatically imported from shot logs generated at the telecine session.

Capturing Video and Audio

Every NLE has a tool or window for logging clips and capturing media into the system. It's important that these tasks be done carefully. If you're using an online-only workflow, the media you capture will be used to generate your final product. If you're using an offline/online workflow, you may be replacing video and/or audio media at a later stage, but it's crucial that the logging information be accurate so that errors aren't introduced later.

See your NLE's manual for details on capturing, but the following are some key items.

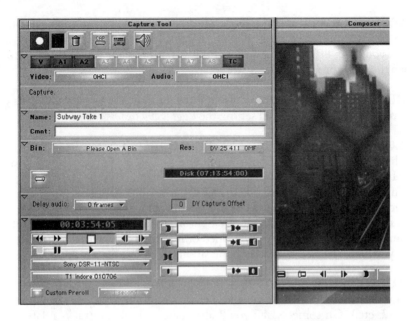

Fig. 14-13. Capture tool in Avid Xpress Pro. (Avid Technology, Inc./Joshua Weinstein)

LOGGING AND CAPTURING. As discussed above, you may prefer to log all the clips on a tape first (marking ins, outs, naming the clip, and saving it to a bin) and then do a batch capture. Or you may mark individual clips and capture them one at a time—sometimes called "capture in to out." (This may result in unnecessary rewinding.) Some people like to mark and name clips while the tape is rolling and capturing—"capturing on the fly." Regardless of which method you use, when marking clips for capture be sure to leave at least five seconds of *preroll* time ahead of the section you plan to use and *postroll* time after your selection.

DECK CONTROL. The capture tool will have controls to control the tape deck or camera (see Input and Output, p. 506). If you're working with a noncontrollable device (say, a consumer VCR), you'll have to find each shot, press play on the VCR, and then start capturing on the NLE.

TAPE NAME. Every tape needs a unique *reel number* or *name*. Depending on your system, you may be able to name tapes however you like. But if there's any chance you will be making an EDL to move the project to another system, it's best to use tape names that are less than six characters with no spaces or punctuation (the name can have numbers and letters but it should start with numbers). A numbering scheme like 0001, 0002 is always safe. In any case, be sure every tape has a unique name/number and that you've indicated the correct name when capturing. If you have a tape with timecode restarts (places where the timecode resets to 00:00:00 because the tape was removed and restarted; see Avoiding Timecode Problems, p. 207) give each section its own tape name, such as 003A, 003B, etc.

DRIVE LOCATION. You must tell the NLE where to store the media files when they're captured. This is called setting the *scratch disk* or *target drive*. As noted above, you'll get better performance if this is not the same physical hard drive on which the NLE program itself is stored.

BIN LOCATION. You must also tell the NLE where to store the clips when they're captured. This is called setting the *logging bin* or *target bin*.

CODEC, RESOLUTION, AND FILE FORMAT. You may have a choice of which codec or what resolution to capture in (see What Format or Resolution to Edit In?, p. 516). In some cases you may want to capture in the codec used for the original recording, then transcode to another codec after capture.

On some systems, you may also have a choice of wrappers (such as MXF, OMF, or QuickTime, see p. 220). Some NLEs work with a particular wrapper and will automatically convert any captured video or imported files to that format. In some cases you may have to use another application to convert the wrapper first.

AUDIO. Several capture settings relate to audio.

You must select which of the audio channels on the tape you want to capture (A1, A2, etc.). On some NLEs you'll also indicate how the tracks relate to each other. (Are they a stereo pair or separate mono channels?) If the audio was recorded with a stereo mic or you're capturing from a mixed stereo tape, then select *stereo pair*. For almost everything else, it's better to capture as separate mono channels (1 + 2). You can pair them in stereo later if needed.

There is a setting to choose audio sample rate (or to allow you to convert to a different sample rate during capture). The current standard for professional broadcast video postproduction is 48kHz at 16-bits per sample. Some DV camcorders are capable of recording at a lower audio rate of 32kHz at 12-bits, which yields noticeably poorer results. If somehow your original DV contains audio at this sample rate, be sure to upconvert it to 48kHz at 16-bits upon capture.

You will have no control over audio level when capturing digital video formats over FireWire. This holds for all cloning and digital-to-digital copying of digital video formats. However, when digitizing an analog format using a capture card or conversion box, you will need to set levels (see p. 527).

With some cameras, captured audio may be out of sync with the video. To address this problem, some NLEs have an audio delay setting to compensate by a frame or two.

When editing material that was shot on film, audio may need to be speed-adjusted before capture; see p. 619.

FRAME RATE AND PULLDOWN REMOVAL. You need to select the proper frame rate for your video. Footage shot in 24p may need to have pulldown removed, p. 565.

Timecode and the Capturing Process

For background on timecode, see p. 22 and p. 203.

Whenever possible, source material (both video and audio) should have timecode. Though you can capture into an NLE footage that doesn't have timecode, several aspects of editing will be limited if you do. For example, if you plan to use an offline/online workflow, this generally requires capturing the material once for the offline, then again at a higher resolution for the online. When video and audio material has timecode, it can be accurately recaptured whenever needed. Without timecode, you would have to try to match the shots by eye (and ear), which can sometimes be done when necessary but is not practical for an entire movie. Without timecode you can't generate an EDL.

Even if you only plan to capture once and finish on the same system, you may find that a drive crashes, or you want to re-edit the project at a later date—yet more reasons why having timecode on your source material is useful.

If your source video doesn't have timecode, consider dubbing it to a format with timecode before capturing to the NLE. For example, if the footage was shot with a consumer analog format like Hi8 or VHS, you could dub it first to DV, then use the DV as your camera tape for the rest of the project.

See above for issues relating to timecode breaks and tapes that have repeating timecode numbers.

TIMECODE ACCURACY. On a timecoded tape, every frame of picture has its own timecode number which is recorded together with the video on the tape. When you capture that into an NLE, the picture and timecode data are separated from each other and may get out of sync (resulting in timecode that can be off by a few frames). It's important to calibrate timecode, especially when using a new NLE or new deck.[9] The easiest way is to capture some video that has burned-in timecode (see Fig. 1-17). Look carefully at the captured video to see if the number in the NLE's timecode display is the same as the burn-in in the picture. If not, adjust the *timecode offset* in the NLE. Do this on a few shots to see if there's drift. When using a VTR with serial deck control (for example, RS-422), accurate timecode requires that deck and the capture card be genlocked with a common sync signal (see p. 509).

With some video formats, timecode may drift from one capture to the next.[10] In other words, a given frame of picture or sound might come in as 1:00:02:10 in one capture and 1:00:02:11 when captured a second time. This would make it difficult or impossible to use an offline/online workflow in which you need to capture material once for the offline, then recapture it for the online and expect it to match perfectly. With these formats, one solution is to capture natively, then transcode to a different codec within the NLE. You use the lower data rate codec for offline editing, then reconnect to the original media that you've saved in the meantime for the online; this should avoid timecode capturing errors, as you're only capturing once.

Adjusting Levels During Capture

When importing compressed digital video and audio in native form, generally you will not adjust the video or audio levels during capture to the NLE. For exam-

9. When using FireWire capture and deck control, this is not necessary with all NLEs.

10. As of this writing, problems have been reported with some HDV and DVHS systems. These may be fixed by the time you read this.

ple, when DV is captured over FireWire, the video and audio are captured as they were recorded, with no adjustments permitted. Later, during editing, you can make changes to the picture or sound.

However, when capturing from analog sources using a capture card or conversion box, the video can be adjusted for proper levels prior to capture. This may be done with controls on the VTR and/or the NLE. Ideally, the source tape has color bars and audio tone recorded at the head of the tape for reference (p. 421). The video levels are checked on the system's waveform monitor and vectorscope (see Figs. 5-2 and 8-3). Follow any instructions in your NLE's manual about making necessary adjustments.

Similarly, you should check the audio level and adjust if necessary. See p. 420 for guidelines in setting audio level.

If your footage lacks bars and tone, you can still use the NLE's waveform monitor and audio level meters to ensure you are within safe video and audio levels, but you'll have to use your judgment about what looks and sounds right.

CREATING AND EDITING SEQUENCES

Now that you've got your material stored on the hard drives, you're ready to start editing. The moment has arrived.

The Editing Interface and Timeline

All NLEs have certain basic things in common, even if they differ in their particulars and in the names used for various parts and actions. The *editing interface* is the main display used to control the system. Usually this is divided into several areas or windows, which may be spread over one or two computer monitors, depending on your setup.

Usually there are two windows that display video (see Fig. 14-14). One of them is for viewing and marking clips you want to use (the equivalent of the source monitor in tape editing; see Fig. 14-7). This may be called the *viewer, source monitor,* or *monitor window.* The second window is for viewing the edited movie or sequence that you are creating. This may be called the *canvas, program monitor,* or *record monitor.*

The *timeline,* where you actually build the movie, shows how the clips are edited together into the sequence (see Fig. 14-15). Most timelines use colored rectangles to represent video and audio clips, often with a *thumbnail* (still frame) showing what the clip contains. Clips are arranged on one or more *tracks,* allowing you to see and move clips in relation to each other. Transitions between clips, such as fades and dissolves, are shown graphically.

Audio clips are represented in another set of tracks. These tracks can be edited independently of the picture or locked together with it. Many systems will display *audio waveforms,* which are a visual representation of the sound signal that aids in finding sounds on the timeline (see Fig. 14-21).

Viewer (source monitor)   Canvas (record monitor)

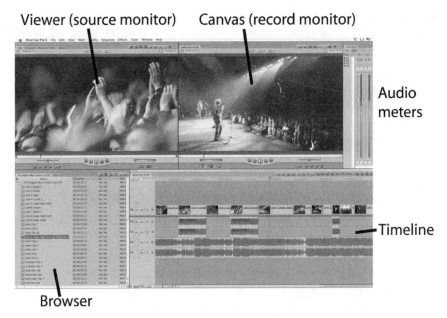

Audio
meters

Timeline

Browser

Fig. 14-14. Final Cut Pro main editing screen. (Apple, Inc.)

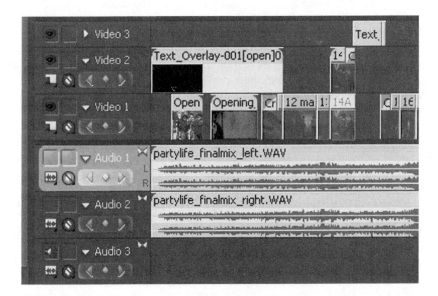

Fig. 14-15. Timeline in Adobe Premiere Pro. Note video clips on the Video 1 track; text on Video 2 and 3. The audio here is a pair of stereo music clips. (Adobe Systems, Inc.)

A long vertical bar on the timeline indicates where the system is playing in "play" mode, or the point at which an edit may take place when you are in "edit" mode. This bar is variously referred to as the *cursor, play line, play bar,* or *position indicator.* On most systems, the cursor moves across the timeline from left to right when you are playing a sequence.

You can *zoom in* on the timeline to see in detail how audio and video fit together at a particular cut or transition, or *zoom out* to see a sequence or the entire movie as a whole, to get a sense of the pacing and overall balance. Once you work with this graphical representation of the movie, you may find it becomes an important tool in how you think about the structure and layout of the film you're making.

Clips and sequences can be played using keyboard commands or by clicking on-screen buttons using the mouse. Professional editors usually rely on *JKL editing,* which is supported by many NLEs. The J key is "play reverse," the K key is "stop" and L is "play forward." Hitting either J or L twice doubles the speed. Often the space bar on the keyboard is both "play" and "stop."

On many systems, the I key is *mark in* (for the start of an edit) and the O key is *mark out.* These are conveniently located above J, K, and L on the keyboard for one-handed operation. Many NLEs allow you to customize the keyboard as you like.

Some editors like to work with a multi-button mouse, trackball, or graphics tablet to control the NLE.

NLEs usually give you several different ways of doing the same task, so you can find the style of working that suits you best. You can use the keyboard, mouse, or a combination. Many pros find that once they know (and have customized) the keyboard, they use the mouse relatively little for basic editing tasks.

You Won't Hurt Anything

As you get started, remember that clips arranged on the timeline are nothing more than pointers to media files stored on the hard drives (see Media Files and Clips, p. 512). You can delete, change, move, or copy clips without in any way affecting or damaging the original media that they point to. Nonlinear editing is thus completely "nondestructive." You can totally mess up a sequence and then return to a previously saved version with no harm done.

To further relax you about the editing process, keep in mind that all systems have undo commands (*Ctrl-Z* on windows or *Command-Z* on Macs), which allow you to easily correct editing mistakes. Some NLEs allow you to select how many "levels" of undo are stored (that is, how many actions in a row can be undone). It's a good idea to set this to at least fifteen or twenty steps so you can fix things that go wrong.

When experienced editors have a sequence they like, but want to experiment with changes, they will *duplicate the sequence*—make a copy of it and park it in the bin. In doing this, you know you can always get back to where you were before. Sequences by themselves take up very little storage space.

Even so, as anyone who has used a computer knows, all sorts of things can go wrong (power outages, crashes, corrupted files) to make you miserable. Be sure to save your work regularly, especially after doing anything complex. Many NLEs have an *autosave* function that stores a backup copy of your project in a location you indicate (on Avids this place is called the *attic;* in Final Cut it's the *vault*). If you set autosave for every fifteen minutes, that's the most work you'll lose in a crash; of course, the more frequently it saves, the more often you'll have to wait while it does.

At the end of each day, be sure to backup your *project file* (which contains all your bins, sequences, and settings) to a separate drive or removable disc. Captured media files are usually not backed up because they're too big, but imported graphics or audio are generally small enough. In the event of a disaster, as long as you have the project file, and your source material has timecode, you can recover your work the way you left it.

Marking Clips and Putting Them on the Timeline

To begin editing, start by identifying the clips you want to use in the bin or browser. On most systems, you can double-click a clip in the bin to view it. You can also drag it to the viewer/source monitor. The entire, uncut clip is the master clip. If you want to use only a portion it, mark an *In Point* (start mark) and *Out Point* (end mark) in the source window. You have just *marked* the clip. It's ready to be put into the movie.

To move the clip to the timeline, your options may include: clicking on it in the source monitor or bin and dragging it directly to the timeline (*drag and drop*); dragging it to an onscreen icon on the canvas/record monitor that selects what type of edit you want to do (more on that below); or using onscreen buttons or keyboard commands to select the edit type.

Some people like to begin editing by assembling entire master clips in a rough order on the timeline so they can view all the material, and then shorten clips later. Others like to view clips individually in the source monitor and shorten them before adding them to the timeline.

Three-Point Editing

When we add clips to shots already on a timeline, four edit points play a part in the process. First we decide which part of each source clip we want to use (by marking an In Point and Out Point on the clip). Then we decide where on the timeline to put it, which involves an In Point and Out Point on the timeline. In Fig. 14-38, you can see the equivalent four points when editing on tape.

To perform an edit, the editing system needs to know any *three* of those points.

Say, for example, we have a wide shot of a woman in a café already on the timeline. We also have a source clip of her sipping coffee in a close shot that we want to add. We could mark the close shot in the source monitor with an In Point just before she sips and an Out Point just after. We then mark an In Point on the timeline, telling the NLE to place the clip just after she lifts her cup in the wide shot. That's three points.

Alternatively, we might mark an In Point on the timeline just before the camera goes out of focus in the wide shot, and an Out Point just after it comes back into focus. Then we mark only an In Point on the closeup of the woman. Again, only three points.

Or, we might choose to mark the timeline the same way, but rather than marking an In Point just before she sips in closeup, we mark instead an Out Point as she puts her cup down. It's still three points. By the way, using the Out Point as the mark is called a *backtimed edit*.

How a new clip interacts with clips already on the timeline is described in the next section. The key idea here is simply that to add a clip to the timeline, the NLE needs to know *any three* In or Out Points in the clip and timeline.

Adding Clips to a Sequence

In nonlinear editing, a timeline containing a group of clips is a *sequence*. With NLEs, the word "sequence" refers to everything on a given timeline, which might mean an entire movie, or just a few shots. Don't confuse this use of "sequence" with the general film usage of "sequence" to mean an individual scene (see p. 323).

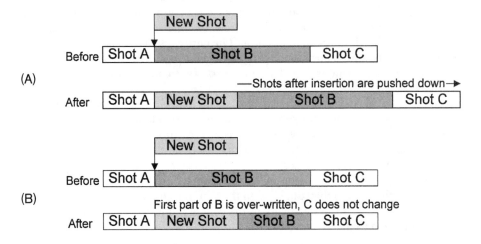

Fig. 14-16. Adding a shot. (A) With an insert or splice edit, adding a new shot causes existing shots after the insertion point to be pushed later in the sequence. (B) With an overwrite edit, the new shot replaces existing material without changing the position of other shots.

As you edit, you build up a clips on the timeline. When you want to add a new clip to an existing sequence, you have two main options about how the new clip will affect the clips already on the timeline. Different NLEs use different terms for these two styles of edits.

Say you've already built a three-shot sequence using clips A, B, and C. Now you want to insert a new shot after clip A (see Fig. 14-16). There are a couple of ways to do this.

INSERT OR SPLICE EDIT. In this type of edit, you *insert* (*splice*) the new clip at the end of clip A. Clip B remains intact, but is pushed back later in the sequence. This is sometimes called a "film-style" edit because it's like the idea of cutting apart a roll of film, splicing in a new shot, and then splicing the roll back together. Note that the sequence gets longer when we add the new clip. If clip B began in the edited sequence at, say, one minute timecode prior to making the edit, it will begin at one minute plus the length of the new clip after we make the edit. Any clips following B will also be pushed back the same amount.

In Final Cut Pro and Premiere Pro this is type of edit is called an *insert*.[11] Avid calls it a *splice edit*. It's sometimes called a *ripple edit* because in video terms, this edit has *rippled* all the clips after the edit point; that is, it has changed where they occur on the timeline.

OVERWRITE OR OVERLAY EDIT. In an *overwrite edit*, when we add the new clip we overwrite (cover over) the existing sequence starting at the edit point and continuing until the end of the new clip. In Fig. 14-16B, the new clip replaces the beginning of shot B. The end of shot B and the rest of the sequence are unaffected. Note that the total length of the sequence does not change. This is sometimes called a "video-style" edit because, in a sense, it "rerecords" a section of the sequence, replacing it with new material. Clips following the edit (later in the sequence) do not ripple; they remain in their original positions.

Insert edits on an NLE are a basic way of adding new material as you construct a sequence. Overwrite edits are useful for changing a sequence you've built without changing its length or the sync relationship between picture and sound. Say you'd constructed a sequence of images edited to a music track, so that cuts in the picture match up to musical beats and the overall sequence is exactly the length of the song. Using overwrite edits, you could add or change shots in the picture without changing the length of the sequence or the basic sync between picture and sound.

Removing Clips from a Sequence

Now, instead of adding a clip to the sequence A, B, C, we want to remove shot B. Again we have two options for doing so (see Fig. 14-17).

DELETE OR EXTRACT EDIT. If we simply want to remove shot B, we can *delete* it. This is a film-style removal, the equivalent of cutting out shot B and attaching the end of shot A to the beginning of shot C. The total length of the sequence is reduced—it becomes shorter by the length of shot B. Some people just call this *delete*; other names include *extract edit* or *ripple delete*. On some NLEs, when a clip is deleted, it is sent to the clipboard (a temporary storage area) and can be easily reinserted elsewhere in the sequence. Even without the clipboard, you can always go back to the original clip in the bin to insert the shot elsewhere.

LIFT EDIT. In a lift edit, when we mark and remove shot B, it is replaced with black filler (see Fig. 14-17B). The filler is really just a place-holder that keeps clips A and C in their original positions, leaving a gap the exact size of shot B between them.[12] The sequence maintains its original length, shot B is gone, and the gap can easily be filled with another shot later. Sync relationships and the total length of the sequence do not change.

---

11. Though this should not be confused with insert editing with a VTR; see p. 556.
12. This is equivalent to slugging a film workprint with leader or fill.

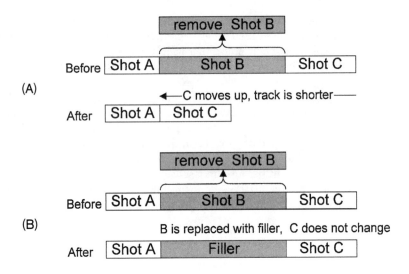

Fig. 14-17. Removing a shot. (A) With a delete or extract edit, removing a shot causes all the following shots to be pulled earlier in the sequence. (B) With a lift edit, any material that's removed is replaced with filler. The rest of the sequence remains unchanged.

Many editing systems offer several other variations on the above-mentioned edits. However, you can perform most editing tasks with these four basic edits. To review: You can bring a clip to the timeline by inserting or by overwriting. You can remove a clip by extracting or by lifting.

Trimming Clips

After clips have been added to the timeline, you need to be able to adjust their length. This is a fundamental part of editing—fine-tuning how one shot moves into the next. In video terms, *trimming* means to adjust an edit point, either to extend or shorten a shot.

There are several ways to trim shots. Most NLEs have a special *trim mode* that helps you to adjust the cut between two shots. Trim mode often has two windows: One displays the last frame of the outgoing shot, the other shows the first frame of the incoming shot (see Fig. 14-18). Once in trim mode, you can extend or shorten the *tail* (end) of the first shot, the *head* (beginning) of the second shot, or both. The trim editor allows you to preview the edit with a looping feature, which can play the transition repeatedly while you adjust it.

You can also trim shots right on the timeline by using keyboard commands or by clicking on the end of a clip and dragging one way or the other with the mouse. With most editing systems you have a choice: You can adjust trims by eye, you can click or use a keyboard command to move the edit point by a preset number of frames, or you can type in any number of frames you want.

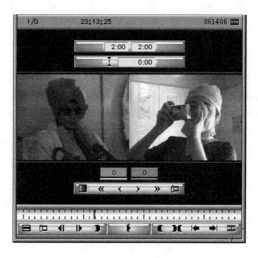

Fig. 14-18. Trim mode. This Avid trim tool displays the outgoing frames of one clip and the incoming frames of the next one. The buttons allow you to trim either or both clips. (Avid Technology, Inc./Joshua Weinstein)

Types of Trims

Like other types of edits, trims also come in different flavors (see Fig. 14-19).

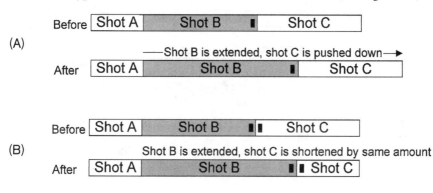

Fig. 14-19. Types of trims. (A) With a single-roller trim (trim tail or ripple edit), the tail of shot B is extended, and shot C is pushed later in the sequence by the same amount. (B) With a dual-roller trim (trim joint or roll edit), the tail of shot B is extended and the head of C is overwritten by the same amount. Shot C becomes shorter, but its position in the sequence doesn't change.

RIPPLE EDITS. Let's go back to our sequence of clips A, B, and C. If we perform a *ripple edit* to the tail of clip B, we can extend the shot (that is, move the tail of the clip to the right, which adds frames). This will push clip C further down, lengthening the overall sequence and rippling all the subsequent clips. Avid calls this a *single-roller trim*; Media 100 denotes this as *trim tail*. If we wanted to shorten the tail of B, we could just as easily delete frames, moving the tail of clip B to the left. This will shorten the entire sequence and bring up all clips following the edit.

ROLL EDITS. Let's start again with the original A, B, C sequence, and apply a *roll edit* to the cut between clips B and C. In this trim, we add frames to the tail of B and delete the same number of frames from the head of C. Clip B is extended and Clip C is shortened. Clip C now starts later, but because the clip has also gotten shorter by the same amount, the clip does not move relative to the timeline. The tail of C remains in the same place and the overall sequence does not change length. Avid calls this a *dual-roller trim*; Adobe calls it a *rolling edit*; on Media 100 this is *trim joint*.

Trimming Entire Clips

Two more specialized trims can be used to trim both ends of a clip at once.

SLIP EDITS. A *slip edit* allows you to use a different portion of a clip without changing its length or position relative to other clips (see Fig. 14-20A). If you slip a clip to the right, you effectively trim back the head of the clip while extending the tail the same amount. This has the effect of allowing you to view a later portion of the shot without changing anything else.

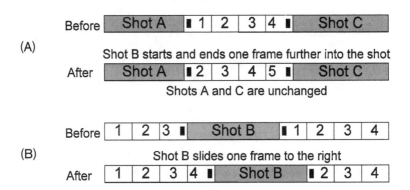

Fig. 14-20. Slip and slide trims. (A) After doing a slip trim, all shots remain unchanged in length and relative position, but we now view a different portion of shot B. (B) With a slide trim, shot B is itself fixed, but its position in the sequence can be changed. As shown here, shot B is slid to the right, which causes the tail of A to be extended and the head of C to be overwritten.

SLIDE EDITS. A *slide edit* allows you to grab a clip and slide it over adjoining clips (see Fig. 14-20B). For example, in the A, B, C sequence, you could grab shot B and slide it to the right on the timeline. The NLE does this by extending the tail of A and trimming back the head of C. Clip B is itself unchanged but is in a new position. The length of the sequence is unchanged. Not all NLEs do slip or slide edits.

Handles and the Limits on Trims

NLEs make it easy to execute your creative ideas. If you want to shorten or lengthen a shot, you just click on it and perform the trim. This is much easier than what it takes to do the same thing with film or with linear videotape.

However, you can't always lengthen a shot when you want to. Say you have a two-minute master clip in the bin and you put the entire clip on the timeline. If you later try to extend the head or tail of the shot, you'll get an error message about having "insufficient media" to do the edit. You've used the whole clip (which represents the entire media file)—there is no more.

You can avoid this situation by trimming back master clips by at least a few seconds at either end before bringing it into the edited sequence. This will also leave some frames available if you later decide to dissolve in or out of the shot. For example, if you want a 30-frame dissolve at the start of a clip, you'll typically need 15 extra frames at the head of the clip to use for the overlap with the previous clip.

When extra media at the head or the tail of a clip is available for use but is not currently visible (or audible) in the sequence, it's called a *handle*. Having handles on your clips gives you the flexibility to extend them or apply transitions when you want (see Fig. 16-10).

It's easy to check whether you have handles on a clip by using the *match frame* command. Put the cursor on the first frame of a clip in the timeline and hit match frame. The master clip will appear in the viewer/source monitor and you can see how much longer it is than the portion you're currently using in the sequence. You will find many other uses for the match frame command—such as hunting for other shots near the one you're matching.

Transitions Between Clips

A *straight cut*, (also called *hard cut* or simply *cut*) is when one shot ends and the other begins cleanly. In NLE terms, any of the other ways of bridging from one shot to another (including a dissolve or fade out/fade in) are called *transitions*. See Cutting Styles, p. 489, for more on the use of transitions in storytelling.

Transitions are easy to do with NLEs. You can select the type of transition, its duration in frames, and its position relative to the cut (centered on the cut, beginning on the cut, or ending on the cut). Some systems let you fine-tune the center of the transition at any point near the cut. As noted above, if you want to do a dissolve you'll need handles of half the dissolve length from each shot (see Fig. 15-9). When doing dissolves, keep in mind that a bright shot will tend to overpower a dark shot, so a brighter shot will seem to dissolve in faster on a dark shot than vice versa.

Moving Clips on the Timeline

There are several ways to move a clip that's already on the timeline. One way is to click on it and drag it with the mouse. Most NLEs have a *snapping* function that makes clips attach "magnetically" to nearby items (including other clips, the play bar, marks you've set, your car keys). Turn snapping on to avoid accidentally leaving a small gap between two clips you want to join. Sometimes you want to position two clips very close to each other but not touching, in which case you'll have more control if you turn snapping off.

Snapping is very handy when you want to mark a clip or area for removal. The play bar will snap to the head of the clip where you can mark an In Point. It will also snap to the tail of the clip (but on some systems you then have to move *one frame to the left* before marking the Out Point to avoid unintentionally cutting a frame from the following clip). In some systems you can click on a clip to select it, or you can *lasso* a clip or a group of clips by dragging around it with the mouse.

The NLE has several options for how clips behave when moved over each other. In one mode, pushing one clip into another will overwrite the second clip. In another mode you can drag one clip ahead of another and make them swap positions. Clips can also be moved numerically by typing in a frame count plus or minus. Consult your NLE's manual for the various options and how to execute them.

The NLE also has *copy* and *paste* functions that can be used to move single clips or many clips on several tracks in a large portion of the timeline. This is a good way to move clips from one sequence to another.

Using Multiple Video Tracks

Most NLEs allow you to create more than one video track. Many effects require two or more layers of video clips stacked together. A simple example is a title *superimposed* over picture. Unless you select otherwise, the top layer is usually the one that is seen "first," so the title goes on the upper track and the picture appears under the letters (see Fig. 14-15). You can adjust any layer's *opacity* (transparency) when you want multiple layers to be visible at the same time.

Using two video tracks can simplify some basic cutting decisions. For example, if you have a continuous shot of a woman talking on the lowest video track and a short cutaway of a man listening on the track above, you can just push the cutaway forward and back, experimenting with placement without having to actually commit it to one spot.

NESTED CLIPS. Complex video effects may require many tracks of video and/or graphics. Sometimes when you need several clips in several layers to accomplish an effect, you'll want to *nest* those clips into a single clip, which is easier to move around. Often this is done by creating a separate sequence that contains only the effects shot and its many clips; you then edit that sequence into the main movie as a single clip on the timeline. The nested clip is like a box that keeps things neatly packaged. You can "step into" the nested clip (often by double-clicking on it) whenever you want to work with the clips within.[13]

Other Types of Edits

In addition to the standard insert and overwrite edits discussed above, there are some more specialized ways of bringing clips to the timeline.

If you have a gap you want to fill on the timeline, but the clip you want to fill it with is either too long or too short, you can use *fit-to-fill*. To do this edit you mark In and Out Points on both the new clip and on the gap. Fit-to-fill will either speed up or slow down the clip to make it fit the gap exactly.

---

13. Note that nested clips don't usually translate to an EDL if you're planning to use one for an online (see below).

If you have a clip on the timeline that's the right length and in the right position but you don't like the picture, you can do a *replace edit*. In Final Cut Pro, this is done by parking the play head at the start of the clip you want to replace on the timeline; going to the viewer and putting that cursor at the head of the replacement shot; then hitting "replace." This saves you having to set any In or Out marks.

BASIC SOUND EDITING

NLEs are powerful tools for editing and mixing sounds. They make many otherwise time-consuming tasks easy and give the filmmaker a lot of control. Let's look at some of the basic ways to work with sound on an NLE.

Working with Audio Tracks

Footage from a video camera typically has one or two channels of audio (and sometimes more). When you capture or import that footage, the NLE creates separate clips for the video and each audio channel, but all those clips are *linked* together to make editing easier (you can unlink them when needed).

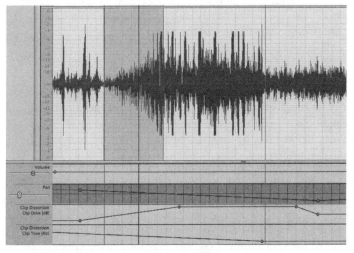

Fig. 14-21. Audio waveforms. A visual representation of the sound, waveforms make some editing tasks easier. This Soundtrack Pro screen also includes tracks to adjust volume and left/right pan using keyframes. (Apple, Inc.)

When you edit a clip from the source viewer to the timeline, the video clip goes to a video track on the timeline and the associated audio clips go to one or more audio tracks (see Fig. 14-15). The NLE has a *track selector* where you can choose which tracks to place the clips on. You can select *not* to include any combination of the clips in the edit.

Audio recorded and captured in stereo (for example, most music) normally has two paired channels, left and right. When you edit a stereo clip to the timeline the audio will appear as a *stereo pair*: A clip containing the left channel will be on one track, and a paired clip containing the right channel will be on the next track playing. Trimming or changing the level of one will automatically affect the other. With many NLEs you can choose to pair or unpair clips whenever you want.

Audio Levels

You may want to adjust the sound level (volume) of clips in a sequence to correct audio that was recorded too loudly or too quietly in the field, or you may want to adjust levels to balance sounds you're editing together (for example, a distant gun shot should be quiet, while a closeup of an explosion should be loud).

When you're editing, what level should the sound be? Most NLEs have a digital audio meter; in no case should the audio level reach the top of the meter. If the peaks (the loudest parts) are reaching the top of the scale, bring the level down. If the meter is set up with 0 dB at the top of the scale, you might keep the peaks (the loudest parts) below about -10 dBFS. For more precise instructions on using meters and setting levels, see The Sound Mix, p. 647.

After you've got a few clips playing normally and showing a good level on the meter, adjust the volume of the speakers (or headphones) to a comfortable level. Then *don't change the speaker level* while you edit. You'll be able to tell a lot about the level just from listening. However, if you constantly raise and lower the speaker level, you won't know if something is really too loud or too quiet.

There are several ways to control the audio level.

CONTROLLING THE AUDIO LEVEL. The sound level of an audio clip can be adjusted by increasing or decreasing *gain*. Many NLEs have a mixing tool that allows you to adjust gain while playing the sequence.

Most NLEs can display the audio gain as a line on the clip itself (see Fig. 16-9). Pushing the line up with the mouse increases the sound level. When *keyframes* are enabled, you can click on the line to set levels at various points in the clip. This is also called *rubberbanding* or *audio gain automation*. Keyframes can be set for simple or complex changes in level throughout the clip.

Sometimes it's easier to use keyboard commands when you want to change the level of a clip, a group of clips, or the setting of a keyframe. Keyboard commands can be very precise when you want to nudge the level up or down a few decibels. The gain is normally 0 dB if nothing has been done to the clip. Raising gain by 6 dB will make the clip sound about twice as loud. (See Chapter 16 for more on sound levels.)

Maintaining Sync

When you play a typical clip in the timeline, the audio and video will be in sync (in other words, when you see someone speaking on the video monitor, you'll hear them correctly at the same time). Depending on how your system is set up, if you're using both a computer monitor and an external video monitor, sync may *not* look correct on both monitors at the same time (see Audio Input and Monitoring, p. 511). Usually, the external video monitor is a correct reference.

As you go about editing your sequence, you need to pay attention to the sync relationship between picture and sound tracks.

When you make an insert (splice) edit, as long as you insert the same amount to every track on the timeline, all the clips that are already on the timeline will stay in sync. For example, if you insert a 15-frame clip into the middle of a sequence, as long you add 15 frames to all the tracks, they will all stay in sync. However, if you were to add 15 frames to the picture but not to the audio tracks, the sound following the insertion would be 15 frames out of sync (that is, 15 frames early; see Fig. 14-22).

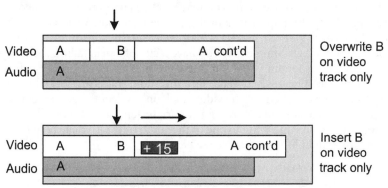

Fig. 14-22. A sync break. (top) If clip B is added *to the video track only* using an overwrite edit, the rest of clip A stays in sync with its audio. (bottom) If clip B is instead added to the video track using an insert edit—and the audio track is locked—the rest of shot A and any clips that follow go out of sync. The +15 indicator tells you that the picture is 15 frames late relative to its audio. Different NLEs use different methods to indicate a sync break.

Most NLEs can automatically add the same amount to all tracks when you make an insertion, keeping the tracks in sync. For this to happen, all the tracks need to be unlocked or enabled so they can expand with the insertion (see your NLE's manual for how to accomplish this with your system). The same idea about sync applies when removing clips via delete (extract) edits. If you delete the same number of frames from all tracks, they'll stay in sync.

Unlike insert and delete edits, when you use overwrite edits to add clips to the timeline, or use lift edits to remove them, you don't have to worry about messing up sync relationships. When you use a lift edit to get rid of a clip, the space where the clip was located remains as a gap, maintaining the original spacing between the other clips on the timeline.

Sometimes you want to put audio and video out of sync with each other for creative reasons, and sometimes it happens by accident. If you do anything that causes a video clip and its associated audio to go out of sync (sometimes called a *sync break*), you'll see a numerical display on the clips showing how many frames you need to move one relative to the other to put them back in sync (see Fig. 14-22). For example, if you see a −7 appear on an audio clip, that tells you that the sound is 7 frames early compared to the picture. One way to fix that is to move the audio clip 7 frames later (to the right on the timeline) to put it back in sync.

Working with Dialogue

Before reading this, see Dialogue Editing, p. 491.

NLEs are wonderful tools for editing dialogue. You can quickly balance levels if one character is louder than another. You can do precision surgery when you need to make a cut in mid-sentence, or remove a breath. You can create multiple tracks for overlapping dialogue.

One very common dialogue edit is when you want the sound to cut before or after the picture cut. For example, you may want to cut away from someone while they're still talking, to help make a bridge to the next shot. Various terms for this effect include *L-cut*, *split edit*, *overlap edit*, or *sound overlap*. Creating an L-cut with a nonlinear system is very simple. Say you have a clip of a man talking, followed by a clip of a woman responding, and you want the picture to cut to her before she's done speaking (see Fig. 14-23). Make sure the audio tracks are locked or disabled (so they won't move). Then, on the video track only, select the picture cut between the man and the woman and do a rolling edit to the left, into the tail of his shot. You might want to do the same thing to one of the audio tracks, so that room tone of the woman's shot is audible as soon as we see her.

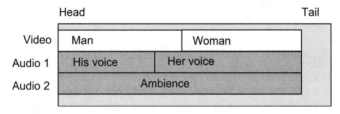

Fig. 14-23. An L-cut. When the audio cut between two shots precedes or follows the picture cut, that's called an *L-cut* or *split edit*. In this case, the audio cut to the woman leads the picture cut by a few frames, which can make dialogue feel more natural. Here, an ambience track is added to reinforce continuity by remaining consistent across the two shots.

Some NLEs can perform an *extend edit*, which is handy for making L-cuts. You simply click on the picture cut, put the play bar where you'd like that cut to be, then hit "extend."

Audio Transitions

The audio equivalent of a dissolve is called a *cross fade*. The outgoing clip fades out while the incoming clip fades in. Like picture dissolves, you can set the length and position of the cross fade relative to the cut (assuming you have sufficient handles). Cross fades come in different styles; often you want to use an "equal-power" version which maintains a constant volume level through the transition. This type of cross fade is sometimes indicated as "Cross Fade (+3dB)."

Sometimes, at a cut between two clips you'll hear a slight click, even though neither clip has a clicking sound in it. If you put a short cross fade (as short as 2 frames) between them, the click will usually go away.

For more on working with sound, see Chapter 16.

BASIC VIDEO EFFECTS

Perhaps no area of video has grown as explosively as visual effects. NLEs are capable of a wide range of video effects, and hundreds of *plug-ins* (standardized, add-on tools that work inside another program) can be purchased for specialized tasks. *Compositing* is the art of building shots from disparate elements that may include live action, *computer generated imagery* (*CGI*), text, graphics, and effects. Compositing applications include Adobe's After Effects, Apple's Motion and Shake, and Discreet's Inferno and Fusion.

The complexity of video effects and compositing is beyond the scope of this book. What follows are some basic effects you might typically use in making a video.

Layers, Alpha Channels, and Keys

When two layers of video are superimposed, you can adjust the transparency (opacity) of each layer to choose which image is more visible. You can also select various composite modes that determine how the layers interact with each other; for example, whether brightness values add or subtract from each other.

Sometimes you want part of an image to be transparent and part opaque. Typically, when you put a title over video you want the title to be opaque where the lettering is and transparent everywhere else so the picture underneath shows through (see Fig. 13-3). Graphics or compositing programs may create video with an *alpha channel*, which is a fourth information channel in addition to the red, green, and blue channels. An alpha channel is a gray-scale image (black-and-white) that defines which parts of a clip are transparent. With some systems, white areas in the alpha channel are opaque and black areas are transparent; gray areas are *partially* transparent. When graphics are created they are often supplied with an alpha channel.

A video layer can include a moving alpha channel, sometimes called a *traveling matte*. A traveling matte allows you to superimpose a moving foreground layer (whether it be an actor or a graphic) on a different background.

One way to modify the alpha channel and create transparency in portions of the image is to use a *key*. When keying, a portion of the image is selected, based on color or brightness, to be made invisible or transparent. In the example of white titles over a video background, a *luma* (luminance) *key* could be applied to the titles. The luma key would identify the brightest part of the frame only (the white letters), make them opaque, and make everything else on the clip transparent.

CHROMA KEYS. In a *chroma key*, a certain color is targeted as the part of the image to be made transparent. A common example is a TV weather forecaster who appears on TV in front of a weather map. This is done by shooting the forecaster in front of a special green background. The chroma key "keys out" everything of that particular green, leaving the person on a transparent background that is then layered over a digital weather map. The green color is a special hue not otherwise found in nature, so you don't accidentally key out, say, a green tie. Chroma keys for film are often done with a blue background. Other names for this are *process shots* or *green-screen* or *blue-screen shots*. To do a process shot, first you film in front of the colored background, then you use software (often included in the NLE) to key out the background.[14] Ultimatte is a common professional chroma key system and is available as a plug-in for various applications.

Chroma keys are used regularly in film and video production to superimpose characters over different backgrounds (see Fig. 14-24). Green-screen shots are not hard to do, but they need to be lit and framed carefully. Green background material is available in several forms, including cloth that can be hung on a frame, pop-up panels for close shots, and paint for covering a large background wall. Try to keep as much separation as possible between the subject and background and avoid green light from the background reflecting on the subject (called spill—most keying software includes some *spill suppression*). Fine details, like frizzy hair, can sometimes be hard to key. Make sure your subject isn't wearing green. The background should be lit as evenly as possible with no dark shadows or creases in the material, though keying programs such as Serious Magic's Ultra claim to be very forgiving of background irregularities. Locked-down shots with no camera movement are easiest. Often, if the camera moves you'll want the superimposed background to move also, which may require motion tracking. As a rule, people will advise you to use a video format with 4:2:2 color sampling and avoid formats like DV and HDV that are 4:1:1 or 4:2:0; however, many successful keys have been done with DV and HDV. Make sure the detail/enhancement on the camera isn't set too high. If you can, bring a laptop with keying software to the set to see how the chroma key looks.

Fig. 14-24. Chroma key. The subject is shot in front of a green or blue background, which is then keyed out. The subject can then be composited on any background. NLEs usually include a chroma key effect or you may get better results with separate software like this Serious Magic product. (Serious Magic)

Wipes

In a wipe, image A replaces image B at a boundary edge moving across the frame. Think of scene transitions in *Star Wars*, which are patterned after old wipe styles that were once popular in Hollywood. There are hundreds of wipe patterns. In some wipes, image A pushes image B off the screen vertically, horizontally, or in

14. For a film shoot, the background is removed in a lab process.

a particular pattern (stars, cross, etc.). The edge of the wipe can be soft or hard or have a colored line.

Speed Effects

Changing the speed of a shot is often used to add an energetic or frantic feel (high speed) or dreamy quality (slow motion). It's very easy to apply speed effects to clips in a timeline. When you double a clip's speed, the system simply skips every other frame; when you slow a clip to 50 percent speed, it plays each frame twice. When slowing down footage shot at normal speed, most NLEs can do *frame blending*, an option that may produce a smoother look by creating transitions between frames. The best slow motion is produced by shooting at high frame rates (see Slow Motion, p. 357).

NLEs that have "fit-to-fill" editing can adjust the speed of a clip to fill a hole in the timeline (see p. 538).

A constant speed effect is one that's applied uniformly to the entire clip. However, some NLEs permit variable speed effects (different speeds in different parts of the clip). In Final Cut Pro this can be done with the *time remapping* feature.

Changing the playback speed of audio will affect the pitch of the sound. The faster you make the clip, the higher the pitch (think of the chipmunk sound when voices are made really fast). Some NLEs or audio editing programs have *pitch shifters* that can be used to try to restore the pitch. Voices and short sounds respond better to this process than long, continuous musical notes which may hiccup after being pitch shifted.

Some NLEs can create time-lapse sequences captured from normal footage by dropping long strings of frames and speeding up the clip by a large amount.

Scale, Orientation, and Distortion

You can always make the picture smaller, so it becomes a frame within the frame. However, if you try to zoom in and enlarge it, the image will become softer and may not hold up. A common example is when combining non-widescreen footage in a widescreen movie. If you try to blow up the non-widescreen footage so it fills the frame, that clip will have lower resolution than the rest of the movie, which may be objectionable. Unfortunately, the option of *not* blowing it up and leaving the image centered in the frame with sidebars—see Fig. 2-15A—may also be unacceptable (some broadcasters won't allow it).

For techniques for zooming in on stills, see p. 548.

An image can be reversed horizontally (mirror image), which is useful when a shot has the wrong screen direction. An image can also be reversed top to bottom. Some people call the former *flipping* and the latter *flopping*, while others call them both *flopping*. A discussion topic for long winter evenings?

There are numerous ways to *distort* the image, squeezing it or changing perspective or wrapping it around a shape like a sphere or a box.

MAKING A LETTERBOX. If you have 16:9 anamorphic SD footage and want to create a letterboxed version for viewing on a 4:3 non-widescreen monitor, you'll need to squeeze the image vertically (visualize Fig. 2-15F being squeezed to look like Fig. 2-15E). This creates the letterbox black bars on top and bottom and restores the image to its proper proportions for 4:3 viewing. On some NLEs this is considered a distortion, and is done by adjusting the aspect ratio setting.

Keyframes and Effect Settings

Many effects are designed to change image size, position, rotation, or speed as the shot progresses. You can start at the beginning of the clip, get the various settings (parameters) the way you want them, and set a *keyframe* (actually you can set a keyframe for each parameter). You then go to a later part of the clip, change the parameters as you please, and set another keyframe. Each keyframe is a waypoint, and the computer will *interpolate* between them, making a transition from one to the next. Sometimes you need to adjust how smoothly the transition happens, using tools such as *Bezier handles*.

Other Image Effects and Controls

There are hundreds of *filter effects*, which process the texture or appearance of the image, such as adding blur or distorting colors.

Image stabilization can be done to smooth out a shot that was filmed shakily or from a bumpy vehicle. Your NLE may have a stabilization feature or you can get stand-alone programs such as iStabilize. Using motion tracking, the program keeps objects in the frame relatively steady while the frame itself moves around them (for example, if the objects go left, the frame goes left too, keeping the objects in the same place on screen). This will result in a constantly moving black border around the frame if you don't enlarge the image to push the border off screen (which lowers resolution a bit). Nevertheless, some image stabilizers are amazingly effective and can even be used to smooth out a jerky zoom.

A *proc amp* (*processing amplifier*) gives control over black and white levels, chroma, and hue. Proc amps are available as a feature within many NLEs and also as separate physical devices used in an editing studio. A *time base corrector* (*TBC*) stabilizes the video signal and can bring a tape from a faulty camcorder or deck up to standards. TBCs often include proc amp controls.

Tape dropout is a momentary loss of recording that can result in artifacts in the image. A *dropout compensator* will fill the error with information taken from an adjacent line of video. *Grain reducers* can minimize video noise, smoothing over the grainy look.

There are various applications used to give a "film look" to video, such as Magic Bullet and Cinelook. The idea of using software to make video look more like film is to create 24p motion effects and simulate the tonal reproduction of different film stocks (including grain patterns, scratches, and even dirt, if you want). Now that 24p video cameras with gamma adjustment are widely available, much of the "film look" can be created in shooting instead of post.

Titles, Graphics, and Stills

Virtually every movie makes use of printed text and graphics of various kinds. NLEs can create text elements as well as shapes, gradients, and other patterns for graphics. For more sophisticated control over text and graphics, programs such as After Effects, Photoshop, Motion, and Avid FX can be used together with your NLE.

Titles

See Titles, p. 499, before reading this section.

Onscreen text in video is sometimes called *CG* (for character generator) or *chyron* (after an early maker of video text devices). NLE packages include basic text generators and often have complex tools for animating titles within the NLE or as part of the NLE suite.

The NLE's title tool should give you simple controls over font choice, font size, color, position, justification, kerning (the space between characters), and leading (rhymes with "sledding"—it's the space between lines). This is all you need to make basic titles. "Supered" video titles (those that appear over picture) generally need drop shadows or some kind of graphic pad under them to set them apart from the background. Another technique is to slightly blur the background under a title to make it stand out more. Usually titles in video shouldn't be overly bright or they'll get noisy.

Bit-mapped titles look best when made at high resolution and with low compression. One reason to do an online in a relatively uncompressed format is to get the best titles (see Online Editing, p. 521). Many NLEs can create titles that are vector-based, meaning that they can be scaled to any size with smooth results. You can build them for an offline edit at one resolution, then import them into an online sequence and rerender them at full resolution. However, titles built separately using a program like Photoshop, whose graphics are bit-mapped at a fixed resolution, maintain a fixed resolution when imported into an offline sequence. They can't be rendered from the timeline to full resolution video with smooth results. They must be individually up-resed in Photoshop and reimported into the higher resolution timeline.

Graphics

For the most control over graphic elements, the NLE is usually not the best tool for the job. Graphic artists often use programs like Photoshop or Illustrator to create graphics that can be imported to the NLE using a variety of file formats. Generally you want to use uncompressed or lossless formats. Depending on your system you might use TIFF (.tif), Targa (.tga), Photoshop (.psd), or highest-quality JPEG (.jpg).

Over time, the process of moving graphics from outside programs to the NLE has gotten simpler, and graphic programs bundled with the NLE are often tightly integrated. However, there are two issues to be aware of when creating graphics on other applications.

First, remember that most graphics programs work in RGB color space while most NLEs work in component (YC_BC_R) color space. See Video Color Systems, p. 192, for more on this. Be aware that colors that may seem dull in RGB on the computer monitor can look very bright on a component video monitor. Avoid choosing rich, saturated colors in the graphics program; they may end up looking garish and noisy in video and exceed the legal range in component 601 or 709 color space (see p. 195).

Another concern is pixel aspect ratio (see Pixel Shape, p. 213). Graphics programs (and all computers) use square pixels. Some digital video formats (NTSC, PAL, and some HDV) use nonsquare pixels. This means that graphics may look distorted if you're not careful (see Fig. 5-17). Fortunately, newer versions of some

NLEs and graphics programs can automatically compensate if you tell them what formats the video and graphics are in. Otherwise, you'll need to build the graphics at a larger frame size so they'll look correct when shown in nonsquare pixels.[15] Consult the documentation with your NLE for suggested frame sizes.

Fortunately, true HD formats use square pixels, so there's no distortion to worry about when importing square-pixel graphics.

Stills

In many situations, you might want to use still images like photographs in your movie. Often, you want to do moves on them, zooming out from a detail to the whole picture, or moving in on someone's face.

Of course, you could just put the photo up on the wall or an easel and shoot it with a video or film camera. However, it's very hard to maintain the steadiness and precision necessary to execute moves on tiny photographic details. In this case, a camera on an *animation stand* (also called a *rostrum camera*) can be programmed to do precise moves. This was once the standard technique for shooting stills and is still used sometimes when shooting on film.

For video, there's an easier way. Using an ordinary scanner you can scan the photo and create a file to import into the NLE. You can then do moves (zooms, pans, rotations) either using motion controls in the NLE, an effects program like After Effects, or a plug-in like Stagetools' MovingPicture, which can simplify programming the moves.

As a rule, you want to avoid enlarging a normal video frame (zooming in) because the image will look less sharp the more you blow it up. With stills, the idea is to scan the photo larger than the video frame, so you can zoom in with no degradation. (If you want to see the whole picture, you can always zoom out with no problem.) When working in SD formats, an image 1000 to 2000 pixels across will give you plenty of room to do a moderate zoom-in. If you scan an eight-by-ten-inch photo at 150 dpi, this will produce an image 1200 x 1500 pixels. If you want to go in very tight (for example, to highlight a tiny detail), scan at a higher dpi to create a still image with more pixels. Similarly, if you're scanning a very small photo, such as a slide, use a higher dpi setting.

With 1080 HD formats, aim for 4000 to 8000 pixels across the image.

Experiment with different moves. Generally, you want to "ease" into a move (ramping up in speed) and then ramp down as the move finishes in a different place. You can set keyframes along a path as waypoints for both zooms and X-Y (horizontal-vertical) moves across the image.

When scanning and editing stills into your movie, bear in mind the aspect ratio of the format you're working in. Vertically oriented stills will leave extra space on the sides if you try to show the whole photo, which could look awkward, especially with widescreen video formats. This is why filmmakers often start tight enough on vertical pictures so the photo fills the frame; then they do a move up or down (such as a move from feet to face on a portrait). Another approach is to put some kind of background behind the picture so the sides aren't completely empty.

15. For example, Apple recommends building a graphic at 720 x 540 in a graphics program so it will look normal when shown in non-widescreen NTSC 720 x 480 DV.

FREEZE FRAMES. Sometimes you want to use a still that comes from your video footage—otherwise known as a *freeze frame*. NLEs can easily generate a freeze frame from any shot on the timeline, which you can then edit back into your sequence as a still. However, don't expect to enlarge part of the freeze frame without it looking soft.

When working with interlaced formats, freeze frames may look ragged or show edge tear (see Fig. 18-8) if there's any movement between the two fields that make up the frame. In this case, you'll want to *deinterlace* the still (this command may be among the video effects). The NLE will discard one of the fields and, if you select the *interpolation* option, will fill in the missing lines with an approximation of what would be there if you had shot with a progressive camera. You'll usually want to deinterlace when making *frame grabs* (still photos) from your movie, say for publicity purposes. For more on deinterlacing moving footage, see p. 720.

FINISHING AND OUTPUT

Now you're done editing (you've "locked" the picture) and you're ready to get the movie out of the NLE and into the world. If you've been working with a simple online workflow (with no separate offline edit) you're ready to export the movie directly from the NLE to videotape, DVD, or to a file. Or, you may be using an offline/online workflow, in which case you're ready to do the online edit. This may involve recapturing your media at a higher resolution on your own machine or you may be moving the project to different system—perhaps at a postproduction facility where you can do the online edit on a more powerful system.

For the basics of offline/online workflow, see p. 41 and p. 514.

If you've already done your online edit, skip ahead to the sections on output. The next section is about the steps needed to make the transition from the offline to the online edit.

Color correction is a central part of finishing a project, and may be done on the NLE before output, during the online or later. This is discussed on p. 573.

FROM OFFLINE TO ONLINE

Planning Your Workflow

As you prepare to finish your project, take some time to plan out your path. You may be working alone on your own system or you may be about to send your project out to sound editors, mix studios, online facilities, and transfer houses. No matter what your route, seek advice about how to accomplish the tasks for finishing. If you're doing the work by yourself, consult manuals, do some research on the Web, and talk to people about the best workflow. There are lots of "gotchas" to be avoided: hidden settings that need to be changed; equipment that's incompatible; technical requirements you're unaware of.

If you're working with outside facilities, it's absolutely essential that you start with them and work backward so you can deliver what they need. Ask them about their preferred workflow, file formats, track layouts, frame rates—anything. Many facilities have instructions posted on their website about how they want materials prepared. There's no "standard operating procedure" when it comes to post-production; it all depends on the particular project, equipment, software, and techniques being used.

Online editing sessions can be very stressful (often a delightful mix of tension and boredom). If you're onlining at a postproduction facility, chances are you're spending more money than you'd like. If you're doing the online yourself, you have the pressure of getting everything right. Be as prepared as possible.

See p. 731 for the business aspects of booking an online edit session.

Trimming and Recapturing Media

Depending on your needs and your system, going from the offline to the online may be done in different ways. The terms used vary with different NLEs. In overview, the process involves these steps:

1. *Prepare the edited sequence (your movie).* The movie you're going to on-line is an NLE sequence made up of clips strung together. Remember that all the clips in the sequence are just "pointers" to the actual media files—the files that contain the video and audio (see Media Files and Clips, p. 512). In the case of your offline edit, those source media files may have been captured at low resolution, or at least not at the maximum resolution of your original camera tapes or files, so you need to replace them with highest-quality, online resolution media files.

    Start by duplicating the sequence in the bin and putting one copy away for safekeeping before you start this process.

    Often, when you're finished offline editing, there are still a number of clips in the sequence that serve no function. For example, audio clips that you made silent, or video clips hidden under another clip that are never seen in the movie. Delete those prior to the online so they don't add unnecessary media and work.

2. *Unlink the clips from their media files.* Prior to the online edit, you want to *unlink* or separate the clips in the sequence from their low-res media files. This is sometimes called "making a clip offline," but this use of "off-line" doesn't refer to offline editing—it just means that the clip is no longer is connected to its media file. When a clip isn't linked to its media, you'll see a message such as "media offline" when you try to play it.

    In some cases you'll leave the offline media files on the hard drives for later use. If you need to free up space, you may choose to delete the original media.

3. *Trim the sequence.* Keep in mind that all the clips in your final movie were edited from longer master clips created when you captured the media originally (before you started the offline edit). Those master clips often represent hours of material you no longer need or want for the online. So, to do the online with *just* the media used in the actual final sequence, you "trim the sequence."

    Your NLE has a media tool or manager in which you can choose to create trimmed master clips that are just the length of the clips in the final movie. In Final Cut Pro, this is done by choosing to "delete unused media" in the media manager (see Fig. 14-25). In Avid, the *decompose* function can be used to create new, shorter master clips.

Since you'll want a little wiggle room to adjust things later, you'll generally choose to add one- or two-second handles to the clips, giving you some extra media at the head and tail of each clip (you won't see the handles in the movie, but they're available for future edits if needed).

4. *Move the sequence to a new project.* For organizational purposes, it helps to move the sequence to a new project folder when trimming it, so that all the new, shorter master clips are easy to find and you don't get them confused with other material. Often you'll want to do this as part of moving to another machine to do the online edit (more on that below).

5. *Recapture clips at high resolution.* Select your new master clips and do a *batch capture* to create new media files at full resolution. Batch capturing is just an automated process in which the NLE puts the clips in order by reel number and timecode, captures them all, and alerts you along the way when to put the next tape into the deck. When everything's captured, you may have to manually *relink* your sequence to the newly captured high-res media.

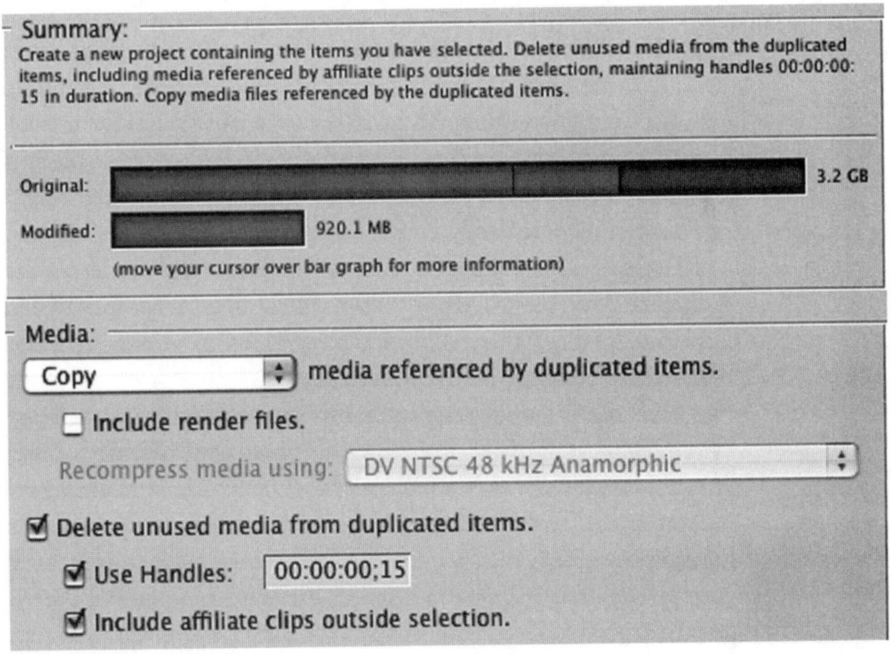

Summary:

Create a new project containing the items you have selected. Delete unused media from the duplicated items, including media referenced by affiliate clips outside the selection, maintaining handles 00:00:00; 15 in duration. Copy media files referenced by the duplicated items.

Original: 3.2 GB

Modified: 920.1 MB

(move your cursor over bar graph for more information)

Media:

[Copy ▲▼] media referenced by duplicated items.

☐ Include render files.

Recompress media using: [DV NTSC 48 kHz Anamorphic ▲▼]

☑ Delete unused media from duplicated items.

☑ Use Handles: [00:00:00;15]

☑ Include affiliate clips outside selection.

Fig. 14-25. Trimming a sequence. This media manager screen from Final Cut Pro shows how unused media can be trimmed from a sequence before copying the media to another drive or location. Note how the lower bar (representing the modified media) is much shorter. As indicated here, 15 frame handles will be added to the new clips. (Apple, Inc.)

This list is deliberately sketchy. There are many options and variations, both in the way various NLEs operate, and in workflow that may be best for your project. Be sure to read the instructions with your NLE. Often, this up-resing process is done only for video, and audio is handled separately (see Preparing for the Mix, p. 640).

Moving from One System to Another

In the workflow described above, for the online edit to work, the editing system needs to be able to read and work with sequences generated in the offline edit. If you're doing the offline and online on the same system, the translation from offline to online can be seamless. Even if you're doing the online on a different machine than the offline, as long as they use the same NLE software (or even sometimes related products from the same maker) getting from offline to online can be very easy.

However, when moving a project from one brand of NLE to another, or between different types of applications (like graphics or audio programs), the translation can get trickier.

What makes nonlinear editing so powerful is that each sequence contains not just information about where each clip begins and ends but also a vast array of instructions about what to do with the clips—effects, transitions, levels, titles, colors—you name it. The layout of the clips and these instructions are the "metadata" (sometimes called data about data, see p. 220). To play the movie we need both the media files (the actual pictures and sounds) and the metadata.

Unfortunately, one brand of NLE can't necessarily read the media or metadata from another NLE, or reproduce the effects created on the other system. There has been a big push in the industry to standardize data so it can be passed from system to system. Wrapper formats such as AAF, MXF, and OMF are designed to create a common language that applications can use to talk to each other. Programs made by Automatic Duck can move metadata between different applications (for example, for importing a Final Cut Pro sequence into an Avid or importing an Avid sequence into Adobe After Effects). For more on wrappers and metadata, see File Formats and Data Exchange, p. 219.

When planning your postproduction workflow, some of your decisions will be based on translation concerns between different systems and different editing or post studios. These are some of the possible situations you'll encounter:

- You can move the sequence and related metadata (sometimes called the *composition*) from one system to another, along with the media files themselves. This "one-stop shopping" can be a real timesaver, but you have to arrange to transport the media, which may be a lot of data.
- You can move the composition from one system to another but not the media. This means you'll have to recapture the media on the second system. If you were planning to recapture media anyway for a high-resolution online, this may be the best way to go. Sometimes you'll actually prefer to send just the composition (perhaps over the Internet) without the media embedded, because the media files are so big.
- You can move the sequence, and possibly even the media, but not *all* the metadata. Often, one system will be able to read a limited set of instructions

from another, but is unable to reproduce *everything* you created in the off-line. One common example is when using OMF to move audio from one system to another in preparation for a sound mix: Sometimes you might be able to send the audio media with the clip lengths and positions, but not any level adjustments you made to individual clips.

- You can send only an EDL. The Edit Decision List (see Fig. 14-39) contains the basic information about clip In and Out points, reel numbers, and a few effects. This is a far more limited information set than what's contained in a sequence, but sometimes it's all one system can take from another. Sometimes the simplicity of an EDL is an advantage as a check against errors. Using the EDL, the online system can recapture the media and position the clips in a sequence. For more on EDLs, see p. 584.

- You can send only the media. When there's no communication between systems, all you can do is send the movie itself. For example, you might output your movie from the offline system to tape, and then capture that as a single clip into the online system. This is only viable if you captured for the offline natively or at high resolution so the picture quality is high (see p. 516). While this saves you the time of recapturing individual clips and avoids recapturing errors, the disadvantage is that you lose all the data about the sequence. So, for example, color correction, which requires knowing exactly where each shot begins and ends, will go a lot slower (and work with effects like dissolves or titles may be limited and/or compromised).[16]

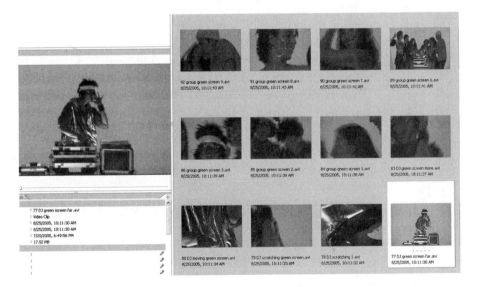

Fig. 14-26. Adobe Bridge provides centralized access to project files and settings for use in a variety of applications. (Adobe Systems, Inc.)

16. Some systems have automatic scene detection, which can at least identify the beginnings and ends of shots.

Nontimecoded Media

When going from one system to another, and particularly when going from an offline editing facility to a postproduction studio for the online, you need to bring copies of any media that doesn't have timecode. This could include music, stills, graphics, and titles. If the titles in the sequence don't translate to the new system, you can often bring them as word processing files to speed up importing them into the new system.

Working with Guide Tracks

Regardless of how you get the offline sequence imported to the online NLE, it's a good idea to also output the offline movie itself for use in the online.

For the video online session, the offline movie can be loaded as one video track in the online sequence. This is sometimes called a *guide track* or a *reference track*. A guide track helps prevent cutting errors and shows the online editor your intentions for effects that may not automatically carry across to the online. The online editor may ask you to supply an output with burned-in timecode.

As noted above, if you captured natively for your offline edit and then output natively back to tape, the material on that tape (and therefore the guide track) should be of *equally high quality* as any other clip in the online timeline (see Native Editing, p. 516). This means that if you create a version of your output *without* burned-in timecode, you can actually use the guide track as a source, if needed. For example, sometimes an effect from the offline, such as variable speed adjustment, doesn't translate well in the online sequence. In that case you could use this section of the guide track for the final film. Most of the time, however, you'll consult the guide track as a check, but leave it invisible on the timeline when not needed.

A guide track can be similarly useful for audio postproduction—to give the sound editor or rerecording mixer a chance to hear what the picture or dialogue editor did in his or her rough mix. This can help as a guide for any level adjustments that didn't translate from the offline editing system to the audio workstation.

Final Products and Versions

Whether you output to tape, file, or DVD, you need to plan ahead for the different versions you'll need and in what forms. For example, if you're working in a widescreen SD format, you may need to make both a full-height anamorphic version and a letterboxed 4:3 version (which may call for different title treatments; see p. 501).

Or, if you hope to distribute in a foreign country, you'll want a *textless version* of the movie that has no onscreen text or titles over picture. Sometimes this is done by attaching a "clip reel" at the end that contains a second copy of any shot that has text over it, but without the text. (Alternatively, you can remove the text from the movie itself, but include those shots with text at the end so a foreign distributor or broadcaster can see how the text should look.) For more on preparing audio tracks for foreign distribution, see Foreign Release, p. 656.

For any version of the movie, plan to make at least one *master version*, and one *protection master* in case something goes wrong with the master.

OUTPUT TO TAPE

For a half century, tape was *the* video recording medium. As hard drives, optical discs, and memory cards fall in price and rise in usefulness, tape will be used less. Even so, tape remains a convenient and inexpensive way to store and transport movies.

This section is about getting a movie out of the NLE and onto tape, which sometimes requires some editing. However, traditional editing between two video-tape recorders is discussed at the end of the chapter.

Different filmmakers and projects have different needs when it comes to getting the movie onto tape (sometimes called doing a *layover*). For a school project, you might need to dump the movie from the NLE to tape so you can screen it for your classmates. However, when creating an *edit master tape* for broadcast or other high-end use, you'll need to position the movie precisely by timecode and be sure there are no flaws in the output, which calls for a high level of care and precision. How you actually do the output depends in part on your approach and in part on the tools you have to work with.

Since a deck for outputting may only be needed for a day or so, filmmakers who don't have one often rent a deck in a particular format or with particular capabilities.

Fig. 14-27. Sony SRW-5000 is a top-of-the-line VTR that records full bandwidth high definition HDCAM-SR. (Sony Electronics, Inc.)

Assemble and Insert Recording

All video decks can do basic *assemble-edit* recording. In assemble mode, the VTR records everything at once: video, audio, *control track* (which helps maintain speed), and timecode (not all decks support timecode). With assemble editing, anything on the tape beginning at the point where you start recording is erased. If you want to record a tape straight through without stopping, assemble mode works fine.

The problem with assemble mode comes when you record one shot, stop, then record a second shot. Whenever you stop recording there is a break in the control track, which can make the picture break up. On older or cheaper analog decks, you get a picture glitch at the beginning of the incoming shot. Newer and better analog and digital VTRs can make that transition smoothly as long as they're used in an editing system that can roll back over the outgoing shot (called *preroll*), get properly up to speed with the control track, then begin the next shot cleanly. However, with "assemble" mode in analog you can never record a shot in the middle of a tape (say to replace a shot in a longer sequence) and expect to have the Out Point of the edit be clean and glitch free.

Another limitation with assemble editing is that you can't edit in just audio or just video. With every assemble edit, *all* the tracks get replaced (audio, video, and timecode) which can be a disadvantage in various situations.

True editing decks whether analog or digital have a recording mode called *insert-edit* recording. In "insert" mode, you have a choice between recording video, any combination of audio channels, and/or timecode. Insert recording does not automatically erase anything on the tape—you get to choose what is replaced and what remains from any previous recording. Insert mode avoids the picture breakup of assemble mode because it does not replace existing control track. Instead, prior to recording you must prepare the tape with continuous control track and timecode. This is variously called *blacking* a tape, *striping* a tape or *blacking and coding* (see below). With continuous control track, you can insert a shot in the middle of the tape and expect it to edit in and out cleanly.

Insert recording is the preferred way to create a master tape. Not all NLEs, decks, and formats support insert recording. In a typical professional editing setup, insert recording is done with RS-422 device control and requires genlock (see p. 508 and p. 509).

NLE Editing Modes

Depending on your NLE and your video deck, you may have various options for how the NLE and VTR interact.

The simplest way to output to tape is to play back the sequence from the timeline and *crash record* to a deck or camera that isn't controlled by the NLE. You put a tape in the deck, manually press "record," then play the sequence on the NLE. Of course, the deck and NLE need to be connected with the proper cables; for DV all you need is a simple FireWire.

A better way to output is to have the NLE control the deck and the recording process (for more on deck control, see Input and Output, p. 506). Different NLEs use different terms for this, including *print to video*, *export to tape*, *edit to tape*, and *digital cut*. This requires a deck that supports timecode. The NLE will usually allow you to mark In and Out Points on the sequence and/or the tape and may have provisions to include countdown leaders, color bars, and other elements before and after the program (see below).

You should be able to use assemble recording with any deck and NLE, but as noted above, your system may or may not support insert recording. Decks that record MiniDV pose a particular challenge. MiniDV was introduced as a consumer format with a tight 10-micron track pitch (distance between tracks), thought to be too fragile for the constant shuttling of linear editing. As a result, Panasonic later introduced a professional version, DVCPRO, with an 18-micron pitch, and Sony offered DVCAM, with a 15-micron pitch. Generally speaking, DVCPRO and DVCAM decks are capable of insert editing (whether they are equipped to do so or not). When JVC introduced its Professional DV, it kept the original 10-micron MiniDV track pitch with no detrimental results and JVC's BR-DV6000 deck, for instance, can make accurate insert edits using either FireWire or RS-422. However, it's difficult to find an NLE that will perform insert edits using FireWire. Final Cut Pro, for instance, doesn't support insert editing over FireWire nor will it support insert editing of MiniDV. Similarly, Avid Xpress Pro permits a rough three-point assemble edit of DV over FireWire (In/Out Point on timeline, In Point on tape; Avid calls it a "digital cut," and doesn't guarantee frame accuracy), but otherwise normal insert and assemble edit functions are disabled. In some NLEs, insert editing of DV and its professional siblings are supported using RS-422 only.

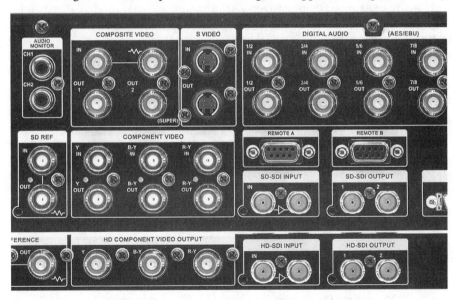

Fig. 14-28. The Edius HDBX1000 breakout box offers many types of input and output for the editing system. Connections shown here include: SD composite, S-video and component (all analog); SD-SDI (digital); HD component (analog); HD-SDI (digital); AES/EBU (digital audio). (Grass Valley)

Preparing the Sequence for Output

The NLE will have a number of output settings, including audio channel assignment, deck control, timecode settings, and others. Consult the manual for your NLE for instructions.

It's imperative that the sequence play out of the NLE cleanly with no *dropped frames*, which appear as a stutter or instantaneous black. There may be a setting to *abort output on dropped frames*, which is a good way to avoid dropped frames you might not see.

Depending on your system and the sequence you're playing, the NLE may be able to play in real time with no problems. Sometimes, however, systems start dropping frames, in which case you want to reduce the load on the computer's processor. There are several steps that can help. Start by rendering all video and audio effects. Do an *audio mixdown*, which essentially creates a single, easy-to-play render file of all the audio. Close all sequences but the one you're playing. Turn off desktop monitoring (sometimes called *mirror to desktop*). See if you can put the deck on a separate bus from the media drives (see Hard Drive Storage, p. 510). Consider breaking a long movie into shorter sequences or reels.

HDV material needs to be rendered (called *conforming* in Final Cut Pro) before it can be output. This can take a *long* time, depending on your system and the project. See p. 226 for possible work-arounds.

Preparing the Edit Master Tape

If you're using insert editing to record the master tape, you need to prepare it by blacking it first. Many NLEs have a setting to do this. Some decks can black a tape by themselves, or with a black signal from an external sync generator. You can also black a tape with a camera by shooting with the lens cap on.

If you're using assemble editing, you don't need to black the whole tape in advance, but you should black at least 30 seconds to provide a clean start point for the recording.

Depending on your system, you may be able to preset a starting timecode for the tape using settings on the deck or in the NLE.

Professional tapes have a fairly standard order of elements at the start of the tape. Depending on your system, you might edit these separately onto the master tape, or you could add them to the head of your sequence on the NLE so they play out already pre-built. Some NLEs can be set to attach them to the head of the sequence as you edit to tape.

The following are typical elements at the head of a master tape:

1. Begin the tape at 00:58:00:00 timecode ("fifty-eight minutes") and record 30 seconds of black leader.

2. Then come color bars and tone (see below) for one minute (from 00:58:30:00 to 00:59:30:00), followed by 10 seconds of black.

3. Then put in a 10-second video slate (create a title card that identifies the project name, production company, running time of the movie, date, aspect ratio, audio channel assignments, etc.).

4. At 00:59:50:00 record a countdown. The countdown displays numbers every second from 10 to 2, with a beep in the audio at each second or at least on the number 2 so you know the picture and sound are in sync. (Since video and audio may get separated and remarried during postproduction, it's nice to have a visual check.) If you don't have a countdown, put black here.

5. The program begins exactly at 01:00:00:00 ("one hour," also called "one hour, straight up"). If you are editing a project that will be finished on film, see Preparing and Delivering Tracks, p. 644, for guidelines on leaders.

Your NLE or deck should be able to generate color bars. Use SMPTE (NTSC) bars or EBU (PAL) bars as appropriate. The audio reference tone is typically set to −20 dB for professional projects (as read on a digital/peak meter); 0 dB as read on an analog/VU meter. Whatever the level of your reference tone, *be sure to note it on the tape box*. For more on reference tones, see p. 421.

At the end of the movie, you should include 30 seconds of black so the program ends cleanly and doesn't cut suddenly to static and snow. You may want to include a few frames of color bars several seconds after the film ends as a signal that it's over and as a tail sync mark.

When outputting to tape, it's very important that you watch the movie as you do so. Look closely for technical problems. Maddeningly, you'll often spot editing or content issues you never noticed before. Hopefully you'll get another chance to correct them! If there are easily fixable problems, you may be able to do a pickup recording, starting from the place where you made the change (but see below for possible problems with edit points).

After recording a tape, be sure to set the *record inhibit* device on the tape cassette to prevent accidental rerecording or erasure.

Frame Accuracy During Output

On p. 526, you'll find information about accuracy and timecode during the capturing process. During output from the NLE to the tape, you'll be dealing with related issues.

If the NLE, the sequence, and the deck are properly prepared, you should be able to record a sequence to tape in one pass with no dropped frames or errors. As long as your equipment is decent, you should get a perfectly accurate output using assemble or insert editing, putting the entire movie on tape, intact, with no problems.

Inaccuracies can occur, however, if you're using FireWire device control, which is commonly used for DV and other formats. FireWire deck control may not be frame accurate, which means if you use it to *make any edits* on the tape they may not be precise.

A common situation is when you've prepared an edit master tape and want to start your sequence exactly at 1:00:00:00 on the tape. With FireWire, the sequence may indeed begin on the tape at one hour straight up, but the first frame that gets recorded may not be the first frame of the sequence—it might start a few frames into the sequence or it may repeat the first frame a few times.

Many NLEs have a calibration setting with which you can offset any consistent errors (some have an offset for audio/video sync errors too). However, keep in mind that when editing with FireWire device control you may get some drift plus or minus at edit points. A partial workaround is to make sure there are no tape edits between the countdown and the start of the movie; at least then you'll know the movie will start cleanly even if the position on the tape's timecode is slightly off.[17] By looking at the countdown, it's easy to see precisely how much you're off.

17. To prevent errors at edit points, avoid *any* edits when you output to tape with FireWire.

OUTPUT TO DVD

The DVD World

See DVDs and Optical Discs, p. 36, before reading this section.

DVDs can be useful at many different points in the filmmaking process. You might burn one from your NLE to output a rough cut. You might have fifty copies of a trailer made for fundraising purposes. Or you might have a replicator manufacture 20,000 units of the finished film for retail distribution. Each of these uses calls for a different approach to making the DVD.

The simplest DVDs can be created with a DVD recorder, which is a standalone unit much like a VCR that can take analog video from a deck or an NLE and record it on a DVD in real time.

Fig. 14-29. DVD recorder. (Califone International, Inc.)

For burning a DVD directly from your computer with more control over the product, you need a DVD burner in the computer or as an external unit. There are many easy-to-use DVD programs (like iDVD, part of Apple's iLife) that are highly automated and have simple drag-and-drop tools for making menus. These days, anyone can burn a DVD.

Authoring a DVD means building a file structure that DVD players can read. In DVD production, the term usually refers to creating menus, setting chapter markers, and dealing with various forms of extras, such as soundtracks in different languages, director commentary, deleted scenes, and all the other features that add value to the DVD.

Prosumer and professional software provide much more control over authoring and offer better digital compression, which impacts picture and sound quality. If you send your project to a professional DVD facility, a *compressionist* may go through the movie, determining the proper compression level for different shots and scenes.

When you need a limited number of DVDs (up to 1000) generally the process is to compress the video using one of a few codecs, then burn that compressed file onto a recordable disc type, such as DVD-R. This is known as DVD *duplication*. This is what you do when you burn your own discs; you can also have duplication done quickly (sometimes overnight) by an outside supplier. With duplication, it's not hard to make changes and recompress when needed. The disadvantages of duplication include higher per-unit costs for discs and the fact that recordable discs may not play in all disc players.

When you're making a large number of discs, rather than record the compressed file directly to disc, a *glass master* is first made, which is then pressed onto commercial grade discs. This is called DVD *replication*. This process takes longer and the glass master is an additional charge, but the manufacturing savings per unit make up for it when dealing with mass quantities. Replication is how standard retail discs are made.

Before 2006, all commercially available DVDs were standard definition (720 x 480 NTSC or 720 x 576 PAL) using MPEG-2 compression (see p. 228). Compressed high definition content can actually be put on an SD disc in the WMV HD format, allowing playback in Windows XP computers, or using the H.264 codec, which plays back in computers equipped with QuickTime 7 (for more on these, see p. 228).

The next generation of true high definition DVDs has arrived in two competing formats: Blu-ray discs (BD) and HD DVD. All players in both formats must support three main codecs: MPEG-4 AVC (also known as H.264), VC-1 (related to Microsoft's WM9), and MPEG-2 (backwards-compatible with SD). As of this writing, it's not clear which disc format will be most popular with consumers.

Discs can be packaged in a number of ways. The classic, folding *Amaray case*, used in most video stores, has a clear plastic sleeve. In it you can insert a cover, which you can print yourself or have a supplier offset for large runs. See Chapter 19 for more on distributing DVDs.

The DVD and Player

The DVD and player together are a remarkably sophisticated system. The DVD communicates to the player through flags in the data stream telling the machine whether the video is widescreen or not, what the frame rate is, and other factors necessary for proper playback. For DVDs encoded at 24p, the player can perform pulldown to feed video to an NTSC or PAL interlaced monitor at 60i or 50i (see Fig. 14-30). Often, movies shot in a 24 fps format (feature films shot on film or on 24p HD) are put onto DVD as interlaced video. A progressive-scan DVD player can deinterlace the picture to reconstruct the original progressive frames (see p. 720 for more on deinterlacing). Because DVD players often perform such complex picture manipulations, there can be real disadvantages to buying a very cheap machine.

DVD audio can be in simple, two-channel stereo or in 5.1-channel surround sound. DVDs can be authored to play multiple soundtracks in different languages or with director commentary. When creating the DVD, you can choose to record the audio with uncompressed PCM tracks, but more commonly Dolby AC-3 is used to compress audio to a smaller file size (see p. 655 for more on these).

Not all DVDs will play on all players. As noted above, recordable disc formats such as DVD-R, DVD+R and DVD-RW (the latter can be rerecorded many times) may not play on some consumer players, particularly older models. You can hire a testing service to verify which players can handle a disc you've made, to avoid playback glitches or *navigation* problems (when the menus don't get you where they should). If you burn your own discs, don't assume that anyone you send it to can play it!

Another compatibility problem comes from the Hollywood studios that divided the world into different DVD "regions" to limit piracy and control markets. DVD players in different parts of the world scan for region codes on the disc and, unless they are multiregion players, may not play another region's DVDs. Region 1 DVDs are made for North America; Region 2 discs play on European machines; and Region 3 is for parts of Asia. Region 0 discs are—in theory—playable everywhere. Note that this coding has nothing to do with differences between actual video standards like NTSC and PAL (which create other incompatibilities when you want to send discs to foreign countries).

Encoding a Disc

Whether you burn your own discs or send your movie out to have DVDs made by a supplier, it helps to understand some of the technical issues involved.

In making a DVD, perhaps the key concern is the compression used to squeeze the movie's data down to a size that can fit on the disc. Not all compressors are the same; seek advice and compare different software applications. As for the particular codec you use, with standard definition DVDs, you're limited to MPEG-2.[18] With high definition DVDs, there's a choice of codecs (see above).

The longer the movie, the more it has to be compressed to fit on a disc, and the more critical it is that compression be done right. For a short movie (say, less than about 50 minutes on an SD disc) compression can be fairly light, which means good picture quality can be maintained without much difficulty.

When you're trying to put a lot of material on a DVD, variable bit rate compression is more efficient but it needs to be done with care. Proper settings for maximum and average data rates will affect picture quality and how smoothly the DVD plays. Consult your software documentation for suggestions. Some editing applications such as Final Cut Pro allow you to set compression markers in the sequence to identify areas with sudden picture changes that may need particular attention. See p. 222 for more about compression, MPEG-2, and constant and variable bit-rate methods.

Noise in the original video will tend to look much worse after compression. Avoid shots with grainy, noisy shadow areas when possible.

When sending out video to a DVD facility, ask how they want it delivered. DLT (digital linear tape) is a common method of delivering data. Some places may *not* want you to deliver on disc.

OUTPUT TO FILE

As video technology develops, we're moving away from storing movies on physical objects such as videotapes and plastic discs. Increasingly, movies are being distributed on networks and over the Web without any physical container, and they're being stored on devices that look less like something from the video industry—like video cassettes—and more like something from the information technology (IT) industry—including memory cards and hard drives.

As a filmmaker, this means that when outputting a movie from your NLE, you'll increasingly be creating a file instead of outputting to videotape or DVD.

---

18. MPEG-1 is sometimes used, but results in lower-quality discs and may not be playable on all machines.

You can think of file outputs from the NLE as falling into two broad categories.

First is the idea of creating a full-resolution file that can be used for additional postproduction work or storage. As an example, a feature film might have editors, animators, and special effects people all working on the same shot. To pass the footage back and forth, a file of the shot may be created using little or no compression for maximum quality. Or, if the file is intended for a TV program, it could be delivered to a network on file in full broadcast quality.

The second category is the creation of highly compressed files for use on the Web, in iPods, or anywhere else that low data rate, fast-streaming video is needed. In this case, picture quality is sacrificed to make the file small and easy to store and transmit.

To understand more about creating video files and compression, see p. 20 and p. 222. Also read about wrappers on p. 220.

Generally speaking, whenever you're creating a file output from the NLE you'll be using one of several codecs to compress the video and you'll be wrapping that in a wrapper format such as QuickTime or MXF. The same wrapper could be used with different codecs at different levels of compression. Here the focus is on QuickTime because it's very common and plays on many platforms, but other wrappers involve similar ideas.

When creating QuickTime files you have a choice between two types of movies. A *self-contained movie* contains all the video and audio in one file, and can be put on disc and played anywhere. A *reference movie* is like a clip in your NLE that points to a separate media file. It's a much smaller file and quicker to create than a self-contained movie because it doesn't duplicate media that already exists on your system. A reference movie can be useful for exporting a sequence from one application to another on your computer, but if you send it to someone else, you also need to send them the original media files it references or they can't play it.

Broadcast-Quality Files

For the highest quality, you want to use the least compression, but this is at the cost of large file sizes. Uncompressed files are often huge. The Animation codec compresses lightly but doesn't create artifacts or degrade quality. Many other codecs are used in broadcast production that compress more but still provide excellent quality. See p. 228 for a partial list. If you're creating files for a particular system, investigate beforehand what codec and what settings are preferred.

When exporting to a system that doesn't recognize QuickTime files, you can output a *numbered image sequence*. This essentially creates a separate numbered file for each frame using a still-image file format such as Targa, TIFF, or PICT and puts them in a folder. This is sometimes done when preparing a film-out, for example. The vast amount of data created by an uncompressed numbered image sequence is often stored on a tape backup system such as DLT. Audio is exported separately.

Compressed Files for Multimedia and the Web

Creating files for Web playback means using a high level of compression to make the files small enough to play quickly. The size of the file should reflect the speed of the end user's Internet connection. Video files can be posted in different sizes, larger ones for users with faster connections and smaller files for slower connections.

Many codecs are used for Web compression, including MPEG-4 and Flash. Start with the highest-quality, lowest-noise video you can and don't reduce quality in editing until you're ready to do the final compression.

Generally you'll want to reduce the frame size to make the picture (and file) smaller. Many Web videos are no larger than 320 x 240 pixels. You can crop pixels outside the picture area, or crop the black bars of a letterbox to reduce the data. Multimedia (computer) video uses square pixels. If you're working with a non-square pixel format (DV, NTSC, or PAL), you need to take that into account when resizing the frame (see p. 213).

Another way to make the file smaller is to lower the frame rate, but this will lower quality. Try to use a frame rate that is evenly divisible into the original rate. If the video is NTSC shot at 30 fps, you might use 15 fps (or use 12 fps for PAL).

When using MPEG codecs with interframe compression, you have a choice of how often to set an I-frame (the distance between I-frames determines the length of the GOP—see p. 225). The farther apart the I-frames (also called "keyframes" in this context), the greater the compression and the smaller the file, but the more you risk artifacts on shots that have a lot of motion or complexity.

Entire books are devoted to video on the Web and in applications like Flash. Get one!

WORKING WITH 24p
SD, HD, AND FILM

Be *sure* to read 24p Video, p. 101, before starting this section.

All motion pictures since the introduction of sound in 1927 were shot at 24 frames per second. Later, NTSC television came along and an industry grew up working at essentially 30 fps (at least in North and South America and Japan), or 60 fields per second taking into account interlace. Then, in the late 1990s, George Lucas asked Sony to develop a new 24p HDCAM format with which to shoot *Star Wars*, and the rest is history. Now filmmakers can shoot video at 24p, and use an NLE to edit material at 24p that originated as SD, HD, or film.

The reason 24p warrants a special discussion is that the process of moving 24p source material into the NLE and then back out again may involve translations in frame rate and timecode. In an ideal world, things would be as simple as shooting at 24p, editing at 24p, and displaying the finished work at 24p. This does sometimes happen. But the reality is, we live in a world where 60i (and 50i) standard def equipment is still used for production and display of 24p movies. For example, in the United States and other NTSC countries, HD footage may be downconverted to 60i SD—perhaps to DVCAM—for offline editing at a lower data rate. Film shot at 24 fps is commonly transferred to 60i in the telecine to make video "dailies" for offline work. Standard definition video cameras that can record 24p do so by embedding it in a 60i stream.[19] So, often, 24p isn't simply 24p.

---

19. 60i is also known as 30i or 59.94i; it means 29.97 fps interlaced, the same as standard definition NTSC.

These are some key considerations about working with 24p in postproduction:

- What frame rate did the camera record in? True 24 fps? 23.976 fps? 24p embedded in 60i?
- Is the 24p footage converted to another frame rate prior to editing?
- What frame rate is used for editing in the NLE?
- What frame rate is used for the output from the NLE?

Bouncing between 24p and 60i is common. There are workflows that involve converting 24p HD or film footage to 60i, then back to 24p for offline editing, then going back to the original 24p footage for online editing, finally converting the master tape to 60i for distribution. Each conversion involves a pulldown process. Keeping track of frame rates and timecode (and keykode for film projects) takes some planning.

There are too many workflows and types of equipment to cover in this book, but if you understand the basic processes involved, you can make sense of your options. For workflows specific to projects shot on film, see Editing Film on Video, p. 605. For pulldown methods used with PAL video see p. 607.

PULLDOWN REVISITED

Pulldown can seem complicated, but remember it's just a tool for translating one frame rate to another. When we use pulldown to convert 24p to 60i, it's a way to maintain the basic look and feel of 24 fps while playing the video at 30 fps. Pulldown allows us to add six frames every second to get from 24 to 30. If we film the hand of a clock sweeping one minute at 24 fps, after pulldown that will still take one minute at 30 fps.

In postproduction there are many situations where pulldown is used to convert 24p footage to 60i, then *reverse pulldown* (also called *reverse telecine* or *inverse telecine*) is used to restore it to 24p. Not all NLEs can do reverse pulldown, and with some formats and NLEs you need a capture card or conversion box to do it.[20] In some cases, pulldown and reverse pulldown can be done with software as a render process after capture (Cinema Tools can do this with Final Cut Pro), but if you have a capture card or external hardware, pulldown can be done during capture on the fly in real time. The advantages of doing reverse pulldown while capturing—as opposed to after the media is captured—are that you save time and reduce the media to be stored by 20 percent.

Let's look at different types of pulldown and how they're used.

Native 24p

As discussed in Chapter 2, a few camcorders can capture native 24p, which means a very straightforward recording of 24 progressive frames a second with no pulldown. Similarly, video formats using *progressive segmented frame* (*PsF;* see below) can record 24p with no additional frames. Formats that use either of these

20. Many Avid systems have an external accelerator board that can do reverse pulldown.

two methods can provide a simple path to shooting 24p and, depending on your NLE and hardware, may allow you to ingest footage into the NLE with no frame rate conversion for editing at 24p.[21]

Similarly, film can be transferred in a telecine to video formats using one of these methods.

However, if during editing you want to view 24p footage on a 60i monitor, or record out to a 60i VTR, then 2:3 pulldown must applied.

2:3 Pulldown

The typical way that 24p sources are converted to 60i is by using *2:3 pulldown* (also known as *3:2 pulldown* or *normal pulldown*). In Fig. 14-30, the top row represents the original 24p footage, which could be film or a 24p image stream in a video camera. We apply pulldown to get to the middle row, which is the 60i (30 fps) stream.

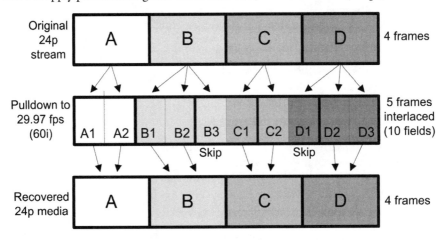

Fig. 14-30. Normal (2:3) pulldown. The top line represents four frames of the original 24p media. The middle line shows how extra fields are added to create five frames of 60i. The bottom line shows how, by deleting two fields, we can rebuild the 24p stream.

Each group of four frames of 24p footage is converted to 5 frames (10 fields) of video at 60i. This is done by creating two extra fields in the 60i stream. Notice that the four original frames A, B, C, and D become five frames in the middle row. Frames A and C are transferred to two fields (which is what we'd expect in an interlaced format—two fields per frame). However, frames B and D are transferred to *three* fields. This pattern or *cadence* is why normal pulldown is also called 2:3 or 2:3:2:3.

Normal pulldown creates smooth motion and is how most film-originated movies have been transferred to video over the years. For productions like television movies that are transferred to 60i and shown in that format (without ever returning to 24p) we can edit the footage essentially like any other 60i video material.

---

21. Unless you shoot at true 24p and edit at 23.976 or vice versa. This is discussed below.

REVERSE 2:3 PULLDOWN. If pulldown has been used to convert, say, 24p HD to 60i SD, we may want to get rid of the pulldown and return to 24p for editing. This is often done while capturing into the NLE. In Fig. 14-30, reverse pulldown or reverse telecine is represented by going from the middle row to the bottom row. The bottom row is the "recovered" or restored 24p stream captured in the NLE.

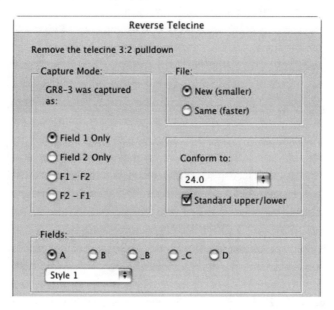

Fig. 14-31. The Reverse Telecine function in Cinema Tools can be used to restore 24p media by deleting the fields that were added in the 2:3 pulldown process. Note that the system needs to know the field order of the footage, and whether you want to create true 24 fps or 23.98 fps media. (Apple, Inc.)

Here's how it's done: The first frame of the 60i has only two fields (A1 and A2), which are combined to restore the A frame in the bottom row. The same thing happens with the next frame of the 60i. But then things get a bit messier. There's an extra field—B3—that gets discarded. Then we find that the two fields of the C frame (C1 and C2) are split across two frames in the 60i. They need to be recovered and combined. Then we have an extra D field to throw away.

For the NLE to do reverse pulldown, it needs to orient itself within the pattern so it knows which fields to save, which to discard, and how to rebuild the 24p timecode. Notice that the A frame is special. It's the only frame of the 24p material that is transferred to exactly one frame of 60i (two fields with no timecode change between the fields). The A frame can be used as a marker to indicate the start of the pattern. Some NLEs can automatically recognize the A frame but in some cases you need to help the system locate the A frames (for more on this, see Managing Pulldown, p. 618).

When working with compressed digital formats that you are capturing natively, one disadvantage of 2:3 pulldown is that it requires decompressing frames 3 and 4 to extract the C frame, then recompressing. That is why *24p Advanced pulldown* was created.

2:3:3:2 Pulldown

Panasonic developed a pulldown pattern called 24p Advanced, which is now used by other manufacturers as well. Like normal pulldown, some frames of 24p are transferred to two fields of 60i and some to three. However, Advanced uses a slightly different cadence. Instead of 2:3:2:3, the advanced pattern is 2:3:3:2 (see Fig. 14-32).[22]

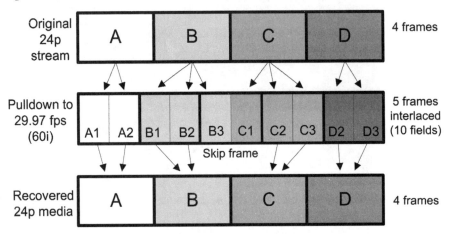

Fig. 14-32. Advanced (2:3:3:2) pulldown. Note the difference between this and Fig. 14-30. Instead of deleting separate fields B3 and C2 to re-create the 24p media, here we delete the entire third frame (B3 and C1) which makes for a cleaner, simpler reverse pulldown process.

The 60i footage that results is not quite as smooth as with normal 2:3 pulldown. However, the benefit of 24pA is found in converting back from 60i to 24p. This reverse pulldown can be done simply and in real time while capturing with a FireWire connection into the NLE. No decompression is required. The camera sets a flag in the data stream, telling the system to simply discard the third frame in the 60i, leaving us with a tidy package of the original A, B, C, and D frames in compressed form.

Other Pulldown Patterns

High definition formats may use other methods to embed one frame rate in another. The progressive segmented frame (PsF) method records 24p in a 48i stream (see p. 104). Each 24p frame is broken into two fields of 48i (see Fig. 14-33). Every

---

22. If you have a 60i clip that came from a shot with 2:3:3:2 pulldown, you can recognize it because every group of five frames has one interlaced frame. Material shot with 2:3 pulldown has two. To tell which frames are interlaced, step through the footage one field at a time and look for unevenness between fields.

frame is treated the same (the cadence is totally regular—2:2:2:2). Reversing this pulldown simply means recombining each pair of fields to a single frame of 24p for playback.

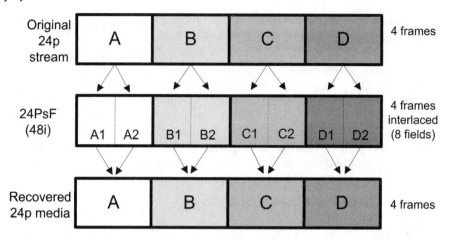

Fig. 14-33. Progressive segmented frame (PsF). Unlike pulldown, here the 24p frames are simply divided into two fields each without adding anything. The 48i fields can simply be recombined without deleting anything to re-create the original 24p media.

DVCPRO HD uses another method to record at a variety of frame rates (this process is described on p. 103). Cameras such as the Panasonic Varicam can shoot at frame rates between 1 fps and 60 fps but are always *recording* at 60p. To shoot 24p, the camera exposes images at 24 fps, then applies 2:3 pulldown internally to repeat one frame twice, then the next frame three times, and so on as it records the 60p stream. The camera flags which are the "true" frames and which are the repeat frames, so the NLE knows what to keep and what to discard during capture to restore the 24p sequence.

If you shoot 60 fps, all of those frames can be captured with no pulldown, creating 2.5x slow motion in a 24p project, much like shooting film at 60 fps.

Some NLEs, such as Avid's Xpress Pro and Media Composer, can do a similar process with standard definition 30p, creating 1.25x slow motion in a 24p project.

EDITING 24p FOOTAGE

How you edit 24p material depends on the kind of project you're doing, the workflow you choose, and the equipment you have.

Working in a 24p Project

When working with footage that originated at 24p (be it film or 24p HD) it's often best to edit at 24 fps on the NLE. This is sometimes referred to as working in a 24p *timebase*. This is a good choice when you're doing an offline edit and want to return to the 24p original material for the online. It's also well suited to making a

24p end product, like a 24p DVD or QuickTime file. If you make 24p HD master tapes, these can be a good source from which many other formats (60i, 50i, 25p) can be created. Not all NLEs support a 24p timebase.

SPEED CONSIDERATIONS. When HD and SD video are shot at "24p" in NTSC countries, that usually means 23.976 fps (often rounded to 23.98). If you recorded sound in the video camera or with a separate audio recorder, you should have no problems with sync as long as you edit using a 23.976 timebase.

However, film projects in the United States are almost always shot at *exactly* 24 fps.[23] Film footage is then slowed down to 23.976 in the telecine or when recorded on SD videotape. Projects shot on film are sometimes edited at 24p and sometimes at 23.976p. The choice will affect the way audio speed adjustment is handled. This is discussed on p. 619. Note that slowing the sound to match the picture is often referred to as "pulling down" or "pulldown," but this is different than the pulldown discussed above that means changing the picture frame rate.

TIMECODE CONSIDERATIONS. In some workflows, 24p HD or film material is transferred to a 60i SD tape before capturing to the NLE. Keep in mind that the 24p timecode used in the original HD footage and in the 24p NLE sequence is not the same as the 30-frame timecode of the SD tape. The count of hours, minutes, and seconds will be the same, but the frame count won't be, since with 24 fps there are 24 frames each second and with 30 fps there are 30. The editing system may be able to make the conversion automatically, but care needs to be taken that pulldown is done correctly and that the timecode of the NLE sequence does indeed match the HD source (ultimately, you'll be doing the online with the original HD material, and it's imperative that timecode of the clips in the sequence is identical). This is especially critical when working with film (see Editing Film on Video, p. 605).

Working in a 60i Project

When producing a project that will be shown in 60i (say, a television movie), or if your movie uses a lot of 60i footage, you may want to edit at 60i instead of 24p. In this case, any 24p material you want to use can have 2:3 pulldown applied and then be treated as 60i footage. For more on working with mixed formats, see below.

Keep in mind that if you edit 24p material at 60i, and then go back to do an online with the original 24p footage, there may be slight cutting discrepancies between the offline NLE sequence and what you end up with in the online. These errors come from the difference between the 30-frame timecode used in the sequence and 24-frame timecode of the original source footage. For more on this concept, see Matchback from 30 fps Projects, p. 622.

For this reason, you may want to plan your workflow to transfer the 24p footage to 60i, then use that as a source for both the offline and the online.

---

23. Unless an NTSC CRT video monitor or TV is being filmed (see p. 723) or unless shot at 25 fps for TV exhibition in PAL countries.

WORKING WITH MIXED FORMATS

These days, it's increasingly common to work on projects that use footage shot in different formats or codecs. For example, you might be working on a documentary in HD that uses archival footage shot in SD. Or you might be working on a dramatic feature shot in HD that has some *B camera* (second camera) footage shot in HDV.

Sometimes filmmakers choose to work with mixed formats as a stylistic device, and sometimes they're forced to do so by circumstances of available equipment or pre-existing footage. There's nothing like hard cuts between different types of source material to accentuate the differences between them in look and feel. This may serve the effect you're trying to achieve, or it may have the unintended result of making some of the footage look worse by comparison.

Some NLEs can play different formats or codecs in the same sequence, allowing you to mix and match. Others require you to choose one format as the base for the sequence, and any footage that's in another format or codec must be rendered before it can be seen. Rendering can slow you down quite a bit. In this case, you might consider converting footage to the same format prior to offline editing. Some systems allow you to edit with mixed formats but require rendering before you can output the movie. You could do your offline this way, then use a pull list (see p. 622) to separate just the shots that need to be converted or transcoded.

Even if the NLE can play different formats, you may still be dealing with differences in frame rate, frame size, aspect ratio, and other factors.

Frame Rate

When you work with a sequence on an NLE, you'll need to select the frame rate or timebase. Some NLEs may be able to accommodate footage in a sequence with different frame rates, but some won't. Several conversion methods can be done.

- As discussed in the previous section, material shot in 24p can have pulldown applied to create 60i. This can be done while outputting from the 24p deck or camera, or by using software in the NLE.
- Similarly, material that's in 60i that originated as 24p can have its pulldown removed so you can use it in a 23.976 sequence. Even material that originated as 60i (and never was 24p) can be converted with software or hardware to 24p (this is done all the time for film-outs).[24]
- Footage shot with 24p Advanced pulldown can be converted to 24p normal using software. Another trick is to capture the 24pA footage to a 23.976 project in the NLE (removing the pulldown), then apply normal 2:3 pulldown while outputting to a 60i deck. Then you can recapture the 60i tape to a 60i project.

24. When you combine regular 60i footage with footage that's been pulled down to 60i from 24p, the two types will have a different motion. You can take the regular 60i, convert to 24p, and add back 2:3 pulldown to make them more similar. Graham Nattress makes an FCP plug-in that does this (www .nattress.com).

- PAL material shot at 25 fps can be slowed down by 4 percent to match a 24 fps timeline. PAL can also be converted to 60i.

Frame Size and Aspect Ratio

When working in HD, there may be times you want to use SD footage, perhaps archival material, in the project. This can create two problems. First, the SD frame has fewer pixels, so it will need to be scaled up to fill the HD frame. This will make it look soft (unsharp) and possibly grainy or noisy in comparison to the HD. This may be unavoidable. Sometimes people display the SD as a smaller box within the HD frame (with some kind of background) to avoid scaling it up. For more on resizing, see Video-to-Video Format Conversions, p. 719.

Another potential problem is cutting together widescreen 16:9 material with non-widescreen 4:3 material. This can happen with SD or HD movies. Several options are available for accommodating one aspect ratio within the other. This is discussed in Aspect Ratio Choices, p. 87.

Field Order

When mixing different interlaced sources, make sure that their *field order* (also called *field dominance*) matches. There are two types of fields in an interlaced frame. The *upper field* (also called *field two* or *F2*) contains the odd-numbered scan lines. (Since some people number scan lines starting from 0 and others start at 1, talking about odd and even can lead to confusion. For the sake of example, however, let's assume here that the upper field starts with line 1.) The *lower* field (also *field one* or *F1*) is made up of the even-numbered lines. Field order refers to which one occurs temporally first in the frame.[25] Digital video formats derived from NTSC and PAL (including DV) are "lower field first" or "lower field dominant." "Upper field first" is found in 640 x 480 video generated by computer graphics systems. See Fig. 18-8 to get an idea of the two fields.

When creating a sequence in the NLE or when doing a reverse pulldown process on capture, it's also important to make sure the setting for field order matches the footage you're working with (see Fig. 14-31). If there's a mismatch between your sequence and some material you want to use, you may need to change the field order of some of your material as you capture it.

There is no field dominance or field order with progressive formats because there are no fields. Mixing interlaced and progressive formats in the same sequence doesn't seem to present any special problems. Since the many existing video displays (meaning CRT TVs) are interlace displays, progressive video is often seen as interlaced anyway—although this is changing with the success of LCDs, plasma screens, and DLP projectors, which are all progressive. If you're mixing interlace and progressive clips specifically for progressive display, you may want to deinterlace the interlaced material using a deinterlacing filter (most NLEs have them). On the other hand, most progressive displays have no problems showing interlaced video. They simply convert interlaced video on the fly into a progressive scan.

25. Raw interlaced video doesn't have frames per se, it's just one field after another. The frame boundary is imposed on the video stream later and determines where timecode is positioned (in SMPTE code it always starts on F1).

Pixel Type

HD uses square pixels, SD uses nonsquare pixels. When mixing formats with different pixel shapes, to avoid distortions in the image you may need to convert some of the footage when importing it to the sequence. See Pixel Shape, p. 213.

WORKING WITH DOUBLE-SYSTEM SOUND

Double-system sound means using an audio recorder that's separate from the camera. Film is always shot double system, and some video projects are too. Recording double system is discussed on p. 434. Speed adjustments needed for projects shot on film are discussed on p. 619. Once the audio has been captured to the NLE at the proper speed for the project, it must be put in sync, that is, lined up correctly with the picture.

If the audio was recorded with timecode, you may be able to line up sound and picture directly with embedded timecode or with the visual display on a timecode slate. Otherwise, you can do it manually. If a slate was used, mark the very first frame where the clap sticks hit in the picture. Then find the first moment that the sound occurs in the audio and mark it. On some NLEs you can identify the position with subframe accuracy, allowing you to slip the clip in tiny increments to get the precise beginning of the sound.

At this point, you want to link the video and audio clips so they'll stay together and display sync breaks if they should get out of sync during editing. Avid has an *AutoSync* function that allows you to simply mark In Points on the sound and picture where the clap sticks hit, then use AutoSync to create a new, merged clip. In Final Cut Pro, you mark In Points on video and audio clips in the viewer, select the clips in the browser, and use the "merge clips" command.

For more on using lip-sync when you don't have a slate, see p. 602.

COLOR CORRECTION

Some people think of color correction as just another video effect, but its importance in the production process warrants special consideration. Adjusting the overall color and brightness values in your movie, and fine-tuning individual clips, can be critical to both how the movie plays for the audience and where it can be shown. Color correction is used to:

- *Establish an overall look for the movie.* Do you want bright saturated colors or are more muted, pastel shades better suited to the story? How much contrast do you like? Is there an overall color cast you want for the film or certain sections of it?
- *Maintain consistency from shot to shot.* Most scenes are made up of several

shots. It's important that these shots feel like they belong together and flow from one to the next (this is especially crucial for dramas). A wide shot of a character might cut to a close-up filmed on a different day, but both are supposed to represent one moment in time. It's essential that the two shots match in color and feel.

- **Correct errors.** A shot may be over- or underexposed, or be too blue because improper white balance was used in shooting.
- **Ensure that the movie is broadcast legal.** Broadcasters have very particular requirements about luma (brightness) and chroma (color) levels. If you're making a video for nonbroadcast use, these levels are useful guidelines.[26] If you're intending to get your movie on TV, video levels must be within specified limits. Similarly, if you're planning a film-out, there will also be target levels.

Color correction is both an art and a science, and a good *colorist* is essential to supporting and enhancing the work of the director of photography, the editor, the art director and, of course, the director. Many filmmakers know the importance of a sound mix not just in polishing the film, but telling the story. Color correction can be equally critical.

Color correction is a delicate thing. You're trying to create a look that reveals the content and expresses the emotion of the movie, while working within technical limitations that can be quite restrictive at times. A shot that looks great to you often exceeds legal levels. Talented colorists find a way to capture the feel you're looking for while keeping the signal "safe." Aesthetically, there's no one "right" color balance—it's up to the filmmakers to decide what serves the story best. Technically, however, there definitely are "wrong" choices that will cause broadcasters or other gatekeepers to reject the project.

How color correction (called *grading* in Europe) is done depends on the project. For a small video project, you might just go through the sequence on your NLE,

Fig. 14-34. Da Vinci Resolve color correction system. (da Vinci Systems, LLC)

---

26. If your project will be shown *only* on computer monitors and never on video, you have more leeway in setting levels.

tuning things up before exporting to tape. For a larger project, rough corrections might be done during the offline edit, with final color correction done in the online edit, where high-end tools, monitors, and external scopes are available. Sometimes color work is done after the online, in a room dedicated to the task, using an image processor such as a da Vinci system (see Fig. 14-34).

Whether you do color correction yourself or have an editor or colorist do it, it helps to understand what's involved. For an overview of terms, see Chapter 8 and the discussion of exposure and contrast in Chapter 5. There is more on color correction for both film and video projects in Chapter 18.

Monitoring the Signal

To do color correction properly, you need a monitor you can trust (see p. 197, also Appendix A). If you're working on a project that will be shown in video or on TV, you must use a video monitor, not a computer monitor, for the job. A professional facility will usually have a high-end reference monitor. At minimum, you need a decent video monitor that has been set up correctly. Having a blue-only setting for calibrating to color bars helps enormously. If the color in your monitor is off, decisions you make about color correction will be too.

For monitoring the video signal, there are two basic tools. The waveform monitor (see Fig. 5-2) can be used to measure luma (luminance) levels which correspond to brightness. A vectorscope gives a visual display of color (see Fig. 8-3). You can use it to read the hue (sometimes called phase) which is a measure of the particular color—for example, to determine whether it is more blue or red. Both vectorscope and waveform monitors can be used to display the chroma level (also called saturation), which is a measure of the intensity of a color. Many NLEs have built-in waveform monitors and vectorscopes which are serviceable if you are outputting from your NLE (see the documentation with your NLE on how to use them). Professionals usually use external scopes that provide more complete information.

Many NLEs have a feature that will flag clips in the timeline that exceed legal video limits for brightness and color so you know what needs fixing.

Guidelines

If you're preparing a movie for broadcast, contact the broadcaster for their technical requirements. In the United States, PBS guidelines are often considered a standard (see the PBS Red Book at www.pbs.org). Technical requirements include a wide range of items (including video levels, aspect ratio, audio levels, and channel assignments) so be sure to discuss them in advance of postproduction.

As a rule, the luma level should stay below about 103 percent on the waveform monitor. The chroma level should also stay below about that level; overall saturation level should be acceptable as long as the signal on the vectorscope doesn't extend past the area marked by the little graticule boxes, which represent the NTSC limit of 75 percent saturation. However, legal level is a combination of luma and chroma, and a very saturated color may sometimes push you over the combined limit of 120 IRE.

PAL, which accommodates 100 percent color saturation, is a different story. No RGB color is illegal as long as luma doesn't exceed 100 percent and chroma 131 percent. (PAL countries use a wider broadcast bandwidth than NTSC's 6 MHz.)

Black level on a digital system should be above 0 percent. If you're working on an NTSC project and using a scope that is being fed *analog output*, blacks should read above 7.5 percent (since 7.5 IRE units is the proper setup level for NTSC; for more on this, see p. 189).

If luma and chroma levels are within legal limits, it's up to you to set the color and contrast. See p. 183 for a discussion of video levels and contrast. Generally speaking, you want to be able to see detail in important parts of the scene, without clipping the highlights or crushing the blacks. Sometimes you have to sacrifice the shadow areas to bring highlights within safe limits. Conversely, you may decide to clip the bright areas in order to bring out shadow detail.

As for color, usually the most important thing is to get the flesh tones right. Warmer flesh tones are often the most flattering, but if Caucasian skin gets too red, cheeks can look flushed or ruddy. Cool tones might be used for a darker or more sinister look.

To establish the overall look, you may choose to increase saturation for more vivid color or desaturate for more pastel shades (extreme desaturation takes you all the way to monochrome). Or you may decide to desaturate only the highlights or shadows to remove a color cast.

Keep in mind that color correction on an NLE is a process of adding an effect to a clip. If you later decide you don't like the look, all you have to do is reset to default settings or simply remove the color-correction effect from the clip altogether.

Tools

NLEs and image processing systems vary widely in their color-correction toolset. You may have a choice between using a very simplified (or automated) set of controls and using a more powerful control panel.

Sometimes there's a set of three controls for blacks, midtones, and whites (highlights). Each might have a color control to adjust hue and saturation and a slider for level adjustments (see Fig. 14-35). Sometimes you can make a simple tweak, such as lowering the level of the whites a few clicks to fix a shot that's too hot, or decreasing the level of the blacks to improve an image that lacks contrast.

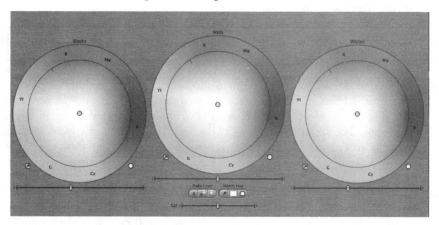

Fig. 14-35. Three-way color correction tool in Final Cut Pro gives you color and level control over the blacks, the midtones and the whites individually. (Apple, Inc.)

For color adjustments, move the color balance toward the color you want or move it directly away from one you don't want. For example, to fix a shot with a green color cast, move the control toward magenta. Experiment with changing saturation and hue separately. Sometimes a color looks off, but the problem isn't the color itself (hue), only that there's too much of it (excess saturation).

Some NLEs include gamma settings which primarily affect the contrast of the midtones. Some NLEs let you manipulate gamma curves in individual color channels. These take some experience to work with.

Often you'll create a color-correction setting you want to use in different parts of the movie (for example, you might have clips from the same shot or reel spread throughout the film). You should be able to drag a customized color correction effect from a clip in the timeline to the bin for storage and reuse on similar clips. It's also helpful to compare previously corrected shots with the one you're working on; some systems allow you to display frames from a few shots at a time.

In some scenes, you'll make an overall correction to get flesh tones right but find that something else (say, clothing or the landscape) no longer looks good. Some systems can do *secondary color correction*, which targets a particular area or color without affecting the scene as a whole.

AUTOMATIC SETTINGS. Many systems have automated controls for setting color and contrast. You can use them as a starting point from which further tweaks can be made, or you can just stick with them if you're uncomfortable making adjustments yourself.

There may be auto-balance buttons for such things as white level, black level, contrast and white balance. Try them and see if you like what they do.

Some systems have an *eyedropper tool* that lets you click on a color that should be white. This can be handy for correcting a shot that has an overall color cast or poor white balance. An eyedropper can sometimes be used to match flesh tones from one shot to another.

Most relatively advanced NLEs have a filter that ensures that luma and chroma levels are within legal limits. In Final Cut Pro it's called *broadcast safe filter*. Premiere

Fig. 14-36. Color correction can be applied to different parts of the frame. Here areas of the background are darkened to add dimensionality. Scenes can be essentially "relit" in post. (Ned Johnston)

Pro's *broadcast colors* effect is similar.[27] This type of filter is an easy and simple way to guarantee levels are safe. One potential drawback is that the filter may clip highlights (resulting in lost detail) in some situations where it would be better to lower the video level manually. Some people adjust levels manually, but throw the broadcast safe filter on the sequence at the very end just to be sure everything's legal.

MEDIA MANAGEMENT

Editing video on an NLE means working with a lot of data. How much data depends on how many hours of material you've captured and what format you're working in. It's easy to have hundreds of gigabytes (or much more) of data without even trying.

There are various points in working on a project where you may want to reduce, reorganize, or move the data. For example, you may be pushing the limits of your storage capacity. Or, if your project contains a lot of material, it may be taking too long to load on your NLE. Or you may want to move the project to another computer.

As discussed earlier in the chapter, an NLE project includes different types of data:

- *Video and audio files (source media files) captured from the camera.* These are very large and therefore the most difficult to store and move around. However, as long as you have access to the original camera tapes or files used to record in the field, you can delete media files and recapture when needed.[28]
- *Clips and sequences.* Clips are created when you capture the video and audio. Sequences are created in editing. Clips and sequences simply "point" to the media files, and take up very little space themselves on a hard drive. It's usually a good idea not to delete them, as they took time to create and might be handy later. However, if there are clips and sequences you rarely use, it can be a good idea to store them in a separate project.
- *Render or precompute files.* These are created during editing and can easily be deleted and rerendered later if needed. Old, unneeded render files have a habit of piling up on the hard drive if you don't occasionally clear them out.
- *Other media.* You may have imported graphics, stills, music, sound effects, and other non-timecoded media that has become part of the project.

Any NLE that's mid-level or higher will have a system for working with media. In the Avid system, it's called the *media tool*; in Final Cut Pro, it's the *media manager* (see Fig. 14-25). These tools can simplify the process of moving or deleting files. Final Cut Pro recommends using the media manager to move or delete media files rather than using the finder. Avid has a *find media relatives* command that can help

---

27. Premiere's filter will also remove unsafe RGB colors that fall outside the NTSC or PAL gamut.
28. Assuming they have timecode; without it, you can recapture but editing is much harder.

you identify which media files on your hard drives are being used by a sequence or clip, in case you want to move or delete unused media.

The following are some tasks you might want to accomplish:

- *Clear out unused media to free up drive space.* If you've been working on a project and want to keep the media actually being used by one or more sequences but delete the bulk of what you originally captured, you can *consolidate* the media. This workflow is similar to the one described in Trimming and Recapturing Media, p. 550, in that you select a sequence (or more than one) and trim it. This is done in Final Cut Pro with *delete unused media*; in Avid it's the *consolidate* command. Instead of unlinking and recapturing the media as you would for an online, you simply copy it to another drive in its shortened, consolidated form. Only after you're sure everything's working, you can then delete the original media files.

  Deleting old render files and audio mixdowns is a painless way to quickly free up space. Final Cut Pro has a *render manager* that can help you see which render files are no longer needed.
- *Move a sequence to a laptop to edit at another location.* As described above, you can consolidate the media and copy it to the second computer.
- *Prepare for an online.* If you're ready for an online and want to recapture only the media used in the final sequence, see the workflow described on p. 550.
- *Archive the project.* You're done editing and have output the final version. Now you want to save the project for the future but take it off the editing system. You'll want to save the project itself (the composition) with all clips and sequences to a disc or drive (this is a fairly small file). You should also store any non-timecoded graphics, music, and media. Though some people save the captured media files, if you have the original camera tapes, this is often not worth the large amount of storage it usually requires. If you've been doing file-based editing without tapes, you'll need to archive the media using DLT tape, DVDs, HD DVDs, Blu-ray discs, hard drives, or other technology. As of this writing, cost-effective file archiving remains a challenge (things were simpler in the "old days" of videotape!).

TAPE EDITING

Traditional video*tape* editing—from one tape deck to another—is used far less than nonlinear at this point. However, it continues to play a role in postproduction. What follows is a brief discussion of tape editing. See Editing on Tape, p. 42, for an overview.

Stages of Tape Editing

Offline and online editing originated with tape editing (see The Idea of Offline and Online, p. 514). If you're doing only a few edits, and need to work quickly, you can use the camera tapes in an online process. However, for a typical long-form project, you'll be spending a lot of time going over your material, shuttling the tapes back and forth, which could damage them. For a tape offline edit, *workdubs* (also called *worktapes* or *workprints*) are made. They are copies of the original camera tapes used for the offline to preserve the camera tapes for the online.

Here are the stages of "traditional" videotape offline/online editing:

1. *Make workdubs.* Play camera tapes straight through and rerecord on another cassette.

2. *Log footage.* View the work dubs and make notes on the material (see The Editing Log, p. 494).

3. *Do offline edit.* During the offline, the workdubs are edited to determine the structure of the movie.

4. *Make an EDL.* This is a list of every shot in the movie, with exact timecode of the first and last frames of each shot. Some systems can generate the EDL automatically; on lower-end equipment you must do it manually.

5. *Do online edit.* During the online, the final *master tape* is created by returning to the camera original tapes and editing them as determined by the EDL.

6. *Mix audio.* For more control over sound mixing, the audio is often *stripped* from the master tape and imported into a digital audio workstation (DAW). After mixing, a *layback* is done to record the final mix on the master tape.

Tape Editing Systems

Tape editing systems are based on the idea of using two or more VTRs and a controller that operates them (see Fig. 14-1). The *source* or *playback VTR* plays the video footage while selected portions are rerecorded on the *record* or *edit VTR*. Usually there are two monitors to view the material: the *source monitor*, which shows what's playing on the source VTR, and the *record/edit monitor* (also called *program monitor*), which shows the edited program. The source and record decks may be in a variety of tape formats. A typical small setup might use two S-VHS, ¾-inch, or Betacam decks. Sometimes the source deck is a lower-cost unit without full recording capabilities. A large production facility might have an editing suite with a variety of VTRs in various formats. Systems with more than one source deck allow you to do dissolves and other effects (these are called *A-B roll systems*; systems that can't do dissolves are called *cuts only*). Some digital tape formats offer a "pre-read" feature that allows dissolves with only two decks.

The controller is the interface between you and the VTRs. *Computer editors* are by far the preferred type of controller since they keep a running list by timecode of every editing decision in the show and can automatically compile an EDL. The simplest type of controllers, sometimes called *control track editors*, can't read timecode. Without timecode, it's much harder to alter or repeat an editing decision or do an online edit. If your editing system does not create an EDL, you can edit with tapes that have burn-in timecode and then compile the EDL manually.

Fig. 14-37. This edit controller offers A-B roll editing (controls up to three VTRs). It includes a video switcher/special effects generator. (Sony Electronics, Inc.)

RECORDING AND PLAYING TAPES

Making Worktapes and Other Dubs

If time and money are very limited, you might risk editing with camera original tapes, but for most productions it is standard practice to make workdubs. You may be able to get low-cost, used tape stock for worktapes. To cut down time spent shuttling to locate shots, keep your worktapes an hour or less.

When making any kind of dub from one VTR to another, try to simplify the electronic path between the two decks. Avoid running the signal through extra equipment such as low-quality switchers, which might add noise. If you're working in a digital format, whenever possible connect the two decks digital-out to digital-in (using a FireWire connection or serial mode), rather than going through the analog video connectors. For analog machines, use component, S-video or "dub mode" connections instead of composite whenever possible (see Video Color Systems, p. 192).

When analog tapes are copied, timecode tracks can become degraded. Use a timecode generator to read the code from the master and regenerate a fresh, clean signal whenever you make a dub. Timecode on digital tapes does not need to be regenerated; it can be copied directly from tape to tape. When doing offline editing, it's often helpful to make worktapes with burn-in timecode (see Fig. 1-17), which is visible over the picture (these tapes are called *window dubs*). If you are editing timecoded source tapes on an editing system that does not read timecode, you *must* have window dubs so you can visually keep track of code.

For insert editing—which is highly preferable to assemble editing when doing tape-to-tape offline or online editing—all edit master tapes must be blacked and coded with control track and timecode (see p. 558).

How Many Generations?

In tape editing, you often need to make copies of copies, which results in lowered picture quality in analog tape formats. Generally, the better the original format, the more generations you can go down before the image is badly impaired. Component formats copy better than composite ones. There is no fixed rule about when analog copies become unacceptable. Rough estimates on maximum generations before significant impairment: Beta SP, four to five; ¾-inch Hi8, S-VHS, two to three; regular VHS, one to two.

Digital tapes can usually be cloned through many generations without noticeable loss. Native clones (made digital-out to digital-in without changing format) are perfect copies; if the signal is converted to analog and then back to digital, there is some deterioration.

Play and Record Settings

Tape editing is based on playing source tapes on one machine and recording the edit master on another. For the video and audio to be properly recorded for each shot, you need to check the whole chain from player to recorder. On some editing systems, this is done by playing a tape on the source VTR and pressing only "record" (not "record" and "play" together) on the edit VTR. This should activate the meters on the record deck without putting the tape into motion (this mode is sometimes called *E-E* ("E to E").

Play some color bars and set up the monitors (see Appendix A). Then roll the source tape to the first shot you want. Check the video level and/or color. If the picture is unsteady, try adjusting the *tracking* (not all formats or machines have tracking control).

Audio levels can be set using a mixer and/or the audio level adjustment on the record VTR. If you're using a mixer, you want the mixer's meter to read at a normal level, neither too high nor too low, but the most important level meter to watch is the one on the record VTR. This is the only meter that tells you the *actual* level that will be recorded on the edit master tape. (See p. 650 for suggestions on setting audio levels, and p. 630 for working with mixers.)

Once you've set the recording level, adjust the speakers (the audio monitor) to a comfortable level. Try not to change the monitor volume during the edit session so you'll be able to judge levels by ear.

OFFLINE TAPE EDITING

You've made your worktapes, prepared the edit master, set levels for proper playback, and gotten a cup of coffee. You've looked through your logs (see Chapter 13) for your first shot, and found it on the source tape. You're ready to start editing.

Making an Edit

Linear videotape editing is a process of building up the movie (or a sequence in it) shot by shot. You start at the first shot and work forward. Go to the first frame you want to use. The edit controller will have a button to mark this frame as the In Point (sometimes called *Mark In*, *Video In*, or just *In*). You then go to the end of the shot and mark the Out Point (also called *Mark Out*, etc.). See Fig. 14-38. Some edit points are easier to determine while running in slow motion, others are easier to judge running "at speed" (regular motion).

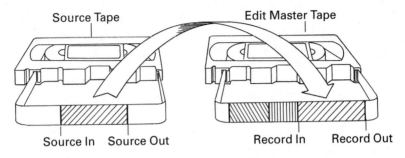

Fig. 14-38. A basic video edit. When editing from the source tape to the edit master, each edit can be described by four points: Source In and Source Out specify which part of the source tape to use, and Record In and Record Out indicate where the shot is to be placed on the edit master. (Robert Brun)

You have just marked In and Out on the source side (*Source In* and *Source Out*), and since you will be rerecording this shot onto the edit master tape, you need to tell the record deck where to put it. You now roll the record deck to the point where you want the shot to begin and mark this In Point. Note that you have now given the controller three points (Source In, Source Out, and Record In). Tape editing systems, like NLE's, work by three-point editing (see p. 531).

Normally you'll be recording using insert edit mode (see p. 556). You can now select *preview*, and the controller will rehearse the edit for you, allowing you to see how it looks. Most controllers will rewind the tapes between three to five seconds from the In Points before starting. This *preroll* is needed to get the machines up to speed before the edit occurs. (If you don't have enough continuous control track or timecode ahead of your edit points for the preroll, the machine may not do the edit.) If you're happy with the preview, you then select *edit* and the controller will perform (execute) the edit. It's always a good idea to check (review) an edit after you make it to ensure that everything worked mechanically and in terms of the picture or audio transition you were hoping for.

Making Changes

After previewing or making an edit, you may find you don't like the timing of the cut. If you want to adjust one of the edit points, you could mark a new In or Out. Alternately, you could use the *trim control* to adjust one of the existing edit points. Trimming in video means adding or subtracting frames from an edit point. It's important to remember that the "plus" and "minus" on a trim control refer to moving the edit point to an earlier or later timecode number. Timecode advances as you go forward in time. People get confused because they may think that trimming plus simply means "extend the shot" and trimming minus means "shorten the shot." If you want a shot to start earlier, you'll be pressing the minus button.

If after you've made an edit you feel that a shot is too short, you can try to pick up the shot where you left off and record more on the tail of it. If your system isn't precise, it may mess up that edit with extra frames or missing frames. This is why it's often a good idea to leave shots a little long in the early stages of tape editing, trimming them tighter as you refine the cut.

After you've edited together a sequence (or several sequences), you almost always want to make changes: lengthen a shot here, lose a shot there, or even drop a whole sequence. Rather than completely starting over, generally what's done during offline tape editing is to take the edit master tape from the record deck, put it in the source deck and edit from that to a new edit master tape. With digital machines connected digitally, quality stays high; with analog systems, you get quality loss at each generation.

THE EDL AND ONLINE TAPE EDITING

At one time, all online editing was done with tape machines. Now, even if you choose to offline edit using tape machines, when you go to a postproduction facility for an online, it will typically be done on an NLE (though you may output from the NLE to tape when you're done).

When you do both the offline and online using an NLE, a lot of information is created in the offline (about effects, titles, color, etc.) that can be carried forward digitally to the online (see p. 552). With tape-to-tape offlines, the information transfer is much more limited. The transfer is done with an *edit decision list* or EDL. The EDL is like a road map used in the online to reconstruct what you did in the offline. It indicates the In and Out Points by timecode of every bit of video and audio that came from the camera source tapes and shows exactly where each piece is to be recorded on the master tape.

If the EDL is done properly, you can go into the online session with the source tapes and, by following your list of numbers, rebuild the edited movie from scratch. The machines should be able to use the EDL to *auto-assemble* (also called *auto-conform*) the show.

Keep in mind that an EDL works only with sources that have timecode. If there's anything in the movie that comes directly from a non-timecoded source (such as music from a CD, scratch narration, computer-generated graphics) you'll have to re-edit these manually in the online session. Whenever possible, rerecord every element that lacks timecode onto a timecoded tape before you edit it into the offline program.

EDLs and Computer Editing Systems

If you've done your offline on a computer editing system, the system should be able to produce an EDL, which you can bring on disk to the online session. There are various standard EDL formats for different editing systems. CMX 3600 is a common standard; others include GVG and Sony. An EDL is just a list of numbers in standard column format. With some systems, an EDL can be created with a word processor or spreadsheet. All EDLs include the following data about each edit (see Fig. 14-39):

1. *Edit number.* A sequential number to help locate edits. Sometimes called event number.
2. *Source reel.* Tells you on which tape to find the source material. This is generally the camera tape number if the movie was shot in video. If shot on film, the source reel is the telecine transfer reel (which may have more than one film camera roll on it). Use numbers, not names for reels (see p. 525).
3. *Edit mode.* Indicates if the source for the edit is *V*ideo, *A*udio, or *B*oth. A1, A2, etc., indicates which audio channel to use.
4. *Edit type or transition.* May be a *C*ut, *D*issolve, *W*ipe, or *K*ey.
5. *Duration.* The length of the transition, in frames. Cuts, being instantaneous, have no duration.
6. *Playback In and Out.* Also called *Source In* and *Out*. These tell you the beginning and end points of the source material to use.
7. *Record In and Out.* These give you the timecode address on the master tape where the source material is to be recorded.

Edit Number	Source Reel	Edit Mode	Edit Type	Dura-tion	Playback In	Playback Out	Record In	Record Out
001	004	B	C		04:22:14:02	04:22:31:15	01:00:00:00	01:00:17:13
002	005	A1	C		05:06:30:11	05:06:31:09	01:00:16:11	01:00:17:13
003	005	B	C		05:06:31:09	05:06:42:02	01:00:17:13	01:00:28:06

Fig. 14-39. Information typically contained in an edit decision list (EDL). The column headings and lines have been added here for clarity. The events in the EDL may be listed in the order they appear in the program (A mode) or be grouped by source tape (B mode).

There are different ways to structure an EDL, which can have an impact on how the online is done. The events in the EDL can be listed in the order they appear in the program (*A-mode*) or grouped by source tape (*B-mode*).[29] In an A-mode assembly, you start at the beginning of the show and work your way down. This allows you to check that everything is right as you progress. This is the best system to use if you did the offline with a non-timecode edit system, or if you want to make any changes during the edit. Doing a B-mode assembly means recording all the shots from a given source reel at a time, putting them where they belong on the master, and leaving gaps where other shots will go. You then put up the next source reel and edit that one to the master. This saves time if there are a lot of source tapes, since switching and setting up tapes can be a hassle, but can cause problems if there are errors in the EDL. Some systems can work with more than one source deck at a time. *C-mode* is a variant of B-mode that records shots from individual source reels but takes them in ascending order on each source reel instead of the order in which they appear in the movie.

29. This use of "mode" is different than the edit mode just discussed.

List Cleaning

An EDL made from an offline edit may contain various errors or unnecessary events. Say during the offline you had recorded a shot, then gone back and added five seconds to it. The system may list that as two separate edits. In the online, you'll want to record that shot in one continuous edit. *List cleaning* is the process by which the EDL is checked to make sure it is efficient and accurate. List cleaning can be done manually or with software. Software can be particularly helpful if you decide at the last minute to add or delete a shot, which may cause all the shots that follow it to ripple (change Record In and Record Out timecode).

Online Tape Editing

The online edit session is the time to rerecord the program at highest possible quality. Use the best equipment you can afford. Tapes should be set up and color balanced carefully. Tape-to-tape color correction can be done during the online or sometimes as an additional step later.

Some editors like to start by recording the offline edit master directly on the online master as a check against errors (sometimes called *blueprinting*). As you do the online, you replace all the shots with newly recorded shots from the camera original tapes. This method adds time to the online, and ceases to be useful if you make changes during the online (which you often want to do when seeing all the shots and effects in place).

CHAPTER 15

Editing Film

The first part of this chapter is about editing projects shot on film the traditional way—using film equipment. The second part is about what has become a more common way of editing film—on video using nonlinear editing systems or linear videotape. See Chapter 1 for an overview of film editing, Chapter 13 for a discussion of editing styles and techniques and Chapter 14 for more on video editing.

TRADITIONAL FILM EDITING

If most people edit film on video, why do it the old-fashioned way? Well, you might be a Luddite and want to cling to low-tech, simpler ways of working. Even if you're not, there are several good reasons to edit film on film. A film workprint gives the best representation of what's in the original camera negative. If you edit film you'll have a better idea of what the movie will look like when printed on film. You may already have film editing equipment and it's cheaper to keep using it than switch. And you may be one of the many people who feel that the tradition and tactile experience of cutting and splicing pieces of celluloid is an important part of working in the medium. Film is the *original* nonlinear editing system.

EDITING EQUIPMENT

The editing bench (see Fig. 1-43) is a table that may be equipped with the following:

Cores, Reels, and Rewinds

In the editing room, film is usually stored on camera cores (see Fig. 6-14). Flatbed editing tables (see p. 593) can accommodate *core-wound* (*tight-wound*) film. Camera raw stock comes in 2-inch cores, but 3-inch cores are better for editing-room use, as they put less stress on long rolls of film. When the film needs to be put on a reel for projection or for work on an editing bench, it is mounted on a *split reel*, which is made up of two halves that screw together. A *flange* is like half of a split reel and allows film to be wound on a core. Some flanges allow film to be wound around itself without a core. Short takes are often stored this way.

Handle core-wound film carefully, especially if it's not very tightly wound. Hold the film flat like a pie, with your palm underneath; otherwise, the center may fall out (*dishing*). If dishing should happen, find a splice, or make a cut, and separate the two halves. Place the half without the core on the plate of a flatbed editing table and tape the inside end of the film to a core put in the empty center. Run the machine so the plate spins, and hold the outer end of the film in place while the inner part of the load winds onto the core. After both halves are rewound, splice them back together.

Double-key reels have two square holes on each side for mounting the reel onto projectors or rewinds. *Single-key reels* in 16mm have one square hole and one round hole. The round hole is "idiot proofing" to prevent the film from being loaded in a projector backward, making single-key reels good for release prints but troublesome in the editing room.

A pair of *rewinds* permit the film to be rewound or searched. Rewinds equipped with a friction or tension adjustment let you increase drag on the feed side to prevent film from *spilling* (unwinding without control) during rewinding. Drag can also be increased if rewinds develop the nasty habit of rotating by themselves. Use the drag adjustment or your hand to put tension on the film as you rewind it. Leave no slack between reels, because the slack may suddenly be taken up and the film broken. Rewinds may be fitted with long shafts to accommodate more than one reel (as when working with sound). Use an end support if more than four 16mm reels are mounted on a shaft. Use reel spacers or camera cores between reels and use clamps to hold the whole assembly in place (see Fig. 15-1).

Fig. 15-1. Moviola rewind with long shaft, spacers, spring clamp and support. (J & R Film)

The Viewer (Action Editor)

Viewers (see Figs. 1-43 and 15-2) are helpful for cutting MOS (silent) sequences and for searching rolls for particular shots. The viewer image is generally not sharp enough to judge the quality of the focus on a shot. Use a projector to evaluate footage for focus and quality. Viewers equipped with a built-in sound head or used with a synchronizer (see p. 591) can play sound and picture together.

If you are editing reversal camera original (not workprint), use a viewer with a simple film path to minimize the chance of scratching film. Never put negative in a viewer, and never whip film through a viewer at rewind speeds. The better-quality viewers allow you to mark the frame on the viewer screen with a grease pencil. Avoid devices on viewers that mark the frame by notching or nicking the film.

The Splicer

In the editing room, virtually all picture editing is done with tape splicers that use clear *Mylar tape* to join pieces of film. During projection, tape splices may throw a couple of frames out of focus at the cut and, over time, the tape may discolor. Forewarn the lab if footage to be printed has tape splices, since ultrasonic cleaning may remove them (see Chapter 17).

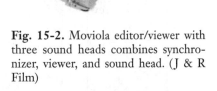

Fig. 15-2. Moviola editor/viewer with three sound heads combines synchronizer, viewer, and sound head. (J & R Film)

You should generally splice on the base side of film to avoid pulling off film emulsion. Splicing on only one side is faster in both making and removing the splice, but some projectors and editing machines will only take picture spliced on both sides (*double spliced*). Single-spliced picture may jam or jump in these machines. Double splices are stronger and do not stretch (*telescope*) as some single splices do.

Tape is available in three basic forms: unperforated in rolls, perforated in rolls, and precut perforated. The *guillotine splicer* (made by various manufacturers) is used with unperforated tape. The tape is stretched over the film and the splicer punches out the perforations. The tape lies across the frame line and is less visible on projection. Some models also have a diagonal cut for sound editing (see below). Unperforated tape is the least expensive, costing about one fourth as much as perforated tape. The splicers themselves are fairly fragile and must be kept clean of glue and punched perforations. The tape is relatively thin, allowing it to pass through projectors well, but splices may telescope over time.

Perforated tape in roll form is used in 16mm and 35mm with the Rivas or Hollywood Film splicers. Some models cut the tape straight, along the frame line, making the physical cut less obvious than on those models that cut with a jagged edge that rests in the picture area. In either case, the tape is fairly thick and is noticeable upon projection. These splicers need less maintenance than guillotine splicers and do not leave little punched perforations to gum up the works. Precut splices, the most expensive of the tape splices, are made primarily for the amateur market. They are very thin, easy to remove, and make the best-quality splice for picture, but are relatively slow to apply and are not often used in the professional editing room. Kodak Presstapes show in the picture area but can be cut with

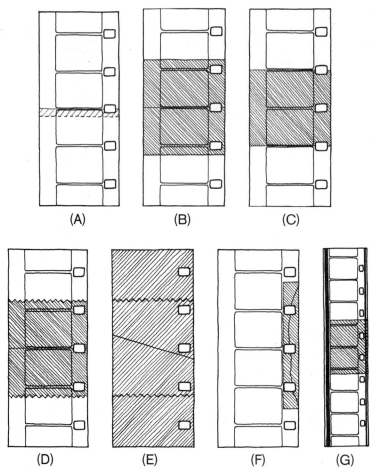

Fig. 15-3. Splices. (A) 16mm cement splice (shown here) extends into one frame. Cement splices in 35mm do not show up in the picture area. (B) Tape splice that extends past the frame line. (C) Tape splice that falls on the frame line. (D) Tape splice on a Rivas splicer showing jagged edge. (E) Diagonal splice on magnetic sound film made with a Rivas splicer. (F) Tape repair of torn perforations. (G) Super 8 guillotine tape splice that does not cover the main magnetic sound stripe but does cover the balance stripe.

scissors to make a splice that extends only to the frame line. They make the least noticeable splice of any and are sometimes used in emergency situations (as when original must be spliced without losing frames). Precut splices may be used with a Rivas splicer or an inexpensive *splicing block*, a grooved block with registration pins to hold the film and a slot to guide a single-edged razor blade for cutting.

   Check each tape splice you make. Remove air bubbles by rubbing. Trim tape that overlaps the edge of the film (which happens with dirty guillotine splicers or poorly manufactured perforated tape) with a razor blade or sharp scissors; otherwise, the film may jam during editing or projection. See p. 600 for splicing mag sound.

CEMENT SPLICERS. Cement splicers are primarily used for splicing nega-tive before printing and for fixing or joining reels of release prints. A cement splice is made by scraping the emulsion off one shot and then bonding the bases of the two shots together with fresh film cement for a strong union. One frame is lost where the emulsion is scraped at each cement splice.

Newer cement splicers should cut into only one of the frames at the splice. *Negative splices* are slightly narrower and cover less picture area than positive splices, but, when properly made, are as strong. In 35mm, the cement splice is out-side the projected picture area, so the splice does not show on projection. In Super 8 and 16mm, on the other hand, the splice does cut into the picture area and is visible on projection. A & B roll printing allows cement splices to be hidden in the smaller gauges (see Chapter 17). Consult Appendix I for techniques of cement splicing.

The Synchronizer

A *synchronizer* keeps film and sound track(s) locked together in the exact same relation to each other as you move from one part of the film to another. A synchro-nizer has one or more sprocketed wheels, called *gangs*, mounted on a revolving shaft. Sound and picture are mounted on separate gangs and are kept in sync frame by frame. You can mount a sound head to reproduce the sound through an ampli-fier and speaker (*squawk box*). If you also use a viewer, place it a standard number of frames from the sound reader and find a point where picture and sound are in sync. Place a point on the sound (like a slate or start mark) under the sound head, and place the corresponding point on picture in the viewer gate. To get decent sound

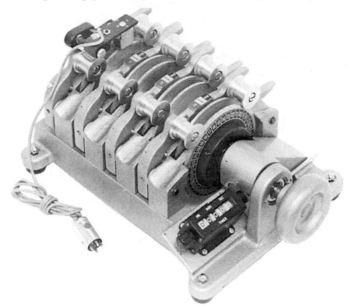

Fig. 15-4. Moviola four-gang synchronizer. The fourth gang is shown with a magnetic sound head attachment. The dial on the first gang is an adjustable frame counter. Most syn-chronizers also have a footage counter; this one has a time counter. (J & R Film)

reproduction, the film has to be cranked at around 24 fps. Synchronizers are available with gangs of different gauges—for example, one 16mm and one 35mm gang.

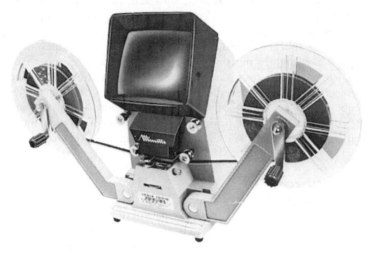

Fig. 15-5. Hervic/Minette Super 8 editor/viewer. (Hervic Corp.)

Fig. 15-6. Moviola six-plate flatbed editing table. (J & R Film)

Flatbed Editing Machines

Flatbed editing machines (sometimes called *editing tables*) are preferred for editing 16mm and 35mm films. Popular flatbeds have been made by Steenbeck, KEM, and Moviola. A *six-plate* editing table has three film transports and allows you to run one roll of picture along with two sound tracks. An eight plate gives you the possibility of two picture and two sound reels (see Fig. 15-7). With an eight-plate you can put the dailies on one pair of transports and the edited sequence on the other pair, making it very easy to search for shots and then splice them into the movie. You could also run one picture reel with three sound tracks. Some flatbeds are modular (for example, the KEM Universal), allowing the machine to be expanded to various combinations of sound and picture heads.

When editing on a flatbed, be sure to project your film on a theater screen as well to check for image defects that aren't visible on the small screen and to get a sense of pacing.

Fig. 15-7. Steenbeck eight-plate flatbed editing table. The model pictured is set up for editing 35mm picture with 16mm sound. (Steenbeck, Inc.)

MATERIALS AND SUPPLIES

Leader and Fill

Blank film for threading and writing information on, called *leader*, should be attached to the beginning (the *head leader*) and the end (the *tail leader*) of every roll of dailies, camera original, magnetic film, assembly, and outtakes. Use at least five to six feet of leader at the beginning and end of each roll and write on every leader the film title, name of production company, and roll number, as well as "head" or "tail," depending on its position in the roll (see Fig. 15-11).

Acetate leader is usually the least expensive and has a dull emulsion and a shiny base. Hold the film obliquely to a light source to distinguish the dull from the shiny side, or place the leader or film between slightly moistened lips or fingers to see which side sticks, the sticky side being the emulsion. *Polyester leader* has no emulsion (both sides are shiny) and is available in a range of colors.

Slug or *fill* is unwanted film footage used to replace damaged sections or to prep soundtracks for mixing. Discarded release prints used to be available from the lab to be used as filler, but copyright fears have reduced this practice.

Leader and slug are available in 16mm, both single- and double-perforated. You can use double-perf leader as head or tail leader only if *everything* on the roll is double-perf. Otherwise, use single-perf so that the film will not be threaded incorrectly and rip the single-perf sections. Because mag film is single-perf, 16mm magnetic film must have single-perf head and tail leaders. Use single-perf slug in mag film rolls, because double-perf slug may cause head wear and unwanted noise. Single-perf leader enables you to distinguish easily when a roll is head or tails out. Because of the advantages of single-perf, some editing rooms use only single-perf leaders and fill. When using magnetic film with leader or fill that has an emulsion side, make sure you splice the emulsion side of the leader to the base of magnetic film to avoid having the emulsion clog the sound heads. Avoid shrunken leader or film; it may chatter and jam during projection.

Other Supplies

Mark your workprint with China marker (grease pencil), which rubs off easily. White and yellow are the easiest colors to see on picture. Using grease pencil on sound can clog the sound heads. Use editing gloves when you handle original or any footage that needs special care to prevent skin oils from getting on the film. Other supplies include splicing tape, fresh film cement, sharp scissors, single-edge razor blades, film cleaner and cleaning felt, masking tape, tape for marking cans, indelible marking pens, and a hole punch.

FILM EDITING PROCEDURES

Handling Film Footage

Most films are edited with workprint, in which case the camera original should not be stored in the editing room. However, some Super 8 and 16mm films shot on reversal stock are edited with the original. Original material is irreplaceable and needs special care. If you are in doubt about whether a piece of reversal film is original or workprint, you can generally distinguish the workprint by looking at the key numbers (latent edge numbers). Original is almost invariably B-wind (see Fig. 7-10) and has key numbers that read through the base. Reversal workprint is A-wind, and its key numbers read through the emulsion. When working with camera original, keep the editing room clean and dust free. But workprint, too, should be kept as clean as possible. At the end of each day's work, cover the tables and bins with plastic. Keep the floor, in particular, clean. Don't allow food and smoking in the editing room.

Hold film by the edges to avoid getting skin oils on the picture or sound oxide. Store rolls in cans or boxes (you can get special cardboard boxes that hold a roll of picture and sound). *Cinch marks* are caused by pulling the end of a loosely wound roll to tighten it. Pushing down on the center of a tight-wound roll that has started to dish will also cause cinch marks.

A clean workprint allows you to judge the film better. It's likely that you'll show the film during the workprint stage to nonfilmmakers—investors, trial audiences, or distributors—who may have little understanding or tolerance for scratched and dirty film. When cleaning a film for a screening, use any of several commercially available cleaners, such as Kodak or Ecco film cleaner. Slightly moisten a lintless cleaning pad or felt with cleaner and sandwich the film in the folded pad as you slowly wind the film from one end to the other. Hold the pad near the feed reel and go slowly enough so that the cleaner will evaporate before the film is wound on the take-up reel; otherwise, there will be a mottle on the film, which can usually be removed by cleaning the film again. Reposition and clean the pad often to avoid the buildup of dirt that may scratch the film.

Assembling Sequences

Like all types of editing, film editing involves going through the rushes or dailies to select shots you want to use, then putting them together in an edited sequence. Like nonlinear video editing, film editing allows you to add or delete shots from the sequence at any point. When removing a shot, you can cut it out and resplice the roll, shortening the sequence. Alternately, you might choose to remove a section of picture or sound and replace it with leader or fill (called *slugging*) to maintain the previous length of the sequence and the sync relationship with the other track(s).

When measuring a length of leader to replace a shot, there are several ways to ensure the two pieces of film are the same length. You can hold the two next to each other to mark the length or put them in a synchronizer. Many editing tables have a frame counter much like a yardstick, on which you can measure frames. You can also use a flatbed's film transports to measure out longer pieces. Put the leader in one of the sound transports, and mark the first frame of leader opposite the first frame of the shot you want to take out. Roll the film forward to the last frame and mark the leader accordingly. On some flatbeds you mark the picture frame that is centered in the picture head and the sound frame that's directly on the sound head. On some machines, like many Steenbecks, you can get a more precise alignment by pulling the film down against the rollers on the side. Have someone show you the proper threading for this.

While editing sequences, individual shots can be hung on pins in a *trim bin* (*film bin*). Some editors put the shots in order in the bin before splicing them into a sequence. As noted above, when working on an eight-plate flatbed, it's easy to take shots directly from the dailies to the rough cut without hanging them in bins first. Some people like to use two flatbeds—one to search footage and the other to run the edited cut.

Trimming and Reconstituting

When you remove an entire shot or a section from the head or tail (a *trim*), hang it in a trim bin. Keep the bin organized by sequence or by edge code number so you can find footage when you want it. On feature films, editors may use *trim tabs* or *cinetabs*, which are small slips of cardboard hung in the bin to identify the shot on a given pin.

Fig. 15-8. Trim bin. You can make your own bin by bolting a wooden rack to a trash can lined with cloth or plastic. (J & R Film)

Footage not being used is considered *outtakes* or *outs*, but many shots will alternately be part of the ins and the outs as you experiment with the rough cut. One way to keep track of outs is to *reconstitute* them—that is, return them to their workprint rolls. Use ink edge code numbers or key numbers to determine their proper order. If the footage has sync sound, reconstitute in sync. It's helpful to have trims accessible in the bins, but the bins should be reconstituted periodically when they get cluttered. Arrange shots on pins in order by edge number before putting them back into the outtake rolls. You'll find that you can locate many shots that have mysteriously disappeared by looking at the bottom of the bin. When moving bins, tape the ends of the pins so shots don't fall off.

Successive fine cuts create their own outtakes. Incorporate these outtakes into the first outtake rolls; otherwise, if a trim roll is made for each version, it becomes difficult to find the extension of a particular shot, since it could be on any one of a number of rolls. It is easy to locate the extension of a shot if all the outtakes are reconstituted by edge number.

Things to Watch Out For

FLASH FRAMES. Check the beginning and end of each shot for *flash frames* (overexposed frames caused by the camera stopping with the shutter open or when the camera changes speed at the beginning or end of a take). Hold the end of the shot up to a white wall or a light box and look for variations in exposure. You must check carefully, since often a drastically overexposed frame is surrounded by several subtly overexposed ones. If you see a slight flashing at cuts when viewing the movie, this may mean you've left in some flash frames.

CUTTING FRAMES. When the negative is cut prior to printing, at least one *cutting frame* (also called *cutback frame*) is needed at the head and tail of each shot to make the cement splice (see Chapter 17). If you are using two parts of the same take (a *split shot*), delete and put aside some frames of workprint between the two shots to allow for the cement splice. Some negative cutters lose only one frame, especially if they are warned that it is a split shot, but others, as a matter of course, leave a frame or more at each end of every shot pulled from the original. To be safe, you may want to leave three or more unused cutting frames between the shots. The number of unused cutting frames is sometimes called the *cut margin*.

FADES AND DISSOLVES. Unless blowups or other special printing is needed, films are generally printed on contact printers (see Chapter 17). Contact printers usually make fades and dissolves in lengths of 16, 24, 32, 48, 64, or 96 frames. Optical printers are not restricted in fade lengths. Check with your lab to see what is available. A 48-frame fade or dissolve is fairly standard. The first and last quarters of these effects often show little noticeable change (that is, the first 12 frames of a 48-frame fade-in look dark, the last 12 have nearly full exposure), so they seem to go by quicker than the frame count would suggest. If one shot is to *dissolve* into another, find the overlapping frames. For example, a 48-frame dissolve has a 48-frame overlap, 24 frames from each shot (see Fig. 15-9). Check the overlap to make sure there are no flash frames or unwanted movements. Store the workprint of the overlap frames in a special place so it can be checked at any time for sufficient length. Too often, the negative cutter comes across a marked dissolve on the workprint and cannot find the extension in the original.

SHOTS WITHOUT KEY NUMBERS. Short shots (those fewer than 20 frames in 16mm) may not have a key number (see Fig. 7-11). Write the closest key number on the shot in grease pencil to aid the negative cutter when he or she is conforming (see Chapter 17). If for some reason an entire roll lacks key numbers, this may be a workprinting error (see p. 663) or because the original lacks key numbers. Consider having ink edge code (see p. 602) applied to the original and workprint before editing. Workprint without key numbers can be matched to the original by eye, but this is very difficult if the location of the shot on the roll of the original is not known. Shots with a lot of camera or subject movement are the easiest to eyeball. Find frames with distinctive movement, line up the original and workprint in a synchronizer, and roll them in sync to find the head and tail of the shot.

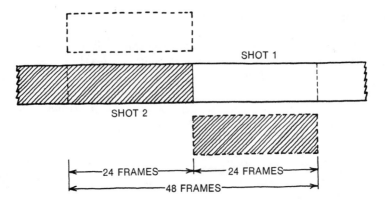

Fig. 15-9. Dissolve. Trim and put aside the workprint extensions of both shots to be used in a dissolve. A 48-frame dissolve needs a 24-frame overlap from *each* shot. This is similar to the idea of needing handles on each clip to make a dissolve on an NLE. (Carol Keller)

FOOTAGE FROM DIFFERENT SOURCES. On some productions, *stock footage* (archival or library footage) is edited with workprint footage from camera original. Sometimes the stock footage is of the wrong wind and will either project flipped or will have to be spliced in base-to-emulsion and will be out of focus during projection. When you use stock footage, be sure the footage is available in a wind that will match the camera original (B-wind). Workprint is usually A-wind. Check the stock footage for wind and, if it is B-wind, send it to the lab to be workprinted or, if it is A-wind, to be duped to change winds. Check frame lines on stock footage to make sure they match the camera original (see p. 251). Sometimes optical printing must be done to correct significant differences. If stock footage has no key numbers, edge code it and its copy for negative matching. If you are using only some of the stock footage, it is sometimes less expensive to do clip-to-clip printing (see Chapter 17).

EDITING 16MM AND 35MM. There are certain important numbers to keep in mind when editing film, and the numbers vary from 16mm to 35mm. It can sometimes get confusing when moving back and forth between the formats (for example, when printing a 16mm film on 35mm). Both formats run at 24 frames per second, but the 35mm frames are physically larger. Thus there are 40 frames per foot in 16mm and the film runs at 36 feet per minute; but there are only 16 frames per foot in 35mm and the film runs at 90 feet per minute (which is 2½ times faster). A 20-minute reel in 16mm is 720 feet; in 35mm it is 1800 feet. You can make the conversion in footage using a special editing calculator like a Reddy-Eddy, a 16/35 synchronizer (just dial the footage in one format and read the equivalent in the other) or by using any hand calculator.[1]

1. To convert a 16mm shot that is 10 feet, 3 frames long, to 35mm footage, start by converting the shot length to frames. 10 feet x 40 frames/foot = 400 frames; now add the extra 3 frames to get a total of 403 frames. 35mm has 16 frames per foot. 400 frames ÷ 16 frames/foot = 25.18 feet, or 25 feet, 3 frames.

REEL LENGTH. Films are divided into manageable lengths for editing, mixing and printing called *reels*. A typical film will be made up of several reels. In 16mm, reels more than 1000 to 1200 feet (27 to 33 minutes) are awkward to work with in the editing room. Though it is possible to print 16mm in longer lengths, some labs prefer that reels not exceed 1200 feet to minimize handling damage. The standard 35mm editing reel is about 10 minutes (1000 feet), though 35mm films are generally printed and released on 2000-foot reels (22 minutes). Talk to the lab and mixing facility for their preferences. If you're cramped for space on the reel, remember that the head and tail of the reel are reserved for printing leaders; the movie itself can't be as long as the reel. When you're done editing, the reels need to be *balanced*, so each reel is full (or nearly so) with the last reel shorter if necessary. Be attentive to the scenes at which reel breaks take place, particularly the first scene on a new reel. Avoid having reel breaks in midscene or where music is playing or before scenes with important information (in case the projectionist messes up the transition from one reel to the next). The heads and tails of reels tend to get a lot of wear and tear, so try to avoid very light scenes which show dirt more.

After a film is printed, the reels are often spliced together for projection or shown alternately on two projectors, using a changeover device. See 35mm Release Prints, p. 687, for inscribing changeover marks on the release prints. See p. 691 for special precautions when preparing sound tracks for multireel films.

MAGNETIC TRACKS AND SYNCHING DAILIES

Sound Transfer
Sound is recorded during production with an audio recorder using one of a variety of formats—hard drive, memory card, ¼-inch tape, DAT, etc. In traditional film editing, the audio is then *transferred* to sprocketed magnetic film (also called *mag stock* or *mag*) for editing with the picture.

In 16mm, editing is done with *fullcoat*, which has sprocket holes like camera film but, like audiotape, is covered on one side with a brown or black oxide for recording the sound. In 35mm, editing may be done with *stripe*, which looks like clear camera film but has a thin strip of oxide for the sound and a balance stripe on the other edge.

Sound transfers may take as long as two hours to transfer one hour of tape. Sound is usually transferred while the picture is being processed. Sound is transferred by playing the original sound and rerecording it on a *magnetic film recorder*, or *dubber*. (The word dubbing comes from "doubling"—that is, "to copy." Dubber is sometimes used to mean a machine that only plays back magnetic film.) Many modern recording devices have precise speed control, but older tape machines will need to be *resolved* to ensure proper speed during transfer. For more on resolving, see Speed Control for Sync Recording, p. 389.

If a reference tone was recorded on the original tape, use it to set the recording level during transfer. The transfer level will normally be set so that the tone reads 0 dB on the transfer equipment's VU meter. But the reference tone is just a starting point; the level needs to be checked on the actual program material. If the transfers

Fig. 15-10. Amega 16mm magnetic film recorder/reproducer. Also known as a dubber. (Rangertone Research. Inc.)

are being done by someone else, warn them of any unusually loud or quiet passages on the tape. Sometimes, a minimal amount of equalization is done during transfer; perhaps to roll off (reduce) low-frequency wind or rumble.

Handling Magnetic Tracks

As noted above, when splicing leader into the sound track, splice the emulsion side of the leader to the base side of the mag film. To prevent misthreading, use only single-perf leader for sound rolls, especially at the head and tail.

Tape splicers designed to cut picture usually work fine with mag film. Sometimes white sound splicing tape is used instead of clear tape, because it is easier to see on the mag film and it may not stretch as much, thereby avoiding sound dropouts. While picture is sometimes double-spliced (that is, taped on both base and emulsion sides) for greater strength and rigidity, never splice the oxide on magnetic stock, or sound reproduction will be interrupted.

Many editors cut 16mm sound on the diagonal, using either a diagonal Rivas splicer or a guillotine splicer equipped with both straight and diagonal cutting blades (see Fig. 15-3). (Note: various makes of diagonal splicers cut at different angles; film cut with one often cannot be butted to film cut with another.) If a straight splice stretches or is badly made, when it passes over the playback head, there will be a brief moment when *no* mag film makes contact with the head. A diagonal splice, on the other hand, even if slightly stretched, ensures that some mag film will contact the head, thus minimizing dropout. A straight cut at the beginning of a loud section of track can sometimes produce a popping or clicking sound; the same can happen if the mag film or splicer is magnetized. Diagonal cuts minimize these effects. The main drawback of diagonal splices is that if you are using the Rivas system, you will need to use two splicers. If noisy splices indicate that your splicer is magnetized, demagnetize it immediately with a bulk eraser or a hand degausser. Make several test splices on blank mag film, and listen closely with the playback volume all the way up. This is best done on a dubber to avoid being misled by mechanical noises at the splice (which are heard on some flatbeds).

Synching Up

When shooting with a video camera, sound and picture are usually recorded together right on the videotape; they are already in sync and ready to be viewed or edited. When shooting film, picture and sound are recorded separately (double system), and the picture has to be put back together with the sound before editing begins. This process is called *synchronizing the dailies, synching the rushes,* or, more commonly, just *synching up* (pronounced "sinking"). When synching is complete, every sync-sound shot on the picture is matched frame for frame to the sound track; each roll of picture has a roll of mag film of equal length that can be played back with it.

In most sync filming, there is more audio recorded than picture. This is because the sound recorder is turned on before and off after the camera and because other wild sound (perhaps for sound effects) is recorded when the camera is not running. (Of course, there is also a certain amount of MOS—silent—picture.) Some editors remove all the wild sound during synching and spool it up on separate rolls. Others leave most of it in place and splice the same length of leader or fill into the picture to keep it even with the sound roll. In general, no footage should be removed from the picture roll during synching unless absolutely necessary: moving picture from one roll to another can result in confusion when searching for footage, and throwing picture away is often regretted later.

Synching up requires an editing machine such as a Steenbeck or Moviola, or an editing bench equipped with rewinds, a synchronizer, viewer, sound head, and amplifier. There are many methods of synching up; one is outlined in Appendix G.

In 16mm, two 400-foot camera rolls are usually spliced together during synching to form one roll for editing, which fits comfortably in a 1000-foot capacity can. Longer rolls can be difficult to handle during editing, resulting in wasted time when searching for a particular shot. When the synching is complete, each roll should have one set of start marks (see Fig. 15-11) at both the head and tail, along with proper labeling so that footage can be easily identified and put in sync when needed.

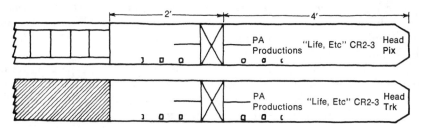

Fig. 15-11. Properly marked head leaders for editing. The start marks are the X's that cover one frame only and are directly opposite each other on picture and sound. (Carol Keller)

Many people find synching up complicated at first and later wonder why it seemed so confusing.

Slates, Accuracy, and Lip Synching

Most double-system sync footage is filmed with the help of a *slate*, whether it be a clapper board, digital slate, slate light, or a microphone tap (see p. 435). When synching up a slated shot, be sure to line up the *first* point in the picture where the slate makes contact and the first point where it is audible in the sound. Sometimes the picture slate occurs between frames. Simply line up the exact point where you think the slate occurred in the picture with the first point where you can hear it on the sound track and then shift them slightly so that the two closest frames line up. Sound that is slightly late relative to the picture is often less objectionable than sound that is slightly early.

If audio has been recorded with a timecode-capable audio recorder and filming has been done with a timecode slate or in-camera timecode (see p. 438), synching can be done by matching the timecode in picture and sound. This is typically done when synching double-system material for video editing.

At some point you will undoubtedly have to sync up a shot that has not been slated. To do this, find a surrogate slate in the scene—the closing of a door or an object being placed on a table. Learn to sync up the movements of people's lips with the sound of their words. Look for words that contain hard labial sounds like *b* and *p* for which the sound becomes audible just as the lips part. The *m* sound can be used, but it is not as precise. After approximate sync has been determined, experiment by sliding the picture two frames ahead or two back to see if you can improve synchronization. Then try moving it one frame each way. A sync error of one or two frames is usually noticeable to attentive audiences. Syncing should be checked carefully (preferably by projecting dailies on a big screen) before edge coding (see below). Sync errors detected after coding are annoying, and after a print is made, very upsetting!

Edge Code (Ink Edge Numbers)

After the workprint has been synched up, an edge coding machine can be used to print identical ink numbers along the edge of the picture and sound rolls (see Fig. 15-12). By lining up the numbers, you can instantly ensure that the picture and sound for any shot are in sync. Also, the numbers allow you to quickly find any section of mag film, which is otherwise hard to do. These numbers are variously called *edge code, edge numbers, ink edge numbers, machine edge numbers, rubber numbers,* or *Acmade numbers* (after one brand of coding machine). They all mean the same thing. Don't confuse edge code with timecode or keycode (see Key Numbers and Edge Identification, p. 271).

In 16mm, edge code is printed every 16, 20, or 40 frames, depending on the setup of the coding machine. In 35mm, code is usually printed every foot (16 frames). There are different numbering systems; one system uses two letters followed by four digits (such as AA1234). Another format uses an eight-digit prefix, a four-digit footage count and a two-digit frame count (AB904434-1428 + 10). Whatever system is being used, indicate a starting code for each roll when submitting the footage to the lab or coding facility. Every pair of sound and picture rolls

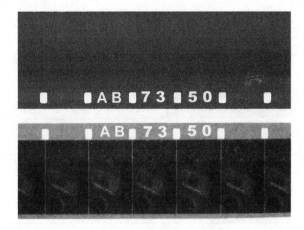

Fig. 15-12. Edge code. After picture and sound rolls have been put in sync, ink edge code is printed identically along the edge of the workprint and the magnetic film.

will then have the same set of numbers printed on them. On some productions, an edge-coding machine is rented for the editing room.

When you get footage back from being coded, put the sound and picture in a synchronizer or editing machine and check that the numbers are in sync with your start marks and that they run continuously without errors from the head of the roll to the tail. On some machines, the ink can occasionally spread into the picture area. In general, ink numbering on the original should be avoided.

MARKING WORKPRINT AFTER PICTURE LOCK

When you're done editing (and the picture is locked or "frozen") the workprint is marked with grease pencil to indicate to the negative matcher how various splices are to be treated:

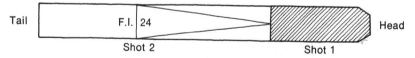

Indicates that shot 2 should begin black and FADE-IN to normal exposure. A 24-frame fade-in is indicated here.

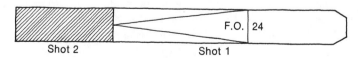

Indicates that shot 1 should begin with normal exposure and FADE-OUT to black. As marked, shot 2 would begin with normal exposure.

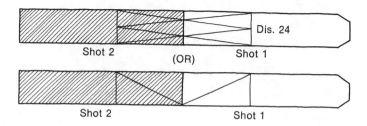

Indicates a DISSOLVE between shots 1 and 2. Note that this is simply a fade-out that overlaps a fade-in.

Indicates a DOUBLE EXPOSURE of shots 1 and 2 so that both will be visible simultaneously. This marking is also used for superimposed titles. The beginning and end of shot 2 are cut and spliced into their proper place, indicating the extent of the double exposure. Include enough frames so that there is a key number in each piece.

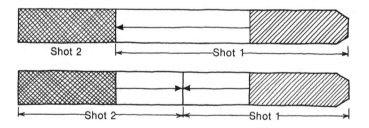

The EXTENDED SCENE marking is used when a piece of workprint has to be replaced with leader because of torn or damaged frames. The arrow indicates to which scene the frames of leader belong.

The UNINTENTIONAL SPLICE mark indicates that a shot has been cut in editing and then put back together, so no cut should be made in the original (normally, the negative matcher will plan to cut the original anywhere he finds a splice in the workprint). A careful matcher should check to make sure all splices are intentional regardless of the mark. You can make splices even clearer by putting vertical lines down the center of all *intentional* splices. It is a good idea to put vertical lines to mark the extent of fades and dissolves and to write their lengths in numbers on the workprint. Some negative matchers prefer the markings on the base, others on the emulsion. See Preparing the Original for Printing, p. 665, for more on this process.

EDITING FILM ON VIDEO

There used to be a fairly standard process of getting a film project from the camera to the screen. Budgets varied, techniques varied, but the workflow (it wasn't called workflow then) of making a workprint, editing it, conforming the negative, and making prints was relatively predictable (see Traditional Film Editing, p. 57, for an overview).

Today, most projects shot on film are transferred to video for editing on a non-linear system and they may or may not return to the original film negative before making prints. Instead of a standard workflow, we now have numerous options and combinations of options. Changing technologies, which include new types of tape and disk recorders as well as evolving digital television standards, are changing how people work. As we move into the future, old assumptions about how things have been done are replaced by new workflows.

Choosing your route through the maze of production and postproduction should be done in consultation with the lab or postproduction facility. At many points you must juggle questions of cost, time, quality, and control over the material. Before you even start shooting, talk to the lab, telecine house, editing facility, audio post facility, and negative cutter. Get the cinematographer and sound recordist in on those conversations too. It's hard to overstate the importance of working out your planned workflow with all concerned parties in advance.

In other chapters you'll find discussions of production techniques, film-to-video transfer, nonlinear editing, and working with the film lab. This section is about issues specific to editing film projects on video. It starts with some possible workflows, then explores working with picture, sound, timecode, and other elements relating to film in the video environment. Many of the same issues apply to working with 24p HD video.

Warning: The material in this chapter may give you a headache or make you consider a different career altogether. Take two aspirin and remember that, though there are a hundred ways to get from the beginning of the process to the end, eventually you only have to pick *one*.

SOME FILM-VIDEO WORKFLOWS

This section examines some possible workflows that can be used for projects that originate on film (or on 24p video). The scenarios are not offered as recommendations, but rather as a way to discuss various options. There are many ways of working and elements from one workflow might be combined with another.

A Note About Frame Rates

Planning a workflow for film production and postproduction involves numerous choices about equipment and methods. Some of those choices hinge on the frame rate(s) you're using for different parts of the process. Which frame rates you use may depend on the part of the world you're working in (NTSC countries or PAL countries), the equipment available to you, and the end product you want to create. It might be helpful to start with a refresher about frame rates.

NTSC COUNTRIES. At one time the only way to edit film-originated movies on video in NTSC countries was at 60i (30 fps). Now we also have the ability to edit at 24p.

If the movie is being made for television and will be broadcast at 60i, it may simplify things to transfer the film in the telecine to 60i video and then just treat it like any other 60i video project. This involves using 2:3 pulldown. See Pulldown Revisited, p. 565, for a discussion of how pulldown and reverse pulldown works.

However, there are advantages to editing at 24p. Doing so can simplify your workflow and increase cutting accuracy if you plan to telecine the film more than once (see below) or release the movie on film. There are also benefits to creating a 24p HD master from which multiple formats and international versions can be derived (PAL, NTSC, DVD, etc.). Editing at 24p may still involve transferring the material to a 60i format beforehand (using 2:3 pulldown), but if this is done, reverse pulldown is used to restore the 24p stream in the NLE.

When working with a 24p format, it's important to keep in mind that the universal standard speed for film cameras is 24 fps and some HD video cameras and NLEs can also operate at true 24p. However, in countries where NTSC video is used, video frame rates are usually 0.1 percent slower than the integer number (see

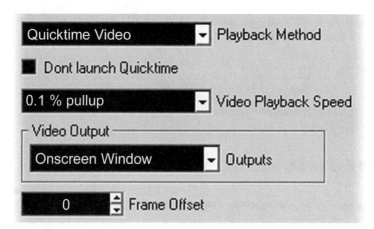

Fig. 15-13. The Nuendo digital audio workstation offers this pullup/pulldown option to increase or decrease playback speed by 0.01 percent or 4 percent for working with NTSC or PAL material. (Steinberg Media Technologies)

The Frame Rate, p. 15). So, when a video camera or deck indicates it's operating at "24p," that usually means 23.976p.[2]

What does this 0.1 percent slowdown mean to you? Well, first of all, you can't hear it or see it. Footage playing at 24p will look the same as 23.976p. However, if sound is running at one rate and the picture is running 0.1 percent faster or slower, they will go out of sync with each other. There are postproduction workflows that involve transferring 24 fps film to 23.976 fps video or to 29.97 fps video. It's essential that the 0.1 percent slowdown involved be taken into account when working with audio (this is discussed more in Importing Audio, p. 619). It's also important to be clear whether you mean 24p or 23.976p as you plan workflows.

PAL COUNTRIES. In countries where PAL has been used, frame rates are simpler. Film can be shot for television at 25 fps and telecined to 25p video in a simple frame-to-frame transfer with no speed change or pulldown. SD or HD video at 25p or 50i runs at *exactly* the stated rate.

When film is shot for cinema projection at 24 fps and transferred to 25p video there are options about how to handle it. The most common method is to speed the film up to 25 fps in the telecine (a 4.1 percent increase), which again provides a simple frame-to-frame transfer. This is sometimes called the *24@25* method. It will cause the audio to rise in pitch slightly (about a half tone), which can be digitally processed later if desired to lower the pitch. Depending on your NLE and your preferences, you may then edit at 25p or slow the NLE down to 24p for editing. When projected in a theater at 24 fps, this will run normally, and when shown on television at 25 fps, it will have a 4.1 percent shorter running time and higher pitched audio.

You can also use pulldown to transfer with no speed change. With the 24 + 1 telecine pulldown method, sometimes called PAL+1, an extra field is added every 12 frames, adding one video frame every second, bringing 24 fps up to 25 fps. With this method, audio remains at normal speed.

Scenario One: Shoot Film, Transfer Once, Finish on Video

This might be used for a project shot on film and destined primarily for video distribution or television broadcast. It is geared toward a relatively quick postproduction schedule. If film prints are needed, they are made by doing a video-to-film transfer from the final video master. See Fig. 15-14.

In this scenario, film may be shot in any format (35mm, 16mm, or Super 8) and production audio on location can be recorded in a variety of formats, using a file-based (disk or memory card) recorder, DAT, or ¼-inch tape machine. Timecode on the audio is highly recommended. If audio is recorded without timecode it may be necessary to post-stripe it with code later.

In-camera timecode or timecode slates (see p. 438) during production will greatly facilitate synching the audio, but timecode on the film is not required.

After shooting, the negative is processed (see Chapter 17) and prepared for the

---

2. People often round 23.976 to 23.98 or 23.97 for convenience.

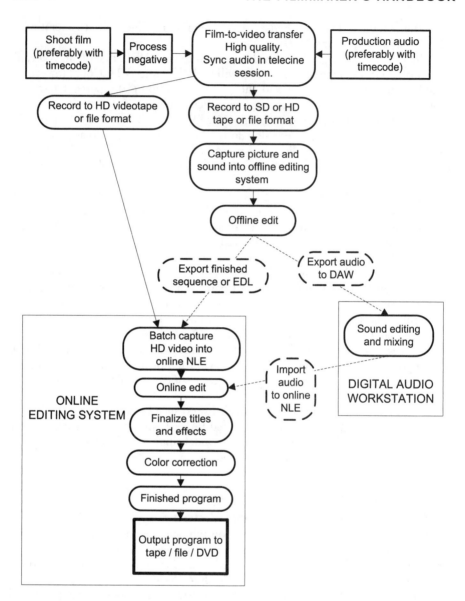

Fig. 15-14. Scenario One. A possible route for shooting film, editing on a nonlinear system and finishing in video.

film-to-video transfer (see Chapter 18). When film workprints (*dailies*) are made for feature films, it is common to separate the *circled* or selected takes (the *buys*) for printing and weed out the other material (*B-negative*) prior to making the work-print. For video transfer, however, often the negative is left intact. Everything may be transferred or the telecine can fast-forward through undesired material to record only the selected takes.

In this workflow, the film will only be transferred to video *once*, so the telecine output is recorded to a high-quality video format, often HD (a high-quality SD format such as DigiBeta is also possible, but has disadvantages). In some workflows, the telecine transfer is done directly to computer drives or disks, bypassing videotape altogether.

Because this is the only video transfer that will be done, a degree of care must be taken in color correction—more than for the "video dailies" used in Scenario Two (see p. 611). Even so, final color correction will be done later in the process.

In this scenario, the sound and picture are put in sync during the telecine session. If the film and audio have proper timecode, there are automated systems that can sync up on the fly during the telecine transfer. However, if picture and sound need to be lined up manually, it can get expensive in the telecine suite. Some facilities have a *layback suite*. Here, you could take a master tape from the telecine that has no audio and sync it up in this specialized room that bills at a lower hourly rate (see Fig. 15-15).

Fig. 15-15. The layback suite is an editing room specifically set up for synching audio sources to video. Less expensive than synching sound in the telecine suite. (DuArt Film and Video).

The reason to sync up at this stage is so that the master videotapes will have sound on them. This simplifies other postproduction tasks and makes it easy to create video dailies for the production team on location or for whoever needs them. In Scenario Two, the sound is synched later, using the nonlinear editing system to do the work. Synching on the NLE may be the most economical and can result in better sync.[3] However, synching on the editing system may delay getting the dailies

---

3. In the telecine, sync is adjusted in one-frame increments; in the NLE you can slide audio plus or minus one quarter frame or less. Also sync errors in the telecine can result from the difference between the 24 fps film rate and 30 fps audio TC rate.

out for viewing and can make it more cumbersome or sometimes even impossible to generate good-quality versions for screening.

In this scenario, you may leave the transfer facility with two sets (or more) of videotapes. One set is the HD master tapes, which will be put aside and used later for the online edit. The second set could be a downconversion from HD to SD (perhaps to 16:9 DVCAM) to be used for the offline edit. The reason to do the offline in SD is to lessen the storage and processing load on the NLE (see p. 520). If you'd prefer not to make a whole set of SD tapes, you could instead set up an HD deck in the editing room and do the downconversion to SD on the fly as you capture the material into the NLE.

If you did the original telecine recording at 23.976 fps, then 2:3 pulldown will be used to create SD tapes at 60i. Reverse pulldown is then done on capture into the NLE if you want to edit at 23.976p or 24p.

Another approach avoids using SD at all. Instead, the HD tapes are captured directly to the NLE using a compressed HD offline codec (such as a low bit rate version of DNxHD) to lighten the load on the NLE. This means no pulldown or reverse pulldown is needed.

After the material has been loaded into the NLE, you're ready to do your offline edit. As mentioned earlier, many projects destined for television in NTSC countries are edited at 60i, but there are various reasons to edit at 23.976p, especially if the initial transfer was done at 23.976.[4]

When you're done with the offline edit and have "locked picture," you're ready to do the online. Often, this is done at a postproduction facility equipped for HD with all the monitors and decks you need. Or, you may be doing the online yourself. Either way, a batch capture is done to bring the original HD media into the online NLE.[5] Then an auto-assemble is done to rebuild the sequence with the HD media (this is a typical offline/online workflow, see p. 516). Color correction may be done at this stage or later on a specialized system.

Generally, audio will be exported to a digital audio workstation (DAW) for mixing in a dedicated sound studio (see Chapter 16). The audio is reimported to the online.

At this point, the show is complete and can be duplicated to various formats and frame rates as needed. If a film negative or prints are required for film distribution, a film-out can be done from the video master.

Scenario Two: Shoot Film, Transfer Twice, Finish via Film

This workflow might be used for a project that is shot on film, edited without a lot of visual effects (*Vfx*), and finished by conforming the original film negative. It allows you to edit with an NLE, then produce film prints in the traditional way, if you choose. Rather than do an online edit to create the final video master, in this scenario you do a film-to-video transfer of the finished film (see Fig. 15-16).

Like Scenario One, this begins with film shot in any format and production

4. In PAL countries you could simply transfer from 50i SD tapes to 25p.
5. Or, if you prefer, you could do an online within a linear tape-to-tape online suite.

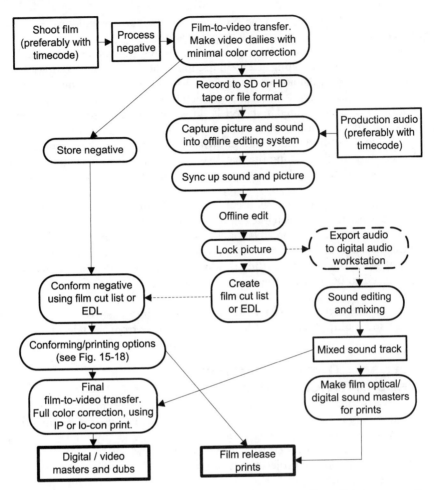

Fig. 15-16. Scenario Two. A conventional route for shooting film, editing on a nonlinear system, and finishing on film. Final video transfer is done from the film (see Fig. 15-17).

audio that has been recorded in one of several possible formats. As noted above, although it is to your considerable advantage to record the sound with timecode and use timecode slates or in-camera timecode, this isn't necessary.

Unlike Scenario One, here the negative is transferred to video for offline editing purposes *only*. These are *video dailies* made as quickly as possible with minimal color correction (one-light transfer). To keep costs down in the transfer, no sound is transferred at this time. The telecine compiles a *shot log*, which is a database that correlates the film keycode numbers and the video timecode generated during the transfer (see p. 705).

Some people choose to record to HD. However, since this video transfer is just for offline editing, let's say instead, an SD recording to tape or file is made using 2:3 pulldown to convert to 60i. At the end of the telecine session you have a set of tapes or files on disk for loading into the nonlinear editing system.

The picture is captured into the NLE and, ideally, reverse pulldown is used (if needed) to restore it to 24 fps or 23.976 fps for editing.

In this scenario, the production audio is transferred directly into the nonlinear editing system. If you're editing at 23.976 fps, the audio must be slowed down by 0.1 percent (see Importing Audio, p. 619). If you're working in PAL, the sound may need to be sped up by 4.1 percent. The sound and picture are then put in sync.

The movie is offline edited in the NLE. Then picture is locked and you're ready for finishing. In this workflow, the next step is to have the original camera negative conformed to the offline edit so you can strike film prints (or make an interpositive first). This may involve cutting the negative into A&B rolls, or stringing takes together for optical printing from a single strand. For more on negative cutting and printing, see Chapter 17.

Some NLEs can generate a film cut list that tells the negative matcher exactly where to cut the negative using key numbers (see Film Cut Lists, p. 622). If your system can't make a cut list, an EDL can be used for the conforming process.

In this scenario, audio is exported for mixing on a separate system. After mixing, an optical soundtrack is created for making film prints. A digital sound track is also produced to be used for the video transfer and any Digital Cinema playback systems.

The final film is then transferred to video from an interpositive or low-contrast film print and multiple versions or formats can be made from the telecine transfer.

Scenario Three: Shoot Film, Transfer Twice, Finish via Film-Out/D.I.

Film is a wonderful medium for shooting. With its unique image qualities, it still holds an important place in production, particularly for feature films. However, when it comes to doing effects, composites, and any number of other things in postproduction, video is far more powerful and easier to work with. It's increasingly common for projects that originate on film to transfer to video for all the post work. Rather than cut the original negative to make film prints, the final online video master becomes the source for a video-to-film transfer (film-out). This gives you an enormous amount of control over the image, and allows you to do things that would be impossible or impossibly expensive any other way. The film-out produces an interpositive or negative from which film prints can be made.

For big-budget films, instead of using a normal telecine to transfer the camera negative to video, a high-resolution film scanner can be used to create a 2K or 4K data file (see p. 713). When working at this resolution, the master version created in the online is called a *digital intermediate* or D.I. (see p. 718). The D.I. is then recorded to film. It's the same idea as doing a film-out, but uses the most sophisticated technology and produces the highest-quality images. Sometimes people use the term D.I. to mean any high-quality video master from which film versions can be made. (A good case can be argued for making a 24p HD transfer at 4:4:4 RGB to HDCAM SR, which is virtually a match for 2K, and it's cheaper.)

This scenario combines various elements of the previous two scenarios (see Fig. 15-17).

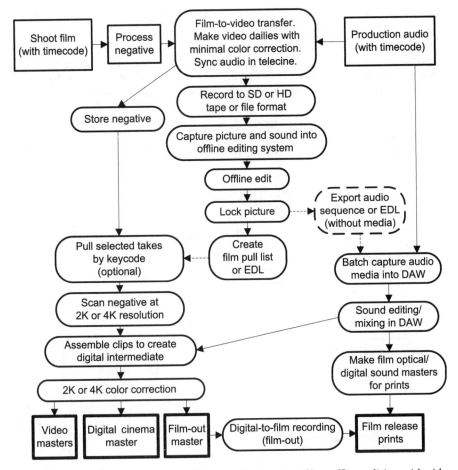

Fig. 15-17. Scenario Three. A possible route for shooting film, offline editing with video dailies, then retransferring the film to create a digital intermediate and online master.

We begin much like Scenario Two, by making video dailies with minimal color correction to SD or HD. Synching is done in the telecine. A shot log of the transfer is generated. An offline edit is done in the NLE at 23.976 or 24 fps. Picture is locked.

Now we go back to the camera original negative, but rather than cut it up to make film prints, we're going to transfer it to video again—at high resolution. This time we'll transfer only the sections that are actually used in the final sequence (the *selects*). This is much like trimming the media in a typical offline/online workflow (see p. 549), and saves hours of telecine time as well as allowing for much better color correction since you know how the sequence goes together.

The NLE generates a pull list (see p. 622) to locate the selected negative that needs to be retransferred. Some systems can do this by film keycode, which is the most reliable way. Alternatively, an EDL can be used to find the shots by timecode. The selects for retransfer may be strung together on a reel; instead of cutting shots precisely to the frame, as you would in the typical negative-matching process, entire scenes can be strung together (flash frame to flash frame). If you shoot Super 16 and don't wish to subject the original negative to the handling that goes with negative cutting (not to mention the extra expense), you might want to inquire whether a particular facility's scanner or DataCine can simply transfer the desired sections from the rolls of camera original negative, fast-forwarding between the desired sections as needed.

For a typical project, this second transfer can be done to HD video. This is a fully color-corrected transfer. An auto-assemble can then be done on a high-powered HD online system to rebuild the sequence with the new HD media.

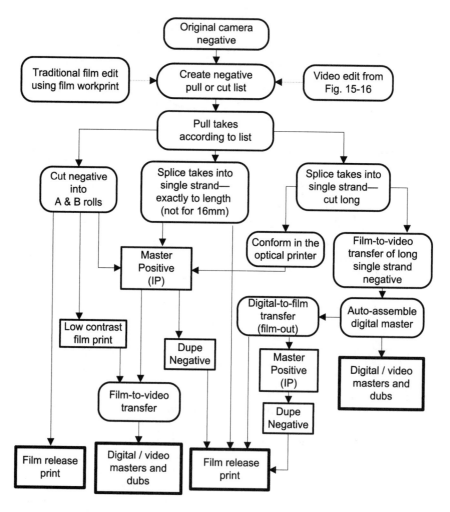

Fig. 15-18. Options for cutting film negative and creating film prints, intermediates, and video transfers. The initial negative pull or cut list may be produced from a video edit (see Fig. 15-16) or a traditional film edit with workprint.

For a high-budget project, this second transfer can be done as a scan to a 2K or 4K data format (which is shown in Fig. 15-17). Again, an online is done to assemble the sequence with the scanned data files to create a digital intermediate.

Either way, the digital master is made. One version is color-corrected for film output (which requires different color settings than for video output). That is sent to a film recorder to create a film negative for making film prints. Another version of the digital master is color-corrected for video and can be output in various formats; still another version is corrected for Digital Cinema projection in theaters via file-based servers.

These days, many SD digital video formats have very good audio quality. This means that production audio recorded in the field that has been transferred to SD video in the editing process can be used for the final audio mix.[6] However, particularly on high-budget films, the sound editors may prefer to use the original production audio disks or tapes as a source for the final mix. This may be because, on a concert film, for example, the production audio was recorded at a higher sample rate or bit depth; or, perhaps because a lower-quality analog format was used in the telecine. In this scenario, rather than export audio from the NLE for the mix, an audio EDL or sequence is used to recapture the production audio into a DAW for mixing. Different mixes may be done for different versions or formats. Afterward, the mixed tracks are recombined with the video master and an optical master is made for film prints.

EDITING METHODS

As discussed above, with projects that originate on 24 fps film or 24p video, there are advantages to editing at 24p (either true 24p or 23.976p). If you offline edit the project on NTSC video at 30 fps, translating back to the negative can be more complex and may introduce errors (see below).

NTSC COUNTRIES. If, as in Scenario Two, you recorded to a 30 fps video format in the telecine, you can still edit at 24p on many NLEs. Some NLEs use reverse 2:3 pulldown to convert from 30 fps back to 24 fps during the capture. Sometimes NLEs capture the full 30 fps stream, but only *display* the 24 frames each second that correspond to the original film frames. Either method should be equally accurate in terms of creating film cut lists, but the second one uses 20 percent more disk storage. If you edit at 24 fps, you can still get a normal 30 fps video output when you need it—for example, to make screening cassettes—by adding 2:3 pulldown on output.

There may also be times when you need a 30 fps EDL (perhaps for sound work or video rerecording). Keep in mind that slight rounding errors like the ones that occur when going from 30 fps to 24 (as described below) also occur when going from 24 fps to 30.

---

6. Quality varies among formats. Uncompressed PCM audio tracks at 48kHz, 16 or 20 bits, are common in video formats and will serve fine if the original audio was recorded at a similar resolution.

PAL COUNTRIES. For projects in PAL countries, if you telecine the film at 25 fps, you can edit at 25 fps in the NLE, or, you can slow the playback to 24p in the NLE (if your NLE is capable of it). Either way, there shouldn't be errors returning to the film.

When You Have a Workprint

Feature filmmakers may make a film workprint of the negative even though editing will be done in video on a nonlinear system. This is because a film workprint gives a better indication of how the finished film will look, and may be preferable for the production team to spot errors and judge lighting and lenses. The workprint may also be used for test screenings. In this case, if desired, the workprint and sprocketed mag film may be put in sync the traditional way (using a film editing machine) prior to the transfer to video. The workprint and mag are edge-coded (see p. 602) after they've been synched, and the edge code is recorded along with the timecode and keycode during the transfer (see Ink Edge Code, p. 705). The edit is done in video on the nonlinear editing system. For the first test screening, the NLE generates an *assemble list* (see p. 622) with which you can conform the workprint to the video edit. You then do your test screening and go back to the nonlinear editor. After you make changes, the system generates a *change list* that highlights exactly where to change the workprint to match the new video version. Change lists are not practical when using an NLE running at 30 fps.

There is always a potential for errors in translating an NLE sequence to a cut negative (and the consequences of screwing it up are great!). Some productions prefer a workprint because it provides old-fashioned safeguards against error. Even so, fewer and fewer projects are spending the money to strike workprints.

Editing Video Assist Dailies

To save time and money, some filmmakers start editing video recorded directly from the film camera's video assist (see p. 247). This allows editing to be done right on the set, giving instant feedback on the shooting and providing quick turnarounds for rush projects. It also allows you to preselect negative that needs to be transferred to video, which can save money in the telecine.

Bear in mind that the video assist image differs from the negative in two major ways. First, you get no reading of whether the exposure, processing, or handling of the negative is okay (you must rely on the lab's report on the negative for this information). Second, the film camera's mirror shutter alternately sends light to the video assist or the film; the film and the video don't both record an image at the same moment. So if you edit the video assist tape, some of your edit points will be off slightly compared to where you might have cut if you were viewing a transfer from the negative.

Editing video assist dailies can be an effective tool for pre-editing material that will be edited in the usual way later. If used as the primary means of editing—for example, on a very low-budget production—it can have serious drawbacks.

CAPTURING SOUND AND PICTURE TO THE NLE

Managing Data

While you're busy editing, putting together clips into a sequence, the NLE is busy keeping track of how those clips relate to the video you captured from, to the film that generated that video in the telecine, and to the audio that was recorded in the field. It's crucial that the relationships between these different types of data be set up correctly when you capture clips into the NLE and that no errors are introduced.

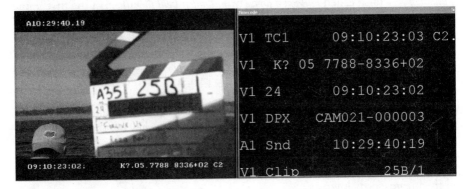

Fig. 15-19. Telecine and video data. This Avid display shows the data that the system is tracking, which includes: the timecode of the offline SD video (09:10:23:03); the pulldown phase (C2); the film keycode (K? 05 7788-8336+02), and the timecode of the production audio (10:29:40:19). As you can see, the 24 fps timecode from the 24p HD master (09:10:23:02) has the same hours, minutes, and seconds as the 30 fps timecode from the SD offline tapes, but the frame count is different because of their different frame rates. Keycode, by comparison, references each original film frame *exactly* because it is recorded on the film's edge by the manufacturer. Keycode is the most reliable common reference among multiple video transfers. (Michael Phillips/Avid Technologies, Inc.)

Part of this job is done by the shot log (see Shot Logs, p. 705). The shot log may be imported into the NLE to guide a batch capture process. As you capture clips, make sure the data in the shot log is accurate. The key numbers and timecode should match in the log, the burn-in numbers on screen, and in the NLE's timecode display.[7]

Michael Phillips, developer of the Avid Film Composer, suggests creating confidence lists to help verify that the numbers are correct. (These instructions are for Avid systems but a similar method can be applied to other systems.) To do this, create columns in each bin with these headings: start, camroll, kn start, kn mark-in, clip name. Then load each clip in the source monitor and mark an In Point at the

---

7. If you're capturing 30 fps material to 24p, the frame count in the burn-in video timecode will not match the 24-frame NLE timecode.

frame where the slate closes. This should bring up the key number for that frame in the kn mark-in column. Do this for every clip and then print out a hard copy of the bin list and send it to the negative cutter. The negative cutter can then check a few takes by running down the slate and examining the actual key number on film. This way, he or she can verify that the key numbers entered into the system are correct.

Managing Pulldown

If you've transferred 24 fps film to 30 fps video (60i) and want to edit at 24 fps in the NLE, reverse pulldown needs to be done to convert back to 24p. To do this accurately, and to track timecode and keycode correctly, the NLE needs to know the *pulldown type* (also called *pulldown phase* or *pulldown field identifier*) of the first frame of each clip. The pulldown type of the first frame of a clip is sometimes called the *pullin*. Pullin information should be included in the shot log and can be imported automatically when batch capturing clips. With some NLEs if you're capturing from a continuous strand of negative with continuous timecode, you can simply set the pulldown type of just one frame on the reel, and then capture whatever you want.

Sometimes there are errors and you need to enter the pullin manually. You should see the pulldown type for any frame following the key number burned in on screen (see Fig. 15-19). Pulldown type is often indicated as A1, A2, B1, B2, B3, etc. If you had an A frame transfer, A frames will have timecode ending in :00, :05, or multiples of five frames. You can also figure out pulldown type yourself by looking at the image (see below).

UNDERSTANDING PULLDOWN TYPE. How pulldown works can be very confusing. To see what's going on, look at Fig. 15-20 (you may also want to look at Fig. 14-30). Figure 15-20 shows a group of four film frames transferred to five frames of 60i video. Notice that film frame A is transferred to two fields of video (A1 and A2). Frame B is transferred to three fields (B1, B2, and B3). Frame C is also transferred to two fields, but they are split between two *different* video frames.

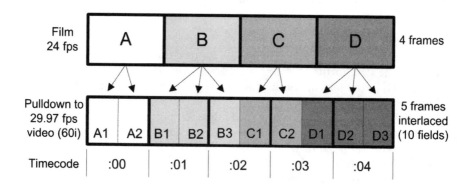

Fig. 15-20. This shows the relationship of pulldown and timecode in an A-frame film transfer using normal pulldown. See also Fig. 14-30.

Here's a way of looking at them:

1. Frame A is transferred to both fields that make up video frame 1. (Two fields total—A1, A2—no timecode change between the fields.)
2. Frame B is transferred to both fields of video frame 2, and to the first field of video frame 3. (Three fields total—B1, B2, B3—timecode change between fields 2 and 3.)
3. Frame C is transferred to the second field of frame 3 and the first field of frame 4. (Two fields total—C1, C2—timecode change between the fields.)
4. Frame D is transferred to the second field of video frame 4 and both fields of video frame 5. (Three fields total—D1, D2, D3—timecode change between fields 1 and 2.)

The pattern shown in Fig. 15-20 is a common way of transferring film (A frame transfer, field 1 dominant). The A film frame is transferred to video frames whose timecode numbers end in :00, :05, and multiples of five frames after that. Thus, the A frame falls on timecode 01:00:00:00, 01:00:00:05, and so on.

If the pulldown type is not indicated, you can figure it out by slowly stepping through the video field by field while watching on a monitor. Find a distinct frame, say a hole-punch or the moment where the clap sticks come together. If two fields are identical and there is no timecode change between them, you're looking at an A frame (note that the A frame is special in having this simple one-to-one relationship between film and video frames). If two fields are identical but the timecode changes between them, that's a C frame. If three fields are identical but there is a timecode change between the first and second field, you're looking at a D frame.

Nondrop timecode should be used when possible. If the video has drop frame timecode, avoid frames where the code jumps. There are transfer patterns other than the one shown in Fig. 15-20 that will vary in terms of where the pulldown type falls relative to timecode.

When working with PAL or other direct frame-to-frame transfers where no pulldown is used, pulldown type doesn't exist. What a relief!

Importing Audio
See Audio in the Telecine, p. 706, before reading this.

NTSC COUNTRIES. Say you shoot double system with a video camera at 23.976 fps (also known as 24p) and a separate audio recorder. You capture the video into the NLE and edit at 23.976 fps (the typical "24p" video rate) or at 60i. The video is running in real time on the NLE. You can capture the audio you recorded separately, and picture and sound should sync up fine, assuming you used an audio recorder with precise speed control.

Now imagine you shoot film double system with a *film* camera running at 24 fps and a separate audio recorder. You transfer the film to video, which is typically running at either 23.976 fps or 29.97 fps (60i). To do this, the film is slowed 0.1 percent in the telecine. You again capture the video to the NLE for editing at 23.976 fps. You try to capture the audio you recorded separately, and you find that picture and sound go out of sync. That's because the audio is running in real time, but the video is running 0.1 percent slower.

There are several solutions to this problem:

If you have the audio synched in the telecine, they will slow it down to match the picture and you can import it normally with the video. This slowing of audio is sometimes also called pulldown (see p. 706).

If your NLE supports it, you can speed the picture up 0.1 percent to true 24 fps before synching the audio. This allows you to import audio digitally at standard 48 kHz sample rate with no frame rate conversion.

If you want to edit at 23.976 fps, you can slow the audio 0.1 percent during capture or after. As noted on p. 435 and p. 706, some audio recorders can be set to 48.048 kHz sample rate. Some editing systems will then "stamp" that as standard 48 kHz, which effectively slows the audio 0.1 percent. Other NLEs use different methods to slow the sound.

As long as you keep in mind whether you're working with real-time media or media that's been slowed 0.1 percent, you can decide if you need to correct for the difference. Discuss workflow plans with the post team.

Projects edited at 24p or 23.976p will need to have pulldown applied to record out to a 60i tape. Some systems have trouble exporting true 24p to 60i, given the 0.1 percent speed difference.

PAL COUNTRIES. When 24 fps film is transferred to 25 fps video in the typical way, there is a 4.1 percent increase in speed. If you slow the video down in the NLE to edit at 24 fps, you can import double-system sound into the NLE with no speed change; if you edit at 25 fps, it will need to be speed adjusted.

SPECIAL CONSIDERATIONS WHEN EDITING FILM ON VIDEO

For some workflows, like the ones described in Scenarios One and Three above, the project is shot on film, but it is finished on video. Even if film prints are eventually made, they come from a video master, not from the traditional method of cutting negative and creating optical effects in a film printer. If you are using such a workflow, this section doesn't apply to you.

For projects like the one in Scenario Two, video is used as an offline editing tool with the goal of cutting the film negative and making film prints. Video and film are different animals, and some things you do in a video edit might not easily translate back to a film finish. There are a number of things to keep in mind.

Dupe Frames and Cutting Frames

When you're editing video you can repeat a shot as many times as you want. For example, you might want to use a certain establishing shot several times in your movie. In film, every shot is based on one piece of negative, which normally can be put in only *one* place in the movie. If you want to use the same shot twice, that footage will usually need to be *duped* (duplicated; see Chapter 17).

Also, at the head and tail of every shot, the negative cutter needs at least a half frame to cement-splice the negative. If you take a shot and cut it into two pieces, you need to leave at least one unused frame between the pieces. This is called a *cutting frame* or *cutback frame* (see p. 597). Many nonlinear editing systems have a "dupe detection" feature that warns you if you've reused any part of a shot or left insufficient cutting frames between shots. When editing at 30 fps on an NLE, leave at least *two* video frames unused so you will be sure to have at least *one* film frame.

If you are printing the negative from a single strand on an optical printer, you may not have to worry about dupes or cutting frames (see p. 671).

Fades and Dissolves

When making fades and dissolves, video editors can choose virtually any length effect. Film contact printing machines (see p. 666), on the other hand, offer a standard set of fade and dissolve lengths and you should try to use one of them. Check with your lab for available lengths. Standards usually include 16, 24, 32, 48, 64, or 96 frames, which (at 24 fps) is .67, 1, 1.33, 2, 2.67, or 4 seconds. If you are working on a nonlinear editing system running at 30 fps, the equivalent video effects are 20, 30, 40, 60, 80, and 120 frames (although some of these are not exact matches). Some nonlinear systems can print out an optical list, which will help you identify any nonstandard effects you may have used.

Bear in mind that fades and dissolves in film may look different than they do in video. In video, a shot being faded up from black or dissolved in over another shot will usually have a steady (linear) increase in exposure. In film, there is usually no visible change in the first quarter of the effect, a steeper "ramp" in the middle, then no change in the last quarter. Some nonlinear systems have a special fade to mimic the film look and the particular way light values mix in film as opposed to video.

Visual Effects

As for more complex video effects and things like titles, you can try to re-create them in film (for example, by using an optical printer, or by filming titles) or you can generate them in video and do a video-to-film transfer of that effect, which can then be cut in with the rest of your negative. This is often done by resing-up the effect shot to HD (if it's not already HD) and outputting a high-resolution file (such as a numbered image sequence or uncompressed QuickTime file; see p. 563). If there are many complex effects, it may be cheaper to do a film-out or D.I. of the whole movie and avoid printing from the original negative at all.

FROM THE NLE BACK TO FILM

As discussed above, in several workflows you do the offline edit on the NLE, then return to the original camera negative to retransfer it to video and/or to conform it so you can make film prints.

If you edited at 24 fps (either true 24p or 23.976p), you should be able to generate a frame-accurate list of the negative used in the final sequence. Sometimes the list is generated from an EDL using timecode. However, it's generally preferable if your NLE can make the list using film key numbers (keycode) from the original transfer. Specialized software is sometimes required. Final Cut Pro uses Cinema Tools to generate lists; Avid uses FilmScribe.

The lab or negative matcher will use the key numbers and/or the timecode to find the negative that corresponds to the clips you used in the NLE sequence.

Film Cut Lists

Several types of lists are used to translate from the NLE to the film negative or workprint. Remember, when talking about negative cutting and film postproduction, an *individual* shot or clip is called a "scene" (as opposed to the meaning of the word in shooting, where a "scene" can be made up of several shots).

- *Assemble list.* Shows all the scenes in their proper order. Includes the beginning and ending footage and frame count of each scene; the first and last key number of each shot; the lab roll number; the camera roll number; and the clip name.
- *Pull list.* Tells the negative matcher which scenes to take (pull) from each camera roll. There are various types of pull lists, including *scene pull lists* and *optical pull lists.* A pull list can be used to string together shots to be retransferred to video after an offline edit.
- *Dupe list.* Shows which material needs to be duplicated prior to conforming the negative because it's used more than once in the movie. A dupe list can be generated at any time during editing to check that no material has been unintentionally duplicated.
- *Optical list.* Shows what source material is needed to create special effects, including freeze frames, slow motion, fast motion, etc.
- *Change list.* Shows only the changes (additions or deletions) that have been made since an earlier version. This is helpful if a film workprint is being cut along with the edited video for test screenings or if the negative has been transferred and edited already and only certain sections need to be changed.

Submitting Materials

When you're ready to have the negative cut or retransferred, find out the preferences of whoever will be working with it. Generally, you'll be submitting an EDL and/or your cut lists on disc and on paper. If the negative is to be cut, they will want a videocassette or file of the final film with burn-in timecode (and key numbers if available). Continuous timecode in the final sequence is important.

Matchback from 30 fps Projects

At one time, film projects edited on video in NTSC countries were routinely edited at 30 fps (60i) on standard NTSC videotape. This was done for many years before NLEs existed. An offline video edit is done, then a 30 fps EDL is generated from the offline, and timecode is used to "match back" to the film negative. In the most simplified example, if a scene begins at 1:02:00:00 timecode, the negative matcher would use a synchronizer to measure exactly two minutes from the start mark on the negative to find the beginning of the shot. Techniques have become more sophisticated, but that's the underlying idea.

While it is still possible to edit at 60i, the problem with doing so is that there often isn't an exact match between the 30 fps timecode and the 24 fps film frame count.

Take a look at Fig. 15-20. You can visualize the lower row as a shot that's five frames long in video and see that it translates neatly and exactly back to four frames of film (the upper row). The same is true of any shot in video that's a multiple of five frames.

Now imagine a three-frame shot in video (say, the first three frames in Fig. 15-20). The six fields that make up the three frames are A1/A2, B1/B2, B3/C1. This could be thought of as two-and-a-half frames of film. If the negative matcher cuts the film using the A and B film frames only, the film shot will be slightly shorter than the video. If she cuts the film to include the A, B, and C frames, the film shot will be slightly longer than the video.

Or consider this more extreme example: Imagine editing together in video a sequence of thirty very short shots that are each one frame long. This sequence will run for one second in video (30 video frames x $\frac{1}{30}$ second per frame = 1 second). Now imagine the negative matcher trying to reproduce this sequence by cutting the film. If she splices together 30 frames of film, the sequence on film will now run 1.25 seconds (30 film frames x $\frac{1}{24}$ second per frame = 1.25 seconds). To create a film sequence that runs one second, she would need to drop 6 frames, making the sequence 24 frames long, losing six of the images you selected.

The software that performs the matchback from 30 fps to 24 fps will drop or add a frame when needed to keep the overall running time the same between the video and film. This may cause slight sync drift, but never more than plus or minus one frame. It can result in some bad edits, such as when you thought you cut something out of the movie (like a flash frame) and you find it's back in after the matchback. You should be able to review the EDL and see where the software made changes to check for potential problems. This is also the reason you should leave *two* cutting frames in the video for the negative matcher so she'll be sure to have at least one in the film.

These kinds of problems *only* apply when going back from a 60i video offline to cut the negative (or to do an online at 24 fps). If you're planning to transfer from film to video only once and stay in 60i, it's nothing to worry about.

Avoiding Sync Errors

When crossing between film and video systems, it sometimes happens that you lose track of a solid sync reference for the sound in the edited movie. For projects in which the film negative will be cut after video editing, it's a good idea to have the negative cut prior to sound editing as a safety precaution whenever possible. You then use a video transfer of the finished movie instead of a dub of the offline edit as the "bible"—the ultimate reference for sync. This way, any sync errors introduced during negative cutting can be compensated for during sound editing. If a film workprint was made during the picture editing stage (see below), the edited workprint can serve as the bible for both sound editing and negative cutting.

Working with Your Negative

In the scenarios discussed earlier in this chapter, some workflows involve re-transferring the negative. This can be done from a pull list, which means you're not cutting the film within a scene, just taking entire shots from flash frame to flash frame and transferring only the frames you need. The benefit is that you don't destroy any footage in case you want to edit another version differently. You might even choose to avoid cutting the negative *at all*, and have the telecine fast forward to the sections you need.

If you're planning to make film prints from the negative (and not from a film-out or D.I.), one approach is to use the traditional method of cutting the film precisely to scene lengths. Customarily, 16mm film is cut into A&B rolls while 35mm may be printed from a single strand. You may want to do the video transfer *before* cutting the negative, or transfer from the finished film print or IP.

Another way to prepare the negative is sometimes called auto conform and is much like the way the video transfer just described is done. It involves stringing the shots in one roll, but leaving individual camera shots "cut long" (taken from flash frame to flash frame). By leaving the shots long, you have more flexibility to make alternate versions of the movie, if needed. You use the EDL or an assemble list from the offline video edit to program an optical printer to "conform" the movie and generate an interpositive. This is more expensive than contact printing, but negative cutting charges may be lower. See Conforming in Camera, p. 671, for more on this method.

CHAPTER 16

Sound Editing and Mixing

The Idea of Sound Editing and Mixing

Sound editing refers to the process of creating and refining the sound for a movie. *Mixing* is the process of enhancing and balancing the sound. On a large production, sound editing is generally done by specialized *sound editors* who are not involved in the picture editing. A *sound designer* may be brought in to create unique textures or effects. On a small production, the same people may do both picture and sound editing.

Sound is often treated as an afterthought, something to be "tidied up" before a project can be finished. But sound is tremendously important to the experience of watching a movie. An image can be invested with a vastly different sense of mood, location, and context, depending on the sound that accompanies it. Some of these impressions come from direct cues (the sound of birds, a nearby crowd, or a clock), while others work indirectly through the volume, rhythm, and density of the sound track. The emotional content of a scene (and the emotions purportedly felt by characters on screen) are often conveyed as much or more by music and sound design as by any dialogue or picture. Even on a straightforward documentary or corporate video, the way the sound is handled in terms of minimizing noise and maximizing the intelligibility of voices plays a big part in the success of the project.

It is said that humans place priority on visual over aural information. Perhaps so, but it's often the case that film or video footage that is poorly shot but has a clear and easily understood sound track seems okay, while a movie with nicely lit, nicely framed images, but a muddy, harsh, and hard-to-understand track is really irritating to audiences. Unfortunately for the sound recordists, editors, and mixers who do the work, audiences often don't realize when the sound track is great, but they're *very* aware when there are sound problems.

The editing of dialogue, sound effects, and music often evolves organically during the picture editing phase. While the dialogue and picture are being edited, you might try out music or effects in some scenes. You might experiment with audio filters or equalization and often need to do temporary mixes for test screenings. Nonlinear editing is *nondestructive*, which means you can do many things to the sound and undo them later if you don't like the effect.[1] For some projects, the picture editor does very detailed mixing in the NLE, which may be used as the basis for the final mix.

---

1. A few effects do in fact alter the captured audio files—avoid those until the final mix.

Fig. 16-1. Mix studio. (Sync Sound, Inc.)

Even so, sound work doesn't usually begin in earnest until the picture is locked and the movie's structural decisions are all made. The job of sound editing begins with the sound editor screening the movie with the director and the picture editor. If you're doing all these jobs yourself, then watch the movie with a pad of paper (and try not to feel too lonely). Every scene should be examined for problems, and to determine where effects are needed and where a certain feeling or quality of sound is desired. If music is to be used, the composer (who will create music) and/or the *music supervisor* (who helps find existing music) are brought in as well. Deciding where to place music and effects is called *spotting*.

The sound editor then begins the process of sorting out the sound. The audio is divided into several different strands or tracks. One set of tracks is used for dialogue, another for effects, another for music, and so on. Portioning out different types of sounds to separate tracks makes it easier for the mixer to adjust and balance them. This process is called *splitting tracks*. Effects are obtained and other sounds are added, building up the layers of sound; this is *track building*.

When all the tracks have been built, a sound mix is done to blend them all back together. Enhancing the way the tracks sound in the mix is sometimes called *sweetening*. The mix may be done in a studio by a professional mixer, or it may be performed by the filmmaker using an editing system or other equipment. A professional mix studio (also called a *dub stage* or *mix stage*) is designed with optimal acoustics for evaluating the audio as it will be heard by audiences. Though more costly, studio mixes are preferable to mixes done in the editing room or other multi-use spaces that may have machine noise, poor speakers, or bad acoustics. For theatrical and ˙ ʳoadcast projects, it's essential to mix in a good listening environment. Also, profes-
ˡ mixers bring a wealth of experience about creating a good sound track that
ᵐakers lack.

mix, the sound track is recombined with the picture for distribution.
ʸpes of distribution may require different types of mixes.

THE SOUND EDITING PROCESS

Like everything else in video and film, sound editing has been transformed by new technology. Where there was once a standard path through the process, there are now many paths and types of equipment. How you do sound editing depends on the project, how it was shot, your budget, and how you plan to distribute the finished movie.

The distinctions between the capabilities of a nonlinear editing system, a digital audio workstation (DAW), and a mix studio have broken down somewhat. For example, some NLEs have very good sound editing capabilities. A DAW, which is a specialized system for sound editing and mixing, might be just another application running on the same computer as the NLE. And a mix studio might be using the same DAW, but with better speakers in a better listening environment.

Fig. 16-2. Digital audio workstation (DAW). Pro Tools system shown with Mackie Human User Interface controller. (Digidesign, Inc.)

For most video projects, the *production audio* (the sound recorded in the field) is recorded in the video camcorder along with the picture. For some video shoots and all film shoots the audio is recorded double-system with a separate audio recorder. For workflows involving double-system sound, see Chapters 14 and 15.

Here are some workflows used for sound editing and mixing:

Projects Shot on Video

BASIC NONLINEAR EDIT. The simplest, cheapest way to do sound work is to just do it on the NLE being used for the offline edit. Audio is captured originally at high quality and can be used for the finished product. Sound editing and mixing are done on the system. Audio is exported as a finished sound track, either with the video or separately (to be remarried to the picture after the online edit is done). This method is best for simple and/or low-budget projects and is usually not a good idea for complex mixes.

NONLINEAR EDIT; TRACK WORK ON DAW; MIX IN STUDIO.
Picture editing and basic sound work are done on a nonlinear editing system. Audio tracks are exported to a DAW for final track work, which gives maximum control over the process. Mixing is done in a mix studio, with good speakers and an optimal environment for judging the mix.

LINEAR VIDEOTAPE EDIT. Offline editing is done with worktapes, followed by online edit with original camera tapes. Simple sound mixing can be done during the online session. More complex audio sweetening is done by stripping the audio from the online edit master and laying it over to a DAW. Effects and music are added, then the mix is done. Audio *layback* is then done to put the final mixed track on the master tape.

Projects Shot on Film

FILM-TO-VIDEO TRANSFER; EDIT NONLINEAR. Film is transferred to video for editing. Production audio is transferred with it, or imported into editing system later. See Editing Film on Video, p. 605, for options.

TRADITIONAL FILM EDIT; FILM MIX. In the traditional method, production audio is transferred to 16mm or 35mm magnetic film for editing. Picture editing is done with one to three mag tracks. After picture lock, sound editing is done by splitting sound into several (or many) more mag tracks. Mag tracks are brought to the mix studio, where they are played on dubbers in sync with the picture while the sound is rerecorded on a master dubber, often in 35mm (see Fig. 16-11). The 35mm fullcoat master is then transferred to whatever formats are needed for distribution.

This method is now rarely used. Even if the film is edited on a flatbed with mag tracks, the sound is often transferred to digital for mixing.

Planning Ahead

Many of the decisions made during picture and sound editing are affected by how the movie will be finished. Some questions that you'll face later on, which are worth considering early in the process, include:

- How will audio be transferred between systems? For example, will you move audio from the NLE used for picture editing to a DAW for mixing? How will you get the audio from the DAW to the master tape or file of the finished movie (see p. 644)?
- How many audio channels will you have in the final mix? There are several audio formats with different numbers of channels (ranging from single-channel mono to 7.1 channel SDDS). Format choice affects every stage of sound editing (see p. 654).
- How will distribution affect mix style? Different types of distribution (including theatrical, television, DVD, or Internet streaming) call for different approaches to sound prep and balancing (see p. 648).
- Will you distribute the project in other languages? This affects track layout and mix (see p. 656).

Some topics in this chapter, such as the sections on sound processing and setting levels, are discussed in terms of the final mix but apply equally to working with sound throughout the picture and sound editing process. It will help to read through the whole chapter before beginning sound work.

SOUND EDITING TOOLS

The Working Environment

Sound work is first and foremost about *listening*, so it's essential you have a good environment in which to hear your tracks. If you're working with video decks or computers that have noisy fans, make every effort to isolate them in another room or at least minimize the noise where you're sitting. Sometimes you can get extension cables to move the keyboard and monitors farther from the CPU, or use sound-dampening enclosures.

The editing room itself will affect the sound because of its acoustics (how sound reflects within it), noise, and other factors. Make sure there's enough furniture, carpeting, and/or sound-dampening panels to keep the room from being too reverberant and boomy.

Speakers are very important. A good set of "near field" speakers, designed for close listening, are often best. They should be aimed properly for your sitting position (often in a loose triangle arrangement with each turned in slightly toward you). Avoid cheap computer speakers. Some people use "multimedia" speakers that have tiny little tweeters on the desktop with a subwoofer on the floor for bass. The problem with these is that they reproduce the high frequencies and the lows, but may be deficient in the midrange where most dialogue lies.

One philosophy is that you should listen on the best speakers possible, to hear every nuance of the sound. Another suggests that you use the same crummy speakers most of the people watching the movie will have. Ideally, you should have a chance to hear the sound on both. The great speakers will have detail in the highs and lows that *some* people, especially theater audiences will hear. The small speakers will create some problems and mask others that you need to know about. Some people use headphones for sound work, which are great for hearing details and blocking out editing room noise, but can seriously misrepresent how people will hear the movie through speakers in the real world. For more, see Audio Input and Monitoring, p. 511. To learn what your movie sounds like, get it out of the editing room and screen it in different environments—such as in a theater with big speakers turned up loud and in a living room on an old TV that has a cheap little mono speaker.

NLE Versus DAW

Picture and dialogue editing are typically done on an NLE, which for many projects is where *all* the sound editing and mixing is done. Some NLEs are bundled with specialized audio applications that have added power (for example, Final Cut Pro and Soundtrack Pro; Avid Xpress can be purchased with a version of Pro Tools).

Professional sound editors and mixers use DAWs with dedicated audio software such as Pro Tools or Nuendo. Among the advantages of DAWs are more sophisticated audio processing, better control over audio levels and channels, and better tools for sample rate conversions. While many camcorders record audio at 48 kHz/16-bits, mixing and audio processing is sometimes done at 24-bits or higher, which may not be supported by an NLE.[2]

It was once the case that NLEs could make trims only in one-frame increments, while DAWs cut at the sample level—less than one thousandth of a frame—for more precise trims. However, now some NLEs offer subframe edits for audio. (The same issue applies to 16mm mag film—which can be cut only on the frame line—versus 35mm, which has four perfs per frame).

On many productions, basic sound editing and track layout is done on the NLE used for picture editing, with refinements and mixing done later on a DAW.

The Mixing Console

The *mixing console* (also called *recording console, mixer,* or *board*) is used to control and balance a number of sound sources and blend them into a combined sound track. Mix consoles range from simple, manually operated boards that may be part of an editing system to massive, computer-controlled systems used on a dub stage that can replay the mixing cues for an entire program. Often, software applications include an onscreen display that looks like a mix board and may be used with an attached console that has physical sliders you can move by hand (a "control surface," see Fig. 16-2).

Because many offline and online NLE setups use a mixer to control various audio inputs, a short discussion may be helpful. The mix board accepts a number of *input channels*, or just *channels*. Each channel is controlled with its own *channel*

Fig. 16-3. Mackie MS1402 mixer. Mackie makes a series of popular, versatile mixers. (Mackie Designs, Inc.)

2. Many film mixes are still done at 16-bits; music mixing is often done at higher bit rates.

strip on the surface of the board that has a *fader* or level control and other adjustments. You might use one channel to input a microphone, another pair of channels to bring in sound from a video deck. The channels can be assigned to various *buses*; a bus is a network for combining the output of two or more channels and sending it somewhere (a bit like a city bus collecting passengers from a neighborhood and taking them downtown). The *mix bus* is the main output of the board, the *monitor bus* is the signal sent to the monitor speakers, and so on. You can send any channel you want to the *main mix*, where a *master fader* controls the level of all the channels together. You might choose to assign some channel strips to a separate output channel. This is sometimes done to create alternate versions of a mix, or when two people are using the board for different equipment at the same time.

One common use for a mixer with an NLE is to route the audio from the video deck or capture card to the speakers (see Fig. 14-2). Or you might use it to adjust levels when recording to or from a second deck.

Figure 16-4 shows a channel strip from a Mackie 121-VLZ mix console. These are the features starting at the top of the strip and working down:

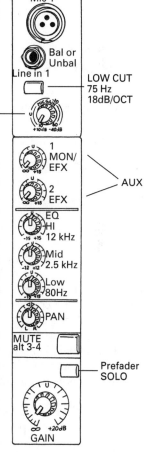

- Jacks for a *microphone input* and a balanced or unbalanced *line level input* (see Audio Connections, p. 401).
- *Low-cut filter* which rolls off low frequencies below 75 Hz (often a good idea, especially for monitoring; see Bass Filters, p. 429).
- *Trim control*, which adjusts the level of the mic or line as it comes into the mixer (see below for setting this).
- *Aux (auxiliary) pots* for sending the signal out for various uses.
- *EQ (equalization)* controls, for high, mid, and low frequencies. Turning each knob to the right boosts that frequency band, turning to the left cuts it. Some mix consoles have "fully parametric EQ," which allows you to fine-tune both the width of the band and where it is centered.
- *Pan pot.* Turning the pan control to the left sends the signal to the left channel/speaker; the other way sends it to the right. When using a mixer to play audio from the NLE, generally you should have the left channel out of the NLE panned fully left, and the right channel panned fully right. If you leave both panned in the middle, both will go to both speakers with no stereo separation.
- *Mute button.* Kills the sound from this channel (so you can hear the other channels without it) and the *prefader solo* which allows you to hear *only*

Fig. 16-4. Channel strip from Mackie MS1202 mixer. See text. (Robert Brun)

this channel, at its original level (before going to any fader). Some boards allow you to select pre- or post-fader.

- *Gain control.* Adjusts the volume level for the channel. Twelve o'clock on the dial is marked U for *Unity Gain* (on some mixers this is marked 0 dB). Setting the level higher than U may add noise.

To set up a channel on a mixer, plug the sound source (say, a video deck) into the channel input. Turn the trim control all the way down, and set the channel gain, the master fader, and the EQ controls to U or 0 dB. Now play the VTR (with nothing else playing) and adjust the trim control until the level looks good on the mixer's level meter. See Chapter 11 for more on setting levels. Now you can set the EQ where you like it, and use the channel strip and master fader to control the level as you choose. Generally, you want to avoid a situation where a channel's gain is set low and the master fader is set very high to compensate. If you're just using one channel, often it's a good idea to leave the channel's gain at U and use the master fader to ride the level (see Gain Structure, p. 423).

SOUND EDITING TECHNIQUE

Editing dialogue and narration is discussed in Chapter 13. Basic sound editing methods are discussed in Chapter 14, for video editing, and in Chapter 15, for projects edited on film.

Evaluating the Sound Track

All the audio in the movie should be evaluated carefully at the start of sound editing. Is the dialogue clear and easy to understand? Is there objectionable wind or other noise? Go through the track and cut out any noise, pops, or clicks that you can, and usually any breaths before or after words (that aren't part of an actor's performance). You can fill the holes later with room tone (see below for more on this).

If you have doubts about the quality of any section of audio, try equalizing or using other processing to improve it. Listen to the original video or audiotape directly to see if it sounds any better. Consult a mixer or other professional for possible remedies. Be critical—if you think you're unhappy with some bad sound now, just wait till you see the movie with an audience. For nondialogue scenes, the remedy may be to throw out the production sound and rebuild the audio with effects (see below). For dialogue scenes, you may need to use other takes, or consider automatic dialogue replacement (ADR; see p. 492). If it's unfixable, you may need to lose the whole scene.

Sound and Continuity

Sound plays an important role in establishing a sense of time or place. In both fiction and documentary, there are many situations in which shots that were filmed at different times must be cut together to create the illusion that the shots actually occurred in continuous time. In one shot the waiter says, "Can I take your order?" and in the next the woman says, "I'll have the fish." These two shots may have been

Fig. 16-5. Steenbeck 16mm six-plate flatbed editing table with two sound tracks and one picture head. An eight-plate is even better for doing sound work. (Steenbeck, Inc.)

taken hours or even days apart, but they must maintain the illusion of being connected. The way the sound is handled can either make or break the scene.

When you're editing, be attentive to changes in the quality, content, and level of sound and use them to your advantage. If your goal is to blend a series of shots into a continuous flow, avoid making hard sound cuts that butt up two sections of audio that differ greatly in quality or tone, especially right at a picture cut. A *crossfade* (sound dissolve) can smooth out a hard cut. Certain differences in quality and level can be smoothed over by adjusting levels and doing some EQ. Sometimes just moving the audio cut a few frames before or after the picture cut helps (see Fig. 14-23).

Audiences will accept most changes in sound if they're gradual. One technique is to add in a background track that remains constant and masks other discontinuities in a scene. Say you had a shot with the sound of an airplane overhead, preceded and followed by shots without the plane. You could add airplane sound to another track (which may be obtained from a sound effects library); fade it in before the noisy shot, then gradually fade it out after it. This progression gives the sense that the plane passed overhead during the three shots. As long as the sound doesn't cut in or out sharply, many discontinuities can be covered in a similar way.

If you're cutting a scene in which there was audible music on location, there will be jumps in the music every time you make a cut in the audio track. Try to position cuts in background sound under dialogue or other sounds that can distract the audience from the discontinuous background.

While gradual crossfades ease viewers from sequence to sequence, it's often desirable to have hard, clear changes in sound to produce a shock effect. Opening a scene with sound that is radically different from the previous sequence is a way to make a clean break, start a new chapter. When cutting from a loud scene to a quiet scene, it often works best to allow the loud sound to continue slightly beyond the picture cut, decaying (fading out) naturally. When a loud scene follows a quiet scene, a straight cut often works best.

When building tracks, don't forget the power of *silence*. A sense of hush can help build tension. A moment of quiet after a loud or intense scene can have tremendous impact. Sounds can be used as punctuation to control the phrasing of a scene. Often, the rhythm of sounds should be used to determine the timing of picture cuts as much as anything going on in the picture.

Sound Effects

For feature films, it's common during shooting to record only the sound of the actors' voices, with the assumption that *all* other sounds (such as footsteps, rain, cars pulling up, or pencils on paper) will be added later. Often, shooting takes place on an acoustically isolated soundstage. Without added sound effects to bring a sense of realism, the footage will seem very flat. Documentaries often need effects as well, to augment or replace sounds recorded on location.

Sound effects (sometimes written *SFX*) are available from a number of sources. You can buy effects on discs or download them from the Web. Most mix facilities keep an effects library. A good library has an astounding range of effects: You might find, for example, 500 different crowd sounds, from low murmurs to wild applause. Libraries such as Sound Ideas or The Hollywood Edge offer effects for specific models of cars, species of birds, types of shoes, guns, or screams.

Fig. 16-6. Foley room. The various floor surfaces are used to make different types of footsteps. Items in background are for generating other sound effects. (Sync Sound, Inc.)

At times, the most compelling effects may not be the obvious library choice. A car zooming by in a dramatic scene could have engine and tire sounds, plus rocket sounds or even musical tones. To create unusual effects, the sound designer will collect, sample, and process all sorts of sounds and textures.

A *foley stage* is a special studio for creating effects while watching the picture. The floor may have different sections with gravel, wood, or other surfaces to simulate different kinds of footfalls. A good foley artist can pour water, make drinking sounds, and do other effects that work perfectly with picture.

Effects can also be used to help define a place or a character and can be used as a narrative element. Some effects are clichéd (the creaking floors and squeaking doors of a spooky old house) but imaginative use of sounds can add a vivid flavor to an otherwise bland location.

Effects are sometimes used to create moods or impressionistic backgrounds that don't relate literally to anything in the image. Creative sound editing may involve burying abstract or unrelated sounds under the more obvious sounds created by people or objects on screen. Sometimes these effects are very subtle. A quiet, very low-frequency sound may be barely audible but can create a subliminal sense of tension. As editor Victoria Garvin Davis points out, often the mark of a good effect is that you never even notice it.

Ambient Sound and Room Tone

The sound track should never be allowed to go completely *dead*. With the exception of an anechoic chamber, there's no place on earth that is totally silent. Every space has a characteristic room tone (see p. 425). There are technical reasons as well as aesthetic ones why the track should always have some sound, even if very quiet. A background of tone or music is sometimes called a *bed*. If the recordist has provided room tone at each location, you can lay it under the scene to fill small dropouts, larger holes, or to provide a sense of "air" which is quite different from no sound. If no room tone has been specifically recorded, you may be able to steal short sections from pauses on the set (such as the time just before the director says "action") or long spaces between words. You may need to go back to the original field recordings to find these moments.

Short lengths of tone can sometimes be looped to generate more tone. When editing mag film, this entails literally splicing the track into an endless loop and rerecording on another dubber. On an NLE, this can be easily done by copying and pasting the same piece more than once. Listen closely to make sure there's nothing distinct that will be heard repeating (one trick is to insert a clip of tone, then copy and paste a "reverse motion" version of the same clip right after it so the cut is seamless).

If you can't get enough tone this way, you could try recording some, but many atmospheres, such as the sound of wind in the trees, are simpler to get from an effects library than to try to record. Another background is *walla*, which is a track of people speaking in which no words can be made out, which is useful for scenes in restaurants, or with groups or crowds.

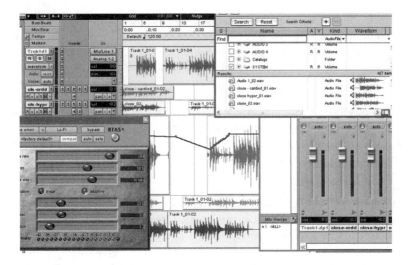

Fig. 16-7. Pro Tools is an industry-standard DAW. Digidesign makes both Pro Tools HD for audio professionals and Pro Tools LE, a more affordable version. (Digidesign, Inc.)

MUSIC

The Score

Music may be *scored* (composed) specifically for a movie or pre-existing music may be licensed for use. An *underscore* (or just *score*) is music that audiences understand as being added by the filmmakers to augment a scene; *source music* seems to come from some source in a scene (for example, a car radio or a pianist next door).[3] Songs may be used over action, either as a form of score or as source music. To preserve continuity, music is almost always added to a movie during editing and is rarely recorded simultaneously with the dialogue. (Of course, in a documentary, recording ambient music may at times be unavoidable.)

Music is a powerful tool for the filmmaker. Used right, it can enhance a scene tremendously. Most fiction films would be emotionally flat without music. But if the wrong music is used, or at the wrong time, it can ruin a scene. Though there are many movies with catchy themes, or where well-known songs are used to great effect, it's interesting how many movie scores are actually quite subtle and nondescript. Listen to the score for a movie you've liked. Often, the most powerful scenes are supported by very atmospheric music that doesn't in itself make a big statement. A case can also be made for times when music should be avoided. In some documentaries and in some moments in dramas, music can have a kind of manipulative effect that may be inappropriate. No matter what music you choose, it unavoidably makes a kind of editorial comment on the action. Sometimes audiences should

---

3. Source music or other sound from within the story's space is sometimes referred to as *diegetic* sound, as opposed to the non-diegetic sound of the movie's score.

be allowed to form their own reactions, without help from the filmmaker (or composer).

Typically, during the rough-cut stage, movies are edited with no music or with *temp (temporary) music*. The editor and/or director bring in music they like and "throw it in" to the movie during editing to try it out. This can be a great way to experiment, and find what styles work with the picture. The problem is that after weeks or months watching the movie with the temp music, filmmakers often fall in love with it, and find it very disturbing to take it out. There are many reasons why the temp music must come out, ranging from it having been used in another movie, to the likelihood that you can't afford it, to the fact that you've hired a composer to write a score. Often, composers have ideas that are very different from the temp music you've picked, and they may not be able or willing to write something like the temp track if you ask them to.

Every composer has his or her own method of working, and the director and composer must feel their way along in finding the right music for the project. *Spotting sheets* (sometimes called *spot lists*, *cue sheets*, or *timing sheets*) should be prepared, showing every needed music cue and its length. The director should discuss with the composer what each scene is about, and what aspects of the scene the music should reinforce. Even if you know musical terminology, describing music with words can be tremendously difficult. Often, the conversation turns to far-flung metaphors about colors, emotions, weather—whatever is useful to describe the effect the music should have on the listener. What makes great composers great is their ability to understand the ideas and emotions in a scene and express that in music. Scoring is often left until the last moment in postproduction, but there is a lot to be gained by starting the process as early as possible.

Licensing Music

If you can't afford or don't want an original score, you can license existing music. Popular songs by well-known musical groups are usually very expensive. Often, a music supervisor will have contacts with indie bands, composers, or others who are eager to have their music used in a movie and which may be much more affordable. Music libraries sell prerecorded music that can be used for a reasonable fee with minimal hassle. Many of them offer tracks that sound *very much* like famous bands (but just different enough to avoid a lawsuit). See Chapter 19 for discussion of copyright, licensing, and the business aspects of using music.

Editing Music

When music is scored for a movie, the composer will generally design each passage to fit perfectly with the picture. If the music has the same timecode as the picture, it's easy to place it in the proper position. Even with a non-timecoded file, if you know the starting timecode you can spot it correctly. Nevertheless, there are times when music needs to be cut or repositioned to work with the edited scenes. Not infrequently, a cue written for one scene works better with another.

When placing music (and when having it composed) keep in mind that in dialogue scenes, the dialogue needs to be audible. If the music is so loud that it fights with the dialogue, the music will have to be brought down in the mix. A smart composer (or music editor) will place the most active, loudest passages of music before or after lines of dialogue, and have the music lay back a bit when people are talking. If the music and the characters aren't talking at the same time, they can both be loud and both be heard.

Cutting music is easier if you're familiar with the mechanics of music. Some picture cuts are best made on the up beat, others on the down beat. Locating musical beats on an NLE may be easier if you view the audio waveform (see Fig. 14-21). With mag film, you can jab at the track with a Sharpie on each beat. With care, you can usually remove notes, phrases, or verses from musical passages if needed. Short (or sometimes long) crossfades help bridge cuts within the music. A musical note or another sound (like some sirens) that holds and then decays slowly can sometimes be shortened by removing frames from the *middle* of the sound rather than from the beginning or end.

In the mix, source music that is meant to appear to be coming from, say, a car radio is usually filtered to match the source. In this case, you might roll off both high and low frequencies to simulate a tinny, "lo-fi" speaker.

Music Creation Software

There are a number of products that allow musicians and nonmusicians to construct music tracks by assembling prerecorded loops of instruments playing snippets of melodies and rhythms. These programs include Sonicfire Pro and Soundtrack Pro. The loops are sampled from real instruments and can be combined in various ways and adjusted for tempo and pitch. These can be used to create an actual score, or to quickly try out ideas as part of a scratch track.

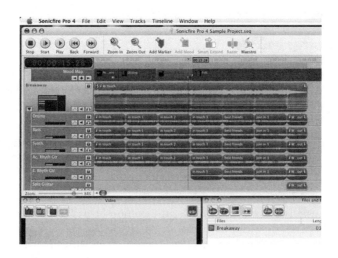

Fig. 16-8. Several programs allow you to create music by stringing together premade loops of different instruments playing various melodies or rhythms. Shown here, Sonicfire Pro. (SmartSound Software, Inc.)

SOME SOUND EDITING ISSUES

POPS AND CLICKS. Often on NLEs, you get a pop or click where two audio clips meet on the same track (even if neither pops by itself). To avoid this, put a two-frame crossfade between them or try trimming one side back by a frame (or less). Some DAWs can routinely add a crossfade of several milliseconds to avoid clicks at cuts. When editing mag film, clicks at splices may mean the splicer is magnetized. Diagonal splices are generally better than straight cuts for minimizing problems at cuts.

AUDIO SCRUBBING. Many sound edits can only be made by listening to the track slowly. The term audio *scrubbing* comes from the use of reel-to-reel tape recorders, where you can manually pull the sound back and forth across the playback head in a scrubbing motion to find individual sounds. Scrubbing on any analog system means that the sound will be much lower in pitch. Some digital systems offer the choice of analog-style scrub (slow and low) and a digital version that plays a small number of frames at full speed. See which works best for you.

STEREO PAIRS. As noted on p. 539, paired stereo tracks include one track that's panned to the left channel and one that's panned to the right. This is appropriate for music, or other stereo recordings, but sometimes two mono tracks from a camcorder show up on the timeline as a stereo pair—in which case you can unpair them, so that both go to both speakers. *Summing* (combining) two identical tracks on the same channel will cause the volume to double (level rises by 6 dB), which may happen when you unpair two identical tracks (you can decrease each track's gain manually, if necessary).

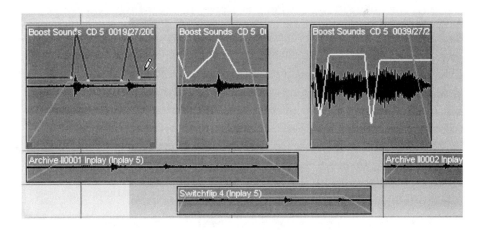

Fig. 16-9. Nuendo is a powerful DAW. Shown here, clips displaying audio waveforms and the "volume envelopes" that control their level. (Steinberg Media Technologies)

You can use summing to your advantage when you can't get enough volume from a very quiet clip just by raising the gain. Try copying the clip and pasting the copy *directly* below the original on the timeline to double the level. While this can work on an NLE, most DAWs have better ways of increasing level.

For more on stereo, see Chapter 11 and later in this chapter.

CODING NEW MATERIAL. Sound editing generally involves bringing new audio material (such as music, effects, narration) into the editing room that didn't originate with the original production sound. When possible, any material on tape should be timecoded or, for a traditional film edit, edge coded before cutting it in to your sound. Lack of code can make it harder to find what you're looking for later.

TRIMS AND OUTTAKES. One advantage of doing at least basic track work on the NLE used for picture editing is to get instant access to outtakes. There are many situations in which you need to replace room tone or a line of dialogue. It's very handy to be able to quickly scan through alternate takes, or to use the match frame command to instantly find the extension to a shot. These things take longer on another machine if you don't have all the media easily accessible on hard drive.

Whoever is doing the sound editing may want access to *all* the production audio recorded for the movie. Crucial pieces of room tone or replacement dialogue may be hiding in unexpected places in the tracks. Be prepared to deliver to the sound editor all the audio, including wild sound, and the logs, if requested.

PREPARING FOR THE MIX

Everything done in sound editing is geared toward the mix. The better your preparation, the better the movie will sound and the faster the mix will go. Regardless of whether the mix will be done by a professional mixer or by you, go through the entire soundtrack and be sure you've provided all the sounds needed. During the mix, changes or new effects may be called for, but try to anticipate as much as you can.

Mixes are done with different types of equipment, but all mixes share the same fundamental process:

1. All of your audio tracks are played back together, in sync with the picture.
2. The relative levels of the tracks are adjusted and various types of EQ and processing are applied as needed.
3. The mixed sound is rerecorded on other tracks for final output.

The *sound mixer*, sometimes called the *rerecording mixer*, presides at the console. Like an orchestra conductor, the mixer determines how the various tracks will blend into the whole. Some mixes require two or three mixers operating the console(s).

Splitting Tracks

During picture editing, the sound may be bunched on a few or several tracks in the editing system. After the picture has been locked, and it's time to prepare for the mix, the tracks are split in a very specific way to facilitate the mix. Sounds are segregated onto different tracks according to the type of sound; for example, dialogue, music, narration and effects are usually all put on separate tracks. Actually, each type of sound is often split into a *group* of tracks (you may need many tracks to accommodate all your dialogue or effects). This layout is used partly so the mixer knows what to expect from various tracks, but also so that he can minimize the number of adjustments made during the mix. Say you have narration in your movie. If all the narration is on one track, and there is nothing else on that track, then the mixer can fine-tune the level and EQ for the narrator's voice and then quite possibly never touch that channel again during the mix. If, on the other hand, the narrator's voice keeps turning up on different tracks, or there are other sounds sharing her track, the mixer will constantly have to make adjustments to compensate.

A simple documentary might be mixed with anywhere from eight to more than 20 tracks; a simple dramatic mix might involve 20 to 40 tracks. A complex, effects-filled drama for 5.1 channel surround sound might have well over 100 tracks. When there are many tracks, often a *premix* is done to consolidate numerous effects tracks into a few that can be more easily balanced with the dialogue and music. Or the composer may deliver the music with many separate tracks of individual instruments that need to be premixed into a stereo pair prior to the main mix (or a few pairs with separate rhythm, melody, and vocal tracks).

Talk to your mixer for his preferences before splitting tracks. Some mixers prefer tracks to be laid out in a particular order. For example, the first tracks contain dialogue and sync sound, the next narration, then music, and the last effects. If there is no narration or music, the effects tracks would follow immediately after the dialogue. If your movie has very little of one type of sound (say, only a couple of bits of music), you can usually let it share another track (in this case you might put music on the effects track).

A common method of labeling tracks uses letters for each track in a group: You might have Dia. A, Dia. B, Dia. C, and SFX A, SFX B, etc. If the movie is divided into reels (see below), each reel is given a number, so a given track might be labeled, say, Reel 3, Mus. A. Ask the mixer for track labeling preferences.

CHECKERBOARDING. To make mixing go faster, tracks within any group are split into a checkerboard pattern (see Fig. 16-10). For example, two characters who are miked differently might be split onto separate dialogue tracks. This makes it easier to adjust the EQ and level differently for the two mics.

In general, if one clip follows another on the same track and you can play them both without changing the EQ, hearing a click, or making a large level change, then leave them on the same track. Tracks should be split when two sections of sound are *different* from each other in level or quality and you want them to be *similar*, or if they are *similar* and you want them to be *different*. Thus, if two parts of a sequence are miked very differently and need to be evened out, put them on separate tracks. If the difference is caused by a change of background tone, it often helps to

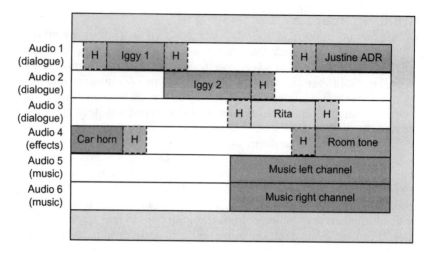

Fig. 16-10. Track work. Prior to the mix, audio is split into separate dialogue, effects and music tracks. Iggy's and Rita's dialogue has been checkerboarded onto three dialogue tracks because they were recorded with different mics and Iggy's first clip needs different equalization than the second one (this kind of checkerboarding is optional; talk with your mixer). The sections marked "H" are handles available for crossfades if needed. Handles are normally invisible on the timeline.

ease the transition by doing a crossfade between the two shots. With a nonlinear system, you can simply add a crossfade (assuming there's enough media). With mag tracks, you can prepare for a crossfade by overlapping the head of the incoming shot with the tail extension of the outgoing shot. The more overlap you provide the mixer, the more flexibility he'll have in controlling the transition.

How many tracks do you need for each type of sound? Say you're splitting your dialogue. You put the first clip on one track, then put the next on the second track. If the next split comes in less than eight to ten seconds, you probably should put that piece on a third track rather than going back to the first. But not necessarily. There are different schools of thought about how much to checkerboard tracks. The idea of splitting tracks originated when mixes were done with mag film dubbers (see Fig. 16-11). With a dubber, for example, it's only possible to do a crossfade between two shots if they're on separate tracks; you *have* to checkerboard them to do the effect. However, with a digital system, it's not hard to set up a crossfade between one clip and the next on the same track (though you do have to stop to create the fade). Mixers differ in how much they want tracks checkerboarded; ask yours for his preferences. Even if he's using a digital system, on the first pass he may be trying to mix by hand—the old-fashioned way—and splitting tracks can make his job easier.

After talking with the mixer, work through the movie shot by shot to determine how many tracks you need. Sometimes you'll want extra tracks for optional effects or alternate dialogue takes to give the mixer more options. You don't want to use more tracks than are necessary; on the other hand, having more tracks could save you time and money in the mix.

Fig. 16-11. Mix studio dubbers. Six playback transports are at left, one master record transport is at right. All can be run in interlock. (Rangertone Research)

Reel Breaks and Reference Tapes

To be absolutely sure that there aren't any sync errors, it's best to do the mix with the *final picture* (either from the online video edit or a video of the printed film). That way, any sync discrepancies can be fixed in the mix.

However, it's often the case that people mix with a *reference tape* or file created from the offline video edit or, for a project shot in film, from the edited workprint. Put your rough offline sound mix on the reference tape as a guide for the mixer.

FOR PROJECTS SHOT IN VIDEO. The mixer will need a tape or file of the offline edit with sequence timecode burned-in (window burn). See Output to Tape, p. 555, for instructions on making a tape with proper leaders, continuous timecode, and no dropped frames. Some mixers want the movie delivered as a QuickTime file (or other format).

Put a *sync pop*[4] (the audible beep in the countdown leader that syncs to the picture exactly two seconds prior to the start of the program) on *all the tracks* as a sync check. Also add a tail leader with visible sync frame and sync pop on all the tracks. This is done on the NLE prior to output.

In some cases, the project will need to be broken into shorter lengths (*reels*) if the entire movie can't be edited, mixed, or finished in one chunk. For example, some NLEs choke when trying to output a full 60-minute or 90-minute sequence. Each reel is made into a separate sequence beginning with a different hour timecode. Accordingly, reel one might begin at 01:00:00:00, with reel two starting at 02:00:00:00, and so on. The reels can be joined together later.

FOR PROJECTS THAT WILL BE FINISHED AND PRINTED ON FILM. See Reel Length, p. 599, for guidelines on dividing up reels. When preparing film projects, each reel should begin with a standard SMPTE leader (sometimes referred to as an Academy leader). This has the familiar eight-second countdown. You can get SMPTE leader from the lab; you can also get a video transfer of it. The leader counts down from "eight" to "two" with two seconds of black following. The frame *exactly* at two should have a sync pop or beep edited into *all sound tracks* (see Fig. 17-8). The sync pops aid in keeping the tracks in sync during the mix and are essential for putting the film optical track in sync with the picture; see Optical Tracks, p. 689. A tail leader with a beep is also recommended.

When editing film projects in video, the SMPTE leader is often edited in before the hour mark, so that the beep at two takes place—for the first reel—at 00:59:58:00 and the first frame of action (FFOA) appears at one hour straight up (01:00:00:00). (This is the way typical video projects are handled.) However, for film projects, some mixers and negative cutters prefer that the SMPTE leader *begin* at the hour mark, so the beep at two would appear at 01:00:06:00 and the FFOA starts at 01:00:08:00.[5] Talk to the mix facility, lab, and/or post house for the way they want the reels broken down.

Preparing and Delivering Tracks

Before splitting your tracks, ask the mixer or sound studio how they like the tracks prepared and delivered. If you're editing on mag film, see Appendix H for a method of preparing tracks on mag.

If you've been editing on an NLE, there are a few options for getting the audio tracks from the edited sequence on the timeline out of your system and into the system used by the sound studio or online edit system. For an overview of this process, see File Formats and Data Exchange, p. 219, and From Offline to Online, p. 549.

EXPORT THE SEQUENCE AND MEDIA. Usually the best way to move the audio tracks to another system is to export the entire sequence with its media.

---

4. In the U.K, it's called a sync *pip*.

5. In 16mm, with the "Picture Start" frame of the SMPTE leader used as zero (01:00:00:00 in video), the first frame of action occurs at exactly 4 feet, 32 frames.

This is typically done by having the NLE export the sequence in a format such as OMF/AAF (see p. 221).[6] When done right, all the audio clips will appear in the DAW or online system in their proper timeline position on their own tracks. Ideally, you'll choose to include the audio media with the OMF composition, so you can give the sound studio a CD or DVD with the sequence and all the sound—what could be handier?

If the audio was not originally captured into the NLE at its highest quality, the mix studio will want *only* the OMF sequence, and will recapture/redigitize the media in their shop from the original tapes.

Depending on the systems involved, not *all* the information in your offline sequence may be translated to the DAW. For example, some or all level adjustments (like rubberbanding) may not carry over from one system to the other. You may also want to remove any filter effects or EQ (see below). Crossfades generally do translate. Automatic Duck makes software that helps translate sequences from one system to another.

Be sure to include ample *handles* on your clips (at least three seconds and up to ten, in some cases). Handles are extensions of clips that remain hidden (inaudible) but are available in case the mixer wants to use them for crossfades or to lengthen a clip (see Fig. 16-10). The OMF export tool should allow you to select handle length.

Be sure all audio clips are at the same sample rate (typically, film and video sessions are done at 48 kHz/16-bit).

EXPORT AUDIO FILES. If your system doesn't support OMF, you can export each track as a separate audio file (in a format such as AIFF or WAV). You *must* have head leaders with a sync pop because, depending on the format, there may be no timecode. This method is cumbersome and doesn't allow for handles. (That is, you can include extensions of shots, as you might when mixing from mag film, but they aren't "hidden" and the mixer will have to manually fade or cut any extra audio that's not needed.)

A similar method is to export the tracks from the NLE to videotape and then capture from tape into the DAW. If you're doing this, you're probably using a video format with only two tracks, so it may take many tapes to get the whole mix. Pretty cumbersome.

EXPORT AN EDL. An EDL contains the basic data about where each clip begins and ends and where it belongs on the timeline (see Fig. 14-39). An EDL contains no media. It's a bit like using OMF but with no media and less information. An EDL is sometimes used when the sound studio prefers to recapture the original production audio instead of using the media from the NLE. An EDL can also be used with systems that don't support OMF.

PREP AND DELIVERY. No matter what method you're using, as a rule you should remove any filters or EQ you've done in the offline edit so the mixer can create his or her own.[7] This is especially the case when exporting audio files like

---

6. Not all NLEs support OMF.
7. Some DAWs, such as Pro Tools, allow the mixer to disregard any plug-in effects on import.

AIFF, because once the effect is applied, the mixer can't remove it later. (When exporting audio files or laying off to tape, you may also want to remove level adjustments you made to clips.)

Some editors put a lot of work into their rough mix and want to maintain the level adjustments they made as a basis for the final mix. If you're using OMF and a system that can translate audio clip level adjustments from the NLE to the mix system, this may indeed save time in the final mix. However, some mixers prefer to start with a blank slate, and don't want the editor's levels at all, as things change a lot once you start sweetening. The mixer can listen to the tracks from the reference tape when he wants to hear what the editor had in mind.

Files can be delivered to the sound editor or mix studio on disc or hard drive. Most files are too big for e-mail, but many facilities have FTP sites that allow you to upload or download large files.

Cue Sheets

In a traditional mix, *mix cue sheets* (also known as *log sheets*) are drawn up. They act like road maps to show the mixer where sounds are located on each of the tracks (see Fig. 16-12). The mixer wants to know where each track begins, how it should start (cut in, quick fade, or slow fade), what the sound is, where it should cut or fade out, and how far the track actually extends beyond this point (if at all). The location

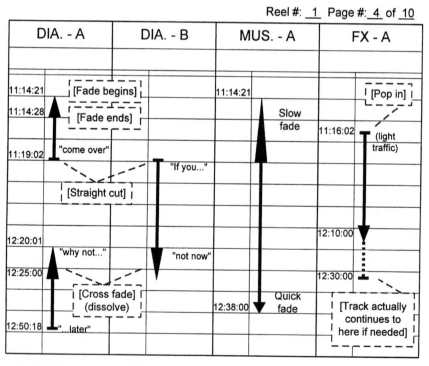

Fig. 16-12. Mix cue sheet. This illustrates one method of notating tracks. The words in quotations are dialogue cues. Bracketed comments are for readers of this book and would not appear on a typical cue sheet. Cue sheets are often not needed anymore.

of sounds is indicated by timecode or, for some film projects, by footage count (see Appendix H). Noting picture and dialogue cues helps as well, especially the last line of dialogue on outgoing tracks. Make notes about any special treatment of a track relative to other tracks (such as "keep low").

These days, few people bother with cue sheets, since the timeline on the DAW shows the mixer where all the clips are.

THE SOUND MIX

This section assumes that you're doing the mix in a sound studio with a professional mixer. However, most of the content applies if you're doing either a rough or final mix yourself.

Arranging for the Mix

Professional sound mixes are expensive (from about $100 to $350 or more per hour); some studios offer discounts to students and for special projects. Get references from other filmmakers before picking a mixer.

Depending on the complexity of the tracks, the equipment, and the mixer's skill, a mix can take two to ten times the length of the movie or more. Some feature films are mixed for months, with significant re-editing done during the process. For a documentary or simple drama without a lot of problems, a half hour of material a day is fairly typical if the work is being done carefully. Some studios allow you to book a few hours of "bump" time in case your mix goes over schedule; you pay for this time only if you use it.

The more time you spend talking, or reviewing sections that have already been mixed, the more it will cost. Sometimes filmmakers will take a dub of the day's work home to review before the next day's session.

Working with the Mixer

The sound mix is a constant series of (often unspoken) questions. Is the dialogue clear? Is this actor's voice too loud compared to the others? Is the music too "thin"? Have we lost that rain effect under the sound of the car? Is the sync sound competing with the narration? Left alone, a good mixer can make basic decisions about the relative volume of sounds, equalization and the pacing of fades. In fact, it's often most efficient to let the mixer rough-in the mix without you there. He'll work faster and when you arrive you can change whatever you want.

Nevertheless, there are many questions for which there is no "correct" answer. The mixer, director, and sound editor must work together to realize the director's goals for the movie. Trust the mixer's experience in translating what you're hearing in the studio to what the audience will hear, but don't be afraid to speak up if something doesn't sound right to you.

Mixers and filmmakers sometimes have conflicts. Mixers tell tales of over-caffeinated filmmakers who haven't slept in days giving them badly prepared tracks and expecting miracles. Filmmakers tell of surly mixers who blame them for audio problems and refuse to take suggestions on how things should be mixed. If you can

Fig. 16-13. Mixer at work. (Sync Sound, Inc)

combine a well-prepared sound editor with a mixer who has good ears, quick re-
flexes, and a pleasant personality, you've hit pay dirt.

MIXING FOR YOUR AUDIENCE

Before an architect can design a building, he or she needs specific information
about where it will be sited, how the structure will be used, and what construction
materials can be employed. Before a sound mix can be done, the mixer will have a
similar set of questions: Where will the movie be shown? What technologies will
be used to show it? How many different versions do you need? Some projects are
designed solely for one distribution route. For example, a video for a museum kiosk
might be shown under very controlled conditions in one place only. But for many
productions, there are several distribution paths. A feature film might be seen in
theaters, on TV, and home video. A corporate video might be shown on a big
screen at a company meeting, then streamed on the company's intranet. Each of
these may call for different choices in the mix. On some projects, more than one
mix is done.

Level and Dynamic Range

How or where a movie is shown affects the basic approach to sound balancing,
in particular the relationship of loud sounds to quiet sounds. Please see Sound,
p. 368, for the basics of dynamic range, and Setting the Recording Level, p. 414.

In a movie theater, the space itself is quiet and the speakers are big and loud
enough so that quiet sounds and deep bass come across clearly. Loud sounds like
explosions and gunshots can be very exciting in theaters because they really sound
big. This is partly because they are indeed loud (as measured by sound pressure) but

it is also due to the great dynamic range between the quieter sounds and the explosions. Our ears get used to dialogue at a quieter level, then the big sounds come and knock us out of our seats. This idea applies to all types of sounds, including the music score, which can include very subtle, quiet passages as well as stunning, full crescendos.

When people watch movies at home, it's a very different story. First, the movie is competing with all sorts of other sounds, including people talking, noises from the street, appliances, air conditioners—whatever. Though some people have "home theaters" equipped with decent speakers, many TVs have lousy little speakers that fail to reproduce either the high frequencies or the lows. And the overall volume level for TV viewing is usually lower than in a theater. Subtlety is lost. If you make any sounds too quiet in the mix, they'll be drowned out by the background noise. Everything needs to punch through to be heard. A common problem happens when mixing music. In the quiet of the mix studio, listening on big speakers, you may think a soft passage of music sounds great. But when you hear the same mix on TV at home, you can't even *hear* the music.

When people watch movies streamed over the Internet, it's usually even worse. The computer may be making noise, the speakers may be small, and the audio may be highly processed for Web delivery. So it's not just the screening environment that limits dynamic range—it's also the delivery format. As another example, 16mm optical tracks are very noisy, and quiet sounds can get lost in the track noise even if the theater itself is quiet.

What does this mean for the mix? For a theatrical mix, you have a lot of dynamic range to play with; for a TV or Internet mix you have much less. One way to visualize it is this: All recording systems have an upper limit on how loud sounds can be. Regardless of the format, you can't go above this level. For a theatrical mix, you can let quiet sounds go much lower than this level. But for a TV mix—or for any format where there's more noise involved—"quiet" sounds should stay much closer to the top.

A useful type of processing for many mixes is *compression*. An audio compressor reduces the level of the loudest sounds to keep them from over-recording.[8] In some mixes, a compressor or peak limiter (see p. 423) might be used just to prevent over-recording of the loudest peaks. But for a TV mix or especially for an Internet mix, compressors and limiters are often used like a vise to squeeze the dynamic range of the sound. The overall level of the sound is raised, making the formerly "quiet" sounds pretty loud, and the compressor or limiter keeps the louder sounds from going over the top (see Fig. 16-14). The result is that everything is much closer to the same level—a compressed dynamic range—so the track will better penetrate the noisy home environment. This also means that the average level is higher than before, which makes the sound track feel louder overall. TV programs may be mildly compressed but commercials are often highly compressed, which is why they seem to blast out of your TV set, even though their maximum peak level is no higher than the seemingly quieter program that preceded it. Pop music is often compressed to the extreme; the average level is pushed way up while the peaks are allowed to rise only a few decibels higher.

8. Don't confuse audio compression with the digital compression used to make files smaller.

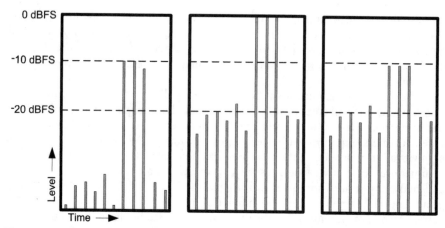

Fig. 16-14. Limiting. (Left) This audio has great dynamic range—note the difference in level between the quietest sounds and the peaks. (Center) If we raise the level so the quieter sounds are loud enough to hear clearly, the peaks are now too high and will be clipped and distorted. (Right) Using a limiter, we can keep the overall level up but ensure the peaks stay under −10 dBFS. Note that we've now reduced the sound's dynamic range. A compressor can be used for a similar effect.

Too much compression can make the track sound flat and textureless. It also makes for an unpleasant experience if you do show the movie in a quiet room with good speakers. Knowing how much compression to use is part of the mixer's art.

In most mix studios, you can switch between full-sized, high-quality speakers and small, not-great speakers which can be extremely useful in helping you judge how the mix may ultimately be heard by viewers. Unfortunately, no matter how careful you are, the aural experience of watching a movie at home will never be as exciting as how the same film sounds in a theater.

SETTING THE MIX LEVEL. If you're working with a mixer, he'll know what level to record the track at. If your program will be delivered to a TV broadcaster, they will have technical specs for average and peak program levels; be sure to show them to the mixer.

If you're doing your own mix, read the discussion on level setting starting on p. 414. If you're using a digital peak meter (where 0 dB is the top of the scale), a common method for broadcast in the United States is to mix so peaks stay below −10 dBFS. Some mixers use a "brick wall" limiter to make sure no peaks go higher. Average level is set around 0 VU on a VU meter. If you only have a peak meter, you can try to keep average level around −20 dBFS (but as discussed in Chapter 11, peak meters aren't very good at indicating the average level). Use a reference tone of −20 dBFS.

In some cases when mixing for non-broadcast video or Internet use, you may want to mix at a higher level, closer to −12 dBFS average level for dialogue, but not let peaks exceed about −6 dBFS (and set reference tone to −12 dBFS).

A typical way to set up the recording system is to play a 1 kHz reference tone on the NLE or DAW (usually at either −20 dBFS or −12 dBFS, depending on your mix level). Then set any equipment that has VU meters—perhaps your mixer or recorder—so that it reads 0 VU. Set the monitor speaker to a comfortable level. Then, *don't change the speaker level while you mix*, so you'll have a consistent way to judge volume level by ear.

Frequency Range and EQ

Another consideration when mixing is the balance of low-, mid-, and high-frequency sounds (bass through treble).

During the shoot, we make every effort to record sound with good mics and other equipment that has a flat response over a wide range of frequencies (see p. 370 for more on this concept). We want to capture the low frequencies for a full-bodied sound and the high frequencies for brightness and clarity. However, in mixing, we often make adjustments that might include: reducing (rolling off) the bass to minimize rumble from wind or vehicles; increasing the midrange to improve intelligibility; cutting or rolling off high frequencies to diminish noise or hiss.

Changing the relative balance of frequencies is called *equalization* or *EQ*. EQ is done in part just to make the track sound better. Some people like to massage the sound quite a bit with EQ; others prefer a flatter, more "natural" approach. It's up to you and your ears.

However, like setting the level, it's not just how things sound in the mix studio that you need to be concerned with. What will the audience's listening environment be? A theater with big speakers or a noisy living room with a small TV? The big bass speakers in a theater can make a low sound feel full and rich. A pulsing bass guitar in the music could sound very cool. The same bass played on a dinky TV might just rattle the speaker and muddy the other sounds you want to hear.

Then you need to take into account the recording or transmission format. Optical soundtracks on film prints may not reproduce frequencies much above 12 kHz and analog TV hits limits around 15 kHz. Digitally compressed audio on the Web may also have a limited frequency range. When frequency range is limited, one common problem is that dialogue that sounds clear in the mix room may lose intelligibility later on. Sometimes it's necessary to make voices a little "thinner" (using less bass and accentuated midrange) so they'll sound clearer to the audience.

This is where an experienced mixer can be very helpful in knowing how to adjust EQ to best advantage for the ultimate viewer.

SETTING EQ. You may want to use some EQ during the picture edit to improve your tracks or you may be doing your own final mix. *Equalizers* allow you to selectively emphasize (boost) or deemphasize (cut or roll off) various frequencies throughout the audio spectrum. The simplest "equalizer" is the bass/treble control on a home stereo. *Graphic equalizers* have a separate slider or control for several different bands of frequencies (see Fig. 16-15). *Parametric equalizers* allow you to select usually low-, mid-, and high-frequency bands, and boost or cut them to varying degrees.

To increase the intelligibility of speech, you might boost midrange frequencies around 2 kHz (2000 Hz) to 4 kHz, and reduce frequencies around 200 to 400 Hz. Also roll off high frequencies above 10 kHz.

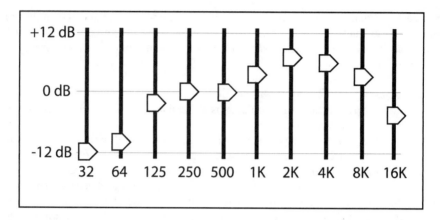

Fig. 16-15. Graphic equalizer. On the version shown here, each slider controls frequencies a half octave above and below the indicated frequency. When a slider is above the 0 dB line, the volume of sound in that frequency band is boosted; below the line, diminished. The equalization indicated here is a basic one for improving the clarity of speech tracks (compare it with Fig. 10-21B). Equalization should be done by ear and not by formula.

Low-frequency cutoff around 75 to 80 Hz or so is often used to reduce the rumble caused by wind and microphone noise (for more, see Bass Filters, p. 429). Since bass rumble can force you to record at too low a level, this is one type of EQ that should generally be done.

High-frequency hiss from tape or system noise may be reduced with a noise-reduction plug-in (preferable) or by rolling off frequencies starting above about 5 kHz or so. The upper-end frequencies can be cut off with a *low pass* or *high shelf filter*. The sound of a voice on the telephone can be simulated by boosting frequencies between about 400 and 2000 Hz and rolling off all others. Good equalization is an art, and should always be done by ear, not by numbers.

Other Sound Processing

Many tools are used to manipulate sound, including the compressors and equalizers just discussed, plus pitch shifters, delays, and noise reduction. In the past, a separate hardware device was used for different effects. Today, many types of sound processing are done with software plug-ins. The following are a few common tools.

NOTCH FILTERS. Also called *dipping filters*, these are a bit like very precise equalizers. They allow you to pinpoint one or two frequency bands and *notch* (cut) them or *peak* (boost) them. Notch filters are useful for isolating and removing specific noises, like the 60 Hz hum caused by fluorescent lights (50 Hz in Europe and Asia), with minimal disturbance to the rest of the track. Many kinds of interference are audible at both fundamental frequencies and harmonics; notching at two or three frequencies may be necessary for complete removal. To get rid of a noise, start by peaking it to make it as loud as possible. Once you've located it, then dip at the same frequency. It sometimes takes a long stretch of sound to find and isolate a noise. On an NLE, you could use a loop function to repeat the clip.

REVERB. The way sound waves reflect off the walls of an enclosed space gives your ear cues about how large the space is. This sound reverberation gives a sense of "liveness" to sound (see Acoustics of the Recording Space, p. 425). A reverb unit can be used to add reverberation to sound after it has been recorded. With more reverb, sounds take longer to decay, making them seem like they were recorded in a larger or more reverberant space. Reverb units can make voices postdubbed in the studio seem more like they were recorded on location. Sound that lacks reverb is sometimes called "dry" or "tight." An *echo filter* repeats the sound as though echoing in a tunnel or canyon.

NOISE REDUCTION. Ambient noise is perhaps the biggest problem in location sound recording. Tape noise can be a big problem with analog recording.

There are various noise-reduction plug-ins that can be very effective in isolating different types of noise and eliminating or reducing them with minimal effect on other sounds.

Another method is called a *noise gate*. Noise gates minimize noise by acting like an automatic gain control in reverse: Whenever there is no clear sound signal (such as speech) they *reduce* the recording level—because it is during the pauses that noise is the most conspicuous. Noise gates can make a noisy track clearer, but a heavily "gated" track will cause the background level to abruptly rise and fall, making it sound noticeably processed. Noise gates can also be used to make an overly reverberant track drier and to change the character of music.

Noise gates, compressors, and other devices share certain types of adjustments. Take the example of using a noise gate to cut out refrigerator noise from a recording of a man talking in a kitchen. Start by imagining the gate as closed, allowing no noise or voice to get through. The *threshold* control determines how loud a sound must be to open the gate; the threshold might be set just lower than the man's voice. The *attack* control determines how fast the gate opens; generally you want a short attack time to open the gate quickly (a slow attack would make the voice fade in). The *hold* control determines how long the gate stays open; it should be long enough not to close during very short pauses. The *release* control determines how fast the gate closes; if this is too sudden, the gating will be obvious. Bringing the *gain* control up slightly allows a *little* refrigerator noise to leak into the silences, helping smooth over the effect.

DE-ESSERS. Compressors used to reduce the sibilance, or whistling, caused by "S" sounds in some people's speech are called *de-essers*. You can hear sibilance distortion sometimes by turning the volume very high on a radio with small speakers. Sibilance can be especially disturbing on a film's optical sound track; the de-esser compresses high frequencies (where sibilance distortion occurs) without affecting much else.

MIX FORMATS

Sound Formats and Audio Channels

Several different audio formats are used when movies are shown in theaters, on TV, DVD, or over the Web. Formats vary in how many channels of audio they can play. In some cases, the producer can choose how many channels to mix for; in others, it's expected that the mix will be produced in a given format. Let's begin with the options in terms of audio channels.

Mono sound means a single channel of audio. For example, 16mm film prints with optical sound tracks reproduce mono sound. The film may be shown on a projector with a single built-in speaker (bad idea) or it may be shown in a theater that has many speakers. Regardless, there is only one channel of sound. Many student films are recorded, edited, and mixed in mono.

Virtually *every other* means of showing a movie today has the possibility of at least two channels of sound. Some have six or more.

In typical home music or TV sound, *stereo sound* means two channels (left and right). Stereo (also called 2.0 channels) adds presence to music and allows you to place sounds on one side or the other, giving a sense of dimensionality. A movie can be released in stereo, even if all the production sound was recorded in mono. In fact, this is often the case. The sound recorded in the field may be taken with a single mono microphone and recorded on one track in the camcorder or audio recorder. During editing, additional tracks are introduced, such as music and effects. Finally, in the mix, the mixer portions the sounds out to either or both of the two stereo channels. Music tracks may have true stereo separation while dialogue is often positioned identically on the left and right (with the pan control in the center), making it essentially "two-channel mono." Many television programs, corporate videos, and other movies are done this way.

In the film industry, "stereo" is understood to include a surround channel. In a movie theater, surround speakers are placed along the sides and rear of the theater. Sounds that are assigned to the surround channel include ambience (atmospheres) and some special effects which surround the audience, adding a sense of realism.

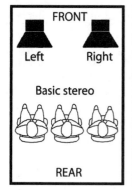 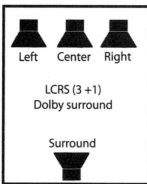 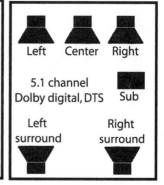

Fig. 16-16. Speaker layouts for different sound formats (as seen from above). The single surround channel in the LCRS format is often sent to more than one speaker. The 5.1 channel format includes a subwoofer for low-frequency effects (deep bass).

Proper theater stereo also has a center channel so that the sound of actors speaking on screen will appear natural, coming directly from the screen instead of seeming off balance for people who are not sitting in the middle of the theater. This format is often referred to as *LCRS* (for left, center, right, surround).

Films mixed for analog Dolby Stereo can have these four channels, with left, center, and right speakers hidden behind the screen, and surround speakers at the rear and sides of the auditorium. The four channels are specially encoded so they can be recorded on just two tracks, so a "stereo" (two-channel) track can carry all the information for the four playback streams. This encoding of four channels in two is sometimes called *LTRT* (for left total, right total).

The *Dolby Surround Pro Logic* format extends the same idea for reproduction in the home. Again, four channels of sound are recorded on two channels of the tape or disc. Dolby Surround Pro Logic provides great versatility for a wide range of playback equipment. If the format is used for a TV broadcast or home video release, people who have only one speaker (say, in an older TV set) receive a mono signal with all the sound. People who have two speakers (in a typical "stereo" TV) will receive a two-channel signal. And people who have a "home theater" setup with left, right, center, and surround speakers and a Pro Logic Decoder in their system can "unfold" the matrix into the four channels for the full effect.

Moving up the food chain, the newer *5.1 channel* standard includes the same left, center, and right channels across the front of the room but the surround channel is split into left and right sides. For really deep bass, an additional channel is added to drive a subwoofer (this channel is called *LFE—low frequency effects*). Since this bass channel uses much less bandwidth than the other five channels, this layout is referred to as having "5.1 channels."

The most common 5.1 channel format is *Dolby Digital (AC-3)*, which is used in a wide variety of applications, including digital broadcasting, DVDs, and theatrical films. Dolby Digital is digitally compressed and can pack all six channels into less space than a single channel of uncompressed PCM audio. *Dolby E* is an improved way of encoding Dolby Digital that can store up to eight channels of audio on two compressed channels.

Other formats add more channels. *Dolby Surround EX* adds a center surround speaker for 6.1 channels, *Dolby Digital Plus* has 7.1 channels (the surround speaker array has four parts—left side, left back, right side, right back) and *SDDS* offers 7.1 channels by dividing the front speaker array into five parts. The goal of adding all these channels is to provide a more dynamic, enveloping sound experience for the audience. How much different they sound from 5.1 is for you to decide. For more on how these formats are applied to film, see Sound for Film Prints, p. 689.

CHOOSING A FORMAT. As a producer, you must decide how you want to take advantage of these formats. In some cases broadcasters or distributors may require programming in a certain format; in other cases it may be optional. Mixing for many channels adds time and complexity to the project and requires a studio equipped with the necessary speaker layout. Some movies are enhanced by multi-channel reproduction; on others it may add very little. A television show, corporate video, or multimedia project might be mixed in basic stereo (just two channels) on the assumption that most viewers will not have a home theater setup and will hear the sound through relatively small speakers on a TV, VCR, or computer. When a theatrical film is to be mixed in Dolby Digital, arrangements must be made to license the format from Dolby, which is not cheap. (Licensing is also needed for nontheatrical products that bear the Dolby logo.) The decision to mix with 5.1 channels or more should be considered in terms of marketing as well: Multichannel sound is considered desirable and may enhance the sales value of your project. However, some independent films are released in basic stereo or even—gasp— mono. Particularly for a non-action, non-special-effects movie, many audiences never notice the difference.

Foreign Release

For foreign distribution, when translation to another language is called for, you will need to supply an *M&E* (*music and effects*) track. The M&E mix contains all the non-dialogue sound that will be used as a bed for dubbed foreign-language voices. On a documentary, the M&E may just be a mix without narration (sometimes called a *DM&E*), since the dialogue is often inextricable from the "effects" (they're all recorded together on location). For a drama, there can also be sync scenes in which dialogue and effects (such as footsteps) can't be separated. In this case, foley work may be needed to create clean effects tracks to which the foreign-language voices can be added, a process that may take several days (see p. 635).

On a documentary, interviews and other scenes are usually subtitled instead of dubbed. If there's narration, it's usually dubbed even if the dialogue is subtitled. Broadcasters may ask for an "undipped" version of the track with no narration. Undipped means a track that has not been lowered or *ducked* as it normally would be whenever the narrator speaks. You can prepare for this by first mixing the entire film with undipped music and sync sound, then returning to the beginning and making a dipped version with narration exclusively for domestic use.[9] See Chapter 19 for more on preparing a movie for foreign release.

DELIVERABLES

At the end of the mix, you may need to create several versions of the material for different uses.

- *Main mix.* The mixed audio is output from the DAW so it can be recombined with the edited picture. This may involve a *layback* process, where the track is recorded directly to the edit master tape (or *several* edit master tapes, depending on how many versions there are). Or the mix may be exported from the DAW as an audio file in OMF or AIFF or other file format to be imported into an NLE and then output with the picture from there.
- *Printmaster.* For projects that will be finished on film, an output is done to create the *printmaster*, which is the source from which the film print's sound track will be created. Sometimes the printmaster needs to be speed adjusted (for example to compensate for 0.1 percent speed slowdown in telecined film

9. DAWs can output undipped tracks simply by removing the added level settings.

in NTSC countries, or the 4.1 percent speedup in PAL countries; see Chapter 15).

- **Compressed files.** You may be making an encoded version of the mix for Internet streaming or other compressed digital formats. The *AAC* codec is used for audio compression in MPEG-4 and H.264 formats.

- **Mix stems.** *Mix stems* (also called *splits*) are the components of the mix, such as dialogue, narration, music, and effects. In the main mix, the stems are combined. Having a file of each stem by itself allows you to use or exclude any stem for making trailers or other versions of the movie (for example, you may use different music in the trailer, or you may later change the music in the movie itself if a music license runs out). Without stems, you have to return to the mix studio and try to split out what you need. On features, music stems without any fader moves are often a required deliverable.

- **M&E.** As described above, you will generally need to deliver an M&E for any foreign markets.

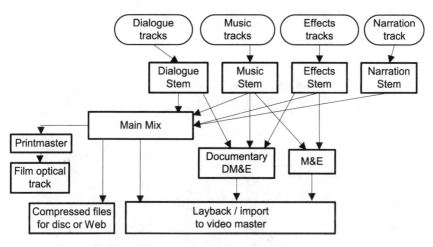

Fig. 16-17. This shows how the mix stems (dialogue, music, effects, and sometimes narration) can be combined and output for various deliverables. A separate M&E mix (or DM&E for a documentary) can often be recorded on additional audio tracks along with the main mix on the final video masters. Sometimes a separate DA-88 audiotape (8-track, same cassette as Hi8 video) is requested as a deliverable for an M&E mix.

CHAPTER 17

The Film Laboratory

T his chapter is about the various stages of processing and printing film, including developing the original, making workprint, conforming the original (negative matching), film printing, and film projection. See Chapter 7 for the basics of raw stock and processing. See Chapter 15 for both film editing and an overview of using film-to-video transfer and video editing for postproduction of projects shot on film. There's more on the specifics of film-to-video transfer in Chapter 18.

Fig. 17-1. Film processing machine. (DuArt Film and Video)

Dealing with the laboratory is, at times, one of the most frustrating technical aspects of filmmaking. To avoid the usual lab problems, know which instructions the lab needs, what can be reasonably expected of the lab, and how to evaluate their work. Although laboratories sometimes do careless work and make errors, their number of errors seldom equals those made by filmmakers. Filmmakers tend to blame all technical faults on the lab, and it is a rare lab that will admit that *it* has made an error.

To choose a lab, talk to filmmakers in your area. In some cities, the nearby labs are fine, but sometimes you are better off working with a lab in another city. You may find a single lab that can do everything you need, which can have advantages when coordinating different aspects of the work. However, on some productions, one lab is used for processing the negative, a video transfer facility does transfers, an optical house does the titles, and another lab makes the final prints. See Chapter 19 for business arrangements when dealing with labs.

THE FILM LAB
DURING PRODUCTION

Shooting Tests

After a lab has been selected, tests are sometimes made of camera, sets, actors (*screen tests*), costumes, and makeup. Particularly important are tests of film stock and processing. For testing, use lighting and locations similar to that used in the final production. Print the tests in the same way you will make the release prints (see below). The production team should evaluate the tests, and the cinematographer should discuss with the lab any adjustments that need to be made in processing, video transfer, or printing.

Processing the Original

Deliver the film to the lab as soon as possible after it is exposed. Pack core-wound film in its black bag and tape down the end so the film does not unravel in transit. Prominently mark "EXPOSED" on the can, so no one mistakes it for unexposed stock. See Camera Film Capacity, p. 242, for unloading magazines and preparing cans for the lab. See Handling Film Stock, p. 273, for general considerations in handling unprocessed film. Each film shipment to the lab should include the following information (labs will often supply a form for these items or use a camera report). The first ten items should be marked on each can of unprocessed camera original.[1] Normally, a letter or purchase order accompanies the shipment. Many of the items below are discussed later in this chapter.

1. The production company name.
2. The working title of the production. Don't change the title in midproduction or the lab may lose your materials.
3. The date.
4. Both the common name of the film stock (for example, Vision 500T) and the emulsion number (such as 7218). See Fig. 7-9.
5. The amount of footage and the gauge. Mark if Super 16.
6. Special processing instructions, including force developing (for example, push one, push two) or instructions for flashing. It's a good idea to discuss any special processing with the lab before ordering the work.
7. The camera roll number. Never repeat a camera roll number.

---

1. As discussed on p. 246, some of this information will normally be written on a piece of tape or a label when the camera magazine is loaded, and the label can be moved to the can when the magazine is unloaded.

8. The approximate location of footage where any camera jams or torn perfs occurred. The lab will do a hand inspection to see that no problems will occur in the processing machines that could ruin your footage and possibly footage from another production.

9. Any tests; for example, fifteen-foot tail exposure test.

10. For a daylight spool on which you wish to save a run-out shot or a darkroom (core) load, mark "OPEN ONLY IN DARK." If the core has popped out, mark "NO CORE" or "AIR WIND."

11. Tell the lab what it should do with the processed original. "HOLD ORIGINAL" means it should be stored in the lab's vault.

12. The name, address, and telephone number of the person to contact in case of questions (or the name of the cinematographer or director, if applicable).

IF YOU WANT WORKPRINT. If you're editing on film, also specify:

13. Workprint instructions:
    a. Color or black-and-white? Any special stock?
    b. Single- or double-perforated? Request print-through key numbers.
    c. One-light print? Standard light? Timed and color-corrected?
    d. For returning workprint: Pickup? Shipped? Insurance?
    e. Request the timing sheet.
    f. Special instructions; for example, day-for-night scenes or unusual color balance.
    g. In 35mm, make sure the camera report details which takes are to be printed.

IF YOU'RE EDITING IN VIDEO. If you're editing in video, you'll need to have a video transfer done (usually from the film negative, but sometimes from the workprint). See Editing Film on Video, p. 605, for an overview of this process and Preparing for the Transfer, p. 699, for ordering instructions for the transfer.

SPECIAL PROCESSING INSTRUCTIONS. In tricky lighting situations, you can make a test to determine if any compensation is needed in processing—for example, by pushing (forced development) or flashing (see Chapter 7 for discussion of these terms).[2] Sometimes, for convenience, the exposure test footage is included on the same roll as other footage. The test can be at the beginning of a roll (*head test*) or at the end (*end test* or *tail test*). Tail tests are preferable and most common, as they avoid the need to rewind the film and are easier to find. Clearly identify the test footage on the can (for example, "end test 15 feet"). Lab personnel will process the test according to your directions; then they'll view it and/or show it to you. After consultation, the whole roll is processed according to the results of the test.

STORING THE NEGATIVE. If you don't have a cool, safe place with low humidity to store the original, have the lab store it until it is conformed or transferred to video. Find out if the lab charges for this service, and get a tour of the lab's vaults—a romantic name for what may be a chaotic, dusty back room. There are

---

2. Not all labs do postflashing.

also warehouses that specialize in film storage where film can be kept in temperature- and humidity-controlled spaces for an added charge.

The Workprint

Workprint is a protection copy of the camera original used for editing. Today, the majority of film projects are edited in video and often no workprint is made. However for student projects and some high-budget features, workprint is still used.

Though one can edit films shot with reversal stocks using the original, generally this is considered too risky except on very low-budget productions. Negative stocks need to be printed just to be viewable. The edited workprint is then used to conform the camera original. The workprinted camera rolls are called *rushes*, or *dailies*, because the lab turns them out quickly. The lab processes the dailies overnight and the filmmakers view them the following day or evening (small labs may not deliver this fast). When a lab delivers the rushes the same day they receive the unprocessed negative, this is sometimes called *daylighting*. The workprint is nearly always an A-wind contact print (see Fig. 7-10).

Timing the Workprint

Workprint is usually made on a contact printer that can make exposure and/or color corrections for each shot (labs usually refer to shots as "scenes"). There are two basic types of workprint that can be ordered—*timed* and *untimed*.

An *untimed print*, also called a *one-light* (or *one-lite*) is made with the same printing light for the entire camera roll; no compensations are made for exposure or color differences from one shot to the next. A one-light print is sometimes made with a *standard light*, which is around the middle of the printer's scale. For example, many printers have a range of lights from 1 to 50 points, the lab's standard light being around 25. Cinematographers working in controlled environments, such as the film studio, often work with the lab to establish a standard light for the entire project, which makes any errors in exposure or color balance immediately apparent (for more on this, see Print Exposure and Color Correction, p. 681).

Another method, sometimes called a *best-light print*, bases the exposure on the first few scenes on the roll and stays consistent for the rest of the roll. If there are gross variations in exposure, sometimes the lab will make a few corrections. In some labs, a best-light workprint is timed for different scenes on the roll (and can be considered a "partially timed" print). Ask the lab how much correction they do on best-light prints.

For a *timed workprint* (also called a *graded* or *color-balanced workprint*), the lab makes scene-to-scene corrections, choosing the best light for each take. There may be a surcharge of 30 percent or more for this service. Don't expect these corrections to be as accurate as those on an answer print (see p. 683). A timed print may be beyond your budget; however, if sections of a one-light workprint are badly timed, it may be worthwhile to have them reprinted, since the workprint is often viewed by many people.

Timing Sheets and Lab Reports

Some labs, as a matter of course, include the *timing sheet* (also called the *exposure report*) with your workprint. The timing sheet is a record of the printer lights used when making the workprint. If a timed workprint is ordered, it's especially important to get a timing sheet and interpret it. Timing corrections may hide mistakes that you need to know about for future shoots. If you know the lab's standard light, it is easy to see which exposure or color balance errors are being compensated for (see p. 681). For example, with negative, if the lab is using more light than standard, then the negative is too dense, that is, overexposed. If your results are consistently overexposed or underexposed, check your equipment.

In feature film production, send the lab a camera report or camera sheets, which, among other things, lists all the takes by footage number and circles those takes to be printed (see Fig. 9-31). To save money, you may print only those camera takes the director feels are usable. Many labs will do this only for 35mm and not for 16mm film. The camera report should also include timing information, for example, exterior ("Ext") or interior ("Int"); special instructions ("print slightly red"). Without instructions, the timer may attempt to bring intentionally underexposed scenes (for example, day-for-night shots) or scenes with colored gels (say, at a nightclub) back to normal. If you shoot a gray card at the head of each scene this can help the timer color balance a normal shot (see Standardizing Color Reproduction, p. 295).

THE LAB REPORT. Many laboratories supply a *lab report* (also called a *negative report*) with the rushes. The lab report lists gross camera errors and damage to the film (for example, significant exposure errors, scratches, and edge fog). When you are filming on location, someone at the lab can read the report to you over the phone or e-mail it.

When you choose your lab, find out which errors the lab will check for in its report. If you can't view the rushes on a daily basis, try to get the lab to include information about bad focus, improper collimation on a zoom lens, dirt in the gate, flicker, breathing, poor image registration, dirt (or "sparkle"), cinching, or static marks. Certainly any processing errors should be noted. The lab report is especially important when no film workprint is made and the movie is being edited in video, which may mask some errors.

Other Workprint Options

In 16mm, workprint may be ordered on double- or single-perforated stock. Double-perf stock is easier to run through synchronizers and other equipment. Single-perf allows the editor to quickly determine which end is heads and which is tails, and he'll be less likely to splice in a short shot upside down. The choice is not critical, but it is better not to mix single- and double-perf on the same production. Most labs routinely print workprint on spliced stock, which means that occasionally there may be a cement splice, which is not too serious, but sometimes there is a color shift or slight fogging of a few frames at the splice. Printing on unspliced stock can be done for a surcharge.

The lab can attach an SMPTE focus leader at the head of your dailies to assist in checking that projectors and editing systems are properly set up and are not cutting off too much or the wrong part of the image.

Edge Numbers on Workprint

Most camera stocks, other than those in Super 8, have key numbers (latent edge numbers) photographed on the edge of the film (see p. 271). Always instruct the lab, in writing, to print these numbers on the workprint. When the workprint is returned, make sure the print-through key numbers are legible. They are essential for conforming camera original and workprint. If the lab forgets to print them, they should make another workprint at no extra charge. They may offer to print matching ink edge code (see p. 602) on original and workprint, but this is not a good practice.

SCREENING THE RUSHES

The cinematographer and director should look at the rushes as soon as possible, preferably the day after shooting. If working with video dailies, use a high-quality, large broadcast monitor whenever possible. If viewing workprint, be sure to project on a good-sized screen, since editing machines may hide errors such as image flicker, slight softness of focus, and bad registration. Sometimes cinematographers like to screen rushes without sound to concentrate on camera issues.

Video dailies are improving a great deal, as are color management systems that help coordinate the color reproduction on different monitors. Nevertheless, it's sometimes difficult to evaluate rushes when transferred to video, as monitors can be very inconsistent in contrast and color. Also, the video may not reveal subtleties that the cinematographer needs to see to evaluate lighting and shooting choices.

Troubleshooting Errors

The following are possible problems that may be evident when screening workprint or a video transfer. Some may be actual problems with the original camera negative, others may be due to the workprint or transfer.

SCRATCHES OR CINCH MARKS. If you see a scratch during the screening, check immediately for its source. The lab report may note whether the scratch is on the emulsion or base (*cell scratch*).

If there's no notation on the lab report, and you're screening workprint, stop the projector and hold the scratched film at an angle to a light source so that you can see the reflection of the light on the film. Twist the film in relation to the reflection to see if the scratch is actually on the film. If it's not on the workprint, the scratch is on the original. If it is on the print, check whether it is also on the projector feed reel. If it is, the scratch was made before projection. If not, the projector is making the scratches. Clean the projector (see p. 694) and check for emulsion buildups or tight rollers before continuing the screening.

Most scratches on original come from the camera, although some come from laboratory or manufacturer errors. A scratch test (see p. 251) prior to filming will usually show a manufacturer error or a camera scratch. If a scratch is precise with no wobble or if it has a slight fuzziness on the edge of the scratch (a sign of a pre-processing scratch), it is probably a camera scratch. Emulsion scratches are usually camera scratches, since most lab rollers touch only the base side.

Further questions to help detect the origin of scratches are: Does the camera scratch now? Do only those rolls shot in a particular mag show the scratch? Did an inexperienced person load the camera? If you're unsure, discuss the matter with the lab and ask (though do not necessarily trust) their opinion. Base scratches can generally be removed by buffing. Liquid gate printing (see p. 682) often hides base scratches and some minor emulsion scratches. You can ask the lab to check whether a scratch is on the emulsion or on the base. A base scratch defracts light (that is, it does not let light pass), so it will appear black on reversal and white (and uncolored) on a positive print from negative. Emulsion scratches let light through; they appear white or colored on reversal and black or colored on a positive print from a negative. *Cinch marks* appear as discontinuous oblique scratches usually caused by handling film poorly, such as pulling unraveled film tight or squeezing dished, core-wound film back into place. Liquid gate printing or buffing may remove cinch marks on the base. Thin camera original (underexposed negative or overexposed reversal) will print with more noticeable scratches and cinch marks.

DIRT ON THE FILM. Dust or dirt that shows black on the screen is less noticeable than when it is white. Dirt on reversal films shows up as black, while dirt on the processed negative original will appear white when printed (called sparkle) or when viewed on video. If a workprint itself is dirty, the dirt shows up black. If you see dirt on a projected print, clean the print by running it through a piece of felt moistened with film cleaner (see p. 595). A noticeable amount of dirt on the felt (assuming this is the first projection) warrants a complaint to the lab. If the dirt is on the original, it may be due to lab handling, dirty changing bags, mags, or cameras. The lab's ability to handle film cleanly, especially in the more critical negative-positive process, is a key consideration in lab selection.

EDGE FOG. *Edge fog* is caused by a light leak that fogs the film before processing. Edge fog lowers contrast, often unevenly, and changes as the camera moves in relation to the light source. The effect is similar to lens flare, but, unlike lens flare, edge fog appears on camera original outside the image area. On color film, it often has a strong color cast. Light leaks can be caused by a loose magazine lid, a loose camera door, a bad magazine-to-camera fitting, a hole in the changing bag, not packing core-wound film in the black bag, or inadvertently opening a can of unprocessed film. Edge fog at the head or tail of spool-wound film is to be expected. See Light Leak Test, p. 252.

STATIC MARKS. Static marks appear as lightning bolts or branches of light (see p. 273).

PROCESSING ERRORS. *Reticulation* is the breaking up of the image into cell-like patterns caused by a sudden change in the temperature of processing solutions. *Chemical staining* appears as blotches, sometimes colored. *Blue comets* are blue streaks that occur on some color stocks when metal reacts with the film in the developer. The metal may come from the camera magazine and may not be the lab's fault. *Uneven development* shows up as waviness in the tonalities and sometimes as an overall mottled appearance. *Exhausted developer* may show up on print as uneven development or, sometimes, as low contrast. *Spotting, mottling,* and *streaking* can be caused by improper drying. Consult the lab immediately to find out if a processing error is on the original. In the event of their error, most labs will only replace stock and refund the cost of processing.

RAW STOCK DEFECTS. Defects in the raw stock are often difficult to distinguish from processing errors. Mottling may come from defects or processing errors. The manufacturer will usually accept responsibility for replacement of defective stock and sometimes processing costs. Out-of-date or improperly stored stock will show increased fog and graininess and decreased contrast and film speed (see Chapter 7).

DIRTY GATE. Dirt and hairs may be in the camera gate or the projector gate, extending out into the image, often from the top or bottom edge. Change the frame line adjustment in the projector. If the dirt moves with the frame line, it means the dirt was in the camera aperture.

CAMERA DEFECTS. For bad registration and breathing in the gate, see Chapter 6. Flicker in the image may be a camera motor defect or a problem with lighting, particularly HMIs or other pulsed lights (see Chapter 12). A partial vertical ghostlike blurring may mean the camera shutter has a timing error. If vertical blurring covers the entire image, most likely the pressure plate was not holding the film in place (lost loop) and the claw never engaged the film. See Chapter 4 for lens problems.

OTHER WORKPRINT ERRORS. Workprint usually projects properly when it's wound base out. If you find that the print must be loaded emulsion out in order to project properly, it may be because the lab has printed the original flipped. An optical print (see below) may be printed in camera original position (which does project emulsion out), but this is extremely rare for workprint. If the film seems flipped and the camera original was reversal, be careful: You may be projecting the original. Sometimes if the overall look or contrast of the print is different from other workprint, the lab may have used a different print stock.

Old shrunken film or recently processed unlubricated film (green film) often chatters during projection. If the workprint makes noise and is unsteady, it may only need lubrication. In any case, the problem generally stops after projecting the film a few times. Check whether the lab forgot to lubricate the film. If you want to do this yourself, use film cleaner with lubricant.

PREPARING THE ORIGINAL FOR PRINTING

This section is about the steps that take place in preparation for printing and/or video transfer after the film has been edited. Let's briefly review the first part of the film editing process. When you buy raw stock to shoot your movie, it already has key numbers (see p. 271) photographically exposed on it by the manufacturer. You then go out and shoot with this stock and give it to the lab for processing. This film, which went through the camera, is called the camera original, the original camera negative (OCN), or just the original. Though some people shoot reversal original, negative stocks are more common.

If you plan to edit the movie using film editing equipment, you generally have a film workprint made from the original, as discussed above. On the workprint, the key numbers from the original are visible alongside the picture. You edit the workprint, and when you're done, you mark it to indicate where you want fades or dissolves (see p. 603). You then give the workprint to a negative cutter, who measures every shot you selected, and, using the key numbers, "pulls" every piece of camera original that corresponds to the parts of the workprint you used in the edited movie. He or she will then splice these shots together in one or more rolls in preparation for making film prints and/or for a transfer to video (this may be the second time the negative has been transferred).

Alternately, if you plan to edit the movie in video, a different procedure is followed. The camera original is transferred to video, at which time a shot log is made that correlates the key numbers on the film to the timecode numbers of the video transfer (see Chapter 18). You then edit your movie on the nonlinear editing system. When you're done editing, a list is compiled of all the shots in the edited movie which correlates the video timecode with the key numbers on the original film (see Editing Film on Video, p. 605). At this point, the shots used in the offline edit are pulled, and can be spliced together for printing. However, these days it has become much more common *not* to make film prints from the original camera negative, but to do a high-quality transfer from the negative to video, finish the film in video, then do a film-out to create a new negative from which film prints can be made (see Chapter 15).

So, if you're going the traditional route and making prints from your original negative, there are several ways the shots can be spliced together ("conformed"), depending on the type of film used, the type of printer to be used, and the way the film will be printed or transferred. Let's look at those now.

Types of Printers

A *printer* is essentially a machine that duplicates one piece of film onto another. The camera original and the unexposed printing stock move past an aperture where the intensity and the color of light exposing the stock can be controlled. Prints can be made either by putting the original in contact with the print stock on a *contact printer* or by projecting the original onto the print stock through a lens on an *optical printer* (see Figs. 17-2 and 17-3). *Continuous printers* move the original and printing stock at a uniform speed, while *step printers* move the two strips past the aperture one frame at a time, holding the strips stationary during exposure. Contact prints are almost always made on a continuous printer, and optical effects on a step printer.

In general, using a contact printer is less expensive than printing optically. Dailies are made on a continuous contact printer—the least expensive printing method. Before the negative is conformed, a decision is made about what type of

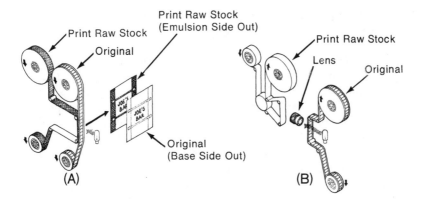

Fig. 17-2. Contact and optical printing. (A) The contact printer: the original is printed in emulsion-to-emulsion contact with the print stock. The inset shows how this changes the wind. Usually the original reads through the base (B-wind), and the contact print reads through the emulsion (A-wind). (B) The optical printer: a lens is used between the original and print stock. The wind can be preserved or changed on an optical printer. (Carol Keller)

printer will be used to make the prints or intermediates. For example, a standard 16mm release print may be made on a contact printer, but if a blowup to 35mm is anticipated, an optical printer will be needed at some point. The original is conformed appropriately for the printer that has been chosen.

Fig. 17-3. Simple optical printer. The camera is at left, the projector at right. The control box advances the camera and projector in sync or independently. The lens is mounted on a bellows to allow you to change the magnification or reposition the image. (J-K Camera Engineering)

CONFORMING THE ORIGINAL (NEGATIVE MATCHING)

Conforming the original must be done with utmost care and precision. The work should be done in a dust-free space, with editing gloves to protect the original from finger smudges. Dirt and scratches must be avoided. Negative stocks are especially vulnerable: dirt on negative prints white, which is more noticeable than reversal dirt, which prints black; negative emulsions are also softer than those of reversal and more easily scratched. Cutting errors made during conforming can be disastrous, and badly made splices can cause serious problems if they jump or come apart during printing. Although some filmmakers choose to do this precise, tedious, and time-consuming task themselves, others gladly pay professionals to do it for them. *Negative cutters* (also called *conformers* or *negative matchers*) may charge a few hundred dollars for a 400-foot reel of 16mm film. Some charge per cut instead of per foot, which may be cheaper or more costly, depending on how the film is edited. If you have a negative matcher do your conforming, you won't need to involve yourself much in the process, but be sure to ask how he or she wants things prepared. Some filmmakers cut and arrange the original but let the lab do the final splicing. The filmmaker normally puts *scribe marks* at the frames to be spliced. Ask the lab how they want the footage prepared. For further information on conforming your own original, see Appendix J.

There are four principal ways of laying out the original for printing (and sometimes video transfer). Each has its advantages.

Single Strand

Splicing the conformed original into a *single strand* (also called *A-rolling*) is simple and straightforward; labs charge less to make prints from a single strand. This is the standard process in 35mm printing, since the frame line is wide enough to make cement splices that aren't visible on screen.

However, when printing from a single strand in 16mm and Super 8, splices—whether made with cement or tape—will show on the screen. Virtually all professionally made 16mm films are printed using a more expensive technique that makes cement splices invisible (see below).[3]

There are some disadvantages to single strand printing. First, depending on the printing machine used, the lab may not be able to make the complete color and exposure corrections for each shot that it could if the film were on more than one strand. Second, when using a contact printer, fades on negative stocks and double exposures, superimposed titles, or dissolves on either negative or reversal stocks are normally not possible, since these effects require the overlapping of two shots. These effects can be done from a single strand if all or part of the film is optically printed.

In 35mm, any effects that would require multiple strands are typically done in an optical printer (or done digitally) and then the effect negative is spliced in with

---

3. If you must print a 16mm or Super 8 film with tape splices, be sure the splices are tight and unstretched. Redo any bad ones. Double-splice the film with guillotine tape or Kodak Presstapes that have been cut on the frame line (see Fig. 15-3). Always inform the lab if a film has tape splices.

the single-strand original for contact printing. As the 35mm image doesn't deteriorate much when duplicated, you can splice second-generation opticals with first-generation original without problems. In 16mm, the two generations may compare badly when spliced together. Even so, some 35mm films are done with multiple rolls.

A&B Rolls

Splices can be made invisible in 16mm by printing from multiple strands of original. *A&B rolling* (also called *checkerboard printing*) is the most common way of printing 16mm films. This involves dividing the shots from the original onto two rolls and spacing them with black leader. Thus, the first shot of the movie is on the A-roll, with black leader opposite it on the B-roll. The second shot is spliced onto the B-roll, and leader of the same length fills the space on the A-roll. To print the A&B rolls, first the A-roll is run through the printing machine with the print raw stock. The shots on the roll are exposed onto the print stock, but wherever there is black leader nothing happens. Then the B-roll is threaded up with the print stock. The shots on this roll occur only where black leader was on the A-roll. They are exposed onto the print stock and the black leader on the B-roll now protects the shots that were already printed from the A-roll. By using completely opaque black leader, you can be sure that although the print stock must be run twice—once for the A-roll and once for the B-roll—each shot in the film will be printed onto unexposed sections of the print stock.

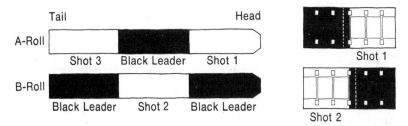

Fig. 17-4. A&B rolling. (Left) Three shots laid out on A&B rolls with black leader as spacing. (Right) The overlap for the 16mm cement splice occurs over the black leader, not over the picture. (Carol Keller)

This technique leads to invisible splices simply because the overlap needed to make the cement splice occurs over black leader, through which no light reaches the print stock. The last frame of shot 1 is clean, and the quarter-frame overlap for the splice occurs on the next frame of black leader. Similarly, the first frame of shot 2 is clean, its overlap being on the preceding frame of leader. For this method to work, the emulsion must be scraped off the original film and never from the black leader; otherwise, light could penetrate the splice.

One major advantage of A&B rolling is that two or more images can be exposed on the same section of print stock simply by putting the images opposite each other on the A&B rolls. Double exposures, dissolves, and superimposed titles can all be accomplished in this way. Sometimes a third roll, or C-roll, is used for triple exposures, for dissolving from one superimposed title to another, for a supered title placed over a picture dissolve or for beginning a second picture dissolve, before the first is completed. Each additional printing roll increases the cost of the print.

Fade-outs and fade-ins with negative stocks are done by splicing a section of clear leader opposite the picture on another roll. Where the picture is supposed to become darker, the light through the clear footage is increased. For color negative films, clear camera original is used instead of clear leader because it contains the orange masking necessary for proper color reproduction. Some labs request that the section of clear film be somewhat longer than the fade it is covering.

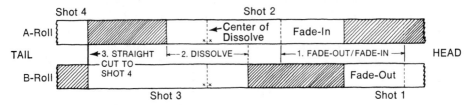

Fig. 17-5. The A&B roll layout for: (1) Fade-out on the B-roll followed by fade-in on the A-roll; (2) Dissolve from A-roll to B-roll; (3) Straight cut from B-roll back to A-roll. The fades indicated in 1 are for reversal film only. (Carol Keller)

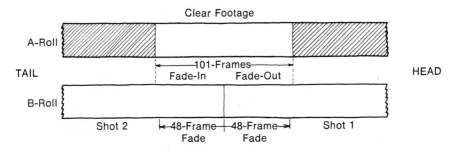

Fig. 17-6. The A&B roll layout for a fade-out at the end of shot 1 followed by a fade-in on shot 2 on negative stocks only. Some labs request that the clear footage be somewhat longer than the fades it is covering. (Carol Keller)

The other benefit of using A&B rolling is that most labs are equipped to make full color and exposure corrections for each shot. If the length of black leader between two shots on a roll is not sufficient for the printer to readjust for the second shot, additional (C or D) printing rolls may be used. Consult with the lab about minimum spacing of shots and effects.

Zero Cutting

Another technique for making invisible splices is *zero cutting*. In zero cutting, the shots are laid out similarly to those in A&B rolling, but with at least a four-frame overlap at each splice (usually the overlap is much greater). When the printer reaches the end of a shot in one roll, its shutter closes very rapidly. When the printer reaches the same frame on the next roll, the shutter opens. If this is done with a continuous printer, the result is a dissolve of one-frame duration, which may be noticeable on some cuts. On a step printer there should be a normal straight cut. Not all labs can do zero cutting; if they can, there is usually an additional charge per cut.

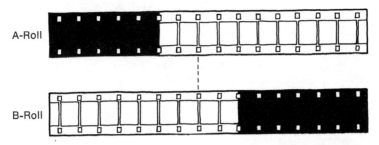

Fig. 17-7. Layout for zero cutting from A-roll to B-roll. The overlap may be far greater than the four frames pictured here. (Carol Keller)

The main advantage of zero cutting is that shots need not be trimmed to conform to the edited version of the film. Instead, shots can be included in their entirety—the way they came out of the camera—with the printer programmed to print only certain sections. This means several different edited versions can be made of one film. Films that are zero-cut in this way often require four or five printing rolls to accommodate all the excess footage. Unlike A&B rolling, opaque black leader need not be used to space the shots on the rolls.

Conforming in Camera

Another method that, like zero cutting, allows for invisible splices and the possibility of making multiple versions of the film involves using an optical printer. The original is spliced into a single strand. Shots may be taken in their entirety (from flash frame to flash frame) or they may be trimmed to nearly their finished (edited) length. The original is loaded in the projector of the printer, and the print raw stock is put in the printer's camera. The printer is programmed by footage count to print only the desired frames. When the chosen end point of a shot is reached, the print stock is held in place while the original is advanced to the beginning of the next shot. Because the original and the print stock can be moved independently of each other, dissolves, double exposures, and superimposed titles can all be done with this single-strand technique. This method, sometimes called *in-camera conform, conforming in camera,* or *auto-conform,* requires the use of an optical printer, which is expensive, but it saves the cost and trouble of conforming the original in the traditional way. Often, optical printing is needed for other reasons anyway (to produce high-quality superimposed titles or when making a blowup), in which case conforming in camera may be the most economical route.

For an in-camera conform to be successful, your negative cutter should be experienced with the particular lab that is completing the work. Not all negative matchers and labs can perform this service.

Printing Leaders

All film original submitted to the lab for printing should have standardized head and tail leaders attached (see Fig. 17-8). A negative cutter will normally prepare leaders; you only need be concerned with them if you are doing the conforming yourself. Information should be written on the leaders in India ink, never grease pencil. The leaders should be spliced emulsion-to-emulsion and base-to-base with the original. The black leader preceding the first image on the film should be replaced with SMPTE head leader, which contains the familiar 8-second countdown (in the case of A&B rolls, the leader is put only on the B-roll). SMPTE, or Society, leader (see Appendix H) should be fresh and of the same wind as the original (normally B-wind). This leader is available at all labs. Sound films should have a beep tone (sync pop) applied to the sound track opposite the number 2 (see Appendix H).

It's simplest to submit sound tracks with the film in *editorial* or *dead sync*. This means that if the sound track and the picture are loaded in a synchronizer with the

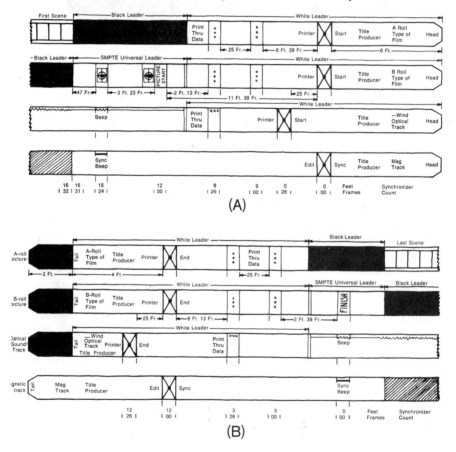

Fig. 17-8. Head (A) and tail (B) printing leaders for 16mm A- and B-picture rolls, optical sound track, and corresponding magnetic track. When the optical track is in edit sync, the three *x*'s on the track line up with the three dots on the picture rolls. When it is shifted into projection sync, the *x*'s line up with the three *x*'s on each picture roll. On the magnetic tracks used for mixing only, a punched start mark is usually made on the frame opposite Picture Start on the SMPTE leader (with no other start mark). Note the sync beep or pop on the sound tracks opposite the "2" on the SMPTE head leader and the "finish" frame on the tail leader. (Carol Keller)

start marks on their leaders in sync, then the first frames of sound and picture will be in sync as well (as the magnetic track is pictured in Fig. 17-8). If a film is submitted along with its optical sound negative, it may be lined up in *projection sync* (also called printer sync). Projection sync takes into account the fact that the optical sound reader on a 16mm movie projector is located 26 frames (20 frames in 35mm) ahead of the aperture where the picture is projected (see Fig. 17-11). If the projection sync mark on the optical sound track is in line with the start mark on the picture, the first frame of sound in 16mm will come 26 frames ahead of the picture (as the optical track is pictured in Fig. 17-8).

All picture leaders should contain only *one* printer start mark. Start marks on sound tracks should be clearly labeled for either edit or projection sync. If you submit all materials in edit sync, the lab will put the track into projection sync for you.

PICTURE CUE SHEETS. When the original is submitted to the lab for printing, a *cue sheet*, which indicates the location and length of each effect, should accompany it. The footage counter is normally zeroed at the printer start mark (although some people zero at the "Picture Start" mark on the SMPTE leader in case the lab changes the head leader to suit their own system). Dissolves are indicated as a fade-in on, say, the A-roll and a fade-out on the B-roll beginning at the same frame. Ask the lab how they want cue sheets prepared.

PREPARING FILM TITLES

Before reading this, see Titles, p. 499.

This section is about making and printing titles for a project that was shot on film and will be printed on film, for those who want to use the traditional methods of generating titles.

Today, many filmmakers create titles digitally, using a nonlinear editing system or dedicated graphics or titling software. Digital titles can be used in video versions of the project and a film-out can be done to put the titles on a negative for making film prints. The power and flexibility of making titles in video far exceeds what you can do the traditional way in film. However, even if you are using digitally created titles, the information below on printing may still apply to your workflow.

Shooting Film Titles

The traditional way to create titles for films is, unsurprisingly, to shoot them directly on film. While professionals generally have a title or optical house do their titles, student and independent filmmakers can often get good results with static (nonmoving) titles by making and shooting their own (crawls and other moves are harder to do yourself). Alternately, you can do the design work and have a professional shoot the titles with an animation camera setup.

The simplest way to make titles is to shoot lettering on paper or cardboard. Titles can be created on a computer and printed with a high-quality laser printer. If you don't have a good printer, you can bring the titles on disk to a copy or printing shop that can print them for you. Of course, you may prefer to do the titles by hand. See p. 501 for guidelines on laying out titles.

If titles are to be superimposed over other film footage (see Fig. 13-3), it's essential that they have high contrast. Light lettering on the title card should be placed against a very dark, uniform background. For a supered title, you want the background on the card to *completely* disappear. Even for nonsupered titles, the background should generally be uniform and fairly dark so as not to draw the eye's attention or show dirt and scratches too much.

Put the titles on a vertical surface and shoot with a tripod-mounted camera (or use a copy-stand arrangement on a horizontal surface). Place lights on both sides of the title at a 45-degree angle from the surface to minimize reflected glare in the direction of the camera. Use a good lens shade and flag the lights off the camera to avoid flare. The title should be illuminated evenly; hold your finger perpendicular to it in the center and in the corners to check that both lights cast equally dark shadows. Steadiness is critical, so use a good camera and tripod. An incident light meter is best suited for checking the exposure for most front-lit titles (use the flat disc diffuser, if possible). If you have enough stock, bracket your exposures (shoot not only at the exposure you think is correct, but a half stop or so above and below it as well). After processing and workprinting, always project the titles on a big screen before cutting them into the original to ensure that they are straight, steady, and well exposed. Many camera film stocks don't have sufficient contrast or sharpness to make high-quality titles. To obtain good contrast, you can use a fine-grained, high-contrast stock like Plus-X. Even better is Kodak's High Contrast Positive 7363 (called Hi Con). Hi Con is designed to produce deep blacks and bright whites, with few of the tonalities in between (see Fig. 7-4). Before you shoot Hi Con, check with the lab to see at what ASA they rate it. Bracket exposures in one-third or one-fourth stop increments and, ideally, run an exposure test at the lab on the same day you plan to process the footage. Hi Con can be developed either as reversal or negative; clear lettering on an opaque background can thus be produced either by shooting black letters on a white field or white letters on a black field. There are disadvantages to processing Hi Con titles as negative if the rest of the film is reversal. The frame line on the titles will be white, and if it does not perfectly match the frame line in the rest of the film, the mismatch will be bothersome.

To get really good contrast, titles should be lit from behind. A printing house will set titles on Kodalith or other high-contrast sheet film in order to produce clear lettering on a perfectly opaque background. Opaquing ink may be used to block pinhole imperfections, and an X-Acto knife is used to scrape any density out of the letters. When a Kodalith is illuminated from behind (usually done on an animation camera setup), maximum contrast between lettering and background is achieved. This technique is especially recommended when you are preparing superimposed titles.

Professionals often have titles shot on 35mm stock (even for 16mm films) to get the cleanest, sharpest lettering. Often, an optical house (see below) is used to design and film the titles.

Printing Superimposed Titles

How superimposed titles (or *supers*) are printed is a subject that confuses many people. Supers appear on screen as lettering over a filmed scene (the "action"). For maximum legibility, the lettering is usually white, or a light color. The simplest supers are those that are *burned in*. Titles are shot with Hi Con stock and developed to appear as clear lettering over an opaque background; they are then spliced into a separate roll to be printed with the rest of the movie.[4] In printing, first the action that appears under the titles is exposed onto the print stock. Then the roll containing the titles is double-exposed onto the same section of print stock. The clear letters burn through to produce white titles on reversal prints or black titles on negative-positive prints (remember, a negative turns dark in areas that receive light).

To produce white supers on a negative-positive print, or black supers on a reversal print, you must *withhold all the light* in the area of the lettering. This may be done by exposing the scene and the titles *simultaneously* on the print stock (not one after the other as described above). Use titles that have opaque lettering on a clear background to mask any light from reaching the print stock where the lettering is. One way to visualize this is to imagine the letters casting a shadow on the print stock. This is often done with an optical printer that has a separate head to hold the titles between the projector (which holds the filmed scene) and the camera (which holds the print stock). Sometimes *bi-packed* titles are made with the titles in the projector and the filmed scene and the print stock sandwiched (bi-packed) in the camera. Using an optical printer is more expensive than contact printing.

Instead of making prints directly from a camera original, often intermediates are made as protection copies from which to strike prints (see Intermediates, p. 684). If the movie was shot with negative stock, this usually means making an interpositive (IP) and dupe negative; for films shot on reversal stock, an internegative may be made. In either case, white supered titles can be inexpensively burned into a dupe negative or internegative using a contact printer. Titles are prepared so that they appear as clear lettering on an opaque background. The titles are then contact printed with the dupe negative. Where the lettering burns into the scene, the image turns black after development. When the dupe negative is then contact-printed onto the release print, these black letters will hold back the light, producing white supers.

For supered titles, you supply the optical house with the negative for the action over which the titles appear and they return to you a second-generation copy of the negative that contains the action and the supers. They also give you a workprint for editing. The new negative can now be spliced in with the rest of your camera original during conforming. Then the movie as a whole can be contact-printed, which is simple and economical.

Laser Subtitles

When subtitling needs to be done for foreign distribution, there are services that can etch subtitles directly into a print with a laser (such as www.lvtusa.com). This may be less expensive for short print runs than preparing subtitles using the methods described above.

---

4. In 16mm, the titles are sometimes spliced into either the A- or B-roll for A&B roll printing or they may be part of a separate C-roll.

OPTICAL EFFECTS

The term *optical effects* (or just *opticals*) refers to a wide range of image manipulations that have traditionally been done using an optical printer (see Types of Printers, p. 666). Today, most complex visual effects are done digitally, then transferred to film when needed. Video effects are discussed in Chapter 14. This section is about effects done the traditional way, on film.

Companies that specialize in optical effects are called optical houses. Some labs have an optical department as part of the lab. Experimental filmmakers often do optical effects themselves, using a camera/projector arrangement (see Fig. 17-3). If you're doing a straightforward film in 16mm, you may never even deal with optical effects.

Optical work is expensive and time-consuming and often has to be redone to get it right; have the optical house give you an estimate before starting work. The optical house should not charge for its own mistakes; however, if you change your mind about an effect, you will, of course, have to pay extra. Fill out a specification sheet (usually supplied by the optical house). Also, mark the effects you want on your workprint or on leader. The lab should return your original film, a workprint of the effects, and the effects themselves in the desired emulsion position (usually they will be negatives, supplied in the same wind as your original). Optical effects that are printed separately from the rest of the film will be at least one generation removed from other scenes in the film (see Print Generations, p. 681). In 16mm, the loss in quality is less noticeable if at least the entire shot (as opposed to just a part of a shot) goes through the same number of generations. In 35mm, however, fades and dissolves are often made optically, spliced in midshot, and the change in generations passes unnoticed by the general audience (but if you watch closely, you can often see a change of color or exposure just before and after a dissolve, especially on older films). Sometimes 16mm optical work is blown up to 35mm and then reduced back to 16mm for superior results, especially when working with supered titles (see above).

If you need to print a section of the original and don't want to cut the roll, you can do *section printing* (also called *clip-to-clip printing*) using either an optical or contact printer. For a surcharge, the lab prints only the sections you indicate in the original.

Optical Effects Between Sequences

FADES AND DISSOLVES. In 16mm, fades and dissolves are usually printed directly from the camera original A&B rolls. This is done with an inexpensive contact printer and keeps the number of generations down. However, fades that are very long (say, more than 128 frames), very short, or very close to one another may have to be done on an optical printer. Optically made fades and dissolves are more precise than those done on a contact printer from A&B rolls. As noted above, 35mm fades and dissolves are often done with an optical printer.

WIPES. In a *wipe*, one scene replaces another at a boundary edge moving across the frame. The variety of wipes is endless; some optical houses offer more than a hundred varieties. In some wipes one image pushes another off the screen along a straight edge. Flip-over or page peel wipes turn one image over like a book page to reveal another image.

Changing Apparent Camera Speed

FREEZE FRAMING (STOP FRAMING OR STOP ACTION). The *freeze frame* is one of the most common optical effects. A single frame is repeated, which makes the action appear to have stopped or frozen. The effect can be used at the beginning, middle, or end of a shot. The dynamic grain pattern of the original is also frozen, so the grain is static and more apparent, giving the image the appearance of a still photograph with visible grain. If there is no movement in the frame, a sequence of a few frames may be alternated back and forth so the grain will change and appear more natural. Sometimes the head or tail of a shot is frozen—not for the effect, but to increase the length of a shot. Freezes are sometimes used to end films, since they suggest ambiguity or holding a moment in time.

FAST MOTION. The apparent speed of the original action can be increased by *skip printing*. Here, every other frame is printed to double the speed or every third frame is printed to triple the speed.

SLOW MOTION. The speed of the original action can be slowed down by *stretch printing*. By printing every frame twice, the speed will be cut in half. Print every frame three times to slow motion by a factor of three. Stretch printing, unlike skip printing, results in some jerkiness in the action. The image seems to alternate between freezing and moving. The effect is very different from slow motion achieved by running the camera at a higher frame rate (see Slow Motion, p. 357). Films shot at 16 fps (the old 16mm silent speed standard) that are to be run at 24 fps (usually to add sound) are stretch printed. To do this, the lab prints every odd frame twice. But, here too, the action is liable to be jerky. Another, more complicated method helps to smooth out the action: odd frames are repeated, but a double exposure is made of the repeat frame with the adjacent even frame. A series of frames 1, 2, 3, 4 . . . would be printed 1, 1+2, 2, 3, 3+4, 4 . . .

REVERSE ACTION. A scene may be printed with the last frame of the original placed first in the print, showing the movements in the shot in reverse (that is, run backward).

Other Image Manipulations

CHANGES IN IMAGE SIZE. The image can be enlarged to change composition, to crop unwanted elements from the picture (for example, a mic boom or dirty aperture), or to enlarge some element. The image can be repositioned to adjust an off-angle horizon line. Sometimes shaky camera movements can be steadied by optically reprinting the scene. Of course, changing image size increases grain and lowers sharpness. In an optical zoom, an area of the frame can be progressively enlarged in successive frames to approximate the effect of a zoom. This will progressively enlarge grain size and decrease sharpness. Optically zooming into a freeze frame exaggerates the effect since the grain pattern of the freeze frame is constant.

If the film will be transferred to video, image repositioning or enlargement can more easily be done during the telecine session.

MATTES. *Mattes* are strips of film with opaque areas that block light from selected portions of the frame. The matte may have a shape like a keyhole or television screen and be fixed, or it may move to follow some action (*traveling matte*). The edges of the matte can be hard or, as in a matte that simulates binoculars, soft. Traveling mattes can be used to insert filmed backgrounds, usually exteriors, for studio shots that are set up in front of blue screen backdrops. Mattes and keys, which are related, are usually easier to do in a video environment (see Basic Video Effects, p. 543).

SUPERIMPOSITIONS. An image can be optically superimposed on one or more images. Superimposition may also be made from A&B rolls or during principal photography. Multiple exposure yields the sum of the exposures. For example, a dark tone exposed on a light tone results in a lighter tone. A bright beach scene exposed with a night scene will wash out almost all the dark tones. In general, multiple exposures work better with darker scenes than with lighter scenes. Whereas in typical multiple exposure the images are consecutively exposed on the print stock, in *bi-pack* exposure—a kind of superimposition made on an optical printer—light passes through two strips of film simultaneously to expose the print. Here a light tone superimposed on a dark tone yields a dark tone. You can approximate the results of bi-packing, but not multiple exposure, by sandwiching two pieces of film and viewing them on a light box or viewer. Bi-packing film is more expensive than using multiple exposures, but usually works better for lighter scenes.

CHANGE OF EMULSION POSITION. As discussed in Chapter 7, contact printing a B-wind original results in an A-wind copy. With optical printing, the change in emulsion position is optional. Optical printing could be used to make a copy that preserves the emulsion position of the original; thus the original and copy could be spliced together without one appearing out of focus relative to the other, as may otherwise happen.[5] Labs sometimes use the expression camera original position instead of B-wind. If optical effects will be cut in with camera original, request that the effects be printed in camera original position. Footage from different sources may not match emulsion positions. One solution is to optically reprint all the shots that read through the emulsion so that they read through the base (B-wind); then all the shots can be printed together.

5. An A-wind copy could also be "flipped" and spliced base-to-base with the B-wind original, which preserves focus but results in a reversed image (mirror image).

BLOWUPS AND REDUCTION PRINTING

Films can be changed from one gauge to another using an optical printer. Enlarging from a smaller gauge to a larger (for example, from 16mm to 35mm) is called a *blowup*. Going from a larger gauge to a smaller is called *reduction printing* or, sometimes, *blowdown*. Blowups must be done very carefully, because all defects are enlarged with the image. Reduction printing is somewhat less critical, though may require image repositioning when going from a widescreen to a non-widescreen aspect ratio (see Fig. 2-15).

Blowups and reduction printing are expensive. If a number of prints are needed, the most economical route is to do the blowup or reduction printing to an intermediate (see Intermediates, p. 684) and then use that to make relatively inexpensive contact release prints. However, sometimes a filmmaker is strapped for cash or needs just one print, say, for a festival screening. Then you might make a *blowup print*—directly from the small-gauge original to the larger-gauge release print. This saves money in the short run, but means starting over from scratch if additional prints are needed.

In some cases, it's a better plan to transfer the original to video, then do a film-out to a larger gauge from the video rather than blow up the negative.

If the shooting ratio is low, it's sometimes less expensive to shoot a movie in the larger gauge to begin with, rather than pay for a blowup later (see p. 68). The quality will be far superior.

16mm and Super 16 Blowups

Blowups from 16mm and Super 16 (see p. 49) are generally done for low-budget feature films that receive theatrical distribution. The Super 16 format, having a larger frame and wider-screen aspect ratio, was basically designed for blowup (see Fig. 1-40). If you know at the start of the project that you will need a blowup, shoot Super 16 whenever possible.

A film originally shot in 35mm will generally have much finer grain than a movie blown up to 35mm from a smaller format. Therefore, when shooting 16mm or Super 16, do everything you can to minimize grain. Use fine-grained film stocks and avoid underexposure of color negative. *Slightly* overexposing color stock up to one stop produces the finest-grain blowup (for more on grain and exposure, see Chapter 7). Avoid very high or very low lighting contrast (see Chapter 12). Avoid flashing and force processing (pushing). Don't do optical effects that add generations to the 16mm original.

REGULAR 16MM. When composing images during the shoot, keep in mind the aspect ratio you intend to distribute the film in. In the United States, most theaters show films at 1.85:1, though some can accommodate 1.66:1, which is a standard used in European theaters. When shooting regular 16mm, be aware that the top and bottom of the frame will be cropped. Some viewfinders are marked for 1.85 aspect ratio (see Fig. 6-7). The lines marked for the top and bottom of the TV safe action area are very close to 1.66 cutoff. Even if the film was not shot with blowup in mind, if the framing is not too tight you'll probably be fine.

When the blowup is made, it's often recommended that a 1.66 or 1.85 hard matte be used, essentially creating a black border at the top and bottom of the image. This way, if a critical part of the image is being cut off, you can reposition the image up or down by scanning. You can decide on a scene-by-scene basis whether to crop from the top, the bottom or both. This allows some flexibility in what is essentially a reframing of the original shot.

SUPER 16. Super 16 provides about 40 percent more picture area than regular 16mm, resulting in increased sharpness and less grain in the blowup. Super 16 is not itself a release format. It extends the 16mm picture area into the area normally occupied by the sound track or by the extra set of perforations on double-perf film. You must therefore use single-perforated film, and the laboratory must be equipped to handle the format. Clearly identify Super 16 film so that it receives proper handling. The full Super 16 camera aperture has an aspect ratio of about 1.69:1. If the framing at top or bottom has not been very tight, theatrical projection can be done at 1.85 without serious cropping (and the camera may have 1.85 frame lines on the viewfinder screen so you can be sure). For non-widescreen TV and video at 1.33, the sides will be cropped. Unless a pan and scan will be done (see Aspect Ratio Choices, p. 87), avoid putting important details at the sides of the frame when shooting.

If you need to make a 16mm print, a 16mm reduction print can be made from the 35mm blowup or a 16mm optical print can be made from the Super 16mm original by recentering and cropping the sides of the image.

PREPARING AND PRINTING THE NEGATIVE. During editing, keep in mind that 35mm is printed in 2000-foot reels, so keep your 16mm printer rolls under 800 feet. If the movie has already been edited and had the negative conformed, some labs can rebalance the reels for 800-foot lengths without difficulty. You may still need to reconfigure the sound track to 20-minute sections to make the optical track (see Sound for Film Prints, p. 689). After editing, the negative must be carefully prepared for printing. Any badly made splices in A&B rolls will tend to jump in an optical printer because the sprocket teeth that hold the film stationary are separated from the printer gate by a few frames (in contact printers the sprocket teeth hold the negative and the print steady right at the area of exposure). Be sure the splicer is properly adjusted. Zero cutting (see p. 670) can eliminate jumping at splices, but may produce a slight dissolve at cuts.

The conventional procedure is to blow up from the 16mm or Super 16mm negative to a 35mm interpositive (IP) and then contact print the IP to a 35mm dupe negative (for more on these terms, see below). This has the advantage of less generational loss (the IP and dupe are both 35mm), which helps minimize grain. Also, if additional dupes are needed, they can be easily contact-printed from the master positive. However, an alternate approach is to make a contact 16mm IP from the 16mm original, and then blow up the 16mm IP to a 35mm dupe negative. This avoids jumping at splices (since the spliced original is run though a contact printer) and is thousands of dollars cheaper for a typical feature. The results can look excellent.

MAKING FILM PRINTS

You've edited your movie. The negative has been conformed, titles and opticals have been cut in, and printing leaders have been prepared. This section is about procedures and options for final printing.

PRINTING BASICS

Print Generations

After the film is edited, the conformed original is printed, which is done either directly onto release print stock or onto intermediate films from which the release prints will be made. Sharpness is lost and grain increased every time a duplicate is made. A print made directly from the camera original is referred to as a *first-generation print*. Copying adds a generation. Thus a print made from a copy of the camera original would be a second-generation print, and so on. Optical effects and stock footage are virtually always at least one generation removed from other scenes in the film. The trained eye can usually distinguish scenes in a film of different generations. The filmmaker has to decide how many generations are acceptable, and then take into account that more generations may be added later by duplicating; for example, a subtitled print is often an additional generation away from the original. There is a point in the duplication process where contrast increases to an unacceptable level and the graininess and fuzziness of the image increase so much that the image appears to fall apart. The difference is greater in smaller gauges—for example, a 16mm print loses more relative to the original than a 35mm print. Special effects often require many layers of images, which is why they're usually done digitally instead of in film. After the effects are created digitally, they can be transferred back to film (see Chapter 18).

Print Exposure and Color Correction

When printing, the amount of exposure for each scene (and color correction for color film) must be controlled to correct exposure errors in the original and to provide creative control for the filmmaker. Printers usually have an exposure scale divided into 1 to 50 steps or *light points* (called variously *lights* or *points*). Color balance is usually controlled by dividing white light into three separate filtered sources (red, green, and blue), which are modulated by light gates and recombined at the printer aperture (*additive printing*)—see Chapter 8.

Different labs use different machines and standards, but as a rule a normally exposed negative will print near the middle of the range, usually between 25R, 25G, 25B and 30R, 30G, 30B. A negative that was overexposed in shooting will need brighter printer lights to compensate. One stop of overexposure will need around +7 to +8 lights correction in all colors.[6]

When printing, changes in the printer light must be made precisely at the be-

6. When doing a quick evaluation of a timing report to see how your negative is exposed, pay particular attention to the green values.

ginning of each shot. Most modern printing machines are computer-controlled and make programmed timing adjustments by footage count without any physical alteration of the original (older machines required tabs or notches on the film to cue the machine). The machine should be able to make timing changes virtually instantaneously between shots (right on the frame line). Sometimes there is lag and you see the change at the beginning of the next frame. Some machines can make gradual changes midscene and may be able to improve a scene that, say, pans from bright sun to heavy shade, by making a timing change within the shot.

Today, many labs use a video color analyzer to time the negative. The timer or grader sees the image projected on a video screen and can set the exposure and color balance, much as a colorist corrects the image during a video transfer (see Chapter 18). The settings are stored and repeated by the printing machine when the print is made. Timing isn't an exact science—the grader must use his judgment about what corrections are needed, and how changes will ultimately translate to the film print.

Even though video technology may be used in timing film prints, the types of corrections available in film printing machines are primitive compared to working in video. In a film printer, an overall color balance must be chosen for each scene. In video, you can change the color of, say, a person's shirt without affecting the skin tone; or you could darken only the sky while leaving the landscape unchanged. This is yet another reason why many film projects are finished in video, then a film-out or D.I. is done to make prints. For more on video color correction, see p. 577.

Liquid (Wet) Gate Printing

Optical printing tends to emphasize dirt, scratches, and cinch marks on the camera original. If the original is immersed in or coated with a liquid of the same refractive index as the film when it passes the printer's aperture, base scratches usually will not show, surface emulsion scratches may be minimized, and graininess is sometimes lessened. This process—*liquid gate*, or *wet gate*, printing—is particularly useful for making optical effects and printing negative original. The improvement of the print can be dramatic. Some telecines are equipped with liquid gates for video transfers. Some labs use wet gate printing as a matter of course for contact and optical prints, some charge extra for wet gate, and others don't do it at all.

Print Stocks

Camera stocks are matched to companion print stocks to produce an image of proper gamma (see Chapter 7). The gamma is usually higher than you might expect to compensate for the loss of contrast due to stray light in the screening room and poor-quality projection systems. Companion stocks are manufactured with the assumption that the scenes on the original have average contrast. If your overall imagery is flatter than normal, consider a print stock with higher gamma or process the stock to a higher gamma. If you are making a print intended for transfer to video, you can order a *low-contrast* (*lo-con*) unspliced print that is optimized for telecine transfer (see p. 709).

Print Color Balance

When making a print, you must instruct the lab whether to balance it for tungsten or xenon projection. Most professional projectors used in theaters and larger institutional screening rooms employ a xenon lamp or other light source with a color temperature of about 5400°K. Amateur projectors or small projectors used in classroom settings often have a tungsten bulb of about 3200°K. Tungsten-balanced prints look slightly blue on a xenon projector, and xenon prints look slightly too warm, or red, on a tungsten projector.

Cleaning the Negative

Use extreme care when handling the negative to avoid dirt, scratches, and cinch marks. The laboratory should clean the negative before making prints. Dust on the film may become embedded in the emulsion and be nearly impossible to remove. The safest cleaning method is *ultrasonic cleaning*. As the film passes through a solvent bath, high-frequency vibrations remove all but the most firmly embedded dust particles. Both ultrasonic cleaning and wet gate printing may destroy tape splices and gradually weaken cement splices. Notify the lab if the printing rolls have any tape splices. Buffing or wet gate printing will often remove base scratches and cinch marks. For badly embedded pieces of dirt, hand cleaning or *spotting* may be needed.

The Dry Lab

Dry labs have no processing equipment, only printing equipment. These labs send the exposed printing stock to another lab for processing. They are sometimes able to turn out release prints in volume at lower prices than conventional labs, and some dry labs will allow you access to a video analyzer for timing. If your film needs this kind of attention (for example, because it has nonstandard color that continually changes), you may want to consider the use of a dry lab. There are disadvantages to their use, however. When a conventional lab does both timing and processing and then makes a processing error, they will redo the work at no extra charge. With a dry lab, you have to work out the various eventualities item by item. Conventional labs make daily test strips to calibrate the analyzer and processing. Inquire at both the dry lab and the lab that does the processing to see if this is done.

ANSWER PRINTS

The Answer Print

The first print from the conformed original is the *answer print*. It is a timed, color-corrected, trial print. Answer prints are made before any intermediates or release prints. All the effects made directly from the original or from opticals (including fades, dissolves, and superimpositions) are on the print except those that may be made on an intermediate.

Answer prints may have an optical sound track (see p. 689) and, if the image is acceptable, may become usable prints. Sometimes a *silent answer print* is made without a sound track if the sound hasn't been mixed yet or for various other reasons.

Generally you should let the timer do the color corrections for the first print on his own. Then screen and/or discuss it with him to make any changes for the next print. Nevertheless, tell the timer in advance of any special timing instructions, such as night scenes or scenes that should have an unusual color cast. Often filmmakers get very accustomed to the timing of the dailies and are shocked by the new timings in the answer print. The lab may take several days to produce the first answer print.

In 16mm, you generally pay for the first answer print at one price, and "additional corrected prints" are made at a lower price. It may take a few answer prints to get everything right. Unless the lab makes gross errors, you pay for each additional print; but generally these prints are usable even if not perfect. In 35mm, some labs will make a certain number of answer prints for a high flat fee until you accept a print, at which time the earlier prints are destroyed. There are methods, mostly used only in 35mm, that allow for corrections to be tested and made without printing the whole film. One method entails printing a few frames from each scene, and another uses trims from each.

Evaluating the Answer Print

View the answer print (or any other print being evaluated) on a projector you know or under standard conditions. The lab will often have a projection room that meets industry standards for image brightness and color temperature. If the print is balanced for xenon projection (see above), view the print on a xenon projector; if balanced for tungsten, be sure the projector is tungsten. Otherwise you will not be able to evaluate the print's overall color rendering.

Carefully check for conforming errors, invisibility of splices, smooth cuts without image jumping, quality and suitability of effects (at this point it's easy to change the length of a fade). Not only should scenes have the desired color balance and density, they should also match within sequences. If the print shows dirt from the original, have the printing rolls cleaned before striking the next print. If there are scratches or cinch marks, you may want to do a test to see if wet gate printing will help. Check the workprint to see if dirt or scratches resulted from the initial processing. If there is a sound track, listen carefully for good sound reproduction without distortion or excess noise. Once you've viewed the film on a projector, you may want to put it on an editing table so you can stop and make notes of needed changes. Some labs have editing machines with either tungsten or "xenon" filtered light sources. Write down a list of shots that need correction. It's best to screen the print with the timer at this point. Otherwise, note errors by footage count from the "Picture Start" mark on the head leader or put masking tape on the problem scenes, so that the timer knows where to correct the next print.

See p. 577 for some color-correction guidelines that apply to both film and video.

INTERMEDIATES

The rolls of spliced original represent the total effort put into the film at this point so it's important to minimize handling. Printing from spliced materials has its dangers; splices can pull apart after repeated cleanings and trips through the printer. Even if handled carefully, the original will start to show wear after several prints. Negative is more vulnerable to damage than reversal. Some labs do not like to pull (make) more than a few prints from color negative original. If more than ten prints are to be made, standard practice is to duplicate the original onto an *interme-*

diate to be used for making *release prints* (that is, the prints for distribution). Intermediates serve several purposes: They protect the original from handling; they serve as an insurance copy; they allow quantity printing at a lower price; they allow some effects to be added more efficiently; and duplicates are available for subtitling in different languages. However, if you are making only a few release prints, printing directly from the original avoids the cost of making an intermediate and achieves the highest quality.[7] Intermediates are sometimes referred to as *preprint elements*.

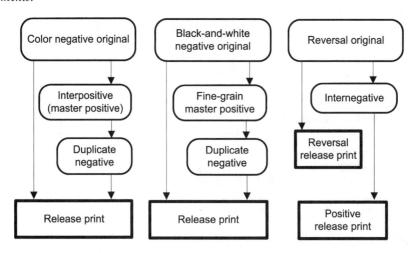

Fig. 17-9. Film printing options. See Fig. 15-18 for negative cutting and video transfer options.

Color Negative Original

Intermediates for original color negative are usually made in a two-step process. The original negative is printed to an *interpositive* (*IP* or *interpos*). IP is the generally preferred term for color intermediates, but *master positive* can be used for both color and black-and-white intermediates. IPs are often done with 5242 for 35mm or 7242 for 16mm. (While 5242/7242 have an acetate base, Kodak also makes a popular version with an indestructible polyester "Estar" base, 2242/3242.) A gamma of 1.0 produces a positive version of the negative without altering the contrast.

After the IP is made, it is printed to the same stock, which reverses tonalities again, to produce a *duplicate negative* (*dupe neg*). Release prints can then be struck from the dupe negative. This not only protects the original negative, but the IP makes an excellent source for a video transfer (see p. 709).

Sometimes dupe negs are made when the same shot is used twice in the movie and you need a second version to cut in with the original camera negative. In this case, be sure to have the dupe neg printed on acetate stock so it will splice well with the OCN.

7. Sometimes an intermediate is made as insurance, but a few prints are still struck from the original.

The IP/dupe neg process allows white supered titles to be done without adding any generations for the titles (see p. 674). Another benefit is that several dupes can be made for striking prints without adding wear-and-tear to the original. Also, printing from the single-strand dupe neg is cheaper than printing from A&B rolls.

There are other forms of intermediates for color negative originals. *Color separation negatives* (also called *YCM masters*) are three separate records of the color original made on panchromatic black-and-white film using red, green, and blue filters, respectively. Each strip contains the color information of one of the three color emulsion layers of the original. Although very expensive, YCM masters use no color dyes and create a permanent, nonfading record of the colors for archival storage.

At one time, a reversal film stock (*color reversal intermediate* or *CRI*) was commonly used to make a one-step duplicate of color negative original. CRIs are rarely used today.

Reversal Original

For films shot with reversal original, an *internegative* (*IN*) can be made from the original. The internegative now serves the same function as a dupe negative (in fact, many people use "IN" and "dupe neg" interchangeably). This allows release prints to be made in the standard negative/positive process instead of trying to strike reversal prints from reversal original, a process that may not be available and often results in lower-quality optical sound tracks (see p. 689).

Black-and-White Negative

To control contrast, black-and-white negatives are duplicated by a two-step process. First, the negative is printed onto a *fine-grain master positive* (usually Kodak 5366/7366) and then the master positive is printed onto a duplicate negative. Ideally, the dupe negative has the same tonal characteristics as the original.

Optical Versus Contact-Printed Intermediates

Intermediates are sometimes optically printed. Optical printing may achieve sharper results than contact printing, and some effects (like freeze framing, supered titles, and repositioning the image) can be made while duplicating. With the IP/dupe process, generally only the IP is printed optically. Sometimes optical printing increases contrast and apparent graininess as unwanted side effects. Wet gate printing, as discussed above, can help a great deal.

Particularly for 16mm films, optical printing sometimes results in slight jumping at splices because of the way the film moves through the printer gate. Sometimes a contact intermediate is steadier, particularly for a blowup (see Preparing and Printing the Negative, p. 680).

If you shot in Super 35, the image extends into the area needed for the sound track. To fix this, the IP will be optically printed to the IN, making the image smaller and sliding it over to make room for the audio tracks. This process is called *formatting*.

Check Prints

At least one answer print is made before making any intermediates such as an IP. After an intermediate or blowup is made, a *check print* is struck to verify that all went well. It may be on the check print that you can see for the first time some supered titles or other printer-made effects. The check print costs less than an answer print but more than a release print.

RELEASE PRINTS

A *release print* is a print intended for distribution—finished and ready to be shown. Minor timing errors on a check print or an answer print can usually be corrected when the release print is made. If the errors are serious, the intermediate materials may have to be redone. If the check print is acceptable, then one-light release prints can be made. Labs generally don't charge for timing corrections when they make release prints. However, if you have an intermediate that can be printed with one printer light, you can more easily change labs. Sometimes labs specializing in release prints offer a better price. However, the best-quality release prints are generally obtained by staying with the original lab. There are price breaks for release prints ordered in quantity. At some labs all the prints have to be ordered at once, while at others the price breaks come as you cumulatively reach certain amounts. The rate-card price is usually negotiable when making several prints.

Fig. 17-10. Release prints being prepared for shipping. (Film-Tech.com)

Today, most movies projected on film are distributed in 35mm. The educational and nontheatrical markets in which 16mm films used to be projected now largely show the same types of movies in video, though film festivals may still accept 16mm.

35mm Release Prints

Usually, 35mm prints are mounted on plastic or metal reels and shipped in plastic cases or heavy-duty *ICC* or Goldberg metal cases. The reels of film should be taped or otherwise secured to prevent unspooling in shipment. The reels are usually about 20 minutes long. Some theaters will splice all the reels into a single *platter* for projection (see Fig. 17-14). The sound should be prepared with pullups in anticipation of the reels being spliced together (see Analog Optical Tracks, p. 689).

Some theaters will keep the reels separate and use two matched projectors. They change over from one projector to the other at the end of each reel to avoid an interruption for reloading. *Changeover marks* are small circles inscribed in the upper right-hand corner of a few frames at the end of each reel to cue the projectionist when to start the next projector. The lab can put marks on the print, or on a dupe negative so they appear on all prints. Counting backward from the last frame on a reel, the marks appear on frames 25 to 28 and 196 to 199. Most labs or projection facilities have a mechanical scriber that makes a neat changeover mark.

16mm Release Prints

You can ask the lab to mount release prints on single-keyed reels, which have the key-shaped center hole on only one side. This is intended as idiot-proofing to ensure that the film is mounted correctly on the projector. Single-keyed reels are inconvenient in the editing room.

You should splice at least 6 feet of single-perforated leader at both the head and the tail of the film. Some people put green leader at the head, red at the tail. Use only single-perf leader to help distinguish the head from the tail and to ensure proper threading. Mark the leader with head or tail, the name of the film, and your name or company name. Most films are printed with SMPTE head leader immediately before the picture. If you splice on SMPTE leader, make sure the leader is of the same wind as the film (B-wind for camera original, A-wind for most prints). SMPTE leader can help the projectionist to focus the projector before the film begins. Unfortunately, many projectionists don't bother to focus until much later.

Films in 16mm that are longer than a half hour (1200 feet) are usually printed in at least two sections, and, if the sections are to be spliced together for projection, the sound should be prepared with pullups (see Analog Optical Tracks on p. 689). Films in distribution are usually mounted on reels of 1600 feet or less. A 2400-foot reel can accommodate a 66-minute film but may be dangerous due to the strain it places on the film in projection. Projection facilities equipped to handle big reels can show a program of a few hours' length in one piece. In this case, the projectionist will splice the reels together. You may want to put changeover marks (see above) on the print for theaters that use two projectors.

All prints get scratched, but 16mm prints are particularly vulnerable. Always clean the projector gate before use (see Adjusting and Operating the Projector, p. 694). Protective coatings to guard the print against scratches, such as 3M Photogard, have sometimes been used.

Print Care and Handling

When labeling print containers for shipment, be sure to put your return address inside the case, since many shippers will cover over exterior labels. Indicate whether a case or reel is part of a set (for example, "Reel 2 of 3"). Prints should be kept clean and free from damage. Broken perforations may be repaired with splicing tape. Preperforated tape can be applied to just the edge of the film without obscuring the picture. Trim it precisely with sharp scissors or a razor blade. A perforation repair device such as the Perf-fix or Cine-Bug systems can restore perfs to a film that lacks an entire edge.

Release prints are generally made on polyester stock. Sometimes a very light coating of wax is applied to the edges of the film to prevent static build-up.

Usually the head and tail of a reel get the most abuse because of handling and dirt. Each time reels are spliced together, frames may be cut off the ends of reels. For distribution, you may want to use a film shipping house (see Chapter 19) that can inspect and repair prints whenever they come back from being shown. For more on film prints and projection, see below.

SOUND FOR FILM PRINTS

Before reading this, see Mix Formats, p. 654, for information about sound mixing and release formats for sound. This section is about putting the finished track on a film print. A film print with sound is called a *composite* or *married* print.

ANALOG OPTICAL TRACKS

Optical Tracks

The traditional and still most common type of composite print employs an *optical sound track*, which uses a photographic process to record and play the sound. Optical tracks are a worldwide standard in 16mm and 35mm. Conventional optical tracks look like wavy lines along the edge of the film (see Fig. 17-12). In the projector, an *exciter lamp* shines a narrow beam of light through the sound track. As the

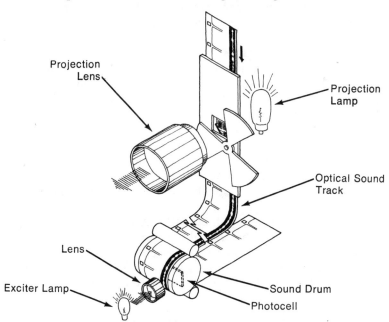

Fig. 17-11. Film projector and optical sound. Light from the exciter lamp shines through the optical sound track. The resulting variations in the light are registered by the photocell (shown in cutaway). In 16mm, the optical sound reader is separated from the film gate, where the image is projected by 26 frames. (Carol Keller)

area (thickness) of the track varies, so does the amount of light that can pass through it. A *photocell* on the opposite side of the film converts the changes in light into a changing electrical signal, which is reproduced as sound. Today, optical tracks use this *variable area* system (an earlier system used variations in track density to modulate the light beam).

Fig. 17-12. Dolby Stereo film prints employ a two-channel optical sound track with four channels of audio encoded on it. They employ Dolby SR noise reduction. (Dolby Laboratories)

MONO OPTICAL TRACKS. In 16mm, optical tracks are mono (one channel of sound), and 16mm optical sound is relatively poor quality. The frequency response only runs up to 5500–7000 Hz. The optical sound track itself is capable of greater range, but few projectors are adjusted to make use of it. Because of their high noise levels, 16mm optical tracks also have limited dynamic range (often less than 40 dB). When the film print gets dirty, the noise, which sounds like a gentle boiling or crackling, increases. Though stereo 16mm optical tracks exist, most projectors work only in mono.

STEREO OPTICAL TRACKS. In 35mm, optical sound may be mono or stereo. With *Dolby SR (Spectral Response)* tracks, four channels of sound (LCRS; see p. 654) can be encoded in one pair of stereo tracks. Dolby SR increases the dynamic range and reduces the noise of optical tracks; it can produce very good quality.

Making Optical Tracks

To make an optical track, you supply the lab or sound facility with the movie's sound track (the printmaster; see p. 656) on disc, DAT, mag film, or other format. They will record it using an optical recorder that exposes the track photographically on a piece of film called an *optical sound negative* or *optical sound master*. After development, the optical sound negative is then contact printed with each release print. At each step in the process, the density of the optical track must be carefully controlled. It is often an advantage to have the optical master prepared by the lab that prints the film. If you have a sound house do it instead, it's imperative that you choose one that has a close working relationship with the lab and has calibrated their equipment in concert with the lab.[8]

Some optical masters are A-wind, others B-wind. An optical master prepared for prints made directly from the original negative should work with prints made from a dupe negative. However, for films shot in reversal, a master made for prints struck from the reversal original normally won't work with prints struck from an internegative. Talk to the lab if you plan to make intermediates.

---

8. They must periodically run a *cross-modulation test*, or *cross-mod*. When you get a low-quality optical track, you can request such a test. The test can be done at the head or tail of your track. It is an exposure and printing check that involves a middle-frequency tone and a low-frequency tone. If the track is properly exposed, the lower frequency should be maximally canceled out.

Traditional optical tracks for color prints require added silver in order to produce enough density. This is done by applying a developer solution to the edge of the film. The applicator sometimes splashes into the picture area, which you should check for when evaluating the print.

Newer projector technology uses an LED instead of a tungsten exciter lamp, which doesn't require silver applicator on the print; instead, a cyan-colored sound track is used. However, these projectors don't read conventional silver tracks well. A compromise *high magenta sound track* may produce acceptable results on either type of projector.

KEEPING OPTICAL TRACKS IN SYNC. When you submit a sound track to the lab to make an optical sound master, it should be prepared according to the standard SMPTE leader format with an audible beep at the "2" (see Reel Breaks and Reference Tapes, p. 643). On the optical master, the beep will appear as a frame of squiggly lines in an area where the track is otherwise quiet and smooth. The lab will position this frame several frames ahead of the "2" when it makes the release print (see Fig. 17-8). The separation is 26 frames in 16mm and 20 frames in 35mm. Without the beep, the lab may have no accurate way to put the track in sync with the picture. Be sure to tell the lab if the movie was edited on video with a non-linear system so they can check that the proper speed adjustments have been made.

WHEN REELS ARE SPLICED TOGETHER. If optical sound negatives or prints with optical tracks need to be spliced together, the splice line can be covered in the track area with a diamond-shaped "bloop" mark that avoids a loud click at the splice. *Blooping ink* or precut *blooping tape* can be obtained at the lab. As discussed earlier, for projection it is common to splice together the various reels that make up a movie and show it in one continuous strand. An interesting thing happens if you splice together two reels of a release print and then run them through a projector. Say you have a 16mm print and you splice the first frame of reel two to the last frame of reel one. When the splice runs through the projector, the picture will cut from one reel to the next, but the sound won't change until about a second later. Actually, you get 26 frames of silence after the cut, at which point the sound from reel two starts with the first 26 frames cut off. Not good.

Why does this happen? Look at Fig. 17-11. The film is moving from top to bottom, so as the cut moves through the projector it first passes the film gate but doesn't reach the sound reader until about a second later. This separation is the reason the optical sound for any frame of picture is located on the print 26 frames ahead of the picture (20 frames in 35mm).

To create a smooth, natural cut in which the sound and picture change in sync, we must repeat 26 frames of sound from the *head* of reel two to the *tail* of reel one. This can be done before, during, or after the mix. It simply means duplicating this short section of sound and adding it onto the tail of reel one's track. Mixers do it as a matter of course at the mix. This is sometimes called a *pullup* (but should not be confused with the use of "pull up" to mean speed up). A pullup should be done to the tail of every reel in the film except the last one. This is *only* needed for film prints and does not apply to editing together reels of video.

DIGITAL SOUND TRACKS

On most modern film releases, digital tracks are used on the film prints to provide better quality and more audio channels.

Dolby Digital

Perhaps the most common digital film print format is *Dolby SR-D*. With this system, a pattern of dots that carry digital data is printed between the sprocket holes of the film print (see Fig. 17-13). Also called *Dolby Digital*, this format can accommodate a 5.1 channel mix (left, center, right; left and right surround; and a subwoofer for low-frequency effects). Dolby Digital prints also include the analog Dolby Stereo optical track described above, for theaters that can't play the digital track. The analog track plays a 4.0 channel mix folded down from the 5.1 channel digital mix.

Dolby Digital requires a license from Dolby for each production as well as certification from a Dolby technician that proper procedures are followed.

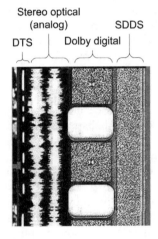

Fig. 17-13. The edge of a 35mm release print showing four types of analog and digital sound tracks that can be put on the same print. (Frank Angel)

DTS, SDDS, and THX

Digital Theater Systems (DTS) uses a CD-ROM disc to play six channels of uncompressed digital sound on a disc playback system interlocked to the film projector. This can be used for a 4.0 channel or 5.1 channel mix. DTS needs to be licensed for your production and works only in theaters equipped with disc playback equipment. DTS can be used on 16mm and 35mm prints and requires a timecode track on the print. In 16mm it replaces the optical track (making the print useless for theaters that lack DTS equipment). With 35mm, the print can accommodate both DTS and an optical track.

Sony Dynamic Digital Sound (SDDS) is an eight-channel digital system that uses a matrix of dots, similar to SR-D, but positioned along the edges of the film outside the sprocket holes. This can be used for 7.1 channel mixes.

On major releases, analog, SR-D, DTS, and SDDS tracks may all be included on the same print so it's usable with any projection system.

Lucasfilm Ltd.'s *THX system* isn't an audio format, but sets standards for the playback environment, regardless of the film format. THX-licensed home theater systems are based on Dolby Pro Logic Surround decoding.

FILM PROJECTORS AND THE SCREENING ENVIRONMENT

Once a satisfactory release print is in hand, you may imagine that you've survived all possible technical surprises in the production process. Don't forget to take into account the variables introduced by screening facilities, projectionists, and audiences, which all greatly affect the way the film comes across on screen.

When films are distributed theatrically, the filmmaker often has little or no control over the projection process. Unfortunately, even in first-run movie houses, the projectors may be badly maintained or adjusted. Even so, the image quality of projected film tends to be much more consistent than video projection, which varies widely with the type of video equipment and how it's adjusted (see Appendix A for adjusting video monitors for screenings).

The Projector

Projectors are usually the weak link in the chain of equipment that transfers the image from the world to the screen. Filmmakers frequently spend thousands of dollars for cameras with steady movement and sharp lenses and then show their films on jittery projectors with cheap, dirty, low-contrast lenses. In fact, poor projection plays a major part in lowering the resolution of the film system when taken as a whole.

When projecting 35mm, the theater will have a set of lenses for different types of prints (flat or anamorphic). For nontheatrical screenings in 16mm, you may be dealing with an ancient, portable projector wheeled in for the screening.

When choosing a projector, look for one that projects a bright, steady image and reproduces sound clearly. Playing a film with a slow music track is often a good test of the projector's reproduction quality. Make sure the projector allows easy access to the film gate for cleaning. The optical sound reader on a 16mm projector needs to be adjusted precisely; this should be checked occasionally by a technician with a test film. Some optical sound readers are set to optimize either A-wind or B-wind release prints, or they may be adjusted in a compromise position. If some films sound better than others on your machine, this may be the reason.

Most larger screening facilities have projectors with xenon arc lamps or other sources with 5400°K color temperature, and you should get release prints color balanced for xenon projection for these venues (see Print Color Balance, p. 682). The small projectors sometimes used in schools and institutions have tungsten bulbs, which are dimmer and yellower in color than xenon sources of comparable wattage.

Typical projectors employ a two- or three-bladed shutter (instead of the

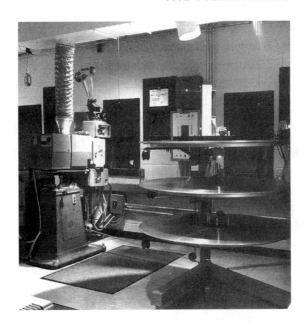

Fig. 17-14. Most theaters use a platter system so that an entire print can be spliced together, fed to the projector in one piece and spooled up again. The projectionist only has to start the projector at the beginning and turn it off at the end. (Film-Tech.com)

halfmoon-shaped shutter used in cameras) to reduce the sensation of flicker. This means each frame is flashed on the screen two or three times, with an instant of darkness between each flash. The more rapid the flashes, the more constant the projector's light seems.

Projectors in 16mm and 35mm run at 24 fps. Super 8 projectors may run at 24 fps or 18 fps (the latter may be indicated as silent speed). Some projectors will run at slow-motion speeds, but this should only be done if the metal screen *heat shield*, which falls between the lamp and the film, is working properly. *Double-system projectors* can play the picture and a separate roll of magnetic film sound track in *interlock* (see Fig. 13-2). These machines are mostly used to screen workprint with its sound track before a composite print is made. Double-system projection can also be done in a mix studio or preview theater.

Adjusting and Operating the Projector

Keep the film path of the projector clean, especially the area of the film gate behind the lens. This is especially important in 16mm and Super 8. Dirt and emulsion dust regularly accumulate in the gate and can easily scratch the film. Use a cotton swab with alcohol or acetone to clean both sides of the pressure plate and the rim of the aperture. Acetone is a powerful cleaner and should never be used on plastic or the cemented metal of sound heads. Clean the gate before every film screening. Clean the projector's lens as you would a camera lens (see p. 176) and if there's a projection room window between the projector and the screen, use some Windex or other household glass cleaner to clean it. Hairs that lodge in the gate during a screening can often be blown out with a can of compressed air while the film runs. If you're running the screening, try to focus the picture and adjust the sound before the audience arrives. Focusing can be done with the naked eye, with binoculars, or with an assistant at the screen if the distance from the projector to the screen (the *throw*) is great. If you focus the projector on the *grain* and not the image itself, you'll be sure to maximize sharpness even if the scene itself was filmed out of focus. As the projector warms up, the focus will drift slightly and will need readjusting.

Most projection systems have a tone quality adjustment (bass/treble). Optical sound tracks often sound best with this adjustment set a bit toward the treble. Adjust the level and the tone with someone standing in the middle of the room who can signal when the sound seems clear but not overly scratchy.

The Screening Room

Films should be shown in rooms that are as dark as possible. Exit lights should be positioned or flagged so that their light does not fall on the screen. Stray light on the screen has the same effect as flashing the film stock before processing: the black tones look lighter and the overall contrast is reduced. Theater walls should be a dark color to prevent light from reflecting back onto the screen.

The size of the projected image is determined by the focal length of the projector's lens and the throw. For any given projector, the larger the image is projected, the dimmer, shakier, and less sharp the image will look. However, a large image—if suitably bright, steady, and sharp—will have more impact on the audience than a small one. It's sometimes recommended that audience seating extend back no farther than six times the width of the screen. The image usually looks sharpest if it is surrounded by a black border; dark curtains are often used to frame the picture.

Screens are available in several types, with various surfaces. Matte screens are made of white cloth or painted wood. A wall can be used for screening if it's painted with a bright, flat white paint. Matte screens usually give the best color reproduction, and they can be viewed from a sharp angle (for example, from the outermost seats in the front rows.)

Lenticular screens are made of a ribbed fabric that acts like a lens, focusing the reflected light back toward the center of the audience. As a result, the image is brighter than that of a matte screen for viewers sitting near the line from projector to screen and dimmer for those sitting at the sides of the seating area.

Whenever possible, the noise of the projector should be dampened or isolated from the audience. Avoid projectors with built-in speakers. In properly equipped theaters, a projection booth with a double glass window isolates the machinery from the audience. For informal setups, the projector can sometimes be placed in another room (projecting through an open door) or in an open closet to block its noise.

Detachable speakers should be separated from the projector and placed near the screen, which gets them closer to the audience and reinforces the sense that the sound is being produced by the action on the screen. In regular movie theaters, speakers are placed *behind* the screen where they project through thousands of perforations in the screen's surface. "Live" or reverberant rooms may make the sound track echo and seem boomy and unclear. Curtains, furniture, sound-absorbent tiles, and the audience in their seats all help reduce reverberation.

CHAPTER 18

Film and Digital Transfers

This chapter is about different types of transfers between formats:

- Transferring film footage to digital video or files
- Transferring from digital video or files to film
- Converting one video format to another
- Shooting video and computer monitors with either film or video cameras

FILM-TO-VIDEO TRANSFER

In contemporary filmmaking, every movie gets transferred to digital video. Most films are edited in digital video using an NLE, but even films that are edited on film the traditional way are transferred to video for broadcast or video distribution.

When transfers are done for editing purposes, they may be done as *video dailies*. Here the goal is to do a quick pass with minimal color correction. After the film is edited, a second transfer can be done with careful tuning of the image. On some projects, the film is transferred only once, sometimes after it's already been finished on film.

This section should be read together with Editing Film on Video, p. 605, which discusses workflows and methods of working with video in the context of editing a movie that was shot on film. This section is about the actual process of doing the transfer from film to digital video or files. For some filmmakers, video transfer is an integral part of their creative control of the image. For others, their involvement is limited to sending the footage to the transfer house and receiving the videotape when it's done.

The Telecine

The *telecine* (pronounced "tele-*sin*-ee") is a device for converting film to video in real time. It has a transport to move film footage smoothly and continuously across a scanner head that reads each frame and converts it to a digital video signal. High-end telecines are very sophisticated. Many can handle a variety of film formats (35mm, 16mm, Super 16, Super 8, and 8mm). The telecine's precision film

Fig. 18-1. Shadow Telecine. CCD scanner. Outputs all common high definition and standard definition resolutions. (Grass Valley)

transport can accommodate either positive or negative film at several different speeds with no danger of scratching. Modern telecines can output in SD or HD video and in some cases higher resolutions of 2K or 4K (not in real time). Most common are telecines are made by Cintel (formerly Rank Cintel) and Grass Valley. Though no longer manufactured, you may still encounter older models by Bosch and Marconi or more recent designs, including ITK's Millennium and Sony's Vialta. In the right hands, all can accomplish professional results.

There are two basic types of telecine: *Flying spot* systems optically superimpose, on the fly, the raster of a small, super-bright monochrome CRT onto each frame of film, which is then digitally sampled through a beam splitter and RGB filters. *Linear array CCD* systems use a bright xenon light to project an image of each frame onto several horizontal rows of linear CCDs, using the vertical travel of the film frame through the telecine gate to create the vertical scan. (Which is why a CCD telecine can't scan a still picture.) A half-century of Cintel telecines exemplify the first approach; Grass Valley's popular Spirit series exemplifies the latter.

Traditionally, each technology has had its "look" and its adherents—as late as the 1990s most filmmakers preferred flying spot telecines, which is no longer the case—but in truth both produce superb results and even experts are sometimes hard-pressed to tell the difference.

Fig. 18-2. Film transport on Spirit Datacine. Precision movement with high image steadiness is crucial for scanning. (DuArt Film and Video)

The *film chain* is a lower-end transfer device made up of a special 16mm film projector that projects the film image directly into a video camera. Film chains are a throwback to the days when local TV stations projected movies on-air from 16mm prints. While film chain transfers are less expensive than telecine transfers, they provide much less control over the film movement and image. The film chain projector's intermittent mechanism is not gentle enough to allow transferring negative.

Sometimes people make a slop transfer by using a video camera to shoot a projected film image or an image off a flatbed editing system. Quality is low, and speed control is not precise enough for reliable editing or matchback to the original film.

At the other end of the spectrum, there's a new breed of film scanners used for HD and for very high-resolution data files (see High-Resolution Film Scanners, p. 713).

The telecine works in concert with several other pieces of equipment in the telecine room or suite. The *color corrector* is a dedicated video processing system that allows the telecine operator or *colorist* to program color and other image settings. Perhaps the best-known is made by da Vinci Systems. A telecine suite will also feature a number of audio and video decks in different formats (see below). An ultrasonic film cleaning machine may be nearby.

In general usage, the word telecine is often used to mean any film-to-video conversion. It's also used to refer to the pulldown process (see Pulldown Revisited, p. 565).

The Transfer Process

In overview, film-to-video transfer involves several items to be aware of:

• *Frame rate conversion.* Film is generally shot at 24 fps. Video is typically recorded at 60i (actually 59.97), 50i, 24p, or 23.976p. Converting from one frame rate to another may involve a pulldown process. See p. 102 and p. 565.

- *Audio speed correction.* When the playback speed of the picture is changed, the audio may need to be sped up or slowed down to stay in sync. See p. 706.
- *Audio synching.* On a film shoot, sound and picture are recorded separately. It's possible to sync the audio during the telecine session. See p. 706.
- *Color correction.* In some transfers, a lot of time and care are put into color balancing; other transfers are done quickly without fine-tuning color.
- *Recording format.* Video may be recorded to tape or to file (hard drive or other method) in a variety of formats. See p. 701.

PREPARING FOR THE TRANSFER

The following are some considerations in planning, ordering, and doing a film-to-video transfer. As noted above, transfers can be loosely thought of in two categories: video dailies, which are made for offline editing purposes, often with the intent of going back to the original camera negative (OCN) after editing to do another transfer; and final transfers, which are done for edited films either from the negative before online editing, or from an assembled source such as a master positive, dupe negative, or low-contrast print after the film is done. Some films, ranging from student projects to television movies, are transferred only once; that transfer is used for the offline edit and for the finished product.

Consult with the transfer facility for their preference. Particularly for video dailies, it's essential that you talk with the video editor and negative cutter before making any arrangements for the transfer.

Booking a Transfer

Film-to-tape transfers are generally billed on an hourly or per-project basis. Transfer time will be longer than the running time of the material; how much longer depends on the material and what's being done to it. Obtain estimates from the transfer facility. As a ballpark, video dailies without scene-to-scene color correction ("one-light" or "best light") may take 1½ to 2 times the running time of the footage; dailies with sound and color correction may take 3 to 6 times the running time; careful color correction of a finished film may take 15 to 20 times. Footage with many short shots may take more time to transfer than material with long takes.

Video Dailies

For video dailies, the negative cutter or lab prepares the footage for transfer and may need to check it afterward. The following items should be specified and/or discussed with the transfer facility when you place your order:

1. *Film format.* Specify whether you shot 35mm, Super 16, 16mm, or Super 8. Flat (nonanamorphic) or 'Scope. Color negative or black-and-white. Manufacturer and film type.
2. *Aspect ratio.* Did you shoot 4:3? 16:9? 1.66:1? 1.85:1? 2.35:1? When

shooting 35mm particularly, it's a good idea to film a framing chart at the head of the reel so that the telecine operator can verify your camera's aspect ratio and exact framing.

3. *Image format.* If widescreen, do you want the video image letterboxed? Or full height and squeezed (anamorphic)? For offline SD editing, it's common to have a widescreen image letterboxed (you can put burn-in timecode info in the black borders).

4. *Video format.* What videotape format are you recording to? Or are you recording direct to hard disk or other data format? What frame rate are you recording to: 24p? 60i? 50i? It's simplest if any interlaced format is field 1 dominant.

5. *Punch head of each camera roll or flat.* A punch mark is made in the negative to serve as a reference point at the zero timecode frame. Some people request that this be at a key number ending in 00 (such as KJ 23 1234 5677+00). Ask for a list of each roll's corresponding key numbers at punch marks. After you have captured the video into the NLE, you can use the list to check against transfer errors. Many people like to have a punch made at the head of each camera roll or wherever there is a break in key numbers (that is, wherever two pieces of film are spliced together). Some negative cutters want only a punch at the head of each *film flat* (also called *lab roll* or *lab reel*) which may be made up of a few camera rolls spliced together.

6. *Pulldown.* When transferring from 24 fps to 60i, specify that you want an "A frame transfer" which should start at the head punch with an even hour of timecode (such as 02:00:00:00). For more on A frame transfers, see Managing Pulldown, p. 618.

7. *Timecode.* This is the timecode that will be recorded on video. For editing purposes, nondrop timecode (ND) is recommended to avoid errors. Specify the starting timecode for each tape (typically a different hour for each). Depending on the video format, you may also specify where you want timecode recorded (such as VITC, see p. 204).

8. *Burn-in numbers.* For video dailies, you generally want burn-in numbers (visible on screen) for film key number, in-camera film timecode (if any), audio timecode (if any), video timecode, as well as parent film frame (A, B, C, D) of each pulldown field, to indicate pulldown cadence. These can be displayed in the black borders of a letterboxed image (see Fig. 15-19). You must specifically request from your postproduction facility inclusion of each of these burn-in data windows in your dailies; you can request where they're placed on the screen and in which order. Don't assume that the post facility will include burn-in numbers unless you request them. You can mask them out later if you prefer not to see them for screening purposes. You can also have two sets of tapes made, one with and one without burn-ins.

9. *Audio synching.* Do you want audio synched in the telecine session (expensive unless it can automatically chase picture) or will you do it later? Is there audio timecode (production timecode)? Timecode slates? Do you want audio code recorded to video?

10. **Color correction.** Do you want the colorist to adjust the image for each scene or just once for the entire roll (which is less expensive). See below for more on this.

11. **Shot log.** You will usually want a shot log (also called *telecine log*, see p. 705) of the transfer. A log file typically includes the timecode, key numbers, and pulldown type of the first frame of each clip that will be captured. When possible, ask to have information logged automatically, which may be more accurate than manual logs. Ask for a file format compatible with your editing system.

12. **Shipping and storage.** Do you want the negative returned to you or stored by the lab or transfer facility? What type of shipping do you want for the videotape and/or negative?

13. **Contact info.** Be sure to include off-hour phone numbers in case of questions.

For video dailies, you have a choice of transferring all the footage so you have easy access to it in the editing room, or you could transfer only "circled takes" that were indicated in the camera report or log as being good. If sound is being synched during the transfer, transferring only selected takes can save money. If sound is to be synched after the telecine, stopping and starting to skip bad takes is sometimes more time-consuming than transferring them. Also, if you find later that you want to use the untransferred takes, you may wish you'd transferred them in the first place.

Generally, video dailies are made directly from the original camera negative. Color correction may be minimal (*one-light* or *best-light* transfer—a single setting for the whole roll, see Timing the Workprint, p. 661). For video dailies, filming a gray card at every scene on location can help expedite rough color balancing (see Standardizing Color Reproduction, p. 295).

Whenever negative is used for any process, handling should be kept to a minimum. Any unnecessary shuttling in the telecine should also be avoided. The negative should be ultrasonically cleaned just prior to transfer.

WHEN YOU HAVE WORKPRINT. On some feature films, a film workprint is still made to allow for test screenings and because the workprint gives a better indication of what's in the negative than a video transfer does (although this is changing with the introduction of HD dailies). In this case, the workprint may be transferred to video for editing, instead of doing the transfer from the negative. When any dailies are done, whether on film or video, the footage needs to be evaluated carefully for camera, stock, or shooting problems. See Screening the Rushes, p. 663, for some of the typical problems.

TELECINE RECORDING FORMATS

There are many video formats you might use to record with in the telecine (though your transfer facility may not have them all). Avoid analog and composite formats when possible.

High-quality SD transfers are often done to Digital Betacam. DV formats with greater compression, such as DVCAM and DVCPRO, may be used for video dailies and are convenient for capturing to disk via FireWire for offline editing. They offer the advantage of being easy to clone as well, if multiple copies are needed. Beta SP, which for years has been popular for offline work, no longer offers any advantages over digital formats and is not recommended.

HD transfer formats include HDCAM, D5 HD, and HDCAM SR. HDCAM SR offers very high-quality HD 4:4:4 RGB recording but is not cheap.

Many telecines can do frame-accurate edits to videotape, allowing you to join reels together or insert retransfers of individual shots without rerecording the whole tape. Bear in mind that telecine transfers are typically billed at a high hourly rate. It often doesn't make sense budget-wise to create more than a few edits while using a telecine.

Increasingly, transfers are done directly to hard drives, using a variety of codecs.

High-resolution 2K and 4K scans (see p. 713) may be done to hard drives or media such as *DLT* (*digital linear tape*).

TELECINE EVENT AND SCENE MANAGEMENT

Telecines rely on several systems to track footage and timecode, and to store and manage event cues like scene changes, effects, and color corrections. Keeping these systems straight isn't simple. The following are the main ones in use, though they're not all used on every production.

Film Key Numbers/Keycode

Kodak and Fujifilm expose eye-readable key numbers and machine-readable bar codes along the edge of camera negative that can be read after the negative is processed (see p. 271). Key numbers identify every frame of the original negative and are essential for match-cutting after editing. The bar code version is called *Keykode* by Kodak and *MR code* by Fujifilm. Most telecines have keycode readers, allowing them to track the negative as it goes through the machine. Key numbers run in an unbroken sequence from the beginning of each camera roll to the end. Unlike timecode in video, film key numbers are permanent in the film and never change, so they're a solid reference for finding and cutting the sections of negative.

In-Camera Timecode (also called Film Timecode)

All Aaton and some Arriflex cameras have the ability to expose timecode along the edge of the negative near the key numbers and keycode (see Fig. 6-16). In-camera film timecode—AatonCode and Arricode are 24 fps versions of SMPTE/EBU timecode—is always set to record the time of day (TOD) at the moment each frame of film is exposed. For sync sound shooting, the audio recorder in the field records identical TOD code. This requires extraordinary crystal sync accuracy in both camera and audio recorder, with drift no greater than one half of a film frame over six hours. During the film-to-video transfer, a special reader in the telecine reads the in-camera timecode. Aaton's Keylink system provides automatic synching by matching the in-camera timecode with the audio timecode (some number crunching is required to reconcile what may be different frame rates). Auto-synching can also be done in some NLEs. In-camera film timecode will have breaks in it every time the camera stops.

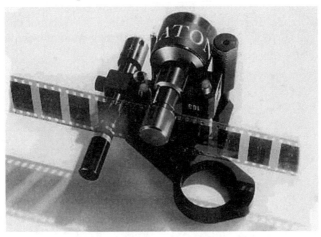

Fig. 18-3. AatonCode reader. Mounted on the telecine, the reader scans the in-camera timecode exposed along the edge of the film (see Fig. 6-16). A similar head on the telecine reads keycode. (AbelCine Tech)

Audio Timecode

Professional audio recorders are equipped to record a timecode track (see Chapter 5). As noted above, when the film camera records the same timecode as the audio recorder, we can easily sync the sound and picture. However, since many film cameras don't record in-camera timecode, a timecode slate may be used for synching (see Fig. 11-17). A timecode slate displays the same timecode as the audio recorder but does so in big red LED alphanumeric characters so that when the film camera shoots it for a few seconds, we have a convenient way to line up picture and sound for synching (see Synching Up, p. 601).

If an audio recording was made without original timecode, it may be necessary to stripe the recording with timecode before going to the telecine session or afterward. Timecode is extremely useful for locating and editing audio, regardless of whether timecode slates or in-camera timecode were used.

Video Timecode (also called Telecine Timecode)

The film and audio timecode discussed above can be referred to as *production timecode*, as this code is recorded in the field during the production. When we transfer the film to video in the telecine suite, a new, separate timecode is recorded on the videotape or to the metadata of a digital file. Sometimes referred to as *telecine timecode*, this is standard video timecode, no different from the timecode you would use for any video recording. It allows each video reel of the transfer to have its own unique, ascending timecode that runs continuously from the beginning of the reel to the end (note that each video reel may contain more than one film camera roll). When recording to a 1080p/24 format like D5 HD or HDCAM in 24p PsF mode, this will be 24 fps timecode. When recording to 60i, it will be standard 30 fps SMPTE timecode. When you capture 60i to a nonlinear editing system, you can either edit at 30 fps or use reverse pulldown to reconstruct the 24 fps frame rate and timecode from the film (see p. 565). PAL transfers will normally be 25-frame EBU code. Together with the key numbers, it's essential that video timecode be tracked correctly for accurate negative cutting and online editing.

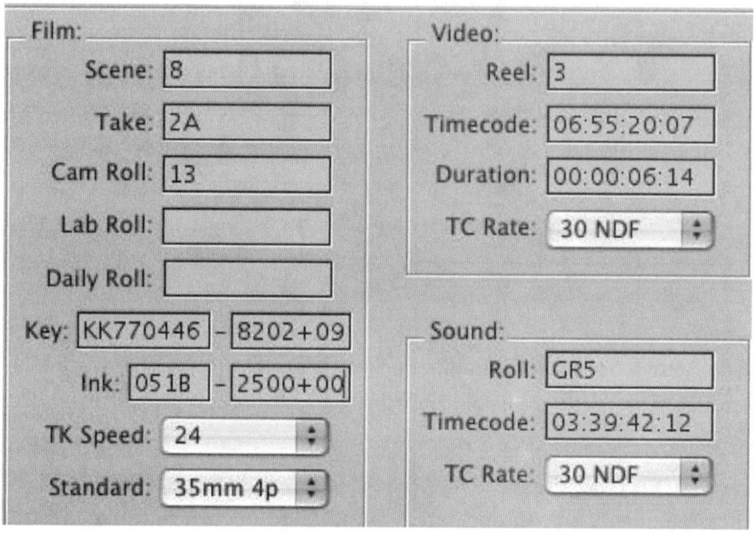

Fig. 18-4. This Cinema Tools screen provides a good opportunity to look at the data associated with a film transfer. (Apple Computer, Inc.)

FILM DATA (from film shot in the field):
SCENE AND TAKE: from slate or log
CAMERA ROLL: original camera negative roll number
LAB ROLL AND DAILY ROLL: each may contain more than one camera roll
KEY: key number read from the keycode exposed in the film when it was manufactured
INK: ink edge code printed on the workprint after it has been synched; used when transferring from workprint.
TK SPEED: telecine transfer speed in fps
STANDARD: film format; 35mm four-perf shown here

VIDEO DATA (the video being recorded in telecine session):
REEL: reel number of videocassette, as assigned by production or facility
TIMECODE: timecode of video
DURATION: length of shot/clip
TC RATE: timecode rate of video; 30 fps nondrop shown here

SOUND DATA (from production audio recorded in the field):
ROLL: sound roll number
TIMECODE: audio timecode recorded in the field (and displayed on digislate)
TC RATE: timecode rate of production audio (see Chapter 11)

Ink Edge Code

On feature films for which a film workprint has been made, identical ink edge code numbers are printed on each roll of workprint and matching roll of mag sound after they have been put in sync by an editor (see p. 602). This is meant to facilitate traditional film-style editing using a flatbed or upright Moviola. With identical eye-readable numbers on both picture and mag track, it's simple to check or re-establish sync when working with many small trims of both picture and sound. Some NLEs can track these numbers to aid in cutting the workprint for, say, test screenings by film projection. Ink edge code numbers must be entered into the NLE by keyboard during logging.

Shot Logs

Without doubt, all these systems create a lot of data! You may wonder what you need it for. If you're planning to edit on an NLE and then return to the original camera negative to do additional video transfers and/or cut the negative for film prints, then you'll want to track the video timecode, key numbers, production film timecode (if any), and the pulldown type of the first frame of each clip. However, if you plan to transfer the negative only once, edit on video, and never return to the negative, you may not need anything more than the video timecode recorded on the master tapes.

Rather than try to keep track of all these numbers manually, you should be able to get a *shot lot* or *telecine log* generated by the telecine at the time of transfer. A telecine shot log might contain information such as scene, take, camera roll number, lab roll number, dailies roll number, key numbers, ink edge code numbers (if any), telecine frame rate, film format, video reel, video timecode, video timecode timebase, transfer duration, audio reel, audio timecode, audio timecode timebase, transfer session, date, production company, and telecine operator's notes.

Like burn-in timecode windows, you must request that the postproduction facility provide this log, and you must specify which types of timecode or keycode you wish to be included. A good policy is to ask that all timecode and keycode data be included in the log, even if there is an extra charge for this. You never know what information about the picture or synched sound might prove to be a lifesaver at a later date.

There are several logging formats, including ALE, ATN (Aaton), Cinema Tools, FLeX, and FTL. The shot log is typically delivered as a database file on disc to be imported into your NLE; you may first need to convert it to a format compatible with your NLE. Avid Log Exchange (ALE) is used to convert logs for Avid systems. Cinema Tools, which is included with Final Cut Pro, does the same for FCP. The numbers from the log file should be checked carefully after capturing the clips in the NLE.

The future of postproduction lies in software that ties together all the data collected about sound and image. Some systems can bring forward script notes made on the set as well as things like color balance information from the telecine and the production team.

AUDIO IN THE TELECINE

Telecine machines cost anywhere from 250,000 to one million dollars, so their owners charge a lot for their use. This makes synching video dailies in the telecine suite an expensive proposition. The exception is when footage has been shot with in-camera film timecode (AatonCode or Arricode) and audio is on a nonlinear medium (CD or hard drive) that can instantly chase (find and keep up with) the picture during the transfer. When this is the case, manual searching for timecode slates, clapper sticks, or other sync points is unnecessary. Such automatic synching of audio during the telecine transfer process imposes no extra time penalty.

When this is not the case, it is usually more cost-effective to transfer the picture first (silent transfer), then sync audio to picture later in a special "layback suite" (see Fig. 15-15). Hourly charges for audio layback are a small fraction of telecine hourly rates. Or you can sync it yourself on your NLE—for free (not counting the cost of the NLE and the editor's time). Make sure you first understand the 0.1 percent audio slowdown in NTSC or the 4.1 percent speedup in PAL, as discussed below. For more on importing audio directly to the NLE, see p. 619.

As discussed in Chapter 15, there can also be definite advantages to synching sound in the telecine room when making video dailies. These include simplifying the workflow, generating screening tapes quickly, and generating a shot log with audio already logged. Working with audio in the telecine involves a few steps.

SPEED CONTROL. First, the sound must be played at the correct speed. Film is traditionally shot at exactly 24 fps, while in NTSC countries, video running at a nominal 30 fps actually runs 0.1 percent slower at 29.97 fps. (See the discussion on frame rates on p. 606.) What this means is that if you're transferring 24 fps film to a video format running 0.1 percent slower, the effective frame rate of the film becomes 23.976 fps and you must also slow the sound down by 0.1 percent. How this is accomplished depends on the type of recorder used to record the sound. Digital recorders are sometimes set to a sample rate of 48.048 kHz in the field and then played back at 48 kHz to slow the playback 0.1 percent. Nagra ¼-inch tape recorders may be resolved to a reference of 59.94 Hz instead of the usual 60 Hz. For more on this process when working with an NLE, see p. 619.

Once the sound has been slowed and put in sync with the picture, they can both be sped up again to exactly 24 fps in the NLE, if desired.

Confusingly, the term *pulldown* is also used to refer to this slowing down of picture or sound, as in, "Don't forget to pull down the sound 0.1 percent in transfer." Similarly, speeding up may be referred to as *pulling up*, as in, "Will this DAT machine pull up from 29.97 to 30?"[1]

There are certain speeds at which a film camera can be run that do not require any pulldown in the audio. Modern crystal sync film cameras can be operated at 29.97 or 23.976 fps. Since these speeds can run on the telecine without being slowed down, real time is maintained, so audio should not be pulled down.

In countries where PAL is used, a different speed adjustment is needed. When film is shot at 24 fps and transferred at 25 fps, the sound must be sped up 4.1 per-

---

1. And the term *pullup* has other meanings as well! See When Reels Are Spliced Together, p. 691.

cent. This results in a noticeable change in pitch, which may be digitally corrected later. If you are using the 24+1 telecine pulldown method, sometimes called PAL +1, in which an extra field is added every 12 frames, audio should run at its normal speed.

TIMECODE. Audio timecode is essential for synching up in the telecine. In NTSC countries, timecode is typically recorded at 30 fps (this is a true 30 nondrop code). When the audio is pulled down 0.1 percent, this timecode rate drops to 29.97 fps, which matches NTSC video perfectly.

In PAL countries, timecode is often recorded at the same rate as the picture.

SYNCHING UP. As noted above, synching up in the telecine can be done in different ways depending on the technology available. If the camera has in-camera film timecode and the audio has matching code, some telecine systems can sync up automatically while the film is running. The telecine needs to be equipped with an AatonCode or Evertz timecode reader, and the audio needs to be on optical disc or hard drive.

If timecode slates were used instead, then the telecine operator must stop at every slate and type in the audio timecode displayed on the slate. The audio can then chase the picture by timecode.

If old-fashioned, non-electronic slates were used, then the operator has to manually locate and match the sync points in picture and sound. Very slow, very expensive.

If you're transferring from workprint that has already been synched, then the entire roll can run uninterrupted from start to finish. This is not practical with negative and raw production audio, since the length of the sound and the picture won't be the same (usually there's more sound).

If you're transferring a finished film, audio may be lined up by timecode, but it's always a good idea to have a countdown leader with an audible sync pop at "2" to check against potential errors.

FINAL TRANSFERS

On some films, a high-quality transfer is done after the offline edit to create color corrected, high-res media for the online. For some films, the high-quality transfer is done after the film has been printed. Understanding how film translates to video is an art, and a good colorist will contribute enormously to the way your film looks. Ask for recommendations to find a good colorist. In a *supervised transfer* you get to be present. In an *unsupervised transfer*—which usually costs less—you let the colorist work alone. Be sure to let the colorist know in advance of any special looks you're going for. Some transfer facilities will charge you per foot instead of per hour for unsupervised work.

Prior to the Online

If video dailies have been used for the offline edit, common practice on many films is to retransfer the negative for the online using just the selected footage from the sequence (see Scenario Three, p. 612). Based on either an EDL (edit decision list organized by video timecode) or a film cut list (organized by key numbers)—both of these generated by the NLE—selected shots are pulled by a negative cutter from the original camera rolls and strung together on a reel for transfer. Sometimes handles of several extra frames are left intact on either end of each clip for flexibility and safety; sometimes instead entire shots are pulled flash frame to flash frame before they're strung together. This avoids physically cutting within a take. It is also possible to forgo cutting the negative altogether. In this scenario, the telecine, on the basis of keycode or timecode, fast-forwards along each camera roll until it reaches a section that needs to be transferred. Shuttling through extra footage may take more time on the telecine, depending upon the shooting ratio (practical for low-budget dramas with low 2:1 or 3:1 shooting ratios, perhaps not with documentaries with 15:1 or more), but the extra telecine expense may be somewhat offset by avoiding the costs of negative cutting. Also, especially in the case of Super 16, transferring from uncut rolls of camera negative ensures less handling and potential damage to the negative.

In all cases, the most accurate retransfer is done with systems that can track key numbers. While locating the selects and retransferring them for the online can also be done with timecode instead of keycode, tracking timecode across different frame rates and transfers can be very complex.

Color correction for final transfers will be done more carefully than with the dailies, with scene-to-scene adjustments made for every shot (which is expensive and very slow). It's essential that the negative be cleaned meticulously to avoid dirt and sparkle. Even so, digital *dustbusting* is often done after the transfer to remove dirt specs.

At this point you will be recording to a high-quality mastering format.

Finished Films

Transferring a finished film is similar to transferring original negative prior to an online session in terms of quality and care that needs to be taken.

Keep in mind that you may need to make several master transfers to different aspect ratios with or without letterboxing and/or pan and scan, different edits (full-length and TV cutdown), or different video standards (NTSC, PAL, or HD). If you have made a distribution deal, these assorted masters are called "deliverables" and are required by contract. Not too long ago this required a separate telecine pass of the entire film for each video standard. Today it is increasingly common to make one master transfer and do your versioning from that. The key to going this route is to make a universal 1080p/24 HD master. From this single master, all broadcast NTSC, PAL, and 60i HD submasters can be generated with no loss in quality.

If you've already cut the negative and done film printing in the lab, you may have some choices about what to use for the telecine transfer.

1. *Original negative.* Using the original negative for the transfer results in the sharpest picture with the most flexibility for color correction in terms of color and tonal scale. Because color negative reproduces a full tonal scale at about half real contrast, all shadow and highlight details are visible (including those power cables on the floor you thought were hidden in the dark corner of the set), details which will be unavailable in later prints that have

higher projection contrast. The negative provides you with maximum choice in how to transfer your film image to video. However, for transfers done after the movie is edited, going back to the original negative entails doing an online edit of the show after it is retransferred to video, which adds cost.

2. *Interpositive.* For movies that have already been edited, an interpositive or IP (formally called a master positive) makes a second-best source for the video transfer. An IP is a single-strand, low-contrast, positive copy of the original negative (see Intermediates, p. 684). It has finer grain than the original negative, possesses the same tremendous latitude, and will already be color and density corrected before it gets to the telecine suite (although more correction will be necessary in the telecine). No online edit is needed after transfer.

3. *Dupe (duplicate) negative.* Kodak 5242/7242 (or 5366/7366 in black-and-white) is a unique motion picture product that is designed for creating IPs, and when the IP is printed onto another roll of the same stock yields a copy of the negative used for long print runs. However, a dupe negative is less desirable than an interpositive as a video transfer element because is it one generation further removed from the original, with consequent loss of sharpness and a build-up of grain and contrast. On the other hand, it is often meant for high-speed, one-light printing, so color and density are well corrected.

4. *Print.* For reasons of cost, a master positive may not be feasible. Standard answer or release prints were once common as transfer elements, but today are considered by many to be too contrasty for good transfers. If a master positive is not available, an economical alternative is a *lo-con* (low-contrast) print made with Kodak Color Teleprint Film 2395/3395. *Lo-con* prints offer less flexibility for color correction than original negatives or master positives; however, they do have the advantage of being already color corrected and edited. Since lo-con prints offer fewer options in transfer, the telecine session may go faster and save you money. Prints are generally complete with all titles and credits, which may or may not be an advantage depending on your needs (foreign broadcasters may want a "textless" version). Note that lo-con prints are too flat in contrast to be used later for regular theatrical projection. In black-and-white, instead of using special lo-con print stock, regular stock can be developed to lower contrast (gamma).

IMAGE CONTROLS IN THE TELECINE

There are many ways to control or manipulate the way the picture looks in the telecine session.

Color Correction

Color correcting (also called *grading* in Europe) a film transfer has a lot in common with correcting material that originated on video. This is discussed in Color Correction, p. 573.

Keep in mind that the image you see on the high-end CRT broadcast monitor

Fig. 18-5. Colorist at work on da Vinci system. (DuArt Film and Video).

or DLP projector in the dark telecine room is far sharper and has richer blacks than what viewers will see on their badly adjusted TVs in brightly lit living rooms.[2] Many telecines have a secondary color corrector that allows you to change specific colors without affecting other colors. You could use this, for example, to warm up skin tones without affecting the overall balance of the scene. Or you could redecorate a set by changing the wall color without affecting the furniture. Most systems allow you to program a gradual, variable change in exposure or color during a shot (called a *dynamic*).

Contrast in the Telecine

The range of brightness in the film negative can be much greater than a video image can reproduce. If during a telecine transfer you make the video image dark enough to read detail in the bright areas of the film, the shadows may be rendered without detail ("crushing the blacks"). Or you could choose to bring the overall brightness up to see detail in the shadows, at the risk of losing detail in the brightest areas. Whichever the case, it's an advantage to use the negative or an interpositive (a "master positive" copy with a low contrast identical to the negative's) for the telecine transfer. This gives the colorist the utmost flexibility to go for detail in either the highlights or the shadows, depending on your needs. If you use a print instead, there is not as much detail to be had in the extremes of shadow and brightness, because the print has much more contrast than the negative (prints are intended to stretch the negative's low-contrast tonal scale to a natural appearance).

2. A DLP projector may not have richer blacks; it depends on the DLP.

With a print, blacks can get really solid or "plugged up" and bright highlights tend to "burn out," neither of which a telecine can recover. Sometimes, however, you may *want* detail to go away, for example, to create inky film noir–style shadows.

Storing and Repeating Corrections

Most telecines can automatically detect cuts in the picture and allow you to store a list of the color corrections for an entire film on disk. You can then go back later and adjust color correction on a shot-by-shot basis, as needed. Bear in mind that color settings in analog telecines, namely flying spot telecines by Cintel, can drift somewhat from day to day or over longer periods of time; it's therefore up to the facility to maintain their flying spot telecine to ensure consistent and repeatable results over time. (CCD telecines are solid-state and inherently stable.) To avoid problems, some colorists prefer to color-correct and transfer one reel at a time; that is, color-correct the reel, clean the negative, lay it off to tape (record it) without stopping, then move on to the next reel. If multiple versions of a transfer are needed (perhaps at different aspect ratios) it may be advisable to transfer all versions of each reel before moving on to the next reel. Your post facility will know the best way to proceed.

Other Telecine Image Controls

Beyond simply reproducing what is on the film, telecines can provide tremendous creative control over the image. Shots can be moved horizontally (*X axis*), vertically (*Y axis*) or resized (*Z axis*). This allows you to pan and scan a widescreen image for conversion to a narrower aspect ratio (see p. 87). You might want to enlarge the image, in order to remove unwanted objects near the edge of the frame, or to zoom in on something important. Flying spot telecines hold a significant advantage here, because they can electronically vary the size, shape, and position of the raster on their CRT to achieve these effects without affecting the resolution of the outcome, while a CCD telecine must always scan at a fixed resolution. To create repositions and zooms, CCD telecines must digitally resize each frame, like enlarging a JPEG in Photoshop. At some scale, the pixels of the original scan will grow evident, although today's CCD telecines sample and interpolate images at a high enough resolution to largely conceal this result.

Many telecines can squeeze or unsqueeze an anamorphic image. Varying the horizontal magnification is sometimes used to creatively distort images.

Telecines offer a variety of frame rates for speeding up or slowing down motion or creating freeze frames. Off speeds can be used for effects on individual shots, or entire films can be time compressed or expanded to fit a certain broadcast length. Speeding up a feature film 3 percent can shave 3½ minutes off the running time without making any cuts. Some movies actually play better if sped up a little for the small screen. With any speed changes, you need to watch carefully for motion artifacts like judder that may be introduced, especially in scenes with fast subject or camera movement. Speed changes will affect the pitch of the sound.

Film may have a certain amount of weave or unsteadiness in the telecine gate, causing the entire image to float slightly. This may go undetected in a straight transfer, but be painfully apparent if nonmoving video titles or effects are later superimposed on the image (titles that are already on the film are not a problem).

Some telecines and scanners use pin registration (see Fig. 6-3) or electronic alignment systems to increase steadiness.

Other image processing includes *enhancement* (also called detail; see p. 137) that increases the apparent resolution by making details stand out more. This should be used sparingly because it also increases visible noise and grain. Many systems are equipped with *grain reducers*, which can help soften the appearance of film grain. Some telecines are equipped with *wet gates*, like those used in film contact and optical printers, which can render invisible scratches and abrasions on the cellulose base of the film (see Chapter 17).

AN ALTERNATIVE FILM-TO-VIDEO TRANSFER SCENARIO

Telecines convert film images to video. In the 1980s and 1990s this meant high-end broadcast videotape, but today it's not uncommon to transfer video dailies to economical DVCAM or even directly to a hard drive. When a hard drive is used, what is recorded is no longer a continuous digital video signal but a series of digital video files compressed using a popular codec like DV or DVCPRO50, then "wrapped" in QuickTime or AVI. The resulting QuickTime or AVI files can then be brought into an editing system by attaching the hard drive to the NLE via a FireWire or USB 2.0 cable.

A new generation of sophisticated software-based "desktop color correction" programs now exist that can perform extensive 32-bit primary and secondary color correction of these files, notably Synthetic Aperture's Color Finesse and Silicon Color's Final Touch (now owned by Apple). Even NLEs offer 32-bit color correction, including Final Cut Pro, Adobe Premiere 2.0, and at the sophisticated finishing end, Avid's Symphony Nitris. Since these programs don't handle real-time video signals but use digital files instead, rendering is always required.

These are not simple tools, and there's a learning curve if you want to use them. Doing color correction is a bit like mixing your own sound track: It's easy to push sliders up and down, but without considerable experience and taste, things can get messed up fast. However, the arrival of professional-grade color correction to the desktop has opened the door to a new workflow in film-to-video transfer.

Instead of a best-light transfer or scene-to-scene correction, some filmmakers are now asking for a "flat" transfer or "flat grade," which is a film-to-video transfer that has visibly low contrast and retains as much of the extremes of exposure as possible at one time. The idea here is that later color correction can occur at the filmmaker's leisure, as it were, since the clock is not running at a post facility. Or another colorist can step in, one not employed by the transfer facility. The trade-off is that the full versatility of transferring from the original negative is lost. Since a "flat" transfer doesn't involve stopping the telecine to make adjustments to picture, it's an economical choice that results in the shortest possible telecine session.

If you choose to go this route, discuss the details with your post facility. Best results for downstream color correction are obtained from 4:2:2 formats with 10-bits per color. DV, DVCAM, and DVCPRO25 are 4:2:0 or 4:1:1 (retaining only 25 percent of the original color data) and 8-bits per color, so they're not ideal for color mastering. DVCPRO50 is a step up, at 4:2:2 and 8-bits. The best quality would be uncompressed standard definition files, which are 4:2:2 and either 8- or 10-bits per color, requiring considerably more disk storage.

On the high definition side, HDV, AVCHD, and XDCAM HD are each 4:2:0 and 8-bits. Avid's open-standard compression, DNxHD, is 4:2:2 and either 8- or 10-bits, while DVCPRO HD is 4:2:2 and 8-bits only. Uncompressed HD files are 4:2:2 and either 8- or 10-bits. Again, considerable disk storage is needed as well as a very fast computer system. An ideal system would be something like Matrox's Axio for editing uncompressed HD—basically a turbocharged NLE using a high-end PC with quad processors, five terabytes of RAID on a fast storage-area network, and Adobe Premiere Pro 2.0 as an NLE interface. A "flat" transfer of negative to uncompressed HD would look spectacular after desktop color correction—in the hands of someone skilled at color correction, of course.

HIGH-RESOLUTION FILM SCANNERS

The limitations of a "flat" telecine transfer are the limitations of video itself: poor resolution and narrow tonal reproduction. What if a device existed to transfer film not to digital video but instead to digital image files that could retain all the resolution and tonal range captured in the original negative?

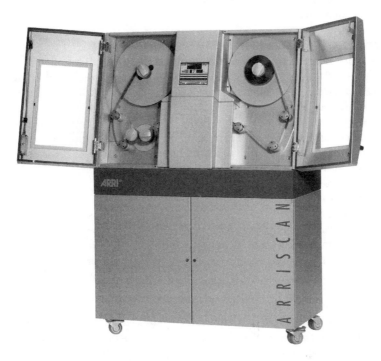

Fig. 18-6. Arriscan high-resolution film scanner. Uses CMOS sensor instead of CCD. Outputs resolutions from 2K to 6K, in DPX and other data formats. (Arriflex Corporation)

Film scanners are film transfer machines capable of transferring film to very high resolution digital files that remove the limitations of video reproduction. If you're familiar with digital still photography, imagine every frame of Super 16 or 35mm film reproduced as a TIFF or RAW file, and you'll have the right idea. Film scanners typically capture film frames to uncompressed *Digital Picture Exchange (DPX)* files. DPX is based on an earlier format devised by Kodak in the 1990s for its pioneering (now defunct) Cineon film scanning and recording system. DPX files are huge and therefore recorded directly to arrays of hard drives called RAIDs (see p. 219) or to digital linear tape (DLT).

The two most common types of scans are "2K" and "4K," which are typically 2048 × 1556 pixels and 4096 × 3112 pixels, respectively. (The exact pixel dimensions of a scan are somewhat determined by aspect ratio and how much of the frame is actually scanned.) The 4K version most closely approximates the original resolution of 35mm negative. However when compared to 2K, 4K requires *four* times the data. This means longer scan times per frame, more processing power, faster networking and data throughput, and four times the disk storage for the larger 50MB/frame DPX files (2K files are 12MB/frame). Rendering a 4K image file takes four times as long too. This translates into at least double the costs of 2K. As a consequence, 2K scans have been Hollywood's budget choice for most 35mm special effects, Digital Cinema applications, and digital intermediate work (see Digital Intermediates, p. 718), although this is changing as the price of high-end computing and fast disk arrays drops. For Super 16 scanning, 2K is considered more than adequate.

Types of Film Scanners

Some film scanners have a continuous film transport similar to that of a telecine. They can transfer film to SD and HD video and also create 2K and 4K scans. Recent examples are Grass Valley's Spirit Datacine and a host of Cintel products, including C-Reality, DSX, Millennium II, and the economical dataMill.

Other scanners are based on the slower, intermittent, pin-registered transports of optical printers. These scanners have no video capability and exist only to create high-resolution film scans. Examples include Arriscan, Kodak Cineon Genesis, Quantel Domino, Cintel diTTo, Oxberry CineScan, and Imagica XE. (Not all are still in production, however.) Some are 2K only, others can achieve 4K. The Northlight Film Scanner can scan a 35mm frame at 6K.

Telecine-type scanners have the advantage of speed. Grass Valley's speedy Spirit Datacine can scan film negative to 2K resolution at 24 fps (real time) and 4K at 7.5 fps. Cintel's dataMill can scan 2K at 15 fps and 4K at 3.75 fps. By comparison, the very best Arriscan can do is 2K at 4 fps (it creates 3K scans for downsampling to 2K, an impressive method) and 4K at 1 fps (downsampled from 6K). Film scanning is typically a slow and costly business.

A 2K or 4K scan can serve as the ultimate "universal master"—a high-resolution 24p source that can be used to generate a digital intermediate for film release (see p. 718), files for Digital Cinema projection, and downconverts to HD or SD at virtually any frame rate and frame size, including NTSC and PAL. One caveat, however, is that storing and retrieving 90 minutes of huge DPX files is expensive, as is accessing and processing them to create downconverts to SD and HD. State-of-the-art technology is required at every step. It often proves more economical to simply transfer the Digital Intermediate negative on a telecine to a 24p HD master, which is then used to make SD and HD deliverables.

DIGITAL-TO-FILM TRANSFERS

A digital video-to-film transfer, or a transfer of digital files to 35mm, is called a *film-out*. These conversions are primarily used by two distinct markets.

At the high end are big-budget feature filmmakers who shoot film and do a high-resolution scan to create a digital intermediate (D.I.; see p. 718). Or they shoot with high-end HD or digital cinematography cameras to capture high definition 4:4:4 RGB or DPX files directly. All of the postproduction and effects are done in the HD or 2K realm, and at the last stage the D.I. is recorded to film to make prints for theatrical distribution in cinemas. Sometimes, instead of transferring an entire movie from digital files to film, only special effects shots are done this way. The new effects negative is cut in with the original camera negative and prints are made the traditional way.

The other transfer market is for independent or television movies that have been shot in SD or HD, but where the filmmakers want to make film prints to show in festivals or for theatrical release. The video is up-resed and converted to 24p if necessary before doing a film-out.

This is an interesting time for digital-to-film transfer. On one hand, new technologies are developing, quality is improving, and the potential market has grown since so many filmmakers are shooting and/or posting in digital video instead of film.

On the other hand, video projection has improved enormously and far more theaters are equipped to show SD or HD video or *Digital Cinema*, which is not a video format but a server-based JPEG2000 file format that conforms to Hollywood's Digital Cinema Initiative (DCI) specifications. Although still a long way off, at some point theatrical distribution will no longer require that images be put on celluloid film.

It used to be that a trained eye could usually tell the difference between film prints made only from film elements and prints made from video-to-film transfers, but some transfers, particularly from 24p HD, are amazingly good. Moreover, telltale signs of digital postproduction are usually undetectable in film that has been scanned to digital files, then output back to film. The goal of D.I., after all, is transparency.

Filmmakers are often unaware that they have a choice of print stocks on which to print their film-out. Kodak, for instance, offers Kodak Vision color print film 2383 and Vision color print film 2393. The 2383 is Kodak's workhorse print stock, but the more contrasty 2393 has richer blacks and more saturated colors—perhaps just the ticket for DV and HDV film-outs that tend toward a flat appearance to begin with.

Digital-to-Film Recorders

There are various technologies for writing digital video or digital files to film, which range in quality and cost. At the highest level currently are *film recorders*. These systems use either a cathode ray tube, a high-res LCD panel, or a laser to record high-resolution 2K or 4K images directly onto a 35mm negative. This process is much slower than real time, though film recorders are getting faster and more affordable as technology develops.

CRT film recorders use a high-resolution black-and-white CRT whose image is projected into a film camera. Each film frame gets three exposures: one each through a red, green, and blue filter. CRT film recorders are slow, especially when photographically "slow" intermediate film stocks like Kodak 5242 (2242 on Estar base) are exposed, which is conventional. Celco's speediest top-of-the-line CRT film recorder, the Fury model, can output a 2K DPX frame with a 1.85 aspect ratio every 1.2 seconds to Kodak 5242 stock. Using a camera negative film, Kodak Vision2 5201 (E.I. 50 daylight), Fury can achieve 1 second per frame. A 4K frame to either film stock is 3.5 seconds per frame. Faster speeds may be possible with faster camera negatives, which filmmakers sometimes prefer because of the natural addition of film grain to the image.

Fig. 18-7. Arrilaser film recorder for making film-outs. (DuArt Film and Video)

The most popular *laser film recorder* is the Arrilaser, which uses three solid-state lasers—red, green, and blue—to write directly to the color negative. It outputs to Kodak 5242 a 2K DPX frame with a 1.85 aspect ratio every 1.7 seconds, or 2.9 seconds per 4K frame.

Most 2K film recorders can also output at native HD resolution, 1920 x 1080, which is slightly lower than 2K—sometimes a modest speed advantage over 2K results.

The original video-to-film conversion method is the 16mm *kinescope*, a device mainly consisting of a film camera shooting a video monitor in real time. Modern kinescopes use a high-quality color monitor and a special film camera with a synchronous motor running at 23.976 fps (for NTSC) with a 288-degree shutter (1/29.97th of a second) and super-fast pulldown to create a two-field-per-frame, flicker-free film image from the video. This type of kinescope (the color negative that results is also called a kinescope or "kine"; rhymes with "skinny") is the most economical transfer method and produces quite good results.

Some facilities use a homebrew kinescope consisting of a 16mm production camera with a 144-degree shutter (often an Auricon, CP16, or Éclair NPR) that captures only one field of video per film frame. "Suppressed field" kinescopes create acceptable results although they throw away half of the video vertical resolution.

The lowest-tech way to get NTSC video on film, which you can do yourself, is to just point any film camera with a variable shutter that includes a setting for 144-degrees at a monitor. This will often result in poor resolution and uneven screen brightness and is inferior to the methods already mentioned, unless you use a high-quality flat-screen professional monitor and a sharp, well-corrected prime lens. (For more details, see Shooting CRT Video Displays with Film Cameras, p. 723.)

Since 16mm has all but died as a distribution format, few people make 16mm kinescopes or choose to film-out to 16mm anymore.

Preparing For and Evaluating the Digital-to-Film Transfer

Before choosing a transfer facility, talk to filmmakers you know and ask to see samples of the facility's work. Once you choose a facility, work closely with them to prepare your video prior to transfer. It's recommended that you do short tests of footage before investing in the full transfer. (Once you sign up with a transfer facility they will do a test anyway.)

The process begins with making your video look as good as possible. When shooting your movie, use a high-quality digital camera at the highest resolution you can afford. Shoot HD or HDV if possible. Shoot at 24p. Professional, high-quality lenses can make a huge difference. Use HD lenses on ⅔-inch B4-mount cameras, even on SD cameras. Favor prime lenses like Zeiss DigiPrimes or Canon HD primes over zooms where possible. Be fastidious about focus, especially in HD. Use a properly set up field monitor (see Appendix A) to avoid unintentional over- and underexposure. (A waveform monitor helps in this regard too.) You may want to use a special gamma in the video camera to preserve as much shadow or highlight detail as possible. Some manufacturers label this a "cine" gamma (see Chapter 5). Before you begin shooting, consult with a transfer facility about the use of nonstandard gammas, to gauge their experience with them.

During editing, project the video on a big screen and look for things like poor focus that may not be noticeable on a small monitor but will be in a theater. Watch for other image defects such as interlace artifacts (in which straight diagonal lines look like stair steps) and color fringing. You may decide to re-edit sections or do some video fixes.

If you shot at 24p, then you're way ahead of the game in terms of the film-out. Since film is also 24p, there should be no problem with motion or interlace artifacts.

If you shot at 25p, the film-out will be made on a frame-for-frame basis, so there won't be motion artifacts, but the projected movie will run 4 percent slower.

When material has been shot at 24p, transferred to 60i video and edited at 60i, then transferred to film, you can get strange motion artifacts unless you use an NLE that can do reverse pulldown so you can edit at the original 24p frame rate.

If you shot at 60i, the footage needs to be deinterlaced (see p. 720) and pulled down to 24 fps. Poorly done, this may result in some scenes looking soft (unsharp) or having judder (stuttering motion). Credit rolls at the end of a film can look particularly bad. Various transfer houses have proprietary software for doing the frame rate conversion and some are superior to others. Desktop software that accomplishes excellent deinterlacing and conversion to 24p include DVFilm Maker, Nattress Film Effects, and Algolith's Algosuite.

Color correction that looks good in video won't necessarily translate directly to film. Video and film possess different color gamuts and tonal scales. Each post facility, moreover, has its particular film recorder tweaked with custom color lookup tables (LUTs), which means that you may not be able take the same set of color corrections from one facility to another. In other words, your video should be specifically corrected for a facility's film-out system. But this is also an area where a lot of creative input can be had in terms of the look on film. If you're on a tight budget, you may be going more or less directly from your color-corrected video with a best-light or minimal correction, but the facility will still have to assign overall values for color correction, gamma, and sharpness. Have the facility put together a test reel of scenes to get a feel for overall density and potential problems.

High-quality transfers are done from 2K and 4K files, and if you shot in SD or HD, your video will be up-resed by the facility prior to the film-out. Some facilities favor high definition 4:4:4 RGB instead of 2K for film-out, maintaining that it matches 2K quality while being more economical. Of course, the higher the resolution you start with, the better it will look when recorded to film. This is why Hollywood features shot digitally often use high-res digital cinematography cameras on the set instead of HD cameras. As of this writing, several manufacturers including Sony are creating 4K cameras for future production.

Titles and graphics created in SD may look soft after being up-resed. You may need to recreate or rerender them in a larger frame size and edit them back into the movie.

Cinema projection is virtually always widescreen, so you need to consider any potential aspect ratio conversions (see p. 87), particularly 1.33 to 1.85.

Just as in any 35mm printing process, the film needs to be broken into reels (see Reel Length, p. 599). If your film is longer than 20 minutes, you and your editor or the facility will need to create reel breaks. Breaking a 35mm feature into reels is an art that involves both picture and sound considerations. Your film lab will be happy to discuss this with you.

See Chapters 16 and 17 for sound track systems used for theatrical projection.

Digital Intermediates

Kodak created the term digital intermediate, or D.I., to describe the process of scanning film to 2K or 4K digital files, doing color correction, degraining, scratch removal, wire removal, special effects, and so forth, in the digital realm, then outputting the results back to film in a seamless, undetectable manner, with no loss of resolution or tonal scale. However, in the years since the term first appeared, its use has widened to encompass virtually all high-resolution digital postproduction, from SD and HD formats to DPX files. Many people use it to refer to a post workflow that results in no film-out at all—for instance, preparing a feature shot on Super 16 and scanned to HD for digital projection at a film festival.

Perhaps the best use of the term is to refer to workflows that involve shooting with high-quality image capture systems (such as 16mm and 35mm film, HD 4:4:4 RGB, or 2K DPX files from digital cinematography cameras) with the intent of doing a high-quality theatrical release, either on film or via the new DCI digital projection specification.

In any case, D.I. ups the technical ante for storage, networking, display, editing, effects, and color correction. A typical D.I. color correction suite might be a small theater-sized room with a Lustre, Quantel Pablo, or da Vinci Systems 2K color correction system and a 2K DLP projector. Networked into the color correction suite might be a Quantel iQ for organizing clips or adding effects. These are expensive toys.

Perhaps as a result, there is also a movement toward "desktop D.I." As desktop computers grow more powerful, many people are asking why expensive D.I. effects work or color correction can't be done more economically. While there's no getting around the stratospheric cost of an HD telecine or film scanner, or the transfer itself, there now exist inexpensive capture cards like the Kona 3 that can input 2K DPX files and 2K QuickTime reference movies directly to hard drive for editing in Final Cut Pro, applying effects, and playing back on 1080/24p HD monitors. Color correction software like FinalTouch 2K offers capabilities equivalent to a da Vinci 2K system, if not the convenience of real time (corrections must be rendered). Popular effects programs such as Adobe After Effects and Shake (owned by Apple) readily handle 2K DPX files.

It will remain the case, nevertheless, that the best colorists will continue to work on professional systems like Lustre and da Vinci 2K, and those most experienced in D.I. workflows and results will be found at the busiest, most progressive D.I. facilities. While desktop D.I. levels the playing field, it doesn't change the rules of the game.

VIDEO-TO-VIDEO FORMAT CONVERSIONS

Given the astonishing number of video formats and variations in use these days, there's often a need to convert from one to another. Many of the issues to consider when converting from, say, SD to HD, or NTSC to PAL are discussed elsewhere in the book.

Conversions can often be done with software or dedicated hardware devices. For example, you might be able to up-res from SD to HD using your NLE at home, or you might send the footage out to a post house to be processed by a high-end hardware conversion system made by Snell & Wilcox or Teranex. For resizing, you might use the NLE itself or purchase a software plug-in such as Digital Anarchy. Both software and hardware solutions vary in their sophistication and in the quality of the output. Read the documentation before choosing software settings and get advice on conversion methods.

Here are some items involved:

FRAME SIZE. Generally speaking, going from a high definition format (many pixels) to a lower-definition format (smaller frame size) works well. Often the image looks better than native images in the lower-def format. Going the other way (up-resing) can cause problems because you're creating new pixels that don't exist in the original. The image may fall apart or look unsharp when converted to a larger frame size.

Going up or down, if you just repeat or delete pixels you can get artifacts (one common up-resing technique is *line doubling* which repeats existing lines of pixels). Better systems use *interpolation* to calculate either a larger or smaller set of pixels based on averaging adjacent pixels. If you started with a column of pixels A, B, C, line doubling would give you A,A,B,B,C,C and interpolation would create new "between" pixels A, A/B, B, B/C, C.

FRAME RATE. Conversions between 24, 30, 50, and 60 fps systems are discussed earlier in this chapter and in Chapters 2, 13, and 14. Frame rate conversions are needed when going between NTSC and PAL/SECAM, or between various HD formats. In some cases pulldown needs to be applied or removed. Not all frame rate conversions can be done successfully without motion artifacts. Again, interpolation (in this case temporal instead of spatial) can help, particularly when going from, say, 60i to 24p. Rather than simply throwing away some fields, which can cause judder, some fields are blended (combined), which can smooth motion. Many NLEs offer frame blending when speeding up or slowing down a clip.

PROGRESSIVE AND INTERLACE. It's very easy to convert from progressive to interlace. One frame is simply divided into two fields (this is PsF; see p. 104). Going the other way requires *deinterlacing*, which is much more complex. Static images aren't a problem—you can just combine the fields. But when there's any movement between two fields they will show edge tear when you combine them (see Fig. 18-8). Some systems just throw away one of the fields and double the other, which lowers resolution and can result in unsmooth motion. Some use field blending to interpolate between the two fields, which may also lower resolution. "Smart" deinterlacers can do field blending when there's motion between two fields but leave static images unchanged.

COLOR SPACE. Different types of color space are discussed in Chapter 5. Some systems can automatically compensate when converting from, say, 601 SD video to 709 HD video. High-end systems may offer custom *lookup tables* (*LUTs*) that map how the color or brightness of the pixels in one format or version will be rendered in another, allowing precise control over color values. Starting with the same master, you might use one LUT when doing a film-out, another when creating a television version.

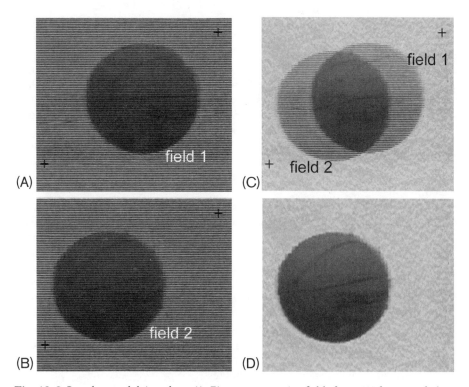

Fig. 18-8. Interlace and deinterlace. (A, B) two consecutive fields from 60i footage of a basketball being thrown. (C) Here we see both fields together as one frame. You can clearly see that each field has half the resolution (half the horizontal lines), and that the ball has moved between the two fields. Makes for an ugly frame. (D) This deinterlaced frame was made by deleting the first field and filling in the gap it left. We can create new pixels for the gap by "interpolating" (essentially averaging) the lines on either side of each missing line. Though this creates a single frame that could be used for a film-out or progressive display, it's not as clean or sharp as true progressive footage shot with a progressive camera. Deinterlacing works best when there's relatively little camera or subject movement. See also Fig. 1-11.

SHOOTING TVs, VIDEO MONITORS, AND VIDEO PROJECTORS

There are many situations in which you might want to shoot a video or computer display with either a video camera or a film camera. You may be shooting a scene in which a character is watching TV or you might be getting shots of a website on a laptop. In some cases shooting video displays is very straightforward. For example, shooting any NTSC display with an NTSC video camera (or PAL display with a PAL camera) requires no special adjustments.

However, whenever the frame rate or scanning rate of a CRT (cathode-ray tube) display does not exactly match the frame rate or shutter speed of the camera, the screen image will seem to flicker. When the camera exposure is only slightly longer or shorter than the time it takes the display to *refresh* (complete the raster pattern), a horizontal *shutter bar* or *hum bar* will appear in the image (misleadingly but commonly called a *roll bar*). The hum bar may appear darker or lighter than the rest of the picture and will slowly creep up or down the screen. If you must pan quickly, a "shearing" effect will sometimes result. Some CRT displays look worse than others in this regard. In some situations you may feel that the flicker or hum bar is acceptable, but in others it can be very distracting. There are various ways to solve this problem, depending on your equipment and your needs. (Note that there is a difference between computer monitors and video monitors; see p. 200.)

The good news is that shooting TVs, monitors, and video-projected images with video or film cameras has become simple with the advent of non-CRT flat-panel displays and projectors based on LCD, plasma, or DLP technologies. These displays modulate brightness at the pixel level, meaning that there is no electron beam to sweep back and forth. No raster pattern to rapidly refresh means no flickering, hum bar, or phasing mismatches. Moreover, LCD pixel response times—the time it takes a pixel to go from full black to full white, then black again—tend to be slower than the decay times of CRT phosphors hit by an electron beam. This LCD "latency" or "lag" acts to further suppress flicker in LCD displays. You can shoot these types of displays with either film or video cameras and usually obtain excellent results regardless of frame rate or shutter speed, at least in most cases. As always, where questions remain, shoot a brief test.

Shooting CRT Video Displays with Video Cameras

Shooting CRT displays with modern video cameras is easy because most professional and prosumer cameras have variable electronic shutters. Some have a specific feature to exactly match the shutter speed of the camera to the display's scanning frequency. Sony's system is called Clear Scan, Panasonic calls theirs Synchro Scan. These provide for a wide range of scanning frequencies (one Sony camera offers a range from 30 to 7000 Hz) that can be dialed in very precisely. Changing the shutter speed of a video camera affects the exposure time, but the basic frame rate is not affected (see p. 134). Don't forget to go back to your normal shutter speed after shooting the screen.

If you can't find a good shutter speed when shooting a CRT computer monitor, you can often go to the control panel on the computer or monitor and choose a different display refresh rate.

When shooting any display, CRT or otherwise, be sure to white-balance the camera on the display and set exposure carefully. If you want the display's image geometry to look flat and rectangular, shoot with a long lens from a good distance away. Or you might try getting very close and letting some parts of the screen be sharp in the foreground with other parts softer in the background. Sometimes when you focus on the screen you see the pixels too clearly or get a moiré pattern. Try throwing the lens *slightly* out of focus.

Some people like to avoid the problems of shooting CRTs altogether by mounting a piece of green- or blue-screen material over the CRT's screen so that video or

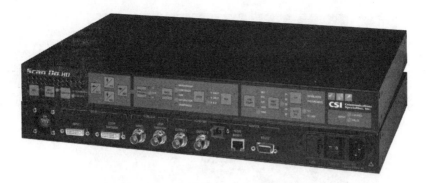

Fig. 18-9. Scan converter. Scan Do HD converts DVI computer video to HD-SDI or SD-SDI at a variety of frame rates. Can be fed to a VTR for recording video. (Communications Specialties)

computer images can be keyed in later.[3] You might also do this if the monitor image isn't available when you're shooting. A caveat—this is much easier to do convincingly if the camera you're shooting with doesn't move.

To obtain the computer screen image for keying, many of today's computers have a handy composite video or S-video output from which you can record. DVI or HDMI computer monitor outputs can also be converted to SD or HD component video with an adapter which can be recorded to a video deck.

Shooting CRT Video Displays with Film Cameras

When Hollywood films include a scene in which a CRT TV is visible, they typically use a special 24 fps video playback system with special 24 fps video decks and CRT TVs. This guarantees a flicker-free image without a hum bar for a film camera operating at 24 fps with a standard 180-degree shutter angle. Note that since a 180-degree shutter at 24 fps results in a shutter speed of 1/48 second, only one field per frame of 24 fps video can be captured using this method. In other words, half of the video image's vertical resolution is missing on film. However, the results of this technique are acceptable, particularly when the TV appears in a wide shot and not in closeup.

Filmmakers working in PAL countries can get a clean image simply by shooting a 25 fps PAL video monitor with a standard crystal sync film camera running at 25 fps with a standard 180-degree shutter. Sometimes filmmakers shooting an NTSC display will adopt a similar strategy and film the NTSC display at 29.97 fps. When transferred to video at 29.97 fps, motion will look normal, but if transferred to video or projected at a standard 24 fps, motion will appear slightly slowed. Therefore, use of this technique hinges on considerations of frame rate and scene content. Be sure to consult with the transfer house in advance about proper speed or timecode settings for the sound recorder to maintain audio sync.

---

3. You can also feed the CRT screen a deep blue or green image instead of putting blue or green material over it, but this sometimes causes keying problems later due to uncontrolled glow and light scatter.

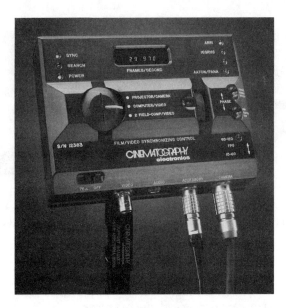

Fig. 18-10. Film/video synchronizing control automatically synchronizes a film camera to another source signal such as a computer, video monitor, projector, or another camera. (Cinematography Electronics)

Another approach to filming a CRT that's displaying NTSC video is to use a film camera with a variable shutter. When filming at 24 fps, a shutter opening of 144 degrees can be used (equals ⅟₆₀ second), at least for short shots. Some cameras provide a precise 23.976 fps frame rate to perfectly match NTSC's 0.1 percent slowdown (from 30 fps to 29.97), which creates a true frame-rate lock. (A shutter opening of 144 degrees becomes 1/59.94 second.) Motion shot at 23.976 will appear normal when projected at 24 fps and the footage can be transferred to video at real time. Again, consult the transfer house on audio.

If you are filming at 25 fps in an NTSC country, then a shutter opening of 150 degrees can be used. (A precise shutter angle of 150.15 degrees would be ideal.)

In truth, the 144-degree shutter technique yields imperfect results. The hum bar is reduced to a few thin lines hardly visible in a wide shot in which the featured CRT TV is small. They're static if the camera's 23.976 fps frame rate is locked to that of the NTSC display. (Some feel that 25 fps at 150 degrees is superior to 24 or 23.97 fps at 144 degrees, because perfect frame-rate matching or "phasing" is not required for smooth results.)

Note that 16mm camera viewfinders will be misleading about hum bars for two reasons: They utilize a 180-degree mirror for viewing even though the shutter is set to 144 degrees; and the ⅟₄₈-second image that you see in the viewfinder or video assist is not the ⅟₄₈-second image exposed on the film.

Nevertheless, if precise speed control is available, either from built-in camera settings or an external unit such as a precision speed control (see Fig. 9-28), the viewfinder can be a useful guide in positioning the hum bar just outside of the CRT's viewable image. The speed control should have a *phase shift* adjustment, which adjusts the exact start of each film frame in time. If you see a hum bar on the video screen when looking through the camera's viewfinder, push the phase button until the bar is no longer visible. If you see two thin darkened bands, push the phase button until the top edge of one band is just off the screen (the other will now appear directly in the middle of alternate frames). If there is no phase shift adjustment, you can reset the phasing of the CRT's and camera's frame rates by turning the camera on and off. To make things easier, Cinematography Electronics makes a Film/Video Synchronizing Control (see Fig. 18-10) that attaches to a monitor and uses video sync to drive the camera at the exact right speed and phase.

When shooting CRT computer monitors with a film camera, things can be especially tricky because computer monitors may run at various refresh rates. You can experiment with a camera's precision speed control or, as noted above, with the refresh rate of the monitor. With no film in the camera, dial the speed control until the hum bar becomes stationary, then, when filming, use the phase control to make sure it's off the screen.

When filming video or computer monitors in closeup, take a reflected light meter reading, not an incident reading, or use a spot meter. The color temperatures of many monitors are close to daylight (6500°K). A color temperature meter can tell you how close. Use an 85 filter for tungsten film if you have enough exposure. Some monitors offer a choice of color temperatures. You may need a fairly fast film to get enough exposure.

CHAPTER 19

Producing and
Distributing the Movie

This chapter is about the business and legal aspects of getting a movie made and getting it shown after it's done. Many of these concerns apply to any kind of film or video project, from feature film to corporate video to student project. The scope of this book allows for only a general discussion of these topics, to help you frame the questions for which you need answers. A proviso for everything that follows: Nothing here should be taken as legal advice or as a substitute for a consultation with an experienced attorney, accountant, or other professional. Also, because laws and customs vary from state to state and country to country, bear in mind that practices may vary where you live. For those who can't afford traditional legal services, organizations such as Volunteer Lawyers for the Arts may be able to assist you.

BUDGETS AND BUSINESS ARRANGEMENTS

Budgets

The *budget* is an accounting of the cost of every aspect of the movie. Prior to production, the *estimated budget* plays a key role in getting the project financed and under way. Not only is the total cost important, but the way the budget is drawn up has an impact too. For professionals, the details of the budget make it clear to funders exactly where the money is going to be spent. For novices, a well-drawn budget helps reassure funders that you understand the production process. That said, when preparing a budget for fund-raising purposes, a certain amount of summarizing is called for. An investor or granting agency may be interested in the line item for equipment, but probably doesn't want to know which camera accessories you plan to rent. For feature films, some production managers and others specialize in reading scripts and drawing up budget estimates based on the use of locations, size of cast, special effects, and the like. Preparing and managing the budget is generally one of the producer's key jobs. During production, the budget is used to track expenses to ensure that the movie remains within the estimate (or, as often happens, to painfully detail how much over budget things have gone).

On a Hollywood feature, the costs of stars, script, salaries, and overhead may be the bulk of the budget; equipment and film or video costs may be less than 10 percent of the total cost. For a student project, on the other hand, if friends donate time and the school has equipment, the cost of film or tape may represent virtually all the cash needed to make a movie. When calculating your film/tape costs, work backward from the estimated length of the finished movie, multiplied by the expected shooting ratio (see p. 320). Sometimes a shoestring fiction film can be cheaper than an unscripted documentary because the action is predictable, entailing a lower shooting ratio and fewer shooting days.

There are many ways to organize a budget. Different types of productions (features, documentaries, corporate projects, multimedia) call for different budget formats. Several software packages (such as Movie Magic Budgeting) will help you lay out a budget and track expenditures. You can make your own using any spreadsheet program. *Film and Video Budgets* (see Bibliography) has many sample formats. Professionals may be reluctant to share complete budgets with you, but may give you the layout they use without the actual numbers filled in.

One type of budget divides expenses into *above-the-line* and *below-the-line costs*. Above-the-line costs are the producer's, director's, and key actors' salaries and those costs incurred before production even begins, such as the story rights and/or script (the *property*). Below-the-line costs include all equipment, materials, and other salaries involved in production. *Negative costs* of a film are all items prior to the marketing and distribution costs. *Distribution costs* include making release prints or dubs, trailers, advertising and promotion, and running the distribution office.

It often helps to divide the budget chronologically, separating the costs of preproduction (research, casting, scouting, planning), production (film or tape costs, equipment rental, location costs, crew salaries, travel, and meals) and postproduction (editing and the various finishing costs: music, mixing, online costs or negative matching, titles and prints or dubs).

Many projects begin with only enough cash to shoot, hoping to raise completion money later. You'll sometimes hear the expression "in the can" used to refer to the cost of production (as in, "We got it in the can for $10,000!"). This figure does not include marketing and distribution costs, and often doesn't include finishing costs like music rights or mixing. Materials, equipment, and labor are sometimes donated to a production (or provided at discount), especially for small or nonprofit projects. It's important to include these in-kind contributions in the budget but indicate that they are not normal cash items. Investors or funding agencies will want to see a budget that includes both types of support, since they are interested in the full value of the production.

Near the bottom of many budgets is an item for *contingency*, which is usually 5 to 15 percent of the entire budget. This figure is intended to cover the unexpected: equipment breakdown and delay, reshooting or unplanned shooting costs (insurance may cover some of these items). Because movies are often budgeted months or years before they are finished, the contingency allotment may also compensate for script or production changes and inflation; some people figure inflation into each budget line item instead.

In addition to the direct costs of getting the movie made, in some budgets the production company adds a fee for overhead and, for commercial projects, profit. Overhead includes the *indirect costs* of running your business independently of the project, such as renting your office space, business insurance, and other related expenses.[1] Profit is money over and above any actual expenses. Some producers list overhead/profit as a percentage of the total budget; sometimes this is listed as a "production fee." Sometimes profit, overhead, and/or contingency charges are buried in the budget by marking up all the *other* line items. For a commercial project, for example, the production company will usually mark up outside labor and materials costs as part of their fee for doing business.

Overhead and profit figures vary widely by the type of project, the total budget, and what the market will bear; talk to producers you know for their suggestions. In some cases, such as corporate or sponsored projects, a fee of 15 to 35 percent (or much more) above the direct costs of making the movie is not uncommon. On the other hand, for nonprofit, grant-funded projects, indirect costs are often not even reimbursable.

Budget Line Items

Following are some expenses to consider when doing a budget. Not all items apply to all types of productions. Some of the headings are for the purposes of this book and would not be used in a typical budget.

PREPRODUCTION
Research
Story/script preparation
Location scouting
Budget preparation
Casting; Hiring crew
Setting up the office

ABOVE THE LINE COSTS
Producer
Director
Story rights
Writer
Principal cast

PRODUCTION PERSONNEL
Production manager
Assistant directors
DP, assistants, camera operator
Sound recordist, boom operator
Gaffer, electrics; Grips
Script supervisor
Makeup/hair
Production designer
Set construction
Art director/stylist; Costumer
Production assistants; drivers
Still photographer
Supporting talent, extras
Benefits on salaries

PRODUCTION EXPENSES
Camera package
Sound package
Lighting package
Grip package; Dolly
Supplies and expendables
Props and sets, costumes
Studio rental
Film and/or tape and/or storage
    media (audio and video)
Catering
FX; Stunts

1. General overhead should not be confused with direct, project-related administrative costs, which could include accounting and legal costs, production insurance, facility rentals, or in-house salaries. These direct expenses of the project are usually specific line items in the budget.

TRAVEL AND LOCATION
Airfares
Excess baggage
Vehicles, mileage, parking, tolls
Lodging
Location fees; Permits
Crew per diems and/or meals

POSTPRODUCTION
Editor
Editing room, supplies
Editing system and
    peripherals/accessories
Workdubs/downconversions
Titles and graphics
Foley; ADR
Visual effects
Online edit, extra machines
Masters and protection masters
Standards/format conversions
Music rights and recording
Narrator and recording
Transcripts
Stock footage or stills
Sound editing, equipment
Sound mix, recording media
Audio layback

FILM FINISH
Titles and opticals
Negative matching or film-out
Fades and dissolves
Optical sound track
Answer print
IP/dupe negative
Check print
Release prints, reels, and cases
Video transfer

ADMINISTRATION
Office rental and expenses
Telephone, Internet, photocopies
Shipping and postage
Insurance (production,
    negative/tape, E&O)
Repairs
Legal and accounting
Contingency

Film Post:
Film processing
Telecine and video stock
Audio synching
    and/or:
Workprint
Sound transfer, mag stock
Edge code

DISTRIBUTION
Film prints and/or video dubs
Screeners (DVDs)
Telephone, postage, shipping
Website, poster, press kits, stills,
    flyers, ad slicks, postcards, trailer
Advertising and promotion
Press screenings, publicist
Mailing lists, study guide
Festival fees, travel

Hiring Crew and Actors

To make a movie, you generally have to get people to work with you, either for pay or sometimes not. A well-planned, well-run production creates a good working environment that can lead to you getting good footage, a good reputation, and a good chance of working with people you like in the future. Craft unions were organized in the film industry as a way to standardize how much personnel are to be paid and to limit what they can be asked to do. Productions range from highly organized (unionized) feature or television movies, to smaller, nonunion film or video projects, to student or independent projects in which no one is paid. Regardless of the type of production, crews work best when they feel they are being treated fairly and the producer is looking out for their needs.

Start by making a workable plan for how large a crew you need (see Chapter 9). Talk to experienced filmmakers for advice. Even on small productions in which everyone is wearing two or three hats, think through who will perform various tasks. Novice producers often neglect tasks (forgetting, say, that props can't get to the set by themselves) or ask too much of the crew (perhaps by failing to schedule enough setup time when the company moves to a new location). To avoid a crisis, discuss with the crew in advance what they will be asked to do, and what resources they need to do it.

Union and other professional personnel usually have a set *day rate* that they charge; rates may differ depending on the type of production. Outside of union productions (where strict rules guide payment schedules), it's important to be clear about what the day rate entails: Some people consider a day eight hours, others ten. On feature films, a day may mean twelve hours or more.

On some productions, after the "day" is over, the overtime period begins. Overtime may be at "time and a half" (1½ times the hourly rate) for a certain amount of time, then may escalate to *double time* or more. Sometimes producers ask for a *flat rate*, which is a fixed day rate with no additional pay for overtime. Another issue is *turnaround*, that is, how much time the crew has between the end of one day and the start of the next; union rules call for penalties if turnaround is too short.

When hiring crew or asking someone to work for free, be up-front and realistic about the schedule. Don't ask someone to work for a flat day rate and neglect to mention that you have eighteen hours of material to cover every day. Be explicit about how overtime will be treated. Draw up a *deal memo* to lay out responsibilities and compensation (union members sign a standard deal form). Union rules are very specific about meals and breaks (with penalties if the time between meals is too long), but even on nonunion shoots remember that an overworked and underfed crew will not perform well. Keep snacks or coffee close at hand.

Producers who are strapped for cash may try to get the crew to work for less money. *Deferred salaries* are paid after the film is finished and has begun to generate income; many consider this a euphemism for free labor. Another bargaining technique is to offer lower salaries in exchange for *points*—a percentage of the film's eventual income. The problem with this is that "income" may be defined as what is left over after many expenses have been deducted (see Distribution, p. 748). Often, personnel will work for less if they feel they're getting a career opportunity: for example, a camera assistant getting a first break to work as director of photography.

Actors are often referred to in the United States as the "talent." Some actors are unionized, some are not. Professional movie and TV actors in the United States generally belong to the Screen Actors Guild (SAG) and/or the American Federation of Television & Radio Artists (AFTRA). The union stipulates a minimum pay rate (*scale*) for different types of productions (depending on budget level and type of distribution) and the prominence of the role (more for lead actors with speaking lines, less for silent extras). Many actors charge more than scale but may lower their rates if they like a project. Contact the union or a casting agent to discuss the many regulations associated with using union talent.

To simplify accounting, many productions hire an outside *paymaster*, which is a service that handles all the paperwork and certifies that proper union payments are made. A paymaster may be necessary when union talent is hired by a production company that is not a *union signatory* (does not have a contract with the union).

Renting Versus Buying Equipment

The advantages of owning a camera or other equipment include certain tax benefits, familiarity with a particular piece of equipment, and the avoidance of rental problems, such as unavailability of equipment, defective equipment, out-of-town rental hassles, and costly short-term insurance policies.

Renting, however, avoids the problems of yearly overhaul and maintenance, interest payments, and yearly insurance premiums. Also, you can choose the most appropriate equipment for a particular shooting situation and not be limited by what you may or may not own. Since technology is rapidly changing, renting keeps you freer to change with it.

Filmmakers can often raise the money to buy equipment when they've been hired to shoot a project over an extended period of time. They can buy the gear and then rent it to the production on which they are working, charging rental house rates. Two or three months of use can pay for half the initial cost of a piece of equipment.

If you plan to rent, research the rates at a number of rental houses. It's often cheaper to rent from a big company even if it is farther away and transportation costs are added; some houses charge no rental while the equipment is in transit. Longer-term rentals are discounted. Typically, the weekly rate is four times the daily rate; the monthly rate may be twelve times the daily rate. Some houses allow you to pick up the equipment Thursday afternoon and return it Monday morning for one day's rental charge. Often you can negotiate deals.

Business Arrangements

During the making of a movie, there are many times when you may need to obtain services, equipment, or materials from organizations like equipment rental houses, studios, labs, postproduction facilities, and mix houses, as well as from independent contractors like animators or graphic artists. Each type of business has a different set of assumptions about the way things are done, yet there are certain ground rules that seem to apply when working with different types of suppliers.

To identify suppliers you want to work with, get recommendations from people who have done projects similar to yours. Watch the end credits of movies and read the trade press for ideas. When talking to a supplier, ask for references of projects they've worked on. If you're lucky enough to find a supplier you like where you live, you can avoid the hassles and risks of shipping and travel and you have the advantage of face-to-face contact, which often makes things go more smoothly. Nevertheless, many filmmakers work with labs and other suppliers in another city. In the United States, the best-known facilities are generally in Los Angeles or New York. Overnight shipping, e-mail, and file exchange over the Web help shorten the distance between you and the supplier.

To deal effectively with a postproduction house, lab, or other organization, find out whom to contact if problems arise. Sometimes a salesperson will be assigned to your account. Sometimes it's better to deal directly with a manager or technical personnel. Some labs have expeditors to personally oversee your production and help usher material through the various departments that may be involved in processing your order.

To minimize the chance of problems, lay out as clearly as you can in advance what you need done and when you need the work performed. Give warnings of impending deadlines and try to get a clear, up-front commitment that the supplier can do the job. If problems do arise, stay cool and try to work through it with the supplier. There are plenty of producers with quick tempers who think that fury and threats are a good way to "get results." If this is your reputation, suppliers may choose not to work with you. Don't be bashful if a supplier has screwed up your order, but maintaining a sense of respect for all involved will usually increase your chances of getting what you want.

Many companies have a *rate card* of standard prices charged for goods and services. You can often get a discount, sometimes sizable, from the rate card prices if the supplier likes the project, if you're a student, or if they need the work. At some facilities, virtually *no one* pays rate card rates. Don't be afraid to negotiate. The worst that can happen is they will refuse to budge on price. You can sometimes get lower rates from a facility by agreeing to work at off hours (like late night) or with junior, less experienced personnel. Sometimes you can get goods and services donated (see Contributions, p. 737).

For jobs that are charged on an hourly basis, be clear about when "the clock is running" and when it's not. For example, in some situations, short breaks and lunch are off the clock; in others, it is assumed to be part of a day's work. Some facilities bill for machine setup time, others start charging only when you actually start work. If a machine goes down or there is a problem caused by the facility, most places will deduct this time from your bill.

Sometimes a supplier will give you a flat bid for an entire job instead of charging you piecemeal for individual items or on an hourly basis. This may be a big cost savings. Flat bids can be problematic, however, if the scope of the job changes as you go along. You might ask for a bid based on, say, three eight-hour days of work. But when the work stretches into long overtime on each of those days because you want things done a particular way, the supplier may want to increase the price. Or the work may be done in the time allotted, just not the way you like it. You have less power to ask for changes when the supplier knows that you're not paying for them. Sometimes suppliers agree to very low bids and later regret them. The work suffers. You may be better off paying a bit more and keeping everyone happy.

Often, one has a choice between contracting with several different suppliers to do different portions of a project. You may get a better deal on one part from Company A and on another part from Company B. These savings have to be weighed against the loss of accountability. If the same company does your titles and online edit, then you won't have to pay for time wasted in the online trying to fix problems with the titles. If two different companies do the work, the title people may fix the problem, but you probably won't get reimbursed for the extra online costs.

PAYING ON CREDIT. Having credit with a supplier simplifies delivery and payments for goods and services. Since filmmakers are notorious for being bad credit risks, you may encounter problems unless you're part of a company with a good credit history or until you establish a clean track record with the supplier. Usually the credit terms are *net* (the full amount) within 30 days. Suppliers will, at times, defer payment until a movie is completed and may waive an interest charge on unpaid balances. If you can't get credit, you must pay COD or in advance. Advance payment avoids the inconvenience of getting personal checks cashed and may expedite the return of materials. If you don't have credit and have to pay for the work before you see it, you lose an important negotiating position if you feel the lab or facility has made an error and the work should be redone. An outstanding balance increases your leverage in negotiations.

Insurance

Many types of insurance are available for film and video production. *Negative/tape insurance* covers damage to the negative or original videotapes from fire, theft, or loss in transit. *Faulty camera, stock, and processing insurance* covers loss or damage to film due to defects. These coverages normally do not include "human" errors, such as setting the exposure incorrectly. *Camera and equipment insurance* covers loss or damage; often only the cash value of the equipment at the time it is lost is recoverable. *Extra expense coverage* provides reimbursement for delays in shooting due to damaged or late equipment, sets, and the like. *General liability* covers bodily injury and suits arising from accidents on the set. *Errors and omissions insurance* is discussed on p. 740. The premiums for these policies are usually determined as some percentage of the film's budget, with specified minimums.

On higher-budget films, it's common to need a *completion bond*, which is a policy taken out by financial backers to protect them in case the film is not finished on time or on budget. The bonding company will monitor the production to make sure things are being done according to their requirements.

FUND-RAISING

Many nonfilmmakers fantasize that the filmmaker's life is one of endless creativity, with days filled with one artistic experience after another. There may be a few filmmakers who live like that, but for most, moviemaking involves seemingly short periods of real creative work and seemingly endless amounts of *business*. And when it comes to business, the biggest item is often finding money for the next project. Unless you're wealthy, if you want to initiate your own projects you'll need to raise money.

"Independent filmmaking" is usually defined as working outside a studio or other large organization that bankrolls and controls your work. But even if you're on salary with a large corporation, you may still need to convince others to fund your project. Raising money can be one of the most arduous and painful parts of making a movie.

How you go about raising money depends on the type of project. A feature film may begin with just an idea (a "concept") or perhaps a *spec script* (speculative—written before a deal is in place). A documentary might begin with an idea, a written proposal, and often some preliminary footage. Generally, the more you can set in place before going to a funder, the better your project will look. This is especially important if you don't have an established track record. Thus, you'll have an easier time getting a drama funded if a well-known actor has agreed to play the lead. Sometimes an endorsement from well-known people helps. On some projects, the producer signs up a group of "advisers" or "consultants" to lend credibility to the proposed project.

Funders—be they film studios, broadcasters, or foundations—love nothing more than sure bets. They want to minimize their risk by putting money into projects that seem likely to offer a return on their investment (in the case of a foundation, return may be measured not in dollars, but in visibility or community outreach). This is why money tends to go to established producers or to fund projects that resemble previously successful projects (hence the production of *Hit Film: The Sequel*). If you are new to the business, or trying to do something new, you'll have an uphill battle. In this case, you may find that funders will support you only after the project is fairly far along or has received other backing ("first money" is always the riskiest). You may have to do a lot of legwork without being paid. This could include writing or commissioning a script yourself, or doing substantial research.

Sometimes seed or development money can be obtained to develop the proposal or script, begin serious fund-raising, or do other preproduction work. Be aware that receiving development money can sometimes require you to give up some or all ownership or control of the project.

If it's feasible to shoot selected scenes of a drama or documentary, you can often improve your chances by preparing a short *trailer* (coming-attractions promo) or sample reel. Some people put together short excerpts with narration, to describe the project and pique interest (for a drama, sometimes a slick theatrical trailer is made to give investors a sense of how the film might be marketed). Another approach is simply to edit together a few selected scenes, which may better indicate the movie's style and the director's ability. Increasingly, broadcasters and funders insist on seeing footage or a sample reel from the project before they'll put down money, particularly for documentaries.

Though you may have a clear idea of what the project will look like and how great it will be, funders can be stunningly unimaginative when it comes to sharing that vision. Examples are legion of successful movies that collected a thick pile of rejection letters along the rocky road to completion. Often, the same funding sources have to be approached more than once before they say yes. But before you approach any potential funder or investor, think hard about whether the project is *really* ready. Surely there are movies that have been bankrolled by distributors on the basis of an unpolished rough cut; but there are probably far more examples of projects that were shown before they were presentable, and ended up turning off the very people the filmmakers hoped to entice. In a crowded marketplace, you may have only *one* shot at many potential backers.

Commercial Funding

Feature films intended for theatrical release are usually financed by studios, film distributors, investor groups, or others who invest in exchange for a share of the film's future earnings. Investor funding is a complex topic; laws governing film investment vary from state to state. If you plan to solicit investors for your project, first consult an attorney familiar with both film investment and tax law. You'll need a *prospectus* that details fund-raising plans, production costs, likely income when the project is done, and the plan for returning the backers' money. If only a few backers are needed, perhaps the simplest arrangement is to form a *limited partnership* (*LP*) or the related *limited liability corporation* (*LLC*), in which the investors supply capital and the filmmaker may retain control and responsibility for the project.

Many fiction films and documentaries, especially those by filmmakers with established reputations, are funded wholly or in part by the entities that will distribute the finished product—this may include film distribution companies, broadcast or cable TV organizations, or publishers (for a multimedia project, for example). Bankable projects, like the sequel to a successful film, can be presold to distributors to raise production money. Frequently, distribution rights are divided so that one distributor buys domestic distribution rights and another buys foreign markets.

Often, independent producers are unable to sell a film prior to production, but may be able to raise completion money after the project is under way if it looks promising. Television networks or stations may be persuaded by a proposal or script to fund all or part of a project, or they may wait until the movie is done. Selling a movie prior to production (or completion) is considered a *presale*; when it's bought after it's done, this is considered an *acquisition*. Ironically, television executives generally offer much more money for a movie that hasn't yet begun—and is therefore a greater risk—than for one that's finished. This usually reflects their desire to get credit for, and have some control over, the project.

Completed movies, especially ones without a strong reputation, often face a buyer's market. Single television shows ("one-offs") are often hard to fit into a broadcast schedule and they are much harder to promote than a series. Unless your project fits into the format of a pre-existing series, sometimes it's easier to raise a lot of money for a *limited series* than it is to raise much less money for a single show. For more on this, see Distribution, p. 748.

While funding for a movie is being arranged, temporary cash shortages can be covered by loans from banks and other sources of credit. Many filmmakers get credit from labs and equipment houses to defer these costs. Credit cards have been used to raise cash quickly for starting or finishing a production. The advantage of a credit card is you don't have to convince anyone to give you the money; the disadvantage is the high interest rate you'll pay if you carry the debt for more than a month.

Getting Grants

The funding sources discussed above are generally only available to projects that are likely to earn a profit or find a sizable audience on television or through other distribution channels. Many documentary, experimental, educational, and short fiction movies never make a profit (or, in some cases, even recoup their costs); some of them are made with a relatively small, non–mass market audience in mind. These projects must usually be subsidized by government, foundations, or private donations. In many countries, there are government-run or private agencies at the national, state/provincial, or local level that give grants for production or distribution. Some grants are given to filmmakers on the basis of their previous work and are not intended to support any particular project. Others are given for specific projects, and the filmmaker's past work is used to determine whether he or she is capable of completing the task. Producers with no track record are always at a disadvantage. If you have no relevant prior work to show, consider teaming up with someone more experienced.

Outright or *direct grants* are cash funds for the project. Sometimes grantors require you to "cost-share" by funding part of the budget with your own or others' cash or with in-kind donations of services, materials, or facilities (see below). *Matching grants* are given with the stipulation that some money be raised first from third-party (outside) sources. A 50 percent match means that the granting agency will give you a dollar for every two dollars you raise from someone else. Often, just the fact that the granting agency has endorsed the project by giving you a grant helps you leverage money from other sources.

For most grants, there is a substantial delay between the time you submit your application and when grant funds are released. Six months or even a year is not uncommon. Plan ahead. As one producer said, "It was three years between the time I conceived of the film and when I was fully funded. By then, I wasn't really interested in shooting it."

Before submitting an application to a granting organization, do your homework and find out what kinds of projects have been funded in the past and what criteria are used to select grantees. If you can, e-mail or contact the agency's staff, both to learn about the organization and so that they know you and your project before the review panel meets. Although the staff usually does not pass judgment on proposals (generally outside reviewers do), they can help in various ways.

When writing a grant proposal, keep in mind that it will be read by panelists who are sifting through many applications; they'll need to understand what you want to do as quickly as possible. Simple, direct, and clear prose is important. Most applications require you to summarize your proposal in a paragraph or two (possibly only a line or two); be sure to formulate a clear and succinct idea of your project and its goals and prepare descriptions of various lengths. Your proposal should be tailored to the guidelines of the agency and the project should be represented in a way that is consistent with their interests.

The budget is a key part of a grant proposal (see Budgets, p. 726). Read the application carefully to see how the granting agency wants it done. As mentioned above, grantors like to see their money put to good use. Many moviemakers take the attitude that their responsibility ends with making the movie (which is no small thing, since many media grant projects are never completed). However, with many grants you can increase your chances of getting funded if you demonstrate a serious commitment to showing the movie when it's done. The more specific you are (and the more interest in the project you can demonstrate from broadcasters or potential users), the better your project looks.

You are often asked to submit a sample movie when applying for grants. A tight, well-made ten-minute piece is usually better than a long, slowly developing feature. In fact, many panels won't watch more than ten minutes anyway. Find out the viewing procedures and cue up a tape to the best scenes or make an edited DVD. You can "set up" the clip with a short, written description.

There are many sources of information on available grants. Search the Internet, or go to your local library for books on granting organizations. The Foundation Center (www.foundationcenter.org) puts out a directory of granting agencies with a tally of projects funded in the past and has branches in many cities. State arts councils often have similar lists. See the Bibliography for suggestions of books, periodicals, and websites.

When searching for a grant, don't just look at the obvious choices for media-related funding. Sometimes you can get money from sources that don't specialize in media, but who have an interest in topics addressed by your project. There are many private foundations or corporate-giving programs that have a particular focus or local interest. A drug company might give a grant for a medical-related project. A bank might give money for a locally produced project as part of their community support. These funders are often looking to maximize the impact of their investment and the amount of publicity they'll get. Be resourceful and prepare yourself for lots of rejection: When they weigh the choice between funding a needed machine at the local hospital and supporting a film or video project, you can guess what many companies will do.

NONPROFIT STATUS. Some grants are available only to nonprofit organizations or indirectly to filmmakers working under the aegis of one. Nonprofit groups in the United States are sometimes referred to by their tax code status *501(C)3*. Nonprofit status doesn't prevent a funded movie from turning a profit. However, the filmmaker must usually establish that the primary goal of the project is social, educational, or artistic—not just profit. As mentioned above, commercial filmmakers can create for-profit corporations solely to produce one movie; this may be for tax or liability reasons. Nonprofit corporations are more difficult to set up. It's usually simpler to affiliate yourself with an existing nonprofit group, which can function as your "conduit" or *fiscal agent* through which to apply for funding. Many organizations, such as film foundations, universities, and church groups, will perform this service. Typically, the supporting group will take 5 to 15 percent of the funds raised as a fee, but this is sometimes waived. Often you can apply for state funds from a state where you don't live, as long as you work with a fiscal agent in that state. Try to find a nonprofit group whose goals or mission are related to the project you're proposing. One advantage of certain types of nonprofit status is that individuals or corporations that support the project may be able to deduct their contribution from their taxes. This factor can be a powerful incentive for wealthy contributors.

Contributions

Resourceful filmmakers (and also desperate filmmakers) are always on the lookout for ways to get goods and/or services donated to a project. Food, air travel, props, and labor may be offered by persons or companies in exchange for a tax deduction, a credit in the film, or the chance to be part of a film in production. A company may support a local film merely to be a good neighbor or, for a larger project, for the advertising. An airline may offer free travel to a project if a shot of one of their planes is included in the film. (Airlines may supply free stock footage of planes in flight, saving you the cost of getting it from a stock footage library.) For a high-visibility feature film, companies will pay a fee or supply advertising to the production if their products are included in scenes. (There are product placement specialists whose job it is to create such tie-ins. Product placement deals are not allowed for projects made initially for TV broadcast.)

Interns will work on productions for experience or sometimes for college credit. Such production assistance can be valuable to both parties but there are also risks for both: Unscrupulous producers often ask too much of unpaid assistants; and, on the other side, free labor often proves the dictum that you get what you pay for.

By putting a notice in the newspaper, you can sometimes get extras to act in crowd scenes for free. It's a good idea to offer them something in exchange for their presence (for example, food and/or entertainment).

Corporate and Sponsored Projects

Many filmmakers earn substantial income (or work full-time) producing projects for corporations. These range from in-house training films, to promotional or marketing pieces, to projects about various topics that the company funds as part of its image building. Frequently, producers will be asked to submit competitive bids to get the job. Be careful of bidding too high or too low—a lowball bid may send the message that you're not very good. Producing a project for a corporate bureaucracy can be fraught with the too-many-cooks problem. Be sure to identify who you are reporting to (and who you actually need to satisfy, which may be an entirely different person or group). Try to structure the deal with payments at clearly defined intervals (completion of script, completion of shooting, and so forth). Have formal *sign-offs* at each stage, to certify that the client finds the work satisfactory; you never want to find out after it's too late that they didn't like a choice you made several steps earlier.

LEGAL AND COPYRIGHT ISSUES

Movies, books, musical compositions, and other creative works are *copyrighted* so that no one may legally duplicate or use material from the work without permission. When you make a movie, you are granted a copyright to protect your work. If you want to use other people's copyrighted material in your movie (for example, a song or a film clip), you need to obtain permission (a *clearance*). Clearing copyrighted material usually involves getting a signed permission or *license*, and paying a fee. There are other types of signed permissions or releases used to establish that you have the right to use someone's appearance or performance, to shoot at a given location, or to tell someone's life story.

Getting required permissions can be a lengthy and expensive process. The permissions themselves may be high-priced, and there may be legal fees and administrative costs in tracking down the rights holders and negotiating a license or other deal. Hollywood studios are often extremely careful to clear all needed rights, and even some that may not be needed. Why? They have lawyers on staff and they're looking for maximum protection. If people know you have a lot of money, they may sue you even if they don't have a legitimate claim. Just defending a suit can cost thousands even if you win.

At the other end of the scale, student and independent moviemakers sometimes don't get the permissions they need, hoping that the chance of litigation is low. While the need for some permissions is clear-cut, other types of clearances fall into a gray area: Even lawyers may disagree about which ones are needed or from whom the permission should be sought. For example, under the fair use laws, you may be able to use some copyrighted material without permission (see p. 744). However, you can't always be sure when fair use covers you. Sometimes lawyers can only offer their opinion. The producer must ultimately make the judgment and take the responsibility. To compound the problem, while claiming ignorance of copyright or privacy law is no defense for wrongdoing, if you ask for permission for something and are turned down by the rights holder—and then go ahead and use the material anyway—you may be in worse legal shape than if you had never asked in the first place (attorneys even disagree about this point).

It's unlikely that anyone will come after you if you put a copyrighted song into a video that you only show privately to friends in your living room. However, as soon as a movie is shown or distributed to the public, especially for a fee, you become vulnerable to a lawsuit if you've used copyrighted material, someone's appearance, or a protected life story without permission. If you lose, you'll pay damages and may also be required to re-edit or stop showing your movie. Distributors, TV broadcasters, and some film festivals may not accept a movie if the required clearances have not been obtained. But even prior to distribution, you will probably need to deal with E&O insurers (see below), who will want to see your permissions.

The greater exposure your project gets, and the more money it generates (or the more money you have), the greater the chance someone will take legal action—justifiably or not. To protect yourself, consult an entertainment or copyright attorney before finishing your movie. For an excellent review of these issues, see Michael Donaldson's *Clearance and Copyright* (see Bibliography).

PROTECTING YOUR WORK

Copyright and Other Protections

When you copyright a movie, the copyright coverage includes dialogue, sound track, music, and photography (film/video footage). Neither the title of a movie nor the ideas or concepts contained in it are protected.[2] Broad ideas for plots and settings cannot be owned, but verbatim excerpts of dialogue can be.

Copyright law has evolved in recent years, and some people are familiar with older, now obsolete statutes. According to worldwide copyright agreements, copyright applies to a script or movie as soon as you commit it to paper, video, or film. This is automatic and immediate and does not require a formal notice or copyright registration with the government (though there are good reasons to register; see below). Sometimes a script is registered prior to casting when the project is in preproduction. Generally, the movie as a whole is registered when it is done.

Another form of protection for scripts and written treatments prior to the making of the movie is to register them with the Writers Guild of America (WGA) script registration service. For a fee, the WGA keeps a copy of your script on file for a period of years. If another project comes out that you feel has plagiarized yours, the registered script can help establish that your material predated theirs. Be

2. While titles can't be copyrighted, they can be restricted on other grounds. A *title search* is done to establish that the title you choose is available for your use.

sure that the WGA registration is noted on the cover of your script when you give it to people to read.

When trying to get a project started you are often in a Catch-22 situation: if you don't tell anyone about the project, you can't generate interest in it; if you do tell, you're vulnerable to people stealing your ideas. When pitching a feature film idea, your ideas are protected somewhat if you are represented by an established talent agency that can help track whom you told your ideas to in case someone later uses them. Even without an agent, you can back up your claims to having pitched ideas for any project by keeping written records of all your conversations and writing follow-up letters after meetings and calls to establish a "paper trail." Whether it will be worth pursuing a lawsuit if you've been wronged is a whole other question.

Registering Your Copyright

As noted above, your work is copyrighted as soon as it exists in tangible form; however, you gain increased protection by registering the copyright. Two steps should be taken as part of the copyright process. First, include a copyright notice in the movie's credits. This is usually something like "Copyright © 2008, [copyright owner's name]. All rights reserved." You can also add "[Your country] is the first country of publication for purposes of the Berne Convention."[3]

In the United States, to register a copyright contact the Register of Copyrights, Library of Congress (www.copyright.gov). You'll fill out an application, pay a small fee, and submit a copy of the movie and a written description of it for archiving. You are asked to submit the "best edition" of the work; for a film project, this would normally be a film print, but you may be able to submit a DVD or tape, which will cost you less. Generally, it's a good idea to register the copyright as soon as you finish the movie. For maximum protection, the registration should take place within three months of the date of "publication," which is defined as the first time the film is offered for distribution to the general public, whether by sale, rental, or loan. Merely showing the film without offering it for distribution is *not* considered publication. Showing your film to a distributor is not considered publication, but making copies and offering it to the public is. Your copyright extends only to the aspects of your movie that are original to your production; material in the movie licensed from other copyright holders remains part of their copyright.

Errors and Omissions Insurance

Errors and Omissions Insurance (E&O) is a policy that protects producers, distributors, and broadcasters from suits arising from libel, slander, invasion of privacy, and copyright infringement claims. It covers legal fees and settlements with a specified maximum per claim as well as a maximum for all claims together. Producers of big-budget feature films may get E&O policies before shooting begins or prior to the film's release. Independents often don't think of E&O at all, especially if there's nothing in the movie that is particularly provocative or risky from a libel or copyright standpoint. However, bear in mind that many distributors and broadcasters will require you to have E&O coverage, and the price of your policy will be partly determined by how carefully you have covered all your legal bases (that is,

---

3. Often the year is indicated with roman numerals. Since this technique probably didn't begin with ancient Roman filmmakers, it may be intended to make it harder for audiences to read how old a movie is.

made sure you have the permissions and clearances you need). Your lawyer can help you through the process and may be asked to sign off that all due procedures were followed. The underwriter of the policy will decide if anything seems risky. Many policies are for three years, made under the assumption that if you haven't been sued by then, you're not going to be. Some policies charge additional fees for each different means of distribution (e.g., festival and/or theatrical, broadcast, home video); try to find one that covers all in one blanket policy.

RELEASES FOR REAL PEOPLE, PLACES, AND THINGS

Talent and Appearance Releases

People appearing in movies customarily sign a release in which they give permission for the filmmaker to use and publicly exhibit their picture, sound, and/or likeness. There are many versions of a release form that the actor or film subject signs. One version is below.

APPEARANCE RELEASE

Person Appearing: _____
Title of Film: _____ (the "Film")
Production Date: _____
Production Location: _____

I authorize _____ (the "Producer"), the Producer's agents, successors, assigns, and designees to record my name, likeness, image, voice, sound effects, interview, and performance on film, tape, or otherwise (the "Recording"), edit such Recording as the Producer may desire, and incorporate such Recording into the Film and all related materials, including but not limited to literary, promotion, and advertising materials. It is understood and agreed that the Producer shall retain final editorial, artistic, and technical control of the Film and the Film content. The Producer may use and authorize others to use the Film, any portions thereof, and the Recording in all markets, manner and media, whether now known or hereafter developed, throughout the universe in perpetuity. The Producer and/or the Producer's successors and assigns, shall own all rights, title and interest, including the copyright, in and to the Film, including the Recording and related materials, to be used and disposed of, without limitation, as the Producer shall determine.

Signature: _____
Address: _____
Date: _____
Social Security #: _____

Put your name or the production company's name as "Producer." For a dramatic, corporate, or other project in which the producer hires or arranges for all persons appearing in the movie, the release may be part of an actor's contract. In this case, the release usually starts "For consideration received. . . ." If the release is not part of a contract, it's a simple matter to have people sign a release when they go on camera.

For some documentaries, it is standard practice to have all subjects sign a release. Usually it's a good idea to get the signing out of the way before shooting. In some documentary situations, however, it's awkward or impossible to get signed releases from everyone. Though a detailed, signed release is preferred by lawyers, it is also possible to use a shorter, less intimidating version, or even to record a verbal "release" on video, audio, or sync-sound film. Explain to the subjects what your movie is about, how you hope to distribute it (that it may be shown on TV, in theaters, on home video, and by other means), and that you're asking for their unrestricted permission to use their appearance. In a group setting, you can explain the project to the group and ask anyone who doesn't consent to let you know or, perhaps, to leave. For concert or crowd situations, sometimes the producer distributes written notices or has an announcement read aloud that states, in effect, that a person's presence constitutes consent to being filmed. There are certain circumstances in which no releases are needed. If you are filming the public goings-on at a newsworthy event, for example, you have the same right as news photographers to shoot without permission (not, however, for product endorsement; see below). If you secretly shoot someone's intimate sidewalk conversation, however, you may go beyond the limit of the public's right to know (though laws vary by country).

E&O underwriters and broadcasters want you to get releases, but experts are divided on the actual value of releases for documentaries. If a subject can establish that he has been defamed by your presentation of him, a signed release may not stand in his way of suing successfully.[4] In a privacy infringement case, on the other hand, the mere presence of a camera crew may be sufficient grounds to establish that the subject was aware that what he said or did would be made public. Court precedents in both libel and privacy law are complex and ever-shifting; when in doubt, it's simplest to ask permission before filming or at least to ask those with objections to leave the area.

For all types of productions, you can't use footage of a person commercially to advertise a product or company (or the movie itself) if you haven't got a release and if the release doesn't specifically grant that permission. The release above includes advertising, but some people prefer the legal language that the person appearing waives *right of publicity*. Some actors will not agree to this clause without additional payment. Many of the rules governing other types of releases and licenses have special provisions when the footage will be used for promotion or advertising.

People, Places, and Things

Whenever a real person, location, or trademarked/copyrighted item is shown or referred to in a movie, there is a chance that someone may object. On feature

4. Some releases contain language by which the subject releases the producer from any claims arising from invasion of privacy, defamation, false light, and all other rights.

films, a *script clearance report* is done by combing the script for references to proper names, addresses, business names, radio stations, etc., and checking to see if these correspond to actual people and places (for example, if there's a character with the same name as a person who actually lives in the city where the script is set). Research services can prepare a report for you or you can do it yourself with a phone directory, the Web, a map, and other sources. Avoid using names of living persons, actual phone numbers, or auto license plates in the area where the story is set. Be particularly careful with negative references: If the criminals in your script run the Acme Corporation in Chicago, and there happens to be an Acme in Chicago, the owners may take action against you. It's safer to make up your own names (and avoid last names whenever possible). Private individuals may give you a written release allowing you to refer to them, but you do not automatically have that right.[5]

You should have a location release signed by the owner of any location where you shoot, specifying his agreement that you are allowed shoot there and that the location can appear in the film. This is particularly important if this is a recognizable business with signs or other visible trademarks. You may be required to replace or not show the signs. When shooting on public streets, in parks, and in other facilities, you generally need city permits and an insurance bond (not to mention a police detail to supervise).

Nevertheless, as attorney Michael Donaldson points out, you have a right to make a realistic film, and including product names or trademarks in a scene may be fair game. Generally, incidental depiction or reference to a trademarked product is okay, as long as the reference isn't derogatory. If the item is particularly featured either by the way it is filmed or commented on, it makes sense to get a written release to do so. It should be noted, however, that some producers, broadcasters, and distributors insist that no commercial trademarks be shown in *any* form (such as on T-shirts) without written permission; so it's always safest to avoid them. In some cases, they are digitally removed or blurred in post.

In documentaries, common practice is often somewhat different than the full legal protections described above. Location releases are not always obtained, trademarked objects appear regularly, and people often refer to or comment on other real people. Whenever the movie makes a negative comment that disparages someone, you should be particularly careful. Either make it clear that this is being offered as opinion and not fact, or, if it is being presented as fact, try to have at least two independent sources to confirm that it is really true.

USING COPYRIGHTED MATERIAL

Many movies use material previously created by someone else, including stories, music, and film clips. These almost always need to be cleared for use. For example, if you want to write a script based on a short story, you need to *option* the

---

5. "Public" (famous) persons have more limited rights of privacy. Deceased persons have no right of privacy. Their estate does retain the right of publicity, to control any advertising related to the deceased. The estate may also control use of film clips showing the deceased.

story from the rights holder (usually the author, who can be found through the publisher). The option gives you the right to develop the script for a period of time. Usually an *option-purchase agreement* is done, which provides for a comparatively lower fee for the option with a specified higher price paid if the movie actually gets made.

There are a few exceptions when you may not need to obtain clearance to use existing work:

PUBLIC DOMAIN. Works that are in the *public domain* are not protected by copyright. The most common type of public domain material is work that was never copyrighted (traditional folk songs) or work for which the copyright has lapsed. Works created in the United States more than seventy-five years ago are likely to be in the public domain. But mere age or traditional history are not proof of public domain status; renditions or arrangements of the work may have newer, applicable copyrights. A copyright report can be obtained from a law firm or done at the Library of Congress to determine public domain status.

FAIR USE. Another way that copyrighted material may be used without permission is through the fair use provisions of copyright law. Fair use is a murky territory, and many people make a lot of assumptions based on a little knowledge. The idea of fair use is to permit (normally short) excerpts of material for the purposes of scholarship, news reporting, and such. The guidelines are somewhat vague. To determine whether an excerpt qualifies as fair use, the law considers whether the purpose is "of commercial nature or is for nonprofit educational purposes"; the nature of the copyrighted work; how much of the copyrighted work is excerpted; and the impact of the excerpt on the potential value and market for the copyrighted work. However, the fact that your film is commercial and intended to make money doesn't exclude the possibility of fair use. Never assume that an excerpt you want to use is covered by fair use unless an experienced attorney confirms that it is.

A group of organizations has drawn up a set of "best practices" when it comes to fair use and documentary film (see www.centerforsocialmedia.org). These guidelines apply to areas such as: using copyrighted material as part of a social or political critique; using copyrighted works of popular culture to illustrate an argument; capturing copyrighted material in the process of filming something else; using copyrighted material in a historical sequence. Hopefully, this set of best practices can help filmmakers understand what is permissible, and can help them defend themselves if someone claims they overstepped the bounds. However, what you can ultimately use may depend on whether the owners of the copyrighted material decide to challenge you; whether insurers, broadcasters, and distributors support these principles; and whether these practices are ultimately affirmed in the courts.

Clearing Music

Many filmmakers have had the following experience. They know a song that would be *perfect* for their movie. They scurry around, trying to figure out how to get permission to use it. Weeks or months later, they get a response back from the holders of the copyrights. They discover that the song is not available, or, if it is, the fee happens to be tens of thousands of dollars more than they have in the budget. Welcome to the world of music licensing.

Clearing music (and movie clips; see p. 747) is one of the thorniest jobs a producer can do. It usually requires extensive research, long delays, and complex negotiations. If you ever have the experience of trying to clear many songs for a movie, you'll probably never want to do it again. Many filmmakers prefer to hire a music clearing service that can shortcut the process with their network of contacts.

If you want to use a pre-existing recording, you'll need to obtain permission to use the musical composition, as well as permission to use the particular recording of it. Often a publishing company controls rights to the composition and a record company controls the recording itself. Sometimes filmmakers can't afford the recording if it's by, say, a famous rock star. They may license the rights to the composition and get someone else to perform the song. If you find a song by a lesser-known band, they may give you a good price as a way to get exposure.

To secure rights to a composition, start by contacting the publishing company. Usually the sleeve for a recording indicates which *performing rights society* the publisher belongs to; these include ASCAP (www.ascap.com), BMI (www.bmi.com) or SESAC (www.sesac.com). If you don't know which one handles the song you're interested in, you can do a search on these sites.

To include a musical composition in your movie, you need *synchronization* or *sync rights*—so named because the music is synchronized to the picture. To perform the music in public, you need *public performance* rights. In the United States, public performance rights for theatrical films are generally included in the deal you make for sync rights; you don't have to pay for them separately, but make sure they're included. For movies that are broadcast on television, the broadcaster usually obtains the public performance rights. If you want to put out a sound track album from the movie on CD or other format, you will also need *mechanical rights*. If you plan to make significant changes to a song (say, to alter the lyrics) you may need to negotiate *adaptation rights*. Some composers or publishers won't permit such changes.

If you want to use a pre-existing recording of the song, contact the owner of the recording—usually the record company (look online or on the sleeve of a CD for the address). You'll need a *master use license* to use the actual recording (performance) in your movie. You should also ask the record company if any *reuse fees* are due the performers on the record. At one time, you would have also needed to arrange to get a copy of the master tape in order to have a high-quality audio dub. Today, you can get the audio recording itself from a consumer CD or other digital format.

NEGOTIATING THE RIGHTS PACKAGE. For the classic situation of trying to clear a recording by a musical artist you like, you will be requesting a sync license with public performance rights from the publisher and a master use license from the record company. Both of them will ask you to submit a written or online request that details the nature of your movie, how you plan to distribute it, and the way the music will be used. You'll pay more if the song is used under the movie's titles or otherwise featured; you often pay less if it will only be background music in a scene.

How the movie will be distributed (by which *media*), where it will be shown (in which *territories*), and for how long (for what *term*) also affect the price of the license fee. Big-budget feature films generally clear music rights for *all media* (theatrical, broadcast, and free cable TV, pay cable TV, home video, and formats not yet invented) in *all territories* (domestic and foreign) *in perpetuity* (forever). This *buyout* of all rights is by far the most desirable in terms of simplifying business arrangements. However, you may not be able to afford it. Getting only the rights you need is usually cheaper. For example, students often make a deal to acquire just *film festival rights*. Or you might get *nontheatrical rights*; or theatrical rights to art houses but not first-run movie theaters (see Distribution, p. 748, for more on these terms). You can renegotiate a more extensive rights package later. Some rights holders will offer only a limited (say, five-year) term. In some license agreements, the term for home video is "in perpetuity," but an additional royalty payment must be made per DVD unit sold. The rights holder will usually have a standard contract for you to sign.

As technologies change, there can be uncertain areas of coverage. For example, video-on-demand (VOD) can be thought of as a service that functions somewhere between cable distribution and home video distribution. However, rights holders may consider VOD a separate area from either of those, to be licensed for a separate fee.

Keep in mind that acquiring rights is a *negotiation*. The rights holder will name a price that may take your breath away; then it's up to you to come back with a lower price. Sometimes they'll consider it, sometimes not. If you're poor and struggling and working on a worthy project, they may make a special exception. If you're too poor (or not part of a reputable organization), sometimes they won't even *talk* to you—it's just not worth their time. If you're negotiating with several rights holders and can find one who offers a lower price, sometimes you can get the others to agree to a lower price too. Often this is done on a *favored nations* basis, which means that for the deal to go through, no one is favored, all parties must agree to the same price. One advantage of using a music clearing service is that they know whom to negotiate with and the standard rates being paid for licenses. You may or may not be able to bargain for a better deal on your own.

Some public broadcasting entities, such as PBS, have blanket agreements and compulsory licenses that may allow you to use music without clearing it with rights holders. This applies only to the television broadcast. You may still need other rights if the movie is shown elsewhere.

Even if the licensing process goes well, it can take months. If a song is integral to the movie (say, if a character sings it), be sure to start as early in preproduction as you can. Increasingly, music publishers and record companies are using online tools on their websites to automate and streamline the process of requesting and paying for a license.

After the movie is done, you must prepare a *music cue sheet*, which details which compositions you used, the performing rights society associated with it, and how the music appears in the movie. This is essential for all parties to collect proper royalties.

LIBRARY MUSIC. To avoid many of the rights issues mentioned above, you can use prerecorded music from a production music library (also called *stock music*). Numerous library collections are available online and on disc with selections in many styles and arrangements. This music is packaged specifically for reuse. A library of stock music may be purchased or leased for a period of time by a production facility or individual tracks may be purchased and downloaded on a *laser drop* basis (what used to be called *needle-drop*, which is a continuous section of a recording used once). The rights for the piece are provided with the fee.

ORIGINAL SCORES. Having an original score written for a movie avoids most of the headaches mentioned above. When producers have an original score composed, often the producer will own the rights to the music, in which case the music is considered a *work for hire*. If, as producer, you own the music, you'll want to set up a publishing entity and register it with one of the performing rights societies (see above) to collect royalties. Sometimes the composer will lower his or her fee in exchange for retaining some or all the music rights, in which case the producer must have a license from the composer to use the music. If the movie is shown widely on television, or in non-U.S. theaters, there can be sizable royalties paid to the holder of the rights. The composer will receive half the royalties regardless of who owns the music.

Clearing Movie Clips

If you want to use a scene from an existing movie in your film (whether it be a full-screen excerpt or something visible on a TV in one of your scenes), you usually need to get written permission. Clearing clips is much like clearing music, and just as much fun. Start by identifying who owns the copyright to the movie you want to use. Sometimes this is the production company, sometimes it is the distributor or television network. Particularly for older films, the film may have been bought and sold several times since it was made. Some companies have a clip licensing department and actively seek deals with licensees like you. Others are extremely protective of their film library, throw up every possible barrier, and may simply refuse you.

As discussed above, you may need to negotiate the fee for the clip. Unfortunately, even after you license the right to use a clip, you may still have to get permission to use various elements in the clip. For example, if there's music in the clip, you generally need to obtain separate licenses for it. The musical composition (even if it is just underscore) may be owned by the studio or by the composer; you need to obtain a sync license (see above), usually for a separate fee. Similarly, the right to use the music recording itself (the master use license) may come with the clip, but sometimes you must license that separately. Some people choose to license the clip without any music and compose their own if necessary.

If there are actors in the clip, SAG and AFTRA (actors' unions; see p. 730) have regulations governing the "reuse" of actors' performances in union productions. Recognizable actors may need to give consent and be paid; stars may waive their fee. The SAG contract governing films made before 1960 is different, and may allow you to use some clips for certain uses without paying actors or getting permissions if you *billboard* the clip by putting the name of the film on screen or having it said verbally each time a clip is shown. You can avoid billboarding by clearing and paying the talent. Contact a SAG office for details. The WGA (Writers Guild of America) and DGA (Directors Guild of America) also have regulations governing the reuse of material.

STOCK FOOTAGE LIBRARIES. There are many *stock footage libraries* or *archives* that supply footage to producers specifically for reuse. These services may specialize in particular types of material, such as sports, historical, nature, or news. Usually the fee is determined by the length of the clip and how you plan to distribute your movie (like music rights, you can license rights to many media or only a few). *Royalty-free* footage means you pay once for any type of use. *Rights-managed* clips require negotiations depending on how you plan to use the footage.

Often, you pay a small fee to get a selection of possible clips; after you edit your show, you pay a higher rate based on the exact number of seconds you use. Keep in mind that while the library supplies the clip, you sometimes need to separately clear what's *in* the clip, including music, actors, news anchors, and such (see above). Some libraries supply pirated footage for which even the clip *itself* is not cleared and you may risk a lawsuit if you use it without the owner's permission.

Several stock libraries are available online, which can be tremendously handy for searching and downloading clips directly to your editing system.

DISTRIBUTION

Distribution refers to the process of getting a movie shown to audiences. There are many different ways to bring movies to potential viewers, including theatrical exhibition, TV broadcast, home video, IPTV (Internet delivery) and multimedia. Some projects make use of several distribution channels, some only a few. New technologies and changing consumer habits are continually changing the distribution landscape. Let's first look at various distribution possibilities, then examine the process of launching a movie into the marketplace.

For the technical concerns of distributing a project, see Chapters 2, 14, 16, 17, and 18.

Theatrical Distribution

Theatrical distribution means showing movies the old-fashioned way: in commercial theaters to paying audiences. Hollywood and independent feature films generally seek theatrical distribution as the first outlet for the movie. However, theatrical distribution can be tremendously risky and for many films it's just not worth the effort or expense. The costs of advertising, promotion, making prints, and running the distribution campaign are high; the chance of making a profit is relatively low. When a studio releases a slate of several films in a year, usually most of them lose money. The one or two blockbusters that make huge profits are counted on to carry the other movies. However, a theatrical run can play an important part in raising public awareness about a movie and garnering reviews. A splashy theatrical release will boost the price of the movie when it is later sold to TV or home video. So a money-losing theatrical experience is sometimes still a good investment in the long run.

Many people feel that the days of theatrical exhibition are numbered, and that a new model based on Internet streaming to homes will make traditional theatrical distribution obsolete. At the same time, theaters are moving toward Digital Cin-

Fig. 19-1. Theatrical exhibition is a tradition that's undergoing big changes. (Film-Tech.com)

ema projection, with satellite delivery of compressed files, instead of the distributor having to manufacture and ship heavy film prints, which is also changing the equation. Whether the communal experience of watching movies in a theater will disappear is a question that only time can answer.

NAVIGATING THE THEATRICAL WORLD. If you're an independent producer interested in theatrical distribution for your project, you have two major hurdles to jump. The first is getting a *distributor*, the second is getting the movie into theaters. Some people choose to *self-distribute*—that is, take on the distributor's duties themselves. Unfortunately, many independently produced feature films never get distributed at all.

What does a theatrical distributor do? Typically, a distributor will *acquire* a movie after it's completed or nearly so (sometimes distributors develop projects from the script stage or earlier). Often, independent movies are picked up for distribution when they're shown at film festivals. If several distributors are vying for a movie, or if strong profits are anticipated, they will offer a sizable *advance* for the film. This is an advance on royalties—whatever the producer is paid as an advance will be deducted from his or her share later. For many low-profile films, the advance is small, or even zero. Even if the advance to the producer is low, the distributor should commit to spending a reasonable amount on *prints and advertising (P&A)*—the basic marketing costs for the picture—and to opening the film in a minimum number of cities.

The distributor then puts together a marketing campaign for the movie. This includes having a poster (*one-sheet*) created and designing newspaper *ad slicks*. A *trailer* (coming-attractions reel) is produced and sent to theaters and posted online in advance of the movie's opening. TV ads and other promotions may be worked up. The distributor then goes about trying to book the movie into various theaters. The theater owners are the *exhibitors*. Exhibitors often need to be convinced to run a particular independent film. Theaters range from large *first-run chains*, which generally show only mainstream Hollywood product, to smaller *independent theaters* and *art houses*, which may also show a variety of other movies, including smaller, older, or foreign films. Independent theaters are currently as endangered as small family farms. Theater chains are programmed from a central office; independent cinemas may hire a *booker* who selects the movies for several theaters.

Novice producers are often shocked by how much of the income generated by their movie does *not* go to them (more experienced producers aren't shocked, just depressed). The total amount of money paid by audiences buying tickets is the *box office gross*. The exhibitor then takes his share and what's left over goes to the distributor (*total film rental*). There are different types of exhibitor/distributor deals. The common 90/10 deal gives 90 percent to the distributor at the start of a film's release, with the exhibitor's share increasing every week the film plays (the exhibitor sometimes deducts his basic expense—the *house nut*—first.) In another arrangement, the exhibitor pays the distributor an agreed-on minimum (*floor*) amount or a fixed percentage of the box office, whichever is larger.

Fig. 19-2. Where the money (and candy) is. Exhibitors may make more from concessions than ticket sales, especially when a film first opens. (Film-Tech.com)

As a ballpark figure for all films, distributors get about half the box office gross. Distributors of independent films may average around 35 to 45 percent of the gross. When you hear that a certain film grossed, say, ten million dollars and cost five million, that movie probably has not broken even when distribution and marketing costs are figured in.

But wait—when do you, the producer, get paid? The exhibitor pays the distributor a film rental and then the distributor deducts *his* fee, often around 25 to 33 percent. Then *all* the distribution costs, including advertising, the costs of film prints, and other promotion are deducted. *Finally*, the producer gets what's left over (if anything); this is the *producer's net*. Ouch. Note that it's in the distributor's interest to spend as much as possible on promotion to create a big splash and try to maximize grosses, but usually that marketing money comes out of your share, not his.

A film can gross hundreds of thousands or even millions of dollars with hardly anything coming back to the producer. This is why it's so important to get the largest advance up front that you can, and not rely on getting your money from the "back end," which may be nonexistent. To avoid all these deductions, powerful stars and directors demand a percentage of the gross. While you probably won't get gross points, you may be able to negotiate payments triggered by the film reaching certain gross amounts.

WHICH THEATRICAL DISTRIBUTOR, IF ANY. If you're lucky enough to have interest from more than one distributor, you may have a hard choice to make. The advantage of large distributors is that they may pay good advances and can afford substantial P&A budgets. One disadvantage is that if your movie is not immediately doing well at the box office, they may drop your film and go on to the next one. A distributor with a smaller slate of films will usually have less money, but may work longer at trying to keep your film afloat (by trying it in different markets or playing in small venues). Sometimes filmmakers get no good offers and choose to handle distribution themselves. No one will give your film more TLC than you, but be prepared to put in many months of full-time work. In several ways, you'll be at a disadvantage compared to regular distributors. They know the good theaters in each city and who books them; you will have to figure it out. Distributors can command the best play dates and can sometimes keep a film in a theater even if it's not doing well. Some exhibitors are notorious for not paying up. A distributor can get payment by threatening to pull his next film, which is leverage you don't have.

Fig. 19-3. The cost and logistics of shipping 35mm prints for theatrical distribution is a big reason Digital Cinema is moving forward. (Film-Tech.com)

Nevertheless, self-distribution may be the only way to get your movie out there. You'll have far more say over how the movie is promoted and you'll get to keep more of the profits. A film shipping house, such as Transit Media (www.transitmedia .net), can simplify your work by storing, shipping, and inspecting the film prints or videos.

A hybrid approach is a *service deal* with a booker or distributor who handles the booking and/or distribution arrangements for a fee. You get the expertise and connections of the distributor but maintain more control (and all the financial responsibility).

One approach sometimes used by both self-distributors and regular distributors is called *four-walling*. Here a theater is "rented" from the exhibitor for a flat fee. Because the exhibitor has no risk, he may take more of a chance on a small film. The distributor then gets to keep the entire box office (less the rental fee).

Television

In terms of sheer audience size, no means of distribution even comes close to TV. Even an unpopular, low-rated TV program can garner millions of viewers. Many filmmakers complain, justifiably, that the type of programming found on television is often conservative and fairly uniform but compared with theatrical distribution, TV is a remarkably democratic medium. TV viewers will tune in to many types of programs, including public affairs, documentaries, nature, and even dramas that they wouldn't go see in a theater. Cable, satellite, and Internet distribution offer a wide selection of programming, but ratings and advertising still drive the industry. For viewers to be aware of a program, money must be spent on marketing. In a kind of vicious circle, marketing dollars tend to go only to shows that are expected to draw lots of viewers.

The majority of television programming is either produced by television entities or commissioned by them. If you work for a network or for a regular supplier of programming, you're aware of the intricacies of getting a new show on the air. If you're an independent producer hoping to sell your project to television, there are a number of ways to approach it. Start by identifying existing series that might make a good fit with your project (whether you have actually produced it yet or not). Some series, particularly on public television and commercial cable networks, actively solicit proposals and works-in-progress from independents. As noted above, single programs can be awkward to distribute and market on TV—you're almost always better off being part of a series.

Consider working with a television *sales agent*. Sales agents know who the key decision makers are and how much has been paid in the past for shows like yours. Sales agents can be indispensable for foreign television markets, as they generally attend the international TV markets (see below) and have contacts in countries where it would be nearly impossible for you to make inroads.

In the United States, the chief outlets for independently produced (or co-produced) programs are cable networks such as HBO, Sundance Channel, IFC and, on the broadcast side, PBS. Actually, PBS is an association of public stations but isn't a traditional, centrally controlled network. This means that only some PBS programming (including the major series) is broadcast on most of the stations around the country on the same date (*hard feed*). Many shows are distributed to stations on an individual basis: Each station chooses when or if to broadcast the show (*soft feed*). The latter makes promotion much more difficult. American Program Service (APS) programming is soft fed, and may offer more opportunities than national series for independently produced shows. If you're trying to get your project on PBS, you can work with an individual PBS station as a *presenting station* to the network, you can go directly to one of the series, or you can try to work through the PBS national headquarters in Washington, D.C. Often, the broadcasters and/ or the producer have to go out and find underwriters, usually corporations, to sponsor the production, acquisition, or promotion of a show. Ironically, producers bringing finished films to PBS sometimes find themselves essentially having to raise the money to get the show on the air.

Nontheatrical Distribution

There are many types of nontheatrical distribution, including *educational* (schools and universities), *institutional* (such as libraries and community groups), and corporate. This is sometimes referred to as *audio-visual (A-V) distribution*. Many projects are made expressly for nontheatrical markets. These include educational pieces designed as curriculum aids, training programs, how-to's, and the like. Nontheatrical distribution is also a significant aftermarket for movies that have already appeared in theaters or on television. At one time, nontheatrical distribution was done with film prints that sold for several hundreds of dollars; now virtually all movies are distributed on DVD or via download for much less. However, prices for DVDs sold to schools and institutions for the A-V market are generally higher than for home video (sometimes a lot higher) and often include public performance rights (which allows the institution to show the movie to groups, though not necessarily to charge admission).

As in theatrical distribution, you may choose to work with a distributor or you may self-distribute. Nontheatrical distribution is a specialized business, and some companies do this exclusively. Some theatrical distributors have a nontheatrical division; others contract with a subdistributor to handle this market. Most nontheatrical distributors have a catalogue of the video and multimedia productions they handle. Distributors have mailing lists of people who have rented or bought similar movies in the past, and they may have a sales force familiar with key personnel in school systems, libraries, and corporations. For some distributors, however, mailing out the catalogue once a year is the extent of their marketing effort. Whereas theatrical distributors generally deduct marketing expenses from the producer's share of the income, many nontheatrical distributors do not deduct expenses. Instead, they pay the producer a flat percentage or royalty for each video sale or rental. The producer might get about 10 to 30 percent of the revenue that comes in to the distributor, depending on the deal.

Home Video and Retail Marketing

Home video distribution refers to selling videos either directly to consumers, to wholesale and retail sales outlets, or to video stores that rent videos to consumers. Some movies are made specifically for this market, others are distributed to home video after playing in theaters or on TV. When some projects go "straight to video" this is the black sign that they failed to find any other distribution. The home video market exploded in the 1980s with the proliferation of VCRs and again about ten years later with DVDs. As the twenty-first century develops, satellite, cable, and Internet video-on-demand technologies will likely shrink the traditional home video DVD market. Eventually, most programming will be delivered electronically with no physical object changing hands.

In a traditional model, videos are released into the home video market in two stages. First they're sold for a relatively higher price to video stores, who rent them to customers. This is the *rental price*. After a period of several months, the price is then dropped to a lower level so consumers will purchase videos directly to keep at home (the *sell-through price*). In recent years, there has been tremendous downward pressure on prices, and the film may be released only at the sell-through price.

Home videos typically retail for around $20 to $25 or so. About half of that goes to the retailer, and half is the wholesale price paid to the distributor. The producer's royalty is a usually a percentage of wholesale; the producer often gets 10 to 30 percent of the wholesale price.

Many filmmakers choose to go with a distributor for home video, in hopes that the distributor can get the movie placed with big retail stores and websites. This can expand the visibility of the project, but the sales price per unit will be determined by whatever retailer is offering the movie at the most discounted rate. If you sell the DVDs yourself (off your website; see below) you can set the price and you will certainly keep a higher percentage of the revenues. If you go with a distributor, depending on the project, you may get a sizable advance, a token advance or nothing at all up front. The distributor should pay for the manufacturing and authoring of the DVD (see p. 560), but may try to deduct some of these costs from your share.

A newer home distribution model involves downloading movies from the Web. Many companies offer movies to download to a computer or an iPod. The website charges users a fee for each download and the producer receives a portion of the download fee.

Self-Distribution for Nontheatrical or Home Video

The chief reasons to self-distribute in the nontheatrical or home video markets are the potential to make (or keep) more money and the opportunity to do individualized marketing for your movie. Self-distribution has been transformed by the fact that you can easily set up a website on which buyers from around the world can directly purchase DVDs or downloads. You may choose to handle the billing and shipping of product yourself, or you can sign up with a *fulfillment house*, which takes the orders and ships DVDs for a fee. Some will manage the whole process (manufacture the DVD, package it, and handle the orders) for a very reasonable price. Usually, the fulfillment house will have a toll-free phone number and can take credit cards for phone orders. You can put a "shopping cart" on your website to take orders or to connect customers directly to your fulfillment house.

There are various ways to drive business to your website. Getting people to link to your site will both increase traffic directly and increase your ranking in search engines.

Self-distributors often do a mass mailing to likely buyers, using purchased mailing lists. This may be done via e-mail or by printing up and mailing brochures. You can buy lists for almost every category of buyer or field of study. For example, you can get a list of all public libraries across the country or teachers in women's studies programs. Your promotional materials should list awards, reviews, and endorsements by people in the field you are targeting. The response rate to a mailing is often only a few percent, but this may be enough to generate a profit.

For nontheatrical distribution, you should also have a poster made that can be distributed for individual screenings. Many nontheatrical movies are accompanied by study guides or training materials. To self-distribute in the nontheatrical market, plan to invest several thousand dollars. It can be a full-time job, especially in the first few months of the movie's release. The campaign requires an initial outlay for DVDs, a website, publicity, business forms, shipping, and costs such as festival entrance fees. There is the ongoing overhead for telephone and promotional mailings. Those self-distributors who have turned a profit have done so by streamlining the mechanical aspects of scheduling, shipping, and billing. Certain costs, like advertising, don't increase much for two films instead of one, so it can be cheaper to work with someone who is distributing a similar film. Distribution cooperatives, like New Day Films, help keep costs down by pooling resources.

Whether you distribute yourself or through a distributor, whenever you're selling through retail outlets expect the retailer to keep half or more of the retail sales price (though if you self-distribute at least you're not splitting the rest with a distributor). If you do decide to go with a commercial distributor, you may still want to retain the right to sell DVDs from your own website.

Other Distribution Issues

FOREIGN DISTRIBUTION. Foreign markets can be very lucrative for both theatrical and TV distribution. Starting when you first plan, cast, or shoot your movie, try to make it appealing and accessible to a foreign audience. To prepare the movie for foreign distribution, there are several things you need to do. The sound must be mixed to allow for translation in other languages (see p. 656). You often need a textless ("generic") version of the movie without any titles (see p. 554). You will also need a transcript (*continuity*) of the finished program, preferably with timecode references, to facilitate translation. Different parts of the world use different video systems and frame rates, and you will need video masters in different formats (see Chapters 14 and 18).

MULTIPLE RIGHTS AND REVENUES. Many projects have the potential to make money in several different markets. How the rights to these markets are handled can make a big difference to your bank account.

When you are making a deal with a broadcaster or distributor, they may ask for many types of rights and territories. For example, a broadcaster may want to share in home video or foreign sales; or a theatrical distributor may want rights to sell the movie to domestic TV. When possible, it's often to your advantage to separate those rights from the deal so you can sell them to another entity for more money. If someone commissions you to do a project, and pays the whole production cost, she will likely expect all rights to foreign, home video, and any subsidiary markets. However, if you initiate a project and the production funds come from several different entities, you're in a better position to retain these other rights, which can be very valuable. An experienced agent or lawyer can help you negotiate the deal.

If you sell a movie to TV and hope to pursue theatrical distribution, try to get the broadcaster to agree to a theatrical *window* prior to the air date (see below for more on this). On the other hand, if you've already sold to TV before you approach a theatrical distributor, he may be much less interested in your project. Normally, the distributor will want to share in the proceeds from a TV sale or home video; this is one of his main hedges against losing money on the theatrical run. Expenses are usually *cross-collateralized*, which means that any new income, say, from a TV sale, goes first to paying off previously accumulated debt before anything is paid to the producer. Be sure the distributor doesn't try to deduct debt from other films they may be handling.

LENGTH. The running time of a movie can have a big impact on its distribution opportunities. For more on this, see p. 499.

Launching a Movie

When a Hollywood studio releases a new movie, there's a well-oiled machine ready to distribute and promote it. The studio has an established network of contacts for theatrical, television, and home video distribution. The studio often has an in-house marketing department to create advertising campaigns and work with the press. For independent producers, on the other hand, releasing a movie can be a bewildering experience of trying to get attention for it and ultimately to find it a home with distributors, broadcasters, theaters, or other outlets.

Different movies have different goals or needs when it comes to distribution. If you've just finished an independent feature, you might be looking for a distributor, press coverage, a theatrical opening, and then aftermarkets of television and home video. But many movies are not intended for theatrical distribution (or just don't get the chance). If you've made a movie intended for TV, you might be looking for a broadcaster (or several in different countries). If your movie has already been bought (or was commissioned) by a TV network, you may only be looking for ways to maximize your press coverage and viewership for the broadcast.

If your movie has the potential to be shown through a variety of distribution channels, it's important to plan the release carefully. When a movie is released to the right markets in the right order and at the right time, exposure and potential profits can be maximized. Traditional distribution models are changing, which affects the sequence of events. The following is an outline for the release of a hypothetical feature film to highlight some of the distribution options.

Often the first step for an independent movie is film festivals and markets (see below). These are used to raise industry awareness about the movie and get some press (but not too much; see below). Distributors attend the major festivals and markets looking for new movies to acquire.

After you sign on with a distributor (or decide to self-distribute), the first commercial release is theatrical distribution. Hollywood films are often released in many cities simultaneously (*wide release*) in order to maximize the effect of advertising and press coverage in national media. Smaller films are often given a *limited release* (also called *platforming*) by playing in a few cities and then expanding to more *play dates* if things go well. Many exhibitors will want to see how a film performs elsewhere before booking the movie themselves. In the United States, opening in major cities such as New York and Los Angeles can be very expensive (advertising costs are astronomical) and very important (everyone's watching the box office).

Because the marketplace is crowded with movies and other entertainment options, you don't want your film to get lost. Independent films tend to be programmed to open in quieter periods, away from the major holiday releases from the big studios. However, with increasing numbers of films on the market, almost *no* time is quiet anymore. Sometimes small films are *counterprogrammed* by deliberately putting them out on holidays, as an alternative to studio fare. The timing of your release should be planned around getting the most press coverage and attention possible. Theaters generally open movies on Thursday night or Friday. Get as many people as you can to go that *first* weekend, because by Monday morning the theater decides whether to pull your film or, if you're lucky, hold it over. Some films open on a Wednesday to increase the chance of press coverage (since so many other films are usually opening—and reviewed—on Fridays.)

The next step typically is home video or perhaps A-V distribution (see above). If a movie has a potential to be used by schools and institutions, it can be released to the nontheatrical market at a higher price than consumers will pay for home video. After several months, you move on to the home video release. Some projects are never released on home video. On the other hand, some movies go directly to home video after a theatrical run to capitalize on any existing public awareness.

Then there is the television release. Some movies are bought or commissioned by free (traditional broadcast) networks, others by pay or premium services (cable or satellite). Some movies play on one and then the other. Some TV executives will commission a film and actively encourage a theatrical run prior to the air date as a way to boost attention and prestige. Others see this as *undermining* their press coverage or prestige and insist on the movie premiering on television. There have been a few notable examples of movies that had a limited TV release on a pay service and then went on to a successful theatrical run, but usually a TV airing means the end of theatrical opportunities. Choosing a good airdate (relative to holidays, elections, major sporting events, ratings "sweeps weeks," and such) is very important. One sequence for release to television submarkets is to start with video-on-demand (right after theatrical), then release on pay cable, basic cable, and finally on free, broadcast TV.

The reason to do home video prior to TV is the assumption that people are less likely to *pay* to watch a movie if they can see it for free on TV. On the other hand, for movies that don't get released theatrically, an upcoming TV broadcast can help land a home video deal. Some broadcast programs have a *tag* at the end of the show telling viewers how they can buy videos, which can be a good marketing device.

THE COMPRESSED RELEASE SCHEDULE. With so many films competing for consumers' attention, marketing and advertising ideally should be done at every stage of release. However, because marketing is so expensive, the industry has been shortening the time between the initial release of a film (with its biggest marketing splash) and the various aftermarkets. At one time, movies came out on home video almost a year after they ran in theaters; now the DVD is released much sooner, while the movie is fresh in people's minds (this also reflects the fact that DVDs are a much larger revenue stream than they used to be). The ultimate compressed release schedule is *day and date* release, in which the DVD is sold and/or TV broadcast is done at the same time as the theatrical release. HDNet Films pioneered the release of Steven Soderbergh's *Bubble* this way. In this case, a financial connection between the theater chain and the broadcaster provided benefits to both. Others are trying day and date release; it's not clear yet how well it works.

Festivals and Markets

Perhaps the best way to get attention for a new project is to enter it in a film festival. The top festivals worldwide include Berlin, Cannes, New York, Sundance, and Toronto. A large group of distributors, agents, and members of the international press attends these festivals, and a successful screening can be a huge boost to a movie. Generating "buzz" can help in many ways. For films that don't have obviously bankable elements like big stars or hot stories, distributors are usually influenced as much by other people's reactions as by their own. (There's a joke about the studio executive who went to see a movie alone. Afterward, a friend asked him what he thought. He said, "I don't know, I saw it by myself.")

The best festivals are very competitive and often require premieres. (If the film has been shown elsewhere in the same country or sometimes the same continent, you may be disqualified.) You can easily lose the opportunity to play at a "smaller" festival while waiting for a bigger one to decide. There are hundreds of festivals around the world, which can provide a fabulous opportunity for you to travel and see your movie with different audiences. Many festivals specialize in particular topics (nature, gay and lesbian, educational, etc.) and festivals often provide a forum for the most interesting discussions about your movie and others. At one time, there was a clear delineation between film festivals and video/TV festivals. This difference is becoming increasingly blurred. Nevertheless, distinctions remain between festivals geared more toward theatrical films and those that accept more television-oriented or nontheatrical fare. There are many websites that list festivals. One of them, www.withoutabox.com, has listings of many festivals and allows you to store your application information, making it easier to apply to multiple festivals. See Bibliography for more sources.

MARKETS. A film or TV market can be thought of as a festival for industry people where the focus is not on watching and enjoying movies but on selling and buying them. Some film festivals, such as Berlin, have a market associated with them. Chief markets in the United States include the Independent Feature Project (IFP) in New York every September, and the American Film Market (AFM), which is geared more toward dramas, in Santa Monica in November. Some markets, such as MIP in France and NATPE in the United States, are primarily for buying and selling television programming. Markets may have selection committees, but are often less selective than festivals. The filmmaker pays a fee and has the opportunity to meet with distributors, broadcasters, and festival programmers about a finished movie, a work in progress, or to discuss a script or proposal.

In some markets, a screening is held in a theater, to which you can invite buyers. In many markets, there's a DVD library for buyers who prefer to watch films by themselves, often on fast-forward so they can "see" lots of films in a short time without being pestered by filmmakers.

Many markets have an organized process to bring producers and buyers together. Some use a "speed dating" method, where short meetings are arranged in which you can pitch your project quickly. Some have a *pitching forum*, in which you get a chance to pitch your project to a large group of assembled buyers. This can be intimidating, but raises the visibility of the project and gives you a very quick idea if there's interest among buyers. One of the key benefits of any market is the opportunity to find many executives in one place at one time.

Publicity

"Publicity" encompasses all the things you can do to raise awareness about your project. Today virtually no theatrical film, TV program, or nontheatrical video can be successfully released without it. If you're rich or backed by a large corporation, you can afford to take out ads to increase awareness of your movie. But publicity, in the form of feature pieces, interviews, reviews, and postings, is a lot cheaper and often more effective. The many types of media available to get the word out include websites, newspapers, magazines, radio, TV, and blogs. For some movies, the goal is to interest the general public. For some projects, such as a corporate or educational video, your publicity may be targeted at a specific market or industry group.

If you can afford it, hire a *publicist*, whose job it is to bring your project to the attention of print, Web, and broadcast entities that might cover your movie. A professional publicist will have a list of editors, writers, and producers to contact. Sometimes publicists are hired for a festival debut, to increase awareness of a film and facilitate its getting a distributor. But be careful about overexposing a movie prior to its actual release in theaters or on television. For example, if a newspaper reviews a movie for a festival, it may decide not to run that review again when the movie is released. For general circulation (as opposed to industry-only) media, insist on short "capsule" reviews at festivals, so the full review can be held off till later. A capsule review, if positive, can be invaluable for preparing posters and marketing materials for the actual release of the project.

Be sure to have plenty *screeners* (DVDs) to give to writers and critics. When possible, hold press screenings or invite reviewers to public screenings so they can see the movie with an audience. Some critics prefer to watch videos by themselves. To improve the chance of a feature piece being done about your movie, emphasize the "hooks" or angles that make your movie special, timely, or relevant. Did you lure a famous actor out of retirement? Is your movie about World War II being broadcast on the anniversary of D day? Did the film make use of local talent? Is there an incredible story about how the movie got made?

Keep in mind that substantial lead time may be needed between when a feature piece is done and the date it actually appears in print or on the air. Contact editors far in advance. If you're going to be in a city, perhaps for a festival, you can sometimes do print or radio interviews and have them "banked" until the movie is released.

Marketing Materials

Having a website for the film is *essential*. Even a simple, basic site can tell people about the film, where they can see it or buy it, and save you huge amounts of money and time. The best way to design a site is to look at what other films have done and decide which features seem useful and which are merely distracting. Try to get as many other sites as possible to link to your site, to drive up traffic and increase your ranking in the various search engines.

You should prepare a *press kit* that can be personally handed to press people and posted on the website. Press notes should include a synopsis, director's statement, list of awards and festivals, credits, and short biographies of the key participants.[6] Some people put several publicity photos in each press kit. One great feature of a website is you can post images (including high-res files) that festivals and press can download when needed.

You'll need a poster and some key art treatments that can be used for ads and other materials. Actually, it's not a bad idea to have a full-sized version of the one-sheet (27 x 39 inches is typical) and some smaller ones that can be put up on bulletin boards and such.

It's extremely useful to have a postcard with basic information about the film (including screening dates and times) that can be handed to people at a festival or market, and left in theater lobbies. You can access many poster and postcard printers online. You send them a digital file and they print out what you need for a few hundred dollars. The larger your print run, the cheaper each copy of the poster or postcard is.

Having a trailer is essential for theatrical distribution and can be helpful for other markets. The trailer will be shown in theaters in the weeks leading up to your run and can be posted online at the film's website and on numerous other sites. For film theaters, you'll usually need both flat and 'Scope (anamorphic) versions. You'll also need a compressed digital version (usually QuickTime, Windows Media, or Flash) for online posting. There are services that specialize in getting your trailer and other "assets" posted on movie websites; it can sometimes be hard to get them out there on your own.

When broadcast critics review your movie, they'll want some short clips from the film to show while they talk about it. They may show the trailer, but you should also prepare a *clips reel* (as of this writing, broadcasters often want this on Beta SP).

The need for good still images cannot be overemphasized. You should have pictures of the actors in role or, for a documentary, the movie's subjects. You'll also need some shots of the production team, especially the director. Having good still images can mean the difference between a paper running your pictures or not. Offer a few to choose from, as competing media may not want to run the same image. Compelling images are also essential for the poster and ad campaign.

On a feature film, stills are usually taken on the set or during production for highest quality. On a documentary or low-budget feature, frame enlargements made from the movie itself may or may not be of high enough quality. High definition formats may reproduce well, but standard definition video often doesn't hold up very well for enlargements. You can improve the quality of standard def frame grabs by deinterlacing and doing other fixes in Photoshop.

For many movies, an *electronic press kit* (EPK) is prepared, including video footage showing the moviemakers on the set.

Selling Your Project and Yourself

A lot of novice filmmakers don't realize how much *selling* they have to do to make movies. It starts at the beginning of the project—getting people interested in your idea—and doesn't stop until long after the film is made and distributed. Some

6. Reviews may be included as well, but generally not for press kits going to other critics.

people are drawn to moviemaking precisely for the commercial aspects, but for many, the constant need to sell feels like a painful distraction from what they really want to do—make movies.

If you've managed to get your movie at least partially under way, you may want to work with a *producer's representative* or a *sales agent* to look for funding and negotiate deals at festivals or markets. The rep or agent has contacts among the potential buyers. Agents and reps have no problem pushing and touting a movie, whereas the people who actually *made* the movie often do. Nevertheless, unless you have a very marketable movie or an established reputation, you may have trouble getting a producer's rep to handle your project. You may do better to look for offers on your own and use an agent or a lawyer to help negotiate a deal when you actually get some interest from a buyer.

Anyone who's tried to sell a movie at a market or festival knows what a demoralizing experience it can be. The doors to the screening room swing back and forth like an old Wild West saloon as buyers rush to catch ten minutes of one movie and five of another (or they don't come at all). A few movies get sold with great fanfare while the other filmmakers are left glumly wondering why they've gotten no offers. Be patient—often a market or festival will lay the groundwork for a deal, but the actual offer may take several months or more to materialize. Sometimes one festival gets you noticed, but it isn't until the next one that someone comes forward with real interest. Unfortunately, the brutal fact is that many films never get distributed or even invited to festivals. Don't be hard on yourself if things don't work out the way you planned.

When you go to a market or festival, do your homework and try to determine which distributors or buyers are most appropriate for your project (often you can get the catalog of buyers in advance of a market, or use the previous year's guide). Find a way to invite the buyers or make them aware of your movie. But treat them with respect. There are stories of aggressive filmmakers who stop at nothing until some executive watches their movie or reads their script. But this kind of harassment is why many weary buyers and programmers, who see hundreds of movies a year, will do anything to avoid having to actually *talk* to filmmakers. Trust the fact that if your movie is good, people will talk about it, and things will start to happen.

A LAST WORD

If you've actually read from the beginning of this book to here, you deserve an award for endurance. You now know a vast amount about creating all sorts of motion pictures. There are many ways to put your knowledge to use. You might decide to work in the "industry" (indust*ries* is more like it), which could mean making dramas, documentaries, industrials, game shows, web videos, or clips for cell phones.

Some people go into film and video with dreams of making a hit and getting rich and famous. If you go into the business, keep in mind that most careers advance much more slowly than the fantasy of being "discovered" and catapulted to the top. A lot of people labor in the trenches for years, and fame and riches may have nothing to do with it. Even if you do well, in the midst of success, there can be plenty of failure. One audience or critic or client might love your film, another might be indifferent. You might have great success with one project and find no takers for the next. Learning to live with uncertainty and risk is essential to surviving. Hopefully, your drive comes from loving what you do.

It may be that you do something completely different in terms of your career. These days, no matter what your vocation or avocation, almost everyone has a reason to create media at *some* point in their lives. In the end, all the technology and technique in this book is meant to give you the power to express your ideas and tell stories. Now it's up to you to decide what stories to tell, and how to tell them. Making movies is hard work, an adventure, and, if you're lucky, a pleasure. Enjoy it!

ADJUSTING A VIDEO MONITOR

The Importance of a Good Video Monitor

We all watch TV and use computers without much thought about how the screens are adjusted for brightness and color. When shooting or editing video, however, having a properly adjusted picture monitor is critical to evaluating and controlling the picture.

While shooting, a monitor displays a likeness of what the camera is capturing, which is not necessarily identical to what the camera is *actually* capturing to tape or disk. The color, shadow detail, contrast, or overall brightness shown by the monitor may or may not match what the camera is actually capturing due to the type and quality of the monitor and the way it is adjusted. The problem here is "seeing is believing"—a concept that's hard-wired into our brains. Whether the monitor is correct or not, we tend to believe what it shows. We'll be tempted to make exposure decisions based on what we see on the monitor, and often make the mistake of giving credence to LCD viewfinders or flip-out screens, only to later discover on a proper CRT picture monitor that the image looks markedly different.

While editing on an NLE, we tend to accept what we see on the computer's monitor, although computer monitors can't accurately reproduce video color space or contrast (see p. 200). Given that NLEs permit sophisticated color correction, this sets the stage for disaster unless color decisions are based on a properly adjusted picture monitor, usually a CRT (though LCDs and plasmas are improving). If you use an NLE's computer screen to color-correct video, you may be in for a nasty shock when the results are played back on a TV.

When your movie is finished and it's time to screen it, video projector adjustment is equally important. A lot of energy goes into producing your project, and you want it to look as good as possible. You want the results on the screen to match all the painstaking color correction you labored over.

In other words, there's no substitute for a good-quality, properly adjusted video picture monitor in production or post. It's a necessity. Video monitors and projectors should always be *set up* (adjusted) using a video signal that contains standard color bars. Today there are many display technologies in use (see Video Monitors and Projectors, p. 197), and the unfortunate fact of the matter is that your movie may look somewhat different on different devices even if they're set up properly. Procedures for adjusting the display, and even terms used for different controls vary between systems.

While theatrical projection is usually done in a very dark room, video monitors are by design brighter than projection and usually look better with a *little* light in the room. Make sure light sources don't fall directly *on* the screen (which washes out the blacks, lowering contrast, and can affect color reproduction). For production work outdoors, a hood or shade can be fitted over the monitor to protect contrast.

An excellent resource for setting up monitors is Joe Kane's *Digital Video Essentials*, which is available on DVD and other formats and includes test patterns and instructions for calibrating video and multichannel audio playback. For instructions on adjusting computer monitors, see the help section in your operating system, video card, or monitor calibration software. Many systems have a simple step-by-step process you can follow to calibrate the display. Bear in mind, again, that computer monitors, however perfectly set up, can not accurately display video color or tonality.

The color bars setup described below applies to video monitors and TVs only. If any terms are unfamiliar, see Chapters 1 and 5.

Color Bars

Once you have your monitor, it needs to be adjusted correctly for color, shadow detail, and contrast using *color bars*—the only method that truly guarantees that what you see is *really* what you get. Most cameras and NLEs generate color bars. You can send a signal directly into the production monitor or NLE video monitor, or you can record the bars for adjustment from playback. If you're shooting a series of tapes, you need only about 30 seconds of color bars at the head of the first tape for later reference.

In NTSC countries, SMPTE ECR-1 bars are used for standard definition video (see Fig. A). This pattern is 4:3 aspect ratio, with the color bars occupying the upper part of the pattern. From left to right these bars are 75 percent white (a light gray), yellow, cyan, green, magenta, red, and blue. Directly below the bars is a thin horizontal band of color rectangles, one rectangle per color bar. The bottom of the

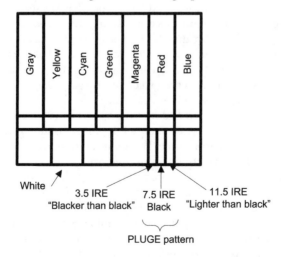

Fig. A. Conventional SMPTE ECR-1 color bars (see also Fig. 3-11).

pattern is mostly occupied by squares of black and white and dark colors. Each of these bars and pattern elements plays a role—as described below—in fast and accurate monitor setup.

Another common color bar pattern, also 4:3, consists of eight vertical color bars alone (the ones described above plus a black bar on the far right). These non-SMPTE "full-field" color bars are often found in consumer cameras and are of limited use for setting up NTSC monitors. Don't bother with them. In PAL countries, however, they are known as European Broadcasting Union (EBU) bars. Note that the left-most bar in NTSC is always 75 percent white (light gray), while the left-most bar in the EBU pattern is always 100 percent white. SMPTE bars have a clever design that allows repeatable monitor setup visually (without using a waveform monitor), which is not possible with EBU bars because of PAL's different signal architecture.

Since 2002 there's a new color bar pattern called SMPTE RP 219-2002, with a 16:9 aspect ratio and a redesigned pattern intended for high definition (see Fig. B). Also called ARIB bars, it looks like the original SMPTE ECR-1 bars, only with an additional 40 percent gray bar on each end. Along the bottom is a new configuration of sample areas, including a smooth gray scale "ramp." The techniques described below for setting up standard definition monitors using the conventional SMPTE color bars apply equally to the widescreen SMPTE RP 219-2002 color bars if you simply ignore the added 40 percent gray bars on the sides.

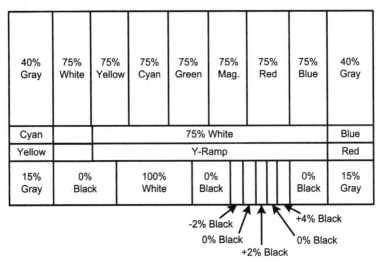

Fig. B. Widescreen SMPTE RP 219-2002 color bars for HD.

Basic Monitor Controls

Two of the main controls on a professional video monitor are *brightness* (sometimes labeled *black level*, or indicated by an icon of the sun) and *contrast* (white level, also called *picture*, and may have an icon of a half-moon). These features are badly named, as the brightness control mainly raises and lowers the blacks, which your eye perceives largely as a change in contrast.

NTSC color monitors also have adjustments for *hue* (also called *tint, phase,* or *chroma phase*) and *color* (saturation, also called *chroma* or *chroma gain*).

Depending on the video system and type of connection, not all of these controls may be used. For example, most PAL TVs and monitors don't have hue (tint) or color (saturation) controls because PAL color stays consistent. Also, when a monitor is connected digitally by DVI or HDMI to the video source, sometimes not all of these adjustments are operative.

Many consumer TV sets have automatic or "smart" settings for color and brightness; turn these off if you are adjusting a TV to color bars.

HOW TO SET UP AN NTSC MONITOR USING SMPTE COLOR BARS

1. **Allow Monitor to Warm Up**
   Run it 15 minutes to stabilize it.

2. **Check Color Temperature**
   Most monitors have a menu setting for color temperature (*white point*), which must be set to a world standard of 6500°K (also called D65) for both NTSC and PAL/SECAM video. If in doubt, check the monitor's menu to confirm the setting. This is not an adjustment you will have to make often.

3. **Set Black Level**
   The control labeled "brightness" on many monitors actually controls the black level, which is the value of the darkest black parts of the image. When brightness is set too low, you lose detail in the blacks (crushed blacks). When brightness is set too high, the blacks look milky or gray.

   In the bottom right-hand corner of the SMPTE bars are three thin vertical gray stripes called PLUGE bars (Picture Line-Up Generating Equipment). Adjusting picture black levels using PLUGE bars takes advantage of the fact that NTSC puts its black level at 7.5 IRE units (instead of at zero as is done with PAL), so it's possible to have an NTSC signal that's "blacker than black." The PLUGE bar on the left represents a 3.5 IRE level ("superblack" or "blacker than black"), the middle one is 7.5 IRE (black), and the right bar is 11.5 IRE (gray or "lighter than black"). Because no NTSC picture detail can truly be blacker than black, all you have to do is to adjust the brightness control until the left and middle bars are indistinguishable. Lower the brightness until the two darker bars merge together, raise it again until you can see three stripes, then decrease it until the darker bars *just* merge again. The gray bar on the right should be just barely visible. That's all there is to it.

   The new widescreen SMPTE RP 219-2002 color bars have a slightly different PLUGE arrangement, with five thin bars that represent -2 percent black, 0 percent black, +2 percent black, 0 percent black, +4 percent black, but the idea is the same. The HD monitor should be adjusted so that the -2 percent black and 0 percent black levels are indistinguishable.

When adjusting a PAL monitor, since PAL uses the full 1 to 100 IRE unit range for picture detail, there is no blacker-than-black signal. You can still accurately set black level on a PAL monitor by displaying the full-field EBU bars described above, putting the monitor in underscan, then visually matching the black color bar on the right to the black level outside of the active picture area.

4. Set Peak White Level

The "contrast" or "picture" control adjusts the level of midtones and bright whites. It sets the distance or separation between the black level and the brightest whites. In the both the classic and new widescreen SMPTE color bars, there's a square in the bottom row that is 100 percent white. (Note that in NTSC, none of the full-sized bars in the upper area is 100 percent white.) Bring the contrast up until the 100 percent square is comfortably bright, but don't set it so high that the white seems to bloom (get fuzzy and larger in size) or other geometrical distortions occur. The 100 percent white square shouldn't spread into neighboring black bars. If you can see scan lines, adjust the contrast for a bright white, then back off slightly until the bleeding together of scan lines diminishes and separate scan lines are clearly visible.

Often, setting the contrast may change your black level, so you may have to go back and forth between the contrast and brightness settings a few times.

5. Set Chroma and Hue

When adjusting NTSC video, hue and saturation (chroma) should be set together. They will affect each other, so you may have to do each more than once.

This is where SMPTE color bars are so handy. If you have a professional monitor, enable the "blue gun" or "blue only" function (sometimes it's a switch or button on the outside, sometimes it is a menu selection). This will turn off the red and green so that the screen turns deep blue (or sometimes black-and-white). If your monitor doesn't have a blue-gun function, you can view the color bars through a Lee 363 blue gel, although this is much less satisfactory.

In blue only mode, adjust chroma (or color) until the two outer SMPTE ECR-1 bars, now both blue, achieve the same intensity or brightness as the small color rectangles directly below them. When this is done, the two outer bars should also match each other (see Fig. C).

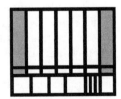

Fig. C. When adjusting color (chroma) on a monitor that displays blue only, these two bars and the patches under them should have the same intensity.

Now adjust the hue (or phase) in a similar way, so the near left and right blue bars and the small color rectangles below them are the same. Counting from the left, these would be bars 3 and 5 (see Fig. D).

All four bars should now match each other and

the small rectangles under them. If this isn't the case, re-tweak chroma/color and hue/phase until you achieve this. The two adjustments are interactive, but it isn't very hard to obtain a good result.

Now leave blue only mode and *voilà!*—perfect color and saturation.

Fig. D. When adjusting hue (tint) on a monitor that displays blue only, these two bars and the patches under them should have the same intensity.

If you have only full-field bars (instead of true SMPTE bars with color rectangles and PLUGE), match the first and seventh bars from the left in blue only mode by adjusting chroma, and match the third and fifth bars from the left by adjusting hue (phase). All four should then match each other. Be sure that you are using NTSC full-field bars with white at 75 percent instead of PAL bars with white at 100 percent.

If you don't have a way to display blue only, look especially at the yellow and magenta bars (second and fifth from the left). There's only one hue setting in which both will be correct. The yellow should be a pure lemon yellow, without any hint of green or orange. The magenta bar shouldn't be red or purple. Color level should be rich but not oversaturated.

Getting accurate color without bars is very difficult, since there is no way to know what colors should look like. The best you can do is to go for the most pleasing skin tones. Make the hue and saturation (color intensity) of the skin as natural as possible.

Another method is to look at a shot of a gray test panel and try to adjust hue until there's no color cast in the gray.

OTHER MONITOR SETUP CONSIDERATIONS

Sharpness
Most video monitors and TVs have a sharpness control (also called aperture or detail) that adds a light line around the edges of things in the scene (see Fig. 3-14). In actuality, this *reduces* fine detail, even though shapes look bolder. Turn this all the way down, then raise it until you just reach the point where added lines appear. Get used to watching pictures without added "sharpness." One exception is that professional camcorders often have a detail adjustment in the viewfinder called "peaking" that can help you focus while shooting. The picture in the finder doesn't look "natural," but you can clearly see what's in and out of focus.

Gamma
Computer monitors and some broadcast video monitors have adjustments for gamma. The standard display gamma in Windows and sRGB (web graphics) is 2.2. This is also a standard for NTSC CRT monitors. The Mac (Apple) standard is 1.8, but some people prefer to set Mac systems higher, closer to 2.2. PAL gamma is up

to 2.8. The gamma of a playback system is determined not just by the monitor's gamma but by the entire chain of image-processing software and hardware in the system.

Lower display gamma makes the image appear to have less contrast. The fact that different playback systems have different gamma can result in contrast looking different, depending on which system you're viewing on. You should try to view your video the way you think most viewers will see it.

Downloadable programs such as QuickGamma can be used for computer monitor calibration. For extremely precise monitor calibration, you can get tools (such as ColorVision OptiCAL and PhotoCAL) with a photometric "spyder" that sits on the monitor surface and measures light output.

Termination

Some monitors have multiple BNC connectors so you can both input and output an analog video signal (composite or component). These can be used to send the analog signal via coaxial cable into the monitor and then out again to connect to another piece of equipment (the signal is then "looped through" or "bridged"). This way, you can connect several monitors together on one line (such as a waveform, vectorscope, and several video monitors). The last monitor on the chain of coaxial cable (or the only monitor if there's only one) needs to be "terminated." Some analog monitors offer automatic termination as a feature. Some instead have a termination switch labeled "75 Ohm Terminator" or just "75 Ω." Switch to the 75 Ω position to terminate. You can also get a special 75 Ω terminator plug to attach to the video-out BNC jack of the last monitor in the chain. Don't use *both* a plug and the switch. An analog monitor not properly terminated will show a noisy, contrasty image with distorted highlights and subtle ghosting. The 75 ohm termination is a requirement of coaxial cable in particular, and therefore affects delivery of SDI and HD-SDI signals too, but monitors that accept these signals are always auto-terminated. Termination is not an issue for short runs of S-Video, DVI, or HDMI.

APPENDIX B

DATA RATES AND STORAGE NEEDS FOR VARIOUS DIGITAL FORMATS*

Frame rate note: "24" = 24 or 23.98; "30" = 29.97; "60" = 59.97

	Video Data Rate (Mbps)	Nominal Compression Ratio[1]	Frame Rate	Chroma Sampling	Bits	STORAGE per minute[2]	STORAGE per hour[2]	Notes
STANDARD DEFINITION[3]								
DVD	3.8[4]	31:1	30, 25, 24	4:2:0	8	37 MB	2.3 GB	MPEG-2 variable bit rate
M-JPEG (offline editing)[5]	8	25:1	30, 25, 24	various[5]	8	60 MB	260 MB	
DV	25	5:1	30, 25[6]	4:1:1 NTSC 4:2:0 PAL	8	217 MB	12.7 GB	
Digital8	25	5:1	30, 25	4:1:1 NTSC 4:2:0 PAL	8	217 MB	12.7 GB	
DVCAM	25	5:1	30, 25	4:1:1 NTSC 4:2:0 PAL	8	217 MB	12.7 GB	
DVCPRO (D-7)[7]	25	5:1	30, 25	4:1:1[8]	8	217 MB	12.7 GB	
Betacam SX	18	10:1	30, 25	4:2:2	8	188 MB	11.3 GB	Sony MPEG-2 tape format
DVCPRO 50	50	3.3:1	30, 25	4:2:2	8	423 MB	24.8 GB	Panasonic DV format
Digital S (D-9)	50	3.3:1	30, 25	4:2:2	8	423 MB	24.8 GB	JVC DV format; ½-inch tape
IMX (D-10)	30	6:1	30, 25	4:2:2	8	227 MB	13.25 GB	Sony MPEG-2 format
IMX (D-10)	40	4:1	30, 25	4:2:2	8	298 MB	17.4 GB	
IMX (D-10)	50	3.3:1	30, 25	4:2:2	8	370 MB	21.7 GB	
ProRes 720 x 486	42	6:1	30	4:2:2	10	320 MB	19.2 GB	Apple editing and finishing codec
ProRes HQ 720 x 486	63	4:3:1	30	4:2:2	10	470 MB	28.2 GB	
XDCAM[9]	—	—	—	—	—	—	—	
Digital Betacam	90	2.3:1	30, 25	4:2:2	10	675 MB	40.5 GB	Sony compression
ITU-R 601 (D-1, D-5)	216[10]	uncomp.	30, 25[6]	4:2:2	8	1.2 GB	71 GB	
ITU-R 601 (D-1, D-5)	270[10]	uncomp.	30, 25[6]	4:2:2	10	1.6 GB	94 GB	

*Table by David Leitner.

	Video Data Rate (Mbps)	Nominal Compression Ratio[1]	Frame Rate	Chroma Sampling	Bits	STORAGE per minute[2]	STORAGE per hour[2]	Notes
HIGH DEFINITION—COMPRESSED								
Where multiple frame rates exist, data rates and storage indicated for highest frame rate.								
DVD— 1280 x 720	6[4]	various	24	4:2:0	8	45 MB	2.7 GB	MPEG-4 AVC (H.264)VC-1
DVD— 1920 x 1080	8[4]	various	24	4:2:0	8	60 MB	3.6 GB	
HD-DVD	36[11]	various	30, 25, 24	4:2:0	8	270 MB	16.2 GB	MPEG-2, VC-1, MPEG-4 AVC (H.264)
Blu-ray	36[11]	various	30, 25, 24	4:2:0	8	270 MB	16.2 GB	
HDV1— 1280 x 720p	19.7	17:1	60, 50 30, 25	4:2:0	8	142 MB	8.3 GB	MPEG-2 constant bit rate
HDV2— 1440 x 1080i	25	22:1	30, 25	4:2:0	8	190 MB	11.3 GB	
HDV— 1280 x 720p @ 24fps	19.7	13.5:1	24	4:2:0	8	142 MB	8.3 GB	JVC only, not HDV standard
AVCHD— 720p	14	16:1	60, 50, 24	4:2:0	8	180 MB	10.8 GB	MPEG-4 AVC (H.264) variable bit rate
AVCHD 1920 x 1080i/p	18	16:1	30, 25, 24	4:2:0	8	180 MB	10.8 GB	
XDCAM HD 1440 x 1080i/p	18	n.a.	30, 25, 24	4:2:0	8	140 MB	8.2 GB	MPEG-2, variable bit rate subsampled horizontally
XDCAM HD 1440 x 1080i/p	25	22:1	30, 25, 24	4:2:0	8	190 MB	11.1 GB	MPEG-2, constant bit rate, subsampled horizontally.Equivalent to HDV 1080i
XDCAM HD 1440 x 1080i/p	35	n.a.	30, 25, 24	4:2:0	8	262 MB	15.3 GB	MPEG-2, variable bit rate, subsampled horizontally
JPEG 2000 1920 x 1080	50	n.a.	30, 25, 24	4:2:2	10	375 MB	22.5 GB	Intraframe wavelet compression. Used in Grass Valley Infinity camcorder.
JPEG 2000	75	n.a.	30, 25, 24	4:2:2	10	563 MB	33.8 GB	
JPEG 2000	100	n.a.	30, 25, 24	4:2:2	10	750 MB	45 GB	
D9 HD— 960 x 720p	100	6.7:1	60, 50, 30 25, 24	4:2:2	8	835 MB	49 GB	
D9 HD— 1280 x 1080i/p	100	6.7:1	30, 25, 24	4:2:2	8	835 MB	49 GB	
DVCPRO HD (D-12) 960 x 720p	100	6.7:1	60, 50, 30 25, 24	4:2:2	8	835 MB	49 GB	
DVCPRO HD (D-12) 1280 x 1080i/p	100	6.7:1	30, 24	4:2:2	8	835 MB	49 GB	subsampled horizontally
DVCPRO HD (D-12) 1440 x 1080i/p	100	6.7:1	25	4:2:2	8	835 MB	49 GB	
AVC-Intra 1440 x 1080i/p	50	n.a.	30, 25, 24	4:2:0	10	375 MB	22.5 GB	Panasonic P2 alternative to DVCPRO HD
AVC-Intra 1920 x 1080i/p	100	n.a.	30, 25, 24	4:2:2	10	750 MB	45 GB	
DNxHD 145 1280 x 720p	145	7:1	60, 50, 24	4:2:2	8	1 GB	56 GB	AVID intraframe compression. Future SMPTE VC-3 standard.

	Video Data Rate (Mbps)	Nominal Compression Ratio[1]	Frame Rate	Chroma Sampling	Bits	STORAGE per minute[2]	STORAGE per hour[2]	Notes
HIGH DEFINITION—COMPRESSED (continued)								
DNxHD 220 1280 x 720p	220	4:1	60, 50, 24	4:2:2	8	1.6 GB	100 GB	
DNxHD 220 1280 x 720p	220	6:1	60, 50, 24	4:2:2	10	1.6 GB	100 GB	AVID intraframe compression. Future SMPTE VC-3 standard.
DNxHD 145 1920 x 1080i/p	145	7:1	30, 25, 24	4:2:2	8	1 GB	56 GB	
DNxHD 220 1920 x 1080i/p	220	4:1	30, 25, 24	4:2:2	8	1.6 GB	100 GB	
DNxHD 220 1920 x 1080i/p	220	6:1	30, 25, 24	4:2:2	10	1.6 GB	100 GB	
DNxHD 36	36	24:1	24, 25	4:2:2	8	270 MB	16.2 GB	offline only
ProRes 1280 x 720 p	147	7:1	24, 25, 30, 60	4:2:2	10	1.1 GB	66 GB	Apple codec. Storage listed is for 60 fps.
ProRes HQ 1280 x 720 p	220	6:1	24, 25, 30, 60	4:2:2	10	1.65 GB	99 GB	
ProRes 1920 x 1080	147	7:1	24, 25, 30	4:2:2	10	1.1 GB	66 GB	Apple codec. Storage listed is for 30 fps.
ProRes HQ 1920 x 1080	220	6.1	24, 25, 30	4:2:2	10	1.65 GB	99 GB	
D5 HD 1280 x 720p	223	4:1	60	4:2:2	8	2.3 GB	135 GB	advanced M-JPEG 4 channels audio
D5 HD 1920 x 1080i	223	4:1	30	4:2:2	8	2.3 GB	135 GB	
D5 HD 1920 x 1080p	223	4:1	24	4:2:2	8	1.94 GB	116 GB	advanced M-JPEG 8 channels audio
D5 HD— 1920 x 1080i/p	223	4:1	25	4:2:2	8	2 GB	121 GB	
HDCAM (D-11) 1440 x 1080i/p	144	4.4:1[1][2]	30, 25, 24	3:1:1	8	1.1 GB	64.8 GB	Sony compression, subsampled horizontally
HDCAM SR (D-16) 1920 x 1080i/p	440	2.78:1	30, 25, 24	4:2:2	10	3.3 GB	198 GB	MPEG-4 Studio Profile
HDCAM SR (D-16) 1920 x 1080i/p	440	4.2:1	30, 25, 24	4:4:4	10	3.3 GB	198 GB	
HIGH DEFINITION—UNCOMPRESSED								
1280 x 720p (8 bits)	353.6		24	4:2:2	8	2.5 GB	149 GB	
1280 x 720p (8 bits)	368.3		25	4:2:2	8	2.6 GB	155 GB	
1280 x 720p (8 bits)	441.9		30	4:2:2	8	3.1 GB	186 GB	
1280 x 720p (8 bits)	737.3		50	4:2:2	8	5.2 GB	310 GB	
1280 x 720p (8 bits)	883.9		60	4:2:2	8	6.2 GB	371 GB	
1280 x 720p (10 bits)	442.4		24	4:2:2	10	3.4 GB	201 GB	
1280 x 720p (10 bits)	460.9		25	4:2:2	10	3.5 GB	209 GB	
1280 x 720p (10 bits)	552.5		30	4:2:2	10	4.2 GB	251 GB	

Video Data Rate (Mbps)	Nominal Compression Ratio[1]	Frame Rate	Chroma Sampling	Bits	STORAGE per minute[2]	STORAGE per hour[2]	Notes

HIGH DEFINITION—UNCOMPRESSED (continued)

Video Data Rate	Nominal Comp. Ratio[1]	Frame Rate	Chroma Sampling	Bits	STORAGE per minute[2]	STORAGE per hour[2]	Notes
1280 x 720p (10 bits)	921.8	50	4:2:2	10	7.0 GB	418 GB	
1280 x 720p (10 bits)	1.10 Gbps	60	4:2:2	10	8.4 GB	501 GB	
1920 x 1080i/p (8 bits)	829	25	4:2:2	8	5.8 GB	348 GB	
1920 x 1080i/p (8 bits)	994.3	30	4:2:2	8	7.0 GB	417 GB	
1920 x 1080p (8 bits)	795.6	24	4:2:2	8	5.6 GB	334 GB	
1920 x 1080p (8 bits)	1.66 Gbps	50	4:2:2	8	11.6 GB	696 GB	
1920 x 1080p (8 bits)	1.99 Gbps	60	4:2:2	8	13.9 GB	834 GB	
1920 x 1080i/p (10 bits)	1.03 Gbps	25	4:2:2	10	7.7 GB	464 GB	
1920 x 1080i/p (10 bits)	1.24 Gbps	30	4:2:2	10	9.3 GB	559 GB	
1920 x 1080p (10 bits)	993	24	4:2:2	10	7.4 GB	446 GB	
1920 x 1080p (10 bits)	2.07 Gbps	50	4:2:2	10	15.5 GB	928 GB	
1920 x 1080p (10 bits)	2.48 Gbps	60	4:2:2	10	18.6 GB	1.1 TB	
1280 x 720p	1.69 Gbps	60	RGB 4:4:4	10	12.4 GB	742 GB	
1920 x 1080i/p	1.58 Gbps	25	RGB 4:4:4	10	11.6 GB	695 GB	
1920 x 1080i/p	1.90 Gbps	30	RGB 4:4:4	10	14 GB	834 GB	

DIGITAL CINEMATOGRAPHY

Video Data Rate	Nominal Comp. Ratio[1]	Frame Rate	Chroma Sampling	Bits	STORAGE per minute[2]	STORAGE per hour[2]	Notes
CineForm RAW 1920 x 1080	96	5:1	24	RAW	10	720 MB	43.2 GB	in-camera wavelet
RAW HD 1920 x 1080	498	uncomp.	24	RAW	10	3.7 GB	224 GB	single sensor Bayer filter
RAW 3K 3018 x 2200[13]	1.91 Gbps	uncomp.	24	RAW	12	14.3 GB	860.5 GB	Arri D-20 single sensor
RAW 4K 4046 x 2048	3.18 Gbps	uncomp.	24	RAW	16	23.9 GB	1.43 TB	Dalsa Origin
HDCAM SR (1920 x 1080p)	880	2:1	24	RGB 4:4:4	10	6.6 GB	396 GB	
1920 x 1080p	1.49 Gbps	uncomp.	24	RGB 4:4:4	10	11.1 GB	667 GB	dual-link HD-SDI
2K (2048 x 1556)[13]	2.29 Gbps	uncomp.	24	RGB	10	17.3 GB	1.04 TB	
4K (4096 x 3112)[13]	9.18 Gbps	uncomp.	24	RGB	10	70.3 GB	4.22 TB	

AUDIO FOR DIGITAL VIDEO

Video Data Rate	Nominal Comp. Ratio[1]	Frame Rate	Chroma Sampling	Bits	STORAGE per minute[2]	STORAGE per hour[2]	Notes
32 kHz—PCM	0.768	uncomp.		2 channels	12	5.8 MB	.35 GB	DV only
48 kHz—PCM	1.536	uncomp.		2 channels	16	11.5 MB	.69 GB	
48 kHz—MPEG1	0.384	Audio Layer II		2 channels	16	2.9 MB	172.8 MB	HDV only
96 kHz—PCM	18.432	uncomp.		8 channels	24	138.2 MB	8.3 GB	

1. Digital video compression encompasses competing techniques from DCT to wavelet compression, constant bit rate to variable, intraframe to interframe. Rarely is compression a simple number or constant ratio, even though we refer to it this way. Each set of techniques may yield a different quality even at the same nominal compression ratio. Compression ratios are therefore unreliable indicators of final picture quality.

2. Where possible, includes overheads for video stream (header and container format) as well as two tracks of 16-bit audio, error detection/correction, timecode, and track information. Actual storage also varies, depending upon factors such as the size and formatting of hard drives. Always keep 25 to 30 percent of disk capacity free as headroom to accommodate variations in disk speeds and data management.

3. Component formats only. Composite digital formats such as D-2 and D-3 not listed.

4. Average video data rate for DVDs is 3.8 Mbps. Compression of standard definition video for DVDs ranges from heavy MPEG-2 compression of 2 Mbps to high-quality compression of 6 Mbps. Maximum DVD data rate is about 10 Mbps.

5. Motion-JPEG (M-JPEG) is not a standardized compression but rather a technique of converting video frames into a sequence of compressed JPEG stills for economical offline editing. There are many variants with different chroma sampling and compression ratios.

6. NTSC 525-line, 29.97 fps digital formats and PAL 625-line, 25 fps formats share virtually identical data rates. The former has a higher frame rate with fewer lines, while the latter has a lower frame rate with more lines. Listing a format as "25, 30" fps in this chart does not imply that all such camcorders and VTRs record and play both standards.

7. Formats with "D" names like D-1, D-5, D-9, etc., are SMPTE standards.

8. Where a single chroma sampling ratio is listed, it applies equally to both NTSC-derived and PAL-derived digital formats.

9. Standard definition XDCAM is not a compression but rather a disc-based capture technology for camcorders. It uses both DVCAM (25 Mbps) and IMX (30, 40, 50 Mbps).

10. These are well-known format rates for Rec. 601 including audio and timecode. The 10-bit data rate of 270 Mbps is the basis of the SMPTE 259M standard that defines the common Serial Digital Interface (SDI). Rec. 601's video bit rates per se are slightly smaller.

11. Nominal baseline bit rate. Blu-ray, for one, can achieve a greater 54 Mbps (1.5x) transfer rate. Forthcoming application of a variety of compression technologies will result in a range of lesser but more practical bit rates to extend programming length.

12. HDCAM MPEG-2 compression is 4.1:1. However, prior to MPEG-2 compression, HDCAM horizontally filters and downsamples an original 1920 x 1080 image to 1440 x 1080. This prefiltering combined with the 4.1:1 MPEG-2 compression creates a cumulative compression of 7.1:1, which is how HDCAM is often described.

13. Aspect ratio is 4:3 like full-aperture 35mm, not widescreen like 16:9 or 1.85. CMOS can omit top and bottom of sensor to output 16:9, dropping data rate by 25 percent.

DEPTH OF FIELD TABLES

See Depth of Field, p. 151, and Depth of Field Charts, p. 158, before using these tables. For faster reference, you may want to get a full set of depth of field charts, such as the ones you'll find in the *American Cinematographer Manual*. This appendix contains two tables to give you an idea of depth of field. The first table is in feet and inches, the second is in the metric system.

To use these tables: (1) Find the lens aperture you are using (expressed as a T-stop) in the Lens Aperture column at upper left. Read across that row to the right until you locate the lens focal length at which you are shooting. This is the column in which the depth of field is indicated. (2) Find the point at which the lens is focused in the Point of Focus column on the left side of the chart. Read across that row to the right until you come to the column you located in (1). These figures indicate the near and far limits of the depth of field as measured from the focal plane. For example (using the Feet & Inches table), at T8, a 100mm fixed focal length lens focused at 10 feet provides a depth of field from 9-0 to 11-4 (that is, 9 feet to 11 feet 4 inches).

This method is used for a $\frac{1}{500}$-inch circle of confusion. For $\frac{1}{1000}$-inch circle of confusion read depth of field two columns to the right. For $\frac{1}{2000}$-inch, read four columns to the right.

Traditionally, the $\frac{1}{500}$-inch circle of confusion was used for 35mm filming, and $\frac{1}{1000}$-inch was used for 16mm. Video cameras with a $\frac{2}{3}$-inch sensor are fairly close to the 16mm image and $\frac{1}{1000}$-inch should be usable. With newer, sharper lenses and film stocks, sometimes a smaller circle of confusion is used. David Samuelson suggests that $\frac{1}{1000}$-inch or $\frac{1}{1400}$-inch should be suitable for most modern lenses and stocks without any diffusion. Sometimes $\frac{1}{2000}$-inch is used for 16mm. Generally, the larger the image will be magnified, the less leeway you have and the smaller the circle of confusion should be. Since 16mm must be magnified more than 35mm to fill the same size screen, a smaller circle of confusion is generally used for 16mm than 35mm.

Depth of field is a geometrical calculation, and the *f*-stop, a geometrical measurement, should be used for depth of field estimations. These charts were calculated with *f*-stops but are expressed in terms of T-stops, allowing $\frac{1}{3}$ stop for the difference. For most lenses, using the T-stop with these charts will be fairly accurate. If your lens is not marked in T-stops, using the *f*-stop will give a slightly stingy figure for depth of field.

Depth of field is not an absolute, and charts only provide an approximation. Rely more on eye focus than charts, especially for very long focal length lenses or regular lenses at close focusing distances and wide aperture.

Depth of Field Tables: Feet and Inches
Nearest and Furthest Point of Acceptable Focus

Lens Aperture (T-stop) — Lens Focal Lengths in Relation to Lens Aperture (mm)

For ⅟₅₀₀ in. circle of confusion use tables as printed.
For ⅟₁₀₀₀ in. circle of confusion transpose focal lengths two columns to right.

T-stop											
T2				21	25	30	35	42	50	60	70
2.8			21	25	30	35	42	50	60	70	84
4		21	25	30	35	42	50	60	70	84	100
5.6	21	25	30	35	42	50	60	70	84	100	120
8	25	30	35	42	50	60	70	84	100	120	140
11	30	35	42	50	60	70	84	100	120	140	170
16	35	42	50	60	70	84	100	120	140	170	200
22	42	50	60	70	84	100	120	140	170	200	240

Point of Focus Measured from Focal Plane (Feet) — Fixed Focal Length Lenses and Most 16mm Type Zoom Lenses

Focus	N/F											
3-0	Near	1-11½	2-2½	2-4¾	2-6½	2-8	2-9	2-9¾	2-10½	2-11	2-11¼	2-11½
	Far	6-7¼	4-8¼	3-11¾	3-7¾	3-5½	3-3½	3-2½	3-1¾	3-1¼	3-0¼	3-0½
3-6	N	2-2½	2-5¼	2-8¼	2-10¾	3-0½	3-2	3-3	3-3¾	3-4½	3-5	3-5¼
	F	9-3¼	6-0¾	5-0¾	4-5¼	4-1¾	3-11	3-9½	3-8½	3-7½	3-7	3-6¾
4-0	N	2-4	2-8½	2-11¾	3-2¾	3-4¾	3-6¾	3-8	3-9¼	3-10	3-10¾	3-11
	F	15-5	7-9¾	6-2½	5-3½	4-10½	4-6¾	4-4¾	4-3¼	4-2¼	4-1¼	4-1
4-6	N	2-6	2-11¼	3-2¼	3-6½	3-9	3-11¼	4-1	4-2½	4-3½	4-4½	4-4¾
	F	25-2	10-1	7-6¼	6-2¾	5-7¾	5-2¾	5-0	4-10	4-8¾	4-7¾	4-7¼
5-0	N	2-7½	3-1½	3-5¾	3-10	4-1	4-4	4-6	4-7¾	4-8¾	4-10	4-10½
	F	75-0	13-1	9-1	7-3	6-5½	5-11¼	5-7½	5-5¼	5-3½	5-2¼	5-1½
6-0	N	2-10½	3-5¾	3-11	4-4½	4-8¾	5-0½	5-3½	5-5¾	5-7½	5-9	5-9¾
	F	Inf	23-10	13-2	9-7¼	8-3	7-5	6-11½	6-7½	6-5¼	6-3½	6-2½
8-0	N	3-3	4-0½	4-8	5-4	5-10½	6-4½	6-9¼	7-1	7-4	7-6½	7-8
	F	Inf	Inf	30-2	16-2	12-8	10-9	9-10	9-2¼	8-9	8-6¼	8-4½
10-0	N	3-6¼	4-5¾	5-3	6-1¾	6-10¼	7-6¾	8-1½	8-7¼	9-0	9-3½	9-5¾
	F	Inf	Inf	Inf	27-6	18-7	14-9	13-0	11-11	11-4	10-10	10-7
15-0	N	3-11¾	5-3	6-4	7-8½	8-10¼	10-1	11-1½	12-0	12-11	13-5	13-10
	F	Inf	Inf	Inf	Inf	50-0	29-6	23-1	19-11	18-2	17-0	16-5
25-0	N	4-5	6-0¾	7-7	9-7¾	11-7	13-9	15-9	17-9	19-3	20-10	21-11
	F	Inf	Inf	Inf	Inf	Inf	Inf	61-0	42-7	36-9	31-4	29-3
50-0	N	4-10	6-10	8-11	11-11	15-0	19-0	23-0	27-4	32-0	35-7	38-9
	F	Inf	Inf	Inf	Inf	Inf	Inf	Inf	Inf	200-0	100-0	70-0
Inf	N	5-4	7-11	10-9	15-7	21-3	30-3	42-3	60-3	80-0	120-0	170-0

35mm Type Zoom Lenses

Focus	N/F											
5-0	N	3-2	3-7	3-10	4-1½	4-3¾	4-6	4-7½	4-8¾	4-9½	4-10¼	4-10¾
	F	19-9	9-9	7-8	6-6¼	6-0¼	5-7¾	5-5½	5-5¾	5-2¾	5-1¾	5-1¼
6-0	N	3-6	4-0	4-4	4-9	5-0	5-3	5-5¼	5-7	5-8¼	5-9½	5-10
	F	177-0	16-2	10-11	8-7	7-8	7-0½	6-8¾	6-5¾	6-4	6-2¾	6-2
8-0	N	3-11	4-7	5-2	5-9	6-2	6-8	7-0	7-3	7-5¼	7-7¼	7-8½
	F	Inf	94-0	23-0	14-1	11-8	10-2	9-10	8-11½	8-8	8-5½	8-4
10-0	N	4-3	5-1	5-9	6-7	7-3	7-11	8-4	8-10	9-1¼	9-4½	9-6¼
	F	Inf	Inf	70-0	23-1	16-11	13-10	12-7	11-8	11-1	10-9	10-6
15-0	N	4-9	5-11	6-11	8-3	9-4	10-7	11-5	12-4	13-0	13-6	13-11
	F	Inf	Inf	Inf	154-0	43-3	26-11	22-2	19-4	17-10	16-10	16-4
20-0	N	5-1	6-5	7-8	9-5	10-11	12-8	14-0	15-5	16-5	17-5	18-0
	F	Inf	Inf	Inf	Inf	195-0	51-0	35-11	28-10	25-8	23-6	22-6
50-0	N	5-8	7-7	9-7	12-6	15-8	19-10	23-6	28-3	31-2	36-0	38-10
	F	Inf	Inf	Inf	Inf	Inf	Inf	Inf	260-0	120-0	82-6	70-3
Inf	N	6-2	8-8	11-5	16-4	22-0	31-9	43-0	61-7	85-6	125-0	170-0

Depth of Field Tables: Metric
Nearest and Furthest Point of Acceptable Focus

Lens Aperture (T-stop) — **Lens Focal Lengths in Relation to Lens Aperture (mm)**

For 0.05mm circle of confusion use tables as printed.
For 0.025mm circle of confusion transpose focal lengths two columns to right.

T-stop				21	25	30	35	42	50	60	70
T2				21	25	30	35	42	50	60	70
2.8			21	25	30	35	42	50	60	70	84
4		21	25	30	35	42	50	60	70	84	100
5.6	21	25	30	35	42	50	60	70	84	100	120
8	25	30	35	42	50	60	70	84	100	120	140
11	30	35	42	50	60	70	84	100	120	140	170
16	35	42	50	60	70	84	100	120	140	170	200
22	42	50	60	70	84	100	120	140	170	200	241

Point of Focus Measured from Focal Plane (Feet)

Fixed Focal Length Lenses and Most 16mm Type Zoom Lenses

Focus												
1-0	Near	0-6	0-72	0-78	0-84	0-88	0-91	0-93	0-95	0-96	0-97	0-98
	Far	2-5	1-65	1-40	1-25	1-17	1-11	1-08	1-05	1-04	1-03	1-02
1-2	N	0-72	0-82	0-89	0-97	1-02	1-07	1-10	1-13	1-15	1-17	1-18
	F	4-41	2-30	1-84	1-58	1-45	1-37	1-31	1-28	1-26	1-24	1-23
1-3	N	0-75	0-86	0-95	1-03	1-09	1-15	1-19	1-22	1-25	1-26	1-27
	F	5-37	2-72	2-1	1-76	1-61	1-5	1-44	1-39	1-36	1-34	1-33
1-5	N	0-82	0-94	1-05	1-15	1-23	1-3	1-35	1-39	1-42	1-44	1-46
	F	18-7	3-82	2-69	2-16	1-93	1-78	1-69	1-63	1-59	1-56	1-54
1-7	N	0-87	1-02	1-14	1-27	1-36	1-45	1-51	1-56	1-59	1-63	1-65
	F	Inf	5-54	3-43	2-60	2-27	2-07	1-95	1-86	1-83	1-77	1-75
2-0	N	0-94	1-11	1-26	1-42	1-54	1-66	1-74	1-81	1-88	1-91	1-93
	F	Inf	11-2	4-98	3-4	2-86	2-53	2-35	2-23	2-15	2-10	2-07
2-5	N	1-03	1-25	1-44	1-66	1-82	1-98	2-11	2-21	2-29	2-35	2-39
	F	Inf	Inf	10-2	5-20	4-02	3-40	3-08	2-88	2-75	2-67	2-62
3-0	N	1-07	1-36	1-59	1-86	2-07	2-28	2-44	2-59	2-71	2-79	2-85
	F	Inf	Inf	33-4	8-03	5-51	4-41	3-89	3-57	3-37	3-25	3-17
5-0	N	1-24	1-65	2-0	2-45	2-84	3-26	3-62	3-94	4-22	4-43	4-58
	F	Inf	Inf	Inf	Inf	21-6	10-8	8-12	6-85	6-15	5-75	5-51
8-0	N	1-36	1-87	2-35	3-0	3-6	4-3	4-95	5-59	6-15	6-61	6-95
	F	Inf	Inf	Inf	Inf	Inf	60-0	21-0	14-1	11-5	10-1	9-42
17-0	N	1-147	2-1	2-71	3-62	4-54	5-73	6-95	8-28	9-56	10-7	11-7
	F	Inf	Inf	Inf	Inf	Inf	Inf	Inf	82-0	35-1	25-0	21-0
Inf	N	1-62	2-42	3-29	4-74	6-48	9-22	12-9	18-4	26-0	37-1	52-0

35mm Type Zoom Lenses

Focus												
1-5	N	0-97	1-08	1-16	1-24	1-3	1-35	1-39	1-42	1-44	1-46	1-47
	F	5-55	2-86	2-27	1-95	1-8	1-69	1-63	1-59	1-56	1-54	1-53
1-7	N	1-03	1-16	1-26	1-36	1-44	1-51	1-55	1-6	1-62	1-64	1-66
	F	13-0	3-94	2-86	2-35	2-11	1-96	1-88	1-82	1-79	1-76	1-74
2-0	N	1-1	1-27	1-39	1-53	1-63	1-73	1-79	1-85	1-89	1-92	1-94
	F	Inf	6-87	4-05	3-04	2-64	2-4	2-27	2-18	2-13	2-09	2-06
3-0	N	1-28	1-53	1-74	1-98	2-18	2-38	2-52	2-64	2-73	2-81	2-86
	F	Inf	Inf	18-9	6-97	5-03	4-12	3-75	3-48	3-33	3-22	3-16
5-0	N	1-47	1-84	2-18	2-61	2-99	3-41	3-72	4-03	4-26	4-46	4-59
	F	Inf	Inf	Inf	Inf	18-3	9-79	7-78	6-64	6-07	5-69	5-49
10-0	N	1-66	2-17	2-68	3-4	4-14	5-05	5-79	6-64	7-32	7-99	8-44
	F	Inf	Inf	Inf	Inf	Inf	Inf	40-4	20-8	15-9	13-4	12-29
20-0	N	1-77	2-38	3-03	4-02	5-12	6-64	8-03	9-8	11-4	13-2	14-51
	F	Inf	Inf	Inf	Inf	Inf	Inf	Inf	Inf	85-2	41-64	32-33
Inf	N	1-89	2-63	3-49	4-99	6-7	9-69	13-1	18-8	26-0	38-0	52-0

HYPERFOCAL DISTANCE TABLE

If the lens is focused at the hyperfocal distance, everything from half that distance to infinity should be in acceptably good focus. See Chapter 4 for limitations on the use of hyperfocal distance and depth of field tables.

To use this table: (1) Find the lens aperture you are using (expressed as an f-stop) in the column at left. Read across that row to the right until you locate the lens focal length at which you are filming. This is the column in which the hyperfocal distance is indicated. (2) Find the circle of confusion you are using on the lower left side of the chart. Read across that row to the right until you come to the column you located in (1). This is the hyperfocal distance for the focal length/aperture combination you are using.

See Appendix C for suggestions on choosing a circle of confusion.

Hyperfocal Distance

Lens Focal Lengths (mm)

f-stop	9	11	12.5	15	17.5	21	25	30	35	42
1	9	11	12.5	15	17.5	21	25	30	35	42
1.4	11	12.5	15	17.5	21	25	30	35	42	50
2	12.5	15	17.5	21	25	30	35	42	50	60
2.8	15	17.5	21	25	30	35	42	50	60	70
4	17.5	21	25	30	35	42	50	60	70	84
5.6	21	25	30	35	42	50	60	70	84	100
8	25	30	35	42	50	60	70	84	100	120
11	30	35	42	50	60	70	84	100	120	140
16	35	42	50	60	70	84	100	120	140	170
22	42	50	60	70	84	100	120	140	170	200

Circles of Confusion / Hyperfocal Distances

Circle of Confusion	Hyperfocal Distances													
0.001in	2ft 6½in	3ft 7in	5ft 3in	7ft 3in	10ft 6in	14ft 9in	20ft 6in	29ft 6in	41ft	59ft	82ft	118ft	164ft	236ft
0.002in	1ft 3in	1ft 9½in	2ft 7in	3ft 7½in	5ft 3in	7ft 4in	10ft 6in	14ft 9in	20ft 6in	29ft 6in	41ft	59ft	82ft	118ft
0.025mm	0.8m	1.1m	1.6m	2.2m	3.2m	4.5m	6.3m	9m	12.5m	18m	25m	36m	50m	72m
0.05mm	0.4m	0.56m	0.8m	1.1m	1.6m	2.2m	3.2m	4.5m	6.3m	9m	12.5m	18m	25m	36m

LENS ANGLE/FOCAL LENGTH TABLES

This chart shows the relationship of focal length and lens angle (angle of view) for different formats. The two video columns on the right refer to ½-inch and ⅔-inch sensors on video cameras. In larger professional video cameras, ⅔-inch CCD or CMOS sensors are often used. Some consumer video cameras have chips as small as ¼-inch. It is the *width* of the image being registered on film or on a video camera's sensor that determines the relationship between focal length and horizontal lens angle.

Start by finding the format you're using in the column headings at top. The lens angle or focal length will be found lower down in the same column. To find a horizontal lens angle, find the focal length you're using in the upper left part of the table and read across until you find the column for your format. To find a focal length for a given lens angle, find the lens angle in the lower left part of the table and read across until you find the proper column.

To calculate the vertical lens angle, divide the horizontal lens angle by the first part of the aspect ratio.

You can also use these charts to compare focal lengths between different formats. For example, say you wanted to find the focal length lens you would need to use with a video camera that has a ½-inch sensor to match the image produced by a 16mm camera with a 25mm lens. Using the top chart, we see that a 25mm lens in 16mm produces a lens angle of 22 degrees. Using the bottom chart, we see that a 22-degree lens angle calls for a focal length between 14mm and 18mm on the ½-inch video camera.

This chart is reprinted by kind permission of David Samuelson and Focal Press from his *Hands-On Manual for Cinematographers* (see Bibliography), which has many useful charts and calculations for image making.

Lens Angle/Focal Length

	Regular 16	Super 16	Academy 35mm	Full Frame	Anamorphic	VistaVision	65mm	½" Video	⅔" Video
				Format					
			Image Width (Projector aperture)						
Inches	0.378	0.463	0.825	0.945	0.838	1.418	1.913	.252	.346
mm	9.6	11.76	20.96	24.0	21.29	36.01	48.59	6.4	8.8
				Aspect Ratio					
	1.33:1	1.66:1	1.37:1	1.33:1	2.35:1	1.5:1	2.2:1	1.33:1	1.33:1

Lens Focal Length (mm) — **Horizontal Lens Angle (°)**

Lens Focal Length (mm)	Regular 16	Super 16	Academy 35mm	Full Frame	Anamorphic	VistaVision	65mm	½" Video	⅔" Video
400	1.4	1.7	3	3.4	6.1	5.2	7	.9	1.2
250	2.2	2.7	4.8	5.5	9.8	8.2	11	1.5	2
200	2.7	3.4	6	6.9	12	10	14	1.8	2.5
150	3.7	4.5	8	9.1	16	14	18	2.4	3.3
135	4.1	5	8.9	10.2	18	15	20	2.7	3.7
100	5.5	6.7	12	14	24	20	27	3.6	5.0
85	6.5	7.9	14	16	29	24	32	4.3	5.9
75	7.3	9	16	18	32	27	36	4.9	6.7
50	11	13	24	27	48	40	52	7.3	10
40	14	17	29	33	60	48	63	9.1	13
35	16	19	33	38	68	54	70	10	14
30	18	22	39	44	78	62	78	12	17
27	20	25	42	48	86	67	84	14	19
25	22	26	45	51	92	72	88	15	20
20	27	33	55	62	112	84	101	18	25
17	32	38	63	70	128	93	110	21	29
14.5	37	44	72	79	145	102	118	25	34
10	51	61	93	100	187	122	135	35	47

Lens Angle (°) — **Lens Focal Length (mm)**

Lens Angle (°)	Regular 16	Super 16	Academy 35mm	Full Frame	Anamorphic	VistaVision	65mm	½" Video	⅔" Video
1	550	674	1201	1375	2440	2063	2784	367	504
1.5	367	449	801	917	1626	1375	1856	244	336
2	275	337	600	687	1220	1032	1392	183	252
3	183	225	400	458	813	688	928	122	168
4	137	168	300	344	610	516	696	92	126
5	110	135	240	275	488	412	556	73	101
7	78	96	171	196	348	294	397	52	72
10	55	67	120	137	243	206	278	37	50
15	36	45	80	91	162	137	185	24	33
20	27	33	59	68	121	102	138	18	25
25	22	27	47	54	96	81	110	14	20
30	18	22	39	45	79	67	91	12	16
40	13	16	29	33	58	49	67	9	12
50	10	13	22	26	46	39	52	7	9
60	8	10	18	21	37	31	42	6	8
80	6	7	12	14	25	21	29	4	5
100	4	5	9	10	18	15	20	3	4

A COMPARISON OF RUNNING TIMES AND FORMATS OF 8MM, SUPER 8, 16MM, AND 35MM MOTION PICTURE FILMS

Running Times and Film Lengths for Common Projection Speeds

Film Format	8mm (80 Frames per Foot)				Super 8 (72 Frames per Foot)				16mm (40 Frames per Foot)				35mm (16 Frames per Foot)	
Projection Speed in Frames per Second	18		24		18		24		18		24		24	
Running Time and Film Length	Feet	Frames	Feet	Frames	Feet	Frames	Feet	Frames	Feet	Frames	Feet	Frames	Feet	Frames
Seconds 1	0	18	0	24	0	18	0	24	0	18	0	24	1	8
2	0	36	0	48	0	36	0	48	0	36	1	8	3	0
3	0	54	0	72	0	54	1	0	1	14	1	32	4	8
4	0	72	1	16	1	0	1	24	1	32	2	16	6	0
5	1	10	1	40	1	18	1	48	2	10	3	0	7	8
6	1	28	1	64	1	36	2	0	2	28	3	24	9	0
7	1	46	2	8	1	54	2	24	3	6	4	8	10	8
8	1	64	2	32	2	0	2	48	3	24	4	32	12	0
9	2	2	2	56	2	18	3	0	4	2	5	16	13	8
10	2	20	3	0	2	36	3	24	4	20	6	0	15	0
20	4	40	6	0	5	0	6	48	9	0	12	0	30	0
30	6	60	9	0	7	36	10	0	13	20	18	0	45	0
40	9	0	12	0	10	0	13	24	18	0	24	0	60	0
50	11	20	15	0	12	36	16	48	22	20	30	0	75	0
Minutes 1	13	40	18	0	15	0	20	0	27	0	36	0	90	0
2	27	0	36	0	30	0	40	0	54	0	72	0	180	0
3	40	40	54	0	45	0	60	0	81	0	108	0	270	0
4	54	0	72	0	60	0	80	0	108	0	144	0	360	0
5	67	40	90	0	75	0	100	0	135	0	180	0	450	0
6	81	0	108	0	90	0	120	0	162	0	216	0	540	0
7	94	40	126	0	105	0	140	0	189	0	252	0	630	0
8	108	0	144	0	120	0	160	0	216	0	288	0	720	0
9	121	40	162	0	135	0	180	0	243	0	324	0	810	0
10	135	0	180	0	150	0	200	0	270	0	360	0	900	0

Typical Running Times of Films

Film Format	8mm				Super 8				16mm				35mm	
Projection Speed in Frames per Second	18		24		18		24		18		24		24	
Inches per Second	2.7		3.6		3.0		4.0		5.4		7.2		18.0	
Film Length and Screen Time	Min	Sec	Min	Sec	Min	Sec	Min	Sec	Min	Sec	Min	Sec	Min	Sec
Feet 50	3	42	2	47	3	20	2	30	1	51	1	23	0	33
100	7	24	5	33	6	40	5	0	3	42	2	47	1	7
150	11	7	8	20	10	0	7	30	5	33	4	10	1	40
200	14	49	11	7	13	20	10	0	7	24	5	33	2	13
220	—	—	—	—	14	40	11	0	—	—	—	—	—	—
300	22	13	16	40	20	0	15	0	11	7	8	20	3	20
400	29	38	22	13	26	40	20	0	14	49	11	7	4	27
500	37	2	27	47	33	20	25	0	18	31	13	53	5	33
600	44	27	33	20	40	0	30	0	22	13	16	40	6	40
700	51	51	38	53	46	40	35	0	25	56	19	27	7	47
800	59	16	44	27	53	20	40	0	29	38	22	13	8	53
900	66	40	50	0	60	0	45	0	33	20	25	0	10	7
1000	74	4	55	33	66	40	50	0	37	2	27	47	11	7
1100	81	29	61	7	73	20	55	0	40	44	30	33	12	13
1200	88	53	66	40	80	0	60	0	44	27	33	20	13	20
1600	—	—	—	—	106	40	80	0	59	16	44	27	—	—

Number of Frames Separation Between Sound and Picture

	8mm	Super 8	16mm	35mm
Magnetic Track	56	18	28	28
Optical Track	—	22	26	20

Figures in the table are for reel-to-reel projection in which the sound precedes the picture.

The speed of 25 frames per second is used for 16mm TV films, and increasingly for other 16mm sound films, in 50 Hz countries.

Reprinted by permission of Eastman Kodak.

APPENDIX G

SYNCHING FILM RUSHES

This is a method for synching sound and picture for projects shot on film and edited using workprint and mag film. For synching in video on a nonlinear editing system, see p. 573.

1. Load the workprint and the mag film in the synchronizer or editing machine. They are usually loaded on the left so that the forward direction is from left to right. For this discussion, it's assumed the material is set up in this way.
2. Use the filmed slate or other point of reference as a guide for putting the sound and picture for the first shot in sync with each other (see Slates, Accuracy, and Lip Synching, p. 602). This requires shifting the position of the rolls with respect to each other.
3. Once the first shot is in sync, move the workprint and the mag film backward (to the left) to the head (beginning) of the picture roll. On the right-hand side of the machine cut off any excess laboratory leader on the picture (although if it contains the lab order number for the roll, you may want to leave that part) and trim the sound roll at the same spot. Splice on about 6-feet of plain, single-perforated leader on both rolls. Anytime you splice leader or fill onto the sound, make sure it is positioned with the base toward the sound head.

   Continue moving backward onto the leader about a foot or so, and mark a start or head sync mark with a Sharpie at the same frame on both rolls (see Fig. 15-11). At the head of the leaders write your name, the name of the film, the camera roll number, and either "head pix" or "head track" on the picture and sound, respectively.
4. Move the picture and sound forward to the end of the first shot. The end can usually be located by the flash frames—overexposed frames that occur when the camera stops between shots. Mark both sound and picture with the number 1 at the same frame.
5. Go forward and sync up the second shot. You will again need to shift the sound and picture relative to each other to accomplish this.
6. After the second shot is in sync, roll the sound and picture backward together to the number 1 you just marked on the picture. Mark a second 1

on the sound at the same frame. Search through the sound roll by hand to find the first 1 you marked on it.

7A. You will usually find the first 1 toward the head of the roll (to the right), which occurs whenever there is more sound than picture (normally the recorder runs longer than the camera). Move both rolls slightly to the right, and cut the sound from the left-hand edge of one of the frames marked 1 to the left-hand edge of the other (for consistency's sake, always cut on the left-hand edge of a marked frame). Splice the sound roll back together, and hang the wild sound you have just removed on a bin or spool it up on a separate roll.

7B. If, instead, you find the original 1 toward the tail (end) of the roll (to the left), this indicates that there is not enough sound to cover the picture (perhaps because the audio recorder started late on the second shot). Cut a piece of leader that is the same length as the distance from the left-hand edge of one 1 to the left-hand edge of the other. Often you can use the editing machine or synchronizer to measure the leader quickly. Splice the leader at the appropriate frame marked 1; this will depend on whether the first or the second shot has insufficient sound. When you've finished, both the first and second shots should be in sync; realign them if necessary.

8. Now go forward to the end of the second shot, and mark it with a 2 on the same frame of both sound and picture.

9. Return to step 5; this time you will be synching up the third shot, and so on.

10. At the tail of the picture roll, cut the sound at the same spot and splice tail leaders on both rolls, marked as before but with tail sync marks and "tail pix" and "tail track" written on the leaders.

This method is fast and leaves a string of wild sound in which each piece is marked according to the shot from which it was removed, which helps in identifying it later. If you prefer to leave any wild sound in the sync rolls, you can do so simply by splicing the same length of leader into the picture at the corresponding spot.

SPLITTING 16MM AND 35MM MAG TRACKS PRIOR TO THE MIX

This section is for people doing film projects that are edited in film with workprint and magnetic film. It describes a method for splitting mag film tracks during sound editing in preparation for the sound mix. See Chapter 16 for guidelines on how and why to split tracks. See Chapter 15 for handling mag film tracks. This discussion is strictly about the physical chores involved in dividing up the mag tracks.

Split mag tracks are a little like A&B rolls for printing picture (see Fig. 17-4); on each roll, sections of mag film alternate with sections of nonmagnetic leader that act as spacers. Clean, unshrunken slug or fill is usually used for this purpose. Splice so the base of the slug is toward the sound heads (meeting the emulsion side of the mag film).

Before setting up to split tracks, you should have already gone through the film and marked the splices where tracks are to be split (see p. 603 for more on this). Tracks can be split on a flatbed editing machine, but it is far easier to use an editing bench with a synchronizer and rewinds. Put the edited sound track rolls on the left. Also put on the left as many rolls of leader as you will ultimately have tracks. This is limited by the number of gangs on your synchronizer; the rolls may have to be done in two or more groups. It's crucial to load up the picture also so you can check for cutting errors.

Put all the rolls in sync on the synchronizer. At the head of each roll, splice about 15 feet of single-perf white leader that is properly labeled with production company name, film title, "head," and the track letter (some people identify tracks by number, not letter).

Only on the picture roll, splice a Society of Motion Picture and Television Engineers (SMPTE) head leader between the first frame of picture and the white leader. SMPTE or Society leader (sometimes called Academy leader, which is actually a different system) contains the familiar countdown from 8 to 2, followed by a short section of black leader (see Fig. 17-8). If you can't get SMPTE leader from the lab, you can fake it by marking the proper frames on your own leader. The frame at 8 is marked "Picture Start"; this is a good point at which to synchronize all the rolls. Use a hole punch (available at stationery stores) to punch the same frame on each of the sound rolls. On the 144th frame after the picture start (that is, 3 feet, 24 frames in 16mm; 9 feet in 35mm) is the 2 frame. This frame should be spliced out on the sound rolls only and replaced with a frame that has a distinctive tone (about 1000 Hz is standard) or, more simply, left in with a stick-on *sync beep* (also called a *sync pop* or *pip*) applied to the track area. In the United States, the track is located in the top quarter of the oxide on the side that has no sprocket holes.

When the film is projected, all the tracks should beep when the number 2 appears on screen, which tells the mixer that all the tracks are in sync, and, if he listens to them individually, that all the tracks are audible. The sync beep is also necessary for lining up the optical track in printing. The first frame of the movie appears on the 192nd frame after the "Picture Start" frame (4 feet, 32 frames in 16mm; 12 feet in 35mm).

Mix dubbers run at high tension. Rivas splicers, which use preperforated tape, make stronger splices than guillotines and should be used for the final splicing if possible. For mixing and printing, films are broken down into segments of convenient length called reels. See Reel Length, p. 599, for more on reel breaks.

If the film will be printed in more than one reel, you may want to prepare 26-frame pullups (for 16mm) while splitting tracks, or you may wait until the mix (see When Reels Are Spliced Together, p. 691). At the end of the film, splice on an SMPTE tail leader and put beeps at the tail sync mark on all the sound tracks to be able to check that all the rolls remained in sync throughout the mix. Add about 15 or 20 feet of white leader after the beeps, which is needed so that the dubbers can be run past the end of the film and then back, and properly label the tail leaders.

Preparing the Picture

These days, most mix studios use video projection. If you've edited with workprint, it will often be transferred to video for the mix (in fact, the mag tracks will probably also be transferred to a digital format).

Whether you're doing a video transfer or actually mixing with the workprint, the workprint should be double spliced and run through a synchronizer or projector to check the splices; with guillotine splicers, the sprocket holes are often incompletely punched out. Many filmmakers make a slop print (a workprint of the workprint) to have a splice-free copy for the mix, since every minute of delay in the mix is very costly. Making a slop print also allows the negative cutter to conform the original to the workprint before the mix is complete.

When doing a cue sheet, indicate the location of sounds by footage count. The footage counter should be zeroed at the "Picture Start" frame on the SMPTE leader. You can usually round off the foot/frame measurement to the nearest quarter foot (for example, in 16mm, 10 feet, 22 frames is about 10.59). Some mixers will want the footage indicated in 35mm feet (see p. 598 for conversion from 16mm to 35mm footage counts) or in timecode.

CEMENT SPLICING

Types of cement splicers range from large foot-operated models to small portable units. Splicers used for acetate-base films use cement to fuse together the overlapping ends of two pieces of film. (For polyester-base films, large, expensive splicers fuse the pieces of film together, generally without the aid of film cement.) Follow the instructions for the particular type of splicer you have and get someone to show you how it works. Before you attempt to splice important material, practice with scrap film until you are proficient. While practicing, test your splices by yanking on them. The film should snap before a well-made splice comes apart. Twisting will make most splices come apart, but will give you a way to compare the comparative strength of test splices.

Hot splicers have a heating element to speed the drying of the film cement, and are faster to use. Since the heating element takes a fair amount of time to warm up, hot splicers are often left plugged in during the whole working day (or, in busy editing rooms, they may never be turned off). However, some editors feel splices made with the heating element on do not last as long. These editors often use hot splicers because of the quality of their construction but use them with the heating element turned off.

The film cement contains a solvent that dissolves film base, and, when dry, will weld together two properly prepared pieces of film. It's important to use a high-quality *fresh* cement. When exposed to air, this solvent evaporates, and the film cement becomes gummy and will no longer make a good splice. To keep the cement fresh: Keep a small working supply of cement in a small well-capped glass bottle, and discard the contents every couple of hours. Store the bulk supply (which generally need be no more than a pint bottle) separately.

Keep the splicer clean of emulsion, properly adjusted and the scraper sharp. Acetone will dissolve both emulsion and film cement. You can use it to clean both the splicer and the small bottle that holds the film cement.

To splice: Place the film in the splicer, emulsion side up. Use the scraper to remove completely the emulsion and binder from the section of film to be overlapped (see Figs. A and B). Make sure the scraped area is clean and dry before applying the film cement. On some splicers you must moisten the emulsion with water or saliva before scraping, and on others you can dry-scrape. You must also remove magnetic striping (if any) in the area to be spliced, either by scraping or by dissolving it with film cement and wiping it away. When scraping emulsion you must be careful not to scrape too deep and gouge the exposed base (see Fig. E).

Any wax or dirt on the base of the overlapping piece of film (that is, the film to be spliced to the area where the emulsion has been scraped) may interfere with a good weld. To remove any foreign material, wipe with an alcohol-moistened cloth or apply a small amount of film cement and immediately wipe it off with a soft cloth. Some editors also lightly scrape the base on the overlapping piece of film. Again, be careful not to scrape too deeply. Apply the cement to the area where the emulsion has been scraped in a thin, even layer. Immediately press the base of the overlapping section onto the scraped, cement-coated area. Open the splicer, and wipe off any excess cement. Rub the splice firmly with a soft cloth to give added assurance of a good splice. Check that the splice is transparent; hazy areas or bubbles are signs of a poor splice.

A properly made splice can be removed from the splicer after ten to thirty seconds (depending on the type of film cement). A hot splicer cuts the time down to five to ten seconds. Though the film can be projected immediately, the splice cures and becomes stronger over time (two or more hours). Causes of poor splices include: emulsion or binder not completely removed; excessive scraping weakening the base, causing the film to break; too great a delay in joining the sections of film after applying cement; too much cement, making a messy splice and also possibly causing the film to buckle in the projector gate; too little cement, making the weld too weak; wax or oil not removed from the base of the overlapping film; old or unsuitable film cement.

Fig. A. If a small section of motion picture film were to be magnified to a great size, you would see the film is made up of more than one layer. In this illustration, the thickness of the various layers is exaggerated.

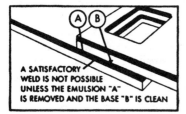

Fig. B. It is impossible to cement the base side of one piece of film to the emulsion of another. The emulsion and binder must first be completely removed so that the two film base surfaces can come in direct contact with each other.

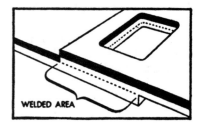

Fig. C. A good motion picture film splice is actually a weld. When a perfect splice is made, one side of the film base is dissolved into the base of the other film. With most splicing apparatus, this requires from ten to twenty seconds.

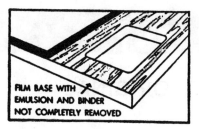

Fig. D. If any emulsion or binder remains on the base in the area where the splice is to be made, a good weld will not result and the splice may not hold.

Fig. E. Scratching or gouging the prepared film base near the emulsion edge should be avoided. Such scratches (A) weaken the weld and may cause the film to break at this point. Fine abrasive scratches are not serious.

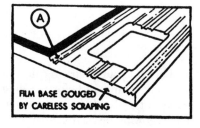

CONFORMING FILM ORIGINAL

This is about preparing film negative (or reversal original) for printing. See Chapters 15 and 17 before reading this section. When you have finished cutting workprint, it should be marked in preparation for cutting the original (see p. 603). The following discussion assumes that the negative is loaded on the editing bench on the left side so that forward movement is from left to right.

The work space should be clean and dust-free. Handle the original only with white editing gloves, which are available at most labs. The cement splicer should be properly aligned and used only with fresh cement (see Appendix I for more on splicing). Never mark the original with a grease pencil; use only India ink or scribe marks (see below). Any black leader used should be fresh and completely opaque. The cans in which the original is stored should be marked with the key numbers (latent edge number) so that any shot can be located by number. It's extremely helpful to have two sets of rewinds. One pair can be used for searching for shots, while the other is used for splicing and, with the aid of a synchronizer, for matching workprint with the original.

Some conformers (also called negative cutters) work by first logging the edge numbers of each shot in the workprint and then pulling *all* the shots from a given roll of original at one time. This cuts down on the handling of the original, since each roll does not need to be rewound every time a shot is taken from it. The shots are then put aside (see below) and assembled in proper order when all the shots have been pulled. Other conformers work by pulling each shot from the original in the order it appears in the workprint. This involves more handling of the original rolls but may reduce confusion. Most conformers find it simpler to first cut all the shots out of the original and then cement splice them rather than trying to do both tasks at the same time.

Place the edited workprint in the front gang of the synchronizer and wind down to the first shot you want to conform until you find the first key number. Lock the shot in place by pushing the lever on the front of the synchronizer. Locate the corresponding shot in the original by its key number and place it in the second gang of the synchronizer in precise frame-to-frame alignment with the workprint.

Unlock the synchronizer and run the two pieces of film back to the head of the shot in the workprint. Mark the frame where the original is to be spliced with *scribe marks*—two small scratches made *outside the picture area* on either side of the sprocket hole where the splice is to be made. Roll both pieces of film to the right slightly until the scribe marks are to the right of the synchronizer. Cut the original with scissors at least a half frame beyond the frame you just marked (which is to the right on most editing setups). This half frame is needed to make the cement splice. Some people routinely leave a frame and a half extra, which is fine as long as the frames aren't needed for another shot.

Now wind down the workprint and original to the tail of the first workprint shot and scribe the original at the last sprocket hole of the shot. Roll the footage slightly to the left of the synchronizer and again cut the original a half frame longer than the workprint shot.

Some conformers wind up each shot separately (either on a core or around itself) and wrap the last few winds in a piece of paper that identifies the shot by its key number. Sometimes white leader is attached with a very small piece of tape to the head and tail of each shot to protect it. The other widely practiced technique is to tape the shots in a continuous strand on a reel. This is feasible only if the shots have been culled in the order they appear on the workprint. Some people feel this is a poor practice, since tape can damage the original and the gum may be hard to remove. Only low-tack masking tape should be used on the original.

When cutting any shots to be used in a dissolve (which is possible only with A&B rolls unless you plan to use an optical printer), don't forget to cut at the *end* of the dissolve mark on the workprint; that is, the shot should be cut one-half the length of the dissolve longer than where the splice occurs in the workprint (the splice is at the center of the dissolve). On the original, sometimes a small x is marked on either side of the sprocket hole at the center of the dissolve (see Fig. 17-5). This should be done outside the picture area on both the A- and the B-rolls, as this helps in aligning the rolls later.

When preparing A&B rolls, it's advisable to have a synchronizer with at least three gangs. Begin by preparing the printing leaders as described in Chapter 17 (see Fig. 17-8). Line up the printer start marks in the synchronizer. The SMPTE leader is usually spliced on the head of the B-roll immediately following the white printing leader. Black leader is spliced opposite it on the A-roll and trimmed to the same length (run both strands in the synchronizer to measure where to cut). The first shot of the cut original film is then placed on the A-roll, with black leader spliced on the B-roll opposite it, and so on.

Remember that fades are laid out differently for reversal films than they are for negative films, while dissolves are laid out the same for each (see Chapter 17).

It is imperative that the emulsion of the black leader never be scraped during splicing, as this will defeat the purpose of checkerboard printing—invisible splices. Scrape only the original film on the overlap you left when trimming each shot. The workprint should be run in the third gang of the synchronizer so you can constantly check that you've correctly positioned shots and effects on the A&B rolls. After the rolls are spliced, they should once again be checked against the workprint for cutting errors. Don't forget to do a cue sheet to instruct the lab concerning fades and dissolves (see p. 673).

See *Cinematography* by Kris Malkiewicz (in Bibliography) for a more detailed description, with illustrations of how to conform original.

BIBLIOGRAPHY

Production and Business Aspects

Academy of Motion Picture Arts and Sciences. *Academy Players Directory* (8949 Wilshire Blvd., Beverly Hills, CA 90211). Photographs of actors with agent listings. Regularly updated.

Association of Motion Picture and Television Producers. *Guide to Location Information* (8480 Beverly Blvd., Los Angeles, CA 90048). Regularly updated.

Directors Guild of America. *Directors Guild of America Directory* (7950 West Sunset Blvd., Los Angeles, CA 90056). Lists members of the Directors Guild. Regularly updated.

Donaldson, Michael, C. *Clearance & Copyright*, 2nd ed. Beverly Hills: Silman-James Press, 2003. As the cover says: everything the independent filmmaker needs to know. Excellent resource, particularly for feature films.

Goodell, Gregory. *Independent Feature Film Production*. New York: St. Martin's Press, 1998. Manual on independent feature film production. Good on unions, casting agencies, budgeting, and distribution.

The Hollywood Production Manual (1322 North Cole Ave., Hollywood, CA 90028). Contains guild and union rules and rates. Lists production facilities in the Los Angeles area.

Honthaner, Eve Light. *The Complete Film Production Handbook*, 3rd ed. Boston: Focal Press, 2001. Comprehensive guide to production management, including setting up a production office, hiring talent and crews, dealing with unions and releases. Includes specific forms needed for all the business aspects of shooting a feature or TV show.

Motion Picture, TV and Theatre Directory (Motion Picture Enterprises, Tarrytown, NY 10591). Useful lists by category of suppliers of production and postproduction services and equipment. Contains listings of such items as negative matchers, labs, and stock footage libraries. Published semiannually.

Simens, Dov S-S. *From Reel to Deal: Everything You Need to Create a Successful Independent Film*. New York: Warner Books, 2003. Practical, useful, down-to-earth advice about producing your first feature.

Wiese, Michael. *Film and Video Budgets*, 4th ed. Los Angeles: Michael Wiese Film Productions in conjunction with Focal Press, 2006. Many sample budget forms with detailed explanations of line items.

Writers Guild, Writers Guild Directory (8955 Beverly Blvd., Los Angeles, CA 90048). Lists members of the Writers Guild and their agents. Regularly updated.

Direction and Writing

Bernard, Sheila Curran. *Documentary Storytelling for Film and Video Makers*. Burlington: Focal Press, 2007. Insights on story, structure, research, and narration, including interviews with filmmakers.

Field, Syd. *Screenplay: The Foundations of Screenwriting*. New York: Dell Publishing, 1994. Oft-cited guide to screenwriting.

Goldman, William. *Adventures in the Screen Trade*. New York: Warner Books, 1983. Wry observations of a master screenwriter.

Katz, Stephen. *Film Directing Shot by Shot: Visualizing from Concept to Screen*. Los Angeles: Michael Wiese Productions, 2001. Guide to production design, composition, storyboarding, and other aspects of planning the visual treatment.

McKee, Robert. *Story: Substance, Structure, Style, and the Principles of Screenwriting*. New York: HarperCollins, 1997. A distillation of McKee's popular screenwriting seminars, with useful insights on creating story, characters, and dialogue.

Proferes, Nicholas. *Film Directing Fundamentals: See Your Film Before Shooting*. Woburn: Focal Press, 2004. Analyzing scripts and films for keys to direction.

Trottier, David. *The Screenwriter's Bible: A Complete Guide to Writing, Formatting, and Selling Your Script*. Los Angeles: Silman-James Press, 2005. Writing the script and getting it out there.

Weston, Judith. *Directing Actors: Creating Memorable Performances for Film and Television*. Los Angeles: Michael Wiese Productions, 1999. Advice on working with actors.

Film Camera and Lenses

American Cinematographer (P.O. Box 2230, Hollywood, CA 90028). A monthly magazine devoted to camera and lighting techniques. Although it has a bias toward large-crew production, there are numerous articles on low-budget film and video.

Burum, Stephen, ed. *American Cinematographer Manual*. Hollywood: American Society of Cinematographers Press, 2004. Camera threading diagrams, 35mm formats, and many useful charts. A standard manual for professional cinematographers.

Carlson, Verne, and Carlson, Sylvia. *Professional Cameraman's Handbook*, 3rd ed. Boston: Focal Press, 2005. Outlines standard industry practice for the camera crew and describes in detail all the professional 16mm and 35mm cameras.

Hart, Douglas C. *The Camera Assistant: A Complete Professional Handbook*. Boston: Focal Press, 1997. Thorough guide to professional camera equipment and the duties of a camera assistant. A must for people seeking crew work as an assistant.

Malkiewicz, Kris I., and Mullen, David M. *Cinematography: Third Edition*. New York: Van Nostrand Reinhold Co., 2005. Covers most technical aspects of motion-picture production. Well written and well illustrated. Includes an excellent section on cutting your own negative.

Samuelson, David W. *Hands-on Manual for Cinematographers*, 2nd ed. Boston: Focal Press, 1998. Excellent resource for camera threading, lenses, special effects, and other aspects. Many useful charts and formulas for optical and film calculations.

Video Cameras and Other Equipment

Millerson, Gerald. *Television Production*, 13th ed. Boston: Focal Press, 1999. Comprehensive guide to television production techniques. Particularly useful for studio and multi-camera productions; doesn't have latest gear.

Poynton, Charles. *Digital Video and HDTV Algorithms and Interfaces*. San Francisco: Elsevier,

2003. Very technical and very thorough engineering guide to digital video. Authoritative resource.

Ward, Peter. *Basic Betacam Camerawork*, 3rd ed. Oxford: Focal Press, 2001. Detailed rundown of Betacam operation and camcorder use in general.

Wheeler, Paul. *Digital Cinematography*. Oxford: Focal Press, 2001. An experienced BBC cameraman discusses his approach to high-definition shooting, with heavy emphasis on Sony HDCAM cameras and menus.

Lighting

Bergery, Benjamin. *Reflections: Twenty-one Cinematographers at Work*. Los Angeles: ASC Holding Company. Interviews, stills, and light setups.

Box, Harry C. *Set Lighting Technician's Handbook*. Boston: Focal Press, 1997. Thorough guide to professional lighting gear and techniques. A must for someone seeking employment as gaffer or a lighting assistant.

Malkiewicz, Kris. *Film Lighting*. New York: Prentice Hall Press, 1986. Examines lighting technique through direct instruction and interviews with cinematographers. A good resource for people with basic knowledge looking to improve their technique.

Millerson, Gerald. *Technique of Lighting for Television and Film*. Boston: Focal Press, 1991. Thorough grounding in lighting theory. Less useful for practical setups.

Sound

Huber, David Miles, and Runstein, Robert. *Modern Recording Techniques*, 6th ed. Boston: Focal Press., 2005. Thorough. Specializes in concerns of studio music recording.

Rose, Jay. *Audio Postproduction for Digital Video*. San Francisco: CMP Books, 2002. Setting up a studio, audio post equipment, tips on audio processing and sound editing.

Rose, Jay. *Producing Great Sound for Digital Video*. San Francisco: CMP Books, 2003. For people who want to really understand digital audio and the recording arts. Lots of practical advice on microphones, camera settings, post tricks, and meters.

Seeberg, Wolf. *Sync Sound for Film and Video*. Los Angeles: Wolf Seeberg Video, 2005. Written for the professional recordist. A wonderfully detailed guide to recording sound with different types of timecode, digital audio recorders, and when doing music videos or shooting monitors. Available at www.Wolfvid.com.

Wyatt, Hilary, and Amyes, Tim. *Audio Postproduction for Television and Film*. Oxford: Focal Press, 2005. Guide to techniques and equipment for audio post.

Laboratory and Postproduction Services

Association of Cinema and Video Laboratories. *Handbook: Recommended Procedures for Motion Picture and Video Laboratory Services*. Bethesda: The ACVL (P.O. Box 34932), 1982. Leader preparation and lab services.

Case, Dominic. *Film Technology in Post Production*. Oxford: Focal Press. 2001. Comprehensive guide to film and laboratory services.

Clark, Barbara and Spohr, Susan. *Guide to Postproduction for TV and Film*. Burlington: Focal Press, 2002. Particularly useful for those managing post for network TV movies and Hollywood features.

Hirschfeld, Gerald. *Image Control: Motion Picture and Video Camera Filters and Lab Techniques*. Los Angeles: ASC Press, 2005. Thoroughly illustrated manual showing the effects of different filters, exposures, and processing on the image. Written by an experienced cinematographer.

Jones, Stuart Blake, Kallenberger, Richard, and Cvjetnicanin, George. *Film into Video: A Guide to Merging the Technologies*, 2nd ed. Boston: Focal Press, 2006. Everything you ever wanted to know about telecines. Readable but mostly for colorists-in-training.

Editing

Avid Technology. *Editing with Avid Express Pro and Avid Xpress DV.* Berkeley: Peachpit Press, 2004. Overview of editing with these NLEs.

Cullen, Sean, Geller, Matthew, Roberts, Charles, and Wilt, Adam. *Optimizing Your Final Cut Pro System*. Berkeley: Peachpit Press, 2006. Technical, detailed guide to postproduction equipment, formats and Final Cut.

DigitalFilm Tree. *Advanced Editing and Finishing Techniques in Final Cut Pro 4*. Berkeley: Peachpit Press, 2004. Guide to effects, color correction, and audio for the experienced user.

Droblas, Adele, and Greenberg, Seth. *Adobe Premiere Pro Bible*. Indianapolis: Wiley Publishing, 2004. Step-by-step guide to the software.

Harrington, Richard. *Photoshop for Nonlinear Editors*. San Francisco: CMP Books, 2005. Tips and tricks for preparing graphics for video.

Hollyn, Norman. *The Film Editing Room Handbook*, 3rd ed. New York: Lone Eagle Publishing, 1998. A guide to the skills needed to be a professional assistant editor. Useful for those seeking employment.

Kauffmann, Sam. *Avid Editing: A Guide for Beginning and Intermediate Users*, 3rd ed. Boston: Focal Press, 2006. An easy-to-read textbook about Avid editing that includes information on HD and script integration.

Murch, Walter. *In the Blink of an Eye*, 2nd rev. ed. Beverly Hills: Silman-James Press, 2001. Insightful views on editing, from the editor of *Apocalypse Now* and *The Unbearable Lightness of Being*.

Oldham, Gabriella. *First Cut: Conversations with Film Editors*. Los Angeles: University of California Press, 1995.

WEBSITES

General

American Film Institute. www.afionline.org. Wide-ranging resource.

eXposure. www.exposure.co.uk. "The internet resource for low-budget filmmakers."

Film Maker. www.FilmMaker.com. How to's and links to many sites.

Filmunderground. www.filmunderground.com. Informal advice and resources.

Foundation Center. www.foundationcenter.org. Database of funders and grants.

Independent Feature Project. www.ifp.org. Organization for filmmakers, festival programmers, and distributors. Hosts annual IFP Market in New York.

International Documentary Association. www.documentary.org. Organization for documentary makers. Resources, screening programs, and also publish *Documentary Magazine*.

Industry News and Magazines

Digital Content Producer. www.digitalcontentproducer.com. Articles and reviews of the latest gear. Useful.

DV Magazine. www.dv.com. Articles and reviews, especially of DV and HDV cameras and editing.

Filmmaker Magazine. www.filmmakermagazine.com. Articles on indie features.

IndieWIRE. www.indiewire.com. News on independent filmmakers, festivals, and releases.

National Alliance for Media Arts and Culture. www.namac.org. Online support for independent media artists.

Television Broadcast. www.televisionbroadcast.com. New technology and practices for the broadcast industry.

Employment and Professional Directories

Craigslist. www.craigslist.org. Listing of freelance and full-time work by region.

Crew Net Freelancer's Directory. www.crew-net.com.

Kemps Film and Television, kftv.com, and Mandy's Film and TV Directory. www.mandy.com. Both are databases of film and television producers, technicians and facilities around the world. Mandy's has help-wanted listings.

Film and Festival Databases

Filmfestivals.com. www.filmfestivals.com. Listings and news of festivals worldwide.

Film Finder. www.filmfinder.com. Database of reviews and recommendations.

Internet Movie Database. www.imdb.com. Comprehensive listing of films and credits.

Rotten Tomatoes. www.rottentomatoes.com. Collects reviews from many sources for hundreds of films. Filmmakers check for their "Tomatometer" rating.

Withoutabox. www.withoutabox.com. Comprehensive listing of festivals with convenient online submission tool.

Technical and Other

Adam Wilt. www.adamwilt.com. Technical articles on DV and HDV.

Creative Cow. www.creativecow.net. Hosted forums and articles on a wide range of cameras, editing systems, and software. A fabulous resource and place to find solutions and post questions.

The Digital Video Information Network. www.dvinfo.net. More forums, specializing in DV, HD, and HDV cameras and editing.

DMN Forums. http://forums.digitalmedianet.com. Another great hosted forum site to find solutions and get specific advice.

Ken Stone. www.kenstone.net. Collected articles and how-to's on various topics, including Final Cut Pro.

Media Lawyer. www.medialawyer.com. Legal resource, with information on entertainment, multimedia, and property law, and with links to other legal and business sites.

Studio Daily. www.studiodaily.com. Technical reviews, articles, case studies. Links to film and video site, HD site, etc.

Manufacturers and Products

AbelCineTech. www.abelcine.com. Film and video cameras. Aaton dealer. Rentals, sales, service.

Adobe. www.adobe.com. Software and products, including Premiere Pro and After Effects.

Apple. www.apple.com. Software and products, including Final Cut Studio.

Avid Technology. www.avid.com. Nonlinear editing systems and other digital products.

B & H Photo Video. www.bhphotovideo.com. Just about any kind of equipment you need.

Canon. www.usa.canon.com. Professional and consumer camcorders.

Coffey Sound. www.coffeysound.com. Professional audio products and links to other audio sites.

Eastman Kodak. www.kodak.com/go/motion. Professional motion-picture films and articles on their use.

Fletcher Chicago. www.fletch.com. Wide range of video and audio equipment, sales and rentals.

Fuji. www.fujifilmusa.com. Professional motion-picture film, video, and digital.

JVC. http://pro.jvc.com/prof/main.jsp. Professional video equipment.

Panasonic. www.panasonic.com/business/provideo/home.asp. Professional video equipment.

Sony Professional Products. http://bssc.sel.sony.com. Professional video and audio equipment.

INDEX

splicing, 486, 589–91, *590*, 600–601, 668–71, 691, 789–91
split edits, 492, 542
split-field diopters, *166*, 167
split focus, 155, *156*
split image range finders, 237
split reels, 587
splitting tracks, 626, 641, 787–88
spotlights, 455–56, *456*, 457
spot meters, 281, *282*, 283, *283*
spotting, 626, 665
spotting sheets (spot lists), 637
spreaders, 345–47, *346*
squeeze images, *88*, 90, 93, *94*, 95
standard definition format, *see* SDTV
standard light, 661, 662
"standby" mode, 128
stand-ins, 343
stand-ups, 333
Star Wars (film), 101, 545, 564
static shots, 325
Steadicams, 51, 353–54, *354*
step printers, 666
step-up rings, 309
stereo pairs, 540, 639–40
stereo sound, 431–34, *432*, *433*, *654*, 654–56
stills, 140, 548–49
stingers, 464
stock footage, 334, 488, 748
stock music, 746–47
stop framing (stop action), *see* freeze frames
stopping down, 150, 154
storage systems, 218–19
story, 312–14
storyboards, 313–14, *314*
straight cuts, 537
streaking, 665
string-outs, 3, 496
stripe, *see* magnetic film
striping, *see* blacking
strobing, *see* judder
styles in moviemaking, 82–108, 332–44
subclips, 523
subtitles, laser, 675
subtractive primaries, 293, *294*
summing audio, 639–40
sun guns, 461
sunlight, 288, 472, 479–80
Super 8, *49*, 247, 281, 289
super black, 179, *190*
Super 8 cameras and film, 46, *46*, *48*, 48–49, 270, 783–84
super-cardioid microphones, *391*, 392, *393*, 406
Super 16 film, 46, 49–51, *51*, 62, 680
Super Grip, *347*
superimposed titles (supers), 499, *500*, 501, 674–75
superimpositions, 678
Super VHS (S-VHS), 38

super white, 179, *190*
supply reels, 387
surround sound, 654, *654*, 655
S-video, *193*, 194, 581
sweetening, 626
swish pans, 348
SXRD projector, 11
sync breaks, 541, *541*
sync errors, 623
sync generators, 509–10
synching up, 56, 434, 601–2, 707, 785–86
synchronization rights, 745
synchronizers, *591*, 591–92
sync pop, 644, 645
sync (synchronous) sound, 54, 235, 434–42, 540–41, 601

T
table stands (for cameras), 345, *346*
tail leaders, 593–94, 601, 671–72, *672*
tail slates, 436
takes, 323
take-up core, 245, *245*
talking heads, 334
tally lights, 129
tape cassettes, 74, *74*, 125
tape editing, 39–40, 42–43, 514, *514*, 579–86, 628
tape focus, 156
tape saturation, 420
tape splices, 589–91, *590*, 600–601
tape stock, 74–75, 124–25
TBC (time base corrector), 546
Techniscope, 52, 93
telecine logs, 617, 705
telecines, 102, 696–712, *697*, *698*
telecine timecode, 703–4
telephoto lenses (tele-lenses), 145, 164–65
teleprompters, 362–63, *363*
television, digital, *see* DTV
television distribution, 3, 61, 63–65, 67, 752–53
termination, 202, 769
test screenings, 497
theatrical distribution, 3, 61–63, 748–52, *749*
35mm film, 46, *46*, 47, *48*, *51*, 51–52, 62, 92–93, 270–72, 272, 598, 624, 687–88, 783–84
30 fps, 615, 622–23
30p, 100–101
three-chip cameras, 17, 136–37
three-color meters, 299
three-perf 35mm film, 51–52
three-point editing, 531–32
three-point lighting, 468–69, *469*, *470*
3/4-inch U-matic, 37–38
three-shot sequences, *487*, 488
3:2 pulldown, *see* 2:3 pulldown
threshold of hearing, 369
threshold of pain, 369
throughput, 216, 510